GREEK ISLAND HOPPING

1999

Written and researched by

Frewin Poffley

Thomas Cook

Publishing

Published by Thomas Cook Publishing
The Thomas Cook Group Ltd
PO Box 227, Thorpe Wood, Peterborough PE3 6PU, United Kingdom

Text & Artwork
© 1999 Frewin Poffley

ISBN 1 900341 52 2

Published annually
ISSN 1362-0002

**Whilst every care has been taken in compiling this
publication using the most up-to-date information
available at the time of going to press, neither the author
nor the Thomas Cook Group Limited as publishers can
accept any liability arising from errors or omissions in the
text or maps, however caused. Readers should note
especially that timings and fares of many Mediterranean
ferry services are fixed only shortly before the beginning
of the season and are often subject to change without
notice. It is therefore strongly advised that all such
information should be checked before beginning any
journey on one of the services listed in this publication.
The views and opinions expressed in this book are not
necessarily those of the Thomas Cook Group Ltd.**

Repro and imagesetting by Z2 Repro, Thetford, Norfolk, UK

Printed in Spain by GraphyCems, Villatuerta, Navarra

Drawn ⌐ & typeset by Frewin Poffley/Thingumajigolo Productions

Contents

ⓘ How to Use this Book

random (though in fact almost all of the boats run the same routes each summer) with the result that the majority of tourists stick to a few well trodden routes while guide books to the Greek islands concentrate on the islands while glossing over the means of travelling between them.

This book attempts to address this inbalance and give you the facts you need to move around with ease. In addition to the more usual sightseeing information, it contains a synopsis of the ferry network around the Greek islands (as well as Aegean and other international services in the Mediterranean east of Venice). As a result, it is very much oriented towards showing you *how* to get around as well as telling you what you will find when you get there. It has been designed to answer the questions:

While everybody has heard of Greek island hopping, if you have yet to try it, the notion of booking a flight to Greece and then wandering between islands one has only vaguely heard of (complete with funny names written in an even more unintelligible looking alphabet) can seem a rather daunting prospect. In fact, once you understand how the Greek ferry system works and how respective islands are linked together, you will find that it is remarkably easy. That said, those who go Greek island hopping (be they novice or a seasoned veteran) can never be said to be lacking a challenge. For Greece is a country apart. Thanks to good international ferry links and a very competitive domestic ferry system (to say nothing of small intimate islands touched by 4000 years of history and populated with friendly islanders long used to speaking English), it offers the best island hopping in the Med. But there are problems, not least of which is Greece's inability to publish ferry timetables despite having a large fleet that carries 10 million passengers each year. Protected by cabotage laws that prevent foreign competition until 2004, ferry companies chop and change boats and services seemingly at

'Where can I go to?'

'How can I get there?'

'What will I find there?'

'Where can I hop to from there?'

In this guide chapters are determined by the main ferry routes. These are followed by a **Port Table** section showing typical High Season departures from the Islands and Mainland Ports covered in the book. At the back of the guide is a **Reference** section containing ferry company information (including a ferry colour key), a **Useful Greek** section and the **Index**.

For ease of use chapters are divided into three sections:

1

Overview & Itinerary

The initial — 'Where can I go to?' — section of each chapter is intended to give you a clear idea of the geographical area covered by the chapter and the best means of tackling the islands and ports within it. On the title page itself you will find a map showing the main ferry route linking the islands, along with approximate sailing times between them and the island name in Greek (in the form — usually the accusative case — that you are most likely to encounter it on ship destination boards and ticket agency timetables). This is followed by a brief description of the characteristics of the group, a map of the area covered, and a model itinerary showing a practical way of tackling the islands in the chain. The itinerary also identifies the best home or 'base' port in the group should you wish to use one island as a springboard to viewing the rest.

2

Ferry Services

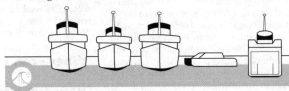

The second — 'How can I get there?' — section is devoted to the ferries that link the islands within each group. (Where a ferry's itinerary includes islands and ports split between several lines-cum-chapters it is described in the chapter in which it plays the most important role.) Each boat's previous High Season route is mapped, and the accompanying text lists the owning company, year of build (and rebuild, if any), and gross registered tonnage (GRT). In addition, there are comments on each ferry's history, reliability and likely changes in 1999. This will give you the means to interpret local advertising and assess the merits or otherwise of the individual boats.

You should find that all ferries are covered bar the four or five last-minute arrivals that turn up out of the blue each summer. Usually these new arrivals are not too much of a problem since they tend to either line up in competition with an existing service or simply replace it. More of a handicap are the periodic fleet reshuffles which can result in up to four or five boats swapping (and adapting) itineraries and giving the appearance of far more substantive change than there really is.

3

Islands & Ports

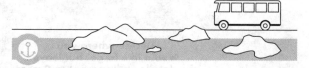

The third — 'What will I find there?' — section consists of a mini A—Z of the Islands and Ports found within the chapter area. All islands, mainland ports and the major sights are briefly described. The 60-odd islands large enough to warrant a ferry link also have an accompanying map showing typical High Season *weekday* Bus and Beach boat services along with town maps identifying the important landmarks and places to stay.

Port Tables

The greatest difficulty in moving around the Greek islands is not knowing the frequency of connections between specific ports. This section of the guide is designed to clue you in on the 'hopping' potential of each port and the ships sailing from them. The Port Tables show *typical* High Season ferry departure times as well as offering **Connections Maps** showing High Season frequency of service to other ports of call. Working within the constraints imposed by much last minute summer scheduling by Greek ferry operators this Port Table section of the book is *not* intended to be a timetable, but a guide that you can usefully employ to hop freely between islands and ports or to adjacent islands from your holiday base. The tables — showing services operating in 1998 (updated with the latest information where available) — are intended to give you the means of determining what is happening and the likely options available when you arrive at any port during 1999, and (given the constraints outlined on p. 32) through to February 2000.

Planning an Itinerary

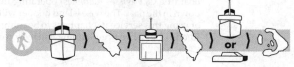

Flexibility is the key to a successful island hopping holiday. Publilius Syrus' natty apophthegm '*It is a bad plan that admits of no modification*' was surely stylused with Greek island hopping in mind. Preplanning an itinerary around the islands is perfectly practical provided a number of points are borne in mind:

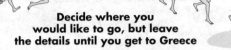

Decide where you would like to go, but leave the details until you get to Greece

Armed with a book like this in the pre-holiday enthusiasm it is very easy to over-plan. It is far better to make a hit list of the four or five islands you simply must get to and then a list of those you would also like to see and thereafter keep your plans reasonably fluid; you can add precise boats and times when you get to your first port of call and establish which are running. Build a 2-week itinerary along the lines of 'on Tuesday we'll arrive at the port at 14.20, giving us a free 20 minutes to sup a pint of ouzo before catching the 14.45 boat', and the chances are you will come unstuck sooner rather than later. You would also end up extremely drunk. Greece is a casual country so an 'on the Tuesday afternoon or evening we'll catch a ferry' approach will be far more successful.

Build itineraries using 'Daily' connections

When pre-planning, use the Port Table Connections maps (in the timetable section at the back of this book) and try to keep as many *6–7 days per week* links in your itinerary as possible; even if this means deviating from your preferred route.

Example: Rhodes to Nissiros. The Rhodes' Connections map below shows that a link exists 2–3 days a week. Closer examination of the Port Table and Ferry description reveals that the primary boat (the C/F *Nissos Kalimnos*) operating this route has broken down in the past. The wise island hopper will note the possibility of using this service if it happens to be running when they get to Rhodes, but when pre-planning will reckon on travelling via Kos

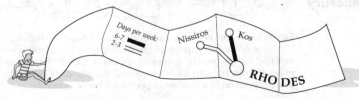

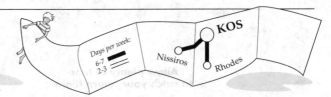

— which has a daily link with both Rhodes and Nissiros (see above). The rule of thumb therefore is that *2–3 days per week* links should always be treated with suspicion: don't build an itinerary that *depends* on them — unless that link comes early enough in your holiday to make alternative plans. Similarly, if the Port Tables show that a route exists courtesy of a single boat it pays to be aware of the potential vulnerability of the link to change.

Always arrive at a port with an Alternative Plan

At some point in the average two week island hopping holiday you will find yourself left high and dry on a quay waiting for a boat that for some reason or other fails to turn up. Life is far more relaxed if you have already preplanned for such an eventuality and can blithely shrug your shoulders and say 'okay we'll do this instead…' The 'this' options usually come down to a later alternative boat, a change of route, and/or the afternoon on the nearest decent beach.

Build in a 2-day 'delay' into your itinerary

One of the great attractions of island hopping is that every island is different and sooner or later you will be washed up on the shores of the one the Gods made for you; tempting you to linger longer than intended. Build this into your calculations: it will also provide you with an extra safety net should weather, a fully booked ferry or lightning strike disrupt your plans.

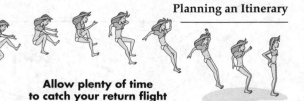

**Allow plenty of time
to catch your return flight**

Always arrange an easily accessible final/return port of call and *allow at least one clear day spare* to ensure that you don't miss your return ferry or flight away from civilisation. This is something that cannot be emphasised enough. If you are starting from a poorly connected airport give yourself two clear days: in short, play safe — there is usually somewhere to play near your starting point so this needn't damage your holiday. If you are moving between chains (e.g. starting from the Dodecanese and moving into one the Cycladic Lines) save the visits to islands near your return destination for the end of your holiday so that your final hops are both short and easy.

When you've used this book ...

... help us update

Greek Island Hopping is field researched each year before being updated. Nevertheless, there will always be instances where up-to-date information was not obtainable at the time of research and we welcome reports and comments from guide users.

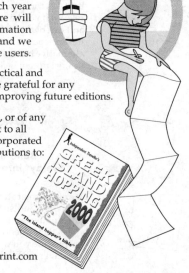

Similarly, we aim to make the Guide as practical and useful as possible to island hoppers and are grateful for any comments, criticisms and suggestions for improving future editions.

A free copy of the next edition of the Guide, or of any other Thomas Cook publication will be sent to all readers whose information or ideas are incorporated in future editions. Please address all contributions to:

The Editor, Greek Island Hopping,
Thomas Cook Publishing,
PO Box 227, Thorpe Wood,
Peterborough, PE3 6PU. United Kingdom.

Or fax us on: 01733 503596
International: +44 1733 503596
e-mail: publishing@thomascook.tmailuk.sprint.com

Symbols, Maps & Tables

Symbols — see inside front cover

Times — see inside back cover

Street Maps

The majority of Greek island towns do not have street names (buildings are numbered instead). The best way of using the maps in this book is to navigate via landmarks (e.g. churches & hotels)

Scale

The maps in this book use the metric system used in Greece. To convert to yards and miles:
1 metre = 1.09 yards
1 kilometre = 0.62 miles

Map Legend

┠┼┼┼┼┨	Railway	░░░	Cliff / Steep Slope
┠─[ ]─┨	Railway Station	∴∴	Map Cross-Section
─○─	Metro Station	∽∽	Waterlogged Land
═══	Street / Path		Open Ground
▭▭▭	Staircase / Muletrack	⤙⤚	Bridge
┈┈┈	Dirt Road	∿∿	City / Castle Wall
▭	Building	⌐≢⌐	Ruins
⌂	Archway	⌐≣⌐	Ruins (roofed over)
○○○	Park / Woodland	⌐┈┐	Line of Lost Walls
░▒▓	Beach	⌐┆┆⌐	Cemetery
∿∿∿	Rocks	🏠🏠🏠	Windmills
⌐⌐⌐	Sports Field / Playground		
⊙	Fountain / Pool		

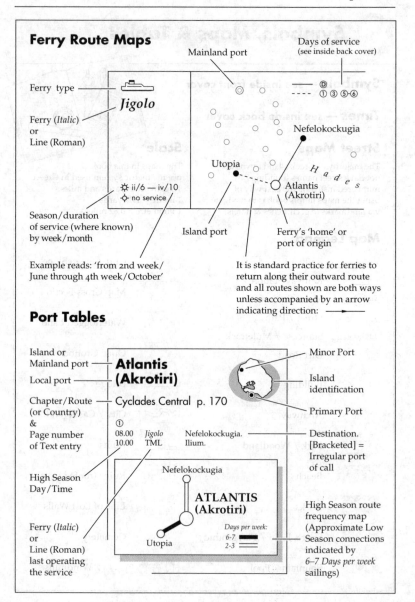

Ferry Route Maps

Ferry type

Ferry (*Italic*)
or
Line (Roman)

Jigolo

Mainland port

Days of service
(see inside back cover)

— ⓓ
---- ① ③ ⑤-⑥

Nefelokockugia

Utopia

Atlantis
(Akrotiri)

☼ ii/6 — iv/10
◇ no service

Season/duration
of service (where known)
by week/month

Island port

Ferry's 'home' or
port of origin

Example reads: 'from 2nd week/
June through 4th week/October'

It is standard practice for ferries to
return along their outward route
and all routes shown are both ways
unless accompanied by an arrow
indicating direction: ⟶

Port Tables

Island or
Mainland port

Local port

Chapter/Route
(or Country)
&
Page number
of Text entry

High Season
Day/Time

Ferry (*Italic*)
or
Line (Roman)
last operating
the service

Atlantis (Akrotiri)

Cyclades Central p. 170

①
08.00 *Jigolo* Nefelokockugia.
10.00 TML Ilium.

Minor Port

Island
identification

Primary Port

Destination.
[Bracketed] =
Irregular port
of call

Nefelokockugia

**ATLANTIS
(Akrotiri)**

Days per week:
6-7 ▅▅▅
2-3 ═══

Utopia

High Season route
frequency map
(Approximate Low
Season connections
indicated by
6–7 Days per week
sailings)

Island Bus & Beach Boat Maps

Island name/s (former name shown in light face).

ATLANTIS / KALLISTE

Symbols (from L to R):

International Ferry Connection

Base Port

Camping

Rooms available

Air, Rail, Bus connecting service

Town, Village or Hamlet (Importance indicated by the size of the text)

0   km   5

Upland Areas

Bus Station/s on accompanying Town Street Map

→ Athens Ⓓ x 3
→ Rhodes Ⓓ x 1

Olympic Airways Domestic Flights

---- Ⓓ 10.00

--- Ⓓ x 6
---- Ⓓ x 4
-·- Ⓓ x 2
······ ⚠ Ⓓ x 3

□ Minosia

Crater Lake

1700 m

Mt. Talos Crater

Fira

Bus and Beach boat routes indicated usually return via the outward route. Frequency given is that found on typical High Season weekdays. Sundays see a major reduction in services. Bus Times (where given) are from the port unless otherwise stated. Significant camping bus services are indicated by a camping symbol as above

Ⓐ Metropolis

Island Citadel / Temple of Cleito & Poseidon

Naval Yards

Gate Towers

Akrotiri

Perissa

Dikta

Built up areas (shaded)

Principal Sights (mentioned in text)

Paved Roads and Important unpaved tracks

Ⓝ All maps in this guide are orientated with North at the top of the page unless otherwise indicated.

INTRODUCTION

- [ ] **GREEK ISLAND HOPPING**
- [ ] **GETTING THERE**
- [ ] **FERRIES AND TICKETS**
- [ ] **HOLIDAY ESSENTIALS**
- [ ] **HISTORICAL BACKGROUND**

SIGHTSEEING ISLES

CYCLADES NORTH	DELOS
CYCLADES CENTRAL	SANTORINI NAXOS ANTIPAROS
CRETE	IRAKLION
DODEC-ANESE	RHODES KOS PATMOS
ARGO-SARONIC	AEGINA
NORTH AEGEAN	THESSALONIKA KAVALA CHIOS SAMOS SAMOTHRACE
EASTERN LINES	CHIOS SAMOS (PITHAGORIO)
IONIAN	CORFU

NIGHTLIFE ISLES

CYCLADES NORTH	MYKONOS
CYCLADES CENTRAL	IOS SANTORINI PAROS
CYCLADES WEST	SIFNOS
NORTH AEGEAN	SKIATHOS THASSOS
IONIAN	CORFU LEFKADA ZAKINTHOS
DODEC-ANESE	KOS RHODES
EASTERN LINES	SAMOS (PITHAGORIO)
ARGO-SARONIC	SPETSES

BEACH ISLANDS

CYCLADES NORTH	MYKONOS ANDROS
CYCLADES CENTRAL	IOS NAXOS PAROS SANTORINI KOUFONISSINI
CYCLADES EAST	KOUFONISSIA
NORTH AEGEAN	SKIATHOS SKYROS THASSOS
IONIAN	CORFU ZAKINTHOS LEFKADA
DODEC-ANESE	KOS KARPATHOS RHODES LIPSI PATMOS
EASTERN LINES	LESBOS
ARGO-SARONIC	AEGINA
CYCLADES WEST	SERIFOS SIFNOS

WINDMILL ISLES

CYCLADES NORTH	MYKONOS
CYCLADES CENTRAL	IOS SANTO ANTIPARO PAROS
CYCLADES WEST	SERIFOS KIMOLOS
EASTERN CYCLADES	ASTIPALEA

QUIET ISLANDS

CYCLADES WEST	FOLEGANDROS SERIFOS SIFNOS
CYCLADES NORTH	KEA ANDROS KYTHNOS
CYCLADES CENTRAL	ANTIPAROS
NORTH AEGEAN	LIMNOS SKYROS SAMOTHRACE ALONISSOS
DODEC-ANESE	NISSIROS TILOS
IONIAN	ITHACA MEGANISI
CYCLADES EAST	ALL OF THEM !

PICTURESQUE 'CHORA' ISLANDS

CYCLADES NORTH	MYKONOS
CYCLADES CENTRAL	IOS SANTORINI PAROS
EASTERN LINES	LESBOS
NORTH AEGEAN	SKYROS
CYCLADES WEST	SERIFOS SIKINOS FOLEGANDROS
EASTERN CYCLADES	ASTIPALEA AMORGOS ANAFI

IDEAL ISLANDS
FOR MAROONING YOUR PARTNER ON WHEN THEY ARE BEING PARTICULARLY IRRITATING

CYCLADES CENTRAL	ANAFI
NORTH AEGEAN	AGIOS EFSTRATIOS
CRETE & EASTERN CYCLADES	GAVDOS
ARGO-SARONIC	ANTIKITHERA

Greek Island Hopping

Guidebooks to Greece are apt to intimidate any would-be island-hopper by observing that the country has some 1,425 islands of which 166 are inhabited. In practice, life is much simpler: Greece has 78 islands connected by regular ferry or hydrofoil, with another 40-odd islets visited by tour or beach boats (the remaining 48 'inhabited' islands being occupied by odd monks, goat-herds and the occasional shipping billionaire). You can therefore get to some 120 islands using commercial boats. Of course, apart from the growing number of island hopping fans devoting holidays toward the goal of doing them all, in the eyes of most tourists not all these islands are *worth* a visit; but which you add to, or cross off, your list rather depends on your vision of the ideal Greek island. Herein lies the fascination of the islands, for the mix of history and geography is different on every one. It is almost as if the Olympian Gods had taken turns at trying their hands at different combinations and then laid the results down side by side to compare each in their turn. Any temptation to linger is tempered by curiosity as to what one is likely to find at the next island down the line.

The Greek islands fall into six named groups. The most popular are the Cyclades. With 26 ferry-linked small islands, this is the group that naturally comes to mind when thinking of island hopping. Following close on behind are the 17 Dodecanese islands running down the Turkish coast. The other groups have less mass appeal and fewer islands, but are growing in popularity. The most frequently visited are the closely bunched Saronic Gulf islands (running south of Athens) as all can be 'done' by day-trippers from the capital, while the widely scattered Eastern and Northern Aegean islands have much to offer if you have more than a fortnight at your disposal. The Ionian islands, distinguished by being the only group to lie outside the Aegean, are poorly connected with the rest of the ferry system but also have their fans.

If you are new to island hopping the first — and most important — thing that you need to appreciate is that the Greek ferry system is not actually geared to moving tourists between islands within any one group, but primarily exists to ferry local Greeks between the islands and Athens (over a third of the population of Greece lives in Athens and many are economic migrants from the islands, returning periodically to their family homes). The ferry network that has developed as a result is best imagined as a wheel, with the 'hub' being Athens (via its ports of Piraeus and Rafina), from which radiate ten 'spokes' or chains of islands, along which ferries regularly steam up and down — usually running 24 or 48-hour return trips from Piraeus. Cross-chain services that enable you to jump between islands on different chains without returning to Athens also exist, but are far fewer in number. It is therefore easy to island hop between the islands along a particular chain or line, but hopping over to an island on another can, on occasions, be quite difficult. The frequency of boats down each line is very tourist-dependent. The standard Low Season daily sailing between the popular islands and the capital can mushroom up to six or more once the summer crowds start arriving. The smaller, less touristed, islands tend to retain an annual twice-weekly subsidized lifeline ferry link with the capital regardless of season.

The first decision that any island hopper therefore needs to make is which 'spoke' or chain of islands they wish to visit. This is a very important decision as the islands collected in each chain combine to offer very different sorts of holidays (individual chains also vary greatly in the opportunities on offer to cross over to another chain). This guide attempts to make this task easier by grouping the Greek islands into chapters according to their regular ferry-linked chain or line (rather than the formal group to which they belong).

The chapter summaries on the next three pages and the chain/chapter map on p. 19 should help you quickly sort out which is the best chain for you. Brief descriptions of the general characteristics of each chain are followed by short sections giving:

1. The Main Islands
These are listed in their normal order of call when sailing from Piraeus.

2. High Season Cross Lines
Crossing between 'spokes' or chains can be difficult at times. This section seeks to highlight those islands most likely to be offering the best chance to cross over to another chain. Note: other islands will also offer irregular cross-line connections via ferries, hydrofoils or tourist boats.

3. Computer Ticket Traps.
This year sees the second year of operation for the new computer ticket booking system for passengers using all large ferries (see p. 38). Partially in operation since 1997, it has resulted in some island hoppers finding that they couldn't travel for a day or two because of fully booked ferries. This list tries to identify those islands and times when high demand for tickets is likely to cause problems in High Season (though it would be unwise to assume that it is infallible!). Apart from the Easter holiday (when most Greeks attempt to return to their home island), computer tickets shouldn't cause you too many problems.

3.
Cyclades Central .... p. 124

Easily the most popular line in Greece (regularly attracting over 40% of island hopping tourists), this line links four very popular islands that offer everything from nightlife to nudist beaches. The chain is characterized by being overcrowded in High Season. Out of the High Season peak-period of mid July to mid August they remain busy, but not oppressively so.

Main Islands
Paros, Naxos, Ios, Santorini.

High Season Cross Lines
Paros — Mykonos (Cyclades North)
Paros — Sifnos (Cyclades West)
Paros — Kos (Dodecanese)
Paros — Samos (Eastern Lines)
Paros — Skiathos, Thessalonika
                        (Northern Aegean)
Naxos — Mykonos (Cyclades North)
Naxos — Amorgos (Cyclades East)
Ios — Sikinos, Folegandros (Cyclades West)
Santorini — Sikinos, Folegandros
                        (Cyclades West)
Santorini — Iraklion (Crete)
Santorini — Skiathos, Thessalonika
                        (Northern Aegean)

Computer Ticket Traps
Frequency of boats should ensure that missing one shouldn't delay you too much. Overnight boats to Athens do tend to fill up fast in August, so you should obtain tickets for these as soon as you know when you are travelling.

4.
Cyclades North .... p. 176

A much visited group thanks to over-popular Mykonos, which shares the same characteristics as the islands on the Cyclades Central Line. The other islands are relatively quiet, most visitors being Greeks. Another feature common to the islands in this chain in High Season is the very strong *meltemi* wind that rushes south down the Aegean; this chain acts as something of a wind break for the rest of the Cyclades. Daily ferries run to these islands from both Piraeus and Rafina.

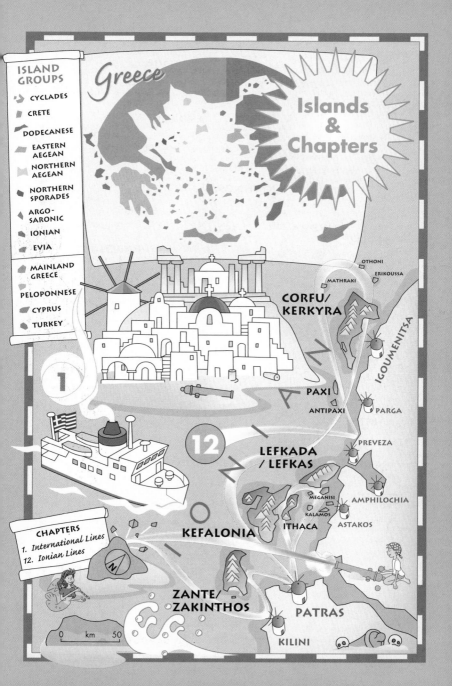

ISLAND GROUPS

- CYCLADES
- CRETE
- DODECANESE
- EASTERN AEGEAN
- NORTHERN AEGEAN
- NORTHERN SPORADES
- ARGO-SARONIC
- IONIAN
- EVIA
- MAINLAND GREECE
- PELOPONNESE
- CYPRUS
- TURKEY

Greece

Islands & Chapters

1

12

IONIAN

OTHONI
ERIKOUSSA
MATHRAKI

CORFU/ KERKYRA

IGOUMENITSA

PAXI
ANTIPAXI

PARGA

PREVEZA

LEFKADA / LEFKAS

MEGANISI
KALAMOS

AMPHILOCHIA

KEFALONIA

ITHACA

ASTAKOS

ZANTE/ ZAKINTHOS

PATRAS

KILINI

0   km   50

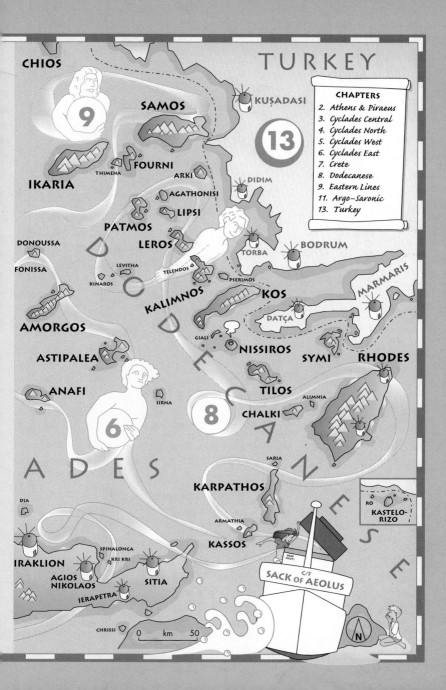

CHIOS

TURKEY

9

SAMOS

KUŞADASI

13

FOURNI

ARKI

THIMENA

DIDIM

IKARIA

AGATHONISI

LIPSI

DONOUSSA

PATMOS

LEROS

BODRUM

TORBA

FONISSA

LEVITHA

TELENDOS

PSERIMOS

MARMARIS

KINAROS

KALIMNOS

KOS

DATÇA

AMORGOS

GIALI

ASTIPALEA

NISSIROS

SYMI

RHODES

ANAFI

6

SIRNA

8

TILOS

ALIMNIA

CHALKI

D

O

D

E

C

A

N

E

S

E

SARIA

A

D

E

S

KARPATHOS

DIA

RO

KASTELO-
RIZO

SPINALONGA

KRI KRI

ARMATHIA

KASSOS

IRAKLION

AGIOS
NIKOLAOS

SITIA

SACK OF AEOLUS

C/F

KEEP
SHUT!

IERAPETRA

CHRISSI

0   km   50

N

Islands & Chapters

THESSALONIKA

KAVALA

KERAMOTI

THASSOS

ALEXANDROUPOLIS

GULF OF THERMAI

NEA MOUDANIA

MARMARAS

MT. ATHOS

AMOULIANI

VOLOS

TRIKERI

ATHENS 2

AGIOS KONSTANTINOS

RAFINA

N

SKOPELOS

SKIATHOS

OTOUGRIA

ALONISSOS

S P O R A D E S

PERISTERA

KIRA PANAGIA

GIOURA

VIPERI

SKANDZOURA

SKYROPOULA

DESPOTI

4

KIMI

EVIA / EUBOEA

SKYROS

ANTIPSARA

PSARA

9

CHIOS

OINOUSSES

LESBOS

10

AGIOS EFSTRATIOS

LIMNOS

SAMOTHRACE

IMBROS

TENEDOS

TROY

DARDANELLES

N O R T H   A E G E A N

ÇEŞME

IZMIR

ALIBEY

AYVALIK

LÁPSEKI

MARMARA

AVŞA

PASALIMANI

BANDIRMA

SEA OF MARMARA

TURKEY 13

km 0   50

Main Islands
Syros, Tinos, Mykonos, Andros.

High Season Cross Lines
Mykonos — Paros, Naxos, Ios, Santorini
(Cyclades Central)
Mykonos — Ikaria, Samos (Eastern Lines)
Mykonos — Skiathos, Thessalonika
(Northern Aegean)
Mykonos — Amorgos (Cyclades East)

Computer Ticket Traps
The holy island of Tinos is subjected to an
invasion of Greeks in the week surrounding
the 15th of August, when ferries are to be
booked solid. Ferries to Tinos on Saturdays
and from Tinos on Sundays are also sure to be
full. Mykonos is the only other island where
you could have problems; links to Paros and
Athens can fill to capacity in High Season.

5.
Cyclades West .... p. 214

A collection of relatively quiet islands increasing in popularity. Most have some nightlife
and at least one good beach. Ferry links with
other lines are relatively poor, but hydrofoils
opened up connections in 1997.

Main Islands
Kea, Kythnos, Serifos, Sifnos, Kimolos, Milos,
Folegandros, Sikinos.

High Season Cross Lines
Serifos — Paros (Cyclades Central)
Folegandros — Ios, Santorini
(Cyclades Central)
Sikinos — Ios, Santorini (Cyclades Central)
Milos — Agios Nikolaos, Sitia (Crete)

Computer Ticket Traps
Kythnos and Serifos are close enough to
Athens to see large numbers of Greeks visiting
at weekends. Ferries to both ports are likely to
be fully booked from Friday evening to
Sundays. Don't try heading north on Sundays.

6.
Cyclades East .... p. 250

The quietest of the Cyclades lines, and also a
sub-line running out of Naxos. The islands are

the least spoilt in the Cyclades, but ferry links
are erratic, hampering easy hopping.

Main Islands
Amorgos, Iraklia, Schinoussa, Koufonissia,
Astipalea, Anafi.

High Season Cross Lines
Amorgos — Naxos, Paros (Cyclades Central)
Amorgos — Mykonos (Cyclades North)
Astipalea — Kalimnos (Dodecanese)
Anafi — Santorini (Cyclades Central)

Computer Ticket Traps
Space limitations on the small, local ferry
running from Amorgos to Mykonos could
result in High Season ticket rationing.

7.
Crete .... p. 272

A popular starting point for island hopping
holidays, Crete sees daily overnight non-stop
ferries from Piraeus (making it an 'empty' —
i.e. island free — spoke from Athens). Crete is
also the termination point for a number of
ferries running down other lines. The island
has something to suit all tastes, with a highly
developed resort packed north coast and a
scenic hinterland and south coast.

High Season Cross Lines
Iraklion — Santorini, Paros (Cyclades Central)
Iraklion — Mykonos (Cyclades North)
Iraklion — Rhodes (Dodecanese)
Iraklion — Skiathos, Thessalonika
(Northern Aegean)
Agios Nikolaos — Milos (Cyclades West)
Sitia — Milos (Cyclades West)

Computer Ticket Traps
Rhodes and Thessalonika-bound ferries often
fill up to capacity in High Season: much depends on the number of ferry sailings.

8.
Dodecanese Lines .... p. 300

Attracting 25% of island hoppers, the Dodecanese islands offer a popular contrast with the
Cyclades. They feel slightly less Greek, but
have much more variety and sightseeing, with
some of the best nightlife and beaches. The

longest single chain in the Greek islands, ferry links are reasonable, though links with other chains are limited. The islands south of Rhodes are poorly connected with the rest of the group.

Main Islands
Patmos, Leros, Kalimnos, Kos, Nissiros, Tilos, Symi, Rhodes, Kastelorizo, Chalki, Karpathos, Kassos.

High Season Cross Lines
Rhodes — Sitia, Agios Nikolaos, Iraklion
                          (Crete)
Rhodes — Paros, Santorini (Cyclades Central)
Kos — Paros (Cyclades Central)
Kalimnos — Astipalea (Cyclades East)
Patmos — Samos (Eastern Lines)

Computer Ticket Traps
Midday ferries running either way between Athens and Rhodes tend to be filled to bursting in High Season and should be booked as soon as possible.

9.
Eastern Lines .... p. 368

A rather quiet line: most visitors tend to be one-island visitors as islands are too large and out of the way to be popular with island hoppers. Ferries from Athens either run to Ikaria and Samos or to Chios and Lesbos, with small ferries connecting the two sections of the chain.

Main Islands
(a). Ikaria, Samos. (b). Chios, Lesbos.

High Season Cross Lines
Lesbos — Limnos, Kavala, Alexandroupolis
                      (Northern Aegean)
Samos — Paros (Cyclades Central)
Samos — Patmos, Kalimnos (Dodecanese)
Ikaria — Paros (Cyclades Central)
Ikaria — Mykonos (Cyclades North)

Computer Ticket Traps
None known.

10.
Northern Aegean .... p. 400

A quiet and very poorly linked line. The small Sporades sub-chain (Skiathos, Skopelos & Alonissos) sees more island hoppers than the rest of the group put together and can be easily reached via ferries from the Cyclades. The North Aegean islands offer a nice mix of quiet beaches and well wooded interiors.

Main Islands
Skiathos, Skopelos, Alonissos, Skyros, Limnos, Thassos, Samothrace.

High Season Cross Lines
Limnos — Lesbos, Chios (Eastern Line)
Skiathos — Paros, Santorini (Cyclades Central)
Skiathos — Iraklion (Crete)
Skiathos — Mykonos (Cyclades North)

Computer Ticket Traps
Limnos—Athens ferries fill up very early: in early August you can get trapped on Limnos for several days if you are not careful.

11.
Argo-Saronic Lines .... p. 442

A group of largely small wooded islands close to Athens and the mainland Peloponnese. The chain is best tackled day-tripping from Athens.

Main Islands
Aegina, Angistri, Poros, Hydra, Spetses, Kithera.

High Season Cross Lines
None. You will have to return to Athens or continue south to Crete.

Computer Ticket Traps
None known.

12.
Ionian Lines .... p. 472

Despite being a chain of large wooded islands with good beaches, this is the least popular group with island hoppers as ferry links are poor (usually requiring a hop to the mainland).

Main Islands
Corfu/Kerkyra, Paxi/Paxos, Lefkada/Lefkas, Ithaca, Kefalonia, Zakinthos/Zante

High Season Cross Lines
None. Buses to Athens from all large islands.

Computer Ticket Traps
None known.

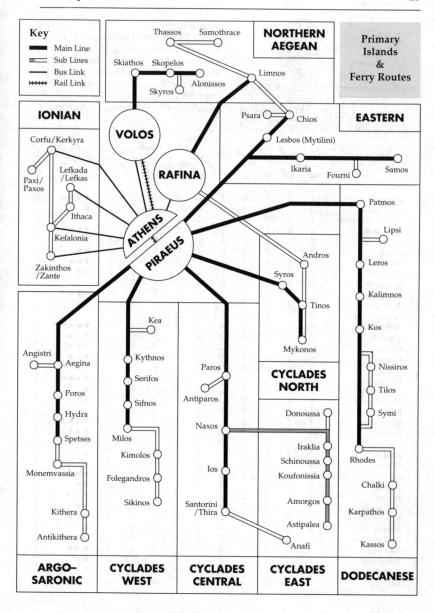

Key
- Main Line
- Sub Lines
- Bus Link
- Rail Link

Primary Islands & Ferry Routes

NORTHERN AEGEAN

Thassos Samothrace
Skiathos Skopelos Limnos
Alonissos
Skyros

IONIAN

Corfu/Kerkyra

VOLOS

Paxi/Paxos
Lefkada/Lefkas
Ithaca
Kefalonia
Zakinthos/Zante

RAFINA

ATHENS / PIRAEUS

Psara Chios
Lesbos (Mytilini)
Ikaria Fourni Samos

EASTERN

Patmos
Lipsi
Leros
Kalimnos
Kos
Nissiros
Tilos
Symi
Rhodes
Chalki
Karpathos
Kassos

Andros
Syros
Tinos
Mykonos

Kea
Kythnos
Serifos
Sifnos
Milos
Kimolos
Folegandros
Sikinos

Angistri Aegina
Poros
Hydra
Spetses
Monemvassia
Kithera
Antikithera

Paros
Antiparos
Naxos
Ios
Santorini/Thira
Anafi

CYCLADES NORTH

Donoussa
Iraklia
Schinoussa
Koufonissia
Amorgos
Astipalea

ARGO-SARONIC | **CYCLADES WEST** | **CYCLADES CENTRAL** | **CYCLADES EAST** | **DODECANESE**

Island Ratings
Having established which island group
you want to visit, the next question you
need to address is which islands within
the group are likely to have most appeal.
Rating the Greek islands is necessarily a
very subjective exercise. Not only are an
island's merits (or otherwise) conditioned

ISLAND RATINGS

	Main Town	Landscape	Tree Cover	Sightseeing	Nightlife	Eating	Peace & Quiet	Beaches	Nudism	Tourism Level	Summary (out of 5)
Aegina	7	4	4	8	7	7	4	4	2	7	●●●●
Agathonisi	0	1	0	0	0	2	10	0	0	1	●
Agios Efstratios	1	3	0	0	0	0	10	4	6	0	
Alonissos	3	6	8	1	2	5	5	5	4	3	●●●●
Amorgos	8	9	3	6	3	6	8	5	5	4	●●●●●
Anafi	4	4	0	2	0	2	8	5	3	1	●●
Andros	4	6	4	1	1	5	6	6	3	3	●●●
Angistri	2	3	7	0	1	3	4	2	0	5	●●
Antikithera	0	2	3	0	0	0	10	1	0	0	
Antiparos	6	4	2	4	5	5	6	7	10	6	●●●●
Antipaxi	2	4	4	0	0	3	6	6	4	3	●●
Arki	0	2	1	0	0	0	10	3	0	1	
Astipalea	8	5	2	6	4	5	7	4	1	2	●●●●●
Chalki	7	3	0	1	2	6	6	3	0	5	●●●
Chios	4	7	6	5	3	7	5	3	2	3	●●●
Corfu	6	6	6	8	10	6	2	9	4	10	●●●
Crete	5	10	6	10	9	7	8	8	5	9	●●●●
Delos	0	4	0	9	0	0	6	1	0	5	●●●●
Donoussa	2	5	2	0	0	3	8	4	0	2	●
Elafonissos	6	5	1	0	0	6	10	7	5	2	●●
Evia	1	7	5	3	1	5	7	4	0	4	●
Folegandros	9	5	1	2	1	7	8	3	2	4	●●●●●
Fourni	4	4	1	0	0	6	10	5	0	1	●●●●
Gavdos	1	5	2	1	0	0	10	3	0	0	●
Hydra	7	4	0	2	7	7	4	1	0	10	●●
Ikaria	2	9	4	1	3	4	6	5	3	3	●●
Ios	7	5	1	1	10	2	3	9	8	10	●●●
Iraklia	2	3	2	0	0	4	7	4	1	2	●●
Ithaca	4	8	4	2	1	6	7	2	0	2	●●●
Kalimnos	3	6	3	3	4	5	3	6	2	6	●●●
Karpathos	4	9	3	5	2	6	6	6	3	3	●●●
Kassos	2	4	0	1	0	2	9	3	0	1	●
Kastelorizo	6	5	3	4	0	5	9	0	0	2	●●●●
Kea	5	4	3	6	2	6	6	4	1	5	●●
Kefalonia	1	8	5	3	2	7	6	7	3	5	●●
Kimolos	5	5	1	2	2	5	10	5	2	2	●●●●
Kithera	6	7	3	3	2	6	9	6	1	1	●●●●

by whether your priorities are beaches and nightlife or peace and quiet, but many islands are apt to leave very different impressions at different times of the year. Ios is a classic example of this; quiet and dreamy in the Low Season, it becomes *the* party island in August; usually attracting very negative reviews in consequence.

Nevertheless, it is possible to give some indication of an island's likely appeal, and the table below should help in this respect. Ratings are given out of ten (*the* place to go if you want this), with zero representing 'forget it'. Summaries are given out of five. Those islands rating less than one are better avoided.

THE TOP 74	Main Town	Landscape	Tree Cover	Sightseeing	Nightlife	Eating	Peace & Quiet	Beaches	Nudism	Tourism Level	Summary (out of 5)
Kos	6	3	2	8	10	3	1	8	4	10	●●●
Koufonissia	3	4	0	1	1	6	10	6	0	2	●●●
Kythnos	2	3	1	1	0	1	8	4	0	1	●
Lefkada / Lefkas	7	7	4	4	5	4	4	6	2	6	●●●
Leros	5	5	2	1	2	5	6	4	0	3	●●●
Lesbos	5	7	3	4	3	7	6	7	3	3	●●●
Limnos	6	6	2	6	3	4	8	7	2	1	●●●●
Lipsi	4	2	1	1	0	5	9	5	3	3	●●
Milos	5	4	2	4	2	6	6	4	1	3	●●●
Mykonos	10	4	0	6	10	8	2	10	10	8	●●●●●
Naxos	10	8	6	6	7	7	5	10	9	10	●●●●●
Nissiros	6	9	4	6	1	4	8	2	0	3	●●●
Oinousses	1	2	3	0	0	2	9	4	0	1	●
Paros	6	5	3	4	9	4	2	8	6	10	●●●
Patmos	8	6	1	6	4	5	7	5	2	7	●●●●
Paxi / Paxos	5	6	5	2	6	5	6	2	0	8	●●●
Poros	4	4	5	2	6	5	3	2	0	8	●
Psara	3	5	0	1	0	4	10	4	0	1	●
Rhodes	8	7	4	10	10	6	1	8	3	10	●●●●●
Salamina / Salamis	0	2	0	1	0	0	2	0	0	0	
Samos	3	7	4	6	4	5	5	8	2	6	●●●●
Samothrace	4	8	5	4	0	6	9	3	1	2	●●
Santorini / Thira	10	10	0	10	8	5	2	4	1	10	●●●●●
Schinoussa	1	3	1	0	1	5	9	5	0	2	●
Serifos	6	6	1	1	2	5	6	7	2	4	●●●
Sifnos	7	7	3	5	5	7	6	6	0	6	●●●
Sikinos	5	4	2	2	0	3	10	3	0	1	●●●
Skiathos	7	6	8	5	8	6	3	9	10	9	●●●●
Skopelos	7	7	7	3	5	5	3	5	8	6	●●●
Skyros	8	5	5	2	1	4	9	4	3	3	●●●●
Spetses	3	4	6	1	7	4	4	3	0	8	●●
Symi	8	5	1	4	5	6	5	4	1	6	●●●●
Syros	5	1	2	2	3	4	4	3	0	4	●●
Thassos	8	9	8	7	6	7	7	10	7	5	●●●●●
Tilos	4	7	2	3	3	5	9	5	0	2	●●●
Tinos	6	7	4	5	3	4	4	3	0	8	●●●
Zakinthos / Zante	3	8	7	3	10	5	3	9	3	8	●●●

Getting There

Part of the key to a successful holiday is getting your documentation, money supply, and entry and exit to and from Greece right. Attention to these details will help acquire the peace of mind needed for carefree island hopping. This can be also encouraged by taking further precautions; i.e.: leave someone an idea of your likely itinerary (along with photocopies of all important documents), and starting out with a clear idea of what you would do if you are one of the unlucky few to hit trouble.

Passports and Visas

Personal documentation is a subject easily dealt with as no visa is required for EU nationals or nationals of Australia, Canada, New Zealand, and the USA for visits to most of the countries on the shores of the Eastern Mediterranean for up to three months; though some countries (such as Turkey) have a small visa/entry charge.

Embassies in Athens

Opening Hours:

Country	Address	Phone	Hours
Australia	37 D. Soutsou	☎ (01) 644 7303	①–⑤ 09.00–13.00
Austria	26 L. Alexandras	821 1036	
Belgium	3 Sekeri	361 7886–7	
Canada	4 Ioannou Gennadiou	723 9511	①–⑤ 09.00–13.00
Cyprus	16 Herodotou	723 7883	
Czechoslovakia	6 G. Seferis	671 0675	
Denmark	11 Vassilissis Sofias	360 8315	
Finland	1 Eratosthenous & V. Kon	701 0444	
France	7 Vassilissis Sofias	361 1663–5	①–⑤ 09.00–11.00
Germany	10 Vassilissis Sofias	369 41	
Hungary	16 Kalvou	671 4889	
Ireland	7 Leoforos Vasileos	723 2771–2	
Israel	1 Marathonodromou	671 9530–1	
Italy	2 Sekeri	361 1723	①–⑤ 09.00–11.00
Japan	2–4 L. Messoghion	775 8101–3	
Netherlands	5–7 L. Vas. Konstantinou	723 9701–4	
New Zealand	15–17 An. Tsoha	641 0311–15	①–⑤ 09.00–13.00
Norway	7 L. Vas. Konstantinou	724 6173–4	
South Africa	124 Kifissias & Iatridou	692 2125	
Spain	29 Vassilissis Sofias	721 4885	
Sweden	7 L. Vas. Konstantinou	729 0421	
Switzerland	2 Iassiou	723 0364–6	
UK	1 Ploutarchou	723 6211–19	①–⑤ 08.00–13.30
USA	91 Vassilissis Sofias	721 2951–9	①–⑤ 08.30–17.00

UK Consulates

Corfu	2 Alexandras	☎ (0661) 30055, 37995
Patras	2 Votsi	☎ (061) 227 329
Rhodes	23 25th Martiou	☎ (0241) 27247, 27306
Thessalonika	8 Venizelou, Eleftheria Sq.	☎ (031) 278 006, 269 984

Since 1993 EU nationals with ID cards have not been required to carry passports within the EU. As the UK has no ID card scheme, UK nationals must continue to travel with a passport. All nationals are recommended to carry passports as they are often required when cashing traveller's cheques or exchanging money in Greece. Passports are always required when taking day excursions to Turkey.

National Tourist Organisation of Greece

One valuable source of information worth tapping before you go to Greece is the Greek tourist service. Usually known by the initials NTOG outside the country and EOT within Greece, their offices provide advice and information on all aspects of the country. Most important for island hoppers are the ferry timetables (see p. 41). There are branches in most major countries including:

UK
4 Conduit Street, London, W1R 0DJ
☎ (0171) 734 5997

Australia
51 Pitt Street. Sydney, NSW2000
☎ (02) 241 1663

Canada
1300 Bay Street. Main Level, Toronto
☎ (416) 968 2220

Money

While it is desirable to have some hard cash always to hand, the safest way of hanging on to your money is to take the bulk in Travellers Cheques (Thomas Cook MasterCard Travellers Cheque 24-hour UK emergency number: ☎ 00 44 1733 502 995). American Express (emergency number: ☎ 00 44 1273 696933) are also well represented in the islands, with a Travel Centre in central Athens (see p. 99). Travellers Cheques, along with Eurocheques, are accepted by banks in Greece (Eurocheques, despite their name, are also accepted in Cyprus, Israel and Turkey). Outside banking hours currency

and cheques can be exchanged at ticket agencies (albeit at a worse rate of exchange). Every year tourist arrive armed with cash cards only to discover that cash dispensing machines are a rarity except on the very popular islands. You are strongly advised to ensure that you have access to your cash via other means (Travellers Cheques remain the most versatile way of carrying money). However you choose to take your funds don't keep them all in one place (this way, if you are robbed you will still have something to fall back on).

Greek banknotes come in 5,000, 1,000, 500, 200 and 100 Drachma denominations; the latter now being replaced by coins. All the nations of the Eastern Med. are 'blessed' with relatively high inflation and running devaluations in exchange rates. This tends to work in the tourist's favour, as there is usually a positive depreciation in the relative value of these currencies against stronger western currencies. Tourist exchange rates to the GB Pound Sterling (US$ 1.62, € 0.704, DM 2.69) at the start of 1999 were:

Cyprus [Pound]	CY£	0.796
Greece [Drachma]	GRD	452.4
Italy [Lira]	ITL	2671.0
Israel [Shekel]	NIS	6.418
Turkey [Lira]	TKL	503799.0

Travelling to Greece

How you get to Greece is going to be largely determined by the nature of your holiday. If you want to maximize your time in the islands the best way is to fly (see overleaf); possibly plugging into the Greek domestic air system (see p. 27) in order to get a flying start. If you doing the European tour then rail (see p. 29) or a combination of train and ferry (the whole of chapter one of this book is devoted to international ferry services) is the most popular route. International bus services have also been popular in the past, but have declined with the Bosnian war.

Flights to Greece
The great majority of visitors to Greece now choose to arrive and depart by air; the market is dominated by a mix of short-haul Charter Flights (most from Europe) and long haul regular services focusing on count-ries with significant ethnic Greek immi-grant populations (the two largest being the USA and Australia).

European Charter Flights
Cheap charter flights from Europe are the most popular (and cheapest) way for island hoppers to get to Greece. Because they are 'piggy-backing' on holiday flights, travellers opting to fly this way have to accept certain limitations. The most important of these are that once booked, these flights cannot be changed, and most require you to return a fortnight later (though with a bit of effort you can find operators who will offer you a 28-day return flight only ticket). Once you are in Greece there is a further dangerous potential pitfall: because charter tickets are cheap concessionary tickets aimed at encouraging tourism to Greece, it is usual condition of issue that you do not stay overnight out of the country. This is particularly relevant should you be tempted to take one of the day-tripper boats or ferries to Turkey. You are likely to be denied your flight home should you — for any reason — be forced to stay overnight there.

Despite recent cut-backs in the number of charter holiday on offer, even in High Season it is possible to visit a Thomas Cook Flight Centre or other travel agent and pick up a last minute return charter flight ticket from around UK£180/US$240. At other times of the year you can do even better with some tickets costing under UK£100/US$150.

Apart from flights to Athens, there are UK and European connections to 17 Greek airports. However, most are of limited use to the would be ferry user. On an island hopping holiday the arrival/departure point is an important consider-ation, since you will have to plan your movements with a view to getting back there. Of the various destinations avail-able, **Athens** remains the safest in this respect, since its port of Piraeus is access-ible on a daily basis from most islands in the Aegean. Naturally, the Cycladic isl-ands of **Mykonos** and **Santorini** are also good starting points (though flights to both are apt to be more expensive than elsewhere) and Crete has a useful and popular airport at **Iraklion** (and to a lesser extent **Chania**) as well. Other regional airports tend to restrict the wider island hopping options available, though the Dodecanese island chain is well served with frequent flights to **Kos** and **Rhodes** — both islands with regular connections with the Cyclades (albeit with long 12-hour sailing times).

Other destinations are often better avoided if you are only in Greece for a fortnight as they do not connect as well into the ferry system. **Samos** and **Skiathos** are the best placed of these and worth considering if you are not planning to venture too far, but **Kavala (Keramoti)** and **Thessalonika** can be hard to return to quickly and shouldn't be considered unless you are planning to pick up a re-turn flight elsewhere. The isolated Ionian group is better served by aircraft than ferries with charter flights to **Corfu**, **Kefal-onia**, **Lefkada (Preveza)** and **Zante**, the first two of which offer starting points for viable small scale island hopping holi-days. Finally, a small number of charter flights also operate to **Patras (Araxos)** and poorly connected **Karpathos** and **Limnos**, but these are not served by all tour operators.

One-way Student/Youth Charter Fli-ghts also operate from the UK and other European destinations. These offer the possibility of staying in Greece over the

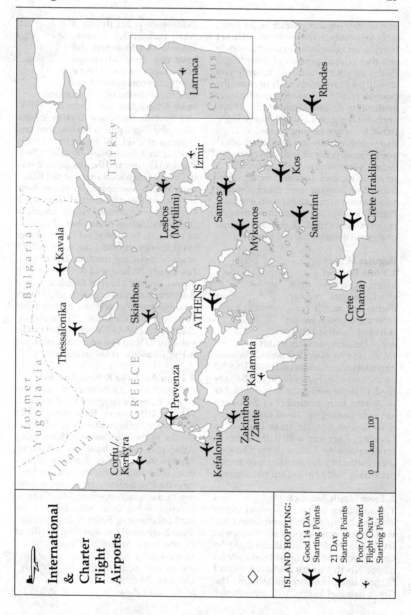

International & Charter Flight Airports

ISLAND HOPPING:

✈ Good 14 Day Starting Points

✈ 21 Day Starting Points

✈ Poor/Outward Flight ONLY Starting Points

one month regular charter flight limit, since you can buy a one-way return ticket (ferry ticket agencies in Greece also widely sell the 'return' portion of these flight deals) at your leisure — though you should take care to buy early or avoid the popular end-of-August flights when seat availability declines dramatically. If you are holidaying on a 2-week charter flight ticket it cannot be emphasised enough that you should always plan to be back at your arrival point at least one clear day before your return flight, otherwise a ferry strike, bad weather, or an over-booked or missing ferry could result in your having to buy an expensive regular flight home via one of the three airports in with scheduled flights to Europe (Athens, Thessalonika and Corfu).

Regular Flights
1. From Europe:

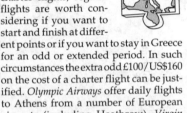

More expensive than charter flights, regular flights are worth con-sidering if you want to start and finish at differ-ent points or if you want to stay in Greece for an odd or extended period. In such circumstances the extra odd £100/US$160 on the cost of a charter flight can be just-ified. *Olympic Airways* offer daily flights to Athens from a number of European airports (including Heathrow). *Virgin Atlantic* also operate from London to Greece in a big way with daily flights to Iraklion and to Athens (from Gatwick and Heathrow). *Easyjet* also operate cut-price daily flights from Luton to Athens.

2. From North America:

The numbers wishing to travel direct between North America and Greece are well down compared with European levels: as a result the only direct flights to Greece are to Athens (as yet there are no direct North America—Greek island flights) and prices are quite high. The Greek national airline, *Olympic Airways*

(address on p. 28), fly out of New York (JFK), Boston, Toronto and Montreal and have one great advantage over other carriers in being able to offer connecting dom-estic flights to the islands from the same Athens terminal. Delta and TWA also fly daily from New York to Athens.

Regular flight return tickets often cost in access of US$1,200 during the summer months; as a result many travellers fly to Western Europe and then make their way to Greece (via a local flight or rail ticket) from there. Low Season fares are more reasonable (usually around US$800). If Greece is your desired North American flight destination (a number of carriers offer flights to Athens via East Coast or West European cities) there are several ways of reducing the financial pain: 1. Book early (tickets sold well in advance attract slightly cheaper fares). 2. Buy a discounted regular or charter flight ticket (taking care to check just exactly what you are getting). 3. Under 24s can pick up cheaper special APEX tickets that can be valid for as long as a year (though travel in High Season is usually not encouraged).

2. From Australia & New Zealand:

Although the total number of visitors to Greece from the southern hemisphere is substantially lower than from North America, there is a wider choice of carrier thanks to the number of airlines using Athens as a long-haul stop-off point. *Olympic Airways* offer flights to Athens from Brisbane, Melbourne and Sydney, most involve two stop-offs—and usually one of these includes Bangkok. *Olympic Airways* flights from New Zealand are via Melbourne or Sydney. In past years there have also been less frequent direct flights from Australia. Other major carriers operating to the region include *KLM*, *Quantas*, *Singapore Air-lines* and *Gulf Air*.

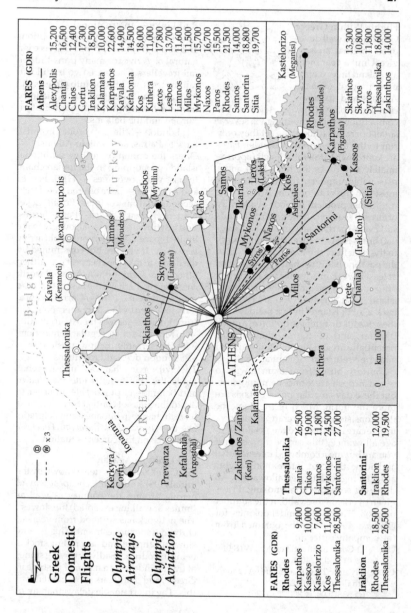

Flights Within Greece
Greece has a well devel-
oped internal air ser-
vice. Until a year or so
ago island links were a
monopoly of *Olympic
Airways* and its asso-
ciated company *Olympic Aviation*, but
competition is now emerging via several
small operators (though as yet they only
run to the more popular islands). Fares
are kept down to tolerable levels (approx-
imately five times the ferry fare) and a
reasonable number of flights are on offer;
most run direct to or from Athens. The
traditional problem of poor availability
of aircraft seats on all the popular islands
still exists (particularly in July and August) but is likely to ease. This could work
to the benefit of the island hopper, as in
the past one has often had to book flights
at least a week in advance via the airline
offices to be found amidst the plethora of
island ticket agents. If you are trying to
pack a lot of islands in to a holiday then
these flights do offer the option of a quick
transfer, and of course, they offer a
potentially invaluable lifeline if you need
a hurried return to the capital.

Courtesy buses from main towns to
island airports were once commonplace,
but these days regular buses or taxis are
more the norm. Much of the domestic
fleet consists of light aircraft, so you have
to take care not to exceed the 15 kilo baggage allowance (this can be a problem if
you are buying a combined international
and domestic ticket: international flights
attract a higher baggage allowance). All
domestic seats are non-smoking. Prices
given overleaf were valid in the summer
of 1998. Timetables and bookings for
Olympic Airways can be obtained from
the company office at:

UK: 11 Conduit Street, London, W1R 0LP
       (☎ 0171 409 2400).
USA: Olympic Towers, 645 Fifth Avenue,
       6th floor, NY 10022
       (☎ 838 3600, ☎ 800 223 1226).

Rail Links — International
Thanks to the many sightseeing options
and its geographical position, Greece is a
natural objective for many trans-Europe
rail travellers. There are two traditional
rail routes from Europe into Greece: the
first (and now most popular) is via ferry
from Italy, the second is through Eastern
Europe and the Balkans.

1: London—Milan—Ancona/Brindisi:
ferry to Patras, and train to Athens.
Offers the option of visiting additional
islands by stopping in the Ionian chain.
In past years two lines — HML Ferries
and Adriatica — have offered free 'Deck'
accommodation to Inter/Eurail ticket
holders on their Brindisi—Patras ferries.
You just turn up at the boat; but given the
limited space available, you should arrive
very early. If you are not constrained by
the desire to take the cheapest route, then
other more scenic options are well worth
considering. Perhaps the best of these the
combination of a Patras/Corfu—Venice
ferry followed by the daily afternoon train
from Venice — across the Austrian Alps
— to Munich and its regular connections
with Paris, Hamburg and Amsterdam.

2: London overland to Athens.
The civil war in what was Yugoslavia has
made the traditional route via Venice
and Belgrade impracticable. In order to
avoid the areas of conflict travellers now
have to change in Budapest and Belgrade.
See the *Thomas Cook European Timetable*
for advice on the current situation.

Rail Links — Aegean
The Greek railway system (known by the
initials OSE) offers the cheapest way of
getting around the country as well as
(mules or walking excepted) the slowest.
The network has suffered from years of
chronic under investment. This is now
slowly changing, and new rolling stock is
being introduced. Sadly, throwing stones
at train windows is a national pastime in
Greece, and many cars show evidence of
this. The interminable delays that are to

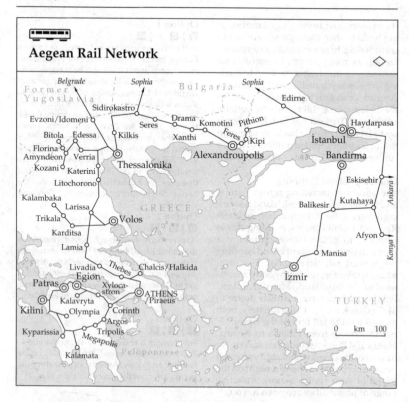

Aegean Rail Network

be encountered when travelling are also a serious disincentive. Most of the system is single track; so trains have to keep stopping to allow oncoming trains to clear the line (it is not unknown for flies to travel down a carriage by hopping in and out of windows as a train crawls along). Timetables are often as much theoretical as factual — the Thessalonika—Larissa/Volos service has been known to leave up to an hour before its stated departure time—and are invariably crowded. Intercity trains are somewhat better, but fewer in number.

In an effort to drum up more tourist custom the OSE have introduced three rail passes. The most useful is the *Vergina Flexipass*. This is for periods of 3, 5, or 10 days travel, and the pass includes other features to increase its appeal (these include accommodation and a city tour of Athens and a one day cruise to Aegina, Poros and Hydra). The second pass is the *Greek Flexipass*. This offers 1st class rail travel for 3 or 5 days. The final pass is the *Greek Flexipass Rail'n Fly* which offers a combination of rail travel and coupons for *Olympic Airways* domestic flights to the islands. This sounds a good idea, though it isn't clear how these coupons can be honoured if a flight is fully booked (as many are).

If you are on a wide-ranging island hopping holiday then these passes are worth considering. In any event the rail system, for all its many faults, is useful, and provides an invaluable back-up to missing ferries when travelling in the Northern Aegean, or in moving between ports on the Peloponnese. Likewise, the equally antiquated Turkish rail link from İzmir up to İstanbul offers a back-up option to the increasingly limited number of ferries running up the Turkish Aegean coast.

One Stop Island Hopping

The appeal of travelling across Europe and hopping on to a Greek island is seemingly very great if the numbers of Inter-Rail and Eurail card users doing this is anything to go by. However, time is a problem since days spent island hopping are wasted rail ticket days. The ideal island is therefore one with good connections to the mainland. Many mainland holiday makers have a similar desire to 'do' a Greek island. Unfortunately, both groups tend to fall foul of the rip-off '3-Island' cruises from Piraeus to Aegina, Hydra and Poros; islands that are largely devoid of the Greek island atmosphere. If you are prepared to spend a night on the island of your choice a more attractive range of possibilities are open to you:

Option 1
1) 2 +) 4 ?

Rail travellers arriving in Greece via Eastern Europe tend to head straight for Athens and then worry about finding a boat once there. Escape the crowds by abandoning your train corridor at Larissa. Frequent connections to Volos will see you a mere three hours from Skiathos — one of the most attractive Greek islands. Daily sea links with Thessalonika mean that you can jump from there as well or return to Eastern Europe without retracing your rail journey. Day trips from Athens are another way to do Skiathos; but the island deserves more time than this. Save a day for hops to neighbouring Skopelos and Alonissos.

Option 2
3) 5) 7

As everybody stops off at Athens it is inevitable that most island-hoppers tend to start from Piraeus and that means a wide choice of possible destinations. Paros is the easiest island to get to. A second day can be spent on Santorini before hopping back to Piraeus overnight.

Option 3
5) 6) 7

For those in a real hurry: Athens then on to Patras stopping over on Corfu for a day before heading on to Italy. Again a popular stopping point with travellers in either direction.

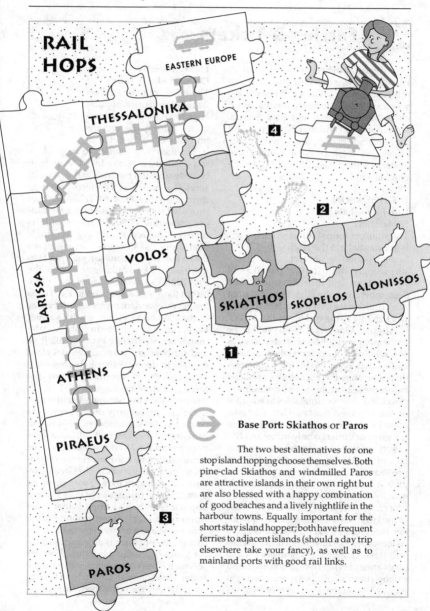

RAIL HOPS

EASTERN EUROPE

THESSALONIKA

4

2

VOLOS

SKIATHOS   SKOPELOS   ALONISSOS

LARISSA

1

ATHENS

PIRAEUS

3

PAROS

Base Port: Skiathos or Paros

The two best alternatives for one stop island hopping choose themselves. Both pine-clad Skiathos and windmilled Paros are attractive islands in their own right but are also blessed with a happy combination of good beaches and a lively nightlife in the harbour towns. Equally important for the short stay island hopper, both have frequent ferries to adjacent islands (should a day trip elsewhere take your fancy), as well as to mainland ports with good rail links.

Ferries & Tickets

Having established which group of islands you want to visit and how you intend travelling to Greece, the next thing you need to take on board are the differences between High and Low Season, ferry, hydrofoil and tour boat types, and the vagaries of the Greek ferry ticket system, as these all have a substantial impact on the ease with which you can more around.

HIGH SEASON
Late June—Late September

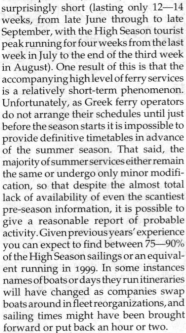

The summer tourist influx is substantial but the High Season period is, in fact, surprisingly short (lasting only 12—14 weeks, from late June through to late September, with the High Season tourist peak running for four weeks from the last week in July to the end of the third week in August). One result of this is that the accompanying high level of ferry services is a relatively short-term phenomenon. Unfortunately, as Greek ferry operators do not arrange their schedules until just before the season starts it is impossible to provide definitive timetables in advance of the summer season. That said, the majority of summer services either remain the same or undergo only minor modification, so that despite the almost total lack of availability of even the scantiest pre-season information, it is possible to give a reasonable report of probable activity. Given previous years' experience you can expect to find between 75—90% of the High Season sailings or an equivalent running in 1999. In some instances names of boats or days they run itineraries will have changed as companies swap boats around in fleet reorganizations, and sailing times might have been brought forward or put back an hour or two.

LOW SEASON
October—Early June

There is a lot to be said for travelling out of the popular High Season period, particularly during the months immediately either side of it, but there is a penalty to be paid, as ferry activity is at a reduced level, with considerable fluctuations in the times of services—and indeed the ferries running them. Low Season Port Tables are not provided simply because in most instances travelling between the islands is merely a matter of catching the single boat every 24/48 hours running up or down the major chains (a rough guide to the likely links available is to take the Port Table Connections Maps and ignore all but the 6—7 days per week links). Times are very dependent on sea conditions, as is the likelihood of any of the smaller boats running; with hydrofoil and catamaran services barely extant at all. June and October are particularly awkward months to describe simply because services are either expanding during the former, or running down in the latter.

During the Low Season reliability also declines. This is partly due to poorer sea conditions (as late as the end of May you can encounter storms that will leave ships port-bound for 24 hours), but economic factors also come into play. Ferry companies are granted licences by the Greek government provided they (i) operate on an annual basis, (ii) regularly visit the less popular islands. The result is that boats run very profitably for four months of the year and at a loss for the remainder. Even though the operator is able to minimize his losses by running a reduced winter service it is very tempting to have a ferry suffer a 'mechanical' failure from time to time, thereby reducing them further.

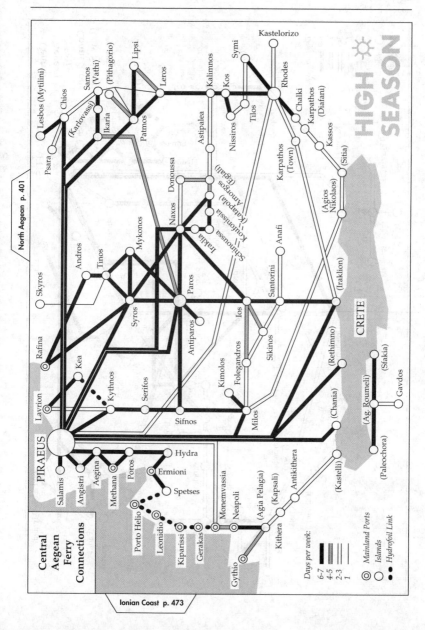

HIGH SEASON

North Aegean p. 401

Central Aegean Ferry Connections

CRETE

Ionian Coast p. 473

Days per week:
6-7
4-5
2-3
1

◎ Mainland Ports
○ Islands
• • • Hydrofoil Link

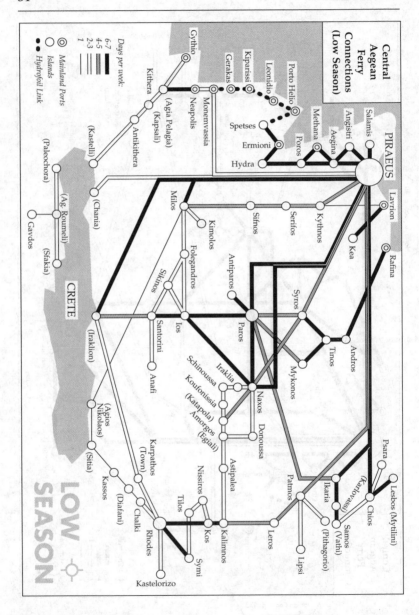

Car Ferries

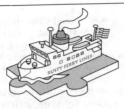

Of the 100-odd larger car ferries licensed to operate in Greek waters, some 50 are engaged on international routes, with the rest operating around the islands. International ferries are on a par with those operating cross-Channel services a few years ago and are slightly better than their domestic counterparts with duty-free shops, swimming pools (filled), and the all-important deck-class shower. Accommodation options range from cabins (prices vary according to the number of berths and their position in the ship), lounges with aircraft-style seats (Pullman class) and basic deck-class facilities (i.e. saloons and open decks).

Most of the large Greek domestic ferries operate out of Piraeus, providing either a daily service (returning overnight) or (if venturing further afield) running a thrice-weekly service. These services tend to be reliable (this means to within 2—3 hours of their scheduled arrival time); the most likely cause of disruption coming from the annual one day strike each summer. Even so, this is normally confined to the daily Piraeus departures/arrivals rather than ferries already at sea. Normally there are a few days' warning of a strike, though unless you hear of it on the grapevine the chances are that you will only find out when you go to buy your ticket.

Conditions on domestic ships vary widely. You can take it for granted that pools will be empty, deck-class showers locked, and that the vessel will have its name in English on the bow and in Greek on the stern. Otherwise anything goes. Class distinctions are somewhat arbitrary, with facilities classed as 'deck' on the better ships classified as 2nd or 'tourist' on the less good. Classes are segregated pretty strictly on board most vessels via a combination of locked doors and barred gates. Unfortunately, there is no similar distinction made between smoking and non-smoking areas (the latter being totally unknown). With a 'deck' ticket you can expect the seating to be divided pretty equally between interior saloons (complete with TVs) and the outside upper decks (where plastic-moulded park bench style seats welded to the deck are the norm). For those who choose to go by 2nd class, cabin accommodation is also on offer on all large boats (prices are comparable to C-class hotel rates); and can be booked when you buy your ticket. Food and drink facilities are always on offer, though this will vary from self-service cafeterias to a hatch providing (along with the all-pervasive smell of burnt cheese) soft drinks, beer, biscuits, toasted sandwiches and microwaved floppy things the locals call pizzas. All foodstuffs are more expensive than those ashore.

If you want more detailed ferry information (previous names, capacity, lengths etc.) you will find most listed in Geoffrey Hamer's excellent *Trip Out in Southern Europe* — available from 'Trip Out', PO Box 1287, London, W4 3LG: £4.40.

Landing Craft Ferries

In sheltered waters where car ferries are needed on short haul routes (usually mainland to island links) small 'Landing Craft' type vessels predominate. The large ferry operators don't have an interest in these local craft, which can carry anything from four to forty vehicles. Passengers are accommodated in the cabin decks at the stern of the ship. These vessels only offer deck-class seats. The bigger boats have a bar. Usually running all year round, High Season sees occasional fights among motorists over the limited space available. In the case of the really small boats, passenger tickets are normally bought on board.

Hydrofoils

Known throughout Greece as 'Dolphins' (i.e. *Delphini*), there are now some 60 of these craft operating in Greek waters. Travelling at twice the speed of the average ferry, they each carry around 140 passengers. Very much fair weather craft, they require reasonably calm sea conditions and so tend to confine visits to islands in more sheltered waters. Consequently services are greatly reduced out of High Season. Rarely operating in the winter or out of daylight hours (their hulls are not strong enough to cope with chance collisions with large pieces of flotsam), they are a fast (if noisy) way of rattling around the Aegean.

All these boats are fitted-out with aircraft-style seats divided between bow, central and rear cabins. The rear cabins (complete with WCs) sometimes have a bar where the crew socialize. As a rule, the further back you go the less bumpy the ride: an important consideration given that these boats often bring out the worst among those inclined to sea-sickness. Between the central and rear cabins there is usually a small open deck over the engine. Here you can stand and admire the view — provided you can cope with the noise, the petrol fumes and (when underway) the 'riding a kicking mule' sensation and occasional cascades of surf. Easily the best seats on a hydrofoil lie at the stern: here there is a small open deck complete with a popular seat offering the smoothest ride and panoramic views.

With tickets (always bought in advance from agencies: they are not on sale on the quayside) costing the equivalent of a 2nd class ferry ticket, it is rare for hydrofoil companies to compete against each other: the market just isn't strong enough. As a result, the standard of service is rather patchy. CERES is the largest line in Greece and have an excellent reputation; offering well thought out timetables published for the year and a good record for reliability and continuity of services between years. Other lines tend to operate in less hospitable areas and are less consistent, with timetables that are only available for the month in hand, if at all, and major variations in their itineraries and schedules each year. In short, you can assume that CERES boats will be operating, but the Port Table entries for other lines are best treated as 'optimistic' projections of what might be around!

Catamarans

The last decade has seen half a dozen of these vessels arrive in the Aegean; several with car-carrying facilities. Offering a fast ride in flat seas and — with the smaller boats — a slow, stomach-churning roll in anything else, they remain very much summer boats. In the past they have not been viewed with much favour by the Greek government as they were seen to siphon off ferry profits during the High Season, but now their numbers are growing steadily, and more on the way. Fares are normally on a par with hydrofoils (except for the odd rare excursion catamarans which are very expensive). The larger catamarans have superior aircraft-style seating and TVs.

Passenger Boats

Increasingly operated as purely tourist boats, these craft range from small car ferry-sized vessels to converted fishing boats known as caïques. Less strike-prone than the large ferries, their main bane are the seas whipped-up by the *meltemi* wind in the summer months and the generally more volatile conditions during the rest of the year. They do, however, provide a useful adjunct to the larger boats though you will encounter wide disparities in fares depending on their 'ferry' or 'tourist boat' status (the latter can be used for one-way island hopping if you are prepared to pay for a return ticket). Some larger 'passenger' boats can also accommodate 2 or 3 cars, or more commonly, motorbikes.

Ticket Agents
In the absence of any central ferry ticket issuing or information authority, ticket agents are to be found at every port, usually occupying offices in buildings near the quay or along the seafront they also frequently offer exchange facilities (albeit at a higher rate of commission), room finding services, and occasionally, unsecured luggage deposit facilities to ticket purchasers. Hours are variable (an attractive feature if you need to change money or cheques out of banking hours) and are often determined by the arrival times of the boats. In Greece most agencies will open up for a short time to sell tickets during the night if a boat is due; however, you cannot count on this, and with the advent of computer ticketing (taking away the option of being able to buy tickets on board ferries) the wisest course of action is to make a habit of buying your ticket from an agent during office hours.

Ticket agents are the only people who seem to thrive on the apparent chaos of the ferry system. Many would argue that they are largely responsible for it. Inevitably they are very keen to relieve you of your money and you should enter an agency with eyes open. The vast majority of passengers do, however, use them without any difficulty. When dealing with an agent bear in mind that:

1. It is rare for a ticket agent to sell tickets for all the vessels calling at a port. The schedules they advertise are therefore incomplete and many will lie blatantly in order to get custom by telling you that their boat is the fastest, next, or the only available. A common dodge is to advertise arrival rather than departure times if this will put 'their' boat ahead of a rival agent's.

2. As fares are regulated by the government there is no difference in the prices ticket agents are able to charge. Any agent's claim that their deck-class tickets are cheaper is rubbish. Another dodge is to advertise prices omitting the port tax and VAT to entice the unwary inside.

3. Outright attempts to sell tourists something they don't want are rare, but do occur; either by selling a higher class ticket than the basic 'deck' fare, or selling a ticket for a boat other than the one wanted, without telling the customer (usually because they don't act for that boat). In vary rare instances tourists have been sold tickets a boat that has just departed.

You can prevent most of these problems by checking that the class, ferry's name, and departure time are on the ticket. Of course, the easiest way of avoiding all problems is to establish which ferry you want before you approach the agent and then simply ask for a ticket for that boat.

International Tickets
International ferry travel in the Eastern Mediterranean is comparatively expensive. This is due to the longer distances involved, the much higher port taxes international boats attract (currently around £5 / US$8 per person and also per vehicle), and partly because in some instances you are obliged to buy a bunk or aircraft-type seating as a minimum rather than a deck ticket. Various discounts are available, depending on the operator. These range from a Student discount (20%), Return ticket discount (5%) — usually advertised as a 10% discount, but in fact only given on the cost of the return part of the ticket — Group concessions (usually 15% for nine or more), as well as reduced Low Season fares. In addition a number of lines operating to Greece offer 'Stop-over'

tickets allowing you to break the journey along the way (though they are quick to point out that during the High Season re-embarkation on a particular boat cannot be guaranteed). However, it is rare for you to be able to travel between two ports in the same country using international boats except as a designated 'stop over' on an international ticket. Fares also tend to be structured on a country to country basis so, for example, if you travel from Greece to Cyprus, the ticket will usually cost the same if you start from Piraeus or a port en route such as Rhodes.

Greek Domestic Tickets
1. Computer Ticketing

Until 1998 it was possible to buy tickets from quayside vendors or on the ferry itself as well as from regular ticket agents. This inevitably led to safety problems as there was no check on the numbers boarding a ferry. Ferry operators were happy to turn a blind eye to this as the odd thousand passengers over official capacity didn't hurt revenues, besides sparing them the expense of buying add-itional vessels to cover the shortfall in capacity during the short High Season period. Things changed in 1995 after a couple of highly publicized incidents of chronic overloading: first, when the C/F *Marina*'s captain received a five-month prison sentence for sailing during the Easter rush with 2,700 passengers aboard (her licensed capacity is 1,447); second, when the C/F *Express Olympia* (licensed capacity 1,200) had her captain arrested at Piraeus on the 31st of July for trying to sail with 2,725 passengers on board. These incidents called into question ferry safety standards in Greece besides attracting damaging international publicity, with the result that a Presidential Decree was issued, requiring ferry operators to bring in a computer ticket system by March 31, 1996 that would ensure that ferries were not overloaded. After protests from ferry operators the start date for the system

was put back, but it is now in force (though you will still find agents selling tickets without phoning the line or using a computer terminal to get an official seat/berth number). To sum up the changes:

1. Passengers can no longer board a ferry without a valid ticket (at all large ports the Port Police are now checking passengers have valid tickets before they board). You should therefore buy a ticket before you arrive at the quay.

2. At the height of the High Season travellers should no longer expect to be able to just jump on the next boat to their desired destination. If the island or ticket agent has used up its allocation of tickets for that boat other would-be passengers will be stuck. Given that ferry operators have traditionally ignored licensed passenger capacities on their boats in order to carry the numbers who want to travel in peak season, this opens up the serious possibility that this summer could see significant numbers of island hoppers facing delays (and possibly missing flights home) as a result. In High Season it is therefore highly advisable to buy the ticket for both the next stage and the final stage of your journey as soon as you have decided what they will be (particularly if your hop would be via a small boat). This will also give you the maximum available time to consider your other options should your chosen ferry be full.

3. Some companies did manage to get computer ticketing up and running in 1996: this highlighted a number of problems, not least of which was double-booking to ensure the ferry sailed fully loaded. If by any chance you are sold a non-computer ticket (this is conceivably possible on some of the smaller islands) be warned you could have to surrender your place should someone else arrive with a computer-generated ticket (this situation could also occur if you buy a basic deck ticket and then seek to upgrade it — as many do — to a berth, once you have boarded an overnight ferry).

International High Season 'Deck' Fares

Long Haul:	UK£	US$	Italy—Greece:	UK£	US$
Ancona—Turkey	62	99	Ancona—Patras	38	61
Brindisi—Turkey	41	66	Bari—Corfu	24	39
Limassol—Haifa	26	42	Bari—Patras	26	42
Limassol—Rhodes	28	45	Brindisi—Corfu	23	37
Piraeus—Haifa	50	80	Brindisi—Igoumenitsa	18	29
Piraeus—Limassol	34	55	Brindisi—Patras	22	35
Rhodes—Haifa	26	42	Trieste—Patras	38	61
Rhodes—Limassol	30	48	Venice—Patras	40	64

Domestic Inter-Island 'Deck' Fares (GDR)

3,400	4,560	4,980	5,740	6,830	8,690	7,360	7,980	9,840	•	**Rhodes**
Kos	1,480	2,200	2,900	4,240	4,550	5,160	6,170	7,625	•	**Kos**
Kalimnos		1,950	2,600	3,970	3,780	5,000	6,010	7,440	•	**Kalimnos**
Leros			1,650	3,580	•	4,930	5,460	7,440	•	**Leros**
Patmos				2,980	3,950	4,400	5,070	7,670	•	**Patmos**
Thessalonika			**Samos**		4,280	3,075	4,250	6,950	•	**Samos**
Skiathos	4,500	**Skiathos**		**Paros**		•	•	•	•	**Paros**
Amorgos	•	•	**Amorgos**		**Chios**		3,420	5,550	7,650	**Chios**
Tinos	9,500	5,700	3,250	**Tinos**		**Lesbos**		4,540	6,600	**Lesbos**
Mykonos	9,800	5,800	3,180	1,200	**Mykonos**		**Limnos**		3,850	**Limnos**
Syros	8,580	5,500	3,580	1,100	1,550	**Syros**			**Kavala**	
Naxos	9,100	6,830	2,420	1,920	1,850	2,150	**Naxos**			
Paros	9,230	6,460	2,760	1,780	1,750	1,570	1,370	**Paros**		
Ios	10,000	7,400	4,440	3,370	3,300	3,830	2,950	2,480	**Ios**	
Santorini /Thira	10,110	8,430	4,620	4,170	3,550	4,150	3,090	3,080	1,700	**Thira**
Crete (Iraklion)	12,500	10,100	•	6,400	6,000	5,650	5,200	4,980	4,400	3,700

Piraeus–Island Fares (GDR)		
(Including port taxes and 8% VAT)		
PIRAEUS to:	Deck	C/M or H/F
Aegina	1,205	2,360
Amorgos	5,260	•
Anafi	6,940	•
Angistri	1,640	2,850
Astipalea	7,050	•
Chalki	9,870	•
Chios	5,770	•
Crete (Agios Nikolaos)	7,740	•
Crete (Chania)	5,850	•
Crete (Iraklion)	7,020	•
Crete (Rethimno)	7,050	•
Donoussa	5,030	•
Epidavros	1,800	3,920
Folegandros	5,340	•
Fourni	5,950	•
Hydra	2,425	4,450
Ikaria	4,900	•
Ios	5,400	•
Iraklia	5,575	•
Kalimnos	7,320	•
Karpathos	8,300	•
Kassos	8,150	•
Kastelorizo	8,300	•
Kea	•	5,250
Kimolos	4,690	9,165
Kithera	5,400	10,950
Kos	7,850	•
Koufonissia	4,850	•
Kythnos	3,200	6,200
Leros	6,670	•
Lesbos (Mytilini)	7,280	•
Milos	5,180	10,160
Monemvassia	•	9,500
Mykonos	5,260	10,300
Naxos	5,100	10,000
Neapoli	•	10,500
Nissiros	7,800	•
Paros	4,700	10,100
Patmos	7,090	•
Poros	2,180	4,300
Rhodes	9,330	•
Samos (Vathi)	6,930	•
Santorini / Thira	6,620	•
Schinoussa	5,100	•
Serifos	3,970	7,750
Sifnos	4,525	8,830
Sikinos	6,250	•
Spetses	3,330	5,950
Symi	9,050	•
Syros	4,580	8,950
Tilos	7,800	•
Tinos	4,900	8,950

2. Ticket Types

Tickets can be bought via the agencies to be found near every quayside or from kiosks on the quay itself. There are three classes on the larger vessels; 1st (Luxury), 2nd, and 3rd (Deck). Deck tickets are the norm and unless you state otherwise you can expect to be sold one. However, there also exists a less well defined 'Tourist' class ticket that is effectively a Deck ticket with a 20% surcharge. Some companies have used this in the past to charge more than the norm for a deck class ticket and this is the reason why there are price differences of several hundred Drachma between boats on some routes. Class numbers are indicated on the ticket using a letter and apostrophe numbering system derived from the classical Greek alphabet. The 'class' (ΘΕΣΙΣ / ΘΕΣΗ) is thus written accordingly: Α΄= 1st, Β΄= 2nd, and Γ΄= 3rd. Signs on ships all use this system. It is standard practice to issue one-way rather than return tickets; though the latter are available (at a saving of 10–15% of the cost of two single fares) provided you don't mind the inconvenience of being locked into using the same line's boats for your return. Groups of 10 or more also can get discounted tickets, and students can occasionally get discounts by waving their student cards at agents.

To date it has not been the practice to buy tickets for journeys unrelated to your starting point (e.g. one couldn't buy a ticket for travel from Paros to Naxos from an agent on Santorini); this is largely because agents on one island haven't had sufficient information about sailing times from other islands. This could well change with the advent of computer ticketing, and is worth looking out for. Past years have also seen a number of failed attempts by ferry operators to introduce a 'Greek Island Pass'. In past years the only ferry line regularly operating an island pass scheme has been Agapitos Express Ferries. Their 1998 passes were valid for two months and offered 4 hops (12,400 GDR),

5 hops (14,450 GDR), or 6 hops (16,150 GDR) using any of its boats. The down side was that passes were only on sale from one ticket agency at Piraeus (located on the main street side of the main ticket agency block). You will also need to confirm your travel arrangements at each port with the local company agent (which might not be easy if the agent anticipates selling his full allocation of tickets).

In Greece it is expected that you will pay for passenger ferry tickets in cash: credit cards are usually only accepted when buying international tickets. The tickets are not transferable to other lines and are only refundable if a ferry fails to arrive. In such instances, standing inside the office of the agent who sold you the ticket until they refund your money is the most effective way of getting it back.

Prices are preset for each island, though local port taxes differ. These are a matter of a few pence on domestic services. 6% VAT is also levied on all tickets in Greece. The average 3rd-class fare, when hopping to the next island down the line, is about £7/US$ 11. 2nd-class tickets cost 50–60% more than deck. 1st-class tickets are not bound by Government regulation so operators can charge what the market can bear. You can expect to pay double the 3rd-class fare. Children between 4 and 10 travel half-fare. Car rates average 4 or 6 times the cost of a deck ticket, depending on whether the length of the vehicle exceeds 4.5 m. Motorcycle rates also go according to size. For a sub-250cc machine the fare is similar to a deck ticket, larger machines are up to double that. However, bicycles are usually allowed free passage.

Excursion boats are not bound by government price regulation and usually charge about twice the regular ferry fare: often because you are buying a round trip (you don't have to use the return leg of your ticket if you are island hopping). Catamaran and hydrofoil ticket prices are Government regulated, with fares akin to 2nd-class ferry rates.

Sources of Ferry Information

Current information on international services can be gleaned from the *Thomas Cook European Timetable* and the *Thomas Cook Overseas Timetable*. A few international operators also have their timetables on web sites (see p. 598-9).

Finding valid times for Greek domestic services is another matter. Greece is an awkward country when it comes to obtaining timetables on the ground. In order to get the maximum information you will need to consult several sources:

(1). **The National Tourist Organisation of Greece** (addresses on p. 23) should be a priority port of call as they give out domestic ferry timetables. These are only distributed outside Greece and come either in the form of the booklet *Greek Travel Routes* (a summer timetable compiled each May) or photocopies of the timetables published in a monthly Greek trade-only publication: *Greek Travel Pages*. The information contained in both is identical (though it is not over easy to consult as ferries and routes are identified by a code system). A second problem is that operators are guaranteed to buy or move up to a dozen ferries between May and mid-summer, so the photocopies of the monthly timetables are far more accurate come August. In an effort to overcome this problem, the publisher of the *Greek Travel Pages* has established a new web site (address: www.gtpnet.com) that gives point-to-point timetables that are updated on a weekly basis.

(2). **In Greece** you will find most ticket agents only display information for their port or island. However, they will have a copy of the *Greek Travel Pages* that you can ask to see. Many also have a second — less comprehensive — timetable publication called *Hellenic Travelling*.

(3). **In Athens** there are additional sources of information. Foremost among these are the National Tourist Organisation of Greece (known locally as the EOT) ferry departure sheets — available from the central Athens (see p. 99) and airport tourist information centres. These contain a list (in English) of the domestic ferry departures from Piraeus to the islands (excluding hydrofoils and Saronic Gulf boats). Issued on a weekly basis, they run from Thursdays through to Wednesday. (Note: if you ask for ferry information in the latter half of this period you will only be given the 'back-half' of these pages.)

If you don't want to venture into central Athens or want information on other mainland port departures you can always do what the locals (and many ticket agents) do and resort to the city newspapers. The best of these is a business daily:

Η ΝΑΥΤΕΜΠΟΡΙΚΗ

which always has Piraeus departures for the following week (usually around p. 39) as well as limited information about departures from other mainland ports. If you are prepared to struggle with the Greek alphabet, it is worth the 200 GDR price and is on sale (before 10.00) at the newspaper kiosk in the Piraeus Metro station among others. Finally, several agents in the central ticket agency block at Piraeus display full departure lists in English inside their 'showrooms'. They also sometimes have ferry company timetables that you can take away.

(4). **On the islands** available information is usually confined to departure times for the island you are on. Sometimes company timetables are available and EOT offices (see individual island entries) also distribute lists of local ferry times. Some agents make up photocopy ferry timetables to augment the billboards to be found outside all agencies advertising boats and current times (these are usually in both English and Greek capitals). In the last resort you can always try the Port Police, who are guaranteed to have a complete list of the day's sailings as well as someone who can't speak English.

Ferry Safety
In the wake of the *Estonia* ferry disaster in the Baltic in September 1994 with the loss of over 1000 lives, the safety record of ro-ro (roll-on, roll-off) ferries has become an issue of considerable concern. As island hoppers largely depend on such vessels, some comments on the safety record of Greek ferries in general, and the pitfalls you could encounter using them are worth making here; not least because one Greek ferry — the *Poseidon Express* (see p. 128) — capsized in 1996 (fortunately without loss of life).

1. Operating Habits & Safety Record
The most encouraging thing one can say regarding Greek ferries is that the way local operators use ro-ro ferries, combined with the local climate, conspire against a major disaster occurring from similar causes. The argument that ro-ro ferries are inherently unsafe because of their liability to capsize if only a small amount of water reaches the car-deck is a formidable one, but against this must be set the fact that the use of ro-ro ferries in Greece make this sort of event a less likely prospect than in other parts of the world.

Both the *Estonia* and the earlier *Herald of Free Enterprise* disasters occurred because of water entering via open front car doors. It is virtually unheard of for a Greek ferry to use the front car door. The standard practice employed by all ro-ro ferries of backing, stern first, up to a quay and then loading cars and passengers via the rear door means that bow doors are rarely opened (except on occasions at Piraeus harbour in order to ventilate car decks when a ferry is idle). In the *Estonia* disaster heavy seas played a critical part in the sinking; causing the front car door to fall off. The Mediterranean is relatively calm most of the year, so door fittings designed for much harsher North Atlantic sea conditions (most large ferries are ex-North European or Japanese boats) are not subjected to the same sort of strains.

This is not to say that Greek ferries are wholly without problems. Age does take its toll (the *Estonia* — built in 1980 — has been described as a ferry 'well into middle age'; yet, with one or two exceptions, every large ferry in the Greek fleet is older), and the last few years have seen several evacuations at sea due to engine room fires. This is the most common problem encountered with Greek boats (roughly one a year). This might seem a lot, but given the fact that Greece has the largest ferry fleet of any country in Europe (over 40% of the EU total), the country has a good safety record.

Of course, there is always room for improvement. It is regrettable that Greece, along with other Mediterranean nations, has opposed the proposed EU adoption of the safety recommendations following on from the *Herald of Free Enterprise* disaster because of the cost of modifying their elderly ferry fleets. Finally, the rigorously enforced class system on some boats means that locked through doors, and iron-gate sun-deck partitions (neither featuring in the original design for the ships in question) could hamper quick evacuations and should be relaxed.

2. Taking Precautions

Without going overboard about safety it is worthwhile taking a moment to consider what you would do if you have to go overboard in a hurry. After all, once you have found a seat, it only takes a couple of minutes to ascertain where the nearest life-jacket is, and, if you are inside, where the nearest exit points are. Those contemplating taking an overnight cabin should also take on board the fact that the chances of surviving a ferry capsize will be greatly reduced. Statistically, the chances of being involved in such an incident are minuscule, and on a day-to-day basis you are safe enough; though a number of — albeit

mundane — dangers unlikely to be encountered on a typical cross-Channel ferry do remain:

1. In order to facilitate rapid ferry turn-around, passenger embarkation/disembarkation is normally via the stern car door. Passengers are often 'invited' down on to the car deck before the ferry has docked, and are usually left standing among the vehicles while the mooring lines are secured. Vehicles are rarely secured to the car-deck — if the ferry was to collide with the quay or another boat, things could get very unpleasant.

2. The time of greatest danger for the foot passenger is when boarding or disembarking. Once mooring ropes are secured, and the stern door lowered, ferries keep their vulnerable stern away from the quay by maintaining sufficient 'slow forward' propulsion to keep their mooring ropes taut. This means that the lowered door is apt to slide along the surface of the quay while passengers are stepping on or off — occasionally trapping feet in the process. When you are caught in a pushing crowd of locals and backpackers (the concept of 'queueing' is unknown in this part of the world) this can become a major hazard, particularly as vehicles load and disembark along with the foot passengers.

3. The lowering/raising cables on the door should also be treated with considerable caution. Get a backpack snagged on one of those in a pushing crowd and as likely as not you'll end up in the water next to those turning propellers.

4. At the height of the summer ferry crews will try to cram everyone on board — even if it means opening up areas of the ship you would not normally expect to find passenger access. The bow deck (complete with anchor chains, capstans, winches and other dangerous equipment) is a favourite alternative passenger deck. Anyone with children should check that areas containing kiddie-crushing contraptions are inaccessible before they are allowed to run free.

Holiday Essentials

Accommodation

Arguably the most challenging part of island hopping is finding accommodation once you arrive. But then this is part of the challenge of this sort of independent holiday. Generalisations on bed availability and price are difficult to make since much depends on when and where you arrive. But in High Season, whatever you are planning to do, it doesn't hurt to take a sleeping bag along so you can decamp to the local campsite should your luck be really out. That said, it is *very* rare to find island hoppers *forced* to resort to roughing it on one of the local beaches.

All types of accommodation are graded by the Greek government (via the NTOG /EOT). Unfortunately, an increasing number of establishments are operating without a licence, or doing their best to evade regulation by understating the number of rooms on offer, or proclaiming themselves to have a higher grade listing than their official one (thus enabling them to charge higher prices). A survey of 25 hotels on Santorini in 1994 showed that all had unlisted rooms and three no operating licence. Other islands produced similar statistics. As a result, some of the hotels mapped in this guide are shown without a class rating, and all those that are shown are given their listed class. Prices also vary greatly between accommodation in the same class group: a reflection of the hoteliers ability to levy additional charges and supplements (e.g. if you stay under three nights you can be charged an extra 10%). Breakfast sometimes must be paid for whether wanted or not. Regardless of where you stay, you should therefore try to ascertain exactly what your total bill will be when you

check in. It also never hurts to ask to see a room before you agree to take it. If you encounter any problems don't hesitate to call in the tourist police (usually the threat is enough to resolve disputes!). It is standard practice for all types of accommodation to hold on to your passport while you are in residence (see 'Scams' p. 56).

The accommodation options in Greece are divided between hotels, pensions, rooms in private houses, the odd youth hostel and numerous campsites.

1. Hotels:

These are categorized by the Greek government into six classes ranging from 'L' (Luxury), followed by 'A' through to 'E'. Prices are very good value by West European standards. Island hoppers usually find that most A to C category hotels are booked en bloc by package tour operators (though if you go in and ask they often have booked, but unoccupied, rooms available). D and E category hotels rely much more on independent clientele.

A-Class:

Singles: 18,000 – 35,000 GDR
Doubles: 24,000 – 45,000 GDR
Top quality rooms with prices to match. You can be virtually certain of finding air conditioning, en suite bathrooms with unlimited hot water, TVs in all rooms and full restaurant facilities within the building. On the down side, A-class hotels are comparatively rare on all but the major tourist islands and are usually inconveniently placed out of town so that they can take advantage of a nearby beach.

B-Class:

Singles: 16,000 – 24,000 GDR
Doubles: 28,000 – 34,000 GDR
Basically cut-down A-class hotels, B-class establishments are more common on the islands. They usually have en suite bathrooms and hot

water but TVs and air-conditioning are less common. Prices are often as high as A-class hotels. Former government-run quality hotels known as 'Xenias' usually fall into this category.

C-Class:
Singles: 10,000 – 20,000 GDR
Doubles: 13,000 – 29,000 GDR
Mid-range hotels offering reasonable rooms. Fairly common all over Greece, they are often the top dollar hotels of twenty years ago. En suite bathrooms are uncommon. No air-conditioning or restaurant facilities.

D-Class:
Singles: 4,000 – 7,000 GDR
Doubles: 5,000 – 10,000 GDR
Once you reach this level then shared bathrooms become the norm (most bedrooms have a sink — minus plug of course). Buildings tend to be much older; usually being converted turn-of-the-century mansions. Popular with backpackers and local Greeks, they offer good basic accommodation, usually close to town centres and ports.

E-Class:
Singles: 4,000 – 5,000 GDR
Doubles: 5,000 – 7,000 GDR
Bottom of the range and very variable. At their best E-class hotels are excellent family run establishments offering attractive clean rooms, at their very worst you will find saucers of rat poison on the landings. Hot water is rare and WCs are usually of the hole-in-the-floor type. Room keys will usually open half the doors in the building. In popular locations hoteliers offer backpackers roof space for a small sum.

Pensions:
Now the popular choice with island hoppers, pensions offer quality rooms at a reasonable price. Like hotels they are graded, but confusingly the grades are A to C and are rated one grade lower than the hotel equivalent (i.e. a B-class pension offers comparable rooms to a C-class

hotel). Clean rooms, usually sharing a bathroom, and with a refrigerator thrown in. Hot water is usually solar-generated; so is only available in the evenings. Friendly and helpful pension owners usually live in the building.

2. Rooms (Domatia):
Mainly on offer in High Season, rooms in private houses sup-up the thousands of independent travellers who haven't hotel accommodation and who don't want to camp. Morning ferries at most islands will be met by eager householders thrusting placards at you as you disembark, adorned with photographs of the room on offer and a price that makes a good starting point for negotiation. Other establishments simply have signs up advertising rooms and await the masses to come knocking on their door (the rooms marked on the town maps in this guide usually display a sign of some kind).

Conditions vary despite government regulation. Officially checked out *domatia* are slightly more expensive and have an EOT plaque on the door:
This is a fair guarantee of quality, as are the rooms advertised as 'Apartments'; which in the main are simply pricier rooms with an en suite bathroom and a refrigerator (though at the upper end of the scale you will find cooking and laundry facilities as well).

If you opt to take advantage of a quayside offer of a room establish exactly what you are getting while haggling over the price: e.g. Where *exactly* is it? (ask them to show you on the map). Is the price for one or two people? (get them to write it down to avoid future arguments). Has the room a private bathroom, shower, hot water?

Many ticket agencies also have lists of rooms and hotels and will push you in the direction of a bed. As with hotel accommodation, room availability does tend to dry up during the day and evening arrivals could have problems.

3. Youth Hostels:

Facilities are basic (i.e. grimy) but usually adequate for the needs of the night. Unlike the rest of Europe, Youth Hostels are something of a rarity in Greece outside the big mainland cities. YHA cards are rarely necessary, but are worth taking if you already have one to hand (though few youth hostels in Greece are recognised as the genuine article by official YHAs elsewhere in Europe). Only three islands have hostels: Crete (7), Santorini (4) and Corfu (2). All offer the cheapest, and therefore popular, 'roofed' option.

4. Campsites:

Most islands boast at least one campsite; the popular islands usually having three or four. Camping is very popular with island hoppers as it not only offers the  cheapest accommodation option, but a guaranteed place to stay in High Season. Competition between sites is intense and most have mini-buses that meet arriving ferries. As with hotels, prices are regulated. Sites are divided up into A, B and C classes. As a rough rule of thumb, trailer-park-type sites are usually A-class while the silent majority are B-class; it is only with the former that the price differential is apparent (most charge around 1300 GDR per person and 800 GDR per tent). Of more relevance are the differing High and Low Season rates: sites are apt to change these without informing campers of the transition (bar a notice at reception). As a result, every July some get caught out by the size of their bill. There is no recognised High Season start date so, sites up prices when they can. A limited number of island sites are signatories to the *Harmonie* and *Sunshine Camping Club* schemes, which offer 10%+ discounts to campers visiting other sites in each scheme (see individual site entries).

Site conditions vary according to the proximity to the port (the nearer, the poorer) and the amount of competition. The time of year can also make a vast difference. Most sites have some tree cover, a mini-market selling basics, and toilet and shower blocks (be prepared for shower doors that don't lock, and salt water at some sites). Where competition is particularly fierce, sites often offer discos and swimming pools as well.

Other characteristics shared by all sites are the bone-hard ground (short, strong tent pegs are strongly recommended) and bamboo roofed areas for the large number of 'sleeping bag sloanes'. Laundry and cooking areas (though the latter activity is rare), safety deposit facilities for valuables, and notice-boards for campers' messages, are also common to all. Outside of the main sites there is a fair amount of freelance camping — though this is technically illegal in Greece. Islands without official sites take a relaxed view of freelancers, and usually have a quiet beach where freelance camping is tolerated.

5. Sleeping on Ferries:

A good way of maximizing your island hopping opportunities, as well as saving on your accommodation bill, is to take over-night ferries wherever possible. All large ferries offer cabin facilities, though on the popular routes and at the peak season period early pre-booking is a necessity as cabins are very popular with travelling Greeks. The price of a night in a cabin obviously varies according to the length of your journey. In most cases a ticket will cost just under double the price of a deck ticket. Travelling on a simple deck ticket is also very popular despite the uncomfortable conditions. In High Season sun-decks and lounges become impromptu dormitories, though the former get quite wet and the latter become stuffy floating smoke holes.

Banks & Post Offices

Greek **banks** are open 08.00–13.00 Mondays to Fridays. On some of the small islands the bank doubles up with the post office, though banking hours remain the same. Through-the-wall cash machines are now arriving in Greece in numbers and all the major islands have at least one. However, if you are relying on cashcards you are likely to encounter problems on the smaller islands. Most islands now have banks — usually a branch of the main bank: the National Bank of Greece. Other banks are rarer: the Agricultural Bank and the Ionian Bank being the most common.

Post Offices (easily identified by their yellow signs showing a horn) are more common than banks. Regular hours are 07.30–13.30 Mondays to Fridays (though local times vary). Until 1996 post offices also served a residual banking role as they cashed Eurocheques. Unfortunately, this arrangement has come to an end thanks to changes to the post office licencing laws. It isn't clear if new arrangements will be put in place to restore the status quo ante this summer. Unless you hear otherwise, it would be wise to assume that Eurocheques can't be cashed in post offices (though some smaller islands with a bank seem to defy this rule); you should, however, still be able to buy stamps! Stamps can also be purchased from street kiosks and newsagents (with a 10% mark-up). Most post offices offer fax machines in addition to the usual poste restante and parcel services. It is normal in Greece to inspect the contents of parcels going abroad before accepting them, so don't seal them up in advance.

Beaches

One of the great attractions of the Greek islands is the abundance of excellent beaches; many conveniently placed near the main towns and ports. Most islands can boast at least one sand beach, and many are blessed with many — the best usually lying on the more protected south or west coasts. A large number of these enjoy Blue Flag status (a widely recognised endorsement of cleanliness), though this is no guarantee that they are as clean as they should be: abuse has occurred — notably at Lindos on Rhodes (see p. 358).

Although for the most part free and easy (going topless is the norm unless the beach is right in the centre of town), on several islands, where the town strand is the only good beach within easy distance, the EOT have turned them into pay beaches (entry usually costs around 200 GDR). They are always crowded, but are kept clean and have showers.

Nudism is very popular in Greece even though it is technically illegal except on very rare licensed beaches. In an attempt to keep popular beaches clothed many islands designate one beach for nudists — these are marked 'FKK' (for 'Freikörperkultur') in this guide — though this isn't going to be much of a legal defence if the police feel like having a crackdown. This happened a couple of years ago on Anafi when the island policeman received considerable publicity after he took to disappearing behind a bush on the camping beach. This in itself was harmless enough (most people disappear behind a bush at some point in their lives), but in this case he did it in order to jump out and arrest young female nudists. The Greek press called him a 'hero'; though there are other, less flattering, nouns that come to mind. Rare incidents like this aside, in practice, provided you are discreet, you are unlikely to be troubled by gawpers or the police. To some extent where you can go nude depends on the time of year: in High Season you usually have to venture further afield as the more accessible beaches get crowded out with beachwear fans.

Bus Services

Greek bus services fall into two types: intercity and local. Intercity buses usually require you to buy a ticket in advance from the bus station. This will have a time and seat number on it and you will be expected to travel on the particular bus departing at that time and to start the journey in the appropriate seat (the number is on the back of your seat). Timetables are strictly adhered to. Prices are low (reckon on paying 20 GDR per km on journeys over 10 km, 50 GDR per km on shorter rides), and the system is extensive, taking in all the major towns around the country. Buses on intercity routes (e.g. Thessalonika—Athens) can get booked solid on weekends and holidays, but by and large you can expect to catch your desired bus. On journeys over two hours the bus will make a 10 minute pit stop (invariably at a restaurant or shop owned by a relative of the driver).

Local, and most island, buses are very different affairs; since you normally pay on the bus and most are so crowded that you are usually doing well to find a seat at all. The majority of island buses are operated as one-vehicle family businesses. Dad will drive while one of the kids weaves their way through the masses collecting the fares. Timetables are strictly adhered to, though this isn't quite as good as it sounds as they change much more frequently. It is also very unwise to expect to find bus services operating on Sundays out of tourist areas. Further problems are posed by the local nature of island buses; they are geared to moving the islanders — not tourists — around. Parties of tourists all settling a 200 GDR fare with a 5000 note are almost made to feel unwelcome. Services tend to finish at the end of the working day and this is often not compatible with the tourist who likes his or her nightlife. Re-routing is also a problem; it is a sad fact of life that

given the choice between driving down a road and an earth track, island bus drivers are irresistibly drawn to the latter. Out of High Season school days add another imponderable to timetables, as buses tour the remoter villages twice a day collecting and delivering the kids.

Electricity

Greece's electrical system runs at 220 volts, with most sockets taking standard 2-pin continental style plugs (most UK and US devices will require adaptors). Each Greek island has its own generation plant (usually whining away on the next bay but one from the main town).

Employment Opportunities

There are a number of employment options open at the student end of the market if you are looking to finance an island-hopping holiday with some casual work. These include the famous ones (notably the donkey dropping collectors on Hydra and the disco dancers employed on Ios to make the outfits seem busy and pull in the punter). Most opportunities, however, are more mundane and are to be found in either doing jobs the locals either wouldn't want to do (many are too busy polishing their Range Rovers to find time to serve customers) or wouldn't want their daughters to do; i.e. cleaning and bar work.

Rates of pay are lousy — hence the rapid turnover in staff. These start at 3000 GDR per night for bar work, and, if you are lucky, up to 5000 GDR per day with a supermarket job. Payment in kind is also sometimes offered: free camping is given by some sites in exchange for a few hours on the quay pulling campers as they come off the ferries. Campsite notice boards occasionally carry advertisements for girls wanted to work in Athens during the winter. What they have to do, and with whom, is never made clear.

Environment

The development of mass tourism has had a major environmental impact on the Greek islands over the last 20 years. Add to this the wider problems faced by the almost landlocked Mediterranean, and you have undeniable problems. The only solace is that, as yet, the islands have exhibited a surprising resilience; most beaches are cleaner than their counterparts in the Western Med. (three quarters of Mediterranean pollution comes from France, Spain and Italy), and the marine damage is, for the most part, indiscernible to the tourist — barring the damage to a small number of species (see p. 61).

Of course, there are spots where things are very bad. Athens is the main casualty, with serious air and marine pollution. The waters of the adjacent Saronic Gulf are very badly damaged and have seen a fall in the number of species of marine fauna from 170 in 1960 to 30 in 1994. Near Piraeus the sea is almost dead: no health-minded Athenian will swim within 15 km of the capital. Things are worse elsewhere. The Turkish city of İzmir pours half a million cubic metres of untreated sewage into the Aegean each year, while the northern Adriatic regularly sees tides of a yellow mucus-like foam on its shorelines. The situation can only deteriorate: problems aren't being addressed and the renewal of sea water in the Mediterranean by exchange with the Atlantic (via the Strait of Gibraltar) takes some 150 years.

The European Union has also been responsible for major terrestrial changes. Most islands have been eligible for grants to improve their previously scenic dirt road networks. A secondary consequence of EU membership has been the relaxing of the restrictions on the ownership of holiday homes by non-Greek nationals in the islands. As the barriers come down so many new buildings are going up.

Food & Drink

Greek cuisine enjoys a rather chequered reputation. At its best it can be very enjoyable and healthy (there are very low rates of heart disease in this part of the world), but there is no disguising the fact that many Greek restaurants fail to do more than provide an acceptable minimum, with a selection of dishes that can only be described as limited (chicken, grilled steak and fish dishes predominating). The general standard of Greek cuisine hasn't been helped by the regular practice of cooking the meal well before eating; the theory being that lukewarm food is better for the digestion. Large quantities of olive oil are also added to 'lube the tubes'. Sadly, the invention of the microwave has only served to further encourage this practice.

All this said, there is plenty of good food around; the trick in finding it is to look for the tavernas and restaurants that are attracting a local clientele: Greeks enjoy good food as much as anyone else, and their patronage is a fair indication that this is *the* place to eat hereabouts. In many cases these aren't the most glamourous looking establishments in town, which are often the sole preserve of the tourist. This doesn't necessarily mean that they are bad. Thanks to the large number of expatriate Greeks returning from the USA and Australia to set up catering establishments in Greece, the number of foreign food outlets is steadily rising on the popular islands. US-style pizzerias are now opening on some of the most unlikely islands (one of the latest is at Katapola on Amorgos), and increasingly exotic establishments are adding further culinary colour to the scene. Paros and Ios have Chinese restaurants, Mykonos a Thai (all looking rather incongruous amidst their whitewashed chora surroundings). At the worst end of the scale, package-tour dominated Kos even has a

Mexican restaurant that requires its customers to wear sombreros: thankfully, such establishments remain very rare.

While Greek food is relatively cheap (you can get a reasonable meal and beer in a restaurant for around 2000 GDR), those on a tight budget doing the islands on the cheap will find they can economise by living out of supermarkets and on Greek fast food. A small supermarket or local grocery store is a standard feature of all island settlements (though by West European standards they are all very small affairs). Except on the islands that see very few tourists, most sell all the essentials. Common to all islands is the much underrated local **fast food**. Sold from small shops and bars it consists of an Arabic bread-style roll (*Pita*) filled either with *Gyros* (spit-cooked layers of meat—usually pork) or *Souvlaki* (kebab), with tomatoes, onions and yoghurt. For a hungry island hopper a plateful of Souvlaki Pita can be a fast-track stairway to heaven, but as with tavernas and restaurants, it pays to look to see where the locals are congregating for they are the ones who really know where to go for the real thing; poor tourist outlets are apt to add handfuls of french fries to the mélange (thus saving on the amount of meat in the pita).

The other great mainstay of the island culinary scene is the ubiquitous **Greek salad**. Known as *choriatiki*, it is made up of sliced tomatoes, onions, peppers and cucumbers, topped with *feta* (goat's cheese) and the odd decorative olive. It is often produced as a side dish to the main course in tavernas. **Main courses** tend to be uninspiring. The most common offerings are spiced meat-balls (*keftedes*), mousaka, and roast chicken.

Seafood is regularly on offer in the islands, though it is now quite expensive as a result of over-fishing; the strings of *chtapodi* (octopus) hung out to dry outside tavernas have traditionally been one of the more photogenic culinary sights. Somewhat less attractive is the sight of the little critters being clobbered until their pips squeak in order to soften them up to the point of being nicely chewy. If this doesn't appeal, you can always eat tender-fried baby squid (*kalamarakia*) instead. **Shell-fish** is also very popular. Crayfish (*astakos*) and Lobster (*kalogeros*) are commonly found on menus. Of the fish proper, the most sought after dishes are grilled mullet (*bouni/barbounia*) and bream (*lithrini*). The small fish of the day's catch are often baked in tomato sauce — a dish known as *Bourthéto*.

Vegetarians will find that the Greek practice of ordering vegetable dishes for both first and main courses ensures that most restaurants will be able to serve up something vaguely palatable. As dairy products are not widely used in Greek cooking it is also perfectly possible to follow a Vegan diet in the islands.

Many islands now have patisseries offering fancy cakes and pastries. These include traditional Greek fare; notably **cheese pies** (*tiropitta*) served piping hot. Island bakeries also sell these and breakfast **doughnuts**, alongside freshly baked bread in the tourist season. Many also now stock soft canned drinks, ice cream and refrigerated chocolate bars (forget about buying chocolate that isn't) as well.

The usual brands of **soft drinks** are all widely available, though shop prices are half what you are charged elsewhere. **Mineral water** is the staple backpacker's day-time drink. On many of the islands it is claimed that you can drink the tap water, but this isn't to be recommended given that summer shortages often result in supplies being heavily adulterated with sea water. Many islands also produce wines, with heavy reds predominating, along with another speciality: *retsina* — a dubious pine barrel 'wine' that doubles up wondrously as turpentine in a pinch.

Greek

One of the most immediate (and often intimidating) problems new visitors to Greece expect to encounter is the apparently strange Greek language with its alien-looking alphabet. Such worries are all but groundless these days. Greece has been on the tourist map for so long that Greek phrase books are now to be numbered among the 'non-essential' items (though they are widely on sale in Greece). In fact, you can be sure of finding someone who can speak English in all the tourist facilities, if only because the language is compulsory in Greek schools, and each summer the country is full of Greek-expatriate families from the USA, Canada and Australia (it isn't usually even necessary to ask the locals if they can speak English). Reading the Greek alphabet on signs and maps is a different matter. Fortunately most road and other tourist-related signs are in both Greek and English, as are most ferry timetables outside ticket agencies. The only exceptions to this are the less touristed islands of the Northern Aegean and the Turkish coast, where German is now the de facto lingua franca (reflecting the nationality of the majority of visitors). Even though you don't need any Greek, any efforts to speak it are appreciated, and a few basic phrases are given on p. 600 along with a summary of the letters and their English equivalents.

Precise transliteration between Greek and English letter forms is difficult as in some instances equivalents are lacking. For example: the Greek for 'Saint' Agiou can be variously transcribed as Agiou, Ag., Ayios, or Aghios. It is also not uncommon to find non-Greek names used alongside their older Greek counterparts. Hence the Cretan town of Agios Nikolaos is known by island bus drivers as 'San' Nikolaos (a hangover from the days of Venetian control of the island). 'Santorini' is another example of a later Venetian name co-existing with an earlier one: 'Thira'. Both are commonly used but

refer to the same island. Just to make life really interesting 'Thira' can also be transcribed as 'Phira' or even 'Fira' and like a lot of Greek islands both the island and its principal town have the same name. This all sounds horribly confusing but it isn't really a major problem provided you look at any unfamiliar name with an eye to the possibility that it could be a variation on the name you are looking for. Thus: Cos = Kos, Lesbos = Lesvos, Siros = Syros, etc. Where an island is commonly known by two names or by a name in a form which does not correspond particularly closely to the form used in Greece (e.g. Rhodes is always referred to locally as 'Rodos', Crete = 'Kriti') both names are given on island maps.

To help aid recognition on each chapter title page you will find the names of the major ports covered by the chapter in Greek. For the most part they are shown in the accusative form as they appear on ticket agency timetables and ship destination boards. E.g. Paros = ΠΑΡΟΣ (nominative) is shown in its more commonly encountered accusative form: ΠΑΡΟ. As a further aid to the language you will find below an old school rhyme (even though it doesn't) used to drum the Greek alphabet into the minds of countless poor kids:

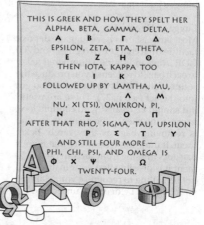

THIS IS GREEK AND HOW THEY SPELT HER
ALPHA, BETA, GAMMA, DELTA,
A   B   Γ   Δ
EPSILON, ZETA, ETA, THETA,
E   Z   H   Θ
THEN IOTA, KAPPA TOO
I   K
FOLLOWED UP BY LAMTHA, MU,
Λ   M
NU, XI (TSI), OMIKRON, PI,
N   Ξ   O   Π
AFTER THAT RHO, SIGMA, TAU, UPSILON
P   Σ   T   Y
AND STILL FOUR MORE —
PHI, CHI, PSI, AND OMEGA IS
Φ   X   Ψ   Ω
TWENTY-FOUR.

Health & Insurance

The countries along the northern shore of the Mediterranean maintain reasonable levels of sanitation and no inoculations are mandatory. However, vaccination against tetanus, typhoid, hepatitis A and polio is a good idea. Minor ailments are often treated by pharmacies, who have a wider remit than in many other countries. All the large islands have 'cottage' hospitals, though most are primitive by West European standards (you should get all injuries treated checked by your own doctor as soon as you get home). These are backed up by at least one doctor on all the islands served by regular ferry and an emergency air service. Reciprocal arrangements for UK NHS patients exist with most countries but the widely mentioned E111 form is of limited value and no substitute for proper insurance. Full medical insurance (including emergency flight home) is very strongly recommended. Amongst the easiest to obtain is the Thomas Cook Travel Insurance Package. This offers comprehensive medical insurance (including the all-important cover for accidents on mopeds 125cc and under) and is available from all Thomas Cook Retail travel shops in the UK. Note: most insurance policies do not provide cover for injury in high risk activities such as bungee jumping.

Luggage Deposits

Most large islands have luggage deposit facilities that charge between 500 and 700 GDR a day and staple a numbered ticket to each bag (to redeem it you produce the counterfoil). Ticket agents have also got into the act (see p. 37). These are useful but should be treated with caution: look to see if any check is being made on who is removing bags as they rarely ticket them. If they don't; be aware that if your bag goes missing from such an establishment it is possible that your insurer will not be willing to recognise your claim as your bag will be deemed 'unsecured'.

Maps & Guides

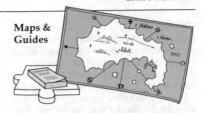

Greece has attracted guide-writers ever since Pausanias put stylus to scroll in Roman times — so much so, that there are few series that don't include the country. If you want to take an additional volume along with you, you will be spoilt for choice. However most are re-researched every second or third year. This tends to be the great weakness of most guidebooks as the Greek islands are changing rapidly: it therefore pays to look at the edition date (not the reprint date) and reckon that the information therein dates from at least a year earlier. Inside Greece it is difficult to obtain West European published guidebooks outside of Athens, and those that are on sale have at least a 25% mark up on their published prices. Individual island guides (in a form of English) are on sale on most islands.

The Greek islands also have a place in the history of cartography; featuring prominently in one of the earliest printed atlases: the *Isolario* of Benedetto Bordone. Published in 1528, it carried woodcut maps based on old books of sailing directions known as 'island books'. The example above is of Mykonos (orientated with Jerusalem at the top) and its accuracy helps to explain the large number of shipwrecks in medieval times. Almost all Greek islands have modern island maps on sale (often with a town plan of sorts on the reverse) — most are about 400 GDR. Unfortunately, the quality of these maps varies greatly. Some of them are excellent, but there are a number that are at best vague, at worst fiction (i.e. with minor tracks shown as major highways), and it is only by trial and error that you can determine the good from the bad.

Moped & Car Hire

In recent years the islands have seen a dramatic increase in moped hire. Any town with a significant tourist presence will have a rental outlet. Prices are low (reckon on £6/US$10 for a day's rental for a low powered machine). Unfortunately, with their increased popularity has come a large rise in the number of tourist deaths and injuries. The former are running at over 100 a year; the latter are too numerous to count. Many of these are the result of inexperienced and ill-equipped riders attempting too much on poor roads using poorly maintained machines. Before succumbing to the temptation to go roaring off into the sunset you should consider the possibility that that sunset could be more final than picturesque.

Even if you are an experienced rider, there are a number of points worth noting. First, insurance: does your holiday insurance cover all the potential risks you run riding a moped or motorbike without a helmet (these can't always be hired along with the moped as few bother with them in Greece)? Secondly, before handing over your day's rental money and your passport (a guarantee that you will bring the machine back) you should: (1) check the condition of the machine, (2) ascertain who is liable for what if it breaks down, (3) check how much fuel you are getting (reputable outlets can often be distinguished by fuel in the tank). Once you have your machine, accept its limitations; most are not powerful enough to negotiate steeper hills and many island roads are all pot-holes. All the above points also apply to car hire. This is expensive: reckon on paying £40/US$65 per day for a Jeep or beach buggy. In order to hire a car you will also need to produce a current driving licence. A Green Card insurance warranty is also strongly recommended.

Newspapers & Books

Most major European papers are available on all but the remotest of the islands — usually via a stationery shop or street kiosk. On the majority of islands they appear a day after publication. In central Athens they are available on the evening of the day they are published. In High Season it pays to arrive early if you want the more popular titles. The difficulty is determining when 'early' is, for it varies according to an island's links with Athens or the nearest island with a direct airport link to Western Europe. On Paros, for example, it is mid-afternoon as the newspapers are carried on the morning ferries from Piraeus. Prices are high: expect to pay double the home country published price. Most newsagents also have a pricey supply of pulp fiction, as well as locally produced maps and guides.

Nightlife

One of the most charming aspects of Greek islands life is the traditional evening promenade around the centre of town. Nights in Greece are the time for the locals to bask in the cooler temperatures and catch up with the gossip. As a result, even the most uninspiring of towns exude an air of companionable bustle that lasts from dusk to 10 or 11 pm. Tavernas take in the lingerers who want to chat (those near the ports also serve as a temporary home for those waiting for night ferries). Most islands also boast at least one disco where you can touch a few more hands in the dance of life. Discos and bars usually stay open until 3 am. Thereafter the streets are often filled with slowly dispersing crowds of the slightly inebriated. This can be a problem time in some parts as a lack of manpower means that there is little by way of a police presence to curb the excesses of the more exuberant revellers.

Photography

Popular makes of film are available on all but the smallest Greek islands. However, if your requirements are in anyway exotic (e.g. brands like Kodachrome 64) you can be certain of encountering considerable difficulty replenishing supplies. The cost of film (generally around 25% more than UK prices) also varies wildly from centre to centre. An extreme example of this is the fact that it is actually cheaper to buy a return ticket to Aegina to buy some brands than it is to buy them at Piraeus. If you want to view the results of your endeavours sooner rather than later you will find that all the popular islands now have at least one 1-hour film processing outlet in the centre of town.

If you want something more than the usual holiday snaps then you should consider using a polarizing filter to combat the brilliant sunlight that bathes the islands. A second constraint on a photographer's prowess are the signs prohibiting photography in military areas. This is particularly true on parts of Kos (and other islands and ports along the Turkish coast) and Crete (home to a major NATO base). Given local sensibilities on this subject it is best to work on the assumption that it is unwise to snap naval craft or personnel no matter where you are.

Police

Greece has three types of police in addition to the usual customs and traffic officials: the regular police, the tourist police and the port police. The islands have a varying number of each depending on their population size. Small or very popular islands have extra officials drafted in to help cope with the tourist season. Islands with a population of under 400 usually only have one permanent official who wears all three hats.

The regular **Police** (identified by a regular police-style blue uniform and peaked cap) have a station on most islands. For the greater part of the year they don't have a lot to do given the very low crime rate among islanders (it is difficult to get away with crime on an island where everyone knows everyone else). For this reason they are relatively few in number and have little opportunity to practice and develop such detection skills as they may possess. Things of course change in the summer when they are faced with a procession of foreigners who have had a couple of dozen beers too many, their possessions stolen (usually by other holiday makers), or worse (see p. 62). Sad to say it, but the reaction to tourists beating at their doors is often one of polite indifference. If you are reporting a crime, the chances are it will be solely for insurance purposes; the probability of the police recovering lost items is very low. It therefore pays to be extra vigilant when it comes to looking after your property. If you are one of the very few who hit serious trouble, then it is advisable to contact your nearest consulate before the police if practicable.

The **Tourist Police** are not to be confused with the regular police (despite having an all but identical uniform: this makes it easier for small island officials to do a quick change act). As their name implies, their function is to look after tourists and ensure that outlets serving them (i.e. hotels, pensions, restaurants, shops, taxis, etc.) are conforming to official regulations. In common with the NTOG/EOT and occasional island tourist offices they also provide maps, island information, travel, and accommodation details. If you ever have difficulty finding a bed or end up embroiled in an argument with a local over a bill, then the tourist police should be your first port of call (often the mere threat of bringing them in is enough to resolve arguments): they are generally very helpful, can speak some English (of sorts) and disposed to be on the tourist's 'side' if there is a just cause for complaint. They can also perform a valuable liaison role if you need to visit the regular police (their offices are often to be found in the same building); so much so, that it is worth taking most problems to them first. Unfortunately, they generally only have officials on islands with a large summer tourist population. Some of these islands (e.g. Santorini) also use summer volunteers as tourist wardens. Armed with a kharki uniform and a smile, they point the masses in which ever direction they are seeking to go.

The third — and most visible — police are the **Port Police**. Decked out in a natty all-white naval officer-like uniform, their sole responsibility is the supervision of the island and mainland ports. Armed with whistles (that are blown constantly) they attempt to keep tourists and locals alike from boarding ferries before those passengers that wish to disembark have done so, as well as keeping both out of the road of cars and lorries attempting to use the same exit/boarding door. They tend to be a fairly frustrated lot as no-one takes a blind bit of notice of them as a rule. On the busier islands quayside passenger sheds have been installed to make the port police's job easier as they enable foot passengers to be corraled behind a locked gate at the end of the shed until the port police deign to release them with a key. On smaller islands they don't bother resorting to such stratagems and just roll up (often on a moped) 20 minutes before

the ferry turns up; armed with ship-to-shore radios, they *know* exactly when a ferry is going to arrive. If you have been waiting several hours for an overdue ferry a port policeman is a very welcome sight.

The port police are usually stationed in a separate building from the regular police. More often than not it is within a couple of hundred metres of the ferry quay and sometimes has a board outside listing the day's ferry departures. Port policemen are not interested in helping you to find a room or anything else for that matter — though they are approachable enough if you want regular ferry information.

Public Holidays

As a rule, public holidays tend to have much more impact on bus rather than ferry services within Greece. Plans to travel on religious holidays should allow for the possibility that services will be reduced or suspended. The Greek Orthodox church still exerts a powerful influence and ferries are sometimes diverted to carry pilgrims to the shrine of the moment (Tinos on August 15 being a good example of this). If you are planning an Easter break in the islands, you should expect to find ferries very busy. In Greece, Easter is the most important holiday of the year and most islanders working in Athens or elsewhere on the mainland try to get back to their island homes to spend the holiday with their families. Public holidays in 1999/2000 are:

March 25 (Independence Day);
April 9, 11, 12 (Easter);
May 1, 30 (Day of the Holy Spirit);
August 15
(The Feast of the Assumption of the Virgin Mary);
October 28
(Ohi Day);
December 25, 26;
January 1, 6;
March 13.

Religion

Thanks to the Greek Orthodox church religion continues to play an important part in Greek society. The result is a profusion of churches and a veneration of things religious no longer seen in Western Europe. This even extends to little old ladies giving up their bus seats to priests just out of theological college — something which might not seem so surprising until you try to get on a ferry along side them, for the little old ladies in black — the notorious black widows — are the original Hell's Grannies of Monty Python fame: kicking and shoving their way aboard with grim determination that refuses to admit defeat. Much of their anger can be put down to the convention that requires them to wear black for years on end. Widowers in Greece get off more lightly, wearing a black armband for a year. Given this strict observance of the traditional dress code, it isn't perhaps so surprising to find that islanders get very upset when tourists attempt to enter churches in shorts or beachwear. Properly dressed (i.e. with torso and legs covered) tourists are made to feel very welcome.

Thanks to a tradition which expects every family to build its own chapel, small room-sized chapels abound on the Greek Islands. Roman Catholic communities are also to be found on some — a remnant from the days of Venetian or Italian rule. Thanks to the population exchanges that followed the Helleno-Turkish war of 1919–22 Islam has all but disappeared from the islands. Athens and a number of island towns still contain mosques sporting increasingly dilapidated minarets, but without exception they have been taken out of use as places of

worship and converted into museums or warehouses. This process has been reversed in the former Greek towns along the Turkish coast.

Scams

The large number of tourists (particularly to Athens) has, sad to say it, produced some sharp practices by an unscrupulous few. These are the most common scams:

1. 5000 Drachma Note Tricks

Version 1: the tourist pays a taxi-driver (airport taxis love this one) or waiter with a 5000 GDR note and by a sleight of hand it is handed back with the protest that it is only a 500 GDR note. *Always* check the size of notes when paying a bill. You can avoid the problem arising by holding the note up before handing it over and saying 'I only have a 5000 Drachma note'. If, however, you do get done, vigorously stand your ground and suggest a visit to the Police: this response is usually sufficient to remedy the situation.

Version 2: the tourist hands over a 5000 GDR note and is given change for a 1000 GDR note. Again, this is a popular ploy on new arrivals in Greece, and a similar response to Version 1 is the best way of resolving the problem.

2. The Passport Trick

Some hotel and room owners charge tourists who have checked-in, found the room unsatisfactory and checked-out again, a fee for the return of their passport. You can avoid this by keeping your passport until you have checked the room. If you do get caught don't hand over any cash: instead call in the tourist police.

3. Bar Tricks

Two bar tricks are common enough to be worth mentioning. The first is the adding of meths or some other tasteless additive to spirits in resort bars (with dire consequences on for the drinker's stomach a few hours latter). The second is the occasional habit of charging of bar/disco entrance fees which can be offset against your first drink. It is only when you get inside that you discover that prices are much higher than elsewhere. Ask about bar prices when buying your ticket.

Sea Sickness

If you fall victim to sea sickness it is more likely as not that it will be thanks to the vessel you are on rather than changes in sea conditions. The Mediterranean is calm compared to the English Channel. Obviously it can get rough — particularly in the Aegean when the *meltemi* wind rushes down from the north — but as a rule on most ferries you are hard put to distinguish any sea movement. Catamarans and hydrofoils can be a different matter.

Sea sickness is caused by the inability of the brain to correlate conflicting information from the eye and ear. The eye perceives the vessel as being a static object while the balance mechanism of the ear is telling the brain that the body is travelling up, down, and all over the place. The easiest way of resolving this cerebral conflict is to: (1) go up on deck where you can keep the horizon, rather than the ship, as the visual static point of reference, thus allowing the brain to accurately interpret the balance information being received from the ear; (2) take up a position in the centre of the vessel about two-thirds the length of the ship from the bow. This will be the optimum point of least vertical and horizontal movement (ferries are designed stern-heavy to ensure that their screws and rudder remain in the water) and is akin to being at the top — rather than the bottom — of a pendulum; (3), eat before you sail and keep nibbling during the journey to keep the stomach occupied.

A number of over-the-counter anti seasickness drugs can be obtained locally in Greece. *Dramamine* is the most widely available but like many of these drugs it is apt to cause drowsiness; for this reason alone it is better to get motion sickness drugs before you travel so that you can be advised as to possible reactions. Alternatives such as adhesive patches, Ginger Root Capsules (the herbalist remedy) and Sea Bands (wrist-bands that rely on Nei-Kuan acupressure point techniques) aren't usually available in Greece.

Shopping

Regular shopping hours in Greece are 08.00–13.30/15.00 Monday to Saturday and 17.30–20.30 on Tuesday, Thursday and Friday. In lucrative tourist towns an open-all-hours (even Sundays) regime is adopted in High Season. Pharmacies in the towns open in the evenings on a rota basis: a sign in Greek on the door would tell you which one if you could read it. Street kiosks are usually open from 08.00–23.00 — so liquid refreshments, snacks and English language newspapers (one day late) are always readily available.

Each island chain has its own specialities (the Cyclades have reproduction Cycladic idols, the Dodecanese duty-free liquor). Leather goods, reproduction statuary, bronzes and ceramics by the score and sponges are common to all. Other islands are noted for individual goods; e.g. the pistachio nuts of Aegina. The more popular islands are 'blessed' with pricey gold and clothing boutiques. A rather incongruous (given the temperatures) and less attractive feature of the more up-market islands are the fur shops now driven to extinction elsewhere.

Sightseeing

Most archeological sites and museums in Greece are regulated by the EOT (the local branch of the Greek National Tourist Board). Opening hours for sites vary, but most operate something akin to a 08.30–15.00 timetable, Tuesdays to Sundays, and are closed on Mondays. Major archaeological sites in Athens and elsewhere usually stay open until at least 18.00 in High Season. You can expect to pay to enter archaeological sites and museums in Greece. Ticket prices are around £2/US$3 to enter a museum, £3–4/US$5–6 for any of the major sites. ISIC-carrying students usually get a

50% discount, and in some instances, gain free admission. In past years Sundays have seen free entry for all visitors to all sites, but many (including the popular sites in Athens) are now charging between 1 April—31 October.

On archaeological sites, tourists are increasingly finding that they are prohibited from entering important individual buildings, or standing on mosaics left in situ (to prevent wear and tear): each usually has strategically sited wardens armed with forbidding whistles, to bring those who step beyond the boundary ropes back into line; as a result a visit to the Athenian Acropolis or Olympia is apt to sound like a school sports day. Site guides are usually on sale at ticket kiosks. For the most part, ruins and exhibits are usually labelled in Greek and English.

Taxis

Island taxis perform a valuable back-up role to the buses; on some islands (e.g. Leros) they have all but replaced them. All are metered, but it is not uncommon for the driver to forget to switch the meter on. Other common practices are similarly weighted against the passenger: it is normal for each passenger to pay the full fare and individual items of baggage also usually attract a small charge. In view of this, you should always endeavour to establish how much the journey will cost before you get going. Finally, don't be too surprised to find locals (who don't pay) grabbing a lift if they know your driver.

Telephones

The Greek telephone system has seen a radical change over the last couple of years thanks to the widespread introduction of the telephone card. As many homes in Greece have yet to be linked to the world by phone, phonecards have become the way to make both domestic and international calls. Phonecards are on sale from street kiosks and the communal telephone offices to be found in every

port and town. Easily spotted by the grey satellite dish that adorns the roof, they are advertised by the initials OTE (ask for the 'Otay'). Usually open from 07.00—

13.00 most contain 6 to 8 booths equipped with meters; you make your call and then pay afterwards at the supervisor's desk. Until the arrival of phonecards the OTE was one of the hubs of island life. These days it is usually empty apart from the staff gloomily contemplating the prospect of impending unemployment in between selling the odd phonecard (1998 prices were 1700 GDR for a 100 unit card, 7000 GDR for 500, and 11,500 GDR for 1000).

Phonecards aside, the Greek telephone system is pretty antiquated. Connections are often hard to make within Greece as most go via undersea cable and you can spend a happy twenty minutes redialing. Phone calls can also be made from the confectionery and tobacco kiosks found in main town streets and from some ticket agencies (in both instances you will have to pay roughly 10% more for your call).

International calls (via satellite) are less of a problem (if you need the International operator dial 161). When phoning from Greece, Cyprus and Italy prefix your home number (after removing any initial '0' in the area code) with:

Australia	0061
Austria	0043
Belgium	0032
Canada	001
Denmark	0045
France	0033
Germany	0049
Ireland	00353
Italy	0039
Netherlands	0031
New Zealand	0064
Spain	0034
Switzerland	0041
UK	0044
USA	001

Time

Greece and the Eastern Mediterranean countries are — apart from a few days during the change-over period to and from summer time in March and October — 1 hour ahead of most European countries, 2 hours ahead of UK GMT/Summer Time, 7 hours ahead of North America Eastern Standard Time, 10 hours ahead of Pacific Standard Time.

What to take

When Phileas Fogg went around the world in 79 days he packed only 2 shirts and 3 pairs of stockings. Admittedly this was backed up with a manservant complete with a carpet bag containing £20,000, but this minor item aside, you could do worse than follow his example and pack as little as you can get away with: the big disadvantage of island hopping is that you have to carry all your luggage with you. Luckily, Greece in the summertime is warm and dry enough for most people to comfortably get by with their beachwear and a couple of changes of clothes. Add to this sundry items determined by your interests in life (those keen on monasteries or churches tend to take more formal clothing, while most young male Italians go for designer sunglasses and five bottles of aftershave lotion), and this is quite enough to be going on with. Some other ideas that are worth considering:

A good **novel**: all island-hopping holidays involve a certain amount of waiting around for boats — a novel will do a lot to reduce any tedium. **Backgammon** is also a popular ferry-waiting pastime. Card games, however, tend to be far less successful thanks to the strong summer winds.

A **pullover** and **windcheater**: ferries are a good way of keeping cool during the day, but a very poor way of keeping warm at night. Deck-class passengers travelling on outside decks (or waiting on quay-sides) will soon regret not having some kind of wind-proof clothing.

Sleeping bags are also commonly seen accoutrements, and a good insurance policy in High Season should you not be able to find a room (as you can make tracks for the nearest campsite). The nights ashore are so mild that it is often only the more amorous (and moany) campers who bother bringing a tent.

Foam mats and **airbeds** are also very popular with deck-class passengers wanting to sleep or lie out on deck. If you are overnighting on a ferry deck they are invaluable, as decks get too wet to place sleeping bags on them unprotected. Both mats and airbeds are available in Greece at a price, along with the cheap straw roll-up beach mats used by almost everyone.

Earplugs are occasionally desirable on some campsites, and if you want to stand on the noisy outside decks of hydrofoils.

A **can opener** is invaluable if you are eating out of local supermarkets (even small grocery shops carry odd tins from the Heinz range, and Kellogg's cereals).

Student Cards: if you have one, take it, as it will get you significant discounts on tours and site entry charges. In some instances they can even get you free entry.

Luxury items are better brought with you than purchased in Greece. Cosmetics, contact lens solutions (the choice is limited outside Athens) and medicines are all notably more expensive than in the UK. Unusual makes of **film** should be brought with you. Regular film is often more expensive , but as keeping your luggage weight down is a priority, this sort of item can be bought as you travel. You should also assume that you will need to carry **lavatory paper** and **mosquito repellent** (there are more mossies than tourists in Greece) and a **sink plug** wherever you go. 'Befores, durings, and afters' (tampax, condoms and nappies/diapers) are available everywhere.

When to go

The Eastern Mediterr-
anean has a similar
climate to Southern
California: hot dry
summers, warm wet
winters and around

3250 hours of sunshine a year. Within the
Aegean there are also significant climatic
variations, with the north — not surprisingly — being a couple of degrees cooler
than average, Rhodes and Crete a degree
above the average and the centre and
west being appreciably drier than the
east. This latter feature is in part due to
the Cyclades, which form a rain 'shadow',
thanks to a ring of hilly islands (notably
Kea, Kythnos, Serifos, Santorini, Ios, Sikinos, Folegandros, Anafi and Amorgos)
obscuring rain-bearing clouds. Though
there has been little apparent change in
climate since prehistoric times, extensive
deforestation has also contributed to the
dryness of the region.

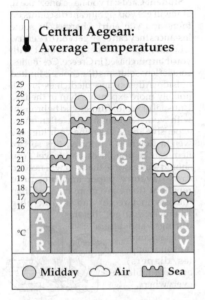

**Central Aegean:
Average Temperatures**

29
28
27
26
25
24
23
22
21
20
19
18
17
16
°C

APR · MAY · JUN · JUL · AUG · SEP · OCT · NOV

◯ Midday   ◠ Air   ⌒⌒ Sea

Although most island hoppers visit
during July and August, the nicest time
to visit Greece is in April and May when
the wild flowers are out, but — sad to say
it — many of the ferries don't run until
the summer crowds come hopping, and
the weather can't always be guaranteed.
September and October also have their
fans, but at some point the first autumn
storms arrive, and when the weather first
breaks these can be positively vicious. It
also rains roughly one day per month
between early June and mid September
in the Northern Aegean and the Ionian
islands, but rarely in July and August
south of Athens.

August is the hottest month of the year,
with average daytime temperatures
around 26° C. July follows a degree behind
but boasts a higher sea temperature. How
hot you end up will depend largely on
where you are: Athens in August is pretty
terrible, along with much of the mainland.
Fortunately, the majority of the islands
(the main exceptions are the Ionian and
Saronic Gulf groups) are spared over-
high temperatures thanks to the summer
meltemi wind and sea breezes.

The *meltemi* (a cooling north wind caused by summer low pressure over Asia)
normally starts up in mid-morning and
blows into the evening. It can be a bit of a
shock if you are not prepared for it: the
Aegean islands from mid-June to October
are *very* windy. This is great for windsurfers (of which there are many), but can
leave beach lovers in sandblasted shock.
Islands such as Mykonos and Paros regularly 'enjoy' over 20 days in July and August with winds over 4 on the Beaufort
Scale, and 12 days when winds go over 6.
(The Beaufort Scale is used to categorize
wind speeds and their influence on the
sea: 4 is a point where paper gets blown
around and waves have small white caps;
6 is the point where telephone wires
whistle, umbrellas blow inside out and
large waves form, preventing smaller
boats and hydrofoils from operating).

☼ Central Aegean: Wind Averages

Days:	Calm	Breezy	Windy
APR	12	11	7
MAY	14	11	6
JUN	11	10	9
JUL	9	10	12
AUG	7	12	12
SEP	9	12	9
OCT	9	14	8
Beaufort Scale	0 – 4	4 – 6	6 +

Wildlife

Sad to say it, the most visible wildlife to be found in Greece these days is human rather than animal (though most animals are pretty wild by the end of the tourist season), for the country is remarkably free of potential pests to tourists. Greece is also lucky in having a dearth of life-threatening species.

Insects are likely to pose the biggest problem for tourists; particularly the large mosquito population that feed along every island promenade. Other terrestrial threats are something of a non-event. A small **scorpion** exists, but possesses a very indifferent sting. **Snakes** play an important part in many island traditions, but are very uncommon in tourist areas besides being — at worst — only mildly poisonous (this doesn't stop the locals going hysterical whenever they see one). Rabies is also known, but isn't a significant problem for tourists.

Marine wildlife is responsible for many of the more painful encounters with nature. The rockier island coasts are home to some painful **Sea Urchins** and **Conger** eels that regularly inflict minor damage. A more serious threat is posed by the **Dragon Fish** (or 'Drakena'), which has poisonous spikes on its spine and gills. It is to be found hidden just off sandy beaches where it burrows under the surface awaiting its prey. Most injuries are incurred while paddling. The symptoms are sharp pain followed by numbness: local doctors are equipped with a serum that will counter the crippling swelling that will otherwise occur over the following days: don't be deceived into believing that the numbness is the extent of the problem — if you are unlucky enough to step on one, seek medical attention.

Greece is also home to a number of attractive species now in decline. Most notable of these is the small colony of **Monk Seals**. Now reckoned to be one of the twelve most endangered species in the world (estimates as to its numbers range from 750 to 300), this poor creature hangs on in its reduced breeding grounds around the small islets east of Alonissos island. **Loggerhead Turtles** on Zakinthos are rapidly going the same way thanks to tourism (see p. 504) and government neglect. In a more enlightened action the Greek government has moved to protect the magnificently horned **Kri-kri** mountain goats of Crete. Sanctuaries have been established on a number of deserted islets around Crete (notably on the island of Dia just north of Iraklion). **Dolphins** also inhabit Greek waters. If half the passengers on a ferry sun deck suddenly rush over to one side of the ship as sure as eggs is eggs the cause will be a school of dolphins swimming alongside. Unfortunately this is not as common an event as it used to be, for Mediterranean dolphin numbers have declined by two thirds in the last decade thanks to a morbillivirus; thought to be one of the symptom of increased pollution (see p. 49).

Women Travellers
There is an old Chinese saying that runs something like 'Ying chu you yong chee choo yee' which roughly translated means 'the difference between a dream and a nightmare is no more than the thickness of the wing of a butterfly'. The Greek islands are often deemed dream country, thanks to their all-pervasive, laid-back atmosphere. However, this appealing feature is a disadvantage when it encourages one to drop one's guard too much. Greece has long taken pride in its long-merited reputation as a 'safe' destination for women travellers, and solo women island hoppers are not uncommon — particularly from Scandinavian countries. However, there appears to be a small, but growing problem of assaults on women.

A *World in Action* TV programme reported the alarming statistic that rapes reported by British women in Greece rose by 112% between 1992 and 1993. Even allowing for the fact that the increased number only totalled 34 (a tiny figure when one considers that over two million Brits visit Greece each year), it is still a worrying trend, given that many assaults undoubtedly go unreported. Part of the trouble is that the past treatment of rape victims by Greek police officers has left a lot to be desired. Even the Foreign Office has been moved to complain that victims have been treated unsympathetically. This is not because officials are indifferent, but more the combination of a lack of language, training and experience in dealing with victims (rape is very rare within Greek society), combined with a conservative outlook that leads them to regard scantily clad young women who party day and night with crowds of young men, both downing alcohol as fast as they can open the bottles, as asking for trouble; it is noticeable that young Greek women have yet to gain a similar degree

of freedom. A further unpalatable fact that local officials are loath to recognize is that a large proportion of reported attacks are by Greek youths or men. This doesn't fit readily with the undoubted fact that, once tourists are taken out of the equation, most islands are crime free zones. The problem is, of course, the old Mediterranean male one of seeing Western girls as (1) loose, and (2) available. Add to this the chaste nature of most of the local girls, and it is inevitable that the unattached Greek male is going to turn the charm on when holidaying alongside zillions of foreign tourists. With a new lot of 'pinkies' arriving every fortnight, they have plenty of opportunity to practise their lines.

In view of all this, the best advice must be to enjoy yourself but take care to avoid potentially dangerous situations. Most attacks appear to take place at the big resorts and party islands. Women walking home alone in the early hours or accepting lifts from locals are particularly vulnerable. Obviously, on holiday one wants a night or two on the town; on these occasions consider splashing out on a reasonable hotel bed near the centre, and don't hang around until closing time when the streets are suddenly awash with inebriated men looking for a good time.

If you are attacked there are a number of things you can subsequently do:
1. Get medical help or, if that isn't available, seek help from women locally, who may lend emotional support.
2. Inform your embassy or consulate (both are very sympathetic) before you talk to the police as they can liaise on your behalf.
3. If you can't be represented by an embassy or consular official, try to go to the police with a companion — preferably someone who can speak Greek.
4. Don't be afraid to curtail your holiday; embassy officials or tour reps can arrange your early return.
5. If you haven't felt up to reporting the attack in Greece, do so when you get back home; inquires can still be pursued.

ⓘ Historical Background

Scattered like confetti on Homer's 'wine dark' Aegean Sea, the Greek islands lie on one of the crossroads of world culture. Almost every Mediterranean civilization has left some mark, resulting in plenty of sightseeing and adding a fascinating dimension to an island hopping holiday. The islands have naturally been influenced by the major periods of Greek history, but being islands they were able to 'enjoy' a greater degree of individual historical variation, and this has added greatly to their separate identities.

Early Cycladic
4500—2000 BC

4500–3200 BC	Early Period
3200–2700 BC	Grotta–Pelos Culture
2700–2300 BC	Keros–Syros Culture
2300–2000 BC	Phylakopi I Culture

The first evidence of human activity in Greece dates from around 8500 BC. The islands appear to have been quickly populated thereafter. Most being wooded, within sight of each other, and of an ideal size for easy defence by small fishing and agrarian communities, they were natural centres of population. The Cyclades in particular flourished during the latter part of this period (3200—2000 BC). Removed from the outside influences of mainland cultures, they developed a distinct and unique sub-culture of their own. Now known mainly through small figurines, this prehistoric Cycladic culture remains tantalizingly elusive. Even the idols carved out of white marble remain a mystery, as their function is far from clear (in this respect, echoes with the massive Easter island figures extend beyond looks). Most have been recovered from graves (though they have also been found in settlements) and depict naked women — usually in a highly stylized form (see p. 253) — standing with arms folded (left above right) and sometimes pregnant. Their 'modernist' appearance has also made them very popular around the

world, with high prices and a large number of fakes typifying the market today. All this is a long way removed from the culture that created them. In the absence of evidence of political or military facets to this society, in retrospect, it looks to have existed in something like the garden of Eden. But clearly it was not all apples and Eves if the depressed, introspective posture of the occasional carved Adam is anything to go by.

Minoan
2000—1500 BC

c. 2000 BC	First sailing ships appear in the Aegean
c. 1900 BC	Palaces built on Crete
c. 1700 BC	Palaces rebuilt after earth-quakes
c. 1500 BC	Santorini eruption fatally disrupts Minoan economy
c. 1450 BC	Knossos Palace destroyed

Around 2000 BC the first major power emerged in the Aegean. Named after a king whose name passed down through legend, the non-Greek Minoans were only rediscovered in the early years of this century thanks to archaeology. Based on a commercial hegemony, the Minoan civilization, with its huge palaces, brilliant frescoes, intricate jewellery, baths, drainage systems, and above all, the first writing, marked a cultural high point that was not to be regained for over a thousand years. Known only through their artifacts, the Minoans never recovered from the economically destructive volcanic eruption of Santorini c. 1500 BC. Taken over by the first Greeks, they disappeared and were forgotten even by the ancient Greeks themselves. They hovered on the edge of memory in dark legends of the sea-king Minos and his labyrinth palace, built to house his half-man, half-bull son (the Minotaur) who lived on a healthy diet of Athenian youths, and the story of Atlantis — an island of bull-worshipping, affluent people who angered their god, who then sank their island into the sea by way of retribution.

64

Mycenaean & Dark Ages
1500—776 BC

c. 1500 BC	Mycenaeans conquer Minoan Crete
c. 1400 BC	Date of the Trojan War?
1200–1100 BC	Mycenaeans superseded by invading Dorian Greeks
1100–750 BC	Dark Ages
900 BC	State of Sparta founded
800 BC	Date of Homer? Greeks adopt Phoenician script
776 BC	First Olympic Games

The successors to the Minoans were the Mycenaeans. Already established on mainland Greece, they were able to rapidly take over the remnants of Minoan power when it collapsed. They also inherited the Minoans' Linear alphabet, but wrote in their own language — Greek. Much more militaristic than their predecessors, these Ionian Greeks rapidly built a trading empire across the Eastern Mediterranean (the odd little 10-year local difficulty over Troy aside). In later Archaic times this period was mythologized into the 'heroic' age given life by the Homeric poems, but latterly the clumsy fortified town walls surviving from this period have been dubbed 'Cyclopic', as they look to have been built by the one-eyed giants who the ancients believed lived on the earth before mankind arrived.

Mycenaean power diminished with the arrival of invading Dorian Greeks (c. 1100 BC): trade and communications fell away, leaving the islands in the thrall of a mini dark age. Painting and writing were forgotten, and, left to their own devices, communities reorganized themselves on a city state basis. This, combined with the arrival of the Phoenicians reopening the trade routes, proved to be the catalyst for change that led to a resurgence in Greek culture. Only the major cities such as Athens and Corinth had held out against the worst of the cultural decline. By the end of the period they were large enough to expand, establishing colony daughter cities as far afield as France, while painting and writing (this time using a variation of the Phoenician alphabet) reappeared. In 776 BC the Olympic Games were established; an event now regarded as marking Greece's coming of age.

Archaic
776—490 BC

650 BC	First tyrants take power in Greece
621 BC	Draco takes power in Athens
594 BC	Solon takes power in Athens and overhauls political system
546 BC	Tyrant Pisistratus rules Athens
530 BC	Start of Persian Wars
508 BC	Cleisthenes takes power in Athens and introduces democratic reforms
490 BC	Persians invade Greek mainland and are defeated at the Battle of Marathon

During the Archaic period Greek art and architecture developed from Egyptian models of heavy pillared buildings and votive statues into the more elegant Greek forms that we know today. Very much an age of transition, these early examples of Archaic painting and statuary — with limbs and features all misproportioned — look to the modern eye like something 'done' by an exhibitor at the Royal Academy's summer exhibition, but the artists of this period increasingly acquired a mastery of basic technique and moved steadily towards a more realistic rendering of their subject matter. The islands were particularly prominent during this period, as their easily defended boundaries produced a number of powerful island city states, with the result that from Aegina to Samos the remains of Archaic structures and statuary can be found. This greater artistic and cultural cohesion was bolstered towards the end of the period by a succession of invasions by the dominant East Mediterranean power of the time — Persia. The first of these attacks came against the Cyclades in 499 and 490 BC. However, the victory by the Athenian-led Greek army at Marathon and then the Athenian naval victory over the Persians at Salamis saw the emergence of regional Greek political supremacy and this brought with it a renewed political and artistic confidence that became the hallmark of the 'Classical' era.

Classical & Hellenistic
490—180 BC

480 BC	2nd Persian invasion: Battles of Thermopylae and Salamis
478 BC	Delian League established
460–457 BC	Athenian Long Walls and Acropolis rebuilding begins

443–429 BC	Pericles rules Athens
430 BC	Plague hits Athens
431–404 BC	The Peloponnesian War
404 BC	Athens defeated by Sparta
399 BC	Socrates executed
359 BC	Philip II becomes king of Macedonia
338 BC	Philip II conquers Greece
333–327 BC	Alexander conquers Persia
323 BC	Alexander dies at Babylon
322 BC	Wars of succession
215–197 BC	Romo–Macedonian wars

The great winner in the Persian wars was the leading Greek participant, Athens. The Aegean islands, weakened by the Persian invasion, agreed to contribute to a fund to maintain a fleet under Athenian leadership to protect them from further aggression. Known as the Delian League, this alliance was used by Athens to exert de facto political control over the islands and prompted leading Greek city states (principally Sparta and Corinth) to fight the Peloponnesian War to prevent Athens emerging as the master of Greece. The islands were reduced to minor players in the larger Greek scene with local art and architecture being neglected in consequence. The islands became more important as sources of revenue and marble than centres in their own right. Islands that dared to oppose Athens (notably Aegina and Milos) also suffered greatly.

Athens, meantime, having been sacked during the Persian invasion, was ripe for redevelopment and under the leadership of Pericles spent (without consent) much of the Delian League contributions on rebuilding the temples on the Acropolis. Accompanied by an equally spectacular literary, theatrical and philosophical cultural explosion, this was the golden age of Greek civilization. However, Sparta's eventual defeat of Athens prevented Greek domination by one city, and the states (none of whom was powerful enough to take overall control) bickered on until Philip II succeeded to the throne of Macedonia. This event marked the transition from the Classical to the Hellenistic periods, for he unified Greece, and succeeded by his son, Alexander the Great, started of a wave of conquest that

was to extend to the borders of India. After the death of Alexander, the empire collapsed and the weakened city states and islands re-asserted their independence in the wars of succession that followed.

The Hellenistic period also left a major mark on Greek culture, though this was more of a natural progression from the symmetry of the classical period than a radical or sudden change. Buildings and artwork became much more decorative and ornamental, while literature and schools of learning grew from the classical foundations. Some of the islands benefited greatly from this, with Rhodes, Kos and Samos exerting greater influence in part as a result of their emergence as major centres of learning.

Roman
180 BC—395 AD

171–168 BC	Third Macedonian War
147–146 BC	Romans impose direct rule on Greece
48–31 BC	Roman civil war
120–150 AD	Period of Roman patronage in Athens under Hadrian
170 AD	Pausanias writes guide to Greece
200–300 AD	Rise of Christianity
395 AD	Alaric the Goth sacks Athens

As Greek power waned, neighbouring Rome gradually came to exercise influence over the divided city states and islands, initially as an arbiter in inter-city disputes, but then as a force in her own right. Having entered Greece in response to an attack by King Mithridates in 88 BC, she never really managed to leave and by 31 BC the whole of Greece had been incorporated into the Roman Empire: the islands divided between five provinces (the Adriatic islands were part of Epirus, the Dodecanese and Eastern Line islands were in Asia, Thassos was in Macedonia, Crete was joined with Libya in Cyrenica–Creta, and the remainder formed part of Achaea along with the Peloponnese, Evia, and the Greek mainland north of the Gulf of Corinth).

Despite the four centuries of stability that followed, the islands went into a slow but marked decline. Reduced to the edges of even provincial centres of power, they saw comparatively little new monumental building (a feature of Roman rule in other parts of the empire) and were increasingly prone to pirate attack. Athens and the islands also saw their first tourists during this period — notably the writer Pausanias (fl. c. 150 AD), who wrote an important guide (beloved by archaeologists wanting to know what specific buildings were called, looked like, and where they stood) to Greece describing the cities and their monuments. Other tourists were more mercenary, and the Roman epoch also saw denudation in local art as many ancient treasures were carted off to embellish the cities and villas of Italy (the occasional shipwrecks that turn up filled with bronze statues are a legacy of this trade). The Greek cities suffered in another important respect; subsumed into Rome's urban culture, they were never able to emerge as major centres of political or cultural power again.

Byzantine
395—1453

527–567	Reign of Emperor Justinian
1050–1200	Sicilian Normans invade Greece Venetians start annexing islands
1204	Sack of Constantinople
1210–1262	Feudal dukedoms established in Greece
1309	Knights of St. John capture Dodecanese islands
1355–1400	Turks conquer Greece
1453	Turks capture Constantinople

By 395 the Roman empire had grown so large that it became unmanageable: the practically-minded Emperor Constantine dividing it into two. Greece came under the control of the Eastern empire and was ruled from Byzantium (later renamed Constantinople and then İstanbul): a city still viewed by many Greeks as a capital under occupation. The islands now began the descent from a period of gradual decline to one of almost total anarchy, suffering considerably in the Slavic and Saracen invasions of the 7th and 9th centuries before becoming embroiled in the general stagnation of the Byzantine empire. Considerable depopulation followed with the destruction wrought by the Crusaders of the 1204 crusade who sacked Constantinople instead of retaking Jerusalem. The islands were part of the spoils and were divided among the plunderers

with the Venetians taking control of Crete, the Genoese of Chios, Lesbos and Astipalea among others. Thus when Constantinople finally fell to the Turks in 1453 many of the islands remained in Christian hands with widespread castle building going on — courtesy of much ancient temple demolition.

Venetian & Ottoman
1453—1830

1453–1469	Turks conquer Aegean islands
1687	Venetians capture Athens
1814	Beginnings of Greek independence movement
1815	Ionian islands come under British rule
1821–1825	Greek war of Independence
1827	Aegina becomes capital of Greece
1830	Frontiers of new Greek state established

During the succeeding centuries the Aegean islands gradually fell to Ottoman Turk rule. Some — such as Rhodes — were lost early (1522) but others under Venetian control held out until the last (Tinos) went in 1715. For the most part Turkish rule was benign. The new landlords were content to appoint island governors and collect taxes. But even as the Turks were completing their conquest of the Aegean their power had begun to wane. The islands became famous either for being the victims of pirates or for becoming their haunts; for they were natural strongholds from which they could attack other islands and the increasing trade between Europe and the Levant.

The years between 1450 and 1750 marked the nadir of the islands' fortunes, with many being abandoned altogether after their populations were massacred or sold into slavery. With Christian, Turkish, Barbary Coast, and local pirates all preying on the islands, the roll call of horrors is a long one. The 1500s saw the worst of it, with Ios being devastated in 1528, and the notorious Barbarossa starting his many depredations in the Aegean by attacking Aegina in 1537; killing all the men and taking 6000 women and children into slavery. In 1570 the Barbary pirate Kemal Reis went on a little slave-gathering expedition and removed the entire populations of Kithera, Skiathos and Skopelos to North Africa.

In the face of these attacks island communities did their best to protect themselves by abandoning coastal settlements in favour of defendable villages (or choras) inland. On a number of Cycladic islands these were built as stockade-like 'kastros' with the houses built on the inside of a defensive wall (these still survive on Folegandros, Kimolos and Antiparos — though in the case of the latter, it didn't prevent the islanders being massacred in 1794). Gradually, however, the more successful 'pirate' islands began to gain a degree of control via their fleets of ships which also took advantage of the growing trade opportunities to enhance their status still further by building impressively mansioned towns (e.g. Hydra, Spetses, and Chios). The arrival of foreign powers (notably the Russians who held control over a dozen islands during the 1770–4 Turkish war) also helped to stabilize the region. By the 19th century Greek nationalism was becoming a potent force: the islands coming to the fore as natural bastions from which insurgents could operate against weak Turkish rule. Less powerful islands demonstrated defiance of Turkish rule by the painting of island houses (heretofore kept an inconspicuous mud brick brown) in the Greek national colours of white and blue (now the hallmark of the typical Cycladic town), while the more powerful islands, via their fleets, gained a notable place in Greek history in the independence struggle; being more than a match for the Turks. This, however, led to reprisals (notably the massacre of 25,000 islanders on Chios in 1822).

Modern
1832—

1833	Prince Otto becomes King
1864	Britain cedes Ionian Islands
1913	George I assassinated
1914–1918	WW1: under Prime Minister Venizelos Greece joins Allies
1920–1923	Turkish War
1940	Greece enters WW2 on the side of the Allies following Metaxas's 'No!' ('Ochi') to Mussolini's demand for right of access
1941	Germans conquer Greece
1945–1949	Greek Civil War
1967–1974	Military rule of the Colonels
1974	Restoration of democracy

Independence in 1832 did not see all of modern-day Greece gain its freedom. The Cyclades aside, the islands remained in foreign hands, only gradually being gathered into the protective arms of the Greek state. Corfu and the Ionian islands were transferred from British control in 1864. WW1 saw the islands of the Northern Aegean come under Greek rule, while the Italians took the Dodecanese from the former Turkey and attempted an unsuccessful Italianisation programme; only to see the islands handed over to Greece at the end of WW2.

Since independence Greece has been engaged in sporadic conflicts with Turkey; notably the war of 1920–23, when Greece attempted to gain control of the ancient Greek cities on Turkey's Aegean seaboard, as well as the former capital of the Byzantine empire — Constantinople (now İstanbul). The war ended disastrously for Greece, culminating with the sack of Smyrna (now İzmir) and a territorial settlement that resulted in 1½ million ethnic-Greeks leaving Turkey for Greece, and some 400,000 ethnic Turks (mainly from the islands) going the other way. Relations between the two countries remain tense. Turkey has failed to recognise Greek sovereignty over the Aegean sea-bed (with its oil deposits) and the Turkish invasion of Cyprus in 1974 has done nothing to heal old wounds. But as both are members of NATO and have economies dependent on tourism they have a vested interest in avoiding outright hostilities. Greece's position has also been bolstered by its emergence as a democracy and membership of the EU (European Union): you can expect to see election posters and EU flags everywhere.

Politically, Greece is now relatively stable after a torrid post-Second World War period which saw a civil war (1945–49) between the government and communist forces, the military dictatorship of the colonels (1967–74) and the formal abolition of the monarchy in 1975 — an institution acquired by modern Greece after the Great Powers (Britian, France and Russia) that had championed her independence installed Prince Otto of Bavaria as King in 1833 after the assassination of the country's first president).

1
INTERNATIONAL LINES

**CYPRUS · EGYPT · GREECE · ISRAEL · ITALY (ANCONA
BARI · BRINDISI · VENICE) · LEBANON · TURKEY**

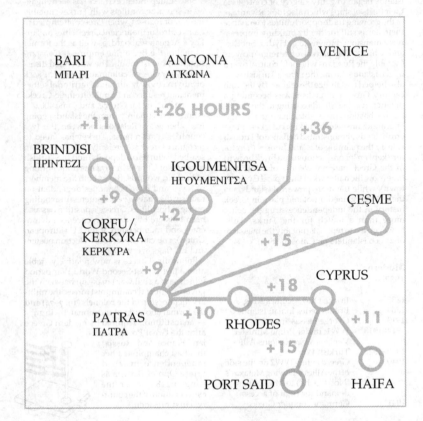

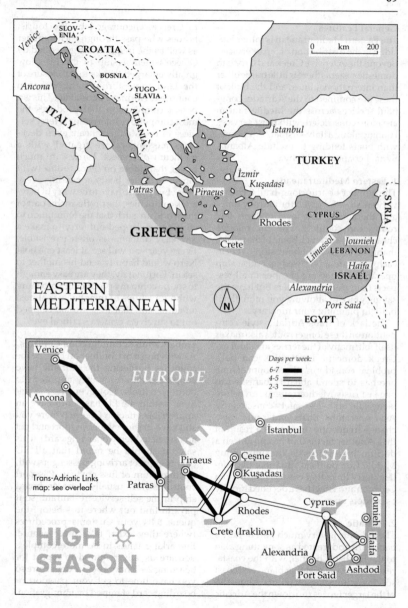

General Features

The Eastern Mediterranean is rather lop-sided in the distribution of ferry services. Beyond the extensive Greek and Croatian domestic systems there is little traffic other than international lines, and the bulk of these are confined to the Adriatic. Long-haul services across the Mediterranean are more constricted, with most services running along a Italy—Israel/Egypt axis, with boats tending to exclude Albania, Syria, Lebanon, and Libya.

1. Eastern Mediterranean

The number of 'true' long-haul ferries is very small — for given the journey times and the subsequent level of fares few routes can compete with the relative cheapness of air travel. Some of the ferries, thanks to six to eight hour stop-overs in each port, are advertised as cruise ship operations. They are cheaper in all respects than true cruise liners but have the saving grace of allowing you more flexibility in planning your itinerary.

The lack of trans-Adriatic style competition on these longer routes also makes itself felt: many of the ferries are older ex-Greek domestic boats (this can be a problem considering the amount of time one has to spend aboard), banished to one last rusty Mediterranean run before being sold off to less safety conscious SE Asia operators. Boats and routes also change frequently; in part as a result of this. Another factor that has produced a decline in services is the improving Middle East political situation: the 'life-line' ferry links that existed to Christian Lebanon and Israel have declined rapidly as borders open up.

2. Adriatic

The Adriatic is very much part of Italy's back yard and treated as something akin to the English Channel, with the coastal resort towns of her rather bland east coast serving as jumping-off points. Almost all of the larger ferries run down the Adriatic to Greece, encouraged by the tourist hordes who pass through each summer as well as the freight trade generated by Greece's membership of the EU (now greatly enlarged thanks to the closure of the land route through the war-torn countries of former Yugoslavia). This is a potent combination that produces the most competitive international ferry services in the Mediterranean: even deck-class passengers are treated with a modicum of respect. Ferries are much larger than those on other routes (with bigger or faster boats appearing every year), but you do have to be wary of maverick companies; the profits in this part of the world are such that the temptation to chuck on a clapped-out ferry to make a few easy drachma is often irresistible. Every year you will see at least one boat Nero would happily send his mother to sea in. Fortunately, they are easy enough to spot; a company producing a brochure without pictures of their boats is almost an admission that they are too clapped out to survive a camera's critical eye.

Embarkation & Immigration Controls

As with much of Continental Europe the countries bordering the Adriatic have adopted a rather low-key approach to border controls. However, their 'abolition' within the EU has yet to have an appreciable effect in Greece (where you still have to show your passport and get an associated ferry boarding card). This said, it should be noted that all EU countries greet arriving passengers with the minimum of fuss anyway. Passport control is now usually done on board ship in the self-service restaurant, so it pays to find out where it is before the queue tells you. Customs procedures (where they exist) take place ashore. Embarking tends to be more complex; you are usually required to report for boarding 2—3 hours before departure so you have time to get your passport or boarding card stamped by immigration.

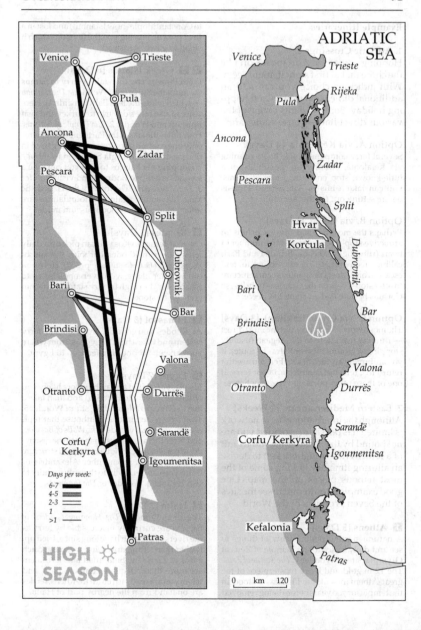

Example Itineraries

1. Adriatic Crossings

Hopping across the Adriatic needn't be the chore that at first sight it might seem. With judicious choice you can add an additional dimension to an island hopping holiday. Some variants to one of the various direct Italy—Patras routes are:

Option A: via Kefalonia [4 Days]

Several ferry companies have boats running via Kefalonia, offering the possibility of a little-known stop en route. Once at Patras, you can take a bus to Athens and Piraeus before setting out for the Aegean.

Option B: via Corfu [4 Days]

Perhaps the most popular route, Corfu is an attractive stop-over point and the number of boats (running to Ancona, Brindisi and Bari) calling ensures that it is easy to get to, and escape from. Most companies seem reluctant to offer stop-overs on the Greece—Italy leg, so Corfu is best visited en route to Greece.

Option C: via Crete (Iraklion) [3 Days]

The most expensive option, but the most direct — running from Italy to the Aegean (usually stopping at Igoumenitsa or Patras en route). If you are buying a return ticket, then you needn't return to Crete, but can pick up your ferry at one of these other ports on your way home.

2. Eastern Mediterranean [4 Weeks]

Although the international ferry network is limited it is possible (provided you are not bound by the constraining time limit of a return charter flight ticket) to devise an alluring itinerary linking some of the most famous places on the map. One good example is to attempt to see the sites of the Seven Wonders of the World:

1 Athens [5 Days]

A natural starting point; plenty of things to see and daily buses to the Temple of Zeus at **Olympia**; site of Wonder 1: *The Statue of Zeus.* The 12 m gold and ivory masterpiece of the great Athenian sculptor Phidias, it stood in the temple for 700 years before being removed

to Constantinople (now İstanbul) and lost in a fire (475 AD), leaving you the floor on which it stood to gawp at instead.

2 3 Greek Islands [6 Days]

From Piraeus you then take a ferry to **Samos** (home of the 8th of the 7 Wonders: *The Heraion* — which made the lists Babylon didn't). Here you can also take a day trip to Turkey and visit Ephesus and Wonder 2: *The Temple of Artemis.* Four times the size of the Parthenon in Athens, only one column survives: most being used in the construction of Agia Sophia in İstanbul.

Hopping via Patmos to **Kos** you can take a second day trip to Bodrum and visit Wonder 3: *The Mausoleum.* The tomb of the Hellenistic king Mausolus; again the foundations are intact, along with a good museum model.

4 Rhodes [3 Days]

On your return to Kos you can pick up a daily ferry down to Rhodes harbour; the site of Wonder 4: *The Colossus* (see p. 352). Here you can wonder along with everyone else as to where this 31 m high bronze statue of the Sun god Helios stood.

5 Limassol [3 Days]

At Rhodes you join the international ferry system and take a boat to Cyprus; from where you can get a connecting ferry on to Egypt.

6 Egypt [7 Days]

Ideally, you'd find a boat (but more likely you will have to ferry to Port Said and then take a bus to Cairo) to **Alexandria**; site of Wonder 5: *The Pharos* (the famous lighthouse that replaced the original wonder, *the Walls of Babylon,* and recently in the news, thanks to the discovery of parts of the earthquake toppled structure on the sea-bed). From either Alexandria or Cairo you can get easily to the only wonder to survive intact: Wonder 6: *The Pyramids.*

7 Haifa [7 Days]

The final Wonder: *The Hanging Gardens of Babylon* are currently inaccessible by ferry as the rivers of Babylon have long since dried up. Rather than sitting down and weeping, catch a bus to Zion. The Sinai road and Jerusalem are more than adequate compensation, and when you are ready to return to Athens, ferries are on hand from the nearby port of Haifa.

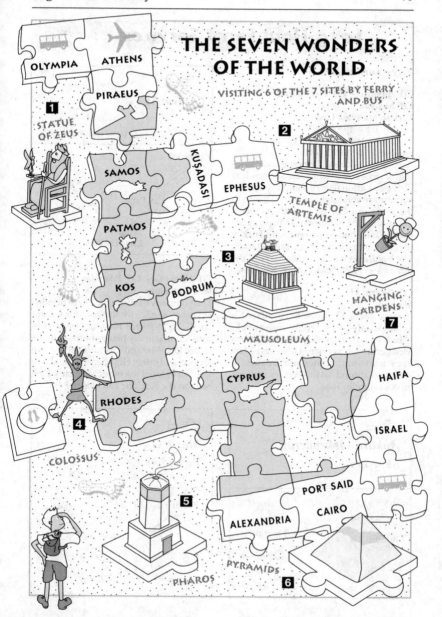

THE SEVEN WONDERS OF THE WORLD

VISITING 6 OF THE 7 SITES BY FERRY AND BUS

Long-Haul Ferry Services

Italy—Turkey Links

C/F *Ankara* - C/F *Iskenderun*
C/F *Samsun*
Turkish Maritime Lines
Ankara; 1983; 10,552 GRT.
Iskenderun; 1991; 10,583 GRT.
Samsun; 1985; 10,583 GRT.

Among the frequent chopping and changing of Eastern Mediterranean services Turkey's national ferry company are one of the more consistent players. Thanks to the large number of Turkish nationals guest-working in Europe, TML provides regular links between Venice and Turkey to cater for this burgeoning travel market. The Venice—İsmir link runs all year, the others are 'High Season only' services.

C/F *Charm M*
Marlines
In past years Marlines have offered a valuable Italy—Crete High Season weekly link as part of a wider-ranging Eastern Mediterranean service. However, Marlines boats and routes are frequently swapped around, so this service may not be operating in 1999.

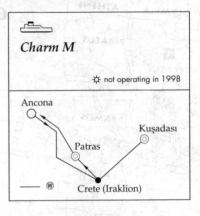

Charm M

☼ not operating in 1998

Ancona — Kuşadası — Patras — Crete (Iraklion)

—— Ⓦ

C/F *Maria G* - C/F *Poseidon*
Med Link Lines
This company has been running a Brindisi—Turkey service for the last four summers. Calls at Patras have not been very consistent, usually being confined to the return leg. When not operating the above service, and out of High Season the above ferries augment the other Med Link Line boat on the Adriatic run (see p. 80).

Ankara - Iskenderun
Samsum

Venice — İzmir — Marmaris — *or* — Antalya — Brindisi — Çeşme

—— Ⓦ
– – – Ⓦ
· · · · Ⓦ

Maria G
Poseidon

Brindisi — Çeşme — Patras

Mediterranean

—— Ⓦ

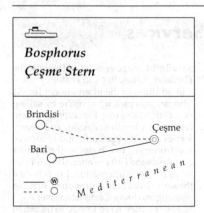

Bosphorus
Çeşme Stern

Sea Harmony - Sea Symphony
Nissos Kypros

C/F Bosphorus - C/F Çeşme Stern
Stern Line
Bosphorus; 1962; 4727 GRT.
Çeşme Stern; 1964; 3984 GRT.
Two old ferries ran an Italy—Turkey service in 1997. Neither has much going for them and offer good examples of how some ferry lines exploit ancient vessels that are no longer allowed in the Greek domestic fleet (courtesy of the 'not more than 30-years old' rule) to make money on international routes.

C/F Sea Harmony - C/F Sea Symphony
Poseidon Lines
Sea Harmony; 1977; 5477 GRT.
Sea Symphony; 1976; 5477 GRT.
These ferries maintain an annual service between Piraeus and Haifa, combining to provide a twice-weekly, no-frills service. In High Season the *Sea Harmony* adds Patmos to her outward schedule and Tinos on her return, while the *Sea Symphony* adds Crete (Iraklion) to her run.

C/F Nissos Kypros
Salamis Lines; 1958; 6103 GRT.
A Scandinavian-built train ferry that still has the railway lines extant on her car deck, the *Nissos Kypros* is now well established on this route. Long familiar to island hoppers (she is the old *Homeros*, a

former NEL ferry that has furrowed the Aegean since the late 70s), she is now on the last leg of her Mediterranean career.

C/F Princesa Cypria -
C/F Princesa Marissa
Louis Cruise Lines
The *Princesa Marissa* combines with the *Princesa Cypria* and P/S *Princesa Victoria* to offer 2/3 day or weekly 'cruises' out of Limassol to Egypt and Israel. Schedules tend to see minor alterations each year, but in the absence of any competition there is little incentive for change.

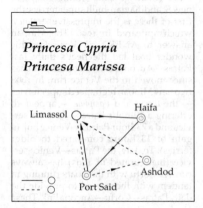

Princesa Cypria
Princesa Marissa

Adriatic Ferry Services

Northern Italy—Greece Links

C/F *Ikarus* - C/F *Pasiphae*
C/F *Aretousa* - C/F *Daedalus*
C/F *Erotokritos* - C/F *Fedra*
Minoan Lines

Ikarus, Pasiphae; 1997, 1998; 31,000 GRT.
Aretousa; 1995; 31,000 GRT.
Daedalus; 1973; 7323 GRT.
Erotokritos; 1974; 12,888 GRT.
Fedra; 1974; 12,527 GRT.

The biggest name on the trans-Adriatic crossing, Minoan Lines are also arguably the best Adriatic line going, with a well merited reputation for a high quality service. Even Deck-class passengers are treated as if they are human beings (though — as is the case with all these international boats — you will find your journey much more comfortable if you book an aircraft-type seat). With a combined fleet of six boats running up the Adriatic, Minoan offer frequent services to Venice (route C) in addition to the traditional daily Ancona departures (routes A and B).

A second major weapon in the Minoan Lines' challenge is the commissioning of new Scandinavian-built super ferries; the first of these is the impressive *Aretousa* which appeared in 1996. The Minoan answer to ANEK's *El. Venizelos*, this wonder boat led the fleet's daily fast Patras—Ancona service (route B), but has since moved to the Venice run. In 1998 two new Minoan high speed super ferries — the *Ikarus* and *Pasiphae* — appeared, offering a 19-hour Patras—Ancona service and a 23-hour Patras—Venice link (a gain of 13 hours compared to older ferries). To date, the Patras—Venice service (inaugurated in 1995) has always run via Corfu with the boats running in tandem with those used to provide the daily Patras—Corfu—Ancona link. These

are all mid-range vessels, and include the *Daedalus, Erotokritos* and *Fedra*.

In addition to the international traffic, Minoan also pick up revenue by selling domestic tickets (e.g. Patras or Igoumenitsa to Corfu) on their Ancona and Venice ferries running via Corfu and Igoumenitsa (route A); two boats — the smaller *Erotokritos* and *Fedra* — offered this service in 1998. Note: international tickets cost the same from both Patras and Corfu, so passengers doing Corfu 'stop-overs' get 'stung' as they have to pay extra when buying a domestic ticket (regular 'stop-over' tickets that allow you to visit Corfu without paying anything on top of the regular Ancona—Patras fare are only available for the Italy—Greece run). It can also pay to keep in mind that if you use these boats you are able to claim a 10% discount on Greek Domestic services provided by Minoan Lines (provided that you buy these tickets along with your international ticket).

C/F *Ionian Galaxy* - C/F *Ionian Island*
C/F *Ionian Star*
Strintzis Lines

Ionian Galaxy; 1972; 9964 GRT.
Ionian Island; 1973; 9547 GRT.
Ionian Star; 1992; 14,398 GRT.

Between 1995–1997 Strintzis Lines joined forces with Minoan Lines to provide joint daily services on several routes. Now that Minoan re-equipped their fleet with three new boats, Strintzis have been left to go it alone again. This hasn't proved easy as they can now only claim to have the forth best fleet on the northern Adriatic routes. In 1997 they ran the *Ionian Galaxy* and *Ionian Island* on the Ancona—Patras route without conspicuous success and both boats moved over to running to Venice in 1998, and further changes are anticipated in 1999.

Both the *Ionian Galaxy* and *Ionian Island* are chunky affairs with distinctive red-and-white striped ski-slope-shaped funnels. They could once claim to offer a new level of facilities for Adriatic travel, but now these facilities are best described as mid-range, being easily outdone by the best of the competition. There is little to choose between the boats, though the *Ionian Galaxy* has the edge with sun-deck sloanes. They have now been joined by the larger *Ionian Star*: an altogether more impressive vessel, though, like her companions, these days rather dwarfed by the competition.

In an effort to improve their competitive edge Strintzis Lines were offering free ferry tickets to Kefalonia or Ithaca (via their domestic boats operating out of Patras) in 1998 for purchasers of international tickets. It is possible that this offer will be repeated in 1999.

C/F *Kriti I* - C/F *Kriti II*
C/F *El. Venizelos* - C/F *Talos*
ANEK Lines
El. Venizelos; 1992; 23,000 GRT.
Kriti I; 1979; 14,385 GRT.
Kriti II; 1979; 14,375 GRT.
Talos; 1975 (rebuilt 1995); 6135 GRT.
Once the main rival of Minoan Lines on Piraeus—Crete routes, ANEK also provide a competing service across the Adriatic, though of late they have rather lost something of their competitive edge. ANEK's last serious attempt to gain the initiative came in 1992 with the introduction of the 3000-passenger *El. Venizelos*. Since then they have struggled: the introduction of two reconditioned ferries — the *Kriti I* and *Kriti II* — running from Patras to Ancona in 23 hours being too little, too late when compared with the competition from Minoan Lines and Superfast Ferries (see overleaf). Despite being overtaken as the biggest and best boat in the Adriatic the *El. Venizelos* is the one real jewel in the ANEK fleet — though she often seems all but empty, even with

Ikarus - Pasiphae
Aretousa - Erotokritos
Daedalus - Fedra

Ionian Galaxy
Ionian Island - Ionian Star

Kriti I - Kriti II
El. Venizelos - Talos

Superfast III
Superfast IV

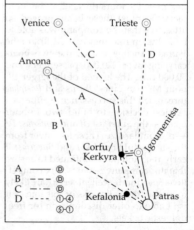

a regular complement of passengers aboard. She has spent the last four years running up to Trieste (route D), thus providing a competing North Italy service to Minoan Lines' Venice run. ANEK's remaining boat is significantly smaller, besides offering an inferior service. The rebuilt *Talos* has been on route A for a number of years (formerly as the *Kydon*).

If you are travelling in anything other than deck-class, then check out respective company fares. In past years ANEK's have tended to be slightly higher than Minoan Lines. The sequence of calls at Igoumenitsa and Corfu has also varied between the companies in past years; if Corfu is your destination then this should be checked out.

C/F *Superfast III* - C/F *Superfast IV*
Superfast Ferries
Superfast III, IV; 1998; 29,300 GRT.
This ferry company arrived on the scene in 1995 with two brand-new, purpose-built Adriatic ferries that took the route by storm. The attraction of two large and well-promoted boats (thanks to their stream-lined look and bright red hulls) offering a fast direct Patras—Ancona sailing (route B). Able to make the crossing in a mere 20 hours (instead of the more usual 30 plus) these boats proved so attractive that the company was able to boast that in 1996 they carried 40% of the Patras—Ancona traffic, the two boats carrying over 220,000 passengers and 50,000 cars. The arrival of the larger 19-hour Minoan Lines' *Ikarus* and *Pasiphae* threatened this success: hence Superfast Ferries' decision to build two 18-hour boats — the *Superfast III* and *Superfast IV* — of a similar size. These took over from the successful *Superfast I* and *Superfast II* early 1998 and have continued to ensure that this company remains very competitive. Speed and excellent service are likely to remain the hallmarks of this line as it isn't able to offer discounts on (or free) domestic tickets.

Bari—Greece Links

C/F *Athens Express*
C/F *Polaris* - C/F *Saturnus*
C/F *Venus* - C/F *Vega*
Ventouris Ferries
Athens Express; 1969; 6416 GRT.
Polaris; 1975; 20,326 GRT.
Saturnus; 1974; 1953 GRT.
Venus; 1976; 14,540 GRT.
Vega; 1975; 2308 GRT.
In past years Ventouris Ferries managed to carve out a nice little position for themselves by concentrating all their resources on the Bari—Patras run and then packing it with boats to discourage competition. This is now changing as the relative shortness of the route has prompted the arrival of a growing number of much better-equipped vessels. In any event, the result is a daily sailing between Bari and Patras (most of the Ventouris ferries run itinerary F). The quality of this company's boats varies greatly. The *Athens Express* is a good example of the pokey end of the scale — being topped with a funnel so weedy that if it had been afloat in Victorian times, photographs of it would have been furtively circulated amongst the members of London clubs as a warning on the dangers of excessively cold baths. The other boats are better, particularly the modern *Venus* which runs the Patras—Kefalonia (Sami) —Bari route in tandem with the above. The *Saturnus* is also unmissable, its port-hole-free and windowless sides giving way to a prefab-like superstructure.

C/F *Countess M* - C/F *Dame M*
C/F *Duchess M*
Marlines
Countess M; 1968; 10093 GRT.
Dame M; 1972; 14015 GRT.
Duchess M; 1970; 2786 GRT.
Marlines have recently joined the Bari ferry throng, transferring boats from their traditional Ancona route where they were proving to be uncompetitive. Their

Athens Express
Polaris - Saturnus
Venus - Vega

Countess M
Dame M
Duchess M

Superfast I
Superfast II

Megistanas

◇

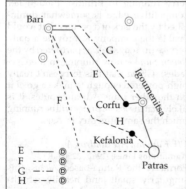

E ——— ⓓ
F - - - - ⓓ
G -·-·- ⓓ
H --- ⓓ

previous attempts to increase custom by adding Ithaca and then Kefalonia to their itineraries on this route, strongly suggests that their boats (now running itinerary E) are finding it difficult to compete. Part of this line's problem is that its fleet consists of elderly ferries that have undergone extensive 'rebuilding'. The *Countess M* is better than the *Dame M*, though this isn't saying much given the superior facilities offered by boats on other routes. At odd times of the year they are joined by the equally indifferent *Duchess M*.

C/F *Superfast I* - C/F *Superfast II*
Superfast Ferries
Superfast I, II; 1995; 23,663 GRT.
Easily the best boats on this route, it is a measure of the intensive competition that boats as new and as impressive as these two vessels (see the Superfast Ferries entry on p. 78) have already been relegated to running on the Bari route. By rights they deserve to clean up and all but did in 1998. This should force the competition into making changes in 1999.

C/F *Megistanas*
Arkadia Lines
Megistanas; 1959; 6530 GRT.
The last decade seen Igoumenitsa emerge as an alternative starting point to Patras for Bari-bound ferries thanks to the growth in trans-Adriatic trade. Arkadia Lines once ruled the route via two ferries that combined to provide a daily link, though they and their elderly ferry — the *Megistanas* — have been absent of late.

Brindisi—Greece Links

C/F *Egitto Express* - C/F *Laurana* - C/F *Palladio* - C/F *Sansovino*
Adriatica
Egitto Express; 1973; 8957 GRT.
Laurana; 1992; 10,000 GRT.
Palladio, Sansovino; 1989; 10,000 GRT.
Adriatica have run several medium-sized ferries on the Brindisi—Patras run (route

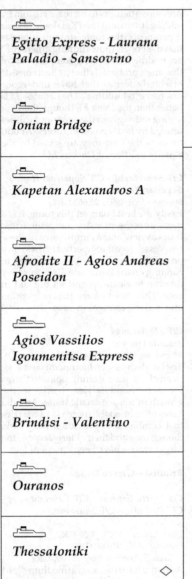

Egitto Express - Laurana
Paladio - Sansovino

Ionian Bridge

Kapetan Alexandros A

Afrodite II - Agios Andreas
Poseidon

Agios Vassilios
Igoumenitsa Express

Brindisi - Valentino

Ouranos

Thessaloniki

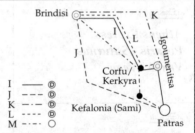

I) on an annual basis, as part of its more wide-ranging Italian Adriatic seaboard operation over the last few years. Packed to bursting with backpackers (taking advantage of Inter/Eurail concessionary rates) and Italian holidaymakers using a national carrier, deck passengers not in one of these categories will probably do better with one of the rival lines. All boats have reasonable on-board facilities that are well maintained.

C/F *Ionian Bridge*
Strintzis Lines
Ionian Bridge; 1976; 12,067 GRT.
Strintzis have managed to remain competitive on this route by moving a comparatively large ferry onto the run. The *Ionian Bridge* is easily the biggest (and best) ferry running to Brindisi, though her competitive edge is somewhat diminished by the lack of a partner that would enable the company to provide a daily service (in 1997 she was partnered by the *Ionian Sun* — now running in the Cyclades). Given that this ferry isn't really high-powered enough to make a go of it on the other trans-Adriatic routes, it is likely that the *Ionian Bridge* will be running much the same itinerary in 1999.

C/F *Kapetan Alexandros A*
Agoudimos Lines; 1962; 3250 GRT.
Formerly the Rafina-based *Alekos*, this singularly small (and heavily rebuilt) ferry moved into this Adriatic route in

1992. She has continued on it ever since — though schedules have been erratic. During the High Season she usually runs a simple, daily one-way Igoumenitsa—Corfu—Brindisi service (itinerary L), while the rest of the year she operates a thrice-weekly Patras—Igoumenitsa—Corfu—Brindisi extended run (itinerary I). Although not as large as some of the other boats on either route, she is a well appointed craft with a very glitzy, if very small, deck-class lounge, and a good track record for reliability.

C/F *Afrodite II* - C/F *Agios Andreas*
C/F *Poseidon*
Med Link Lines
Agios Andreas; 1969; 10178 GRT.
Afrodite II; 1967; 4190 GRT.
Poseidon; 1971; 8980 GRT.

A relatively new company to the Adriatic scene, Med Link are building up a fleet of elderly, but reasonable boats, on the Brindisi route (running itinerary J from April to September) in addition to their long-haul Turkey service (see p. 74). Since 1996 this company's ferries have made additional stops at Kefalonia during the High Season (a feature which suggests they are having difficulty drumming up tourist traffic). A comparative lack of publicity means these boats have a relatively low profile.

C/F *Agios Vassilios*
C/F *Igoumenitsa Express*
AK Ventouris
Agios Vassilios; 1962; 2977 GRT.
Igoumenitsa Express; 1961; 2455 GRT.

Another of the newer companies on the route, AK Ventouris were the new arrivals in 1993 (running itinerary K). Their first boat — the *Anna V* — had the misfortune to sink at her moorings in early 1996 and the company hasn't really recovered since: in fact no boats were running during the 1998 high season. Prior to last year a reliable service was maintained. Even after the *Anna V* disappeared in 1996 via

the *Agios Vassilios* and an old Aegean ferry, the *Igoumenitsa Express* (formerly the *Sifnos Express*). Given that this company has appeared and then vanished before it could be the case that AK Ventouris has gone back into hibernation.

C/F *Brindisi* - C/F *Valentino*
Vergina Ferries
Brindisi; 1968; 5169 GRT.
Valentino; 1972; 4469 GRT.

These two ferries offer an annual Patras—Brindisi service (itinerary J), though schedules include Igoumenitsa at the height of the summer. Their main source of income is derived from the transportation of commercial vehicles rather than foot passengers (these boats are just too ugly to make the attractive brochure propositions). The *Brindisi* is the ex-Mediterranean Lines' *Raffaello*. The romantically named *Valentino* is singularly ill-named, looking like a floating municipal car-park.

C/F *Ouranos*
Fragline; 1969; 3777 GRT.

After the best part of a decade running in tandem with a feebly small companion, the *Ouranos* has run solo on route L since 1995. A reasonable enough boat, she isn't sufficiently high-powered enough to make a go of it on any of the other Adriatic routes, and is looking extremely dated. With a ferry nearing the end of its working life, Fragline (a company with a reputation for providing a consistent service) must surely be tempted to make substantial changes in the near future.

C/F *Thessaloniki*
Unknown Owner; 1966; 10,499 GRT.

A former Greek domestic ferry — the D.A.N.E *Kamiros* — too long in the tooth to still be competitive in Greece, the *Thessaloniki* is definitely a boat to avoid if she is still on the route in 1999. Unfortunately, the Brindisi run attracts at least one rust bucket each year — though they never last very long.

C/M *Catamaran Dados I*
C/M *Santa Eleonora*

Since 1996 catamarans have operated up-market Italy—Greece services. The Brindisi—Corfu—Igoumenitsa service is run by the *Catamaran Dados I*, leaving the *Santa Eleonora* operating to Corfu and Paxi. Very expensive, and catering for affluent Italians, scheduling tends to be 'elastic'.

C/F *Apollonia II* - C/F *Egnatia II* - C/F *Media II* - C/F *Panther* - C/F *Poseidonia*
Hellenic Mediterranean Lines

Apollonia II; 1964; 3950 GRT.
Egnatia II; 1973; 11,481 GRT.
Media II; 1964; 3680 GRT.
Panther; 1967; 4269 GRT.
Poseidonia; 1967; 4479 GRT.

HML Ferries, one of the mainstays of the Brindisi—Patras route, are one of the most competitive lines in the Adriatic. Their innovative itineraries take in a number of Ionian islands otherwise inaccessible except by domestic ferries. In 1995 Zakinthos was added to itineraries that have long included useful calls at Kefalonia (Sami) and Paxi — otherwise ignored by ferry operators. Much of this enterprising scheduling is due to the fact that HML rely on very dated, small ferries and need to have some means of competing with other lines. However, the period 60s on-board facilities are kept commendably clean and ensure that the boats have more character than most. The only quibble is the swapping around of boats and times in annual fleet reshuffles that means you are faced with the least consistent time-table in the Adriatic, which means you have to ascertain the name of your boat when buying your ticket.

P/S *Petrakis* - P/S *Sotirakis*

Despite Albanian pirate attacks on this coast, tour boats run to the Albanian port of Sarandë, undertaking the 90-minute run several days a week (these are apt to change each year). Tickets must be booked a day in advance for visa processing.

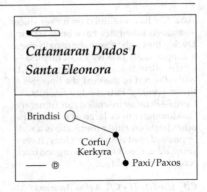

Catamaran Dados I
Santa Eleonora

Brindisi

Corfu/
Kerkyra

—— Ⓓ

Paxi/Paxos

Apollonia II - Egnatia II
Media II - Panther
Poseidonia

Brindisi

Corfu/
Kerkyra

—— Ⓓ
---- Ⓓ
—·— Ⓓ
—·· Ⓞ

Paxi

Kefalonia
(Sami)

Patras

Zakinthos/Zante

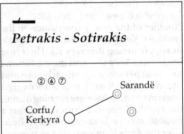

Petrakis - Sotirakis

—— ②⑥⑦

Sarandë

Corfu/
Kerkyra

Trans-Med Ports (Non-Adriatic)

Alexandria

Egypt is too far removed from the rest of the ferry network to figure widely on schedules. Services that do exist are rather irregular with most operating via the Cypriot port of Limassol. Alexandria is an attractive neo-colonial city with good bus and rail links to the capital Cairo, some three hours drive to the south. The port area is very extensive, though ferry traffic has declined with the reopening of the Suez Canal and Port Said.

Ancona

The number two destination for north-bound Patras ferries, Ancona is a substantial — but thanks to its commercial activities not particularly attractive — city on the upper Italian Adriatic coast. It sees considerable ferry traffic thanks to good road connections north (and hence is a natural departure point for holidaying Italians from the northern cities) and trans-European rail links (daily departures for Frankfurt and Munich). Nearby Rimini also has a daily overnight express train to Milan, Bonn and Amsterdam.

Those mad enough to want to stay will find several cheap hotels opposite the railway station, which is home to a tourist information kiosk that issues free city maps along with accommodation information.

Ashdod

Very nearly Israel's second port, lying just north of the Gaza Strip, Ashdod very occasionally appears on cruise/ferry schedules. Links are very erratic indeed. Given the troubled state of the Gaza Strip an increase in ferry activity is unlikely.

Bari

An attractive — if unspectacular — city, Bari is too far south down the Italian boot to be an appealing port of call for travellers heading on to Northern Europe, nor is it sufficiently north to appeal to holidaying Italians either. As a result, it is very much the number three west-Adriatic ferry port. On the same rail line as Brindisi, but a longer journey by ferry, your chances of finding a train seat in summer are likely to be limited.

Brindisi

This pleasant city is the destination for the majority of the Patras—Italy ferries. This is due to the easy turn-around time (22 hours); thus allowing two ferries to combine and offer a daily service in each direction. This is the best arrival point if Rome or southern Italy is your next port of call. However, if you are passing through Italy you will still be faced with a long drive or rail journey north.

Accommodation can be a problem thanks to occasional waves of boat people from Albania (most of whom are temporarily housed in local hotels before being returned).

Cyprus

Offering an interesting mix of sun, sand, and antiquities — to say nothing of Greek and British military cultural lifestyles happily co-existing side by side — Cyprus offers a worthy stop-over should you be hopping between Greece and Israel or Egypt. Since the 1974 Turkish invasion the Cypriot Republic has been confined to the southern 60% of the island. Despite this the south has prospered while the isolated Turkish-occupied north (set up as an unrecognised Turkish Cypriot republic) remains stagnant. The UN–monitored Green Line between the two sides of the island cannot be crossed at any point. A peace process of sorts has been crawling along for years, but was all but wrecked with the fatal shooting of two Cypriot protesters in August 1996. It would be unrealistic to expect the situation to improve in the foreseeable future. Given that northern Cyprus can only be accessed via Turkish ports, those services are covered in Chapter 13. You should also note the potential pitfall of having a Turkish-Cypriot stamp in your passport. This can (though not always) cause severe difficulties when entering Greece, since you can be deemed to have inevitably been in receipt of 'stolen property' (e.g. by staying in a hotel owned by a displaced Greek Cypriot), your new 'criminal' status will go

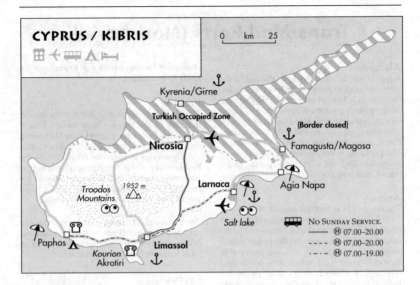

CYPRUS / KIBRIS

0   km   25

Kyrenia/Girne

Turkish Occupied Zone

Nicosia

(Border closed)

Famagusta/Magosa

Troodos Mountains 1952 m

Larnaca

Agia Napa

Salt lake

Paphos

Kourion Akrotiri

Limassol

 No Sunday Service.
——— 07.00–20.00
- - - - 07.00–20.00
- - · - 07.00–19.00

down even less well if attempting to enter Greek Cyprus: you could well be denied entry.

With the division of the island has come a shift in the focus of Cypriot life, from the divided capital of Nicosia, to the south coast ports. **Limassol** (a seemingly un-planned concrete town) has became the de facto centre of Greek Cyprus as well as the ferry hub of the Eastern Mediterranean beyond Greece. The centre is quite pleasant in a garrison town sort of way; the nearby British forces base at Akrotiri dominating the local economy. Helpful tourist offices at both new ferry terminus building (linked to the centre by city bus #1) and Limassol waterfront have free maps showing all hotels and guest houses.

The island's second port is at **Larnaca**. A prosperous resort that has grown up since the invasion thanks to the new international airport and the need to replace lost Famagusta. The Costa del Sol atmosphere of the seafront (complete with an awful beach) contrasts greatly with the ghost town ferry terminus (Larnaca is one of the quietest international ferry ports in the Med.) 2 km east of the centre.

Λ

Geroskipou Camping: Only island site, on the beach 3 km to the east of Paphos.

∞

Tourist offices carry information on all the easily accessible sights from Limassol. These are the ruined cities at Kourion and Paphos and the Troodos mountains: a cool retreat from the heat of the coast.

Durrës

The principal port of Albania and its nearby capital of Tirana, ugly Durrës is not a leading candidate for an increase in ferry activity in the near future. Until the recent wave of liberalisation the thrice-monthly ferry link to Trieste was one of the principal means of entering the country.

Haifa

Haifa is a large (and not particularly attractive) port on the northern edge of Israel's Mediterranean seaboard. Conflict with her neighbours means that the country has no land route to Europe, and this is reflected in the relatively high level of ferry traffic linking Haifa with Limassol, Rhodes and Piraeus. This link operates three days a week in High Season and is maintained at twice-weekly level throughout the rest of the year. Since the peace treaty with Egypt irregular services to

Alexandria and Port Said are also on offer, but most are tourist/cruise ship vessels with prices to match. Most casual non-vehicle traffic on both these routes is gleaned from the ranks of the backpacker and Kibbutz brigade. Security problems within the country are reflected on ferries that include Israel in their itineraries. This is tighter than on other boats (particularly since the terrorist attack on the Greek tourist ship *City of Poros* in 1988) and even if your destination is not Israel you can expect rigorous questioning on boarding

Jounieh

A small port set safely in the Christian enclave of the Lebanon in a wide bay 20 km north of Beirut. A ferry link was established on the outbreak of the civil war that left Beirut port in ruins. For the bulk of the last 20 years operating a 'rat' run to Larnaca on Cyprus. Services were suspended in 1994.

Otranto

Cornered on the heel of Italy, Otranto is too remote to attract ferry traffic bar the odd maverick boat, and even then only because it offers the shortest (a beguiling advertising point) Adriatic crossing from Corfu and Igoumenitsa. Poor road and rail connections with the rest of Italy.

Port Said

Lying on the north-eastern entrance to the Suez Canal, Port Said has regained its role among Egypt's premier commercial ports following the re-opening of the waterway. Good bus links with Cairo, which is just as well since — canal excepted — there is little of interest here. Fortunately the Cairo road follows the bank of the canal (free sightseeing) so that arrival here has some advantages. That said, if you are arriving as an independent traveller outside a cruise/tour visit, you should allow 3–4 hours to negotiate the tortuous local immigration and customs processing operation.

Sarandë

This shop and restaurant-free town on Albania's southern coastline is now visited by Corfu tour boats four days a week. Passengers must pre-book at least four days in advance: this is to enable visas to be prepared. When

booking you will be asked to provide your surname, forenames, father's name, place of birth, date of birth, nationality, and occupation. Fares are quite high: 7000 GDR one way, 12,000 GDR return (plus a US$ 30 visa). A one-way ticket out of Albania to Corfu sees the price rise to US$ 40 (it never hurts to have the odd dollar in your pocket when venturing off the tourist trail). Given the current shortages in Albania you are also advised to take absolutely everything bar drinking water with you.

Trieste

Argued over by Yugoslavia and Italy after the last war, Trieste voted to join the latter in a UN plebiscite. Despite this, it retains strong connections with the Slovenian Istrian peninsula and is awkwardly linked with the rest of Italy (though it is the terminus for several trans-Europe trains — notably to Budapest and Geneva). The northern gateway to Slovenia and Croatia, the city remains a ferry backwater tucked away at the head of the Adriatic and unlikely to see an increase in traffic in 1999.

Valona

Albania's third, and most northerly port, it saw its first regular ferry service in 1993. A town with few facilities, it is unlikely to develop in the future. Conditions of passage as for Sarandë above.

Venice

Considering how great an impact Venice has had over the history and culture of the Mediterranean it is surprising how little it figures on ferry schedules. To some extent this is due to the same geographical difficulty that affects Trieste: being at the head of the Adriatic the city does not figure prominently on trans-European road or rail routes. Since motoring around Venice is somewhat handicapped by the canal system, and the fact that former Yugoslavia (only a couple of hours away by road) is no longer on the tourist map, it is inevitable that the *Stazione marittima* is under-utilised. This is a pity, as arriving by boat is one of the best ferry landfalls going. It is almost worth waiting for one of the few ferries that visit simply to enjoy this experience. In practice, however, Venice remains the preserve of long-haul travellers, with the majority of boats voyaging to Patras or Turkey.

2
ATHENS & PIRAEUS

ATHENS · PIRAEUS (GREAT HARBOUR) · (ZEA)
LAVRION · RAFINA · SALAMIS

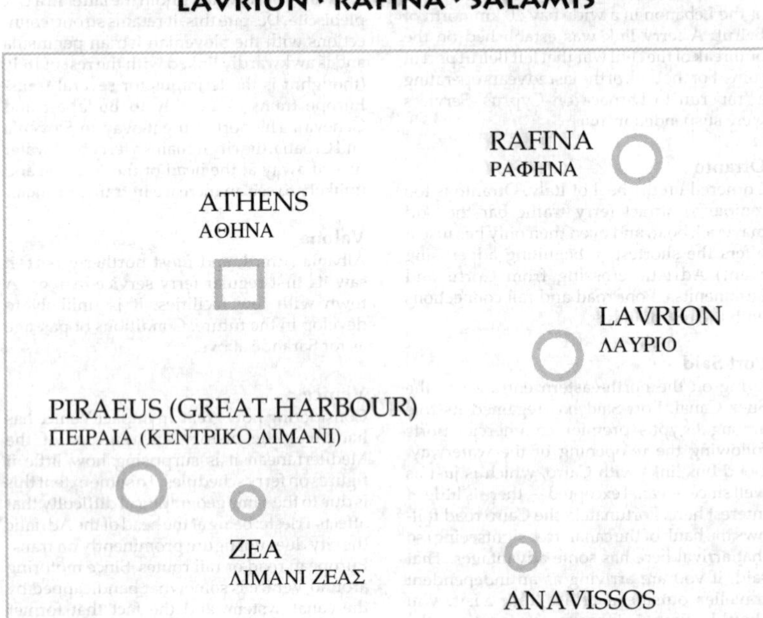

RAFINA
ΡΑΦΗΝΑ

ATHENS
ΑΘΗΝΑ

LAVRION
ΛΑΥΡΙΟ

PIRAEUS (GREAT HARBOUR)
ΠΕΙΡΑΙΑ (ΚΕΝΤΡΙΚΟ ΛΙΜΑΝΙ)

ZEA
ΛΙΜΑΝΙ ΖΕΑΣ

ANAVISSOS
ΑΝΑΒΙΣΣΟ

SALAMIS
ΣΑΛΑΜΙΝΑ

General Features

Lying at the centre of the Eastern Mediterranean ferry web, and still the most popular charter flight entry point into Greece, Athens sees more tourists passing through than any other port of call. Unfortunately, the rise in the city's population from 12,000 in 1820 to over 4 million today has done nothing for one of the greatest cities in the world. The ancient heart is now lost amidst a grimy concrete urban sprawl. Athens is a Bette Davis-at-80 sort of city; looking like an ugly spider, but graced with the remains of a pair of wondrously beautiful eyes. Consequently, most visitors profitably fill a couple of days doing the Acropolis and the National Museum and then get out fast. This chapter can thus be said to cover the 'damaged' area of Greece. Like most tourists, its gaze is firmly directed on the ancient city centre and the Athenian ports of Piraeus, Rafina and Lavrion, as well as mentioning in passing the ugly suburb island of Salamis. If sightseeing is not your thing (or if you want to retain the relaxed frame of mind that idling around the islands has wrought), a final day or two in or around Athens waiting for your flight home can come as something of a shock to the system and it is worthwhile considering the alternative of flying to one of the island airports and then island hopping to the city for a long weekend from there.

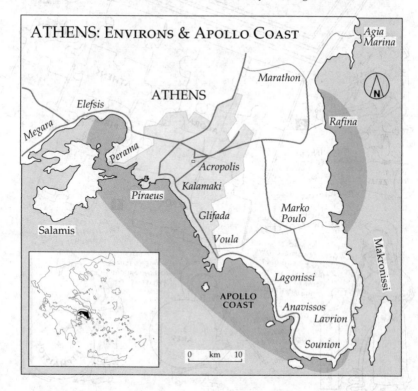

ATHENS: Environs & Apollo Coast

Agia Marina
Marathon
ATHENS
N
Elefsis
Megara
Rafina
Perama
Acropolis
Kalamaki
Piraeus
Marko Poulo
Glifada
Salamis
Voula
Makronissi
Lagonissi
APOLLO COAST
Anavissos
Lavrion
Sounion
0   km   10

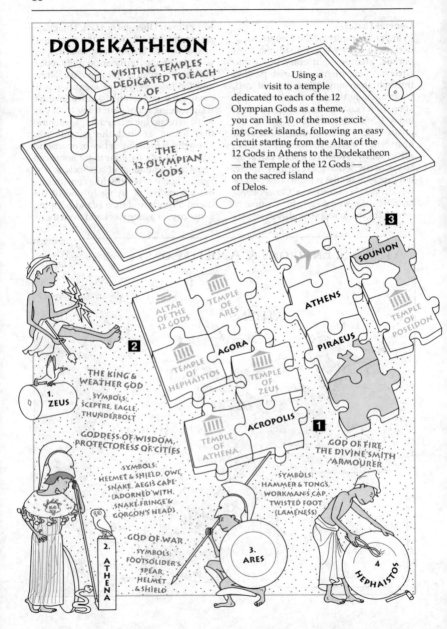

DODEKATHEON

VISITING TEMPLES DEDICATED TO EACH OF

THE 12 OLYMPIAN GODS

Using a visit to a temple dedicated to each of the 12 Olympian Gods as a theme, you can link 10 of the most exciting Greek islands, following an easy circuit starting from the Altar of the 12 Gods in Athens to the Dodekatheon — the Temple of the 12 Gods — on the sacred island of Delos.

3

SOUNION

ATHENS

TEMPLE OF POSEIDON

ALTAR OF THE 12 GODS

TEMPLE OF ARES

AGORA

PIRAEUS

2

TEMPLE OF HEPHAISTOS

TEMPLE OF ZEUS

THE KING & WEATHER GOD

SYMBOLS: SCEPTRE, EAGLE, THUNDERBOLT

1. ZEUS

1

TEMPLE OF ATHENA

ACROPOLIS

GODDESS OF WISDOM, PROTECTORESS OF CITIES

SYMBOLS: HELMET & SHIELD, OWL, SNAKE, AEGIS CAPE (ADORNED WITH SNAKE-FRINGE & GORGON'S HEAD).

GOD OF FIRE, THE DIVINE SMITH/ARMOURER

SYMBOLS: HAMMER & TONGS, WORKMAN'S CAP, TWISTED FOOT (LAMENESS)

2. ATHENA

GOD OF WAR

SYMBOLS: FOOTSOLDIER'S SPEAR, HELMET & SHIELD

3. ARES

4 HEPHAISTOS

QUEEN GODDESS /
GODDESS OF
MOTHERHOOD
(WIFE OF ZEUS)

8. ARTEMIS

SYMBOLS:
DIADEM / SCEPTRE

6. HERMES

7. HERA

PARIS
2060 KM

THE
MESSENGER GOD,
BRINGER OF LUCK,
CONDUCTOR OF SOULS

SYMBOLS:
WINGED BOOTS,
HERALD'S STAFF,
WIDE BRIMMED HAT,
CHLAMYS CLOAK

GODDESS OF VIRTUE
& THE HUNT
(TWIN SISTER OF APOLLO)

SYMBOLS:
BOW & ARROWS /
LONG HUNTING BOOTS

4

TEMPLE
OF
HERMES

TEMPLE
OF
HERA

5

EPHESUS

SAMOS

GODDESS
OF
LOVE

PATMOS

TEMPLE
OF
ARTEMIS

KOS

6

9. APHRODITE

GOD OF THE SEA
EARTHQUAKES
& HORSES

CRETE
IRAKLION

RHODES

TEMPLE
OF
APHRODITE

SYMBOLS:
DOVE /
CUPID SON
EROS

SYMBOLS:
TRIDENT /
DOLPHIN

7

GOD OF WINE & PLEASURE

SYMBOLS:
IVY CROWN / BRANCH,
THYRSOS, DRINKING CUP,
DRUNKEN SATYRS & MEANADS
PANTHER

5. POSEIDON

10. DIONYSOS

The Dodekatheon
Example Itinerary [3 Weeks]

In the Greco-Roman world many deities were worshipped but only the 12 Gods with thrones in the palace above Mt. Olympus (and therefore known as the 'Olympians') had temples built to them on a wide scale. They were the national gods; transcending the political boundaries of the city states. The later Romans (whose capacity for original ideas didn't extend much beyond roads, concrete and killing people in circuses) adopted the Olympians wholesale, contenting themselves with giving them new names (with the exception of Apollo). Widely depicted in all forms of ancient art, each of the 12 Olympians had their own symbol/s to aid recognition (a fortunate circumstance as 'god spotting' will enliven many a vase-filled museum visit today). The remains of their temples also offer a light-hearted excuse for some excellent island hopping. The following itinerary offers an easy circuit around the Aegean islands seeking out the ghosts of the gods.

Arrival/Departure Point

Athens is the best starting point because you will encounter the only weak link in the itinerary (Samos to Patmos) early in the loop. But you can also join the circuit at Kos, Rhodes, Crete (Iraklion), Santorini or Mykonos should you so choose.

Season

This itinerary can be successfully executed at any time from June to September as it runs down the two most popular lines in the Greek ferry system — the Dodecanese and Cyclades Central lines.

1 Athens: The Acropolis

The centre of Athens offers an easy way to notch up a handful of the twelve temples without difficulty. If you join the circuit at the Thissio Metro station and walk to the north entrance of the Agora you will pass the site of the **Altar of the Twelve Gods**. It is now not clear if these included all the Olympians but the altar served as the *omphalos* (navel) of the city. The milestone for measuring distances throughout Attica, it is the logical starting point for the itinerary. Walking east around the north and east sides of the Acropolis you will come to the largest temple ever built in Greece; the Olympieion or **Temple of Zeus**.

Zeus (Roman **Jupiter**), the king of the Olympian gods, was also the god of the sky, or weather god. He walked around with a handful of thunderbolts and was wont to give any passing nymphs a quick flash if his wife Hera was out of sight. He passed the rest of his time upon a throne of black marble set upon a pedestal of the seven rainbow colour steps keeping a moody eye on the affairs of gods and men.

Turning west, a walk along the south side of the Acropolis will bring you to the western entrance. The Acropolis includes the Parthenon among several **Temples of Athena**.

Athena (Roman **Minerva**), the goddess of wisdom, was the most popular of the goddesses (thanks to her role as the protectress of cities). She also enjoyed a secondary role as a patroness of the feminine arts and crafts — notably spinning and weaving. She frequently appears in ancient art, usually wearing the distinctive Aegis cape (made out of snake's scales, fringed with snake's heads and sporting a Gorgon's head) showing her association with the hero Perseus who killed the Gorgon Medusa with the goddess's help.

2 Athens: The Agora

Assuming you haven't broken your leg on the slippery marble of the Acropolis then you next head for the nearby south-east entrance of the Agora site. Walking across the Agora to the northern entrance, turn west to the mound that is all that remains of the **Temple of Ares**. Believed to be almost identical to the nearby complete temple of Hephaistos, it originally stood elsewhere only to be re-erected here during the Roman infilling of the Agora.

Ares (Roman **Mars**) was the god of war and thus not the most popular of deities. Feared rather than revered, worshippers sacrificed dogs to him. Nauseatingly handsome and usually naked, he was the paramour of Aphrodite, possibly siring her son Eros.

On the hillside to the west lies the complete **Temple of Hephaistos**. Once surrounded by artisan and craftsmen's workshops it is the most complete temple surviving in Greece.

Hephaistos (Roman **Vulcan**), the workman's god, was arguably the unhappiest deity. Not only was he once thrown (literally) out of Olympus by Hera (laming himself when he landed on the island of Limnos), he was also married to Aphrodite and thus forever hopping mad with her hopping into bed with just about everybody and then coming up with all sorts of lame excuses. He is easily identified by his tools and is often riding a mule.

3 Sounion

Athens sightseeing can be wound up with a day trip to Cape **Sounion** and the impressive **Temple of Poseidon** on the hillside overlooking the Aegean Sea.

Poseidon (Roman **Neptune**) was another moody god, swimming around with a chip on his shoulder because he lost out to his younger brother Zeus when the three brothers divided the universe between them by lot after defeating their father **Kronos** (Roman **Saturn**). Poseidon got the sea, Zeus the heavens, and Pluto the underworld (they shared the earth). The god of the sea, earthquakes and horses, he is often only distinguishable from Zeus by his trident and dolphin.

4 Piraeus to Samos

Returning to Athens, head on to Piraeus and your first island hop to the ugliest island port on the itinerary — Samos (Vathi). Buses here will take you on to Samos (Pithagorio) and the nearby Heraion — the largest Greek-built temple in Greece. Just to the east of it lie the foundations of two tiny **Temples of Hermes**.

Hermes (Roman **Mercury**) always managed to come in as 12th man when listing the Olympians in order of importance. His natty winged boots and traveller's hat hardly encouraged respect. Temples to him were thus thin on the ground, and although he was revered as the conductor of souls to the underworld, his reputation as a trickster and cheat confined his following to the ranks of merchants, traders and thieves. Easily identified by his herald's staff he is frequently pictured taking Hera, Athena and Aphrodite to the first ever Miss Universe contest; the judgement of Paris.

The **Temple of Hera**, although only one column remains standing, is a much more

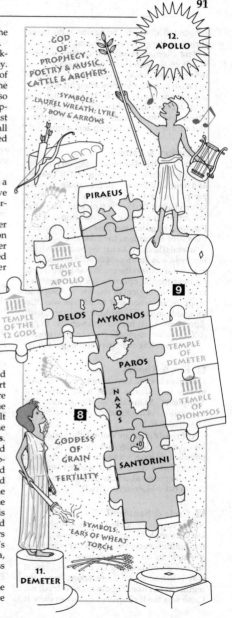

GOD OF PROPHECY, POETRY & MUSIC, CATTLE & ARCHERS.

SYMBOLS: LAUREL WREATH; LYRE; BOW & ARROWS

12. APOLLO

PIRAEUS

TEMPLE OF APOLLO

TEMPLE OF THE 12 GODS

DELOS

MYKONOS

9

PAROS

TEMPLE OF DEMETER

TEMPLE OF DIONYSOS

N A X O S

8

SANTORINI

GODDESS OF GRAIN & FERTILITY

SYMBOLS: EARS OF WHEAT; TORCH

11. DEMETER

substantial affair: this being one of the major shrines to the goddess in Greece.

Hera (Roman **Juno**), the queen goddess, was both the sister and wife of Zeus. They never got on, thanks to his constant attempts to ravish passing nymphs. Their life together was a litany of attempts by Hera to catch him in the act. This thwarted voyeur's symbol was a heifer but she is usually depicted with Zeus and adorned with a diadem and sceptre.

5 Turkey & Patmos

Samos (Vathi) is also the jumping-off point for day trips to Ephesus in Turkey and its **Temple of Artemis**. With one column standing it looks pretty similar to the Heraion. If you don't fancy visiting Turkey then pick up one of the few ferries or a tourist boat and hop down to Patmos. The monastery here was also built on the site of a temple to the goddess.

Artemis (Roman **Diana**), the beautiful virgin huntress, was goddess of all wild places, with a secondary role as the moon goddess. Having no time for the opposite sex she spent her hours protecting female chastity — along with mopping up when that failed (she was also the goddess of childbirth). Often pictured with Apollo, she used her bow and arrows to put suffering animals painlessly out of their misery — thereby acting as a sort of anti-cupid figure.

6 Kos & Rhodes

From Patmos you have very easy hops down to Kos and Rhodes. Both were home to a **Temple of Aphrodite** — though only the foundations of the Rhodes Town example are identifiable today.

Aphrodite (Roman **Venus**), the goddess of love, beauty, fertility and the sea, was very popular for obvious reasons. Usually depicted with either a dove or her winged son Eros (often depicted as a fully grown man rather than a baby-blobs style cupid).

7 Crete & Santorini

Alongside the Rhodian Temple of Aphrodite stood a temple of Dionysos. However, little of this building survives. For a better example of a temple to this god you have to do some serious island hopping on to Naxos. Easiest way is to bounce off Crete, taking one of the regular ferries from Rhodes to Crete (Iraklion). Crete was the birth-place of Zeus so there is

some logic in the hop. After touring Knossos, from Iraklion you can then pick up a Cyclades Central Line ferry stopping off at Santorini for more sightseeing before hopping on to Naxos.

8 Naxos & Paros

Naxos is home to a large Archaic temple on the small islet of Palatia just north of the ferry port. Thought to have been dedicated to either Apollo or Dionysos, visit it on the possibility that it is a **Temple of Dionysos**, since Naxos was this god's island and where he married the abandoned Ariadne.

Dionysos (Roman **Bacchus**) was the god of fun; inventing wine and orgies. Often shown accompanied by Satyrs (naked bald men with horse's tails and large what-nots), nymphs or maenads (frenzied women dressed in fawn and panther skins) he started out as the god of the fruit of the trees. He was not originally one of the Olympians but gained admission when **Hestia** (Roman **Vesta**) — the old maid goddess of the hearth — stepped down in his favour.

From Naxos you have an easy hop on to Paros: the Kastro at Parikia being built on the site of a **Temple of Demeter.** Its surviving wall is made up of stones from the building.

Demeter (Roman **Ceres**) was famous for not smiling. The goddess of fertility, she was particularly associated with the crops of the soil such as grain and corn. She is often depicted holding the torch carried when she went down into the underworld (Hades) to recover her daughter Persephone whom Zeus had ordered to be married to their brother Pluto.

9 Mykonos & Delos

From Paros you have another easy hop on to Mykonos: the starting point for excursion boats to the island of Delos — home to the foundations of an important **Temple of Apollo**.

Apollo the god of poetry, music and prophecy, was the most popular of the Olympian gods. He was also thought by some to be the sun god Helios. His popularity ensured that plenty of temples were erected in his name. He is often pictured as a naked and beardless youth holding a lyre.

Delos is also home to smaller temples to Aphrodite, Artemis, Demeter, and Hera as well as the **Dodekatheon** itself. Having visited Delos and returned to Mykonos you can complete the island circuit by taking a ferry back to Piraeus for your return flight home.

Athens: City Links

Getting Around

Athens has a large and overcrowded public transport system made up of buses, trolley-buses, a single line metro and 1000 of the most uncooperative taxi drivers in Europe. The metro offers the cheapest and quickest means of moving around — unless you want to get to the airport or intercity bus stations. For these you will have to take either an expensive taxi or resort to the great Athenian bus system. The NTOG/EOT office in Syntagma Square provides the timetables and route summary sheets on request. Athens' buses come in two colours: Blue, the city buses, running from the centre to the suburbs (books of tickets bought in advance from street kiosks), and Orange, running further afield within the local province of Attica.

Airport Buses & Taxis:

Athens airport — 9 km south-east of the centre — has three terminals:

1. West Airport (Olympic Airways and Domestic Flights only).

2. East Airport (all foreign airlines and some charter flights).

3. Charter Flights (most charter flights). Note: some charter flights arrive at one terminal and depart from the other, so check your return terminal carefully.

Buses run to all three terminals (though, as they are not always visited in the same sequence, it is best to check with the bus driver that you are at the correct one):

#091: runs from Athens (Syntagma Square and/or Omonia Square — see p. 96) every 30 minutes from 06.00–01.30, and hourly through the night. The journey takes 30 minutes; the fare is 160 GDR.

A bus service (**#19**) also exists between **Piraeus** (see p. 119) and the airport; running to all three terminals roughly every fifty minutes 05.00–22.00, then hourly to

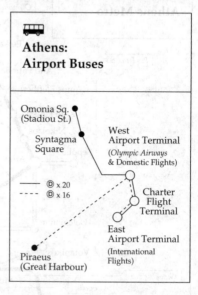

Athens: Airport Buses

Omonia Sq. (Stadiou St.)

Syntagma Square

West Airport Terminal
(*Olympic Airways & Domestic Flights*)

—— Ⓓ x 20
- - - Ⓓ x 16

Charter Flight Terminal

East Airport Terminal
(*International Flights*)

Piraeus (Great Harbour)

01.00. Journey time 40 minutes; 200 GDR.

Taxis also prey on the unsuspecting at the airport. They will rook you if they can, so be sure to establish the fare in advance as 'official' fares and reality are very different. A good example of this is the airport to Piraeus run, where the 'official' 2000 GDR fare (double at night) usually ends up around 5500 GDR!

Buses to Intercity Bus Stations:

City buses run from the centre to the two main bus stations:

#024: Runs between the Intercity Bus Station serving Evia and Northern Greece (**Terminal B**) at Liossion St. and Amalias Ave. (entrance to the National Gardens).

#051: Runs between the Intercity Bus Station serving Patras and the Peloponnese (**Terminal A**) at 100 Kifissou Street and Omonia Square.

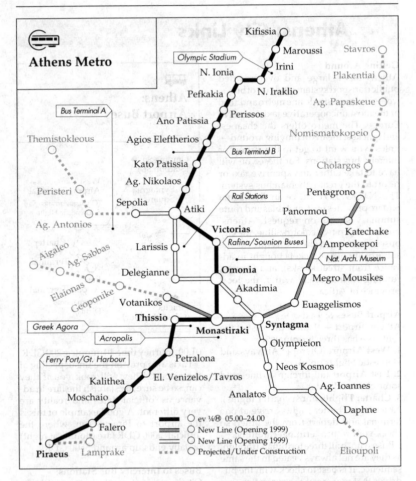

Athens Metro

Kifissia
Maroussi
Stavros
Olympic Stadium
Irini
N. Ionia
Plakentiai
Pefkakia
N. Iraklio
Ag. Papaskeue
Perissos
Ano Patissia
Nomismatokopeio
Agios Eleftherios
Bus Terminal B
Kato Patissia
Cholargos
Ag. Nikolaos
Pentagrono
Sepolia
Atiki
Panormou
Victorias
Katechake
Larissis
Rafina/Sounion Buses
Ampeokepoi
Nat. Arch. Museum
Delegianne
Omonia
Megro Mousikes
Akadimia
Votanikos
Euaggelismos
Thissio
Syntagma
Monastiraki
Greek Agora
Olympieion
Acropolis
Neos Kosmos
Ferry Port/Gt. Harbour
Petralona
Ag. Ioannes
Kalithea
El. Venizelos/Tavros
Moschaio
Analatos
Daphne
Falero
Piraeus   Lamprake
Elioupoli

Themistokleous
Bus Terminal A
Peristeri
Ag. Antonios
Aigaleo
Ag. Sabbas
Elaionas
Geoponike
Rail Stations

○ ev ¼⊕ 05.00–24.00
○ New Line (Opening 1999)
○ New Line (Opening 1999)
○ Projected/Under Construction

Athens Metro

The easiest way of moving between the centre of Athens and Piraeus is via the metro system. Largely above ground, the service is efficient, if crowded in the rush hours. The only minor problem you are likely to encounter is finding the station entrances, since they are not sign-posted.

Tickets are obtained from manned kiosks or ticket machines (these require you to select your ticket before the coin slot opens). Once you have your ticket, it pays to remember to insert it in one of the date-punching machines sited at platform entrances: you will face a heavy fine if caught travelling with a virgin ticket. The fare from the centre of Athens to Piraeus is 120 GDR. Trains run roughly every 20 minutes from 05.00–24.00 (the last train leaves Piraeus promptly at midnight).

Athens—Mainland Port Bus Links

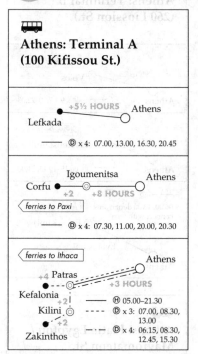

Athens: Terminal A (100 Kifissou St.)

+5½ HOURS · Athens

Lefkada

—— Ⓓ x 4: 07.00, 13.00, 16.30, 20.45

Igoumenitsa · Athens

Corfu ● ——◎—— +2 · +8 HOURS

⟨ ferries to Paxi ⟩

—— Ⓓ x 4: 07.30, 11.00, 20.00, 20.30

⟨ ferries to Ithaca ⟩ · Athens

+4 Patras

Kefalonia · +3 HOURS

+2

Kilini · ◎

+2

Zakinthos

—— Ⓗ 05.00–21.30

---- Ⓓ x 3: 07.00, 08.30, 13.00

—·— Ⓓ x 4: 06.15, 08.30, 12.45, 15.30

Lying at the centre of the Greek bus system, Athens has a number of wider-ranging bus services of value to the island hopper. These bus routes link the capital with ports not served by Piraeus or Rafina-based ferries but which have ferry links of their own to adjacent islands. For the most part important centres in their own right, these ports have bus links from Athens timed to connect with ferries, so that buses can take passengers on to island capitals (you buy a ferry ticket along with your bus ticket). Some ferry companies also run private Athens—mainland port buses for the benefit of their passengers.

The largest bus station in Athens (Terminal A) at 100 Kifissou St., lies an inconvenient 4 km from the centre of the city, buried behind a block of semi-derelict buildings on the east side of one of the city's freeways (home to innumerable run-down scrap-yards and warehouses). From the road it would be impossible to spot were it not for the constant procession of buses mysteriously disappearing down adjacent side-streets. The terminal is in fact a warehouse-like building filled with numbered bus bays and lined with confectionery stalls. Only the ticket hall

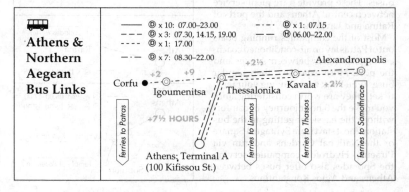

Athens & Northern Aegean Bus Links

—— Ⓓ x 10: 07.00–23.00
--- Ⓓ x 3: 07.30, 14.15, 19.00
---- Ⓓ x 1: 17.00
—·— Ⓓ x 7: 08.30–22.00

--- Ⓓ x 1: 07.15
—— Ⓗ 06.00–22.00

+2½ · Alexandroupolis

Corfu ● –◎– +2 · +9 · Thessalonika · Kavala +2½

Igoumenitsa

⟨ ferries to Patras ⟩ · +7½ HOURS · ⟨ ferries to Limnos ⟩ · ⟨ ferries to Thassos ⟩ · ⟨ ferries to Samothrace ⟩

Athens: Terminal A (100 Kifissou St.)

is new, contrasting vividly with the surrounding decrepitude. The terminal serves most intercity buses (including buses to Thessalonika) as well as the west coast ports (Patras and Igoumenitsa), the Ionian islands and the Peloponnese.

Terminal B at 260 Liossion St. is a much smaller and altogether friendlier affair 800 m NW of Ag. Nikolaos metro station. A similar distance out from the centre as Terminal A, it is equally badly signposted; both are best reached via taxi. Connections from Terminal B are much more limited with port/island links confined to Evia and the Sporades. Buses from both these stations usually stop in one or two of the larger towns en route but are otherwise difficult to board from the roadside (the notable exception being the popular Patras buses — which are flagged down just north of the Corinth Canal bridge as they do not enter Corinth itself). All the important bus times are listed on GNTO bus information sheets and in the *Greek Travel Pages*.

The third terminus of note in Athens is near Areos Park north of the National Archaeological Museum at the junction of Platia Egyptou and Mavromateon St. (running down the west side of the park). There is no terminal building here, just a small bus park with bus stops. Buses departing from here are orange suburban buses. These provide a frequent service between central Athens and the ports of Rafina and Lavrion.

Most of the companies running boats out of Patras lay on air-conditioned coaches for passengers between Athens and the port. More expensive than regular buses (you book when buying your ferry ticket), they are worth considering since you make the 3 hour journey in comfort without the hassle of getting to the bus station (most start from Syntagma Square or the National Gardens and run via Piraeus). Hydrofoil companies serving the Sporades also offer buses between Athens and Agios Konstantinos.

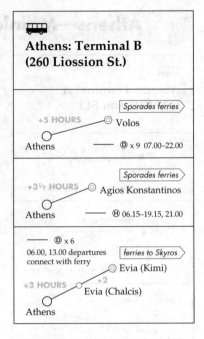

Athens

Parthenon
(East Façade)

Mosque of the Bazaar
(with the Acropolis in
the background)

WELCOME TO THE ATHENS
FLEA MARKET
OPEN THROUGHOUT THE WEEK

ΚΑΛΩΣ ΗΛΘΑΤΕ
ΣΤΟ ΔΗΜΟΠΡΑΤΗΡΙΟ
ΣΩΜΑΤΕΙΟ ΠΑΛ...
"ΑΓΙΟΙ ΑΠΟ...

OLD SIGN
2000
DRACHMA

Monastiraki Square
(the only good bits)

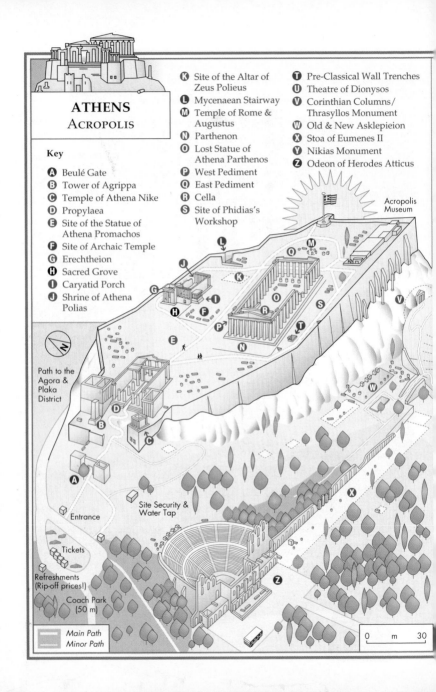

ATHENS
ACROPOLIS

Key

- **A** Beulé Gate
- **B** Tower of Agrippa
- **C** Temple of Athena Nike
- **D** Propylaea
- **E** Site of the Statue of Athena Promachos
- **F** Site of Archaic Temple
- **G** Erechtheion
- **H** Sacred Grove
- **I** Caryatid Porch
- **J** Shrine of Athena Polias
- **K** Site of the Altar of Zeus Polieus
- **L** Mycenaean Stairway
- **M** Temple of Rome & Augustus
- **N** Parthenon
- **O** Lost Statue of Athena Parthenos
- **P** West Pediment
- **Q** East Pediment
- **R** Cella
- **S** Site of Phidias's Workshop
- **T** Pre-Classical Wall Trenches
- **U** Theatre of Dionysos
- **V** Corinthian Columns/ Thrasyllos Monument
- **W** Old & New Asklepieion
- **X** Stoa of Eumenes II
- **Y** Nikias Monument
- **Z** Odeon of Herodes Atticus

Acropolis Museum

Path to the Agora & Plaka District

Site Security & Water Tap

Entrance

Tickets

Refreshments (Rip-off prices!)

Coach Park (50 m)

Main Path
Minor Path

0   m   30

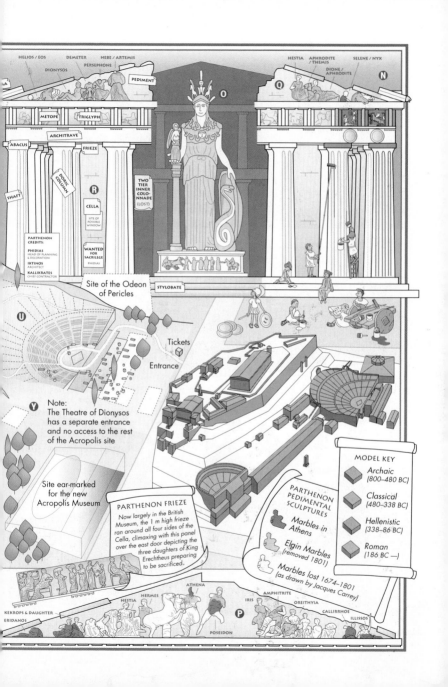

HELIOS / EOS   DEMETER   HEBE / ARTEMIS   HESTIA   APHRODITE / THEMIS   SELENE / NYX

DIONYSOS   PERSEPHONE   DIONE / APHRODITE

PEDIMENT

O   **Q**   **N**

METOPE   TRIGLYPH

ARCHITRAVE

ABACUS   FRIEZE

DORIC COLUMN

SHAFT

R

CELLA

SITE OF POSSIBLE WINDOW

TWO TIER INNER COLONNADE (LOST)

PARTHENON CREDITS:

PHIDIAS
HEAD OF PLANNING & DECORATION

IKTINOS
ARCHITECT

KALLIKRATES
CHIEF CONTRACTOR

WANTED FOR SACRILEGE
PHIDIAS

Site of the Odeon of Pericles

STYLOBATE

U

Tickets

Entrance

Y   Note:
The Theatre of Dionysos
has a separate entrance
and no access to the rest
of the Acropolis site

Site ear-marked
for the new
Acropolis Museum

PARTHENON FRIEZE
Now largely in the British
Museum, the 1 m high frieze
ran around all four sides of the
Cella, climaxing with this panel
over the east door depicting the
three daughters of King
Erechtheus preparing
to be sacrificed.

MODEL KEY

Archaic
(800–480 BC)

Classical
(480–338 BC)

Hellenistic
(338–86 BC)

Roman
(186 BC —)

PARTHENON PEDIMENTAL SCULPTURES

Marbles in
Athens

Elgin Marbles
(removed 1801)

Marbles lost 1674–1801
(as drawn by Jacques Carrey)

KEKROPS & DAUGHTER   HESTIA   HERMES   ATHENA   AMPHITRITE   OREITHYIA   CALLIRRHOE

ERIDANOS   IRIS   ILLISSOS

P

POSEIDON

Waterfront Fishmonger
RAFINA

Main Ticket Agency Block
PIRAEUS

NAIAS EXPRESS

Rumour has it that this is what
happens to backpackers who
dare to enter the
Deck-class
saloon ...

Piraeus

Quayside
Breadseller

Athens: Centre & Ports

Athens

AΘHNA; pop. 4,000,001.

CODE ☎ 01
NTOG INFORMATION DESK ☎ 322 2545
TOURIST POLICE ☎ 171
POLICE ☎ 100
FIRST AID ☎ 166

Given her fantastic historical pedigree and world-wide reputation as a premier sightseeing destination, Athens is apt to disappoint. The transition from quaint Turkish town to a city housing a quarter of Greece's population has been an ugly one, producing a glorious (if very touristy) city centre surrounded by a sea of grime. Air pollution is also a serious problem. The Athenian conurbation is home to half of Greece's cars and 90% of the country's industry, and while the beauty of the Acropolis buildings can go to your head, so do the smog clouds (the *nephos*) that periodically force the government to ban motorists from the streets. In High Season Athens is hot and steamy, protected by the surrounding hills from the cooling summer winds that bathe the islands. However, for all this, the city offers a couple of days of excellent sightseeing, and has good links with the islands via the ports of Piraeus and Rafina.

When visiting Athens, priority should be given to an early visit to an NTOG/ EOT information office. This excellent tourist service provides free city street maps along with information sheets on hotels, buses and ferry departure times for the ferry ports at Piraeus and Rafina. There are several offices in the city. The easiest to find is housed in the National Bank on Syntagma Square. In addition to the head office in Amerikis Street there are also desks in the various airport terminal buildings, the long distance bus station, and the main railway station.

Most visitors negotiate Athens without problems, but you should be aware that the impact of 4 million tourists a year has had an unfortunate effect on a minority of the locals. There have always been two types of Athenian: the hospitable and charming individuals on a par with most of the Greek islanders, and the other kind — who in days past ordered the death of Socrates, amongst others. Sadly, most of the descendants of the latter class have become waiters or taxi drivers. In Athens many of the taxi drivers are something else — it pays to get into a taxi before stating your desired destination: most drivers have their own patch and aren't interested in going anywhere else ('anywhere else' being where you want to go). Requests for the airport or Piraeus are seen as a licence to overcharge to excess. All in all, when in Athens it pays to keep your eyes open (see also: 'Scams' p. 56).

Modern Centre

The centre of Athens lies some 6 km from the coast, thanks to the Acropolis. This landmark stands at the heart of the city as it has always done. The modern centre, however, is made up of three distinct parts. First is the Ancient City, now slowly making a reappearance as a growing number of archaeological sites (and described in the sightseeing section of this chapter). These are in the process of being united into one archeological park, which is due to be completed early in the next century. The second section of the modern centre lies to the north of the Acropolis, and comprises the remaining buildings and narrow winding streets of the Turkish city (now known as Old Town or simply the 'Plaka' district). Surrounding both, and the part of town most visitors first encounter via the rail, bus and metro links, is the post-1832 Greek

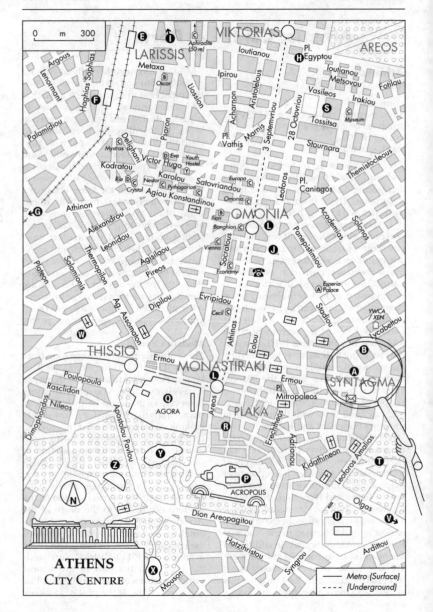

ATHENS
CITY CENTRE

Metro (Surface)
(Underground)

Key

- **A** Syntagma Square / National Bank
- **B** EOT Tourist Information Office
- **C** Thomas Cook *Bureau de Change*
- **D** American Express Travel Centre
- **E** Railway Station (Eastern Europe)
- **F** Railway Station (Corinth/Patras)
- **G** Bus Terminal A (Main Bus Station)
  (100 Kifissou St: 2 km W.)
- **H** Bus Stop (Rafina/Lavrion/Sounion)
- **I** Bus Terminal B (Evia/Kimi)
  (260 Liossion St: 1.5 km NW.)
- **J** Airport Bus Stop (Omonia)
- **K** City Information Kiosk
  & Airport Bus Stop (Syntagma)
- **L** McDonald's
- **M** Bookshop
- **N** Museum of Cycladic Art (100 m)
- **O** Parliament Building
- **P** Acropolis
- **Q** Agora
- **R** Roman Agora / Plaka (map: p. 101)
- **S** National Archaeological Museum
- **T** National Gardens
- **U** Olympieion & Arch of Hadrian
- **V** Stadium (50 m)
- **W** Kerameikos Park
  (Ancient City Cemetery)
- **X** Mousieon / Filopapou Hill
- **Y** Areopagus (Ancient 'Senate' Hill)
- **Z** Pnyx (Ancient 'Parliament' Hill)

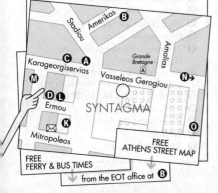

independence new centre (largely constructed in the century before 1940). When Athens was chosen — for largely sentimental reasons — as the capital of the newly independent Greece, it was little more than a minor garrison town (thanks to the heavily fortified Acropolis) with a few thousand inhabitants. The new Bavarian-born king of Greece took advantage of the opportunity to construct a fitting West European-style capital of wide boulevards outside the old city (which was intended to be demolished, excavated, and preserved as a vast archaeological park). All went well with this scheme until the disastrous Helleno-Turkish war of 1920–22, which resulted in a flood of refugees into Athens, overwhelming the planners with their impromptu building. As a result, the post-independence city has its wide boulevards (graced with blocks up to a dozen storeys high) defiantly ignoring the hilly terrain, but beyond this, chaos reigns, in the form of the encircling kilometres of concrete suburbs bisected by traffic-choked freeways.

The Post-Independence City

Often similarly jammed with traffic (thanks to the four-times-daily rush hour in Athens), the post independence city (the map opposite only shows the major streets) isn't the perfect tourist destination, and has little appeal beyond the large numbers of hotels, the National Archaeological Museum, and the pleasant National Gardens to the east. Its one saving grace is that the grid-iron street system at least makes it easy to walk between the major points via the main streets without getting too lost. The most important of these streets are **Stadiou**, **Athinas** and **Ermou**, which run between the three main squares. **Syntagma** (Constitution) Square — the tourist 'hub' of the city and home to the Greek Parliament — is the most important and attractive of these. **Omonia** — the very grimy traffic hub that sits spider-like in the centre of the web of new city streets has less appeal. Adopted as a meeting point for the men of Athens, it is an even less attractive spot at night. **Monastiraki** is the smallest of the three squares and is currently one huge building-site thanks to the construction of the new metro line. It is not surprising, therefore, that most tourists prefer to stick to Syntagma Square (this is also a glorified traffic island, partially closed by the building of a new metro station, but at least it has the merit of possessing both restaurants and some greenery) and the old town streets nestling around the base of the Acropolis that make up the Plaka district.

Recent encouragement to venture further has come via a pedestrianization scheme. This started in early 1995, with the closure to vehicles of most streets in the triangle between Omonia, Monastiraki and Syntagma squares. This has been taken further with a programme and re-paving these streets. Quite why this particular area has been so designated is more of a mystery. Admittedly, there are a large number of stores, but this isn't a noted hotel district, and overall, grime is the order of the day. Sadly, this on-going programme of public works is likely to get a lot worse before it gets better: Athens has been awarded the 2004 Olympic games and this is sure to generate considerable building activity. This is likely to prompt tourists to venture into the greener parts of the city. These include the National Gardens and the Likavittos and Filopapou (alias Mouseion) hills with their views across the city. The Likavittos is reached via a cable car, while the Filopapou is in the centre of a pine-wood park to the south-west of the Acropolis.

Readers should be aware that, although Athens is a relatively safe capital city, visiting parks and wooded areas is dangerous at night. In the crowd-free Low Season tourists have also been mugged at mid-day on the Filopapou; so take care.

Plaka District / Old Town

Plaka is the last remnant of pre-Greek-independence Turkish Athens, and the only part of the city with any great appeal. A warren of 17th and 18th c. red-tiled town buildings mixed with earlier small Byzantine churches, small leafy squares and excavated archaeological sites, it roughly occupies the large north-east quarter of the ancient city, and is bounded by the Acropolis and Olympieion to the south and the Agora to the west. Originally, the old town extended over the

---

Key

Ⓐ Syntagma Square (map: p. 99)
Ⓑ McDonald's / American Express Travel Centre
Ⓒ English Bookshops
Ⓓ Cathedral
Ⓔ Kapnikarea Church
Ⓕ Monastiraki Square
Ⓖ National Gardens
Ⓗ Old Bazaar Street
Ⓘ Flea Market
Ⓙ Restaurant Area
Ⓚ Agora Ticket Kiosks
Ⓛ Library of Hadrian
Ⓜ Roman Agora
Ⓝ Tower of the Winds
Ⓞ Roman Baths (Two sites)
Ⓟ Monument of Lysicrates
Ⓠ Arch of Hadrian
Ⓡ Olympieion site ticket kiosk
Ⓢ Olympieion
Ⓣ Temples to Kronos & Rhea, Apollo, Hera, and Zeus
Ⓤ Agora Viewing Mount (with lethal, slippery marble steps)
Ⓥ Acropolis Ticket Kiosks (50 m)
Ⓦ Parthenon
Ⓧ Propylaia to the Acropolis
Ⓨ Erechtheion
Ⓩ Acropolis Museum

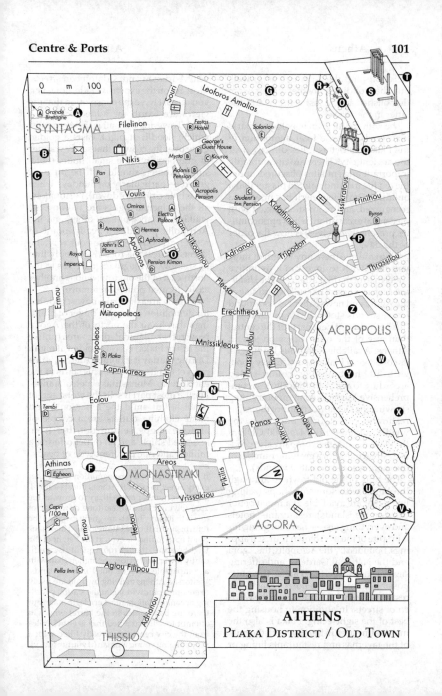

ATHENS
PLAKA DISTRICT / OLD TOWN

Acropolis and the Agora areas as well, but the buildings on the former were demolished in the last century and the latter in the 1930s.

The 19th century 'archaeological park' plan envisaged the total demolition of the Plaka district as it lies directly over the ancient city. There are undoubtedly important ancient sites obscured under the red tile roof and painted plaster Plaka buildings, but their merit has now been recognized, and renovation mixed with piecemeal excavation (when opportunities present themselves) is now the order of the day.

If you are in Athens any length of time, you may wish to invest in a definitive street map of the Plaka district. The *Historical Map of Athens* (1000 GDR), on sale at the Agora and newspaper kiosks around town, sounds stuffy, but is much better (for both old and new parts of the centre) than any of the other maps on sale in Athens. Available in various languages, its coverage of Plaka is particularly good, with all the buildings colour-coded according to age. A historically less comprehensive, but more contemporary, map showing the location of many of the larger restaurants and tourist outlets, is the vividly coloured *Sky Map* (500 GDR)of the Plaka district (this company also produces street maps for a growing number of the more resort-orientated islands).

The bulk of the old town — although throbbing with souvenir shops (selling items that are available at a much better price on the islands), restaurants, hotels and everything else — has a lot going for it in spite of the overblown tourist trappings. Bounded by the Acropolis, the Agora and the National Gardens, and offering several shady tree-filled areas, it is quite possible to forget the horror that is the rest of Athens while you explore the warren of streets. In addition to housing the best of the sightseeing, Plaka is also the main eating area in the city, with the bulk of the tavernas and restaurants lining or

near Adrianou and Kidathineon streets. Most are on the expensive side; however, you at least have the consolation that the views are worth the added costs of a meal. Towering over all is the Acropolis, which, floodlit at night, casts a golden glow over the crowds that safely wander in numbers into the small hours (note: single women should still be on their guard — particularly on Sundays when the whole city shuts down). Fortunately, all the principal sights are within easy walking distance of each other, and the Acropolis provides a ready point of reference should you lose your way; the streets nearest the rock rise steeply into its shadow. Syntagma Square lies to the north-east of the old town and is another easily located point of reference.

The only area the Plaka now scheduled for demolition is the thin finger of buildings that lie to the north of the Agora. Now rather dilapidated, this area (unlike the rest of Plaka) is best avoided at night. During the day it is home to the city's flea market (on Ifestou St.). This starts at the entrance to Monastiraki metro station. For the most part it sells the worst sort of rubbish, but amid the imitation brand name clothing outlets are a couple of antique shops selling detritus from scrapped ships, and an outlet offering a million and one different type of beads.

▶

It is not much of an exaggeration to say that every street in central Athens boasts a hotel, and their number are is likely to grow as the 2004 Olympics draw near (one downside of this is that many hotels are going to have to be refurbished in the meantime). A bed in Athens is not hard to find — even at the height of the High Season — though room quality is significantly lower, and prices are higher, than with a comparable class of hotel in the islands. Visitors to Athens arriving by train are likely to encounter individuals at the station peddling accommodation: most are legitimate, but there are bad apples in the barrel who will attempt to sell you a bed that is either miles from the city centre, or already filled with a very obliging young woman (if you are lucky).

In the perfect world the visitor to Athens should seek to stay in or near the Plaka district. Even though this is a very noisy part of the world, it is conveniently close to all the sights — so much so that it is worth booking ahead to secure a room. The antiquated nature of the buildings mean that top-end hotels are relatively scarce, with the notable exception of the A-class *Electra Palace* (☎ 324 1401), and the B-class *Plaka* (☎ 322 2096) and *Amazon* (☎ 323 4002). There are a number of B-class pensions in the middle price range. These include the nice *Adonis* (☎ 324 9737) and *Acropolis* (☎ 322 2344), along with the small and popular *Byron* (☎ 325 3554). If you are looking for a reasonable C-class hotel, then the *Hermes* (☎ 323 5514) and the *Aphrodite* (☎ 323 4357) are good bets. At the budget end of the range are the C-class pension *John's Place* (☎ 322 9719), the E-class *Solonion* (☎ 322 0008) along with several places offering rooms south of Syntagma Square. Plaka also has a number of dubious unclassified establishments. The streets running north from **Ermou St.** also have a number of cheaper hotels that are adequate for a night or two. The best are along Eolou St., notably the *Tembi* (☎ 321 3175) with its impressive street views of the Acropolis, and the poorly sited C-class *Pella Inn* (☎ 325 0598) in the more dangerous, run-down part of Plaka.

Omonia Square also has a fair number of budget establishments tucked away in the backstreets. Most in the immediate area of the square are pretty ropy, and contrast greatly with the large number of excellent mid-range hotels that line the streets to the north-west. Agiou Konstandinou St. is one of the most fertile hunting grounds, with the C-class *Pythagorion* (☎ 524 2811), and *Nestor* (☎ 523 5575). Two blocks to the north, along Victor Hugo St., there is also the D-class *Eva* (☎ 522 3079) and a new *Youth Hostel* (☎ 524 1708).

The railway station also has several reasonable hotels within easy reach. These include the expensive B-class *Oscar* (☎ 833 4215) and the C-class *Aphrodite* (☎ 323 4357) and *Mystras* (☎ 522 7737).

A

Athens has several poor trailer sites in the outer environs that are better avoided. The best sites are a longish bus ride away along the Apollo coast near Cape Sounion, including the popular *Camping Sounio Beach* (☎ 0292 39358) and *Camping Varkiza* (☎ 0189 74329).

Athens has some 40 museums or historic sites, but the main ones can be covered in a couple of days — the big four being:
1. The Acropolis.
2. The Agora (the ancient market / city centre).
3. The Plaka District / Old Town.
4. The National Archaeological Museum.
As a book for island hoppers this guide assumes that the reader won't be spending more than a couple of days in the capital and therefore only these major sights are described in detail in the following pages. If, however, you are staying longer you might care to consult a detailed city guide — the *Blue Guide to Athens* (Black / Norton) is easily the best, but adequate alternatives are on sale from local bookshops.

Ancient Athens

Considering how great a cultural and military powerhouse Athens was, the size of the ancient city comes as a surprise, for it is very small by modern standards (see map between pages 112–113). It has been calculated that the walls contained 6,000 houses for an estimated population of some 36,000. However, this figure is misleading, as a good half of the population of 'Athens' lived and worked at the Athenian port of Piraeus. Piraeus soon developed as a city in its own right, and by the classical period people were openly talking about the 'upper' and 'lower' cities (Athens being the former). The historian Thucydides wrote that the Athenian leader 'Themistokles thought Piraeus more useful than the upper city', and this comment reflected Piraeus's growing role as the military, business and commercial base — Athens itself being viewed as more of the political, religious and cultural centre. This was natural enough given that Athens — represented on all her coins by her symbol, the owl of wisdom — was home to the traditional sites for worship (the Acropolis), law (the courts in and around the Agora) and learning (the three Gymnasia: including the Academy, beloved by Plato, and the recently discovered Lyceum, founded by Aristotle).

Defending this odd urban structure took some doing, particularly as Athens was primarily a maritime power (the Peloponnesian War lasted 30 years simply because Athens was dominant at sea while Sparta and her allies controlled the mainland). After the Persian sack of Athens in 480 BC, Themistokles rebuilt the city walls protecting Athens and Piraeus. Moreover, the two were connected by two walls running parallel to each other several hundred metres apart; known as the 'Long Walls', they — along with the short-lived outer Phaleron Wall — added up to a formidable defensive system that from the air would have looked like a giant dumbbell. Following the Athenian defeat in the Peloponnesian War in 404 BC, the Long Walls were demolished, only to be later rebuilt. By the Roman era they had gone for good, Piraeus was in decline, and the focus of Athens moved north and east, with the building of the Roman Agora and the Hadrianic Wall.

The surviving remains of the ancient city are substantial, but not very representative. The Athenians built their houses and the greater part of the city walls out of adobe bricks, and over the millennia these have reverted to mud. Many of the marble buildings do survive in part, though you would never guess that they were all once brightly painted. As for the 3000 bronze statues observed by Roman writers; well, the National Archaeological Museum is now home to the surviving odd finger or two.

Historical Background

Athens was once the most powerful of all the Greek city states. It is best known for the work of a mere three generations in the 5 C. BC when it first stood alone as a bulwark against the massed forces of the Persian Empire (its citizens playing a crucial part in the battles of Marathon in 490 BC and Salamis in 480 BC) and then, under the leadership of Pericles and his successors, became the fountainhead of European civilization, playing host to the sudden flowering of the Greek genius that gave the western world its first theatre, greatest art and architecture, and first true history and philosophy. However, the dynamic that had set the city apart soon faded, and Athens had to settle for becoming a major centre of learning during the Hellenistic and Roman periods, then a minor town under the Turks, before emerging as the capital of Greece in the 19th century.

Thanks to the protection offered by the Acropolis, Athens has been occupied since Neolithic times. During the Mycenaean period the Acropolis was fortified, and this served the city well during the dark ages that followed as it was able to repulse the waves of Doric Greeks pouring into Greece. By the 8 C. BC

Athens had gained control of the surrounding province of Attica and emerged as one of the major art centres in Greece. This developed into a leading cultural role in the 6 C. BC under the patronage of Pisistratus who initiated the Great Dionysia (a semi-religious eisteddfod) as part of the annual Panathenaic festival. This gave the world the first established texts of Homer, and later produced the birth of drama; for it was in Athens that most of the great plays of Greek tragedy and comedy were conceived and first performed. A succession of leaders — Draco, Solon and Cleisthenes — also instituted constitutional reforms that led to Athens emerging as the champion of democracy. Rule by orators in turn prompted debate, and enquiry into words and their meanings; which in turn extended the debate to wider ideas and concepts of morality. As a result, Athens developed as a centre for debate, attracting the great philosophers — Socrates, Plato and Aristotle among them. Athens also emerged as a major economic power — largely thanks to the profits derived from the substantial silver mines at nearby Lavrion.

Athenian victories over the Persians gave the city the role of leading protector of the Greeks and, on this basis, the islands contributed funds for the maintenance of the Athenian trireme fleet. Unfortunately, Athens rapidly turned these contributions into a tribute, and the islands into a de facto empire, and used the excess monies to build the Acropolis temples. Fearful of Athenian domination, the cities of Sparta and Corinth were soon embroiled in the Peloponnesian war, which Athens lost after 30 years of struggle. Never regaining her military pre-eminence, Athens fell to Philip of Macedon in 338 BC. and came under Roman control in the 2 C. BC. The city was sacked by Sulla in 86 BC, saw a brief renaissance (thanks to the patronage of Hadrian), and finally faded from the scene when it was sacked by the Herulian Goths in 267 AD.

Reduced to cowering behind the Valerian wall (which confined the city to the Roman Agora and the Acropolis), Athens was a minor town in the Byzantine Empire. It was ruled by the Franks and the Venetians before the Ottoman Turks gave it four quiet centuries (their rule being only briefly interrupted by the disastrous Venetian conquest of the city in 1687) prior to Greek independence in 1833.

The Acropolis
The greatest attraction in Athens is the Acropolis (see map between pages 96–97). The name means 'the city on the rock'. Standing some 90 m above the surrounding plain, the rock proved easily defensible, later becoming the focus of religious activity, before its defensive value again came to the fore. The buildings constructed on the rock add up to one of the most important archaeological sites in the world. Even in their ruined state, the Parthenon and the Erechtheion remain architectural wonders, forming the nucleus of an ensemble of buildings that led the Roman writer Plutarch to say of them that 'they were created in a short time for all time ... a perpetual newness blooms upon them untouched by the years, as if they held within them some everlasting breath of life and an ageless spirit intermingled in their composition'. These days this effect is somewhat diminished by the presence of three million visitors a year, but if you arrive early, you can avoid the worst of the crowds. The site is open ⊚ 08.00–18.30 (entrance fee 2000 GDR). Coach tour guides have the right to push to the head of the ticket-kiosk queues. Tourists are not allowed to venture inside the Acropolis buildings.

The Acropolis has evidence of occupation dating back to Neolithic times, though later building has destroyed most traces. It is known that in the Mycenaean period it had a palace and saw its first major fortifications. In the Archaic period the Acropolis emerged as the religious centre of the city, with a succession of temples erected on the rock before the Persians fired them in their invasion of Greece in 480 BC. Calamitous at the time, this event proved to have a happy outcome, as it cleared the way for the massive rebuilding programme inspired by the Athenian leader Pericles some 30 years later — just as the flower of Greek culture was busting into full bloom; it is the ruins of these buildings that remain today.

Through the Hellenistic and Roman periods the Acropolis saw little further building (apart from on its outer slopes), and it was only from the 7 C. AD on that the area around the temples was in-filled with other buildings, as the rock was again used as a fortress. This state of affairs continued through the period of Turkish rule (one of the early European visitors describing the Acropolis mentions that there were two streets of whitewashed houses between the Parthenon and the Erechtheion).

Once Athens became the capital of an independent Greek state, the Acropolis was rapidly converted from a fortress-town to a museum. In 1833 work began in stripping away the detritus of 2000 years (this included the removal of several streets of houses and a 30 m tower built atop the Propylaea) to reveal the ancient buildings in all their ruined glory. However, restoration of the Classical buildings resulted in unwitting damage due to poor techniques. The worst of these was the use of iron staples in rebuilding that rusted and caused many marble blocks to split (the ancients coated the original staples with lead to prevent this process occurring). This has resulted in all the buildings requiring major attention in the last few years, and quite a lot of controversial new 'white' marble is visible. The nature of such restorations is a subject of much argument. Current rebuilding is limited to work needed to ensure the structural integrity of the monuments and all new blocks are dated to ensure there is never confusion between old and new material. All the additions are also reversible. Previous restoration has been more substantial; notably the rebuilding of the centre columns on the north facade of the Parthenon in 1933. It has been suggested that the south side be similarly 'repaired', but this is a contentious idea and has been shelved while other worries — notably the growing threat of acid rain damage — are discussed.

Acropolis Entrance / West Side
Modern visitors approach the Acropolis from the same side as the ancients: though the first building encountered is a late construction. ⓐ the **Beulé Gate** (named after its excavator) formed part of the defensive wall constructed in the 3 C. AD. It replaced a large processional stairway constructed by the Emperor Claudius in 52 AD. Today the path winds up to the Acropolis much as it did in classical times. After the Beulé Gate you are confronted by two bastions projecting out from the Acropolis proper. On the northern one is ⓑ the distinctive **'Tower' of Agrippa** (C. 178 BC). A Hellenistic plinth 8.8 m high, it bore a succession of bronze statues (including a chariot carrying Antony and Cleopatra), and takes its name from a statue of Marcus Agrippa erected on it in 27 BC.

The south bastion is more appealing, being home to ❸ the lovely small **Athena Nike Temple** (427–424 BC). Designed by Kallikrates, it was dismantled in 1686 by the Turks so that the bastion could be used to house cannon. Fortunately, all the stones were preserved on site and it was re-erected in 1836–42. The building has a frieze running right around it, and contained a statue of Athena with Nike (Victory). Unfortunately, the lack of tourist retaining walls on the bastion means that it is fenced off: the steps to the Acropolis offer the best view you can get of it. Like all the Acropolis buildings, it is built of pentelic marble. Thanks to small deposits of iron in the marble, the colour has gradually mellowed from white to a creamy yellow as the iron has gradually oxidized over the millennia.

Extending out onto the bastions are the wings of ❹ the **Propylaea** (438–432 BC): the ceremonial gateway to the Acropolis. Deemed to be the best of its kind by the ancients, it was never fully completed. The outbreak of the Peloponnesian war and Athenian defeat ensured that its decoration was never finished. Designed by Mnesikles, the building was famous for its five massive doors and painted ceiling. The north wing was also a noted picture gallery. The building was used as a bishop's palace in the 13 C., and in the 17 C. became a magazine for the Turkish garrison, suffering severe damage when a passing lightning bolt struck. The Venetian bombardment of 1687 finished the job of demolition by putting paid to the famous ceiling. South-east of the Propylaea (and now represented only by scattered stones) are the foundations of a double-winged stoa; a votive shrine to **Artemis Brauronia** (the bear goddess), and nearer the Parthenon, the **Chalkotheke** or **Magazine of the Bronzes**.

The North Side

Surprisingly, the magnificent Parthenon temple was not the holy of holies on the Acropolis. It was more of a glorious ante-chamber to the true religious centre — the Erechtheion — which was located on the north side, on the probable site of the Mycenaean palace. This building was guarded by a large bronze statue that stood at ❺ facing the Propylaea. Known as the **Athena Promachos**, this famous figure is long lost, but part of the stone base has been identified. The path takes you past the site where it stood, and then divides. One branch takes you along the north side of the Parthenon

(the traditional approach route to this temple), the other runs northward past foundations at ❻. This is the site of a **Temple of Athena Polias**. Built c. 530 BC, it originally stood alongside another limestone temple — the melodiously named **Hekatompedon** — meaning 'one hundred footer' (c. 566 BC), which stood on the Parthenon site. Sometime around 508 BC this building was demolished. Its incomplete successor — the **Pre-Parthenon** — was destroyed by the Persians. Its column drums were later used to close off the other entrances to the Acropolis and are still visible in the north wall when viewed from street level. After the Persian sacking, the Athenians swore never to rebuild the temples. They later got around this vow by levelling the Athena Polias temple site, and having made a gesture in this direction, proceeded to rebuild the other buildings.

Not least among these was the **Erechtheion** (c. 421–405 BC). This complex of shrines is a four-chambered building (❼) that conformed to an ancient and irregular plan. It was home to several ancient and venerated wooden figures — notably a statue of Athena Polias — that were removed (along with the population of Athens) to the island of Salamis during the Persian sacking. The path approaches the building running past ❽ the site of the **Sacred Grove** (which was home to the olive tree offered by Athena, when winning her contest for the patronage of the city with Poseidon) and then turns east at the **North Portico** (fronting a shrine to Poseidon). Designed by Kallikrates, the Erechtheion is graced with delicate Ionic columns. It became a church in the 6 C. and later the harem for the Turkish commander — an idea no doubt inspired by ❾, the **Caryatids** — the famous maiden-column porch. All the figures are now copies: the originals are in the Acropolis Museum (barring the one in the British Museum). The east portico fronted the main shrine to Athena Polias and now has a **Restored Column** (❿) at the north end. Added in 1981 (most postcard photos are still without it), it has attracted criticism thanks to its 'fake' weathered finish. In fact, it is an accurate copy of the original — now in the British Museum.

To the south east of the Erechtheion stood a large stepped altar at ⓚ dedicated to **Zeus Polieus**, of which little remains. Instead, the path runs east of the site past a deep well in the floor of the rock at ⓛ. Known as the **Mycenaean Stairway**, it was one of two stairways up the north side of the rock that were closed off in the classical period (the Persians gained access to the Acropolis via a second, to the north of the Erechtheion). From here the path then runs east to the flag bastion and its views of the city. On its way it passes the scanty remains of  the tiny, round tholos **Temple of Rome and Augustus**; a late and clumsy addition (27 BC) to the Acropolis monuments, all but ignored by ancient writers.

The Parthenon

The main temple cum city treasury dedicated to Athena Parthenos (the Virgin Athena), the Parthenon (**N**) dominates the Acropolis. Built between 447–432 BC, the building is remarkable for not having a straight line in it. The platform is deliberately convex to allow rainwater to drain off. The columns are also convex — a feature designed by the building's architects Iktinos and Kallikrates to correct the optical illusion that makes straight columns appear thinner in the middle. The simple Doric columns also lean in slightly — were they tall enough, their centres would meet at a point some 2.5 km above the building — as well as being abnormally tall and placed closer together than was traditional. Tradition was also defied in the size of the building; most temples were built 6 columns wide — the Parthenon has 8. Its length was determined by a standard formula (2 x the number of width columns + 1) producing 17 columns down the sides: thus retaining regular proportions yet making it appear unusually long. The result is a building that makes all other Greek temples look small and clumsy by comparison.

Intact for over 2000 years, the Parthenon has had a chequered history. Highlights include a couple of passing rulers using it to put a finger up (among other things) at the city population by using it as a brothel. In the 6 c. it was converted into the church of St. Sophia: a change which inflicted major structural damage as the orientation of the building had to be turned 180 degrees (the main entrance was originally on the east side to allow the rising sun to shine in upon the statue of the goddess), and an apse was added to the east end. In the Ottoman period the Parthenon became a mosque, with a minaret poking through the roof on the south-west corner. It met its end in 1687, when a Venetian army besieged the city. On hearing that the Turks were using the Parthenon as a hiding place for their arsenal (they assumed their attackers would never bombard a former church) the Venetian commander Morosini did just that. A shell landed on the building, blowing it apart, and leaving fragments of the roof, cella and the 300 women and children sheltering inside all over the Acropolis.

In its ruined state, the Parthenon continued to suffer. Reduced to two unconnected gable ends, it was used as a quarry for a mosque that was built in the shell (described by one visitor as looking like 'an ugly cork in a beautiful bottle'). Its remaining sculptures were removed by Lord Elgin (see p. 110), and poor restoration and pollution have taken their toll since. The Parthenon is currently having quite a lot of work carried out on it, but this is not nearly enough for some archaeologists, who have called for the re-roofing of the building to save the foundations (protected until 1687) from increasing rainwater damage.

In its prime the Parthenon was ornately decorated, with sculpture and other decorative features brightly painted in gaudy 'Mickey Mouse' colours. As much a statement of civic pride as a temple, it housed a treasury in the smaller room in its west end, but its main function was to house the 12 m high chryselephantine (gold and ivory) statue of **Athena Parthenos** (**O**). This remarkable figure cost more than the Parthenon itself, and its designer, Phidias, his reputation and almost his life. Known now through small copies bought by ancient tourists, it stood 12 m high and represented the goddess holding a shield in her left hand and a man-sized, winged Victory in her right. Her helmet was topped by a sphinx and two griffins, and her shield was decorated with scenes from the mythical battle between the Athenians and the Amazon women. It was this shield that brought about Phidias's downfall. His pre-eminent position as the supervisor of the Acropolis rebuilding programme brought him enemies, who took advantage of a perceived likeness in the faces of two of the figures on Athena's shield to himself and his mentor, Pericles, to have him charged with sacrilege. Forced to flee the city, he took sanctuary at Olympia and there created one of the seven wonders of the world — his chryselephantine statue of Zeus. The Athena was deemed to be the inferior of the two, though she was impressive enough, with clothing made of sheets of gold tacked onto a wooden frame. Her flesh was sculpted ivory, and her eyes; precious gems. The figure stood, facing east, before a pool of sea-water (to reflect light from the door) at the back of the Parthenon's main room. In its prime it must have been over-whelming. To the ancients, walking into the dimly lit chamber, it must have seemed as if the goddess herself was standing before them. The figure survived until c. 400 AD when it was removed to Constantinople and later destroyed by fire.

The Parthenon also boasted other major art treasures that survive in part. The **Pediment Sculptures** are the most obvious of these. Now reduced to fragments in museums (those now on the building are copies), by great luck, they were drawn in 1674 by Jacques Carrey, a French painter, a few years before they were damaged. **P** the **West Pediment**, was the best preserved until 1687. Its theme was the contest between Athena and Poseidon for the patronage of the city. Sadly, when the Venetians captured Athens, Morosini decided to remove the central figures and horses as war trophies, but they fell and were smashed in the attempt to take them down. The central **East Pediment** (**Q**) figures were lost in the 4 C. AD when the Parthenon was turned into a church. According to Pausanias the theme was the birth of Athena, but he gives no further details. A 1–2 c. AD altar from Spain, thought to be based on this pediment, shows Athena and Zeus standing in a similar pose to the main figures on the west pediment (studies of floor marks suggest they were similarly framed by pairs of horses).

The other great Parthenon art treasure is the **Frieze**. Over 159 m long, it is a high point of Greek art. It ran around the outer wall of **R** the **Cella** (the 'building' inside the ring of columns). Long thought to depict the Panathenaic procession to the Acropolis in honour of the goddess, it is now believed to be a representation of a myth; the sacrifice of the daughters of Erechtheus (a king of Athens). Just over half of the panels were recovered by Elgin and are in the British Museum. Along with the majority of the surviving pedimental figures, they are the most important of the 'Elgin Marbles'.

The South Side

The area to the south of the Parthenon contains a couple of oddities. Now unmarked, is the site of **S** **Phidias's Workshop**, used for the construction of the gold and ivory statue. Fragments of the materials used have been found in this area. Walking along to the west end of the Parthenon you will come to **T** the **Pre-Classical Wall Trenches**. These pits were natural fissures in the rock inside the Acropolis walls. In the Classical period they were used as 'graves' for the damaged sculptures from the temples destroyed by the Persians (and are now in the Acropolis museum). Left open, with low skirting walls, they form a minor hazard. The Acropolis wall is also dangerously low, but looking over it you are able to take in the layout of the buildings lining the southern slope better than you can at street level.

Looking down from left to right, the first, and largest of the south slope structures is **U** the **Theatre of Dionysos** (c. 330 BC). Marking the spot where most of the great plays of Greek tragedy and comedy were first performed in annual competitions, the site now has a separate entrance on the south-east corner of the Acropolis area (entrance fee 400 GDR). In the Classical period the theatre stage and seating occupied the lower tiers and were made of wood. With the rebuilding, the seating was extended right up the slope, though this has now gone. Above the theatre and close under the walls stand **V** two **Corinthian Columns** (320–310 BC). These were erected by sponsors of winning dramatic performances — the west one is known as the **Thrasyllos Monument**. Cut into the rock below is a small shine — now the chapel of Panagia Spiliotissa. To the left of the theatre stood a major classical hall-like building known as the **Odeon of Pericles** (little survives), while to the right are the foundations of two healing sanctuaries; **W** the **Old Asklepieion** (c. 420 BC), and the **New Asklepieion** (c. 300 BC). A number of minor shrines lay between these buildings and the west Acropolis slope. Running east of the theatre is **X** the **Stoa of Eumenes II** (c. 197–159 BC), the back wall of which has survived as part of the later city wall. At its eastern end lie the foundations of **Y** the **Nikias Monument** (320–319 BC) which was demolished to build the Beulé Gate. Finally, **Z** the **Odeon of Herodes Atticus**, is the best preserved building on the Acropolis slopes. Built in 160–174 AD, the inner section of its façade survived by being incorporated into the later city wall that ran around the Acropolis. The interior seating was lost thanks to the same reason, but has since been replaced to allow performances in the theatre. The rooms behind the stage have also been rebuilt from the foundations.

Acropolis Museum & Elgin Marbles

After looking at the buildings on the Acropolis, the museum nestling in a natural hollow in the rock behind the Parthenon is apt to be something of an anti-climax. A small building, it is due to be replaced by a more substantial affair in several years time. With the best site exhibits now in the British Museum (thanks to Lord Elgin), and the more interesting smaller Acropolis-related pieces (notably the marble copy of the statue of Athena Parthenos) housed in the National Archaeological Museum, the Acropolis Museum has to make do with the residue — principally the remains of the pre-classical sculpture from the buildings destroyed in the Persian sack of the Acropolis and the handful of sculptures and reliefs that escaped Elgin and other collectors. This said, the museum does merit a visit (if only to see close up the original Caryatids — now housed behind protective glass). The archaeologically minded might also consider buying a detailed Acropolis guide as, unusually, few of the exhibits are labelled, and are spread over nine rooms:

Rooms I–III: Persian Rubble Rooms

These rooms are devoted to the sculptures damaged by the Persians in 480 BC and later ceremonially buried by the Athenians. These include: **Ⓐ** the **Lioness and Calf**: the latter creature is being torn to flesh (6 c. BC); **Ⓑ** a **Gorgon's Head** (550 BC); **Ⓒ** part of a pedimental sculpture depicting **Herakles fighting the Triton**; **Ⓓ** the **Calf Bearer**, one of the most influential and important Archaic works of art; and **Ⓔ** the **Lion Group**, also from the pediment of an Archaic temple (570–560 BC).

Room IV: Phaidimos Room

Devoted to sculptures (not all from the Acropolis) by this artist. Primary exhibits are **Ⓕ** the **Equestrian Statue**: the torso of the first European equestrian statue known, and **Ⓖ** the **Peplos Kore**: a woman named after her clothing, with traces of her original paint (530 BC).

Room V: Gigantomachia Room

Lined on one side by **Ⓗ** the **Showcases**. Behind the glass, running from left to right are ceramics from south slope buildings, archaic marble fragments from the Acropolis, small masonry and clay sculptures and wooden blocks from the holes of the Parthenon column drums. This room also contains **Ⓘ**, the **Gigantomachia**. The battle between the Olympian Gods and the giants was a popular theme in Ancient

Greek art; this example shows Athena fighting a giant and comes from the Archaic temple that proceeded the Parthenon.

Room VI: Late Archaic Works

This room contains a mixed collection of items, notably **Ⓙ**, the **Mourning Athena**, c. 460 BC, (see pose of Athena on p. 88): a famous relief, it was discovered in 1888 south of the Parthenon; and **Ⓚ** the **Kritios Boy**; 480 BC, (illustrated below) a statue of a youth in Parian marble.

Room VII: Parthenon Fragments

This rather thin collection is dominated by **Ⓛ** the **West Pediment figure**; a male figure —

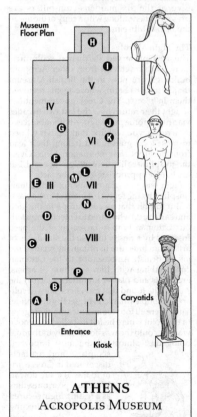

Museum Floor Plan

ATHENS
ACROPOLIS MUSEUM

possibly the river god Ilissos, and  the **East Gable figure**: the torso of a woman—thought to be the moon goddess Selene driving her chariot toward the sunset.

Room VIII: Parthenon Frieze fragments

Most of the surviving frieze is now in the British Museum, but several weathered slabs are here: **N** the **East Frieze** depicts a procession with sacrificial animals and athletes, and **O**, which shows **Youths with Amphorae**. This room also contains **P**, the **Nike Relief**, from the Temple of Nike, showing Athena undoing a sandal (409–406 BC).

Room IX: The Caryatids

Five of the six maidens-cum-pillars are preserved here, along with a copy of the one in the British Museum.

The Elgin Marbles

The best preserved Parthenon sculptures, along with fragments from other Acropolis buildings, are now in the British Museum thanks to Lord Elgin, whose agents removed them in 1801–4. The Greek government has sought their return over the last two decades via a high profile campaign—without success. As a result, you will find that Elgin is vilified in most local guides and (taking their lead from these) not a few international ones. Over-the-top phrases like 'looter Elgin' abound, but are hardly appropriate given the facts.

Elgin was one of a number of individuals (inspired by the revival of interest in the classical tradition that swept Europe in the 18th and early 19 c.) who dared to enter the mysterious Ottoman Empire in search of the past. Inspired by a desire to raise the standards of art and architecture in Britain, he secured the job of British Ambassador to the Ottoman court, taking with him a retinue of artists, architects and plaster moulders. Once in the Aegean he found that travellers' tales of collapsing temples thanks to neglect by the 'infidel Turk' were all too true and his ambitions grew to the point where he felt impelled to remove what he could (he was not the only individual doing this: almost all the most important sculpture and artifacts discovered in Greece prior or to the 20 C. are now in West European museums as a result). Elgin secured a written firman directing the Ottoman

authorities who had been ruling Athens for over 350 years to allow his agents to remove 'inscriptions and sculptures' from the derelict Acropolis buildings. He only narrowly beat his French counterpart to the marbles, and indeed, other Parthenon sculptures are now in the Louvre and Vatican museums. The Greeks have never accepted the legitimacy of Turkish rule, and perceive these agreements as being akin to one thief passing on stolen goods to another.

Given the uniqueness of the Parthenon and its universal recognition as *the* symbol of Greece, a strong emotional case can be made for the return of the marbles (it is difficult to remove them in London and not feel considerable qualms on this score). However, Elgin bashers hardly help their cause by failing to acknowledge that his motives were hardly on a par with a looter's, or that plaster casts made by his workmen of sculptures he didn't remove show that they deteriorated significantly before their importance was recognized. In this respect, Elgin's claim that he was 'saving' the marbles was borne out by events (though the 1998 revelation that the many of the marbles had been 'skinned'—by over zealous cleaning by poorly supervised British Museum staff in the 1930s — has somewhat eroded this).

The impact the sculptures had in London is also not readily acknowledged (beyond the fact that they helped bankrupt Elgin — he spent £74,240 recovering the marbles). Widely admired (the poet Keats gazed at them for hours at a time like a 'sick eagle looking at the sky'), they have been very influential, occasionally in quite bizarre ways. Most important was their contribution to the pro-Greek romanticism sweeping Europe that led to the Great Powers (Britain, France and Russia) supporting Greek nationalism and the foundation of the Greek state. At the other end of the scale, fashionable London dandies made total fools of themselves adopting a posture (known as the 'Grecian bend') supposedly based on the figures. However, the most delightful fall-out from Elgin's acquisitions came with the horse's head removed from the north corner of the Parthenon's east pediment. Subsequently used as the model for what has become the standard international chess-set knight, it has acquired an unassailable status as the most copied piece of sculpture in history.

The Agora

Within easy walking distance of the Acropolis lie a number of important archaeological sites. The most important of these is the **Agora**, the ancient marketplace, to the north-west. An open square during classical times, bounded by all the major administrative buildings in the city, it was in-filled with buildings in the Hellenistic and Roman periods. Add to this 3000 years of continuous occupation and the result is the confused jumble of foundations that one sees today. The Roman travel writer Pausanias described all the major buildings, so most of those unearthed have been identified. Problems, however, do remain. The north side of the Agora still lies under the modern city (the buildings here are dilapidated, with the sword of demolition hanging over them), hindering a comprehensive assessment of the site's history. Moreover, two important buildings — the **Theseion**, the major shrine of the city's founder, and the **Stoa of Herms** — are known to have been in the vicinity of the Agora, but remain undiscovered.

The area so far exposed has been excavated since the 1930s when the Turkish buildings covering the Agora were demolished. The metro line cutting off the northern third of the site is a legacy of the last century (1891) when its importance was unrecognized. Today the Agora is heavily planted with trees, offering a shady retreat from the hot city streets.

The North and East Sides

There are two entrances to the Agora; one on the Acropolis side, and the main entrance, sited on a bridge over the metro line. The street leading to the latter (Adrianou) offers you a glimpse of several inaccessible buildings. Most notable of these is the corner of **A**, the **Painted Stoa** or **Stoa Poikile** (c. 460 BC), currently being excavated by students from the American School of Archaeology. Once the most famous secular building in Athens, it was a natural meeting place for the city intelligentsia. Its reputation was based on the paintings that adorned its walls (it was the Louvre of the ancient city) and the bronze shields hung about it (captured from the Spartans at the battle of Sphakteria in 425 BC — one is now in the museum). As a result of the chattering crowds that gathered here, it

became the only building to give its name to a school of philosophy; as those that followed the philosopher Zeno regularly met in the building and thus became known as 'Stoics'.

Turning to the other side of the road, you can look down on the foundations of the small, winged **Royal Stoa** (c. 500 BC) at **B**, where the city magistrates took their oath of office. Hereafter, the road runs to the railway bridge. From the ticket kiosk on the bridge, the main path descends onto **C** the **Panathenaic Way**. Running south-east to the Acropolis, this was the most important road in the city. It was the ceremonial route for the annual procession depicted on the Parthenon frieze. Nowadays, it runs to the south end of **D** the **Stoa of Attalos**. Rebuilt between 1953–56 by the American excavators, it is now the **Agora Museum**. The original was a gift from the king of Pergamum c. 145 BC. It replaced an earlier row of shops and is a typical example of this type of building, with two storeys and 21 square rooms at the back that functioned as shops. A pillar with a statue of Attalos in a chariot stood in front of the stoa, with **E** a **Bema** (a speaker's platform), directly in front of that. Nearby are the circular remains of **F** a Roman **Fountain**. To the north stood the classical law courts, but the surviving foundations (straddled by the railway line) are of a later **Hadrianic Basilica** (**G**) with an **Augustan Colonnade** (**H**) running west from it.

The Central Area

The centre of the Agora was an open square during the classical period. Now it is dominated by **I**, the **Odeon of Agrippa** c. 15 BC. Rebuilt several times (largely on account of the massive vaulted roof that collapsed now and again) it was later rebuilt as a vast gymnasium c. 400 AD. The most prominent feature today are the three colossal statues of tritons and giants that formed part of the entrance of the original building. The triton heads are of particular significance, as ancient sources say that they were modelled on the (now lost) pedimental sculpture of Poseidon on the Parthenon. To the north of the Odeon lies the remains of **J** the **Altar of Ares** (c. 420 BC). It was here that dogs were sacrificed in honour of the god. To the west was **K** the **Temple of Ares** (c. 435 BC). Now no more than a low mound, it was originally very similar in design to the Hephaisteion on the hill to the west (it is thought to possibly be the work of the same architect). The building wasn't originally located here: all the surviving stones are numbered (indicating it was moved from a different site); the foundations are Roman, and some of the guttering seems to have come from the Temple of Poseidon at Sounion. The original location of the temple isn't known (suggestions range from the Roman Agora to Acharnai outside the city), but this sort of movement wasn't uncommon in the Roman period, when many outlying shrines were abandoned due to urbanization.

North of the Temple of Ares, and now tucked against the metro line wall, lies a corner of the boundary wall that surrounded the small **❶ Altar of the Twelve Gods** (6 C. BC). Now all but lost under the track, this was one of the most important monuments in Athens. The altar was not only venerated as a place of sanctuary (particularly for the destitute) but also served as the *Omphalos* or navel of the city and the province of Attica. As such, it was the official starting point, from which all distances were measured.

The West Side

Travelling west, the path then emerges at **❿**, the **Stoa of Zeus Eleutherios** C. 430 BC, which was an early (and therefore small) stoa with projecting wings. Ornately decorated, it was the base for the official in charge of religious ceremonies and trials for murder or impiety. It is better known in literature as the favourite stoa of the philosopher Socrates. It was in this building that he was wont to argue with his fellows, taking the line that he knew nothing and then proceeding to demonstrate that those who claimed to know something 'didn't know nuffin' either. Showing up large numbers of people who thought that they were intelligent didn't exactly endear Socrates to those in power, and he was tried and executed on trumped-up sacrilege charges in 399 BC.

South of the stoa of Zeus lie the foundations of **❶ the Temple of Apollo Patroös** (4 C. BC). One of the oldest temples in Athens, it was destroyed and rebuilt several times. The colossal statue of Apollo (now in the Agora museum) once stood in it. On the other side of the path, and to the south, stands a replica of the torso of a **Statue of Hadrian (❶)**, notable for the breast-plate adorned with the delightful mix of Athena (accompanied by a snake and owl) standing on the back of a wolf suckling Romulus and Remus.

Behind the buildings on the west side of the Agora and overlooking all is **❶** the **Hephaisteion** (449–444 BC). The best preserved temple in Greece, it is the only temple to retain its roof substructure substantially intact (the inner cella now has a medieval roof over it). Built just before the Parthenon (but not with money raised by the islands for the Delian League: this temple hadn't a predecessor to be destroyed by the Persians), for many years it was thought to be another important temple — the Theseion (hence the metro station of that name nearby) — but this notion has now been discredited. Inside it still contains the bronze cult statues of Hephaistos and Athena. Around it are trees planted in their classical positions; the original pots were unearthed when the site was excavated. This excavation also revealed that to the north of the Hephaisteion stood **❶** the **Arsenal** of ancient Athens, now known only through post holes.

The steps leading up to the Hephaisteion also marked the boundary between the religious and secular buildings on this side of the agora. To the south stood **❶**, the **Metroön** (430 BC); theoretically a temple dedicated to the mother of the gods, it became the repository for the government archives. It was built on the original site of **❸**, the **Bouleuterion** (5 C. BC). This was the council chamber for the city senate house, and was rebuilt a number of times during its working life, gradually increasing in size, and each time further back from the main line of buildings. This allowed the Metroön to be expanded south to **❶** the circular **Tholos** (C. 470 BC). One of the most important buildings in Athens (being the headquarters for those charged with the running of the city) it was manned 24 hours a day (and had its own kitchen). It is a controversial structure, with widely differing reconstructions being put forward (in part because it was rebuilt several times). In its last incarnation, it had a conical roof with diamond-shaped tiles. Opposite this collection of buildings was **❶**, the long narrow monument of the **Eponymonus Heroes**. Adorned with the statues of the founders of the political tribes of Athens, it was used to display public notices.

The South Side

The southern boundary of the Agora was dominated by a series of stoas that gradually encroached north to the point where they added to the in-filling of the classical Agora

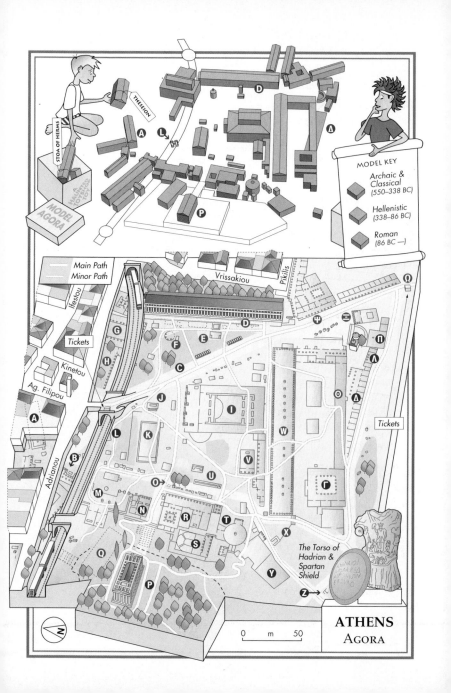

MODEL KEY

Archaic & Classical (550–338 BC)

Hellenistic (338–86 BC)

Roman (86 BC —)

THESEION

STOA OF HERMS

MODEL AGORA

Main Path

Minor Path

Vrissakiou

Piklis

Tfestou

Tickets

Kinetou

Ag. Filipou

Adrianou

Tickets

The Torso of Hadrian & Spartan Shield

ATHENS
AGORA

0   m   50

N

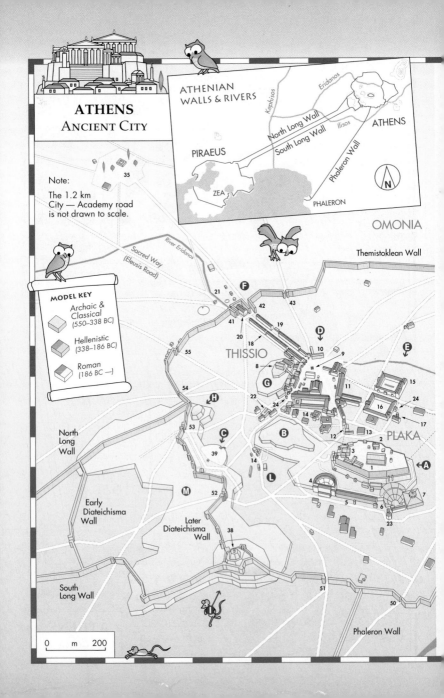

ATHENS
ANCIENT CITY

Note:
The 1.2 km
City — Academy road
is not drawn to scale.

35

ATHENIAN WALLS & RIVERS

Eridanos

Kephisos

North Long Wall

South Long Wall

Ilisos

ATHENS

PIRAEUS

ZEA

Phaleron Wall

PHALERON

N

OMONIA

Themistoklean Wall

Sacred Way
(Eleusis Road)

River Eridanos

MODEL KEY

Archaic &
Classical
(550–338 BC)

Hellenistic
(338–186 BC)

Roman
(186 BC —)

THISSIO

North
Long
Wall

Early
Diateichisma
Wall

Later
Diateichisma
Wall

South
Long
Wall

PLAKA

Phaleron Wall

0   m   200

21 F 42 43
41 19
20 18 D 10 9
55 8 E
G 11 15
22 24 16 24
14 13 17
12
3 2
B 1 A
C 39 4 7
14 L 5 6 23
M 52
38
51 50

Key

- **A** Acropolis
- **B** Areopagus
- **C** Pnyx (Parliament)
- **D** Agora (Marketplace)
- **E** Roman Agora Area
- **F** Kerameikos
- **G** Kolonos Hill
- **H** Hill of the Nymphs
- **I** Mouseion Hill
- **J** Ardettos Hill
- **K** Roman 'New City'
- **L** Early City Centre
- **M** Early Residential Area

CITY LANDMARKS

1. Parthenon
2. Erechtheion
3. Propylaea
4. Odeon of Herodes Atticus
5. Stoa of Eumenes
6. Theatre of Dionysos
7. Odeon of Pericles
8. Hephaisteion
9. Altar of the Twelve Gods (City Centre)
10. Stoa Poikile
11. Stoa of Attalos
12. Eleusinion
13. Diogeneum
14. Private Houses
15. Library of Hadrian
16. Roman Agora
17. Tower of the Winds
18. Stoas lining the Panathenaic Way
19. Euboulides Monument
20. Pompeion
21. Main Cemetery
22. Classical Prison
23. Public Bath-houses
24. Public Latrines
25. Lysicrates Monument
26. Palladion
27. Arch of Hadrian
28. Temple of Kronos & Rhea
29. Olympieion
30. Delphinium
31. Temple of Tyche
32. Tomb of Herodes
33. Temple of Artemis Agrotera
34. Stadium
35. Academy (Gymnasium)
36. Lyceum (Gym)
37. Kynosarges (Gym)
38. Monument of Philopappus
39. City Parliament Platform (Pnyx)
40. Garden of Theophrastos

MODERN DISTRICTS

LIKAVITTOS

N

Hadrianic/Roman Wall

SYNTAGMA

River Eridanos

River Ilisos

CITY GATES

41. Sacred Gate
42. Dipylon Gate
43. Eriai Gate
44. Acharnian Gate
45. North-East Gate
46. Diochares Gate
47. Hippades Gate
48. Diomeian Gate
49. Itonian Gate
50. Halade-Gate
51. South Gate
52. 'Dipylon above the Gates'
53. Melitides Gate
54. Demian Gate
55. Peiraic or Piraeus Gate
56. Roman Gates

Main Road
Minor Road
Line of the Valerian Wall

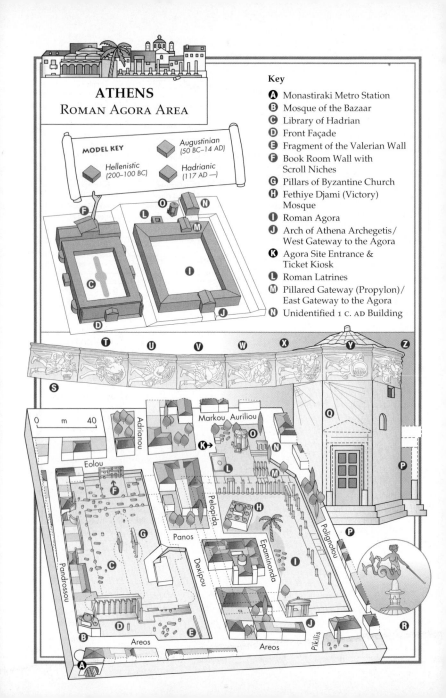

ATHENS
ROMAN AGORA AREA

MODEL KEY

Hellenistic
(200–100 BC)

Augustinian
(50 BC–14 AD)

Hadrianic
(117 AD —)

Key

- **A** Monastiraki Metro Station
- **B** Mosque of the Bazaar
- **C** Library of Hadrian
- **D** Front Façade
- **E** Fragment of the Valerian Wall
- **F** Book Room Wall with Scroll Niches
- **G** Pillars of Byzantine Church
- **H** Fethiye Djami (Victory) Mosque
- **I** Roman Agora
- **J** Arch of Athena Archegetis / West Gateway to the Agora
- **K** Agora Site Entrance & Ticket Kiosk
- **L** Roman Latrines
- **M** Pillared Gateway (Propylon) / East Gateway to the Agora
- **N** Unidentified 1 c. AD Building

0   m   40

Adrianou

Markou Auriliou

Eolou

Pelopida

Panos

Dexipou

Epaminonda

Pandrossou

Areos

Areos

Pikilis

Polignotou

square. Temples were also added at this later stage. They included the small **South-West Temple** at **ⓥ**, with an altar (of Zeus Agoraios) 30 m to the north, and a small stoa-like building to the south (used by the Athenian civil service). Behind these lies the foundations of **ⓦ** the **Middle Stoa** (2 C. BC). The largest stoa to be built in Athens, it took the form of a double-aisled hall open on both sides. It was later incorporated into the 4 C. AD gymnasium along with the nearby Odeon. Abutting it to the west was **ⓧ**: a block of **Small Buildings** that included a cobbler's shop and a latrine, and **ⓨ** the **Stratagion**. Only tentatively identified, this building was probably the Pentagon of ancient Athens, and used as both the military headquarters and home of the supreme commander. Conveniently located near the city prison, its incumbents tended to move from one to the other with alarming regularity — particularly during the Peloponnesian war when the 30-year stalemate between Athens and Sparta lead to a succession of commanders being executed for failing to win the war. The classical **Prison** (**❷**), just outside the Agora, was where Socrates was executed (a clay miniature of the philosopher was found on site).

South of the Middle Stoa lie the foundations of the classical south Agora buildings. These include **ⓕ** the **Heliaia** (C. 470 BC), the original city courthouse, and **ⓖ** the **South Stoa I** (5 C. BC). Now overlain by **ⓗ** the **South Stoa II** (2 C. BC), the former is of greater interest as the surviving fragment contains the foundations of

the small dining rooms (the walls being no more than a dining couch and a doorway wide) that stood at the back of this stoa.

Beyond this the remains are largely Roman, consisting of: **ⓐ** the **South-East Fountain House** (C. 470 BC); now partly overlain by a Byzantine church. The back walls also survive from **ⓘ** the **Athens Mint** (C. 400 BC) where the famous owl coins were struck. To the east lies **❸** the **South-East Temple** (1 C. BC). This was another Roman import; the materials being taken from a classical temple of Aphrodite at Sounion. The other side of the Panathenaic way was also embellished in the Roman period with **ⓙ** the **Library of Pantainos** (102 AD) and **ⓚ** the **South-East Stoa** (1 C. AD): yet another shopping mall on the path to the later **Wall of Valerian**, which was constructed out of the remains of Agora buildings following the Herulian sack of the city in 269 AD.

The Roman Agora

Sandwiched between 18 C. mansions in the Plaka district are the remains of several important ancient structures: notably the **Roman Agora**, the adjacent **Library of Hadrian** and the Hellenistic **Tower of the Winds**. Unfortunately, an unsympathetic medieval street plan makes interpretation of the remains difficult, running as it does across the lines of the ancient ground plan.

The **Library of Hadrian** (2 C. AD) is usually the first building encountered thanks to the nearby Monastiraki metro station. Sadly, the library is still undergoing excavation and tourists have to make do with peering through the iron railings of the fence surrounding the site. The most prominent feature of the extant remains is the north side of the front façade. This was abnormally high to counter the fact that the library is lower down the Acropolis slope than the adjacent market: the library was therefore made to appear the same height. The façade consists of seven columns, each of which would have been surmounted with a statue. The main peristyle court behind was, according to the Roman travel writer Pausanias, graced with a 'hundred splendid columns' — none of which have survived. The quad had an ornamental pool in the centre (later replaced by a 6 C. basilica, several columns from which still stand) with lecture rooms down the sides. Books took up a relatively small part of the library's space and were housed in a scroll room at the back of the

---

ⓞ The Tower of the Winds (also called the Horologion of Andronikos Cyrrhestes)

ⓟ Entrance Portico

ⓠ Sundial Lines

ⓡ The Lost Triton Weathervane

The Winds:

ⓢ NW: **Skiron** (holds charcoal cauldron)

ⓣ W: **Zephyros** (showers lap of flowers)

ⓤ SW: **Lips** (holds stern of trireme-like ship)

ⓥ S: **Notos** (emptying an urn of raindrops)

ⓦ SE: **Euros** (mantled, with arm cloaked)

ⓧ E: **Apeliotes** (showers lap of fruit)

ⓨ NE: **Kaikias** (holds shield of hailstones)

❷ N: **Boreas** (mantled, and holding a conch)

building; by lucky chance, the surviving wall has the storage niches extant.

The **Roman Agora** (1 C. BC) is known to stand on the site of the classical commercial market, but of earlier structures there is no trace. In the Roman period, it was linked to the classical Agora via a couple of stoas running east behind the Stoa of Attalos. The surviving remains are equally diverse as those of the library; in this case consisting of a reasonable number of columns arranged as picturesquely as possible around the two surviving sides of the peristyle court. Behind them lie the foundations of a number of stoa style shops. The gateways have survived; the main entrance is reduced to an arch standing in glorious isolation (now fenced off; access to the site is from the rear: tickets 500 GDR). The rear gate only exists as a series of square columns bounded by a drain on the outer side.

As you enter the Roman Agora site you are confronted by two contrasting structures. On your right are the remains of a 1 C. AD **Roman Latrine**; built to seat the masses in comfort, it offered a secluded spot to sit and chat while getting on with the business of the day. To the east stands the wonderfully preserved 2 C. BC **Tower of the Winds**. A remarkable building, cute and approachable in size, it has survived against all the odds in various guises (not least as a dervish clubhouse during the years of Turkish rule). A marble octagon, the tower was a waterclock, sundial, and weather-vane combined, and possibly the city planetarium. On the north-west and north-east sides were porticoed doors, while up the south side climbs the remains of the clock mechanism in the form of a semicircular turret. Quite how this worked is still not understood. Given that the ancients measured time by dividing the daylight hours into 12 (so an 'hour' was never the same length on any consecutive day) it, presumably, caused its designers a headache and a half too. The 8 cardinal winds are aligned to their respective points of the compass. Favourable winds are shown as youths; hostile winds are bearded, older figures. Each holds an appropriate object. Most are self explanatory, with the exception of Lips (responsible for blowing an enemy fleet ashore: hence the ship's stern), and Skiron (the charcoal cauldron symbolised drought). The Roman writer Vitruvius records that the tower was topped with a bronze Triton weather-vane, holding a wand which pointed to the prevailing wind.

National Archaeological Museum

One of the great cultural treasure houses of the world, this is one attraction that should figure prominently on the itinerary of every visitor to Athens. Among the principal exhibits are the **Minoan Frescoes** from the excavations on Santorini, the **Mask of Agamemnon** and other gold work uncovered by Schliemann at Mycenae, and **Sculpture** from all the important sites in Greece. Supposedly open ① 12.30–19.00, ②–⑤ 08.00–19.00, ⑥, ⑦ 08.30–15.00 (tickets 2000 GDR), times do vary a bit, depending on the numbers of attendants who turn up (no room is left without a guard). Some rooms (usually the less important ones) are occasionally closed off for an hour or two if they can't be manned. If you really want to get the most out of a visit you should consider buying a copy of the detailed museum guide (these are on sale in Room 3, which contains the ticket kiosk, sales desk and cloakroom, where bags and cameras must be deposited).

Room 4 is the first visitors enter, and one of the most dramatic in the museum. Known as the **Mycenaean Hall**, it contains the magnificent **Mask of Agamemnon** among its impressive gold collection culled from the graves at the palace of Mycenae in the Peloponnese.

Room 5 contains Neolithic and Pre-Mycenaean artifacts, though island hoppers will find **Room 6** of more interest — known as the **Cycladic Room** as all the exhibits have been recovered from the Cyclades. The haul adds up to a pretty disparate collection. At the main entrance end are the early Cycladic figures — including the largest figurine yet discovered (see p. 257) and the better known **Harpist** (see p. 268) and **Flautist** (illustrated overleaf). At the other end of the gallery you will find the **Flying-Fish Fresco** fragments recovered from Milos: though the described 'blue cloth' on the display label is now thought to be a net.

Rooms 7–8 and **11–12** are devoted to **Archaic Sculpture** (**Rooms 9–10** being devoted to smaller works). Room 9 has a number of pieces from Delos and a very Egyptianesque-looking kouros from Milos. **Room 13** contains more such figures including the **Aristodikos** figure that gives the room its name. Used to mark graves, it is logical to find next door, in **Room 14**, a collection of **Early Classical Gravestones**.

Room 15 is known as the **Poseidon Room**, thanks to the large bronze of the God that dominates it. Some believe the figure to be the

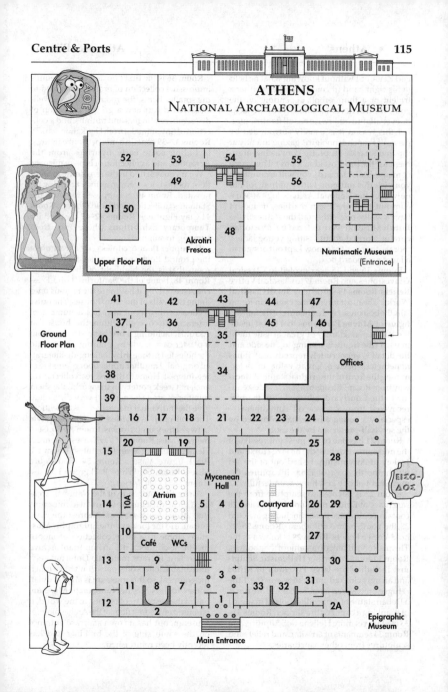

ATHENS
NATIONAL ARCHAEOLOGICAL MUSEUM

Upper Floor Plan

52 53 54 55
49 56
51 50
48

Akrotiri Frescos

Numismatic Museum
(Entrance)

Ground Floor Plan

41 42 43 44 47
37 36 45 46
40 35
38 34
39

Offices

16 17 18 21 22 23 24
20 19 25
15 28
14 10A
Atrium
5 4 6 Courtyard 26 29
10
Café WCs 27
13 9 30
11 8 7 3 33 32 31
12 2 1 2A

Mycenean Hall

ΕΙΣΟ-
ΔΟΣ

Epigraphic Museum

Main Entrance

god Zeus, but without knowing what he held in his right hand (it could have been either a trident or a thunderbolt depending on the god), we will never be sure. The figure lacks its eyeballs but otherwise has all its attributes. For this reason it is usually surrounded by packs of French schoolgirls gazing intently at the god's tackle (a pretty convincing argument for the pro-Poseidon lobby). This is one of many similar hazards you will encounter if you visit this museum with children; for not only does the National Archaeological Museum not have the Elgin marbles, it doesn't have a 'willie box' either (all the statues in the British Museum were defaced by a Victorian curator worried about visiting young ladies' morals; the results are now kept out of sight in a large cardboard box).

Rooms 16 and 18 are devoted to Classical Gravestones, and Room 17 to Classical Votive Reliefs. Rooms 19–20 display Small Classical Works. The most interesting exhibit in Room 20 is the best preserved miniature of the famous figure of Athena Parthenos that stood inside the Parthenon. Hardly of great artistic merit in itself (the figure is leaning to one side and the detail is very crudely reproduced), it has nonetheless been of great value in determining the form of the original statue. A doorway from Room 20 leads to a staircase descending to the Courtyard, adorned with marbles recovered from a wreck off Antikithera — especially a young athlete, half-corroded by the sea, half-preserved by the mud.

Room 21 has one of the most impressive of the museum's exhibits; the bronze Horse and Jockey of Artemision. Fished out of the sea off the north coast of Evia, it captures the movement of boy and horse wonderfully.

Room 22 is devoted to sculpture from the sanctuary at Epidavros. Rooms 23–24 and 28 contain 4 C. BC gravestones (including in Room 28, the Youth from Antikithera), Rooms 25–27 hold Votive Reliefs. Room 29 is known as the Themis Room thanks to a statue of the goddess. Room 30 contains further Hellenistic Sculpture, including the large Poseidon of Milos and an ugly cloaked child, known as the 'little refugee', recovered from Turkey. More fun is a Delian statue of Aphrodite, poised in the act of spanking a cupid with a slipper. Rooms 31–33 contain yet more Hellenistic Sculpture, and Room 34 remnants of an Altar, and reliefs and sculptures from other sanctuaries.

Room 36 is the first housing the museum's impressive collection of bronzes. Devoted to the smaller items, the room includes a well-endowed dwarf and a grizzly collection of dismembered fingers and thumbs, and a collection of tiny animals (from Deukalion's ark?). Rooms 37–39 contain a mix of bronze figures, including some early figurines from the Acropolis, and a collection of bronze mirrors.

What you will find in the remaining ground floor rooms is less certain as they are being renovated. Room 40 is supposed to house the Stathatos Collection and Gold Objects; Room 41 Clay Figurines. Rooms 42–47 are used for Temporary Exhibitions (these vary from summer to summer).

The upper floor occupies only a fraction of the ground floor area, yet they include one room that is the highlight of the museum; Room 48, home of the Santorini/Thira Frescoes (see p. 170), it has more of the famous ones lining the walls of mock-up houses. The outer section of this room also has a number of artefacts discovered within the houses at Akrotiri, including a bed reconstructed from a plaster cast, made by pouring plaster into the holes left in the ash by the long-disintegrated original. The other upper floor rooms are of less interest. Home to the greatest collection of ancient Greek pottery in the world, the sheer number of artefacts makes it very difficult to give the individual pieces their just attention. The collection is divided by date and style between the various rooms: Room 49–50: Geometric Vases; Room 51: Vari Vases; Room 52: Heraeum of Argos and Sophilos; Room 53: Black-figure Vases; Room 54: Red-figure Vases; Room 55: White Background Vases, Room 56: 4 C. BC Vases.

Along the south side of the National Archaeological Museum are two related museums that attract fewer visitors. Nearest the main entrance to the former is the Epigraphic Museum. Home to a large collection of monumental inscriptions, it is an important archive of ancient literary material. Unfortunately, unreadable letters on stones don't have much mass appeal, so this museum is always quiet. Somewhat busier is the Numismatic Museum; one of the best coin collections in the world, it is housed on the first floor of the Archaeological Museum, but has its own staircase entrance on the south side of the building and has recently been refurbished.

Other Athenian Sites

In addition to the 'big four', there are plenty of other sites worth investigating. The first port of call for Greek island fans should be the **Museum of Cycladic & Ancient Greek Art**, as its more notable exhibits include a large collection of Cycladic idols (some showing evidence of having once had painted features).

Among the other sites east of the Acropolis is the small circular **Monument of Lysicrates** (335 BC). Three metres in diameter, it was erected to display the bronze tripod won at the Dionysia festival of that year by Lysicrates. A glorified pot-stand, it is a rare survival, and the Corinthian columns that adorn it are the oldest examples in Athens.

The skimpy **Arch of Hadrian** (2 C. AD) stands nearby. Built to mark off the old city from the Emperor Hadrian's Roman additions, it is adorned with inscriptions. On the Acropolis side: 'This is Athens, ancient city of Theseus'; on the reverse; 'The city of Hadrian and not of Theseus'. Built of pentalic marble, it provides a gateway to the largest temple built in Greece.

The massive **Olympieion** (515 BC–132 AD) — the Temple of Olympian Zeus — took just under 650 years to build. Replacing an earlier temple built near the site of the plug hole that Zeus opened in the earth to abate Deukalion's (the Greek Noah) flood, it was started by the tyrant Pisistratus in 515 BC but abandoned after his overthrow. Thereafter, it was left incomplete through the Classical and Hellenistic periods. Work resumed in 174 BC, when Antiochos IV of Syria commissioned the Roman architect Cossutius to begin work on a modified design (the columns now on the site date from this revised building). Unfortunately Antiochos died before the building was finished, and the temple added to its record as the longest building site in history. It even saw some of its columns removed to Rome by the general Sulla. Hadrian finally completed the building, adding a gold and ivory statue of himself and Zeus for good measure. Of the original 104 columns, 15 remain standing. The fallen 16th collapsed during a storm in 1852, and a 17th was demolished in 1760 by order of the Turkish governor and burnt to make lime for the construction of a mosque. It is thought that the other 4 of the 21 columns recorded standing in 1450 suffered a similar fate. There is a 1000 GDR entry fee to the site.

To the east of the Olympieion lies the **Stadium** (143 AD), rebuilt in 1870 for the first modern Olympiad in 1896. With seating for 70,000 spectators, it takes advantage of the slopes of two hills to avoid the need for expensive earth banking. It is thought that the site (initially using just the bare hillsides) was used as the stadium from the 4 C BC.

The **Hills of Athens** played a very important part in city life. Apart from the Acropolis (with its theatres built in the natural hollows on its south side) there are two lesser hills of note. The nearby **Areopagus** was the hill of justice. Here the supreme court of the city had its home. In addition, it was reputedly used by the Amazon women, the Persians, and St. Paul during their attacks on Athens. Today, very slippery steps take you up to a good view over the Agora. A better viewing point is the **Mouseion** (alias Filopapou Hill). The spot on which the cannon that blew up the Parthenon stood (this is where the best postcard shots are taken as well), it does not have a rodent problem as its name implies. In fact, 'the hill of the Muses' (for this is what Mouseion means) was quite a mystical spot. Today, it is home to the ugly funerary **Monument of Philopappos** (114 AD), and some foundations of the **City Wall**. These run down past another hilltop viewing point to the oddly named **Pnyx**. This was an artificial platform, built out of the side of the hill, where the Athenian democracy held its citizen's meetings. Today it plays host to the more prosaic *son-et-lumière* shows. The final hill of note lies east of the old city at **Likavittos**. Blessed with good views of the Acropolis, it is accessed by cable-car (1000 GDR).

The final major archeological site, **Kerameikos** (the name means 'potter's district'), the cemetery of Ancient Athens, is now a replica tomb-filled park (complete with bubbling brook filled with turtles and frogs). Little visited — in part because of its location in the down-at-heel part of Plaka — it also has the remains of two of the city gates (the **Sacred Gate** and the **Diplyon**) and the **Pompeion**, the building from where the great Panathenaic processions to the Acropolis started.

Outside Athens is one major site within easy reach. Few regret taking the 2-hour bus ride to **Sounion**, the cape on the southern tip of Attica that is home to the photogenic **Temple of Poseidon**. Built in 444–440 BC, it functioned as a landmark, guiding sailors towards Athens (it lies about 90 minutes sailing from Piraeus).

Piraeus
ΠΕΙΡΑΙΑΣ

CODE ☎ 01
PORT POLICE ☎ 4511 311, 4172 657
TOURIST OFFICE ☎ 4135 716

The main port of Athens for some 2800 years, Piraeus is the hub of the modern Greek ferry system. Lying 8 km south-west of the Acropolis, it was once a town in its own right, but in the years since Greek independence it has been reduced to a suburb by the capital's urban sprawl, and a frenetic, less than pleasant place at that. In fact, it is difficult to conceive of a spot more removed from the dreamy idyllic island most tourists are in search of. This is one port of call where it pays to know in advance roughly what you are trying to do and where you are going.

Once an island itself, Piraeus is a hilly peninsula decked with anonymous, tall apartment blocks laid out in a strict grid fashion, and with harbours on each side. This is where the fun starts: for Piraeus has three harbours of note. By far the largest is the **Great Harbour**; situated on the western side, it is departure point for all car and passenger ferries as well as the Aegina hydrofoils. **Zea**, the second harbour (500 m over the hill on the eastern side), is primarily a yacht marina, but the quay (Zea Marina) near the entrance is also the departure point for the hydrofoils and catamarans running to the Saronic Gulf islands. The third, **Flisvos**, is an excursion-boat port 7 km to the east of Zea: vessels departing from here are sure to be expensive and to be avoided.

The Great Harbour
Regardless of how you get to Piraeus you are likely to find yourself dumped at the north-east section of the Great Harbour; home to the bus, metro and railway stations. The waterfront consists of a wide quay, separated by a hedge-cum-wall from the ten-lane streets behind (so clogged with traffic that in the rush hour motor-bikes resort to the pavements). Piraeus is a commercial town and this is reflected in the buildings on the waterfront; most of these are shipping offices or branches of banks with maritime interests. Food shops, tourist facilities and hotels are thin on the ground. For these reasons, Piraeus is not a place to arrive at the last minute or in the small hours. All this makes Piraeus a pretty insufferable place to be at the best of times; never mind if you un-lucky enough to be here during one of the — fortunately rare — ferry strikes (if you are caught, try heading for Rafina with its hydrofoils and campsite).

On the plus side, plans are now being implemented to turn the Great Harbour into one huge passenger terminal, with improved waiting and transit facilities (free airport-style buses now run between the terminal and the western side of the harbour). However, in some respects things are getting worse: Piraeus — along with some large islands — is also experiencing a serious pickpocket problem: the thieves join the crowds bustling to get on ferries (who reveal the whereabouts of their wallets as they take out their tickets). Be careful!

The focal point for ferry travellers is the square housing the bus station just south of the railway and metro stations (Platia Karaiskaki). In the billboard-encrusted, dilapidated block next to the Port Police building (which has a full ferry departure list posted up by the front entrance) you will find the nucleus of the **ticket agents**. Most are sharks. Step within hailing distance of an agency door and you'll get hassle. A chorus of 'Where are you going?' rings out from the moment the agencies open at 05.00. So it helps to be both prepared (the NTOG ferry information sheets are invaluable in this respect) and not over trusting. Likewise, you should note that although ticket agents in the islands can be very useful for changing money out of banking hours, if you use the Piraeus agencies you can be sure of

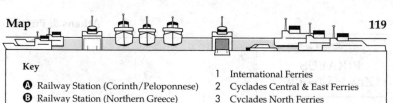

Map 119

Key

- **A** Railway Station (Corinth/Peloponnese)
- **B** Railway Station (Northern Greece)
- **C** Metro Station / WCs
- **D** Bus Station
- **E** Ticket Agency Block
- **F** Domestic Passenger Terminal & WCs
- **G** Athens Airport Bus Stop
- **H** Large Supermarket
- **I** McDonalds
- **J** International Ferry Terminals
- **K** Free Quayside Bus Halts

1 International Ferries
2 Cyclades Central & East Ferries
3 Cyclades North Ferries
4 Cyclades West Ferries
5 Dodecanese Ferries
6 Crete Ferries
7 Samos & Ikaria Ferries
8 Chios & North Aegean Ferries
9 Saronic Gulf Ferries & Catamaran
10 Hydrofoils (to Aegina only) & *Mega Dolphins* (Cyclades West)
11 Salamis Taxi-boats / Hydrofoils

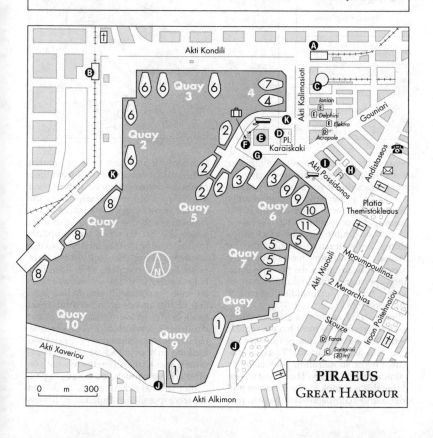

PIRAEUS
GREAT HARBOUR

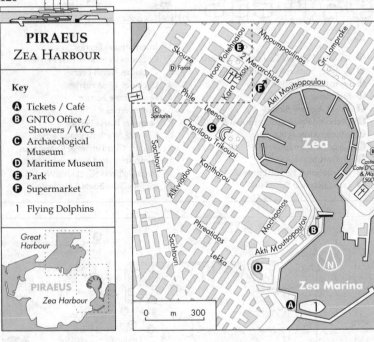

PIRAEUS
ZEA HARBOUR

Key

A Tickets / Café
B GNTO Office /
    Showers / WCs
C Archaeological
    Museum
D Maritime Museum
E Park
F Supermarket

1 Flying Dolphins

Great
Harbour

PIRAEUS

Zea Harbour

0   m   300

being ripped off. An increasing number
of them offer free (unsecured) baggage
storage facilities if you buy a ferry ticket;
if you want to store your luggage securely
there is a regular luggage deposit in the
passenger terminal building. The 'see a
tourist and double the price' snack shops
along the waterfront should also be
treated with caution; food-hunters are
better off heading for the produce stalls
and supermarket that look onto the small
square behind McDonald's (just east of
the ticket block).

Ferries are loosely grouped according
to destination, and most have a regular
berth (though these change from year to
year and aren't marked). To be on the
safe side you should allow yourself thirty
minutes to find a ferry. The easiest way of
doing this is to look for the funnel or hull
logo as most companies only have four or

five boats. It also pays to be aware that
ferries might not arrive back from their
previous excursion much before their
listed Piraeus departure time. Given the
limited number of access points in the
wall-cum-hedge, it is advisable to walk
inside this barrier when ferry hunting;
for boats can be berthed anything up to a
kilometre along the dock. Many have
ticket booths (complete with computer
ticket issuing facilities) somewhere nearby on the quayside. If you do buy from
one of the agents in the central ticket
block (and most tourists happily do), ensure that the service is as direct as possible:
in High Season rooms disappear fast and
arriving an hour ahead of the other boats
often makes all the difference to what's on
offer and how much you'll have to pay.

International tickets should be bought
as early as possible. All international boats

dock on the south side of the Great Harbour. There are several customs and immigration buildings — the dilapidated Quay 9 shed being the most used.

Zea Harbour

Zea (the ancient trireme war-fleet base) is much more attractive than the Great Harbour, with seats on the rampart-like waterfront overlooking the shoal of yachts in the basin below. The waterfront buildings are also less commercial and there is the added bonus of a reasonable super-market not too far from the waterfront. Near Zea Marina itself you will find a minuscule EOT / NTOG office (note: they don't have ferry departure information) sited at the posh end of the yacht marina. Catering for the yachtsmen it is something of a boon, since the back of the block contains public showers and WCs.

⋈

Few tourists attempt to stay in Piraeus as the available accommodation is either downright horrible or inconveniently located. The most obvious clutch of hotels are near the Great Harbour in the backstreets south of the metro station. For the most part they are to be avoided as most are more like sailor's dosshouses, lacking even a modicum of comfort (of either mattress or maid variety). If desperate however, try the *Electra* (☎ 417 7057) just off Gouniari Street. Those who are prepared to walk should find a better bed at the *Santorini* (☎ 452 2147) just off the south-east end of the Great Harbour. Meanwhile, plush establishments shun the Great Harbour altogether, and lie on and behind the up-market waterfront to the east of Zea Harbour. These include the expensive *Kastella* (☎ 411 4735), *Cote D'Oro* (☎ 411 3744), and *Mistral* (☎ 411 7094).

∞

Amidst today's grime one is apt to forget that Piraeus was once an important centre in its own right. In fact, during the 5 — 4 c. BC it was seen as substantially more than just the Athenian harbour-cum-naval base, becoming an embryonic sister city in all but name. Unbelievably (when one looks around today), ancient Piraeus was also regarded as a very beautiful city — and given the proximity of Athens for comparison, the modern town has obviously lost a great deal. Part of this reputation was due to town planning; for unlike Athens it was designed by one of the greatest of Greek city planners, Hippodamos, and boasted a grid-like street system of the kind now associated with North American cities (the streets between the Great Harbour and Zea still follow the ancient pattern).

In addition to all the regular city accoutrements (i.e. temples, public buildings and even two agoras) Piraeus was heavily fortified; with skirting walls protecting the city and harbours. However, the Roman era saw a shift in trade routes, and with it began a period of prolonged decline — so much so, that by 1833 Piraeus had a recorded population of only 22.

Time and 19 c. building has obscured most traces of the ancient city, with few of the buildings described by Pausanias located to date. Visible remains are scanty: the best being the fragments of a Hellenistic **Odeon** west of Zea. The famous trireme sheds have been found, but are locked away in the basements of buildings around Zea harbour. The **Maritime Museum** (on the waterfront of Zea) ② to ⑥ 08.30–12.30. has one on view. Archaeological finds (including bronzes fished out of the harbour) are currently housed in the **Archaeological Museum** ② to ⑦ 08.30–15.00.

Lavrion

ΛΑΥΡΙΟ; pop. 8,000.

CODE ☎ 0292
PORT POLICE ☎ 25249

A small, sun-touched commercial port famed in classical times for its silver mines Lavrion (or Lavrio) offers little today apart from fishing boats, a blackened pier, and a view of the sad island of **Makronissi**; used to detain political prisoners for much of this century. Lavrion is now the main ferry port for the island of Kea. Occasional services head further south to Kythnos by way of Kea. A town of wide and dusty streets, the most important thing you need to know in Lavrion is that the bus stop lies on the roadside of the square next to the fishing quay. Buses do the 1½ hour Athens run hourly as well as heading south to Cape Sounion and the nearest campsite (8 km).

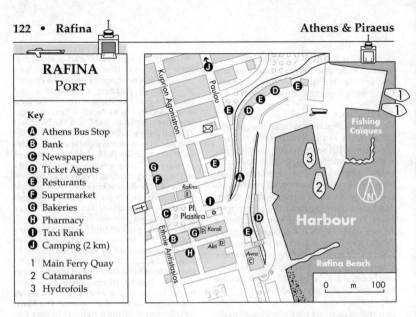

RAFINA
PORT

Key

- **A** Athens Bus Stop
- **B** Bank
- **C** Newspapers
- **D** Ticket Agents
- **E** Resturants
- **F** Supermarket
- **G** Bakeries
- **H** Pharmacy
- **I** Taxi Rank
- **J** Camping (2 km)

1 Main Ferry Quay
2 Catamarans
3 Hydrofoils

Rafina
ΡΑΦΗΝΑ

CODE ☎ 0294
PORT POLICE ☎ 28888

Some 27 km from the centre of Athens, Rafina is a pleasant leafy suburb town on the west coast of Attica with a reputation for good fish restaurants (courtesy of its role as the main fishing port for the capital). The port also has another — and growing — role as the second departure point from the capital to the islands: notably destinations on the Cyclades North Line (some island agencies even go so far as to list Rafina as 'Athens' on their schedules). Now being enlarged, the port lies below the town's main square cum park, and offers a much more attractive starting point for island hopping than Piraeus. Instead of grime and hustling ticket touts you wade through fresh fish stalls (at their busiest in the evenings) to reach the boats. Furthermore, boat fares to and from Rafina are 20% cheaper than Piraeus, and although the bus fare into

Athens erodes most of this saving on short hops, there are gains to be made on longer journeys. Connections with Athens are good, with hourly buses departing from the port slip road (extra buses gather on the quay and meet ferries). The catch to all this is that the number of ferries is far fewer and travellers are often forced to repair to the scruffy, but popular, beach just south of the port while they wait for an evening sailing. Rafina departure times are listed on separate NTOG information sheets. Athenian papers also carry them.

🛏

Most tourists are in transit so there are no rooms. Of the hotels, the *Korali* (☎ 22477) in the main square is reasonable and inexpensive, if not inspiring, as is the *Rafina* (☎ 23460). More pokey is the *Atki* (☎ 24776), while the large *Avra* (☎ 22781/3), above the port, offers the nearest you will find to the high life.

Δ

A well-signed beach site 2 km north of the port (though the walk seems longer). Excellent facilities, but usually empty: the Balkan war has depleted the numbers motoring from central Europe. A second site on the Athens road isn't worth the hassle of finding it.

Salamina / Salamis

ΣΑΛΑΜΙΝΑ; 93.5 km²; pop. 23,000.

CODE ☎ 467

Cowering behind the shipyards and rows of rusting ships anchored west of Piraeus lies the famous, but lamentably ugly, island of Salamis (known these days as Salamina). Its great claim to fame comes via the battle between the Greek and Persian trireme fleets in 480 BC which took place in the narrow straits between the north-east side of the island and the mainland. This encounter, one of the great naval battles in history, prevented the Persian conquest of Greece and in so doing altered the destiny of European civilisation. Unfortunately, Salamis has been in decline from this high point ever since and after 2500 years this means that things are pretty bad. The close proximity of Athens has resulted in it becoming little more than a smoggy suburb of the capital. Not the cleanest water to swim in

either (this is one of the few places in the Aegean where bathing is a health hazard), so unless you are clocking-up islands, ferry hops, or are a student of military history, then sadly, it is worth giving a miss. None of the settlements has much to offer; the capital, Salamina, is dusty and lacking even a modicum of town planning, while Selinia (the nearest thing Salamis has on offer to a 'resort') is rather scruffy. Nicer, in a very quiet way, are the villages of Eantio and Peristeria.

Bus services are good along the limited routes run, but the south of the island (easily the nicest part with even the odd patch of forest cover on the hillsides) is not served. The main ferry link runs from the mainland suburb of **Perama** to **Paloukia** on the east coast, while a second operates from **Steno** to **Nea Peramos**. In addition, commuter boats run frequently to Piraeus Great Harbour.

⊨

No rooms. Budget hotels at Selinia and Eantio.

SALAMINA / SALAMIS

0   km   3

Nea Peramos ⚓
Faneromeni monastery
Batsi
Nafstathmos
Steno
Salamina ⚓
Perama
Paloukia
Battle of Salamis 480 BC
Ambelakia
Selinia ⚓   PIRAEUS
Eantio
365 m
Paralia
Kaki Vigla
⊕ x 8 ⟡19.00
Karakiani   Perani
Peristeria

⊙ ev ½⊕ 08.00–00.30
⊕ 00.30–03.30
⊙ ev ½⊕ 06.30–23.00

⊙ ev ½⊕ 05.30–00.30
#8   ⊙ ev ½⊕ 05.30–23.30
#12   ⊙ ev ½⊕ 06.00–22.00
#11   ⊕ 06.00–21.00

3
CYCLADES CENTRAL

ANTIPAROS · IOS · NAXOS · PAROS · SANTORINI / THIRA

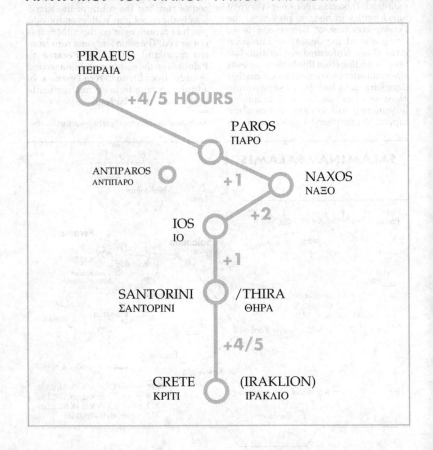

PIRAEUS
ΠΕΙΡΑΙΑ

+4/5 HOURS

PAROS
ΠΑΡΟ

ANTIPAROS
ΑΝΤΙΠΑΡΟ

+1

NAXOS
ΝΑΞΟ

IOS
ΙΟ

+2

+1

SANTORINI
ΣΑΝΤΟΡΙΝΙ

/THIRA
ΘΗΡΑ

+4/5

CRETE
ΚΡΙΤΙ

(IRAKLION)
ΙΡΑΚΛΙΟ

General Features

The Cyclades derive their name from being said to 'circle' the island of Delos — birthplace of the god Apollo. In practice, they lie in a semi-circle south of a line running from the north-west to the south-east drawn just north of Delos.

Within the Cyclades the islands fall neatly into four subgroups with Paros and the Central Cyclades line islands now forming the true centre of the group. The Central Cyclades consist of a number of islands that are known by name to most visitors to Greece. Among these, volcanic Thira/Santorini is deservedly

popular, being identified with the legend of Atlantis; disco-laden Ios is known by repute to every student under the sun; Paros has a happy mix of almost everything; and Naxos has an excellent blend of atmosphere and golden beaches.

However, unspoilt islands these are not. Given that most new island hoppers make for an island that they've at least heard of, it is inevitable that this group should have become the main artery in the ferry system, seeing more visitors than the rest of the Cyclades put together. Out of High Season they are fine, but during the summer these islands feel very overcrowded.

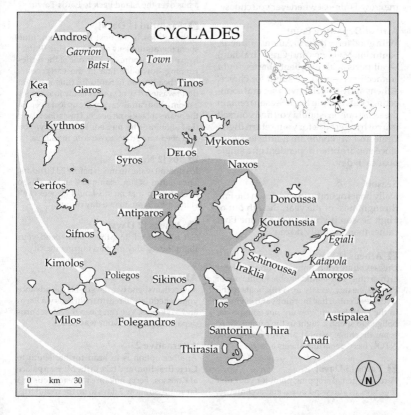

Example Itinerary [2 Weeks]

A justifiably popular group of islands forming the backbone of the Greek ferry system. High Season connections are so frequent that they make for extremely relaxed island hopping. With ferries almost as frequent as red buses down Oxford Street, even the most timid of travellers can wander without fear. The main islands can be done in any order since there are boats up and down the line at all times of the day. You won't be short on company either. Even so, with a little effort, you can escape the worst of the crowds almost whenever you choose.

Arrival/Departure Point

With good ferry links to Athens/Piraeus, Santorini, Mykonos and Crete (Iraklion) — all ports with excellent charter flight connections — you are spoilt for choice. Athens and Santorini (with several connecting boats daily in High Season) remain the safest options should you find yourself in a rush to get back for your return flight. Crete and Mykonos are a little less easy since you are often dependent on a single boat each day.

Season

Daily boats operate up and down the line through most of the year, though out of High Season it will be just the one boat rather than the daily dozen.

1 Athens [1 Day]

Unless you are really unlucky with your flight arrival time, you should be able to ship out of Piraeus the day you fly in. With boats to the Cyclades Central line mornings and evenings in the High Season, you are not going to be obliged to spend a night in the capital. Grab some drachma, a meal and, of course, the NTOG ferry departure sheets and go.

2 Paros [3 Days]

Paros is a genial stopping point for your first few days, as you wind down and acclimatise.

Plenty of beaches, nightlife and that all-important Greek island atmosphere, and, when you want to avoid the worst of the sun, the cave on Antiparos makes an interesting excursion easily to hand.

3 Naxos [2 Days]

More relaxing than Paros, Naxos is the next stop down the line. If you don't want to stay you can always visit as a day trip from Paros; a morning boat will set you down in time for lunch and you can then pick up a Paros-bound evening Santorini—Piraeus boat. If you visit on one of the days that the small *Express Skopelitis* (p. 254) heads to Amorgos you can take her as far as Paros (Piso Livadi) and then a bus over the island back to Paros Town.

4 Santorini [4 Days]

Although Ios is the next in the chain, time spent there is unlikely to leave you in a fit state to explore Santorini. Pick up one of the ferries running down the line in the early hours when heading on to Santorini (this way you don't waste a day of your holiday looking for a room). You can always make up lost sleep on the nearest black sand beach. This is one island that shouldn't be missed. Realistically, you will need three days to explore the sights.

5 Ios [2 Nights]

Ios doesn't wake up much before 23.00 hours. The mixture of sun, 'slammers' and sand is so over the top that most island hoppers can't stand it for more than a day or two.

1 Athens [2 Days]

Get a boat back to Athens and spend your flight 'safety' day in hand touring the city.

Alternative 1

Rather than spend two days on Naxos, advance your schedule and return to Piraeus via Paros and **Mykonos**. You can glean the latest Paros departure times on your way south.

Alternative 2

Another option is to head further south to **Crete (Iraklion)** and take in the Minoan palace at Knossos. Ferry links are more tenuous this far south, so allow 3 days to do the round trip.

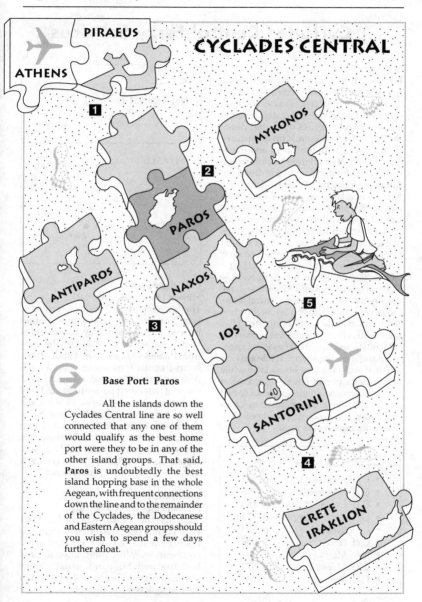

CYCLADES CENTRAL

ATHENS **PIRAEUS**

1

MYKONOS

2

PAROS

ANTIPAROS

NAXOS

3

IOS

5

Base Port: Paros

All the islands down the Cyclades Central line are so well connected that any one of them would qualify as the best home port were they to be in any of the other island groups. That said, **Paros** is undoubtedly the best island hopping base in the whole Aegean, with frequent connections down the line and to the remainder of the Cyclades, the Dodecanese and Eastern Aegean groups should you wish to spend a few days further afloat.

SANTORINI

4

CRETE IRAKLION

Cyclades Central Ferry Services

Main Car Ferries

Because all the islands on this line are popular tourist destinations, ferries are geared to moving large numbers of passengers — fast. The rich pickings result in a dozen regular ferries operating down the line in High Season, with departures from Piraeus both mornings and evenings. Even out of High Season there are usually two boats a day in each direction. Complementing the Cyclades Central Line ferries are a large number of hydrofoils and regular ferries heading on to Samos, Crete, Rhodes and the Dodecanese, which pick up extra drachmas by making stops along this line (these boats are described in the chapter most appropriate to their overall itinerary and are listed below).

Over the past decade two companies — Ventouris Sea Lines and Arkadia — have dominated the Cyclades Central Line. However, this changed in 1996 when Ventouris had its fleet impounded after their owners found themselves in financial difficulties, and Arkadia's *Poseidon Express* — hit rocks during a storm while arriving at Paros and sank five hours later while tied up at the harbour quay. Over the last two summers a new regime has established itself, with the excellent Minoan Lines and, sadly, less good Agapitos boats now firmly dominating the route.

🚢 See also:	
• C/F *Anemos*	p. 372
• C/F *Dimitroula*	p. 406
• C/F *Express Athina*	p. 183
• C/F *Golden Vergina*	p. 372
• C/F *Ionian Sun*	p. 183
• C/F *Leros*	p. 306
• C/F *Marina*	p. 304
• C/F *Milena*	p. 372
• C/F *Romilda*	p. 305

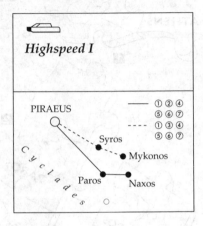

Highspeed I

C/M *Highspeed I*
Minoan Lines; 1996; 4480 GRT.
This large catamaran was a new arrival of 1997, offering very fast journey times between Athens and the Cyclades islands. With a top speed of 36 knots, she runs from Piraeus to Paros in just under three hours (regular ferries take around five). Able to carry 620 passengers (in bland rows of aircraft-type seating) and 150 cars, she offers a glimpse of what the Greek ferry scene might be like in a few years time. However, this window into the future comes at a price: fares are on a par with hydrofoils (i.e. roughly double regular deck fares); though you get a 20% discount if you buy a return ticket.

C/F *Ariadne*
Minoan Lines; 1967; 7748 GRT.
Although the *Ariadne* will see her 32nd birthday this year, this reliable, large ferry is still more than a match for most of the competition. With international class facilities and Minoan's usual higher standard of customer care, she remains a boat to look out for. Brought over from

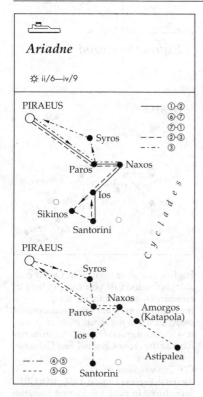

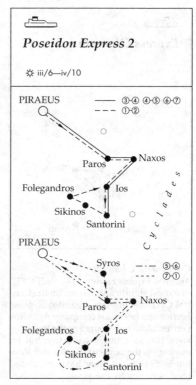

the Adriatic Patras—Ancona route to cover for the missing VSL boats in 1996, she has run a little changed summer schedule ever since. Given her age (she is only three years away from the 35-year limit for Greek domestic ferries), there is a possibility that she will be replaced by another Minoan vessel in 1999.

C/F Poseidon Express 2
Arkadia Lines; 1973; 5284 GRT.
Formerly the trans-Adriatic *Dimitrios Express*, the *Poseidon Express 2* was an unintended traveller on the Cyclades Central Line at the start 1996. Renamed and chucked on the route at short notice to cover for

the ill-fated *Poseidon Express*, she was forced to modify her popular predecessor's itinerary to take in a wider range of ports, as she is significantly smaller, and less well suited to running a no-frills straight run down the line six times a week. Arkadia Lines are one of those rare companies that like to keep timetable changes to a minimum, and this boat's 1996 summer schedule has been repeated every year since. Although not the largest ferry on the route, *Poseidon Express 2* is a popular boat: her main weakness is her layout; built for colder climes, she is over-endowed with cabins, and her public rooms are small and awkwardly placed.

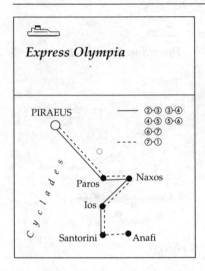

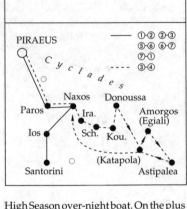

C/F *Express Olympia*

Agapitos Express Ferries; 1973; 4657 GRT.
The most significant players on the Central Cyclades line are Agapitos Express Ferries and her sister company Agapitos Ferries. Until four years ago the two lines were run as a single company, but by buying up the boats of the defunct Ventouris Seas Lines they have expanded their services to the point where they have something approaching a monopoly on the line. Unfortunately, the Agapitos fleet is the worst in Greece and these companies seem to be the main offenders when it comes to discriminating against foreign tourists (see p. 143). The *Express Olympia* has a crew that appears to regard all backpackers (Marilyn Monroe look-a-likes aside) as being somewhere between gorillas and monkeys in the evolutionary chain and not to be allowed in the saloons until every seat has a Greek. This ferry also enjoys chequered reputation, as Low Season finds her spacious and comfortable, while High Season sees her reduced to an dirty over-crowded grime-bucket (see p. 38); this is definitely *not* a good

High Season over-night boat. On the plus side, her saloon (if you can get into it) conspires to add a touch of the bizarre to the island hopping experience; decorated with murals of the white cliffs of Dover, it is an incongruous hang-over from her days as the cross-Channel *Earl Granville*.

C/F *Express Santorini*

Agapitos Express Ferries; 1974; 4590 GRT.
Introduced in 1994, the *Express Santorini* (formerly the French *Chartres*) operates in tandem with the *Express Olympia* down the Cyclades Central Line, but with a once weekly run into the Eastern Cyclades. Again, anti-backpacker discrimination is the norm on this boat. Although a fraction smaller than the *Express Olympia*, the *Express Santorini* is arguably the nicer boat once you manage to get inside.

C/F *Express Apollon*

Agapitos Express Ferries; 1973; 5101 GRT.
Formerly the Ventouris Sea Lines' *Apollo Express 1*, the *Express Apollon* has been one of the premier boats on the Central Cyclades Line since the 1980s. Originally

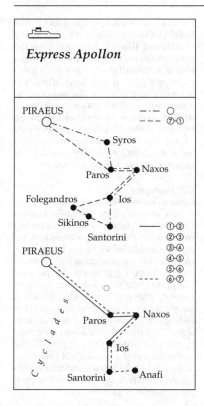

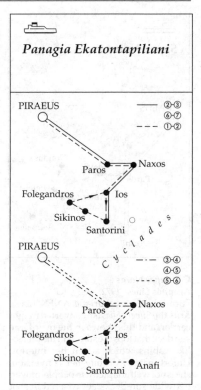

the cross–Channel *Senlac* (she was named after the hill on which the Battle of Hastings was fought), her new Greek owners re-christened her after the god of archery. This is surely one in the eye for all those who maintain that ferry owners have no sense of humour. Larger than the other Agapitos Express boats on the route, she saw minor adjustments to her timetable in 1998, and her 1999 High Season itinerary could see further tweaking.

C/F *Panagia Ekatontapiliani*
Agapitos Lines; 1972; 5590 GRT.
Formerly the Ventouris Sea Lines' *Apollo Express 2*, the awkwardly re-christened

Panagia Ekatontapiliani is named after the important church at Parikia on Paros. All but identical in external appearance to her sister ship, the *Express Apollon* (company colours aside), she started out life as the cross-Channel *Hengist*. Marginally the bigger and better boat, she even has an arcade games room on board. As with the *Express Apollon*, her 1998 summer itinerary saw minor variations from the previous year. The remarkable similarity in the combination of routes between these two boats also nicely demonstrates how these two seemingly separate Agapitos-named companies are still working as one in all but name.

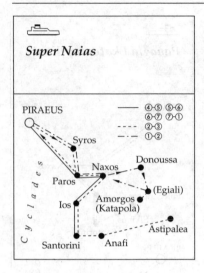

C/F *Super Naias*
Agapitos Lines; 1972; 6843 GRT.
Formerly the ex-Adriatic ANEK Line's *Kriti*, the *Super Naias* is a converted freight carrier, and this shows in the over-large sun deck that tops the ship, and the prefab-like cabins which adorn her interior. Unfortunately, despite her conversion, she is not well adapted as a people-mover: her wide sun-decks get covered in soot

from her inadequate smokestacks, while her deck-class internal seating is horribly insufficient (backpackers will face the usual problems with this line in getting a look in here). All in all, this is not a good overnight ferry if you can't afford the price of a berth. In 1998 she was offering cheap berths (1000 GDR on the price of a deck-class ticket) in an effort to increase her appeal. She does, however, keep well to time, and her unique runs from Santorini to Anafi and Astipalea considerably enhance hopping options there.

C/F *Maria PA*
Golden Ferries; 1964; 1698 GRT.
A new arrival on the Cyclades Central Line in 1998 (she spent 1997 running from the southern Peloponnese to Kithera), this small Golden Ferries boat sought to capitalize on the large numbers of tourists hopping between the popular islands to make a quick drachma. Unfortunately, the only thing golden about this ferry is the rust along the waterline on her hull, glinting in the bright Aegean sunlight. The truth is that this boat is a clapped out tub that doesn't run to time (by the end of the day she is usually at least three hours late). Definitely a vessel to be avoided, she is likely to see itinerary changes if she is running again in 1999.

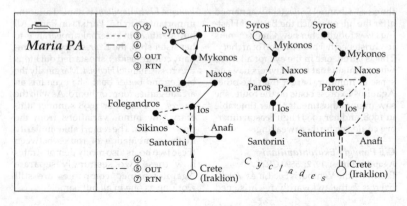

C/F *Express Paros*
Amorgos Ferries; 1965; 1365 GRT.

Formerly the Ionian island *Kefallinia*, this small car ferry replaced the *Paros Express* (the ex *Elli*, ex *Schinoussa* — which had run around the Cyclades since the late 60s) in 1994. Far too small to cope with the summer crowds and too slow to run her predecessor's itinerary to time, she has made a lot of people very late over the years and surely cannot survive long on the route before a replacement is found. Her only redeeming feature is that she is a character ferry, conspicuous by the absence of a funnel. Her Greek architect also had a passion for narrow stairwells and low doorways, which means that she is difficult to board and disembark from. Her itinerary changes every other month, and can only be fully gleaned by the destination sheets posted up on board. Until 1996, her main role was to provide a morning Mykonos to Santorini service, but since 1997 she has run a much more erratic weekly itinerary that suggests her owners are either getting pretty desperate or that she is manned by a crew undergoing therapy from the 'it's 16.00 on Friday, so this must be Santorini' nature of most Greek ferry services.

C/F *Syros Express*
Amorgos Ferries; 1970; 1070 GRT.

A new arrival in the Cyclades in 1995, the diminutive *Syros Express* has been wandering in Greek waters for a number of

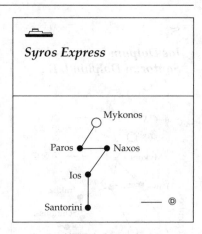

years without ever finding a successful role: first in the northern Aegean as the *Aegeus*, then as the *Zephyros* in the Ionian islands. In 1995 she ran an between the Cyclades Central and West lines, only to take over from the ancient *Mykonos Express* morning departure from Santorini—Mykonos. In 1997 she replaced the *Syros Express*, which ran the other way (Mykonos—Santorini). Unfortunately, she is too small to cope comfortably with high seas whipped up by the *meltemi* wind, and it is not uncommon to find her confined to port in High Season; and even in moderate seas, passengers will find themselves spending the voyage going up and down like a bride's nightie.

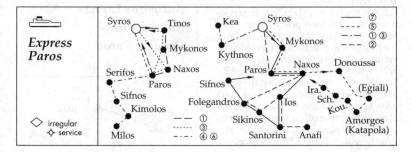

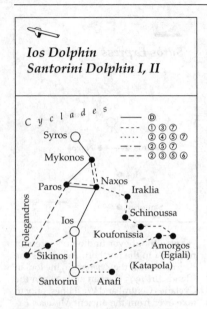

Ios Dolphin
Santorini Dolphin I, II

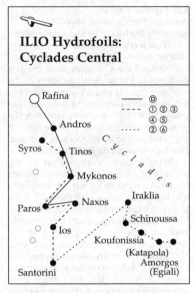

ILIO Hydrofoils:
Cyclades Central

H/F *Ios Dolphin - Santorini Dolphin*
Speed Lines

New arrivals in the Cyclades in 1997, the three Speed Lines boats run out of Santorini, Ios and Syros to neighbouring islands. With schedules orientated to serving island-hopping day-trippers, they offer unique opportunities to take in some of the smaller islands via their twice daily links to Anafi, Sikinos and Folegandros.

ILIO Hydrofoils

ILIO attempt to provide a Cycladic service out of the mainland port of Rafina and Santorini with their *Delphini* fleet. As ever with small boats in the Cyclades in summer, the *meltemi* wind plays havoc with schedules, so it is a case of seeing what is going on the day of travel (refunds are given without question if boats don't run). Given the history of chopping and changing, further adjustments to itineraries are probable in 1999. Services are also greatly reduced out of High Season.

Paros—Antiparos Taxi boats

Three small boats roll from Paros to Antiparos Town, providing an hourly 40-minute 'tourist' link in High Season. Don't be surprised if you have to take the Punta ferries (see opposite) back, because of over-choppy afternoon seas. One way tickets cost 430 GDR in 1998.

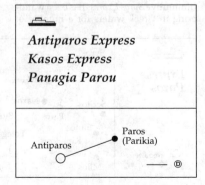

Antiparos Express
Kasos Express
Panagia Parou

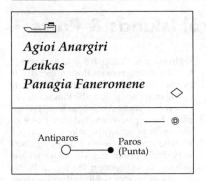

Agioi Anargiri
Leukas
Panagia Faneromene

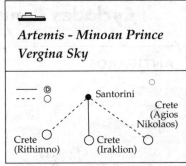

Artemis - Minoan Prince
Vergina Sky

C/F Agioi Anargiri
Several small ferries provide a vehicle-link across the straits between Antiparos Town and the quay at Paros (Punta). Their only redeeming feature is the fare:; at 150 GDR it is 70 GDR cheaper than the Paros town boats, even allowing for the Punta—Parikia bus fare (190 GDR).

C/F Theoskepasti - C/F Nissos Thirassia
Two boats operate a 'life-line' ferry service to Thirasia disguised as a Santorini caldera tour. Tickets for the *Theoskepasti* are bought from a one-off agent housed just north of the Port Police office in Fira town. This boat also runs a twice-weekly day return service (departing 07.45 from Fira Old Port) that offers a much cheaper way (1100 GDR Rtn.) of spending 5 hours on Thirasia than via their daily tourist day tour, though they insist that you use the 13.30 return service in the hope that day-trippers will opt for the tour.

Tour Boats
The large number of ferries conspire against the existence of Cyclades tourist boats. These only exist where ferry links are weak. There are a number of vessels of note; the largest run daily day trips from various port on Crete to Santorini. The biggest of these are the *Minoan Prince*, the *Artemis* and the *Vergina Sky*; all rely on package-tourists who are willing to

pay their extortionate fares. Two light-weight tourist boats (the *Aphrodite Express* and the *Agios Nektarios*) also operate in the Central Cyclades. Not for sea-sickies, and expensive, they occasionally offer hops that are rarely possible by regular ferry: in 1998 this included Paros to Delos (8000 GDR) and Paros to Serifos three times a week (7000 GDR).

Theoskepasti

Nissos Thirassia

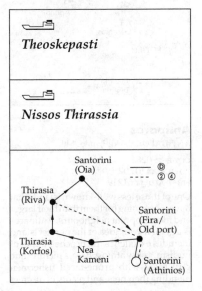

Cyclades Central Islands & Ports

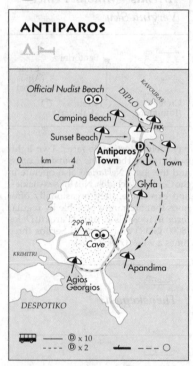

ANTIPAROS

Official Nudist Beach

KAVOURAS

DIPLO

Camping Beach

FKK

Sunset Beach

Antiparos Town

0   km   4

Town

Glyfa

299 m.

Cave

KRIMITRI

Apandima

Agios Georgios

DESPOTIKO

Ⓓ x 10

---- Ⓓ x 2

Antiparos
ΑΝΤΙΠΑΡΟΣ; 55 km²; pop. 540.

CODE ☎ 0284
POLICE ☎ 61202
FIRST AID ☎ 61219

One of those less well-known islands that have more going for them than their larger and more popular neighbours, Antiparos is a gem. If your idea of the perfect island includes excellent sand beaches, a spot of nudism, a cosy atmosphere, a picturesque port filled with prune-faced fishermen mending their nets, and plenty of discreet

nightlife then Antiparos is it. As a result the island attracts many day-trippers from nearby Paros who head either for a beach or the other attraction, the famous cave.

In many ways Antiparos is a strange place, having been severed from Paros as the result of an earthquake around 550 BC. The straits between it and Paros are very shallow (which is why all ferries are obliged to sail around the top of Paros when heading for Santorini) and narrow with the fields on the western side of the island rolling into the sea. The only settlement — **Antiparos Town** — straddling the flat northern tip of the island and with a fortress at its centre forms the focus of island life. Enough of the old town survives to give plenty of atmosphere; though the environs are dominated by establishments offering accommodation. Apart from the tavernas and boutiques lining the winding main street, the town's great attraction lies in its beaches. Within easy walking distance there is one guaranteed to suit most tastes. Families head for the shallow and sheltered beach to the north of the port, while the good sand beach opposite **Diplo** island (reached via the track to the campsite and then a 100 m path to the right) is the preserve of windsurfers (boards can be hired) and nudists (this is one of only three official nudist beaches in Greece). More hardy types in search of solitude head for Sunset Beach; windswept and with an abandoned air, it is the place for contemplating the meaning of life (and what one is doing with it) and for quietly drowning oneself if one isn't happy with the conclusions. Drowning one's sorrows back in town is even easier as bars aplenty cluster around the fortress and trickle down the main street. The town is also well equipped with discos (notably establishments in the inland town windmill and near the Galini hotel).

The rest of the island is relatively un-developed; a decent road has only recent-ly been completed, allowing buses to run south to the cave, and occasionally to Agios Georgios on the south-west coast. There is a comfortable scatter of holiday homes along the coast road, as well as taverna-backed sand beaches at **Glyfa** and at **Apandima** (the old mooring point for boats bringing visitiors to the cave).

The beach at **St. Georgios** is remote, but if you hire a car or moped, it is worth the effort of getting to. The hills behind are nothing to look at, but are nonetheless notable. Home to a major early Cycladic settlement, the first to have ever been explored, they have yielded up a large collection of Cycladic figures (excavated by one of the first modern tourists to visit the Cyclades — James Theodore Bent — in 1833–34, they now form the nucleus of the British Museum's impressive collect-ion). Most notable are the early highly stylised 'violin' figurines (see p. 253).

⊨

There is plenty of hotel accommodation in Antiparos Town, though it is on the pricey side. Top of the range is the C-class *Artemis* (☎ 61460) with good views over the harbour. Equally good, but rather less well-placed, is the inland *Galini* (☎ 61420). The remainder of the hotel accommodation is cheaper. This includes the waterfront D-class *Mantalena* (☎ 61206), and a collection of E-class establish-ments in the backstreets between the tourist and ferry quays — the *Korali* (☎ 61236), *Antiparos* (☎ 61358) and *Chrisoula* (☎ 61224). Budget travellers should note that the E-class *Begleri* (☎ 61378) is more expensive than the C-class establishments! Room availability in town is also good, but many are booked on a long-stay basis so arrive early in High Season.

Λ

Camping Antiparos (☎ 61221): a nice site (bar a poor site store) — with trees and a series of bamboo compounds — 1 km along a dirt track north of the town. Mini-bus meets boats.

👓

Nudist beach aside (which in High Season sadly attracts more timid than enlightened fans), Antiparos has two sights of note. The first is a small medieval **Kastro** (c. 1440) at the heart of Antiparos town: though until one is inside it one is hard put to recognise it at all. Sited at the end of the high street, it is a rectangular structure that in its heyday looked akin to a three-storeyed Alamo-like stockade, with houses lining the inside walls. In the years since it has been painted white, the top storey has gone, and windows and doors have been let into the outside wall. As a result, from the outside, the walls now look like any typical white cubist Cycladic row of buildings. On the south side, however, you will find a small unpainted Gothic archway — the original single doorway in the walls. Even today it is the only way you can gain access to the courtyard of the stockade-cum-castle without going through one of the houses. This ensures that something of the original enclosed atmosphere remains (though better examples of this type of fortification exist on Kimolos and Folegandros).

The second — and well hyped — sight on the island is the **Antiparos Cave**. A couple of centuries ago this cave was one of the most famous in the world; so much so that it inspired many by its reputation alone. Not least among these was Johann Wyss (the author of *Swiss Family Robinson*) who — picking up on the juxtaposition of an island and a cave — appears to have derived the idea for the Rock House from reading of the Antiparos cave, acknow-ledging the debt by having the narrator say:

'I had … read the description of the famous grotto of Antiparos'

After this build up the cave itself inevitably suffers in comparison with both the myth and some other caverns accessible today. However, even allowing that discriminating troglodytes are likely to be disappointed, for most the cave is a gentle and rewarding introduction to the underworld. Certainly there are enough buses and agency tours hell bent on getting you there (and making an equally big hole in your pocket). For this reason you should exercise caution; for if you are not careful the cave is not the only pitfall that you could en-counter. You should be aware of the following:

(1). In the summer of 1998 the round bus trip to the cave was 1200 GDR. One-way tickets cost 600 GDR. Several agency buses and the island bus run to the cave but tickets are not interchangeable; it therefore pays to buy single tickets so that you can return on the first available bus back.

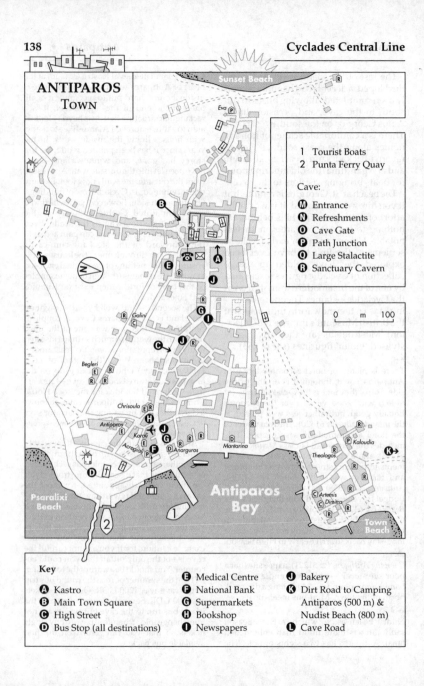

ANTIPAROS TOWN

Sunset Beach

Eva

1 Tourist Boats
2 Punta Ferry Quay

Cave:
Ⓜ Entrance
Ⓝ Refreshments
Ⓞ Cave Gate
Ⓟ Path Junction
Ⓠ Large Stalactite
Ⓡ Sanctuary Cavern

0   m   100

Galini

Begleri

Chrisoula

Antiparos

Koroli

Acrogiali

Anarguros

Mantarina

Kaloudia

Theologos

Psaralixi Beach

Artemis

Dimitra

Town Beach

Antiparos Bay

Key

Ⓐ Kastro
Ⓑ Main Town Square
Ⓒ High Street
Ⓓ Bus Stop (all destinations)
Ⓔ Medical Centre
Ⓕ National Bank
Ⓖ Supermarkets
Ⓗ Bookshop
Ⓘ Newspapers
Ⓙ Bakery
Ⓚ Dirt Road to Camping Antiparos (500 m) & Nudist Beach (800 m)
Ⓛ Cave Road

(2). Tours and bus tickets do not include the cave ticket price of 600 GDR.

(3). All buses decant passengers on a bend of a road half-way up an apparently isolated mountain-side. Here you will be met by mules with touting owners. Those taking up the offer to be taken for a ride are apt to feel bigger asses than their mounts when they find that the cave entrance is only 150 m up the path.

(4). Low Season sees buses reduced to a trickle; so expect delays when both departing and returning. In addition, the cave is often locked, prompting further delays.

Once inside Mt. Agios Gianni you will find yourself in a cave that has been on the tourist map almost as long as the Parthenon, and unfortunately, it is as badly damaged. Many of the stalagmites and stalactites (sexist mnemonic: tights come down) are broken. In times past the cave's fame ensured that stalagmites were carried off by the Russian navy to the Kremlin. More recent damage was inflicted during the last war when German soldiers used the stalactites for rifle practice. The walls are also covered with graffiti dating back 300 years: the more notable vandals including King Otho of Greece (who visited in 1840), and Lord Byron. Rumours persist of a stalactite inscribed by some failed assassins of Alexander the Great hiding in the cave. Graffiti is less of a problem today as movement in the cave is restricted to a narrow stairway barely wide enough for two people to pass (in High Season rotund visitors have been known to commit mass murder simply trying to pass by on the other side). Rusty iron handrails are provided for midgets, but at several points the stairs are built onto stalagmites and taller vertigo suffers could be in for a heady time (for these reasons photography in the cave is forbidden). The cave is floodlit, but it might be worthwhile bringing a torch as power cuts are not unknown in this part of the world.

Pottery has been found in the cave indicating occupation back to archaic times, though the nearest it has ever come to fame was in 1673 when a potty Frenchman (one M. de Nointel) organised a Christmas Day mass (complete with fireworks) in the main chamber — the congregation being 500 of the bemused population of Paros (who were paid to indulge this exhibition of antiquarian eccentricity). Just over a century later — in 1774 — the locals built the chapel at the cave entrance to prevent anything like this happening again.

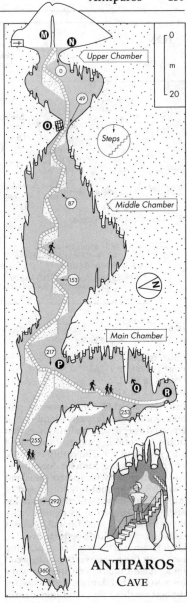

ANTIPAROS
CAVE

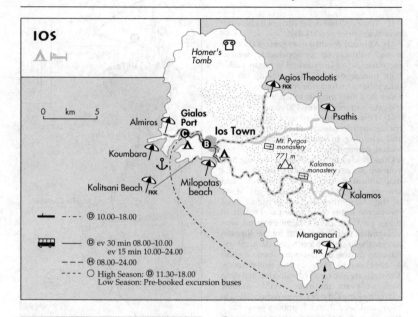

Ios

IOΣ; 108 km²; pop. 1,650.

CODE ☎ 0286
PORT POLICE ☎ 91264
POLICE ☎ 91222
HOSPITAL ☎ 91227

Ios (pronounced *EE*os) has gained a reputation and a half as *the* party island since it emerged as a popular student destination in the 60s, offering a heady cocktail of sun, sand and sex. The reality is a little more complicated, for a lot depends on when you go and which part of the island you visit. From mid July to the end of August the crowds pour in, and Ios attempts to live up to its reputation — those looking for a traditional, unspoilt Greek island would do better to avoid it, but for the rest of the year, even if partying isn't your thing, it is worth paying a call for Ios has a lot going for it. In many ways Ios is an ideal holiday island; it has two of the best beaches to be found anywhere in

Greece, a picturesque old chora, good connections for day trips to other islands, and — most importantly of all — a buzz about it that you just don't find anywhere else. It is difficult not to get caught up by the atmosphere, and, as you don't have to join the all-night party, it is possible to turn a blind eye to the excesses of those that do and simply embrace those aspects of the island that appeal to you. In some respects the island's reputation is rather overblown, for although the days of the youthful hanger-out are not exactly over, a growth in the number of families visiting (thanks to the thirty-somethings returning to the haunts of their giddy youth) is beginning to restore the balance a bit. The telling fact that Parikia on Paros and Fira Town on Santorini both now have more night-spots is also rarely acknowledged, in part because the nightspots on Ios are heavily concentrated in the centre of town and not obscured among a plethora of competing attractions.

Not all is sweetness and light, however, and Ios does have a less appealing side that the island's more passionate fans are loath to accept. The height of the season sees it ludicrously over-crowded, with the attendant problems of noise, poor sanitation, alcohol abuse and theft — all of which are more evident than on other islands. The locals have got in on the act as well, with some of the bars adding god-knows-what to spirits and cocktails, invariably with dire consequences for the drinker a few hours later. Violence is also a problem: the rumour mill regularly churns out rape figures running at over a dozen each summer (occasional victims being male). How much truth there is in such sobering bar talk is hard to establish, as the police are not keen on highlighting this aspect of island life.

Describing the geography of Ios is easy enough, for there are only three main points of reference, with a bare 4 km between them: the Port, the chora set up on the hill behind (known as the Village), and the Beach (Milopotas) on the other side of the chora hill. At first sight the island seems innocuous enough, for the port of **Gialos** is quite sleepy — give or take a dozen bars. Indeed, it is positively quiet compared to its counterparts on Paros and Santorini, besides being far more attractive than either of them. For this reason it attracts those who want to be able to escape the worst excesses of the island's nightlife, and has a good supply of hotels, along with an excellent bakery and several restaurants. It is only when you step inside the supermarket and discover that the check-out racks are filled with condoms that you first get a hint that something, somewhere, could be up.

Behind the port climbs the old mule **stairway** up to the Chora. This offers an appealing alternative to the new road, but thanks to slippery, sloping steps that are awkward enough when you are sober (never mind when one is totally sozzled and in the dark), it accounts for the fact

that there is always someone hopping around with a leg in plaster and the widely advertised doctors' practices in the town. Most visitors prefer to use the two island buses instead. These are more crowded than buses elsewhere — and this is really saying something. Until you have tried travelling on an Ios bus in one of the 'rush hours', you haven't fully enjoyed the Greek island experience. The sardine-tin times are between 11.00–14.00 when heading for the beach, 15.00–18.00 returning from the beach, and after 21.00 heading for the village. The buses do nothing else except run from the port to the chora and then down to Milopotas and Koumbara.

Ios Town (alias the Village) at the top of the stairs is a real contradiction: the islanders having made a far better job of combining a pretty chora village with a heavy bar and disco scene than their counterparts on the other popular islands. During daylight hours it retains much of its former small village atmosphere, and at first sight you would be hard put to know that it was anything more. Come dusk, the windows and doors of the lower town buildings open to reveal a profusion of bars and boutiques.

All the large clubs (which need more space) now lie along the road and strip of building-free ground (thanks to ownership disputes) that divide the old and new halves of the town. Things don't get really going much before 22.00 (it is a truism of Ios that the sun sets as a new day dawns), after which life gets wilder by the hour. Shutting — or rather falling — down time is usually 03.00. If you are young, and male, and have come to Greece looking for the girl of your dreams, you will probably find Ios disappointing; not only has the author had a good look around first and found nothing,

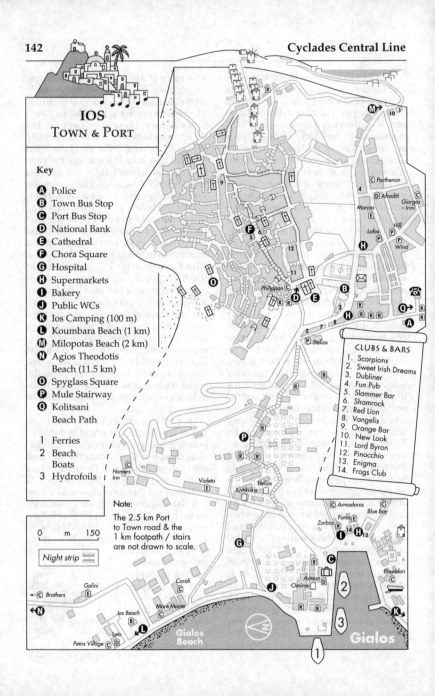

IOS
TOWN & PORT

Key

Ⓐ Police
Ⓑ Town Bus Stop
Ⓒ Port Bus Stop
Ⓓ National Bank
Ⓔ Cathedral
Ⓕ Chora Square
Ⓖ Hospital
Ⓗ Supermarkets
Ⓘ Bakery
Ⓙ Public WCs
Ⓚ Ios Camping (100 m)
Ⓛ Koumbara Beach (1 km)
Ⓜ Milopotas Beach (2 km)
Ⓝ Agios Theodotis
    Beach (11.5 km)
Ⓞ Spyglass Square
Ⓟ Mule Stairway
Ⓠ Kolitsani
    Beach Path

1 Ferries
2 Beach
   Boats
3 Hydrofoils

CLUBS & BARS

1. Scorpions
2. Sweet Irish Dreams
3. Dubliner
4. Fun Pub
5. Slammer Bar
6. Shamrock
7. Red Lion
8. Vangelis
9. Orange Bar
10. New Look
11. Lord Byron
12. Pinocchio
13. Enigma
14. Frogs Club

Note:
The 2.5 km Port
to Town road & the
1 km footpath / stairs
are not drawn to scale.

0   m   150

Night strip ▬▬

Parthenon
Afroditi
Giorgos – Irini
Marcos
Lofos
Hill
Wind
Philippon
Stefios
Homers Inn
Violeta
Krinkakis
Helias
Armadoros
Blue Boy
Zorbas
Faros
Poseidon
Brothers
Galini
Ios Beach
Leto
Petra Village
Mara Monte
Corali
Omiros
Acteon
Gialos Beach
Gialos

but most nightspots seem to find males outnumbering females by two to one. Nightspots catering for those with minority sexual orientations are also all but non-existent: there are no sheep on Ios. The popular bars change with the year and season, so positive recommendations are difficult. Of the big dance clubs, *Scorpions* seem to have had the edge of late, but the *Dubliner* and *Sweet Irish Dream* also draw crowds. The smaller bars in the old part of town are more intimate and serve food (notably *Pinocchio's*, which doubles up as a pizzeria). Finally, there are a good collection of quieter bars in the port; the *Frog's Club* being the patently obvious place to stop if you are waiting to hop aboard a ferry.

After bars, beaches are the great attraction of Ios. **Milopotas Beach** is one of the best in the Aegean; a long stretch of golden sand, it is large enough to accommodate even the High Season crowds and is backed by a scatter of bars and tavernas. However, in summer it is wind-blasted by the *meltemi*. Visitors to Ios of a decade ago will mourn the arrival of a road running the length of the beach that has destroyed the nudism at the far end.

The rest of the island — being arid and hilly, with poor dirt roads — is quiet, though regular buses (starting at the port) now ferry people to the main beaches. The best of these is the superb stretch of sand taking in several bays at **Manganari** on the south coast (beach boats also visit). **Agios Theodotis**, on the east coast, is almost as good, with the skimpy ruins of a Venetian kastro in lieu of the former's disco / taverna and windsurfing school. Both are predominantly nude, unlike the official nude beaches at oily **Koumbara** (which is now very restrained thanks to arrival of hotels and a regular bus service) and at **Kolitsani**. This latter beach is in a small cove (favoured by yachts as a quiet mooring point) that is best reached is via the path that runs east from the town post office road.

Are **YOU** a victim of ANTI-TOURIST DISCRIMINATION?

Over the last three years a small — but increasing — number of ferries are discriminating against non-Greeks. At embarkation time crew members are positioned at the entrance to Deck-class saloons where they divert foreigners (particularly backpackers) to the open sun decks, while admitting Greek speakers to the areas with interior seats. Contrary to these crew members' claims, there is no such thing as an 'outside only' passenger ferry ticket in Greece, and this practice amounts to anti-tourist discrimination.

The author has brought the problem to the attention of the Greek tourist authorities in the hope that they will be able to prevent it recurring. If you find you are a victim in 1999 please take a moment to tell us by sending a postcard (to the address on p. 10) giving:

1. The FERRY NAME
2. The EMBARKATION PORT
3. The DATE.

This information will enable us to bring the problem to the attention of the Greek Minister of Tourism and 'name and shame' the worst companies and ferries in next year's edition.

📇

Rooms are plentiful on Ios; though the usual caveat about arriving early in the day applies to Ios as well. Life has been made easier of late by the building of an accommodation office on the ferry quay. If you are staying more than a fortnight (it is not unknown for people to get off a ferry and then ask in the nearest ticket agency where they can stay for three months!) it is worth trying to negotiate a reduced rate. If you are staying for several weeks you will be expected to pay your bill on a weekly basis (this applies on campsites as well).

The **Port** is well equipped with several good mid-range hotels (though the noise from the ferries can be a problem). These include the C-class *Armadoros* (☎ 91201), *Blue Bay* (☎ 91533) and the *Poseidon* (☎ 91091). There is also the somewhat noisy D-class *Acteon* (☎ 91207) over the ticket agency, and the E-class *Faros* (☎ 91569). Nearby **Gialos Beach** offers some of the most relaxed (and quietest) rooms on Ios. These include the beach-side C-class *Corali* (☎ 91272) and *Mare Monte* (☎ 91564), the expensive *Petra Village* (☎ 91409) and B-class *Ios Beach* and the D-class *Leto* (☎ 91279).

The **Chora** has a plentiful supply of rooms — mostly in the old part of town — and, a number of reasonable hotels. Best among these are the D-class *Afroditi* (☎ 91546) and the C-class *Parthenon* (☎ 91275). The C-class *Giorgos* —*Irini* (☎ 91527) is also very popular, as is the *Philippou* (☎ 91290) near the Cathedral, and the E-class *Marcos* (☎ 91060).

The road to and behind **Milopotas Beach** also has a large number of pensions and hotels perched along it. These include the C-class *Far Out* (☎ 91446), *Delfini* (☎ 91340), and *Nissos Ios* (☎ 91306), and the E-class *Aegeon* (☎ 91392). Milopotas is also home to the expensive B-class *Ios Palace* (☎ 91269). Finally, if you are really seeking the quiet life on Ios, there are also some rooms at **Agios Theodotis Beach**.

Å

Thanks to the high student numbers, Ios is well equipped with three campsites, but even this is not enough at the height of the season when you will find tents pitched peg to peg by the early evening. The rest of the year there is space aplenty. Regardless of when you visit, you should take extra pains to secure all valuables as petty theft is depressingly common (all the sites have safety deposit facilities). Thanks to the number of long stay

(i.e. a couple of months or more) visitors — many of whom are strapped to find the funds to party *and* pay their camping bills — it is all but impossible to stay a week at a campsite without either hearing of someone losing their travellers' cheques or cash from their tent, or worse, overhearing fellow campers debating as to which is the most profitable tent to 'do over'. As for the sites:

Ios Camping (☎ 91329), complete with a new swimming pool, lies opposite the ferry quay. Its convenient port location is not the money-spinner that it should be, as most campers prefer to be near the beach and head for one of the sites behind Milopotas beach:

Camping Stars (☎ 91302) nearest the village road, is a well-established, if small site, showing its age. Popular with long-stay visitors, it has plenty of tree cover and friendly staff.

Far Out Camping (☎ 91468) at the end of Milo-potas is a member of the *Harmonie* camping scheme. Its 'far out' location and good amenities combine to make it a social venue in its own right. Facilities include a pool complete with rock music and DJ. There is even a pool-side ear-piercing service if the loudspeakers haven't already done the job for you.

👀

The official and oft-quoted island sight is **Homer's Tomb** — or rather the alleged stones from which it was made — is all but impossible to get to and, frankly, not worth the effort of the difficult journey. As a result most visitors justifiably prefer to get stoned in the bars and discos of Ios Town instead.

The one Ios sight not to be missed is the view from the top of the **Chora Hill**. Finding your way up through the warren of streets is, admittedly, half the fun of it (a couple of stair-ways that disintegrate into steep tracks on the western side of the Chora will eventually get you there), but there is usually a steady trail of sunset watchers heading in the same direction to help you. The top, adorned with several chapels and a scree slope of pebbles, offers fantastic views of the port framed with the island of Sikinos behind in one direction, and the Chora and distant Santorini in another. The best time to visit is at sunset, when the port is bathed in a golden glow, and the wine-dark harbour sea is furrowed by a procession of ferries running up from Santorini en route to Piraeus; the combination offers one of the best panoramic views in the Greek islands.

Milopotas –
the most popular beach
on Ios

Every Sunday morning and
evening a hapless youth is
sent up into the highest
campanile in Ios Town to
ring the bells …

IOS

Chora Hilltop Views of the Campanile
& Evening Ferries calling at Ios Port
(with Sikinos on the horizon)

Ios Town: the Chora Hill

ANTIPAROS
Main Street & Kastro

PAROS
Morning Ferries Arrive
at Paros (viewed from
Parikia Beach)

Sightseeing on
Parikia Beach

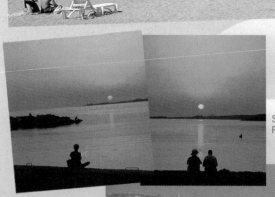

How to make mad,
passionate, erotic
love on the back
of a Great Striped
Man—Seating
Whale ...

PAROS
Parikia Town

Temple Site Kastro Church

Paros Ferry Quay (with Passenger
Sheds & Windmill)

NAXOS
Town/Chora

Cyclades Central

Naxian Ferry Ticket Agency

The C/F *Syros Express* arrives at Naxos

Cyclades Central

The Doorway of Ariadne's Palace often prompts speculation over the size of her lover — the god Dionysos ...

Temple of Apollo / Ariadne's Arch
NAXOS

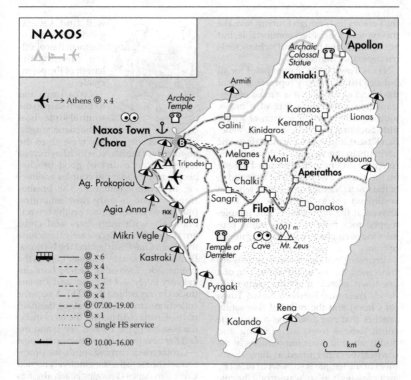

NAXOS

→ Athens Ⓓ x 4

Naxos Town /Chora

Archaic Temple

Archaic Colossal Statue

Apollon

Komiaki

Armiti

Koronos

Keramoti

Lionas

Galini

Kinidaros

Melanes

Moni

Moutsouna

Tripodes

Ag. Prokopiou

Chalki

Apeirathos

Agia Anna   FKK

Sangri

Filoti

Danakos

Plaka

Damarion

Mikri Vegle

Temple of Demeter

Cave

1001 m

Mt. Zeus

Kastraki

Ⓓ x 6
Ⓓ x 4
Ⓓ x 1
Ⓓ x 2
Ⓓ x 4
Ⓗ 07.00–19.00
Ⓓ x 1
Ⓞ single HS service
Ⓗ 10.00–16.00

Pyrgaki

Rena

Kalando

0   km   6

Naxos

ΝΑΞΟΣ; 448 km²; pop. 18,000.

CODE ☎ 0285
PORT POLICE ☎ 22300
POLICE ☎ 22100
FIRST AID ☎ 23333

Naxos can lay claim to being one of the most popular Greek islands — at least with island hoppers. Not only are the numbers visiting higher than for any other island, but the average length of stay is also greater than that for other popular islands. This isn't surprising given that Naxos offers an alluring mix of an attractive port town, a succession of wonderful, easily accessible sand beaches (complete with proper sand-dunes), an interior

landscape of lush valleys and ruin-topped sky-lines, and good links with other islands. Writers — ancient and modern — have regularly labelled Naxos as the most beautiful of the Cyclades.

Not only is it the largest island in the group, but it is a popular day-trip destination, and the primary jumping off point for Amorgos and the Little Cyclades. Thanks to a prosperous agricultural base Naxos has long been able to ignore the tourist market, but this is now changing. The last decade has seen the opening of an airport, and a large increase in the number of tourists. Fortunately, their impact has been relatively benign, as the tourist strip is confined to Naxos Town and its environs. At the moment Naxos thus enjoys just enough tourism to make the 'typical' tourist feel comfortable, but not so much that the island's character is irredeemably damaged.

Naxos Town is the arrival point for all but air visitors. Hardly representative of the island as a whole, it is a mass of contradictions, offering a mix of a brash, touristy waterfront, a warren of lovely little backstreets winding up to a Venetian Kastro, and one of the most dramatic harbours in the Aegean — thanks to the romantic skyline arch of a ruined temple on the causeway-linked islet at the edge of the town (Naxos is one island where it is difficult not to know that you have arrived at the right place). The temple-topped rock provides a beguiling promise to arriving ferry passengers of things to come.

Surprisingly, as far as most tourists are concerned, Naxos is still something of a one-town island; most are content to divide their time between Naxos Town (or Chora) and the miles of fine sandy beaches that run down the coast to the south, where freelance camping and nudity abound. First impressions of the town can be rather mixed, as the enchantment of the temple is somewhat offset by an increasingly glitzy waterfront; the cute old hardware shops of just a few years ago have now given way to tourist shops and cash dispensing machines. Most of the town's amenities are to be found here, including a good bookshop and a bus station complete with timetables for the island. The municipal authorities have also woken up to the tourists' occasionally more pressing needs and have installed a WC and shower house on the main street behind the promenade. Once you step into the streets behind the main street and wander into the chora, you will discover the older and more attractive face of the town. The combination of castle, Greek chora and Venetian houses combine to make for shady, and interesting wandering, and near the castle walls you

will find several good restaurants to augment the collection running the length of the promenade.

Naxos Town and its beach strip to the south also play host to the island's nightlife. This is surprisingly tame given the popularity of the island, which has thrived regardless on a diet of good beaches peopled by holidaying couples wallowing in dreamy romance. The brasher singles scene is only now emerging (though so far its impact on the town is minimal), with more bars and clubs arriving each year. Recent arrivals include the *Ocean Club Disco* behind the National Bank and the nearby *Musique Café* on the promenade. Two other nearby bars can get very lively — *Mike's Bar* and *The Jam* (tucked away behind the OTE). A popular collection of nightspots lie along the main port—Grotta road just off the ferry quay; the best being the *Empire, Seven* and the *Loft Bar* near the police station on the port —Grotta road. Turning south, the promenade is home to the imaginatively named *Greek Bar*. Agios Georgios beach also has the popular *Asteria Disco* attached to the hotel and other bars in the nearby streets.

The coastline south of Naxos Town is a **beach strip** without equal in the islands. Running for kilometres between headland and cove are a succession of excellent sand beaches. The nearest lies on the edge of town at **Agios Georgios**. This is a good family beach, even if the large numbers visiting mean that it isn't the cleanest. A small headland to the south divides it from the low 'dam' that was built (at great cost to the wildlife) to prevent the salt flats behind — that are now home to the island airport — from flooding. A very windy beach has grown up along the north side of the dam, which is popular with windsurfers and ignored

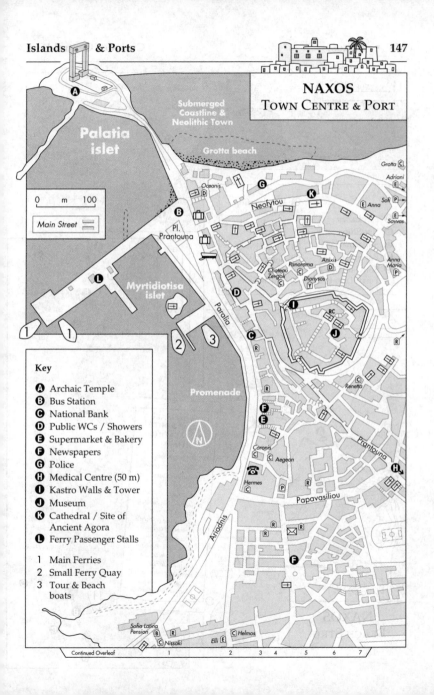

NAXOS
TOWN CENTRE & PORT

Palatia islet

Submerged Coastline & Neolithic Town

Grotta beach

Grotta C
Adriani E
Sofi P
Anna E
Savvas E

Oceanis D
Neofytou
G
K

0 m 100
Main Street

B
Pl. Prantouna

Chateau Zevgoli C
Panorama C
Anixis
Dionysos Y
Anna Maria P

Myrtidiotisa islet

L

D
I
RC
J

Paralia

C
R
Renetta C

1 1
2 3

Promenade

R
F
E

N

Caronis C
C Aegean

Hermes C
P
R

Prantouna
H

Papavasiliou

Key

- **A** Archaic Temple
- **B** Bus Station
- **C** National Bank
- **D** Public WCs / Showers
- **E** Supermarket & Bakery
- **F** Newspapers
- **G** Police
- **H** Medical Centre (50 m)
- **I** Kastro Walls & Tower
- **J** Museum
- **K** Cathedral / Site of Ancient Agora
- **L** Ferry Passenger Stalls

- 1 Main Ferries
- 2 Small Ferry Quay
- 3 Tour & Beach boats

R
R
F

Ariadnis

Sofia Latina Pension
R
C Nissaki
Elli E
C Helmos

1 2 3 4 5 6 7

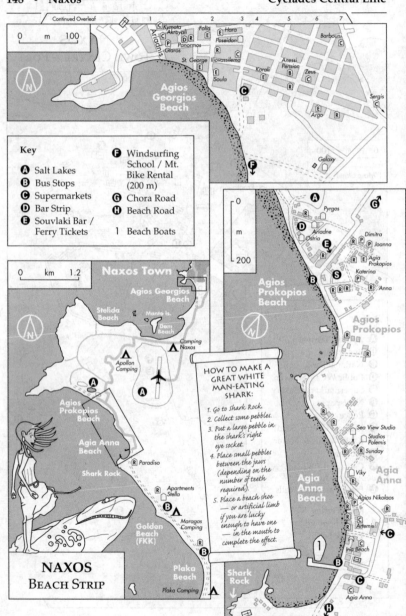

Continued Overleaf

0 — m — 100

Agios Georgios Beach

Kymata
Akreyali
Folia
Hara
Poseidon
Panormos
Glaros
St. George
Iliovassilema
Soula
Korali
Anessi Pension
Zeus
Barbouni
Argo
Sergis
Galaxy

Key

Ⓐ Salt Lakes
Ⓑ Bus Stops
Ⓒ Supermarkets
Ⓓ Bar Strip
Ⓔ Souvlaki Bar / Ferry Tickets
Ⓕ Windsurfing School / Mt. Bike Rental (200 m)
Ⓖ Chora Road
Ⓗ Beach Road
1 Beach Boats

0 — m — 200

Agios Prokopios Beach

Pyrgos
Ariadne
Ostria
Dimitra
Joanna
Agia Prokopios
Katerina
Anna

Agios Prokopios

0 — km — 1.2

Naxos Town

Agios Georgios Beach

Stelida Beach
Manto Is.
Dam Beach
Camping Naxos
Apollon Camping

Agios Prokopios Beach

Agia Anna Beach

Shark Rock

Paradiso
Apartments Stella
Maragas Camping

Golden Beach (FKK)

Plaka Beach

Plaka Camping

NAXOS BEACH STRIP

Sea View Studio
Studios Polemis
Sunday
Viky
Agios Nikolaos
Artemis
Ina Beach
Agia Anna

Agia Anna Beach

HOW TO MAKE A GREAT WHITE MAN-EATING SHARK:

1. Go to Shark Rock.
2. Collect some pebbles.
3. Put a large pebble in the shark's right eye socket.
4. Place small pebbles between the jaws (depending on the number of teeth required).
5. Place a beach shoe — or artificial limb if you are lucky enough to have one — in the mouth to complete the effect.

Shark Rock

by everyone else. **Stelida** beach to the west is more popular and has a taverna.

South of the Stelida headland lie the bigger beaches (now sadly being marred by unsympathetic hotel and holiday home development). **Agios Prokopios** is the first of these. Home to a motley collection of establishments offering beds, the only paved street in town is the main road. Be sure to take a look at the small salt lakes behind the beach to the north of this beach 'resort'; dry in summer, the beds are caked with a layer of salt. Travelling in the opposite direction the coast road runs as far as **Agia Anna** beach. Thereafter a dusty track leads you to the increasingly quiet **Golden** and **Plaka** beaches. Beach boats also run from Agia Anna and Naxos Town to the isolated beaches of **Kalando** and **Rena** on the south coast.

In spite of its attractive main town, Naxos's fame has always rested on its verdant, but hilly hinterland where an attractive rural Greek atmosphere pervades. Farming is still an important feature of the local economy (the island is noted for its wines and cheeses), and indeed, has been so profitable that it is only now that Naxos is really jumping on the tourism bandwagon. Sadly, roads have yet to catch up with this trend and are in a positively lethal condition in parts (this is one island where it is better to stick to buses rather than resort to mopeds). Most tourists tend to compromise and see the interior via a daily tour bus that heads along the meandering mountain roads (that run through pretty **Komiaki** — the highest village on the island) to the small developing northern 'resort' of **Apollon**. With an indifferent beach and little nightlife, few people stay here, however, and the fishing village subsists on the tour parties taking in the local sight — the giant Kouros (see p. 151) and lunch before returning to civilization.

Two settlements en route also attract attention. The first is the attractive hillside village of **Filoti**, which, in addition to lying at the centre of the fertile Tragaia Valley and offering a view of an appealing unspoilt Greek island community, is also starting point for the 2-hour trek to the summit of **Mt. Zeus** (the highest peak in the Cyclades). Serious hikers will find that it is worth attempting the ascent (despite the poorly marked paths), to marvel at the view of the archipelago, and the cave half-way up, where the god was supposed to have been born, and then nurtured by an eagle. The second village of note is **Apeiranthos**. Arguably the most attractive on the island, it has several Venetian towers and streets paved with the island's famous marble. The village is also home to a small Archaeological Museum housing some Early Cycladic figures. The village school also houses a small Geological Museum which charts the area's 17–19 c. emery mining industry. This was responsible for the road to the former port of **Moutsouna** — now a quiet beach backed by holiday homes. The remainder of the east coast of Naxos is very quiet, with tourists something of a rarity. This is in part due to the open-cast mining south of Lionas.

The various ticket and travel agencies on the waterfront road are a good starting point when bed hunting (assuming you escape the room owners besieging the ferries). **Naxos Town** is home to the bulk of the island accommodation, with an easily located batch of hotels in the northern town. Nearest the ferry quay is the D-class *Oceanis* (☎ 22436), with the E-class *Anna* (☎ 22475) and *Savvas* (☎

HOW TO MAKE MAD, PASSIONATE, EROTIC LOVE (IN THE DARK) ON THE BACK OF A GREAT WHITE MAN-EATING SHARK:

SEE p. 609–22

22213) down the street behind. There is also a nice hotel in the C-class *Grotta* (☎ 22215) beyond the *Apollon* (☎ 22468). In addition to several places offering rooms, the promenade has a cluster of C-class hotels at its southern end: the *Hermes* (☎ 22220), the *Aegeon* (☎ 22852), and the *Coronis* (☎22626). The warren of streets around the castle is also home to a number of hotels. At the top of the range is the C-class *Renetta* (☎ 22952) to the south; the maze of streets to the north containing the *Panorama* (☎ 22330) and the pricey *Chateau Zevgoli* (☎ 22993), along with the D-class *Anixis* (☎ 22112) and a youth hostel/pension, the *Dionysos* (☎ 22331).

The **Agios Georgios Beach** area is also well endowed with hotels and pensions including the E-class *Soula* (☎ 23637) and *St. George* (☎ 23162). On the town road to the beach stands the C-class *Helmos* (☎ 22455), with the E-class *Folia* (☎ 22210) to the south. Two other hotels of note are nearby: the E-class *Korali* (☎ 23092) behind the beach supermarket, and, hidden three blocks behind, the C-class *Zeus* (☎ 22912).

The beach strip is gradually being developed; at **Agios Prokopios** there are a scatter of pensions and the E-class *Agia Prokopios*. **Agia Anna** is more up-market with three C-class hotels near the beach; the *Iria Beach* (☎ 24178), the *Agia Anna*, and the *Artemis* (☎ 24880).

Λ

There is very fierce competition between the four sites that lie on the beach road running south of Naxos Town; so much so that is not unusual to be approached on ferries by students (working off their camping bills) handing out promotional flyers in High Season. The sites have very different attractions, so it is worthwhile deciding what your priorities are before choosing between them:

Naxos Camping (☎ 23501) is the nearest site to Naxos Town (2 km). This makes it the most convenient for nightlife fans. The down side is that, knowing that they will get the town fans, they don't bother to provide much else. Even so, the site is large, with plenty of shade, clean facilities and a roadside pool. Agios Georgios beach is a 1 km walk up the road.

Apollon Camping (☎ 24117), a member of the *Sunshine Camping* scheme, is 4 km from the town. It is inconveniently placed for both the town and the wilder end of the beach strip. It offsets these disadvantages by providing better facilities than the competition. These

include a fair mini-market, washing machines in the laundry block and a pool. Buses stop outside the gates en route to the beach strip.

Maragas Camping (☎ 24552), a member of the *Harmonie* camping scheme, is 7 km from the town, is a typical (if large) beach site. The absence of anywhere else to go ensures that the beach fronting bar is well patronized.

Plaka Camping (☎ 42700) is the newest site on Naxos (opening in 1997). Despite having immaculate facilities it was all but empty during its first summer of life. The site is probably going to struggle, thanks to its isolated position. Tucked behind the sand dunes of Plaka Beach, it is miles from anywhere and not for campers without their own wheels.

∞

Naxos Town offers the best sightseeing options. First of these is the **Archaic Temple** (6 c. BC) and its remarkably well-preserved cella doorway on Palatia islet. Reached by braving a surf-kissed causeway (that was home to half-a-dozen windmills in medieval times), it is now expected of most visitors that they will come away with at least one photograph of themselves standing astride the base stones inside the arch (this isn't quite as famous a shot as being snapped holding up the leaning tower of Pisa, but it runs it pretty close). Little remains of the rest of the temple apart from the floor and assorted stones. Originally having 12 Ionic columns on each side and 6 at each end, the building was later converted into a church, and — until the late Middle Ages — was surrounded by houses.

The temple is something of an enigma, as no surviving literature from antiquity mentions it. With no inscriptions from the site recovered either, debate rages as to whom it was dedicated; the main candidates being Dionysos or Apollo. Sentiment favours the former, but its age and the particular affinity that the Archaic Naxians enjoyed with Delos and its Apollo sanctuary suggests the latter. What is known is that it is a contemporary of similar massive temples built during this period at Athens and Samos. The fragments that survive also testify to the fact that this impressive temple was never finished: the stone 'knobs' adorning some of the larger stones on the archway were left by the builders on otherwise finished blocks to help hoist them into position. Their removal was one of the last acts in a temple's completion: it never happened here.

The temple arch was initially believed by antiquarians to be the doorway of Ariadne's palace, for tradition has it that Naxos was the home of the god Dionysos. It was on Patatia that he is supposed to have ravished Ariadne, the beautiful maiden abandoned here by the Athenian hero Theseus after their escape from Knossos on Crete. Quite why Theseus dumped the girl who — with her ball of thread — gave him the means of escape from the Labyrinth after killing the Minotaur isn't known. Three millennia on, attempts to unravel the threads of this relationship are dangerous; however it is a fair bet that Ariadne was both very highly strung and apt to whine. Dionysos, the God of wine and pleasure, loved both a good wine and Ariadne and built her a palace, only to find that she (being a mere mortal) inconsiderately went and died on him; whereupon he got the hump, threw her bridal crown of seven stars into the night sky (these now form the constellation Corona Borealis) and went off and invented orgies.

The **Old Town** (largely a product of the period of Venetian rule between 1207–1566 when members of the Sonudi family set up shop as the Dukes of Naxos) runs around the 13 c. castle walls and is filled with geraniums and — particularly on the northern side — a lovely warren of little streets to get lost in. The **Kastro**, built on the site of the ancient acropolis,

contains a Roman Catholic cathedral and a **Museum** (one of the few where you can see some of the Early Cycladic marble figurines so sought after by art thieves). The Kastro is well preserved (and graced with the escutcheons of various Venetian noble families), though its heart has a somewhat antiseptic feel to it: this is in part because the ruling Venetian community that lived here constructed it as their own non-Greek part of town and the islanders have not managed to shake off their ambivalent feelings towards it since.

The windswept northern shoreline of the town, known as **Grotta**, is also of interest, thanks to a couple of caves and the submerged remains of an Early Cycladic town (presumably complete with drowned figurines) just off the beach. Remains of the Classical and Roman town are harder to spot. Some excavation is going on in the Grotta area, but major buildings — such as the theatre — have yet to be located. The site of the agora is known; it stood, north of the kastro, on the site of the current cathedral square.

Around Naxos are a number of archaeological sites of varying merit. The most visited of these are the ancient marble quarries at **Melanes** and **Apollon**, where there are the partially carved remains of large male statues known as **Kouroi**. These are stylised figures which were abandoned half-completed due to faults in the stone. The colossal **Apollon Kouros** (7 c. BC) is easily the best of the three; 10.5 m tall (making the figure four times life-size), it is a giant rough sketch in stone of a god — probably Dionysos. The two **Melanes Kouroi** — despite being abandoned in something nearer their intended final form, are much smaller (being only just over life size) and of a much cruder design than the Apollon figure. The remains of a finished Naxian colossal figure of similar size to the Apollon Kouros can be seen on the nearby island of Delos (see p. 194). Naxos was a major exporter of sculpture during the Archaic period (the

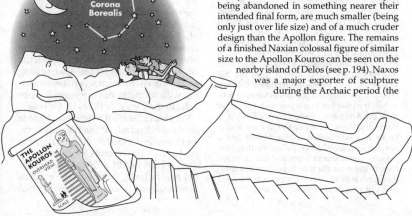

Corona Borealis

THE APOLLON KOUROS OVERHEAD VIEW

famous lions on Delos were also carved from Naxian marble), but as with Paros, export — rather than local construction — was the order of the day, so Naxos itself has comparatively little Archaic material on show.

Remains of ancient structures are to be found in remoter areas of Naxos. The most noteworthy of these is a **Temple of Demeter** that lies halfway down the road from Naxos Town to the beach hamlet at Pyrgaki. Dating from the 6 C. BC, it was unusual in having a square floor plan and 5 Ionic columns on its pedimental side, and a roof made up of marble beams and thin marble tiles that allowed a diffused light into the interior. The building survived until the 9 C. AD, when it was destroyed and the site abandoned. Now recognised as important because of the uniqueness of its architecture, the temple is currently fenced off while archaeologists attempt to rebuild as much of the structure as they can.

Naxos is also noted for its **Towers** (over 30 in number, they are known as 'Pyrgi' and are the remains of fortified manor houses), **Castles**, and even the occasional fortified monastery for good measure. These litter the interior; most date from Medieval times. The closest one to the tourist strip is well-preserved **Paleopirgos Castle** one hour's walk inland via a track running from Plaka beach. Most of the Pyrgi require hard walking if you want to visit them, but they do offer a good starting point for those who enjoy walking holidays, and Naxos is a popular island among walkers. Anyone else taking time to explore the island by foot should step first in the direction of the bookshop on the promenade and buy a copy of Christian Ucke's excellent *Walking Tours on Naxos* (4000 GDR); this offers 16 suggested routes and a lot of background detail.

The final great sight on Naxos is the **Mount Zeus** and **Cave of Zeus** combination. Not a trek for the faint hearted, the walk (described in detail in the guide above) from the hill village of Filoti to the summit takes in the cave where, tradition has it, Zeus was raised. Truth to tell, the cave isn't on a par with the larger cave on Antiparos. Relatively shallow, it is more of a sloping cavern 150 m deep and is home to a substantial colony of bats and a curious species of large yellow spider. Few visitors venture much beyond the entrance (where there are the remains of a rough altar) if only because most don't appreciate the need to bring a torch until they get into it.

Paros

ΠΑΡΟΣ; 194 km²; pop. 7,900.

CODE ☎ 0284
PORT POLICE ☎ 21240
POLICE ☎ 21221
FIRST AID ☎ 22500

A large and well-placed island, Paros has become the de facto hub of the Greek ferry system in recent years, and it is now difficult for Cycladic island hoppers to avoid calling at some point during their holiday. As a result, Paros is apt to get horribly over-crowded at the peak of the High Season. In part this is due to the charms of the island itself, for it is ringed with good sandy beaches, is fertile inland (in a dusty sort of way), and now has plenty of nightlife into the bargain.

Paros' main port and tourist centre is at **Parikia** (though you find that except on the island itself all ticket agents and schedules simply refer to it as 'Paros'). Occupying a sheltered bay on the west coast, it has been the main island centre since the Bronze Age when an early Cycladic village existed on the site. It briefly lost its role as the island capital during the Ottoman period, when inland Lefkes took over (being far less vulnerable to pirate attack). Today the port town has re-emerged as the undisputed centre on the island, ribboning ever further along the shore. At its heart lies a typical Cycladic chora, complete with the odd wall of a Venetian kastro built on the site of the ancient acropolis in 1207. Neither are the best examples of their type (though the chora manages to retain a surprising amount of charm even when it is swarming with tourists), but are suitable symbols, in their way, of Paros as a whole.

Very much tied to the shoreline, Parikia does not extend inland to any great extent, and is neatly divided by the road running south from the recently extended ferry quay (Prombona St.). To the west lies the old part of town, to the east the modern hotel and beach strip. Between the two

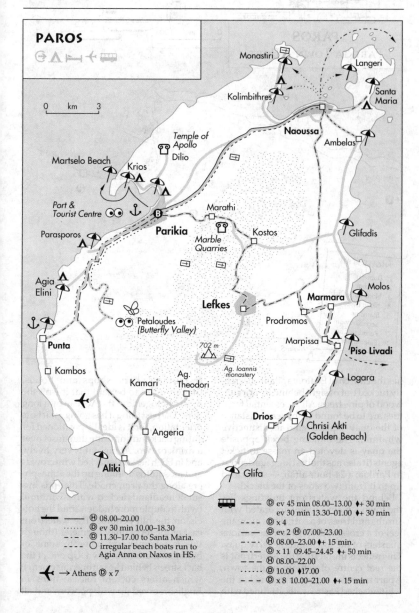

PAROS

0   km   3

Monastiri
Langeri
Kolimbithres
Santa Maria
Naoussa
Ambelas
Temple of Apollo
Dilio
Martselo Beach
Krios
Marathi
Glifadis
Port & Tourist Centre
Parikia
Marble Quarries
Kostos
Parasporos
Agia Elini
Petaloudes
(Butterfly Valley)
Lefkes
Marmara
Molos
Prodromos
Marpissa
Piso Livadi
Punta
702 m
Ag. Ioannis monastery
Logara
Kambos
Kamari
Ag. Theodori
Drios
Angeria
Chrisi Akti
(Golden Beach)
Aliki
Glifa

⊖ 08.00–20.00
..... ⓓ ev 30 min 10.00–18.30
–·–· ⓓ 11.30–17.00 to Santa Maria.
– – – ⭕ irregular beach boats run to Agia Anna on Naxos in HS.

✈ → Athens ⓓ x 7

— ⓓ ev 45 min 08.00–13.00 ♦+ 30 min
     ev 30 min 13.30–01.00 ♦+ 30 min
– – – ⓓ x 4
— ⓓ ev 2 07.00–23.00
–·–· ⊖ 08.00–23.00 ♦+ 15 min.
–··–·· ⓓ x 11 09.45–24.45 ♦+ 50 min
— ⊖ 08.00–22.00
..... ⓓ 10.00 ♦17.00
– – – ⓓ x 8 10.00–21.00 ♦+ 15 min

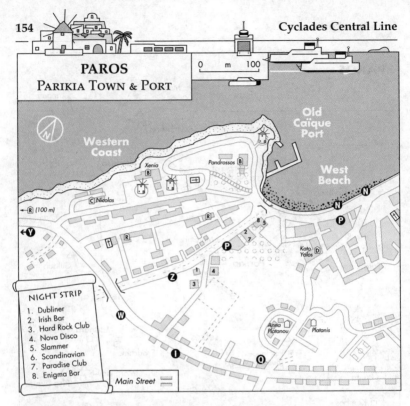

PAROS
PARIKIA TOWN & PORT

0   m   100

Old Caïque Port

Western Coast

West Beach

Xenia

Pandrossos

Nicolas

R (100 m)

Kato Yalos

Anna Platanou

Platanis

NIGHT STRIP

1. Dubliner
2. Irish Bar
3. Hard Rock Club
4. Nova Disco
5. Slammer
6. Scandinavian
7. Paradise Club
8. Enigma Bar

Main Street

lies the church of Ekatontapilani, discreetly tucked out of sight behind a park cum wood of pine trees. All the essential facilities are to be found within easy distance of the quay 'square' amd its distinctive windmill. The building block opposite the quay is devoted en masse to ticket agents (it also has the best luggage deposit in Parikia: a 24-hour affair — stairs lead up to it from two sides of the block).

Behind the waterfront buildings lies the town's main square; decorated with shrubs and trees of a sort, it has more the feel of a crossroads between the various quarters of the town and the ferry quay. This reflects the fact that the waterfront is the real centre of activity in the town. Apart from the section composed of the whitewashed kastro walls, it is lined with restaurants, bars, shops and hotels, though it has to be said that it isn't the most photogenic in the Aegean by a long way. The best thing it has going for it is its orientation; for it is ideally positioned for sitting back and admiring the sunset over a drink or two. At night it is very lively, and in High Season is packed with crowds and mosquitos drinking up the atmosphere along the promenade. This ends in a small headland decked with a windmill (with a couple more hidden amid the hotels on the hill behind). The waterfront east of the ferry quay is quieter (though this is relative) and home to some of better restaurants in town. Up one of the backstreets behind lies an open air cinema, which offers current release films in English, served up with popcorn and all

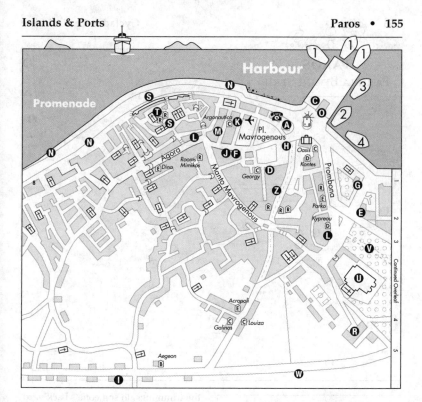

Key

A Tourist Information Office
B Bus Station (15 m)
C Hotel Information Kiosk
D Police / Tourist Police
E Hospital / Clinic
F National Bank of Greece
G Public WCs
H Taxi Rank
I Supermarket
J Bakery
K Pharmacy
L International Press
M Paros Craft Shop
N Tavernas

O Ferry Passenger Stalls
P Night Strip
Q Cinema Rex
R Archaeological Museum
S Frankish Kastro Walls
T Foundations of the
        Temple of Aphrodite
U Ekatontapiliani
        Cathedral &
        Baptistry
V Pine Wood Park
W Ring Road
X Naoussa Road
Y Punta Road
Z Street / River Bed

1 Ferries
2 Antiparos Town
     & Cave Tour
     Boats
3 Hydrofoils
4 Krios Beach &
     Camping
     Taxi Boats

*Panagia
Ekatontapiliani —
The Cathedral Church*

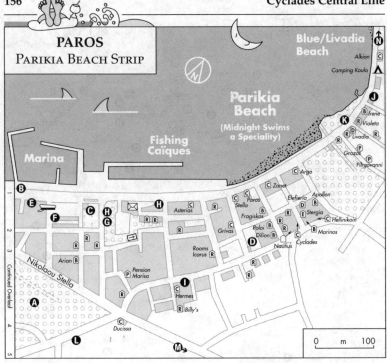

PAROS
PARIKIA BEACH STRIP

Blue/Livadia Beach

Parikia Beach
(Midnight Swims a Speciality)

Fishing Caïques

Marina

Nikolaou Stella

Continued Overleaf

Key

- Ⓐ Pine Wood Park
- Ⓑ Bus Station (All destinations)
- Ⓒ Excavated Classical & Hellenistic Cemetery
- Ⓓ Open Air Cinema
- Ⓔ Books & International Press
- Ⓕ Large Supermarket
- Ⓖ Mountain Bike Rental
- Ⓗ Moped Rental
- Ⓘ Supermarket
- Ⓙ Pizzeria
- Ⓚ Bar Strip
- Ⓛ Parikia Town Ring Road
- Ⓜ Naoussa Road
- Ⓝ Krios & Dilio Roads

---

the trimmings, in someone's back yard. A second cinema — the *Rex* — lies on the ring road that skirts the back of the town.

Nightlife in Parikia is dominated by the growing collection of cocktail bars along the waterfront, and the complex of bars and nightclubs lying off the riverbed-cum-road (dry in summer) that emerges behind the beach at the western end of the promenade. These start with the *Slammer Bar / 7 Muses Disco* and *Paradise Club*, continue past the *Nova Disco* bar before arriving at the real hot spot in Parikia; the large *Dubliner/ Cactus Shots/Down Under* and *Hard Rock Club* complex where almost everything goes on behind high walls and bamboo screens.

Parikia also has a number of beaches within easy reach. The best and most popular is the main town beach, opposite the tourist hotel and restaurant strip east of the ferry quay (during the small hours it plays host to drunken bathers kitted out in their underclothes). There is another — albeit more skimpy — beach on the east side of the bay that is also crowded, and a less attractive strand on the west end of the town promenade. All are adequate for the odd day of sunbathing, but are pretty inferior compared to some of the other beaches on Paros. One of these, a collection of coves a boat ride across the bay at Krios, is easily accessible from Parikia, and has many fans thanks to the opportunity it offers to remove more beach-wear than is acceptable nearer the town (i.e. everything). Buses from Parikia are usually very crowded, and geared to moving tourists to beaches further afield. Both the bus station (in the form of a dinky little kiosk) and the beach boats operate from points just to the east of the ferry quay.

The fenced-off ferry quay is one of the largest in the Cyclades and in High Season sees ferries queuing up to berth during the midday and midnight busy periods. Waiting ferry passengers are corralled in three quayside passenger stalls. At the ferry end of each is a gate that is unlocked when the ferry calls; it therefore pays to be in the correct stall (the port police chalk up the names of the next three boats due in on blackboards on the town side of each). When arriving at Paros you should also note that the quay exit gate is on the west/old town side of the passenger stall block (this is kept locked until the first arrivals reach it, to prevent stall-jumping by departing passengers). On Paros the sheer number of tourists also dictate that it is advisable to buy your tickets well in advance if you are planning to take one of the smaller ferries in High Season. Apart from the crowds, the only problem you are likely to encounter is the delightfully

large choice of connections available. During the Low Season Paros remains the best served Aegean island, though daily departures rarely reach double figures.

Around Paros there are a number of tourist resorts and beaches that are easily accessible thanks to the good (but invariably very crowded) bus service. The picturesque chora town of **Naoussa**, set in a bay on the northern coast and dominated by a tall Orthodox church, has rapidly expanded to become the island's second major tourist centre. Smaller and prettier than Parikia, it shares one thing in common, in as much as it is also bursting at the seams with tourists during the summer months. At the height of the season numbers get quite oppressive as its capacity to absorb the numbers is not nearly so great. At the centre of the town is a white-washed chora. Laid out in an almost grid-like pattern, it is more boutique-filled than its Parikia counterpart. In spite of this, it is the taverna-lined waterfront that is the great draw, with a charming caïque harbour backed by pretty Venetian houses (now doubling as dreamy tavernas) and protected on the seaward harbour wall side by the remains of a kastro-cum-tower — now reduced to a surf-kissed breakwater. Running through, and dominating, the centre of town is a dry (in summer) river bed that is home to the town bus stop.

The chora lies to the east, gradually ascending the hillside to the dominating church and a handful of derelict windmills to the north. West of the river bed the town is reduced to a ribbon of houses running a mere two or three blocks deep along the coast. This coast road is home to the OTE and Police station as well as the best Naoussa can offer by way of a beach; be warned, this isn't a lot. As a result, boats run from the waterfront to beaches around the bay, and round the headland to the beach at Santa Maria (also reached via a daily bus from Parikia or a local bus from Naoussa).

The number three resort town, **Piso Livadi**, is a quaint village gathered around a cute little harbour on the east side of the island, with a thrice-weekly link to Amorgos, besides being a nice place to stay if you want to escape the worst of the crowds. It is also conveniently close to the island's best beach (all the best beaches on Paros are to be found along this stretch of coast) at **Chrisi Akti** (Golden Beach). As the name suggests, this is an excellent stretch of sandy coast and is popular with wind-surfers (despite the pretensions of less attractive Santa Maria beach to the north). Nearby lies the village of **Drios**; now rapidly being spoilt by ugly uncontrolled hotel development, it is the destination of Parikia buses.

The fourth centre of note is at **Aliki** on the south coast. Little more than a quiet beach village, it offers a peaceful alternative to the main resorts. In High Season it also has an irregular taxi boat service to Antiparos (sometimes continuing east to a beach on the islet of **Despotiko**). Other destinations have less going for them.

The inland chora village of **Lefkes** developed as the island capital during the days when pirates ruled the seas, forcing the abandonment of the traditional centre at Parikia. Built in the shape of a vague amphitheatre in the hills, it is well worth a look and is an appealing hang-over from the days before Paros was irredeemably changed by tourism. Access is easy via the frequent Parikia—Piso Livadi buses; though it is better to avoid them when the masses are either travelling to or from the east coast beaches.

Parikia buses also run hourly to the middle of nowhere. This is the lonely quay at **Punta**; landing place for the regular Antiparos car ferries (times are posted up on the chapel wall near the quay).

◢

A–C class island hotels and pensions on Paros are listed (along with their prices) in the Accommodation Office on the ferry quay. The staff will phone around for you. Plentiful

offers of rooms also greet the early boats (many by room owners from nearby Antiparos), but prices rise in High Season when the morning ferries from Piraeus start arriving after midday. From then on you will have to be prepared to pay up or look further afield. Naoussa is the best bet, as the town is plastered with 'Rooms' signs. Piso Livadi also has a reasonable supply.

Well-endowed **Parikia** is home to the greatest number of the island's hotels. These are divided between the old part of town (mostly smaller, budget establishments) and the new, tourist dominated suburb to the east (which is home to the bulk of the package tour hotels). Other hotels lie around the town environs — including the pricey *Xenia* (☎ 21394) located 100 m west of the town's west beach behind a couple of windmills.

Mid-range hotels mostly cater for package tourists, but they are quick to snap up island hoppers to fill any empty beds. Some even have signs outside indicating vacancies. The waterfront east of the ferry quay includes the C-class *Asterias* (☎ 21797), *Stella* (☎ 21502) and the *Argo* (☎ 21367). Quieter hotels lie in the streets behind, including the *Cyclades* (☎ 22048) and the new *Hotel John* (☎ 22797). If you want to splash out at the middle end of the range, the C-class *Argonautica* (☎ 21440) is conveniently placed behind the main town square with attractive, if pricey, rooms. Near the ferry quay are a couple of reasonable D-class establishments that are also easy to find: the *Kontes* (☎ 21096) and the *Kypreou* (☎ 21383). The latter is the cheaper of the two.

Another popular group of hotels lie along the river bed cum road: the C-class *Galinos* (☎ 21480), *Louiza* (☎ 22122) and E-class *Acropoli* (☎ 21521). Other E-class hotels in town include the *Dina* (☎ 21325) and the *Parko* (☎ 22213). At the budget end of the market are a number of establishments offering rooms (these are effectively backpackers' pensions), notably *Rooms Icarus* (☎ 21695) in the new strip and the better *Rooms Mimikos* (☎ 21437) in the chora part of town.

Other towns also have hotels on offer (again details are available from the Accommodation Office in Parikia). **Naoussa** is the best equipped, with the B-class *Naoussa* (☎ 51207), overlooking the waterfront, standing out from the rest. Another town with a good hotel named after it is **Piso Livadi** which has the C-class *Piso Livadi* (☎ 41309) near the town bus stop.

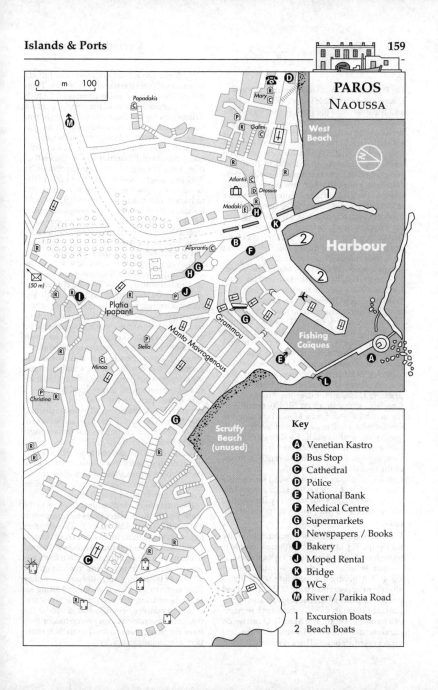

PAROS
NAOUSSA

West Beach

Harbour

1 Excursion Boats

2 Beach Boats

Fishing Caiques

Scruffy Beach (unused)

Platia Ipapanti

Manto Mavrogenous

Grammou

Papadakis

Mary

Galini

Atlantis

Drossia

Madaki

Aliprantis

Stella

Minoa

Christina

0   m   100

Key

 A Venetian Kastro
 B Bus Stop
 C Cathedral
 D Police
 E National Bank
 F Medical Centre
 G Supermarkets
 H Newspapers / Books
 I Bakery
 J Moped Rental
 K Bridge
 L WCs
 M River / Parikia Road

1 Excursion Boats
2 Beach Boats

A

On Paros there are a large number of sites:
Camping Koula (☎ 22081): nice olive-grove site
and the nearest to the port. A member of the
Harmonie camping scheme, the site cashes in
on its convenient location, though the down
side is that sleepers can expect more disruption
than most from 03.00 ferry arrivals and disco
returnees. This site is unusual in having a
computer that logs your arrival time and then
calculates your bill when you leave. This can
work to your advantage if you check in after
midnight (you get a night's free camping), but
take care to check your bill; it has been known
for campers newly arrived in Greece to find
that the computer has recorded their checking
in five hours before their plane left London
(and then charged them accordingly).
Camping Krios (☎ 21705) is one of the newer
sites on the beach opposite the port. It is sadly
let down by a lack of regular cleaning. The
taxi-boat link to Parikia is also not conducive
to nightlife or catching an early morning ferry.
Parasporos Camping (☎ 21394), is a better site 3
km south of the town with mini-buses that
provide campers with a free service to and
from town. Past years have seen free tents
provided to campers out of High Season.
Camping Naoussa (☎ 51398) is one of the better
sites on Paros if a frenetic nightlife isn't a
priority; again, mini-buses meet boats.
Camping Surfing Beach (☎ 51013), nestling in
the scrub behind Santa Maria beach, is the
newest site on Paros. Popular with windsurfers using the beach. Facilities are good,
with a free shuttle service to and from Parikia.
Camping Agia Elini is an indifferent site on one
of the best island beaches.
Captain Kafkis Camping (☎ 41392), 1 km outside
Piso Livadi, is for those who like a quiet life;
you have to make your own way here as this
site doesn't send mini-buses to meet ferries.

∞

Considering that Paros was famed in antiquity
for the quality of its marble (Parian marble is
more translucent than other types in Greece
— that is to say, light penetrates further
through it, giving it a sparkling white, light-
absorbent appearance) it is sad that the island
boasts no classical archaeological site of importance (though there is the scanty remains
of a temple at Dilio). The **Marble Quarries** do
survive just outside Marathi, though few
visitors venture beyond the cave-like entrance.

The **Venetian Kastro** at **Parikia** was largely
constructed from the remains of archaic **Temples of Demeter & Apollo**, remnants of which
can be seen in the form of the circular column
drums now embedded in the surviving kastro
walls and the black foundations of the temple
base. The town does, however, have one notable architectural monument: the 6 c. AD cathedral church of **Ekatontapiliani**. This rather
odd name (thought to be a corruption of 'in
the lower town') now means 'Our Lady of the
100 doors' — for the building was supposed
to have had as many. Truth to tell you would
be hard put to know it today; though a number
of students of architecture have managed to
trace a dozen on their first attempt and 99 after
a few ouzos. The 100th is widely believed to
have been carried off by the Turks (a delightful
notion as it suggests in a subtle way that the
old enemy is completely unhinged along with
it). Tradition also claims that the church was
designed by Isidore of Miletus; with the
construction carried out by his pupil Ignatius.
When it was completed, Isidore is said to have
been so jealous of the church's beauty that he
attacked his pupil on the roof with the result
that both fell to their deaths in the ensuing
struggle. Given that Isidore was one of the
architects responsible for the infinitely more
wondrous Agia Sofia in İstanbul/Constan-
tinople one suspects this is local hyperbole.
The oldest part of the building is Roman
anyway. The **Archaeological Museum** behind
the church has part of the Roman pavement
uncovered in the church on display amongst
other island exhibits.

South of Parikia, the old town of **Lefkes** is
the main destination for tour buses thanks to
its old chora atmosphere. The main sights in
town are the churches — notably the white
marble church of the Holy Trinity.

The final tourist destination of note is to the
Valley of the Butterflies (alias tiger moths) at
Petaloudes (from May to July). These gather
before dying to mate in this quiet spot. Unfortunately, the poor creatures are now subjected
to clapping and shouting exhibitions by tourists — thus alarming them into flight: the
clouds of butterflies are, after all, what they
have come to see. This is very debilitating for
animals nearing the end of their lives and
trying to conserve energy, and is producing
dire consequences; as every jump means they
have the energy for one less hump their numbers are declining rapidly.

Santorini Taxi Boat

Caldera View from Oia/Ia

SANTORINI /THIRA

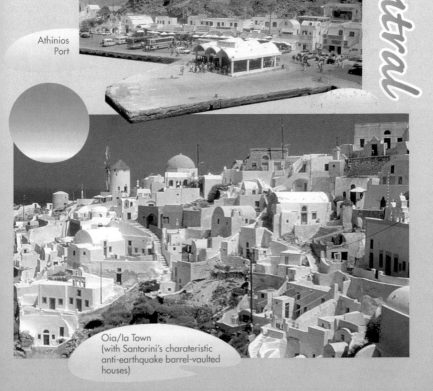

Athinios Port

Oia/Ia Town
(with Santorini's charateristic anti-earthquake barrel-vaulted houses)

SANTORINI
AKROTIRI Excavation

Boxing Children Fresco

Building Delta (East Side)

West House & Triangular Square

BUILDING TYPES

Large Ashlar Block Buildings

Large Town Houses

Appartment Type Buildings

Commerical Buildings

Unexplored Buildings

AKROTIRI C. 1750 BC

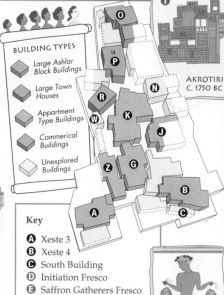

Key

- **A** Xeste 3
- **B** Xeste 4
- **C** South Building
- **D** Initiation Fresco
- **E** Saffron Gatherers Fresco
- **F** Adorants Fresco
- **G** Building Beta
- **H** Boxing Children & Antelope Frescoes
- **I** Blue Monkeys Fresco
- **J** Xeste 2
- **K** Building Delta
- **L** Stone Sacral Horns
- **M** Lilies or Spring Fresco
- **N** Xeste 5
- **O** Sector Alpha
- **P** House of the Ladies
- **Q** Fresco of the Ladies
- **R** West House
- **S** Fisherboys Fresco
- **T** Miniature Fresco
- **U** Bathroom
- **V** Triangular Square
- **W** House of the Anchor
- **X** Propylon
- **Y** Telchines Road
- **Z** Building Gamma

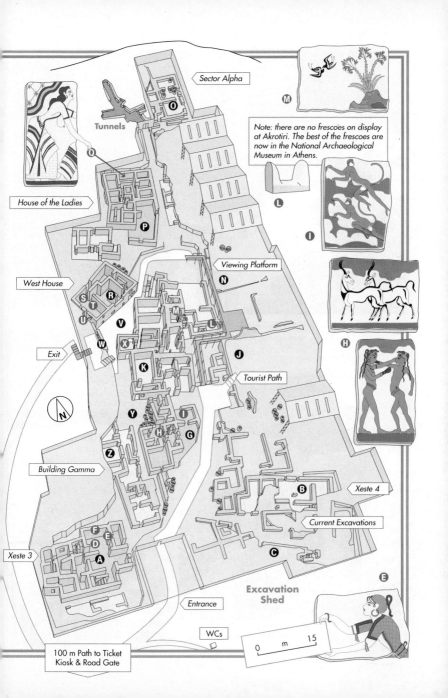

Sector Alpha

O

M

Tunnels

Q

Note: there are no frescoes on display at Akrotiri. The best of the frescoes are now in the National Archaeological Museum in Athens.

L

House of the Ladies

P

I

Viewing Platform

N

West House

S **T** **R**

M

U **V**

L

W **X**

J

H

Exit

K

Tourist Path

N

Y

I

H **G**

Z

Building Gamma

B

Xeste 4

F **E**

Current Excavations

D

C

Xeste 3

A

E

Excavation Shed

Entrance

WCs

0   m   15

100 m Path to Ticket Kiosk & Road Gate

SANTORINI/THIRA
View of the Volcano/Kameni Is.
from Fira Town

SYROS
Ermoupolis

Cyclades

THIRASIA
Main Street in August

Santorini / Thira

ΣΑΝΤΟΡΙΝΙ / ΘΗΡΑ; 73 km²; pop. 7,100.

CODE ☎ 0286
TOURIST POLICE ☎ 22649
PORT POLICE ☎ 22239
HOSPITAL ☎ 22237

The most spectacular (and one of the most expensive) of all the Greek islands, Santorini is subject to ever increasing waves of tourists drawn by the landscape, the archaeological discoveries at Akrotiri, and the legend of Atlantis. The island is commonly known by two names: the Venetian 'Santorini' (after the 3 C. AD St. Irene who died in exile hereabouts) or its Classical name of 'Thira' (now reinstated as its official name). 'Santorini' is more popular with tourists. Ferry operators usually prefer 'Thira' (also transcribed as 'Fira'), in the interests of brevity on ship destination boards.

The island is the largest fragment of a volcanic archipelago made up of the broken remnants of the largest caldera on earth. It is now thought by many to be the origin of the Atlantis legend; the in-pouring of the sea into the caldera during a massive eruption circa 1500 BC giving early sailors the impression that the greater part of the island had sunk, taking the Minoan settlements on the island with it. Within the caldera, subsequent volcanic eruptions (the last in 1925–26) have spawned new islets of ominous, black, razor-sharp lava. The volcano is now quietly simmering with sulphur emissions and hot springs. If this wasn't enough by way of icing the tourist cake, the caldera rim is frosted with scenic white cubist towns that take a tumble every time an earthquake hits. The island also has a reputation as a home for vampires. All this ensures that Santorini is on the itinerary of every cruise ship, day-tripper and casual tourist within range, and usually full to overflowing, regardless of the time of year (a major problem in itself as the island has no fresh water springs;

supplies are tankered in daily from the mainland).

The centre of activity on Santorini is **Fira Town** (also transcribed as 'Thira' and 'Phira'). This large island capital is perched precariously on the edge of the caldera rim, with a switchback staircase (carpeted with donkey droppings) down the crater wall, and a cable-car for those who don't care for the donkey rides or the 587 awkward steps. These run to the old port of Skala Fira — and its mooring buoys for cruise ships — below the town. Now unashamedly a tourist centre, Fira has preserved enough of its charm to make a visit enjoyable. This might not seem to be the case if you arrive in the early hours when the main town square is thronged with nightlife fans and is literally ankle deep in litter, but once the surprisingly efficient sweeps have done their stuff and revealed once again the black lava stone used to cobble the streets, a vague semblance of the Greek island idyll is restored, and even enhanced by the weird nature of the place. For Fira Town rolls dramatically with the landscape, falling fast from the caldera rim to the coastal plain, with its views of neighbouring Anafi. The rim itself is by no means level, and has the buildings rolling up and down every photogenic step of the way.

The great attraction in town is the view over the caldera and the volcano (principally from Ipapantis St.). Bars and telescopes clutter up the best viewing places, fronting the warren of boutique-filled backstreets behind. Hidden away in these are several museums. The town currently has two Archaeological Museums: the old museum, filled largely with post-Minoan artifacts, and a new museum. Built several years ago to house the Minoan frescoes found on the island, it is only now being completed. Standing by the town bus station, it is *just* possible that it will finally open its doors in 1999. Finally, Fira has a privately run town museum —

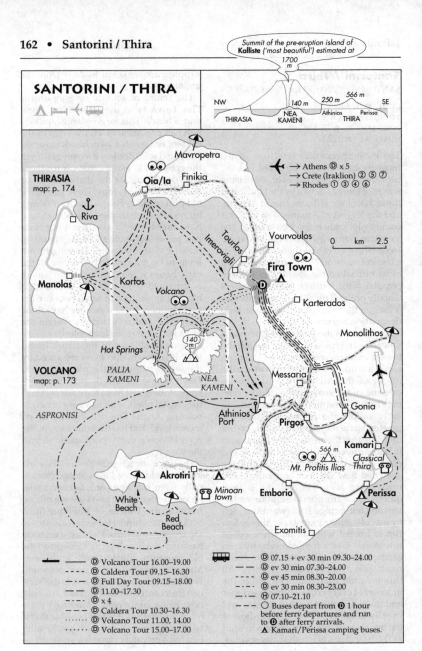

Summit of the pre-eruption island of **Kalliste** ('most beautiful') estimated at
1700 m

NW — 140 m — 250 m — 566 m — SE
THIRASIA — NEA KAMENI — Athinios — THIRA
Perissa

SANTORINI / THIRA

Mavropetra

THIRASIA
map: p. 174

Riva

Oia/Ia   Finikia

→ Athens Ⓓ x 5
→ Crete (Iraklion) ② ⑤ ⑦
→ Rhodes ① ③ ④ ⑥

Tourlos
Imerovigli

Vourvoulos

0 — km — 2.5

Fira Town

Ⓓ

Manolas   Korfos   *Volcano*

Karterados

Monolithos

Hot Springs

140 m

VOLCANO
map: p. 173

PALIA KAMENI

NEA KAMENI

Messaria

ASPRONISI

Gonia

Athinios
Port

Pirgos

Kamari

566 m

Classical Thira

Mt. Profitis Ilias

Akrotiri

Minoan town

Emborio

Perissa

White Beach

Red Beach

Exomitis

— Ⓓ Volcano Tour 16.00–19.00
--- Ⓓ Caldera Tour 09.15–16.30
–·– Ⓓ Full Day Tour 09.15–18.00
— — Ⓓ 11.00–17.30
–··– Ⓓ x 4
···· Ⓓ Caldera Tour 10.30–16.30
······ Ⓓ Volcano Tour 11.00, 14.00
······ Ⓓ Volcano Tour 15.00–17.00

— Ⓓ 07.15 + ev 30 min 09.30–24.00
— — Ⓓ ev 30 min 07.30–24.00
---- Ⓓ ev 45 min 08.30–20.00
--- Ⓓ ev 30 min 08.30–23.00
— — Ⓗ 07.10–21.10
— — Ο Buses depart from Ⓓ 1 hour before ferry departures and run to Ⓓ after ferry arrivals.
▲ Kamari/Perissa camping buses.

known as the Megaro Gyzi — which is a repository for odds and ends. Its most interesting exhibits are unlabelled photos of the pre-earthquake town (Fira was all but levelled on the 9th of July 1956 by a tremor that killed 53 people and destroyed 2400 homes). Along the rim you will find occasional fragments of buildings that fell into the caldera during the 1956 earthquake (one is apt to wonder if the restaurants perched precariously on the rim are really such a good idea). If losing many of its old buildings wasn't bad enough, Fira has suffered further disfigurement thanks to the large pumice quarry at the southern edge of the town; a gaping hole in the caldera wall that has been excavated to the pre-eruption level, revealing the stumps of petrified trees.

To get the most out of Fira you have to pick your moment. Early mornings are the best time to explore for is it cooler, the rising sun gives the buildings a lovely warming glow, ferries glide silently across the caldera over a cobalt-blue sea, and the streets are free from the camera-clutching hordes and the moped packs that cruise round looking for someone to mow down. As the sun sets the town comes into its own again as the vibrant nightlife scene takes over. Radiating out from the main square are a profusion of bars and clubs that have one characteristic in common — they are all expensive. As Santorini will make a huge hole in your pocket you could do worse than dance in one; the *Tithora Club*, near the top of the port stairway, offers a dance floor in a 15 c. pumice cave and troglodyte male dancers. There are also three other large disco/clubs in town: the *Dionysos*, the *Enigma* and the *Koo Club*. Popular bars in Fira include the *Backpackers'* (aptly sited near the youth hostels), the *Blue Note* (a bar turned pool hall) and the very expensive *Tropical* (on the caldera rim).

The island ferry terminus is at **Athinios**, 4 km south of Fira. Little more than a long quay — complete with a passenger shed — at the bottom of the caldera cliff face, it is backed with ticket agencies, tavernas and a WC at the far end. It exists here solely because it was at this point that it was possible to cut a switch-back road down the cliff-side. In spite of this, access is still very limited; in High Season the number of vehicles attempting to reach the quay can result in major traffic jams, and it is not unknown for bus passengers to have to walk down the cliff to join their boats. These often hang around for a few hours: Santorini's popularity is reflected in the ferry schedules; some 9 hours sailing from Piraeus, the island is an obvious terminus for boats doing a regular daily round trip.

The caldera rim also has other settlements clinging to it. The most important of these is the pretty small northern town of **Oia** (otherwise transcribed as 'Ia' and pronounced as 'EEa'). Also badly damaged by the 1956 earthquake, the town has been rebuilt after a fashion. Promoted as the 'Paris of the Aegean' for no apparent reason other than its photogenic nature (the best picture postcard caldera rim views are invariably of Oia), it has fewer crowds and a nicer atmosphere than Fira; this along with a reconstructed windmill, an excellent Naval Museum, and superb sunset views, brings in the tour parties by the coach load. Sunsets aside, Oia is best explored during the day. Relatively cheap buses run from Thira (though the road is a disappointment as it runs too far inland for travellers to enjoy sweeping caldera views), leaving you to explore at your own pace. When you are tired of walking you always have the option of descending one of the two cliff-side stairways to the tiny port below the town. This has seen ferries decant passengers into taxi boats in past years, but now relies on fish-dish tavernas for its income. There is also a cliff-side path running back into the

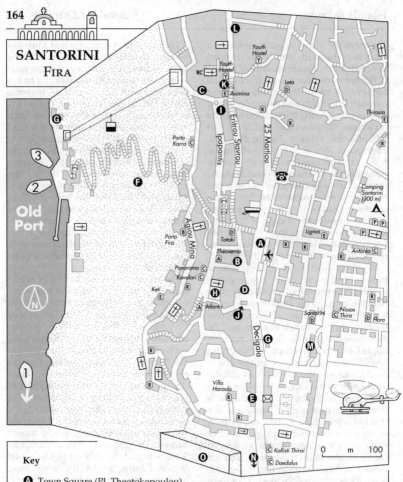

SANTORINI
FIRA

Key

- **A** Town Square (Pl. Theotokopoulou)
- **B** National Bank of Greece
- **C** Cable Car Ticket Office
- **D** Bus Station (all destinations)
- **E** Police
- **F** Stairway / Mule track to Old Port
- **G** Public WCs
- **H** Cathedral
- **I** Old Archaeological Museum
- **J** New Archaeological Museum
- **K** Megaro Gyzi Museum
- **L** Old Style (unwhitewashed) Street
- **M** Medical Centre
- **N** Road to Port (4 km) & Heliport (2 km)
- **O** Pumice Quarry

- **1** Athinios Port / Ferry Terminal (4 km)
- **2** Old Port Tour Boats & Thirasia ferry
- **3** Cruise Ship taxi boat arrival point

caldera basin and ending at swimming rocks with a small — chapel topped — lava stack 20 m offshore.

Following the rim around there are several other small villages that are increasingly filled with expensive tourist accommodation, but which are still noticeably less spoilt than the main towns. The biggest of these are **Finikia**, just outside Oia, and **Tourlos** and **Imeravigli**. These last two run into the residential northern section of Fira Town (not shown on the map opposite).

Turning inland from the caldera rim, the bulk of the island slopes steeply away and looks rather scruffy, being dry and treeless; the land being given over to producing tomatoes and ground-crawling vines that provide the wine for which Santorini is famous. The most accessible vineyards — with imaginative names like 'Volcano' — are to be found near Kamari and they thrive on a procession of tour coaches that bring the masses to get their tongues around labels like 'Lava'. The reds certainly live up to the billing; giving the taste-buds a big bang that rapidly dwindles to an ashy nothing.

Dotted around the grey volcanic landscape between the vines are a number of whitewashed villages, which these days serve to mop up the tourists who can't find beds elsewhere. The largest of these — such as impressive hilltop **Pirgos**, and less dramatic **Emborio** and **Gonia**, have become minor centres in their own right. The best, however, is the dusty village of **Akrotiri** on the southern wing of the caldera rim. Only now opening up to tourism, it still retains much of its traditional character, thanks to the odd windmill, though the nearby Minoan town excavation is helping to change this. The town also offers good views of the volcano set against the backdrop of the towns of Fira and Oia on the caldera rim (telescopes are provided on the headland to the west of the town). The down side to Akrotiri is the lack of a convenient nearby beach.

Volcano islands are not generally noted for having brilliant beaches, and Santorini is no exception. Beaches there are in profusion, but most are strewn with black pebbles or pumice. However on the southeast coast, the beaches consist of wide stretches of black sand which, although it lacks sparkle and gets painfully hot (leaving sun worshippers looking like so many rows of pink sausages in a Teflon frying pan), has prompted the emergence of two large and successful beach resorts at Perissa and Kamari. Both are unashamedly tourist centres and nothing more, but they cater for very different markets. **Perissa** is very much the haven of the independent and budget traveller with a host of pensions, rooms and bars running along a main road running inland from the beach. **Kamari** is better established and more up-market, with a lot of package tour hotels and a sophisticated waterfront. It is also conveniently placed for the island's airport. The two resorts are separated by an iron-curtain of a headland which is topped by the ruined Classical and Roman capital of the island. Access on the Perissa side is via a well-trodden, but poor, path that requires a good hour's hard walking. On the Kamari side there is a longer switch-back road (built for the coach tours) that is serviced by minibuses. Both road and path arrive at a roundabout of sorts, usually complete with a van selling refreshments.

Other beaches on Santorini are to be found near the Minoan excavation at Akrotiri. The site — and its bus link to Fira — is only a short walk from the southern shore and caïques to two more of the island's beaches; Red Beach and White Beach. Both are named after the colour of their cinders-cum-sand. Oia also has an indifferent beach nearby, at Mavropetra.

⊢

The supply of beds dries up early in High Season on Santorini. Even if you arrive on the first of the Piraeus morning boats (berthing around 15.00), you could have to settle for a

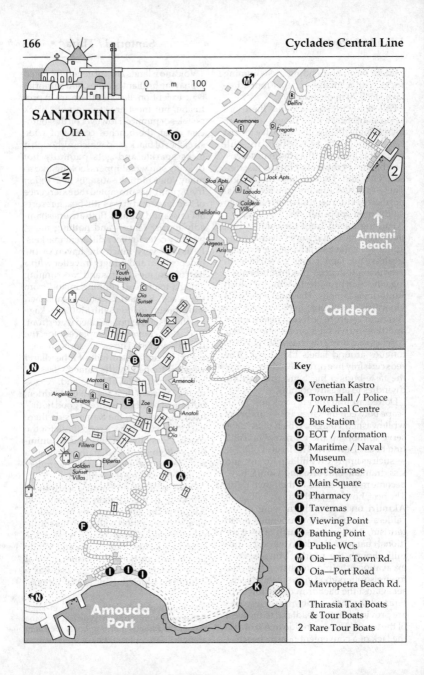

SANTORINI
OIA

0 m 100

Caldera

↑ Armeni Beach

Key

A Venetian Kastro
B Town Hall / Police / Medical Centre
C Bus Station
D EOT / Information
E Maritime / Naval Museum
F Port Staircase
G Main Square
H Pharmacy
I Tavernas
J Viewing Point
K Bathing Point
L Public WCs
M Oia—Fira Town Rd.
N Oia—Port Road
O Mavropetra Beach Rd.

1 Thirasia Taxi Boats & Tour Boats
2 Rare Tour Boats

Amouda Port

night in a campsite or hostel before finding something more to your taste. The more expensive hotels tend to lie on the caldera rim (if you choose to stay in one, it pays to forget both your bank balance and the fact that when the last earth-quake struck most of the rimside buildings ended up a lot nearer sea level than they were before). Top of the range, and a landmark in its own right, is the chunky A-class *Atlantis* (☎ 22232) near the cathedral. Nearby lies the B-class *Porto Fira* (☎ 22849). To the north of this is the C-class *Porto Karra* (☎22 979), while two more C-class hotels lie up the slope: the *Panorama* (☎ 22481) and *Kavalari* (☎ 22455).

The east side of Fira Town offers the best prospect of finding a bed in High Season, with a number of 'cheaper' hotels. These include the C-class *Nissos Thira* (☎ 23252) and *Antonia* (☎ 22879), the D-class *Santorini* (☎ 22593) and *Flora* (☎ 81524), and the E-class *Lignos* (☎ 23 101) and *Thirasia* (☎ 22546). The road to the campsite is also worth trying as it is lined with pensions. Other hotels lie to the south of the town, including the C-class *Kallisti Thirai* (☎ 22317) and the *Daedalus* (☎ 22834). More hotels are being built to the south, overlooking the ugly old pumice quarry — pretty desperate stuff. The cable-car area of town also has a number of cheaper establishments. These include three youth hostels — the *Youth Hostel* (☎22722) on Eritrou Stavrou being easiest to find — and the E-class *Asimina* (☎ 22034). Inland the D-class *Leta* (☎ 22540) stands near the main road. A final option is to head for the village of **Karterados** which sups up the tourist overspill at the cost of a thirty minute walk into town.

Perissa is also popular with two large hostels on the outskirts of town. There are also plenty of pensions and small hotels offering relatively cheap beds. These include the E-class *Meltemi* (☎ 81325), *Boubis* (☎ 81202), and *Marouisana* (☎ 81124) on the main road. Rather more up-market is the D-class *Marianna* (☎ 81286), complete with pool.

Kamari has less non-pre-booked beds on offer, and outlets offering rooms are decidedly thin on the ground. The better bets here are the C-class *Akis* (☎ 31670) and *Adonis* (☎ 319 56), the D-class *Blue Sea* (☎ 31481) and *Andreas* (☎ 31692), and the E-class *Dionysos* (☎ 31310).

Other towns with hotels and rooms include **Oia** — complete with a good *Youth Hostel Oia* (☎ 71465), and **Pirgos** on the road to the port.

A

There are four campsites on Santorini; most have mini-buses meeting ferries:

Camping Santorini (☎ 22944) lies down the hill from Fira Town, and is easily the most convenient if you want to be close to the island's transportation hub and nightlife. The site has a small swimming pool, an excellent mini-market and reasonable tree cover. Prices are typical for Santorini: (i.e. 200 GDR more expensive than sites on Paros but still cheaper than Mykonos). In High Season the site can be very crowded: the numbers attempting illegal entry has resulted in heavy camping pass checking in past years. The site is a member of the *Harmonie* camping scheme.

Perissa Beach Camping (☎ 81343) is an equally expensive and crowded beach site right in the centre of the Perissa. The camping entrance also acts as a general information centre. With a fair amount of tree cover, the site is great if you want to stagger straight from bar to sea via a tent. The down side is the noise level and the saltwater showers.

Caldera View Camping (☎ 82010), outside the village of Akrotiri, is the newest site on Santorini. A member of the *Sunshine Camping* scheme, the site has a swimming pool and new facilities, it has bungalows on site as well. On the wrong side of the road to actually have a 'view' of the caldera and too far from the island's beaches or nightlife, this campsite appears to be struggling to bring in the crowds.

Kamari Camping (☎ 31453) is a municipal site (which means poorer facilities and fewer campers). Located on the main road out of Kamari, it suffers from being 1.7 km from its namesake beach and looking half abandoned. Only open from June to September, it does have plenty of shade. No mini-bus service.

∞

The whole 'Thira' archipelago is one vast tourist attraction, and there is sufficient sightseeing to fill a good four days, though tour buses — all taking in the inevitable winery — manage to cram a lot into a few hours. In addition to the caldera rim towns of Fira and Oia there are three major sights — the Minoan town of **Akrotiri**, the Hellenistic town (known as **Ancient Thira**) on the headland between Perissa and Kamari, and the caldera **Volcano** islands and rim villages. Although the first two of these offer only a couple of hours exploration, if you are using local transport, it is best to allow a day to visit each.

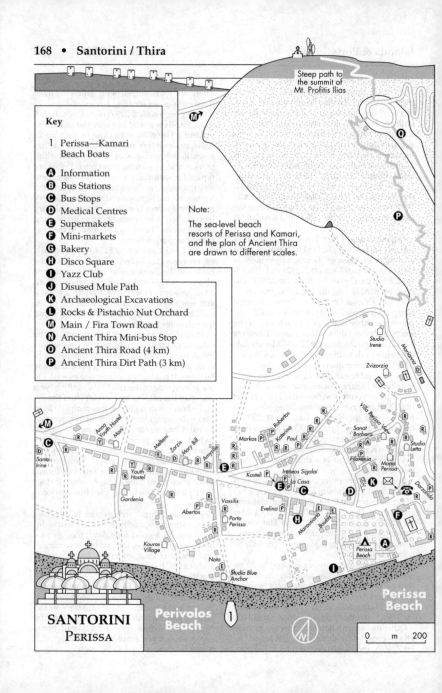

Key

1 Perissa—Kamari
  Beach Boats

Ⓐ Information
Ⓑ Bus Stations
Ⓒ Bus Stops
Ⓓ Medical Centres
Ⓔ Supermakets
Ⓕ Mini-markets
Ⓖ Bakery
Ⓗ Disco Square
Ⓘ Yazz Club
Ⓙ Disused Mule Path
Ⓚ Archaeological Excavations
Ⓛ Rocks & Pistachio Nut Orchard
Ⓜ Main / Fira Town Road
Ⓝ Ancient Thira Mini-bus Stop
Ⓞ Ancient Thira Road (4 km)
Ⓟ Ancient Thira Dirt Path (3 km)

Note:

The sea-level beach
resorts of Perissa and Kamari,
and the plan of Ancient Thira
are drawn to different scales.

Steep path to
the summit of
Mt. Profitis Ilias

SANTORINI
PERISSA

Perivolos Beach

Perissa
Beach

0   m   200

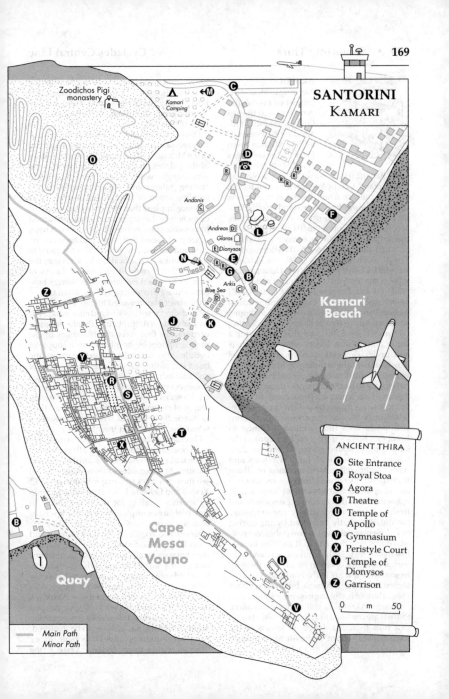

SANTORINI
KAMARI

Zoodichos Pigi
monastery

Kamari
Camping

Andonis

Andreas
Glaros
Dionysos

Arkis
Blue Sea

Kamari
Beach

Cape
Mesa
Vouno

Quay

ANCIENT THIRA

O Site Entrance
R Royal Stoa
S Agora
T Theatre
U Temple of
Apollo
V Gymnasium
X Peristyle Court
Y Temple of
Dionysos
Z Garrison

0   m   50

Main Path
Minor Path

Akrotiri

Nestling in an undistinguished ravine that runs down to the sea beyond Akrotiri village, lies the Pompeii-an-like Minoan town (map between pages 160–161) that has elevated Santorini to the top of the archaeological world map. A complete town buried by the ash and pumice from the massive eruption that blew the pre-Santorini island apart, Akrotiri is a sightseeing 'must' — even though the accessible area is quite small (you will be hard put to make a visit to the excavation last half an hour). Buses run direct to the site from Fira Town. Open ②–⑦ 08.30–15.00, the entrance fee is 1200 GDR. If you really want to appreciate what is on view you can't do much better than read *Art and Religion in Thera* (2000 GDR) beforehand; this is an excellent guide (complete with reconstructions of the fresco rooms) and is on sale in tourist shops in Fira Town.

Protected by a tin roof that makes for a stuffy atmosphere, the 35-century-old site is still under excavation. Archaeologists are slowly unearthing an amazing Minoan town, with all the attributes of high civilization that have come to be the hallmark of this remarkable pre-Greek people. These range from the humble street drains (that didn't appear elsewhere in the Mediterranean for a millennium) and inside WCs (that weren't a feature in European homes until a century ago) to the surprisingly modernist appearance of their houses (equipped with large windows and central light wells). Most amazing of all are the large number of wall frescos — most reduced to fragments that have to be painstakingly reassembled — that exhibit a spontaneity and freshness that seems wholly contemporary (an illusion greatly enhanced by the boxing boys fresco, which depicts two pubescent naked youths sporting Michael Jackson look-a-like hairstyles). Sadly, until the new archaeological museum opens in Fira Town, all the frescoes on view are in the National Archaeological Museum in Athens, but even without them, the site is still impressive enough.

Because Akrotiri is still under excavation, tourists are confined to a predetermined route that runs though a couple of streets of the town. Some 10,000 m² of the site has now been excavated. Estimates as to the town's size

range from 30,000 to 200,000 m². Neither the harbour (thought to lie in a now pumice-filled inlet west of the current excavation) nor any overtly public buildings (if they exist) have been unearthed.

Discovered in 1967, the site was the reward for years of searching. Following the discovery of the Minoan civilization (with the excavation of the palaces on Crete) archaeologists were increasingly wont to ask why they were finding palaces and villas but nothing resembling towns or commercial centres. Their absence implied that they must have existed elsewhere in the Aegean and attention turned to possible sites; notably to Santorini where, in 1867, a fresco-filled house had been uncovered and subsequently lost. Akrotiri came to light thanks to its location in a ravine; the stream that formed it eroded the layers of pumice to reveal evidence of buildings beneath. Once a prospering 16 C. BC town that — if the street plan revealed to date is typical — looked similar to Greek island choras today, it was abandoned (probably thanks to early earthquakes that were the harbinger of the main eruption) by its inhabitants a couple of decades prior to the explosion that ripped the heart out of the island. Covered by layers of volcanic ash, the quake-damaged buildings, some several storeys high, have been preserved. Frescoes aside, the houses are relatively empty of contents, as the townsfolk had time to hurriedly collect all removable valuables when they abandoned their homes.

On entering the excavation shed, you arrive in an open area from which a path runs north along the line of the former stream that exposed the site. On either side of the entrance you can see the remains of two major buildings — ❹ **Xeste 3** and ❺ **Xeste 4** — that are often ignored by tourists heading for the ticket check. In fact, both are examples of the most important building type uncovered to date. They are large mansions with ashlar block façades, and notable for possessing removable interior wooden panel walls in the major front rooms along with 'lustral basins', which appear to have had some religious use. **Xeste 4** has only been partially excavated (work stopped in 1974 when Professor Marinatos — Akrotiri's discoverer — died in a wall collapse, has just resumed). A further house at ❻, known as the **South Building,** has also yet to be explored. All these buildings appear to have major frescoes within them. Indeed, **Xeste 3** (the only one fully excavated to date) has provided the richest haul of frescoes recovered from one building. These include the **Monkey Musician Fresco** (depicting blue monkeys — a sacred animal in Minoan art — playing lyres and pipes), **The Initiation Fresco** (portraying youths preparing for a coming of age ritual), **The Saffron Gatherers Fresco** (showing young girls picking blooms) and **The Adorants Fresco** (which depicts a number of young women and a 'Demeter-like' mother-earth goddess).

Once you pass the ticket check visitors arrive at **Building Beta**. Badly damaged by the stream, it is an example of the second type of building uncovered, being a large structure filled with small rooms. The layout and the lack of kitchen facilities (there is usually only one per block) suggests that the inhabitants lived in a communal, rather than family, unit. These houses appear to represent the lowest housing rank. They did, however, have frescoed rooms like the other buildings, and Building Beta has provided us with several of best known Akrotiri frescoes; the **Boxing Children and Antelope Frescoes**, and the **Blue Monkey Fresco**. At the end of this structure the path arrives at a small square and the **Xeste 2**, a third large ashlar block mansion (as yet unexplored).

From this point, tourists have to walk along a viewing platform that runs past the central area of the excavation. This is dominated by the block at known as **Building Delta**. Easily identified by the **Stone Sacral Horns** now sitting on the wall beside the walkway (they are believed to have once adorned the top of the building), this is another of the communal-living-type buildings. Within it archaeologists discovered the almost complete **Lilies** (or **Spring**) **Fresco**, depicting a landscape of lilies and swallows. The swallows provide a poignant insight into the changed conditions on the island, for Santorini is now one of the few Aegean islands not to see swallows nesting in the summer (the dry volcanic ash isn't adhesive enough for them to build their mud nests), though they do still wistfully fly around looking for suitable sites. To the east of Building Delta are the tops of the walls of the unexplored building **Xeste 5** at .

At the end of the viewing platform the path turns west, taking you past the northern section of the site. Currently roped off, it is inaccessible to tourists beyond tiptoe views. Following the

line of the former torrent bed, this open area leads to , the most northerly part of the excavation. Known as **Sector Alpha**, it is the site of a **Pithoi Jar Storehouse** several storeys high, and apparently some kind of communal food warehouse or shop. It marks the spot where digging commenced at Akrotiri in 1967, and where the first fresco fragments were found. These include a fragment showing a North African man and a palm tree and a swallow fragment (illustrated below). Just visible at stands the **House of the Ladies**. An important town house (it is the only building so far discovered with a light well), it has yielded up the **Fresco of the Ladies** (depicting some well-endowed women robing a lost figure), and the **Papyrus Fresco** (deftly painted with yellows, blues and reds as the painters of the Akrotiri frescoes had no green pigments at their disposal). This fresco suggests trade links with Egypt as this plant is not native to Greece. Unfortunately, the House of the Ladies looks a bit of a mess because, in the eruption, the ground storey collapsed; the upper floor falling, largely intact, on top of it.

After running past the northern façade of Building Delta (notable for having a stairwell filled with 'karate-chopped' stairs), the tourist path turns south-west, following the path of one of the ancient town's streets now known as the **Telchines Road**. On the opposite side of the path to the Building Delta stairs is a small pithoi jar display against the wall of the **West House**. Along with the House of the Ladies, this is an example of the third type of building on the site: being a large independent town house for the middle rank of Akrotiri society (though again interpretations differ as —judging by the contents—the large upstairs window belonged to a 'weaving room'; this suggests some commercial activity was taking place in the building). Smaller than the ashlar block mansion type, this house is nonetheless well adorned with frescoes; yielding up , the famous **Fisherboys**, and the tapestry-like river and nautical festival scenes on the **Miniature Fresco**. This narrow strip fresco is of particular importance as it appears to be a pictorial narrative of a voyage between four towns (ending at Akrotiri itself). Its information on the ships and houses of the period is invaluable and unique.

Another unique feature of the West House — though it is not possible to see this wonder — is the upstairs bathroom at ❶ (complete with a latrine connected to a pipe running down inside the external wall). This led to a mains drain under ❷ the **Triangular Square**. This is the most impressive part of the site, thanks to the height of the buildings.

The tourist path currently ends at the Triangular Square (the exit stairs run up over ❸ the unexcavated **House of the Anchor**). You can, however, look through the windows of ❸ the **Propylon**, or entrance hall, of Building Delta, and look down ❷, the Telchines Road to the **Pithoi Jar Display** at the edge of the so-called **Mill-House Square**; another of the tiny open areas that appear to have played an important part in the town's life. From this square, the street narrows, running between Building Beta and a similar type of building at ❷: **Building Gamma**. Still only partly excavated (only the street side rooms have been explored so far), this structure has also yielded up its first fresco fragments.

Ancient Thira

A few centuries after the eruption that destroyed the Minoan settlement on Santorini, the fertile volcanic soils brought colonizing Doric Greeks to the island. The new centre emerged on the east coast, on the easily defendable high headland north of Perissa (see map on p. 169), and the remains of the town (dating from the Archaic to the Roman era) can be explored. The site has yet to be fully excavated; the exposed remains mainly consisting of nondescript foundations and a poorly preserved theatre. The site is more of scenic rather than archaeological merit. Its main attractions are a number of faint carvings of an erotic — well, okay, 'porno' — nature on some of the buildings (be warned; you have to look pretty hard to find them), and, on the end of the headland, an early Archaic temple of Apollo Karneios that has a ground plan more in common with a town house than a traditional temple. The town also has an agora, a long royal stoa and the remains of a number of large Hellenistic town houses.

Open ⊛ ex ① 09.00–15.00 (last admissions at 14.30) entrance is free, though the expensive mini-buses that run to the site from Kamari cost 1000 GDR one-way, 1500 GDR return. Given this, it isn't very surprising that Ancient Thira is popular destination for island walkers along with nearby Mt. Profitis Ilias, which is topped by a radar station and monastery.

The Volcano / Kameni Islands

Since the Santorini eruption circa 1500 BC, new islands (the 'Burnt Islands') have risen out of the caldera in subsequent eruptions. The largest, the volcano islet of **Nea Kameni** (Great Kameni), is a popular sight on the itineraries of all the boat tours; though the sun-baked 20-minute walk to the George I crater that does nothing more than give off a bad smell, is not the idyll that it seems from Santorini (where fake postcards are on sale depicting this crater as a glowing inferno). This said, excursions are justifiably popular, for the burnt islands offer a unique opportunity to walk over the cinder black lava of a sleeping volcano. Visitors find a daunting, frying-pan-hot landscape lacking refreshment facilities, and all but the most hardy vegetation (the only tree is on Palia Kameni) and populated by a small number of invisible rabbits.

Tour boats also make a call to the hot springs — for a popular swim session — off the smaller and older island of **Palia Kameni**. This was the first island to emerge during an eruption in 196 BC. A second briefly put in an appearance in 46 AD, before Mikra Kameni emerged in 1573. Nea Kameni appeared in 1711, was enlarged in the great eruption of 1866–8 when the St. George I crater appeared, and was finally joined with Mikra Kameni in the 1925–26 eruption. As Santorini must be due for another one sooner or later, you should note that before the last two, the waters around the islands turned a milky colour thanks to underwater sulphur emissions. If this phenomenon were to recur, catching the next ferry to anywhere is probably a good idea.

Meantime, the popularity of the offshore sights provides plenty of custom for small orange and white tourist boats. These craft run various itineraries; all include visits to Nea Kameni and the hot springs. There are three basic tours on offer: the Full Day Tour (09.15–18.20) costs 5,500 GDR and takes in the works, including a sail out of the caldera to Cape Akrotiri. The Caldera Round Trip (09.15–16.30) excludes this run and is slightly better value at 4,500 GDR, while the two half-day burnt islands (alias 'Volcano') trips — the first also taking in the hot springs (15.20–19.30); the second, the town of Oia (10.30–16.30) are a more rushed 3,500 GDR. Students armed with proof of their status receive a 20% reduction on all trips. It also pays to be aware that tickets are up to 1,000 GDR cheaper at the port.

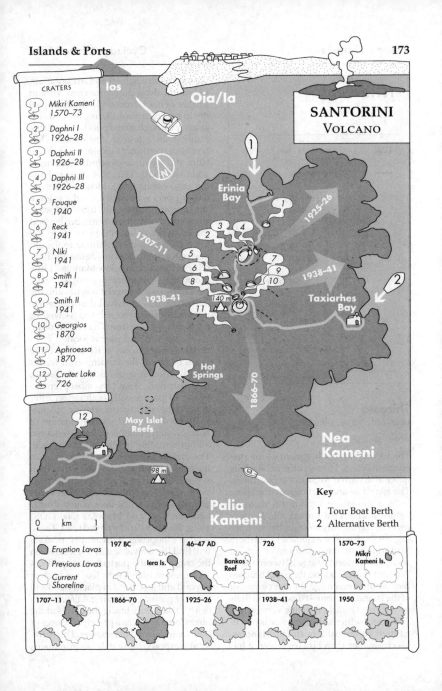

SANTORINI
VOLCANO

CRATERS

1 Mikri Kameni 1570–73
2 Daphni I 1926–28
3 Daphni II 1926–28
4 Daphni III 1926–28
5 Fouque 1940
6 Reck 1941
7 Niki 1941
8 Smith I 1941
9 Smith II 1941
10 Georgios 1870
11 Aphroessa 1870
12 Crater Lake 726

Ios

Oia/Ia

Erinia Bay

1925–26

1707–11

1938–41

1938–41

Taxiarhes Bay

140 m

1866–70

Hot Springs

Nea Kameni

May Islet Reefs

98 m

Palia Kameni

0   km   1

Key

1 Tour Boat Berth
2 Alternative Berth

Eruption Lavas
Previous Lavas
Current Shoreline

197 BC — Iera Is.
46–47 AD — Bankos Reef
726
1570–73 — Mikri Kameni Is.
1707–11
1866–70
1925–26
1938–41
1950

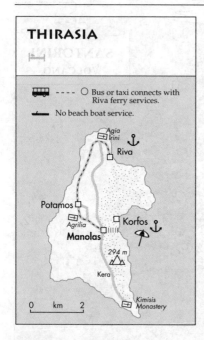

THIRASIA

🚌 ---- ◯ Bus or taxi connects with
        Riva ferry services.

⚓ No beach boat service.

Agia
Irini
Riva ⚓

Potamos

Agrilia

Korfos ⚓

Manolas

294 m

Kera

0   km   2

Kimisis
Monastery

Thirasia

ΘΗΡΑΣΙΑ; 9 km²; pop. 260.

CODE ☎ 0286

The second largest fragment of the pre-eruption island, Thirasia offers a blissfully quiet alternative to Santorini's crowds. The island — and particularly the chora — is a miniature version of Santorini before tourism swamped all. Thirasia owes its tranquillity to an earlier swamping; for the island was joined to northern Santorini until an eruption in 236 BC collapsed the land bridge between them. Without it, and lacking the good beaches that would encourage the development of the island as a tourist destination in its own right, Thirasia remains very quiet.

The only settlement of any size is perched high on the caldera rim at **Manolas**. Much smaller than Fira (of which it has

views), it is an irregular and stringy affair, ribboning along the caldera rim without a maze of backstreets behind. Its appeal lies in its size; for wandering around is to journey through an unspoilt island village rather than a tourist destination. Odd houses carved hobbit-like into the pumice cliffs and a couple of windmills simply add to its charm (Fira lost all its mills in the 1956 earthquake). Most visitors are day-trippers who arrive via the caldera rim staircase (boasting the usual awkward steps and donkey transport), but beyond the existence of several tavernas in the town their impact is confined to the old port of **Korfos** tucked inside the northern wing of the caldera below Manolas. Little more than indifferent shingle beach backed by half-a-dozen tavernas and the odd shop, it is the usual destination for the small caldera tour boats as well as regular taxi-boats from Oia on Santorini.

Thirasia's second port is located in an isolated northern bay at **Riva**. This is the usual berth for the landing-craft ferries (that also double up as caldera tour boats). Unfortunately, it isn't the most prepossessing of places with nothing on offer beyond the odd taverna, a string of houses and a dusty road, its only feature of note is a long pebble beach that is rendered all but unusable by the oil that mars it. The exposed quay is the usual home of the island bus that does little other than serve caldera tour parties during their brief sojourn on the island. Other boats are met by two truck-taxis which shuttle between Riva and Manolas (500 GDR) along the island's only paved road. Those who are hopping with empty pockets will find the walkable dirt track between the chora and the port a better option.

The rest of island feels like the back of beyond and is scarred in places thanks to years of pumice quarrying. In fact much of Thirasia is now lining the banks of the Suez Canal as it was a principal source of both materials and manpower. This activity also exposed the first 'Minoan' remains to be discovered in the archipelago (in 1869); alerting archaeologists to its potential. Unfortunately, the site is lost. Tours try to make up for this by stopping at the diminutive hamlet of **Potamos** (home to an ugly multi-coloured campaniled church) and at even smaller **Agrilia**.

🛏️

The only hotel on Thirasia is the excellent, purpose-built *Cave Mare* (☎ 23349); complete with pool, it stands on the crest of the island with stunning views for the caldera in one direction and the wild surf-kissed outer shores of the island on the other. During the High Season tavernas in the town also offer rooms.

👓

Unless you opt to stay on Thirasia you won't have time to take in more than a port and the town. Those that do stay shouldn't miss the walk along the caldera rim to the southern tip and its 1851-built Kimisis monastery. Running from Manolas, the path passes through the abandoned pumice-cliff house village of **Kera**. Riva also has a 'sight': to the west of the bay lies the church of **Agia Irini**: a structure of no great distinction, it is notable for giving neighbouring Santorini (literally 'Saint Irene') its Venetian name.

THIRASIA
MANOLAS

Note:
The stairs and Korfos port are drawn to half the town scale.

Beach

Fishing Caïques

Korfos Port

Manolas

Cavo Mare

0   m   100

Key

- Ⓐ Town Hall
- Ⓑ Riva Bus & Taxi Square
- Ⓒ Cardphone & Medical Centre
- Ⓓ Mini-Market
- Ⓔ Bakery & Pastry Shop
- Ⓕ Pumice-Cliff Houses
- Ⓖ Mule Stables
- Ⓗ Tavernas
- Ⓘ Restaurant Panorama
- Ⓙ Nick's Restaurant
- Ⓚ Candouni Resturant
- Ⓛ Manolas—Riva Road
- Ⓜ Dirt Track to Riva Port
- Ⓝ Stairway
- 1 Ferries / Tour Boats & Oia Taxi Boats

200 m

4

CYCLADES NORTH

ANDROS · DELOS · EVIA · MYKONOS · SYROS · TINOS

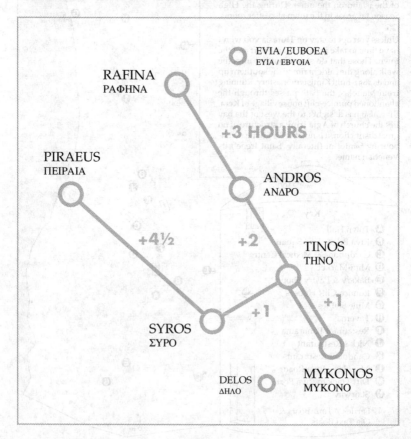

EVIA/EUBOEA
EYIA / EBYOIA

RAFINA
ΡΑΦΗΝΑ

+3 HOURS

PIRAEUS
ΠΕΙΡΑΙΑ

ANDROS
ΑΝΔΡΟ

+4½   +2

TINOS
ΤΗΝΟ

+1   +1

SYROS
ΣΥΡΟ

DELOS   MYKONOS
ΔΗΛΟ   ΜΥΚΟΝΟ

General Features

The Northern Cyclades Line covers those Cycladic islands to the east of Piraeus and the 'Athenian' port of Rafina and is served by daily boats from both. The islands lying along this line include the former Mecca of the Greek World — the sacred island of Delos (birthplace of the God Apollo) and its modern equivalent; the island of Tinos (home to the most important shrine of the Orthodox church in Greece). Delos, lies in theory if not in fact, at the centre of the Cyclades. While all the islands vary greatly in their characteristics, the one feature common to all is a tendency to be extremely windy. The *meltemi* 'hits' these Greek islands the hardest and they form something of a buffer for the rest of the Cyclades.

Cosmopolitan Mykonos and its satellite Delos remain the best known islands on this line, the former being numbered among the most popular of all the Greek islands. Syros is often mentioned in older guide books as being the hub of the Cycladic ferry network as its 19 c. commercial port of Ermoupolis is the formal capital of the group; however, the island has faded into relative obscurity and can now only boast half the number of ferry sailings of its southern neighbour Paros. The remaining islands are very much orientated to Greek rather than international tourism. Andros and Evia (now little more than an extension of the Greek mainland) remain well off the beaten track. Tinos is less so, thanks to the constant stream of locals enjoying a spot of religious pilgrimage and has hordes of little old ladies descending upon it to join the — mainly package — tourists at the height of the season for the feast of the Assumption of the Virgin Mary. As for little Giaros, it does not figure on ferry schedules as it is now an assault course for the military, with access prohibited.

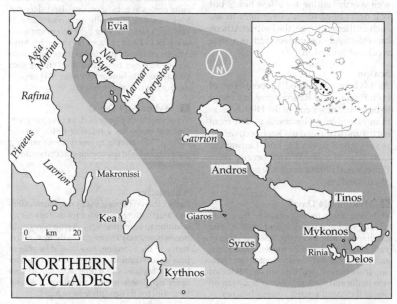

Example Itinerary
[2 Weeks]

The two ferry routes running out of Piraeus and Rafina that meet at Mykonos combine to provide a nice island hopping circuit that is both easy and for the inexperienced reasonably safe. Boats are sufficiently frequent down both lines for you to be sure of a daily boat up and down at least one of the lines even out of High Season.

Arrival/Departure Point

Two easy alternatives: Athens and Mykonos. Athens is usually the cheaper of the two and with far more frequent flights into the bargain. You can do the loop easily from either base. Mykonos is chosen here as it offers a more relaxed start and end to a holiday and a pleasant alternative to arrive at and rushing back to Athens. The other ports en route are well worth visiting for a few hours but you don't need to stay overnight to see such as there is to see; the loop to Athens can effectively be undertaken as a long weekend excursion.

Season

As Mykonos is served by boats out of both Piraeus and Rafina, ferry links tend to be better either end of the High Season than elsewhere. The result is that from early June to the end of October coverage is very good down the line. During the Low Season a single ferry service from Piraeus and Rafina normally operates on alternate days.

■ Mykonos [4 Days]

Mykonos offers the opportunity for a very relaxed start to a Greek Island holiday. You can happily idle away the first few days of your stay with day trips to Delos and Paros and even Tinos if you want to cut corners later on. In-between you can tilt at Mykonos windmills and start an all-over body tan on one of the island's many naturist beaches.

■ ■ Tinos/Andros [1 Day]

If you take the daily 08.00 Mykonos—Rafina ferry to Tinos you'll arrive in time for a late breakfast. An interesting day stop, you can either stay overnight or have the option of picking up the afternoon boat to Andros (note; accommodation is thin on the ground there) or on to Rafina where you can take an evening bus into Athens.

■ ■ Rafina/Athens [4 Days]

If you are not tied to budget accommodation it will be to your advantage to pre-book your Athens hotel accommodation while on Mykonos via one of the ticket agents. It will be hard not to arrive in the capital at any other time than the evenings (hardly an ideal time to start hunting for your bed). Thereafter you will be free to explore at your own pace and adjust the length of your stay as your fancy takes you.

■ Syros [1 Day]

On the schedule of Piraeus—Mykonos ferries, Syros offers an interesting day out. The difficulty comes in getting off the island since the Mykonos link is usually only once daily. If you don't fancy staying here you might have to repair to Tinos or Paros for the night. After Athens you could find Syros something of an anti-climax; but the island does ensure that you appreciate how much nicer Mykonos is during the rest of your stay.

■ Mykonos [4 Days]

Returning with plenty of days to spare gives you the scope for a relaxing finish to your holiday. Not having to worry about missing your return flight is something not to be underestimated.

Alternative

Rather than returning via Syros, **Paros** offers an attractive alternative (or for that matter an addition to your itinerary). A stop here could necessitate a stay overnight — though, if you arrive in the morning, you should be able to pick up a hydrofoil or ferry on an evening run back to Mykonos. A Paros stop would also open up possible calls to Naxos, Ios and Santorini for those with time to hand.

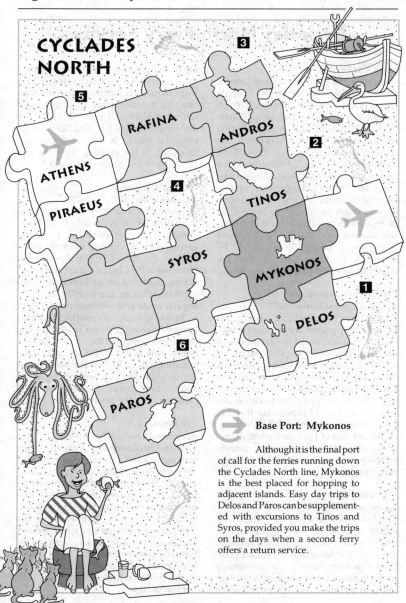

CYCLADES NORTH

Base Port: **Mykonos**

Although it is the final port of call for the ferries running down the Cyclades North line, Mykonos is the best placed for hopping to adjacent islands. Easy day trips to Delos and Paros can be supplemented with excursions to Tinos and Syros, provided you make the trips on the days when a second ferry offers a return service.

Cyclades North Ferry Services

Main Car Ferries
Although the Cyclades East Line is defined within this section as a single line, in practice it is not a complete through route. Daily ferries run both from Piraeus (to Syros, Tinos and Mykonos) and Rafina (to Andros, Tinos, and Mykonos); the combination of the two sub-lines effectively forms the 'line'. Ferry times are reasonably well established. More problematic are the fewer longer-haul vessels that run down the line and then continue on into other groups. Here there have been considerable fluctuations in the last few seasons, and the 2—3 day a week island-direct linkings listed should be treated with some caution, as they are dependent on comparatively few boats.

C/F *Express Aphrodite*
Agapitos Express Ferries; 1977; 11500 GRT.
Formerly the UK ferry *Stena Hibernia*, this large ferry appeared in mid August 1997 on the Cyclades North Line, taking one of the regular two morning slots out of Piraeus and quickly establishing herself as the best ferry on the Piraeus branch of the line (though this isn't saying a lot as most of the boats are grimy Agapitos vessels — a fact that could explain the thriving catamaran links down the Rafina branch). In the summer of 1998 the *Express Aphrodite* ran daily down the line. If she remains on this route times are unlikely to change much in 1999.

C/F *Naias II*
Agapitos Lines; 1966; 4555 GRT.
The *Naias II* is a real veteran of the Greek island ferry scene, having run on this route for many years, first as an independent ferry, and latterly as part of the Agapitos Line fleet. Sister to the notoriously awful *Golden Vergina* she is equally slow and (outside at any rate) grimy and is, for many tourists, a less than happy introduction to the Greek ferry system (if you want to make the best of a bad job then head for the large Deck-class passenger saloon amidships). On the plus side, her day-time schedule has seen little change over the years; though 1996 saw the dropping of her evening runs and her calling at Syros on alternate days.

C/F *Naias Express*
Agapitos Lines; 1971; 3715 GRT.
The new arrival on this route in 1996 was the rather small but comfortable *Naias Express*. Until 1995 she sailed as the G.A. Ferries' *Dimitra*, having formerly operated as the cross-Channel *Earl Harold*. Since her arrival in Greece she has produced a steady trail of confusion thanks to her name change, her inability to find a regular route and — most spectacularly — breaking from her moorings in Paros harbour during a storm in April 1996; causing the sinking of the *Poseidon Express*, which was holed while trying to take avoiding action. In 1998 she managed to get through the year without incident, and ran a summer schedule that was little changed from the previous two years.

C/F *Penelope A*
Agoudimos Lines; 1972; 5109 GRT.
The flagship of a one-boat company which sails out of Rafina, this ferry has operated the route since 1992 — latterly in tandem with the *Bari Express* and *Superferry II* (see p. 182). In the summer she also makes one extended run into the Eastern Cyclades. Formerly the cross-Channel *Horsa*, the *Penelope A* is a sister of the *Express Apollon*, and insignia aside, looks identical. Onboard facilities however, are a touch above her former stable-mate; the competition on this route has forced Agoudimos to fit her out in style.

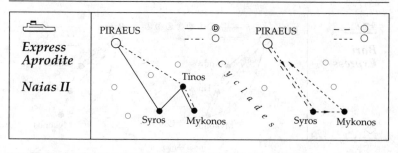

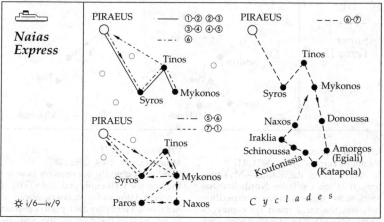

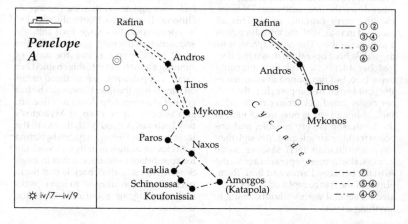

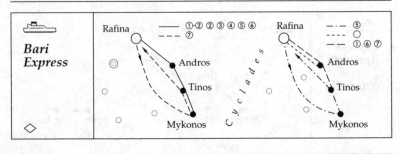

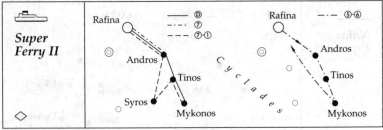

C/F Bari Express
Ventouris Ferries; 1968; 3397 GRT.

In recent years the Rafina—Mykonos branch of the Cyclades North line has seen some quite vicious competition between the three main ferry players. This involved ferries literally racing each other down the line, with local TV interviewing ferry captains et al. This all changed in 1994, with the introduction of a joint timetable. The *Bari Express*, now the oldest boat operating down the line, lost her lucrative Mykonos morning departure, but has gained in as much as she isn't forced to compete directly with her better fitted out former rivals. This said, although she is now rather long in the tooth, she is very reliable, and on-board facilities are adequate (though they have a utilitarian feel). As her name implies, she formerly operated across the Adriatic between Patras and Bari. Rumours that she is to be replaced have circulated for several years without coming to anything as yet.

C/F Super Ferry II
Strintzis Lines; 1974; 5052 GRT.

Now undoubtedly the premier boat on the line, the well-equipped *Super Ferry II* is an escalator and a patisserie ahead of her rivals. Her open-deck plan is also far in advance of the competition and she feels ten years newer than the *Penelope A*, although barely two. Distinctly 'chunky' in appearance, this large boat initially encountered docking problems in the small island ports. Before the days of running a joint timetable this enabled her rivals to consistently nip in ahead of her on runs down the line. However, she has got her manoeuvring down to a fine art, and is quite zippy even in Mykonos's tiny harbour. A good boat, thanks to the large amount of interior space (the Rafina—Mykonos route is usually far too windy for comfortable sun-deck travel in High Season), her sole drawback is that backpackers are 'encouraged' to leave packs in the tiny luggage room at the top of the escalator.

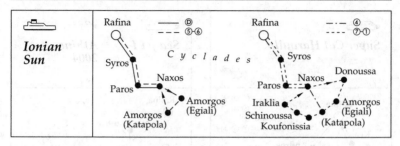

Ionian Sun

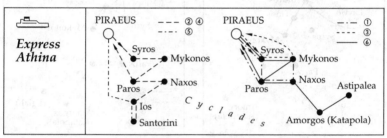

Express Athina

C/F *Ionian Sun*
Strintzis Lines; 1978; 11,179 GRT.
Formerly running across the Adriatic, this large ferry moved into the Aegean in 1998, operating out of Rafina. She sought to fill a gap in the market by providing a regular daily link between the islands of the Cyclades North line and the Central Cyclades line. How well this works remains to be seen, however, timetable changes are more than likely in 1999; Strintzis Lines have a history of experimenting with odd ferries out of Rafina and then either seriously modifying their schedules or removing them all together the following year.

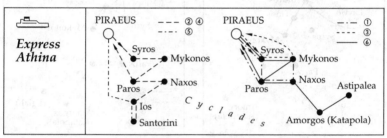

See also:
- C/F *Dimitroula*   p. 406
- C/F *El Greco*   p. 406
- C/F *Express Paros*   p. 133
- C/F *Syros Express*   p. 133
- P/S *Express Skopelitis* p. 254

C/F *Express Athina*
Agapitos Express Ferries; 1973; 5071 GRT.
Formerly the Ventouris Sea Lines boat *Panagia Tinou 2*, this ferry reapperaed at the end of the 1998 season in Agapitos colours. Her major fault is a propensity to bob around like a cork in even calm conditions; this is one Greek ferry on which you could end up feeling sea-sick the moment she leaves Piraeus. In poorer conditions mass throw-ups are not unknown. Thanks to her late arrival last year her itinerary was built around percieved gaps in the existing timetable; it is therefore likely that 1999 will see significant timetable changes.

C/M *Super Cat Haroulla*
Goutos Lines; 1994; 5000 GRT.
The *Super Cat Haroulla* is the largest catamaran operating in the Eastern Mediterranean. Painted in an unmissable bright red and white, she is a vehicle-carrying, passenger-ferry sized boat, with better than average deck-class facilities. The new

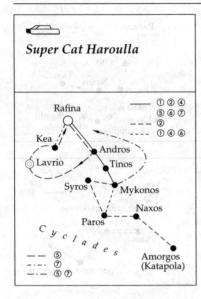

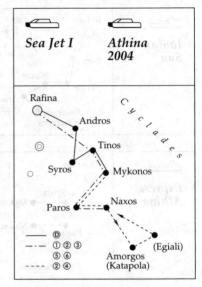

arrival on the Cyclades North line in the summer of 1996, she made a faltering start thanks to a lack of timetable advertising. This has been compounded by with an apparent lack of speed that makes her little faster than her rival ferries — though the reality is that she is a significantly faster boat (and has the same fares), but she loses much of this advantage due to her lengthy docking times. One of the few catamarans with sun-deck, she still offers speed advantages if your destination is the next island down the line.

C/M *Sea Jet I*
Seajet; 1995; 499 GRT.

The new arrival on the line in 1995, this large, passenger-only catamaran offers a taste of the good life for half the time you would have if you took a ferry, and for comparatively little extra money. A large craft (i.e. of a similar size to the Saronic-Gulf *Sea Cat I*), she really is propelled by water jets; a feature that even has the locals queuing up to travel on her (though

she is acquiring an unhealthy reputation for failing to dock in rough seas). Even allowing for her waning novelty value, she should continue to be popular. Her itinerary is unambitious, her speed ensures that she can make both morning and afternoon return runs to Tinos and Mykonos. On board facilities are very good (partly because she is relatively new). Loud rock music is played all the way and the large number of TV screens add to the cheer by repeatedly showing a film demonstrating how to abandon ship.

C/M *Athina 2004*
Goutos Lines

Named in honour of the awarding of the 2004 Olympic Games to Athens, this small red catamaran was the new arrival on this line in 1998. Described as a 'turbo cat' and with an advertised speed of 50 knots it was obviously trying to cream off some of the passenger traffic that might otherwise gone by air. Her itinerary is similar to the *Sea Jet*, though days differ.

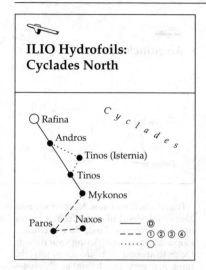

**ILIO Hydrofoils:
Cyclades North**

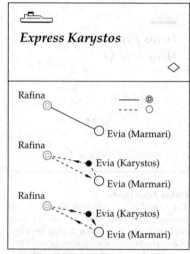

Express Karystos

ILIO Hydrofoils

Among the ILIO services running out of Rafina are a number specific to the Northern Cyclades. Given their track record of constant chopping and changing, ILIO will probably change things around again in 1999. The only consistent feature to date has been a daily service down the Rafina branch of the Cyclades North line to Mykonos. These runs include occasional calls at the otherwise unconnected Tinos village of Isternia.

C/F *Karystos*

Mililis Lines; 1968; 830 GRT.

A tiny Greek-built ferry that rattles daily between Rafina and Karystos on Evia, the *Karistos* changed hands in 1996, changing from a Goutos Lines boat into the flagship of the diminutive Mililis Lines. If she wasn't providing an 'essential' link service she would be a leading candidate in the 'next tub for the scrapyard' stakes; as it is, she is set to crawl for another five years. As with the C/F *Express Karystos* timetables see regular monthly changes.

C/F *Express Karystos*

Local; 1971; 3017 GRT.

A small ferry brought in to replace the elderly *Marmari I*, which had run this route for many years, the *Express Karystos* has happily taken over her predecessor's schedules with little change. Slightly larger than the C/F *Karistos*, she operates out of (Evia) Marmaris to Rafina with occasional visits to (Evia) Karystos. Not on a tourist route, her on-board facilities are distinctly utilitarian.

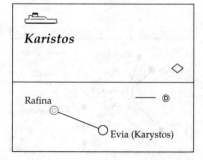

Karistos

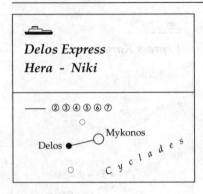

Delos Express
Hera - Niki

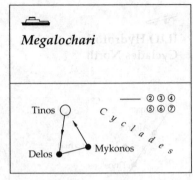

Megalochari

Delos Tour Boats

The island of Delos is only accessible via tourist boats. The best run direct from Mykonos several times a day in High Season (you can pick up your boat on any of its return runs, so you can spend up to five hours on Delos). The *Hera* is the largest and most comfortable of the three Mykonos boats; the *Niki* and *Delos Express* run more frequently but, being smaller, roll about much more. Return tickets cost the same (1500 GDR) for all three boats, but are not interchangeable. Boat tickets do not include the entrance fee for the archaeological site.

Tour boats from Tinos, Naxos and Paros also visit Delos, but suffer from a couple of disadvantages. First, they include a stop at Mykonos, restricting your time on Delos to around 1½ hours. Secondly, the fares are very much higher (Naxos—Delos trips cost around 6000 GDR).

The *Ariadne of Naxos* is the best of these boats; the *Naxos Star* being rather on the small side. Their timetables change frequently. The Tinos-based *Megalochari* is a 1959-built rust bucket. Top-side seating gives tourists a 'hole' new experience; those carrying planks of wood will find themselves at a distinct advantage.

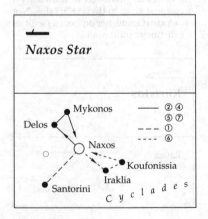

Naxos Star

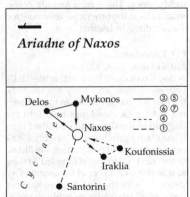

Ariadne of Naxos

Cyclades North Islands & Ports

Andros

ΑΝΔΡΟΣ; 380 km²; pop. 9,020.

CODE ☎ 0282
GAVRION POLICE ☎ 71220
ANDROS TOWN POLICE ☎ 22300
HOSPITAL ☎ 22222

Despite being the second largest and most northerly of the Cyclades, Andros is only slowly edging its way onto the tourist map. A combination of rich vegetation and mountains have failed to bring the crowds. The only obvious reason for such a paradox is the lack of any notable population centre, for Andros really has a lot going for it if a downbeat, understated beach holiday is your kind of thing. The

locals of course have long been in the know, and like Kea, Andros has been the preserve of Greek, rather than foreign, tourists, with many of the better-off Athenians having villas on this appealing island. Despite the fact that Andros is on a major ferry route, independent island hoppers don't visit in large numbers; the great majority of visitors are package tourists who spend their time on the south coast, split between the port of Gavrion, and the tourist resort village of Batsi to the east. Relatively few venture across the island to the capital at Chora, a symptom of the limited bus service; Andros is another of those islands that are best explored with your own transport.

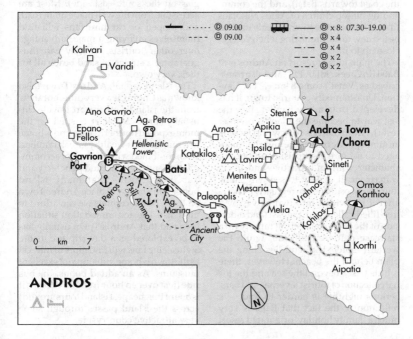

Most visitors arrive by ferry and thus find themselves deposited at the port of **Gavrion**. Set in a deep inlet, it consists of an intimidatingly large (and very dusty) ferry quay, backed by a little port village strung along the waterfront behind. All the usual facilities (including an information office housed in an old dovecot) lie along the shore: Gavrion is one of those 'what you can't see isn't there' sort of places, besides being very windy. Island buses (centred on Andros Town; Gavrion times are posted up in shops and ticket agents) turn around by the ferry quay before running back along the coast to the capital. More often than not they take any arriving tourists with them as Gavrion offers little incentive to linger. The port beach is a sadly indifferent affair (most people who stay in town migrate to the excellent sand beaches that run down the coast towards Batsi), and the commanding hilltop church of Agios Nikolaos that dominates the town reveals itself to be too new to be interesting when you get close up to it.

The main tourist resort on Andros is at **Batsi** (in Greek 'ΜΠΑΤΣΙ', and also transcribed as 'Vatsi') some 8 km east of Gavrion. Unashamedly a tourist town, it has developed from a tiny hamlet since the last war to become the island's premier resort. Given that it is so new and lacking an atmospheric centre, the town has managed to acquire a surprising amount of character with an attractive and lively waterfront (it is easy to see why some tourists choose to return regularly). Thereafter it is divided into two halves by a tree-filled valley, with the east (and older) side of the town clambering rapidly up a staircase cluttered hillside, while the western 'hotel strip' end lies along the plain behind the beach. However, there is little to see beyond the sea and the usual collection of tourist tavernas and bars. Serious nightlife is harder to find — a reflection of the fact that Batsi is very much a 'family holiday' orientated resort

— and you don't have to wander around for long to come across bored-looking teenagers (dreaming wistfully of Ios Town, Faliraki on Rhodes, and Malia on Crete) who are just not quite old enough to be allowed on parent-free vacations. Nightspots tend to be located out of town; these include the *Placebo* on the Gavrion road and the *Sunset* disco on the hill behind the hotel strip, north of the town.

Batsi's importance to tourists has grown of late, as it has taken over Gavrion's role as the island's hydrofoil and catamaran port; no doubt because these vessels offer the only means by which the town's large tourist population can go day-tripping to other islands. It is also the base for the island's beach boats, with daily departures to a number of good sand beaches in the coves and bays either side of the town (these include a nudist beach at Delavogias on the south-east side). Most are accessible from the well made main road, and moped or car hire fans will find themselves enjoying a major advantage over other tourists, as they can thus guarantee a stretch of sand beach all for their very own.

The island capital, **Andros Town** (also known as **Chora**), is a very different affair from the island's other port towns. Unusually for a capital, it is sited on the more exposed northern coast, and is home to a number of a wealthy Greek families. This, combined with the lack of accommodation and nightlife, and poor ferry and bus links, means that many island hoppers are happy to place Andros Town on their 'island capitals we can afford to miss' list. The accommodation situation is so bad that Andros Town usually has to be explored as a day trip excursion. Sightseeing fans will find more of interest as the town is home to a couple of excellent museums. As an added bonus, the bus ride (just over an hour from Gavrion — it is one of the cheapest island tours around) across the island passes through some very attractive countryside.

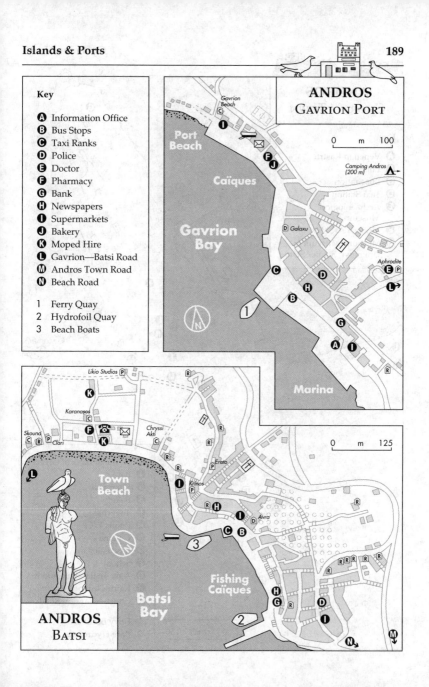

Key

- **A** Information Office
- **B** Bus Stops
- **C** Taxi Ranks
- **D** Police
- **E** Doctor
- **F** Pharmacy
- **G** Bank
- **H** Newspapers
- **I** Supermarkets
- **J** Bakery
- **K** Moped Hire
- **L** Gavrion—Batsi Road
- **M** Andros Town Road
- **N** Beach Road

1 Ferry Quay
2 Hydrofoil Quay
3 Beach Boats

ANDROS
GAVRION PORT

0   m   100

Gavrion Beach

Port Beach

Caïques

Gavrion Bay

Camping Andros (200 m)

Galaxu

Aphrodite

Marina

ANDROS
BATSI

0   m   125

Likio Studios

Karanasos

Skouna

Clari

Chryssi Akti

Town Beach

Erato

Krinos

Avra

Batsi Bay

Fishing Caïques

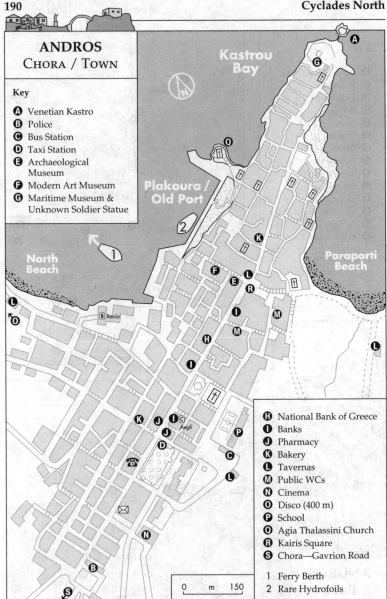

ANDROS
CHORA / TOWN

Key

- **A** Venetian Kastro
- **B** Police
- **C** Bus Station
- **D** Taxi Station
- **E** Archaeological Museum
- **F** Modern Art Museum
- **G** Maritime Museum & Unknown Soldier Statue

Kastrou Bay

Plakoura / Old Port

North Beach

Paraporti Beach

Xenia

Aegli

- **H** National Bank of Greece
- **I** Banks
- **J** Pharmacy
- **K** Bakery
- **L** Tavernas
- **M** Public WCs
- **N** Cinema
- **O** Disco (400 m)
- **P** School
- **Q** Agia Thalassini Church
- **R** Kairis Square
- **S** Chora—Gavrion Road

1 Ferry Berth
2 Rare Hydrofoils

0   m   150

Sited on a wind-buffeted, finger-narrow peninsula, the majority of the buildings in the town are typical neo-classical 19 c. piles. The main street dominates the town, running its length and dotted with shops and up-market boutiques. It ends in a small square adorned with an ugly bronze (entitled 'The Unknown Sailor') waving out to sea, and a Maritime Museum that is usually closed. The sailor's view of the horizon is blocked by an islet topped by the remains of a long abandoned Venetian kastro. Known as the Mesa Kastro, it was built between 1207–33, and is reached via a narrow, arched bridge. The whitewashed buildings and the backstreets behind this square are the most appealing part of town, and are all that remains of the medieval capital of Kato Kastro. At the landward end of the old part of town are a notable Archaeological Museum and a Museum of Modern Art. Both have enjoyed the patronage of the wealthy Goulandri family — Andros is another of those islands that has among its sons a family of benevolent shipping millionaires.

The rest of the island remains virtually tourist free, thanks to the lack of a decent bus service and the comparatively low number of tourists on the island: Andros is a good island to visit if unspoilt hill villages filled with dovecots (a legacy of the period of Venetian rule) appeals. The most visited inland settlement is **Mesaria** on the Andros Town road. This village retains a number of medieval buildings, including several ruined tower houses. Mesaria also has a 10 c. Byzantine church. Just up the road is the more picturesque village of **Menites**, a settlement with an even greater ancestry: the main church stands on the site of a temple of Dionysos. In the mountains south of Andros town stands the Monastery of Panachrantou. Founded in 961, it is home to St. Panteleimon's skull. Armed with healing powers, this relic packs quite a bit of pilgrim-pulling power. The monastery is just one of many possible destinations for walkers on Andros; other suggested island walks can be found in a local guide — *A Practical Guide to Andros* — which is on sale locally.

📫

Accommodation is thinly spread around the island. In **Gavrion** the waterfront *Galexu* (☎ 71228) offers rooms for the desperate along with the better *Gavrion Beach* (☎ 71312). **Batsi** is host to the bulk of the island's accommodation, with the *Chryssi Akti* (☎ 41236), *Skouna* (☎ 41240) and *Karanasos* (☎ 41480) — complete with restaurant — being augmented by several pensions and plenty of hillside rooms. In **Andros Town** options are fewer. Best bet is the C-class *Egli* (☎ 22303), just off the High St. There is also and expensive *Xenia* (☎ 22270) overlooking the beach and port on the north side of the town.

Å

Camping Andros (☎ 71444): a reasonable site just behind Gavrion, it tries to make up for its odd location by providing all the facilities; these include a swimming pool, restaurant and pool table.

👓

Sightseeing is limited on Andros as the major archaeological sites have yet to be seriously explored. The most accessible object of interest is a 20 m high **Hellenistic Tower**: a 3 km hour long hike inland from Gavrion. Known as the 'Tower of Agios Petros', conjecture varies wildly as to its purpose and age, with Mycenaean to Byzantine dates being suggested.

The remains of the ancient city of **Paleopolis** offer an attractive boat excursion from Batsi. Largely unexcavated, the ancient capital (from 600 BC to 500 AD) is sited down a steep path off the town road and also under the sea (the site has one beach, where visitors are not encouraged to carry a bucket and spade). Tourists visit to enjoy the pretty valley walk between the beach and the modern village. Of ruins there are few signs; the most notable discovery is a 2 c. BC marble copy of a bronze statue of Hermes by Praxiteles. Unusually, the island has managed to retain this major sculpture and it is the prize exhibit in the Andros Town **Archaeological Museum**. The **Museum of Modern Art** is also worth exploring (despite having several works by the sculptor of the Unknown Sailor), if only for the strange 'sound' exhibits that follow you around.

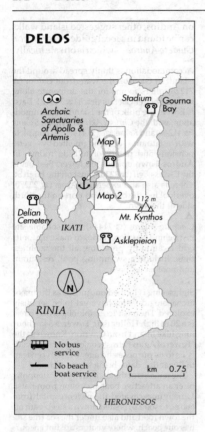

Delos

ΔΗΛΟΣ; 3.6 km²; pop. 20.

Easily the smallest of the Cyclades islands (anything smaller is deemed to be a mere islet), Delos is also one of the most famous. Home to one of the most important sanctuaries in ancient Greece, the island is now one of the great classical archaeological sites of the Mediterranean, not least because it was all but abandoned during the Roman era and thus remains unspoilt by the gradual accretion of later buildings.

Historical Background

Tradition had it that in an effort to escape the amorous attentions of the god Zeus, a wench named Asteria ignored the maxim that no woman is an island and contrived to metamorphose into one, thereafter drifting where tide and current would take her, sometimes above the surface, other times submerged. Not unnaturally, this did nothing for ancient ferry schedules, and Poseidon finally intervened and anchored the island of 'Asteria' to the sea-floor. As a result it was thereafter known as 'Delos' or 'visible'. Years passed only for another of Zeus's escaping lovers — Lato — to land on the island, disguised as a swan, and give birth to the twin deities Apollo (the most popular of all the Greek gods) and his sister Artemis. This set Delos up nicely: with a background of divine sex and religion Delos not unnaturally became a leading spiritual centre in Ancient Greece. This role was bolstered by a quadrennial games festival on a par with the Olympics, and the island's emergence as the trade centre of the Aegean. In its later years, during the Hellenistic period, its trade markets came to overshadow the sanctuary, and the excavated complex of temples and markets are an impressive testament to this double life. That said, the extant structures are confined to jumbled foundations, thanks to a history of systematic demolition.

A major Mycenaean site, Delos took off as a sanctuary with the construction of a Temple of Apollo in the early 7 c. BC (largely under Naxian patronage). As the sanctuary grew in importance, it underwent various stages of ritual purification. This started in 540 BC with the removal of all graves to neighbouring Rinia island. This was followed in 426 BC with an edict making it illegal to give birth or die on Delos (this policy is maintained today via a ban on overnight stays, and if that was not discouragement enough, the only hotel has been in ruins for 1600 years). The 426 BC edict prompted the growth of a town on Rinia (otherwise known as 'Larger Delos') — where one could be born or die and not get blamed for it. On the political front, such moves helped Delos emerge as a non-partisan sanctuary — a sort of mini-Switzerland amid the warring Greek city states, under the control of none.

With the rise of the 4 c. BC Persian threat Delos was chosen as the nominal centre of the anti-Persian alliance of Greek city states, and it was to Delos that each sent contributions to

MYKONOS
Town Waterfront & Windmills

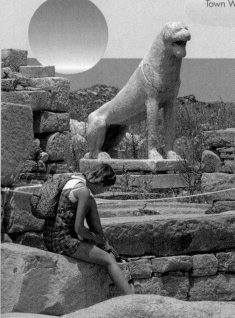

DELOS
Delian Lioness

Rubble Field & Mt. Kynthos

Paraportiani Church
& Little Venice House

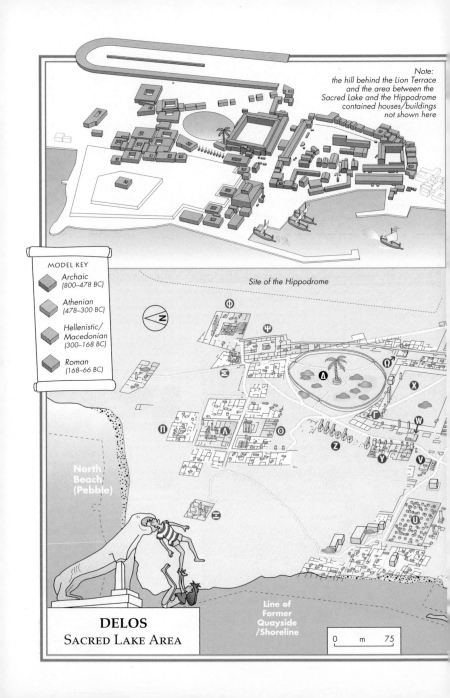

Note:
the hill behind the Lion Terrace
and the area between the
Sacred Lake and the Hippodrome
contained houses/buildings
not shown here

MODEL KEY

Archaic
(800–478 BC)

Athenian
(478–300 BC)

Hellenistic/
Macedonian
(300–168 BC)

Roman
(168–66 BC)

Site of the Hippodrome

N

North
Beach
(Pebble)

DELOS
SACRED LAKE AREA

Line of
Former
Quayside
/Shoreline

0   m   75

Key

A Agora of the Competialists
B Stoa of Philip V
C South Stoa
D Propylaea
E Oikos of the Naxians
F Base of the Colossal Statue of the Naxians
G Stoa of the Naxians
H Great Temple of Apollo /Temple of the Delians
I Temple of the Athenians
J Porinos Naos of Apollo
K Treasuries

L Neorion/Monument of the Bulls
M Altar of Zeus Soter & Polieus
N Agora of the Delians
O Sanctuary of Dionysos
P Stoa of Antigonos
Q Minoa Fountain
R Artemision & Colossal Statue of the Naxians
S Thesmophorion
T Agora of Theophrastos
U Hypostyle Hall
V Dodekatheon Temple
W Letoon/Temple of Leto

X Agora of the Italians
Y Granite Monument
Z Terrace of the Lions
Ⓣ Sacred Palm Tree
Ⓐ Sacred Lake
Ⓞ Koinon of the Poseidoniasts of Beirut
Ⓝ House of the Diadumenos
Ⓗ Hillside House
Ⓣ House of the Comedians
Ⓔ House of the Lake
Ⓖ Palaestra of Granite
Ⓟ Palaestra of the Lake
Ⓐ Temple of Anios

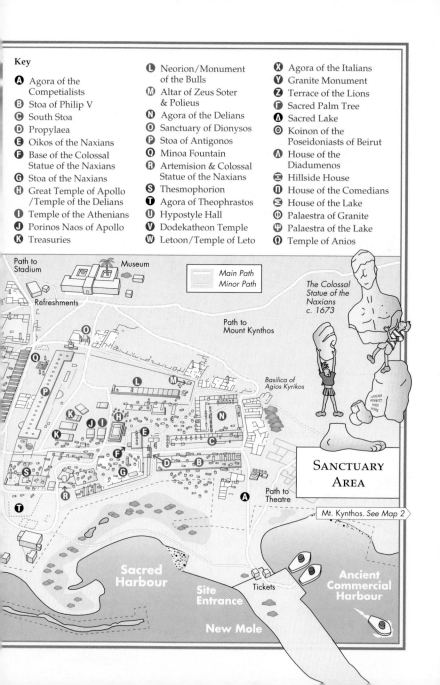

Path to Stadium

Museum

Refreshments

Main Path
Minor Path

The Colossal Statue of the Naxians *c. 1673*

Path to Mount Kynthos

Basilica of Agios Kyrikos

LORENA HORWITT WAS HERE

SANCTUARY AREA

Path to Theatre

Mt. Kynthos. *See Map 2*

Sacred Harbour

Site Entrance

Tickets

Ancient Commercial Harbour

New Mole

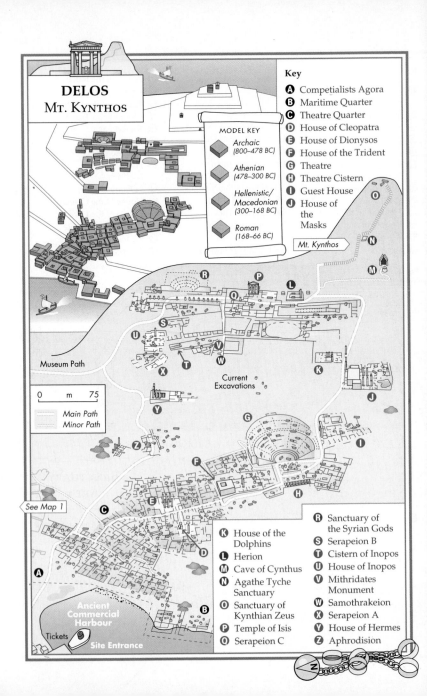

DELOS
MT. KYNTHOS

Key
- **A** Competialists Agora
- **B** Maritime Quarter
- **C** Theatre Quarter
- **D** House of Cleopatra
- **E** House of Dionysos
- **F** House of the Trident
- **G** Theatre
- **H** Theatre Cistern
- **I** Guest House
- **J** House of the Masks

MODEL KEY

Archaic
(800–478 BC)

Athenian
(478–300 BC)

Hellenistic/
Macedonian
(300–168 BC)

Roman
(168–66 BC)

Mt. Kynthos

Museum Path

| 0 | m | 75 |

Main Path
Minor Path

Current
Excavations

See Map 1

- **K** House of the Dolphins
- **L** Herion
- **M** Cave of Cynthus
- **N** Agathe Tyche Sanctuary
- **O** Sanctuary of Kynthian Zeus
- **P** Temple of Isis
- **Q** Serapeion C

- **R** Sanctuary of the Syrian Gods
- **S** Serapeion B
- **T** Cistern of Inopos
- **U** House of Inopos
- **V** Mithridates Monument
- **W** Samothrakeion
- **X** Serapeion A
- **Y** House of Hermes
- **Z** Aphrodision

Ancient
Commercial
Harbour

Tickets

Site Entrance

a common war chest. However, the Delian League (as the alliance was known) was soon dominated by Athens, and this led to political control of the island passing to Athens, and the neutering of Delian influence. Thereafter, under Athenian patronage, the commercial aspect of Delos became ascendant.

After 250 BC Delos came under the control of the kings of Macedonia, and gradually emerged as the largest slave market in the Mediterranean. The historian Strabo estimated that on a typical day 10,000 slaves would change masters. The wealth that came with this trade brought about the island's downfall. After coming under Roman control in 168 BC, it was sacked in 88 BC by Mithridates Eupator, king of Pontos, in his war with Rome. Having lost 20,000 of its population in the attack, Delos was sacked again 69 BC by the pirates of Athenodoros, an ally of Mithridates. Delos never recovered. Abandoned by her rich patrons, and her trade functions re-centred elsewhere, she settled into a period of long decline that culminated with the arrival of Christianity — an event that destroyed her tarnished remaining religious role. From the 6 c. AD Delos appears to have been abandoned. In 1566 the Turks occupied the island, the tiny population doing a brisk trade selling much of the masonry, and burning the fine marble to make lime, before being driven away by the establishment of a pirate base on the island that survived into the early 19 c.

Visitors to Delos should bring a sunhat, good shoes and beverages (refreshments are scandalously expensive on Delos; e.g. a can of cola costing 150 GDR in a supermarket will set you back 1000 GDR here). Local visitors from Mykonos also wear stout shoes for fear of deadly snakes, but this is just paranoia; there aren't any deadly snakes in Greece. All tour boats arrive at a mole (complete with barrier and ticket kiosk on the island side) built out of the debris from the excavations. In poor sea conditions boats berth on the other side of the island in Gourna Bay.

There is a site entrance fee of 1200 GDR (this is included in the price of *some* agency tours — it is advisable to check when buying) which also includes the museum. Establish carefully boat return times. You will need 2—3 hours in order to visit all the major features on the site — all are marked with stones inscribed in Greek and French (most of the excavation has been carried out by the École Française D'Athènes). Unfortunately, there isn't a set route to follow when exploring Delos. Tourists peel off in all directions as soon as they pass the ticket kiosk. Given the summer heat, an anticlockwise circuit is recommended as you can attempt the summit of Mt. Kynthos while still fresh; this means starting with Map 2, and then taking in the sites on Map 1 and the museum as you find them.

The rather ugly site museum is the most imposing building on the island. Fortunately, once you gain admission (you will have to show your entrance ticket) you will find that inside it is among the better archaeological museums in Greece. The eight galleries are home to a good collection of sculpture, mosaics, plaster wall paintings, household utensils and jewellery.

The Sanctuary Area

The heart of ancient Delos was made up of the central Sanctuary and Sacred Lake areas (see the double-page colour map between p. 192–193). On arriving at the site most tourists head for the enormous rubble field that once was the Sanctuary Area. In its prime it was the heart of Delos, containing the main shrines to Apollo and a collection of holy sites dating back to Mycenaean times.

All arrivals to Delos start from ❹ the Hellenistic **Agora of the Competialists**. This was a market dividing the religious and commercial

DELOS
SLAVE MARKET
SPECIALS !

ORGY GIRL —
10,000 TALENTS !
WITH FREE
PET HUNK
ATTACHED !

areas of Delos; it is adorned with the bases of monuments erected by guildsmen. The main path from this crossroads ran north. This was the **Sacred Way** (or **Dromos**), the processional road to the sanctuary, and bounded by **B** the **Stoa of Philip V** (150 C. BC); named after a king of Macedon, and **C** the **South Stoa** (3 C. BC). Both were filled with shops.

The religious part of the site began with **D** the **Propylaea** (2 C. BC). This was the ceremonial gateway to the main sanctuary precinct (the **Hieron of Apollo**). It boasted three doors and four pillars (the bases of which survive, along with a statue base on the west side that has the footprints left by some long lost bronze hero). Just inside stood one of the oldest buildings on Delos: **E** the **Oikos of the Naxians** (7 C. BC), an odd shrine with open ends and a roof supported by a row of internal pillars. Along its north wall stands **F** the **Base of the Colossal Statue of the Naxians**. This famous sculpture (see **R**) was a 6 C. BC **Kouros** of Apollo that stood over 10 m high. The broken base is inscribed 'I am of the same marble, both statue and base' on its east side and 'The Naxians to Apollo' on its west. The statue looked out to sea, over the monuments within **G** the L-shaped **Stoa of the Naxians** (6 C. BC). First among these was the **Bronze Palm Tree of Nicias** (417 BC) which was lost when the Apollo fell on it during a storm; only its base survives.

North of the Oikos lie the foundations of three Apollo temples. Delos is unusual, in that later temples were built alongside (rather than replacing) earlier buildings. This had the side effect of leaving the site with a series of small temples, rather than acquiring one great major temple, as other major shrines did. The focus provided by the sacred harbour also prompted another change in tradition, as all the temples have their main entrances on their west sides, instead of the usual east (it was normal building practice for the main door, opening on the statue within, to face the rising sun). The largest and newest of these temples was **H** the **Great Temple of Apollo (Temple of the Delians)**. Built on the founding of the Delian League in 478 BC., this was the only temple on Delos to have columns on all four sides. North of it lies **I** the **Temple of the Athenians** (425–417 BC). Built out of Pentalic marble by Athenian workmen, it was highly decorated with sculptures. **J** the **Porinos Naos of Apollo** (6 C. BC) was the oldest temple, with columns only across its west front.

Running in an arc north and east of the three Apollo temples are the foundations of **K** the **5 Treasuries**. All date from the 6 or 5 C. BC, and lead round to several more important sanctuary precinct buildings. First among these is **L** the 3 C. BC **Neorion** (otherwise known as the **Monument of the Bulls** because of its decorative reliefs). This is one of the most unusual buildings known from ancient Greece. A stoa with a two-storey north end, it housed a trireme in its lower southern half. This glorified warship shed was built by Antigonos Gonatas to commemorate a naval victory over the Ptolemies. To the east lie the remains of several buildings housing minor cults, the **Bouleuterion** (6 C. BC) and the **Prytaneion** (3 C. BC). To the west lies **M** the **Altar of Zeus Soter & Polieus** (3 C. BC).

South of the precinct boundary lies the **Agora of the Delians**. This was lined with 2 C. BC stoas on its north and east sides and a 3 C. BC stoa on its south. Behind this complex stood a late Christian **Basilica of Agios Kyrikos**, along with a series of houses, including the **House of Kerdon** (marked by a couple of columns). The precinct boundary street runs north from here to **O** the **Sanctuary of Dionysos**, a popular tourist venue (thanks to the two broken giant phalli on pillars) and the nearby **Monument of Gaius Billienus** (1 C. BC), the marble torso of a Roman general. This backs onto **P** the foundations of the massive **Stoa of Antigonos** (3 C. BC), a ceremonial building surrounded by monuments. These include **O** the water-and-frog-filled **Minoa Fountain** (6 C. BC) on its north side and, on the south, the semi-circular **Graphe** or **Oikos**, the Mycenaean tomb of Arge and Opis (the maidens who supposedly attended Leto at Apollo's birth).

Artemis was worshipped in the north-west corner of the sanctuary; **Q** the **Artemision** (C. 175 BC) was built on the site of an Archaic temple which was built over a Mycenaean shrine. It is easily located as it is now the home of the divided white marble torso of the **Colossal Statue of the Naxians** (this was cut in two and its head lost in pre-18 C. AD attempts to remove it — one of the statue's hands is in the site museum, and a foot is in the British Museum). South of the Artemision lie the confused remains of several buildings: the

Keraton (4 C. BC); a building that was used in a crane-dance ritual first stepped by Theseus, the **Oikos of Andrians & Heiropoion** (otherwise known as the **Monuments of the Hexagons**), and 🅢 the **Thesmophorion**, a 4 C. BC shrine complex that included a **Temple of Demeter**.

The Sacred Lake Area

Lying north of the Apollo temples precinct and the Stoa of Antigonos is the Sacred Lake Area. The Sacred Lake (so called because it was on its banks that Apollo and Artemis were born) marked the boundary of the Archaic sanctuary. With the rise of Delos as a trading centre, the area later became an up-market mansion district.

The main street leading to the Sacred Lake runs from 🅞 the **Agora of Theophrastos** (126 BC) on the north side of the Sacred Harbour. When commercial forces were in the ascendant even the Sacred Harbour was put to commercial use with the building of 🅤 the **Hypostyle Hall** or **Stoa of Poseidon** (3 C. BC), a many pillared merchants' exchange that was open on the harbour side. Now reduced to a field of capitals and bases, it was graced by 44 Doric and Ionic pillars (their absence is a clear sign of deliberate demolition). To the east stood 🅥 the **Temple of the Dodekatheon** (4 C. BC), dedicated to the 12 gods, it replaced an earlier Archaic structure.

Around the corner lies 🅦 the **Letoon** (or **Temple of Leto**) Built in the 6 C. BC, it honoured the mother of Apollo and Artemis, and — unusually — faced south, in order to face their temples. The surviving base of the building is easy to miss, thanks to the more impressive remains that stand either side, namely 🅧 the **Agora of the Italians** (2 C. BC); a large two-storey peristyle building named after its excavators, and 🅨 the **Granite Monument** (2 C. BC), a large building constructed out of granite blocks that is thought to have been a religious meeting house.

The high point of any tour of Delos is undoubtedly 🅩 the **Terrace of the Lions** (7 C. BC). Powerful, deftly-carved, archaic figures, now reduced to a weathered minimalist perfection, they stood guard, looking over the Sacred Palm from which Leto hung to give birth to Apollo and Artemis. Thought to have once been up to 16 strong, only 5 lions survive in situ. The body of a 6th was removed in the early 18 C. to guard the Arsenal in Venice.

Unfortunately, the locals touched it up, replacing the original head with something more in keeping with the traditional Venetian Lion (complete with mane). The result is best summed up by the poor creature's expression of pained surprise; a case of being not so much maned as maimed. The Greek government has requested the torso's return and it is difficult not to sympathize given the poor beast's obvious distress (see below).

The site 🅕 of the **Sacred Palm Tree** is probably the circular trunk-sized hole amid the foundations next to 🅐 the **Sacred Lake**. Dry since 1925 (when it was drained for fear of malarial mosquitos), it was originally perfectly circular and graced with swans. However, during the Hellenistic period, when the mansion district was built, the secular merchants (no doubt still being broken on a wheel in Hades) had the street to the harbour widened — prompted the narrowing of the lake and leaving it with the current oval shape. When it was drained the existing wall was erected to mark its perimeters, and a commemorative palm tree planted in the centre.

North of the Sacred Lake are the remains of 3 C. and 2 C. BC mansions. Two have yielded up statues: 🅖 the **Koinon of the Poseidoniasts of Beirut** was built by Syrian merchants (a statue of Aphrodite whopping a cupid with a slipper — now in the National Archaeological Museum in Athens — was found here); 🅐 the **House of the Diadumenos** was named after a 2 C. BC copy of Polykleitos' Apollo. Other houses have more to see; 🅔 the **Hillside House** has been excavated out of the hill and gives an overhead view of the typical internal layout, while 🅞 the **House of the Comedians** has a good example of a central cistern (complete with water and Kermit-green frogs) with part of its roof-   cum-floor intact.

Some way north of this house stands the **House at Scardana** — the only one of a number of houses in this area to be excavated. Turning east brings you to ❸ the **House of the Lake**, which has a pretty little peristyle court, while ❿ the large **Palaestra of Granite** (2 C. BC) behind it is dominated by a large water-filled cistern divided into quarters. ⓫ the **Palaestra of the Lake** (3 C. BC) is more nondescript, but also has a cistern. Behind it lies the line of the **Wall of Triarius** (66 BC), built by a Roman legate to protect against pirates. The wall ran over demolished ancient buildings past ❶ the **Temple of Anios** (7 C. BC), a small temple dedicated to a mythical king of Delos. Outside the line of the wall are the foundations of various unidentified buildings. From here a path runs north-east, past the site of the long vanished U-shaped **Hippodrome**. Built C. 200 BC, it was later demolished to build defensive walls. Its predecessors, the **Gymnasium** (3 C. BC) and **Stadium** (C. 274 BC) survive in part on the east side of Delos, but see few tourists. Beyond them are the remains of a number of houses and a large 2 C. BC **Synagogue**.

Mount Kynthos

The Mount Kynthos area (see the colour map facing p. 193) contains a diverse mix of buildings that reflect the diverse history of Delos. The theatre and residential buildings are the main attractions; some of the latter are among the best preserved 3 and 2 C. BC houses in Greece. Most retain walls up to chest height (these are not shown on the map for fear of rendering it unusable) and many adorned with mosaics have undergone some rebuilding. The mosaics — many quite famous — are something of a disappointment as they need watering to bring out their colours.

Along with visitors heading for the central sanctuary district, ❶ the **Agora of the Competialists** is the starting point for exploration of the Mount Kynthos district. Running down to the south is ❷ the **Maritime Quarter**. Little visited today (though the foreshore has a path of sorts running along it), this area is made up of warehouse buildings. Most are only partly excavated, but enough has been discovered to show that this was where the Delian slave market flourished. The tourist path, however, moves in the direction of ❸ the **Theatre Quarter** (the residential area near the theatre), where all the buildings have been explored. A walk up the ancient main street will bring you to a

marked side-street leading off to ❹ the **House of Cleopatra & Dioscurides** (137 BC); named after the statues of two wealthy Athenians to be seen within (this Cleopatra is not the queen of Egypt with the famously lovely nose: in fact, this lady hasn't even got a head), it has the remains of a typical peristyle pillared central courtyard. The statues on site are reproductions: the originals are now standing in the site museum. Further up the main street lies ❺ the **House of Dionysos**. The first of the 'mosaic' houses, it is named after the impressive mosaic of Dionysos riding side-saddle on a panther. Similarly, ❻ the rebuilt **House of the Trident** has a trident mosaic. Both houses can be locked and are only open if sufficient site staff have turned up for guard duty.

The main residential street finally emerges at ❼ the **Theatre** (4 C. BC). Now badly preserved in detail (its seating proved too tempting to masonry thieves) it is still impressive in its size and atmosphere. Climbing to the level of the higher tiers, it is easy enough to imagine it filled with a 5,500 capacity crowd. It is unique among ancient theatres in having a stage building constructed on its circular orchestra or stage: the **Skene**. Possibly three floors high (to allow the 'gods' to appear from above) it had colonnaded lower storeys. Only foundations remain, with rubble running back to ❽ the **Theatre Cistern**. This stored rainwater running off the theatre. 22.5 m long and 6 m wide, it is filled with water; its roof is missing, though the supporting arches remain.

The tourist path ascends the hill south of the theatre past a marble-lined doorway that marks ❾ the **Guest House**. Thought to have been an inn, it is notable for having the deepest cistern of any house on Delos. It is 8.3 m deep and without protective rails. Those that don't fall in will find the path continuing up to ❿ the **House of the Masks** (named after a mosaic illustrating a series of actor's masks). A large building, it had shops along its street side. Nearby stands ⓫ the **House of the Dolphins**, a smaller, richer structure with mosaics depicting cupids riding dolphins.

Once past the House of the Dolphins the tourist path emerges at an upper sanctuary level. This area contains a number of small temples, as well as shrines devoted to eastern deities (a reflection of the island's days as an international trading centre). The first recognisable building is ⓬ the **Herion** (C. 500 BC). A small temple dedicated to Hera, its columns survive, along with an altar. This temple also marks the point where the main path divides. One branch steps up to the summit of **Mt. Kynthos** (don't miss the tiny path running to the mysterious **Cave of Cynthus** or **Grotto of Hercules** at ⓜ. Dating from the 3 C. BC, it contained a statue of the hero under its roof of pitched granite slabs, and has a circular marble altar outside the door). The main path runs up past the foundations of ⓞ the **Sanctuary of Agathe Tyche** (of which little survives) before reaching the summit. Here stood ⓞ the **Sanctuary of Kynthian Zeus & Athena** (7 C. BC). Once similar in size to the Herion, the only surviving remains are a few slippery foundation stones from which you get blown into next week trying to take in the superb panoramic views.

Returning to the Herion, the next building of note is ⓟ the heavily restored **Temple of Isis** (3 C. BC), complete with a headless statue of Isis standing within its walls. Nearby is ⓠ **Serapeion C**, a small stoa-lined court. Further along this terrace is ⓡ the **Sanctuary of the Syrian Gods** (C. 100 BC) which included a religious amphitheatre for witnessing ceremonies. Below this terrace is the site of a second stoa-lined court: ⓢ **Serapeion B** (2 C. BC), and below that, ⓣ the **Cistern of Inopos** (3 C. BC). Still filled with green water, it was built to collect the fountain-head waters of the Inopos, the sacred river of Delos. Legend had it that had its source in the Nile (hence the location of all 'eastern' shrines in this area). Nearby is ⓤ the **House of Inopos**. South of the cistern lie the remains of ⓥ the **Monument of Mithridates Eupator** (C. 100 BC), a king of Pontos. This stood in front of ⓦ the **Samothrakeion** (4 C. BC) a temple to the Great Gods (the Kabeiroi) of Samothrace.

East of the cistern, in the largely unexcavated area, lie other buildings of interest; notably ⓧ **Serapeion A** (3 C. BC), a third stoa-lined court, and — accessed via a narrow path branching off the museum path — ⓨ the **House of Hermes** (4 C. BC). This two-storey house is the best preserved peristyle court mansion on Delos and not to be missed, as it gives the visitor an excellent impression of what many of the houses must have looked like. Further along this path lies ⓩ the **Aphrodision** (4 C. BC), a tiny temple of Aphrodite. From here the path passes discarded rails from the narrow railway used by early excavators to remove debris, and rejoins the main sanctuary area.

Evia / Euboea

EYBOIA; 3580 km²; pop. 165,000.

CHALCIS: CODE ☎ 0221
POLICE ☎ 22100
KIMI: CODE ☎ 0222
POLICE ☎ 22555
FIRST AID ☎ 22322

The second largest island in Greece, mountainous Evia (or Euboea) is not a member of the Cyclades; it is included in this chapter thanks to its links with the North Cycladic islands via hydrofoils running to both and ferries running out of Rafina. In fact, Evia isn't popular with island hoppers and remains well off the tourist map, lacking the beaches or sights that would bring the crowds. The island's position on the north-east coast of Attica does little to help, as linked by a bridge and motorway to Athens it is often seen as merely an adjunct to the mainland it hugs so closely. Even the main town can't seem to make up its mind and clings to both island and mainland. Ferry connections are poor, being confined to a number of minor crossing points to the mainland at intervals along the coast (this tells you all you need to know about the island's roads) and the main Skyros—'mainland' link. These are all local services and times vary little during the year.

The island capital is at **Chalcis**, located half-way up the west coast at the narrowest point of the Evian Strait (known as the Euripus Channel). The town was an important centre in ancient Greece, thanks to its strategic position on the straits, but is now an ugly commercial centre with only a distinctive Turkish quarter, and a popular, up-market waterfront to redeem it. The old fashioned swing bridge that straddles the 30 m strait marks the boundary between the chic northern and southern commercial quarters; the straits are too narrow to admit cargo vessels north of the bridge. Not unnaturally the town is also the hub of the island bus services. These are wide ranging, but infrequent, and on difficult roads. This, and the distances involved, means that Evia is not really a moped island either. If getting around is not very easy, getting to Evia is: bus and rail links with Athens are very good.

Around Evia are a number of towns or villages with little in common. **Eretria** is the most notable of them, and is now emerging as a poor tourist resort. Like Chalcis, it was a major ancient city in the 6 C. BC, before Athens dominated the region and it fell into decline. Indeed, by the beginning of the 19 C. the population was so small that the town was used to re-house those inhabitants of Psara that managed to escape the 1824 Turkish devastation of that island. As a result Eretria is also known as **Nea Psara**. Set on a dry dusty plain, it is a garden of Eden short of beautiful thanks to the half-empty grid layout of the incomplete new town, but the plentiful archaeological remains of the ancient city are some compensation, as is the good beach east of the harbour.

Other centres have less going for them. **Loutra Edipsos** is Greece's premier spa, emerging as a popular holiday destination in the late 19 C. However, it has yet to emerge as a modern tourist resort and is marred by the rather dismal air of a faded watering hole. More cheerful spots are to be found elsewhere. **Limni** is a coastal village turned resort, as is **Pefki** on the northern coast, but even so, there is little disguising the fact that neither are worth flying all the way to Greece for. The latter does, however, receive occasional visits from Sporades' hydrofoils.

The southern half of Evia is dominated by two port villages, **Karystos** and **Marmari**. Both have direct ferry links with Rafina and tend to clog up with escaping Athenians during the weekends. Karystos is the nicer of the two, set in a wide bay with a Venetian-built harbour. Marmari has less charm but does offer regular boat trips to the small wooded Petali Islands (**Megalo Petali** & **Xero**) 1 km to the south.

Kimi Port (as distinct from Kimi town, a hillside village 4 km inland), is the principal jumping off point for Skyros and its links with the other Northern Aegean destinations. It is tucked beneath the mountain range that makes up the backbone of Evia, and is a very pretty little place with an excellent beach just below the harbour. Unfortunately, beds are thin on the ground. Thanks to Evia's motorway link with Athens, Kimi is a de facto mainland port with regular buses, and most visitors pass straight through. The link with Skyros is the mainstay of ferry activity. Other departures (usually a twice weekly to the Sporades in High Season) are poorly advertized, and remain easier to arrive than depart on.

⊨

Considering its size, Evia is poorly equipped with hotels, and rooms are a rarity. **Chalcis** offers the greatest choice of beds thanks to its hotel-littered waterfront. Unfortunately, the majority are pricey, top end of the market, establishments. Top of the range is the A-class *Lucy* (☎ 23831). Budget hotels lie nearer the bridge. These include the *Kentrikon* (☎ 71525) and the very noisy (and somewhat primitive) *Kymata* (☎ 21317) and *Iris* (☎ 22246). Meantime, on the mainland side you will find the quieter *Hara* (☎ 25541) is very reasonable.

Eretria has several mid-range hotels including the good C-class *Xenia* (☎ 61202). As it stands alone on a causeway-linked islet on the east side of the town (recently re-named **Dream Island**) noise is not a problem. **Kimi Port** has rooms and two hotels, the best being the C-class *Beis* (☎ 22604).

A

There is camping on Evia, but the sites are poorly placed and geared to motor-campers. Island hoppers are likely to find that the site near **Pefki** (☎ 0226 41161) of most use. There is also a motorpark site 5 km north of Eretria.

ᏀᎧ

If you discount the attractive pine-clad mountain scenery, the **Euripus Channel** in **Chalcis** is Evia's most noteworthy sight, and boasts a 2500 year pedigree as a tourist attraction thanks to the odd combination of land and currents which make the tide change eight times a day. Since the building of the first bridge over the

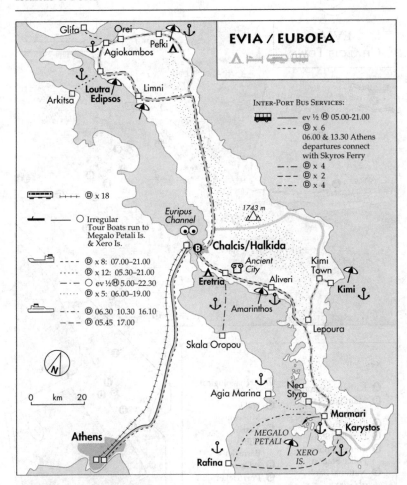

EVIA / EUBOEA

INTER-PORT BUS SERVICES:

— ev ½ Ⓗ 05.00-21.00

- - - Ⓓ x 6
06.00 & 13.30 Athens
departures connect
with Skyros Ferry

—·—· Ⓓ x 4

- - - Ⓓ x 2

—··— Ⓓ x 4

⊢⊣⊢⊣ Ⓓ x 18

○ Irregular
Tour Boats run to
Megalo Petali Is.
& Xero Is.

- - - Ⓓ x 8: 07.00–21.00
········ Ⓓ x 12: 05.30–21.00
—·—· ○ ev ½Ⓗ 5.00–22.30
—·—· ○ x 5: 06.00–19.00

—·—· Ⓓ 06.30 10.30 16.10
- - - Ⓓ 05.45 17.00

0   km   20

Glifa • Orei • Pefki • Agiokambos • Loutra Edipsos • Arkitsa • Limni • Euripus Channel • 1743 m • Chalcis/Halkida • Ancient City • Eretria • Aliveri • Amarinthos • Kimi Town • Kimi • Lepoura • Skala Oropou • Agia Marina • Nea Styra • Marmari • Karystos • Athens • MEGALO PETALI • XERO IS. • Rafina

30 m-wide narrows in the 5 c. BC, the locals have wondered over the phenomena. Aristotle is reputed to have drowned when he threw himself into the sea in exasperation at his inability to explain it. His successors still haven't come up with the answer but, given the murky state of the water, have generally opted for cleaner forms of suicide. Signs of the ancient city are as well hidden as the sea-bed, and archaeology fans will do best to head for the

Archaeological Museum, which houses finds from all over the island. The remains of ancient **Eretria** offer better sightseeing; the great rival of Chalcis (the two cities fought a succession of wars for control over the plain that separates them) has a notable theatre (largely denuded of stone), the foundations of a number of important houses and a section of city wall, complete with the best preserved Archaic period gate in Greece.

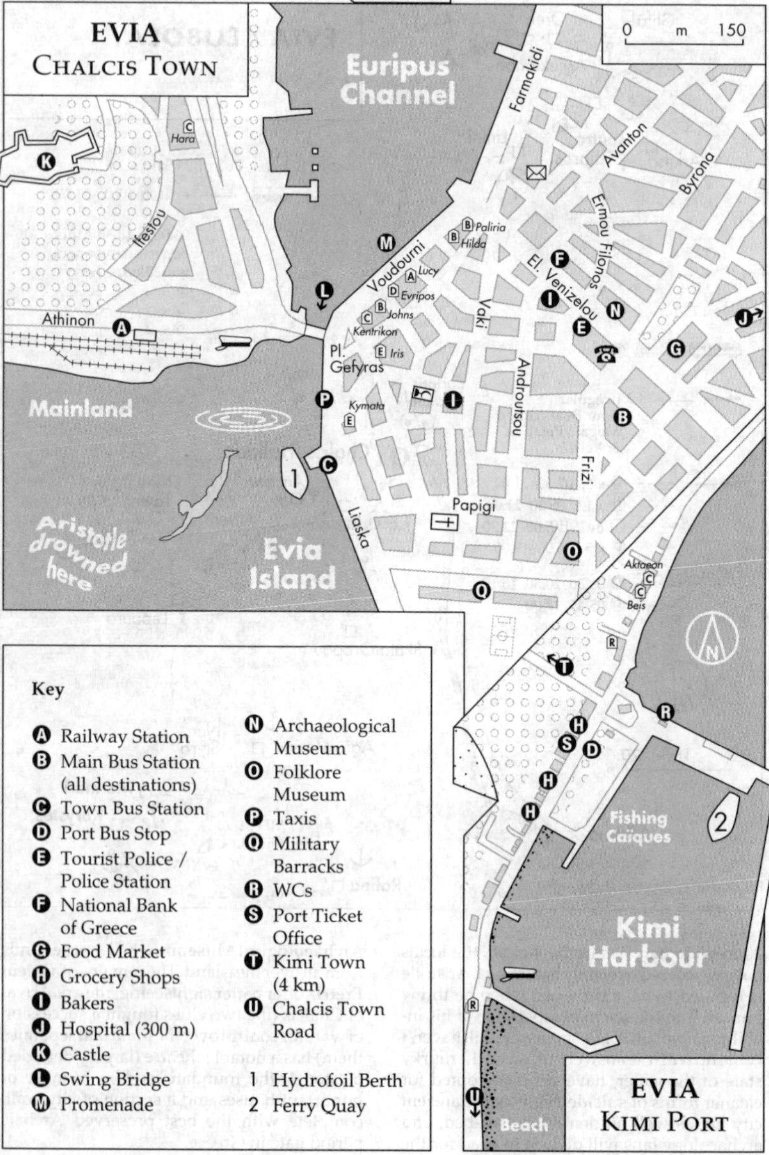

EVIA
CHALCIS TOWN

Euripus
Channel

Farmakidi

Avanton

Byrona

0   m   150

C
Hara

K

Ermou Filonos

El. Venizelou

Voudourni

M

B Paliria
A Hilda

F

Lucy

I

N

A Evripos

E

G

B Johns

Iflsou

Athinon

A

L

C Kentrikon

Vaki

E Iris

J

Mainland

P

Pl.
Gefyras

Kymata
E

Androutsou

B

Aristotle
drowned
here

C

1

Frizi

Iliaska

Papigi

O

**Evia
Island**

Aktaeon

C
Beis

Q

N

T

R

Key

Ⓐ Railway Station
Ⓑ Main Bus Station
   (all destinations)
Ⓒ Town Bus Station
Ⓓ Port Bus Stop
Ⓔ Tourist Police /
   Police Station
Ⓕ National Bank
   of Greece
Ⓖ Food Market
Ⓗ Grocery Shops
Ⓘ Bakers
Ⓙ Hospital (300 m)
Ⓚ Castle
Ⓛ Swing Bridge
Ⓜ Promenade

Ⓝ Archaeological
   Museum
Ⓞ Folklore
   Museum
Ⓟ Taxis
Ⓠ Military
   Barracks
Ⓡ WCs
Ⓢ Port Ticket
   Office
Ⓣ Kimi Town
   (4 km)
Ⓤ Chalcis Town
   Road

1 Hydrofoil Berth
2 Ferry Quay

S
D

H

H

R

Fishing
Caïques

2

**Kimi
Harbour**

R

U

Beach

**EVIA
KIMI PORT**

Mykonos

ΜΥΚΟΝΟΣ; 88 km²; pop. 5,700.

CODE ☎ 0289
PORT POLICE ☎ 22218
POLICE ☎ 22482
FIRST AID ☎ 23994

Now among the most heavily touristed (and expensive) of all the Greek islands and the location for the get-away-from-it-all film *Shirley Valentine*, Mykonos is one of those islands that are superb at the quieter times of the year but which descend into the realms of the truly awful at the height of the High Season (with over 750,000 visitors a year some of the residents even go island hopping to get away from the chaos — especially in mid-July to mid-August). The island has been near the top of the Greek island tourist map since the mid 1960s courtesy of one of the most scenic harbours in the Mediterranean, a profusion of good sand beaches tolerating nudism, and the nearby premier sightseeing island of Delos. Sadly, the prolonged exposure to heavy tourism is reflected in the terrible damage wrought on the landscape — thanks to the excessive amount of hotel and holiday home building — and on the local tourist industry (the attitude on Mykonos to tourists is increasingly reminiscent of darkest Athens: i.e. forget the old fashioned Greek ideal that 'visitors are guests' and screw them for every penny you can get out of them instead). Sadly, on Mykonos you need to check your change carefully — even on buses — and keep an eye out for double-charging in supermarkets.

Formerly a preserve of the world's jet-setters, Mykonos always has exhibited wildly inflated prices, thanks to a scene dominated by expensive boutiques and night clubs where French and the male gay scene thrive. A procession of cruise ships calling provides little incentive to keep prices down (you should reckon on paying a 25% premium for the pleasure of a stay on Mykonos). Notwithstanding the cost of living, backpackers also swarm over the island each summer in increasing numbers; their great redeeming function being to make the island much safer for the single male who, in years past, was apt to find out what the fairer sex have to put up with. Unfortunately, Mykonos also attracts a goodly number of rowdy urban Greeks, seemingly attracted by the island's reputation for loose living. At their best they clog the roads with mass moped displays; at their worst they included a rapist with a rather nasty knife in 1995, and a mass convention of graffiti artists in 1996. All this sounds pretty dire, but if you are careful when here, and come at the right time, Mykonos is still a very rewarding place to visit.

The only large settlement on a small island, **Mykonos Town** is the over-burdened hub of all this activity. Centred on the famous crescent-shaped harbour bay with its headland topped with windmills, it is an attractive maze of white-washed cubic houses riddled with alleyways deliberately contrived to distract both would-be pirates (to say nothing of tourists) and the *meltemi* wind that attacks Mykonos very hard each summer. The largest of its kind in the Cyclades, the chora street maze is so intricate that it happily baffles seasoned visitors. It is in the nature of things that sooner or later you will be obliged to head for either the hills and the roads that surround the town, or the chaos that is the bus square at Plati Yailos, or the harbour itself, simply in order to re-establish your bearings.

The harbour, naturally the focal point of the town, is stunningly attractive when viewed from the hill behind the ferry quay, and among the prettiest in Greece. However, the heavy waterfront mix of tavernas, souvenir and (expensive) gold and silver shops, backed by bars, night-clubs and restaurants, quickly dispels any pretence that this is an unspoilt island town. This is not to say that Mykonos Town doesn't exude Greek island charm,

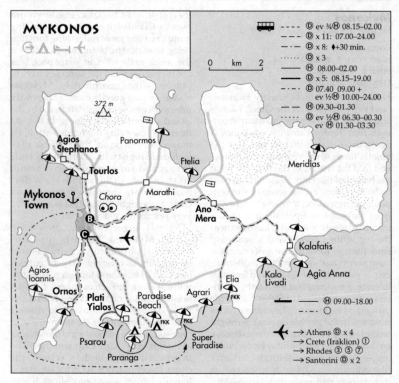

MYKONOS

----	Ⓓ ev ¾Ⓗ 08.15–02.00
---	Ⓓ x 11: 07.00–24.00
--	Ⓓ x 8: ♦+30 min.
......	Ⓓ x 3
――	Ⓗ 08.00–02.00
▬▬	Ⓓ x 5: 08.15–19.00
-·-·-	Ⓓ 07.40_09.00 + ev ½Ⓗ 10.00–24.00
― ―	Ⓗ 09.30–01.30
······	Ⓓ ev ½Ⓗ 06.30–00.30 ev Ⓗ 01.30–03.30

0   km   2

372 m

Agios Stephanos
Tourlos
Mykonos Town
Agios Ioannis
Ornos
Plati Yialos
Psarou
Paranga
Paradise Beach
Super Paradise
Agrari
Elia FKK
Kalo Livadi
Agia Anna
Kalafatis
Meridias
Ano Mera
Marathi
Chora
Ftelia
Panormos

Ⓗ 09.00–18.00
Ⓞ

✈ → Athens Ⓓ x 4
→ Crete (Iraklion) ①
→ Rhodes ③ ⑤ ⑦
→ Santorini Ⓓ x 2

---

for it does — almost to excess. But it is difficult to escape the impression that it is contrived and done purely for the tourists' benefit. This can be seen in the spate of windmill rebuilding on the hills around the town (leaving postcard manufacturers struggling to keep pace). Further building work is now going on in an effort to relieve the pressure. A ring road around the town is due to open in 1999, and a new ferry port is being built up the coast at **Tourlos** to replace the existing town quay, as ferries have great difficulty manoeuvring in the small harbour (it is unclear if this will open in 1999).

Fortunately, amidst the tourists and building, echoes of the old Mykonos can still to be found; the locals who aren't in the tourist industry somehow manage to carry on with their daily routine, seemingly oblivious to the mayhem around them, and still walk down to the waterfront each morning to buy produce and freshly caught fish. Tourists also get in on the act by relieving the fishermen of any part of their catch that they can't sell, so that they can throw fish to the very photogenic pelican that is allowed to flap the streets at will. Actually, the history of the Mykonos pelican (the island's famous mascot, and a beast that is snapped in virtually every photo-orientated Greek island guide book) is worth a brief mention as it provides a good insight of how the island has gone ever down. The original pelican landed on Mykonos in 1956 during a storm, and rapidly emerged as a premier attraction just when the island was taking off as a tourist destination. The locals persuaded it to stay by clipping its wings and naming it Petros. In the event this was a slight misnomer as it was pe*trol* that did for it: the poor thing was run over in 1985 — an victim of the island's traffic injury boom. Fortunately, its killer — a passing taxi driver — also fancied himself as a taxidermist and attempted to recover the situation by stuffing his victim. This was not an unqualified success, as the deception was noticed; the islanders thereafter deciding to install Petros in the Craft and Folklore Museum and get in a couple of replacements (now usually to be found near the waterfront, looking vainly for a refuge from the camera-snapping crowds) hoping that no one would notice the difference.

If the pelicans have got any sense, they keep their feathers well down at night, for Mykonos after dark is something else; in High Season the town literally throbs. Unfortunately, some hereabouts throb too much; particularly when confronted by an unattached female, and Mykonos has had more than its fair share of problems (those who find all this difficult to square with the fact this is the *Shirley Valentine* island should note that the film was produced well out of season when the pretence of a dreamy, idyllic Greek island could be maintained). Nightlife is

scattered around the town. The hottest venues change with each year, though there are regular favourites. These include the big *Hard Rock Café* complex on the Ano Mera road (reached via free mini-buses from the town) and a cluster of bars near the Paraportiani church. These include the *Windmill Disco*, the *Irish Disco* and the *Scandinavian Bar*. More up-market venues are to be found behind Little Venice and the yacht marina near the ferry quay.

The beaches are the island's other big draw — particularly those on the south coast, which offers an appealing mix of windy headlands and bays decorated with long strands of sand. These start at **Plati Yialos**, a crowded, hotel-backed beach with a small quay from which caïques shuttle along the coast to Paradise, Super Paradise and Elia beaches. All bar Plati Yialos have their nudist end. **Paradise Beach** is the most famous (and crowded), though it is somewhat over-rated. The beach bar attached to the campsite really goes to town when it comes to charging rip-off prices. Nudism is confined to a few brave women and a clutch of posing gay men on the western end. **Super Paradise** has traditionally been the gay beach, but these days it has a pretty even mix of sexes and more nudity than Paradise. **Elia Beach** is the best of the four and is predominately nude. All four are linked by a rough path. Taking the overspill from these crowded strands are the windy north coast beaches. However, most are only good for sunbathing fans as offshore currents can be dangerous. The best of these beaches are at **Panormos** and **Ftelia**.

The interior of Mykonos is hilly and barren with surprisingly few villages. However, farms and the massive numbers of new holiday homes now under construction and ruining every skyline, leave

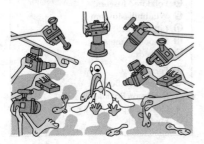

the landscape cluttered with white-washed cubic architecture in abundance. Other centres are small; the most visited being **Agios Stephanos**, which has a sub-standard (for Mykonos) beach that is nonetheless popular because it is easy to get to. The only village of any size inland is at **Ano Mera**. Home to a museum and a 6 c. church, it is the centre of one of the few remaining unspoilt parts of the island.

Buses run frequently around Mykonos, particularly between the town and all the popular beaches. Unusually for a Greek island they operate into the small hours during the summer months. Ferry links are also good, for Mykonos is an import-ant bridging port for those wanting to travel onto or from the Cyclades Central line. Sailings to Rafina (usually labelled 'Athens') are widely advertised without mention of the stops at Tinos and Andros.

Mykonos has a hotel and room information office on the ferry quay; this makes life relative-ly easy, but not that easy as beds fill up early in High Season. Perhaps more than with any other island it pays to arrive before noon.

The town has a number of C and D 'standard' (one hesitates to say 'priced') hotels including the waterfront *Apollon* (☎ 22223) and a varied collection on Kaloaera St., including the C-class *Zorzis* (☎ 22167) and *Marios* (☎ 22704) and the D-class *Maria* (☎ 24212) and *Philippi* (☎ 22294). The hills behind the town are another fertile hunting ground, and include the noisy *Olympia* (☎ 22964) and the better placed *Nazou* (☎ 22626) and C-class *Zanni* (☎ 22486) and *Pelican* (☎ 23454). *Paradise Beach Camping* also offers popular chalets. At the top end of the market is the poor A-class *Leto* (☎ 22207) which earlier in the century played host to the King of Greece, but sadly, hasn't been upgraded since. A better bet if you want everything from satellite TV to saunas and jacuzzis are the *Petasos Hotels*: there are three on Mykonos; one in the town (☎ 22608), and two at Plati Yailos (☎ 23437).

A

Mykonos has two sites five minutes walk from each other (via the coast path). Compet-ition between the two ensures considerable rivalry in grabbing campers off the boats.

Both charge the same rates and are among the most expensive in the Aegean in High Season (reckon on paying at least 300 GDR more per day than on other island sites).

Camping Mykonos (☎ 24578) is a newish site on a headland overlooking Paranga beach. Now the best site on the island, it has clean facilities, friendly staff and is served by hourly buses en route between Mykonos Town and Paradise beach. Let down by an pricey mini-market.

Paradise Beach Camping (☎ 22852): forget the 'Paradise' bit — this is the site that threatens to give Hell a good name. The site's proud boast that it has been around since 1969 is fully borne out by its awful washing facilities which clearly haven't been upgraded since. Add to this some very unenthusiastic staff and a mini-market that charges double the rates found in most supermarkets, and one is left wondering why anyone chooses to stay here.

Key

A Accommodation Office / Tourist Police / Camping Bus pick-up point
B Bus Station (N. & Central Mykonos)
C Bus Station (Pl. Plati Yialos)
D Police
E Tourist Police
F National Bank of Greece
G Supermarket
H Newspapers / Bookshop
I Ferry Passenger Stalls
J Public WCs
K Moped Rental
L Paraportiani Church
M Archaeological Museum
N Maritime Museum of the Aegean
O Folklore Museum
P Windmill Museum
Q Little Venice
R School of Fine Arts
S Cathedral

1 Ferry Quay
2 Delos Tour Boats
3 Excursion Boat Berth
4 Cruise Ship mooring point
5 Hydrofoils

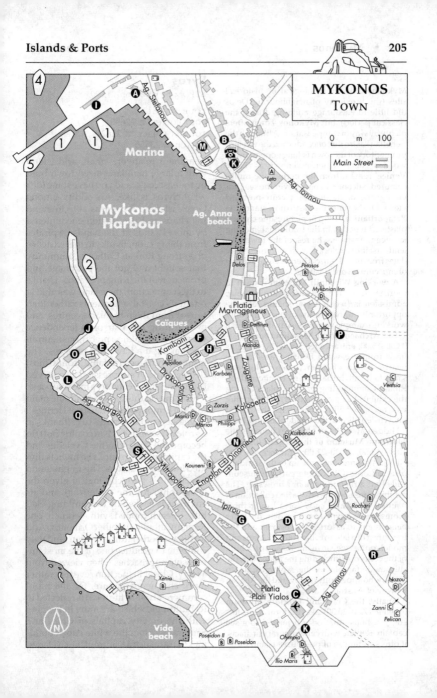

MYKONOS
TOWN

0   m   100

Main Street

Marina

Mykonos
Harbour

Ag. Anna
beach

Ag. Stefanou

Ag. Tonnou

Leto

Delos

Petasos

Mykonian Inn

Platia
Mavrogenous

Delfines

Caïques

Kambani

Apollon

Manda

Karboni

Drakopoulou

Dilou

Zougane

Zorzis

Maria

Philippi

Marios

Kaloaera

Ventsia

Karbonaki

Ag. Anargiron

Kouneni

Enoplion

Dinameon

RC

Mitropoleos

Ipirou

Rochari

Xenia

Platia
Plati Yialos

Nazou

Zanni

Pelican

Vida
beach

Poseidon II   *Poseidon*

Olympia

Ilio Maris

N

〇〇

Mykonos lacks archaeological or historical sites (the proximity of neighbouring Delos did little to encourage building during the classical period), but **Mykonos Town** offers plenty by way of compensation. Although the Venetian kastro that once adorned the western promontory of the town is long gone, a row of wooden galleried houses known as **'Little Venice'** remain from the period; the multi-coloured balconies hanging over the sea providing one of the town's picture-postcard views. On the site of the kastro now stands the **Paraportiani**, a group of picturesque chapels plastered together in the traditional 'melting ice cream' fashion. The rest of the town also lends itself to exploration, though most only dates from the 18—19 c. There are also a clutch of museums worth visiting:

A working **Windmill Museum** is open to tourists on the hillside east of the harbour; admission is free and you should take the opportunity to have a look (this is the only working example you can visit in the islands).

The **Archaeological Museum** (open ②–⑦ 08.30–15.00; entrance fee 500 GDR) contains finds from excavated Delian graves on the nearby island of Rinia (when Delos was sanctified, all burials were re-interred on Rinia). Commanding pride of place among the exhibits is a 7 c. BC red terra-cotta pithoi vase decorated with a relief that is the earliest known depiction of the wooden horse of Troy.

Hidden away in an old town house is the **Maritime Museum of the Aegean** (open ⑩ 10.30–13.00, 18.30–21.00; entrance fee 200 GDR). Although not quite up to the standard of its Santorini (Oia) counterpart, the museum still offers a rewarding hour's browsing. The exhibits consist of a pretty varied collection of nautical odds and ends spread over three rooms, and a lawned back garden (the latter being home to assorted gravestones and the top 20 feet of a late 19 c. lighthouse). Maps and models on an Aegean theme make up the bulk of the collection (including the *Endeavour*, the ship made famous by the explorer Captain Cook; who apparently discovered the Aegean by way of Australia).

Finally, the **Craft and Folklore Museum** (open ⑩ 17.30–20.30) takes the form of a restored 17 c. house that once belonged to a sea captain. Replete with contemporary artifacts, it offers a glimpse of pre-tourist island life.

Syros

ΣΥΡΟΣ; 86 km²; pop. 21,000.

CODE ☎ 0281
PORT POLICE ☎ 22690
TOURIST POLICE ☎ 22620
POLICE ☎ 23555

Imagine a relatively small, arid island with a large mainland-sized town built on the east coast, and you have some idea what Syros is like. An oddity among Greek islands, Syros was able to avoid the chaos and destruction encountered by most islands at the hands of pirates from the 17 c. on, thanks to the existence of a strong Roman Catholic community that sought and got the patronage and protection of the King of France. Thanks to this connection, the island was able to retain its coastal settlements rather than retreat from them to inland centres, and even during the War of Independence was able to maintain a precarious neutrality, making it a haven for refugees. The influx of refugees (notably from Chios) fleeing Turkish suppression also served to give the town economy a massive boost.

Building on this background, the main town of **Ermoupolis** ('The city of Hermes') developed rapidly in the 19 c. (thanks to its role as *the* mid-Aegean coaling port) to become the largest in the Cyclades and the capital of the group. The town is divided into three quarters. This might sound Greek but is perfectly logical given the geography; for the waterfront and its environs is backed by two building-clad hills — each topped with a church, one Roman Catholic, the other Orthodox. Add to this a superb natural harbour, and they combine to produce one of the most impressive approaches when viewed from a ferry. Closer inspection reveals a rather more chequered picture, for the rapid commercial rise of the town is reflected in its buildings, which are more in keeping with the dowdy capitals of Chios and Sami rather than the white cubist buildings that are such a feature of the Cyclades.

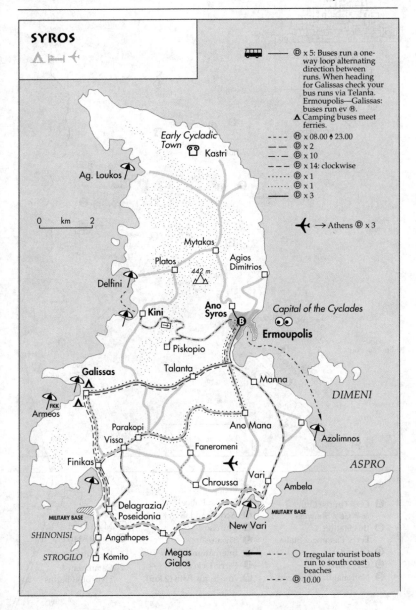

SYROS

⊞ x 5: Buses run a one-way loop alternating direction between runs. When heading for Galissas check your bus runs via Telanta. Ermoupolis—Galissas: buses run ev ⊕.
▲ Camping buses meet ferries.

- - - - Ⓗ x 08.00 ◊ 23.00
— — Ⓓ x 2
—·— Ⓓ x 10
— — Ⓓ x 14: clockwise
······· Ⓓ x 1
······· Ⓓ x 1
——— Ⓓ x 3

✈ → Athens Ⓓ x 3

Early Cycladic Town
Kastri
Ag. Loukos

0   km   2

Mytakas
Platos
442 m
Agios Dimitrios
Delfini
Kini
Ano Syros
Ⓑ
Capital of the Cyclades
◉◉
Ermoupolis
Piskopio
Talanta
Manna
DIMENI
Galissas ▲
Armeos FKK ▲
Parakopi
Vissa
Ano Mana
Azolimnos
Faneromeni
Finikas
ASPRO
Chroussa
Vari
Ambela
MILITARY BASE
Delagrazia/ Poseidonia
New Vari
MILITARY BASE
SHINONISI
Angathopes
STROGILO
Komito
Megas Gialos

▬—·— ○ Irregular tourist boats run to south coast beaches
- - - - Ⓓ 10.00

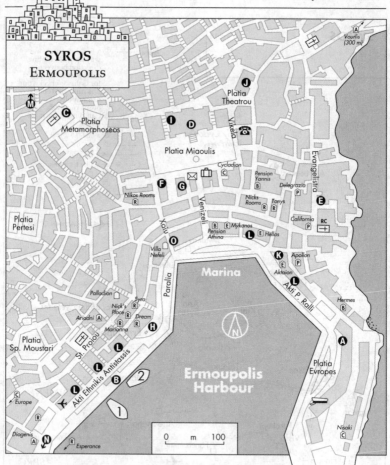

SYROS

ERMOUPOLIS

Vourlis
(300 m)

Platia
Theatrou

Platia
Metamorphoseos

Platia Miaoulis

Cycladian

Pension
Yannis

Delegrazia

Nicks
Rooms

Tonys

California

Nikos Rooms

Pension
Athina

Mykonos

Hellas

Platia
Pertesi

Villa
Nefeli

Apollon

Aktaion

Marina

Palladion

Nick's
Place

Syra

Ariadni

Dream

Marionna

Hermes

Platia
Sp. Moustari

**Ermoupolis
Harbour**

Platia
Evropes

Europe

Diogenis

Nisaki

Esperance

0   m   100

Key

- **Ⓐ** EOT Tourist Office
  & WCs / Showers
- **Ⓑ** Bus Station &
  Ferry Passenger Stalls
- **Ⓒ** Cathedral
- **Ⓓ** City Hall
- **Ⓔ** National Bank of Greece
- **Ⓕ** Police
- **Ⓖ** Tourist Police
- **Ⓗ** Accommodation Kiosk
- **Ⓘ** Museum
- **Ⓙ** Theatre
- **Ⓚ** International Press
- **Ⓛ** Ferry Tickets
- **Ⓜ** Ano Syros Path (2 km)
- **Ⓝ** Main Road
- **Ⓞ** Street Market
- **1** Ferry Quay
- **2** Catamaran &
  Hydrofoil Berths

Fortunately the islanders have made a conspicuous — and largely successful — effort to improve the appearance of the waterfront in recent years and the all new polished up Ermoupolis is now beginning to exude something of a buzz in High Season. Even the staircase-choked back-streets are gradually losing the air of dilapidation, though they are still home to an intriguing collection of down-at-heel shops and a lively street market of sorts along Xiou St. All this might not sound very encouraging, but for this very reason Ermoupolis does offer some interesting sightseeing as it sports a faded neo-classical charm of sorts that neighbouring islands cannot match: it is worth a visit just to capture the contrast with the cute Cycladic village look that dominates elsewhere.

The two town hills also contrast greatly with each other and the lower town. Catholic **Ano Syros** is easily the more interesting as the buildings on its upper slopes form the nucleus of the original island chora. On your left hand side as you enter the harbour, it has a meandering staircase running down to the lower town. Attempting this climb is the most popular sightseeing trip in town, and you can take in the British Cemetery half-way up the hill (where the victims of a WW1 troopship sinking are interred). The Orthodox hill town on **Vrontado** only dates from the 19 c. and, bar the domed church that marks it out from the more Kastro-like church topping Ano Syros, it has little of interest.

The recent tourist influx has yet to make much impact on the rest of the island. North of Ermoupolis, tourists will find they have become the main local attraction; though ever increasing numbers of hill walkers head for the area. The main resort (courtesy of the best island beach) is at **Galissas** on the west coast. Between maintaining traditional agriculture and catering to the tourists, the patchwork village is a curiosity, with reed-beds and rural farming lying uneasily alongside a

decidedly incongruous and little used concrete pitch and putt course, oddly isolated hotels and a couple of camp sites. Weekends find the tree-backed beach packed with islanders, so if you like solitude you will do better going elsewhere. One possible option — provided your body is up to it — is to take the track over the southern headland to the island's nudist beach at Armeos (though voyeurs shouldn't get their hopes up as there are usually as few nudists as clothes on view).

South of Galissas is a second resort strip running from **Finikas** down to **Delagrazia** (alias **Poseidonia**). However, the beaches are much more scruffy, and one has to search pretty hard to justify stopping here with so many other good beach islands close to hand. The remaining southern half of Syros is, if truth be told, best seen from a bus: merely a collection of small villages scattered over low-lying countryside and lacking tourist appeal.

Ferry links with Syros are adequate but no more: long gone are the days when the Ermoupolis was the hub of the Cycladic ferry system. In fact Syros is somewhat out on a limb these days, seeing a greater number of odd-ball calls than most islands. The Port Police have a complete list of the day's sailings chalked up in the doorway of their barrack-like building. In the past ferries and hydrofoils have docked at various points around the harbour, but with the introduction of computer ticketing you can expect all boats to berth near the passenger stalls on the west side quay. The town bus station has also moved here. Frequency of buses to the main centres is good, but dominated by a large number of one-way services.

➤

There are beds aplenty in **Ermoupolis**; most are at the budget end of the market, and are advertised by a forest of signs. Given the comparatively small numbers of tourists visiting Syros, finding a bed is rarely a problem and there is now a quayside kiosk to help you. The relocation of the ferry berth to the west side of the harbour is prompting a rash of new hotel and room conversions. These include the plush A-class *Ariadni* and the quayside *Dream Rooms*. At the bottom end of the market are *Tony's*, buried in the warren of streets behind the waterfront and the better located *Apollon* (☎ 22158) and *Athina* (☎ 23600). More up-market hotels are not so centrally placed. Nearest is the B-class *Hermes* (☎ 28011) with its own tiny section of private beach. On the west side of the port is the C-class *Europe* (☎ 28771), and to the north-east stands the A-class *Vourlis* (☎ 28440). Elsewhere on Syros beds are few except at **Galissas** which has a supply of rooms.

Λ

Two sites exist on Syros at **Galissas**. Set in a pistachio nut-tree grove, *Two Hearts Camping* (☎ 42052) — a member of the *Harmonie* scheme — is the better of them. Don't be put off by the romantic pitch to their advertising — broken single hearts are also admitted. *Camping Yianna* (☎ 42418) is nearer the beach, but rather run down. Mini-buses from both meet all boats.

𝒢𝒪

Ermoupolis offers the main sightseeing on Syros, and unusually for a Greek island town is well endowed with street names (the west European influence coming to the fore again). Several blocks up from the waterfront is the impressive **Miaoulis Square**. Adorned with a statue of the Greek hero of the War of Independence after which it is named, and a bandstand, it acquires a cosmopolitan air once evening falls. To the west side of the town hall that dominates the square is a small **Museum** housing exhibits (courtesy of this being the capital of the Cyclades) from other Cycladic islands too small to possess one (the exhibits include a few Cycladic figures from Keros and Amorgos). Just north-east of the square you will also find a miniature version of the La Scala **Opera House**: built in 1862, it has been closed for refurbishing ever since.

The hills north of **Kastri** offer possibly the most intriguing and (unless you like hard hill-walking) inaccessible sites on the island. Ringing one of the hilltops are the walls of one of the largest of the **Early Cycladic** culture villages yet discovered. Built towards the end of the period, it clearly was defensive in function (the odd horseshoe-shaped bastion aside, the surviving 'ramparts' look just like typical hill farm walls the world over), and was accompanied by a large cemetery that has yielded up a number of important Cycladic figurines.

Tinos
ΤΗΝΟΣ; 193 km²; pop. 7,730.

CODE ☎ 0283
PORT POLICE ☎ 22348
POLICE ☎ 22100
FIRST AID ☎ 22210

The spiritual centre of modern Greece, mountainous Tinos even outshines Patmos for raw pilgrim-pulling power. Billed as the Lourdes of the Aegean, Sundays and the Virgin Mary-related festivals on the 25th March (Annunciation), and particularly the 15th of August (Feast of the Assumption), see the main centre of Tinos Town jam-packed with the faithful. If you plan to stay, then you should try to avoid arriving on Tinos on Saturdays and in the week preceding these festivals. The focus of all this activity is an icon housed in the church that dominates the town: the Panagia Evangelistra (or Megalochari, meaning 'Great Joy'). However, the religious dimension is only one aspect to the spiritual importance of Tinos; for the island is also a focus of Greek nationalism, thanks to its history of being the last of the Greek islands to succumb to Turkish rule (when the Venetians finally abandoned it in 1715). The torpedoing of the visiting Greek warship *Elli* on Assumption Day 1940 by an Italian submarine (before Greece had formally joined the war on the side of the allies) was an outrage that also served to encourage Greek resistance during WW2. As a result of this background, Tinos has thrived on Greek rather than foreign tourism (something all too evident in the all-Greek timetables outside ticket agencies), and it is only now starting to emerge as a foreign tourist destination.

Coated with a sprinkling of small villages and over 1200 picturesque dovecots (the island speciality) Tinos is very attractive. However, it remains very much of a 'one town' island and is best explored via excursions from the port and centre of **Tinos Town**. A largely modern affair, it owes its existence solely to the church and icon; and this shows, for as you approach by ferry, the seemingly thin scatter of buildings looks to have a rather tenuous hold on the foreshore. Once within the confines of the harbour mole the town reveals itself to be a substantial but largely modern settlement — no old world chora charm here. Its most conspicuous feature is the main street that runs up the hillside from the waterfront to the impressive walls and ornate plaster façade of the church at the back of the town. In fact, Tinos Town is dominated by three streets: the waterfront (replete with ticket agencies, restaurant, and a good supermarket south of the Port Police office), the pedestrianized Evangelistrais (lined with a number of particularly tacky souvenir shops that sell plastic bonsai trees among other things) and Leoforos Megalocharis, the main processional road to the church: on feast days devout pilgrims process up it on their knees, stopping off only to buy

candles — some up to 2 m high — from shops along the way. This all sounds serious stuff, yet the town feels a very relaxed, laid-back sort of place, and is a nice base for exploration.

Tinos Town also has a couple of beaches reasonably close to hand. The closest — Ag. Fotias beach — is a walk away; 500 m past the town's camp site. However, the best is at **Kionia** (now the island package tourist centre). Buses run frequently from Tinos Town, or if you are feeling energetic you can walk along the coast past the scanty remains of a temple to Poseidon and Amphitrite and a small stoa. Poseidon was the island's favourite deity after he relieved Tinos from a plague of snakes by sending along a flock of hungry storks ('Tinos' is derived from the Phoenician word for snake: *tenok*). These days finding a snake is very difficult and on a par with working out where your ferry is going to dock in Tinos Town. Depending on wind conditions, ferries can dock at one of

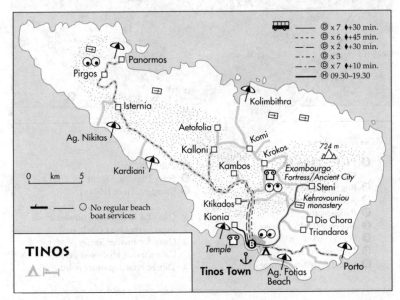

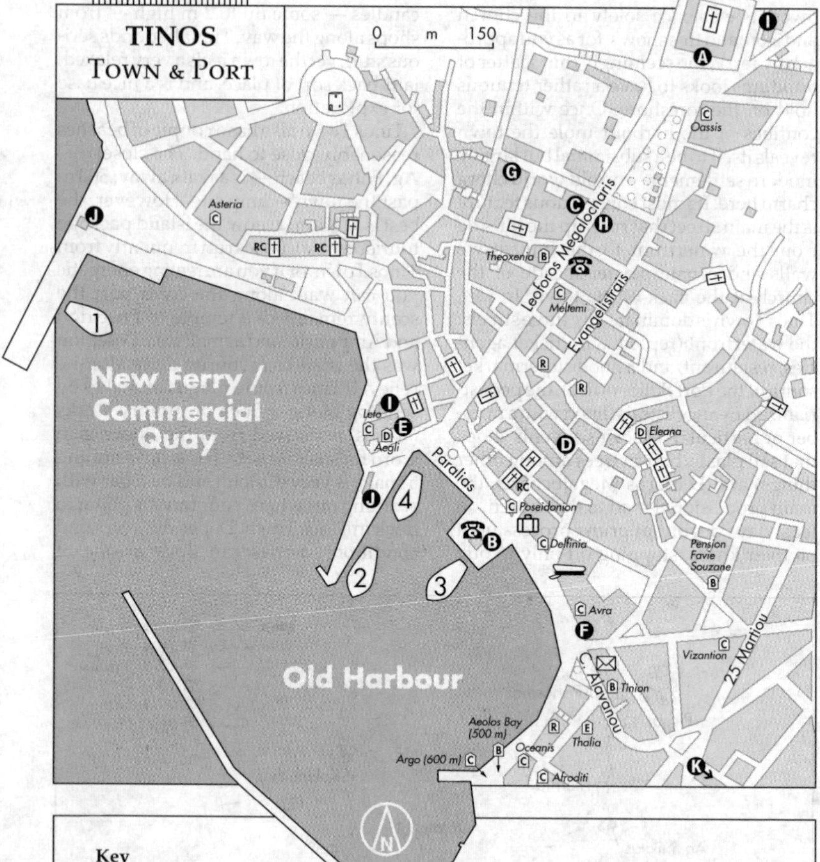

TINOS
TOWN & PORT

0   m   150

New Ferry / Commercial Quay

1

2

3

4

J

Paralias

Old Harbour

Asteria

Oassis

Theoxenia

Leoforos Megalocharis

Evangelistrais

Meltemi

Lela

Aegli

Poseidonion

Delfinia

Eleana

Pension Favie Souzane

Avra

Vizantion

25 Martiou

Alavanou

Tinion

Aeolos Bay
(500 m)

Argo (600 m)

Oceanis

Thalia

Afroditi

N

Key

Ⓐ Panagia Evangelistra Church (Megalochari)
Ⓑ Bus Station (all destinations)
Ⓒ Archaeological Museum
Ⓓ Police Station
Ⓔ National Bank of Greece
Ⓕ Supermarket
Ⓖ Cultural Centre
Ⓗ Clinic / Medical Centre

Ⓘ Public WCs
Ⓙ Ferry Passenger Stalls
Ⓚ Camping Tinos (150 m)

1   Quay for large ferries (unsheltered)
2   Inner Ferry Quay (sheltered)
3   Quay for smaller ferries / Catamaran / Hydrofoil Berth
4   Tourist boat departure point

three quays; you'll have to ask where your boat will berth.

Tinos Town aside, the island is very quiet (apart from the billing of tourists and the cooing of the doves). The former capital lay on the upper slopes of **Mt. Exambourgo**. If you care to attempt the steep walk, you will find the remains of the Venetian fortress behind a monastery and part of the Archaic city wall. The summit was an important landmark in ancient times, when sailors navigated by always keeping in sight of land. Local tradition had it that, when it was obscured by cloud, it was a sure sign that unsettled weather was on the way, but you should take this with a pinch of salt as even in High Season the island peak is often hidden from view.

The villages of Tinos are, in the main, pretty mountain-side affairs little visited by tourists, with the notable exception of the attractive northern centre of the island, the hill village of **Pirgos**. Now home to a substantial sculpting community — which thrives in these parts thanks to several quarries producing high quality marble — it is a very attractive place in its own right. Most of the local marble is exported via the nearby small port village of **Panormos**, which is redeemed by a passable beach and a few rooms. Buses run to both daily (other villages have irregular bus calls), though Sunday services are not good. Buses also provide good links the 12 c. village-like monastery at **Kehrovouniou**; another popular excursion destination. If you are easily irritated by other people's personal habits then avoid sitting next to priests or little old ladies on the island buses. These delightful souls indulge in the practice of crossing themselves every time they pass a chapel or roadside shrine. There are said to be 643 chapels on Tinos.

⊨

Tinos Town has plenty of hotels and some rooms. Prices are slightly higher than average, but on pilgrimless nights you can usually haggle advantageously. Arrive at festival time, however, and well … you may have heard of the 'feeding of the five thousand', but the streets of Tinos Town sees an annual re-enactment of the less talked about 'sleeping of the five thousand' that came after that memorable nosh-up. Budget beds are limited to a scatter of rooms and two D-class hotels; the quayside *Aigli* (☎ 22240) and the backstreet *Eleana* (☎ 22561). The majority of hotels are C-class; the more appealing being those along the waterfront. These include the *Oceanis* (☎ 22452), the *Avra* (☎ 22242), the *Delfinia* (☎ 22289) and the B-class *Tinion* (☎ 22261).

A

Tinos Camping (☎ 22344): A reasonable site. Blown clean daily, it has plenty of tree cover, and a dovecot in lieu of a mini-market. It is a member of the *Harmonie* camping club scheme. ◌◌

The stucco plastered church of **Panagia Evangelistra** (complete with the icon causing all the fuss) is the main sightseeing destination on Tinos; though the latter is so encased in gold and glass that it is difficult to get anything other than a brief impression. The **icon** is reputedly the work of St. Luke (the time involved in pursuing a second career as a painter no doubt explains why the author of the third gospel copied roughly 60% of Mark's gospel into his own), and if true shows a remarkable anticipation of later Byzantine art. Reputedly from a church destroyed by pirates in the 10 c., it is widely believed to be endowed with healing powers. It came to light in 1822 after a passing nun saw a hunky bronzed workman digging in a field and had a vision (of what, history hasn't recorded). Given instructions where to dig he unearthed the icon, miraculously uninjured. The church was built on the discovery site. The icon's appearance during the birth throes of the Greek state has further enhanced its symbolic importance to the Greek people. Take care to observe the church dress code; it is very strictly enforced here.

Tinos Town is also host to the island's **Archaeological Museum**; the exhibits include a late Hellenistic sundial and odd fragments recovered from the temple of Poseidon and the Mt. Exambourgo Kastro. **Pirgos** also has a couple of museums; one devoted to the current crop of local artists; the other to the town's most famous son: the leading Greek sculptor of the 19 c., Ianoulis Chalepa.

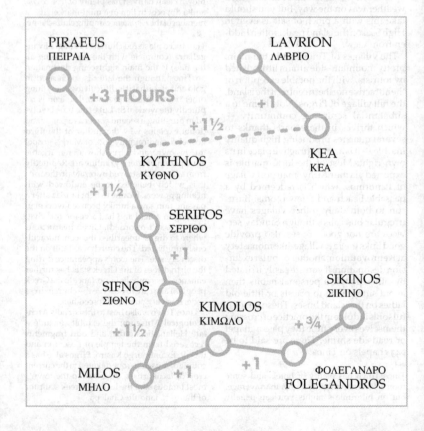

5
CYCLADES WEST

**FOLEGANDROS · KEA · KIMOLOS · KYTHNOS
MILOS · SERIFOS · SIFNOS · SIKINOS**

PIRAEUS
ΠΕΙΡΑΙΑ

LAVRION
ΛΑΒΡΙΟ

+3 HOURS

+1

+1½

KYTHNOS
ΚΥΘΝΟ

KEA
ΚΕΑ

+1½

SERIFOS
ΣΕΡΙΘΟ

+1

SIFNOS
ΣΙΘΝΟ

SIKINOS
ΣΙΚΙΝΟ

KIMOLOS
ΚΙΜΩΛΟ

+¾

+1½

+1

+1

MILOS
ΜΗΛΟ

ΦΟΛΕΓΑΝΔΡΟ
FOLEGANDROS

General Features

The Western Cyclades Line runs in an irregular 'L'- shaped chain around the rim of the group. A paucity of camping sites and budget accommodation produces the odd combination of fewer backpackers and greater numbers of Greek holidaymakers than elsewhere; thus helping to keep the islands free from the worst trappings of mass tourism. In fact out of the High Season foreign tourists are thin on the ground. The chain is peculiar in that the nearer the island is to Athens, the fewer foreign tourists it tends to see. Northerly Kea — served by the mainland port of Lavrion — is very much of an Athenian's get-away-from-it-all weekend island, but very quiet in midweek. Kythnos and Serifos are quite off

the beaten track despite the frequency of Piraeus ferries. Sifnos, on the other hand, is the only island in the group that comes close to being labelled 'touristy' and even this is mild by Central Cyclades standards. Milos — famous as the island where the Venus de Milo was discovered — attracts tourists by virtue of name recognition rather than the limited appeal that it has in its own right. Neighbouring Kimolos makes an interesting day excursion but is very much of a minor island as are the two at the tail end of the line; Sikinos and Folegandros. Bridging the Central and Western lines, they do not fit comfortably into either, being serviced by boats steaming down both; but as they are more characteristic of the Western Cyclades they are covered here.

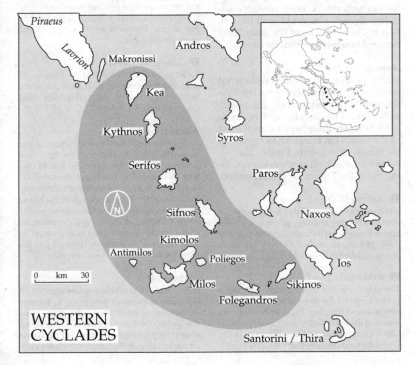

Piraeus

Lavrion

Makronissi

Andros

Kea

Kythnos

Syros

Serifos

Paros

Sifnos

Naxos

Kimolos

Antimilos

Poliegos

Ios

Milos

Sikinos

Folegandros

0   km   30

WESTERN
CYCLADES

Santorini / Thira

Example Itinerary
[2 Weeks]

Those looking for a fortnight's holiday
that combines the sights of Athens with
some relaxed island hopping without
huge crowds of backpackers could do
worse than the Western Cyclades. An
atmosphere of quiet romanticism rules.
The islands are close to the capital and
fairly quiet, yet with enough going on so
that you don't end up feeling as if you
had been washed up at the back of beyond.

Arrival/Departure Point
None of the islands boast an international
airport, and connections with other island
groups are so poor that Athens is the only
viable starting point. During the High
Season Santorini becomes another possibility; though you could well have to
hop to Paros for one of the daily boats
running into the line from there.

Season
Daily services operate (somewhat
irregularly) down the line from late June
through to late September. The month
either side of this sees ferries five days a
week falling to three days during the rest
of the year. Don't depend too much on
the Sifnos—Paros or the Piraeus (Zea) —
Kythnos — Kea hydrofoil services operating out of the June to September period.

1 Athens [2 Days]
Since you can't spend all day in the sun at the
start of a holiday anyway, you might as well
take in the sights of the capital over a couple of
days (picking up the NTOG ferry departure
sheets/Hydrofoil timetable at the same time).

2 Kythnos [1 Day]
The quietest island in the group; you might
prefer to spend the day elsewhere if you are
new to island hopping. Experienced hoppers
weary of the hurly-burly of the more popular
Greek islands will find more to savour in the
somnolent atmosphere that pervades here.

3 Serifos [2 Days]
A day is all that is needed to take in the port
and dramatic Chora hanging on the hill behind.
After this you can retire to the beach and wait
— if needs be for an extra day — for a *morning*
ferry to Sifnos; enabling you to take your pick
of the accommodation on arrival there.

4 Sifnos [4 Days]
As this is the best beach island in the group
(and by this stage you should be better conditioned to enjoy spending more extended time
in the sun), Sifnos offers the opportunity to
enjoy a few days of complete relaxation.

5 6 Milos/Kimolos [3 Days]
Milos provides the best sightseeing in the
Western Cyclades. Three days can be happily
spent between the catacombs, beach and if
you are really feeling adventurous, a day-trip
to Kimolos via the Apollonia-based taxi-boats.
(Don't leave a Kimolos trip until the last day
just in case high seas result in you getting
stuck for the night).

1 Athens [2 Days]
Finally, take a boat direct to Piraeus —
spending the recommended clear day spare
before your return flight finishing your
exploration of the capital.

Alternative 1
Rather than returning direct to Piraeus, if you
have the time available, you can take
advantage of the new hydrofoil link to visit
Kea. Once one of the most important of all the
Greek islands it offers some good sightseeing.
Ideally, you should aim to explore the island
in mid-week as rooms disappear as the
weekend approaches. You are also recommended to visit Kythnos in passing earlier in
your itinerary (to establish times) if you are
planning to catch the irregular ferries.

Alternative 2
In July and August **Folegandros** appears on
schedules sufficiently frequently to become
an alternative destination. However, boats
and hydrofoils do not run every day, and you
should be prepared to return to Piraeus via
ferries running up the Central Cyclades Line.

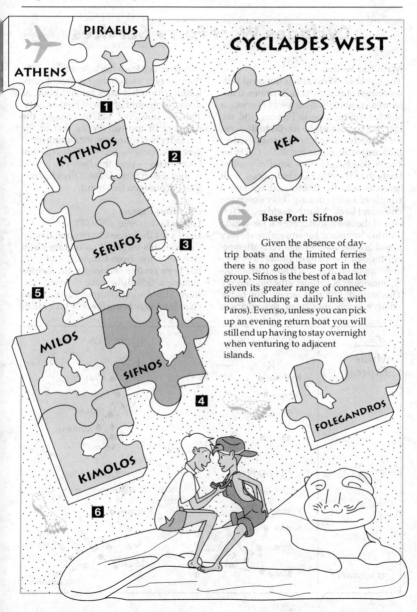

CYCLADES WEST

PIRAEUS

ATHENS

1

KYTHNOS

2

KEA

SERIFOS

3

Base Port: Sifnos

Given the absence of day-trip boats and the limited ferries there is no good base port in the group. Sifnos is the best of a bad lot given its greater range of connections (including a daily link with Paros). Even so, unless you can pick up an evening return boat you will still end up having to stay overnight when venturing to adjacent islands.

5

MILOS

SIFNOS

4

FOLEGANDROS

KIMOLOS

6

Cyclades West Ferry Services

Main Car Ferries

The Cyclades West line is the most self-contained of all the Cycladic routes, thanks to a combination of fewer tourists, a shorter sailing time to Piraeus, and the fact that the islands lie too far to the west for ferries heading for other chains to feel inclined to call in. As a result, the Cyclades West islands rely on a smaller pool of boats than the other Cycladic lines, with services usually dominated by just a couple of boats running daily down the chain and back. A further odd characteristic of the line is that there isn't anything akin to a 'standard' itinerary; almost every possible combination of ports is attempted, though the pattern of services sees only minor changes each summer (mostly, one suspects, to relieve the monotony). This state of affairs is largely due to the relative unpopularity of the northern

islands which leads ferries to either ignore them or only call on their outward runs. Links with other lines remain poor, as does the amount of tourist boat activity. This is, however, set to change; the pressure of tourism in the rest of the Cyclades is encouraging increasing numbers of visitors — and Cyclades Central Line ferries — onto this line. The arrival of the CERES *Mega Dolphin* fleet has further encouraged this trend.

C/F *Milos Express*

Lindos Lines; 1969; 4797 GRT.

Until 1995 the largest ferry operating on the line, this elegant Lindos Lines boat (formerly the cross-Channel *Vortigern*) has been on this service for the last ten summers. Schedules have changed relatively little during this time, but this could change in 1999: being the only boat in this

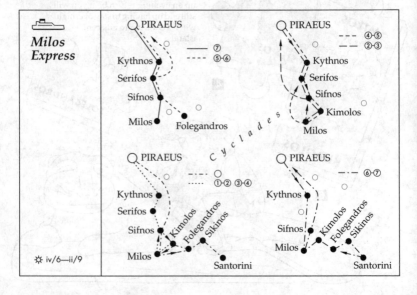

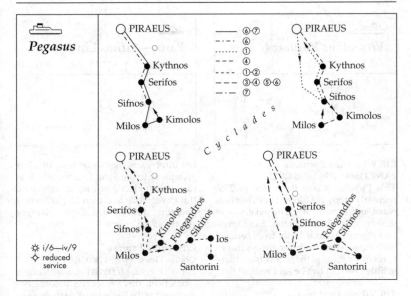

Pegasus

☼ i/6—iv/9
◇ reduced service

company's 'fleet' she is particularly vulnerable to a competitor should one appear (as she can't be replaced by a better Lindos Lines boat). A second factor that could conspire against her running in 1999 is her age: this is now starting to show. Deck-class facilities are adequate, with a large saloon, but her external seating is on the utilitarian site. However, her summer itinerary is so well established that, if she goes, the probability is that a successor will run a similar service.

Assuming she is running as normal you will find this boat providing not only a reliable service down the line, but also an invaluable cross-line service with the islands at the southern end of the Cyclades Central line. These remain intact whatever else changes each summer — though minor variations to the ports of call are to be expected from the previous year. Out of High Season the *Milos Express* operates less frequently on this line and occasionally deputises on others (e.g. running down the Peloponnese to Crete).

C/F *Pegasus*

Ventouris Ferries; 1977; 4810 GRT.

On the route since 1996, the Ventouris Ferries' *Pegasus* moved across from the Patras—Bari international route. Although quite a small vessel, her international class facilities make her easily the best vessel on the line (though the competition to the *Milos Express* invariably is). Her limited capacity is, however, something of a liability in High Season: unfortunately, this is one of those boats whose crew attempts to prevent non-Greek backpackers from entering the deck-class saloons on boarding. This particularly true during the busier weekend runs. Those able to argue their way inside will find the usual TVs and aircraft-seating in her saloon, along with locked WCs and air-conditioning that often leaves the boat feeling like a floating freezer. Since 1996 her itineraries have been pretty wild even by Cyclades West line standards, and it is difficult to believe that this summer will not see the changes rung yet again.

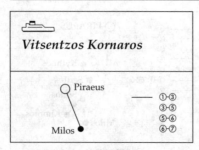

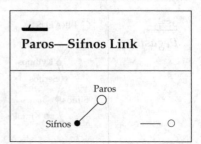

C/F *Vitsentzos Kornaros*
LANE Lines; 1976; 9735 GRT.

This Piraeus—Crete ferry (see p. 276) regularly stops at Milos on both her outward and return runs. The existence of this service explains why the *Milos Express* and *Pegasus* exclude Milos from some of their runs. Apart from her always inconveniently calling in the small hours, there is little else that can be said against her.

T/B *Nikos - Pantanassa*
These Apollonia-based taxi boats make the crossing to Kimolos three times daily in High Season. At 500 GDR it's cheaper — if somewhat more choppy — than taking a ferry from Adamas.

Cyclades West—Paros Link
In past High Seasons there has always been an invaluable inter-line connecting service five days a week between Paros and Sifnos. Unfortunately, the vessel providing this link keeps changing. Over the last three years the caïque *Margarita* has given way to the *Syros Express*, which in turn was replaced in 1997 initially by a ILIO hydrofoils and then *Mega Dolphins* operating out of Milos. Expect changes again in 1999.

C/F *Mirina Express*
Goutos Lines; 1975; 1168 GRT.

The best regular ferry in the small Goutos Lines fleet, this vessel has become the mainstay of the Lavrion—Kea route, usually mooring overnight on Kea. Greek built, she has the traditional, but now rare, external staircases for passengers at her stern. Otherwise she is rather characterless, though the presence of a reasonable deck-class saloon means that there is no need to buy a higher class ticket to travel in reasonable comfort on this boat. Despite

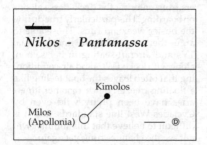

the arrival of hydrofoils in 1992, she has maintained her practice of previous years of providing a once weekly Kea—Kythnos service (though it has to be said that these trips see her running all but empty as this service is barely advertised at all). Her only weakness comes with the weekend rush, when Athenian commuters (rushing to cottage retreats in Kea) fill her to bursting, despite additional sailings.

H/F *Flying Dolphin*

In 1992 Kea finally emerged from its isolation from the rest of the Greek ferry system courtesy of a daily hydrofoil link with Piraeus (Zea Marina) and Kythnos. This was modified during the summer of 1998 to a *Mega Dolphin* service to Kea and Andros. Whatever the final destination, this service makes an Athens—Kea day trip is a practical option. This is worth considering as you have the safeguard of a guaranteed late ferry to the mainland. Changes are possible in 1999, though the Zea—Kea High Season link is almost certain to be operating again.

H/F *Mega Dolphin*

CERES moved onto the Cyclades West line in a big way in the summer of 1997 with the arrival of their *Mega Dolphin* fleet. Otherwise known as 'Italian' hydrofoils or dolphins (most hydrofoils in Greece are Russian-built), these boats are much more powerful two-deck affairs, with a bar sited on the lower level. Their extra size means that they are better able to cope with the more exposed sea conditions that, when poor, put regular hydrofoils out of action. Needless to say, ticket prices are fairly high and to date these three boats (numbered XXX–XXXII) don't seem to have done much more than cream off some of the first class passenger traffic (the lack of airports on most of the islands in the Cyclades West chain means that this is greater than on other lines). Scheduling has proved erratic so far, and changes should be expected in 1999.

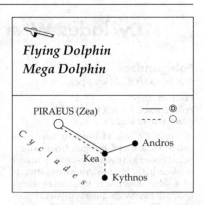

Flying Dolphin
Mega Dolphin

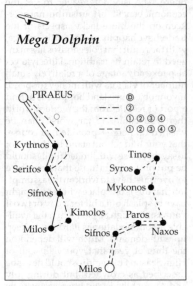

Mega Dolphin

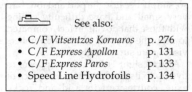

See also:
- C/F *Vitsentzos Kornaros*   p. 276
- C/F *Express Apollon*   p. 131
- C/F *Express Paros*   p. 133
- Speed Line Hydrofoils   p. 134

Cyclades West Islands & Ports

Folegandros

ΦΟΛΕΓΑΝΔΡΟΣ; 32 km²; pop. 650.

CODE ☎ 0286
PORT POLICE / POLICE ☎ 41249
FIRST AID ☎ 41222

A 'romantic' island boasting one road and no large shops, Folegandros has long been known as a get-away-from-it-all sort of place. In the last few years it has attracted a select clientele of up-market island lovers drawn by the quiet laid-back atmosphere. The islanders, eager to get the economic benefits of tourism but not over-keen on the more tacky aspects of the trade, have happily promoted this image, with the result that Folegandros has managed to retain its traditional lifestyle yet also take advantage of a relatively small number of visitors with money to spend. If your object in island hopping is to find a port of respite from the modern world then you could do far worse than be washed up here — provided, of course, that your budget can stand it. This is not to say that those with limited funds should be put off visiting (those that are miss a lot); you just have to work on the assumption that this is one place where you might have to splash out a bit for a day or two if you visit in High Season when the available accommodation is hard put to keep up with demand. Much will depend on the time of year that you visit. Out of High Season Folegandros could never be described as crowded, but during July and August the island often seems to be so, simply because the port and town are very small and have difficulty coping with those that do call. In fact, compared to any of the 'popular' islands the numbers visiting are surprisingly low.

At first sight Folegandros appears to live up to its historical role as a place of exile, courtesy of its arid and rocky landscape, but as is so often the case with Greek islands, first impressions can be misleading. The dusty little port in Karavastasis bay doesn't do the island justice. Relatively new, it is little more than a motley collection of tourist-generated buildings trailed around a rather poor beach. Now used as the island caïque harbour, the fishermen weighing their catches and mending nets on the quay inadvertently add some colour, and with each season the port becomes a little more lively. The locals have tried to tart it up as best they can (latterly by adding an elaborate staircase down to a second, very poor, beach over the quayside headland), but it remains more of a place to pass through rather than stay in. Two roads run out of the port. The first skirts the port beach and then round the bay and over a headland before running down to Livadi beach (an indifferent strand of sand) with the campsite on the hillside behind. The second is the main island road, running up to the Chora and the settlements behind. Buses run regularly between the two (times are posted up at the 'bus station' on the ferry quay).

Chora (also known as Folegandros Town) is the only large centre and lies 4 km from the port. One of the most attractive of the traditional whitewashed cubist Cycladic villages, it is a mini Mykonos Town without the crowds, and feels like the sort of place where everybody obviously knows everybody else and everybody else's grandmother besides. Part of the secret of its appeal is its location. Set atop a 200 m cliff on the northern coast it shares that 'living on the edge of the world' feeling common to the caldera towns on Santorini. However, unlike the latter, Chora doesn't look the dizzy views in the eye (though there are several good vantage points) but for the most part

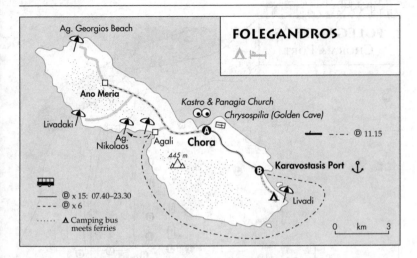

FOLEGANDROS

Ag. Georgios Beach

Ano Meria

Kastro & Panagia Church

Chrysospilia (Golden Cave)

Livadaki

Ag. Nikolaos

Agali

Chora

445 m

A

Ⓓ 11.15

B

Karavostasis Port

Livadi

Ⓓ x 15: 07.40–23.30

Ⓓ x 6

Ⓐ Camping bus meets ferries

0   km   3

turns in on itself. The result is a cosy huddle of houses and churches centred on a couple of leafy squares (thanks to a number of large plane trees) decked with pots of red geraniums and check-cloth taverna tables that leave one feeling that one is tucked away in the heart of a provincial French hill village. Chora is a great place for romantic evening meals (to say nothing of futile cliff-edge gestures if all you end up with is a spot of unrequited love or the taverna bill). Joking aside, Folegandros has figured in press reports of late thanks to several tourists disappearing off cliff paths without even the consolation of a broken heart to justify their fall. Visitors who manage to stay topsides will find that the old Kastro quarter is the best part of town. This neatly hides the cliff-edge from view, besides offering the most attractive example of the medieval house-stockade forts built to defeat Cycladic islands from pirate attacks. Its interior is a real delight; the flower-filled aisles of whitewashed houses being adorned with brightly painted balconies and ranks of external staircases (each with its own cat). New

development in the town (largely up-market hotels and apartment blocks) is confined to strips along the access roads; the liveliest being along the dusty Ano Meria road which has several bars and a disco en route to the Fani Vevis pension.

After passing by Chora the main road runs west along the spine of the island. Although there is a bus service of sorts along it, it is also a ready made excursion if you are up to the walk. There are several possible destinations: the first being the excellent sand beach at **Agali** (also known as Vathi, and just under an hour's walk from Chora) complete with a couple of tavernas offering rooms. From here a coastal path winds its way to a second good beach at **Ag. Nikolaos**. Both can also be reached by a daily beach caïque running from the port in High Season. If beaches aren't your thing you can continue to walk west along the windmill-clad island spine road (complete with superb views of Serifos and Crete) to **Ano Meria**: a very quiet little village that does little more than hug the island road it is hardly a major attraction in itself, but it at least provides a destination to aim for.

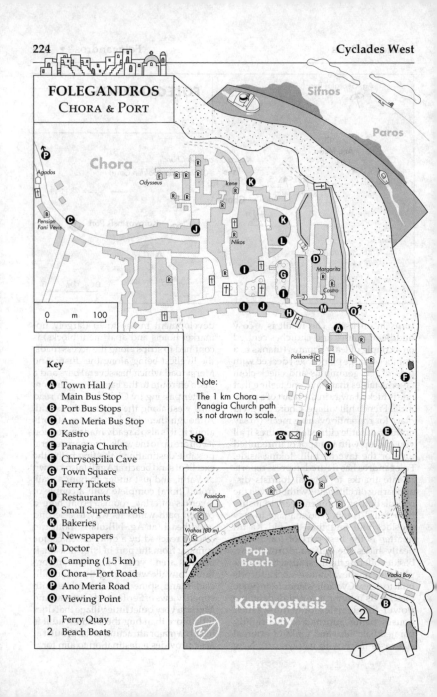

FOLEGANDROS
CHORA & PORT

Sifnos

Paros

Chora

Agados

Pension Fani Vevis

Odysseus

Irene

Nikos

Margarita

Castro

0   m   100

Key

Ⓐ Town Hall / Main Bus Stop
Ⓑ Port Bus Stops
Ⓒ Ano Meria Bus Stop
Ⓓ Kastro
Ⓔ Panagia Church
Ⓕ Chrysospilia Cave
Ⓖ Town Square
Ⓗ Ferry Tickets
Ⓘ Restaurants
Ⓙ Small Supermarkets
Ⓚ Bakeries
Ⓛ Newspapers
Ⓜ Doctor
Ⓝ Camping (1.5 km)
Ⓞ Chora—Port Road
Ⓟ Ano Meria Road
Ⓞ Viewing Point

1 Ferry Quay
2 Beach Boats

Note:

The 1 km Chora — Panagia Church path is not drawn to scale.

Polikania

Poseidon

Aeolis

Vrahos (80 m)

Port Beach

Vadia Bay

Karavostasis Bay

🛏
Rooms are available to rent in the port, but most tourists take the bus that meets all boats to **Chora**, which is both prettier and has more options. The most appealing of these are in the old kastro; the small B-class *Castro* (☎ 412 30) and the *Margarita Rooms* (☎ 41321). More rooms are scattered around the town with hotels confined to the outskirts. The best of these is the new C-class *Polikania* (☎ 41322) on the port road. The Chora—Panagia Church path also has some plush furnished apartments along it. Somewhat more down-market rooms lie on the east side of town, along with the E-class *Odysseus* (☎ 4139). The Chora—Ano Meria road also has a couple of pensions including the deceptively dour-fronted B-class *Fani Vevis* (☎ 41237). **Karavastasis Port** also has several hotels including the C-class *Aeolis* (☎ 41205). There are also several signs advertising rooms though most turn out to be for establishments elsewhere on the island.

▲
Camping Livadi (☎ 41204); 2 km west of the port along the coast path. Lack of competition (and water) all too evident with the very poor washing facilities — hence the freelance camping on the adjacent beach. Bring foodstuffs with you as the campsite restaurant takes full advantage of the longish walk to the port (a mini-bus meets ferries). Tents are available for hire, but view before you pay: some of the 'two person' jobs are *very* small.

👓
The only major island sights regularly visited are the **Chora** and its **Kastro** (built in 1212 AD). The attractive whitewashed **Panagia Church** lies on the cliff-hill on the north-east side of the Chora and stands on the foundations of the ancient city wall that stood on the site. Although it is quite a climb to the church the wonderful views over the town and island are more than worth it.

A further walking option is to head along the road to **Ano Meria**. Although little more than a string of houses (and the odd windmill) strung along the spine of the island, the scenery is worth the effort. Ano Meria is also home to a small **Folk Museum** — the only museum on the island. In past years rare excursion boats have also headed for **Chrysospilia** (Golden Cave), set in the base of the cliff below the Chora, just above sea level. However, the cave is now off limits and likely to remain so.

Kea
KEA; 131 km²; pop. 1,700.

CODE ☎ 0288
PORT POLICE ☎ 21344
POLICE ☎ 21100
FIRST AID ☎ 22200

Despite being only three hours from Athens, Kea (also transcribed as 'Tzia') is one of the hidden pearls of the Aegean, retaining much of its rural charm and now popular with those who like walking holidays. This is something of an unfamiliar role for an island that was home to an important Minoan outpost and was one of the cradles of Greek civilization. Kea has always been, and remains, an island set apart from the rest. Not only did it manage to support four city states where most islands could barely manage one, but it was also a pioneer of social change by introducing a compulsory celebratory cup of hemlock when its citizens reached retirement age at 70. These days the locals buy holiday homes instead. As a result, the island tends to fill up quickly on weekends with Athenians escaping the city smog: Kea is comparatively fertile for a Cycladic island and is graced with countryside that is noticeably greener than neighbouring Kythnos. If you intend to stay during High Season then plan for a mid-week arrival. Foreign tourists are comparatively thin on the ground, and nightlife is sparse and scattered.

All ferries and hydrofoils dock at the small port of **Korissia**, a tapering port-village that is now emerging as the island's main 'resort', sited on the west side of Agios Nikolaos bay. On the south is a long sand beach and the largest collection of accommodation on the island. However, apart from these attractions there is little incentive to linger. In truth, the waterfront lacks interest thanks in part to the bland topography of this part of the bay. The port beach also isn't the world's greatest, being quite awful at the quayside end (it improves noticeably as you progress around the bay). Korissia is also more substantial than it looks from the sea, with more building in the valley floor behind the waterfront. This part of town is dominated by the red brick chimney of a derelict Victorian enamel and metallurgy factory. This sounds rather dour, but it doesn't impact on the touristy areas. Further evidence of late 19 c. activity lies on the north side of Korissia bay: an excellent natural harbour, the bay was an important coaling station in the years leading up to WW1 and the roofless coal stores still stand at Kokka near the village of **Vourkari** — laid out like a miniature version of Korissia and now a growing up-market resort thanks to a large yachting marina located here.

Buses run from the port to Vourkari and, more frequently, to the red-tile roofed main town of **Ioulis** or **Chora**. Visible from the port, it sits in a natural amphitheatre in the hills; overlooked by a handful of ruined windmills that are all that remain of the 26 that once topped the so-called Mountain of Mills. The town is built around nine springs (now decorated with mule troughs) and clings to a couple of hillsides; the old Kastro dominating one, and the Chora the other. The streets are too narrow to admit vehicles, and this remains a very attractive working town packed with tiny houses, though most visitors simply pass through in search of the famous Kea Lion. Ioulis is also the best base for exploring the rest of island.

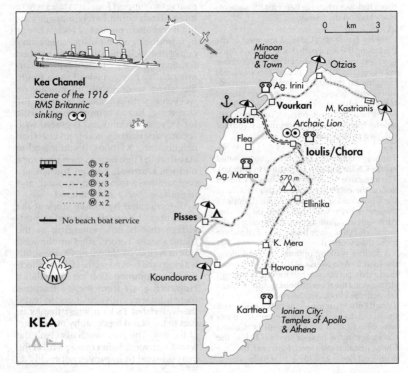

The rest of Kea is an odd mix of unspoilt countryside and holiday-villa filled villages. Best of these is the delightfully named **Pisses**. In the normal course of things one would assume that this name was just an unhappy accident, but the existence of another hamlet baring the equally appealing name of 'Flea' suggests that the islanders have really got this place-naming thing down to a fine art. With a good sand beach backed by a prosperous market-garden valley, Pisses is served by a very inadequate once-daily bus service. The northern hamlet of **Otzias** is better served, but, filled with holiday villas, it is of little interest, as is the south-west coast 'resort' of **Koundouros**; now tarted up with distinctive pseudo wind-mill homes near the tiny quay, it sees hydrofoils en route to Korissia. Walkers meantime, will find bus-free **Flea** has more buzz as a destination than most thanks to its location in a ravine with 13 watermills.

⋈

Rooms are on offer in Korissia and the Chora. Hotel / pension options are thin on the ground: though this shouldn't mean difficulty in finding a bed in mid-week. **Ioulis** has one superbly placed B-class pension (on top of the old kastro site), the *Ioulis* (☎ 22177) — complete with a terrace restaurant and an owner who is happy to add the odd extra to your bill (you are usually told exactly what you are paying for on arrival), and a small E-class hotel charmingly placed on one of main town alleys: the *Filoxenia* (☎ 22057). **Korissia** has the C-class hotel *Karthea* (☎ 21204) on the waterfront and a B-class 'motel', the *Tzia Mas* (☎ 21305) at the better end of the beach. However, the best hotel in town lies down a dusty track behind the beach; the newish B-class *Korissia* (☎ 21484, 21355). **Koundouros** also has one hotel: the pricey B-class *Kea Beach* (☎ 31230).

Λ

Camping Kea (☎ 31335). A nice site on the best island beach at Pisses 16 km from the port, it suffers somewhat from its isolated location.

෴

Oldest and most accessible of the Kea sites is on the promontory north of the port: the foundations of a **Minoan Palace** at Agia Irini.

As usual with Minoan sites, there is little here but a jumble of thick-walled foundations. In this case there are the remains of half-a-dozen elaborate houses (with cellars complete with drains), streets with public benches, and defensive walls. The site takes its name from the red-tiled church on the promontory.

The most impressive sight on Kea — the grey granite 6 c. BC **Lion of Kea** —lies on a olive-groved hillside on the far side of Ioulis; 6 m long, it is carved sphinx-like from an outcrop of rock and looks back across the valley towards the town wearing an enigmatic smile. This often seems to wear a little thin when the inevitable parties of tourists queue up to be photographed bestriding his head.

Of the four classical cities surprisingly little remains except at remote **Karthea** (for which you will need your own transport) where there are the dramatic cliff-side remains of a late Archaic temple of the Pythios Apollo. **Ioulis** (home of the 5 c. BC poet Simonides) has the remains of a **Venetian Kastro** built out of the ruins of a second temple to Apollo. There is also an **Archaeological Museum** housing island finds in the town. The third city (Korissia) produced a famous Kouros statue (now in Athens) but otherwise (like the fourth of Kea's cities Poiessa — near Pisses) there is little extant on the ground today. Elsewhere on Kea you will find the substantial remains of a **Hellenistic Watchtower** at **Ag. Marina** and a monastery at M. Kastrianis.

One final site of interest is the steamy, mirror-smooth **Kea Channel**. Although there is nothing to see except sea, sea, sea, the strait is the last resting place of the *Britannic* (sister-ship of the *Titanic*). Originally laid down as the *Gigantic*, she was renamed after the *Titanic* disaster. Launched in 1914, she struck a mine off Kea on the 21st of November 1916 — while serving as a hospital ship during the WW1 Dardanelles campaign — and sank with the loss of 30 lives (her lifeboats were sucked into her rotating propellers as her captain vainly headed for Korissia in a last-gasp attempt to beach her). Like her sister, she was the largest vessel semi-afloat at the time of her sinking, and still holds the record as the largest liner on the sea-bed. Lying on her starboard side in

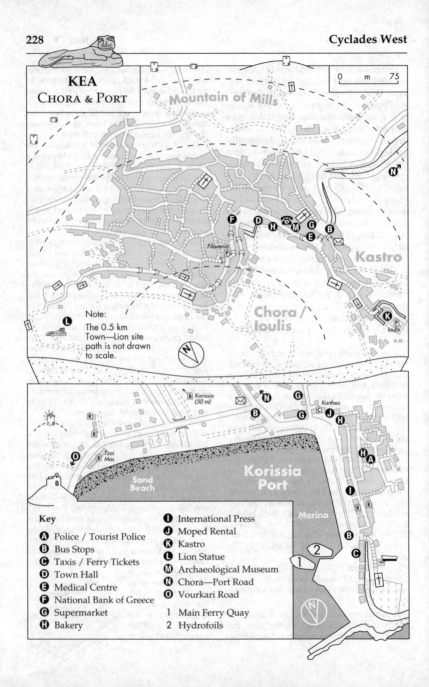

KEA
CHORA & PORT

0   m   75

Mountain of Mills

Filoxenia

Kastro

Chora /
Ioulis

Note:
The 0.5 km
Town—Lion site
path is not drawn
to scale.

Ioulis

Korissia
[50 m]

Karthea

Tzai
Mas

Sand
Beach

Korissia
Port

Marina

Key

Ⓐ Police / Tourist Police
Ⓑ Bus Stops
Ⓒ Taxis / Ferry Tickets
Ⓓ Town Hall
Ⓔ Medical Centre
Ⓕ National Bank of Greece
Ⓖ Supermarket
Ⓗ Bakery

Ⓘ International Press
Ⓙ Moped Rental
Ⓚ Kastro
Ⓛ Lion Statue
Ⓜ Archaeological Museum
Ⓝ Chora—Port Road
Ⓞ Vourkari Road

1   Main Ferry Quay
2   Hydrofoils

110 m of water, she can now only be viewed via a Jacques Cousteau video. This is set to change: during August 1995 Dr. Robert D. Ballard — the discoverer of the *Titanic* — explored the site and found the ship excellently preserved with even her smokestacks extant (albeit separated from her hull). The TV programme has already been broadcast, and the wreck is pictured in *Lost Liners* (Hodder & Stoughton/Madison Press). Dr. Ballard has expressed a desire to take things further and use the wreck to establish 'the world's first undersea museum' with tourists visiting the site live via the internet. Laudable though this ambition is, don't hold your breath: in Greece the state telephone company is so inefficient that it can take six years to have a household (never mind a wreck's hold) telephone line installed — hence the excessive popularity of mobile phones in this part of the world.

Kimolos

ΚΙΜΟΛΟΣ; 38 km²; pop. 800.

CODE ☎ 0287
PORT POLICE ☎ 22100
POLICE ☎ 51205
FIRST AID ☎ 51222

A good island to escape the crowds and the more commercial trappings of tourism, Kimolos is named after the 'kimolia' or chalk that was mined here before Fuller's Earth (used in the manufacture of porcelain) took over as the dusty mainstay of the local economy: ferries running along the north-east side of the islands pass hillsides badly scarred with open cast mines. This sounds singularly uninviting, yet the sea view creates a very false impression, for the southern half of Kimolos has a nice sleepy backwater atmosphere with a number of fine sand beaches (notably at Aliki). In addition, the islanders are among the declining number that treat visitors as honorary members of their large extended family. Those looking for a tranquil holiday in traditional surroundings will find Kimolos to be a minor gem. More cautious island hoppers will find that in High Season Kimolos can also be visited as a

KIMOLOS

0   km   4

Prassa

397 m

Ellinika   Klima

AGIOS   FKK   **Chora**
ANDREAS   Ancient   Remma
                     City
                          Aliki   **Psathi**
Kambana

AGIOS
EFSTATHIOS

🚌 No bus service
⛵ No beach boat service

day-trip destination; weekly tour boats run from Milos, and ticket agents on Sifnos have recently taken to advertising ferry day trips (taking advantage of those boats running down the line to the Central Cyclades and then returning, such services typically gave day hoppers just over five hours on Kimolos).

All ferries (and the 4 x ⊕ caïques that make the 30-minute run to and from Apollonia on the north coast of Milos) dock at the small port of **Psathi** on the south-east coast. Little more than a quiet bar-backed quay beside a beach lined with odd trees and fishermen's houses, it looks suitably like the back of beyond; though this is somewhat deceptive as it is often quite lively, thanks to a couple of tavernas, a bar and a very popular beach restaurant. The air of abandon is greatly enhanced by the crescent of hills behind the port, most topped with derelict windmills. This is relieved by the attractive hilltop chora that trickles down the hillside toward the port. The chora and

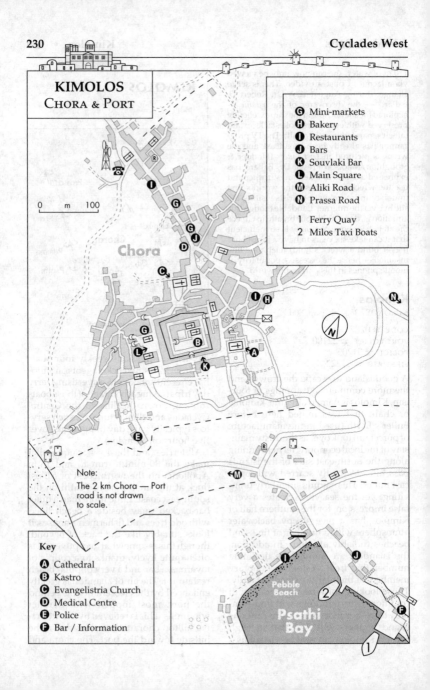

KIMOLOS
Chora & Port

G Mini-markets
H Bakery
I Restaurants
J Bars
K Souvlaki Bar
L Main Square
M Aliki Road
N Prassa Road

1 Ferry Quay
2 Milos Taxi Boats

Chora

0   m   100

Note:
The 2 km Chora — Port
road is not drawn
to scale.

Key

A Cathedral
B Kastro
C Evangelistria Church
D Medical Centre
E Police
F Bar / Information

Pebble Beach

Psathi Bay

port are linked by an easily walked 1.5 km road — islanders will often offer visitors a ride on the back of a truck in the absence of any public transport (Kimolos is this sort of a place).

Chora itself is a pretty, unspoilt, working island village complete with a dominating 'cathedral' (a disappointing 20 C. building). Deftly hidden away in the ramshackle streets in its centre is another of those stockade-type kastros built to protect the inhabitants from the marauding pirates of four centuries ago. The town has grown up around this, and latterly along the valley floor road to the north. Consisting mainly of housing there is no obvious centre of town (most of the important services have been added on at the edges). There are various small squares where the inhabitants gather (the one on the west side of the kastro being the most 'cosy'). Shops are spread equally thinly all over town (and choice of goods tends to be limited as tourism has yet to reach a point where retailers stock up with outsiders in mind).

The rest of Kimolos is very quiet, though somewhat noisier than in past years thanks to another of those large EU road-building grants (in this case 150,000,000 GDR). This has seen Kimolos acquire the less than idyllic tarmac roads that have scarred many of the smaller Greek islands. In this case the upgraded roads run from Chora to the rather ugly mining hamlet of **Prassa** on the north-east corner of the island, and the much more appealing beach hamlet of **Aliki** on the south coast.

🛏

The lack of hotels reflects the small number of overnight visitors to Kimolos. Fortunately, accommodation isn't as thin on the ground as it looks from the map opposite (rooms are not advertised; locals either meet boats or rely on tavernas to refer customers on). Most rooms are in **Chora** (or in the case of the *Meltemi Bar Rooms*; on the far side of it). The nearest the island has to a hotel is the large purpose-built rooms outlet on the port—Chora road. Tavernas backing on to **Aliki** beach also offer

beds; notably *Taverna Aliki* (☎ 51340). Freelance camping is tolerated on the remoter beaches.

👓

Kimolos has, from its earliest history, been dominated by its large neighbour Milos. This limited development on the island, and with it possible sights. These do exist, but most are located in the remoter parts of the island and take some effort to visit. The **Chora** is the exception; it has some notable buildings (not least the Cycladic stockade-type kastro), and — if you are up to the climb — superb panoramic views of the chora, port and nearby islands (including large Poliegos opposite the port, which is used for grazing goats) from the top of the windmill lined hill behind the town.

Sharing similar features with the stockade kastros on Antiparos and Folegandros, the Kimolos **Kastro** is in many ways the best of the three, as it hasn't been modified by later openings in its walls, or painted to a picture postcard perfection. The interior houses are much as they originally were (in a run down sort of way), lining the inner walls and with characteristic rows of external staircases. All are inhabited, and look on to the central block of buildings that make up the core of the kastro. The core buildings (the churches aside) are ruinous. From the ground the kastro appears to share a similar symmetrical shape as its Antiparos counterpart. However, from the air its north wall can be seen to bulge out to meet the summit of the chora hill (the kastro is built against the summit rather than atop it). Access is via two original gateways; the one on the east side offset from the centre and baring the date 1556. Some of the internal features come from a 13 C. fortification. The **Chora Churches** are also worth a look. The best of these is the lovely old **Evangelistia** (1608) just outside the north walls of the kastro; bare of plaster, it stands in warm contrast to the surrounding whitewashed buildings.

The Chora aside, the main points of interest are a sulphur spring at the northern hamlet of **Prassa**, a surviving **Tower** of the ubiquitous ruined Venetian kastro (built on the slopes of the island's highest mountain, Paliokastro), and the site of the island's **Ancient Capital** on the west coast; now largely submerged between Kimolos and Agios Andreas islet (otherwise known as Daskaleio) near Ellinika beach. Finally, near Kambana beach are the remains of a number of **Mycenaean Tombs**.

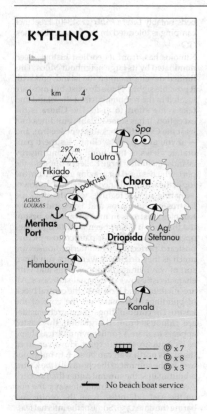

KYTHNOS

0   km   4

Spa

297 m   Loutra

Fikiado

Apokrissi   **Chora**

AGIOS LOUKAS

Merihas Port

Flambouria

Driopida   Ag. Stefanou

Kanala

🚌 ——— Ⓓ x 7
---- Ⓓ x 8
—·— Ⓓ x 3

←— No beach boat service

Kythnos

ΚΥΘΝΟΣ; 86 km²; pop. 1,500.

CODE ☎ 0281
PORT POLICE ☎ 32290
POLICE / TOURIST POLICE ☎ 31201
FIRST AID ☎ 31202

A friendly, rocky little place three hours sailing south of Athens with few tourist facilities, Kythnos (also often transcribed as 'Kithnos') is not the sort of island where the casual island hopper will be tempted to linger. The main attraction of the place is its very lack of attractions: a feature more likely to appeal to the jaded palette of the experienced island hopper than a novice. None of the island centres (primarily the port, the Chora and Driopida) can offer excessive amounts of tourist appeal beyond the undeniable attraction of being 'unspoilt' communities, while the rest of the island is spectacularly undramatic.

The port of **Merihas** is untidily strung around three sides of a small bay on the west coast and is very slowly emerging as a resort village in lieu of better alternatives elsewhere. Truth to tell, things haven't got very far; it has a pebbly-sand beach of sorts backing onto a tree and taverna lined waterfront that is also home to a number of rather down-at-heel looking small stores and not a lot else beyond growing clusters of holiday homes and rooms on the hillsides and valley behind. Things aren't helped by one over-large hotel — the *Possidonion* — totally out of character and scale with the other buildings, now being reduced to a derelict hulk and the preserve of the occasional squatter. This is hardly the stuff of romantic quayside evening strolls — unless you are a new town architect from a former communist bloc country. However Merihas isn't all bad; almost all the island accommodation worth knowing about is here and there are better beaches concealed beyond the two headlands to the north of the ferry quay; the best being a long tree-backed strip of sand two headlands along the Port— Chora road.

An erratic bus service links the port with the main towns (times are posted in the front windscreens). Inland there are two settlements of note; the capital at Chora, and the village of Driopida. In ancient times Kythnos was divided between them, and even today they manage to all but ignore each other (an attitude made easier by the need to take different roads from the port to each of them).

Set amid a gently undulating plain of brown stubble fields and low hills topped with windmills **Chora** (also known as

Kythnos), for all its lack of 'sights', offers an attractive destination, with friendly inhabitants and plenty of whitewashed charm. It more than makes up for Merihas. The island's comparative lack of popularity has ensured that it has remained surprisingly unspoilt, with no tourist accommodation and only two or three small souvenir shops marring the main street that runs the length of the town. The side streets are also appealing, with a donkey lingering around every other corner. Fortunately, in this part of the world they earn their keep in the traditional way instead of lugging well-heeled tourists around. Chora also does its bit for Greek island church architecture; churches here add to the variety by having their bells hung on the outside walls (usually near the door). At various points in the town you will find signs to the wind park that sits on the hills rising behind the far end of town. A destination worth attempting as it requires you to explore the length of the town, don't go expecting Disneyland: there is nought there but several modern power-generating windmills poignantly positioned alongside derelict traditional mills.

Other towns on Kythnos have less going for them. First among these (at least with the elderly Greeks who make up the bulk of the island's visitors) is the 19 c. spa resort and fishing port at **Loutra** on the north coast. Unfortunately, a thimbleful of the thermal waters has more fizz than all the tourists here put together and if you want to be spared a depressing experience then avoid the town. **Driopida** is more up-lifting; located in a fertile hill valley, its houses are topped with red tile roofs reminiscent of town houses on Kea. Sadly, accommodation is non-existent.

The rest of Kythnos is very low key; consisting mainly of arid treeless hills, highly terraced, and speckled with the thyme from which the rich island honey derives its distinctive flavour. Given that Kythnos barely recognizes the existence of tourists (because it sees so few), it is almost superfluous to add that the best island beach — on the east coast at **Ag. Stefanou** — is not served by buses and thus inaccessible; unless you fancy the dusty walk down the hillside from Driopida. A more practical option is to walk up the western coast from Merihas to the isolated beach at **Fikiado**; a golden causeway of sand that links Kythnos with the islet of Agios Loukas.

🛏

Even in High Season you can't walk far from the ferry quay without islanders calling out 'Room?' The comparative lack of tourists all but guarantees a cheap bed on demand. Most rooms are to be found at **Merihas**, though it is worthwhile ascertaining where your bed is before finally accepting an offer: some are at the top of very taxing hillside staircases that one wouldn't want to tackle more than once a day. If you want to phone ahead, try the rooms near the dentist — complete with early morning calls (well, screams) from 08.00 (☎ 32 284, 32104) or the second establishment offering rooms past the small chapel on the south side of the bay (☎ 32105). Hotel accommodation is much thinner on the ground; being confined to the mid-range *Kythnos* (☎ 32092). The island also has three C-class establishments all in the wrong place — i.e. the spa 'resort' of **Loutra**. At the bottom end of the range is the relatively inexpensive *Xenia Anagenissis* (☎ 31217). This is followed by the pricier *Kythnos Bay* (☎ 31218) and the *Meltemi* (☎ 31271).

👀

Visitors don't come to Kythnos for the sightseeing and it is pretty limited. Chora has some fragments from ancient buildings tucked away in a small 'garden' just off the main street, and Driopida lays claim to the notable **Katafiki Cave** at the head of its valley. The cave extends for over a kilometre and has several lakes. Sadly, it is currently closed due to the lack of funds needed to employ guides (one of the tourist shops at Merihas has a cave guidebook on sale). Hill walkers will (hopefully) find a **Venetian Kastro** on the northern tip of the island that is notoriously difficult to get to. A more practical walk runs between Chora and Driopida. Finally, there are many **churches** littering the hillsides, but an increasing number are locked following a series of icon thefts.

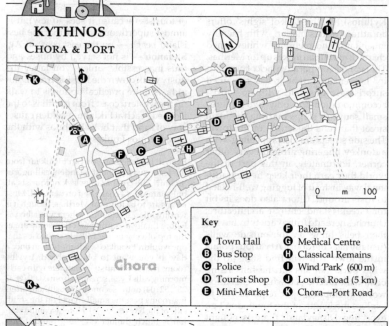

KYTHNOS
CHORA & PORT

Chora

Key

A Town Hall
B Bus Stop
C Police
D Tourist Shop
E Mini-Market
F Bakery
G Medical Centre
H Classical Remains
I Wind 'Park' (600 m)
J Loutra Road (5 km)
K Chora—Port Road

L Information Kiosk
M Pharmacy

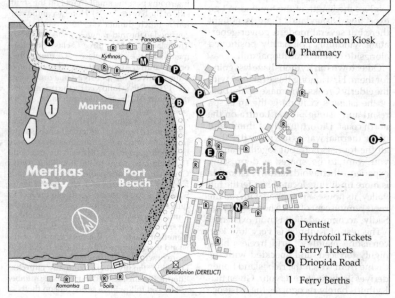

Panorama

Kythnos

Marina

Merihas
Bay

Port
Beach

Merihas

Possidonion (DERELICT)

Romantsa   Solis

N Dentist
O Hydrofoil Tickets
P Ferry Tickets
Q Driopida Road
1 Ferry Berths

Milos

ΜΗΛΟΣ; 161 km²; pop. 4,500.

CODE ☎ 0287
PORT POLICE ☎ 22100
TOURIST OFFICE ☎ 22445
POLICE ☎ 21378

Like its more scenic neighbour Santorini, Milos is volcanic in origin — with its primary port of Adamas located in the flooded interior of an old caldera. Comparisons however, are apt to end there for Milos has no dramatic scenery to draw the crowds and relies on mining as the mainstay of the local economy. This has not helped the development of the tourist trade, for although the island is famous thanks to the discovery of the beautiful Hellenistic statue of Aphrodite (the Venus de Milo), mining and the workings of archaeologists looking vainly for the statue's arms have left the island looking sadly scarred. At first sight Milos is apt to disappoint those looking for typical Greek island charm, but this is misleading, for the island has its moments and if you are on a sightseeing holiday has enough of interest to make it worth stopping over for a couple of days.

Thanks to its large sheltered harbour Milos was an important centre in ancient times rivalling Naxos as a centre of Pre-Hellenic civilization with an important Minoan settlement developing on the northern coast at Filiakopi. Prior to this Milos appears to have been a major trading post thanks to the availability of obsidian, a volcanic glass that could be cut to make sharp tools. Mycenaean and Archaic settlement followed apace, and by the Classical era Milos was one of the more notable of the minor players in the internecine struggles of the Greek city states. The island's great moment in history occurred in 416 BC when Milos refused to join Athens in her war with Sparta and Corinth (an event later immortalised by the historian Thucydides in the Melian Dialogue in his *History of the Peloponnesian War*). By way of a reprisal the Athenians voted for the execution of all the adult males on the island. With the women and children sold into slavery and the island repopulated with Athenians, Milos kept a low profile from then on — apart from a short period in the 17 c. when it emerged as a notorious pirate centre, and WW I when it was used as an Allied naval base and coaling station.

With the exception of the north side of the island, Milos is very sparsely populated. Few tourists venture beyond the triangle of settlements made up of Adamas, Plaka (and its associated villages) and Apollonia. The port of **Adamas** is now the biggest of the three, and this is not saying a lot: like the island itself, at first sight it doesn't impress, but it grows on most who stay for a day or two. Built upon a weathered plug of magma, it is distinctive, even if the waterfront is not the prettiest in Greece — the views across the bay (which looks more like a lake as the entrance is hidden from view) are marred by the commercial ships serving the mining industry. Either side of the town are several small sandy beaches. There are also several discos in town that are the sum total of the island's nightlife.

North of Adamas lies the classical centre of Milos. This part of the island is dominated by a cluster of four villages the prettiest of which, **Plaka**, is the island capital. Easily the most photogenic part of Milos, it is an unspoilt whitewashed chora with the usual warren of streets to get hopelessly lost in, and with superb views and a couple of museums worth visiting. Dominating the town is another volcanic mound topped with a number of chapels: all that remain of the old Venetian Kastro-cum-town. The other villages in the quartet are close enough to walk to: the best being **Tripiti** running down from a windmill topped hill to the remains of the ancient island capital and the lovely string of waterfront fishermens' houses that make up the tiny old port of **Klima**.

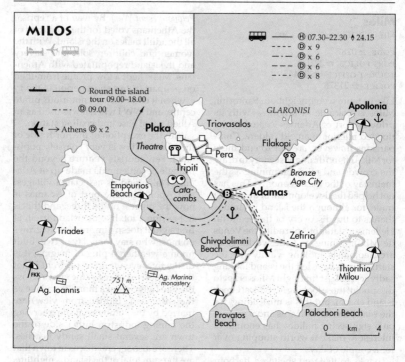

A second village of note lies on the north-east coast at **Apollonia**. An attractive village lining a sheltered bay, it is emerging as a tourist resort. Even in spite of the inevitable open-cast mining eating away an overlooking hillside, it is one of the more scenic parts of the island with an attractive windswept northern headland. The availability of caïques to neighbouring Kimolos also helps (along with some nice tavernas and rooms) to draw such tourists as come to Milos. Backing the bay is a sand beach complete with a few trees, tents and a long neglected WC.

Around the rest of the island are a scatter of good and scantily occupied beaches — those in the monastery and goat inhabited west of the island inaccessible without your own transport. The best of these ser- ved by the reasonable bus system is the pebble beach at **Palochori** with several buses running daily in High Season. If you have your own transport you can do better, for Milos is blessed with a plentiful supply of attractive, but remote, beaches that are ideal for indiscreet nudism. A beach boat runs across the main bay to one at **Empourios**, and the island boat tour gives you a glimpse of the rest.

The ferry quay Information Office (☎ 22445) hands out information sheets showing the location of all hotels. Rooms tend to be 10% more expensive than elsewhere in the group. There are no campsites but unofficial summer beach camps spring up at Adamas (over the headland west of the port) and Apollonia.

Most of the hotels and pensions are in **Adamas**. These include the spiffy, pricey C-class

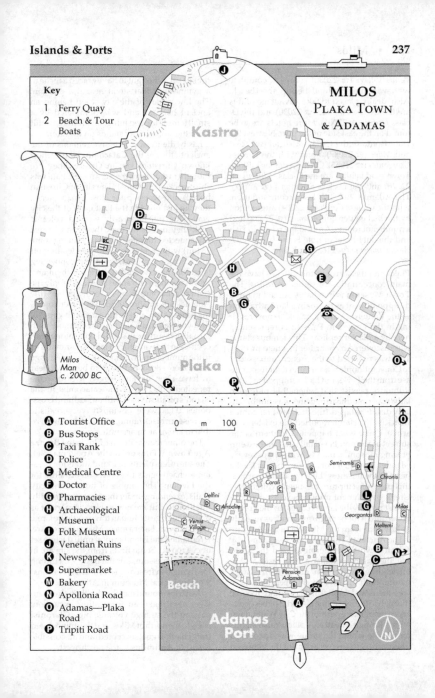

MILOS
Plaka Town & Adamas

Key
1 Ferry Quay
2 Beach & Tour Boats

Kastro

Milos Man c. 2000 BC

Plaka

Ⓐ Tourist Office
Ⓑ Bus Stops
Ⓒ Taxi Rank
Ⓓ Police
Ⓔ Medical Centre
Ⓕ Doctor
Ⓖ Pharmacies
Ⓗ Archaeological Museum
Ⓘ Folk Museum
Ⓙ Venetian Ruins
Ⓚ Newspapers
Ⓛ Supermarket
Ⓜ Bakery
Ⓝ Apollonia Road
Ⓞ Adamas—Plaka Road
Ⓟ Tripiti Road

0   m   100

Semiramis
Delfini
Corali
Afrodite
Chronis
Georgantas
Miles
Meltemi
Venus Village
Pension Adamas

Beach

Adamas Port

Venus Village (☎ 22030) complex, complete with swimming pool and the port's best beach. Also ideally placed to take advantage of this are the C-class *Afrodite* (☎ 22020) and the D-class *Delfini* (☎ 22001). More hotels are to be found on the east side of the port. Nearest the waterfront are the C-class *Meltemi* (☎22284) and *Milos* (☎ 22087) along with the D-class *Georgantas* (☎ 21955). On the Adamas—Plaka Town road behind are the C-class *Chronis* (☎ 22226) and the D-class *Semiramis* (☎ 22117). The Adamas 'hill' has less accommodation; with the C-class *Corali* (☎ 22204) augmented by the B-class pension *Adamas* (☎ 22322) and a number of rooms. Around the rest of the island the only hotel of note is the friendly D-class *Panorama* (☎ 21623) at **Klima**.

∞

Plaka and the surrounding villages have the main concentration of sights on Milos. The **Town Museum** is inevitably something of a disappointment as the main island attraction — the **Venus de Milo** (C. 320 BC) is now residing in the Louvre in Paris (it is represented here by a plaster replica). This famous statue was discovered by a farmer in a field in 1820. This was reported to the French ambassador to Constantinople who arranged for its purchase from the Turks and had it shipped to Paris. Rumours persist that when this plumpish lady was first unearthed she was not brachially disadvantaged (the first two Frenchmen who saw the statue reported the existence of arms). Quite what happened to them is the subject of any number of tall tales; the best embracing ransom demands, with almost every islander having, if not an arm, then at least a hand in the business. Like the Elgin marbles, this piece of sculpture has been exploited by Greek government ministers seeking a popularist profile, the latest request to the French government for her return coming as recently as July 1994 from the Minister of the Aegean.

The **Ancient City**, down the road at nearby Tripiti, is worth wandering around; though to call the extant remains a city casts a very misleading impression given their scanty nature. Built on a relatively steep hillside, it was the island capital from around 1000 BC through to the Byzantine period. The best preserved remains are parts of the **City Walls** along with a **Roman Theatre**. A plaque also stands on the site where *the* statue was discovered (there are plans to erect a copy of the Venus on

the site): it is thought to have graced a niche in a gymnasium that stood near the stadium. The lower part of the city stood behind an ancient harbour and was dominated by a small temple topped hill (a small church, built from the stones, now stands on the site).

Easily the most impressive remains of the ancient city are the **Catacombs**; the earliest known Christian site in Greece (they are thought to date from the 1 C. AD — St. Paul was shipwrecked on Milos). The site of Christian burials and worship for close on 400 years, they lie just outside the East Gate of the city wall. Dug into the easily worked volcanic rock they originally took the form of three unconnected tunnels (the longest being some 184 m) with secondary chambers leading off them. Since their discovery in 1840 connecting corridors have been dug between them and two of the three entrances closed off. Only the central catacomb is open to the public (the Adamas information office has current opening times). Once inside the catacomb you will find yourself in a long, floodlit chamber with burial niches in the walls and floor, along with cavities in the walls for oil lamps. Estimates as to the numbers interred in the catacombs range from 2000—8000, but as 'dem bones' appear to have risen up and legged it during the repeated pillaging of the catacombs in the island's piratical years (Milian skull and crossbones flags were obviously very realistic exercises in black humour), it is all but impossible to arrive at an accurate figure.

The other major site on Milos is the **Bronze Age Town** at **Filakopi** on the Apollonia road. The site offers plenty of foundations for passing archaeologists to ponder on but little for the layman. The jumble of houses and city walls (extending under the sea) are not readily intelligible, but are nonetheless important as one of the largest Minoan towns outside Crete and Santorini. Later a major Mycenaean centre, it remained the island capital until decline set in c. 1100 BC. Some finds from the site are in the Plaka museum, but the best — including the flying fish fresco — is now in the National Archaeological Museum in Athens.

Boat trips around the island, although expensive, also make an interesting excursion; passing the strange volcanic pipe **Glaronisi** islets to the north of Milos, and the uninhabited (rare chamois goats excepted) and inaccessible island of **Antimilos** to the north-west.

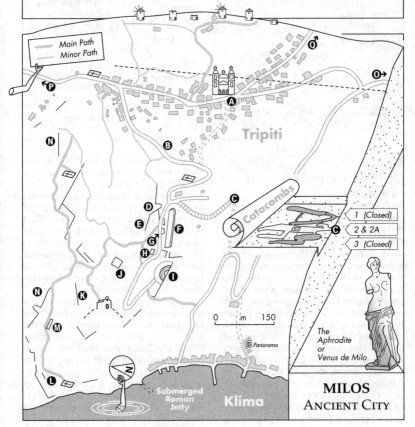

Key

Ⓐ Tripiti Village Bus Stop
Ⓑ Main Path to Archaeological Site
Ⓒ Entrance to the Catacombs
Ⓓ Circular Bastion
Ⓔ Internal Defensive Wall
Ⓕ Stadium
Ⓖ Discovery site of the Venus de Milo / Gymnasium
Ⓗ Foundations of Baptistry & Early Christian Font

Ⓘ Roman Theatre
Ⓙ Site of Main City Temple?
Ⓚ Roman Baths
Ⓛ Private Houses
Ⓜ 'Hall of the Mystai' Mosaic
Ⓝ Sections of City Wall
Ⓞ Road to Triovasalos Village (1 km)
Ⓟ Road to Plaka Village (1 km)
Ⓠ Road to Adamas Port (4 km)
Ⓡ Current hiding-place of the Venus de Milo's arms

Main Path
Minor Path

Tripiti

Catacombs

1 (Closed)
2 & 2A
3 (Closed)

The
Aphrodite
or
Venus de Milo

Panorama

0   m   150

Submerged
Roman
Jetty

Klima

MILOS
ANCIENT CITY

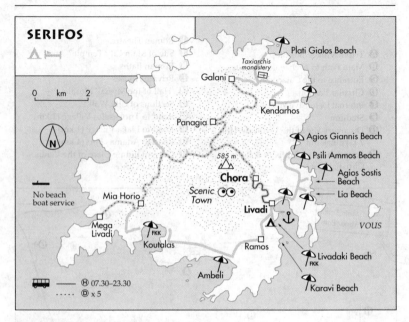

SERIFOS

Plati Gialos Beach

Taxiarchis monastery

Galani

Kendarhos

Panagia

Agios Giannis Beach

Psili Ammos Beach

585 m

Chora

Agios Sostis Beach

Scenic Town

Lia Beach

Mia Horio

Livadi

No beach boat service

Mega Livadi

VOUS

Koutalas

FKK

Ramos

0   km   2

N

Livadaki Beach

FKK

Ambeli

Karavi Beach

🚌 —— Ⓗ 07.30–23.30

····· Ⓓ x 5

Serifos

ΣΕΡΙΦΟΣ; 70 km²; pop. 1,100.

CODE ☎ 0281
PORT POLICE ☎ 51470
POLICE ☎ 51300
HOSPITAL ☎ 51202

Serifos is one of those islands that always seems to end up near the top of the list of 'one of those places the ferry calls at on the way to the island you are heading for'. This is a pity, because in many respects the island has more going for it than its more popular neighbour Sifnos. Equally distressing, a goodly number of the citizens of Athens are in the know about this and descend like a plague of locusts for weekends and summer holidays: be warned, ferries departing Serifos for Athens on Sundays are almost certain to be booked solid before you get a chance to buy a ticket. Athenians aside, sunbaked Serifos is blessed with a laid-back, relaxed ambience. During Low Season weekdays, at least, the island offers a tantalizing glimpse of what Ios might have been like if it hadn't been discovered by the partying masses; the set-up is not dissimilar, with a small port over-looked by an appealing chora, coupled by a good beach a headland away. Serifos is as barren and with as poor a road system as Ios, too; as a result few visitors venture beyond the closely connected port—chora—beach combination.

The only means of arrival and escape is the cosy beach and pine-fringed harbour of **Livadi**. Set in a deep-cut bay on the south coast, it is home to most of the island's facilities from the bank, supermarket and nightlife (don't expect too much on this score: discos on Serifos invariably notch up a greater tally of discs played than dancers through their doors) to almost all the accommodation options. However, for all this, the port is

Cyclades West

Chora Square Taverna
Menu & Chair

SERIFOS
Chora Houses

How to keep cool in Greece:
Example 21

MILOS
Apollonia Beach

KEA
Archaic Lion
& Tourist Circus

Cliff-top Chora Views on
Folegandros

Kastro Houses & Main Square Church
FOLEGANDROS

Cyclades West

Cyclades East

KOUFONISSIA
Port Village Beach & Fishing
Caïques

SCHINOUSSA
✝ Chora Church

IRAKLIA
Quay & Village

ANAFI
Chora Square

AMORGOS
Chora

Chora Bus Station
Square

Waterfront at
Katapola

Amorgos:
Conch-blowing
fishermen sell
their catch in
the streets of
Chora

ASTIPALEA
Chora Windmills
& Kastro

Cyclades East

very small and charmingly primitive. The one feature of note is the over-large ferry quay built onto the headland that protects the harbour bay.

The bay itself is lined by hotels and houses offering rooms. These look onto a passable sand beach (though the dust thrown up by cars negotiating the port's one-way traffic system means that it pays to walk to the east of the hotel strip). A better beach lies to the west of the ferry quay at **Lavadaki**. This is supposedly designated as one of the island's two nude beaches, but the crowds turn this into an all family affair during the summer months. Those looking for the chance to reveal more to fewer people should consider talking the short path that runs from the end of Lavadaki beach over the headland to **Karavi** beach. The more energetic might also consider taking the track that runs from the far end of the harbour beach to the succession of charming beaches on the east coast. These start with **Lia** and run up to **Agios Giannis** — passing en route the island's best beach — a long stretch of sand backed by a couple of tavernas at **Psili Ammos**. About an hour's walk from the port bay it can also be reached via a track running down from Chora. Beyond Psili Ammos is a longer beach at Agios Giannis; usually very quiet, it tends to be the sole preserve of the occasional nude hiker.

A second walking option (provided you are prepared to keep your clothes on) is the old mule path running from the road behind the port up a steep hillside to the island's only town. The path and modern road repeatedly meet and turn away all the way up the hillside — like a pair of virgin lovers' furtive glances; with mule water troughs taking the part of occasional tears along the way. Unless you attempt it during the heat of the middle of the day it is an easy and pleasant walk, though at some points where path and road meet you have to look quite hard to pick up where the path continues.

Just over 2 km long, the path finally wanders into the lower slopes of the island capital at **Chora**. Straddling the slopes of finger of rock pointing skyward (complete with a whimsical small chapel placed deftly on the tip) Chora is not to be missed. It deserves a visit for it is one of the most photogenic choras around: a mini-Astipalea Town, complete with a ridge of windmills, and a hill topped with whitewashed chapels and the scanty remains of a kastro. The views over Chora and the port bay from the top are suitably breathtaking, and worth the effort of finding your way through the narrow warren of streets (many in a poor state of repair).

The main hill aside, Chora neatly divides into two quarters. The older section runs in an arc north along the hill spine until it reaches the windmills (most of the houses run down the east slope before farming terraces take over). The 'new' town cascades down the south slope of the chora hill, and there is limited access between the two. Still very much a residential town with few concessions to tourism, Chora lacks landmarks (thereby guaranteeing you will get lost in it for a street or two). Fortunately, it is not so big that this is much of a problem and some relief is to be gained by the provision of working water taps at strategic points on the edge of the chora and the old road.

The rest of Serifos is not visited by the great majority of visitors. Consisting of arid, stone-littered hills ('Serifos' means 'stoney') that are relieved only by odd patches of vegetation (like equally dry Santorini the island's principal crops are tomatoes and ground-creeping vines) and a scatter of isolated farms, it doesn't exactly invite exploration; though ambitious walkers will find plenty to please them. The dull red brown landscape isn't really enhanced by the litter of rusting remains from the island's —now defunct — the iron mining industry. This thrived a century ago but declined between the world wars: its only lasting impact being in the field of Greek industrial relations: a 1916 miners' strike saw the deaths of several strikers before workers' rule was established. More appealing are the small villages connected by poor roads. These lead variously to the island's other official nudist beach at Koutalas, and to the **Taxiarchis** monastery on the north coast.

An earlier island attraction is presumably still lying around somewhere and, if discovered, is probably better left where you find it; for Serifos was the childhood home of Perseus, the Greek hero who cut off the head of the Gorgon Medusa (a personified shriek who, if looked at directly in the eye, would turn the viewer into stone). Armed with this little trinket, Perseus went around the island flashing it at anyone who didn't take his fancy; this included the king and most of the island population. This seems to have left the modern inhabitants in a quandary: on the one hand this mythological hero provides the only event in the history of the island worth talking about, yet he presumably did to death many of their ancestors. As a result Perseus, although a Greek hero, is all but ignored here.

Elsewhere Perseus was a popular figure in ancient art. Not to be confused with the god Hermes, he was armed with a mirror shield (provided by his patron Athena), a pair of winged boots, a head-satchel and cap of invisibility (donated by nymphs), and a sickle (a gift from Hermes). His foe Medusa was one of the horror stories of Greek mythology. Noted for having a head of snakes instead of hair, early representations of her play on her popping eyes and also add wings, a belt of boars' teeth and show her running with protruding fangs and tongue. During the Classical period subtlety took over, and she was made infinitely more terrible by being represented as a beautiful maiden. Her beheading and Perseus's subsequent pursuit by her two sisters (Sthenno 'the Strong' and Euryale 'the wide-leaping') was a popular theme in Archaic art.

The Myth of Perseus & the Gorgons

Once upon a time Acrisius, the king of Argos, was warned by an oracle that his daughter Danaë would produce a son who would kill him. Whereupon he imprisoned her in a bronze chamber (an ancient variation on the chastity belt). Needless to say the god Zeus — disguised as a golden shower (of what it is probably politic not to ask) — visited her and nine months later Perseus appeared. Loath to kill his grandson Acrisius promptly put him into a chest with his mother and cast it out to sea. It drifted to Serifos where mother and son were received cordially by the local king Polydectes, who fell violently in love with Danaë, allowing both mother and son to live in his palace. Danaë, however, successfully rejected the king's advances until Perseus was fully grown. Polydectes then sought to get him off the scene while he pursued his mother by sending him off on a seemingly impossible task — to fetch the head of the Gorgon Medusa. This Perseus did with a little help from his friends; notably the goddess Athena the god Hermes, and some Gorgon-hating sea nymphs. On returning to Serifos, Perseus turned Polydectes and his courtiers into stone by producing the head of Medusa after he discovered that the king had attempted to force his mother into marriage. After returning the gifts of Hermes and his patron Athena (who thereafter wore the Aegis cape, adorned with the Gorgon's head and fringed with snakes) Perseus and his mother decided to return to the mainland, where en route to his home, he mis-threw a discus while competing in some funeral games; accidentally killing a member of the crowd — his grandfather.

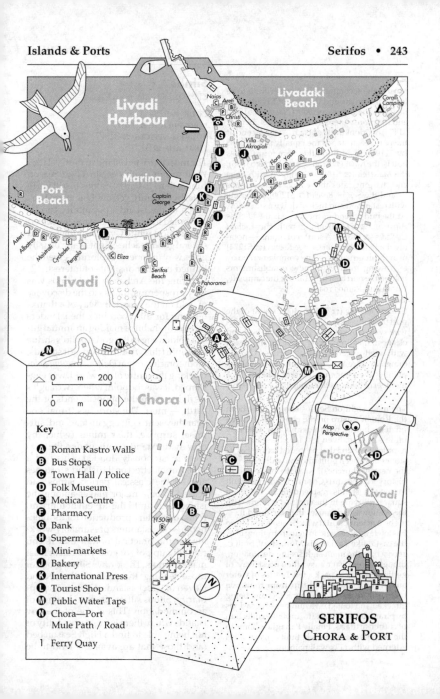

Livadi Harbour

Livadaki Beach

Coralli Camping

Naias

Areti

Christi

Villa Akrogiali

Flora Yasso

Helios Medusa Danae

Marina

Captain George

Port Beach

Livadi

Asteri

Albatros

Maistrali

Cyclades

Pergola

Eliza

Serifos Beach

Pahorama

Chora

Map Perspective

Chora

Livadi

SERIFOS

CHORA & PORT

Key

- **A** Roman Kastro Walls
- **B** Bus Stops
- **C** Town Hall / Police
- **D** Folk Museum
- **E** Medical Centre
- **F** Pharmacy
- **G** Bank
- **H** Supermaket
- **I** Mini-markets
- **J** Bakery
- **K** International Press
- **L** Tourist Shop
- **M** Public Water Taps
- **N** Chora—Port Mule Path / Road

1 Ferry Quay

(150 m)

ᕦᕤ

Most of the accommodation on Serifos is to be found in and around the port of **Livadi**. This includes the B-class pension *Naias* (☎ 51585) and the more expensive B-class hotel *Areti* (☎ 51479) overlooking the beach. At the far end of the port beach stands the equally pricy *Asteri* (☎ 51191). In addition there are four C-class hotels: the *Naias* (☎ 51585), the *Eliza* (☎ 51763), the *Maistrali* (☎ 51381) — topped with flags and charging rates above most B-class hotels — and the *Serifos Beach* (☎ 51209), complete with restaurant and tucked down a side alley. At the budget end of the range is the D-class *Albatros* (☎ 51148) along with the E-class *Cyclades* (☎ 51315). A scatter of rooms — notably the faded *Captain George Rooms* (☎ 51274) near the main square — are complemented by a growing number of new establishments behind the port beach and along the campsite, Chora and Ramos roads.

Λ

Coralli Camping (☎ 51500): 400 m west of the port (mini-buses go 2 km around the port one-way system to get there). One of the best and cleanest sites in Greece; right on the beach with well-watered shady shrubs. On-site bungalows are also rented out. The only weak point is the poor mini-market. The site is a member of the *Sunshine Camping Club* scheme.

∞

The main sight on Serifos should have been the **Roman Kastro** on the chora hill. Unfortunately, it was reduced to a few walls by pirates in 1210. Even less is to be seen of the temple of Athena that preceded it (most of its stones have been built into the walls of two of the nearby churches). Near the other end of history's spectrum is Chora's Town Hall. Built in 1909, it stands resplendent in the main square, glorying in the contrast it offers with the whitewashed houses that surround it.

The **Ancient Capital** which was at Mia Horio has left few traces, and in lieu of anything else, the castle-like **Taxiarchis Monastery**, built c. 1600 AD, is the main sightseeing destination, though access isn't easy; the surest way of getting there is to pack a few bottles of water and walk it: the round-trip from the town takes a little over four hours. Despite being attacked and looted on a number of occasions by pirates it is still home to a notable collection of church artifacts. Finally **Panagia** is home to the island's oldest church. Built c. 950 BC, it is adorned with 14 c. wall paintings.

Sifnos

ΣΙΦΝΟΣ; 89 km²; pop. 2,200.

CODE ☎ 0284
PORT POLICE ☎ 31617
TOURIST OFFICES ☎ 31977, 32190
FIRST AID ☎ 31315

The most touristed island in the Cyclades West group (with regular High Season connections to Paros), Sifnos is still fairly quiet by Central Cyclades Line standards. Much of the island's popularity can be attributed to its hilly landscape, sprinkled with typical white Cycladic villages and several good beaches; sightseeing usually gives way to general exploring, given the limited number of sights of interest.

During the Archaic period Sifnos was very prosperous, thanks to the discovery of gold on the island. By way of a thanks offering for this good luck the islanders were in the habit of making an annual gift of a golden egg to the god Apollo's shrine at Delphi (this wasn't as odd as it sounds, for the oracle stone at Delphi, the *Omphalos* marking the centre of the world, was egg-shaped; it was the point where two eagles — flying from the opposite ends of the earth — met). The story has it that one year they sent a gilt egg instead and, surprise, surprise, their mines (which by now had extended out under the sea) were mysteriously flooded. This had a catastrophic effect on the island's fortunes and by the classical period Sifnos had ceased to be a major player among the islands and (until the advent of tourism) relied on pottery production for its livelihood — the islanders presumably working on the practical notion that if you can't dig up pots of gold you can at least make the pots. These days Sifnos is one of those leading the pack in the second eleven of Greek islands. Despite its popularity, Sifnos suffers from a shortage of accommodation. This is one of the few islands where there is a real possibility of not being able to find a High Season bed (and those that are available tend to be expensive); it pays to arrive on a morning boat if you haven't phoned ahead and booked your bed.

All ferries dock on the 'wrong' side of the island where a narrow gorge provides a natural harbour at **Kamares**. Considering how small the port is, it is a surprisingly lively place thanks to its de facto role as the tourist centre, defying the stark hills that climb high above it, seeming to almost bundle it into the sea. Clinging to the shoreline you will find waterside tavernas by the score, a growing number of bars which are acquiring quite a reputation of over-sharp dealing, several travel agents and a sand-and-pebble beach of some length and dubious quality. Accommodation is spread thinly but evenly around the back of the settlement; and is, for the

most, part hidden behind clumps of trees and the half-hearted attempt to turn the road behind the beach into a promenade. Near the ferry quay there is also a helpful tourist information office. Frequent buses run from a turn-around point near the quay into the interior, making escape very easy — though most journeys seem to require you to change at Apollonia. All buses run east and south as the northern third of the island is all but unpopulated; the gold mines now being inaccessible even to the archaeologically minded. The bus ride itself is something of a revelation as the road runs up a valley filled with olive and fig trees; for Sifnos is not the barren island that the sea views suggest, and agriculture still pays an important role in its economy.

SIFNOS

Ⓓ x 4 10.30–17.30

Ancient Gold Mines

0   km   3

Ag. Marina

Kamares ⚓

C

Scenic Village

Artemonas

Pano Petali

Kastro

Apollonia /Chora

B

Kato Petali

680 m

Faros

Taxiarchis monastery

Vathi Beach

Platis Gialos

Chrisopigi Monastery

Ⓓ x 24 07.00–24.00
Ⓓ x 24 07.00–24.00
Ⓓ x 20 07.00–24.00
Ⓓ x 22 07.00–24.00
Ⓓ x 3
Ⓓ x 6
Ⓓ x 5

BUS ROUTES:
Sifnos has a good bus system built of some 11 routes criss-crossing the island. All pass through Apollonia: their combined frequency is shown on this map. Expect to change at Apollonia. There are three bus stops in the town:
1. In front of the Post Office (for Kamares)
2. In front of the Hotel Anthoussa (for Platis Gialos, Faros)
3. Opposite the Hotel Anthoussa (for Artemonas, Kato Petali & Kastro)

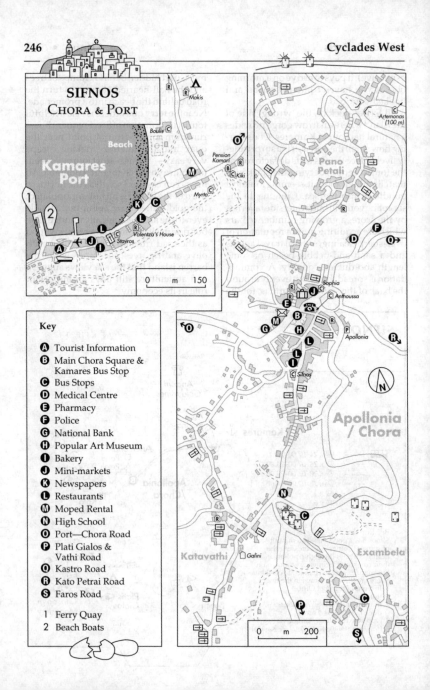

SIFNOS
CHORA & PORT

Kamares Port

Beach

Boulis

Makis

Pension Kamari

Kiki

Myrto

Valentza's House

Stavros

0   m   150

1 Ferry Quay
2 Beach Boats

Sophia

Anthoussa

Apollonia

Pano Petali

Artemonas (100 m)

Silfos

Apollonia / Chora

Galini

Katavathi

Exambela

N

0   m   200

Key

- **A** Tourist Information
- **B** Main Chora Square & Kamares Bus Stop
- **C** Bus Stops
- **D** Medical Centre
- **E** Pharmacy
- **F** Police
- **G** National Bank
- **H** Popular Art Museum
- **I** Bakery
- **J** Mini-markets
- **K** Newspapers
- **L** Restaurants
- **M** Moped Rental
- **N** High School
- **O** Port—Chora Road
- **P** Plati Gialos & Vathi Road
- **Q** Kastro Road
- **R** Kato Petrai Road
- **S** Faros Road

The modern 'capital' of **Apollonia** lies 5 km inland. As island capitals go it is a regular odd-ball; being merely one of four closely placed hill villages that has grown (by virtue of its role as the island's crossroads) to become the de facto nucleus. Lacking a historical heart of note, the settlement has grown along the roads to the neighbouring villages rather than in a traditional manner; creating an unusual village-cum-suburb web of buildings. Tourist activity is centred on the bland square in the heart of this jumble; little more than a road junction fringed with houses it is doesn't do the town justice; though all essential services are conveniently to hand. In fact, the tourist-shop cluttered street behind the square is supposed to be the true centre of the universe hereabouts. For Apollonia to have any appeal you have to enjoy walking; if you do so, and you can be rewarded with an interesting day clambering up and down the white-washed streets. The best views are to be found on the windmill-topped hill above **Pano Petali** — the mills themselves being rather fun thanks to their fish-shaped weather-vanes (a more interesting piece of religious symbolism than the more usual cross). The farmyard-backed backstreets behind **Exambela** are also quaint in a down-beat sort of way. Both offer excellent views of the comparatively isolated east coast former capital of Kastro, which is just within walking distance is you are not tempted by the bus.

The string of beaches along the south coast are the islands other great attraction. Of these, the best is at taverna-backed **Vathi** and is now visited by a new road and regular buses as well as caïques from Kamares port. A dirt track also runs from Vathi to the south-coast beach resort at **Platis Gialos**. Made up of tavernas, rooms and the odd hotel strung along the foreshore, it is the main beach on Sifnos. Further east lies the less popular small village of **Faros**; complete with three small beaches lined with a grubby brown sand.

▶◀

Good tourist offices on the port waterfront and Apollonia main square are of major help finding accommodation. There are four hotels in **Apollonia**, and all are C-class. Nearest the town square is the *Anthoussa* (☎ 31431), with the *Sophia* (☎ 31238) tucked away in a nearby street. Quieter than both is the *Sifnos* (☎ 31624) away to the south. The *Artemonas* (☎ 31303), 1 km to the north-east, is nice, but inconveniently placed. There is also a good pension in town — the *Apollonia* (☎ 31490).

Kamares also has accommodation in the form of the C-class *Stavros* (☎ 31641), the *Myrto* (☎ 32055), *Kiki* (☎ 32329), *Boulis* (☎ 321 22), and the B-class pension *Kamari* (☎ 31710). There are also some rooms — including some half-a-dozen establishments on the north side of the bay (not shown on the map opposite): these will appeal to worshippers of Aphrodite as they will have to undertake romantic moonlit walks along the length of the beach when their partner needs feeding and watering.

Other settlements also have a scatter of hotels: **Faros** has the D-class *Sifneiko Archontiko* (☎ 31822) along with the expensive B-class *Blue Horizon* (☎ 31442), and **Platis Gialos** the B-class *Platys Gialos* (☎ 31324) and the D-class *Filoxenia* (☎ 322212).

▲

Kamares has a friendly site behind the beach with outside washing facilities and little space: late arrivals in July and August are often reluctantly turned away. *Camping Plati Gialos* (☎ 31786) is a bigger olive-tree hill site on the south coast, west of the village bus stop.

෴

The most popular sight is the small **Chrisopigi Monastery** sited on a small islet (linked to Sifnos by a causeway) lying west of Faros. Equally photogenic is the former island capital at **Kastro**. Largely built between the 14 — 19 C., it is now an impeccably kept little village that has retained most of its medieval character and shouldn't be missed. Not least among its sights are the old whitewashed houses complete with brightly painted wooden huts on their balconies: a Greek variation of the outside privy. Best of all is the unspoilt atmosphere; though tourists are now arriving in increasing numbers. Of the other small villages around Apollonia, Venetian-built **Artemonas** is the most attractive, with the Kohi church built on the foundations of a Temple of Artemis.

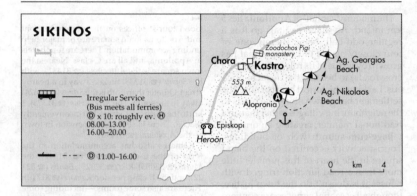

Sikinos

ΣΙΚΙΝΟΣ; 41 km²; pop. 330.

CODE ☎ 0286
POLICE ☎ 51222
FIRST AID ☎ 51211

If you want to experience an 'unspoilt' Greek island you can't pick much better than Sikinos. A hilly gem close to Ios, it is only in recent years that a ferry quay, road and a hotel have appeared; changing the scruffy beach port bay but otherwise unspoiling the working island atmosphere. After Anafi, Sikinos is the least touristed large island in the Cyclades, and offers a unique insight as to what Ios and other popular islands were like in pre-tourist days. For apart from a restaurant in both village and port, there are few concessions to tourism and much of the island's attractiveness stems from the fact that the donkeys constantly processing through the only town are carrying water rather than tourists. Another plus is the hospitality of the islanders, who have the unusual distinction of being of Cretan stock (their ancestors re-populated the island in the 16 C.).

Sikinos is visited via Cyclades East and occasional Cyclades Central ferries which call at the tiny bay port of Aloproina; home to summer caïques (running to several good south coast beaches) and buses to Kastro / Chora; a settlement consisting of two closely sited villages. Climbing up the spines of opposing hillsides, they are delightful, picturesque examples of their kind. **Kastro** is the larger and its lower quarter is now the de facto 'town' centre. Shrunken **Chora** is a suburb, with a trail of ruined houses and mills running up the hillside behind.

⊨

A reasonable supply of rooms scattered around the port is augmented by a fewer number in Kastro / Chora. Few in the latter have signs: owners meet boats instead. The only hotel, *Porto Sikinos* (☎ 51220), is new and expensive: rooms start at 13,000 GDR.

∞

Kastro / Chora aside, the only sights on Sikinos are two unusual defunct (and locked up) monasteries. The closest is **Zoodochos Pigi**, overlooking the main town. Once fortified, it gives Kastro its name. The donkey path up to it is not in the best condition, but those without broken legs are rewarded with superb views. More ambitious sightseers have the option of making the scenic and windswept walk across the island to **Episkopi**, a delightfully adapted Roman templet now masquerading as a monastery. Originally thought to be a small Hellenistic temple to Hera (hence Heroön), it is now deemed more likely to have been a 3 C. AD mausoleum. It is the only surviving remnant of the ancient centre of the island which was here rather than at Kastro. Virtually intact, it was converted into a monastery in the 17 C.

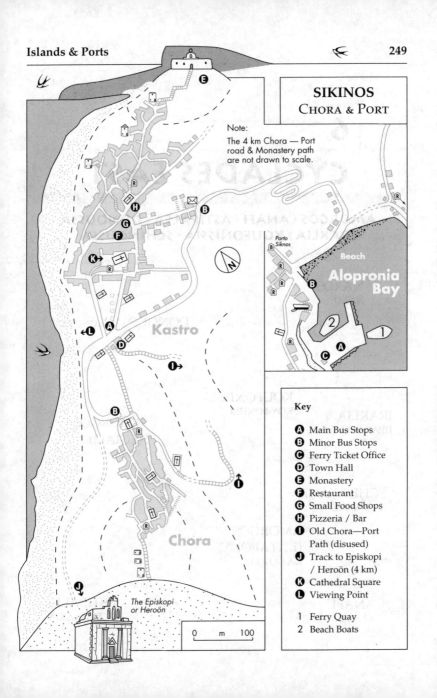

SIKINOS
CHORA & PORT

Note:

The 4 km Chora — Port road & Monastery path are not drawn to scale.

Porto Siknos

Beach
Aloptonia Bay

Kastro

N

Chora

The Episkopi or Heroön

0   m   100

Key

Ⓐ Main Bus Stops
Ⓑ Minor Bus Stops
Ⓒ Ferry Ticket Office
Ⓓ Town Hall
Ⓔ Monastery
Ⓕ Restaurant
Ⓖ Small Food Shops
Ⓗ Pizzeria / Bar
Ⓘ Old Chora—Port Path (disused)
Ⓙ Track to Episkopi / Heroön (4 km)
Ⓚ Cathedral Square
Ⓛ Viewing Point

1 Ferry Quay
2 Beach Boats

6
CYCLADES EAST

**AMORGOS · ANAFI · ASTIPALEA · DONOUSSA
IRAKLIA · KOUFONISSIA · SCHINOUSSA**

NAXOS
ΝΑΞΟ

+1½

DONOUSSA ΔΟΝΟΥΣΑ

+1

+1¼

KOUFONISSIA
ΚΟΥΦΟΝΗΣΙ

IRAKLIA
ΗΡΑΚΛΕΙΑ

+½

AMORGOS
(EGIALI)
ΑΙΓΙΑΛΗ

+¼

+1

SCHINOUSSA
ΣΧΟΙΝΟΥΣΑ

+1

+3 HOURS

AMORGOS
(KATAPOLA)
ΚΑΤΑΠΟΛΑ

ANAFI
ΑΝΑΦΙ

+2

ASTIPALEA
ΑΣΤΥΠΑΛΑΙΑ

General Features

In the centre of the Aegean lie a number of islands that do not fall easily into chapters organised by ferry routes. Rather than distort the reader's perception of those routes by describing them elsewhere, these islands are gathered together here. All are relatively untouristed: the last redoubt of the pre-tourist era, and all the better for it. The fact that they are untainted by mass tourism is their great charm: in many ways these are the *real* Greek islands!

The best known (and most accessible) is scenic Amorgos. It lies at the end of the line for most ferries that call — as does quiet Anafi to the south. To the east lies Astipalea; administratively one of the Dodecanese, but more characteristic in appearance of the Cyclades and usually served by ferries visiting the other islands in this chapter (hence its inclusion here).

The minor Cycladic islands running east of Naxos to Amorgos make up the balance of this chapter. Variously known as the 'little', 'lesser', 'minor', or 'small' Cyclades, they are all little gems. Only four are inhabited (Iraklia, Koufonissia, Schinoussa and isolated Donoussa), and all are small enough to make you feel as if you really are on an island; since it is almost impossible not to lose sight of the sea. These islands are a true delight — if you can live without banks and discos. All have small, friendly populations that subsist on fishing.

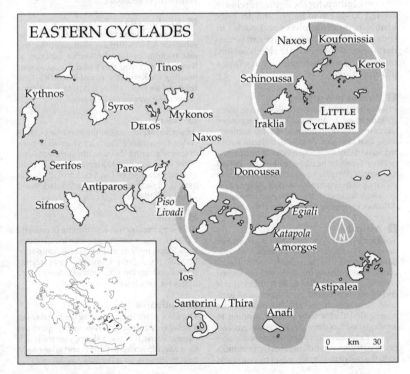

EASTERN CYCLADES

Example Itinerary [2/3 Weeks]

This chapter covers two islands — Amorgos and Astipalea — widely hailed as amongst the most attractive and unspoilt in the Aegean. Lying off the main ferry routes, they are passed over as impracticable by most island hoppers restricted to a fortnight's travelling. Yet, in fact they can easily be incorporated in to a tight timetable. The trick is to tackle them as primary objectives. By visiting them first you can easily build them into a wider ranging island-hopping holiday, and as Amorgos was a major centre of the Early Cycladic culture, the itinerary below takes in other islands similarly blessed. However, don't expect to find idols standing on every hilltop, for the figures rarely exceeded 30–40 cm in height and are only visible as museum pieces and copies in souvenir shops. The itinerary can be undertaken in two weeks in the High Season, outside it, abandon Koufonissia or take a leisurely three.

1 Piraeus to Astipalea

Piraeus is the obvious starting point when seeking to get to Astipalea simply because of the comparative frequency of ferry connections. That said, you could still be faced with a two-day delay awaiting a boat. If your prospective ferry is heading elsewhere before arriving at Astipalea you can hop ahead and pick it up at the intermediate port. Alternatively, you can spend the time sightseeing in Athens or hopping south to nearby Aegina.

2 Astipalea

Your length of stay on Astipalea is going to be delimited by the paucity of a means of escape. Beyond saying that the overall pattern of ferry connections remains the same each summer it is difficult to generalise as ferry times at this end-of-the-line island tend to change each year. You should be able to plan on the assumption that a ferry will be running to Amorgos within three days. If Amorgos and the Cyclades have less appeal you should also find that ferries run to Kalimnos (with its links with the rest of the Dodecanese) twice a week.

3 Amorgos (Egiali)

The great majority of visitors to Amorgos head for Katapola, but if you didn't encounter a long delay at Athens, those who like quiet island ports should find themselves with plenty of time to stop off at Egiali first. When you are ready to move on you have the option of taking either a bus or ferry on to Katapola.

4 Amorgos (Katapola)

Once at Katapola you are effectively plugged back into the ferry mainstream. With daily boats to Naxos you are within easy striking distance of the Cyclades Central Line. Katapola is also the best jumping off point on Amorgos for the Little Cyclades and Koufonissia, but if the *Skopelitis* isn't running daily, you should allow for the possibility of being stranded on the beach a day longer than intended either here or on Koufonissia.

5 Koufonissia

Koufonissia offers a fair degree of small island escapism — but with the reassurance of having just enough by way of tourist facilities to hand. Even if you can't find a caïque-tour heading for Keros, the island is worth taking time out to visit. Allow a day in hand for a connecting service on to Naxos.

6 Naxos

An arrival at Naxos after the previous ports of call can be a bit of a shock for you will be back in tourist country. Even so, the northern coast of the town was host to a major Early Cycladic village, the museum has a clutch of idols, and a souvenir shop near the promenade is devoted to selling little else.

7 Paros

Although Parikia was also the site of an early Cycladic village the main reason to call now is to pick up a ferry or tour boat on to Antiparos. Besides, if you have found the other islands restful and idyllic you won't be tempted to linger for long here anyway.

8 Antiparos

The ideal place to while away the last days of a holiday, Antiparos is reasonably quiet yet close to Paros. It is easy to lounge on the beach for a day, nip across to Parikia and take a night boat to Piraeus for a final day in Athens.

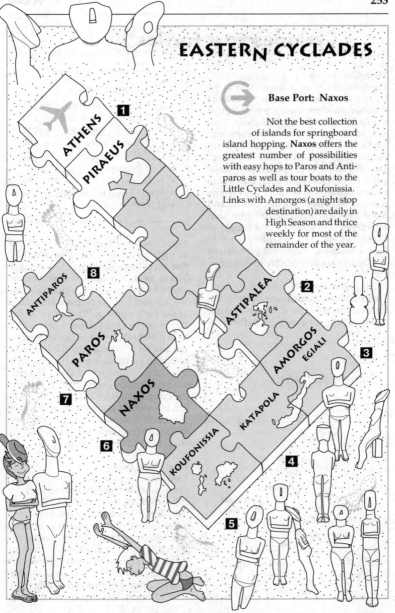

EASTERN CYCLADES

Base Port: Naxos

Not the best collection of islands for springboard island hopping. **Naxos** offers the greatest number of possibilities with easy hops to Paros and Antiparos as well as tour boats to the Little Cyclades and Koufonissia. Links with Amorgos (a night stop destination) are daily in High Season and thrice weekly for most of the remainder of the year.

ATHENS

PIRAEUS

ANTIPAROS

PAROS

NAXOS

KOUFONISSIA

ASTIPALEA

AMORGOS

EGIALI

KATAPOLA

Cyclades East Ferries

Main Car Ferries

The isolated nature of the islands in the Eastern Cyclades has conspired against the emergence of vessels solely dedicated to providing services to this chain. Instead, boats that normally run elsewhere take time out to make an extended run that includes various islands in the group. This means that services and boats change quite a lot each year, though the overall pattern changes very little; with ferries running from the Cyclades Central and North lines running on to Amorgos (and sometimes Astipalea), and a couple of Cyclades Central boats adding Anafi to their schedules. Occasional catamarans and hydrofoils also venture to Amorgos.

C/F Express Skopelitis

This invaluable, small car ferry is the local bus for the Little Cyclades and like most Greek buses is apt to get ludicrously

See also:
- C/F *Express Olympia*   p. 130
- C/F *Express Paros*   p. 133
- C/F *Express Santorini*   p. 130
- C/F *Naias Express*   p. 180
- C/F *Nissos Kalimnos*   p. 307
- C/F *Penelope A*   p. 180
- H/F *Sea Jet*   p. 184
- Speed Lines Hydrofoils   p. 134
- ILIO Hydrofoils   p. 134

over-crowded. The current vessel arrived in 1998; replacing the smaller *Skopelitis*. She runs from Amorgos (Katapola) to Naxos six days a week in High Season. Out of High Season, this is cut to a twice-weekly run. Her predecessor also called at the Parian port of Piso Livadi on her Mykonos runs, but the new boat is unable to negotiate the shallow harbour and is waiting for it to be dredged before restoring this part of the regular itinerary. On board conditions on the *Express Skopelitis* are significantly better than on her predecessor, but this isn't saying a lot as this she is less than comfortable when fully loaded. If Katapola is your destination you should also note that this boat is very slow; rarely arriving before 22.00.

Anafi Mail Boats

Two caïques — the *Alkyon* and *Ag. Nikolaos* — provide a twice weekly mail service to Santorini on the days that ferries don't call. They only take passengers from Anafi to Santorini (Athinios port). Latest times and tickets are obtained from Anafi port's Jeyzed Travel. The down side is the time taken (two hours to a ferry's one), the price (an extra 500 GDR), and the frequency (they don't run on windy days, which is most days in July and August).

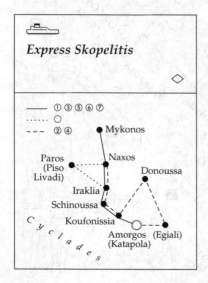

Express Skopelitis

◇

—— ① ③ ⑤ ⑥ ⑦
······ ○
– – – ② ④

Mykonos

Paros (Piso Livadi) Naxos Donoussa

Iraklia
Schinoussa
Koufonissia
Amorgos (Egiali) (Katapola)

C y c l a d e s

Cyclades East Islands & Ports

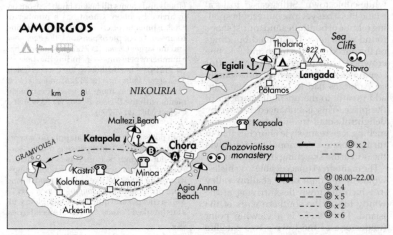

AMORGOS

Tholaria · 822 m · *Sea Cliffs* · Stavro
Egiali · Langada
NIKOURIA · Potamos
0 km 8
Maltezi Beach
Katapola · **Chora** · Kapsala
GRAMVOUSA · Chozoviotissa monastery
Kastri · Minoa
Kolofana · Kamari
Arkesini · Agia Anna Beach

⊕ 08.00–22.00
Ⓓ × 4
Ⓓ × 5
Ⓓ × 2
Ⓓ × 6
Ⓓ × 2
Ⓞ

Amorgos

ΑΜΟΡΓΟΣ; 117 km²; pop. 1,720.

CODE ☎ 0285
PORT POLICE ☎ 71259
POLICE ☎ 71210
FIRST AID ☎ 71208

The most easterly of the Cyclades, Amorgos has been one of the least touristed of the large Aegean islands. This is rapidly changing as its reputation grows, for Amorgos *should* be on the itinerary of any Cycladic island hopper. It is rugged, mountainous, often battered by choppy seas, and at first sight more intimidating than many other islands. But once ashore, it turns out to be very friendly and charmingly unspoilt. The 'Amorgos' experience is dominated by the island's hilly terrain. One consequence of this is that the road system has been very poor, the two main settlements at each end of the island only recently being connected by a good road and regular bus. As a result, ferries call at both centres (ticket agents also use port names in lieu of 'Amorgos' on timetables),

and even the islanders tend to think of their end as separate from the other half.

Katapola, the principal port, lies on the more populous western half of Amorgos. Tucked into a suitably scenic bay on the north coast, it is rapidly acquiring all the trappings of a mini resort (a patisserie has just opened) besides offering the best facilities on offer on the island. This isn't saying a great deal as shopping — as elsewhere on Amorgos — is rather limited. However, you will find tavernas and a road running the extent of the bay, along with various establishments offering rooms. The port beach is more for show than lying on (such surf as there is looks curiously soapy), and a regular taxi boat chugs across the bay to a much better beach behind the eastern headland. Fanning out behind Katapola is a fertile plain bisected by a road that winds steeply up the hills behind to the island's capital at Chora (as ferries steam toward the bay it is just possible to make out the Chora windmills and satellite dish towers on the skyline). Frequent buses run between the Chora and port (Katapola, incidentally, means 'below the town').

Chora is a superb example of a Cycladic white-cubic town. Still geared to local island life, it has yet to acquire the bespoiling retinue of boutiques and tourist shops found elsewhere. The ruined buildings on the outskirts of the town and a skyline crowned with derelict windmills (for some unclear reason each extended family on Amorgos had to have its own mill) add greatly to the unspoilt character of the place. This is enhanced further by delightful small tree-filled squares and melting ice-cream-style churches that in turn generate a cosmopolitan touch via the odd artist sketching in dreamland.

The main street (inaccessible to vehicles) winds up the floor of the shallow valley in which the town lies, arriving at the windy top of the southern cliffs of the island. Here there is a viewing point (under one of the town's two satellite dish towers) and the top of the staircase that winds down to both the main tourist attraction on Amorgos: the monastery of Chozoviotissa and the road to the island's most popular beach — at **Agia Anna** — a tiny pebble affair known for nudism (both can also be reached by island bus). To the north looms Mt. Protitis Ilias which, even in summer, is usually accompanied by a playful cloud chasing its tail around the upper slopes. This intimidating spectacle sets the tone for the island hinterland that is little frequented by tourists thanks to the paucity of bus services.

Egiali, the island's second port, is smaller but, thanks to a better beach and a hilly skyline topped with several villages, is more picturesque than Katapola. Set in a wide sandy bay with an absurdly long quay, it is overlooked by two hill villages. In past years backpackers have predominated, but it is cultivating a more up-market image. Much more accessible than even five years ago, it is very quiet and is a destination more likely to appeal to seasoned island hoppers, but then this sense of friendly solitude is the reason people come here.

⊨

Hotels and rooms fill fast in High Season: try to arrive by noon. **Chora** has a number of establishments (often without signs) offering rooms and a couple of pensions; the *Panorama* and the larger *Ghaias* (☎ 71277). **Katapola** has a number of pensions — including the *Amorgos* (☎ 71214) — in addition to the C-class hotels *St Georgie / Valsamitis* (☎ 71228) and *Minoa* (☎ 71480). **Egali** has more up-market establishments with the B-class *Egialis* (☎ 73393) and C-class *Mike* (☎ 73208).

Λ

Both ports have sites: at **Katapola** is *Camping Katapola* (☎ 71257): inexpensive, and reasonable out of High Season, it gets crowded in August. Popular with French school groups, it can sometimes feel like a playground during a fire drill. **Egiali** has *Camping Amorgos* (☎ 73 333): a cheaper and quieter site complete with a bus (marked *Pension Askas*) that meets ferries.

👓

The island sight is the spectacularly impressive 11 c. **Chozoviotissa Monastery** complete with a miraculous icon of the Virgin (open ℗ 08.00–13.00). Plastered into the side of a cliff 300 m above sea level, it justifies adding Amorgos to any itinerary; 'formal' clothing must be worn by those seeking admission.

Chora itself is more scenic than sight-filled. The best it has to offer is the finger of rock poking up from the whitewashed buildings: this is home to an unimpressive wall of a tiny 13 c. Venetian **Kastro**. Other sights are harder work. Near Katapola at **Minoa** are the remains of a classical town (a temple and the agora are visible). **Kastri** also has a poor classical site.

Hill Walking is also another island sightseeing — particularly on the east side (Egiali has one agent offering 'Herb Tours'). Amorgos shops sell plain white maps showing the paths and suggesting itineraries and journey times. Topping the list is the 5–7 hour walk along the island spine from Katapola to Egiali; this offers sumptuous views — including the ex-leper colony islet of **Nikouria** (Egiali boats visit) and the beach islet of **Gramvousa** (Katapola boats visit), and the hillside at **Kapsala** where the largest **Cycladic Idol** yet discovered was unearthed. Almost life size, it is now in the National Archaeological Museum in Athens.

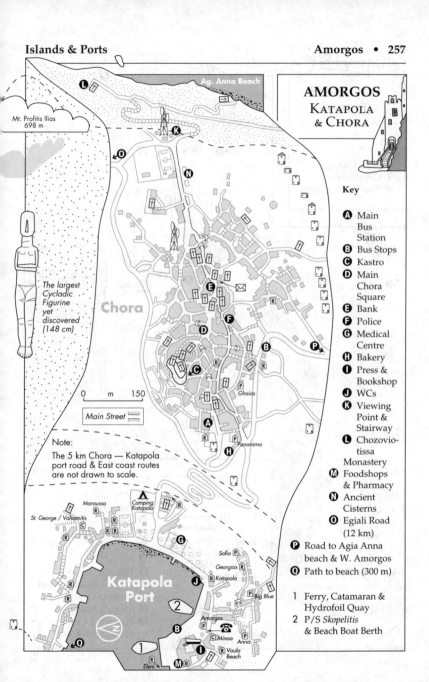

Mt. Profitis Ilias
698 m

Ag. Anna Beach

AMORGOS
KATAPOLA
& CHORA

The largest
Cycladic
Figurine
yet
discovered
(148 cm)

Chora

0   m   150

Main Street

Note:
The 5 km Chora — Katapola
port road & East coast routes
are not drawn to scale.

Ghaias

Panorama

Key

Ⓐ Main
Bus
Station

Ⓑ Bus Stops

Ⓒ Kastro

Ⓓ Main
Chora
Square

Ⓔ Bank

Ⓕ Police

Ⓖ Medical
Centre

Ⓗ Bakery

Ⓘ Press &
Bookshop

Ⓙ WCs

Ⓚ Viewing
Point &
Stairway

Ⓛ Chozovio-
tissa
Monastery

Ⓜ Foodshops
& Pharmacy

Ⓝ Ancient
Cisterns

Ⓞ Egiali Road
(12 km)

Ⓟ Road to Agia Anna
beach & W. Amorgos

Ⓠ Path to beach (300 m)

1 Ferry, Catamaran &
Hydrofoil Quay

2 P/S *Skopelitis*
& Beach Boat Berth

Maroussa

Camping
Katapola

St. George / Valsamitis

Sofia

Georgias

Katapola

Big Blue

Amorgos

Minoa

Anna

Voula
Beach

**Katapola
Port**

Eleni

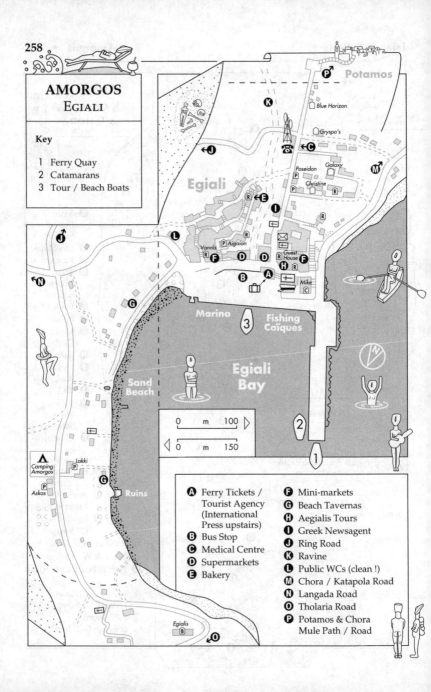

AMORGOS
Egiali

Key

1 Ferry Quay
2 Catamarans
3 Tour / Beach Boats

Potamos

Blue Horizon

Gryspo's

Galaxy

Egiali

Poseidon

Christine

Vannis

Aigaion

Guest House

Mike

Marina

3 Fishing Caïques

Egiali Bay

Sand Beach

0   m   100

0   m   150

2

1

Camping Amorgos

Lakki

Askas

Ruins

Egialis

🅐 Ferry Tickets / Tourist Agency (International Press upstairs)
🅑 Bus Stop
🅒 Medical Centre
🅓 Supermarkets
🅔 Bakery
🅕 Mini-markets
🅖 Beach Tavernas
🅗 Aegialis Tours
🅘 Greek Newsagent
🅙 Ring Road
🅚 Ravine
🅛 Public WCs (clean !)
🅜 Chora / Katapola Road
🅝 Langada Road
🅞 Tholaria Road
🅟 Potamos & Chora Mule Path / Road

Anafi

ΑΝΑΦΙ; 38 km²; pop. 340.

CODE ☎ 0286
POLICE ☎ 61216
TOURIST OFFICE ☎ 61253
MEDICAL CENTRE ☎ 61215

One hour's sailing east of Santorini, at first sight it seems something of a paradox that Anafi is one of the least accessible islands in the Aegean: so much so, that 'Anafi' is the Greek word for 'Timbuktu'. Tradition has it that the island sprang up out of the sea by order of Apollo when the legendary Argonauts were in need of a berth. This was as near as the island has ever got to a spring; apparently the Argonauts didn't need water as the island isn't furnished with any. Covered by a 25 m thick blanket of pumice from the eruption of Santorini, it has never been a prosperous place. Those who are washed up on Anafi's mountainous shores will find a barren island with one hilltop chora village overlooking a diminutive port; but the atmosphere is superb. So much so, that the island is attracting increasing numbers of visitors drawn to the laid-back isolation, the low cost of living and a succession of sandy crowd-free beaches.

The Chora can lay claim to be one of the last truly unspoilt Cycladic choras, and is a pretty place in a downbeat sort of way; with Santorini-style anti-earthquake barrel-roofed houses and exterior baking ovens. However, although its setting is little short of majestic, it lacks an obvious centre of focus (the hilltop at its heart is missing an all-important kastro—though it offers superb views over the town). Instead, the main centres are the bus squares at each end of the chora; the eastern seeing more activity, the western a quiet picture-postcard affair. Needless to say there is no bank; but there are a couple of tiny food-cum-tourist shops and a restaurant in the centre of town. A new 4 km road has brought with it a pint-sized bus that scuttles frequently between the chora and port (the old 1.5 km mule track

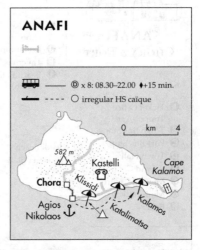

ANAFI

🚌 —— ⓓ x 8: 08.30–22.00 ✦+15 min.
⚓ - - - - ○ irregular HS caïque

0 ——— km ——— 4

582 m
Kastelli   Cape
                            Kalamos
Chora Klisidi
Agios ⚓   Kalamos
Nikolaos   Katalimatsa

still exists for energetic traditionalists).

The tiny cliff-backed port of Agios Nikolaos is — rather surprisingly — the real hub of Anafi life (such as it is). Everyone seems to pass through at some point during the day and as a result it has several tavernas and a travel agency that acts as a money exchange. A short cliff-side path walk away is attractive tree-backed Klisidi beach: in summer it now quite crowded (the far end seeing the odd nudist).

🛏
No hotels, but rooms are on offer at the chora, port, and beach. If you are phoning ahead try *Jeyzed Travel* (☎ 61253), *Ta Plagia* (☎ 61308) or *Villa Apollon* (☎ 61237) behind Klisidi beach.

Λ
August sees anything up to 80+ tents lining Klisidi beach. Camping is free, but there are no facilities bar the tavernas behind the beach.

👓
If you are seeking a genuine unspoilt Greek island Anafi is it. If nightlife is more your thing then the best sight on offer is apt to be the ferry arriving to pick you up. The more adventurous will find a ruined **Venetian Kastro** at Kastelli, and a deserted monastery (built on the supposed site of a **Temple of Apollo** set up by the Argonauts) atop the hill that dominates the eastern end of the island. Beach boats visit quiet beaches en route.

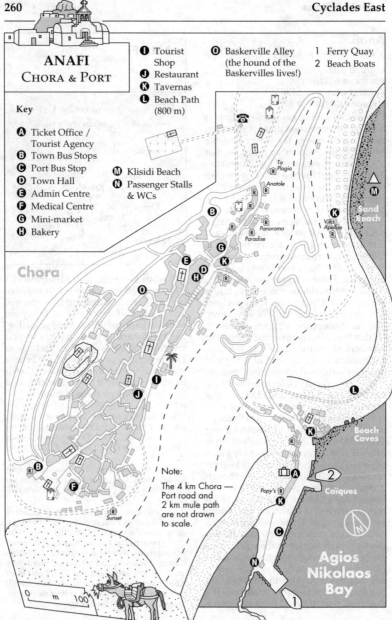

ANAFI
CHORA & PORT

Key

Ⓐ Ticket Office /
    Tourist Agency
Ⓑ Town Bus Stops
Ⓒ Port Bus Stop
Ⓓ Town Hall
Ⓔ Admin Centre
Ⓕ Medical Centre
Ⓖ Mini-market
Ⓗ Bakery

Ⓘ Tourist
    Shop
Ⓙ Restaurant
Ⓚ Tavernas
Ⓛ Beach Path
    (800 m)

Ⓜ Klisidi Beach
Ⓝ Passenger Stalls
    & WCs

Ⓞ Baskerville Alley
    (the hound of the
    Baskervilles lives!)

1 Ferry Quay
2 Beach Boats

Chora

Ta
Plagia

Anatole

Panorama
Paradise

Villa
Apollon

Sand
Beach

Ⓜ

Ⓑ

Ⓖ
Ⓔ Ⓚ
Ⓗ Ⓓ

Ⓞ

Ⓘ

Ⓙ

Ⓛ

Beach
Caves

Ⓑ
Ⓕ

Sunset

Note:
The 4 km Chora —
Port road and
2 km mule path
are not drawn
to scale.

Popy's

Ⓐ

2

Caïques

Ⓝ

Ⓒ

Agios
Nikolaos
Bay

1

0   m   100

ASTIPALEA

✈ → Athens ② ④ ⑥ ⑦

Ⓓ x 10 08.20–19.20
Ⓓ x 4 10.30–16.30
③ ⑥ 09.10

FOKIONISIA

Vathi

Maltezana
Vai

Ag. Theologos
monastery
Ag.
Andreas

Chora

HONDRO

GLINO

KOUTSOMITI

AG.
KRIAKI

Ag.
Ioannis

482 m.

*PONDI-
KOUSA*

Livadia

Agios Constantinos
Beach

KOUNOUPI

0   km   5

Vatses
Beach

Kaminakia
Beach

Ⓓ 10.30–16.00
Ⓓ 11.00–16.00
③ ⑥ 09.10 ♦16.30

Astipalea

ΑΣΤΥΠΑΛΕΑ; 95 km²; pop. 1,150.

CODE ☎ 0243
PORT POLICE ☎ 61208
TOURIST OFFICE ☎ 61217
POLICE ☎ 61207
FIRST AID ☎ 61222

Administered from Kalimnos, butterfly-shaped Astipalea is technically a member of the Dodecanese group. Yet, in both appearance and frequency of ferry links, the island has far more in common with the neighbouring Eastern Cyclades, with a white-cubist house chora (complete with windmills and castle) and typical barren, arid hillsides. Its relative remoteness, lack of nightlife (there are only three discos!) and reasonable — but not spec-tacular — beaches have all conspired to keep the masses at bay. All this is now changing; for one only has to sail between the folds of Astipalea's wings and see the castle-topped chora for a certain fascin-ation to take hold. The end-of-the-world sense of

introspection that pervades is enhanced by the combination of the island's beachcomber scruffiness (there are insufficient tourists to fund municipal cleanups here) and the picturesque litter of islets around the coastline.

Astipalea is a perfect spot to quietly unwind and soak up the Greek island atmosphere, free from crowds, yet in tangibly exotic surroundings. Folks come here to clamber up the hillsides behind the town and drink in the views. Buffeted by the wind, this is an island which encourages you to feel exhilaratingly alive. Rich, blue sea-filled vistas drenched in a dreamy bright sunlight worthy of an Alpine ski-slope and all that sort of stuff.

Coming back down to earth, the only settlement of any significance is the main **Chora** and port complex; an odd mix of staircases and new buildings running up to one of Greece's nicer old towns. Finding your way around is not particularly difficult: just keep climbing and sooner or later you arrive at the castle entrance

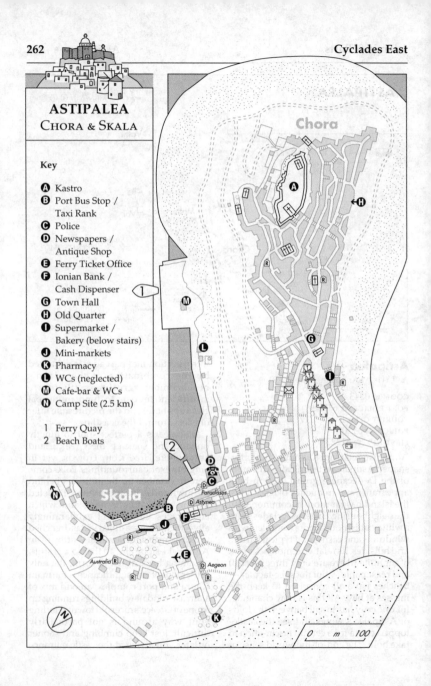

ASTIPALEA
CHORA & SKALA

Key

- **A** Kastro
- **B** Port Bus Stop / Taxi Rank
- **C** Police
- **D** Newspapers / Antique Shop
- **E** Ferry Ticket Office
- **F** Ionian Bank / Cash Dispenser
- **G** Town Hall
- **H** Old Quarter
- **I** Supermarket / Bakery (below stairs)
- **J** Mini-markets
- **K** Pharmacy
- **L** WCs (neglected)
- **M** Cafe-bar & WCs
- **N** Camp Site (2.5 km)

1 Ferry Quay
2 Beach Boats

Chora

Skala

Paradissos
Astynea
Australia
Aegeon

0   m   100

which offers a shady (and wind-free) retreat in the form of a passage that burrows quaintly under one of the two surviving whitewashed interior churches to the forecourt, and spectacular views of the coastline and beach islets to the south.

Most tourist facilities are to be found fringing the port, in the saddle-top windmill square above, and strung along the stairways and roads between the two. The popular port beach is lined with tavernas and mini-markets and is the nearest thing you will find to the centre of town: the chora square is usually too windy for those left standing to want to linger in it for long. After years of waiting Astipalea finally acquired its first bank —a waterfront branch of the Commercial (complete with cash dispenser) — in 1996. The National Bank of Greece also has a 'representative' next to the *Aegeon* hotel.

Reliable buses run from both the port and chora squares. The prime destinations are **Livadia** to the west of the port; site of the island's best beach and backed by a fertile valley that gave the island renown in classical times as a source of market garden produce, and east to **Maltezana** (also known as **Analipsis**), a former pirate lair noted as the spot where a French captain died in 1827 by firing his corvette to avoid capture; the closest Astipalea has to a resort beach, the nearest thing you'll see to skulls and cross-bones are paraded by elderly nudists.

The rest of the island lacks decent roads; buses crawling to Astipalea's second port at Vathi only twice a week. Blessed with a good beach and set in a deep fjord-like cove, this is a scenic village with a good cave, but it really only comes into its own during the winter months when heavy seas occasionally force ferries to berth here. Hill paths lead to several hilltop monasteries on the island and to a number of narrow tree-filled valleys.

⤶

Room supply is good, with owners meeting the boats and three inexpensive, but reasonable, hotels (all D-class) in the lower part of the town. The best of these — notably the clean but spartan *Paradissos* (☎ 61224) — and the *Astynea* (☎ 61209) are on the waterfront. The *Aegeon* (☎ 61236) lies on the chora road. Rooms are also available in the houses on the north side of the port bay (these have great views of the floodlit Kastro at night) and also in the beach villages of Livadia and Maltezana.

A

Camping Astipalea (☎ 61238): a pleasant and well shaded — if isolated — pebble beach site 2.5 km east of the port. Mini bus meets ferries.

∞

Astipalea's great attraction is its imposing **Kastro**. Built on the site of the ancient acropolis, it is a 9 c. Byzantine fortification, later rebuilt after a fashion by the Venetian Quirini family that ruled Astipalea between 1207 and 1522. Never a traditional castle, it thereafter evolved into a medieval apartment block of sorts during the centuries of piracy that followed. In its prime it was home to some 4000 people: its walls containing a labyrinth of staircases and four-storey buildings (if contemporary accounts of it are anything to go by then the island has lost a quite amazing tourist attraction). This was extant until the 1920s, when the Italian building of the port shifted the axis of settlement away from the chora, prompting partial demolition. An earthquake in 1956 destroyed those buildings that hadn't been demolished along with the north-east wall, leaving the interior little more than a shell, with only the churches and the fragmentary remains of the houses that nestled against the window-choked walls (now a storey lower than in times past) surviving.

Little of pre-medieval Astipalea survives, thanks in part to the island's most famous son, an Olympic boxer by the name of Kleomedies. Disqualified for killing his opponent at the games he returned to Astipalea in disgrace and did a Samson; pulling down the pillars of the island school and killing all the children along with himself (his late opponent obviously got in at least one good head blow). The fact that the school had pillars is about the only thing known of the island's classical architecture. Odd fragments of buildings are to be found in the Kastro walls and the island has yielded up a number of important inscriptions. The best remains are found at Maltezana, where a series of well-preserved zodiac mosaics from a **Roman Bathhouse** are on view.

Donoussa

ΔΟΝΟΥΣΣΑ; 13 km²; pop. 100.

CODE ☎ 0285

Rising steeply out of the sea east of Naxos, isolated Donoussa is the second largest and least visited of the Little Cyclades. Tucked behind the untouristed east coast of Naxos, it lies too far north to be a convenient stop for ferries serving the other islands in the group. Tourist boats are also notable by their absence. For these reasons it pays to work out how you are going to leave before you hop over.

Once ashore, you will find that Donoussa is a tranquil, friendly place that has a growing reputation among those looking to 'enjoy' a tranquil week or two in a largely unspoilt Greek island community. For good measure the island has several good sandy beaches on the south coast and three hamlets on the girdling coastal road. The largest settlement lies in a bay

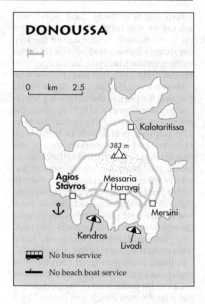

DONOUSSA

0   km   2.5

☐ Kalotaritissa

383 m

Agios Stavros   Messaria / Haravgi

⚓

☐ Mersini

Kendros   Livadi

🚌 No bus service

No beach boat service

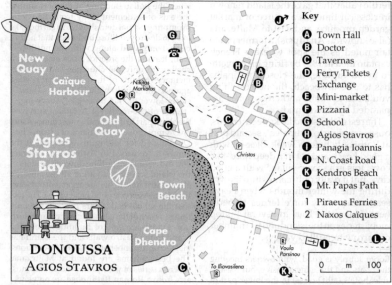

New Quay

Caïque Harbour

Agios Stavros Bay

Old Quay

Nikitas Markolas

Town Beach

Cape Dhendro

DONOUSSA
AGIOS STAVROS

Christos

P

Voula Parsinou

To Iliovasilena

Key

ⓐ Town Hall
ⓑ Doctor
ⓒ Tavernas
ⓓ Ferry Tickets / Exchange
ⓔ Mini-market
ⓕ Pizzaria
ⓖ School
ⓗ Agios Stavros
ⓘ Panagia Ioannis
ⓙ N. Coast Road
ⓚ Kendros Beach
ⓛ Mt. Papas Path

1 Piraeus Ferries
2 Naxos Caïques

0   m   100

on the south-east coast at **Agios Stavros**. Although it is a rather scruffy settlement, it is home to most of the available tourist accommodation. However, outside the half dozen tavernas, little English is spoken, and there is only one general store. A souvenir shop/ticket agency on the waterfront also offers exchange facilities with rates so bad that it is more advantageous to head back to Naxos for a couple of days and visit a bank there instead.

The rest of Donoussa offers rewarding walks and several excellent empty beaches at Kendros and Livadi. The hamlets are studies in unspoilt rural communities, **Mirsini** being the most prosperous thanks to the existence of a spring which is the island's main water supply. Isolated **Kalotaritissa** has appeal as a walking destination. In past years the coastal walk was the main activity Donoussa had to offer. Unfortunately, the road is now in the process of being coated in tarmac — courtesy of an EU grant (this will enable the the island's two vehicles to have grand prix races); so the 16 km circumambulation is unlikely to be as appealing as it once was.

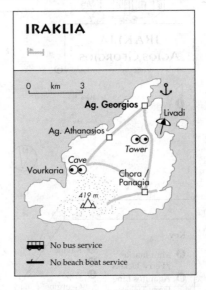

Rooms are not over-abundant (take up offers made when ferries arrive). The pension *Christos* (☎ 51555) is complemented by several establishments offering rooms. These include the waterfront *Nikitas Markolas* (☎ 51566) and the *Voula Parsinou* (☎ 61455). There is also some freelance camping on Kendros beach.

Iraklia

ΗΡΑΚΛΕΙΑ; 17.5 km²; pop. 110.

CODE ☎ 0285

A hilltop sticking out of the sea that tapers away into low hills to the north, Iraklia (usually pronounced 'Heraklia', and not to be confused with Heraklion / Iraklion, the capital of Crete) is marginally the most accessible of the Little Cyclades, thanks to occasional tour boat trips from Naxos Town. Like Donoussa, the island has a growing reputation for 'get-away-from-it-all' fans but, unlike the other Little Cyclades, isn't building extra facilities to meet growing High Season demand.

All ferries call at the north coast port of **Agios Georgios**. Set in a deep inlet, it is a rather scruffy, ramshackle affair with two main streets of sorts, bisected by a small ravine that winds up the most fertile valley on the island. The village boasts all the usual lack of amenities with a scattering of tavernas and a single food shop (that sells bread and milk imported from Naxos and ferry tickets for all but one line). Additional pluses are a sandy harbour beach backed by shady trees, and friendly locals who treat those staying more than a day or two as honorary villagers (though most rooms are carefully sited on the outskirts of town). This is not without advantages as most visitors find themselves nicely placed to walk to Iraklia's best sand beach at **Livadi**. This is a wide, taverna-backed strand with views across the narrow strait to Schinoussa (10 minutes sailing time away).

IRAKLIA
AGIOS GEORGIOS

Key

- **A** Mini-market /Ferry Tickets
- **B** Agapitos Line Ferry Tickets
- **C** Cardphone
- **D** Tavernas
- **E** Town Hall
- **F** Mule Troughs
- **G** Passenger Shed
- **H** Panagia Road
- **I** Livadi Beach
- **J** Ravine
- **K** School
- **L** Agios Georgios Church
- **M** Taxiarchis Church
- **N** Agios Athanasios Path
- **1** Ferries
- **2** Caïques

Anna
Maria
Alexandra
Dimitris
Manolis
Anthi & Angelos
Melissa

Town Beach
Agios Georgios Bay
Fishing Caïques
New Quay

0   m   100

The rest of the island offers an ideal retreat for leisurely walks though past visitors will be disappointed to find that the Port—Panagia mule path has been replaced with an EU-sponsored road wide enough to pass for a runway. Little used beyond Livadi, it runs past a hill overlooking the beach on which stands the impressive remains of a tower — dating from the days when these islands were notorious pirates' nests — to the old hillside chora at **Panagia** (now home to a mere half-a-dozen houses and a church). A surviving mule path runs from the back of Agios Georgios up the west coast and on ⌄ to a cave (complete with stalactites) near Vourkaria Bay.

Room supply is okay out of peak season (owners meet boats) but in July and August there are days when late arrivals can't find a bed — it pays to either phone ahead or arrive early. Prices are high regardless of season (1000 GDR more than on Naxos). All the beds on Iraklia are in Agios Georgios — the largest group include the *Maria* (☎ 71485), the *Alexandra* (☎ 71482), and the nearby *Anna* (☎ 71145). Rooms in the village itself include the *Anthi & Angelos* (☎ 71486), the *Melissa* (☎ 71539) and the *Manolis* (☎ 71569). There is also some freelance camping at the far end of Livadi beach.

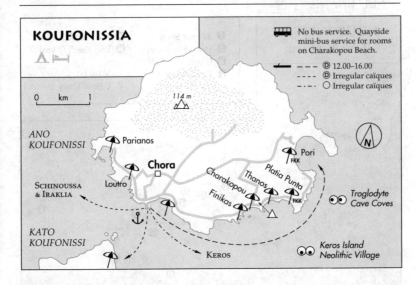

Koufonissia

ΚΟΥΦΟΝΙΣΣΙ; 3.8 km²; pop. 280.

CODE ☎ 0285

This being Greece, it is not surprising that the smallest inhabited island in the Little Cyclades is the most heavily populated, and indeed, touristed. Koufonissia is becoming quite a trendy place to visit, for although it can offer only the usual mix of beaches and mule tracks, the former are of a high quality and the generally cosy beach island atmosphere gives it an edge over its companions. If you have time to visit only one of the Little Cyclades, or are a little wary of venturing too far from the tourist trail then Koufonissia is probably the island to go for. Truth to tell, part of its attraction is that it does have at least a modicum of facilities (i.e. a post office, tavernas, a hotel and plenty of rooms), and ferry connections are as good as any in the group.

Koufonissia is, in fact, the collective name for two islands: Ano (upper) Koufonissi and Kato (lower) Koufonissi —

though these days the name is generally taken to mean the former. Ano Koufonissi is the main island (its low-lying companion being little more than a reef rising a few metres above sea level and used for grazing goats), and is home to the only settlement and the ferry quay. Hemmed in by Kato Koufonissi and Glaronissi, with mighty Naxos dominating the northern horizon and the much taller island of Keros close by to the south, Koufonissia has a wonderful little-kid-in-the-playground feel about it. The island is easily identified thanks to the white-roofed windmill to the left of the quay as you view it from the ferry. In addition, it is low and flat, tapering gently down to the sea on the south side. Moreover, you will usually find a picturesque flotilla of fishing caïques moored in the sandy bay to the east of the ferry quay.

Standing on the gentle hill behind the quay is the chora. This has all the essential facilities (with the exception of a bank and a good supermarket: the food stores on Koufonissia are very poorly stocked

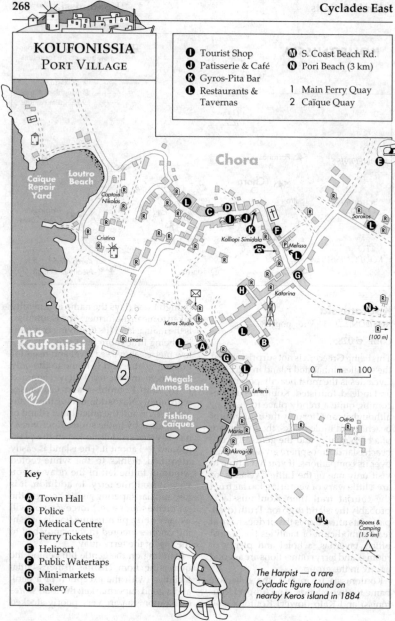

KOUFONISSIA
PORT VILLAGE

I Tourist Shop
J Patisserie & Café
K Gyros-Pita Bar
L Restaurants & Tavernas

M S. Coast Beach Rd.
N Pori Beach (3 km)

1 Main Ferry Quay
2 Caïque Quay

Chora

Caïque Repair Yard

Loutro Beach

Captain Nikolas

Cristina

Ano Koufonissi

Megali Ammos Beach

Fishing Caïques

Sorokos

Kalliopi Simidala

Melissa

Katarina

Keros Studio

Limani

Lefteris

Maria

Akrogiali

Ostria

(100 m)

0   m   100

Rooms & Camping (1.5 km)

Key

A Town Hall
B Police
C Medical Centre
D Ferry Tickets
E Heliport
F Public Watertaps
G Mini-markets
H Bakery

The Harpist — a rare Cycladic figure found on nearby Keros island in 1884

compared to most) and is pretty enough in a ragged sort of way, but in truth, it is a rather tame affair compared to most island choras. The old-style main street aside, most of the newer buildings are holiday homes or tavernas.

Fortunately, no-one comes to Koufonissia for much other than the beaches. Most of these are wonderful crescents of golden sand gracing a series of wide coves running south from Parianos on the west coast to Pori on the east. All are accessed via dirt tracks. The beaches get progressively better the further east you go. Charakopou and Thanos are the busiest thanks to the rooms, taverna and campsite. The very limited tree cover on Koufonissia is also at its poor best here. Nudism is supposedly banned on the island, but the islanders seem very laid back about this, and Platia Punta and Pori are de facto nudist affairs thanks to their comparative isolation. Both are reached by a dirt path that meanders along the edge of the low-cliffed coastline. This has been badly eroded by the sea, producing a succession of coves each with a tiny cave under the cliff path. In August each is usually home to a latter-day troglodyte couple whose presence can be deduced by the scent of evaporating suntan oil wafting up to the cliff path. Pori is the best beach and worth the effort of getting to it, but be warned: the coastal path walk is much longer than it looks thanks to the indented coastline. There is an inland mule path to Pori but this is less picturesque thanks to the lack of the magical turquoise seas, caves, coves and nudists. Instead you have to make do with the low scrub that covers the island.

⊨

The port village is increasingly devoted to providing rooms for summer visitors. If you are phoning ahead there is plenty of choice. Harbour views are offered by the *Maria* (☎ 71436), the *Akrogiali* (☎ 71685) and the *Keros Studio* (☎ 71600). In the centre of town is the pension *Melissa* (☎ 71454), the *Katarina* (☎ 71455) and the *Kalliopi Simidala* (☎ 71462).

Those looking for some thing more tucked away shoud try either the *Sorokos* (☎ 71453) or the *Ostria* (☎ 71671). In addition to rooms in the port village, a number of rooms are also available behind Charakopou beach.

Λ

Free camping is provided by a taverna between Charakopou and Thanos beaches. However, you pay for the use of the very limited washing facilities, and the tiny WC block is better imagined than described. Very limited shade.

ᏨᏣ

Caïques regularly make the crossing to Kato Koufonissi (there are several isolated farmsteads near the shore) and also make occasional trips to the Neolithic village site on neighbouring **Keros**. This large hilltop poking out of the water is far more impressive a sight than Koufonissia, looking as if it ought to be the most important of the Little Cyclades. However, apart from the obligatory mad monk, it is uninhabited, and used for grazing. This is all something of a come down from its days as a major centre of the Early Cycladic culture (c. 3000–2000 BC). Excavations on the west coast at the end of the last century produced over 100 Cycladic figures — the largest group found to date, including the famous harpist and flautist (both are now housed in the National Archaeological Museum in Athens). This reflects the island's apparent role as a manufacturing centre for these idols. If you charter a caïque (expect to pay at least 15,000 GDR for a day round-trip) to take you across, take care you don't end up instead at the remains of a medieval village on the north coast.

Schinoussa

ΣΧΙΝΟΥΣΣΑ; 8.5 km²; pop. 100.

CODE ☎ 0285

Once in a while a Greek island appears on the horizon that is so nice that it is almost a shame to tell people about it: dreamy and diminutive Schinoussa (pronounced 'Skinoussa') is one of these. Unfortunately, it needs hordes of *Greek Island Hopping* readers dropping in every year like a hole in its ferry quay; its charm comes from being so delightfully unspoilt. How long it will remain this way is another matter. To date it has been well served by its poor

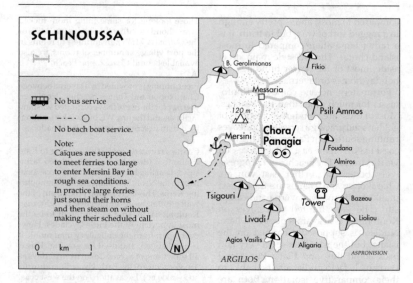

SCHINOUSSA

No bus service

— ·—·— ○

No beach boat service.

Note:
Caïques are supposed
to meet ferries too large
to enter Mersini Bay in
rough sea conditions.
In practice large ferries
just sound their horns
and then steam on without
making their scheduled call.

0   km   1

B. Gerolimionas

Fikio

Messaria

120 m

Psili Ammos

Mersini

**Chora/
Panagia**

Foudana

Almiros

Tsigouri

Tower

Bazeou

Lioliou

Livadi

Agios Vasilis

Aligaria

ASPRONISION

ARGILIOS

harbour which for many years dis-
couraged visitors by forcing ferries to
dump passengers into taxi boats, and
even now a proper quay has been built,
still discourages casual island hoppers
by looking so intimidatingly quiet (the
inlet has only with only three buildings
to its name). All this hides a multitude of
gifts, for once you venture inland, Schinoussa is all charm.

The only settlement of any size is known
variously as '**Chora**' or '**Panagia**'. Skill-
fully sited on a low ridge between the
island's low hills, it commands good
views without being too obvious itself —
a hangover from the pirate days which
saw the island depopulated several times
(the current inhabitants are descendants
of Amorgos stock who repopulated Schinoussa in the early 1800s). For the most
part, Chora is a single street affair and,
despite having few older buildings, has a
very appealing small-town character. It
has its fair share of characters too —
notably the owner of the tiny two room
'Tourist Centre'-cum-village store, who

usually offers lifts from the port in lieu of
an island bus service. The store also sells
ferry tickets (also available just before
departures at the port) and has an unreliable timetable posted up on the opposite
side of the street. The rest of the street is
home to the usual litter of tavernas (most
offering rooms) and occasional small
shops, and finally peters out into a couple
of tracks that wander down to the popular
beach at Livadi and to the east coast
beaches. In fact, Schinoussa is well endowed with beaches; there are up to a
dozen around the coast. However, although adequate, they are made of grey,
coarse sand and are not on a par with the
golden strands to be found on neighbouring islands — a fact that partly explains
Schinoussa's relative unpopularity.

The rest of the island can best be
described as looking like a group of
interconnected low rock dunes. Schinoussa is made up of some nine hillocks
(the northern two topped with derelict
windmills, with another on the hill
between Tsigouri beach and the chora).

SCHINOUSSA
CHORA & PORT

Key

A 'Tourist Centre'/
Exchange/Tickets/
Mini-market
B Ferry Timetable
C Main Sq./Cardphone

D Supermarket
E Mini-market
F Tavernas
G Bar
H Café-Bar Margarita
I Passenger Shed
J Chora—Port Road
K Messaria Road
L Livadi Beach Path
M Almiros Beach Path
N Tsigouri Beach Path

1 Large Ferries
2 C/F *Express Skopelitis*
& Hydrofoils

Note:

The 1.2 km
Chora—Port
road is not
drawn to scale.

With the notable exception of the port—Chora road, all the roads on the island are dirt track affairs and the preserve of the island's mule population, which seems to outnumber the human inhabitants. The only other settlement is the hamlet of **Messaria**, north of Chora, which is home to some 20 people. Ironically, given the comparative lack of inhabitants and visitors, Schinoussa has the best water supply of any island in the Little Cyclades, thanks to the existence of three springs. In the absence of tourists, they feed the wild chewing-gum bushes (mastica) that cover the hillsides instead.

🛏

Given its size, Chora has a surprising number of rooms on offer and more are being built. As with Iraklia, expect to pay 1000 GDR above rates on other islands. Accommodation in Chora starts with the *Pension Pothiti* (☎ 71184) and the *Dream Studios* (☎ 71175). At the other end of town are the *Meltemi* and the *Anesis* (☎ 71180). Other options lie on the Messaria road with the *Anna* (☎ 71161) and the solitary *Provaloma* (☎ 71185). There is also some freelance camping behind Livadi beach.

7
CRETE

AGIOS NIKOLAOS · CHANIA · IRAKLION · KASTELI
PALEOCHORA · RETHIMNO · SFAKIA · SITIA

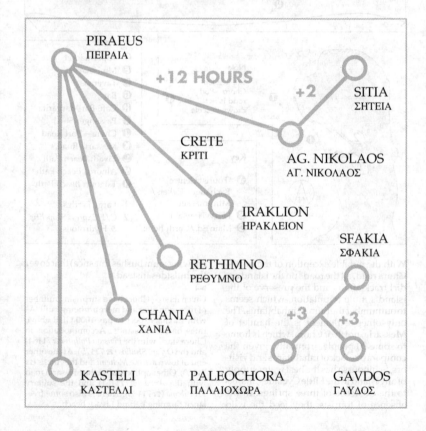

PIRAEUS
ΠΕΙΡΑΙΑ

+12 HOURS

+2

SITIA
ΣΗΤΕΙΑ

CRETE
ΚΡΙΤΙ

AG. NIKOLAOS
ΑΓ. ΝΙΚΟΛΑΟΣ

IRAKLION
ΗΡΑΚΛΕΙΟΝ

SFAKIA
ΣΦΑΚΙΑ

RETHIMNO
ΡΕΘΥΜΝΟ

CHANIA
ΧΑΝΙΑ

+3

+3

KASTELI
ΚΑΣΤΕΛΛΙ

PALEOCHORA
ΠΑΛΑΙΟΧΩΡΑ

GAVDOS
ΓΑΥΔΟΣ

General Features

Crete is such a large island that it justifies a separate volume in several popular guide series. A goodly number of island hoppers also sample the island in passing: for the most part restricting their visits to the string of port cities along the northern coast. These are worthy destinations in their own right and play such an important role in Cretan life that it is almost better to think of Crete as half-a-dozen 'city-states' sharing the same island. The modern capital of Iraklion is the most visited thanks to its good ferry and air links though it doesn't have half the atmosphere of the former capital of Chania or nearby Rethimno. The remaining cities of Agios Nikolaos, Sitia and Kasteli have less going for them, but they do have important ferry links for wide-ranging island hoppers. In addition to the north coast ports, the south west coast has a miniature ferry system of its own that invites exploration — as do the odd collection of associated islets scattered around the Cretan coast.

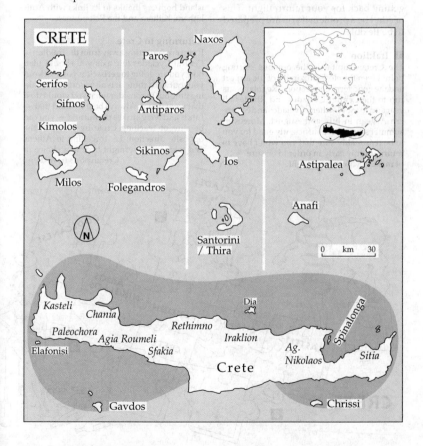

CRETE

Serifos
Sifnos
Kimolos
Milos
Paros
Antiparos
Sikinos
Folegandros
Naxos
Ios
Santorini / Thira
Anafi
Astipalea

N
0   km   30

Kasteli
Chania
Paleochora
Agia Roumeli
Elafonisi
Sfakia
Rethimno
Iraklion
Dia
Ag. Nikolaos
Spinalonga
Sitia
Crete
Gavdos
Chrissi

Crete-based Itineraries

Many regular island hoppers choose to avoid annual visits to Athens by flying to and from Crete. This is an attractive option (by any standards Crete is a much more appealing destination), but you do have to be careful given the limited nature of the ferry links between Crete and the islands. Not only is there the very real possibility that you will have to wait a day or two before being able to jump across, but you also have the problem of getting back for your return flight. This needn't be a problem if you are prepared to be flexible.

1 Iraklion
The Cretan capital is the obvious starting point given the close proximity of the airport and the good ferry connections. Regular boats run to the Central Cyclades and Rhodes all year and to the Northern Cyclades and Northern Aegean in July and August. Moreover, summer services are sufficiently good for you to be reasonably sure that you won't have to return unduly early in order to be sure of making your return flight.

2 Agios Nikolaos & Sitia
The two east Crete towns of Agios Nikolaos and, to a lesser extent, Sitia are also worth considering as starting points; having regular links with the Cyclades West island of Milos and the south Dodecanese islands to Rhodes. However, they are not particularly frequent: if you are flying into Iraklion visit the EOT / NTOG office and get their current timetable before heading for these towns.

3 Kasteli
The small port of Kasteli on the west side of Crete also has options for really ambitious island hoppers thanks to its links with Antikithera, Kithera and the Peloponnese.

Returning to Crete
If you are venturing away from the Iraklion—Central Cyclades line axis you should plan how you are going to get back as you work out your outward route. It is also worthwhile taking time out to consider what you would do if that went down. Always bear in mind that — funds and ferry strikes permitting — you can be sure of reaching Crete by going in the opposite direction: i.e. travelling to Athens and taking an overnight boat to a choice of Cretan ports from there.

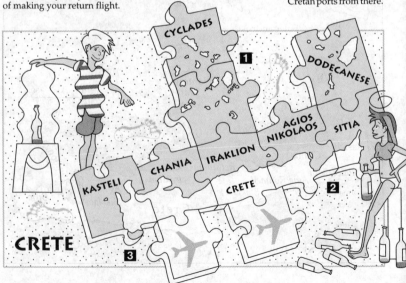

Cretan Ferries

Main Car Ferries

Crete is used as a springboard by long-haul ferries, as well as being well served by direct boats. The latter are reliable and can be timed to the minute. However, it is not uncommon for indirect ferries to be up to four hours late; Crete is often at the end of scheduled routes and thus delays (thanks to the distance from Piraeus) tend to be longer than elsewhere in the system. Such ferries either steam down from the Central Cyclades or ricochet off Crete en route to Rhodes. In High Season Cretan links are significantly enhanced by boats running a thrice-weekly service between Thessalonika and Iraklion, via the Sporades and Cyclades island chains. In 1998 the *Dimitroula* and *El Greco* ran on the route. As they provide a unique service into the Northern Aegean, they are described and mapped in that chapter.

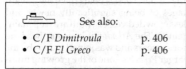

See also:

- C/F *Dimitroula*   p. 406
- C/F *El Greco*   p. 406

King Minos - N. Kazantzakis
Aptera - Rethimno   ◇

C/F *King Minos* - C/F *N. Kazantzakis*
Minoan

King Minos; 1972; 9652 GRT.
N. Kazantzakis; 1972; 10500 GRT.

These direct ferries are the primary link between Piraeus and the capital of Crete, Iraklion. They derive the bulk of their revenue from freight and vehicles. Tourist traffic, although important in the summer months, seems to count more as a bonus than a prerequisite for the existence of this annual service. That said, Minoan have announced that they are planning to run two high speed catamarans between Iraklion and Piraeus. Along with ANEK, Minoan already shares an effective duopoly on the route. Both companies possess large fleets and ferries are switched around at intervals so you could see other vessels running the service. Departure times can vary by an hour or so depending on the time of year. High Season also sees occasional extra morning departures from Piraeus, when demand is high.

C/F *Aptera* - C/F *Rethimno*
ANEK

Aptera; 1973; 7058 GRT.
Rethimno; 1971; 7291 GRT.

ANEK have run two boats on the Piraeus—Iraklion service for many years, though like Minoan they swap their boats about from time to time. The *Aptera* moved over from the Piraeus—Crete (Chania) service to partner the *Rethimno* in 1997. Both are significantly smaller vessels than their Minoan counterparts, and thus somewhat less competitive. Even so, they are reasonably well-appointed craft, if rather elderly. As with the Minoan boats, the overnight nature of these services means that, in High Season, sleeping cabins are rapidly booked up. Schedules are unlikely to change in 1999, whichever two boats ANEK choose to run the service.

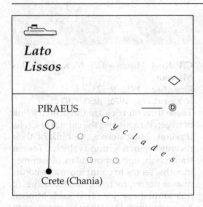

Lato
Lissos

PIRAEUS
Crete (Chania)

C/F *Aptera* - C/F *Lissos*
ANEK
Aptera; 1973; 7058 GRT.
Lissos; 1972; 9893 GRT.
Given the size of Crete, ANEK have found a profitable niche offering a daily service to the north-western town of Chania (via its port at Souda). In past years Minoan Lines devoted a single ferry to this route, but this service stopped in 1996. Both ANEK boats have run on this route for a number of years, and there isn't likely to be much change in 1998. Given this route is less popular than the Iraklion service, these boats might be a better bet if you are seeking a cabin booking and are planning to visit Chania while you are on Crete.

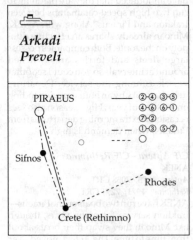

Arkadi
Preveli

PIRAEUS
Sifnos
Rhodes
Crete (Rethimno)

C/F *Arkadi* - C/F *Preveli*
Cretan Ferries (Rethimno SA);
Arkadi; 1983; 4097 GRT.
Preveli; 1980; 5683 GRT.
If Iraklion isn't your objective, the two boats offering a daily link with Rethimno offer an attractive alternative. Although smaller than their rivals on other routes, the Cretan Ferries boats have the advantages of being significantly newer and less crowded vessels. Both are well maintained. The *Arkadi* has been on the route for six years and was joined in 1995 by the larger *Preveli* — one of the growing number of ex-Japanese ferries in Greece. Schedules don't change much, though you do find the odd variation on some summer sailings; in 1997 this was a one-off run to Rhodes, and in 1998 odd calls at Sifnos.

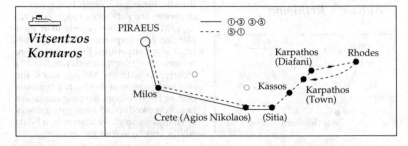

Vitsentzos
Kornaros

PIRAEUS
Milos
Karpathos (Diafani)
Rhodes
Kassos
Karpathos (Town)
Crete (Agios Nikolaos)   (Sitia)

C/F *Vitsentzos Kornaros*
LANE Lines; 1976; 9735 GRT.

In past years Crete has seen several subsidised ferry runs, notably a thrice-weekly link from Piraeus to Agios Nikolaos and Sitia via Milos. Unfortunately, neither port offers lucrative pickings and several lines have tried and failed to make the route pay (the bulk of the traffic consists of lorries running between these ports and the capital). The latest company to have a go is the one boat operation LANE Lines. Armed with a large well-equipped vessel — the *Vitsentzos Kornaros* (the ex-cross Channel *Pride of Winchester*) — they are keeping the thrice-weekly service going, and even trying to make the route more attractive by running an extended run beyond Crete to Kassos, Karpathos and Rhodes in 1998. This replaced a failed attempt to run a four-times weekly service in 1997. Cabin space on this boat is usually readily available.

Low Season Links
Out of the High Season Crete sees irregular ferries calling in en route to Rhodes. Unfortunately, it is impossible to predict these services in advance; however, if you are travelling in the early spring or autumn, they are worth looking out for. Most combine calls with ports in the Cyclades (usually running down the Western Cyclades Line and stopping off at Santorini).

South Crete Line
Five small ferries operate along the south-west coast of Crete from the ports of Paleochora and Sfakia/Chora Sfakion. Their primary role is ferrying tourists disgorged from the mouth of the Samarian Gorge to adjacent coastline towns, but they also offer an irregular service to the remote island of Gavdos to the south (the bulk of the weekday services have lately been from Paleochora, while weekend runs have been out of Sfakia). Timetables are available from the EOT branch in Iraklion. Although these boats are

🚢	See also:	
•	C/F *Daliana*	p. 132
•	C/F *Romilda*	p. 305
•	C/F *Kantia / Candia*	p. 451
•	P/S *Minoan Prince*	p. 135

supposed to service the mountain-locked fishing hamlets they remain very tourist dependent, and only a limited service — April to October — operates out of the July—August peak. A weekly Sfakia—Gavdos service operates all year round (formerly this ran from Paleochora). Most of the boats are small passenger 'ferries', too small to survive commercially elsewhere; the exception being a small car ferry charged with the vital task of bringing refrigerated ice-cream lorries to the roadless, but tourist-full, Agia Roumeli.

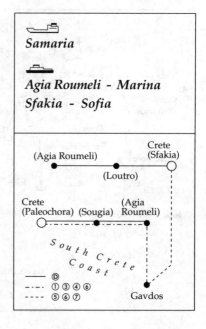

Samaria

Agia Roumeli - Marina
Sfakia - Sofia

⚓ Cretan Ports

Crete
KPITI; 8259 km²; pop. 460,000.

The fifth largest island in the Mediterranean and the largest in Greece, Crete is larger than some independent island states and has plenty to occupy the visitor. Geography and history have combined to mark the island out as one of the most diverse in Greece. Long and mountainous, it marks the southern boundary of the Aegean Sea, supping up the contents of any rain-clouds that might have otherwise attempted to venture further north as well as acting as a giant breakwater for the southern Aegean as a whole. Crete is also an island of great strategic importance, for without control of it no power was able to fully command the rest of the Aegean. As a result, the island is littered with the remains of all the great powers from the region, and indeed, appears to have been the power-base of the earliest of them all — the bronze age Minoan civilization. Their palaces are among the top sightseeing destinations; though later Greek and Roman temples, Byzantine churches, Venetian fortresses, Ottoman mosques, and WW2 German battlefields also lie thick on the ground.

If this was not enough, Crete is also very fertile and following in the tradition of its role as an important grain producing island in the ancient world, now is the major supplier of market garden produce to Greece. The self-sufficiency gained by

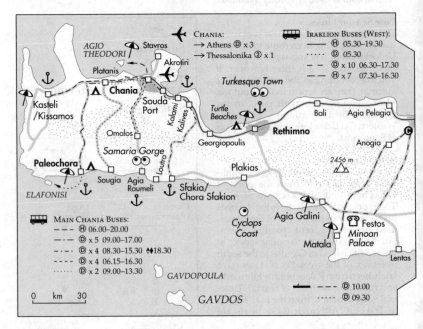

CHANIA:
→ Athens ⑩ x 3
→ Thessalonika ② x 1

IRAKLION BUSES (WEST):
—— Ⓗ 05.30–19.30
···· ⑩ 05.30
– – ⑩ x 10 06.30–17.30
— — Ⓗ x 7 07.30–16.30

AGIO THEODORI — Stavros — Akrotiri — Platanis — Chania — Souda Port — Kalami — Kalives — Kasteli/Kissamos — Omalos — Samaria Gorge — Paleochora — Sougia — Agia Roumeli — ELAFONISI — Loutro — Sfakia/Chora Sfakion

Turkesque Town — Turtle Beaches — Bali — Agia Pelagia — Rethimno — Georgioupolis — Anogia — Plakias — 2456 m — Cyclops Coast — Agia Galini — Matala — Festos Minoan Palace — Lentas

MAIN CHANIA BUSES:
– – – Ⓗ 06.00–20.00
– · – ⑩ x 5 09.00–17.00
– ··· – ⑩ x 4 08.30–15.30 ◆◆18.30
– – – – ⑩ x 4 06.15–16.30
······ ⑩ x 2 09.00–13.30

GAVDOPOULA
GAVDOS

0   km   30

– – – ⑩ 10.00
····· ⑩ 09.30

this has given the Cretans a reputation for hot-headed independence and radical politics. Tourism, although not vital to the economy, is now rampant thanks to good beaches, impressive sightseeing and a climate befitting an island lying further south than the northern coast of Tunisia. All major settlements now lie on the north coast which has developed into an English-speaking tourist strip that looks increasingly closer to Benidorm rather than the bucolic, unspoilt Greek island idyll. Fortunately, the south coast (the resort town of Ierapetra aside) and greater part of the hinterland — rugged and mountainous, covered in pine forests and wildly beautiful — remain remarkably untainted and invite exploration; though comparatively few visitors to Crete venture beyond the spectacular walk down the longest gorge in Europe at Samaria. This winds down to the nicest

part of the island — the collection of small port villages and dreamy shoreline of the south-west coast from Matala (with its history of 1970s hippy troglodytes) to the dusty town of Paleochora and its caïques to the exquisite islet of Elafonisi with its sandy beaches and turquoise seas.

The size of Crete has resulted in ferry links with the mainland developing to six ports on the northern coast. All significant towns in their own right, they provide good bases for exploring the adjacent coastlines and hinterland. They are linked by the island's main road (which runs the length of the northern coast, with feeder roads running south from the main towns to the mountain villages and the south coast) and are served by frequent buses. The island bus service is excellent; making travel on Crete both easy and cheap; besides providing a valuable link between ferry routes.

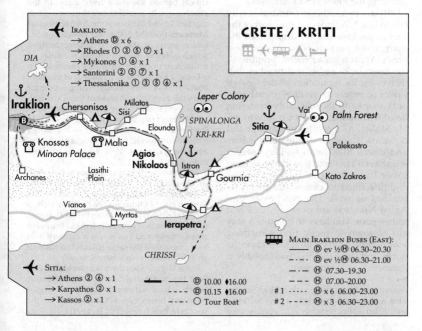

Agios Nikolaos

ΑΓΙΟΣ ΝΙΚΟΛΑΟΣ; pop. 19,000.

CODE ☎ 0841
TOURIST POLICE ☎ 22321
POLICE ☎ 22338
TOURIST INFORMATION ☎ 22357

The premier port of eastern Crete (though given the paucity of ferry connections this isn't saying a lot), Agios Nikolaos is an attractive — though all too obviously tourist — town perched on a tiny headland deep within the Mirambelou Gulf. Named after the patron saint of sailors, the town's name is a common one, and not to be confused with other ports in the Gulf of Corinth or on Anafi. In fact, for most of its life it was known as Lato, but the Venetians chose to rename it and the modern authorities have simply opted for a Hellenised version of the name (though you will still find local bus drivers referring the town as San Nikolaos).

Only a couple of hours from Iraklion by bus, Agios Nikolaos is at the heart of the Cretan package-tourist strip. Of all the north coast ports it is easily the most brash. Apart from a general 'prettiness', the town lacks sights and beaches, but thrives on its reputation as the 'Ios' of Crete (i.e. where the youth element hangs out), thanks to its role as the watering hole for a number of nearby resorts (notably Malia). As a result, the harbour and downtown area is dominated by bars and discos filled with holiday makers who haven't realized that if they were on Ios or Paros they could enjoy a similar nightlife filled to excess and plenty of beaches as well. The beaches around Agios Nikolaos are over-crowded and rather poor: you have to go quite a way out of town to really find something worthwhile. The best lie at Elounda to the north, and along the Sitia road (notably at Ammoudi and Almyros).

⊨

Accommodation fills up early in High Season. This is also one town where it pays to have a well-filled wallet: certainly in July and August

this is not the place to prevaricate if your boat or bus is met with offers of a room. The easiest hotels to find lie on the waterfront on the opposite side of the harbour to the ferry quay. These include the C-class *Alcestis* (☎ 22454) and (250 m north-west) the B-class *Coral* (☎ 28363) and the B-class pension *Lida* (☎ 22130). Finally, the C-class *Mandraki* (☎ 28880) lies north of the bus station.

A

Nearest site to the town, *Gournia Moon Camping* (☎ 0842 93243) is well away from the town at Gournia, near a Minoan palace.

👀

The town itself has no buildings of particular merit thanks to the Turks who demolished the Genoese fortress. Instead the heart of the town is dominated by a **lagoon**-like, sea-lake inner harbour of reputedly measureless depth. The reality doesn't live up to the mystique: the 'lake' (which is some 55 m deep) was only connected to the sea in 1907 when the existing channel was dug. It is lined by expensive tavernas whose prices are only matched by the rip-off bar on the main ferry quay. In the absence of a historical centre the one notable sight in Agios Nikolaos is the **Archaeological Museum** (located 500 m up Paleologou St., which starts at the inner harbour bridge), which is home to an impressive display of artifacts recovered from nearby Minoan sites.

Being a tourist town, a number of pleasure boats — festooned with advertising — operate from the port, though most of them are ludicrously expensive, given the distances involved. The most popular of these excursions is to the Cretan version of Alcatraz — the former Knight's fortress turned leper colony island of **Spinalonga** (see p. 299), which is invaded most days a week.

Taxi boat services also operate to the resort of **Elounda** and the quiet village of **Plaka**. There are also excursions to the remains of the Roman city of **Olous** up the coast, as well as Bird and Kri-Kri (named after the local species of goat) islands. If you really feel like throwing money away you can go on a mystery boat tour (these visit the same islands but without an explanation as to where you are).

In the High Season there is a weekly bus and boat trip to **Chrissi** (see p. 298), the exotic beach island off south-east Crete. Agios Nikolaos buses connect with boats at the southern beach resort of **Ierapetra**.

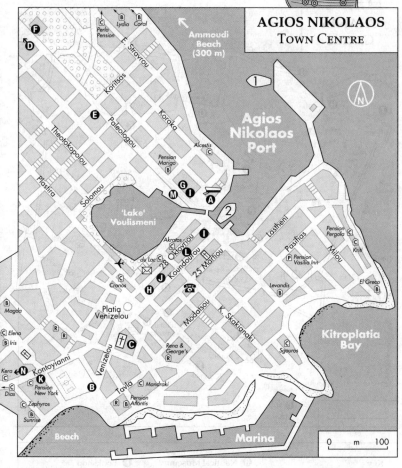

AGIOS NIKLAOS
TOWN CENTRE

Ammoudi
Beach
(300 m)

Agios
Nikolaos
Port

Perla
Pension
E. Stravrou
Koritsos
Koraka
Theotokopolou
Paleologou
Plastira
Solomou
Alcestis
Pension
Marigo

'Lake'
Voulismeni

Akratos
28 Oktovriou
Koundourou
25 Martiou
dv Lac
Cronos

Lostheni
Pasifias
Milou
Pension
Pergola
Krifi
Pension
Vasilia Inn
Levandis
El Greco

Modatsou
K. Stakianaki

Platia
Venizelou

Magda
Elena
Iris
Kera
Dias

Kontoyianni

Zephyros

Venizelou

Pension
New York
Tavla
Mandraki
Pension
Atlantis
Rena &
George's

Sunrise

Sgouros

Kitroplatia
Bay

Beach   Marina

0   m   100

Key

A Municipal Tourist Office
B Bus Station
C Cathedral
D Hospital (150 m)
E Tourist Police Office
F Archaeological Museum
G Folk Museum
H National Bank of Greece
I Bank
J English Bookshop
K Moped Rental
L Ferry Tickets
M Taxi Rank
N Sitia Road
1 Ferry Quay
2 Tour Boats

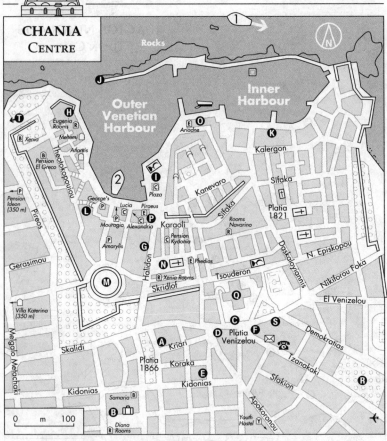

CHANIA CENTRE

Rocks

N

Outer Venetian Harbour

Inner Harbour

Eugenia Rooms

Xenia

Meltemi

Atlantis

Pension El Greco

Theotokopoulou

Pension Ideon (350 m)

Pireos

Gerasimou

Villa Katerina (350 m)

Meglalo Melachaki

Ariadne

Plaza

Kanevaro

Sifaka

Kalergon

Platia 1821

George's

Lucia   Piraeus

Mouragio   Alexandria

Amarylis

Karaoli

Rooms Navarino

Pension Kydonia

Sifaka

N. Episkopou

Daskaloyannis

Nikiforou Foka

Halidon

Phedias

Xenia Rooms

Skridlof

Tsouderon

El Venizelou

Demokratias

Skalidi

Kriari

Koraka

Kidonias

Platia 1866

Samaria

Diana Rooms

Kidonias

Platia Venizelou

Tzanakaki

Stakion

Apokoronou

Youth Hostel

0   m   100

Key

- **A** NTOG / EOT Office
- **B** Main Bus Station
- **C** Souda Bus Stop
- **D** Youth Hostel Bus Stop
- **E** Tourist Police Office
- **F** National Bank of Greece
- **G** Archaeological Museum
- **H** Nautical Museum
- **I** Mosque of the Janissaries (Old EOT)
- **J** Venetian Lighthouse
- **K** Venetian Arsenal
- **L** Renieri Gate
- **M** Shiavo Bastion
- **N** Cathedral
- **O** Police
- **P** Bookshop
- **Q** Turkish Market
- **R** Gardens
- **S** ANEK Ticket Office
- **T** Beach & Pool (200 m)

1   Ferry Terminal (6 km East at Souda)
2   Beach & Tour Boats

Chania

XANIA; pop. 50,000.

CODE ☎ 0821
TOURIST POLICE ☎ 24477
NTOG ☎ 26426
EMERGENCY ☎ 22222

The capital of Crete until 1971, Chania (pronounced Hanya) is now the number two city on the island. As such, it is the beneficiary of the second daily direct service between Crete and Piraeus. Chania boasts one of the most attractive town centres on Crete, retaining much of its Venetian/Turkish heart and offering an attractive caïque-filled harbour lined with tavernas (complete with expensive package tourist orientated menus). Unfortunately, some of the outer suburbs are pretty ropy, and the town's modern port (thanks to the inability of the old harbour to handle large vessels) is located an inconvenient 6 km to the east of the town centre — across the Akrotiri headland at Souda. In addition to the heavy package tourist trade, local prices are pushed up by the military personnel from the nearby Akrotiri NATO air and naval base. The military presence is strong in the area (i.e. 'photography banned' notices abound, and there are always plenty of unattached males in the local discos), but in the main it doesn't detract from the town. Inevitably, the harbour is the main centre of activity. Used as the set for the film *Zorba the Greek*, it is easily the most attractive on Crete — even with the crowds. Taxi boats run from here (ferry fans shouldn't miss the free raft across the harbour to the Fortella restaurant) to local beaches and the small islet of **Agio Theodori**. The winding streets behind the waterfront are inevitably very boutique laden, but also contain a fair number of easily found pensions. All the main services are to be found in the centre apart from the bus station which lies outside the old city walls, some five blocks in from the waterfront. Chania is the main junction for the Eastern Crete bus system with good links to Paleochora and the ports on the south Cretan coast as well as the villages in the White Mountains that rise behind the town.

🛏

Rooms are in limited supply, but pricier beds are less hard to come by. The NTOG / EOT office can help you find a bed. The B-class *Samaria* (☎ 51551) is right next to the bus station and easily located; so too is the E-class *Piraeus* (☎ 54154) on the Old Port waterfront. Like all the hotels and pensions in this area it is rather noisy. Tucked behind the Nautical Museum are the much more expensive B-class *El Greco* (☎ 904 32) and A-class *Palazzo* (☎ 43255). The Old Harbour and the main street (Halidon St.) between the Old Harbour and the bus station have a number of pensions in the side-streets behind them. There is also a *Youth Hostel* (☎ 53565) at 33 Drakonianou Street, south of the town centre.

A

Camping Chania (☎ 31138). A reasonable site 3 km on the road to Kasteli is backed up by *Camping Agia Marina* (☎ 68555) further west (take the Kasteli bus and ask for the camping).

👓

Known as the 'Venice of Greece' the town itself is the main sightseeing attraction. Needless to say, this being Greece, it is without a single canal; the city acquiring the label by virtue of its largely Venetian-built centre. Although heavily bombed during WW2, the heart of Chania is graced with a remarkable collection of Venetian buildings (now protected by government decree). First among these are the **City Walls**; built c. 1590 after the Barbary pirate Barbarossa sacked nearby Rethimno. The city fathers' fear was such that they added a 15 m deep moat to the outer side for good measure. The harbour was also fortified (the ruins of the **Arsenal** can be seen on the waterfront), and a **Nautical Museum** is now housed in the old walls.

Within the old town there are a number of 16 c. **Venetian Churches**: the one on the main street now housing the city **Archaeological Museum**, which contains material from the town's early Minoan settlement through to the classical period. Two centuries of Turkish rule have also left their mark; most notably in the form of the lovely multi-domed waterfront **Mosque of the Janissaries** — built to mark the Ottoman conquest of the city in 1645.

IRAKLION
CITY CENTRE & PORT

Old Port

Ferry Port

Sophocles Venizelou

Xenia (A)

(N)

(R) Pension Karpathos (P)

(R) Vironos

(R) Youth Hostel (Y)

(D) Rea

(C) Pension Marys

Hania Kroneou (E)

(D) Palladion

Kydonias

(G)

(J) (I)

Platia Kallergon (R)

(D) Hellas

25 Augoustou

Idhomeneos

Ag. Titou

OLD TOWN

Mirabellou

Pension Ilion (P)

(B) Makariou

(P)

Beaufort

(A)

(M)

Platia Venizelou

Dedalou

Pension Hadjidakis

(C) (D) Daedalos

Astoria (A)

Ikarou

(Q)

Cretan Sun (E)

Dikeosinis

(E)

(E) (F)

(E) Ionia

(D)

Platia Eleftherias

NEW TOWN

(H)

Odhos 1821

Odhos 1866

Averof Othonos

Dimokratias

(O)

Olympic

0   m   300

Key

A NTOG / EOT Office
B Main Bus Station / WCs
C SW Bus Station (Festos / Ag. Galini)
D Bus Stop (Hotels & Camping)
E Tourist Police Office
F Police
G El Greco Park
H Cathedral
I Loggia
J Turkish Fountain

K Venetian Fortress
L Venetian Arsenal
M Archaeological Museum
N Historical Museum
O Venetian City Wall
P Port (Vehicle Entrance 300 m)
Q Airport (4 km)
R Thomas Cook *Bureau de Change*

1 Ferry Quay (Ferry Terminal Building 200 m East)
2 Hydrofoil / Catamaran Berth

Iraklion
ΗΡΑΚΛΕΙΟ; pop. 102,000.

CODE ☎ 081
PORT POLICE ☎ 282002
TOURIST POLICE ☎ 283190
EOT / NTOG OFFICE ☎ 228203
EMERGENCY (FOR MOST OF CRETE) ☎ 100

The main port and modern capital of Crete, Iraklion (alias Heraklion) does its best to equal Athenian grime at its worst, but doesn't quite make it. Instead, the city has to settle for looking as if it is suffering the effects of a catastrophic explosion at a local cement factory. However, it is not all dust and grime: the mollifying existence of the well-preserved Venetian city walls, waterfront fortress and arsenal do something to redeem the ambiance, and the Archaeological Museum (home to the largest display of Minoan artifacts in the world) is enough to justify adding the city to any itinerary.

Iraklion is a very popular starting point for Greek island hopping holidays, thanks to the international airport on the city limits. In fact many regular island hoppers prefer to start from here, just to avoid the horrors of Athens airport (Iraklion airport is one of the leading charter flight destinations in Greece). The city is also the hub of the island bus system and an important ferry junction. Ferry links are adequate, if not brilliant. In addition to the daily service to Piraeus, in High Season you can also be fairly sure of at least one boat every other day to Santorini and the Cyclades, and a ferry every third day to Rhodes. Ferry arrivals will find themselves on a long commercial quay; the east end being reserved for international boats. On the west side of the fence that separates this international section, you will find a ferry passenger terminal with ticket offices (most are only open for a few hours each day). Boats arriving in the early hours berth here regardless of line. Behind the commercial quay stands the New Town; an ugly expanse of concrete that is best ignored. A short walk west, however, will bring you to the main city bus station and the old town.

The old town was the Venetian capital of Crete (the later Turks preferring Chania) and is easily identified by the massive city walls that surround it. Built during the 16th and 17th centuries, they are so substantial that they enabled the inhabitants of Candia (the city only acquired the ugly name of Iraklion with Cretan independence) to withstand a Turkish siege for over two decades before the city capitulated in 1699. Better still, they have even managed to defy the combination of WW2 bombing and later property developers who have done much to destroy the heart of the old town.

Today the old centre is dominated by 25 Augoustou Street (home to many ferry ticket agencies and not much else) which runs up from the old port to the main square — Platia Kallergon; this is the hub of the old town (though, if truth be told, the attractive and shady El Greco park to the east is a more pleasant spot), and home to a number of tavernas popular with the locals. Once night falls, the square ceases to be a frenetic road junction and marks instead the boundary of the pedestrian zone, opening onto the side streets south of Dikeosinis Street which are home to the best of the tourist-orientated restaurants and shops.

Apart from sightseeing and ferry links, Iraklion has little to offer, and although a large number of tourists pass through, they rarely stay long: Iraklion remains very much a city for Greeks. Nightlife is poor (for foreign tourists at any rate) and as a beach destination it doesn't score highly either. If you are looking to wash off the dust, the hotel strip (starting 4 km west of the centre) bus takes you to a sandy strip of sorts. To the east, there is a fair sand beach at Amnissos (take the #1 bus), 8 km from Iraklion centre: plane spotters will love it as it is directly under the airport flight path.

☙

There are few rooms on offer in Iraklion but plenty of hotel accommodation. Top of the range are the A-class *Xenia* (☎ 284000) on the waterfront and the *Astoria* (☎ 229002) overlooking leafy Eleftherias Square. C-class hotels lie pretty thick on the ground. These include the *Olympic* (☎ 288861) and the *Daedalos* (☎ 224391). Being old and dusty, the old town also has plenty of D-class establishments close to the centre. There are three worth trying: the *Hellas* (☎ 225121), the *Palladion* (☎ 282563) and the *Rea* (☎ 223638). E-class hotels are a bit more dubious but will do for a night in a pinch. The *Cretan Sun* (☎ 243794) is too noisy for comfort, though the rooms are pleasant enough. Finally, in addition to a number of pensions, there is a good *Youth Hostel* (☎ 286 281) at 5 Vironos/Cyronos St. complete with fairly priced rooms, a café/bar, and baggage storage facilities.

A

The size of Cretan towns ensures that sites are inconvenient distances from centres. Iraklion is no exception; the nearest being an excellent beach site: *Camping Creta* (☎ 0897 41400) lying 30 minutes east via a #18 bus, then a 20-minute walk.

⚅⚅

Iraklion boasts two attractions that draw the crowds. The **Minoan Palace** at **Knossos** (see opposite) is the big pull: 5 km from the town centre, it is an easy bus ride (#2 bus runs every 20 minutes from the bus station: tickets from the kiosk by the bus stop) and is the most important Minoan site on the island. The **Archaeological Museum** (open ① 12.30–19.00, ②–⑦ 08.00–19.00; entrance fee 1500 GDR) in Iraklion is rich in associated finds, and offers a shady, fresco-filled retreat from the midday heat of the city streets. Star exhibits include the best of the Knossos frescos and a model reconstruction of the palace, as well as finds from the smaller Minoan palace complexes at Festos and Milia.

Iraklion also has second museum: the less frequented **Historical Museum**. This houses exhibits ranging from Byzantine icons of saints to memorabilia of the heroes of the independence struggle (Crete only joined Greece in 1913) to photos of the German occupation in WW2. The museum is also home to the only painting now in Greece of the country's most famous painter — El Greco (alias Domenikos

Theotocopoulos) — who was born in pre-concrete Iraklion in 1541.

Hunting around the town, you will find a few architectural lights amid the grey modern buildings. First and foremost is the **Rocco al Mare** — the wonderfully well-preserved Venetian 16 c. kastro that stands at the entrance to the old harbour; its front portal is still adorned with a Venetian winged lion. It is open ⑩ 08.00–15.00; entrance fee 500 GDR. Inside you will find assorted dank halls filled with cannon, a mule stairway to the upper levels and a delightful capless miniature minaret added by the Turks (tourists can ascend for views over the fortress). Near the Rocco al Mare are the remains of the **Venetian Arsenal**, now reduced to a few heavily restored arches (often used by local fishermen for storing nets) that herald the seaward end of 25 Augoustou street, which runs up to the main square (Platia Kallergon). This is dominated by the ornate **Morosini Fountain** (1625), a charming lion-inspired work commissioned by the nephew of the vandal who blew up the Parthenon in Athens. To the east of the fountain is a reconstructed contemporary **Venetian Loggia**, which was heavily damaged by bombing in the last war.

Thanks to its position as the central Crete bus hub, Iraklion is also a good jumping off point from which to visit the Minoan palace sites on **Malia** and **Festos** (also transcribed as 'Phestos'). Regular buses run past Malia and some five a day venture to Festos. Both sites are open ⑩ 08.00–19.00; entrance fee 1200 GDR. Unlike Knossos neither site has undergone 'reconstruction' and both are as excavated. For this reason alone, a visit to one of them is worthwhile as you will get a good insight into what newly excavated Knossos looked like. Malia is the better preserved of the two and is unusual in its coastal plain location. The palace at Festos is much more dramatically sited on a hill top above the Messara plain, and has a more sophisticated theatre-cum-dancing floor than the famous example at Knossos.

Iraklion buses also run across the island to the southern coast town of **Matala**. Famous in the 1960s as a hairy hippy haven (who took to getting as high as possible while living in the local beach-cliffs — these are honeycombed with caves that have been inhabited by men and cyclops since Neolithic times), the town is now a much tamer family resort.

Knossos

The Palace of Knossos (see colour map between pages 288–289) was the centre of Minoan civilization between 3000–1400 BC. Its fame was such that faint memories of it, and its name ('Knossos' is of pre-Greek origin) lingered on in Greek myth long after the site of the palace and the Minoan civilization were forgotten. By the Classical period, a thousand years after its destruction, beyond the myths and a belief that a Golden age had given way to an age of Iron, no recollection of the pre-Greek Minoans had survived. As a result, when garbled tales came out of Egypt of a wonderful bull-worshipping maritime island-based civilization that lived 'in the far west' Plato looked around, saw no evidence of it, and, with a greater knowledge of geography than the Egyptian story tellers of a millennium earlier, placed this lost power in the 'far west' of his day — the Atlantic; hence 'Atlantis'.

Incredibly, beyond the odd pot and some clay tablets bearing a strange script, the Minoans remained completely unrecognised until Sir Arthur Evans began excavating at Knossos in 1900. His discovery of a massive, elaborate, surprisingly modern looking palace adorned with modernistic frescoed walls, pillared light wells and drains (a feature not found in other European civilizations for a millennia), yet lacking defensive walls (suggesting an awesome military command of the region), was equal to any other archaeological discovery this century. Apart from an interruption during WW1, Evans continued to excavate at Knossos until the 1930s. As part of this exercise he undertook considerable rebuilding. This involved replacing the lost wooden pillars and beams with concrete substitutes — had his sponsors not balked at providing additional funds for concrete he would probably have rebuilt the whole complex. The result gives you plenty to see (even if this sort of 'reconstruction' is nowadays regarded as over-enthusiastic) and offers a nice compromise between the impression given of the former palace as it was and the warren of foundations that recall the palace of Greek legend: the famous Labyrinth where the Athenian hero Theseus fought the dreaded Minotaur before running off with the King's daughter, Ariadne. Worth recalling, it ran something like this:

The Myth of Theseus & the Minotaur

Far away and long ago there lived a King called Minos. He presided over a powerful maritime empire. Unfortunately for Minos, his wife, Queen Pasiphae, took a fancy for the idea of a night in bed with a large white bull that the king had refused to sacrifice to Poseidon (a strange desire which rather suggests that King Minos was King Minus-an-inch-or-two when it came to the tackle department). Pasiphae sought out the chief craftsman — Daedalus — and ordered him to devise some kind of heifer-shaped sex aid that would allow her to… Well, anyway, one hell of a night and nine months later she gave birth to the Minotaur; the monstrous creature with the body of a man and the head of a bull. King Minos then ordered Daedalus to construct the labyrinth in which the Minotaur was hidden away. Here it lived on an annual diet of 14 Athenian youths and maidens who were pushed into the entrance and never seen again. Daedalus, meantime, was imprisoned to prevent him from divulging the secret of the labyrinth (to say nothing of indulging the queen's fancies) whereupon, with his son Icarus, he made some wings out of feathers and wax and flew to Sicily by way of Ikaria (where Icarus died after flying too near the sun). Meantime, back at the labyrinth, Theseus, the son of the king of Athens, disguised as one of the annual sacrificial youths, killed the Minotaur with the help of Ariadne, who gave him a ball of thread that enabled him to escape from the labyrinth. The couple then fled to Naxos where the highly strung Theseus unceremoniously dumped his love, returning to Athens alone.

The palace uncovered by Sir Arthur Evans is multi-layered and complex, the structure being built around the four sides of a flattened hilltop. Originally built in the Middle Minoan period c. 1950 BC, the palace was destroyed (along with all the other early Minoan palaces) c. 1700 BC, probably as the result of a massive earthquake. Rebuilt in the opulent style reproduced by Evans, the succeeding structure boasted the staircases, light wells and plaster-coated walls that make it so distinctive, although to call it a 'palace' is rather misleading, for the building complex at Knossos appears to have not only been the focus of political and religious life, but was also the centre of judicial, administrative, commercial and industrial activity. The hectares around the site contain the remains of a number of associated Minoan villas and houses, and a small town.

The massive eruption of Santorini c. 1450 BC triggered the collapse of the Minoan civilization, with all the Cretan palaces being destroyed—Knossos among them (seemingly by fire). Partially rebuilt by alien Mycenaean Greeks, it was the only Minoan palace site that wasn't abandoned. However, it didn't survive for long; being finally destroyed — possibly as the result of a raid by invaders — c. 1400 BC. Thereafter, the palace hill (still known as 'Knossos') was home to a small undistinguished Archaic settlement that survived through into the Roman era.

Visitors to the palace today no longer need a ball of string to find their way around. From the moment they arrive at Knossos, life becomes very easy: you just follow the crowds. These start at the main road (lined with tavernas and tourist shops) which runs between the palace site and the small modern village of Knossos (where a limited number of rooms are available). Iraklion buses stop near the large coach park (complete with WCs) at the site entrance.

Open ® 08.00–19.00, the entrance fee is 1500 GDR (ISIC-holding students can usually get in free). Now surrounded by large pine trees, the site is accessed from the west. Most visitors explore the features of Knossos in the sequence given overleaf, but you are free to wander (though rumour has it that plans are in hand to confine access to parts of the site due to heavy tourism wearing down the floors: you may therefore find that the traditional route around the site described below has changed).

On entering the site, visitors first pass along a tree-lined avenue which ends with a bust of Sir Arthur Evans. This stands on the edge of the palace **West Court** that is dominated by ❹ three tree-filled circular **Offering Pits** used in Minoan worship. In to these were thrown ceremonial pottery vessels (an odd habit curiously replicated by the later Greeks with their passion for smashing platters after meals). Behind the West Court stands the reconstructed west façade of the palace. Although roped off, doorways enable you to peer into ❸ the **Pillar Hall**, the first of the palace's estimated thousand rooms. Next door, and just about visible, are ❻ the **West Magazines**. These are long storage pits containing the large pithoi jars used to store oil and wine (the palace seems to have served a secondary role as a communal warehouse for the region). Originally they were unlit rooms deep in the bowels of the building. Passing these, the path brings you to the **Western Propylon** (porch) and ❹ the **Corridor of the Procession** (which takes its name from the fresco depicting gift-bearers and a goddess figure).

From the Western Porch the path divides: one branch runs off to the roped-off ❺ **South /High Priest's House**, outside the palace walls. This is currently closed while it awaits restoration, but it is possible to observe the rebuilt characteristic red, tapered Minoan pillars that adorn the building. Meanwhile the main tourist route turns back, past the partially reconstructed ❻ **South Propylon** or gatehouse (complete with a fake white, tapered column). To the east of this structure stands a pair of large **Sacred Horns** (now a popular seat for tourist photos); part of the almost obsessive Minoan bull-cult, they were replicated many times over in a smaller form as a decorative device along the tops of the palace building walls. From the back of the South Propylon run ❻ the **Stairs** that led into the religious wing of the palace (follow them up today and you are able to get a better view of the pithoi in the West Magazine).

A second path from the South Propylon runs east to ❻ the **Central Court Corridor**, which now contains a reproduction of the famous **Prince of the Lilies Fresco**. One of the most famous frescoes found at Knossos, it shows a kilted youth wearing a crown of lilies and peacock feathers. From his posture it is probable he was leading a sacred animal of some kind, but these days he stands alone,

Crete

IRAKLION
Venetian Harbour &
Kastro Runway

Minoan Palace:
North Entrance Bastion
& Racing Bull Relief

KNOSSOS

Venetian Kastro/
Rocco al Mare:
Capless Minaret

Minoan Palace:
Sacred Horns

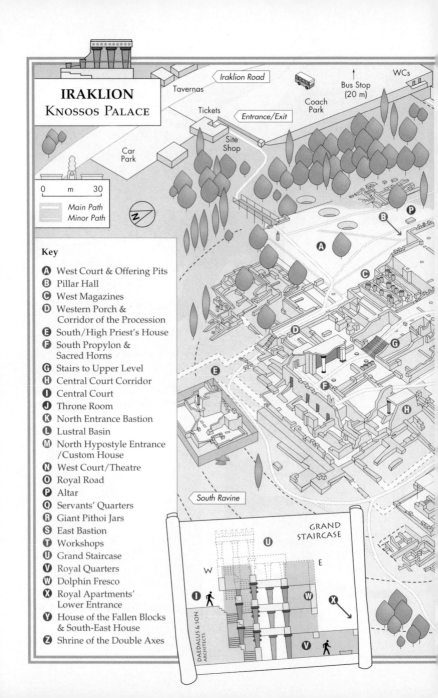

IRAKLION
KNOSSOS PALACE

Iraklion Road
Tavernas
Tickets
Entrance/Exit
Coach Park
Bus Stop (20 m)
WCs
Site Shop
Car Park

0   m   30

Main Path
Minor Path

Key

- **A** West Court & Offering Pits
- **B** Pillar Hall
- **C** West Magazines
- **D** Western Porch & Corridor of the Procession
- **E** South/High Priest's House
- **F** South Propylon & Sacred Horns
- **G** Stairs to Upper Level
- **H** Central Court Corridor
- **I** Central Court
- **J** Throne Room
- **K** North Entrance Bastion
- **L** Lustral Basin
- **M** North Hypostyle Entrance /Custom House
- **N** West Court/Theatre
- **O** Royal Road
- **P** Altar
- **Q** Servants' Quarters
- **R** Giant Pithoi Jars
- **S** East Bastion
- **T** Workshops
- **U** Grand Staircase
- **V** Royal Quarters
- **W** Dolphin Fresco
- **X** Royal Apartments' Lower Entrance
- **Y** House of the Fallen Blocks & South-East House
- **Z** Shrine of the Double Axes

South Ravine

GRAND STAIRCASE

W   E

W

X

DAEDALUS & SON ARCHITECTS

I

V

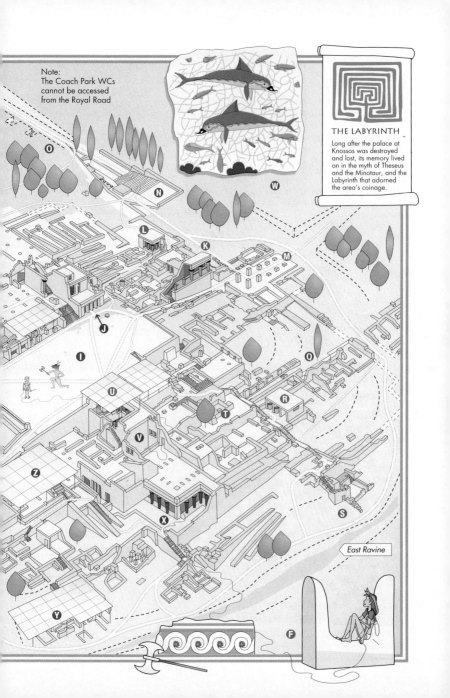

Note:
The Coach Park WCs cannot be accessed from the Royal Road

THE LABYRINTH

Long after the palace at Knossos was destroyed and lost, its memory lived on in the myth of Theseus and the Minotaur, and the Labyrinth that adorned the area's coinage.

East Ravine

**C/M Supercat
Haroulla**,
C/F Super Ferry II &
H/F Mega Dolphin
at Mykonos Town

C/F Rodanthi
Departs from Santorini

C/F Ariadne

**C/F Express
Apollon**

A typical High Season ferry embarkation scene
on one of the smaller islands
(in this case Koufonissia)

and has to make do with a new role as the symbol for the Minoan Lines ferry company.

The corridor leads to ❶ the **Central Court** —a feature common to all Minoan palaces but implemented at its best at Knossos. This formed the centre of palace life, with the various quarters of the palace opening out onto it. The court is also thought to be the place where the famous bull-leaping contests, or rites, were performed. Artwork found on the site suggests that young men would grab the lowered horns of a charging bull, then, as the animal attempted to free itself by rearing its head, would use the momentum of that movement to somersault over the horns, landing on their feet on the animal's back before jumping clear. This must have been quite a spectacle and was clearly a far more sophisticated exercise than modern bull-fighting (the act of strutting around waving a red blanket seems singularly pathetic by comparison).

The **West Side Buildings** adjacent to the Central Court appear to have contained the religious centre of the palace. The most famous of the remains being ❷ the **Throne Room**. Arguably the most interesting room on the site, it is viewed via a basin-filled anteroom (complete with a second dummy throne placed so tourists can photograph each other sitting on it). The throne you can't sit on was originally thought to be that of the ruler at Knossos (hence its title: 'the throne of Minos'), but is now believed to have seated a High Priest. Made of gypsum, it has gypsum benches on either side, above which are frescoes of griffins and lilies (the design dating from the Mycenaean occupation). The throne's shape is also of interest as it mimics a wooden ceremonial chair design.   The Throne room is also a good   example

of the degree of reconstruction undertaken by Evans: photographs of the excavation show that the throne's back stood several feet above the height of the surrounding walls, with only the griffin's feet surviving from the frescoes. All of this room (and the storey above) from seat height is, therefore, 'fake'. The frescoes, along with most of the others found, have been reconstructed from tiny fragments. Applauded at the time, they have come in for criticism since, following the discovery of the better preserved Akrotiri frescos on Santorini. By comparison, the Knossos reconstructions (produced by a French father-and-son artist combination with the name of Gillieron) look curiously lifeless, and in some instances the fragments were completely misinterpreted (in the most notorious 'reconstruction', the remains of a blue monkey ended up being rebuilt as the figure of a boy).

Directly to the south of the Throne Room are the remains of the **Central Staircase** that served the west wing of the palace. Today it ascends to the rebuilt floor level at the top of the South Propylon stairs, and then further on up to nowhere (though the panoramic views of the site are good from the top). Ascending to the first level and then weaving your way around the back of the staircase you will come to the small, reconstructed chamber over the Throne Room. This contains the light well that descends to the south side of the Throne Room and a number of fresco fragments on its walls. The covered-over ruins to the south of the Central Staircase are also of note as they yielded up the famous statuettes of the topless, snake-waving ladies.

Returning to the Central Court and then heading north, the path leads down past the most the most photographed architectural feature on the site: the rebuilt tapered columns of ❸ the **North Entrance Bastion**. Easily the most impressive of the entrances to the palace complex (thanks in part to the steepness of the hillside corridor at this point), it is home to the reconstructed **Racing Bull Relief**. Although the notion is perhaps a trifle fanciful, it has been suggested that this wall remained visible among the rubble of the palace into the Archaic period, helping to give rise to the legend of the Labyrinth and the Minotaur. Behind it are yet more rooms and storage chambers and, ❹ the **Lustral Basin**: a small reconstructed sanctuary complete with tapering pillars.

BULL LEAPING

Following the path down past the North Entrance Bastion brings you into the square-pillared chamber known as **⓪** the **North Hypostyle Entrance** or **Custom House**. It is believed that this room served as an accounting point where goods (brought up from the harbour 5 km away) and personnel were checked into the palace. Turning west from the Custom House, the path runs on to a feature of greater fame: **⓪** the **West Court** or **Theatre**. Truth to tell, it doesn't conform much to modern ideas as to what a theatre should look like, being merely an earthquake damaged paved area with a flight of steps and no seating. It has been identified as a 'theatre' for want of any other feature at Knossos that could serve as the 'dancing floor which Daedalus made for Ariadne in broad Knossos' described by Homer. In reality it is more of a terminus for **⓪** the **Royal Road** that runs west from it. Described as the oldest paved road in Europe, the road dates from the earliest palace period. Originally, it was lined with houses and led to the **Little Palace** (a large Minoan villa that stood nearby) and the town that is thought to have built up outside the palace complex. Today, the deeply excavated path runs into the supporting wall of the site coach park, and has partially excavated buildings on its south side. Nearer the palace, excavation has opened up a path that runs back to the entrance court past **⓪**, one of two **Altars**. A second excavated Minoan road runs north of the Custom House to an inaccessible building known as the North Pillar Hall.

East of the Custom House, the site path drops away sharply (all the east-side rooms of the palace were built on the slope of the hill. The north-east corner of the palace was home to **⓪** the **Servants' Quarters**, now little more than a jumble of foundations. The singular exception to these incomprehensible ruins is the re-roofed room on the edge of this quarter containing **⓪** the **Giant Pithoi Jars**. These stand over 2 m high, and are the largest found at Knossos. The 'room' they are in was once part of the complex of eastern storage rooms in the palace. The best means of seeing these is to take the staircase running from the central court to **⓪** the **East Bastion**. The stairs divide the servants' quarters and storerooms from **⓪** the **Workshops**, where the palace craftsmen did their stuff. Individual rooms (directly opposite the Giant Pithoi

Jars) have been identified as potters' and stone-cutters' workshops. The craftsmen in this latter workshop carved stone utensils out of blocks of basalt imported from the Peloponnese.

The south-east sector of the palace containing the royal quarters was the most luxurious part of the complex. Unfortunately, the reconstructed buildings have been closed for several years, undergoing restoration, and are unlikely to be open during 1999 (the 1900s concrete has flaked and cracked and proved no durable substitute for the wood and stone it replaced).

Until this building is reopened, visitors have to make do with standing at the Central Court entrance and peering down into **⓪** the reconstructed **Grand Staircase**, that in its prime stood five storeys high (only the bottom two of the three rebuilt storeys contain a significant amount of original material). Built around a light well adorned with the usual colonnades of tapering pillars (originally up-turned trees) and spacious verandas adorned with frescoes, the Grand Staircase is the single most impressive architectural feature of the palace, besides marking Knossos out as a royal residence above the rest (other palaces on Crete had nothing to match it). It formed a royal approach to **⓪** the **Royal Quarters**, with bathrooms on each floor (off the south-west corners) and doorways leading off into shrines and private rooms. The rebuilt staircase has been used to display reconstructions of a number of frescoes found in nearby rooms, notably the Mycenaean-period figure-of-eight shields and **⓪** the lovely **Dolphin Fresco**. Fortunately the original fragments of these frescoes are on display in the Iraklion Archaeological Museum, so not all is lost if the Grand Staircase is still closed when you visit.

Sadly, if the staircase is closed you will miss out on the Royal Quarters which are closed along with it. The nearest you will get to seeing them is to glimpse

GRAND STAIRCASE & QUEEN'S APARTMENTS

CLOSED
for rennovation

into ❸ the **Royal Apartments Lower Entrance** (this is reached via the path that runs around the site or — from the Central Court — via the East Bastion steps). From here you can just make out the **Hall of the Double Axes** (now thought to be the King's Audience room as the remains of a throne — complete with a four-pillared canopy — were discovered here) and the **King's Megaron**. This private royal room had a private balcony and was the original home of the figure-of-eight shield frescoes. Evans believed the room contained another throne. Another room leading off the Hall of the Double Axes leads to the **Queen's Megaron**. Smaller than the King's Megaron, it was also adorned with frescoes — the most famous being the Dolphin Fresco. From this room runs a gallery complete with a triple window that opens out onto a light well. On this gallery stands the **Queen's Bathroom** (complete with a small painted hip-bath) and the **Queen's Toilet Room** which served as a dressing room. It, too, had a window and door into the light well (the door providing access to another small room off the light well that served as her most private of throne rooms).

The floor of the light well is also known as the **Court of the Distaffs**, after a symbol carved on the walls. From it runs a second corridor that leads to the **Treasury Room**. In this room Evans discovered a number of fragments from gold and ivory objects. These are believed to have fallen from a room immediately above. The private royal living quarters are also lost; they are thought to have been located on the upper floors of the royal quarter of the palace.

The eastern edge of the palace now sits at the base of a small pine-shaded valley formed by the excavation of the lower hill rooms. From the Royal Quarters, the path runs on to the covered-over remains of the south-east corner of the palace. These include a number of 'private' apartments now named after their excavated remains: ❹ the **House of the Fallen Blocks** (no guesses as to what you will find here), the **House of the Channel Screen**, the **House of the Sacrificed Oxen**, the **House of the Monolithic Pillars**, the **South-East House**, and west of that ❷ the **Shrine of the Double Axes**. The double headed axe was another popular Minoan motif; known as a 'Lavrys' it is thought by some to be the origin of the word 'Labyrinth' — meaning 'palace where the Lavrys is worshipped' (though others claim this is a load of bull).

Kasteli

ΚΑΣΤΕΛΛΙ; pop. 2,800.

CODE ☎ 0822
PORT POLICE ☎ 22024

A small, rather drab, town on the western edge of Crete offering all the essential facilities but no more, Kasteli is often called, by ticket agents and maps alike, by its older name of **Kissamos**. The only ferry connections are the subsidised services to Kithera, Piraeus and the southern Peloponnese; a fact reflected in the location of the ferry quay, over 2 km west of the town centre on a particularly quiet stretch of coastline. The solitude of the surrounding countryside — particularly to the Gramvoussa Peninsula to the west — is the only real attraction, given that the town (complete with a uninspiring centre and a comparatively poor beach) itself lacks zip at all times of the day. Despite being the local transportation hub, the absence of frequent buses means you will need to hire a moped or car to explore the wilds.

🛏

Plentiful supply of rooms are on offer in the town square and waterfront, even at the height of the season. There are also a number of reasonable hotels including the C-class *Kissamos* (☎ 22086), *Castle* (☎ 22140) and the *Peli* (☎ 22343). There is also a B-class hotel/pension, the *Astrikas*, and one D-class outlet with expensive apartments, the *Mandy* (☎ 22825).

Λ

Camping Mythimna (☎ 31444): very quiet, 5 km east of the town centre on an excellent beach (take a Chania-bound bus and ask to be dropped at the campsite). There is also a semi-official site closer to hand — *Camping Kissamos* (☎ 23444). Complete with pool, it lies 200 m west of the town centre.

👓

Sightseeing is a bit thin on the ground if you don't have your own wheels. The best thing on offer is the 7 km trek (buses are rare) inland to the village of **Polirinia** which has the substantial remains of an **Ancient City** (complete with an aqueduct commissioned by Hadrian) on the hillside above the current centre.

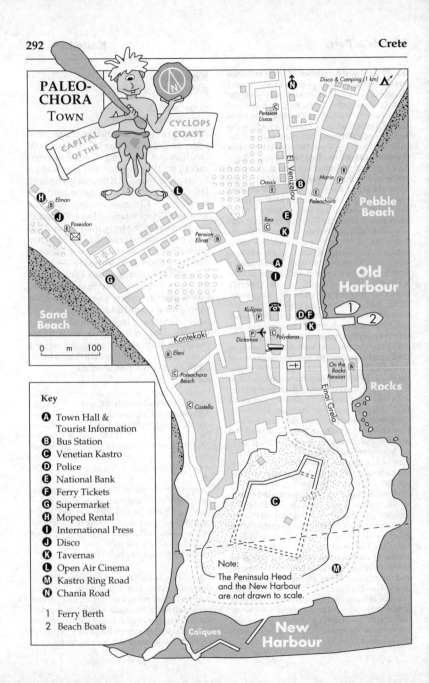

PALEO-
CHORA
Town

CAPITAL
OF THE

CYCLOPS
COAST

Disco & Camping (1 km)

Pension
Lissos

El. Venizelou

Maria Ⓡ Ⓟ

Ⓔ Paleochora

Pebble
Beach

Oassis Ⓔ

Ⓗ Elman
Ⓑ
Ⓙ
Ⓔ Poseidon

Ⓡ Rea
Ⓒ

Ⓔ
Ⓚ

Ⓖ

Pension
Eliras Ⓑ

Ⓡ

Ⓐ
Ⓘ

Old
Harbour

Sand
Beach

0   m   100

Kalipso
Ⓟ ☎

Ⓓ Ⓕ
Ⓚ

1

2

Kontekaki

Dictamos

Ⓒ Polydoros

Ⓡ Eleni

Ⓒ Paleochora
Beach

✝

On the
Rocks Ⓑ
Pension

Rocks

Einai Grela

Ⓒ Castello

Key

Ⓐ Town Hall &
   Tourist Information
Ⓑ Bus Station
Ⓒ Venetian Kastro
Ⓓ Police
Ⓔ National Bank
Ⓕ Ferry Tickets
Ⓖ Supermarket
Ⓗ Moped Rental
Ⓘ International Press
Ⓙ Disco
Ⓚ Tavernas
Ⓛ Open Air Cinema
Ⓜ Kastro Ring Road
Ⓝ Chania Road

1   Ferry Berth
2   Beach Boats

Ⓒ

Ⓜ

Note:
The Peninsula Head
and the New Harbour
are not drawn to scale.

Caïques

New
Harbour

Paleochora

ΠΑΛΑΙΟΧΩΡΑ; pop. 3,000.

CODE ☎ 0823
PORT POLICE ☎ 41214
POLICE ☎ 41111
FIRST AID ☎ 41211

The south-west coast of Crete is characterized by cliffs, ravines and a number of small, isolated settlements. The region is also famed as Cyclops country; though there is little sign of these one-eyed giants today. The main town on the coast is at **Paleochora**, a dusty peninsular town (built beneath a Venetian Kastro constructed in 1279 and destroyed by Barbarossa) with beaches on either side and a daily boat to the idyllic brush-covered beach islet of **Elafonisi** to the south-west.

Sfakia (also known as **Chora Sfakion**) is the next in size and lies at the other end of the line (its main attraction being the bus service with Chania). **Agia Roumeli**, at the mouth of the Samarian Gorge, is a tourist trap of little merit. Now living off the large number of tourists walking the gorge, it is still a half abandoned shadow of its former self. The tiny fishing hamlets of **Lutro** and **Sougia** have fared somewhat better, but see few tourists.

A second 'resort' has developed at **Matala** (accessed by bus from Iraklion), home to a good beach backed by cliffs pockmarked with caves that look to have once been home to a colony of Cyclops. During the 1960s these hapless giants failed to keep a spare eye out for squatters and the hippy brigade moved in, changing all the boulders on the caves, and generally making a nuisance of themselves. Most are now company executives so things have calmed down a bit. Even so, this part of Crete is still an odd mixture of local conservatism and discreet foreign liberalism.

⊢

Rooms available in all ferry ports, but supplies are necessarily limited. Most are to be found in Paleochora. At the budget end of the range are the E-class *Paleochora* (☎ 41023) and *Oassis*

(☎ 41328), the C-class *Polydoros* (☎ 41068) and *Rea* (☎ 41307), and some pensions including the dangerously named *On the Rocks* (☎ 41713).

Λ

Camping Paleochora (☎ 41120); 2 km east of the town in olive grove behind pebble beach. A beach disco keeps campers awake several nights a week in summer.

ᏀᎧ

Paleochora is the best jumping-off point for the **Samaria Gorge**. 18 km long and ranging from 3.5 km down to 3 m wide, the gorge is Crete's Lilliputian Grand Canyon (and the longest canyon in Europe). One of a number of deep ravines that run down the southern slopes of the White Mountains, it has been a national park since the 1960s. The gorge — which takes its name from an abandoned village within it — is open from the 1st of May to the 31st of October (at other times of the year the rivers are high and the danger from falling rocks is too great) when it is patrolled by National Forest Service staff whose function is to ensure that visitors don't come to grief, attempt to stay overnight, or enter outside the permitted hours (the gorge is open from 08.00–15.00: from 15.00 to sunset visitors are only allowed to visit the first 2 km of each end).

Buses run daily from Iraklion (05.30) and (at more reasonable hours) from Chania to the village of **Omalos** at the northern entrance to the gorge. The trek down the gorge takes some six hours with good shoes, and is very pretty — particularly in the spring. High Season travellers will find the walk less attractive; the numbers of trekkers turning a communion with nature into a noisy hobbit's walking party. It is best to do the walk early in the day to be sure of picking up a Sfakia-bound ferry from **Agia Roumeli** in time for the last bus (usually 18.30). The great highlight of the walk is to be found 3 km from Ag. Roumeli — at **Sideropontes** ('the iron gates') where the gorge narrows to only 3 metres, while rising to a height of over 300 m.

Local ecologists are becoming increasingly concerned by the numbers visiting the gorge (an average of 2,000 a day now do the walk in the summer months). Paths are being eroded, and the rare horned Cretan ibex (the Kri-Kri) and the golden eagles that once thrived here have departed for less noisy hillsides (the Samaria gorge is only one of five great gorges along this coast).

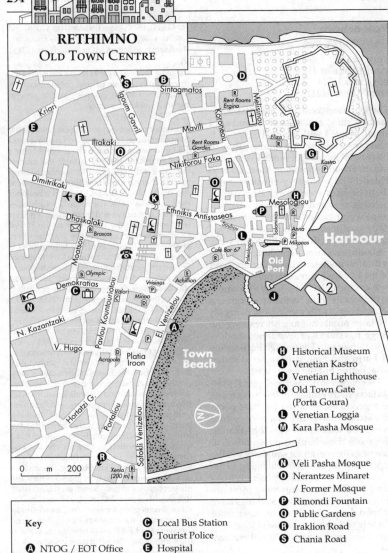

RETHIMNO
OLD TOWN CENTRE

Key

A NTOG / EOT Office
B Long Distance Bus Station
C Local Bus Station
D Tourist Police
E Hospital
F National Bank of Greece
G Archaeological Museum

H Historical Museum
I Venetian Kastro
J Venetian Lighthouse
K Old Town Gate (Porta Goura)
L Venetian Loggia
M Kara Pasha Mosque

N Veli Pasha Mosque
O Nerantzes Minaret / Former Mosque
P Rimondi Fountain
Q Public Gardens
R Iraklion Road
S Chania Road

1 Ferry Quay
2 Tour Boats

Rethimno

ΡΕΘΥΜΝΟ; pop. 20,000.

CODE ☎ 0831
TOURIST POLICE ☎ 28156
POLICE ☎ 25247
NTOG OFFICE ☎ 29148

Of the major port towns along Crete's north coast, Rethimno is the jewel in the crown; for not only can it claim to have the best preserved historical centre — German bombing in WW2 left it comparatively unscathed — packed with an interesting mix of Venetian and Ottoman buildings (the particularly rich Turkish overlay adding much to the exotic atmosphere of the town), but is unique in having a very good town beach into the bargain.

Complemented by a very attractive harbour (complete with a very helpful NTOG / EOT office on the waterfront), and the largest Venetian castle in Greece, it is not surprising that Rethimno is developing as a popular package tourist resort destination. Hotels are mushrooming up all over the place — particularly along the coast east of the town — and doing little to enhance the ugly suburbs (one of the few negative points) around the old town.

If it wasn't for the tourists the old town would offer the chance to walk back a few centuries thanks to the narrow streets lined with unspoilt buildings (some of the Turkish houses have even retained their original wooden balconies), to say nothing of a couple of minarets attached to buildings that started life as Venetian churches. In spite of its being laid out in a regular fashion it is easy to get lost in the maze of the old town (it is worth allowing for this before you start exploring); fortunately you don't have to go far in any direction before coming upon a recognisable landmark. The taverna-lined Venetian harbour in particular is a visual delight, but also the town's bane. Too small to accommodate large boats, and prone to silting up, it accounts for the town's relative obscurity in the last couple

of centuries. Ferry connections reflect this state of affairs and are scanty — consisting of boats running direct to Piraeus augmented with occasional more expensive tourist boats to Santorini.

⊨

The popularity of Rethimno leads to higher prices than in other towns, so you could have to ask around; though there are rooms and pensions aplenty — most within a block of the town beach or waterfront. There is also a Youth Hostel (☎ 22848) at 41 Tombasi St. With some forty hotels in the town or its environs finding a bed isn't difficult. Finding a cheap bed is a bit more tricky. The best bets are the D-class Minoa (☎ 22508), Kastro (☎ 24973), Acropole (☎ 27470) and the E-class Achillion (☎ 22581). Higher up the range is the C-class Valari (☎ 22236) near the National Bank and the B-class Olympic (☎ 24761) by the bus station.

A

Camping Elisabeth (☎ 28694) and Camping Arkadia (☎ 28825): reasonable sites 4 km east of the town. There is also a third site further out: Camping Agia Galini (☎ 91386).

👓

The **Venetian Kastro** is the most obvious attraction in the town. Known as the **Fortezza** it was built in 1574 after repeated Barbary pirate raids on the town. One of the best preserved Venetian castles in Greece, in its prime its walls almost held a town in themselves, but most of the interior buildings have gone now (apart from the former church that was later converted into a mosque) and you have to make do with the lovely views over the town.

Somewhat surprisingly (considering how much of the old centre has survived) the Venetian town walls have all but disappeared; the only remnant being one gate known as the **Porta Goura** (1572). Within the alleyways of the old town stands a Venetian **Loggia**. Built c. 1600, it originally served as a meeting place for the town's officials. Nearby flows the 17 C. **Rimondi Fountain**; a late Venetian addition to the town. The later Turkish presence offers another sightseeing option; the climb to the top of the minaret of the 18 C. **Nerandzes Mosque**, with its views over the castle and town.

Rethimno also has **Archaeological** and **Historical Museums** housing a variety of (sadly indifferent) finds from its Minoan origins to its later role as a haven for scholars fleeing the Turkish conquest of Constantinople.

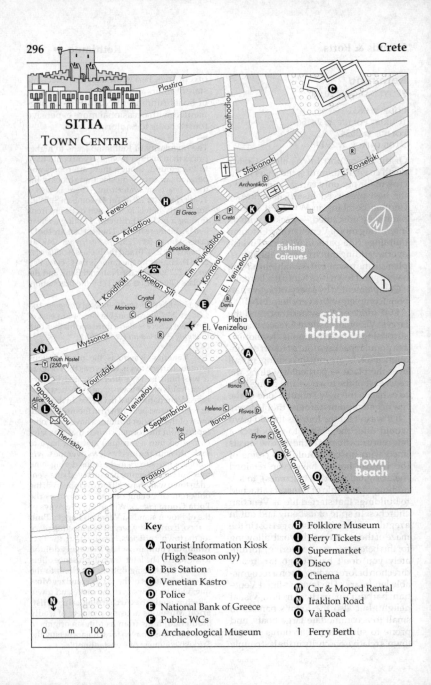

Plastira

SITIA
TOWN CENTRE

Xanthiodiou

C

E. Rouselaki

R

I. Sfakianaki

Archontikon

D

R. Fereou

H

El Greco

C

R

P

K

Creta

I

G. Arkadiou

R

Apostilos

Em. Foundalidou

V. Karnarou

El Venizelou

Fishing
Caïques

Kapetan Sifi

R

I. Konditaki

Crystal

C

Mariana

C

D

Mysson

E

B

Denis

**Sitia
Harbour**

Myssonos

R

Platia
El. Venizelou

← **N**

← Youth Hostel
Y (250 m)

D

Paponastassiou

Alice

C

L

G. Vourlidaki

J

A

Itanos

C

M

F

El. Venizelou

4 Septembriou

Helena

C

Flisvos

D

Therissou

Itanou

Vai

C

Elysee

C

Konstantinou Karamanli

B

Praisou

**Town
Beach**

G

N
↓

0   m   100

O
↓

1   Ferry Berth

Key

A Tourist Information Kiosk
(High Season only)

B Bus Station

C Venetian Kastro

D Police

E National Bank of Greece

F Public WCs

G Archaeological Museum

H Folklore Museum

I Ferry Tickets

J Supermarket

K Disco

L Cinema

M Car & Moped Rental

N Iraklion Road

O Vai Road

Sitia

ΣΗΤΕΙΑ; pop. 8,000.

CODE ☎ 0843
PORT POLICE ☎ 22310
TOURIST POLICE ☎ 24200
POLICE ☎ 22266
FIRST AID ☎ 24311

The most easterly port on Crete, scenic Sitia is very much the poor relation compared to the other towns along the northern coast when it comes to ferry connections. However, it beats the pants off Agios Nikolaos as an attractive destination. Set in a wide bay, the Venetian-built town (that none-the-less manages to feel more like a regular island chora; being all white houses and staircases) attracts its share of tourists in High Season, thanks in part to its lovely fishing port atmosphere and a three-day annual August wine festival (grapes and raisins are the region's principal exports). The town, which is built like an irregular amphitheatre around the port, is also blessed with a reasonable sand beach that extends east for over a kilometre, and has a couple of days of sightseeing for those who want it. The municipal tourist information kiosk that opens every summer in the main square offers information on the sights and accommodation options.

Sitia is the north coast port for the finger of land that makes up the eastern extremity of Crete. The windmill-cluttered hinterland known as the Lasithi plain is very quiet, with poor roads: you usually have to double back to Agios Nikolaos to get to the other population centres on the south coast. Fringing the Libyan Sea, they escape the attentions of *meltemi* wind that slams into Crete's northern coast and thus enjoy calmer seas during the summer months. The only large town is at **Ierapetra** (pop. 11,000). This rather ugly tourist resort (like Sitia served by regular buses from Agios Nikolaos) has an excellent beach, a fair amount of nightlife

on the noisy promenade, the odd campsite and not a lot else. High Season, however, is not the time to come, for in July and August it gets insufferably hot; though during the winter months it offers some of the best temperatures in Greece. The main reason island hoppers visit the town is to join one of the caïques — filled with tourists seeking to escape the crowds — that run to **Chrissi** island (see overleaf).

⊨

In **Sitia** rooms are plentiful (except for the end of August Sultana Festival), with over a dozen hotels in the centre. For a reasonable bed try the B-class pension *Denis* (☎ 28356) on the waterfront. At the budget end of the range is the D-class *Archontiko* (☎ 22993), and the *Pension Artemis* (☎ 22564). There is also a *Youth Hostel* (☎ 22693) 500 m from the town centre (towards Iraklion) at 4 Therissou St.

Ierapetra (phone code 0842) also has some accommodation despite being a package tourist resort town: notably, the D-class *Cretan Villa* (☎ 28522) near the bus station, the beach front D-class *Iris* (☎ 23136) and C-class *El Greco* (☎ 28471). In the centre of town are the noiser D-class *Coral* (☎ 22848) and the pensions *Gorgona* (☎ 23935) and *Diagoras* (☎ 23898).

᠙

Thanks to a good **Archaeological Museum** (housing finds from the Minoan palace at Zakros), and a passable **Folklore Museum** in the town, there is enough to keep one occupied if you have to wait for a boat. The only building of note is the restored **Kastro** on the hill behind the town. Really a glorified fort rather than a full blown castle, it was built in 1204 and later enlarged by the Venetians, repelling a Barbary pirate raid in 1538 before falling to the Turks in 1651. In the absence of any significant Turkish remains (the town lay in ruins for the two centuries following its capture), popular tourist buses also head east to the good sand beach (graced with islets offshore) at **Vai**: the beach, however, isn't the reason the tourists come, for behind the sand is the only natural **Palm Forest** in Europe. Looking like a piece of transplanted North Africa it is now a national park.

Ierapetra has a tiny **Archaeological Museum**, a small **Turkish Quarter** and a **Venetian Fort** protecting the harbour. The town lies on the site of an important ancient city, though few remains have come to light.

⚓ Crete: Minor Islands

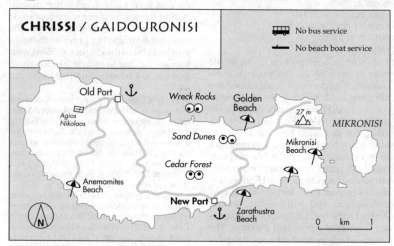

CHRISSI / GAIDOURONISI

🚌 No bus service

⛵ No beach boat service

Old Port

Wreck Rocks

Golden Beach

27 m

MIKRONISI

Agios Nikolaos

Sand Dunes

Mikronisi Beach

Cedar Forest

Anemomites Beach

New Port

Zarathustra Beach

0   km   1

Chrissi
ΧΡΥΣΗ; 6 km²; pop. 0.

Formerly known as Gaidouronisi ('donkey island'), the small island of Chrissi is a nature reserve (now without donkeys) and beach island sitting in the Libyan sea 10 km to the south of the Cretan town of Ierapetra. Daily excursion boats (500 GDR) run from the town in High Season.

Blessed with an intriguing mix of good clean sandy beaches, backed by sand dunes and a small forest of cedar trees, Chrissi is the nearest thing in Greece to a plausible desert island. Usually uninhabited, it has a couple of tavernas (located at the new harbour) that open during the tourist season and freelance camping has been tolerated in the past. Chrissi is traversed via a dirt track that links the new harbour with its predecessor (complete with a nearby chapel and lighthouse) to the north-west and the best of the beaches — Golden Beach — to the north-east.

Gavdos
ΓΑΥΔΟΣ; 34 km²; pop. 50.

The most southerly part of Europe, Gavdos is worth a visit if only for curiosity value. Sun-baked and isolated (visitors should bring their own food and essentials), it is home to about forty fishermen living on in otherwise abandoned villages (the former population once exceeded 8,000). Normally sitting in the Libyan Sea in quiet obscurity, the island hit the headlines in June 1996 when Turkey — in the wake of the argument over the sovereignty of Imia (see p. 317) — claimed Gavdos was 'disputed territory'; a delicious piece of nonsense as Turkey is hundreds of kilometres away.

Despite its tiny population Gavdos has a post office/OTE, a doctor and — somewhat bizarrely — a policeman; all housed in the capital of Kastri. The island has quiet beaches at Korfos (at the mouth of a small fertile valley) and at Sarakiniki.

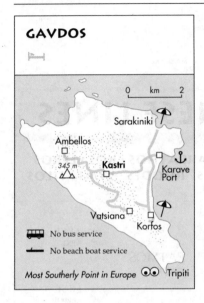

GAVDOS

0   km   2

Sarakiniki

Ambellos

345 m   **Kastri**

Karave
Port

Vatsiana   Korfos

🚌 No bus service

⊢ No beach boat service

Most Southerly Point in Europe   👀 Tripiti

⊢

A few rooms are available in both Karbre and Kastro (pre-booking is possible via travel agents in Paleochora). Freelance camping is also tolerated in season.

👀

The nearest Greece has to a ghost-town island, Gavdos lacks sights beyond an air of wild abandon. However, it does offer some interesting walks. Those trekking to the end of Europe at Tripiti will, however, be able to enjoy the rather incongruous sight of large oil tankers passing by like spook ships from another age. Occasional caïques also venture to uninhabited **Gavdopoula** to the north-east.

Spinalonga

ΣΠΙΝΑΛΟΝΓΑ; 1 km²; pop. 0.

Spinalonga is a small rock islet guarding Mirabello bay on the coast of Crete. A Greek version of Alcatraz, the island is billed by tour boat operators running out of Agios Nikolaos as the 'island of the living dead' thanks to its history as a

former leper colony. The island is dominated by a well-preserved Venetian Fortress. Built in 1579, it achieved fame for holding out against Turkish attack for thirty years after the rest of Crete had succumbed (it finally fell in 1715). When the island came under Greek rule in 1903, it was turned into a leper colony that closed with the death of its last inhabitant in 1955. Although Spinalonga was supposedly a hospital, in reality it was a dumping ground, with lepers of all ages (including children) marooned on the island, living in the former Turkish village built within the fortress's massive curtain walls. Guided tours (usually included in the tour boat price of 6,000 GDR) around the island are standard as the derelict buildings are now in a poor state of repair. Complete with poignant stories of the poor souls left here, they also take in the leper's cemetery and battlements.

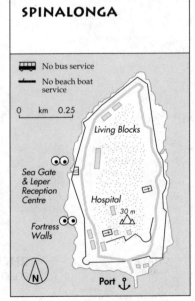

SPINALONGA

🚌 No bus service

⊢ No beach boat service

0   km   0.25

Living Blocks

👀
*Sea Gate
& Leper
Reception
Centre*

Hospital

30 m

👀
*Fortress
Walls*

Ⓝ

Port ⚓

8
DODECANESE LINES

CHALKI · KALIMNOS · KARPATHOS · KOS · LEROS
LIPSI · NISSIROS · PATMOS · RHODES · SYMI · TILOS

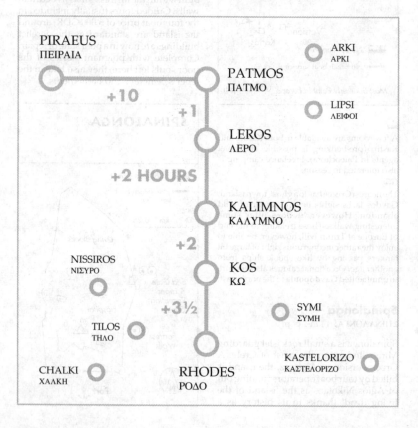

PIRAEUS
ΠΕΙΡΑΙΑ

PATMOS
ΠΑΤΜΟ

ARKI
ΑΡΚΙ

LIPSI
ΛΕΙΦΟΙ

+10

+1

LEROS
ΛΕΡΟ

+2 HOURS

KALIMNOS
ΚΑΛΥΜΝΟ

NISSIROS
ΝΙΣΥΡΟ

+2

KOS
ΚΩ

SYMI
ΣΥΜΗ

+3½

TILOS
ΤΗΛΟ

KASTELORIZO
ΚΑΣΤΕΛΟΡΙΖΟ

CHALKI
ΧΑΛΚΗ

RHODES
ΡΟΔΟ

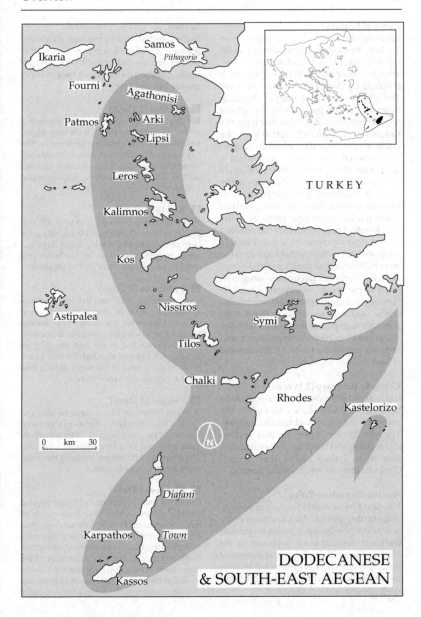

Ikaria

Samos
Pithagorio

Fourni

Agathonisi

Patmos

Arki

Lipsi

Leros

TURKEY

Kalimnos

Kos

Astipalea

Nissiros

Symi

Tilos

Chalki

Rhodes

Kastelorizo

0   km   30

N

Diafani

Town

Karpathos

DODECANESE
& SOUTH-EAST AEGEAN

Kassos

General Features

Running down the Aegean coastline of Turkey, the Dodecanese chain derives its name from the Greek 'dodeka' or 'twelve', after the major islands in the group which revolted against Turkish rule in 1908. The islands possess a unique character thanks to a combination of the strong architectural heritage inherited from the Knights of St. John (who left at least one castle on every island), the Italian occupation between 1913 and 1943 (when a deliberate attempt was made to Italianize the islands), the allure of day trips to the Turkish mainland (visible from most islands), and the duty-free status that has accompanied their late entry into the Greek state. The tourist influx has resulted in the development of a considerable pleasure boat industry that augments the ferry infrastructure, making island hopping easy. Ferry connections — once confined to the group — increasingly overflow beyond the geographical boundaries of the Dodecanese, while isolated Astipalea, though part of the group, has more in common in history, appearance and ferry links with the Eastern Cyclades and is thus included in Chapter 6.

Example Itinerary [2 Weeks]

If you aren't the most adventurous island hopper the Dodecanese chain offers the prospect of an easy and relaxed holiday. The islands offer a popular mix of good sightseeing and beaches. The only down side is an Italian rather than typical Cycladic atmosphere in many towns.

Arrival/Departure Point

Rhodes, Kos or even Piraeus are reasonable starting points. All have good entry points into the group. Rhodes is perhaps the most popular (so it is chosen in the example here); though lying at the end of the chain with poorly connected islands immediately north of it, it is an indifferent springboard/base port island.

Season

Early June through to the end of October sees a high level of services. Out of this period ferries only run 3—4 days per week and the all-important tourist boats are far less evident.

◼ Rhodes [2 Days]

Rhodes is a good starting point if venturing up the Dodecanese chain; with easy flights and plenty to see while you acclimatise. The city tourist office also distributes current ferry schedules and with these in hand you can start to fill in the details of your intended itinerary.

◼ Kos [4 Days]

Arriving on Kos you will find yourself well placed to take advantage of the island's good base port options by staying a few days and alternating between days on the beach and day hops to Nissiros and Turkey (Bodrum).

◼ Kalimnos [2 Days]

Can be happily 'done' as a day trip from Kos if you don't want to change your accommodation. Otherwise, it is an easy hop and you can head on to Mirities and spend a couple of days between the beach and the islet of Telendos. Kalimnos also has the best beach boats to the island of Pserimos should you want to try out the beach there.

◼ Patmos [3 Days]

A suitably spectacular island to aim for, Patmos has a nice lazy mixture of sights and beaches. You can also add other islands to your tally and take boat trips to Lipsi and Marathonisi/Arki before catching the overnight ferry back to Rhodes.

◼ Rhodes [3 Days]

One of the great advantages of flying direct to the Dodecanese is that your final couple of days are spent in far nicer surroundings than those offered by Athens. Returning to Rhodes with plenty of time to spare before your return flight means you can take advantage of the many tourist boats down the coast to Lindos, as well as day trips to the islands of Symi and — with a little more circumspection — Chalki.

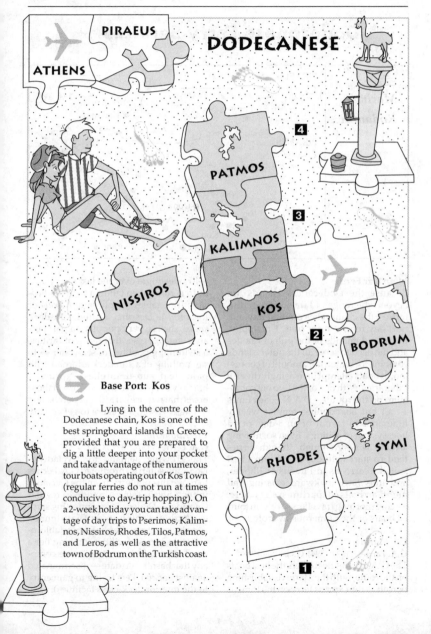

PIRAEUS

ATHENS

DODECANESE

4

PATMOS

3

KALIMNOS

NISSIROS

KOS

2

BODRUM

Base Port: Kos

Lying in the centre of the Dodecanese chain, Kos is one of the best springboard islands in Greece, provided that you are prepared to dig a little deeper into your pocket and take advantage of the numerous tour boats operating out of Kos Town (regular ferries do not run at times conducive to day-trip hopping). On a 2-week holiday you can take advantage of day trips to Pserimos, Kalimnos, Nissiros, Rhodes, Tilos, Patmos, and Leros, as well as the attractive town of Bodrum on the Turkish coast.

RHODES

SYMI

1

Dodecanese Ferry Services

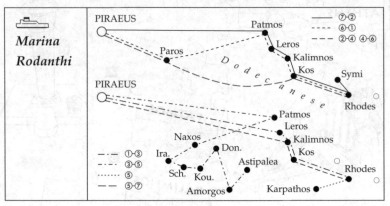

Marina
Rodanthi

PIRAEUS
Patmos
Paros
Leros
Kalimnos
Kos
Symi
PIRAEUS
Rhodes
Patmos
Leros
Naxos
Kalimnos
Ira.
Don.
Kos
Astipalea
Rhodes
Sch. Kou.
Amorgos
Karpathos

⑦-② ⑥-① ②-④ ④-⑥

①-③ ③-⑤ ⑤ ⑤-⑦

Main Car Ferries

Because the Dodecanese islands are beyond the range of Piraeus day-return ferries, the chain relies on 'first day out, next day return' ferry runs. Unhappily, the twin demands of the pull of Rhodes and the need to serve all the other islands combine to create a fair amount of confusion, as boats attempt increasingly diverse itineraries, with one of the two big companies on the route — D.A.N.E. Sea Lines — all but abandoning regular weekly itineraries in favour of an 8-day, or ad hoc, system of sailings. Even so, moving around is easy enough, though ferries tend to start with departure times best suited to arrivals in Piraeus or Rhodes, and thus have awkward evening and night arrivals/departures elsewhere, forcing morning travellers to rely on tourist boats or the numerous hydrofoils.

C/F *Marina*

G.A. Ferries; 1971; 5941 GRT.

The G.A. Ferries fleet offers the best boats on the route, with the *Marina* establishing herself as the express ferry on the Piraeus

—Rhodes route over the last four years; in 1998 running in tandem with the *Rodanthi* (timetables simply said '*Marina* or *Rodanthi*'). Despite limited sun-deck space, she is a very popular; in part because she possesses that rarest of rarities, a swimming pool full of sea-water — to say nothing of a sun deck adorned with palm leaf sun-umbrellas. Normally horribly over-crowded, she is one of those boats that require early ticket purchasing in High Season, if you are to get aboard.

C/F *Rodanthi*

G.A. Ferries; 1974; 8273 GRT.

The growing demand for Cyclades—Dodecanese ferries prompted G.A. Ferries to move this big ferry from the Cyclades in 1997. She has since provided a regular Cyclades—Dodecanese connecting service. A comfortable ferry, but with limited sun-deck seating, she has comfortable interior deck-class facilities, making her a good overnight ferry (this is one company that hasn't—to date—discriminated against backpackers trying to gain entry to the interior deck-class facilities).

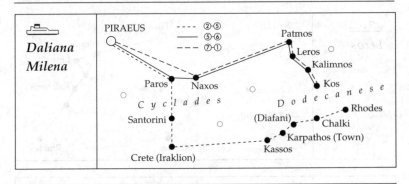

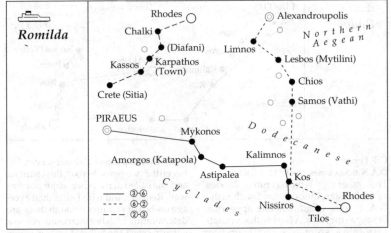

C/F Daliana

G.A. Ferries; 1970; 5528 GRT.

The *Daliana* has offered an alternative escape route to and from the Dodecanese via her Cyclades—Crete—Rhodes itinerary. This route has existed since 1990 courtesy of a number of G.A. Ferries' vessels. An ex-Japanese boat, the *Daliana* is joined on odd-ball runs to this island chain by her almost identical sister: the *Milena* (see p. 372). Both ferries have small smoke-stacks astern, comfortable interior deck class facilities, and sun-deck bench seats for sleeping bag fans.

C/F Romilda

G.A. Ferries; 1974; 5169 GRT.

The *Romilda* (the former cross-Channel *Pride of Canterbury*) is a large vessel with an excellent deck-class interior. Her only weakness is the limited amount of sun-deck space. Since 1997 she has operated out of Rhodes, running a High Season link to the North Aegean coast, a supplementary Crete service, and a convoluted itinerary to Piraeus via assorted Cyclades islands. These are subsidised 'lifeline' services, and if the *Romilda* isn't on them in 1999 another ferry is sure to be.

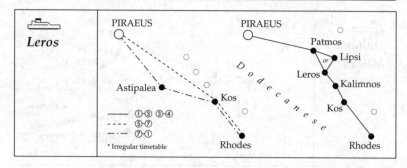

Leros

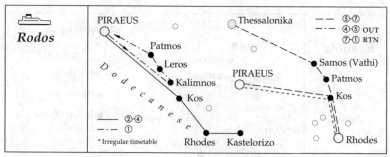

Rodos

C/F *Leros*

D.A.N.E Sea Lines; 1968; 5257 GRT.

This rather ugly ferry has run to Rhodes as the Strintzis Lines' *Ionian Sea*, then the G.A. Ferries' *Dimitra*, before appearing in 1997 as the *Leros*. A boat with a reputation for always running several hours late, her on-board atmosphere reflects her age, and feels rather old fashioned. Originally the Italian *Canguro Bruno* ('*Brown Kangaroo*') her sun decks and deck-class saloons are adequate, if not among the best in Greece. Each year sees significant tampering to her High Season itinerary, so expect changes in 1999.

C/F *Rodos*

D.A.N.E Sea Lines; 1973; 6475 GRT.

Another D.A.N.E ship running an eight-day Piraeus—Rhodes itinerary (schedules are irregular as a result), the *Rodos*

formerly ran a direct 12-hour service between the two ports. In 1997, this changed and she called at the other major ports as well. Reliable, and with better than average on-board facilities (though these are deteriorating with her increasing passenger turn-over), she suffered a major engine fire in 1991, forcing passengers to be transferred in mid-Aegean to a rescue boat. In 1998 the *Rodos* took over much of the itinerary of the missing *Patmos*, so if that ferry is back there could be major changes in 1999.

C/F *Ialyssos*

D.A.N.E Sea Lines

Ialyssos; 1966; 8586 GRT.

A *Canberra* look-a-like ferry (in a very small way), the old and grubby *Ialyssos* has been a depressing mainstay on this line for over a decade. She survives thanks

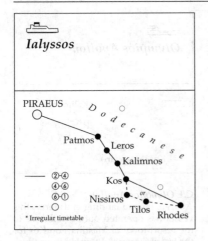

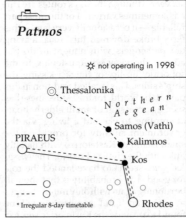

to the comparative lack of High Season ferry provision down the Dodecanese, running a very irregular series of itineraries over the last three summers. Only to be recommended for short journeys or emergencies, she is due to be replaced sometime in the next three years.

C/F *Patmos*
D.A.N.E Sea Lines; 1972; 7480 GRT.
The new boat down the Dodecanese in 1992, the *Patmos* — when she is around (she was missing in 1998) — is a large, if rather boring, ferry. The only 'interesting' that can be said of her is that she never appears to call at her namesake island.

She is nonetheless a cut above the rest of the D.A.N.E fleet in the deck-class facilities on offer. Her Rhodes—Thessalonika route was a new addition to schedules, though an irregular schedule, which resulted in her running alternate eight and then five day weeks, was rather confusing.

C/F *Nissos Kalimnos*
A. N. E. Kalimnos Sea Lines; 1988; 754 GRT.
The only small car ferry sailing solely within the Dodecanese, this Greek-built vessel operates out of Kalimnos and provides an invaluable service to adjacent islands. Run by a one-boat company, her itinerary has barely changed over the last

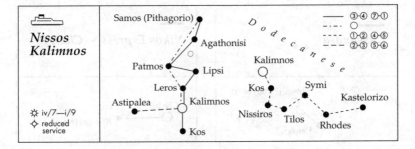

six years (though the days routes are run has sometimes varied). For the most part reliable — if occasionally very late — this ferry broke down in July 1992, leaving her passengers with nought to do but admire the view while listening to the soporific 'lip-lip' of the sea kissing the ship's sides. This is called tradition in this part of the world, for the Dodecanese has seen a succession of small elderly boats attempting to eke out a living, via the government subsidy for providing the small island of Kastelorizo with its only link with the civilized world. The *Nissos Kalimnos* seems to have landed the role for good. The probability is that she will be running again with only minor changes in 1999, and if not, a substitute will be found to provide the Kastelorizo service. Unfortunately, the minor changes are unlikely to include improvements to her shabby interior, seriously awful WCs and a lack of air-conditioning.

Samos—Dodecanese Links
Cross-line links between Samos and the Dodecanese exist via a weekly summer service (in past years a boat from the NEL fleet running down from Lesbos and latterly by the *Anemos* — see p. 372), and daily High Season hydrofoils. A second and more reliable connecting service that also runs during the Low Season is provided by the *Cassandra*: a small 1956-built tour-boat that rolls further than many stomachs care for.

C/F *Olympios Apollon*
A large, insipid landing-craft ferry, this vessel has operated out of Kalimnos to the resort town of Mastihari on Kos for the last eight years. Running three times daily, she exists to serve charter holiday makers running to and from the airport on Kos. At the same time, she also provides a useful evening service for any day-trippers who have missed their tour boat and are marooned on Kalimnos or Kos.

T/B *Nikos Express* - T/B *Chalki*
Two caïques turned tour boats provide the Chalki with its main link with the wider world, running daily to Rhodes (where they connect with the daily bus service to and from Rhodes Town). The *Nikos Express* is the best of the two, though both are apt to roll for the full 90-minute crossing. Tickets are bought on board.

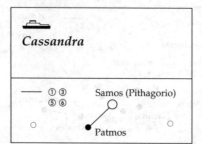

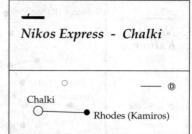

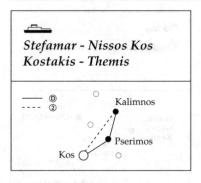

Stefamar - Nissos Kos
Kostakis - Themis

Stefamar - Nissos Kos
Kalypso - Kostakis
Themis

Dodecanese Tour Boats

The inconvenient departure times of many ferries in the Dodecanese means that most island hoppers resort to at least one of the tourist craft shown on this page. Although they cost a bit more, the convenience value makes them worth it, and they partly exist to provide one-way journeys for those not enamoured with day-tripping. Kos is the main base for these tour boats, with two large and comfortable vessels — the *Stefamar* and the *Nissos Kos* — augmented by several smaller boats. They swap destinations several times a week, but, in practice, combine to run a daily service to Nissiros, Kalimnos and Pserimos; a quick wander around the town's travel agents or along the waterfront in the evening will enable you to find out which one you want. Tickets are sold on the quayside prior to

departure as well as at regular travel agents. You can also pick these vessels up on their return runs, if they have spare capacity (when tickets are sold on board). The same is true of the smaller boats operating out of Patmos to Lipsi, and the larger Rhodes—Symi tour boats. The most useful of these is the *Symi I*: a small passenger ferry that carries several cars in a pinch. Worth looking out for as — charging ferry rates — she is cheaper than other tourist boats, usually running an early morning Symi—Rhodes service. She returns to Symi filled with tourists (most suffering from the lack of on board air conditioning). The more expensive catamaran *Symi II* runs in tandem with her, starting from Rhodes. Both boats are now suffering following the arrival of hydrofoils (see overleaf), which cream off much of the route's tourist traffic.

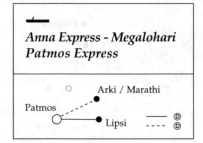

Anna Express - Megalohari
Patmos Express

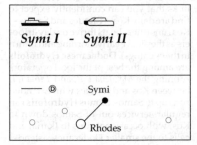

Symi I - Symi II

Samos Hydrofoils

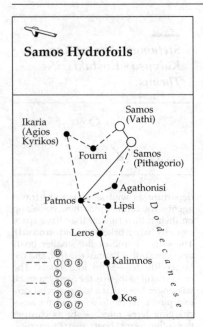

Dodecanese Hydrofoils

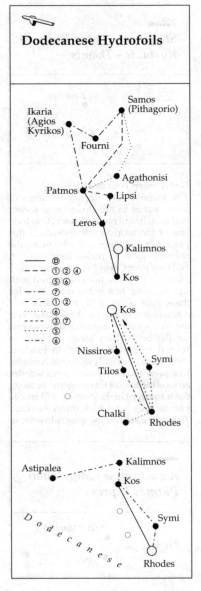

Hydrofoils

Local hydrofoils provide an invaluable addition to ferries if only because they don't require night travel. The down side is that most of these boats are quite old and there are considerable fluctuations in levels of activity with little happening outside the late June — September period, so it is very much a case of looking to see what is running when you arrive. The links that you can confidently expect to find are daily Kos—Rhodes and Samos—Kos runs (these boats thrive on day-trippers as they leave early morning and return in the evenings). **Dodecanese Hydrofoils** are among the best of the local operators running the *Mazilena I, II,* and *Tzina I, II* between Kos and Rhodes with extended runs up to Samos. **Samos Hydrofoils** run regular services out of Samos down to Kos, with occasional runs to Ikaria, and calls to the smaller Dodecanese islands.

Dodecanese Islands & Ports

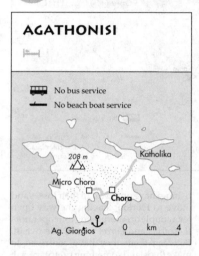

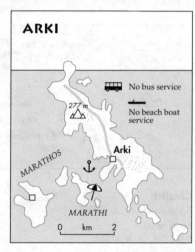

Agathonisi

ΑΓΑΘΟΝΗΣΙ; 13 km²; pop. 110.

CODE ☎ 0247
PORT / REGULAR POLICE ☎ 23770

Poorly connected Agathonisi is home to a small fishing community, six islets (all uninhabited), and a large ferry quay. An uninspiring hilly island covered with thorn bushes, it remains the preserve of the odd northern European grimly determined to get away from it *all*. The best reason to visit is the sense of elation that comes on leaving it; you can guarantee that you will return from your holiday feeling you have really achieved something. Unfortunately, the sum of the parts is considerably less than the whole. The two hamlets aren't worth spending three days on the island for and the only activity on offer is walking the donkey path to an abandoned village at Katholika.

Two port pensions offer a total of 12 beds.

Arki

ΑΡΚΟΙ; 7 km²; pop. 50.

CODE ☎ 0247

Consisting of scrub-covered dune-hills unrelieved by anything of interest, one dour fishing village and a dozen odd islets, Arki is not on the tourist map. The island also has no ferry quay, so boats steam aimlessly around on the off-chance of meeting a passenger-filled caïque. More important, there is no regular caïque to nearby uninhabited islet of **Marathi** (complete with a delightful beach backed by a couple of seasonal tavernas) — the destination for most 'Arki' advertised Patmos boats (check your exact destination if taking one of these). Marathi excepted, visitors should bring their own food, shelter, spade and nut-bucket.

Accommodation is limited to two tavernas offering rooms in Arki village. One of the tavernas on Marathi also offers summer rooms.

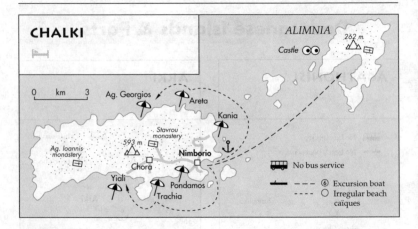

Chalki

ΧΑΛΚΗ; 28 km²; pop. 300.

CODE ☎ 0241
PORT POLICE ☎ 45220
POLICE ☎ 45213
FIRST AID ☎ 45206

If you are seeking out that elusive Greek island that just isn't like any other Greek island then Chalki (pronounced 'Hal-key', and often transcribed as Khalki, or Halki) should be pretty high up your hit list. A small, barren, undistinguished island to the south-east of Rhodes, Chalki is little more than a bone-dry rock (the island takes its name from the bronze that was once mined on here). Indeed, Chalki has no fresh water supply, and as a result, all produce and fresh water is tankered in from Rhodes twice a week. To help conserve stocks, tap water is heavily adulterated with sea water: drink from a tap on Chalki and you'll end up thirstier than before you started. Add to this a touch of early 1900s sponge-blight and a failed 1980s attempt to turn the island into a summer UNESCO youth conference centre and it is enough to ensure that most of the islanders (who formerly eked out a living via sponge

fishing) have opted to cut their losses and move to Florida; leaving the way open for a couple of enterprising tour operators (*Laskarina* and *Direct Greece*) to move in. Between them they have contrived to make the island something pretty special: for the truth is that Chalki is really an up-market tourist resort in the middle of nowhere masquerading as an unspoilt Greek island.

At first sight everything seems pretty normal, for the island has only one settlement of note in the form of a typically picturesque, semi-dilapidated port town backed by neglected hinterland, but when you look closer it is clear that the port of **Nimborio** is by no means a typical Greek island town despite initial appearances. A trail of red tiled Venetian (or if you prefer Symi or neo-classical) style mansion houses set around a horseshoe-shaped bay, and with a skyline topped by three ruined windmills, it is quite attractive, but when you start walking the streets it quickly becomes clear that many of the properties have been converted into holiday villas. Add to this the diminishing number of houses still in ruins and it is doubtful if more than a third of the houses are actually occupied by islanders. This

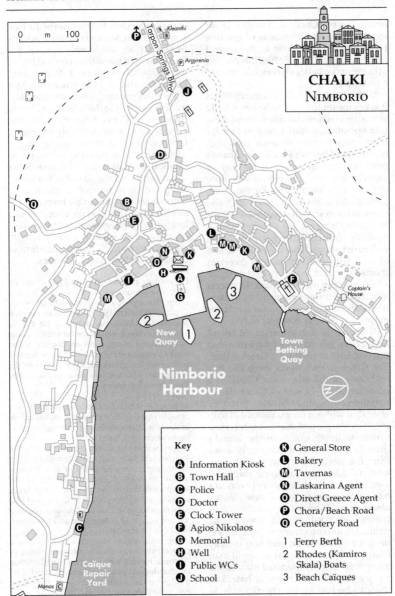

0   m   100

Kleanthi

Tarpon Springs Blvd

Argyrenia

CHALKI
NIMBORIO

B

J

D

Q

B

E

L

M **M** **K**

N

O **K**

M

I

H **A**

F

Captain's
House

M

G

3

2

2

1

New
Quay

Town
Bathing
Quay

**Nimborio
Harbour**

R

C

Manos **C**

Caïque
Repair
Yard

Key

A Information Kiosk

B Town Hall

C Police

D Doctor

E Clock Tower

F Agios Nikolaos

G Memorial

H Well

I Public WCs

J School

K General Store

L Bakery

M Tavernas

N Laskarina Agent

O Direct Greece Agent

P Chora/Beach Road

Q Cemetery Road

1 Ferry Berth

2 Rhodes (Kamiros
    Skala) Boats

3 Beach Caïques

is not to say that Chalki is all about tourism for there is a small nucleus of genuine town life adding colour to the several hundred upper-middle class Brits playing at being make-believe Greek villagers for a fortnight.

All this might sound unduly critical but it is not meant to be so: to be fair, Chalki would be in serious trouble without these tour operators, as the island is just too far off the popular ferry routes to rank high on the island hopper's hit list, and hasn't really enough going for it by way of either beaches or sightseeing to have more appeal in its own right. Furthermore, there is a lot to be said in favour of Chalki as a holiday destination if you don't want to do anything except unwind with a book for a fortnight (there is no nightlife, no tourist shops, and no bank), or are blessed with children able to entertain themselves and want a quiet holiday where you can let them roam the streets at will without worrying about their safety (there are no watersports, and no cars or mopeds as there is nowhere to go).

Of course, as any experienced island hopper can tell you, the problem is that this just isn't normal for a Greek island. The Greek islands never were like this and none of the others are: Chalki is a glorious fake — a sort of Greek island variation on Agatha Christie's *Bertram's Hotel* (but without the excitement of having Miss Marple and an organising crime syndicate living in). Even the island's main beach — a 15-minute walk away from the town at Pondamos — is now artificial (courtesy of some imported sand); the original being swept away in a bad winter storm in 1995. Worse still, the absence of a 'normal' mix of tourists contributes to a rather odd atmosphere: painted in tour brochures as the ultimate unspoilt island, in an odd sort of way Chalki ends up feeling more spoilt than many more heavily touristed islands. It is a place you will either love or hate, and this can be bad news. The flip side to

escapist islands is that they can be difficult to escape from. Most islands offer a choice of alternatives within easy reach if you find your own is less than you had hoped for: sadly, Chalki doesn't. If you don't like it then you could be in real trouble: it is not unknown for disenchanted holiday-makers to take the daily boat and bus to Rhodes City (a two-hour trip each way) several times a week simply to enjoy a few hours back in the normal world.

Of course it is possible to escape on Chalki itself; walkers not afraid of rougher terrain will find the island offers something and the waterfront is enlivened by half-a-dozen tavernas that hum into the small hours. This is in part because of a lack of beds for independent travellers (many end up beating a hasty retreat) and the awkward 05.30 departure time of the daily 'lifeline' boat to Rhodes.

🛏

Unless you are travelling well out of season then you should phone ahead and book a room. The options are limited to the small *Captain's House* (☎ 45201), the B-class pension *Kleanthi* (☎ 45334), the *Argyrenia* (☎ 45205), and the C-class hotel *Manos* (☎ 45295). None have distinguishing signs on display. Villas run by *Laskarina* or *Direct Greece* are pre-booked well in advance but both have agents on the waterfront who will be able to advise if they have any spare rooms.

👓

Nimborio (alias Emborio) does have one notable sight in the form of the tallest campanile in the Dodecanese. The only 'sightseeing' destination on Chalki is the former **Chora**, topped with a chapel-filled castle built by the Knights of St. John and complete with a derelict monastery nearby. Set safely inland, it is now all but abandoned, and sees almost as few tourists as it did pirates: faced with the choice between a very steep walk from the port (the road rises 300 m in 2 km) and caïques heading for tiny scraps of beaches around the island, most opt for the latter.

The main sightseeing excursion is also a caïque ride away on the adjacent island of **Alimnia**. Blessed with some excellent beaches, an abandoned village, and a castle straddling a ridge on the south-eastern side, the island has more going for it than Chalki.

Kalimnos

ΚΑΛΥΜΝΟΣ; 111 km²; pop. 14,500.

CODE ☎ 0243
PORT POLICE ☎ 24444
POLICE ☎ 22100
HOSPITAL ☎ 28851

A number of Dodecanese islands have laid claim to being the sponge-fishing centre of the Aegean — Symi not least among them — but relatively quiet Kalimnos has a better claim than most. Yet to embrace mass tourism, Kalimnos is a medium-sized island north of Kos that hides its attractions behind superficially forbidding mountains and one of the largest and most dour of island towns (population 11,000) in the Aegean. First impressions are, however, misleading, for between the mountains lie dark pockets of verdant vegetation, and there is certainly enough on the island to see if you don't mind poking around in dark holes to find it. In fact, holes are something of an island speciality. Not only are they abundant in the island's sponges, but Kalimnos has three caves visited by irregular excursions, and a whole lot more scattered around the island in which you can risk getting irrecoverably lost.

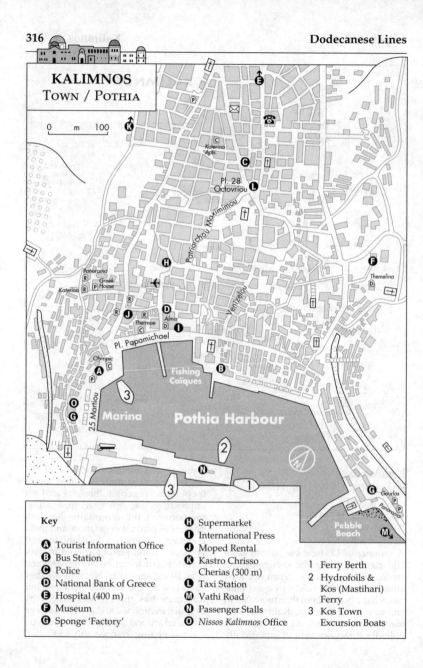

KALIMNOS
TOWN / POTHIA

0   m   100

Katerina
Apts.

Pl. 28
Octovriou

Patriarchou Maximimou

Panorama

Katerina   Greek
House

Thermae   Alma

Pl. Papamichael

Olympic

Venizelou

Themelina

Fishing
Caïques

25 Martiou

Marina   **Pothia Harbour**

Gourlas

Panorama

Pebble
Beach

Key

Ⓐ Tourist Information Office
Ⓑ Bus Station
Ⓒ Police
Ⓓ National Bank of Greece
Ⓔ Hospital (400 m)
Ⓕ Museum
Ⓖ Sponge 'Factory'

Ⓗ Supermarket
Ⓘ International Press
Ⓙ Moped Rental
Ⓚ Kastro Chrisso
   Cherias (300 m)
Ⓛ Taxi Station
Ⓜ Vathi Road
Ⓝ Passenger Stalls
Ⓞ *Nissos Kalimnos* Office

1 Ferry Berth
2 Hydrofoils &
  Kos (Mastihari)
  Ferry
3 Kos Town
  Excursion Boats

Kalimnos hit the headlines in 1996 thanks to a dispute with Turkey over the neighbouring islet of Imia. Used by Kalimnot farmers to graze goats, Imia saw groups of Greek and Turkish marines landing on the island in order to tear down each others flags and raise their own. Add to this a couple of gunboats, and the incident threatened to become a very nasty affair until mediating US diplomats negotiated a joint stand-off.

Gunboats notwithstanding, ferries call at the capital, **Pothia** (also known as **Kalimnos Town**), which fills the floor of a sheltered bay on the mountainous south coast. Also the object of daily excursion boats from Kos Town, the Italianesque waterfront is arguably one of the best of its type in the Dodecanese. Lined with trees and tavernas, it manages to offset the unappealing size of the town that sprawls behind it surprisingly well; offering an attractive spot in which to watch the world go by. Sadly, the rest of the town has too much of the world going by for comfort: the locals treat the narrow streets as if it were a motorbike rally course and this makes exploration uncomfortable to say the least. The only consolation is that the lack of sights means that Pothia offers little temptation to linger.

Most tourists seem to spend a day in the capital and then rapidly head on over the hills to the expanding resort/beach strip running along the north-west coast, opposite the island of Telendos. At the centre of this strip is the resortified village of **Mirties** which has little to offer besides a pretty dire pebble beach and regular caïque services to Leros and Telendos (there are better beaches along the coast to the south). From Mirties the hotel strip dribbles along the coast to become the resort of **Masouri**. Thereafter the road takes you to the northern finger of Kalimnos which is very quiet, with a limited bus service. Despite this, it is worth visiting thanks to an interesting cave just outside the village of **Skalia** and the

blissful isolation of the pebble beach village of **Emborio** which is attracting a growing number of those in the know.

The rest of Kalimnos tends to be little explored. The best and most popular alternative destination is the deep inlet of **Vathi** on the east coast. Set in a citrus-filled market-garden valley, the harbour of **Rena** offers a hotel, a few rooms and a notable sea cave (visited by tour boats from Pothia). If you fancy spending four hours getting to Vathi the hard way you can always attempt the walk from Pothia over the top of the island (the old dirt track runs up from behind the museum) in the happy knowledge that there is a bus that will get you back. Walking is also the only way to take in some of the island's other caves, though if you are without a guide you will be wise to *Cave* all of them. Faint-hearted troglodytes can see the best of them by ferry; courtesy of the *Nissos Kalimnos*, which has photos of a number of them adorning one of the pillars of its saloon.

ᵇᵉᵈ

Surprisingly for such a large island Kalimnos lacks a campsite or freelance camping area. There are, however, plenty of beds available, most in Pothia and Mirities, and in the former you can easily seek help via the helpful tourist office housed in an old beach hut 200 m from the ferry quay behind a bronze statue of Poseidon. **Pothia** has a pretty mixed collection, starting with the waterfront C-class *Olympic* (☎ 28801) and *Thermae* (☎ 29425), along with the D-class *Alma* (☎ 28969). A quieter D-class hotel — the largely package tour *Villa Themelina* (☎ 22682) stands near the museum. A clutch of establishments lie up in the backstreets rising behind the harbour. These include the C-class *Panorama* (☎ 23138) and *Katerina Rooms* (☎ 22532) — not to be confused with the package tourist-dominated *Katerina Apartments* near the back of the town — along with the excellent pension *Greek House* (☎ 22559).

Mirities also has over a dozen hotels including the D-class *Myrties* (☎ 47512) and E-class *Paradise*. Finally, **Rena** has the C-class *Galini* (☎ 31241) and the pension *Manolis* (☎ 22641), and **Emborio** also has a few rooms.

∞

Pothia was built on the back of the sponge fishing industry and has little by way of sights, excepting the inevitable small **Archaeological Museum** that is home to odd finds (from several barely explored sites around the island). Of failed sponge industry there is now little sign, bar the inevitable waterfront sponge seller pestering tourists and a small **Sponge Factory** just off the ferry quay where you can see the bleaching process under way. The sponge industry all but collapsed after WW2 thanks to advances in diving technology that enabled the local fleet to fleece the sponge-beds from Kalimnos to Libya to near extinction. Long considered to be part of the plant kingdom, sponges have only recently been re-classified as animals (for over two thousand years the locals had been wondering why the little critters squeaked when they hit them): the sponges are, in fact, the fibrous excreta of colonies of micro-organisms. In the sea they are an inconspicuous black, but once they have been boiled alive and then bleached in vats of nitric acid they soon pail to a creamy-yellow colour. At the factory you can buy all shades (depending on the amount of acid used), though the locals aren't keen on going into too much detail as to what is going on —

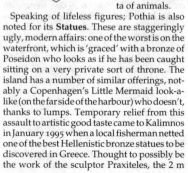

it is doubtful if many tourists would be over keen to buy the little things if they realized that they were rubbing themselves with the boiled bodies and excreta of animals.

Speaking of lifeless figures; Pothia is also noted for its **Statues**. These are staggeringly ugly, modern affairs: one of the worst is on the waterfront, which is 'graced' with a bronze of Poseidon who looks as if he has been caught sitting on a very private sort of throne. The island has a number of similar offerings, notably a Copenhagen's Little Mermaid look-a-like (on the far side of the harbour) who doesn't, thanks to lumps. Temporary relief from this assault to artistic good taste came to Kalimnos in January 1995 when a local fisherman netted one of the best Hellenistic bronze statues to be discovered in Greece. Thought to possibly be the work of the sculptor Praxiteles, the 2 m

high figure of a woman, clothed and with one arm folded across her chest, was a major find. Dating from the late 4 c or early 3 c BC, it has been described as the only example of its kind to survive from the period. A very grateful government gave the fisherman a million drachma by way of a reward for not trying to sell it on the black market. Unfortunately, it also rapidly took the lady in question to Athens for conservation; and given the statue's importance, the betting is that it is unlikely to see Kalimnos again.

Pothia is also the starting point for tour boats that run to the main sea cave: **Kefalas's Cave**. Famous for its stalagmites and stalactites, this cavern is said to be that in which the god Zeus hid from his immortal father before killing him (gods can do *anything*). These boats also often stop off at the islet of **Nera** to the south-west, where there is a small monastery. Other tour boats irregularly visit the **Daskalio Cave** at Vathi. If you fancy venturing further afield, Pothia has also lately seen the arrival of regular day-trips to **Kos** (courtesy of the P/S *Kouronis*), and to **Bodrum** in Turkey (via Kos) with the P/S *Agia Ekaterina*.

Elsewhere on Kalimnos you will find two reasonable castles: the **Castle of the Knights of St. John** (alias **Kastro Chrisohera**) complete with it own monastery, outside Pothia, is the better preserved, but a better excursion is to be had visiting the second: the abandoned fortress-village (complete with nine preserved whitewashed chapels) of **Pera Kastro**, just outside the old capital of Chorio, thanks to its impressive views. **Mirities** below has little to offer except an indifferent beach and a diminutive harbour of sorts.

One of the best reasons to visit Kalimnos is the opportunity the island offers to take a taxi boat across the narrow straits to the small, volcanic, and largely unspoilt island of **Telendos**. Sitting like a giant boulder offshore (the island is supposed to resemble a petrified princess, but you need to have an appreciative eye for the local sculpture to see this) and offering a nice beach, a few rooms and a castle besides, this is one of the best small islands going. Originally joined to Kalimnos, Telendos was born in 554 AD when an earthquake struck: the ancient capital of the island doing a 'Port Royal' and sinking under the straits in the process. If you take a caïque at the turn of the tide, 'tis said you can hear them bells' tolling from the city on the sea-bed.

Karpathos

ΚΑΡΠΑΘΟΣ; 301 km²; pop. 5,400.

CODE ☎ 0245
PORT POLICE ☎ 22227
TOURIST POLICE ☎ 22218
POLICE ☎ 22222
HOSPITAL ☎ 22228

Along with Kassos to the south and Saria to the north, the island of Karpathos forms a small archipelago midway between Rhodes and Eastern Crete. A appealing destination if you are looking for a quiet, relatively unspoilt Greek island, it remains a tricky spot to get to: the great majority of visitors are package tourists flying in direct from Europe. Given the low level of ferry links (the 'two boats in each direction' pattern of weekly services has been running for over seven years now), you should allow a couple of days in hand if you visit, to make your escape.

Like Amorgos, Karpathos enjoys a history of division with the two sides of the island effectively separated by inhospitable terrain, with the result that ferries call at two island ports. The similarities end there, however, because Karpathos has higher mountains, much more tree cover (though this has been sadly diminished by recent forest fires), is graced with some excellent beaches and — thanks to the large expatriate community (many now in the US) who send back funds — is now among the most affluent islands in the Aegean. In spite of the appearance of regular charter flights, tourism has yet to take off, with the somewhat paradoxical effect of creating a High Season surplus of demand for what limited facilities do exist. Buses run to the most popular island beach at Ammopi, but the service is otherwise generally very poor. Other transport options are pretty dire, the taxis being too expensive except for the shortest journeys, and car and moped hire limited by the poor quality of the road network and the lack of fuel stops outside the capital.

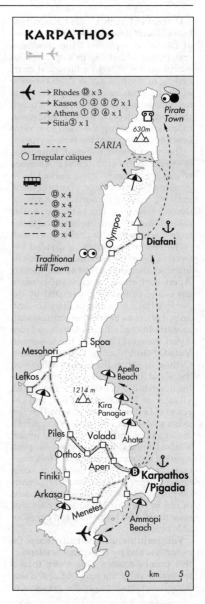

KARPATHOS

→ Rhodes ⒹD x 3
→ Kassos ① ③ ⑤ ⑦ x 1
→ Athens ① ③ ⑥ x 1
→ Sitia ③ x 1

Pirate Town

630m

SARIA

○ Irregular caïques

Ⓓ x 4
Ⓓ x 4
Ⓓ x 2
Ⓓ x 1
Ⓓ x 4

Olympos

Diafani

Traditional Hill Town

Spoa

Mesohori

Apella Beach

Lefkos

1214 m

Kira Panagia

Piles

Volada

Ahata

Orthos

Aperi

Finiki

Karpathos /Pigadia

Arkasa

Menetes

Ammopi Beach

0   km   5

The capital, **Pigathia** (called 'Karpathos' by locals and timetable writers alike) lies at the more populous flatter southern end of the island. Surprisingly for an island capital, it lacks a historical heart and is, in truth, a rather drab concrete affair. Its main assets are a picturesque harbour setting and a 4 km sandy beach that runs north of the town. High Season caïques also run up the coast to several beaches ending up at the best — Apella.

The main tourist resort on Karpathos lies to the south of the capital at **Ammopi** where three sandy bays, backed by a growing taverna village, play host to the growing number of tourists. If Ammopi doesn't take your fancy, then irregular caïques also run from the beach to quieter coves backing onto the drab airport road.

The rest of Karpathos is divided between a dozen villages (most of which lie in the southern half). First among these is **Aperi**, the former chora and still home to the island cathedral: dominated by expensive holiday homes built by US émigrés, it offers an interesting contrast with more traditional villages elsewhere. From Aperi the road climbs to the less spoilt **Volada** before topping the island spine at **Orthos**, at 510 m the highest village on the island (bring a pullover) before running down to one of the most attractive hill villages on Karpathos at **Piles**, and the resort of **Lefkos**. However, a rival to Piles exists at **Menetes**, which offers an interesting mix of old mansion-style and white-washed houses (depending on how posh a part of town you are in) and a folk museum. Beyond Menetes lies the growing resort village of **Arkasa**. Straddling a narrow gorge, it is home to the scanty remains of one of the four Mycenaean cites that once thrived on Karpathos and a reasonable beach.

Villages in the northern half of Karpathos are few and far between; the island at this point becomes little more than a mountain ridge sticking out of the sea. Rough dirt roads (more the preserve of hikers than vehicles) do extend north from the hill villages of Mesohori and Spoa, but caïques running between Pigadia and the small northern port of **Diafani** remain the principal means of travelling between the two halves of the island. In fact, quiet Diafani largely owes its survival to the package-tourists en route to explore the famous hill village of **Olympos**. Easily the most photogenic village on the island, lofty Olympos — complete with restored windmills galore — straddles a steep ridge, is notable for retaining a traditional village lifestyle (with the women conspicuously decked-out in 19 C. dress). Sadly, this is increasingly a show for the tourists' benefit. This is not to say that the local girls all dive for the nearest pair of jeans the moment the tourist bus heads down the hill, but the town now does have more suspiciously non-traditional souvenir shops than most.

◢

There is no camping on Karpathos bar an unofficial site 30 minutes walk north of **Diafani**. Fortunately, beds are plentiful, even in High Season. Most budget accommodation is in **Karpathos Town**. At the bottom end of the range are a of couple pensions offering rooms: *Harry's Rooms* (☎ 22188) north of the bus station, and *Carlos Rooms* (☎ 22477) along with two E-class hotels: the *Zephyros*, and the *Avra* (☎ 22388), a block inland. Moving up the price range, the D-class *Coral* and *Anessis* (☎ 22100) are topped by the C-class *Karpathos* (☎ 22347) and *Atlantis* (☎ 22777). In **Diafani** you will also find offers of rooms, pensions and several hotels including the quayside E-class *Chryssi Akti* (☎ 51215).

∞

Sightseeing is very limited, the best thing on offer being the High Season taxi boats (the *Adelais* and *Chrisovalandou*) that run up the coast to **Diafani**. The latter boat also visits the uninhabited island of **Saria** beyond, complete with a deserted 'pirate' town noted for having the remains of some oddly shaped houses (i.e. cone-like roofs). This can also be reached via caïque from Diafani, which has a bus link to Olympos: a tour bus in all but name, its Karpathos town counterparts offer the best way of seeing the southern villages.

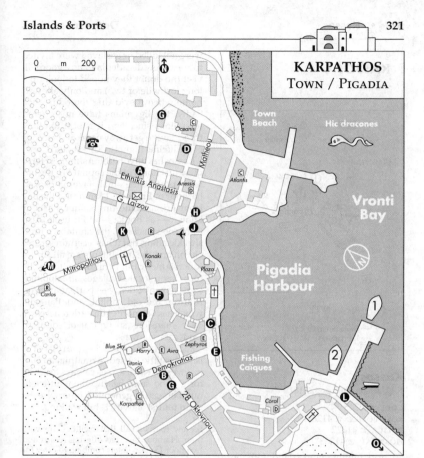

KARPATHOS
TOWN / PIGADIA

0 m 200

Town Beach

Hic dracones

Vronti Bay

Pigadia Harbour

Fishing Caïques

Town Beach

Oceanis

Matheou

Atlantis

Anessis

Ethnikis Anastasis

G. Laïzou

Konaki

Plaza

Mitropolitou

Carlos

Blue Sky

Harry's

Avra

Zephyros

Titania

Demokratias

Karpathos

28 Oktovriou

Coral

1

2

Key

- Ⓐ Tourist & Regular Police
- Ⓑ Bus Station
- Ⓒ National Bank of Greece
- Ⓓ Hospital
- Ⓔ Waterfront Clock Tower
- Ⓕ Town Hall
- Ⓖ Supermarket
- Ⓗ Pharmacy
- Ⓘ Bakery
- Ⓙ Newspapers
- Ⓚ Moped & Car Hire
- Ⓛ WCs
- Ⓜ Airport & Menetes Road
- Ⓝ Aperi, Spoa & Diafani 'Road'
- Ⓞ Ammopi Beach Road

- 1 Ferry Quay
- 2 Beach & Excursion Boats

KASSOS

🚌 —— Ⓓ x 2

—— - - - - ○ Irregular caïques

ARMATHIA

✈ → Rhodes Ⓓ x 1
→ Athens ③ x 1
→ Crete (Sitia) ③ x 1
→ Karpathos ① ② ③ ④ ⑥ x 1

Kassos

ΚΑΣΟΣ; 66 km²; pop. 1,184.

CODE ☎ 0245
PORT POLICE ☎ 41288
POLICE ☎ 41222
HOSPITAL ☎ 41333

An arid, mountainous island with more cliffs than beaches, Kassos is definitely not on the tourist map and has seen ferry services dwindle over the last five seasons and its population over the last two centuries. It has an odd history, having been subjected to an attack by a band of marauding Egyptians who carried off most of the women and children in 1824 with the thanks of their Ottoman overlords (Kassos was another of those small islands with a large fleet that enthusiastically joined the 1824 bid for Greek independence only to see savage retribution). The few male members of the population who

were not killed or enslaved were invited to Suez a few decades later on a goodwill visit (no doubt they hoped to look up a long lost wife or two) and only allowed home when they'd dug the odd canal. Sadly, the Egyptians have not offered ferry links since and it is best to allow three days to get away or take advantage of the lifeline flights to Rhodes and Crete.

Kassos has three harbours: the new ferry quay just north of the capital **Fri**, the old ferry port at the small taverna-backed harbour of **Emborio** 1 km round the bay from Fri, and the tiny caïque harbour known — as Bouka — at Fri itself. Also transcribed as Phry, the capital is a ramshackle affair, but it has a certain scruffy charm and the inhabitants are all smiles (often American). Behind the 'town' lie four closely located villages, all exhibiting signs of gentle decay — particularly **Ag. Marina**, the old capital, and **Panagia**, which has yet more of those derelict early 19 c. mansions so typical of southern Dodecanese towns.

Lacking roads or beaches the rest of the island is little visited. **Armathia**, an islet just west of Kassos, sees caïques heading for a good sand beach when sufficient numbers can be generated, otherwise the main tourist activity is hill walking.

╠═╣

So few tourists call that facilities are very poor. Harbour tavernas offering rooms and two poor C-class hotels combine to cater for the few that do call (they can more than handle the number of visitors, even in High Season). Best is the *Anagenissis* (☎ 41323), with the *Anessis* (☎ 41201) limping in behind.

👓

Kassos is not noted for its sightseeing. That said, there are sights of a sort. Most notable is the **Sellai Cave** near the airfield, complete with all the usual subterranean accoutrements. The village of **Poli** is also of some interest; being located (as its name suggests) on the site of the **Ancient City** (complete with Acropolis). A Byzantine church now adorns the site. A second church of note is that at **Arvanitohori**, which is partly carved out of the bedrock of the hillside.

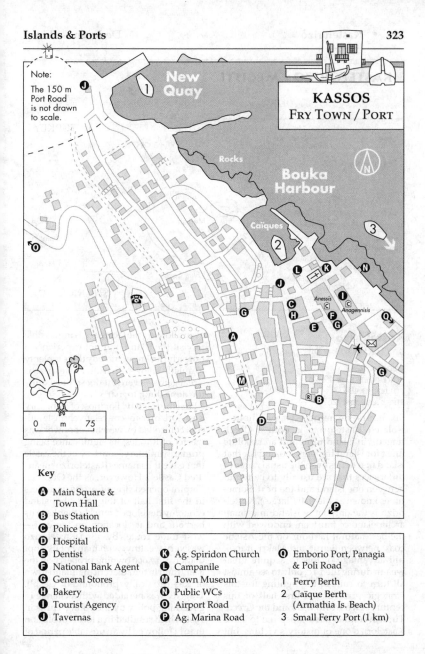

Note:

The 150 m
Port Road
is not drawn
to scale.

New
Quay

Rocks

Bouka
Harbour

Caïques

KASSOS
Fry Town / Port

N

3

1

2

J

O

L

K

N

J

C

G

H

E

F

I

G

A

M

R

B

D

Q

G

P

0   m   75

Key

Ⓐ Main Square &
Town Hall

Ⓑ Bus Station

Ⓒ Police Station

Ⓓ Hospital

Ⓔ Dentist

Ⓕ National Bank Agent

Ⓖ General Stores

Ⓗ Bakery

Ⓘ Tourist Agency

Ⓙ Tavernas

Ⓚ Ag. Spiridon Church

Ⓛ Campanile

Ⓜ Town Museum

Ⓝ Public WCs

Ⓞ Airport Road

Ⓟ Ag. Marina Road

Ⓠ Emborio Port, Panagia
& Poli Road

1 Ferry Berth

2 Caïque Berth
(Armathia Is. Beach)

3 Small Ferry Port (1 km)

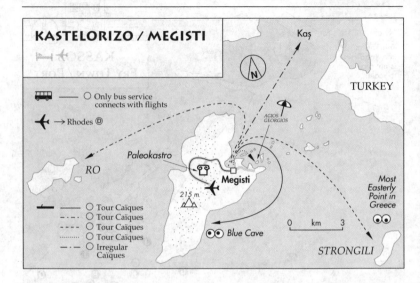

KASTELORIZO / MEGISTI

Kaş

N

TURKEY

🚌 —— O Only bus service
connects with flights

✈ → Rhodes Ⓓ

AGIOS
GEORGIOS

Paleokastro

RO

Megisti

215 m.

*Most
Easterly
Point in
Greece*

—— O Tour Caïques
-·-· O Tour Caïques
---- O Tour Caïques
········· O Tour Caïques
—·— O Irregular
        Caïques

0   km   3

◉◉ Blue Cave

◉◉

STRONGILI

Kastelorizo

ΚΑΣΤΕΛΛΟΡΙΖΟ; 9 km²; pop. 210.

CODE ☎ 0241
PORT POLICE ☎ 49270
POLICE ☎ 49333
FIRST AID ☎ 49267

Six hours steaming east of Rhodes, isolated Kastelorizo is both a Greek tragedy in island form and an absolute must for island hoppers looking for that island that defies even the usual range of differences that are usually to be found between one island and the next. Sometimes known as Megisti ('large'), Kastelorizo is the only large island in a small archipelago of fourteen. Endowed with the best natural harbour on the Asiatic coast between Beirut and Makri, it took full advantage of this to acquire great wealth during the 19 c. only to see almost all turn to ruin in the fighting for this strategic prize in the first half of this century. Two world wars and the Greco-Turkish conflict have conspired to leave Kastelorizo one of history's victims, but

even allowing the fact that it is impossible to visit the island and not experience a powerful feeling of tragedy there is plenty to quietly enjoy — in truth Kastelorizo is a real gem — even if it doesn't feel quite the done thing to 'party' here.

First the tragedy. For most of its history Kastelorizo was been a relatively insignificant controlled by whichever power was master of Rhodes; its significance being primarily military, courtesy of the castle that gave it its name (Kastelorizo means 'Red Castle'). However, as the Ottoman Empire opened up to European traders in the first half of the 19 c. the island economy developed quickly thanks to its harbour and its location on the east—west trade route. By 1850 Kastelorizo was very wealthy; with many of its population of 17,000 owning property on the island and in the adjacent mainland town of Kaş (ironically pronounced 'Cash'). Tragedy was heralded with a change in governing policy by the ruling Turks in 1908 which resulted in a local revolution in 1913 followed by an unstable period of self rule that saw the island cut off from the Anatolian mainland and economic decline setting in. Worse was to follow with the arrival of WW1. The French occupied the island in 1915, turning it into a naval base. This prompted Turkish forces to blockade the island and shell the harbour and town in 1917. In 1921 the French handed over Kastelorizo to the Italians under the Treaty of Sevres that gave the Dodecanese islands to Italy, thereby condemning the island's economy to a prolonged period of decline: the lack of any contact (never mind trade) with the mainland and changes in shipping routes proving to be a fatal double blow. The Italians attempted to turn Kastelorizo into a passenger seaplane base (serving Rome—Beirut flights) but this wasn't successful. Their integration policy, which sought the Italianization of the Dodecanese islands by banning the speaking of Greek in schools and public places, proved an even greater disaster, being fiercely resisted by the islanders. This left the Italians ill-disposed to help rebuild the town after it was badly damaged by an earthquake in 1926. As a result of all this, the town's population fell from 9,000 in 1910 to 1,400 in 1940.

In 1941 WW2 came to Kastelorizo when the British briefly captured the island only to see the Italians rapidly retake it. With the Italian surrender in 1943 the British regained control, and the town was then subjected to dive-bomb attacks by German planes. This resulted in massive damage and the decision to evacuate the remaining island population to Cyprus. Following their departure, in 1944 a fire completed the devastation of the town; the burnt-out buildings being bulldozed by the British for safety reasons. Some islanders asserted it was to cover up looting by the garrison: a hard claim to substantiate given the years of decline that proceeded the war and the bomb damage to the town during it. The final tragedy was yet to come: in 1946 the British ship *Empire Patrol* — overloaded with 500 returning islanders—sank after a fire broke out on board: 33 of them died.

Union with Greece in 1947 has brought a measure of quiet stability, but lying 90 km east of Rhodes and under 3 km from Turkey, Kastelorizo — the most easterly part of Greece — is very isolated. The brutal truth is that the island isn't really viable without close contact with the Anatolian coast, yet that isn't really a practical proposition given the politics of the region and the exclusively Greek inhabitants. As a result it floats in a sort of limbo sea, with its tiny population encouraged to stay by a mix of subsidies and new housing provided by a government afraid that if the population declines much more Greek sovereignty could be called into question. A strong sense of identity felt by expatriate islanders and their descendants (who contrive to book solid all available accommodation at the height of the season) is also a powerful source of sustenance.

Megisti or **Kastelorizo Town** has less than a third of its former buildings still standing. Old postcards and guidebooks on sale from waterfront shops reveal the pre-WW2 town to have looked very like a second Symi with similar tiers of mansion-style buildings crowding around the magnificent, wide, U-shaped harbour bay. Only the houses behind the back of the harbour survive in any numbers: the castle hill that once formed the centre of town now being reduced to bulldozed rubble. The waterfront — shorn of many of its buildings by German bombing — is on the verge of being rebuilt. One new house (presumably a copy of its predecessor on the site) has appeared in the 'gap' backing onto the new ferry quay and concrete footings for several more houses have been marked out (this is a way of registering

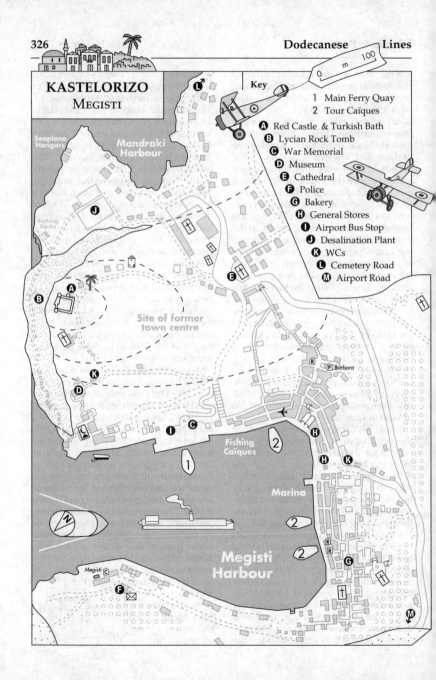

KASTELORIZO
Megisti

Key

1 Main Ferry Quay
2 Tour Caïques

Ⓐ Red Castle & Turkish Bath
Ⓑ Lycian Rock Tomb
Ⓒ War Memorial
Ⓓ Museum
Ⓔ Cathedral
Ⓕ Police
Ⓖ Bakery
Ⓗ General Stores
Ⓘ Airport Bus Stop
Ⓙ Desalination Plant
Ⓚ WCs
Ⓛ Cemetery Road
Ⓜ Airport Road

Seaplane Hangars

Mandraki Harbour

Bathing Rocks

Site of former town centre

Fishing Caïques

Barbora

Marina

Megisti Harbour

Megisti

N

plots by expatriate islanders). The attractive pastel mansioned waterfront buildings that have survived are home to the new 'centre' of town and here you will find the bulk of the town's shops and tavernas (which happily sprawl to the edge of the harbour as the quayside street is too narrow to admit vehicles).

The backstreets are more sobering: for the most part rows of semi-derelict houses and blocked off alleyways, they have a distinct ghost town feel to them. The only one of any length runs up the periphery of the castle hill; once a backstreet, it is now the main town artery between the waterfront and the partially rebuilt main square (now home to the cathedral, several churches, odd houses and a barracks). Paths also lead across the hill to the former main stairway (now reduced to an impressive flight of steps ascending into demolished oblivion) and to the castle. The castle is now the only significant survival from the old town centre (bar a small redundant Turkish bath and a ruined windmill), and is really little more than a glorified tower (albeit a pretty impressive one). Access is via a steep metal staircase that runs up against one of the side turrets. Walking on, the path passes a new museum and then runs down to the pitiful collection of houses around the locked mosque. On the other side of the hill is the small harbour of Mandraki, semi-derelict and home to a desalination plant it is backed by hills now being developed with government-built homes. A road of sorts also leads to a headland that is home to the town cemetery.

Kastelorizo not only enjoys very high summer temperatures (without the cooling influence of the *meltemi* these are regularly over 40° C) but also has a high military presence. The main garrison lies on the airport road and does much to add to the frontier-town feel of the place. When tensions with Turkey are running very high, armed patrols parade along the waterfront and helicopters occasionally

pass low overhead; in serious anticipation that Kastelorizo — an isolated Greek thorn in the soft underbelly of the Turkish Mediterranean coast — will be the first victims of a Turkish attack on Greece. All this sounds pretty grim, but Kastelorizo is actually a cheerful place in High Season. This is largely thanks to the many Australian expatriate visitors who do much to add to the vitality of the town. 80% of those able to claim Kastelorizian ancestry are now settled in Australia (in this part of Greece a man doesn't bring a phrase book; he just brings his Sheila). The only down side is that with so many ex-pats around, others can end up feeling a bit like outsiders.

The rest of the island is difficult to visit unless you like hiking. Walkers will enjoy Kastelorizo thanks to an excellent walking guide *Capture Kastelorizo* (2000 GDR) by Marina Pistisonis (who describes herself as 'A Greek Aussie but always a Kassie at heart'). Available in a waterfront shop, it is also a good introduction and guide to the island as a whole. The main destination is the ancient acropolis at Paleokastro.

◄

Accommodation in August is in very short supply: if you haven't booked you are cooked. Out of High Season you can always find a bed and will be met with offers when ferries dock. The only hotel is the expensive B-class *Megisti* (☎ 49221). This is augmented by several pensions. Most easily found is the *Barbara* (☎ 29295); others are signless and include the *Kristallo* (☎ 41209) behind the main square and the *Paradisos* (☎ 49074) near the west end of the harbour. Rooms are an option; notably opposite the *Barbara* (☎ 29074). There isn't a campsite and freelance camping isn't an option given the high miliary presence. Roughing it in the small patches of woodland on the outskirts of town isn't viable as their floors are littered with pine-needles and spent cartridges: both are deadly, though the former are surprisingly toxic and will leave those foolish enough to make an impromptu bed out of them looking like a walking example of some strange boil-covering disease a day or two later.

∞

The 1380-built **Castle** is the main sight in town, followed by the **Museum** which is free and worth a look. It contains an odd assortment of finds from the ancient acropolis at Paleocastro, earthernware from a medieval wreck off the south-west coast, and the usual collection of local house artifacts and costumes. Cut out of the rock beneath the castle is the only **Lycian Tomb** to be found in Greece (though there are plenty on the coast opposite). If you feel minded to attempt the short clamber up the steep cliff-side steps you will find a tomb with a view with room for six. Finally, although the **Cathedral** only dates from the last century it is also of interest as the columns in the nave were taken from the temple of Apollo at Patara in Lycia (back in mainland contact days).

Thanks to a roadless, and hilly interior, sightseeing is limited to Paleocastro and boat excursions to Fokiali Cavern — the best sea-cave in Greece if not the Med. Tour boats are dotted around the harbour, from where they make irregular runs to Turkey and to the outlying islands of **Strongili** and **Ro** (which has passed into Greek nationalist folklore thanks to its last inhabitant — a little old lady — who heroically ran up the Greek flag each day until her death in 1986. Her grave is one of the first things you see on landing on the island).

As is the case with many Greek islands, some of the more interesting 'sights' are no longer there to see. Kastelorizo has its sightseeing ghost in the form of the aircraft carrier *Ben My Chree* (Manx for 'girl of my heart'). One of the first half-dozen carriers in the Royal Navy, she was launched in 1908; starting out as passenger steamer running between Liverpool and Douglas. On the outbreak of WW1 she was rebuilt as a carrier, with addition of a flight deck and a prominent stern hangar (that housed 4 Sopwith camels and 2 Short seaplanes). Between 1915–16 she served in the Dardanelles during the Gallipoli campaign, and in January 1917 she sailed to Kastelorizo to replenish the supplies of the French garrison. Forced to use the main harbour because of her size (she was 375 feet long), she was shelled by the Turkish artillery batteries on the mainland. Her hangar received a direct hit on January 9 1917 at 2:13 pm, setting it on fire. Within half an hour the ship had been abandoned and continued to blaze until she finally sank on the morning of the 11th. In late 1919 the hulk was refloated and towed to Piraeus where she was sold to a German scrap merchant.

Kos

ΚΩΣ; 290 km²; pop. 21,500.

CODE ☎ 0242
PORT POLICE ☎ 26594
TOURIST POLICE ☎ 28227
POLICE ☎ 22222
HOSPITAL ☎ 22330

Thanks to an attractive mixture of sand and sights Kos (often transcribed as Cos) is a justifiably popular package tourist destination. A long tapering island with a high spine of mountains running along its southern side, it lies mid-way down the Dodecanese, and is the de facto hub of ferry activity on the chain, with virtually every ferry putting in an appearance and an unsurpassed number of tourist craft operating to neighbouring islands and the Turkish coast.

Large for a Greek island (45 km long), Kos was an important centre in the ancient world. Unlike Rhodes, Kos was never quite large enough to be a major force in its own right, leaving it more prone than most of the larger islands to the vicissitudes of history: it variously relied on the patronage of Egypt (under the Ptolemys), Rome (from 130 BC) and Rhodes (from 1 C. AD) for its protection. Its shaky geology has also played a major part in its development: it was devastated by massive earthquakes on several occasions; notably in the 6 C. AD. and again as recently as 1933. As a result, much of its fame was derived from an odd mix of figures and famous associations rather than economic or military prowess. First among the historical figures were Hippocrates (460–357 BC) — the so-called 'Father of Medicine' — who was born and had his school here (at the Asklepieion), and a famous painter contemporary of Alexander the Great by the name of Apelles. The island was also a noted producer of fine wine, and scandalously, in the Roman era, see-through silk garments beloved by Senators' wives and the transvestite Roman Emperor Caligula.

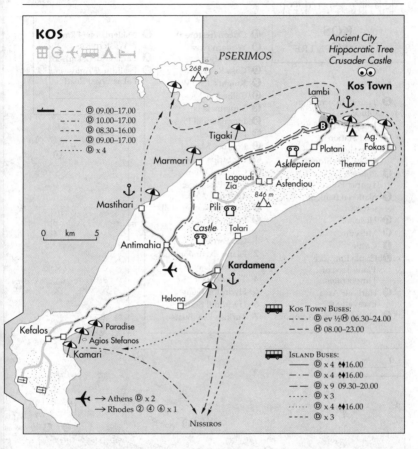

Kos Town, the main port and capital of the island, lies on the sandy east coast with views across to Turkey. It is a gentle, wide-avenued centre of flowers and trees that would be very restful if it wasn't for a spot of mass tourism. For the most part the more scenic parts of town have stood up to this remarkably well, but the streets north of the castle-dominated old harbour (and indeed, the coastline north and south) are dominated by a heavy concentration of hotels, discos and tee shirt shops

that will either be your idea of holiday heaven or a variation of hell: this is the secret for the town's success for there is something here to appeal to all tastes — unless you like solitude. The centre is very Italianesque in feel, having been largely rebuilt during the interwar occupation years (courtesy of the massive 1933 earthquake). Some consolation for the loss of any tangible 'Greek' atmosphere is to be found in the Italian disinclination to rebuild over any archaeological

KOS
TOWN CENTRE

Key

A Tourist Information Office
B Island Bus Station
C Taxi Station
D City Hall, Customs & City Bus Stop
E Police & Tourist Police
F National Bank of Greece
G Hospital
H Museum
I Castle
J Castle Entrance / Plane Tree of Hippocrates
K Harbour Area Excavations
L Site of Ancient Acropolis

M Odeon (restored)
N Western Area Excavations
O Casa Romana
P Knights' City Wall
Q Cathedral
R Supermakets
S International Press
T Pharmacies
U Produce Market
V Bar Strips
W Cinema Orfeus
X Ferry Passenger Terminal / WCs
Y Ferry Passenger Stalls
Z Public WCs

1 Car Ferries
2 Island Excursion Boats
3 Bodrum Day Boats
4 Tour Boats
5 Hydrofoil Quay
6 Hydrofoil Berth
7 Turkish Day Boats

F Asklepieion (4 km) & Western Kos
A Lambi Rd. (2 km)
O Psalidhi & Agios Fokas Coast Road

ANCIENT CITY
10. Temple of Pandimos Aphrodite
11. Temple of Heracles
12. Small Temples
13. Roman Agora
14. Stoas (4c. BC)
15. City Wall
16. Site of East Wall Gate
17. Harbour Baths
18. North Baths
19. Roman House

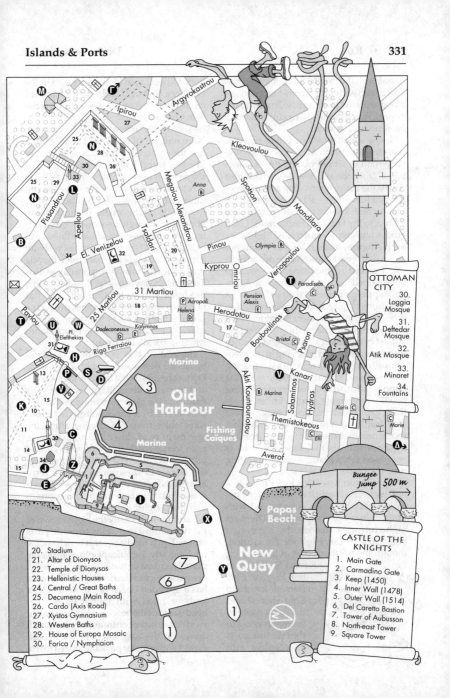

Ipirou

Argyrokastrou

Kleovoulou

Spotson

Mandilara

Anna

Megalou Alexandrou

Tsaldari

Pinou

Olympia

El. Venizelou

Pissandrou

Apellou

Kyprou

Omriou

Veriopoulou

Paradissos

31 Martiou

25 Martiou

Acropoli

Pension Alexis

Herodotou

Helena

Boubolinas

Psaron

Dodecanessus

Kalymnos

Riga Ferraiou

Bristol

Pl. Elefthekias

Marina

Akti Kountouriotou

Kanari

Salaminos

Hydras

Marina

Old Harbour

Themistokeous

Karis

Marie

Fishing Caïques

Marina

Elli

Averof

Bungee Jump

500 m

Papas Beach

New Quay

OTTOMAN CITY

30. Loggia Mosque

31. Deftedar Mosque

32. Atik Mosque

33. Minaret

34. Fountains

20. Stadium
21. Altar of Dionysos
22. Temple of Dionysos
23. Hellenistic Houses
24. Central / Great Baths
25. Decumena (Main Road)
26. Cardo (Axis Road)
27. Xystos Gymnasium
28. Western Baths
29. House of Europa Mosaic
30. Forica / Nymphaion

CASTLE OF THE KNIGHTS

1. Main Gate
2. Carmadino Gate
3. Keep (1450)
4. Inner Wall (1478)
5. Outer Wall (1514)
6. Del Caretto Bastion
7. Tower of Aubusson
8. North-east Tower
9. Square Tower

remains that came to light, leaving Kos Town with wide, open, ruin-topped vistas along with the boulevards. To add to the appeal, much of the town centre has now been pedestrianized.

Hotels are strung out along the east coast from Lambi to Ag. Fokas. This hotel-strip road is served by city buses (timetables from the office at ❻), which also run to the main sightseeing attraction — the Asklepieion — a healing sanctuary that became a major focus for pilgrimage thanks to the fame of Hippocrates. Local guides will give you a detailed life history of this figure, though his story is rather elusive. The earliest advocate of a 'scientific' practice of medicine, he seems to have gained fame by travelling the Aegean, stopping plagues and other little mass infections by advocating the novel ideas of boiling drinking water and the isolation of the sick from the healthy. Thereafter, almost every medical saying and practice was ascribed to him, glorying in the association, and leaving scholars wondering if he ever said anything notable at all (the Hippocratic Oath — see the map facing p. 337 — probably started life as something like: 'I wish this pesky snake would stop following me around'). The most recent manifestation of this hero-worship by association is the ancient tree he is supposed to have taught under, standing near the castle.

Nightlife on Kos often looks to be in a not dissimilar condition to the tree: by the early hours the town is festooned with limp limbs propped up by bars. The main nightclub area lies on the north-east boundary of the Harbour Excavation, though the northern part of town along Kanari St., home to the *Playboy Club* (famed for disco light shows) and the *Beach Boys* bar (arguably home to the best music), is also replete with

bars. Other discos in town are also in the northern Kanari/Lambi district and include *Disco Heaven*, the *Kalua* (both on the beach) and the *Disco Rock Club*.

Much of the appeal of Kos town is the large number of good sand beaches that line the east coast either side of the town. The beach and hotel strip to the north of the centre is now very developed and one is often hard put to see the sand for sun umbrellas and tourists. The beach strip to the south of the castle is much more appealing (though it is slowly deteriorating), with emptier strands, and lined with palm and eucalyptus trees and a cycleway running alongside the main road. Bicycle hire is deservedly very popular in Kos Town as the layout is well suited to this mode of transport (indeed, the flat northern side of the island has proved so popular with cyclists that a number of roads now have designated cycle lanes running parallel to them).

The rest of Kos is fertile (the island boasts the best water supply of any of the Dodecanese islands) but is rather scruffy and littered with military encampments thanks to the close proximity of Turkey. It is served by very overcrowded buses (timetables from ❻) running along the one main road down the island spine, with feeder roads linking it with coastal villages. Kardamena and Mastihari are the largest of these, with regular ferry links to Nissiros and Kalimnos respectively. Both have become tourist resorts in their own right.

Kardamena is easily the bigger town of the two, almost managing to outdo parts of Kos Town for discos and beach shops. Lacking any significant old centre, the place is a mass of hotels some six blocks deep and over a kilometre long. The town has a crowded beach on its west side, a harbour filled with tourist boats (that head daily for the beaches along the south-west coast) in the centre and several small quays on the east side. As one would expect with a major package tourist town, all the important facilities are readily available: most are in the blocks that line the promenade. The bus stop is 150 m up the main street running up behind the ferry quay. Nightlife isn't hard to find either, with the *Tropicana* disco in the block at the east end of the promenade and *Disco Starlight* on the landward side of the main road into town.

Mastihari, the largest settlement on the north coast, also has a good sand beach but is much quieter than Kardamena and offers a better mix of tourism and regular town. Built on a wide, flat promontory, it has a small harbour and a single major street running directly inland. The best beach in town lines the wide bay to the west of the centre, while the eastern half of town is dominated by several large hotel complexes. In this respect it mirrors the north coast village of **Tigaki**. This small settlement offers a popular alternative to the Kos Town beaches, via its impressively large expanse of sand that is popular with windsurfers. Like adjoining Mastihari, it consists of a promenade (complete with a disco – the *Annabella*) and a main street that runs directly inland to the main island road.

Inevitably, the more attractive destinations are harder to get to. The best beaches are tucked away under the western 'fin' of the island beneath the hilltop windmilled village of **Kefalos** (site of the pre-Kos Town ancient capital of the island) 45 km from Kos Town. This is easily the best part of Kos, quieter and more fertile than the rest of the island. This area has some notable pine woods south-west of Antimahia known as Plaka. These are now an attractive picnic spot for island coach tours and those with their own transport. Although hotel development has also encroached onto the landscape, the area is still relatively unspoilt. The largest beach centre is at **Kamari**. This is a resort village with a lovely sandy strand, the remains of an ancient Agora, a couple of discos and a large *Club Med* complex behind

Agios Stefanos beach (named after a ruined early basilica on the small headland that separates the beach from the village. Just offshore is the attractive chapel topped islet of Agios Nikolaos. To the east are a series of beaches reached via boats or bus stops along the main road. These include Paradise, Sunny and Magic beaches.

The inland towns on Kos have less going for them. The majority of visitors to Kos end up passing through **Antimahia**. Distinguished by having the only working windmill on Kos, the town is better known for being the jumping off point for the island's charter flight airport. To northeast is the village of **Pili**, built alongside its beautiful, ruined medieval counterpart, it is more worthy of a look.

High Season sees a rush for the available hotel space and rooms, and understandably so for Kos, an island overloaded with upper and mid range package tour hotels, is poorly supplied with budget accommodation, given the number of visitors it sees. It thus pays to arrive on a morning boat (i.e. Rhodes hydrofoil rather than afternoon ferry). The limited budget rooms available in **Kos Town** are divided between seven establishments. To the south of the ferry quay the D-class *Hara* (☎ 22500) lies one block behind the beach road that is home to package tour hotels for a kilometre each side of the town (if funds aren't too much of a problem then finding a bed in one of them is never very difficult). Alternatively, you can try the C-class *Maritina* (☎ 23241) near the OTE. Although it is on a busy street, it is not as noisy as the clutch of hotels overlooking the Old Harbour. These consist of the E-class *Kalymnos* (☎ 22336), the D-class *Helena* (☎ 22986) and *Dodecanessus* (☎ 28460) and one good pension — the *Acropoli* (☎ 22244). To the north lies a second, the *Alexis* (☎ 28798). There are also a limited number of rooms around the town: owners are in the habit of only meeting the major boats.

Each of the main tourist villages on Kos has more hotels than most islands can muster. At the budget end of the range: **Mastihari** has the D-class *Faenareti* (☎ 51395), the E-class *Zevas* (☎ 22577) and some good rooms on the waterfront: *Panorama* (☎ 59145), **Kardamena** the D-class *Paralia* (☎ 51205) and the E-class *Olympia*, and **Kefalos**, the D-class *Sidney* and E-class *Eleni* and *Maria* (☎ 71308). Rooms are also available at all the above as well as at **Tigaki** and **Kamari**.

Δ

Camping Kos (☎ 23275): 3 km south of Kos Town on the main beach road. A well maintained and friendly family-run site (complete with reasonable mini-market) set in an attractive mix of a flower garden and orchard. Minibus meets ferries, but campers arriving by other craft will have to take the coast road bus or walk (the site is at the end of the long straight section of road, bounded by the cycleway).

∞

Kos is one of the best islands going when it comes to sightseeing. First and foremost there is the **Asklepieion**, one of the greatest shrines in Greece (described overleaf). Kos town itself is the other big crowd-puller. By mixing sightseeing, shady trees, and the occasional drink at a passing taverna, the town offers a relaxed and interesting day's sightseeing.

The most obvious attraction is the **Castle of the Knights** (open ②–⑦ 08.30–15.00). Started in 1450 it initially consisted of just the keep and the inner enceinte (curtain wall). Following the unsuccessful Turkish assault of 1480, in 1495 the Grand Master of Rhodes, Pierre d'Aubusson, had the outer enceinte constructed, the task being completed by his successor Fabrizio Del Carretto in 1514; their coats-of-arms (see the Rhodes City map between pages 352–353) are carved on the walls at various points. Most of the masonry used in the castle was pillaged from the ancient city and Asklepieion. It was also used to construct the **Knight's City Wall**, a fragment of which survives on the north side of the Harbour Area Excavation, and includes a gateway and the south-west tower. The castle also had a moat, which now houses the road that runs under the bridge.

Standing opposite the castle bridge is the impressive 14 m girthed (and now hollow) **Plane Tree of Hippocrates** — its not so plain limbs artistically supported with scaffolding and cut-up tractor tyres. Supposedly the one he taught under, it is only in fact about 500 years old. It shades a Turkish fountain (dry) constructed from fragments of ancient buildings, and the best of Kos Town's several mosques: **Gazi Hassan Pasha Mosque** (1786).

Immediately to the south of the mosque lies the largest excavated area of the ancient city;

the **Harbour Area Excavation**. This roughly corresponds with the site of the medieval city. The bulk of the excavation consists of foundations and the inner stone cores of temples (only the long gone exteriors were faced with marble); it is the preserve of lizards during the day and couples serenading the moon at night. Amid the rubble are the remains of a temple of Aphrodite and a couple of reconstructed columns from the Roman Forum. More interesting is the town **Museum**, housing the finds not shipped by the Italians to Rhodes.

The **Western Excavation** area to the east of the town centre is (thanks to Italian restorers) the best of the ancient sites. A number of pillars that formed the gymnasium's peristyle court have been 'reconstructed', and the streets still bear the ruts worn into the stones by ancient carts. The site also has walls complete with original painted plasterwork, though the ancient Acropolis isn't visible, its position marked only by the mosqueless minaret on the hill. To the south of these excavations lie two other attractions: the restored **Odeon** and also a rebuilt example of a Roman Villa (the Italians not surprisingly opted to reconstruct this building rather than one of the Hellenistic houses nearby), the **Casa Romana**, a mixture of pools and mosaics. Worth a look: don't be put off by the singularly ugly cement exterior of the building: Roman houses always were decorated with pretty plain exteriors.

Additional minor sites are scattered around Kos. The most impressive of these is the **Antimahia Castle**. Sited atop a hill north of the airport and Kardamena, it can be reached either via a 3 km path from the airport—Kos Town road or a 10 km track that starts 700 m east of Kardamena (tourist buses are too busy visiting the Asklepieion to venture in this direction). Built by the Knights of St. John in the first half of the 16 c., it is triangular in shape, with corner turrets. Within the ruined walls are the remains of a number of houses and a couple of churches. A second site worth taking in lies at at **Therma** — a 4 km walk from **Ag. Fokas** — where hot springs run down to the sea.

Finally, Kos has boat excursions aplenty, with craft running across the 5 km straits to **Bodrum** in Turkey and to all the adjacent islands, including the beach islet of **Pserimos**. This is a crowded beach island reserved for day-trippers seeking (in vain) to escape the crowds. Boats berth at a small quay serving the small settlement on the west coast.

The Asklepieion

The remains of one of the most imaginative and effective creations of Greek architecture lie on a hillside 4 km west of Kos Town. Overlooking both the town and the Turkish strait, the Asklepieion (open ②–⑦ 08.30–15.00) was the leading medical sanctuary in the Greek world. Dedicated to the God of Healing, Asklepios (a son of Apollo whose symbol was a snake curling up a staff), it was — thanks to the revenue that accompanied the pilgrims that flocked there — an architectural and cultural centre. The sanctuary was founded a century after the death of Hippocrates (357 BC) and because of his associations developed thereafter. Built on four terraces carved out of a gentle hillside adorned with a sacred wood, it was considered a masterpiece of Hellenistic architecture in its day and boasted a series of famous paintings by Apelles to heal the spirit when they couldn't manage the body. Offices to the latter were undertaken by a priestly order supposedly descended from the god. The sanctuary also offered a much-used right of asylum.

Despite losing some of its most notable art works to Rome, the Asklepieion thrived until the 6 C. AD when it was reduced to rubble either by the Anatolian attack on Kos in 554 AD or an earthquake. The ruins lay undisturbed until 1450 when the Castle of the Knights was constructed in Kos Town: the need for building blocks being sated by the readily available ancient masonry in the town and at the Asklepieion. As a result, the site was all but stripped bare of architectural members and its location passed out of memory.

One of the lost great shrines known only through literary sources, the search for the Asklepieion began in 1896; the site eventually being pinpointed by an English archaeologist W.R. Paton in 1902 — though it was left to a local antiquarian, G. E. Zaraphtis, and his German archaeologist sponsor Rudolf Herzog to crudely excavate the site. From 1904 on Zaraphtis began a systematic excavation that continued until his death in the 1933 earthquake. Thereafter Italian archaeologists did as much building as excavating; rebuilding the impressive terrace walls (with tuffstone blocks in lieu of marble) and staircases, and adding a pillar or two for good measure. The site is therefore as much of a 'fake' as the Minoan

palace at Knossos on Crete, but as in that case, the reconstruction is inspired and of great value to those seeking an appreciation of its former grandeur.

Today the Asklepieion is approached via a pleasant suburb road that emerges through an avenue of cypress trees at a large coach and bus park. A short path takes you past a drinking water tap to the ticket kiosk at the entrance to the site. At this point you have to choose between taking the path up the south side of the site and then walking down the terraces from the upper terrace or taking the ancient route (i.e. walking up the staircases). The description below assumes the latter; if only because it is easier to climb, rather than descend, stairways without hand rails.

Directly inside the site entrance are the foundations of a small Roman bathhouse (with hypocaust floor in the hot room and a beautifully preserved plunge pool complete with steps) where pilgrims would cleanse themselves before entering the sanctuary proper. The modern path runs past this to **Ⓐ** the **Entrance Stairs**. Consisting of 24 steps they climb to the **Lower Terrace** and the site of the formal gateway to the sanctuary: **Ⓑ** the **Entry Propylon**; now marked only by a pillar base under a shady tree. The vision — on passing through it — of the wedding-cake terrace layers ascending to the main temple, is now only to be dimly gleaned. So too is the enclosed 'courtyard' atmosphere of the Lower Terrace created by **Ⓒ** the **Galleries** — pillared, stoa-like buildings which once ran from either side of the gate to the middle terrace wall. Even so, the Lower Terrace retains the wide, open aspect that graced it in antiquity and it was probably on this terrace that athletic contests associated with festivals honouring the god were held. Unfortunately, the votive statues that were such a feature of this terrace have long gone. All that remains are **Ⓓ** the rebuilt **Statue Niches**. In one of these niches stood a very famous statue of antiquity now lost — the Aphrodite by the even more famous sculptor Praxiteles. The only figures remaining are the **Torsos** at **Ⓔ**, propped against the **Middle Terrace Wall**. On the stoa side of the path at **Ⓔ** you will also find one of the few remaining statue bases (complete with the ghostly footprints of its owner) that adorned this terrace.

Walking along to the north side of the terrace wall you arrive at **Ⓕ** the **Fountains**. Fed by both sulphurous and iron-rich springs, these were revered for the supposed healing properties of the water. The later Romans debased the atmosphere by building **G** the **Latrines** nearby (no doubt the steady tinkle of water dribbling into the sacred pool prompted too many to go in search of a sacred tree or two).

Returning back along the terrace you come to **O** the **Second Staircase**. Running up to the Middle Terrace via 30 steps it brings you on to the real heart of the sanctuary; for directly in front of you is **I** the **Great Altar of Asklepios** (4 C. BC), the oldest building of the Asklepieion. Now reduced to its foundations, it was similar (albeit on a smaller scale) to the Great Altar at Pergamon, with a central stairway running up to the winged base. The base was also roofed, and one of the ornate roof coffers lies on the edge of the foundations. To the north lies the oldest temple in the sanctuary: **J** the **Asklepios Small Temple.** Dating from the 4 C. BC, it was built in the Ionic style (two of the columns have been restored) and functioned as the sanctuary treasury after it was replaced as the main shrine on the site. In this capacity it housed a series of wooden panel paintings by Apelles. One — the Aphrodite Anadyomene — was widely regarded as a masterpiece of ancient art. It was carried off to Rome by the Emperor Augustus. On the Lower Terrace side are the bases for lost votive statues, while tucked away on the Upper Terrace side is a Roman building on Greek foundations **K**, believed to have been the **Priest's Quarters**.

Opposite the Priest's Quarters are the semi-circular foundations of **L** the **Exedra / Public Platform**. An odd building, with no clear function, suggestions as to its purpose have ranged from a public bench to an assembly point for priests or doctors. The terrace wall behind it has several more statue niches. To the east, the Romans in-filled the terrace by building **M** an irregularly orientated **Temple of Apollo**; now the most visible of all the buildings on the site thanks to the seven fake columns erected by the Italians to give you something to look at. Two of them contain fluted fragments of the original drums.

To the south, now little visible and partly overgrown with trees, are the foundations of **N**, usually known as the **Lesche** or **Conference Hall** — though the precise function of the building remains unclear.

Given the snake cult associated with the god Asklepios, it is somewhat surprising that the Asklepieion does not appear to have possessed a snake house (its counterpart at Epidavros had a magnificent Tholos built for this purpose); so perhaps this was it. Snake rooms were common at medical shrines, for these lovely little critters were deemed to have healing powers — given the numbers of lame men who suddenly acquired the ability to run very fast when faced with one (to say nothing of the numerous compulsive stammerers suddenly able to say 'Asklepieion' three times in as many seconds at the first time of asking).

Behind the buildings on the Middle Terrace is **O**; the first stage of the double **Upper Terrace Wall**. In fact, the Middle Terrace can be divided into two (hence the four terraces), but as the upper part of the Terrace is too small to contain buildings, it is viewed as merely a half-way point up **P** the **Monumental Staircase**. This consists of two closely positioned flights that rise in 60 steps to the **Upper Terrace** and its superb views over both the site and Kos Town.

Dominating the centre of the Upper Terrace is **Q** the **Large Temple of Asklepios**. Built in the 2 C. BC, this was the main temple on the site to the god. Doric in style, it was an irregularly shaped 6 x 11 columned building, notable for having the lowest of its three steps made of black marble. Today only the foundations and part of the interior floor survive. Around the side and back perimeter of the terrace ran **R** the **Galleries**, forming an peristyle backdrop to the temple. At some later date the side galleries were extended to provide, what are thought to have been **S** Patients' Rooms.

From the back of the terrace a path winds into **T** the **Sacred Wood** — a delightful, shady canopy of pine trees that surrounds the site — emerging a hundred metres later in a small grove adorned with the remains of a tiny temple of unknown attribution. Returning to the main terrace, another path runs to the southern end and joins the main path running down the south side of the site. This takes you past a disused museum and the back of the **Large Roman Baths**. Dating from the 1 C. AD, this is a late, but major structure, again boasting hypocaust floor pillars. The walls have been extensively repaired (though one of the front rooms — at **U** — retains some original painted plaster). From here the path returns past the small bathhouse to the site entrance.

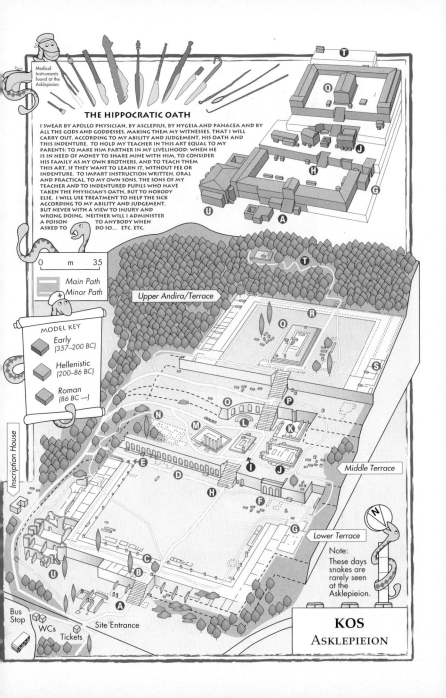

Medical Instruments found at the Asklepieion

THE HIPPOCRATIC OATH

I SWEAR BY APOLLO PHYSICIAN, BY ASCLEPIUS, BY HYGEIA AND PANACEA AND BY ALL THE GODS AND GODDESSES, MAKING THEM MY WITNESSES, THAT I WILL CARRY OUT, ACCORDING TO MY ABILITY AND JUDGEMENT, HIS OATH AND THIS INDENTURE. TO HOLD MY TEACHER IN THIS ART EQUAL TO MY PARENTS: TO MAKE HIM PARTNER IN MY LIVELIHOOD: WHEN HE IS IN NEED OF MONEY TO SHARE MINE WITH HIM, TO CONSIDER HIS FAMILY AS MY OWN BROTHERS, AND TO TEACH THEM THIS ART, IF THEY WANT TO LEARN IT, WITHOUT FEE OR INDENTURE. TO IMPART INSTRUCTION WRITTEN, ORAL AND PRACTICAL, TO MY OWN SONS, THE SONS OF MY TEACHER AND TO INDENTURED PUPILS WHO HAVE TAKEN THE PHYSICIAN'S OATH, BUT TO NOBODY ELSE. I WILL USE TREATMENT TO HELP THE SICK ACCORDING TO MY ABILITY AND JUDGEMENT, BUT NEVER WITH A VIEW TO INJURY AND WRONG DOING. NEITHER WILL I ADMINISTER A POISON TO ANYBODY WHEN ASKED TO DO SO… ETC. ETC.

0   m   35

━━━ Main Path
┅┅┅ Minor Path

Upper Andira/Terrace

MODEL KEY

◆ Early (357–200 BC)

◆ Hellenistic (200–86 BC)

◆ Roman (86 BC —)

Inscription House

Middle Terrace

Lower Terrace

Note: These days snakes are rarely seen at the Asklepieion.

N

Bus Stop

WCs

Tickets

Site Entrance

KOS

ASKLEPIEION

Asklepieion:
View from the
Upper Terrace

Statue Niches in the
Middle Terrace Wall

KOS
Kos Town:
Main Square Mosque

Old Harbour
Waterfront

Chora & Monastery of
Saint John the Theologian

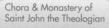

View of Chora
& the Ferry Quay

PATMOS

Greece is a great
place for girls who
break up with their
boyfriends — there
are bronzed hunks
to be had on every
island waterfront ...

SYMI
The C/F *Nissos Kalimnos*
Docks at Gialos Port

Sponge Diver
Bronze

RHODES
Lindos Acropolis &
Faliraki Shop Sign

EXCHANGE
RENT HERE
FANS WHEEL CHAIRS
WALKING STICKS
CRUTCHES

KASTELORIZO
Megisti at Dawn
(with mainland Turkey in the
background)

LEROS
Windmill at
Agia Marina

Dodecanese

EVENING ARGOS
WELL-WISHERS
FLOOD
AEGEAN
TOURISTS BLAMED
FOR LOSS OF AT
GREEK ISLANDS !

DELPHI ORACLE
LATEST
Glub, glub, glub,
glub... glub, glub,
glub...

NISSIROS
Town Well

Leros

ΛΕΡΟΣ; 53 km²; pop. 8,200.

CODE ☎ 0247
PORT POLICE ☎ 23256
POLICE ☎ 22222
HOSPITAL ☎ 23251

Leros is a real oddity among the Greek islands. Conveniently placed between the popular islands of Patmos and Kos, it is sufficiently attractive to deserve its fair share of the crowds — even despite its lack of sights — and yet, although it is well served by ferries, the island remains stubbornly off the tourist trail. There is, of course, a reason and that is its rather unsavoury reputation. This is so bad that leaflets issued to tourists by the Municipality of Leros are, unusually, forced to acknowledge the problem thus:

'In 1958 the Community of Psychopaths was established at Leros, which is still here today, under the name of 'State Therapeutical Hospital of Leros'. Stemming from that, by mistake or sometimes in purpose, an infamous picture of Leros has been promoted, which in no way can identify with the island and its people. Since 1989 various press reports in Greek and foreign press presented in excess the negative sides of such an establishment'.

In short, a past Greek government came up with the idea of conveniently placing all lunatics and severely mentally handicapped adults in one location — Leros. The media reports in question were humiliating accounts, widely publicized across Europe, that patients in the hospital were being kept in concentration camplike conditions. Further damage was done when it was revealed a year or so later that the improvement in those conditions promised by the authorities had not materialized. Happily, thanks to international pressure, things have now improved, though the legacy of this episode lives on in the lack of visitors. Greek tourists tend to avoid the island anyway (its name has become a byword in Greece

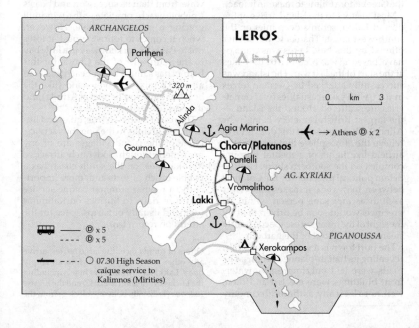

carrying much the same resonances that 'Bedlam' has acquired in English). In many ways this is unfortunate, because Leros has a fair bit going for it in a downbeat sort of way, and you are likely to find that the islanders are both welcoming and almost pathetically grateful that you are mad enough to have paid them a visit (Note: take care not to look *too* mad).

Its reputation not withstanding, Leros is not by any means a typical Greek island. Superficially, it is not dissimilar to Patmos; being small and hilly, with a deeply indented coastline offering a number of sheltered bays complete with beaches. However, the years of Italian rule between the world wars have left a greater mark than on any other islands in the chain, and it is fair to say that Leros still retains the atmosphere of an Italian island. This is largely because the crumbling plastered 1930s buildings, the harbour works and military roads (lined with plane trees) are Italian built, with the tiny nucleus of the Greek chora failing to make an impact.

Most visitors to the island arrive at the port of **Lakki**, set in a deep inlet on the south-west coast. Thanks to the shelter offered by this bay, Leros was a major naval base and was occupied by the Allies at the start of the last war. The island was successfully attacked by German forces in 1943, with 5,000 casualties (war cemeteries are scattered around the island — the largest British cemetery being near Alinda). The memory of this does little to relieve the atmosphere that is set by the airfield-like lights of a mental hospital complex on the southern shore. Used to detain political prisoners by the Colonels between 1967–1974, it makes the perfect asylum as any sane person within its precincts would soon be driven mad by the sight of the means of escape constantly steaming in and out of the harbour.

The port town is a very artificial affair, revealing its Italian-planned origins. The roads were laid out, impressive waterfront buildings were erected and then, well, not a lot really, as the local economy

has never grown enough to allow a town to fully develop in the space provided. The result is a mix of odd buildings and clumps of trees that is a bit ghost-townish. On the plus side, accommodation is easily found here (even if the views are not very appealing), along with all the essential services, and in summer the promenade has been known to play host to a travelling circus, complete with little top.

The bus service on Leros is so poor that taxis thrive along the walkable 3 km road to the chora at **Platanos**. Slightly more Greek in appearance, it lies under the protecting walls of the imposing Kastro, but is somewhat spoilt by indifferent buildings, a rather dingy atmosphere and the busy road running through the centre. All the main services lie on the street which runs down to the little port of **Agia Marina.** The 19 c. main port, Agia Marina is now rather neglected (though it is still used by hydrofoils and by the island's excursion boats). It has a more attractive waterfront than its successor, and boasts a pebble beach complete with a windmill gracing a submerged mole. However, when it comes to tourist appeal, it loses out to **Pantelli**, tucked away in a little bay to the south-east of the Chora, for this hamlet has a much better beach that is an attractive mix of pebbly sand (like the beach at the resort hamlet of **Alinda**) and the odd fishing boat besides.

The rest of Leros is fertile, quiet and little visited, thanks to the poor bus service. None of the island villages are of any great merit, though moderately attractive **Xerokampos**, on the south coast, has a pebble beach of sorts and, more importantly, a regular summer caïque service that runs daily to Mirities on Kalimnos (demand usually outstrips space for the afternoon return trip).

⊨

Offers of rooms meet the large ferries; arrive any other way and you will find an empty quay. **Lakki** has a number of hotels including the D-class *Miramare* (☎ 22043) and the E-class *Katerina* (☎ 22460), both one block in from the

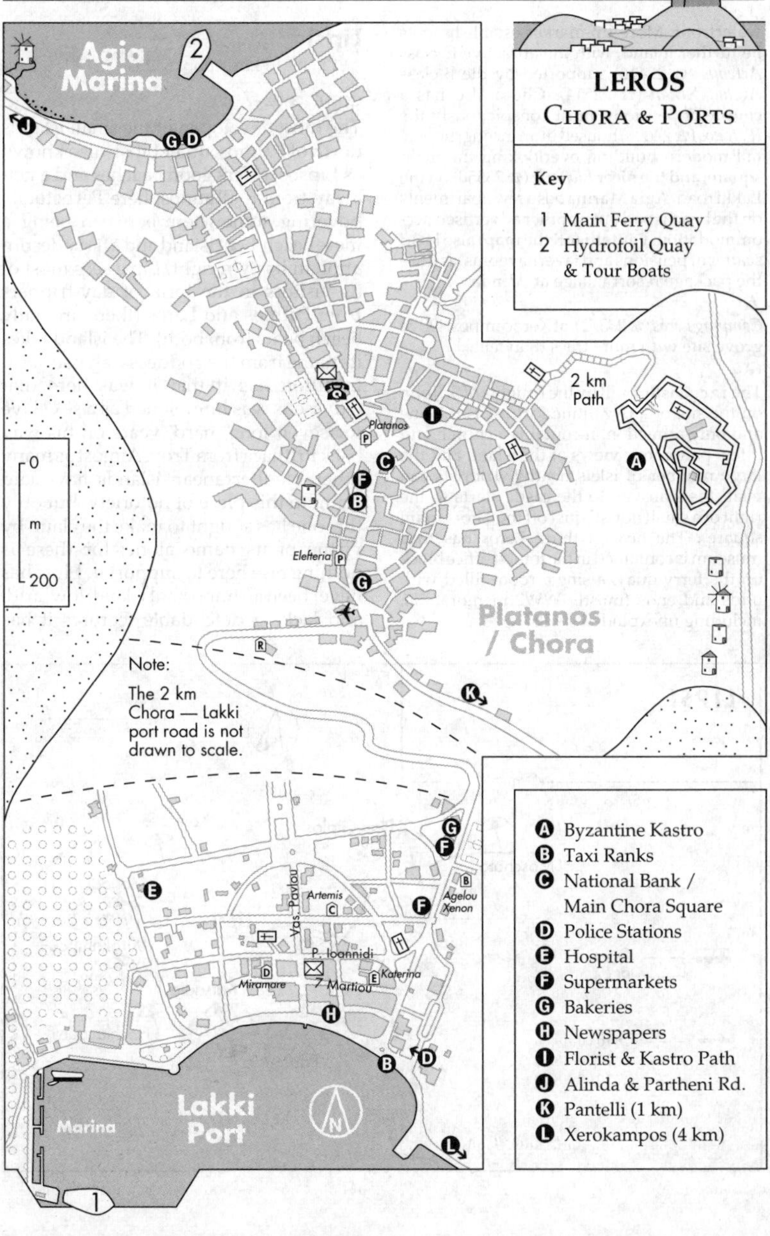

Agia Marina

2

J

G **D**

LEROS
CHORA & PORTS

Key

1 Main Ferry Quay
2 Hydrofoil Quay
   & Tour Boats

2 km Path

I

Platanos **P**

C

F

B

A

Elefteria **P**

G

Platanos / Chora

R

Note:

The 2 km Chora — Lakki port road is not drawn to scale.

K

G
F

E

Yas. Pavlou

Artemis **C**

B
Agelou Xenon

F

P. Ioannidi

D
Miramare

7 Martiou

Katerina

H

Marina

B **D**

Lakki Port

N

1

L

A Byzantine Kastro
B Taxi Ranks
C National Bank / Main Chora Square
D Police Stations
E Hospital
F Supermarkets
G Bakeries
H Newspapers
I Florist & Kastro Path
J Alinda & Partheni Rd.
K Pantelli (1 km)
L Xerokampos (4 km)

waterfront. More up-market establishments lie further inland, with the attractive C-class *Artemis* (☎ 22416) supported by the B-class *Agelou Xenon* (☎ 22514). **Chora** also has a couple of pensions: most conspicuously the *Platanos* (☎ 22608) housed in an incongruously tall modern building overlooking the main square, and the nicer *Elefteria* (☎ 23550) on the Lakki road. **Agia Marina** has a few apartments on the beach road but no other advertised accommodation. **Pantelli** (off the map) also has a scatter of pensions and taverna rooms, as does the package resort village at **Alinda**.

Λ

Camping Leros (☎ 23372): at Xerocampos. Olive grove site with more trees than tents.

∞

The 12 c. **Castle** built by the Knights of St. John on the site of a Byzantine fortress is the one and only attraction. It contains a church and offers panoramic views of the island and the large number of islets nearby. Tourists can visit (the stairway to the castle starts to the right of a small florist's just off the Chora main square). The nearest thing Leros has to a museum is contained in the tourist office block on the ferry quay: a single room filled with odds and ends (mostly WW2 memorabilia, including unexploded shells).

Lipsi

ΛΕΙΨΟΙ; 16 km²; pop. 650.

CODE ☎ 0247

The most developed of the small islands north of Patmos, quiet Lipsi (also known as Lipsos) offers good beaches and a getaway-from-it-all atmosphere. Perpetually hovering somewhere between being a mere beach-boat island and a ferry destination in its own right, Lipsi sees most of its visitors in the form of day-trippers from Patmos and Leros (there are daily beach boats from both). The island takes its name from the goddess Calypso: local tradition has it that it was here that Odysseus was imprisoned as a sex slave for seven long, hard, years on his way back to Ithaca from Troy. Almost as many other Mediterranean islands have laid claim to this piece of notoriety, but only this one has sought to make the claim by virtue of its name alone; for there is nothing else here to support it. Lipsi has never been an important island; low, arid, and lacking defendable features it has

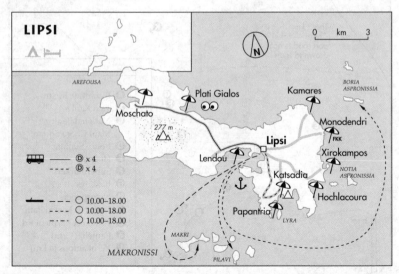

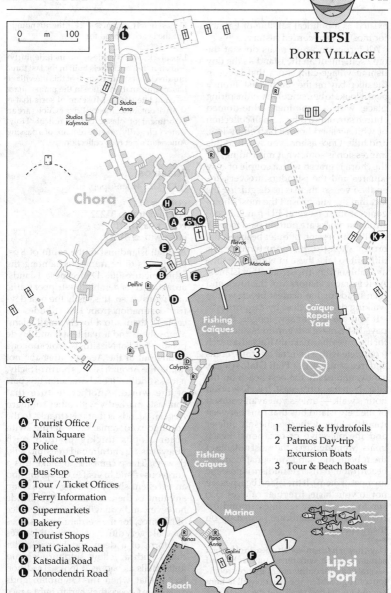

LIPSI
PORT VILLAGE

0   m   100

Studios Anna

Studios Kalymnos

Chora

Flisvos

Manoles

Delfini

Fishing Caïques

Caïque Repair Yard

Calypso

Fishing Caïques

Marina

Renas

Pano Anna

Galini

Beach

Lipsi Port

1 Ferries & Hydrofoils
2 Patmos Day-trip
   Excursion Boats
3 Tour & Beach Boats

Key

- **A** Tourist Office / Main Square
- **B** Police
- **C** Medical Centre
- **D** Bus Stop
- **E** Tour / Ticket Offices
- **F** Ferry Information
- **G** Supermarkets
- **H** Bakery
- **I** Tourist Shops
- **J** Plati Gialos Road
- **K** Katsadia Road
- **L** Monodendri Road

existed as a political satellite of Patmos for most of its recorded history.

All ferries and tour boats dock at the only settlement on the island — the tiny fishing village-cum-chora that is set in the deep bay on the south coast. From a boat it looks to be a singularly uninspiring place; with a prominent blue-domed church surrounded by a small collection of whitewashed houses backed by low, arid hills. Once ashore you will find this impression is somewhat misleading, for the chora is graced with a couple of cosy squares and the islanders are very friendly. Even so, there is no disguising the fact that the village isn't the most photogenic around (several EU-funded construction works are putting paid to this): it is the succession of quiet beaches that bring visitors to Lipsi. Unfortunately, it is difficult to take these in within the time available on day-trips from other islands. As it is, most visitors 'do' the town and then head for the nearest beach within walking distance (close by the port).

If you are able to stay longer, then it pays to be more adventurous and head for the coves that make up **Katsadia** beach (complete with a taverna offering rooms and free camping), or **Plati Gialos** (wide, sandy, and easily the best beach on the island) on the north coast. It is close on an hour's walk — unless you avail yourself of the new island bus that runs between it and the town. Other beaches are quieter and the objective of occasional beach boats. **Monodendri** is the most notable of them, being the island's designated nudist beach (though discreet nudism is possible on most of them). If the island beaches are not to your taste, irregular caïques also run to several tiny satellites around the coast of Lipsi (details are posted up on the caïque quay).

🛏

Day-tripper tourism has left a dearth of budget accommodation, with the result that beyond several quayside outfits offering pricey rooms (out of High Season you will do well to hunt around for the best deal) and the waterfront D-class hotel *Calypso* (☎ 41242), there is nought but the beach to head for.

∞

Lipsi lacks sights (unless you include thirty-odd churches or chapels built in the last three hundred years), but in spite of this the village has an information office in the main square — complete with a **Museum** of sorts that is short of notable contents. Prize exhibits are an assortment of plastic bottles full of 'Holy' water (allegedly) and the remains of a passing American's pet rock collection.

Nissiros

ΝΙΣΥΡΟΣ; 41 km²; pop. 1,100.

CODE ☎ 0242
PORT POLICE ☎ 31222
POLICE ☎ 31201
FIRST AID ☎ 31217

A small island just to the south of Kos, Nissiros is to be numbered among the more picturesque Dodecanese islands; attracting considerable day-tripper traffic and worthily so. It is easily the best day-trip destination from Kos (Rhodes excepted); thanks to a lovely small island atmosphere and a real Jekyll and Hyde personality. For Nissiros is a volcano cone jutting out of the Aegean. In shape not unlike the Aeolian islands north of Sicily, it looks oddly out of character in this part of the world. Another feature that contrasts markedly with other southern Aegean islands is that it is (thanks to the volcanic soil) remarkably fertile, with outer slopes thickly planted with vineyards, fig and almond trees and wild flowers. These combine to make this a gorgeous island to visit in the spring and an excellent shady walking destination any time of the year. Climb the hill-side however, and you will see the other face of Nissiros, for the verdant outer slopes conceal a very different interior: this takes the form of a deep and barren crater caked with a yellow sulphurous mud that smells as bad as it looks. Tradition has it that when the Olympian gods arrived in Greece they had to fight a race of giants for control of the earth. Nissiros was formed as the result of a battle between Poseidon and the giant Porphyris; the god speared a lump of Kos and dumped it on the giant, burying him alive — hence the volcano's rumblings as he periodically tries in vain to break free.

Nissiros has one town of note — the port of **Mandraki** — and a number of minor villages; including two (Emborio and Nikia) on the crater rim. Mandraki is an attractive centre that to date has managed to cater to the tourist hordes without losing its whitewashed narrow street charm. Not very large, the port side of town is just a main street ribboning along the northern shore. The promenade, however, is not the centre of Mandraki life: the town almost has its back to it, preferring instead to huddle in the valley between the volcano and the headland that plays host to the small Venetian castle that stands guard over the town.

Just about large enough for the casual visitor to get lost in for a hundred metres or so, Mandraki invites relaxed exploration. In addition to the castle and shoreline, the town has some lovely unspoilt streets and small squares (the main square — Ilikiomeni — lying on the inland edge of town). The atmosphere reflects the gentle, unhurried island village life, and even if the islanders no longer draw water from the picturesque town well that stands in Pilaoulli square, Mandraki offers a blissful contrast with the brash commercial bustle of Kos and Rhodes.

This is not to say that Nissiros is slow to sell itself. Thanks to the volcano, the quayside is lined with tour agents selling trips to the crater and there is even a island-cum-volcano model for good measure. Tour buses run from quay to the crater floor and the crater rim villages. Island buses also start from here, but go no further than the crater rim, as well as to other inhabited hot spots around the island (there are hot water springs to be found outside **Nikia** and also at **Loutra**;

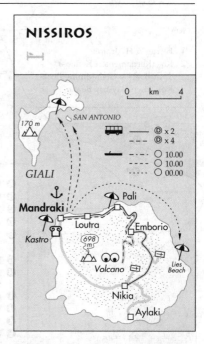

now the home of a rather run down spa).

Both the crater rim villages of **Nikia** and **Emborio** have viewing points along with steps/paths down into it. Nikia is the better of the two, both as a viewing station and in the degree of inhabitation. Thanks to the building of a number of holiday homes it is quietly thriving, while Emborio is now half abandoned (the population having retreated to the small beach village of Pali).

Like Santorini, Nissiros has black or red sand beaches, but in the main these are poor affairs (people generally come to Nissiros to have a day off from burning on a beach), the best being **White beach** near **Pali** (the only white sand beach of any size on the island), followed by **Lies** beach (made up of tiny grey pebbles). The nearest beach to Mandraki (**Koklaki**) lies below the cliffs on the west side of

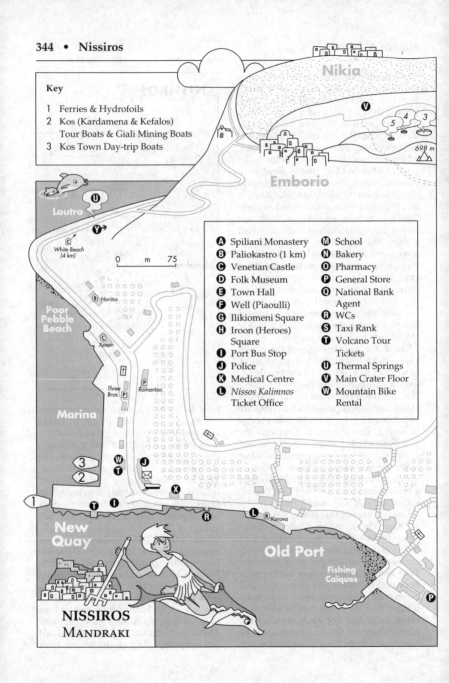

Key

1 Ferries & Hydrofoils
2 Kos (Kardamena & Kefalos)
   Tour Boats & Giali Mining Boats
3 Kos Town Day-trip Boats

A Spiliani Monastery
B Paliokastro (1 km)
C Venetian Castle
D Folk Museum
E Town Hall
F Well (Piaoulli)
G Ilikiomeni Square
H Iroon (Heroes) Square
I Port Bus Stop
J Police
K Medical Centre
L *Nissos Kalimnos* Ticket Office
M School
N Bakery
O Pharmacy
P General Store
Q National Bank Agent
R WCs
S Taxi Rank
T Volcano Tour Tickets
U Thermal Springs
V Main Crater Floor
W Mountain Bike Rental

Nikia

698 m

Emborio

Loutro

White Beach (4 km)

0   m   75

Poor Pebble Beach

Haritos

Xenon

Three Bros.

Romantzo

Marina

Karava

New Quay

Old Port

Fishing Caïques

NISSIROS
MANDRAKI

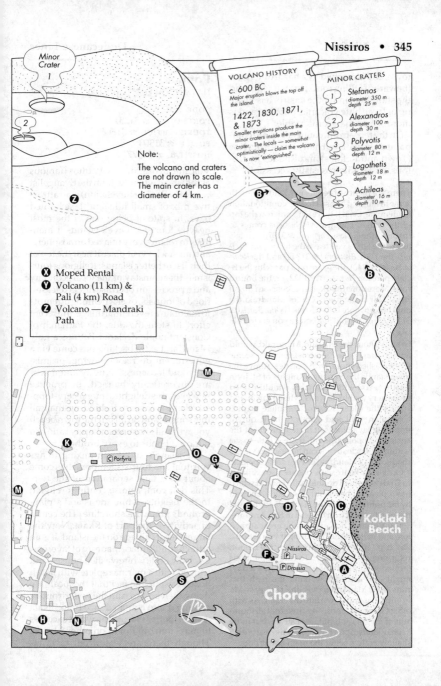

VOLCANO HISTORY

c. 600 BC
Major eruption blows the top off the island.

1422, 1830, 1871, & 1873
Smaller eruptions produce the minor craters inside the main crater. The locals — somewhat optimistically — claim the volcano is now 'extinguished'.

Note:

The volcano and craters are not drawn to scale. The main crater has a diameter of 4 km.

MINOR CRATERS

1 *Stefanos*
diameter 350 m
depth 25 m

2 *Alexandros*
diameter 100 m
depth 30 m

3 *Polyvotis*
diameter 80 m
depth 12 m

4 *Logothetis*
diameter 18 m
depth 12 m

5 *Achileas*
diameter 16 m
depth 10 m

X Moped Rental
Y Volcano (11 km) &
Pali (4 km) Road
Z Volcano — Mandraki
Path

Minor Crater 1

Porfyris

Koklaki Beach

Nissiros

Drossia

Chora

town, and is reached by a hazardous path (beware of falling rocks) that runs around the shoreline under the kastro. It is made up of large blue volcanic 'pebbles' and is more scenic than comfortable.

On the ferry front, connections are comparatively poor, but daily boats from Kos (Town and Kefalos) and Rhodes hydrofoils, make Nissiros easily accessible.

There are plenty of rooms in Mandraki, with some in Pali and Nikia. Hotel accommodation is adequate, even if there isn't much at the top of the range. The nearest Nissiros comes to luxury is the C-class *Porfyris* (☎ 31376). Hotels just to the left as you leave the ferry quay include the *Three Brothers* (☎ 31344) and the *Romantzo* (☎ 31340), these are on a par with the B-class pension *Haritos* (☎ 31322) on the Loutro road. More down market is the pension *Drossia* (☎ 31328) in the town. Out of Mandraki the only hotel of note is the C-class *White Beach* (☎ 31497/8) on the hill just before you get to Pali.

Even without the volcano **Mandraki** would attract tourists to Nissiros; being a scenic whitewashed chora with 2 castles. Above the town stands the Venetian Knights of St. John **Castle** (1315) which contains a multi-iconed monastery within its walls, while 1 km inland stands the older **Kastro**: complete with a Cyclopian wall and gateway built out of imposing lava blocks, it marks the site of the ancient acropolis (though there is little to see within the enclosure. It can be reached via the road south of Mandraki or via a cliff-top track.

Occasional boat excursions are also available to **Giali** — a small double-hilled island which has a pleasant beach surprisingly unmarred by the pumice quarrying in the hillside behind it— and to a beach on the islet of **San Antonio**. The **Volcano**, however, is the great attraction, and better done first thing if you are on a day trip. Tour buses run to the crater floor, returning 2–3 hours later. The more ambitious (armed with plenty of water and half a day) might also consider walking the path that runs from Mandraki, over the rim, past Mt. Profitis Ilias and down into the crater. As with other Greek volcanos, Nissiros is not all fountains of magma and pillars of steam, but more a lunar landscapey hole — in this case with 5 shallow craters set in the main crater floor.

Patmos

ΠΑΤΜΟΣ; 34 km²; pop. 2,600.

CODE ☎ 0247
PORT POLICE ☎ 31231
TOURIST OFFICE ☎ 31666
POLICE ☎ 31303
HOSPITAL ☎ 31577

Volcanic in origin, cosy Patmos (famous as the island where St. John the Evangelist wrote the Book of Revelation) is an attractive mix of small hills and beach-lined bays. In spite of being one of the most heavily touristed Greek islands it manages to retain a very relaxed atmosphere, and most who visit place it near the top of their list of better islands. Religious tourism is the mainstay of the local economy and a procession of cruise liners release a flood of tourists, overwhelming attempts to maintain a reverential image. In a recent effort to stem the tide, the Patriarch of Constantinople declared Patmos a holy island, and extra backing has come via a government decree outlawing 'promiscuity and looseness'. Nudity and discos are theoretically banned. In practice however, this delightful monastery-topped island is far less forbidding than all this sounds and on all but the town beach you will still encounter a happy ratio of a hundred boobs to every brother.

The island's success in mixing things spiritual and tourists temporal has come about by a tacit separation of the two. This deft compromise confines religion to the heights, while the island's playgrounds grace the shoreline. The centre of activity is the port of **Skala**. Now the largest resort village on the island, it is an attractive little place made up of tavernas, Cycladic-style whitewashed houses, and fringed with a marina replete with beach boats. Despite the fact that the locals are doing their best to ruin the waterfront by turning it into a moped race track, Skala is still a long way from the worst excesses of mass tourism found on other islands. Though there are waterfront tavernas aplenty, there are no large hotels and Tinos-tacky souvenir shops here. The only obvious concession to the numbers visiting is the inordinately large quay built to accommodate the cruise liners whose tear-and-bunting departures enliven evening promenades along the waterfront. Most only stay long enough for passengers to be whisked by bus up to impressive looking Chora for a quickie tour of the monastery.

Skala is also home for most of the hotels on the island. Fortunately, these do not mar the town, as they are judiciously spread around, and are all low-lying. The second bay behind the north headland (graced with a church and an early Christian roadside tomb) is home to the island's noisy oil-powered electricity generator, the town graveyard (disconcertingly illuminated with candles during the evenings) and a number of hotels. A

large yachting marina has also recently been constructed in the adjacent bay.

Chora is a very insipid sort of place — lacking shops, rooms for rent and any 'lived-in' sense at all. A maze of white-washed mansion-style buildings skirting the high, dark, buttressed walls of the monastery, it is too quiet for its own good, and filled with churches, has become little more than a glorified outer precinct to the monastery itself. Many of the larger houses (most dating from the 18 c.) have been bought up as holiday homes by wealthy outsiders and are closed up for most of the year. Only the row of windmills crowning the ridge at the edge of the town remind one that the chora once had a less sanitized role. The monastery aside, the best reason to visit Chora is the excuse it gives to walk the old 3 km mule path that runs up from the port (not that you really need one, for the

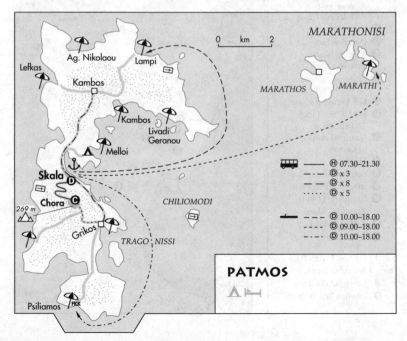

PATMOS

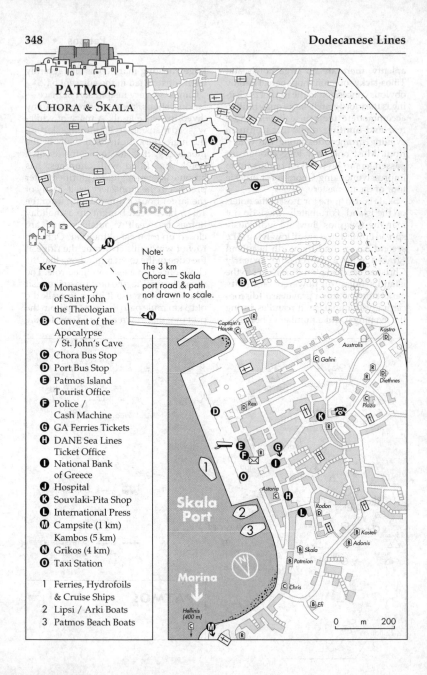

PATMOS
Chora & Skala

Chora

Note:
The 3 km
Chora — Skala
port road & path
not drawn to scale.

Key

- **Ⓐ** Monastery of Saint John the Theologian
- **Ⓑ** Convent of the Apocalypse / St. John's Cave
- **Ⓒ** Chora Bus Stop
- **Ⓓ** Port Bus Stop
- **Ⓔ** Patmos Island Tourist Office
- **Ⓕ** Police / Cash Machine
- **Ⓖ** GA Ferries Tickets
- **Ⓗ** DANE Sea Lines Ticket Office
- **Ⓘ** National Bank of Greece
- **Ⓙ** Hospital
- **Ⓚ** Souvlaki-Pita Shop
- **Ⓛ** International Press
- **Ⓜ** Campsite (1 km) Kambos (5 km)
- **Ⓝ** Grikos (4 km)
- **Ⓞ** Taxi Station

1 Ferries, Hydrofoils & Cruise Ships
2 Lipsi / Arki Boats
3 Patmos Beach Boats

Captain's House

Australis

Kastro

Galini

Diethnes

Plaza

Rex

Astoria

Rodon

Skala Port

Kasteli

Skala

Adonis

Patmion

Marina

Chris

Hellinis (400 m)

Efi

0   m   200

journey is a very attractive one). An easy walk (though most people prefer to bus up and then return on foot), it is an excellent way of taking in the island.

The rest of the island has much more going for it; being a lovely mix of bays and beaches tucked away within the folds of an intricate coastline. Beach caïques run from Skala to the best of these — **Psiliamos** to the south and the multi-coloured pebble **Lampi** on the north coast, as well as to the adjacent beach islands of Lipsi and Arki (most 'Arki' taxi boats in fact go to a beach and taverna on the adjacent islet of Marathi). The only other settlements of any size at all are at **Kambos** — which is a pleasantly unspoilt hill village complete with a pebble beach — and **Grikos**; billed as a 'resort' village (though it has fewer hotels than Skala).

In addition to the beach boats, Patmos has a good bus service running between the main centres. Photocopied timetables for these and all regular ferries are available from the information office located in the quayside post office building.

⊨

Plenty of rooms available, thanks to the island's pilgrim status. Offering hordes meet all boats. The island tourist office in the block behind the ferry quay also has lists of hotels. The majority are to be found in Skala, which is also the name of the premier hostelry — the B-class hotel *Skala* (☎ 31343). At the north end of the port, it is close by other up-market establishments including the waterfront *Patmion* (☎ 31313). Best of the mid-range hotels are the C-class *Chris* (☎ 31001) and *Hellinis* (☎ 31275). Cheaper hotels are also plentiful. Just off the quay is the D-class *Rex* (☎ 31242), and behind the town are the *Kasto* (☎ 31554), the *Plaza* (☎ 31217), and cheaper *Rodon* (☎ 31371).

A

Camping Stefanos alias *Patmos Flowers Camping* (☎ 31821) lies 2 km away; around the harbour and over the hill at Melloi. A bambooed site — one of the best in Greece, but suffers from the island's water shortages in High Season. The new mini-bus only ventures to the port in High Season and usually has to make two journeys to the site when large ferries come in.

👓

The main attraction is impossible to miss: the castle-like **Monastery of St. John the Theologian** standing majestically atop Mt. Kastelli. Founded in 1088, it started out as merely a hilltop monastery, but repeated pirate raids prompted its fortification. This process continued when the island fell under the rule of the Dukes of Naxos (from the 13 c. to the 16 c.) who allowed it an unusual degree of autonomy, so that when the Turks finally took control of the Aegean Patmos — like Mt. Athos — was able to retain semi-independent status. The present castle layout is relatively recent: a damaging earthquake in 1956 that brought down a tower and several walls prompted its partial rebuilding. Open daily, precise times vary, but it is always open ①–⑥ 08.30–13.00, ⑦ 10.00–12.00. Entry is free: though you have take care to be modestly dressed (no shorts or bikini tops). Surly monks do wonders for the atmosphere — successfully repelling all boarders since the monastery's foundation. As a result it is a treasure house containing over 890 early Christian manuscripts (notably an early 6 c. version of St. Mark's Gospel), a large collection of icons, and the most important display of monastic artifacts in Greece. Built on the site of the ancient acropolis, fragments of a temple of Artemis also litter the building.

Halfway up the Skala—Chora road and mule-track you will come to the second major monastery on Patmos: the **Convent of the Apocalypse,** (opening times as above) built over the cave where St. John saw and dictated (to his disciple Prochoros) all. Banished to the island in 95 AD by the Roman Emperor Domitian for winding up the population of Ephesus, he spent 15 years in a cave writing the Book of Revelations. Quite why he was disposed to conjure up such happy notions as 'And I looked, and behold a pale horse: and his name that sat on him was Death, and Hell followed with him' remains a mystery; modern Patmos encourages far happier thoughts, and the island in St. John's day (complete with a picturesque temple in place of the forbidding monastery) had even more going for it. Perhaps the excellent hole-in-the-wall souvlaki-pita shop on the main street leading to the OTE had yet to set up in business? Finally, when you have had enough of Patmos, boat trips offer a taste of freedom. Daily boats head from the harbour for Lipsi while regular hydrofoils visit Samos.

Rhodes

ΡΟΔΟΣ; 1398 km²; pop. 68,000.

CODES: (TOWN) ☎ 0241
      (REST OF THE ISLAND) ☎ 0244
PORT POLICE ☎ 28888
NTOG / EOT OFFICE ☎ 23255
TOURIST POLICE ☎ 27423
POLICE ☎ 7423
HOSPITAL ☎ 22222

The largest island in the Dodecanese, Rhodes (known locally as 'Rodos'), is one of the most touristed islands in Greece thanks to an attractive mix of good beaches, plenty of sightseeing, an unspoilt interior, and a sound reputation for being the sunniest island in the Aegean (it sees over 300 days of sunshine a year). This is probably just as well, for myth has it that when Zeus divided up the world he forgot to allocate a portion to the sun god, Helios, who promptly took for his own the fertile island of Rhodes that was just then emerging from the sea.

Even allowing for repeated earthquakes and invasions, Rhodes has been pretty much sunny side up ever since, for the island has something for just about everyone. The main tourist strip runs down the east coast: a necklace of sand beaches hung between the two sightseeing jewels of Rhodes City and the acropolis-topped town of Lindos. Inevitably there is a down side to this: with package-tourists descending all year round, Rhodes also comes more expensive than many other Greek islands, and the island clearly doesn't feel the need to cater for independent travellers in great numbers. On the plus side, the heavy tourist presence has encouraged a proliferation of pleasure boat services augmenting the ferries that call — thanks to the island's role as a terminus on the domestic ferry network and point of call for international services to Cyprus, Israel and Egypt. The combination makes Rhodes an attractive point from which to start an island-hopping holiday.

Sightseeing fans will find rich pickings on Rhodes thanks to the island's colourful history. For most of the classical period Rhodes was — like most others — a bit player in the wider struggle between Greek and Persian and Athens and Sparta, swapping sides whenever it was deemed politic to do so. She first left her fingermarks on the pages of history following the death of Alexander the Great when she sided with Ptolemy in the wars between his successors, prompting one of his rivals, Demetrius Poliokretes to lay siege to Rhodes City in 305 BC. The siege failed in spectacular fashion (the townsfolk selling the abandoned siege engines and using the money to build the mighty Colossus). Inspired by the victory and growing success as a trading centre, Rhodes came into its own as a Hellenistic power centre, boasting an artistic school that produced works of the calibre of the famous Winged Victory of Samothrace and gave — according to Strabo — Rhodes City over 2000 statues, and a navy that controlled the Eastern Aegean.

However, Rhodes was eclipsed by the rise of Roman power, paying the price for supporting Julius Caesar (by way of retribution she was captured in 44 BC by Cassius and stripped of her art works), and finally becoming part of the Empire in 70 AD. Further damage followed with regular earthquakes and invasions of Goths (269 AD), Persians (620), Saracens (653), Fourth Crusaders (1204). Stability of a sorts came with the arrival of the crusading Knights of St. John in 1309, who fortified Rhodes City, establishing it as the home of the Knights Hospitallers, and the European front line against the Ottoman Turks. Besieged in 1444 and 1480, Rhodes City finally fell in 1522. Treated comparatively badly by the Turks (who tended to stigmatize islands that had resisted them), Rhodes was occupied by the Italians (most of them architects and archaeologists) between the world wars, finally joining Greece in 1947.

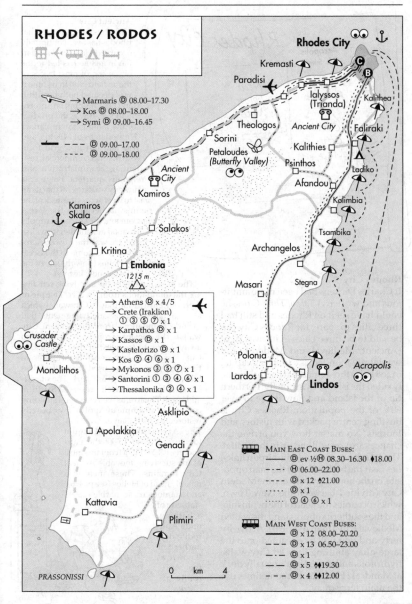

RHODES / RODOS

→ Marmaris Ⓓ 08.00–17.30
→ Kos Ⓓ 08.00–18.00
→ Symi Ⓓ 09.00–16.45

--- Ⓓ 09.00–17.00
--- Ⓓ 09.00–18.00

Rhodes City

Kremasti

Paradisi

Ialyssos
(Trianda)

Kalithea

Theologos

Ancient City

Faliraki

Sorini

Kalithies

Petaloudes
(Butterfly Valley)

Psinthos

Ancient
City

Afandou

Ladiko

Kamiros

Kolimbia

Kamiros
Skala

Salakos

Tsambika

Kritina

Archangelos

Embonia
1215 m

Masari

Stegna

→ Athens Ⓓ x 4/5
→ Crete (Iraklion)
   ① ③ ⑤ ⑦ x 1
→ Karpathos Ⓓ x 1
→ Kassos Ⓓ x 1
→ Kastelorizo Ⓓ x 1
→ Kos ② ④ ⑥ x 1
→ Mykonos ③ ⑤ ⑦ x 1
→ Santorini ① ③ ④ ⑥ x 1
→ Thessalonika ② ④ x 1

Crusader
Castle

Polonia

Acropolis

Monolithos

Lardos

Lindos

Asklipio

MAIN EAST COAST BUSES:
—— Ⓓ ev ½Ⓗ 08.30–16.30 ♦18.00
–·– Ⓗ 06.00–22.00
--- Ⓓ x 12 ♦21.00
···· Ⓓ x 1
···· ② ④ ⑥ x 1

Apolakkia

Genadi

MAIN WEST COAST BUSES:
—— Ⓓ x 12 08.00–20.20
--- Ⓓ 13 06.50–23.00
–·– Ⓓ x 1
—— Ⓓ x 5 ♦♦19.30
--- Ⓓ x 4 ♦♦12.00

Kattavia

Plimiri

0   km   4

PRASSONISSI

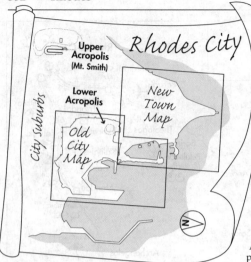

Rhodes City

Upper Acropolis (Mt. Smith)

Lower Acropolis

New Town Map

Old City Map

City suburbs

Ancient City

Unfortunately, the fact that Rhodes has been continually occupied since its foundation in 408 BC has led to the obscuring of most traces of the ancient city. In its time it was deemed both beautiful and notable. Built on a greenfield site, it was the product of the famous town planner Hippodamos of Miletus, and was laid out in a grid form with distinct commercial, residential, administrative and religious quarters. Fragments of the city walls reveal that it ran east to west across the neck of the peninsula between the Great Harbour and the Upper Acropolis (which stood outside the city walls). At its centre was the Lower Acropolis, which was home to the Great Temple of Helios (now the site of the Palace of the Grand Masters).

The most notable of the surviving remains are the foundations from a 3 c. BC **Temple of Aphrodite** just inside the Old City walls (which also contain other assorted fragments that include foundations from the Ancient City walls). The ancient acropolis is also hidden away. Lying to the west of the current Old City, it is also known as Mt. Smith (after an English Admiral who used it as a spyglass hill) and is now laid out as a park. The site offers a shady view of a well-preserved **Stadium** and small **Theatre**, as well as several standing columns of a **Temple of Apollo** (over-heavily restored by its Italian excavators).

The **Archaeological Museum** (open ②–⑦ 08.30–15.00: the entrance fee is 1200 GDR) contains most of the surviving movable Ancient City remains. These include a notable head of Helios (see p. 356), and a famous 1 c. BC marble statuette of a bathing, nude Aphrodite drying her hair (known as the 'Aphrodite of Rhodes').

APHRODITE OF RHODES
1 C. BC

GLUE

Rhodes City

If Charles Dickens had been more ambitious and written *A Tale of Three Cities*, he could have set it on Rhodes and still had three cities to spare; for Rhodes City can be said to be three cities in its own right (Ancient, Medieval and Modern), and was jointly founded as a unifying capital in 408 BC by three cities that had previously ruled the island. Lying on the northern tip of the island and now home to over 60% of the population, Rhodes City is bustling centre packed with history and tourists. No matter how you arrive, the chances are you will end up in the capital. The main bus terminus (with airport links) lies near the bottom left of the map opposite, on the boundary between the Modern City (divided between the New Town, which occupies the head of the peninsula, and the southern suburbs) and the walled Medieval City (map overleaf). Arrive by ferry and you will be decanted onto the large quay abutting the Old City walls; hydrofoils and tourist boats usually dock at Mandraki Harbour, but sometimes use the main ferry quay.

Harbour Windmills

19 c. Clock Tower
(Offers good views
over the Old City)

Marine Gate

Choosing Lunch at an
Old City Taverna

OLD CITY
Ippokratous Square Fountain
& Socratous Street

Rhodes

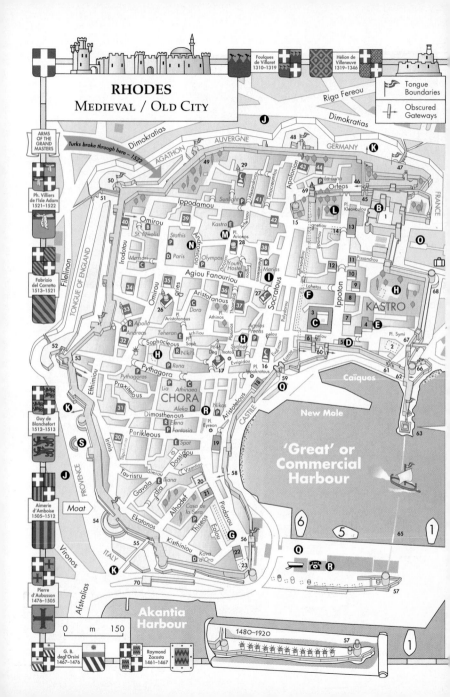

BYZANTINE CHURCHES

30. Agia Ekaterini
31. Agia Triada
32. Aghii Theodori
33. Agia Kyriaki
34. Archangelos Michaii
35. Agios Fanourios
36. Agios Spiridon
37. Archangelos Michaii
38. Agios Konstantinos
39. Agios Nikolaos
40. Agios Athanasios
41. Agia Paraskevi
42. Aghii Apostoli
43. Agios Georgios
44. Agios Marcos

OLD CITY GATES & TOWERS

45. Artillery Gate
46. St. Anthony Gate
47. Amboise Gate
48. St. George Tower
49. Tower of Spain
50. St. Mary / Virgin Tower
51. St. Athanase Gate
52. Koskinou / St. John's Gate
53. Koskinou / St. John's Tower
54. Tower of Italy / Carretto
55. Italy Gate (1924)
56. St. Catherine's / Mill Gate
57. Tower of the Mills / France
58. Port Gate (1924)
59. Marine Gate
60. Arnardo Gate
61. Arsenal Gate
62. St. Paul's Gate
63. Nailac Tower Base
64. Lost Nailac Tower
65. Harbour Chain Line
66. St. Paul's Tower
67. Liberty Gate (1924)
68. St. Peter's Gate
69. Clock Tower
70. Akantia Bastion

Key

Ⓐ City Tourist Office
Ⓑ Grand Masters Palace Museum
Ⓒ Archaeological Mus.
Ⓓ Byzantine Museum & National Bank
Ⓔ Folk Art Museum
Ⓕ Kastro Inner Wall
Ⓖ Ancient City Wall
Ⓗ Classical Excavations
Ⓘ Drinking Fountain
Ⓙ Moatside Park
Ⓚ Moat Access Points
Ⓛ Turkish Library
Ⓜ Turkish Baths
Ⓝ Folk Dancing Theatre
Ⓞ Son-et-lumière
Ⓟ Italian Cathedral
Ⓠ Taxi Stations
Ⓡ Public WCs
Ⓢ Moat Theatre

1 Piraeus Ferries
2 International Ferries
3 Tour Boats
4 Hydrofoils
5 Cruise-ships
6 Turkish Day Boats

Dieudonné de Gozon 1346–1353

Pierre de Corneillon 1354–1355

Roger de Pins 1355–1365

Raymond Béranger 1365–1374

Robert de Juilly 1374–1377

Ferdinand d'Hérédia 1377–1396

Philibert de Nailac 1396–1421

Antoine Fluvian 1421–1437

Jacques de Milly 1454–1461

Jean de Lastic 1437–1454

Makariou

Platia Vas. Georgiou II

Plessa

Pl. Eleftherias

24

Mandraki Harbour

Marina

Akti Boumbouli

25

64

The Colossus of Rhodes (attempting the pose favoured by 15 c. illustrators)

CITY LANDMARKS

1. Palace of the Grand Masters / Temple of Helios Site
2. Temple of Aphrodite
3. Hospital of the Knights
4. Inn of Auvergne
5. 'Our Lady of the Chateau' Church
6. Inn of England
7. Inn of Italy
8. Inn of France
9. 'Palace of Zizim'
10. Chapel of France
11. Inn of Provence
12. Inn of Agathon / Spain
13. Loggia
14. 'St. John of the Collachium' Site
15. Suleymaniye Cami Mosque
16. Chadrevan Mosque
17. Ibrahim Pacha Cami Mosque
18. Castellinia
19. Admiralty / Bishop's Palace
20. 'Our Lady of the City' Church
21. Hospice of St. Catherine
22. St. Pantaleon

23. 'Our Lady of Victory'
24. Site of Ancient & Medieval Dockyards
25. St. Nicholas Fortress / Site of the Colossus?
26. Redjeb Pasha Mosque
27. Agha Mosque
28. Mastapha Mosque
29. Hamza Bey Mosque

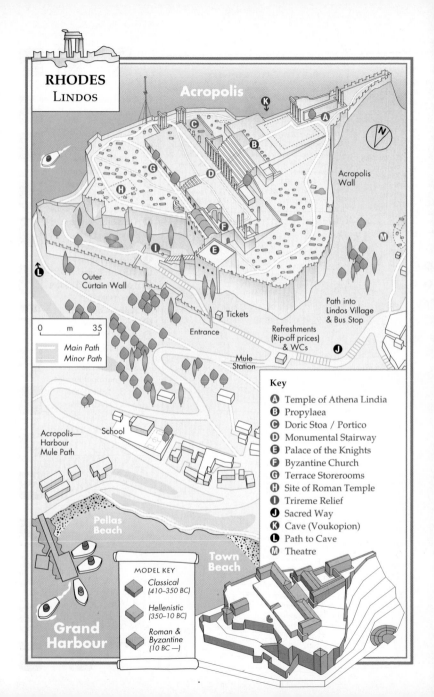

RHODES
LINDOS

Acropolis

Acropolis Wall

Outer Curtain Wall

Tickets

Entrance

Refreshments (Rip-off prices) & WCs

Mule Station

Path into Lindos Village & Bus Stop

0 m 35

Main Path
Minor Path

Acropolis—Harbour Mule Path

School

Pellas Beach

Town Beach

Grand Harbour

Key

- **A** Temple of Athena Lindia
- **B** Propylaea
- **C** Doric Stoa / Portico
- **D** Monumental Stairway
- **E** Palace of the Knights
- **F** Byzantine Church
- **G** Terrace Storerooms
- **H** Site of Roman Temple
- **I** Trireme Relief
- **J** Sacred Way
- **K** Cave (Voukopion)
- **L** Path to Cave
- **M** Theatre

MODEL KEY

- Classical (410–350 BC)
- Hellenistic (350–10 BC)
- Roman & Byzantine (10 BC —)

Medieval / Old City

Many Greek island towns offer a dramatic contrast between the ancient centre and modern quarters, but Rhodes City takes this to extremes with the character-packed, moated and walled medieval Old City seemingly floating apart from a quintessentially Italianesque New Town. This not to say that the Italians didn't leave their mark on the Old City, for they did in a big way, repairing the walls and medieval buildings and allowing the locals to tear down the forest of minarets that the Turks had added to the Byzantine city churches that had been converted into mosques. Occupying the eastern half of the ancient city, the Old City also contains reminders of its more illustrious past, including a hint of the former grid street layout that is still visible in the position of the main thoroughfares — now rather distorted by centuries of encroachment by buildings repeatedly rebuilt after earthquakes.

The Old City offers several days of sightseeing and plenty of opportunity to get lost time and time again in the warren of narrow streets. To get the most out of your wanderings you can't do better than to buy the detailed Old City guide: *The Knights of Rhodes — The Palace and the City* (2000 GDR).

Bounded by a moated wall breached by 11 gates, the Old City was divided by an inner wall (now largely lost) into two sections, from the Byzantine period on; the smaller northern section forming the inner defensive core of the fortified city. Known as the **Kastro** or **Collachium**, it contained most of the important buildings during the 14 and 15 c., when the city housed the West European Knights of St. John; the lowly Greeks lived in the larger southern part of the city, known as the Chora.

Surrounding both sections of the town are the impressive **City Walls**. Rebuilt several times by the Knights of St. John, they represent one of the best preserved medieval fortifications in Europe. In their day they proved a formidable barrier to Turkish ambitions to take the island, protected by a deep, dry moat, and divided into defensive sections known as **Tongues** (the Knights of St. John recruited members to their order right across Europe, and they were grouped in units according to language). After several unsuccessful assaults, it finally took a 6-month siege by 200,000 Turks to capture the city, held by 290 Knights supported by 6,000 local Greek soldiers. The losses were equally impressive, with 50,000

Turks killed compared to only 2,000 defenders. The defenders' casualties were so low in part because, once the Turks finally breached the wall, the Knights negotiated a strategic withdrawal in return for leaving the city intact.

Beyond exploring the various gates and towers, the walls also offer various attractions. The best of these is the guided tour that allows you to walk along the walls (②, ⑦ 14.15. 1200 GDR). This runs anti-clockwise from the courtyard of the Palace of the Grand Masters to the stairs beyond St. John's Gate. It is also possible to walk the length of the moat (there are access points at intervals in the walls). Below the north wall is a daily *Son-et-lumière* that tells the story of the 1522 siege.

Protected by the moat against land attack, the seaward side of the city wall circuit was also formidably fortified. The walls here bounded the **Great Harbour** (now significantly diminished by the building of a seaward side road, a new mole and the enlarged ferry quay), with the impressive **Marine Gate** providing the main entrance to the city. The ancient moles built on both sides of the harbour were also utilized, with the construction of impressive towers that guarded a massive chain, that closed off the entrance. Today only one of these towers survives (the **Tower of the Mills**); its much more romantic-looking partner, the lost **Nailac Tower** (named after a Grand Master and adorning many early drawings of the city), collapsed in an earthquake in 1863. The Italians did plan to rebuild it, but WW2 put paid to that ambition, so tourists have to make do with standing on its base instead.

Within the walls, the biggest pull is **The Palace of the Grand Masters**. Sadly, the current building is a fake. The original — converted into a prison by the Turks — blew up in 1856 after some bright spark (no doubt a warder determined to prove that cigarettes do kill) ignited a thousand tonnes of forgotten gunpowder that the Knights had left in one of the dungeons. Rebuilt in the 1930s as a palace for Mussolini, the building (open ②–⑦ 08.30–15.00. 1200 GDR) is home to many Kos Town mosaics.

To the south-east of the Palace stands a **Loggia** that once covered the way to the lost cathedral church of the Knights (also demolished in the gunpowder explosion). The Loggia archway opens out into one of the best preserved medieval streets in Europe; cobbled **Ipaton Street**, which was once the ancient processional street from the Temple of Helios to the harbour. Lined with the **Inns of the Knights** (meeting houses for each Tongue), it has been restored by the Italians, though the result is curiously lifeless. At the harbour end of the street stands the impressive **Knights' Hospital**: the Knights of St. John were not known as the Hospitallers without reason. The hospital now houses the **Archaeological Museum**. Nearby is a **Byzantine Museum** housed in the **'Our Lady of the City' Church**.

A short walk south of the museum brings you into **Socratous** — the main shopping street cum souk that is now filled with tacky tourist shops. At the west end is the pink **Suleymaniye Cami Mosque**, built on the site of a church by the victorious Suleiman in 1522. Now disused, older postcards show it with an impressive minaret. Recently taken down for structural reasons, the locals don't seem keen on restoring it, preferring to devote their energies to renovating the many Orthodox churches converted into mosques. Depending on their age, local guidebooks refer to these buildings by their mosque or saint names (it is only recently that their original dedications have become apparent — as covered-over frescos and mosaics are exposed).

The last great building from the medieval period lies outside the Old City on the mole of **Mandraki Harbour** (with its two bronze deer). This is the turret fort of **St. Nicholas** (now adorned with a lighthouse). This fort also guarded a harbour chain. Unfortunately, it is currently closed for restoration.

New City
Needless to say, the largest and most boring of the cities that have made Rhodes City what it is today is the modern bit, the only part that is worth bothering with at all is the section that occupies the head of the peninsula, and known as the New Town. It takes its name from the earlier Greek settlement that emerged here during the Ottoman period (when Greeks were banned from living within the Old City). Following WW1, the occupying Italians embarked on an extensive building programme, adding as many grandiose buildings as they deemed necessary to accurately reflect the town's status as the capital of the Italian Dodecanese. These days package-tourist hotels and bars (over 200) dominate. Otherwise the New Town has little to offer, bar a bracing sunbathe on aptly named Windy Beach and a sea-level **Aquarium** that is worth a visit.

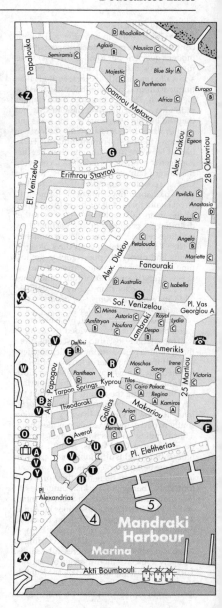

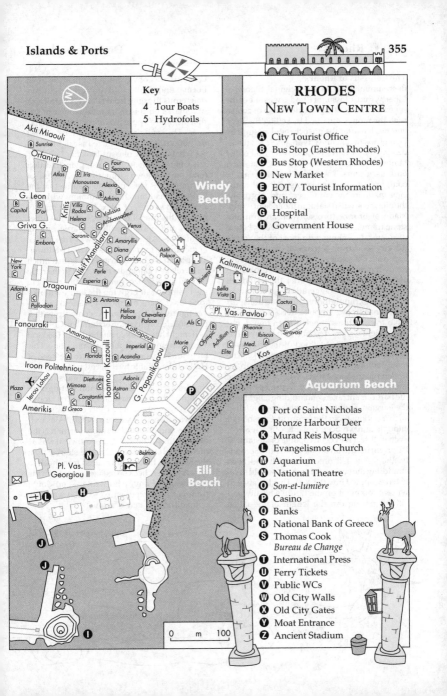

Key

4 Tour Boats
5 Hydrofoils

RHODES
NEW TOWN CENTRE

- **A** City Tourist Office
- **B** Bus Stop (Eastern Rhodes)
- **C** Bus Stop (Western Rhodes)
- **D** New Market
- **E** EOT / Tourist Information
- **F** Police
- **G** Hospital
- **H** Government House

- **I** Fort of Saint Nicholas
- **J** Bronze Harbour Deer
- **K** Murad Reis Mosque
- **L** Evangelismos Church
- **M** Aquarium
- **N** National Theatre
- **O** *Son-et-lumière*
- **P** Casino
- **Q** Banks
- **R** National Bank of Greece
- **S** Thomas Cook *Bureau de Change*
- **T** International Press
- **U** Ferry Tickets
- **V** Public WCs
- **W** Old City Walls
- **X** Old City Gates
- **Y** Moat Entrance
- **Z** Ancient Stadium

Windy Beach

Aquarium Beach

Elli Beach

Akti Miaouli
Orfanidi
Sunrise
Four Seasons
Atlas
Iris
Manoussos
Alexia
G. Leon
Kritis
Villa Rodos
Athina
Capitol
D'or
Valissia
Helena
Ambassadeur
Griva G.
Saronic
Venus
Embona
Amaryllis
Astir Palace
New York
Diana
Carina
Atlantis
Perle
Esperia
Dragoumi
Palladion
St. Antonio
Helios Palace
Chevaliers Palace
Fanouraki
Amarantou
Kathapouli
Eva
Florida
Imperial
Acandia
Iroon Politehniou
Ioannou Kazoulli
Diethnes
Adonis
Plaza
Mimosa
Ierou Lahou
Constantin
Astron
Amerikis
El Greco
G. Papanikolaou
Pl. Vas. Georgiou II
Belmar
Nikif Mandilara
Coral
Rimini
Bella Vista
Kalimnou – Ierou
Cactus
Pl. Vas. Pavlou
Als
Olympic
Achillion
Marie
Phoenix
Ibiscus
Med.
Elite
Siravast
Kos

0   m   100

The Colossus of Rhodes

Best summed up as the original Statue of Liberty, the Colossus of Rhodes was one of the seven wonders of the world. Built c. 290 BC with the money obtained by selling the siege engines left after the unsuccessful attempt by Demetrios to take the city in 305/4 BC, it was designed by Chares of Lindos, a pupil of the famous Lysippos (Alexander the Great's favoured sculptor). The figure took 12 years to complete and was the largest colossal statue ever made in ancient Greece and, arguably, the most renowned statue in the ancient world. Made of bronze (probably on an iron and stone frame), it only stood for 63 years before it collapsed — along with most of the rest of the city — during a massive earthquake in 227/6 BC. Thereafter it lay as a wondrous ruin for over nine centuries until it was broken up and removed in 653 AD, after the island fell under Arab rule: exaggerating legend having it that it took nine hundred camels to transport the bronze from Aleppo to Syria.

No trace of the statue has been found, nor did ancient writers describe its pose. This has opened the way for a flood of theories as to where it stood and what it looked like. The most famous of these was dreamed up by Italian renaissance artists, who opted for the compelling image of giant figure bestriding the harbour entrance, and holding a light into the harbour. Sadly, all the evidence is against such a notion. First, the figure just wasn't tall enough to have been capable of such a feat even if its feet had been capable of sustaining it upright in such an unstable posture. Secondly, the statue fell onto land (if it had been straddling the harbour entrance it would surely have toppled into the sea). Thirdly, ancient writers comment on the figure's beauty and height (pacing out the length of the fallen

Colossus was obviously a popular pastime) but make no mention of its posture. It is always dangerous to argue from silence, but the lack of remarks on this score means one can say that the figure's pose was literally 'unremarkable'. This same argument also tells against the notion that the figure acted as a lighthouse. So, what did the Colossus look like?

If Chares kept to the Lysippian tradition (and he is known primarily as a pupil of Lysippos) it is reasonable to assume that the Colossus had much in common with the Lysippian statues of Alexander that rapidly became the model for statues of many other heroes and gods (Apollo not least among them). This 'Alexander' pose was a derivative of the kouros form with the left foot traditionally placed slightly forward but with a much more relaxed gait and a reduction in the ratio of head to body size from the traditional 7:1 to the Lysippian 10:1 (giving the figure a hunky torso look). Using fragments of various Lysippian figures, it is possible to come up with a plausible reconstruction of the fallen Colossus as it might have looked on the day of the local Vestal Virgin Brass-Rubbing Club outing. This bit of fun is made easier thanks to the head of Helios (identifiable by the crown of holes that would have held the gold sun-rays) in the Rhodes Archaeological Museum. Dating from within a hundred years of the construction of the Colossus (it could possibly be a copy of it), it is a variant of the Lysippian head of Alexander. A second great aid to reconstruction is the fact that the statue's height is known: it was 31 metres high (making it a metre shorter than the Statue of Liberty, measured from head to toe). A further check on its size comes from the comment of Pliny, who wrote — no doubt from personal experience — that it was only with difficulty that a man

could put his arms round the figure's thumb (he is curiously reticent about what Mrs Pliny could just about get her arms around).

Where the Colossus stood is also the cause of much debate. Colossal statues traditionally stood either near the temple of the god to whom they were dedicated (e.g. the statue of Apollo on Delos) or at port entrances; usually on the end of man-made moles. On Rhodes, the Temple of Helios stood on the site now occupied by the Masters' Palace. During the 1930s, the Italians extensively excavated before rebuilding the palace, and found nothing that to suggest that the Colossus stood in this area. The port alternatives also present problems as there were five ancient harbours, and all Rhodian moles are man-made. In order to visit the site of the Colossus, you therefore need to take in the Tower of the Mills, the base of the lost Nailac Tower, the landward entrance of Mandraki harbour and the Fort of St. Nicholas on the Mandraki harbour mole. This last location is arguably the most likely site for the Colossus. The site's champions point to the existence of a number of curved marble blocks built into the walls of the circular central tower of the fort that appear to come from a Hellenistic structure with the same 17 m diameter; the suggestion being that the tower is built directly onto the remains of the base of the Colossus.

Helios: The Sun God

The deity that inspired the Colossus of Rhodes has left his mark in more tangible ways beyond the memory of his statue. Widely respected in the Eastern Mediterranean (Apollo occupied his role as the god of light in the rest of the Greek world) from the Archaic period on, Helios was particularly associated with beginnings, rebirth and light coming up out of darkness. The ancients believed that he rode a chariot of fire across the sky each

day before spending the night sailing around the dark side of the world in a giant cup. From the Hellenistic period on, his cult developed from basic superstitions (it was considered very dangerous to turn one's back on the rising sun) to a point from the mid-2 C. AD when it became the de facto religion of the Roman world. Even the Emperor Constantine — who made Christianity the state religion of the Empire — combined worship of the 'Unconquered Sun my companion' with his Christianity, for the first decade of his rule.

As a result, the church ended up inadvertently adopting holy days that had no biblical significance, merely because they had already become established as holy days in the Empire. Not least of these was the use of Sunday as the day of worship rather than the Jewish Sabbath. Sunday — as the first day of the week — was literally 'Sun'-day: the day of the Sun god. (Note: this guide adopts the European timetable convention of numbering Monday — the first working day — as ①). Helios's birthday was also absorbed into Christianity. The 25th of December (the first day that could be shown to be getting longer after the winter equinox) was a popular feast day in the Eastern Mediterranean from the 5C. BC on. Not content with nabbing the sun god's birthday and day of worship, the early church made off with his symbol too. All ancient gods had an identifying symbol (see p. 88–91); Helios's was a sunburst — represented as an orb, or points of light around the god's head — the original halo: all of which leads one to wonder how many clergymen have looked forlornly across ranks of empty pews of a Sunday morning and mourned the fact that Helios wasn't also the god of orgies.

THE COLOSSUS OF RHODES
RECONSTRUCTED FROM THE LYSIPPIAN-STYLE HEAD OF HELIOS IN RHODES, THE TORSO OF A LYSIPPAIN BRONZE OF ALEXANDER. AND THE FEET AND GOOLIES OF A LYSIPPIAN APOLLO.

SOUVENIRS

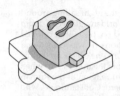

Lindos

After Rhodes City the next great centre and sightseeing attraction is the picturesque, acropolis-topped village of Lindos. Although it isn't the capital of Rhodes, Lindos has a pedigree that puts most Greek island capitals to shame. Of three early Doric Greek cities of Rhodes, it was the only one that had sufficient going for it to survive the collective decision to found a new capital at Rhodes City. This was, in large part, due to its having a major shrine that remained the premier shrine on the island even after Rhodes City was built. Indeed, the famous Temple of Athena Lindia that stood atop the dramatic coastal acropolis was famed throughout the Greek world. Gradually fortified during the Roman and Byzantine eras, the acropolis ensured that the ancient city beneath its walls remained occupied, developing in the last few centuries into a scenic white-washed village complete with narrow cobbled streets (now protected from further development by a government decree).

Even without the acropolis, the village would be a sightseeing destination of note, and it is not surprising that Lindos has emerged as a premier day-trip destination, with a procession of tour buses and boats running down from Rhodes City and arriving at the small leafy town square or the pitifully small harbour quay. Even with the crowds lining up to take donkey rides or being ripped off by the local refreshment prices, Lindos defiantly manages to retain a fair measure of charm.

In addition to the acropolis and the foundations of a 4 c. BC. theatre, the village also has a number of notable 17 c. mansion houses with ornately carved doorways, and a Byzantine church decorated with frescos. Most visitors, however, seem to find the tourist shops and the sandy beaches either side of the village more interesting (this is partly because the mansions are not easily identifiable).

Lindos village lies in a hollow, sandwiched between the seaward acropolis and the hills that surround the village. Either side of the acropolis are beach-lined bays. The northern bay — usually known as the Grand Harbour — is home to the town beach, and the small quay where the day-tripper boats from Rhodes City berth. The southern bay is reputedly the point where St. Paul arrived on the island in 43 AD and is now known as St. Paul's, or the Small Harbour. Legend has it that the bay was formed when the rocks opened up to protect St. Paul, as his ship battled against seas that threatened to shipwreck him. This was no doubt a wonderful event for the saint, but it must have left the owners of the land pretty browned off.

Lindos also has problems beyond passing saints knocking holes in the coastline, and the crowds. In the summer of 1994 the village received considerable publicity for flying a EU Blue Flag (these are awarded to beaches that reach a high standard of cleanliness), while independent scientific tests made in 1992 revealed that 'the waters of Lindos Bay and its surrounds are heavily contaminated with bacteria specifically associated with human sewage'. Bacterial levels were recorded up to 100 times more than is allowed by EU regulations. The problem was an obsolete sewage system. Lindos received an EU grant to replace it and it should be in operation by now. That said, the flag-waving local authorities have made it all but impossible to believe in their claims that all is now safe, and the wise reader would do well to avoid bathing in the two town bays for the foreseeable future (part of the sewage problem was deemed to be the fault of yachts emptying their tanks in Lindos Bay, and the village sewage system isn't going to clean up this part of the problem).

The Acropolis

Open ②–⑦ 08.30–15.00 and ① 12.30–15.00, (the entrance fee is 1200 GDR), the acropolis (see the colour map opposite p. 353) is one of the most spectacular archaeological sites in Greece; so much so, that the 116 m rock has been drawing tourists since antiquity, thanks to **Ⓐ** the **Temple of Athena Lindia**. Built in 348 BC, the surviving structure is a tiny affair with its end columns and side walls (it never had columns down its sides) partially reconstructed. It replaced earlier temples (including its immediate Classical predecessor, which burnt down) dating as far back as the 10 C. BC. As the sanctuary grew in importance, other buildings were added; the most notable being **Ⓑ** the formal gateway or **Propylaea** (407 BC) to the temple precinct, and **Ⓒ** a large, 42-column, double-winged **Doric Stoa** (208 BC) that formed the entrance to **Ⓓ** a **Monumental Stairway**. The construction of this majestic Stoa heralded a phase of Hellenistic sanctuary embellishment on the grand scale, and was a precursor to the major development along similar lines of the Asklepieion on Kos. As with the Asklepieion, the Italian excavators attempted a considerable amount of reconstruction (rescuing many of the stones that were reused in later buildings on the site). Unfortunately, like the poor reconstruction at the Rhodes City acropolis, the touch is not so deft, and the overall impression, although positive, is one of excess (the amount of tastelessly added new material is apt to leave the visitor with the unfortunate impression that these are the remains of bombed WW2 buildings).

During the Byzantine period, the acropolis was fully fortified, a process completed with the construction work carried out by the Knights of St. John. Within the walls they also rebuilt **Ⓔ** a medieval castle on a grand scale, turning it into a fortified **Palace** (complete with the now ruined Byzantine church of Agios Ioannis). This final phase of fortification saw the best survival on the site brought within the walls: the **Trireme Relief**. Measuring 4.6 m long and 5.5 m high, it was carved by Pythocretes on the cliff wall and shows the stern and rudder of an ancient Greek warship. The relief served as the base for a statue of a priest named Hagesandros.

Finally, outside the acropolis walls on the seaward side, there is a large cave. Lying almost directly underneath the main temple, it seems to have added to the religious significance of the site during the Dark Ages.

The Rest of the Island

1. East Coast

While Rhodes City and Lindos dominate the tourist industry on Rhodes, the rest of the island also has much to offer. The east coast sees regular boats running down each morning, stopping at resorts and sand beaches en route to Lindos. Provided you can afford them, they are preferable to taking a bus (and cooler), as the coast road does not hug the shoreline. The first port of call is usually the faded 1920s spa town of **Kalithea**: built by the Italians, it offers a delightfully quixotic collection of pseudo-Moorish buildings set in odd landscape of small park areas between the rocks of the seashore. These days, the world has moved on (in every sense) down the coast to one of the nightspot Meccas of Greece — the youth-and-disco dominated resort of **Faliraki**. As such centres go this one isn't bad and offers everything from a very wild — 'girls, don't tell your mothers' — nightlife to bungee jumping. The resort is quite widely spaced out and dominated by a long sandy beach offering plenty of water-sports. Not surprisingly, the cuisine and atmosphere is 'international' rather than Greek. You should also be aware that the resort is beginning to acquire a very unhealthy reputation for sex attacks.

The next major beach down the coast is rocky **Ladiko**. The place where much of *The Guns of Navarone* was filmed, it has been known as 'Antony Quinn' beach (after the former filmstar who played the lead), but this is now changing as too many visitors are simply asking '*Who?*'. South of Ladiko come the resort beaches of **Kolimbia** and **Tsambika** (which has a monastery-topped hill behind the beach, offering good views of the coast-line), and the far less spoilt beach at **Stenga**. This is best reached via a track that runs down from the inland village of **Archangelos**. After Lindos, this is perhaps the most interesting settlement on the east coast (it is also the largest 'village' on the island). Set in a valley noted for its orange groves, Archangelos is made up of typical white-cubist houses, but has the added bonus of a very impressive Castle of the Knights (built in 1467) and a fresco-decorated late Byzantine church (1377). The village is also on the tour-bus circuit as it is a leading hand-woven carpet and leather boot manufacturing centre.

South of Lindos the only significant resort is the pine-tree backed beach village at **Pefki**. Thereafter the coast is very quiet (though the beaches are good enough), with buses reduced to a trickle: **Kattavia** sees a service only three times weekly. However, if you have your own transport, then this part Rhodes is a delight — particularly the beach islet of **Prassonissi**, which is linked by a sandy beach causeway to the southern tip of the island.

2. The West Coast

The west coast of Rhodes is greener, quieter and less popular than the island's east coast. The winds that hit this side of the island have blown away any chance of it becoming a major package tourist strip. Beaches tend to be pebble rather than sand, and littered with driftwood; escapist beachcombers will love them. Tourist development on this side of Rhodes is largely confined to the coast between Rhodes City and the airport at **Paradisi**. This is as developed as the top half of the west coast. Thereafter, you are into country dominated by farms and vineyards rather than hotels. In spite of this, many visitors to Rhodes venture down this coast during island excursions for the coast road is the jumping off point for a number of sightseeing destinations. Regular — but infrequent — buses also run down this coast to the sights. The best served of these is **Trianda**, the stop for the ancient city of Ialyssos and, to the south, **Mount Filerimos**. This latter destination is a low hill picturesquely clad in pine trees and a mix of Byzantine and Knights of St. John era churches.

Beyond the airport, the west coast highway is joined by the road to **Petaloudes**. This is the inland butterfly valley where millions of tiger moths are scared into flight by almost as many tourists between late June and early September. Like the similar site on Paros, the numbers of moths are declining each year, thanks to the numbers of tourists. The next notable destination after Petaloudes is **Kamiros**. This is the second abandoned west coast ancient city and the third most popular sightseeing destination on the island. Thereafter the road continues along an ever quieter coast: a single daily Rhodes City bus gathers passengers at the rather sad hamlet of Kamiros Skala en route to Monolithos. **Kamiros Skala** (not to be confused with the ruined city) has a daily caïque link to Chalki (times on the ferry timetable sheet issued free in Rhodes City). **Monolithos** is the most important village on the southern half of the west coast. In truth it is a rather poor beach resort redeemed by a Castle of the Knights perched on an overlooking hill. Arguably the most impressive castle on the island, it was built in the 15 c. Today it offers stunning views across the sea to the island of Chalki, and some dangerously crumbling walls on its sea-cliff side. Beyond Monolithos, the island is very sparsely populated. Like much of the mountainous interior of Rhodes, it remains surprisingly untouristed. Those wishing to visit these unspoilt parts of the island will need a good road map and their own transport; car hire comes into its own when exploring an island the size of Rhodes.

Rhodes City is the best place to stay, as it is at the hub of the transportation network. The city has a good supply of rooms (the tourist office also offers a room-finding service). The New Town is dominated by block-booked package tourist hotels (though they often have empty rooms). Most of the independent travellers' accommodation is to be found in the best part of town — in the old city, but rates are at least 10% higher than on other islands.

At the bottom end of the range you will find pensions aplenty, among the best being the *Nikos* (☎ 23423) and the *Aleka* (☎ 33701) — both within easy distance of the port (look for 'CHORA' on the Old City map). A street to the north-east is home to the good *Rena* (☎ 26217), and tucked quietly away on the south side of town are two more good-value establishments; the *Andreas* (☎ 34156) and the *Apollo Rooms* (☎ 35064). Thanks to the competition, E-class hotels are all pretty reasonable. These include the *Spot* (☎ 34737), the *Sydney* (☎ 25965) and the *Teheran* (☎ 27594). The cheap *Kastro* (☎ 20446) near the Turkish baths has noisy rooms overlooking a square. D-class hotels include the excellent, if out of the way, *Kava d'Oro* (☎ 36980) and the better placed *Paris* (☎ 26356).

Λ

Rhodes has one east coast camp site — *Camping Faliraki* (☎ 85358) — that offers easy access to both Rhodes City and Lindos. A nice site 16 km south of the former, with a superb mini-market and washing facilities, it can easily be reached by bus (take the Rhodes City bus for Lindos and *not* Faliraki as the site lies 2 km beyond the centre of Faliraki, and ask the driver to let you off at the camping: the site lies 500 m down a side road that leads off toward the coast from the main highway). One of the best maintained sites in the islands, it is popular with Brits, and boasts a swimming pool.

ᏀᏯ

Most island hoppers, if they are island hopping, will have their work cut out just taking in the sights in Rhodes and Lindos without having time to venture further afield, though Rhodes has sufficient sightseeing to fill a 2–week holiday. Top of the list are the other two pre-408 BC cities (both accessible by bus). **Kamiros** is, in fact, the best preserved of the three former centres of power. Abandoned after Rhodes City was built, much of the city plan is still visible, but sightseeing suffers considerably thanks to the lack notable major buildings. The remains at **Ialyssos** are far more fragmentary and consist of the remains of a 3 C. BC. **Temple of Athena Polias and Zeus Polios** on the site of the ancient acropolis. Unlike Kamiros, a settlement of sorts survived at Ialyssos until comparatively recently. Its close proximity to Rhodes City ensured that it was a natural centre of operations for besiegers of the city: both the Knights of St. John and Suleiman used it as a base prior to their conquests of the island.

Symi

ΣΥΜΗ; 58 km²; pop. 2,500.

CODE ☎ 0241
PORT POLICE ☎ 71205
TOURIST OFFICE ☎ 71215
POLICE ☎ 71111
FIRST AID ☎ 71290

A small island half tucked within the folds of the indented Turkish coast, hilly Symi (inappropriately pronounced 'Sea-my') is both a popular day-tripper destination from Rhodes, and the prized objective for an exclusive few able to find overnight accommodation. There are two stories as to how the island got its name. The first is that Symi is named after a little known goddess daughter of Ialyssos who was carried away from Rhodes by a passing boat-builder who thereafter upset her by doing nothing but ignore her while he built boats. This story is as boring as he was and not worth going into further. The alternative tale, has it that the island was originally called 'Simia' or 'monkey island'. Besides being far more appealing, this explanation is also much more plausible given the hilly nature of the terrain (you almost need to be a monkey to get around here). Of course, day-trippers from Rhodes aside, there isn't a monkey in sight: the simian bit comes from Prometheus (the man who stole fire from Zeus) who — myth would have it — was subsequently imprisoned and died here after the wrathful god zapped 1.6% of his DNA, thereby turning him into a monkey.

Symi was once one of the most prosperous islands in the Aegean, thanks to the combined industries of shipbuilding and sponge fishing. Its pre-WW2 history is not unlike nearby Kastelorizo; for Symi likewise enjoyed considerable prosperity coupled with political autonomy during the period of Ottoman rule, only to see its fortunes dramatically wane with the rise of the steamship and the island's isolation from the Anatolian mainland, following the Italian take over of the Dodecanese after WW1. Having long since cut down its trees (which once covered the island), barren Symi depended on timber from mainland Turkey to maintain its output of over 500 caïques a year; once this was lost, and the sponge fishing declined, the island fell into comparative poverty. Salvation of a sorts came with the Turkish invasion of Cyprus in 1974, when Symi emerged as a popular Rhodes' day-tripper excursion (in lieu of Turkish Marmaris, which was necessarily out of bounds). Since then it has become ever more popular; overly so in the eyes of many island hoppers.

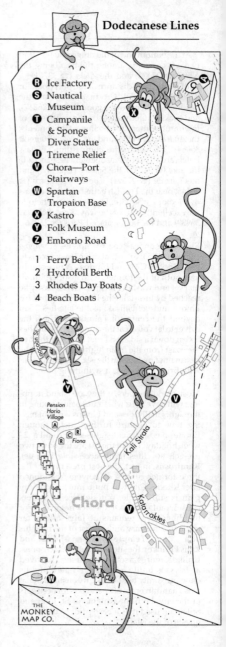

R Ice Factory
S Nautical Museum
T Campanile & Sponge Diver Statue
U Trireme Relief
V Chora—Port Stairways
W Spartan Tropaion Base
X Kastro
Y Folk Museum
Z Emborio Road

1 Ferry Berth
2 Hydrofoil Berth
3 Rhodes Day Boats
4 Beach Boats

Lagoon St.

Pension Horio Village **A**

C **R**
R Fiona

V

Kali Strata

Chora

V Katarraktes

THE MONKEY MAP CO.

W

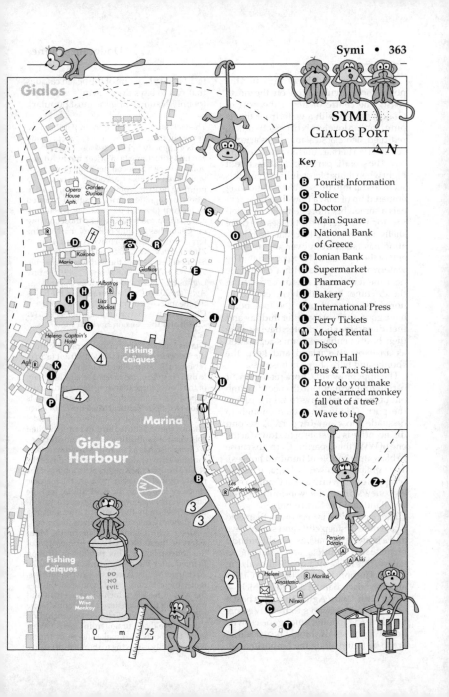

Gialos

Opera House Apts.
Garden Studios

SYMI
GIALOS PORT

△ N

Key

- **B** Tourist Information
- **C** Police
- **D** Doctor
- **E** Main Square
- **F** National Bank of Greece
- **G** Ionian Bank
- **H** Supermarket
- **I** Pharmacy
- **J** Bakery
- **K** International Press
- **L** Ferry Tickets
- **M** Moped Rental
- **N** Disco
- **O** Town Hall
- **P** Bus & Taxi Station
- **Q** How do you make a one-armed monkey fall out of a tree?
- **A** Wave to it

Kokona
Maria
Glafkos
Albatros
Lisa Studios
Helena
Captain's Hotel
Agli

Fishing Caïques

Marina

Gialos Harbour

Fishing Caïques

DO NO EVIL
The 4th Wise Monkey

0   m   75

Les Catherinettes

Pension Dorain
Aliki

Heleni
Anastasia
Marika
Nireus

0   m   75

The only large settlement on Symi is the port—chora combination on the north coast. The centre of life is the port of **Gialos**, graced with a waterfront that is pure magic: a lovely mix of pastel painted, red-tiled, neo-classical mansions arranged in serried tiers around an amphitheatre bay. The scene is particularly attractive at night when the banks of dull orange lights seem to roll into the sea like the glowing embered lip of a lava flow. Daylight reveals a somewhat more complicated picture, for a number of the houses are mere shells, reflecting the fact that the population has fallen from over 30,000 at the end of the 19 C. to under 3,000 today. The waterfront (complete with a campanile near the ferry quay) is crowded during the daytime, but quickly reverts to its normal sleepy self once the tour boats have gone; these arrive after midday and then depart four hours later, having done their best to enhance Symi's reputation as an expensive island and keep the sponge and herb shops in business.

The upper town of **Chora** retains an air of tranquillity, thanks to the need to climb one of the two stairways running up from the port. This is more than enough to dissuade most day-trippers. A second disincentive is the state of the town (at the end of WW2 the departing Germans chose to blow up a couple of hundred houses). The remaining town is large, if rather scrappy, but is worth a visit thanks to the bay views from the windmill topped headland and the Kastro hill.

The rest of Symi is very quiet, thanks to a coastline of steep cliffs and sandy bays and a hinterland that has nought but odd farmsteads, hamlets and goat-tracks galore; this makes it a good hill-walking island. The only bus runs between Gialos and the beach hamlet at **Pedi**, which — along with sandy **Agios Nikolaos** beach — sees most of Symi's tourists. Visitors not choosing to loiter among the crowds or brave the small shingle beaches that are to be found along the **Emborio** road, head instead for one of the beach caïques that run to bays down Symi's east coast (pebbly **Nanou** being the most popular).

The lack of accommodation (in part because of the shortage of water) puts great pressure on bed capacity in High Season. Usually you can find something (at a price), but in August you can expect to encounter huge problems if you haven't booked ahead or arrived on a morning boat: it is common for late arrivals to resort to roughing it on the mosquito-haunted waterfront to await the next day when they can snap up rooms vacated by those moving on. **Gialos** has the bulk of the rooms. Near the ferry berth are the expensive A-class *Akiki* (☎ 71665), *Nireus* (☎ 72400) and the *Dorian* (☎ 711 81). Best bets behind the harbour are the *Albatros* (☎ 71707), the *Kokona* (☎ 71549), the tiny *Glafkos* (☎ 71358) and the pricier *Opera House Apts* (☎ 72034). On the chora side of the bay is the cheapish *Agli* (read 'ugly') *Rooms* (☎ 71665). **Chora** also has a few rooms, the hotel *Fiona* (☎ 72088) and the pension *Horio* (☎ 71800).

Gialos has a number of sights ranging from the **Trireme Relief** on the waterfront (a 1945 replica of the ship relief at Lindos on Rhodes) to the *Les Catherinettes* taverna where the Treaty of the Dodecanese (handing the islands to the Allies) was signed that same year. There is also a two-floor **Nautical Museum** (250 GDR); the exhibits consist of half-a-dozen model caïques, the odd stuffed bird and an unlabelled collection of nautical bric-a-brac (mostly brac).

Chora also has a fair **Folk Museum** (follow the blue arrows) along with the remains of the **Kastro** built by the Knights of St. John, but the most original things in town are the majestic stairway known as the **Kali Strata**, and the large circular base of a **Tropaion** (victory monument) set up by the Spartans after a nearby naval victory over the Athenians in 411 BC.

Along with Gialos, **St. Panormitis Monastery** on the south coast is the prime target of the tourist boats. This palatial institution (named after the patron saint of sailors, the Archangel Michael) seems to exist for tourists. It also owns the largest of Symi's satellites — the islet of **Seskli**, which provides fruit and produce for the monastery's lone monk. Some tours have visits in their itineraries, including a twice-weekly excursion from Gialos. Occasional taxi boats also make the short trip to **Nimos**, a hilly islet lying to the north of Gialos.

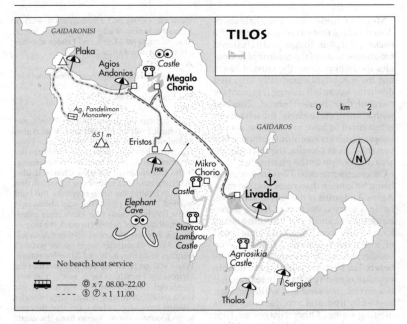

Tilos

ΤΗΛΟΣ; 63 km²; pop. 320.

CODE ☎ 0241
PORT POLICE ☎ 44350
POLICE ☎ 44222
FIRST AID ☎ 44210

A sleepy island even in High Season, Tilos is a place of hills topped with castles, quiet orchard valleys and empty beaches. For years it has been all but ignored by tourists, perhaps because at first sight it looks rather dull compared to almost every other island in the Dodecanese. Other factors also come into play, with rumours of internecine feuds between the islanders (resulting in few tourist facilities emerging) whispering up and down the Dodecanese; reflecting past antagonism between the two communities on the island. Happily today there is nothing on Tilos to support them: the islanders are generally very friendly and

welcoming. Even better, unlike many small islands in the region, you can be reasonably sure of finding a room of some sort no matter when you visit.

Having abandoned several tiny hill villages, the island population is now divided between the port of Livadia and the tiny capital of Megalo Chorio: the two being linked by a recently paved road.

Livadia is the more vibrant of the two centres with a plethora of new hotel and apartment building going on behind the old waterfront. Although tourism is the only economic god now worshipped in town, Livadia has managed to retain much of its former homely small island appeal, with a leafy central square, sleepy tavernas (that only come to life once darkness falls) and a handful of friendly shops. The port quay also gives way to a long clean beach, that unfortunately, is little used as it is made up of large pebbles that are just a bit too big for comfort.

Megalo Chorio is a small, half-abandoned village that sits on a foothill at the back of a flat plain. In ages past it clustered around the walls of the castle that dominates the hilltop above the current town, but the inhabitants gradually migrated down the kastro hill leaving fragmentary ruins of their houses behind. Touched with a hint of melancholy, the settlement is too small to have much in the way of shops, which are easily out numbered by tavernas. As at Livadia, the town doctor also doubles up as the pharmacist.

Other settlements on Tilos are tiny; most being little more than names on the map. **Agios Andonios** is the only one of note, being a sorry collection of half-a-dozen houses near a small jetty huddling near a long scruffy 'beach' backed by the turret of a derelict windmill. **Eristos** is even smaller, but is set to grow thanks to its beach. The best on the island and doubly popular as nudity is happily tolerated, it is a mix of grey sand and white pebbles, backed by trees and a couple of tavernas offering rooms. Other villages on Tilos are now ruinous, notably derelict **Micro Chorio**, abandoned in the 1950s.

The main roads on Tilos have recently been made up with concrete and tend to keep to the valley floors. These are surprisingly fertile, with lovely shady, mature oak trees, fields of silage and collections of hives (the island is known for its honey). With the improved road system has also come a new blue bus (a cut-down regular bus type). Bus times are hard to find (they are only listed on the information kiosk on the quay at Livadia), but in summer services are frequent enough.

ᕮ

Livadia has the bulk of the accommodation including two hotels: the C-class *Irini* (☎ 44293) (hidden away in a jungle of a garden) and the E-class *Livadia* (☎ 44266). There are also a number of apartments charging hotel rates — including the good C-class *George Apartments* — and pensions. The bulk of the island rooms are also at Livadia. **Megalo Chorio** also has establishments offering rooms, including the

Milou (☎ 44204) and *Elecantakia* (☎ 44213). **Agios Andonios** of all places also has the B-class *Australia* (☎ 44296), and **Eristos** also has a hotel: the new *Eristos Beach*.

A

There is no official campsite on Tilos: however, freelance camping is tolerated at both Plaka and Eristos beaches.

👓

Main sightseeing destination on Tilos is the 1470-built fortified hill **Monastery of Agios Panteleimon** on the north-west side of Tilos. The island bus runs twice a week in the summer and waits an hour before returning.

The **Castle** above **Megalo Chorio** is also worth the effort of a visit; though the path that runs up behind the town is not for the faint hearted. At some points the way ahead isn't immediately obvious (the locals have piled-up small cairns of pebbles to mark the way — though these are more obvious when descending). Allow 45 minutes to get up the path, 15 minutes to do the castle and 30 for the return. When you get to the top you will find that the fortress isn't nearly as large, nor is it as well preserved, as it appears from the town: some walls are all but missing and a couple of water cisterns have unguarded holes that descend to god-knows-where. Views from the castle are spectacular — both of Tilos and across the straits to Nissiros, which from this vantage point really looks like a volcano.

A few years back, a small island off the coast of Siberia received considerable publicity after the discovery that the island was home to a species of **Dwarf Mammoth** a couple of hundred thousand years earlier. What is less well known is the fact that they came to Tilos for their summer holidays (the fossilized bones of those killed in moped accidents litter caves on the island). The town hall at Megalo Chorio is home to a small bones **Museum**.

Finally, hikers will love Tilos. Armed with a good island map (two are on sale in Livadia: go for the good blue rather than the poor white one), it is possible to wander at will, exploring the series of little castles that run down the spine of the island, including one at **Mikro Chorio** which is worth the walk anyway. A walk to the monastery also enables you to take in **Agios Andonios Beach**. This has a sobering reminder of the dangers of over-exposure thanks to the petrified remains of three 7 c. BC (Pompeiian?) sailors who were caught napping by an eruption of Nissiros c. 600 BC.

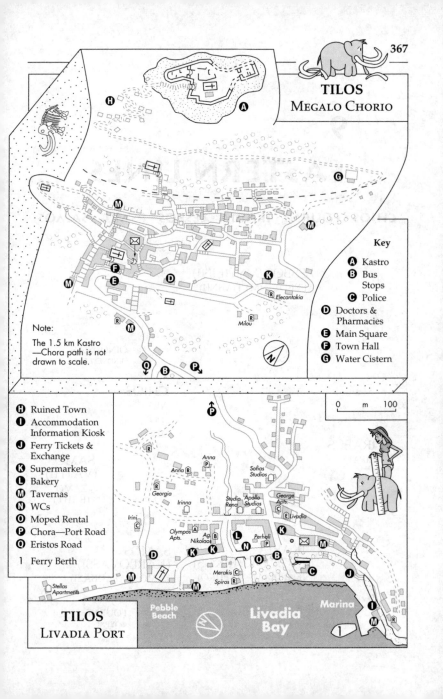

TILOS
MEGALO CHORIO

Key

Ⓐ Kastro
Ⓑ Bus Stops
Ⓒ Police
Ⓓ Doctors & Pharmacies
Ⓔ Main Square
Ⓕ Town Hall
Ⓖ Water Cistern

Note:

The 1.5 km Kastro —Chora path is not drawn to scale.

Elecantakia

Milou

Ⓗ Ruined Town
Ⓘ Accommodation Information Kiosk
Ⓙ Ferry Tickets & Exchange
Ⓚ Supermarkets
Ⓛ Bakery
Ⓜ Tavernas
Ⓝ WCs
Ⓞ Moped Rental
Ⓟ Chora—Port Road
Ⓠ Eristos Road
1 Ferry Berth

0   m   100

Anna

Anna

Sofias Studios

Georgia

Irinna

Studio Rena

Apollo Studios

George Apts

Livadia

Irini

Olympos Apts.

Ag. Nikolaos

Perholi

Merakis

Spiros

Stellas Apartments

TILOS
LIVADIA PORT

Pebble Beach

Livadia Bay

Marina

9
EASTERN LINES

CHIOS · FOURNI · IKARIA · LESBOS · PSARA · SAMOS

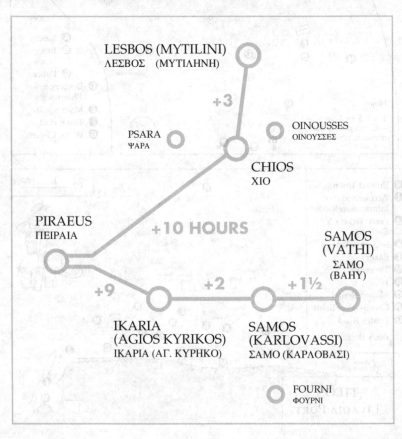

LESBOS (MYTILINI)
ΛΕΣΒΟΣ   (ΜΥΤΙΛΗΝΗ)

+3

PSARA
ΨΑΡΑ

OINOUSSES
ΟΙΝΟΥΣΣΕΣ

CHIOS
ΧΙΟ

PIRAEUS
ΠΕΙΡΑΙΑ

+10 HOURS

SAMOS
(VATHI)
ΣΑΜΟ
(ΒΑΗΥ)

+9

+2

+1½

IKARIA
(AGIOS KYRIKOS)
ΙΚΑΡΙΑ (ΑΓ. ΚΥΡΗΚΟ)

SAMOS
(KARLOVASSI)
ΣΑΜΟ (ΚΑΡΛΟΒΑΣΙ)

FOURNI
ΦΟΥΡΝΙ

General Features

The Eastern Aegean Line is made up of two separate routes running from Piraeus east across the Aegean to those Greek islands adjacent to the Turkish coast north of the Dodecanese. All the ferries operating Eastern Line services follow the natural geographical division of the islands into the two sub-groups, either running Piraeus—Ikaria—Samos, or Piraeus—Chios—Lesbos (Mytilini).

The more southerly route takes in the large and increasingly popular island of Samos as well as the less well known Ikaria. Each boast two regular ports at which ferries can call, giving scope for alternations in schedules. The more northerly route runs across to Chios and then running along the Turkish seaboard to Lesbos (Mytilini); both are large islands

which have remained economically independent of the tourist hordes but which are increasingly attracting Grecophiles jaded by the over-tourism encountered elsewhere. Northern route sailings are almost exclusively confined to the major ports of Chios Town and Lesbos (Mytilini), but a number of ferries then continue on into the northern Aegean to varying ports of call. Both groups also include minor islands little visited by tourists: Fourni and Samiopoula off Samos, Oinousses and Psara accessible from Chios. Links between the two lines remain poor, but are slowly improving with a connecting Chios—Samos service three days a week. Equally indifferent are connections with the Dodecanese which are so thin on the water that locals utilize Patmos-bound tourist boats.

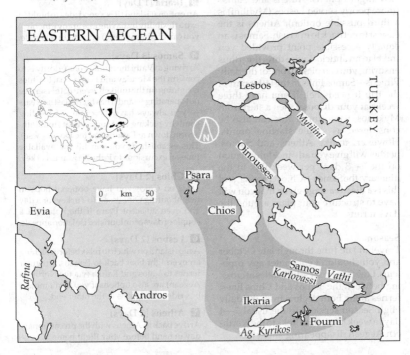

EASTERN AEGEAN

TURKEY

Lesbos

Mytilini

N

Oinousses

Psara

0   km   50

Evia

Chios

Rafina

Samos
Karlovassi   Vathi

Andros

Ikaria

Fourni

Ag. Kyrikos

Example Itinerary [2 Weeks]

An itinerary based on the Eastern Lines is for those who prefer a scattering of trees rather than High Season crowds with their Greek islands, and are happy to settle for quiet taverna eating and making their own entertainment. It is unlikely to appeal to those who like to boogie between boats. The islands en route are comparatively quiet thanks to a mix of fewer ferry connections and the need to get a bus to the nearest reasonable beach (on the popular Cycladic islands you only have to fall overboard near to port to find yourself on one). The crowds are missing more than they realise.

Arrival/Departure Point

On a fortnight's holiday there are two easy flight options: Athens and Samos (more poorly served Lesbos (Mytilini) is a third possible option). Athens is the easiest to get back to in a rush. Samos is an equally accessible point provided you travel in an anticlockwise direction (thus ensuring you can pick up one of the daily Piraeus—Samos links in the latter part of the trip if needs be). If you have three weeks at your disposal then a start from Mykonos, Santorini or Kos can also be considered as viable starting points. However, unlike Athens and Samos, neither will give you advance information on the 2—3 days per week link in the itinerary: the Samos—Chios crossing, and this is a disadvantage given that you will have to structure your plans around the days it runs.

Season

Travel in late June through late October and you shouldn't encounter any problems. Low Season sees difficulties in crossing between the Samos and Chios lines; ferries along both decline from the daily High Season services to the usual 3—4 days a week level, with links to the Northern Aegean disappearing altogether.

■ Athens [2 Days]

Quite apart from the city sights, Athens offers agents in Piraeus who do anything if there is the prospect of getting you to buy a ticket, including showing you the latest Miniotis Brothers Co. timetable when you ask about ferry links between Chios and Samos. With this information you can then work out how many days you have either side of this weak link and allocate nights and stops accordingly.

■ Paros [2 Days]

As there are not usually morning and evening boats out of Piraeus along the Samos line it is often more convenient to make for better connected Paros and then jump from there onto a Samos boat. It also breaks up an otherwise 12-hour voyage and offers a quick dash down to Naxos and the Cyclades Central Line if you have a third week to hand.

■ Ikaria [1 Day]

An optional island (it is a good idea to build in extra flexibility by having one in any itinerary) you can fit (time willing) into a tight schedule.

■ Samos [3 Days]

Arriving at Vathi the number one priority is to confirm the Monday and Friday boat to Chios is running (in the unlikely event of this service not operating — and it has for the last six years — you always have the option of heading south by picking up a tourist boat from Pithagorio down to Patmos and the Dodecanese). This established, you can fill the available time on excursions to Pithagorio and Turkey.

■ Chios [2 Days]

Once on Chios you have optional hops to neighbouring Oinousses, to Turkey for a day and even adjacent Psara if the notion of a couple of days of untouristed isolation appeals.

■ Lesbos [2 Days]

A nice island on which to relax before catching an overnight boat back to Piraeus. Irregular ferries to Volos and Rafina (via the Northern Aegean) are also options if you don't mind a bus ride into Athens at the other end.

■ Athens [2 Days]

Arrive back in Athens with the precautionary day in hand before your flight home.

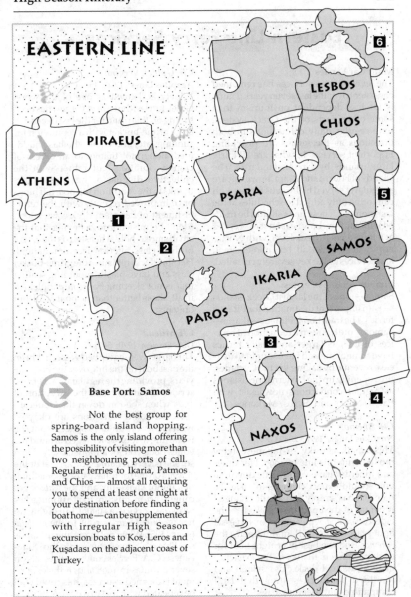

EASTERN LINE

1 ATHENS PIRAEUS

6 LESBOS

CHIOS **5**

PSARA **2**

SAMOS

IKARIA

PAROS **3**

4

NAXOS

Base Port: Samos

Not the best group for spring-board island hopping. Samos is the only island offering the possibility of visiting more than two neighbouring ports of call. Regular ferries to Ikaria, Patmos and Chios — almost all requiring you to spend at least one night at your destination before finding a boat home — can be supplemented with irregular High Season excursion boats to Kos, Leros and Kuşadası on the adjacent coast of Turkey.

Eastern Line Ferry Services

Main Car Ferries

The level of ferry services has remained consistent over the last seven years. Traffic is far less dependent on tourism than some other parts of the Greek system, with regular daily connections in both directions as the ferries are providing important services to what are all fairly large islands by Greek standards. The islands of Fourni and Psara, however, are irregularly served by Piraeus ferries with calls often only added to schedules at the last moment. These links should be treated with caution. Low Season sees services at a four-days-a-week level, with Northern Aegean links all but non-existent, and services to Turkey severely curtailed.

Piraeus—Samos Ferries:

Samos — one of the largest Greek islands — is an important destination for Piraeus ferries. The traditional Piraeus—Ikaria—Samos route has seen a reduction of services of late, as larger and faster ferries have come along and have sought to increase revenue by calling via the Cyclades; thus opening up the Eastern Lines islands as regular connections now exist with Paros/Naxos and Syros/Mykonos.

C/F Anemos

Nomikos Lines; 1976; 2889 GRT.

This small, chunky ex-Japanese ferry moved onto this line in 1997. Her times and itinerary have yet to settle down, so you should expect changes in 1999. To date she has simply run a little changed itinerary of the boat she replaced — the elderly *Samaina*. A pleasant enough vessel and reasonably well maintained, the *Anemos* isn't the best overnight boat for deck passengers thanks to the existence of only a small deck class saloon and moulded sun-deck seating that isn't compatible with sleeping bags.

C/F Golden Vergina

Agapitos Lines; 1966; 4555 GRT.

Widely acclaimed as one of the worst Greek ferries, the *Golden Vergina* has been sailing on this route for the last decade. A large grime-bucket with a reputation for running late, in the past she has shuddered along; not thanks to an excess of engine vibration, but rather with the collective disgust of her passengers thanks to the conditions on board. Things have improved recently with the refurbishment of her main deck class saloon (don't be misled into believing that the small smoke-hole at her stern is the extent of deck class interior accommodation). Her sun-decks remain in the grime-bucket class and have plastic moulding seating that is not sleeping-bag compatible. All in all, she is better than no boat at all, but only just.

C/F Milena

G.A. Ferries; 1970; 5491 GRT.

This large, well-equipped vessel has been the best boat on the line over the last nine years, providing the regular G.A. Ferries' service to Samos (with the exception of 1995 when she ran down the Dodecanese). On board conditions are okay — with plenty of sun-deck space — but she is starting to look a bit ragged around the edges once you look more closely. Even so, she is very reliable. The arrival of the *Anemos* on the route has caused something of a minor shake-up, and the *Milena* got caught up in this; in 1998 running her weekday services as usual, but giving up her weekend Samos runs to the *Daliana* (see p. 305). When not operating to Samos the *Milena* again ventures into the Dodecanese. G.A. Ferries combined vessels on several routes in 1998 and, if the experiment is deemed a success, this could well be repeated with these two boats in 1999.

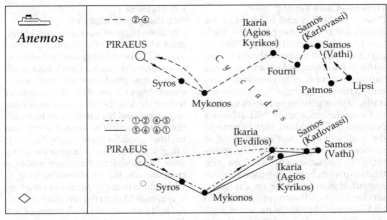

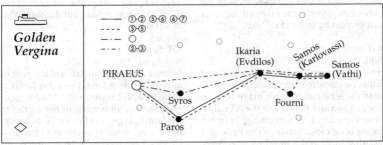

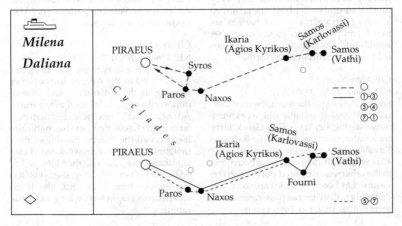

Piraeus—Chios Ferries:

Piraeus to Lesbos and Chios links are dominated by one company: the Maritime Co. of Lesbos (NEL Lines). This is, in part, the result of the lack of heavy tourist traffic in the northern Aegean: there are a sufficient number of large islands to require a fleet of big ferries but not enough traffic to prompt other operators to move in. Given their monopoly, NEL achieve a commendable standard, both in terms of the quality of their fleet and the level of service. The company is, however, something of a timetable compiler's bane, as it tends to pool its boats, with the swapping around of boats running on any given service, and the adjusting of timetables in mid-summer (though the pattern of services is little altered). For these reasons the services opposite are mapped together rather than by individual boat.

C/F Agios Rafail

NEL Lines; 1968; 2262 GRT.

This small ferry (complete with lopsided funnel and scaffolding sun decks) is arguably the least comfortable major ferry in the Aegean and the runt of the NEL fleet (the experience is something between being on a cross between the back of a floating lorry and a building site). Very much the number five boat, she is shoved around from year to year. Changes are more than possible in 1999, though her weekly odd-ball run from Lesbos to Volos is likely to remain in some form.

C/F Alcaeos

NEL Lines; 1970; 3930 GRT.

Somewhat long in the tooth, the medium-sized *Alcaeos* is reliable old workhorse now passing her days in a Greek ferry backwater, running the lifeline Rafina—Kavala route several times a week (see p. 407), with additional runs from both ports to the otherwise unvisted port of Sigri on Lesbos. On-board facilities are okay, but distinctly utilitarian: her passenger saloon seems older than her 1970 vintage.

C/F Mytilene

NEL Lines; 1973; 6702 GRT.

One of the biggest Greek domestic ferries, the *Mytilene* is now the number two boat in the NEL fleet. Once aboard, it is difficult to imagine one is on a Greek boat at all, such is the plush interior. Her size is something of a problem; the search for the sun deck or the WCs is apt to be hard on the feet, and her turnaround times are not good due to the limited entry/exit facilities given the numbers she can carry. Long standing island hoppers rushing aboard may well find a certain nostalgia creeping on; the escalators waiting to whisk them to the upper decks are a long way removed from the antiquated external hull staircases of Greek ferries of old. The company had problems getting her up and running in 1992, but she has settled down since.

C/F Sappho

NEL Lines; 1966; 6500 GRT.

Named after the famous Lesbian poet of antiquity, this old maid was displaced as the largest NEL boat in 1992. As a consequence she lost all bar one of her sorties to the North Aegean in favour of the workhorse role, running overnight Piraeus—Chios—Lesbos services. Now running for the last seven years, this pattern is unlikely to change much in 1999.

C/F Theofilos

NEL Lines; 1975; 19212 GRT.

The new super ferry in the NEL fleet, this boat arrived in the Aegean in 1995 after running as the Australian *Abel Tasman* (followed as by a brief spell as the trans-Adriatic *Pollux*). Now the largest domestic ferry in the Greek fleet, she has naturally taken on all the 'heavy' passenger runs (notably the glamourous weekend Thessalonika service). As with the *Mytilene*, life on board isn't exactly cosy: she is just too big for comfort. That said, she is an excellent overnight ferry with good value cabins.

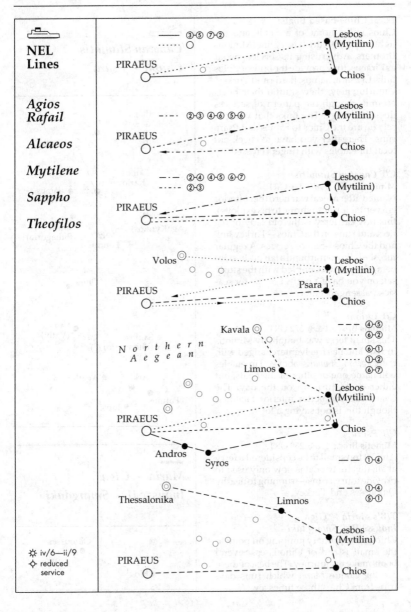

NEL Lines

Agios Rafail

Alcaeos

Mytilene

Sappho

Theofilos

☼ iv/6—ii/9
◇ reduced service

Local Chios-based Boats:
Chios is the home of a small, and delightfully amateurish ferry line: Miniotis
Brothers. Advertising its services as far
as Piraeus, they provide the bulk of Chios
links to Psara, Samos, Ikaria and Turkey.
Unfortunately, they shuffle their boats
around; though the pattern of services
doesn't change. The links that you can
rely on are the Chios to Samos and Psara
runs. Thereafter you have to check out
local timetables with fingers crossed.

C/F *Capetan Stamatis*
Miniotis Bros.; 1967; 436 GRT.
Named after a local war hero (her interior
is a veritable photo shrine to his exploits),
this tiny car ferry is the old lady of the
fleet and runs on the Chios—Turkey link
and the Chios—Samos service. A regular
tub, she is thrown around a fair bit, besides
being very slow. Coupled with the stuffy
saloon you have a perfect recipe for sea-
sick passengers galore.

C/F *Chioni*
Miniotis Bros.; 1968; 572 GRT.
This small ferry was bought by Miniotis
in 1991 and has freely interchanged with
the *Capetan Stamatis* above. Timetables
will name one or other of the boats, but
either could turn up on the day. The
Chioni has the better interior facilities,
though this is not saying a lot.

C/F *Psara*
Miniotis Bros.; 1963; 250 GRT.
Almost too small to be considered a ferry
at all, this rusty boat is now only used to
provide tourist runs—running to nearby
Oinousses and Turkey.

**T/B's *Maria - Olga -
Inousse II - Smargdaki***
Chios is the primary jumping off point to
the small island of Oinousses. Several
boats make the journey. The best of these
are the caïque *Maria* which runs day-
trips from Chios three times a week.

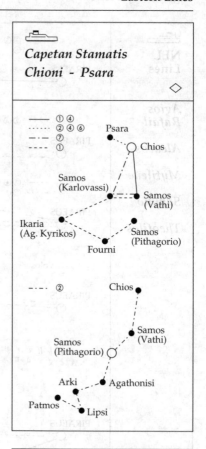

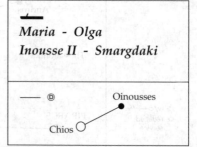

Eastern Line Islands & Ports

Chios

ΧΙΟΣ; 852 km²; pop. 54,000.

CODE ☎ 0271
TOURIST OFFICE ☎ 24217
TOURIST POLICE ☎ 26555
PORT POLICE ☎ 44433
FIRST AID ☎ 23151

Relatively untouristed (thanks to an ugly main port with no good beaches close by) nor offering much in the way of photogenic sightseeing, the large island of Chios remains quiet with its low-key attractions hidden away. To do the island justice you need to take time to explore away from the capital for Chios has a merited reputation for having some of the most fertile and attractive terrain to be found in the Aegean. Indeed, in many ways the landscape is the best thing about Chios, as well as being the source of its quiet affluence: thanks to the growing of mastica (the sticky stuff used to make paint adhere to walls and chewing-gum to everything else). Most of the island is mountainous, with the mastica bush crop covering much of the south, while the north is forested — though major fires in 1981 and 1987 inflicted considerable damage to this region. A more recent and lucrative contribution to the local economy has come via the sea; for almost every Greek shipping tycoon in sight seems to hail from here or the neighbouring satellite of Oinousses.

A bastion of quiet prosperity, Chios has enjoyed a very low-key history for much of its existence. Most of its population appear to have been too busy making a mint through growing and chewing gum to have had time for philosophical speculation or political struggle. This only changed in the 19 c. and the devastating impact of the island's brief sojourn into the limelight haunts Chios still. Like many islands located close to the Turkish coast

Chios suffered in the struggle for Greek independence. Having joined the rebellion by a number of islands against Turkish rule in 1822, Chios was singled out (along with neighbouring Psara) — largely for convenient geographical reasons — for the most severe retribution. On the orders of the Sultan the entire island was sacked, with its buildings burnt. Over 30,000 islanders were massacred in the process and a further 70,000 (mainly women and children) were enslaved and deported. A devastating earthquake arrived in 1881, just in time to nicely set back the island's recovery. This is now complete, though the scars of the last two centuries are still very evident.

The capital, **Chios Town**, has retained its late 19 c. industrial port waterfront and this has little to recommend it. Demolished by the 1881 earthquake, subsequent rebuilding has left the town an inadequate harbinger to the attractiveness of the rest of the island. As one might expect on Greece's premier chewing-gum growing island, Chios Town is home to a large expatriate North American community that returns to the island each summer. The back streets behind the waterfront offer an incongruous mix of crumbling mansions, pool bars and New Yorker run pizza bars. The quayside is more reminiscent of a mini (and empty) version of Piraeus than any other harbour in Greece. The centre of activity lies near the northwestern corner: this is where all the large ferries dock, with the most scenic part of the town behind (complete with a closed mosque and a large tree-filled square/ park). In an attempt to humanize the waterfront, the western side is now pedestrianised during the evening; the local mosquitos taking full advantage of the humans taking in the night air (this is one harbour where it can be quite potent).

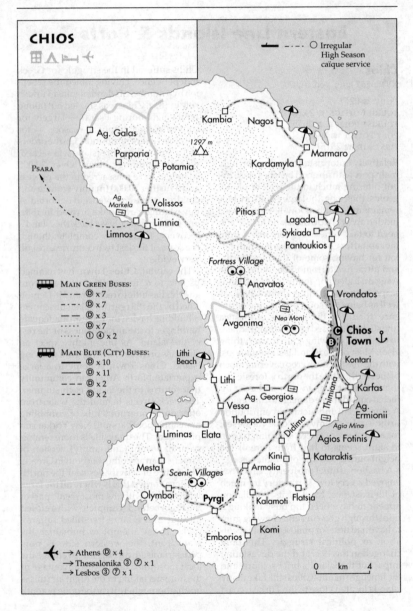

CHIOS

Irregular High Season caïque service

Kambia
Nagos
Ag. Galas
1297 m
Marmaro
Parparia
Potamia
Kardamyla
Psara
Ag. Markela
Volissos
Pitios
Lagada
Limnia
Sykiada
Limnos
Pantoukios
Fortress Village
Anavatos
Vrondatos
Avgonima
Nea Moni
Chios Town
Kontari
Lithi Beach
Karfas
Lithi
Ag. Georgios
Ag. Ermionii
Vessa
Thelopotami
Agia Mina
Didima
Liminas
Elata
Agios Fotinis
Kini
Kataraktis
Mesta
Scenic Villages
Armolia
Olymboi
Pyrgi
Kalamoti
Flatsia
Komi
Emborios

MAIN GREEN BUSES:
— ·· — Ⓓ x 7
— · — Ⓓ x 7
— — Ⓓ x 3
······ Ⓓ x 7
········ ① ④ x 2

MAIN BLUE (CITY) BUSES:
——— Ⓓ x 10
——— Ⓓ x 11
— — Ⓓ x 2
- - - Ⓓ x 2

→ Athens Ⓓ x 4
→ Thessalonika ③ ⑦ x 1
→ Lesbos ③ ⑦ x 1

0   km   4

Commendable though this effort is, the waterfront just doesn't lend itself to romantic evening strolls (it is too smelly for one thing), and once the crowds have departed taxis and motor-bikes use it as a race track into the small hours, when they give way in turn to packs of stray dogs which chase each other along its length instead. All this is rather a pity because the town does have enough in it to justify a short visit once you get behind the grubby, down-at-heel feel of the place, thanks to a castle, a warren-streeted old quarter and several small museums.

Getting away is easy as most of the major villages on Chios are linked by the island bus services. Blue city buses — in their eagerness to escape the capital — run well beyond Chios town environs to cover the whole central portion of the island, while less consistent Green long distance buses (both start from their own terminals near the town park) serve the rest. Timetables for both services (and ferries) are provided by an official NTOG /EOT office on Kanari St. (a side-street off the north-east corner of the harbour).

Southern Chios has most to offer the tourist thanks to a series of scenic medieval fortress villages in the mastica growing region. These settlements, known as the 'mastic villages' (mastichoria), should be a must on the itinerary of anyone spending more than a day on Chios. Their numbers vary according to which local guidebook you happen to pick up, but the total is in the high teens. They share a number of common characteristics; with a line of houses built around their perimeter that doubled to form a defensive wall (the populations of the mastic villages were the only ones to escape alive in the 1822 destruction of Chios), protective watch towers are built on any exposed corners along the wall, and the streets within adopt the Cycladic warren pattern; deliberately designed to confuse any enemy that managed to get in. In the centre of most of the villages is

a well protected church or tower that provided a final point of refuge. **Pyrgi** is the biggest and prettiest of these villages, and is noted for the whitewashed houses that adorn its streets and a main square that is over-painted with a wide variety of geometric blue patterns that extend even to the underside of the balconies. Nearby lies the smallest of the mastichoria; **Armolia** — a noted pottery production centre. **Mesta** is also worth exploration, for although not as pretty as some, it retains more of its medieval buildings (including the largest church on the island) and with it, its old world atmosphere. **Olymboi**, on the road between Pyrgi and Mesta, is in many ways the best preserved, with little building beyond its almost rectangular walls and a well preserved central tower. It also has a port at **Liminas** that until a few years ago saw the occasional ferry. Nowadays only the occasional tourist boat disturbs the waves.

To the east of Chios Town is one of the most northerly of the mastic villages at **Vessa**. Built on the side of a hill, it offers an easy half day's excursion. While just to the south of Chios Town are a couple of other popular destinations: **Karfas**—now rapidly developing as the island's premier tourist resort — also offers the nearest reasonable beach, and the monastery of Agia Mina — site of another massacre by the Turks.

North of the town, buses run frequently to **Vrondatos** and the Daskalopetra or 'teaching rock', which tradition associates with Homer (Chios — an island without many ancient notables of its own — is yet another of those islands that claim him as a son). North of this resort the island is a quiet, tourist-free zone. The largest village is at **Kardamyla**; though it isn't much bigger than its equally rustic and undisturbed neighbours. Whitewashed Volissos on the west coast has more to offer, with remnants of a fortress and a pretty little harbour at **Limnos** with caïques to Psara.

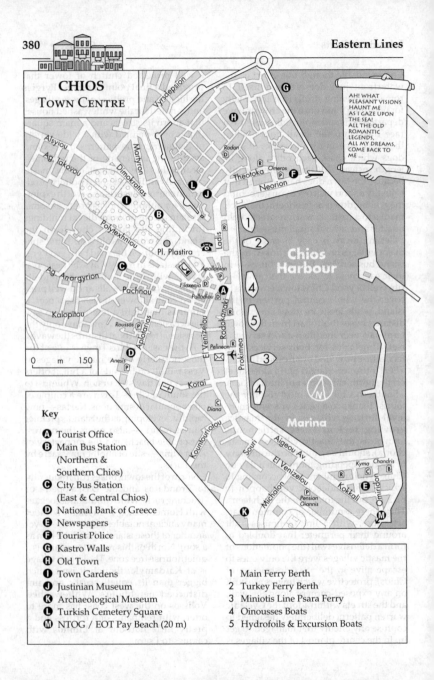

CHIOS
TOWN CENTRE

AH! WHAT
PLEASANT VISIONS
HAUNT ME
AS I GAZE UPON
THE SEA!
ALL THE OLD
ROMANTIC
LEGENDS,
ALL MY DREAMS,
COME BACK TO
ME ...

Chios Harbour

Marina

Vyrsdepsion
Alsyiou
Ag. Iakovou
Dimokratias
Martyron
Rodon
Theotoka
Omeros
Neorion
Polytekhniou
Pl. Plastira
Ladis
Apollonian
Filoxenia
Pachnou
Palladiou
Ag. Anargyrion
Radakanaki
El Venizelou
Kalopitou
Roussos
Apolonias
Pelineon
Prokimea
Anesis
Koral
Diana
Koumouriou
Souri
Aigeou Av.
El Venizelou
Kyma
Chandris
Michalon
Kokkali
Pension
Giannis
Omirou

Key
- **A** Tourist Office
- **B** Main Bus Station (Northern & Southern Chios)
- **C** City Bus Station (East & Central Chios)
- **D** National Bank of Greece
- **E** Newspapers
- **F** Tourist Police
- **G** Kastro Walls
- **H** Old Town
- **I** Town Gardens
- **J** Justinian Museum
- **K** Archaeological Museum
- **L** Turkish Cemetery Square
- **M** NTOG / EOT Pay Beach (20 m)

1 Main Ferry Berth
2 Turkey Ferry Berth
3 Miniotis Line Psara Ferry
4 Oinousses Boats
5 Hydrofoils & Excursion Boats

0   m   150

ㅂ

The lack of tourists means that accommodation options are adequate but not vast. Chios Town has the most beds, but in High Season finding an empty one come the evening can be a problem; ticket agencies will phone around for you. Best (and most expensive) hotel in town is the *Chandris* (☎ 25761), hiding in the street below the harbour. Nearby is the popular mansion *Kyma* (☎ 44500). The *Radon* (☎ 24335) in the old town also offers a quiet atmosphere and reasonable prices. Noisier, but clean are the *Diana* (☎ 24656) and cheaper *Filoxenia* (☎ 22813). Rooms along the waterfront are also popular and generally good value for money though the best lie in the old town. Most of the main island towns also have several hotels (Karfas being the best served with five) along with a scatter of rooms in Pyrgi and Mesta.

A

Completely off the backpacker trail, Chios isn't well endowed with camping facilities. The only site of note is *Chios Camping* (☎ 741 11) and this isn't up to much. An exposed, isolated beach site 14 km north of Chios Town, it is too remote to send a bus to meet ferries. Would-be campers are better off finding a hotel in town.

👓

Lacking any notable sites from the Classical, Hellenistic or Roman periods, the main attraction on Chios is an 11 c. **Byzantine Monastery** at **Nea Mona**, 15 km west of Chios Town. Carefully tucked away in the foothills, it is founded on the spot where shadowy myth says three passing hermits discovered an icon. Quite what three hermits were doing in each others' company in the first place isn't clear, nor is the picture of how they happened upon the icon any clearer. This remains an event more weird than wonderful. Be this as it may, the monastery thrived and is now home to some of the finest Byzantine frescos and mosaics known. Many date from the monastery's foundation in 1042, though a fair number were lost in a damaging earthquake in 1881. The monastery's charnel house is also home to a ghoulish display of skulls, tastefully arranged in glass-fronted bookcases. Victims of the 1822 massacre of the island's population by the Turks (who axed to death those members of the population who had sought refuge in the church, along with 600 monks), they stare at visitors in serried rows like a hungry

crowd of evangelicals looking for converts. Another relic of Greek nationalism housed in the monastery is a grandfatherish clock that was carried away by the Greek inhabitants of Smyrna (modern İzmir) when they fled the city in 1923. Note: the clock is melodramatically set to Constantinople time; so it doesn't do to check your wristwatches by it.

East of the monastery lies another popular sight: the abandoned cliff village of **Anavatos** whose inhabitants did a collective jump as the Turks approached (sightseeing on Chios is not for the squeamish). Chios Town has a few sights worth hunting out including the remains of the Genoese **Kastro** (1433) housing the **Turkish Quarter** to the north of the harbour. The only part of the town to survive the 1881 earthquake, it was badly damaged, still boasts an impressive moat. Less inspiring are the **Archaeological Museum** and Cathedral. The town is also home to the **Justiniani Museum** (devoted to church art). Those with more cash in hand can also splash out on a day-trip to Turkish **Çeşme** on the coast opposite.

Fourni
ΦΟΥΡΝΟΙ; 37 km²; pop. 970.

CODE ☎ 0271
PORT POLICE ☎ 44433
POLICE ☎ 44427
FIRST AID ☎ 112

Fourni is the largest island in small rocky archipelago lying between Ikaria, Samos and Patmos. If you are looking for something close to an unspoilt island, then look no further; for Fourni is one of the few genuine articles left in Greece. Formerly the home of Byzantine pirates, the island is quiet even in High Season, only recently emerging as a regular ferry destination and still lacking proper roads. Unfortunately, as word gets around, this is starting to change and Fourni now sees regular day boats from Ikaria dropping in to augment the tourists that seek it out.

The bulk of the population lives in the chora town of **Fourni**. Home to a large fishing fleet, Fourni is very much a working town: its waterfront is usually covered with mounds of yellow nets, and

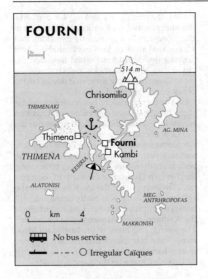

FOURNI

514 m

Chrisomilia

THIMENAKI

Thimena □ □ **Fourni**

THIMENA   □ Kambi

KESIRIA   AG. MINA

ALATONISI

                                MEG.
                                ANTRHROPOFAS

0   km   4

                                MAKRONISI

No bus service

----- O Irregular Caïques

the well supplied fish tavernas behind
stand cheek by jowl with a tiny ice factory
(the production lines run from late afternoon). At the end of the harbour is a usa-
ble beach (the two combining to form the
centre of town life). Littered with caïques
all year round, the beach becomes a
playground for the local kids in summer
— offering an appealing change to the
usual monotonous rows of tanning tourists encountered elsewhere.

The town itself is unusual without
having tangible sights on offer (beyond
the inevitable derelict windmills). The
narrow, over-straight, mulberry tree-
lined main street is an odd mix of quaint
provincial Greece combined with a rare
— for the islands at any rate — grid
layout (this pattern gives way to the usual
chaotic street arrangement once the land
rises behind the main square). Most of
the few facilities in town are located in
either the main street or the square (bar
the anonymous medical centre which is
marked only by the presence of an
ambulance parked outside).

Thanks to a combination of inbreeding
and eating excessive amounts of fish the
— very friendly — locals are apt to be a
bit eccentric at times. The Fourni versions
of those notorious little old ladies in black
have been known to jump fully clothed
into the sea (black hat and all) in order to
play with bathing kids (looking like something out of Roland Dahl's *The Witches* in
the process). It is also not uncommon to
find parents feeding toddlers with bowls
of runny white yuk while they walk along
the town beach of an evening. If you like
fish/shellfish then don't be put off by
such exhibitions of madness, for fish lovers will find that Fourni is the next thing
to paradise. Prices, however, are surprisingly high; with a fleet sending most of its
catch to Athens, the locals have come to
accept city prices as normal. Even so, it is
difficult to resist giving one's wallet a nip
when confronted with a waterfront taverna bathed in the glow of the setting sun,
its tables heaving with red lobsters (this,
and the heaving toddlers on the beach,
add up to a really colourful spectacle).

Emptier beaches lie to the north and
south of the village if you are prepared to
negotiate the rough tracks that run to
them. The locals aren't terribly keen on
island walking and prefer to take taxi caïques to the only other villages on Fourni
at Chrisomilia and Kambi. The second
inhabited islet in the archipelago — **Thimena** (complete with one untouristed hillside hamlet) — is also visited by caïques,
but strangers are not made over-welcome.

Fourni village is home to all the available
accommodation. There are no hotels, but even
in August you can be sure of being greeted
with offers of rooms.

Fourni has little sightseeing, bar the lidless
Hellenistic Sarcophagus that stands in the
town square acting as a litter bin, and a few
blocks south of the town, at **Marmari** cove: a
relic from the days when Fourni was used as
a marble quarry for the city of Ephesus on the
adjacent Turkish coast.

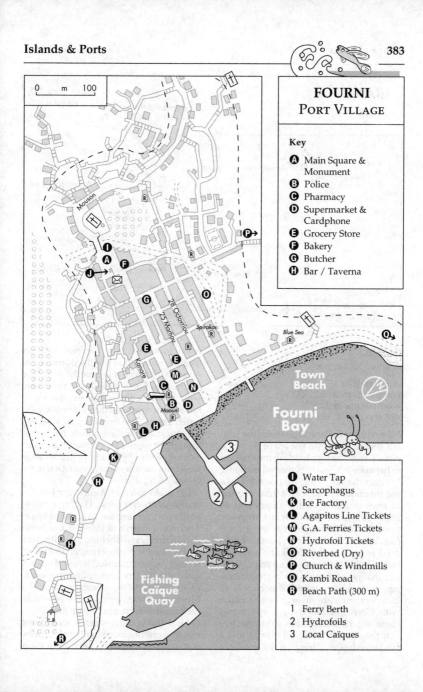

0 m 100

FOURNI
PORT VILLAGE

Key

A Main Square & Monument
B Police
C Pharmacy
D Supermarket & Cardphone
E Grocery Store
F Bakery
G Butcher
H Bar / Taverna

Mouson

28 Octovriou

25 Martiou

Kanare

Spirakos

Blue Sea

Town Beach

Fourni Bay

Maouni

Fishing Caïque Quay

I Water Tap
J Sarcophagus
K Ice Factory
L Agapitos Line Tickets
M G.A. Ferries Tickets
N Hydrofoil Tickets
O Riverbed (Dry)
P Church & Windmills
Q Kambi Road
R Beach Path (300 m)

1 Ferry Berth
2 Hydrofoils
3 Local Caïques

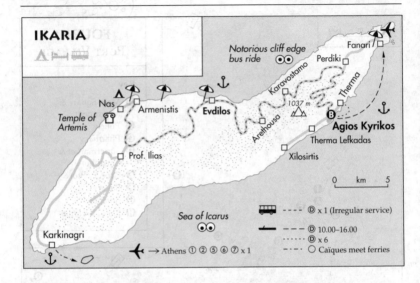

IKARIA

Notorious cliff edge bus ride

Fanari

Perdiki

Karavostamo

1037 m

Therma

Nas

Armenistis

Evdilos

Arethousa

Agios Kyrikos

Temple of Artemis

Therma Lefkadas

Prof. Ilias

Xilosirtis

0   km   5

Sea of Icarus

Karkinagri

→ Athens ① ② ⑤ ⑥ ⑦ x 1

---- ⓓ x 1 (Irregular service)

--- ⓓ 10.00–16.00

···· ⓓ x 6

·-·- ○ Caïques meet ferries

Ikaria

IKAPIA; 260 km²; pop. 9,500.

CODE ☎ 0275
TOURIST OFFICE ☎ 22222
PORT POLICE ☎ 22207
HOSPITAL ☎ 22330

Named after the unfortunate Icarus who fell and drowned (in the sea of the same name), after the wax holding the feathers to his man-made wings melted on flying too near the sun, wing-shaped Ikaria is a mountainous island with a thin covering of trees standing on the slopes like so many pins in a cushion. In fact, the view from the ferry is almost the most comfortable thing about the island. Often used as a place of exile, Ikaria seems to lack a coherent sense of identity. With five changes of name in the last two thousand years, a three-month existence as an independent state in 1912 before union with Greece, a failed 19 c. spa resort (boasting thermal springs so radioactive that they had to be closed down), and a freelance hippy colony on the northern

coast monopolizing the best beaches (besides seeming to put the islanders off tourism for good) this is perhaps not too surprising. But it does leave the island with a decidedly faded air: the locals haven't got much and don't seem to expect much either. The few tourists who call are often left feeling much the same; though, if you are prepared to grub around, with a bit of effort Ikaria can at least offer an 'interesting' variation of the Greek island theme.

The main town of **Agios Kyrikos** lies on the south-east coast. Having evolved as the port serving the 19 c. resort spa of Therma, it hasn't developed much beyond a street or two behind the waterfront and is filled with the cheaper and uglier type of Aegean mansion house. The only quarter with any atmosphere lies north of the *Hotel Adam*: a warren of streets filled with shoeshops. On the plus side, the backstreets clambering up the hillside behind the boulder-strewn waterfront, exude an air of quiet, small town domesticity (Agios Kyrikos is another of those

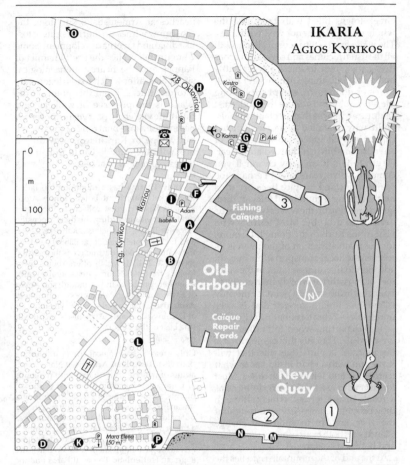

IKARIA
AGIOS KYRIKOS

Key

A Main Square
B Bus Stop
C Police Station
D Hospital
E Bank
F Newspapers
G Pharmacy
H Supermarket
I Bakery
J Pizzeria
K Rex Cinema
L Moped Rental
M Sculpture of Icarus
N Passenger Stalls
O Evdilos Road
P Xilosirtis Road

1 Ferry Berth
2 Hydrofoil Berth
3 Therma/Fourni Caïques

Greek towns filled with cats), and the whole town is well endowed with trees. The waterfront is the focus of all life; with all the usual facilities and several tavernas doing their best to inject a (very) little bonhomie into things. There isn't much to see or do in town, except stroll along the ferry quay and admire the modernist sculpture of Icarus that greets all arrivals. Quite why the failed aviator is depicted caught in what appears to be the beak of an enormous bird isn't immediately clear. (Truth to tell, it isn't any clearer if you come back five years later.) Perhaps the sculptor decided to spice the story up a bit by adding a mythical Halcyon bird, quietly nesting on the waves when Icarus decided to drop by. Most tourists who visit Agios Kyrikos are doing little more, for the main attraction of the town is its role as the local transportation hub. In addition to the caïques (and, in the summer of 1995, thrice-weekly hydrofoils) to Fourni, it is the starting point for the only island bus link: a service that is very unreliable — often terminating at Evdilos — and departing when full rather than on schedule. The only thing going for it is the journey: a cliff-edge ride that will leave you with a vivid insight as to what Icarus saw and felt as he fell to sea. Most tourists who use this bus are doing so as a result of the ferries, which although they provide a daily service throughout the year, are apt to chop and change island ports both from summer to summer and between seasons.

At the end of the mountain road lies the more appealing north side of the island (home to pine-forests, vineyards, and the island's final beaches). **Evdilos**, the bus's final destination, is Ikaria's second port, but sadly, is a village in decline. Huddled around a small hilly bay, it offers few temptations to linger. Ferry links remain good thanks to the hippy hoppers who collar this side of the island during the High Season. Most disembarking here are those in the know — heading for the

beaches at Armenistis, 8 km along the coast, now witness to the first signs of Ios-like disco and taverna development. Some 2 km further on lies the pretty hamlet of Pappas and the nearby archaeological site at **Nas**, after which roads degenerate into dirt tracks. From this point on the island is the preserve of walkers, and thus little visited. In past years rare ferries have made a taxi-boat rendezvous off the hill village of **Karkinagri**, providing a link with the outside world in lieu of a terrestrial means of access.

🛏

Gloomy Therma has a monopoly on faded up-market waterfront hotels, while Agios Kyrikos has a motley collection of cheaper establishments including the B-class pension *Adam* (☎ 22418), the C-class *O Karras* (☎ 22494) and E-class hotel *Isabella* (☎ 22839) — all on the waterfront. More attractive is the pension *Kastro* (☎ 22474), which offers rooms overlooking the town. Rooms are generally scarce elsewhere on the island — though some exist at Evdilos and there are a goodly number at **Armenistis**. There are also unofficial campsites at Evdilos (at Livadi), Armenistis and at Nas (the best of the three).

👀

Only great archaeological site of interest on Ikaria is a **Temple of Artemis** at Nas: foundations of which survive along with remnants of the ancient harbour. In the last century a marble statue of the goddess Artemis was unearthed at the site but an enlightened priest put paid to the island's chances of making it as a major sightseeing destination by burning it on the grounds that it was a pagan idol. Other archaeological points of interest on Ikaria are a 3 C. BC **Hellenistic Tower** at Faros and the very scanty remains of the ancient island capital at Kambos.

Agios Kyrikos sees frequent water taxies running to the ugly spa and hotel hamlet of Therma 4 km from the town, a reasonable beach at Fanari, and more interesting daily High Season caïques to the Fourni archipelago. Waterfront signs pointing out the town museum (150 m south of the hospital) take you on a town walk to a long abandoned building. On the west side of Agios Kyrikos lies a second spa village, at Therma Lefkadas.

LESBOS

	MAIN GREEN BUSES:
——	⑨ x 4 ⬧18.00
— —	⑨ x 6 ⬧18.00
–·–·–	⑨ x 2/3
–··–··–	⑨ x 2/3 ⬧13.15
– – –	⑨ x 1 13.15

	MAIN BLUE (CITY) BUSES:
– – – –	⑭ 07.00–20.00
· · · ·	⑭ 07.00–18.00
········	⑭ 06.30–20.00

0   km   10

Skala Sikamias
Castle — Molivos/ Mithimna
Petra
Mantamados
Anaxos
Agios Paraskevi
Moni Perivolis
Kalloni
Temple of Aphrodite
Spa
Pirgi Thermis
Moni Limona
Aqueduct
Castle & Theatre
Sigri   Andissa
Petrified Trees
Lambou Mili
Mytilini
Eressos
Gulf of Kallonis
Varia
Skala Eressou
Agiassos
Gulf of Gera
968 m
Paleokipos
Loutra
Feminist Beach
Polihnitos
Skopelos
Agios Ermoyenis Beach
Temple of Dionysos
Vrissa
Vatera
Ag. Isidoros
Plomari
Tarti Beach

✈ → Athens ⑨ x 4
→ Thessalonika ⑨ x 1
→ Limnos ⑨ x 1
→ Chios ③ ⑦ x 1

⬥——— ⑨ x 2
–·–·– ⑨ x 2
········ ○ Irregular Service

🚢——— ⑨ x 8

Lesbos

ΛΕΣΒΟΣ; 1630 km²; pop. 104,600.

MYTILINI CODE ☎ 0251
NTOG TOURIST OFFICE ☎ 22776
PORT POLICE ☎ 28888
HOSPITAL ☎ 28457

The third largest Greek island, Lesbos (pronounced Les*vos*) is more popular with locals rather than with foreign holiday-makers (this latter category largely confined to those individuals who go everywhere, and sundry loving couples — usually female — searching out their feminist roots). Thanks to good olive oil and ouzo (the aniseedy national drink) brewing industries, the island is economically self-sufficient, with little need to develop tourism. This is somewhat intimidated anyway by the size of Lesbos and the nature of bus services, which are inconveniently centred on the east coast capital of Mytilini, and infrequent, making quick movement difficult without your own transport. Given that sights are spread inconveniently around the island and that much of the stark landscape reflects the island's volcanic origins, it is perhaps not surprising that most island hoppers confine themselves to Mytilini and the lovely northern resort town of Mithimna/Molivos.

Mytilini, the island capital, is the destination for all ferries and is one of those ports which operators prefer to refer to direct in preference to the island name. At first sight very appealing, straddling a promontory adorned with a impressive castle and a busy harbour crowned with a prominent pineapple-domed church, this large town is something of a disappointment on closer inspection: being little more than a conglomeration of drab, dusty streets that are filled to bursting in the week, but dead to the world on Sundays. One of these, Ermou — running from the harbour to the northern town bay — doubles as the town bazaar with a suitably bizarre collection of junk shops.

All the facilities are within a drachma's throw of the inner harbour waterfront. Along the quay to the west lie the city bus station (with a frequent service to Pirgi Termis — a popular spa and beach resort to the north), a Folk Art Museum, a Byzantine Museum and the main bus station. This latter landmark is the best way out of town with daily links to all parts of the island. You may wish to take advantage of this sooner rather than later for although the Mytilini townsfolk are friendly enough they are more superstitious than most, and leapt into the world's press in 1994 when, during an excavation of a 19 C. Muslim cemetery, a stone-lined crypt hollowed out of the city wall was found to contain a vampire's coffin. The inhabitant, a middle-aged man, had been nailed through his neck, pelvis, and ankles to the casket base in order to prevent him from rising again. This was a common enough practice in Greece at the time (as was the habit of nailing horseshoes to a deceased's hands and feet so that if they were to go walkies the locals would hear them coming). Quite what this particular unfortunate had done to deserve his fate

is not known. Rumour, probably malicious, has it that he was a misogynist who rashly spoke out of turn in a lesbian bar; but this is unlikely given that he appears to have been dead before he was nailed down.

Thanks to the olive-grove lined Gulfs of Gera and Kallonis, Lesbos is effectively divided into three parts, with Mytilini and the peninsula below hanging on like the island's tail. Links between the three are all but non-existent: hence the difficulty in moving around by public transport without returning to Mytilini. To date, the northern part of the island has been the focus of the tourist industry, thanks to the attractive castle-topped northern coast town of **Molivos** (officially known by its older name of **Mithimna**) 62 km from Mytilini. Once Mytilini's great rival for control of the island it has benefited immeasurably from losing out and not ending up the home of innumerable grimy 19 C. mansions. Instead, cobbled streets, a pebble beach and photogenic houses are the order of the day. The village of **Petra** 5 km to the south is also emerging as a resort thanks to its better beach.

The best island beaches, however, lie elsewhere. The surprisingly quiet resort village of **Vetera** has an amazing 7 km stretch of sand and can be reached direct by bus or beach boat from the indifferent southern resort of **Plomari**. The bus route is better as it takes in the lovely old (and government protected) hill village of **Agiassos** carved out of a pine forest with cobbled streets and old timber houses, and the objective for regular package-tourist excursions.

The west side of Lesbos is visibly less fertile than the east and comparatively quiet with the singular exception of **Eressos** and its impressive beach at Skala Eressou (and site of ancient Eressos). Home to the feminist poet Sappho and the island's lesbian movement, the long sandy beach is comparable with that at Vetera — apart from the scattered bodies

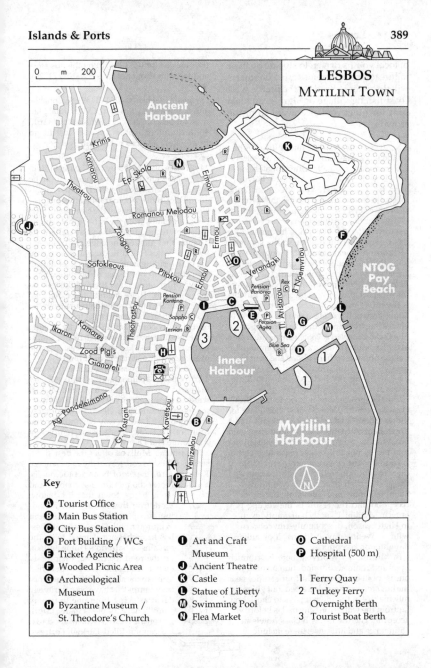

Key

- **Ⓐ** Tourist Office
- **Ⓑ** Main Bus Station
- **Ⓒ** City Bus Station
- **Ⓓ** Port Building / WCs
- **Ⓔ** Ticket Agencies
- **Ⓕ** Wooded Picnic Area
- **Ⓖ** Archaeological Museum
- **Ⓗ** Byzantine Museum / St. Theodore's Church
- **Ⓘ** Art and Craft Museum
- **Ⓙ** Ancient Theatre
- **Ⓚ** Castle
- **Ⓛ** Statue of Liberty
- **Ⓜ** Swimming Pool
- **Ⓝ** Flea Market
- **Ⓞ** Cathedral
- **Ⓟ** Hospital (500 m)
- 1 Ferry Quay
- 2 Turkey Ferry Overnight Berth
- 3 Tourist Boat Berth

of local youths driven to suicide by their failure to chat up foreign fluff. Lone males will do better to head for the pretty, west coast fishing village of **Sigri** — an ideal spot for quiet romance away from the crowds.

☙

A semi-friendly Tourist Police office lies just off the ferry quay offering (if you ask nicely) accommodation details. Unfortunately most of it is well away from **Mytilini Town**. In town (which is where you often need to be thanks to ferry departure times that prohibit sleeping elsewhere) options are more limited. Out of High Season the scatter of rooms around the town offer the best value for money; for this reason they fill quickly in the summer. Most are on or near Ermou St., though the best lie on the south side of the harbour. The hotels are a pretty diverse collection. The B-class *Blue Sea* (☎ 23994) just off the ferry quay offers the prospect of an easy, if pricey, bed, but this is deceptive thanks to a 'strictly no riff-raff' admissions policy (note: if you are under forty or wearing a backpack then *you* are 'riff-raff'). The C-class *Sappho* (☎ 28888) on the other side of the harbour is much more accommodating, but too popular by half (phone ahead in High Season). If you can afford the odd 15,000 GDR a night, the nearby B-class *Lesvion* (☎ 22038) offers an attractive option.

Usually the last hotel in town to fill is the C-class *Rex* (☎ 28523): a leading candidate for the weirdest hotel in Greece, it looks like a down-beat Addams Family mansion, and boasts hollowed mattresses so old that getting into bed is not unlike getting into a coffin. Add to this the cloves of garlic embellishing the wrought iron trellis of the front door and the photograph of a naked two-headed Siamese infant boy adorning the hotel reception and the result is the cheapest hotel in Mytilini. Usually half empty, even in High Season, it is a family-run concern with a 'Wednesday Addams' look-alike daughter on reception.

In **Mithimna / Molivos** there is so much hotel and room accommodation on offer that one is spoilt for choice . The tourist office near the bus stop can help find a bed, but given the hilly nature of the town it pays to check how far from the waterfront any bed is before you accept it. The town has B-class hotels in abundance and little else; these include

the *Poseidon* (☎ 0253 71570) by the bus stop, and the waterfront *Sea Horse* (☎ 0253 71320).

△

Camping Mithimna (☎ 0261 71169): reasonable, and popular site: 2 km east of Mithimna, 1 km from the beach. *Camping Dionysos* (☎ 0252 613 40), on the other hand, is a new site just inland from Vatera and has yet to really get going.

◉◉

Mytilini is dominated by the **Castle**, built in 1373 on the site of the old acropolis; it can be visited, but, overlooking the Turkish coast, is another of those photographically sensitive sites. Impressive views of the castle can, however, be gleaned from the hillside that is home to the bowl (sans seats) of the 3 c. BC **Hellenistic Theatre** that marked the edge of the ancient town. Mosaics found in excavations nearby are now residing in the good **Archaeological Museum** 50 m north-east of Mytilini's ferry quay. Other undoubted town sights are no longer extant. These include the canal that once separated the castle peninsula from the rest of the island (Ermou street follows much of its former course) and the wacky looking tower (see illustration below) that once adorned the end of the — just visible — eastern mole of the now defunct northern harbour.

Elsewhere on the island: the hamlet of Moria, 4 km outside Mytilini, has the impressive remains of a 3 c. AD **Roman Aqueduct** that watered the ancient city at Mytilini. Odd fragments survive along its 20 km length notably at Lambou Mili. Some way beyond Lambou Mili are the scanty remains of Temples of Aphrodite and Dionysos.

Mithimna / Molivos offers the best sightseeing on Lesbos courtesy of the 14 c. Genoese **Kastro** built on the site of the ancient acropolis, and the almost too picturesque cobbled and stone house town that lies below. Finds from the ancient town (including sarcophagi) are in the **Museum** in the town hall. The west side of Lesbos has what are claimed to be the remains of **Sappho's Home** and, on off the road to Antissa, the grossly over-rated remains of a petrified forest in the shape of three desultory tree stumps that have been variously dated as being from one to twenty million years old. Finally, **Sigri**, on the west coast has a good 18 c. cannon-filled **Turkish Fortress**.

Oinousses

ΟΙΝΟΥΣΣΕΣ; 16 km²; pop. 420.

CODE ☎ 0272
POLICE ☎ 55222

Oinousses (also commonly transcribed as 'Inousses') is the collective name for a group of nine tiny islands that lie off the north-east coast of Chios. The only inhabited island — the largest in the group — goes under the same name and is the object of regular High Season day-tripper boats from Chios Town.

Blessed with several good beaches, attractively clear seas and one large town that feels more like a city suburb on the slide than an island capital, Oinousses has the distinction of being the birthplace of several of Greece's richest shipping owners. Summers therefore see luxury yachts in the harbour; their owners visiting luxury villas tucked discreetly away in an otherwise attractive, but declining, town. The strong seafaring tradition hereabouts sees many of the menfolk working away: the result is a curious mix of affluence combined with boarded-up summer holiday homes. For this reason tourism is all but ignored as the remaining islanders (many of whom work in fishing-related industries) have enough coming in to be able to resist the temptations to turn their home into a resort island. The most obvious consequence of all this is that tourist facilities are scarce to the point of being non-existent (beyond the normal bank-cum-post office), and the usual welcoming attitude typical of most Greek islanders is thin on the ground if you try to sleep on it (you will as likely as not be rounded up by cadets from the island's nautical school). Those that recourse to the only hotel fare somewhat better.

The lack of tourists has in its turn made an attractive island difficult to visit, as the local Chios boats are mostly based on Oinousses itself; forcing you to stay overnight. This state of affairs improved considerably during the summer of 1996, but

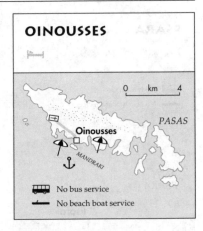

OINOUSSES

0   km   4

PASAS

Oinousses

MANDRAKI

🚌 No bus service
⛴ No beach boat service

the island is still best visited by the Chios Town day-tripper boats (frequency varies greatly according to the time of year). In addition to visiting Oinousses proper, these boats often also stop at the privately owned harbour mouth church islet of **Mandraki** 300 m from the town quay.

🛏

No rooms, but one nice, if pricey, C-class hotel in the town — the *Thalassoporos* (☎ 55475) — usually has rooms available all year round.

👓

Oinousses is relatively bereft of things to see or do other than lie on the beach (the best lie in quiet coves to the west of the town). The town can only boast a **Maritime Museum** (that is invariably closed) filled with mementos donated by local shipping millionaires. This means that most visitors are reduced to doing the coastal walk to the **Evangelismou Convent** on the western tip of the island. Home to the mummified corpse of a shipping billionaire's daughter who snuffed it shortly after becoming a nun, the monastery was rebuilt as a shrine to her memory by her father (who has now joined her in her mausoleum). The fact that her body hadn't decomposed after its traditional three-year stint underground (in Greece graves are re-used, so once the flesh has rotted the bones of the deceased are removed and interred elsewhere) was taken as a (fortuitous — for the monastery's finances at any rate) sign of sainthood.

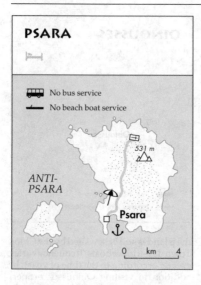

PSARA

[bed symbol]

🚌 No bus service
⛵ No beach boat service

ANTI-PSARA

531 m

□ **Psara**
⚓

0　　　km　　　4

Psara

ΨΑΡΑ; 45 km²; pop. 460.

CODE ☎ 0274.

Barren and dusty Psara rarely figures on tourist itineraries and, ignored by most ferry operators, wallows quietly in the shadows of its own grim history. An obscure island in ancient times, it came to prominence (along with the Saronic islands of Hydra and Spetses) in the early 19 c., thanks to an indigenous fleet of merchant adventurers. Psara was thus well placed to play a prominent part in the early liberation struggle of the independent Greek state, but — lying just off the Turkish mainland — very badly placed when it came to avoiding the wrath of the Turks that came after. By way of setting an example to would-be rebellious islands the Turks laid waste to the island in 1824; killing the bulk of the population (inflated by refugees from other islands) of 20,000 (3,000 escaping by boat to found a town on Evia: Nea Psara). Psara has never really recovered from the event the

Greeks call the 'holocaust'. Some survivors drifted back, the island has never prospered. Almost all live in the only town of **Psara**. Traversing a headland on the south coast, it is hardly the typical island town. Photographs suggest that it is quite developed, but the reality is rather different. With few made up roads and not much in the way of shops, the town feels like an undeveloped version of Lipsi. Town buildings — which for the most part are gloriously undistinguished — are pretty scattered, as there is no pressure on space. Most of the town life — such as it is; for the settlement feels like one large suburb — centres on the waterfront square which is home to one bar, a couple of shady trees and a memorial adorned with miniature cannon. A gun-manned bastion of sorts has also been built on the northern headland of the caïque harbour which is also home to a couple of tavernas. On the plus side the typical 'family' small island atmosphere pervades, and there are a reasonable number of American-English speakers in the backstreets thanks to expatriates returning 'home' each summer.

The rest of the island is barren and has little to offer apart from walks to distant windmills or empty beaches (sadly, most of poor quality: the best lie along the road to the north-east of the town) and an 18 c. monastery on the north side of the island.

[bed symbol]

The thin supply of beds on the island are dominated by a prison converted to a hotel by the EOT, the B-class *Miramare* on the north side of town, and the *Xenonas Pension* (☎ 612 93). There are also a few rooms.

∞

Sightseeing on Psara is thin on the ground. The Turks took a lot of trouble to ensure that there was nothing left to look at, totally demolishing the castle that stood on the headland still known as **Paleokastro**. Now topped by a couple of chapels it offers sunbaked views across to Antipsara but little more. A few ruinous pre-holocaust buildings survive, and there is a small museum on the outskirts of town that is usually closed.

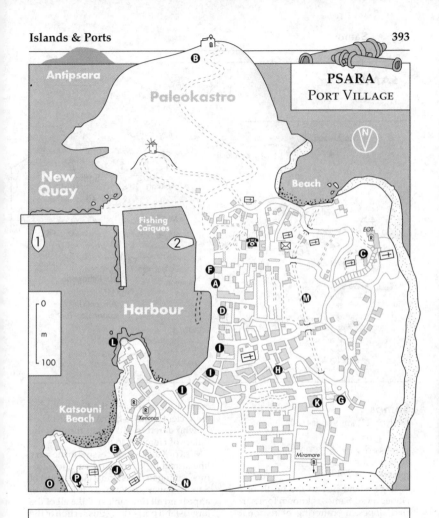

PSARA
PORT VILLAGE

Antipsara

Paleokastro

New Quay

Beach

Fishing Caïques

EOT

Harbour

Katsouni Beach

Xerionas

Miramare

Key

Ⓐ Town Square
Ⓑ Site of Venetian Kastro
Ⓒ Police
Ⓓ National Bank of Greece
Ⓔ Museum
Ⓕ Main Square Bar &
   Ferry Tickets

Ⓖ Supermarket
Ⓗ Bakery
Ⓘ Tavernas
Ⓙ School
Ⓚ Old Water Wells
Ⓛ Cannon Memorial
Ⓜ Ravine (dry in summer)
Ⓝ Village Ring Road

Ⓞ Lazoreta Beach
Ⓟ Dirt Track to:
   Lakka Beach &
   Limnos Beach

1 Ferry Berth
2 Berth for (rare)
   Excursion Caïques

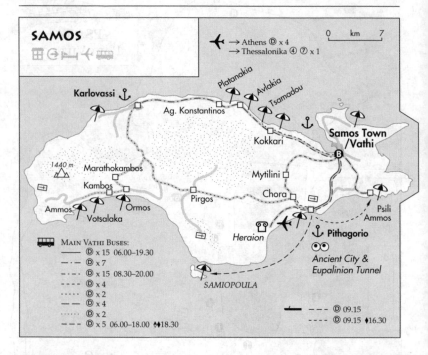

Samos

ΣΑΜΟΣ; 472 km²; pop. 41,500.

CODE ☎ 0273
TOURIST OFFICE ☎ 28530
PORT POLICE ☎ 27318
HOSPITAL ☎ 27407

A large island just to the north of the Dodecanese, Samos is known for its tree-clad slopes, a scattering of reasonable sand beaches, and top end of the package tourist market (island-hoppers are not noted for visiting in large numbers). The island was one of the most important in the ancient world and particularly noted as a centre of learning. This reputation was derived from her most famous sons, notably Aesop (of fable fame), Pythagoras, Epicurus, Aristarchus (the astronomer who worked out that the earth revolved

around the sun), and the Columbus of the ancient world — the navigator Kolaios — who dared to sail a ship through the Pillars of Hercules in 650 BC.

Most of Kolaios's successors in the ferry line attract little fame and even less fortune sailing to the island's largest port of **Samos Town** (or **Vathi** as it is wont to appear on all timetables). Like all of the large island ports along this section of the Turkish coast it is commercial in appearance (i.e. a drab and dingy collection of 19 c. buildings) without the obvious charm of the harbours of the smaller islands that make up the Dodecanese. This said, it is the sort of place you can happily spend a few hours in — though you wouldn't travel across Europe just to visit it. This is something of a surprise if you venture here by way of Pithagorio to the south, as from the hills overlooking the town, Vathi looks to be a very attractive place. As it is, most tourists confine their wanderings to the waterfront, the streets running in parallel to it, and the small, but pleasant, town park abutting the post office and the town's archaeological museum. Despite this, Samos Town figures on the itineraries of most island hoppers who venture into the Eastern Aegean north of the Dodecanese as Vathi is the terminus for all Piraeus—Ikaria—Samos ferries, with small (but invaluable) linking services on to Chios. Turkey and the well preserved ancient Greek city of Ephesus is also a popular hop away from here, as you will find if you venture into the multi-stepped ticket agency near the ferry quay: they aren't over interested in selling anyone trips to anywhere else. As usual in this part of the world political tensions are evident: the Port Police are very sensitive when Turkish boats are in, and are quick to shepherd interested spectators away from these boats. Sleeping on the ferry quay is also a non-starter thanks to the attentions of mice and men (or in Vathi's case rats and policemen). Tourist activity in the town is low key; with most of the package tour hotels being located along the coast at the pretty beach resort of **Kokkari**, an easy bus ride away.

The second of the island's ports is commercial **Karlovassi**. Also on the north coast, but an hour's steaming closer to Piraeus, it had its heyday during the late 19 c. when boats were slower and it formed the nearest convenient link with the mainland. Even today most Vathi-bound ferries call en route, though few tourists disembark. The run-down 19 c. neo-classical warehouse backdrop to the port (inconveniently placed on the outskirts of the town) is neither prepossessing nor relieved by an equally drab town beyond. It does, however, have residual value as both a place to pick up boats after touring the length of the island, and where you can sure of finding a High Season bed.

The third Samian port of **Pithagorio** on the south coast offers a complete contrast to the northern ports. Now the centre of the island's tourist industry, it has a very attractive atmosphere and the bulk of the island sights, but bar a few tourist boats and a daily summer hydrofoil (most heading for Patmos) it is poorly connected with the ferry network with only a couple of regular departures each week. The modern town lies over the ancient capital of the island. Known at the time as 'Samos', it is not to be confused with the modern capital with that name on the north coast. In fact, Pithagorio has changed names several times, and the current name only dates back to 1953 when the town was re-christened in honour of the island's most famous son: the mathematician Pythagoras (from the Middle Ages until 1953 the town was called Tigani).

Despite the large numbers of package tourists in town, Pithagorio manages to retain a surprisingly dreamy air (at least until evening falls), with a snug taverna and tree-lined small harbour backed by red-roofed town behind. Unfortunately, all this means that Pithagorio is very expensive by Greek standards — a reflection of the top-island-resort status it enjoys (hotels line the beach-lined coast along its western side) and the number of sightseeing day-trippers calling. Tourism has at least ensured the existence of regular taxi boats to Psli Ammos beach as well as to **Samiopoula** islet (visiting a north-side beach and taverna).

Buses run from Samos Town calling at almost all the main island towns and villages twice daily. The busy routes however, are along the north coast to Karlovassi and south to Pithagorio. The north coast buses thus pass through the resort at Kokkari, the beach villages at Tsamodou and Avlakia before arriving at Ag. Konstantinos (an ugly tourist town better seen from the bus) and Karlovassi. Karlovassi is also the jumping off point for the south-west coast. This is in many ways the most attractive part of the island; an appealing mix of taverna-lined beaches and fishing villages that form a relaxed and unexploited backwater. **Votsalakia** and **Ammos** beaches are easily the best and usually quiet, even in High Season.

Samos is unusual for a popular Greek island in having no camping facilities. Budget accommodation is also thin on the ground in the popular towns. As a result Samos can be a very tricky island on which to find a reasonably priced bed in August — particularly if you arrive in the latter part of the day: at this time of the year it pays to phone ahead. Ticket agencies have lists of accommodations as do the Tourist Police.

Vathi, the capital, is not really a primary tourist destination and this is reflected in the accommodation; with most of the beds in hotels strung along the coast well away from the town centre. In the town are a number of better placed establishments. The waterfront has a number of hotels including the B-class *Xenia* (☎ 27463) at the south-east end of the harbour and the better placed *Aeolis* (☎ 28904), and the C-class *Samos* (☎ 28377) which occasionally has reasonably priced rooms and always boasts a main staircase with overhangs designed for midgets. Nearer the budget end of the range is the waterfront E-class *Artemis* (☎ 27792). The hilly backstreets behind the harbour are also a rich source for beds with the E-class *Parthenon* (☎ 27234) and several pensions (principally along Stamatiadou St.).

Pithagorio has a tourist office/booth just off the main street with accommodation information. The quayside has a number of pricey but justifiably popular hotels hidden behind the tavernas, including the B-class hotel / pensions *Tarsanas* (☎ 61162) just off the ferry quay, and the *Acropole* (☎ 61261), along with the almost as pricey C-class *Damo* (☎ 61303) and *Delphini* (☎ 61205). The streets behind offer the prospect of better hunting. On the main street is the B-class *Fillis* (☎ 612 96) and behind, the budget D-class *Alexandra* (☎ 61429) and E-class *Paris* (☎ 61513). These are augmented by several minor pensions and a limited number of rooms.

Karlovassi is an ugly place and finding a bed is rarely a problem. Cheapest option is the Youth Hostel behind the large Panagia Church,

but there are some 14 hotels in town. At the bottom end of the range are the D-class *Morpheus* (☎ 32672), the *Astir* (☎ 33150) and the *Aktaeon* (☎ 32356) near the port. At the top end of the range is the A-class *Arion* (☎ 92020).

Given that Samos was one of the better endowed islands with monuments in ancient times, the extant remains are something of a disappointment: much has gone and the remainder can comfortably be taken in during the course of a day trip to the island.

Pithagorio is the sightseeing town on Samos; though at first sight this might seem rather surprising as there doesn't initially appear to be much to see beyond the exhibits in the **Archaeological Museum** (though the best of the local finds are to be found in the **Vathi Archaeological Museum**). In fact during the 6 c. BC it was the island capital and ruled by the tyrant Polykrates, who seemed intent on leaving a series of monumental works behind him. No doubt it was a considerable source of satisfaction to him when, crucified (by the Persians in 522 BC) on the Turkish coast opposite the town, he hung around and surveyed the wondrous constructions he had commissioned. All survive — in various states of repair — today. These include the **Temple of Hera** (usually known as the **Herion** and described overleaf) and the best preserved of the Polykratic monuments; the **harbour mole**; now the ferry quay, most tourists walk its length without knowing it to be any different from quays the islands over. The quay reflects the fact that Pithagorio hides all but scant remains of the ancient city of Samos. Beyond odd collections of stones and the foundations of some Hellenistic houses behind the **Castle of Legothetes** (built in 1824 by a hero of the independence movement) only the ruinous **Theatre** and **City Walls** skirting the tops of the hills behind give a hint as to what was here before. The oddest of the Polykratic monuments is well hidden (though signposts give the game away today); the 1034 m **Tunnel of Eupalinos** (named after its architect and completed in 524 BC), hewn through the mountain, it was designed to guarantee water supplies to the city as well as offering a means of escape (though Polykrates failed to take advantage of it). The first claustrophobic 70 metres of the tunnel is open to the public ⑨ ex① 9.00–14.00, the entrance fee is 500 GDR.

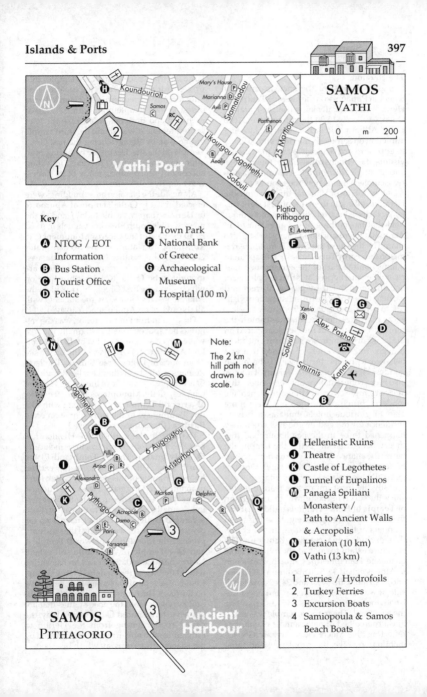

SAMOS
VATHI

Koundourioti

Mary's House

Marianna

Avli

Samos

Parthenon

Platia Pithagora

Artemis

Vathi Port

Likourgou Logothethi

Stamatiadou

25 Martiou

Aeolis

Sofouli

Key

A NTOG / EOT Information
B Bus Station
C Tourist Office
D Police

E Town Park
F National Bank of Greece
G Archaeological Museum
H Hospital (100 m)

Xenia

Alex. Pashali

Sofouli

Smirnis

Kanari

0   m   200

SAMOS
PITHAGORIO

Logothetou

Fillis

6 Augoustou

Anna

Aristarhou

Alexandra

Pythagora

Markou

Delphini

Acropole

Damo

Paris

Tarsanas

Note:
The 2 km hill path not drawn to scale.

I Hellenistic Ruins
J Theatre
K Castle of Legothetes
L Tunnel of Eupalinos
M Panagia Spiliani Monastery / Path to Ancient Walls & Acropolis
N Heraion (10 km)
O Vathi (13 km)

1 Ferries / Hydrofoils
2 Turkey Ferries
3 Excursion Boats
4 Samiopoula & Samos Beach Boats

Ancient Harbour

The Heraion

Lying 8 km west of the ancient capital of Samos at Pithagorio is the massive **Temple of Hera** — more usually known as the **Heraion**. Open ②–⑥ 08.30–15.00, the entrance fee is 1000 GDR. Although it is the main sightseeing attraction on Samos, the Herion is more likely to appeal to archaeological fans than casual visitors; the remains consisting of foundations and a single incomplete column (hastily reassembled) that is now the island's totem.

One of the most unusual things about the Heraion is the site itself: for at first sight this major shrine is bizarrely sited in an anonymous field that has nothing of the grandeur of an Acropolis to enhance it (a characteristic also shared by the site of the Great Temple of Artemis on the nearby Turkish coast). This apparent whimsy on the part of the ancients becomes clear when one appreciates that temples were usually surrounded by groves of trees and gardens (a fact now lost on most modern visitors to what are usually dry, dusty treeless excavation sites) and these factors came to the fore with the siting of the Heraion. Placed on the banks of the Imbrasos stream in a meadow of lygos trees (a variety of willow) that was believed to be the birthplace of the queen goddess Hera, its location so far out of town is also more coherent once one remembers that ancient temples were not the equivalent of the modern church or mosque but were more akin to glorious hotels, built as a private residence for the god or goddess when they happened to be in the neighbourhood (the theory being that the better the temple, the better the chance that the patron deity would be tempted to visit and then stay): worship generally took place at nearby altars.

Easily the most impressive feature on the site is the surviving column of ❶ the **Heraion** or **Temple of Hera**. A famous building, it had the odd role of being the eighth of the seven wonders of the world (getting into later lists that excluded inaccessible Babylon). The structure extant today was the fourth temple on the site. Four times the size of the Parthenon in Athens, it had 3 x 8 30 m columns at its east end, 3 x 9 along the west and 24 x 2 down each side, it was built in the 6 C. BC, but never finished; though the Romans added steps along the east front. The massive temple was really like a roofed bed of nails: a mass of columns reflecting the concreteless Archaic Greeks' inability to solve the problem of bridging large internal spaces. The three temples that preceded it stood more to the east, the first only recently surrendering the claim to be the oldest known temple built with columns at each end and down its sides. Like the later second temple it was small: the third temple built 6 C BC by Rhoikos being the first Great Temple on the site. Destroyed by fire c. 525 BC after standing for only 25 years, its extant successor (incorporating many of its stones) was built by Polykrates.

Alongside the Heraion other buildings were erected, notably ❸ the **Temple of Aphrodite** or **Hermes** (barely visible today), and ❹ the now invisible **South Stoa** now vaguely marked by ❺ the base of the **Ciceros Monument** (2 C. AD); home to statues of the Roman orator Cicero and his brother Quintus. To the east stands an enigmatic group of stones that are thought to be ❻ the **Kolaios Ship Base** on which stood the first Greek ship to sail on the Atlantic (it was viewed by the ancients with all the awe of an Apollo space capsule).

The area in front of the Herion was the religious hot spot on the site. Originally the area was a paved square bounded by ❼ the **Rhoikos' Altar** (6 C. BC) which was built on the site of an ancient **Lygos Tree Shrine**. The later Romans in-filled — as they usually did, adding ❽ a **Temple** (on the site of the earlier Heraion temples), ❾ the **Monopteros Altar / Temple**, ❿ a second **Temple** (2 C. AD) along with ⓫ a tiny **Bathhouse**. In the early Christian era a **Basilica** (ⓚ) was also constructed.

The area to the north of the Heraion has revealed traces of several structures including ⓛ a **Mycenaean Tholos Tomb** and ⓜ the **North Stoa**. This is the site of the earliest known example of this uniquely Greek form of architecture. Originally a wooden structure, it was replaced in stone in the Hellenistic period. A small town grew up to the east of it and several ⓝ **Hellenistic Houses** have been excavated. Temples however, lined the sanctuary precinct; the foundations of two: ⓞ **Temple A** and ⓟ a **Temple of Aphrodite** still extant. Nearby lie the foundations of an Archaic shrine with ⓠ the base of the **Genelos Statue Group**. Copies of several of the statues have be erected on the base. The originals are the only significant survivals from the 2000 statues that are known to have graced ⓡ the **Sacred Way**, the paved road running from the Herion to Pithagorio, and now irreparably damaged by the island airport runway which bisects it.

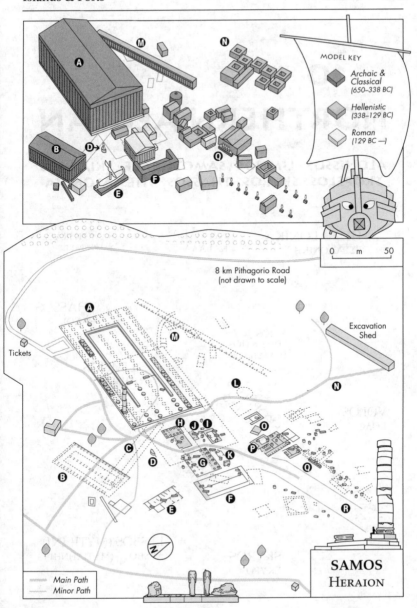

MODEL KEY

Archaic & Classical
(650–338 BC)

Hellenistic
(338–129 BC)

Roman
(129 BC —)

0 m 50

8 km Pithagorio Road
(not drawn to scale)

Tickets

Excavation Shed

Main Path
Minor Path

SAMOS
HERAION

10
NORTHERN AEGEAN

ALONISSOS · LIMNOS · SAMOTHRACE · SKIATHOS
SKOPELOS · SKYROS · THASSOS · THESSALONIKA

THESSALONIKA
ΘΕΣΣΑΛΟΝΙΚΗ

KAVALA
ΚΑΒΑΛΑ

SAMOTHRACE
ΣΑΜΟΘΡΑΚΗ

+1½

+6½

THASSOS
ΘΑΣΟΣ

AGIOS
EFSTRATIOS
ΑΓ. ΕΦΣΤΡΑΤΙΟ

+6

LIMNOS
ΛΗΜΝΟ

VOLOS
ΒΟΛΟ

SKOPELOS
ΣΚΟΠΕΛΟ

+5 HOURS

+3

+1 +1

ALONISSOS
ΑΛΟΝΝΗΣΟ

SKIATHOS
ΣΚΙΑΘΟ

+3

SKYROS
ΣΚΥΡΟ

LESBOS (MYTILINI)
ΛΕΣΒΟ   (ΜΥΤΙΛΗΝΗ)

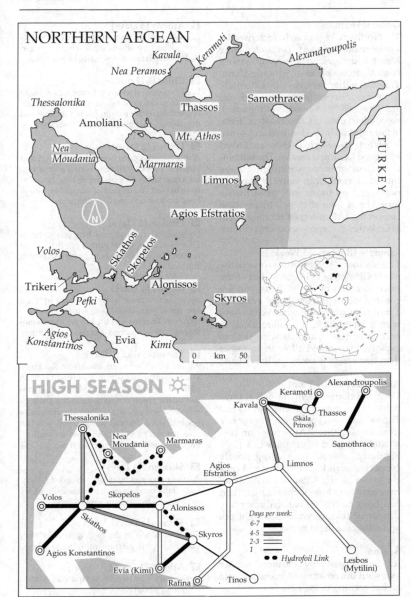

General Features

The Northern Aegean is characterised by a combination of poorly connected large islands and mainland ports, coupled with an easily accessible small Sporades chain. Travel is either very easy or extremely problematic depending upon where you are. The 'easy' part consists of the small, wooded islands off the coast of Evia: Skiathos, Skopelos, Alonissos and — to a lesser extent — Skyros. These are linked by a good hydrofoil service. The remainder of the northern network requires more time and really can only be happily negotiated by those with more than a fortnight at their disposal. In the Low Season the lack of ferries running north of Lesbos curtails non-Sporades options.

Example Itinerary [3 Weeks]

The Northern Aegean offers some of the nicest Greek island hopping, but at the price of a loss of flexibility as you are constrained by the few boats available. This itinerary has been achieved in 8 days with a lot of luck. It is more usual to encounter delays, and allowing time to explore, you should allow three rather than two weeks to complete the circuit.

Arrival/Departure Point

There are charter flight airports at three points on the circuit: Athens, Kavala and Thessalonika and you can happily operate from any of them. Athens is the best should you need to get back in a rush. Similarly, as you are visiting poorly connected ports it is better to travel anti-clockwise as the latter destinations all have easy ferry links to the mainland and bus links to the capital: reducing any danger of finding yourself caught out and missing a flight home.

Season

July and August only : the months either side see reduced services sinking away to all but nothing in the Low Season.

■ Athens [3 Days]

An easy starting point with access to NTOG ferry departure sheets from which you can deduce departure times further up the line.

■ Chios [2 Days]

Well worth a stop-over, Chios has a lot to offer. You can establish in Athens when subsequent boats are running down the line and thus deduce the times of Chios—Lesbos ferries.

■ Lesbos [2 Days]

A nice island, which is just as well given that you will probably have to wait a day or two for a boat north. Depending on how long you have to wait you can either stay in Mytilini or head up to much prettier Mithyma.

■ Limnos [2 Days]

Unless you have to change here you can treat Limnos as an optional port of call that can be missed if your Lesbos boat north leaves you running late.

■ Kavala [4 Days]

An attractive town in which to rest up for a few days. You should take advantage of the ferries to Thassos and the less regular Samothrace boat — stamina and time permitting.

■ Thessalonika [1 Day]

Athens buses run every hour from Kavala so you can run across at your leisure and pick up either hydrofoil or ferry to Skiathos. This is one of the weak connections in the chain as weekend services out of Thessalonika can be booked solid. Should this happen you can take a train to Volos and then a Skiathos-bound hydrofoil or ferry from there.

■ Skiathos [3 Days]

Another nice resting point with good Athens links if the need arises via Volos. Even so, try to find time to continue on to Skyros.

■ Skyros [2 Days]

The final island in the loop with daily ferry links with Kimi and the waiting bus to Athens.

■ Athens [2 Days]

Arrive back with two days to spare if you have a flight pre-booked.

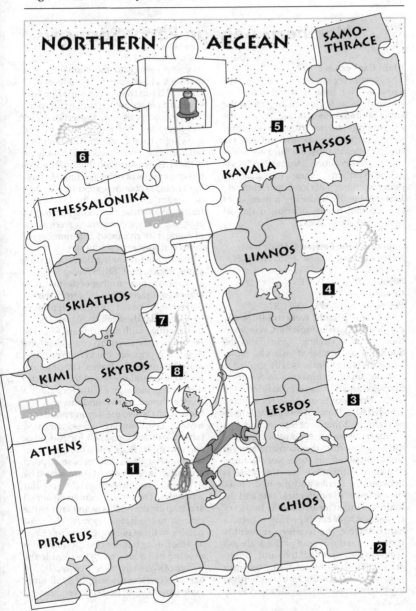

Northern Aegean Ferry Services

Main Car Ferries
The North Aegean ferries fall into four groups. The first is a collection of diminutive car ferries bustling along the small Sporades line, the second is made up of large ferries running summer services from Thessalonika to Crete via the Cyclades islands, the third are wide-ranging ferries running to mainland ports in the Northern Aegean (the majority being summer services operating via Lesbos). Finally, there are a number of shorter-haul ferries offering mainland links to adjacent islands.

Sporades Line Ferries & Hydrofoils
Nomikos Lines; *Lemnos*; 1976; 1787 GRT.
Macedon; 1972; 1974 GRT.
Skopelos; 1965; 1414 GRT.
Goutos Lines;
Papadiamantis II; 1973; 1060 GRT.
The Greek islands were traditionally divided into two groups: the Cyclades or those islands 'circling' Delos, and the Sporades or 'scattered' islands. Nowadays the latter term is usually applied to just the small archipelago of Skiathos, Skopelos and Alonissos (also referred to as the Northern Sporades). These small wooded islands attract considerable tourist traffic and therefore ferry activity.

Four small car ferries run along the line, most starting from the mainland town of Volos, but some from Agios Konstantinos. The only competition on the route is between the ferries and the hydrofoils: the advent of computer ticketing and the hydrofoil threat means that the two ferry companies have combined forces to run a joint timetable. This sees regular monthly changes, but the overall package always seems to end up much the same. Itineraries A and B (see opposite) are the most widely run. Most ports see a ferry berthed overnight in order to provide a very early morning service to the mainland — a feature that accounts for schedules of C and D. E is run twice weekly in High Season but days are apt to change each year.

Strong competition to the ferries down the Sporades line is provided by the growing hydrofoil system. Although they only operate a restricted service outside of the High Season, with the usual hydrofoil constraints of being confined to daylight hours and calm sea conditions, they do cream off considerable passenger traffic (so much so, that in the summer of 1995 the ferries companies were complaining bitterly about the number of hydrofoil runs on the route).

In addition to running the same routes as the ferries, the CERES *Flying Dolphins* also operate to a number of destinations otherwise inaccessible by ferry, with a daily High Season morning departure from the islands south to Skyros (H) — usually filled with day-trippers — and to ports along the northern coastline of the Aegean. A popular, but very expensive, daily hydrofoil (I), leaves Thessalonika for Skiathos and the rest of the Sporades during the summer, calling four days a week at the town of Moundania en route. Moundania is also the starting point for a hydrofoil (J), four days a week, heading (after a call at Marmaras) for Alonissos and ending at either Volos or Agios Konstantinos. Finally, a number of small ports around Evia and Volos (G) are served by hydrofoils running otherwise regular schedules. These calls seem to be aimed at attracting the odd local and are of little interest to the island hopper. The most notable of these ports are Pefki (on Evia) and the fishing hamlet-clad islet of Trekeri nestling like a lone tooth just inside the mouth of Volos bay. Note: hydrofoil ticket agencies can usually supply a full timetable (covering all ports) on request.

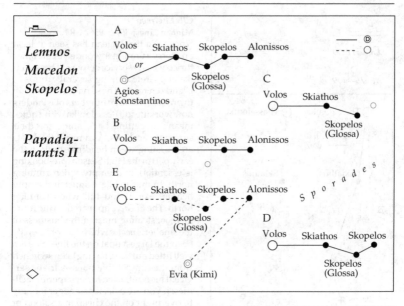

Lemnos Macedon Skopelos

Papadiamantis II

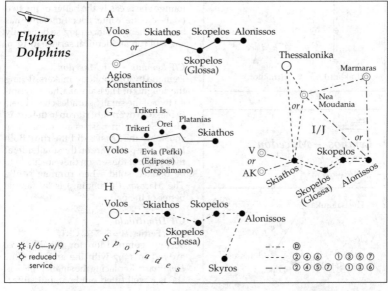

Flying Dolphins

☼ i/6—iv/9
◇ reduced service

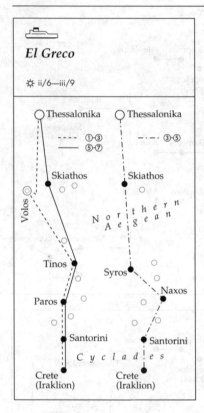

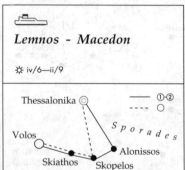

C/F *El Greco*
Minoan Lines; 1972; 9562 GRT.
Since 1989 the Aegean has seen at least one ferry running a wonderful summer thrice-weekly service between Thessalonika and Crete, linking several groups of islands en route. The service exists solely to provide the large numbers of islanders now working in Thessalonika with a quick means of getting back home for their summer vacations. As a result the boats are bursting when heading south in the early part of the High Season (pre-booking is essential), and empty when running north. In mid to late August and empty heading south and full when running north. The *El Greco* appeared on the route in 1996, stealing most of the business of the smaller *Anemos* which had previously been the largest boat on the line. She is a well fitted out boat, having been switched from the competitive trans-Adriatic service. This is reflected in her superior facilities: if you are a deck passenger looking to overnight on the cheap in a saloon or lounge she is easily the better of the two boats on the route. Her timetable has been unchanged since 1997, so hopefully she will run an identical service in 1999.

C/F *Lemnos* - C/F *Macedon*
Demand by local holiday-makers, fleeing the delights of Thessalonika, has prompted two of the small Sporades chain boats to make an overnight run up to the city in High Season in past years (though in 1998 only the *Lemnos* did the run). Both ferries (see p. 404) are on the small side; at the height of the season they are likely to be booked solid when running south. The *Macedon* (if running) is by far the better of the pair.

C/F *Dimitroula*
G. A. Ferries; 1978; 7222 GRT.
Serious competition for the *El Greco* arrived in 1997 with the arrival of the *Dimitroula*. Replacing the smaller *Anemos*, she is a well fitted out boat, but suffers

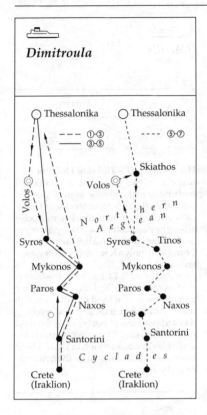

Dimitroula

from being smaller than her rival and the fact that she only runs this route in July and August. She is also slower, though this is due to her happy habit of calling at more Cycladic islands. This makes her a valuable boat for island hopping — though her itinerary could well change in 1999, given G. A. Ferries' habit of tinkering with schedules. Like the *El Greco*, the *Dimitroula* makes a point of calling in at the Northern Sporades island of Skiathos (note: in 1998 neither boat called at Skyros as the *Anemos* had regularly done), opening up the possibility of returning to Athens from the Cyclades via this attractive, wooded island.

C/F *Alcaeos*
NEL Lines; 1970; 3930 GRT.

The mainland ports of Rafina and Kavala have been connected for a number of years by a regular 'lifeline' ferry service that takes in the poorly connected islands of Agios Efstratios and Limnos (in past years with occasional calls at Skyros as well). There has been much chopping and changing on this route of late, with the elderly, but adequate, *Alcaeos* (see also p. 374) being only the latest of a number of ferries to take a turn at providing the thrice-weekly service. Now on the route for five years, this ferry seems older than she is: she hasn't enjoyed the refits

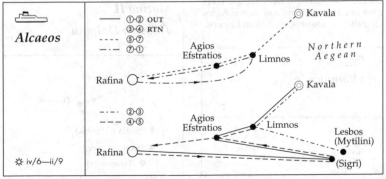

Alcaeos

☼ iv/6—ii/9

that have given her contemporaries a new lease of life. She could be moved in 1999 as she is booked solid on some of her summer runs. If you are heading for Lesbos check where the ferry will dock; every other year (including 1997) she has operated to the small port of Sigri rather than Mytilini, and in past years has occasionally provided a High Season weekly connecting Dodecanese link with a run to Patmos. Athens' newspapers carry current times of Rafina and Kavala departures.

C/F Lykomides
Skyros Line; 1973; 1169 GRT.
A small car ferry operated by a one-boat company, the *Lykomides* runs solely between the ports of Evia (Kimi) and Linaria on Skyros. A little-changing daily 'lifeline' service runs throughout the year, with a second and an occasional third trip in High Season. Reliability is good and facilities are reasonable given the lack of competition. Athens buses link up with Kimi sailings (see p. 96).

C/F Aeolis
Local; 1968; 135 GRT.
The minuscule *Aeolis* operated for many years between Lesbos and Turkey. Now serving out the few remaining years before age limitations dictate her retirement from Greek domestic waters, she runs an irregular service out of Agios Efstratios to Limnos, ferrying islanders who need to do business there: Agios Efstratios is administered from Limnos.

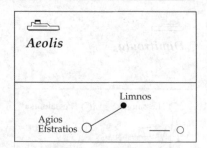

H/Fs Marina II – Thission Dolphin
Kavala is the home of a couple of hydrofoils that combine to provide a six times daily High Season service to Thassos Town. Popular with tourists and locals alike (they are faster than taking a ferry to Skala Prinos and then a bus on to Thassos Town, with only a few pence/cents difference in the price). The *Thission Dolphin* is operated by ANET Line, while the *Marina II* is owned by NEL Lines. During the summer season at least one of them will make additional morning and evening day-tripper runs to ports down the west coast of Thassos. Operated in much the same way as a bus service, tickets for both boats are usually bought on the quayside or on board.

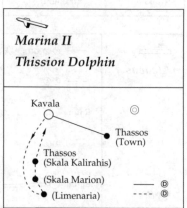

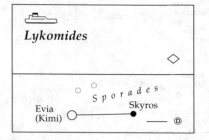

Thassos — Mainland Ferries
A service provided by nine landing-craft car ferries. Most are run by the local A.N.E.T. Line and are named along the lines of *Thassos I*, *Thassos II* etc. Tickets are bought from kiosks on the quayside or on board. The main service is the 70- minute crossing between Kavala and the Thassos port of Skala Prinos. A 30-minute crossing between Thassos Town and Keramoti attracts more vehicles. Reliability and frequency (every 2 hours) of these boats is good. Skala Prinos ferries also provide a four times daily (mainly commercial vehicle) service to the roadside hamlet of Nea Peramos 20 km west of Kavala.

C/F *Arsinoe*
Arsinoe Lines; 1980; 800 GRT.
Named after a temple on Samothrace, this is the only ferry linking the island and Alexandroupolis with the rest of the Greek ferry system. A bit of an odd boat all around; not least because she retains one of those — now rare — traditional Greek chapels on her sun deck. Secondly, it is not locked, but open to the passengers and their prayers. Finally, the WC sinks are regularly polished with a Greek version of 'Flash': proving that even the most wistful of prayers can occasionally be answered in one. During the last year she has been joined by two hydrofoils:

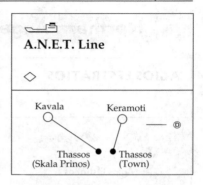

A.N.E.T. Line

the *Niki* (also operated by Arsinoe Lines) runs to Samothrace and occasionally to Kavala and Limnos, and the *Thraki III* (a Thracian Lines vessel) that also makes the Samothrace trip several times daily.

C/F *Saos*
Local; 1964; 707 GRT.
One of those little car ferries reduced to eking out an existence in a remote corner of the Aegean, this boat is due to be replaced in 1999. Operating a daily Alexandroupolis—Samothrace service, she covered for the *Arsinoe* when she was headed for Kavala. She also ran an odd-ball, once-weekly, run down to Limnos (Moudros) during the High Season. It isn't clear if her successor will continue this service.

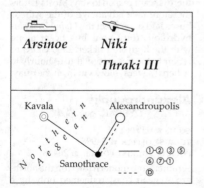

Arsinoe *Niki*
Thraki III

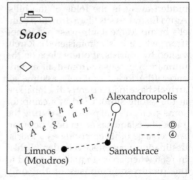

Saos

⚓ Northern Aegean Islands & Ports

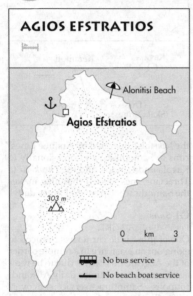

AGIOS EFSTRATIOS

Alonitisi Beach

Agios Efstratios

303 m

0   km   3

🚌 No bus service
🚤 No beach boat service

Agios Efstratios

ΑΓΙΟΣ ΕΥΣΤΡΑΤΙΟΣ; 43 km²; pop. 300.

A remote, sunbaked island with vegetation (mostly scrub and scattered oak trees) hidden away in the folds of the hills, Agios Efstratios sits like a drowned camel's hump to the south-west of Limnos (from where it is administered). Rarely visited by tourists, it offers close on the ultimate in 'get-away-from-it-all' experiences (the locals routinely assume all arrivals have inadvertently disembarked at the wrong stop). Used as a camp for some 5000 political prisoners during the 1930s, the island has never been popular. Any chance of its emerging as a tourist destination was effectively demolished in 1968 when an earthquake put paid to the picturesque houses of the only settlement on the west coast. This in itself was unlucky enough, but unfortunately the military junta ruling Greece at the time decided to help out and sent the army to the rescue. Helpfully demolishing the damaged town, they rebuilt it with ugly concrete prefabricated buildings laid out in military formation. They also bulldozed the town beach beyond repair in the process. The islanders have been in mourning ever since.

Given the attractions of the town, most visitors take to walking, as the island is criss-crossed with goat tracks that wander into hidden folds in the hills and down to deserted beaches. The best is a long strand of volcanic sand on the north coast.

A tiny pension and some tavernas offering rooms are the sum of the island's facilities.

Agios Konstantinos

ΑΓΙΟΣ ΚΩΝΣΤΑΝΤΙΝΟΣ

Figuring larger on ferry schedules than in real life, this port is a distinct nonentity as a destination in its own right. Little more than a stopping point on the main road to Athens, four blocks deep and backing onto the mountains of Attica, there is scant reason to stay. Most visitors therefore take advantage of the Athens buses laid on to meet the *Flying Dolphins* hydrofoils (buy your bus ticket along with the hydrofoil ticket: 2500 GDR) or repair to the bus station (buses hourly to Athens) several blocks in from the quay.

Alexandroupolis

ΑΛΕΞΑΝΔΡΟΥΠΟΛΗ; pop. 34,600.

CODE ☎ 0551
TOURIST OFFICE ☎ 24998
POLICE/TOURIST POLICE ☎ 26418

A rather drab modern town on the northern Aegean coast redeemed only by a lively promenade decked with a light-house, Alexandroupolis is named after an obsure 19 c. king of Greece rather than Alexander the Great (who renamed half the cities of Asia after himself during his campaigns). This fact eloquently sums the place up, and not even the annual July through August wine festival can dispel the 'okay, but not a great place' impression. On the plus side, this port is quite difficult to get to (thanks to its location near the Turkish border), and from a ferry point of view this is definitely the end of the line. No reason to come here apart from the daily boat to Samothrace.

Most non-Greek tourists are just passing through via the seven Kavala buses a day and the Athens railway link.

The wine festival produces considerable pressure on the limited accommodation available in High Season. The Tourist Office has lists of rooms in the town, but if you arrive after midday the only option likely to be open to you is an expensive waterfront B-class *Egnatia Motel* (☎ 37630), 2 km west of the ferry quay. There are, however, a number of hotels in town worth a try first; the best bets being away from the waterfront. These include the D-class *Ledo* (☎ 28808) and *Majestic* (☎ 26444) and the C-class *Alex* (☎ 26302) and *Alkyon* (☎ 23593/5).

Key

Ⓐ Main Square & Lighthouse (1880)
Ⓑ Bus Station
Ⓒ Railway Station
Ⓓ Police / Tourist Police
Ⓔ National Bank of Greece
Ⓕ Pharmacy

Ⓖ Cathedral / Ecclesiastic Art Museum
Ⓗ WCs
Ⓘ Ferry & Hydrofoil Tickets
Ⓙ Road to Komotini & Kavala
Ⓚ Road to Kipi & Turkey

1   Ferry Berth
2   Hydrofoil Berths

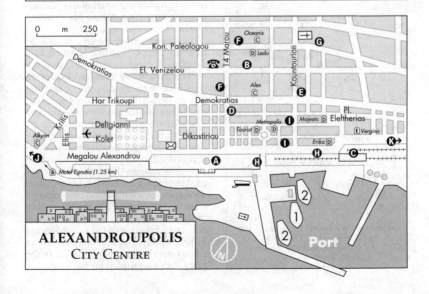

ALEXANDROUPOLIS
CITY CENTRE

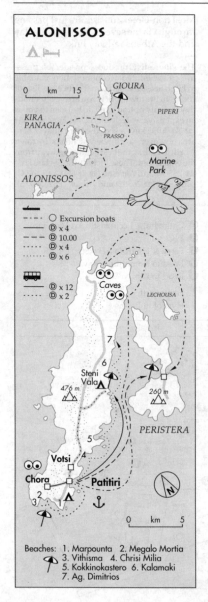

ALONISSOS

0 km 15

GIOURA

PIPERI

KIRA
PANAGIA

PRASSO

ALONISSOS

Marine
Park

---- ○ Excursion boats
—— Ⓓ x 4
--- Ⓓ 10.00
—— Ⓓ x 4
···· Ⓓ x 6

—— Ⓓ x 12
···· Ⓓ x 2

Caves

LECHOUSA

7

6

Steni
Vala

476 m

260 m

PERISTERA

5

Votsi

Chora

Patitiri

2

3   1

0   km   5

N

Beaches: 1. Marpounta 2. Megalo Mortia
3. Vithisma 4. Chrisi Milia
5. Kokkinokastero 6. Kalamaki
7. Ag. Dimitrios

Alonissos

ΑΛΟΝΝΗΣΟΣ; 64 km²; pop. 1,500.

CODE ☎ 0424
PORT POLICE ☎ 65595
POLICE ☎ 65205
MEDICAL CENTRE ☎ 65208

The least populated of the larger Sporades, Alonissos is a popular destination
for daily day-tripper boats from Skiathos
and Skopelos thanks to an attractive port
lined with low cliffs garnished with pine
trees, a pretty hilltop chora and a nearby
marine nature reserve that is one of the
few remaining homes for the threatened
Mediterranean Monk Seal. The island is
also rapidly developing as a rather chic
holiday destination in its own right. The
fact that it is less touristed than its neighbours makes it appealing to increasing
numbers of visitors attracted by the quiet
beaches (accessible only via a flotilla of
caïques thanks to the dirt track roads),
the friendly islanders and the overwhelm-
ingly cosy ambiance of the place. Given
this, it is best to allow for extended stays
here when planning your holiday: seduct-
ive Alonissos is one of those places where
one can't help but linger.

The largest settlement on Alonissos is
now the port of **Patitiri**. Nestling in a
delightfully piratesque cliff and taverna-
decked cove, it has managed to acquire
considerable charm despite the fact that
it is modern village from roof to cellar;
thanks to a disastrous earthquake in 1965
which left it in ruins and the hilltop capital
of Chora badly damaged. Coming after
extensive depopulation that followed after the island's vineyards were wiped out
in 1950 by disease, the earthquake prompted the Junta then ruling Greece to dictate that the remaining islanders be rehous-
ed in the rebuilt port. Thanks to tourism,
prosperity has returned and Alonissos is
now quite busy when the tour boats are
in. Fortunately, they don't stay more than
a few hours so the dreamy nature of the
place isn't interrupted for too long.

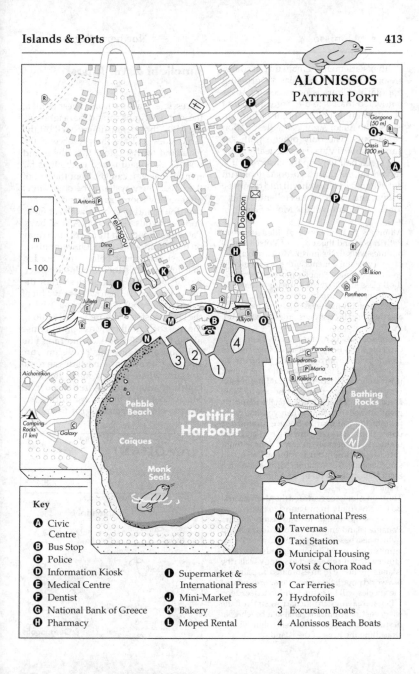

ALONISSOS
PATITIRI PORT

Gorgona (50 m)

Oasis (300 m)

Antonis

Pelasgou

Dina

Ikon Dolopon

Julieta

Aichontikon

Camping Rocks (1 km)

Galaxy

Ikion

Pantheon

Paradise
Liadromia
Maria
Kabos / Cavos

Alkyon

Pebble Beach

Patitiri Harbour

Caïques

Monk Seals

Bathing Rocks

3 2 1 4

Key

- **A** Civic Centre
- **B** Bus Stop
- **C** Police
- **D** Information Kiosk
- **E** Medical Centre
- **F** Dentist
- **G** National Bank of Greece
- **H** Pharmacy
- **I** Supermarket & International Press
- **J** Mini-Market
- **K** Bakery
- **L** Moped Rental
- **M** International Press
- **N** Tavernas
- **O** Taxi Station
- **P** Municipal Housing
- **Q** Votsi & Chora Road
- **1** Car Ferries
- **2** Hydrofoils
- **3** Excursion Boats
- **4** Alonissos Beach Boats

Other settlements remain tiny in comparison. Thanks to the island's growing popularity **Chora** is now seeing houses renovated thanks to the large number of people wanting holiday homes. The town is also the major sightseeing destination hereabouts. The only other significant hamlet is **Steni Vala**. Tucked neatly away in a creek half way up the east coast it is served by the daily taxi-boats than run out of Patitiri. Here you will find tavernas, a shop, and the HQ of the Hellenic Society for the Protection of the Monk Seal.

▬

Alonissos has 14 hotels divided between **Patitiri** port and the suburb of **Votsi** some 20 minutes walk to the north. Most are B and C category establishments with prices at the top end of the range. Among most expensive is the B-class *Alkyon* (☎ 65450) on the waterfront, but the east cliff-top hotels offer better views for less; notably the E-class *Liadromia* (☎ 65521), and the pricer B-class pension *Cavos* (☎ 65216).

Α

Alonissos has two small, very basic sites. *Camping Rocks* is the most accessible, and lies 1.5 km from the port. An idyllic, mature pineforest site (albeit with rudimentary facilities), it is rarely crowded. Come 22.00 the reason why becomes clear thanks to the nearby *Rocks Disco*; the largest and loudest on the island, its great attraction is that, when you and your partner are too beat to bounce around the dance floor, you can retire to a tent and then bounce to the beat on the forest floor without suffering any loss in music volume. The second site, *Camping Ikaros* (☎ 65258) is at isolated Steni Vala, but can fill up in August.

◠◠

Tours on Alonissos centre on the **Marine Park**. Boats leave daily from Patitiri to north coast sea caves and then on to a monastery on **Kira Panagia** island and a beach on **Gioura** island (which also has yet another of those 1000 stalagmite caves with Cyclops legends attached). However, don't go expect to see any seals; the islands are home to an estimated 20 pairs out of a world population of 800. Pessimists predict the species will be extinct within a decade.

  Peristera, lying across a narrow strait off the east coast of Alonissos, is also a beach-boat destination. There is also a small fishing village straddling the neck of the island.

Amoliani & Mt. Athos

Accessible via bus from Thessalonika, the island of Amoliani and the neighbouring Mt. Athos peninsula are well off the ferry lanes and are the preserve of the mainland tourist rather than the island hopper. Amoliani island is about as far removed as you can get from the rest of the Greek ferry system. The one hamlet offers a few rooms as well as dirt roads over the island to good beaches at Ftelis and Tsarki (also known as Alikes) bays. Passenger boats run from Tripiti, a quay on the Ouranopolis road. **Ouranopolis** is the last settlement before the 'border' that delimits Mt. Athos (the closed collection of medieval monasteries) from the rest of the world. The town is now a bit of a tourist trap, but does offer boat trips to the Dhenia islets offshore as well as along the coast of Mt. Athos. Most simply cruise along the coast, but each morning you will find one doing the 'provision' run, stopping at various monasteries en route to Dafni where the few males (females, both human and animal, are banned from Mt. Athos) with the almost impossibly hard-to-obtain permits to visit disembark.

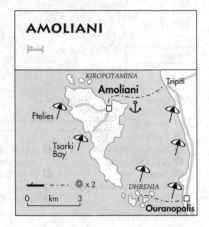

AMOLIANI

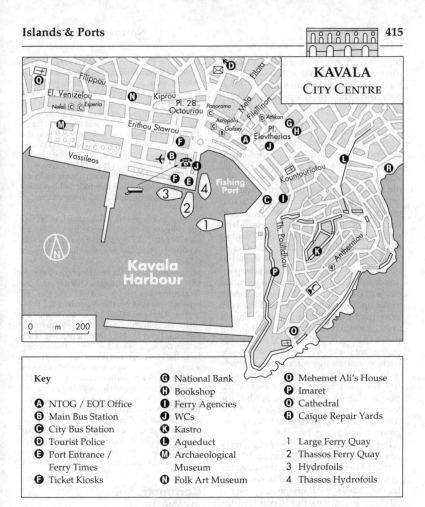

KAVALA
CITY CENTRE

Key

A NTOG / EOT Office
B Main Bus Station
C City Bus Station
D Tourist Police
E Port Entrance / Ferry Times
F Ticket Kiosks
G National Bank
H Bookshop
I Ferry Agencies
J WCs
K Kastro
L Aqueduct
M Archaeological Museum
N Folk Art Museum
O Mehemet Ali's House
P Imaret
Q Cathedral
R Caïque Repair Yards

1 Large Ferry Quay
2 Thassos Ferry Quay
3 Hydrofoils
4 Thassos Hydrofoils

Kavala

ΚΑΒΑΛΑ; pop. 57,500.

CODE ☎ 051
NTOG/EOT OFFICE ☎ 222425
POLICE ☎ 222905
HOSPITAL ☎ 228517

If you exclude hydrofoils from the equation, Kavala (ancient Neapolis) is easily the premier port of the Northern Aegean, with good links to the otherwise unconnected islands of Thassos and Samothrace, and also — in High Season — the Athenian port of Rafina, the Dodecanese and Rhodes. If this wasn't reason enough to venture in this direction, the city itself is one of the nicest in Greece; set against a backdrop of rolling hills, it nestles snugly between their lower folds and the shoreline, with a picturesque Turkish quarter topped with an imposing castle, an aqueduct and traditional caïque-building thrown in for good measure. Sadly, however, the strong tourist presence is very evident in local prices.

The city centre is surprisingly compact, dividing into two quarters. To the east lies the old town dominated by the castle set upon the building-clad promontory ringed by the old city wall (known as the Panagia Quarter). Outside the walls, the old town continues to the north under the arches of the delightful aqueduct that once took water to the castle. The inlet to the east is littered with boat-builder's yards. To the west lies the old fishing harbour. Still home to a fair number of working caïques, they sit somewhat incongruously against a backdrop of 'modern' buildings (and the ugly main city square — Pl. Elevtherios) that now make up the new town behind the very busy road that divides the two. Things are a bit more relaxed on the west side of the old harbour, with several reasonable restaurants with views over the castle backing onto a long promenade, complete with sun-bleached lawns and the odd tree for good measure. The rest of the new town isn't up to much, but has the merit of a reasonable scatter of shops (though supermarkets are thin on the ground) and a very busy bus station.

The absence of many competing ferry companies means that ticket agents are confined to three outlets on the quayside serving the large boats and ticket kiosks for the Thassos boats on the quay. Buy in advance if you can, but if you find the kiosks closed then tickets are bought on board after the ferry has departed. The quay has ferry times up at the entrance gate kiosk (in Greek) and a procession of large landing-craft type car ferries and a hydrofoil heading for Thassos. The Samothrace ferry berths on the east side of the harbour under the castle walls.

⊨

A good NTOG/EOT office on the edge of Eleftheria Sq. has free city maps and will help you find where the one empty bed is to be located. Hotel accommodation is rather limited, and at the bottom end of the scale very poor; this is one city where it pays to look up-market a bit. Within an easy walk of the waterfront there are a number of C-class establishments: the *Acropolis* (☎ 22 3643) and *Panorama* (☎ 22 4205) — both near the old harbour, and the *Esperia* (☎ 22 9621) and *Nefeli* (☎ 227441) near the museum. Best of the down-market options is the D-class *Attikon* (☎ 22 2257) a couple of blocks behind the EOT office. If you can afford to splash out then the waterfront B-class *Galaxy* (☎ 22 4521) is the best hotel in the centre.

A

Nearest to the port is a poor, treeless NTOG site 3 km to the west. 5 km to the east is *Irini Camping* (☎ 22 9776): a good trailer park site. A better bet is to hop over to a site on Thassos.

👓

Main sights in Kavala are the maze of streets that make up the **Panagia Quarter** and the **Byzantine Kastro** (℗ 10.00–17.00), the old quarter spanned by the **Aqueduct** (c. 1550) and an **Archaeological Museum** (home to a disparate collection culled from sites around Kavala). There is also a **Municipal Museum** full of the usual round of bric-a-brac dating from the early 19 c. on. If you have more than a day in Kavala then you should consider venturing 15 km north-east of the city to the remains of the ancient city of **Philippi**: the site of the battle in which Octavian (later the Emperor Augustus) defeated the murderers of Julius Caesar, Cassius and Brutus in 42 BC. Straddling the main road, the remains are substantial and include a well-preserved latrine (this is more than modern Kavala can boast). Buses run every ½ hour from Kavala.

Keramoti
ΚΕΡΑΜΩΤΗ

An isolated 'port' that owes its existence solely to the fact that it is the nearest point on the mainland to Thassos. Definitely not a foot passenger's destination, there is little more here than a quay, a quiet beach and a motor-park-style campsite. Package tourists often pass through via the landing craft ferries serving Thassos Town en route for Keramoti airport some 20 km to the north-west.

Limnos

ΛΗΜΝΟΣ; 477 km²; pop. 16,000.

CODE ☎ 0254
PORT POLICE ☎ 22225
TOURIST OFFICE ☎ 22315
POLICE ☎ 22200
HOSPITAL ☎ 22203

The home of Hephaistos, the divine smith, Limnos (also commonly transcribed as 'Lemnos') is a fertile, volcanic island opposite the entrance to the Dardanelles — a strategic location that inevitably attracts a strong military presence. An accompanying lack of tourists (who are missing a lovely island) has ensured a continuation of the traditional island culture now sadly absent elsewhere. This, coupled with good beaches, very friendly islanders and an attractive (in a weird volcanic molehill, lumpy, sort of way) main port of Myrina, are all the more reason to visit. Somewhat less appealing is the reputation of the curative properties

of the local soil; indeed, Limnosian mud pills were viewed as a sort of Viagra-like wonder drug by much of the ancient world. These days the locals seem less adept at weaving money-spinning yarns to ensnare gullible visitors.

Myrina (also known as Kastro, thanks to the floodlit castle built on the ancient acropolis) is very much the centre of island life and is a prosperous little working town with an interesting warren of backstreets leading off from the main street that snakes its way from the cute little square backing on to a small caïque harbour near the constantly enlarging ferry quay, under the castle walls and then east into the suburbs. Lined with an odd mix of hardware shops, discos and men's clothing outlets (it is difficult to forget that Limnos has a large army garrison), it is very much the focus of town life. Either side of the castle are the town's sandy beaches; the one to the north being decidedly more up-market.

LIMNOS
MYRINA / KASTRO

Key

- **A** Venetian Kastro
- **B** Bus Station
- **C** Police
- **D** Hospital (20 m)
- **E** National Bank of Greece
- **F** Ferry Ticket Office
- **G** Main Sq. / Taxi Station
- **H** Supermarket
- **I** Bakery
- **J** Pharmacy
- **K** International Press
- **L** WCs
- **M** Moped & Car Rental
- **N** Turkish Fountain
- **O** Museum

  1   Ferry Berth

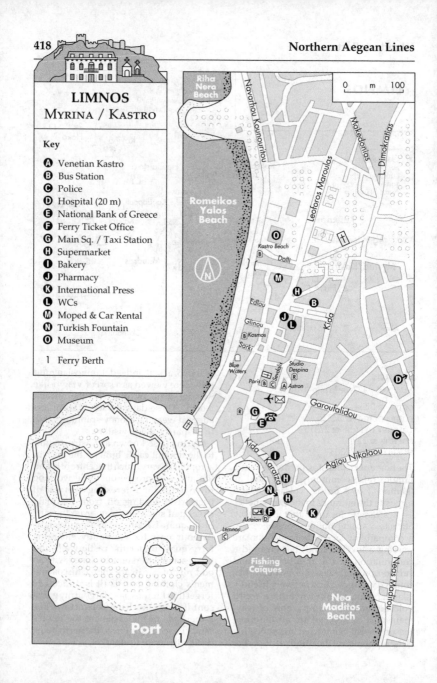

Limnos is a lovely island to visit if you have your own transport and very frustrating — given the almost non-existent bus service — if you haven't. The two halves of the island contrast greatly. The east side is flat and fertile, with two lakes adding to the oddly un-Greek landscape of cornfields and grazing cattle, while the west has a starker rocky volcanic terrain and the bulk of the best beaches. Apart from Myrina the only large settlement is at **Moudros** (the forward Allied military base during the ill-fated Gallipoli campaign; thanks to the sheltered bay, it also safely housed the Allied generals). Buses link the town with the capital, but unfortunately, the service is geared to moving islanders into Myrina for work in the mornings and returning them at night. With only two services offering a same day return to Myrina, buses are all but useless for tourism purposes. Short of hiring a moped, the best way to see the remote sites of interest on Limnos is to take the once-a-week bus excursion (unfortunately, the day varies).

⊢

In High Season a Tourist Police office is open in Myrina's town hall which will help you find a bed. This usually means directing you to one of the **Myrina** hotels (of which there is a reasonable selection). On the waterfront the D-class *Aktaion* (☎ 22258) and the C-class *Lemnos* (☎ 22153) are easily found and reasonable. Harder to find is the C-class *Sevdalis* (☎ 22691), which lies in a side street one block beyond the OTE square on the town's main street. More up-market establishments tend to lie near the beaches. These include the B-class *Paris* (☎ 23266) and the expensive *Kastro Beach* (☎ 22148), which lies at the east end of the town's north beach.

👓

Limnos was an important island during the Archaic period: the primary archaeological site at **Poliochni** predates Troy on the adjacent Turkish coast. Tours visit this rather confused site along with the site of the classical city at **Hephaisteia**, built on the spot where the god Hephaistos landed and lamed himself after Hera threw him from the summit of Mt. Olympus in a fit of 'peak'. The tangible remains include a temple to the god and an odeon.

Marmaras
ΜΑΡΜΑΡΑΣ

A resort on the middle fork (known as Sithonia) of the Halkidiki peninsula, Marmaras (alias Nea Marmaras) is on hydrofoil itineraries. An pricey resort with a reasonable beach, bus links to Thessalonika, and a campsite, the main incentive to visit is the boat tour along the coast offering a glimpse of the monasteries of Mt. Athos. Marmaras is the easiest departure point for island hoppers wanting a look; the daily excursion costs 7,000 GDR.

Nea Moudania
ΝΕΑ ΜΟΥΔΙΑΝΑ

An over-touristed small town on the Northern Aegean's west coast just north of the left hand fork (alias Cassandra) of the Halkidiki peninsula, Nea Moudania is the weekend getaway resort for Thessalonika, and now sees a number of hydrofoils calling en route to the Sporades. Beyond the crowded beach, some over-expensive hotels and a crowded campsite, it has very little to recommend it — unless you are in a hurry to continue onto Cassandra. Hourly buses to Thessalonika offer frequent means of escape.

Nea Peramos
ΝΕΑ ΠΕΡΑΜΟΣ

Unless you have a vehicle, this mainland port 15 km east of Kavala is not really a practical proposition given the 'inter-city' nature of local buses. However, host to several daily landing-craft ferries running to Thassos, it offers a short-cut to motorists arriving from or departing west. Set in a cosy, open-mouthed bay, this hamlet (complete with beach, kastro and campsite) is an infinitely more relaxing jumping off point to Thassos than Kavala. If you are prepared to stop overnight, Nea Peramos is worth considering as a quiet overnight excursion for Thassos trippers.

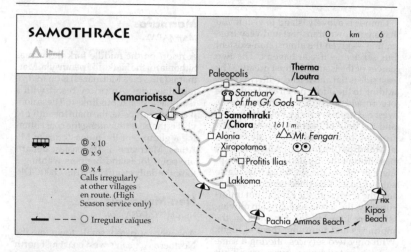

Samothrace

ΣΑΜΟΘΡΑΚΗ; 178 km²; pop. 2,800.

CODE ☎ 0551
PORT POLICE ☎ 41305
POLICE ☎ 41203
FIRST AID ☎ 41217

A dramatic heavily wooded mountain peak rising from the sea, Samothrace was an island of spiritual pilgrimage in the ancient world; partly, one suspects, because it was as difficult to get to then as it is now. First impressions of a comparatively bleak and mountainous island are enhanced by the almost apologetic way the main island town and port of **Kamariotissa** clings to the foreshore against a backdrop of undulating hills devoid of vegetation bar the odd wind-broken tree and stubbly cornfields. A couple of horribly modern electricity-generating windmills on the long western spur do nothing to relive the almost forbidding sense of isolation. This tends to do Samothrace something of a disservice for once ashore it is quite a friendly place. All the nightlife and essentials are to be found in the port along with most of the accommodation. For once on a Greek island, English is

little spoken as most visitors are German or Scandinavians.

Almost all tourist activity is confined to the northern coast thanks to the impressive archaeological remains of the Sanctuary of the Great Gods at Paleopoli and the spa-village at Therma. Other island villages see few tourists. Buses run regularly to the whitewashed island capital at **Chora**; a jumble of whitewashed houses tucked comfortably out of sight in a fold in the foothills, it is devoid of hotels and all the other trappings of modern tourism and topped with the remains of a lovely castle. Equally attractive is the pretty hill village of **Profitis Ilias** (buses also head for here calling irregularly at other villages en route). Buses also run direct to the campsite via **Therma** (also known as Loutra). As the name implies, this is a spa resort of sorts and now the main tourist centre on the island, though trees out-number tourists for the greater part of the year. Not really a beach island, Samothrace does have two excellent examples that are sadly only accessible by dirt track or irregular caïque on the south coast at Pachia Ammos and delightfully remote Kipos.

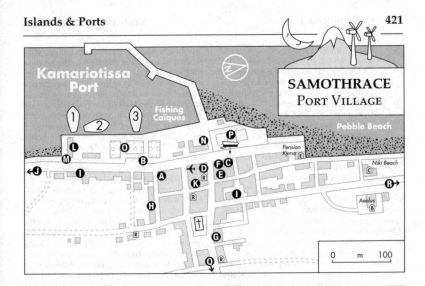

SAMOTHRACE
PORT VILLAGE

Key

Ⓐ Information / Bus Office
Ⓑ Bus Stop
Ⓒ Police
Ⓓ National Bank of Greece
Ⓔ Pharmacy
Ⓕ Supermarket
Ⓖ Grocery Store

Ⓗ Bakery
Ⓘ Moped Rental
Ⓙ Disco & Promentory
Ⓚ Bar / Ferry Tickets
Ⓛ Passenger Stalls
Ⓜ WCs
Ⓝ Old Lighthouse
Ⓞ Waterfront Park

Ⓟ Beach Square
Ⓠ Chora Road
Ⓡ Therma Road

1 Ferry Berth
2 Hydrofoil Berth
3 Irregular Beach
   Caïques

⊢

Rooms and hotels are scattered thinly between the port, Paleopolis, Therma and Chora. Low numbers of visitors means low prices. At the **Port** you will find, at the northern end of the waterfront, the C-class *Niki Beach* (☎ 41561), with the pricey B-class *Aeolis* (☎ 41595) close by, along with a pension — the *Kyma* (☎ 412 68). **Paleopolis** has the B-class *Xenia* (☎ 41230) and the C-class *Kastro* (☎ 41850) close to hand. **Therma** is also blessed with a couple of reasonable establishments: the B-class *Kaviros* (☎ 41 577) and the C-class *Mariva* (☎ 41759).

▲

There are two High Season only sites on the north coast: *Camping Loutra* (☎ 41784), a poor site 3 km east of Therma. *Multilary Camping* (☎ 41759) is a much better site 2 km further on.

◌◌

Samothrace offers two great attractions: the most obvious being **Mt. Fengari** (the 'Mountain of the Moon'). Used by Poseidon as a seat while he observed the Trojan war, mortals seeking serious hill walking (via Therma) find that when they get to the summit after a day's climb that the ground is still warm.

The **Sanctuary of the Great Gods** at Paleopolis sees far more visitors. The remains of one of Greece's premier places of pilgrimage (the first historian, Herodotus, was initiated into the rites, and Alexander the Great's parents met and fell in love here), it is sadly diminished, but is located in a marvellous woody ravine setting that more than makes up for the limited remains. The sanctuary was pre-Greek in origin, being originally dedicated to the

Great Mother Earth goddess Axieros and a fertility god, Kadmilos. The Greeks quickly conflated these figures with their own Demeter and Hermes and so kept local traditions going for the best part of a millennia. What those traditions were is still something of a mystery. Ancient writers were loath to mention them thanks to the belief in shadowy demon figures (known as the Kabeiroi) who were thought to harbour implacable wrath towards any that divulged the sanctuary's secrets. However, it is known that anyone could be initiated into the sanctuary's mysteries and that the torch-lit night-time ceremony had two stages (the first involving purification, the second, initiation into the rites). Despite earthquakes and the odd pirate attack, the sanctuary (politically independent throughout its life) was only abandoned with the formal adoption of Christianity by the Roman Empire, and most of the important buildings were rebuilt several times during the course of their working life.

Access to the site today is via a footpath running inland from the main coast road. Walking past the hotel and the museum along the path running parallel with the central ravine stream, on your right you will see the remains of **Ⓐ** the **Milesian Building** (so called because of an inscription associated with it), and behind it **Ⓑ** the remains of a **Byzantine Fort** built from stones from the sanctuary.

The most important buildings were all located on the 'island' of land bounded by the (usually dry) streams running down the ravines. Crossing the stream brings you to **Ⓒ**; the rotund **Arsinoeion** was also an important structure though of much later date. Built c. 285 BC, it was the largest circular building ever constructed by the ancient Greeks. Commissioned by Queen Arsinoe of Thrace, it was used for public sacrifice. To the north is **Ⓓ** the **Anaktoron** (also known as the 'Hall of the Lords'); it was one of the oldest buildings on the site, being in continuous use from the 6 c. BC to the 4 C. AD. It was used for the first stage of the initiation rites. In the Roman period a robing room, (**Ⓔ** the **Sacristy**) was added to the building, when it was substantially rebuilt.

Turn south of the Arsinoeion and you come to **Ⓕ** the **Temenos** (an open air precinct with a ceremonial entrance on the north-east side), and **Ⓖ** the **Hieron**. Now the most prominent

building on the site, thanks to its columns (re-erected in 1956), the temple was the location for the second stage of the initiation. The remains of spectator seating line the interior walls. On its west side lie the scanty foundations of **Ⓗ** the **Hall of Votive Gifts** (c. 540 BC), little evident now, but important in that it survived for close on a thousand years without rebuilding. Next door is the much better preserved **Altar Court** at **Ⓘ**, dedicated by a half-brother of Alexander the Great. The path now crosses a culvert that ran under the theatre stage. **Ⓙ**, the site of the **Theatre** is now just a tree-covered depression and barely recognisable, as almost all the seats were removed for the construction of later fortifications.

Once you have passed the theatre, the paths divide. The eastern path wanders over the stream and a hill (that was home to **Ⓚ** the **South Necropolis**) before coming to the substantial foundations of **Ⓛ** the **Propylon of Ptolemy II**, a formal gateway constructed for the use of the local townspeople (the ancient capital — Paleopolis proper — stood to the east of the sanctuary). When originally built it had the stream channelled to emerge through it. On the west side of that stream are two rather obscure buildings: **Ⓜ** a **Circular Building** and **Ⓝ** a **Doric Structure** dedicated by Phillip III and Alexander IV.

The western path turns west up the hillside behind the theatre, bringing you to the foundations of **Ⓞ** the **Nike niche**: a small building cut into the hillside that was built specifically to house **Ⓟ** the famous **Winged Nike (Victory) of Samothrace**. Made of Parian marble, this sculpture is the site's greatest archaeological find, and (bar the missing head) is now in the Louvre. It takes the form of an 'angel' standing on the prow of a ship. The Nike niche was in fact a fountain house, and the prow stood in a double-level floor basin filled with water.

From the Nike building the path continues up the hill to the higher level behind the theatre and **Ⓠ** a **Stoa**. Plenty of fragments of this large structure lie scattered around but nobody has yet found the time to reassemble them. Between the stoa and the central ravine stream at **Ⓡ** lie scanty remains of **Hellenistic Buildings** (purpose unknown). Finally, returning to the main path you come back to the **museum**; well laid out and worth a visit, though the most important sculptures found on the site are now in French and Austrian museums.

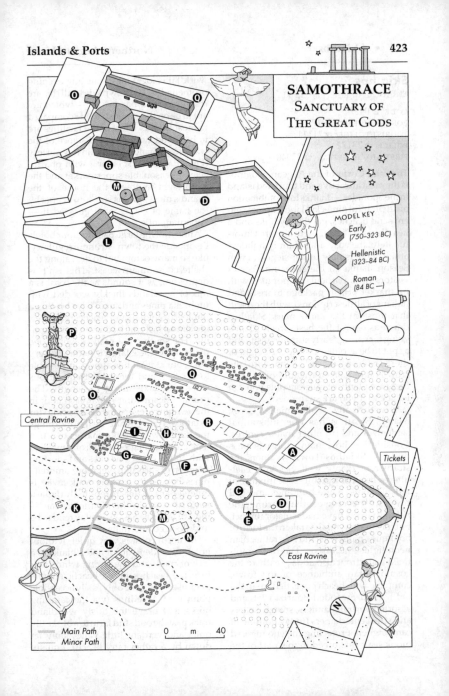

SAMOTHRACE
SANCTUARY OF THE GREAT GODS

MODEL KEY

Early
(750–323 BC)

Hellenistic
(323–84 BC)

Roman
(84 BC —)

Central Ravine

Tickets

East Ravine

Main Path
Minor Path

0   m   40

Skiathos

ΣΚΙΑΘΟΣ; 61 km²; pop. 4,900.

CODE ☎ 0427
PORT POLICE ☎ 22017
TOURIST POLICE ☎ 21111
POLICE ☎ 23172
FIRST AID/HOSPITAL ☎ 22040

The mini-Corfu of the Aegean, Skiathos is the most attractive and touristed island in the Sporades — thanks to a combination of a delightful pine-clad landscape, excellent sand beaches, good ferry links and a heavily used charter flight airport. Unfortunately, the cosy 'ideal family holiday' atmosphere is now under siege in High Season thanks to the sheer number of visitors (it is particularly popular with up-market British package tourists and Italians of all descriptions), with the result that those in the know mark Skiathos down as one of the best Greek islands going for spring/early summer visits and a spot to be avoided during the height of the season. That said, even with the crowds it remains a friendly place, and there are plenty of quieter spots you can escape to if you are so minded.

As with many of the smaller Greek islands Skiathos has one substantial settlement and no other major centres. Considering how many tourists pass through, **Skiathos Town** weathers the storm remarkably well. Set in an islet-littered bay, it is a picturesque mixture of red tile roofs, white buildings and bell towers. The crowds that throng the narrow streets have had a major impact, but fortunately, this has taken the form of boutiques, patisseries and bars rather than neon lights and discos. The restaurant-lined waterfront also adds greatly to the cosmopolitan ambiance of the town; complete with beach boats tied up in the old harbour, wooded Bourtzi islet, and assorted portrait painters, sponge sellers and street entertainers (to say nothing of campaigners protecting the endangered monk seals that breed in this part of the world) it is ideal for interesting evening promenades. The downside to all this are restaurant and bar prices — which are apt to be on the expensive side compared to most islands. Most of the facilities are to be found within easy distance of the waterfront or along the main town artery (Papadiamantis St.) along with pharmacies, a reasonable supermarket and the main sight in town: the house of the island's most famous son; a 19 c. poet by the name of — yes, you guessed it — Papadiamantis.

Almost all the large package tour hotels lie outside the town, strung irregularly, like so many octopi out to dry, along the sheltered southern coast. This isn't as depressing as it sounds as the coast is a mix of headlands thickly wooded with umbrella pines and small bays hosting a number of golden sand beaches; the hotels are almost lost amidst this attractive jumble. The south coast road (the only one made up on the island) is naturally very busy, but at least it is almost impossible to get lost, and there are frequent bus stops and taxis along its length. The primary destinations lie at each end; in the evenings everyone is heading for Skiathos Town, while in the mornings the big draw is **Koukounaries** beach; a long crescent-shaped stretch of sand filled with bodies of various hues and sporting a lagoon of sorts with yet more umbrella pines behind it. A short walk away is quieter **Banana Beach**, reputedly the best naturist beach in the Mediterranean — most of the bananas on display tend to be middle-aged and Italian.

The north coast is very quiet, without hotels or settlements of note, thanks to a lack of roads and the strong winds that turn the beaches into a beachcomber's paradise. In fact, the only easily accessible point is at **Asselinos** (via the camping buses that brave the dusty woodland track past the odd stud farm to a blissfully quiet and verdant little valley only let down by a rather tatty beach). Equally

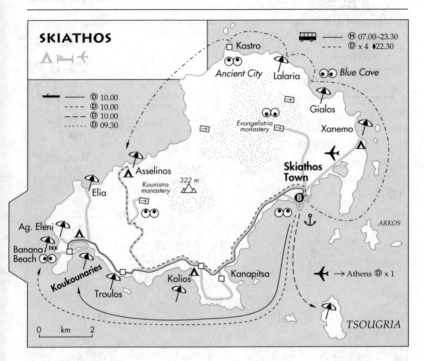

underdeveloped is the wooded interior of the island which is popular with hikers and those who have found the frequent, but horribly overcrowded, bus service too much to cope with. The east coast is similarly the preserve of those looking for a quiet life; the one blot on their happiness being the island airport (see sights). There is a poor beach and campsite at **Xanemo**, but you will have to recourse to beach boats if you want to do better. **Lalaria** on the north-east corner is the best bet; a very picturesque tapering pebble beach at the base of a cliff, it is more Beachy foot than head.

⊨

Rooms can be very hard to come by in High Season; you might have to rough it a bit on your first night. A quayside kiosk just north of the ferry quay offers accommodation advice.

Offers of rooms made when getting off the boat are not to be ignored. Hotels there are aplenty on Skiathos. Most are block-booked by package tour operators. Seeking out untaken up rooms is an option, though you will find almost all the A to C class hotels are well out of town bar the B-class *Alkyon* (☎ 22981) on the airport road. Within Skiathos Town there are a number of budget establishments; the poor D-class *Avra* just off the waterfront, the *San Remo* (☎ 22078) at the other end of the harbour and the *Kostis* (☎ 22909) behind the post office. E-class hotels are to be found on or near Papadiamantis St. These include the *Ilion* (☎ 21193), the *Morfo* (☎ 21737), the *Australia* (☎ 22488) and the *Karafelas* (☎ 21236).

Λ

There are four sites on Skiathos: nearest to the port is a municipal campsite at Xanemo. Under the airport flight path, it does a roaring trade but attracts few campers. The newest site is at *Koukounaries Camping* (☎ 49290) and is easily

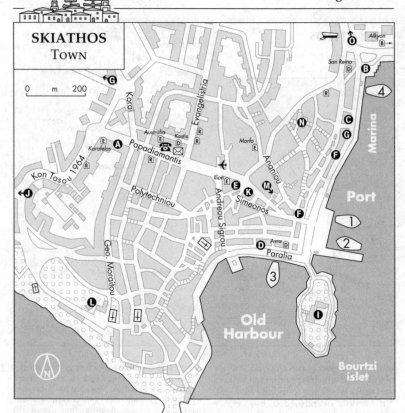

SKIATHOS TOWN

0   m   200

Alkyon

San Remo

Marina

Port

Koraí

Evangelistria

Australia

Kostis

Karafelas

Papadiamantis

Morfa

Ananiou

Kon Tasou 1964

Polytechniou

Ilioti

Andreou Sigrou

Simeonos

Paralia

Avra

Geo. Moraitou

Old Harbour

Bourtzi islet

Key

A Police Station
B Bus Station
C Asselinos Bus, Car Rental & Taxi Rank
D Newspapers & Books
E National Bank of Greece
F Nomikos Lines Ticket Offices
G *Flying Dolphin* Ticket Office
H Car Rental (50 m) & Cinema (200 m)
I Site of Old Kastro (replaced with school: now a theatre)
J Junction with Ring Road (20 m)
K Pharmacy
L Hospital
M Papadiamantis House Museum
N Spyglass Church with Campanile
O Town Ring Road to all destinations

1 Ferry Quay
2 Hydrofoil Berth
3 Tourist & Beach Boat Quay
4 East Coast Beach Boat Quay

the best for the beach of the same name and buses to Skiathos Town, though it is expensive. If camping in green pastures (with nought but fellow campers' nocturnal impressions of the birds and the bees to distract you) is more to your taste, then laid-back *Asselinos Camping* (☎ 49312) is to be recommended (served by orange buses; tickets from the travel agent near the bus pick-up point). Unfortunately, this cannot be said of *Camping Kolios* (☎ 49249), a very poor site that takes full advantage of its roadside position between the beaches and Skiathos town to prey on the unwary.

∞

Skiathos Town is the island's main attraction. The only 'sight' as such is the well-preserved turn-of-the-century home of the poet **Alexandros Papadiamantis**. A sort of Greek Lord Tennyson without the title, you will find a simple islander's homestead likely to appeal to minimalists and creaky floorboard fans. Unfortunately, this poet had as few possessions as his fellow islanders and the house reflects this wonderfully. Most tourists visit Skiathos Town at least once a day if only to pick up the daily tour boats heading on to Skopelos and Alonissos, the beach boats (most heading for Koukounaries, Banana and a beach on the adjacent islet of **Tsougria**), or the anticlockwise island boat tour.

The island boat tour also stops briefly at the **Blue Cave**, a sea cave on the east coast, and at **Kastro**, site of the medieval centre of the island until it was abandoned in the last century after piracy was no longer a threat to the islanders' security. Set on an all but impregnable headland, it is now a picturesque ruin of houses, streets and churches. Excursions also run to two monasteries: **Kounistra** to the west (for the view) and to **Evangelistria** (a popular donkey ride destination north of Skiathos Town, famed throughout Greece as the place where the Greek flag was first raised in 1807 by a group of conspiring independents).

Finally, if you want some really inspired sightseeing try the beach road running past the end of the airport runway. Supposedly closed every time a flight leaves (via warning traffic lights) it made headlines in 1996 after three tourists unwittingly stood behind a departing 747. When it took off they did as well; one landing on a nearby beach, a second waist-deep in the sea and the third ending up on a mainland-bound hydrofoil with a broken jaw.

Skopelos
ΣΚΟΠΕΛΟΣ; 96 km²; pop. 4,700.

CODE ☎ 0424
PORT POLICE ☎ 22180
POLICE ☎ 22235
FIRST AID/HOSPITAL ☎ 22220

The largest island in the Sporades group, Skopelos has less sparkle than neighbouring Skiathos. The beaches are not as good (most are pebble), there is less sightseeing, and the main town has far less going on. Even so, it is an attractive island — covered in pine forests and (thanks to flatter terrain) more agriculture as well. With the easy links to the airport on Skiathos, Skopelos has seen a dramatic rise in tourism as package tour operators have moved in; promoting the island as an ideal quiet family-holiday destination. Independent travellers are far less visible, but their numbers are on the increase as the appeal of over touristed Skiathos wanes, and many are apt to rank it ahead of Skiathos thanks to its more relaxed, laid-back atmosphere.

The main settlement is **Skopelos Town**, tucked beneath a ring of sheltering hills in a deep bay on the northern coast. This is something of a disadvantage as, lying on the exposed side of the island, ferry and hydrofoil services can be subject to disruption. On windy days these, and other tourist boats, are often diverted to a small inlet quay at **Agnontas** on the sheltered south side (free buses into town are laid on in this event). Skopelos Town has retained much of its whitewashed traditional appearance despite being badly damaged in the 1965 earthquake that put paid to the Chora on neighbouring Alonissos. Repairs have been sympathetic, and the town is undeniably attractive, but somehow the total adds up to less than the sum of the parts. Easily the best part of town is the old quarter that rises from the tree-lined waterfront steeply up the slopes of the kastro hill on the west side of the bay: a collection of labyrinthine streets

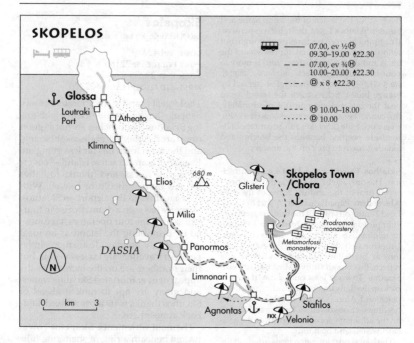

chock-a-block with steep staircases, chapels and attractive houses — many with overhanging wooden balconies and red-tile roofs. The streets abutting the waterfront are now devoted to the tourist industry, but the heart of the old town remains the preserve of the locals. One knock-on from this is that almost all the tourist accommodation is either elevated to the ring road which skirts the lower slopes of the hills that make a natural boundary to the town or relegated to the newer part of town at the back of the bay. This latter area is also home to the main town beach; running the width of the bay, it offer ringside views of the procession of docking hydrofoils and ferries. Unfortunately, it as it is made up of grey sand that becomes increasingly pebbly the further along you go. It does have one redeeming feature; the sea floor hereabouts is shallow and rock-free; making it a passable kiddie beach.

Given that there is only one metalled road and a good bus service, visiting the rest of the island is very straightforward. Most of the bus stops are at beach hamlets. **Stafilos** can lay claim to being the over-crowded main island beach: it owes this role largely thanks to being a walkable 4 km from Skopelos Town. **Panormos** is the next beach, and popular with wind-surfers (there is also unofficial camping in the coves on either side). **Milia** offers a long strand of pebbly sand and is usually quiet. while **Elios** is home to the nearest thing Skopelos possesses to a resort village. Buses venturing this far then run to **Klima**, an semi-abandoned village that has never recovered from the 1965 earthquake, before arriving at the island's second major settlement of **Glossa**. A small

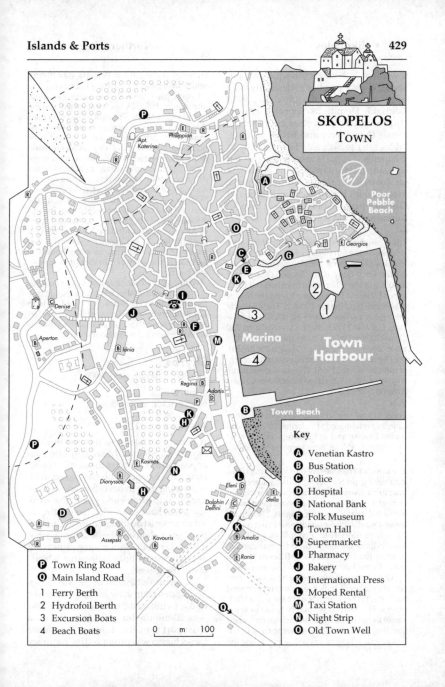

SKOPELOS
TOWN

Poor
Pebble
Beach

Marina

Town
Harbour

Town Beach

Key

- **A** Venetian Kastro
- **B** Bus Station
- **C** Police
- **D** Hospital
- **E** National Bank
- **F** Folk Museum
- **G** Town Hall
- **H** Supermarket
- **I** Pharmacy
- **J** Bakery
- **K** International Press
- **L** Moped Rental
- **M** Taxi Station
- **N** Night Strip
- **O** Old Town Well

- **P** Town Ring Road
- **O** Main Island Road

- **1** Ferry Berth
- **2** Hydrofoil Berth
- **3** Excursion Boats
- **4** Beach Boats

0   m   100

town that is both picturesque and unspoilt, Glossa perches majestically on a hillside 3 km above the tiny drab port of **Loutraki.** Despite its appeal it attracts surprisingly few devotees but plenty of ferries (Note: ferry and hydrofoil timetables refer to Skopelos Town simply as 'Skopelos'; Glossa is usually listed as if it were an island in its own right). Elsewhere on the island, caïques run to otherwise inaccessible, but attractive, beaches at **Glisteri** from Skopelos Town and to **Limnonari** from Agnontas.

🛏

There are plenty of rooms in **Skopelos Town** (a kiosk on the ferry quay offers information). Hotel beds are also reasonably plentiful. Nearest the ferry quay is the E-class *Georgios* (☎ 22308), but like other waterfront hotels it is apt to be a bit noisy. For a quieter life try the cluster of hotels behind the town beach. These include the pricey C-class *Delfini* (☎ 23015), the D-class *Eleni* (☎ 22393), the E-class *Stella* (☎ 220 81) and *Rania* (☎ 22486). At the upper end of the market are the B-class *Amalia* (☎ 22688), the *Dionyssos* (☎ 23210) and, nearer the centre of town, *Ionia* (☎ 22568). **Glossa** also has some rooms on offer, as well as a hotel: the C-class *Avra* (☎ 33550).

Λ

There are no official campsites, but freelance camping is tolerated at Velonio (the unofficial nudist beach), and at Panormos beach; now the recognised 'camping strip' on Skopelos.

👓

The town and beaches are the main attractions; sightseeing on Skopelos tends to come in a poor third. **Skopelos Town** provides just about enough to justify a day-trip from a neighbouring island, but lacks specific sights. The **Kastro** is a serious disappointment; now being reduced to little more than a couple of walls that hardly grab the eye. The only museum in town is the tiny **Folk Art Museum** hidden away in the backstreets, and largely passed by. Once you start wandering (well okay, given the number of staircases, climbing) around backstreets the churches offer the main landmarks. The town is reputably home to some 120 of them, but it isn't clear which clubs and bars the person doing the counting frequented before embarking on his task. First among the

churches is the cliff-top **Panagia ston Pirgho** which overlooks the harbour entrance.

Coach trips around the island are quite popular, and usually take in at least one of the island monasteries. Three of these open their doors to visitors, **Prodromos** and **Evangelismou** (both dating from the 18 C. and now occupied by nuns) and 16 C. **Metamorfossi** (now uninhabited; so you can be a bit more uninhibited when it comes to observing the dress code). In addition, tour boats operate daily out of Skopelos Town to Alonissos and Skiathos. Alonissos boats often stop at the islet of Agios Georgios between Skopelos and Alonissos and after beating up the east coast of Alonissos run around the Marine Park (see p. 408) islets. Ticket Agencies also offer day trips to Athens (via early morning hydrofoil and coach) for a day of quickie sightseeing — at a price.

With plenty of shade and scenery Skopelos is a good walking island. Walkers should buy the snappily titled 'Sotos Walking Guide to Local Beauty Spots & Places of Historical Interest' by Heather Parsons (2000 GDR), which is on sale in several waterfront shops.

Skyros

ΣΚΥΡΟΣ; 208 km²; pop. 2,900.

CODE ☎ 0222
PORT POLICE ☎ 96475
POLICE ☎ 91274
FIRST AID ☎ 92222

A gem of an island to the east of Evia, Skyros (pronounced Sk*ee*-ros) offers an appealing mix of one of the best Cycladic-style choras and a history laced with everything from transvestism and a Greek Excalibur to pirates and poets. The weak spots that have prevented it emerging as a major tourist destination are the limited number of good beaches and the fact that it is too far from regular ferry routes (out of High Season links with other islands are non-existent).

The main settlement of **Skyros Town** lies hidden from view from the sea in the folds of a hill on the east side of the island — a 20-minute bus ride from the west coast port hamlet of **Linaria**. This desire for seclusion was prompted by the piracy

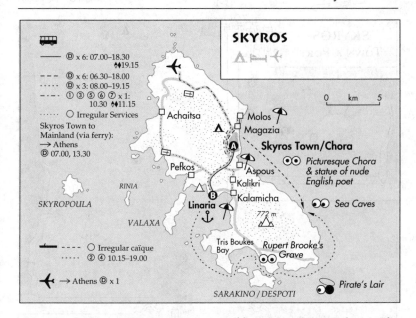

of the 16 and 17 c., but did not prevent 'Three Entrance Bay' at the southern end of the island becoming a notorious Pirate Lair. During the Heroic Age the warrior Achilles had much the same hideaway idea with equally little success; for foreseeing his death at Troy, he hid on Skyros disguised as a girl only to let his frock slip when Odysseus (offering a particularly heroic sword for sale) discovered him and dragged him by the heel to its date with destiny (see p. 511). Surprisingly, there is nothing commemorating this event in the town. Instead, you will find a bronze of another poetic warrior who died with a sore point — Rupert Brooke, the First World War poet, who came off worse in a fight with a mosquito, dying unheroically here of his wound in 1915, en route to Gallipoli. If he sauntered around the island wearing as little as his statue it is not surprising that he was smitten and, all things considered, was lucky not to share the fate of the third

notable to come a cropper here — the hero Theseus who was thrown over a cliff onto a nudist beach by the then king of Skyros, Lykomides. These days the townsfolk are more friendly, in part because the chora has managed to retain much of its unspoilt charm thanks to the bulk of the island accommodation being located a bus ride away on the beach. The chora — a car free zone — is dominated by the castle and the main street which winds up the hill towards it, and is particularly appealing in the evenings when the streets are thronged with gossiping locals. It is, however, often quite windy.

Rupert Brooke's grave aside, the rest of the island is little visited by tourists: most visitors to Skyros confine themselves to the chora and the relatively close resort villages of **Magazia** and **Molos** which are linked by a good sand beach (the island bus service isn't geared to getting tourists anywhere else). Those hiring their own transport to explore further will find the

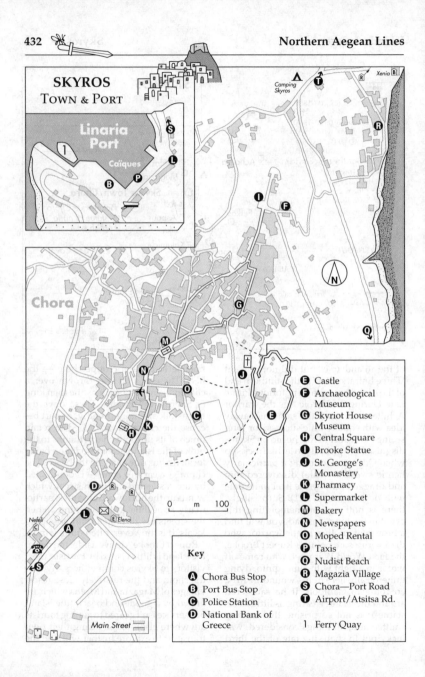

SKYROS
TOWN & PORT

Linaria
Port

Caïques

Camping
Skyros

Xenia Ⓑ

Ⓣ

Ⓡ

Ⓢ

Ⓛ

Ⓑ   Ⓟ

Ⓘ

Ⓕ

N

Chora

Ⓖ

Ⓜ

Ⓠ

Ⓝ

Ⓞ

✝

Ⓙ

Ⓒ

Ⓔ

Ⓗ Ⓚ

0   m   100

Ⓓ Ⓡ   Ⓡ

Nefeli
Ⓒ

Ⓛ ✉ Ⓔ Elena

Ⓐ

Ⓢ

Key

Ⓐ Chora Bus Stop
Ⓑ Port Bus Stop
Ⓒ Police Station
Ⓓ National Bank of
    Greece

Ⓔ Castle
Ⓕ Archaeological
    Museum
Ⓖ Skyriot House
    Museum
Ⓗ Central Square
Ⓘ Brooke Statue
Ⓙ St. George's
    Monastery
Ⓚ Pharmacy
Ⓛ Supermarket
Ⓜ Bakery
Ⓝ Newspapers
Ⓞ Moped Rental
Ⓟ Taxis
Ⓠ Nudist Beach
Ⓡ Magazia Village
Ⓢ Chora—Port Road
Ⓣ Airport/Atsitsa Rd.

1 Ferry Quay

Main Street

expense well worth it. The southern half of Skyros is mountainous, the north flatter and more fertile, and the whole delightfully unspoiled and well wooded with pine trees (making this magnificent hill walking country). The only down side to the island is the sometimes intimidating heavy military presence — though there is no obvious reason for the numbers of soldiers stationed here beyond the obvious charm of the island.

Skyros has also attracted media attention thanks to a 'holistic holiday community' that has established itself at remote **Achaitsa** (or Atsitsa) on the north-west coast (with a centre in Chora). Offering mind/body/spirit courses (brochures from your local GNTO) for those asking questions like 'What is stopping me from being who I really am?', the community has been accused of encouraging marital breakdown thanks to the allegedly high number of subsequent divorces by holiday makers. This is very unfair, because anyone who chooses to spend a holiday apart from their partner 'painting the soulscape' is obviously in a marriage that is in pretty serious trouble anyway. To do the community justice, most people who go on these courses return swearing by them and the impact on the island is far less obtrusive than most tourist-related activities. However, this doesn't stop some of the locals asking 'Why us?' First someone erects a bronze nude of a poet they have never heard of in the middle of town (at a time when most chaste village maidens wouldn't have known what a poet's lyric metre was, still less seen one), and now they have ranks of skinny-dipping middle management types asking 'Where am I going?' On Skyros, this question at least, is easy to answer as ferry connections are confined to the link with Kimi and hydrofoils to the Sporades.

There is a reasonable supply of rooms on Skyros spread between the town and the beach villages of Magazia and Molos. Hotels are thin on the ground and rather pricey; though

the island is worth it. The best establishments are also in the beach villages to the north. **Molos** has the new A-class *Skyros Palace* (☎ 91994) on the beach (a large apartment complex on the beach with its own pool), the B-class *Angela* (☎ 91764), and the new C-class *Paradissos* (☎ 91220). Closer to the town lies the B-class *Xenia* (☎ 91209), a lovely hotel on the beach under the kastro at **Magazia**. Hotel options in Chora are limited; your best bets being the C-class *Nefeli* (☎ 91964) on the road just before you enter the town and the E-class *Elena* (☎ 91738) behind the Post Office. Chora also has a good supply of rooms — though these tend to be offered by owners on the ferry quay rather than baring identifying signs in town.

A

Although backpackers are not thick on the ground there are two sites on Skyros. *Skyros Camping* (☎ 92458) is near the chora. A field site located between the beach and the chora hill, it isn't very popular due to the poor facilities on offer. A second — and more attractive option — is provided by an unofficial site operated by a taverna on the beach in the bay just to the north of Linaria port.

The **Chora**, with its traditional Skyrot houses and blue and white 'Delftware' pottery (a noted Skyrot product) is the main attraction on the island. The streets are so narrow vehicles are confined to the outskirts, and like all good choras just invites you to get lost and then lost again. The town climbs to an impressive **Venetian Kastro** of Byzantine origin with fantastic views over the town and island as well as housing a small **Archaeological Museum**. Below the castle walls is the **Monastery of St. George**. The chora also has a folk museum in the form of a traditional house (known as the **Faltaits Museum**) decked out with examples of the island wares (though most of the town houses retain the fittings and platters that give the museum its atmosphere).

The grave of **Rupert** ('If I should die, think only this of me: That there's some corner of a foreign field that is forever England') **Brooke** is set under a small grove of olive trees in the **Pirate Bay** on the south of Skyros, and is the premier destination of tourist caïques (which occasionally also visit the pirate base — once one of the largest in the Aegean — of **Despot's Island**) and island bus tours (easily the most accessible way of seeing Skyros). The east coast cave was also a **Pirate Grotto** in its day.

Thassos
ΘΑΣΟΣ; 398 km²; pop. 16,000.

CODE ☎ 0593
PORT POLICE ☎ 22106
POLICE / TOURIST POLICE ☎ 22500
TOWN HALL ☎ 22118
FIRST AID ☎ 22190

A large, beautiful island tucked against the northern Aegean seaboard, Thassos is the most northerly island in Greece. Mountainous and green; with over half of its surface covered with cedar, oak and pine forests (now criss-crossed with bulldozed fire gaps to keep any forest fires under control) and fringed with good sand beaches, the island has emerged as a popular (if somewhat pricey) north European package-holiday destination, as well as attracting caravaners willing to motor through the Balkans. Fortunately, hotel development, although evident, is by no means over-conspicuous thanks to reasonable spacing around the attractive 95 km coastline, and the island is further improved by being out of the reach of the backpacking hordes that so damage the dreamy Greek island idyll elsewhere.

The main settlement at **Limenas** (also popularly known as **Thassos Town**) lies in a large bay on the north coast—offering the shortest crossing point to the mainland (12 km). A very pleasant mix of modern town and ancient city ruins, it reflects the island's history as a quietly prosperous state during the ancient period (its wealth generated by gold and silver mines and marble quarrying). With a scatter of later Turkish houses, in-filled with modern (invariably tourist related) buildings, the town is probably akin to what Kos Town would have looked like today if both Crusaders and Italians had not come a-building. Even the presence of tourist outlets and discos accompanying the holidaymakers fails to diminish the appealing relaxed atmosphere.

Activity naturally centres on the waterfront, which is surprisingly diverse with three distinct zones: the ferry quay (home to most of the services and shops), the ancient harbour (base for tour and beach boats, starting point for town tours, and offering leafy night-time waterfront promenades), and the popular town beach (backed by restaurants and tavernas). The tree-filled streets behind are thinly lined with buildings that are rarely more than one deep.

Movement around Thassos is dominated by the coast road that runs in a rough circuit around the island. Most buses travel in an anticlockwise direction to connect with the main port of **Skala Prinos** perched on an east coast spit: a tourist dominated hamlet, but with more going for it than many Greek ports with a number of tavernas and holidaymaker orientated shops, a goodly number of trees dividing the outlets offering accommodation and a working caïque repair yard. South of Skala Prinos the west coast is fairly quiet with the bulk of the island's low-key agriculture and scattered beach villages until it reaches **Limenaria** on the south coast. The island's main resort (courtesy of a long, narrow sand beach) and the only other large town, it is largely a product of the mining industry in the early years of this century; though this fact is somewhat misleading as the only dark holes these days are provided by the local discos. These exist in numbers, as if trying to compensate for the damaged landscape around the town: this southern part of the coast is the most spoilt part of Thassos thanks to extensive forest fire damage in recent years. Those in search of scenery will do better to head on to neighbouring resort villages of **Pefkari** and **Potos** which have quieter beaches. Potos is also a convenient place to pick up buses heading inland to the island's medieval capital at **Theologos**. Now reduced to a quiet, whitewashed hill village, Theologos has only benefited from its isolation.

The beach at **Makriammos** aside, the east coast of Thassos is the best on offer.

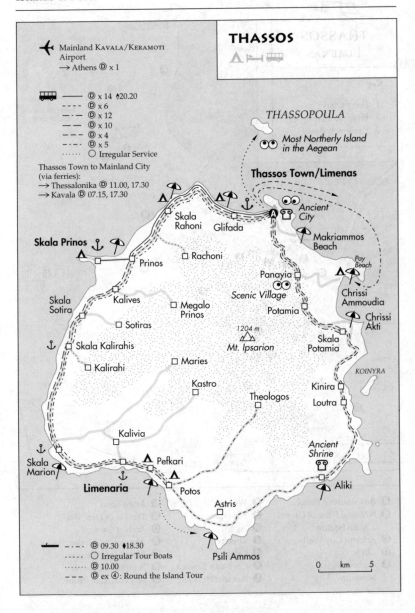

THASSOS

Mainland KAVALA/KERAMOTI Airport
→ Athens Ⓓ x 1

——— Ⓓ x 14 ♦20.20
- - - - Ⓓ x 6
—·—·— Ⓓ x 12
—— Ⓓ x 10
— — Ⓓ x 4
—·—·— Ⓓ x 5
········· ○ Irregular Service

Thassos Town to Mainland City (via ferries):
→ Thessalonika Ⓓ 11.00, 17.30
→ Kavala Ⓓ 07.15, 17.30

THASSOPOULA

Most Northerly Island in the Aegean

Thassos Town/Limenas

Ancient City

Makriammos Beach

Pay Beach

Skala Rahoni   Glifada

Skala Prinos

Prinos   Rachoni

Panayia

Scenic Village

Potamia

Chrissi Ammoudia

Chrissi Akti

Skala Sotira

Kalives

Megalo Prinos

Sotiras

1204 m
Mt. Ipsarion

Skala Potamia

KOINYRA

Skala Kalirahis

Kalirahi   Maries

Kastro

Theologos

Kinira

Loutra

Kalivia

Ancient Shrine

Skala Marion

Pefkari

Limenaria   Potos

Astris

Aliki

Psili Ammos

0   km   5

—·—·— Ⓓ 09.30 ♦18.30
········· ○ Irregular Tour Boats
········· Ⓓ 10.00
— — Ⓓ ex ④ : Round the Island Tour

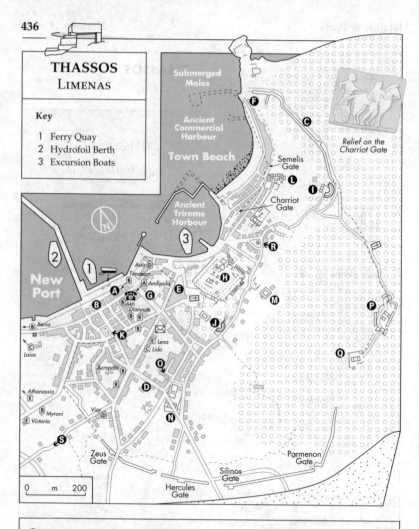

THASSOS
LIMENAS

Key

1 Ferry Quay
2 Hydrofoil Berth
3 Excursion Boats

Relief on the Charriot Gate

Submerged Moles

Ancient Commercial Harbour

Town Beach

Semelis Gate

Charriot Gate

Ancient Trireme Harbour

New Port

Astir
Timaleon
Amfipolis
Akti Dionysos
Xenia
Laios
Lena
Lido
Acropolis
Athanassia
Myroni
Victoria
Vissy

Zeus Gate

Hercules Gate

Silinos Gate

Parmenon Gate

0   m   200

- **A** Bus Station / Police
- **B** National Bank of Greece / Main Square
- **C** Ancient City Walls
- **D** Clinic
- **E** Archaeological Museum
- **F** WCs
- **G** Newspapers
- **H** Agora
- **I** Theatre
- **J** Odeon
- **K** Christian Basilica
- **L** Ancient Houses
- **M** Artemision
- **N** Temple of Hercules
- **O** Arch of Caracalla
- **P** Acropolis / Medieval Castle
- **Q** Temple of Athena
- **R** Temple of Dionysos
- **S** Road to Skala Prinos

More scenic (the road deviates from the coast to take in the lovely mountain villages of **Panayia** and **Potamia**; the latter is a popular tour destination in consequence) it runs down to the picture-postcard village of **Aliki** and, arguably the most attractive part of the island: the long golden sand pine-backed beach running from **Kinira** to **Psili Ammos**.

➡

Thassos Town is the best place to stay on the island. Rooms are around but are never plentiful in High Season. You shouldn't ignore offers on disembarking. There are also a wide range of hotels in Thassos Town, most behind the ferry quay. Prices are higher than average, and the balance of accommodation is towards the upper end of the range. At the top is the A-class *Amfipolis* (☎ 23101). B-class hotels include *Xenia* (☎ 71270) and the pensions *Acropolis* (☎ 22488), *Myroni* (☎ 23256), *Akti* (☎ 22326) and *Dionysos* (☎ 22198). C-class hotels are confined to the *Lido* (☎ 22929) and *Laios* (☎ 22309). At the bottom end of the range are the D-class *Astir* (☎ 22160), and E-class *Victoria* (☎ 22556), *Lena* (☎ 22793) and *Athanassia* (☎ 22545).

A

There are several sites at Skala Prinos including a pleasant NTOG / EOT site: *Camping Prinos* (☎ 71171) 700 m west of the ferry quay. Complete with its own pebble beach, it is the easiest site to get to without your own transport, but like other sites on Thassos it is geared to the trailer/camper market and full of young families in High Season. Other sites are more isolated and invariably have a full range of facilities (including reasonable mini-markets). *Camping Ioannidis* (☎ 71477) and *Camping Perseus* (☎ 81352) at Skala Rahoni are well placed and worth considering. Even better — if you can live with the isolation — are south coast *Pefkari Camping* (☎ 51595) and east coast *Chryssi Ammoudia Camping* (☎ 61207).

👓

Thassos Town offers an easy day's sightseeing, along with a readily accessible beach. Ancient remains are scattered liberally around the town, though in almost every case nothing but foundations survive. Most obvious of these is the **Agora**, which backs onto the ancient harbour and houses the remains of a couple of Roman stoas, a tholos (a small circular temple) and several monumental altars. Nearby is a

small **Archaeological Museum** (it has a notable 3 m high Archaic kouros, various pieces of sculpture, labels in French and no entry fee). To the south lies a small **Odeon** fronted by a tiny remnant (50 m) of a paved **Hellenistic Street**. This led to the triumphal **Arch of Caracalla**, now reduced to some impressively large foundations. Other survivals consist of temples to assorted gods along with a well-preserved **Theatre**. Hidden away in the forest, this theatre is one of the most appealing in the Greek islands. However, the number of pine trees enthusiastically growing amid the tiers of bench seats does suggest that the occasional performances put on here for the tourists' benefit are a bit on the wooden side.

Perhaps the most impressive feature of the ancient town is the well preserved 4 C. BC **City Wall** that skirts the hills around the modern town and includes the old Acropolis. The wall fragments are in varying states of repair, along with the gates that each take their name from the Archaic reliefs carved on them. A wooded path (complete with street lamps) runs from the theatre up to the **Acropolis** — its ancient remains now incorporated into the walls of a ruined **Medieval Castle** (built in 1259). From the Acropolis the path runs on to a **Temple of Athena**. Little remains of the building, but the views over Thassos Town are worth the walk.

The buses that run around the scenic coast road are also very popular with visitors. Twice a day (mornings and late afternoons) they make a circuit of the island — thus offering tourists the opportunity to make 'day trips' to the destination of their choice. Most make for the east coast villages of **Panayia** and **Aliki** (the latter offering the remains of a small Doric shrine and ancient marble quarries).

Thessalonika

ΘΕΣΣΑΛΟΝΙΚΗ; pop. 406,500.

CODE ☎ 031
PORT POLICE ☎ 531504
NTOG OFFICE ☎ 263112
TOURIST POLICE ☎ 544162
POLICE ☎ 522589

The 1997 European City of Culture and the second city of Greece, Thessalonika (often abbreviated to plain 'Salonika') commands attention as an important bus and rail junction, but the city has to work hard to keep the many tourists passing through. With a population approaching half a million, along with all the smog, crowds and concrete of the capital Athens — but without the mitigating grace of an Acropolis complex — Thessalonika has limited appeal unless you are prepared to venture well away from the waterfront.

Founded in 316 BC by the Macedonian commander Cassander (husband of Alexander the Great's half-sister), the city, unlike most other important centres in Greece, was never a major city state in its own right (hence the lack of classical antiquities); instead, ideally placed on the trade route between the Levant and the Balkans, it has thrived as a major staging post from the Roman era (when it became the capital of the province of Macedonia) to the present day. Its history, therefore, is one of repeated changes in ruler as the warring powers in the region through the centuries have fought to secure its strategic position, leaving a legacy of impressive Byzantine churches and an even more spectacular city wall. Poets and philosophers are conspicuous by their absence: Thessalonika just wasn't their sort of town. Trade has always been the order of the day and with it came waves of immigrants (notably 1492 when 20,000 Spanish Jews settled in the city, and 1923, when Greeks emigrating from Turkey arrived in numbers).

The last hundred years have not been particularly kind to the city. Victim of a devastating fire in 1917 (which resulted in the waterfront and commercial centre being totally destroyed and then reconstructed on a grid system, with only the odd rebuilt church or ancient monument poking incongruously amid the new buildings giving a reminder of the city of old), Thessalonika saw its commercial stuffing all but knocked out during WW2 when the occupying German forces deported the large Jewish population to the death camps. This was followed by a major earthquake in 1978 that inflicted

considerable damage to the rich legacy of Byzantine churches (many only recently rebuilt after the fire). These three events have combined to take much of the zip out of the city's step, and the pervading down-town atmosphere is one of a utilitarian, if cosmopolitan, commercialism; this is all rather a pity given that this city is often the first port of call for visitors to Greece — courtesy of its position on the main railway line to Europe. Even so, while this isn't Greece at its best, there is certainly enough sightseeing to fill a couple of leisurely days. If you are looking for something more, then you would be better advised to move on, for although the city has an active nightlife, swimming is a non-starter: tucked up in the Thermaic Gulf, the seas hereabouts are not as clean as they might be.

No matter how you arrive, the easiest way of getting your bearings is to head for the waterfront (which would be attractive enough were it not for the harbour seemingly doubling up as the city's primary sewage disposal system). Those that brave the brown waves and murderous traffic that bedevil the promenade will find a helpful NTOG/EOT office located mid-way along it offering free city maps (though finding your way around the centre is easy enough provided you stick to the main streets). Most of the sights are to be found in the north and eastern sections of the city. The former (just to the north of the area on the map opposite) includes the well-preserved city walls and the only part of the pre-1917 town to survive the flames. Now known as the Kastra district, it is an atmospheric maze of tiny streets more reminiscent of a Turkish town and offers a considerable contrast with the bland wide boulevards (albeit fairly leafy ones) running between the large city squares of the rebuilt centre.

As befits a major city, bus links are good all year, though the bus stations are poorly marked, hard to find and are best reached via taxi. However, Thessalonika is not

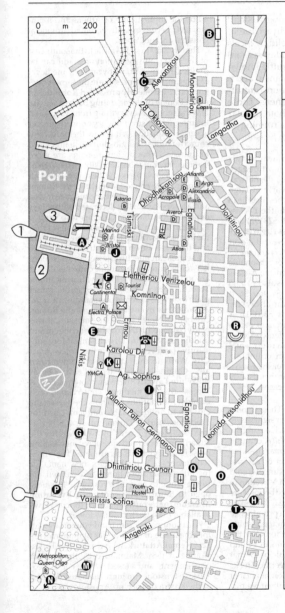

THESSALONIKA
CITY CENTRE

Key

A Port Entrance /
Customs Building

B Railway Station
(all destinations)

C Main Bus Station:
Athens & West
(700 m)

D Bus Station:
Kavala & East
(1 km)

E NTOG / EOT Office

F British Consulate

G US Consulate

H Hospital

I Tourist Police

J Banks

K Cathedral

L University

M Archaeological
Museum

N Folk Museum
(800 m)

O Rotunda
(Ag. Georgios)

P White Tower

Q Arch of Galerius

R Roman Agora

S Palace of Galerius

T Acropolis & City
Walls (500 m)

1 Domestic Ferries
2 International Ferries
3 Hydrofoil Berth

well served by ferries; though island hoppers can justify a visit by virtue of those boats (often booked solid by locals at the start of the local holiday season) that do run. Thessalonika is a little-known jumping off point for the islands, and a preferable alternative to an uncomfortable night train-bound to Athens. Those prepared to pay will find both regular ferries and daily hydrofoils running to the Sporades islands in High Season.

⊨

As the nearest camping is 25 km away at Agia Triada (via a #72 or #73 bus), most budget travellers head for the hotels near the railway station. These usually fill up early in High Season. Phone ahead if you can; best bets lie in the centre of town and include the D-class *Alexandria* (☎ 536185), *Ilisia* (☎ 528492) and *Atlas* (☎ 537046), and the E-class *Argo* (☎ 519 770) and *Atlantis* (☎ 540131). Near the port both the D-class *Marina* (☎ 538917) and the C-class *Continental* (☎ 277563) offer reasonable rooms. To the east lies the expensive A-class *Electra Palace* (☎ 23 2221). There is also a *Youth Hostel* (☎ 225946) at 44 Alex. Svolou St. If things get really desperate you can always try the port area D-class *Bristol* (☎ 530351). A remarkable survival of both fire and earthquake, this dilapidated dump offers corridors that would not be out of place in a 19 c. mental hospital and rooms filled with crumbling plaster glued together with squashed mosquitos. For some unknown reason they usually have spare beds even in High Season.

∞

If you only have a short time in Thessalonika then you should abandon all other sightseeing for the **Archaeological Museum**. Housing the contents of Phillip II of Macedon's (Alexander the Great's father) tomb at Vergina (closed to tourists) it contains a collection of art and goldware not to be missed, including the gold casket decorated with the star of Macedon in which Phillip's partially cremated bones were interred. They are now laid out near the casket. The museum has gained, in both prominence and the number of visitors, from the dispute over the use of the name Macedonia by the former Yugoslav republic to the north. Phillip II's remains are seen as irrefutable proof that 'Macedonia is Greek'; in this respect the Greeks do have a point, as the population of ancient Macedon were Greek speakers (albeit regard-

ed by the sophisticates of Athens and mainstream Greece as quaintly accented provincial cousins) and not Slavs.

The city's main sights all lie to the south-east of the port/railway station area and can be divided into ancient and Byzantine / medieval categories. Most impressive in the former category is the excellently preserved **Rotunda**: an intact Roman building dating back to 306 AD. Having served as everything from a museum to a mosque (the surviving abandoned minaret is very conspicuous), it is now the university church of Agios Georgios, but is usually closed to tourists. Other ancient remains are more fragmentary but more accessible. The **Arch of Galerius** (303 AD) is the best preserved of them, and was erected to celebrate the Roman Emperor's victory of the Persians at Armenia and Mesopotamia. It is decorated with reliefs depicting the battles. Galerius also built a **Palace** in the city but only foundations of this, the Roman **Agora** and **Hippodrome**, are extant and there is little on public display.

The great architectural jewels in Thessalonika's crown are the Byzantine churches dotted around the city and the Medieval fortifications. Most famous of the churches is the rather plain looking **St. Demetrius** standing near the Agora (it lies over the remains of the Roman city baths). Noted for its fine mosaics, it was badly damaged in the 1917 fire, and the current building is a copy in all but name. More substantive (and venerable) are the largely intact **City Walls** to the north of the down-town area. Originally they extended east as far as the **White Tower**. Otherwise known as 'Lefkos Pirgos', this is a medieval construction built on older foundations, and now the nearest the city has to an identifiable emblem. Used for executions during Turkish rule it was christened the 'Bloody Tower' by the locals after the sultan imprisoned and massacred his rebelling personal bodyguards here in 1826. The sultan took umbrage at the burgers' new name for his little home from home and painted the tower white by way of a response. It is now open to tourists, and contains a **Byzantine Museum** that is put to shame by the city views available from the top of the tower.

With your passport to hand you can also get into the home of the founder of modern Turkey, **Kemal Attaturk**, who was born in Thessalonika in 1881. Maintained by the Turkish government, and closed whenever Greco-Turkish tensions run high, the house lies east of the Kastra district, on Apostolou St.

Volos

ΒΟΛΟΣ; pop. 71,400.

CODE ☎ 0421
PORT POLICE ☎ 38888
NTOG OFFICE ☎ 23500

The number four city of Greece, Volos (or Bolos) is set deep in a bay north of Evia, and is the mainland jumping-off point for the Northern Sporades island chain. Long an important port, the modern town lies atop the ancient city of Iolkos, home of Jason the Argonaut, from whence he set out in search of, and returned with, the mythical Golden Fleece. Sadly, there is little to show of this pastoral ancestry these days — except the ugly appearance of a city that looks as if it ought to be the sort of place which manufactures sheep dip. As a result, most visitors just pass through, being either day-trippers from the islands or Athens-based groups 'doing a Greek island' or using the town as a jumping off point for the very attractive oak-wooded Mount Pelion peninsula rising up behind. This popular tourist attraction (hence the helpful NTOG tourist office in Volos town centre) was home to the half-men, half-horse Centaurs that have long since hoofed it from the city-clad foothills to quieter parts, despite the existence of a good Archaeological Museum on Volos's bustling waterfront. The means of getting away are very good; with a dozen buses a day to Athens as well as a rail link to Larissa. Ferry connections with the Sporades are good all year, though other sea connections (including the uninspiring fishing hamlet-clad islet of **Trikeri** to the south) are less consistent.

🛏

Both the D-class *Iassson* (☎ 26075) and E-class *Europa* (☎ 23624), just off the ferry quay, provide indifferent rooms that serve in a pinch. Private room availability is very poor.

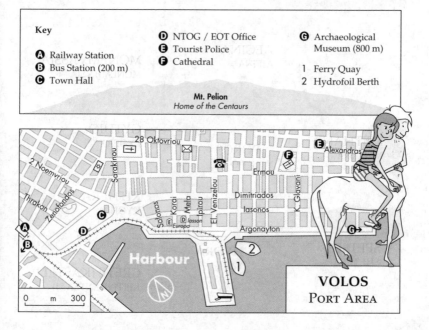

Key

A Railway Station
B Bus Station (200 m)
C Town Hall
D NTOG / EOT Office
E Tourist Police
F Cathedral
G Archaeological Museum (800 m)

1 Ferry Quay
2 Hydrofoil Berth

Mt. Pelion
Home of the Centaurs

28 Oktovriou
2 Noemvriou
Thrakon
Zenofondos
Saraknou
Solonos
Korai
Mela
Spirou
El. Venizelou
Dimitriados
Iasonos
Argonayton
K. Glavani
Ermou
Alexandras
Iasson
Europa

Harbour

VOLOS
PORT AREA

0   m   300

11
ARGO-SARONIC LINES

**AEGINA · ANGISTRI · ANTIKITHERA · GYTHIO · HYDRA
KITHERA · MONEMVASSIA · NEAPOLI · POROS · SPETSES**

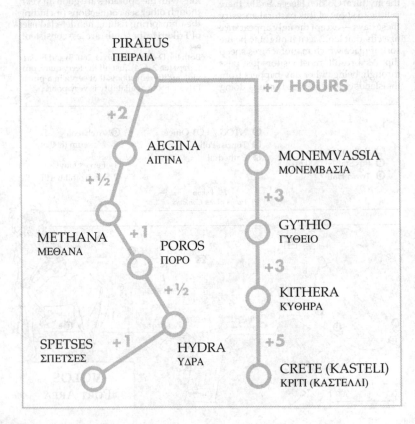

PIRAEUS
ΠΕΙΡΑΙΑ

+7 HOURS

+2

AEGINA
ΑΙΓΙΝΑ

MONEMVASSIA
ΜΟΝΕΜΒΑΣΙΑ

+½

+3

METHANA
ΜΕΘΑΝΑ

+1

POROS
ΠΟΡΟ

GYTHIO
ΓΥΘΕΙΟ

+3

+½

KITHERA
ΚΥΘΗΡΑ

SPETSES
ΣΠΕΤΣΕΣ

+1

HYDRA
ΥΔΡΑ

+5

CRETE (KASTELI)
ΚΡΙΤΙ (ΚΑΣΤΕΛΛΙ)

General Features

This 'Argo-Saronic' chapter encompasses ferry services to islands within the Saronic Gulf proper, as well as those running down the so-called 'Argoid' or East Peloponnesian coast to Kithera and Crete. Ferries confine their runs within one of the two branches, the all important linking services being provided by hydrofoils. The islands and ports also reflect this divide and range from among the most heavily touristed in Greece (within the Saronic Gulf, where the short distance to the capital provides a ready tourist and commuter market), to coastal hamlets further south that hardly deserve to be on the ferry network at all, and only are so thanks to subsidies. Connections reach their nadir on Antikithera, the small island most poorly served by regular ferry in the Aegean. There is thus little middle ground between the two groups. Ports are either over-touristed with a veritable procession of landing-craft type ferries and hydrofoils running around (Aegina, Poros, Hydra, and Spetses all qualify for this category thanks to their popularity as day-tripper and European package tour islands), or they can be almost too quiet for comfort (the Peloponnese and island of Kithera) relying on a couple of infrequent ferries and an occasional long-range High Season hydrofoil. Aristotle and his golden mean clearly never found much favour in these parts.

If you like the idea of island hopping against a background of such extremes, then this route offers a happy mix of days when you can visit up to eight ports in 24 hours (if you feel mad enough to try it), with others when you have to wait as long for a ferry. One set of boats definitely to be avoided are the widely advertised 'three-island' day cruise trips starting from Piraeus and taking in Aegina, Poros and Hydra. You can do this yourself using the hydrofoils for half the price, and save even more using the local ferries.

1 Angistri
2 Methana
3 Souvala

4 Ag. Marina
5 Kosta
6 Porto Helio
7 Galatas

0 km 30

SARONIC GULF &
EAST PELOPONNESE

Example Itinerary [2 Weeks]

The mix of over-touristed and relatively inaccessible ports of call offers an interesting holiday for those who like variety. Even so you will have to be prepared to compromise and adjust your schedule (particularly the latter part). Arrive on a favourable day and it is quite possible to get down the group (returning either via Crete and a direct boat back to Piraeus or by bus back up the Peloponnese). Otherwise you will have to skip a port.

Arrival/Departure Point

Athens is easily the best airport on offer. If you are offered a cheap flight to either airports on the Peloponnese or Crete ignore the temptation; they are just too difficult to get back to in an emergency.

Season

If you are prepared to give it an extra week then this itinerary could be followed all year round or you could return via the Central Cyclades Line. Otherwise the usual High Season advantages in terms of frequency of service apply.

1 Athens [2 Days]

An easy starting point and an easy first hop: all the boats start from the same quay at Piraeus and offer frequent starts for Aegina so you won't have to hang around for long.

2 Aegina [1 Day]

An interesting first port of call with enough to fill a day with sightseeing. But the inescapable evidence of mass tourism does little to nurture a get-away-from it all Greek island atmosphere. Accommodation can also be a problem so if you are having real difficulty you could take an evening boat on down the line or alternatively, pick up an evening ferry to the neighbouring small beach island of Angistri.

3 Poros [1 Day]

The town itself can be done in a couple of hours but this does make a good base of operations if you prefer to 'do' the adjacent islands as outings from one base. Mainland excursions to Mycenae and the famous theatre at Epidavros are possible from here too.

4 Spetses [2 Days]

The best beach island in the group and thus the best place to rest up for a couple of days while you wait for a hydrofoil or ferry south. The mainland village of Kosta is also easily accessible, with buses to nearby tourist sites.

5 Monemvassia [2 Days]

After being pampered by the profusion of services thus far the jump to Monemvassia can come as something of a shock. It seems like the end of the world but in fact it is quite a civilized little place. If a hydrofoil or the ferry is not offering your required hop on south you can always take a bus to Napoli and pick up the ferry from there.

6 Kithera [2 Days]

This quiet island offers a complete contrast with its northern Saronic sisters and is a worthy destination to aim for in its own right. That said, the first priority on arrival must be establishing when you can get off. If the wait for a boat on to Crete is too long you always have a boat to Gythio or Napoli on the Peloponnese (both offering bus links with Athens) as a safety option to fall back on. Alternatively, if you have tarried too long in the Saronic Gulf you can give the island a miss and head directly on to Crete.

7 Crete [2 Days]

Dumped on the eastern end of Crete you will have to get a bus from Kasteli to Chania and then another on to Iraklion. Here you can take time out to visit Knossos and the Archaeological Museum before taking the overnight boat back to Piraeus.

1 Athens [2 Days]

If you are planning to venture as far down this line as Crete you could do worse than skip a day in the capital at the beginning of your holiday to give you an extra day's safety at the end of your trip. Either way, as usual give yourself at least one clear day back in Athens before your return flight.

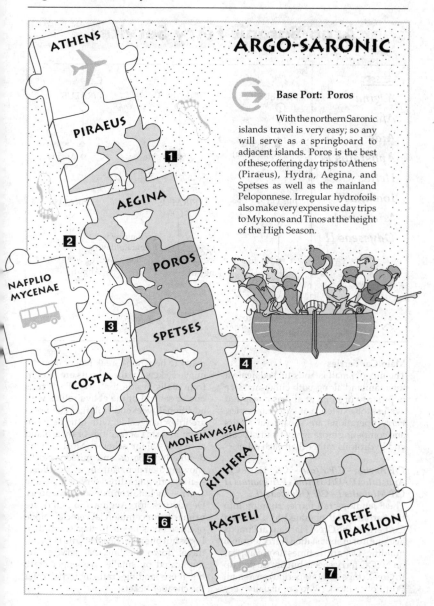

ARGO-SARONIC

Base Port: Poros

With the northern Saronic islands travel is very easy; so any will serve as a springboard to adjacent islands. Poros is the best of these; offering day trips to Athens (Piraeus), Hydra, Aegina, and Spetses as well as the mainland Peloponnese. Irregular hydrofoils also make very expensive day trips to Mykonos and Tinos at the height of the High Season.

Argo-Saronic Ferry Services

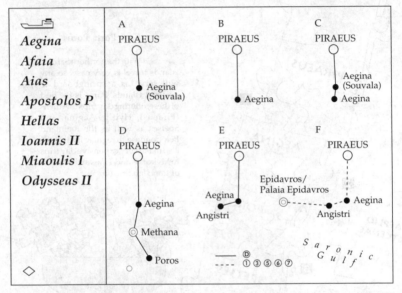

Aegina
Afaia
Aias
Apostolos P
Hellas
Ioannis II
Miaoulis I
Odysseas II

A
PIRAEUS
○
● Aegina
(Souvala)

B
PIRAEUS
○
● Aegina

C
PIRAEUS
○
Aegina
(Souvala)
● Aegina

D
PIRAEUS
○
● Aegina
◎ Methana
● Poros
○

E
PIRAEUS
○
Aegina
● ●
Angistri

F
PIRAEUS
○
Epidavros/
Palaia Epidavros
◎------ ● ● Aegina
Angistri

S a r o n i c
G u l f

---- ⒹΌ
① ③ ⑤ ⑥ ⑦

Main Car Ferries

The mix of small islands tucked against the mainland along with either massive popularity or none at all has conspired against the existence of large car ferries. Ferry operations are short-haul affairs and competing more against tourist boats and hydrofoils rather than each other.

C/F Aegina - C/F Afaia - C/F Aias - C/F Apostolos P - C/F Hellas - C/F Ioannis II C/F Miaoulis I - C/F Odysseas II

The 8 landing-craft ferries running into the Saronic Gulf operated by Poseidon Co. berth in the Great Harbour at Piraeus just south of the bus station/ferry terminal building. Departure times do not appear on NTOG ferry sheets but are posted up in Greek (for a 48-hour period) on a small Port Police kiosk (who are usually very

ready to help non-Greek readers) on the quay. Tickets for these boats are bought from stalls beside the ferry. Each runs one or several of the above routes with additional weekend sailings. The boats are interchangeable, with little between them in terms of facilities or their bland all-white colour scheme. Most display destination boards and nursery clocks showing their departure time. Most boats —if not offering a direct service to Aegina Town—include it on extended schedules. Departures for Aegina (Souvala) are primarily for commercial vehicles. None of these boats heads further south than Poros but offer the cheapest (and slowest) travel down the line. All services are duplicated by smaller passenger craft, but these landing-craft car ferries offer the cheaper tickets.

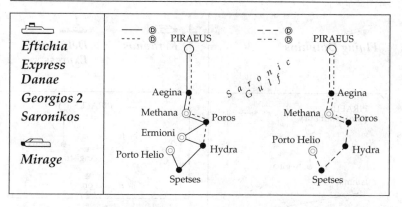

In addition to the fleet of landing-craft ferries, the Saronic Gulf is served by a number of small regular ferries. Faster than the landing-craft types, they venture further down the line, but are primarily on the route to ensure that a ferry service can be maintained during the winter months when poor sea conditions confine the landing-craft ferries to port.

C/F Express Danae
Agapitos Express Ferries; 1972; 1903 GRT.
Long standing island hoppers will know that once upon a time there was a little ferry — the *Kyklades* — that every three weeks left Piraeus on a wondrous voyage to almost every island you could name; running via Crete to Kavala on the North Aegean coast. After years being laid-up she reappeared in 1994 as the *Methodia*, running to Porto Helio while managing to retain both her external staircases and her reputation for running late. Now firmly established on the Porto Helio route as the *Express Danae*, her refurbished interior is starting to resemble that of its shabby predecessor.

C/F Georgios 2
Local
The largest and best of the small ferries on the Porto Helio route has, for a number of years, sailed under the name *Georgios*. The latest incarnation — the *Georgios 2* — appeared in 1997, running a similar service to her predecessor and offering a reasonable on-board facilities.

C/F Eftichia
Argo–Saronic Line; 1974; 869 GRT.
The sharp-nosed, but reliable, *Eftichia* — a passenger boat converted over to a full car ferry — is the smallest fully-fledged ferry on the line. Usually overcrowded to busting as a result, she offers a less relaxed journey than most of her rivals.

C/F Saronikos
Argo–Saronic Line; 1974; 1126 GRT.
A roofed-over landing-craft ferry, the *Saronikos* runs in tandem with the *Eftichia*; the two vessels make alternate runs, with one boat going all the way to Poros while the other starts later and turns back at Aegina.

C/M Mirage
Strintzis Line
A newcomer on the route in 1998, this medium-sized catamaran used her speed to provide a twice-daily service to Porto Helio with trips in-between to Aegina. Her on board facilities are similar to those on the CERES hydrofoils (see p. 450).

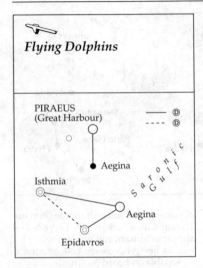

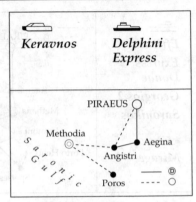

H/F *Flying Dolphins*
CERES

For reasons that aren't clear, hydrofoils heading direct to Aegina depart from Piraeus (Great Harbour) rather than from Zea Marina. Tickets are bought from a kiosk on the quay (see p. 119). The boats tend to be very popular in the rush hours and weekends, so it pays to book your return if it is going to coincide with these times. The island of Aegina is also developing as a jumping off point for additional hydrofoils to Epidavros. These run mornings and evenings in High Season, for the benefit of tourists wanting to continue onto the famous archaeological site. In 1998 an additional link ran to the entrance of the Corinth Canal, at Isthmia, ferrying tour parties to nearby ancient Corinth.

C/M *Keravnos* — P/S *Delphini Express*

For the last few years, a tatty catamaran has run around the upper reaches of the Saronic Gulf. Similar to the tiny *Nearchos* that once ran to the Central Cyclades from Crete, she is equally the worse for wear, her schedules are inconsistent (they

are posted up daily on the ticket booth on the quayside at Piraeus). These usually consist of a prosaic Piraeus—Aegina—Angistri service. More popular with locals rather than tourists, she was joined by the small *Delphini Express* tour boat in 1998.

H/F *Falcon I—III*
Sea Falcon Lines

A new hydrofoil service emerged in 1996 with the arrival of an hourly service to the resort of Agia Marina on Aegina. The limited popularity of the route has forced changes since the addition of Souvala, and latterly Paros and Hydra to some itineraries. Further changes could well occur in 1999.

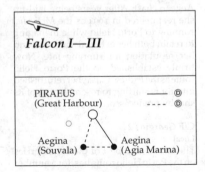

Argo-Saronic

AEGINA
Temple of Aphaia

The C/F *Aias* arrives at Aegina (with the Hidden Harbour in the foreground and Angistri Is. on the horizon)

HYDRA
Main Street & Cannon

ANGISTRI
Main Ferry Quay & Church at Skala Port Village

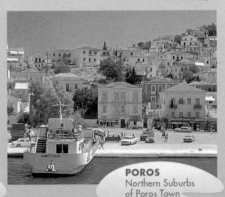

POROS
Northern Suburbs of Poros Town

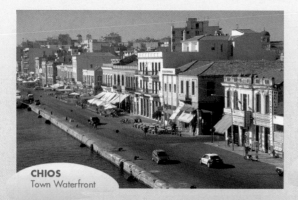

CHIOS
Town Waterfront

The P/S *Fourni Express*
Departs from Fourni
Village Beach

SAMOS
The Roman Catholic
Church on Vathi
Waterfront

Northern Coast east of
Karlovassi

Eastern Lines

FOURNI
Village Beach

SKOPELOS
Panagia ston Pirgho
at Skopelos Town

The C/F *Macedon*
Moored at Skopelos Town

ALONISSOS
Alonissos' Beach Boats
in Patitiri Bay

A CERES *Flying Dolphin*
hydrofoil — a common
visitor to the Sporades &
Argo–Saronic islands

THASSOS
View of Thassos Town
from the Acropolis

Northern Aegean

Ionian

KEFALONIA
Sami Beach & Tide Mill
Wheel

CORFU/KERKYRA
Old Town & Palace Wall
Staircase

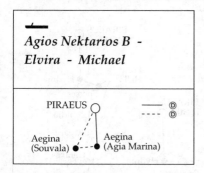

*Agios Nektarios B -
Elvira - Michael*

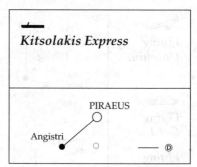

Kitsolakis Express

Small Passenger Boats

In addition to the regular ferries, hydrofoils and catamarans, a number of smaller passenger craft operate to the islands of Aegina and Angistri. For the most part small vessels incapable of journeying far, they rely on commuters and day-tripping tourists for their custom; each boat runs several times daily to its own set destination. Departures for the following 48-hours are posted up on the Saronic Gulf quay Port Police kiosk (they are listed separately at the end of the regular ferry departure times). Tickets for these boats are either bought on board or from ticket 'desks' on the quayside.

Most likely to be of use are flashy *Elvira*, the **P/S** *Agios Nektarios B* (not to be confused with her larger namesake, this is a tiny boat boasting an upturned tin bath

masquerading as a dummy smokestack) and **P/S** *Michael*: all three providing a link with the resort of Agia Marina on Aegina. Also of interest is the **P/S** *Kitsolakis Express* which heads direct to the 'beach' island of Angistri. A more popular means of access is via a large caïque — the **T/B** *Moschos Express* — that runs (well, okay, rolls) from Aegina Town, calling at both the main ferry quay at Skala as well as Megalochorio along the coast. Finally, there is the **P/S** *Manaras Express*; she also ventures to Angistri (via Aegina) but is less prepossessing, being a tiny tub of a boat that looks to have been cobbled together out of old banana boxes. She runs for the benefit of those who like to live dangerously and is usually filled with locals visiting Athens on shopping expeditions.

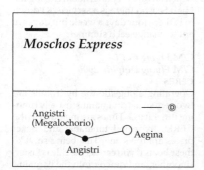

Moschos Express

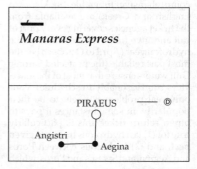

Manaras Express

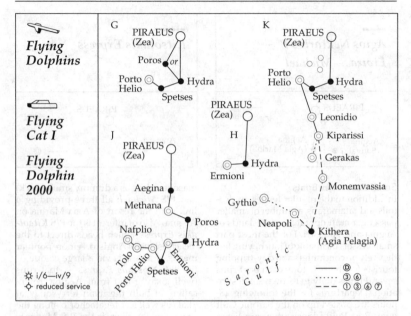

H/F *Flying Dolphins*
CERES

Provided your budget will stretch to a hydrofoil ticket, the yellow and blue CERES *Flying Dolphins* are both the most versatile and quickest way of hopping around the Saronic Gulf. So much so, that some islands (e.g. Hydra) largely depend on them. Easy to use, if only because comprehensive timetable booklets (in English and Greek) are available from the ticket agencies covering every port of call and give times for the whole of the hydrofoil year (April to October). For the most part reliable (the protected Saronic Gulf waters ensure that most of these services run reasonably to schedule), your only real problem is likely to be their popularity; in some instances it pays to buy a return ticket: this is particularly true for (1) last hydrofoils from any given port, and (2) hydrofoils between Poros and Aegina, and Spetses and Poros, which

are relatively few in number. Apart from the services to Aegina (see previous page) which use the Great Harbour, all services arrive and depart from Piraeus (Zea Marina). Itinerary G is the most consistent of the routes run, but the timetables are dominated by one-off irregular itineraries. Most of these take in ports along J, which is run every afternoon. During the High Season there is a service (K) down to Kithera four days a week: but days are apt to change each summer.

C/M *Flying Cat I* –
C/M *Flying Dolphin 2000*
CERES

Operating alongside the hydrofoils are two very swish catamarans; usually running itinerary G. Times are included in the CERES hydrofoil timetable and ticket prices are the same. This being so, take these boats if you can, as the ride is faster, smoother, and quieter into the bargain.

Southern Peloponnese Ferries

One of the few subsidized ferry routes left in Greece runs down the Peloponnese coast and on to Crete (Kasteli). Until 1997 the itinerary had changed little in years; though the days of operation and ferries on the route did. However, since then the company running the two boats on the route — the *Theseus* and smaller *Martha* — has run into financial difficulties and other boats have been drafted in to cover. The vessel providing the Piraeus—Kasteli link is ANEK's *Kantia*, while the *Martha* has been replaced by the *Nissos Kithera*: a small ferry bought by the islanders of that name to keep a maintain a daily link with the mainland. Not surprisingly, consistent timetabling has been a rarity with all these changes, and further modifications can be expected in 1999. It remains to be seen if the Piraeus—Kasteli boat will resume calls to the small ports down the Peloponnese, though the thrice weekly runs from Crete to Gythio and Kalamarta look to be secure, as are the essential lifeline links to Antikithera which exist for the locals benefit (mass tourism has yet to reach this part of the world).

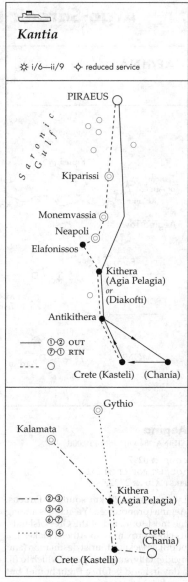

Kantia

☼ i/6—ii/9   ◇ reduced service

Nissos Kithera

Argo-Saronic Islands & Ports

AEGINA

🚌 ── ○ ev ¾ ⊕ 06.15–20.30
     ---- Ⓓ x 13: 06.15–20.30
     -·-· Ⓓ x 11: 06.15–20.30
     ···· Ⓓ x 5

Souvala
Vagia
Agii
Mesagros
Kipseli
Palaiochora
Temple of Apollo
Kolona
Temple of Aphaia
Aegina Town
Kontos
Alones
Ag. Marina
Faros
Marathon
Portes
Ⓓ x 12
Mt Oros/ Temple of Zeus
532 m
MONI
Perdika
Sfentouri
0   km   2

Aegina

ΑΙΓΙΝΑ; 84 km²; pop. 10,000.

CODE ☎ 0297
TOURIST POLICE ☎ 23243
FIRST AID ☎ 22222

Lying a mere 20 km south of Piraeus, Aegina (pronounced 'Ye–nah') is among the most touristed of the Greek islands. Its close proximity to Athens makes it a popular package tourist destination (and incidentally, an ideal spot in which to fill a day in hand before a flight home), but despite this, out of August it is not noticeably overcrowded. If you don't mind commuting each day, the island is actually quite a nice base for 'doing' the capital, besides offering pleasant wooded, low-lying mountain scenery and plenty of sand beach coves for (given the cleanliness of the water) somewhat dubious bathing.

Aegina has had an up and down history: emerging during the 5 c. BC as a serious rival to Athens, it lost the inevitable regional power struggle that followed. Forcibly re-populated by the Athenians, the new inhabitants deemed it safer to grow pistachio nuts rather than dream of power: Aegina is now the nut capital of Greece. In 1829 Aegina Town briefly again came to the fore when it became the first capital of the Greek state (before losing out to Athens for a second time).

Aegina Town, complete with its neo-classical frontage from its days as the capital, is the main centre and by far the best of the possible ferry destinations. The waterfront is lined with tavernas and tourist shops (pistachio nuts figuring prominently in the displays of wares) near the ferry quay, but once you move along the waterfront or inland a street or two, Aegina Town reveals itself to be a surprisingly unspoilt small island town surrounded by nut orchards and offering a day of gentle tourism. The town is very much centred around the ferry quay, the tourist presence all too evident by the existence of horses and carriages standing along the promenade awaiting a fare. But either side of this the waterfront is attractive despite a busy road.

To the south, in the ancient commercial harbour, you will find full-to-overflowing caïques selling fruit and veg. (note: *no* pistachio nuts) with a fresh fish market housed in a quayside alley opposite. To the north lies the remains of the ancient trireme harbour. This was famous in the ancient world; though its name — it was known as the 'hidden harbour' — has caused more than one scholar to scratch his head because it isn't, well, exactly 'hidden'; even after two and a half thousand years. Behind it rises the lightly wooded former acropolis at Kolona (with good views over the Saronic Gulf and the town and the fine beach to the north). Along the beach road lie the bus ticket kiosk and several budget hotels and restaurants. Ticket agencies are surprisingly thin on the ground; the quayside Port Police kiosk has ferry departure times posted up daily (in Greek), with ticket kiosks (often only staffed half an hour before the ferry is due to depart) either

side. Note: if you are planning to return to Athens via late afternoon/evening hydrofoil you should buy your ticket on arrival as they tend to get booked up.

Aegina's bus service is limited but good, running frequently along the northern coast to the island's second town of **Agia Marina**. Linked by small passenger ferry to Piraeus, it is an unabashed package tour resort with all the trimmings. Even so, so far as disco-cities on the sand go it is better than most. If night-life is a priority then it will appeal, otherwise the walk up the pine-forested hill to the Temple of Aphaia is likely to be of greater interest (the 2 km path looks to have been made by a runaway bulldozer). If you are visiting Aegina for a day it is worth considering taking the ferry to Agia Marina, walking up to the temple then taking a bus to Aegina Town and a ferry back to Athens from there.

Other coastal villages are less developed, but gradually falling to the tourist hordes, or failing this, have become villa-filled suburbs for the more affluent Athenians. The small fishing port of **Perdika** on the south-west coast is the most attractive, and surprisingly unspoilt, with some rooms on offer besides boats to the delightfully quiet pine-clad islet of **Moni**. The third of Aegina's ports, **Souvala**, is a resort village with a reasonable beach and a large quay used by lorries unwilling to negotiate the streets of Aegina town.

⊨

Most of Aegina's hotels are pre-booked by tour operators or inconveniently placed. In town there are plenty of options in the middle price range. The best of these are: the *Brown* (☎ 22271) at the south end of the town, along with the hotels north of the port; the *Marmarinos* (☎ 23510) just has the edge, though there is little between the *Plaza* (☎ 25600), *Avra* (☎ 22303), *Artemis* (☎ 25195) and the budget *Togias* (☎ 24242). Those looking for something a little different should try the *Pension Pavlou* (☎ 22 795); which offers pricey, but atmospheric, rooms in an old town house. Regular rooms fill up quickly; so arrive early.

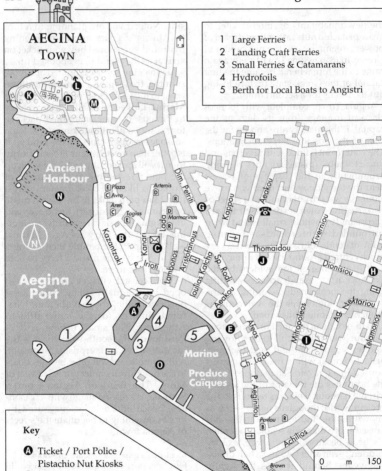

AEGINA
TOWN

1   Large Ferries
2   Landing Craft Ferries
3   Small Ferries & Catamarans
4   Hydrofoils
5   Berth for Local Boats to Angistri

Ancient Harbour

Aegina Port

Marina

Produce Caïques

Key

Ⓐ Ticket / Port Police /
    Pistachio Nut Kiosks

Ⓑ Bus Station (All destinations)

Ⓒ Regular & Tourist Police

Ⓓ Archaeological Museum /
    Site of Ancient Theatre

Ⓔ National Bank of Greece

Ⓕ Newspapers

Ⓖ Medical Centre

Ⓗ Hospital

Ⓘ Cathedral / Former Museum

Ⓙ Markello's Tower

Ⓚ Acropolis & Temple of Apollo

Ⓛ Road to Beach (50 m) & Aphaia (10 km)

Ⓜ Site of the Ancient Stadium

Ⓝ Remains of the 'Hidden Harbour'

Ⓞ Ancient Commercial Harbour

∞

The crumbling lone column of the **Temple of Apollo** stands as a marker indicating the site of Aegina's ancient acropolis on the northern edge of the town. The walls were demolished by the Athenians so little but jumbled foundations remain. The temple once resembled the temple of Aphaia but you would be hard pressed to know it now. This site (known as Kolona or 'column') is also home to Aegina's reasonable **Archaeological Museum** (08.30–15.00 ex ①), which houses finds from around the island, notably coins (Aegina was the first island to mint its own currency — its symbol was the turtle) and the 6 c. BC 'Aegina Sphinx'. The rest of Aegina Town is stronger in atmosphere than sightseeing detail; the one exception being the oddly turreted **Markello's Tower**. Built in 1802, it was the office/home of Greece's first Governor and the tiny ground floor is now a home for local art exhibitions.

The island's major draw is the 5 c. BC **Temple of Aphaia** (a minor daughter goddess of Zeus ignored elsewhere); set atop a pine tree-clad hill 10 km from Aegina Town, it is one of the best preserved in Greece with a unique 2-storey inner colonnade (it is one of the few temples to retain its interior columns). The pedimental sculptures, however, now reside in Munich. Similarities with the Acropolis in Athens extend beyond 'lost' sculptures: it is advisable to visit as soon as the site opens (℗ 08.00–15.00/17.00) to avoid the crowds. On the plus side, the site is excellently signboarded, and the temple is very appealing; being a more approachable size than the later temples in Athens. Its charm extends beyond its size and location: built around 490 BC, it reflects the transition between the Late Archaic and Classical traditions. The terrace setting with its views and lightning mast (one set of gable sculptures in classical times and the western end seem to have been demolished by lightning strikes — the last was in 1969) also help to give the building a character all its own. Note: only limited refreshments (i.e. beer and orange juice) are available from a taverna at the site.

Aegina also had another major temple of interest — the **Temple of Zeus** on the peak of Mt. Oros. Only the foundations survive, with few tourists venturing up the mountain path. The final site of note on Aegina is the monastery of **St. Catherine** on the road east of Aegina Town. It lies west of the abandoned former hill capital of **Palaiochora** on the site of a Temple of Aphrodite.

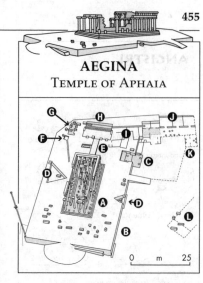

AEGINA
TEMPLE OF APHAIA

0   m   25

Key

- **A** Temple of Aphaia
- **B** Rebuilt Sanctuary Precinct Wall
- **C** Classical Propylon (gateway)
- **D** Foundations of 6 c. BC Precinct
- **E** Ceremonial Ramp & Altar
- **F** Cistern & Base of Sphinx Column
- **G** Remains of Archaic Altar
- **H** Classical Altar
- **I** Archaic Priest's Quarters & Baths
- **J** Classical Priest's Quarters
- **K** Outer Propylon
- **L** Anti-peribolus (precinct) Building

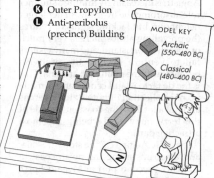

MODEL KEY

Archaic (550–480 BC)

Classical (480–400 BC)

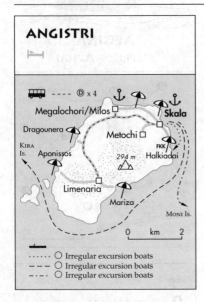

Angistri

ΑΓΚΙΣΤΡΙ; 17 km²; pop. 530.

CODE ☎ 0297

A satellite of Aegina, pine-clad Angistri is a popular day-excursion destination for beach-loving Athenians too afraid of the pollution in the Saronic Gulf to venture to beaches closer to home. In addition, Angistri is increasingly finding a summer role absorbing the overflow of her larger neighbour, but lacking sights or centres the prevailing atmosphere is very much of a beach resort island, and many visitors fail to venture beyond the prettyish beaches near the main port at Skala. This is the de facto island centre, and is made up of a collection of hotels and tavernas and not a lot else (the coast either side of the ferry quay easily being the most attractive part).

The daily Aegina caïque stops at Skala, and also runs along the north coast to Angistri's second port at Megalochori/

Milos. The island's diminutive bus calls here en route from Skala to the 'capital' at Limenaria. This is an untouristed village; the only attraction is the escape from the coastal crowds.

∽

There is little to see on Angistri, but the island is a viable base for day-tripping to Athens. Caïques visit offshore islands and tour agents offer excursions to nearby Epidavros at a price.

⊨

Reasonable supply of rooms and some 22 D and E-class hotels, but these are apt to fill with Athenian 'weekenders' from Friday on.

Antikithera

ΑΝΤΙΚΥΘΗΗΡΑ; 29 km²; pop. 115.

Occupying the straits between the Peloponnese and Western Crete, this island is a dry rock that would only appeal to extreme get-away-from-it-all fanatics. The tiny population lives in two dusty hamlets and see few strangers. In fact, Antikithera is best known for its shipwrecks; one of which yielded up the bronze Ephebe of Antikithera now in the National Archaeological Museum in Athens. The Elgin marbles were also temporarily sunk here en route to Britain. Most ferries steer well clear and out of High Season links are reduced to one a week; so the island is inaccessible for all

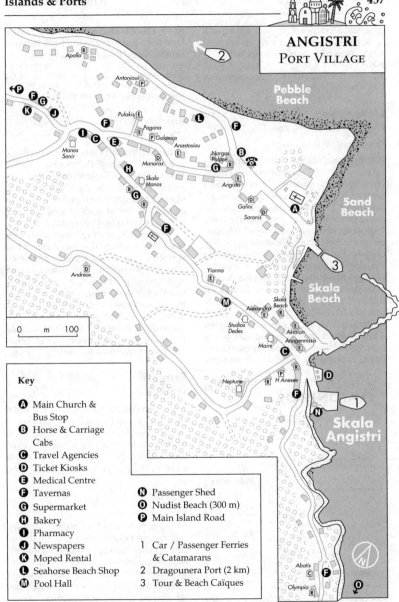

ANGISTRI
PORT VILLAGE

Pebble Beach

Sand Beach

Skala Beach

Skala Angistri

Apollo

Antonioui

Pulakis

Pagona

Galaxias

Anastasiou

Manaras

Nargos Palace

Skala Manos

Angistri

Galini

Saronis

Manos Sonir

Andreas

Yianna

Skala Beach

Alexandro

Studios Dedes

Maire

Anagennissis

Aktaion

Neptune

H Anesee

Abatis

Olympia

0   m   100

Key

A Main Church &
  Bus Stop

B Horse & Carriage
  Cabs

C Travel Agencies

D Ticket Kiosks

E Medical Centre

F Tavernas

G Supermarket

H Bakery

I Pharmacy

J Newspapers

K Moped Rental

L Seahorse Beach Shop

M Pool Hall

N Passenger Shed

O Nudist Beach (300 m)

P Main Island Road

1 Car / Passenger Ferries
   & Catamarans

2 Dragounera Port (2 km)

3 Tour & Beach Caïques

practicable purposes. If you want a quick look you can visit via a ferry en route to Crete, returning north 6 hours later.

Ⓜ

Take a room here and you will double your host's annual income!

Elafonissos

ΕΛΑΦΟΝΗΣΙ; 19 km²; pop. 270.

CODE ☎ 0734

An attractive, isolated, beach island lying off the southern Peloponnese coast town of Neapoli, Elafonissos ('deer's island') was linked to the mainland by a causeway until 1677. The only settlement lies at the site of this divide: a church now standing in glorious isolation (along with Elafonissos's only tree) from the other buildings on a spit of land tapering towards the mainland. Elafonissos town is a pretty fishing village that offers an ideal base if your notion of getting away from it all includes an absence of banks and other tourists. In addition, the island is blessed with clean seas and a superb sand beach 4 km south of the village (accessible via an irregular boat). Caïques augment ferry links, running to Neapoli (30 minutes

ELAFONISSOS

No bus service

━ ╌ ╌ Ⓓ 10.00–16.00

east). There is also a landing craft mainland service operating to a track running off the Neapoli—Peloponnese road.

Ⓜ

Some rooms and 2 B-class pensions in the village: the *Asteri Tis Elafonissou* (☎ 61271) and the cheaper *Elafonissos* (☎ 61268).

Epidavros

ΕΠΙΔΑΥΡΟΣ

So named on timetables, this resort village is actually the small Peloponnese port of **Palea Epidavros**. Host to three campsites, and a dozen hotels, the main reason to stop off here (the beach aside) is the archaeological site of ancient Epidavros 15 km away (taxis and buses run direct; the latter also to nearby Ligourio en route for **Nafplio** — which also has a direct bus service to the site). An important sanctuary to the healing god Asclepius (of staff and serpent fame), the site is home to a theatre (4 c. BC) that was recognised by the ancients themselves as the most perfect ever constructed. Fortunately, it is also the best preserved, and with seating for 14,000 it is a sightseeing must. Tours run weekly from all the nearby islands.

Ermioni

ΕΡΜΙΟΝΙ

A suburb commuter town on the Peloponnese coast. Tourists with any sense avoid disembarking here as there is nothing to see or do: the town lacks even a serviceable beach. Majority of vessels calling are hydrofoils.

Gerakas

ΓΕΡΑΚΑΣ

Located in a mini-loch half-way down the eastern Peloponnese, this small and uninspiring hamlet (without buses or a beach) has little but a road into the interior. In past years regular hydrofoils and rare ferries have called at the port (none of the latter were operating in 1998).

Gythio

ΓΥΘΕΙΟ; pop. 4,950.

CODE ☎ 0733
PORT POLICE ☎ 22262
TOURIST POLICE ☎ 0731 28701
POLICE ☎ 22271

The most important town on the south coast of the Peloponnese, Gythio offers an attractive Venetian house-fronted promenade, decked out with fish restaurants and set against the green foothills of Mt. Laryssion. A good base for exploring the region, it is a pretty — if somewhat over-touristed — port with quite a history. Sparta's naval base during the Peloponnesian war, it was sacked by Athens in 455 BC, (relations are now on a friendlier footing, with 4 buses daily via Sparta). During the Roman era the town became an important production centre for murex — the imperial purple dye — extracted from sea molluscs by a method now lost. Most of ancient Gythio is now equally invisible: the only survival of note being a small theatre 400 m north of the current town. Ferry links are also rather poor as Gythio lies tucked 2/3 hours steaming up the Gulf of Lakonia. Along with the occasional tourist boat, they combine to provide an almost daily service to Kithera and its links with the outside world.

⊨

A dozen hotels, but they tend to be expensive: this is package tour country. The cheapest are the waterfront D-class *Akaion* (☎ 22294) and *Kranae* (☎ 22249). Fortunately rooms are on offer and well sign-posted around the harbour area of the town.

Å

Several quiet olive grove sites lie just off a good beach 5 km south of the town. Buses run hourly past the camping strip.

∞

The main sight lies just to the south of the promenade: the small causeway-linked islet of **Marathonisi** (ancient Kranai). Famed in antiquity as the spot where Paris spent his first night with Helen (whose face launched the first thousand Greek ferries) while carrying her off to Troy, the islet attracted the curious

from the first, prompting the erection of a Hellenistic temple of Aphrodite and a number of other shrines. As late as 1770, garbled tales of the Jolly Roger prompted the islet's Turkish masters in far away Istanbul to sanction the building of a fortress tower (newly restored) to keep nonexistent local brigands in hand. Apart from this construction, a couple of chapels, and a suitably phallic lighthouse, Marathonisi has no other buildings but is disappointingly covered in shrubby trees and hosts an annual summer pan-Hellenic mosquito convention so large that one wonders if any mortal has ever managed an untroubled night's sleep here.

Hydra

ΥΔΡΑ; 52 km²; pop. 3,000.

CODE ☎ 0298
PORT POLICE ☎ 52279
TOURIST POLICE ☎ 52205
TOWN HALL ☎ 52210

A hilltop sticking out of the Aegean lacking roads or beaches, Hydra (pronounced 'EE-dra') has overcome the disadvantages of a generally dour appearance to become one of the most touristed spots in Greece. This is due to a combination of a very

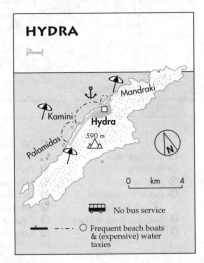

HYDRA

Mandraki

Kamini

Hydra

590 m

Palamidas

N

0   km   4

🚌 No bus service

- - - ○ Frequent beach boats & (expensive) water taxies

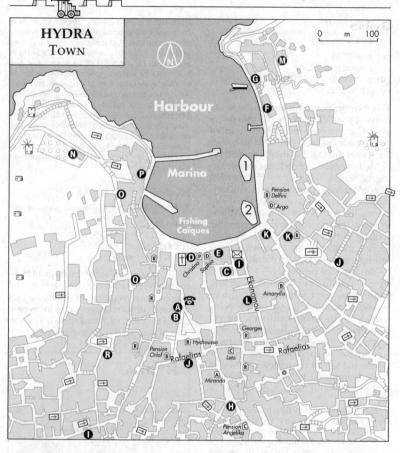

HYDRA
TOWN

Harbour

Marina

Fishing Caïques

Pension Delfini

Argo

Christina

Sophia

Economou

Amaryllis

Georges

Amaryllis

Hydroussa

Pension Orlof

Leto

Rafaelias

Rafaelias

Miranda

Pension Angelika

Key

A Tourist Police
B Hospital
C Market
D Panagia Monastery / Clock Tower
E National Bank of Greece
F Museum
G Old Arsenal / Port Police
H Doctor
I Supermarket
J Pharmacy
K Bakery
L Cinema
M Kriezis Mansion
N Koundouriotis Mansion
O Tombasis Mansion
P Voulgaris Mansion
Q G. Voulgaris Mansion
R L. Koundouriotis Mansion

1 Ferry / Hydrofoil Berth
2 Taxi Boats

attractive fortified harbour town and the close proximity of Athens (making it a perfect day-tripper island). Sadly, the numbers calling have turned the place into a tourist trap and the island is now arguably the least idyllic in the whole Aegean, with a constant procession of hydrofoils and tour-boats bringing in the crowds and encouraging the most expensive island prices in Greece. Poor and insignificant in ancient times, Hydra's transformation into a gold and jewellery boutique has its origins in the 17th and 18th centuries, when, lying on the periphery of both Turkish and Venetian spheres of influence, the island bred a succession of autonomous buccaneer flash Harrys who successfully exploited the growth of Euro-Levantine trade. The town thrived and grew to support a population of 28,000 before post-independence decline reduced the numbers to around 3,000, eking out an existence by sponge fishing until tourism took off.

Apart from the town, with its harbour walls adorned with cannon, Hydra has little to offer. Decked with steep hill paths and a scattering of monasteries and with a car and motorbike ban, it is often touted as a hill walking destination given the absence of anything else to do. Bathing areas are confined to three northerly beaches that are small, poor, crowded and served by expensive taxi boats.

ᵬ⊷

Pricey hotels and rooms. Book ahead if at all possible. The A-class *Miranda* (☎ 52230) and B-class *Hydroussa* (☎ 52217) are the premier hotels in town and with prices to match. Those on a tighter budget will fare better trying the C-class *Leto* (☎ 53385), the pension *Angelika* (☎ 53202) or the D-class *Argo* (☎ 52452). Also on the waterfront is the rather run down D-class *Sophia* (☎ 52313). Right under the monastery belfry, certain disadvantages become apparent on the hour, every hour.

⚭

For most tourists **Hydra Town** is Hydra. Very photogenic, it is snugly tucked into a fold in the barren hills and consists of neo-classical mansions built during the years of prosperity

fanning up the hillsides behind the port. The packed-to-bursting waterfront is distinguished by the 18 C. **Panagia Monastery**; built from the stones of the famous Temple of Poseidon on Poros. On the hillsides either side of the harbour are the early 19 C. mansions built by the leading pirate families of the day. The **harbour fortifications** are also impressive and do wonders for the feel of the town. Carefully restored (boutiques aside), it is worth stopping off for a look before catching a hydrofoil to the next port of call when you feel a comparatively inexpensive drink coming on.

Kalamata
ΚΑΛΑΜΑΤΑ; pop. 41,910.

CODE ☎ 0721
PORT POLICE ☎ 22218
TOURIST POLICE ☎ 23187

The second city of the Peloponnese (after Patras), Kalamata is a sprawling conurbation well off the regular ferry trail. Tucked away in the deepest recess of the Messiniakos Gulf, it has a rail link with the rest of Greece and regular buses to both Athens (8 daily) and Patras (2 daily). The bad news is that the bus station is 3 km from the port, which saw its first ferry service at the end of the 1993 summer season. From the island hopper's perspective Kalamata is thus an unattractive destination. To be honest, from any perspective Kalamata is a very ugly city. Badly damaged by a massive earthquake in 1986 it has never really recovered from the loss of buildings and the exodus of inhabitants that followed from it.

ᵬ⊷

Limited number of budget hotels on or near the waterfront including the *Plaza* (☎ 82590) *Nevada* (☎ 82429) and the *Pension Avra* (☎ 82759). Offers of rooms are very rare.

Α

Camping Patista (☎ 29525): 2 km east of the ferry quay; an okayish beach site.

⚭

With most of the Venetian/Turkish buildings flattened by the earthquake, the only site of note that the city has left is a **Frankish Kastro** on low acropolis just north of the bus station.

Kiparissi
ΚΥΠΑΡΙΣΣΙ

An idyllic hamlet on the Peloponnesian coast offering a pleasant mixture of red-tiled houses, trees and a good shingle beach that attracts the occasional day-tripper hydrofoil. The ferry only seems to call in order to pick up the occasional stranded motorist who — having braved the mountain track to get here — finds himself without the nerve to drive back.

Kithera
ΚΥΘΗΡΑ; 278 km²; pop. 2,600.

CODE ☎ 0735
PORT POLICE (AGIA PELAGIA) ☎ 33280
PORT POLICE (KAPSALI) ☎ 31222
POLICE ☎ 31206
FIRST AID ☎ 31243

Arguably deserving of the title of the last unspoilt large Greek island, Kithera lies in glorious isolation from other island chains like a lump of rare meat falling off the Peloponnese fork. Unfortunately, there are few eaters; the remoteness of the place means that ferry connections are very limited, and most visitors are not island-hoppers but travellers to the Peloponnese. The lack of an island chain to call its own has always left Kithera at something of a loose end. Historically it was administered as part of the Ionian group, but although sharing a similar history (of Venetian rather than Turkish rule), its appearance is more in common with the Cycladic islands. These days local schizophrenia is further enhanced by the additional complications of the island now being administered direct from Athens and a largely migrant population: like Kastelorizo in the Dodecanese, this is another Greek island where everyone seems to own an Australian passport. This results in Kithera being either appealingly full or uncomfortably empty as the number of town houses converted into holiday homes grows.

However, bucking this trend, an increasing number of expatriates are choosing to retire on the island. While welcoming, they are not keen to see their dream island degenerate into yet another tourist resort. A more serious handicap to enjoying the island is, in part, a consequence of the lack of tourists; a fact reflected in the level of services. Public transport is poor (the school bus runs down the road bisecting the island twice daily in the summer; with frequent, but expensive, taxis making the most of this). If you want to make the most of Kithera then you need to bring or hire your own transport.

Most visitors arrive via the northern hamlet of **Agia Pelagia** (though of late ferries have been arriving at various ports). A dreamy — if rather unprepossessing — sort of place, Agia Pelagia has emerged over the last decade as the island's primary port and now sees the bulk of the ferry traffic as well as any calling hydrofoils. On the back of the ferry traffic have come a growing number of tavernas and outlets offering rooms, but these are so spread out that they do little to encourage a cosy atmosphere. In this respect, the over-long quay hardly helps either. On the plus side, there are several small coves either side of the port with quiet, sandy beaches. This is just as well as Agia Pelagia isn't really the best base from which to explore Kithera. If this is what you have come to do, then moving south opens up more options.

Tourists bent on sightseeing usually head straight for the scenic hilltop capital of **Chora** (home to a lovely, quiet, white-washed village with a notable number of oddly-shaped chimneys) that meanders up the spine of a hill to an impressive, but ruinous castle, or the resort port of **Kapsali** that lies below. Kapsali now sees few ferries — except when conditions prevent boats docking at Agia Pelagia. It has to rely on to two pebble beaches in a bay divided by a small chapel topped headland, plus its bar life for its appeal. The islands best sand beach lies beyond Kapsali on the south-east coast at Fryiammos; though without a moped it is a long dirt track walk away.

The rest of Kithera is home to empty villages on rolling low hills with little vegetation; the best of these lies along the main island road at **Potamos**. Now slowly emerging as a convenient halfway-house between the settlements at each end of the island (though it lies well to the north), Potamos is home to the island's regular Sunday market and larger shops.

🛏

Hotels are scattered thinly around the island, but the majority of beds are now to be found at **Agia Pelagia**. The D-class *Kytheria* (☎ 33321) and the B-class *Filoxenia* (☎ 33610), both close to the ferry quay mop up evening arrivals, but you will find plenty of other offers of beds. Potamos also has some rooms and the *Pension Porfyra*(☎ 33329). **Chora** meantime, has the pricey, but lovely, B-class *Margarita* (☎ 31694) and a couple of cheaper pensions — notably *Pension Keti* (☎ 31318) and some unsigned rooms. **Kapsali** has the luxury B-class pension *Raikos* (☎ 31629), both rather pricey. Budget accommodation — notably the D-class *Aphrodite* (☎ 31328) and rare rooms along the beach — is usually snapped up in season.

Λ

Camping Kapsali (☎ 31580): a nice (pine-wood) site on the outskirts of Kapsali, but only open mid-June through to mid-September.

👓

The **Chora**, straddling a narrow 500 m ridge, and the Venetian **Kastro** (built in 1503) are the most accessible attractions that Kithera has to offer. The latter looks impressive from a distance but the remains are rather 'bitty'. The best reason to visit are the panoramic views of Kapsali and the coast. In Chora there is also a small town **Museum**. The most popular excursion is to the pretty village of **Milopotamos** with its impressive **Cave of Agia Sophia**, and nearby, a Venetian castle and town.

Between Chora and Milopotamos lies the village of **Livadi**, complete with a bridge dating from the period of English rule (1814–1864). Looking incongruously out of place on a Greek island, it would happily pass as a railway viaduct anywhere in southern England. Kithera was noted in antiquity as the

KITHERA

0   km   7

→ Athens ⓓ x 4

Agia Pelagia ⚓

Potamos

Paleochora ⚓

Diakofti

Cave

Milopotamos

Paleopolis

506 m

City & Temple of Aphrodite

Karvounades

Livadi

Kalamos

Chora

Fryiammos

Cycladic Style Chora & Venetian Kastro

Kapsali

Resort Village

🚌 ···· ⓓ x 2: Ag. Pel: 09.00, 14.30
Kapsali: 11.00, 17.00

No beach boat service

place where the goddess Aphrodite was born (or drawn) out of the sea (a claim also made by Cyprus). Kithera's claim was not disputed in antiquity and the centre (at **Paleopolis**) was home to a **Temple of Aphrodite** that the travel writer Pausanias deemed to be the oldest, most beautiful, and most venerated in the world. A church constructed from the temple stones now stands on the site. The final site of note is the medieval town of **Paleochora** — abandoned after the island's entire population was sold into slavery by the pirate Kemal Reis in 1537.

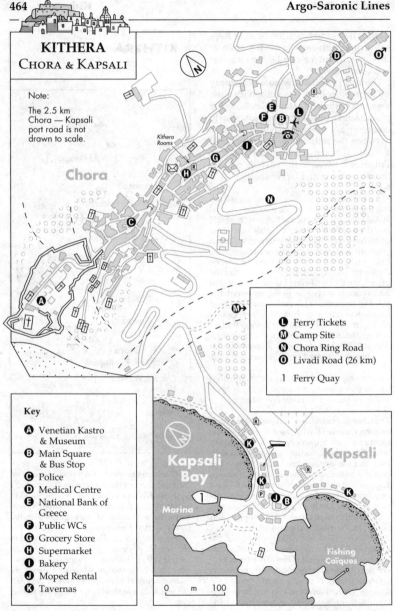

KITHERA
Chora & Kapsali

Note:

The 2.5 km
Chora — Kapsali
port road is not
drawn to scale.

*Kithera
Rooms*

Chora

Kapsali Bay

Marina

Kapsali

Fishing
Caïques

L Ferry Tickets
M Camp Site
N Chora Ring Road
O Livadi Road (26 km)

1 Ferry Quay

Key

A Venetian Kastro
    & Museum
B Main Square
    & Bus Stop
C Police
D Medical Centre
E National Bank of
    Greece
F Public WCs
G Grocery Store
H Supermarket
I Bakery
J Moped Rental
K Tavernas

0   m   100

Leonidio
ΛΕΩΝΙΔΙΟ

A small coastal town served by hydro-foils in the summer months. Commuters and the odd tourist escaping the crowds are the only beneficiaries of the service: there isn't any reason to stop off here.

Methana
ΜΕΘΑΝΑ; pop. 998.

Another small port — this time on a peninsula jutting north from the Pelo-ponnese into the Saronic Gulf. Ferries as well as hydrofoils call but most of the traffic is local rather than tourist. Like Leonidio most visitors ship out on the same boat they arrive on.

Monemvassia
ΜΟΝΕΜΒΑΣΙΑ

CODE ☎ 0732
PORT POLICE ☎ 61266
POLICE ☎ 61210

A distinctive small town at the southern end of the Peloponnese, Monemvassia (or rather its adjacent mainland town of Gefira) lives off the tourism generated by the mini Gibraltar-cum-boulder offshore. From the ferry both look a bit austere but this is deceptive: there are souvenir shops and tavernas aplenty on the mainland, while the boulder town lies on the south-ern flank out of view. They are linked by a causeway that also provides a conven-ient quay for both the single ferry that calls and High Season hydrofoils.

⊨

Plenty of rooms available as well as a number of hotels. These include the E-class *Akroyali* (☎ 61306) and D-class *Aktaeon* (☎ 61234); both are near the causeway along with the C-class *Minoa* (☎ 61209). The A-class pension *Kastro* (☎ 61413) provides a more pricey alternative.

Λ

Camping Paradise (☎ 61680): a lovely and relatively quiet site 3½ km south of the town.

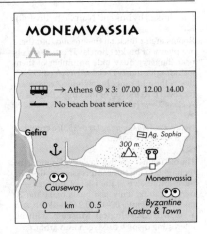

MONEMVASSIA

Λ ⊨

🚌 → Athens Ⓓ x 3: 07.00 12.00 14.00
⛴ No beach boat service

Gefira
⚓
Causeway
0   km   0.5

Ⓗ *Ag. Sophia*
300 m ⛰
🏛
□
Monemvassia
👀
Byzantine Kastro & Town

👀

The 350 m '**Rock**' looks barren from the north, but once the ferry steams past the eastern side the remains of a fortress (dating back to Hom-eric times) and a medieval village dominate the rock. The main Byzantine centre on the Peloponnese, its (largely abandoned) upper and lower towns offer an interesting day's exploration, besides being the site of an important event in the struggle for Greek independence: an unjustifiable massacre of every man in the Turkish garrison in 1821.

Nafplio
ΝΑΥΠΛΙΟ; pop. 10,700.

CODE ☎ 0752
PORT POLICE ☎ 22974
POLICE ☎ 28131

Tucked into the Peloponnese coastline, stately and popular Nafplio — also tran-scribed as 'Nauplion' — was briefly cap-ital of the embryonic Greek state (1827–34) between Aegina and Athens and is visited by occasional hydrofoils. The tourist presence is high, thanks to the combination of a building programme which stalled when 'capital' status was lost, leaving the best preserved Venetian town in Greece, along with the daily influx from the nearby beach resort of **Tolo** (also linked by bus and Nafplio hydrofoil).

⊨

Rooms aren't thick on the ground, but there are plenty of budget hotels. The side streets near the ferry quay hide a number of them including the musty D-class *Acropole* (☎ 27796). Best of the mid-range hotels is the *Agamemnon* (☎ 28021). At the top of the range, there is an A-class *Xenia* (☎ 28981) in the town.

▲

Nearest is *Tolo Camping* (☎ 59133); a crowded site 8 km to the east.

👁

The old town is worth a day's exploration; the highlights being three impressive castles (the most impressive is the islet of **Bourtzi** — a mini Alcatraz; daily taxi boats make the 20 minute crossing 09.00–13.00, 16.00–19.00), and a small **Archaeological Museum** with an interesting display of Mycenaean artifacts.

Neapoli
ΝΕΑΠΟΛΗ

CODE ☎ 0734
PORT POLICE ☎ 22228
TOURIST POLICE ☎ 0731 28701

The most southerly port on the Peloponnese, Neapoli is tucked in the lip of the Gulf of Lakonia. Not that there is much to be laconic about, for there is nought here but a poorly connected and dusty town. The austere, 'end of the known world' feeling that pervades (that led to the ancients believing that the entrance to Hades — the underworld — lay at the southern tip of the Peloponnese) will do little for the tourist who likes his nightlife, though this is a resort town of sorts thanks to the long narrow beach bisected by the ferry quay. Most holiday-makers seem to be Greeks escaping the crowds elsewhere. If you are looking to get away from it all then Neapoli might have appeal — and nearby Elafonissos offers some attractive consolation.

⊨

Limited rooms, and three B-class pensions: the *Alivali* (☎ 22287), the *Arsenakos* (☎ 22991), and the *Limira Mare* (☎ 22208).

Poros
ΠΟΡΟΣ; 28 km²; pop. 4,500.

CODE ☎ 0298
PORT POLICE ☎ 22274
TOURIST POLICE ☎ 22462
HEALTH CENTRE ☎ 22222

Poros marks the limit for the landing-craft ferries running out of Piraeus. It is actually made up of two islands (**Sphalria** and **Kalaureia**) separated by a narrow canal and connected by a bridge, and takes its modern name from the narrow strait that separates it from the mainland: 'Poros' meaning 'passage'. In fact Poros is an extremely odd island; for the straits — rather than the island itself — are the focus of activity, with settlement running along the shores on either side and the bulk of the island relegated to hinterland. The 'island' sensation is strangely thin, with an atmosphere more reminiscent of a large coastal town ribboned around a narrow bay. Perhaps because of this and a lack of good beaches, Poros attracts less tourism than her neighbours. However, it is a nice base for doing the mainland sights and adjacent islands.

Poros Town is the only settlement of any significance; occupying most of Sphalria Island. It consists of whitewashed and red-tile houses banked between the long quay and a stubby hill topped with a campanile. On first arriving, the water-front can come as a bit of a shock; for not only is it the third smelliest in the Aegean (after Piraeus and Chios) but is adorned with several of the tackiest tourist shops to be found in Greece. Fortunately, the further you walk south from the ferry quay the better it gets; developing into an attractive mix of tavernas and yachts, with a myriad of taxi-boats and small car ferries scuttling across the straits to the mainland village of Galatas (the path ends at some rocks where the town children bathe). The backstreets are also reasonably attractive in a downbeat sort of way: but it is difficult to imagine anyone coming to Poros for the architecture. One suspects the main reason some tourists come back year after year is the low-key 'niceness' of the island: though if truth be told you don't have to go far to find better. Perhaps this is why cycle hire is so popular on the island — as they offer easy access to better mainland beaches.

Settlement on the wooded main island is largely confined to tourist developments along the straits (served by frequent buses). The coast south of the town is the busiest, with the bulk of the island's poor beaches (all pebble) and the now unused but pretty monastery of **Kalavrias** (alias Zoodochos Pigi). At the other end of the strait lies Russian bay; home to a 1828 nautical conference in which Britain, France and Russia discussed the future of the independent Greek state. En route you will pass the beach at Neorio: arguably the best of the island's poor collection. Walk inland, and Poros improves considerably; the abundance of trees being some

compensation for the demolition of the WCs on the waterfront of Poros Town.

Galatas is much more dowdy than Poros Town; though some efforts have been made to tart up the waterfront. Unless you are heading for the campsite there is no great reason to venture here.

ᕄ

Poros Town offers the best chance of finding a Room south of Aegina. There are also a number of easily located hotels along the waterfront. Closest to the ferry quay is the B-class *Latsi* (☎ 22392), the *Saron* (☎ 22279) and the C-class *Aktaion* (☎ 22281). More expensive hotels tend to be out of town on Kalavrias; the largest being the B-class *Poros* (☎ 22216). There are also several waterfront hotels in **Galatas** if you draw a blank in Poros Town. These include the D-class *Saronis* (☎ 22356) and the C-class *Galatia* (☎ 22227) and *Papasotiriou* (☎ 22841).

Δ

Camping Kirangelo (☎ 24520): friendly small mainland site 1 km inland on the road north of Galatas. Avoid the tent village on the coast north of Galatas: this is a hospital resort run by the Greek health service for the elderly insane.

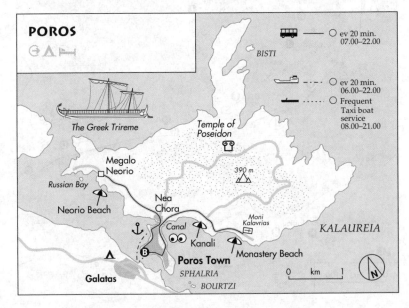

POROS

The Greek Trireme

BISTI

Temple of Poseidon

Megalo Neorio

Russian Bay

Neorio Beach

Nea Chora

Canal

Kanali

Moni Kalavrias

KALAUREIA

Poros Town

Monastery Beach

Galatas

SPHALRIA

BOURTZI

390 m.

🚌 ——— ○ ev 20 min. 07.00–22.00

⛴ –·–·– ○ ev 20 min. 06.00–22.00

▬▬ ······ ○ Frequent Taxi boat service 08.00–21.00

0   km   1

N

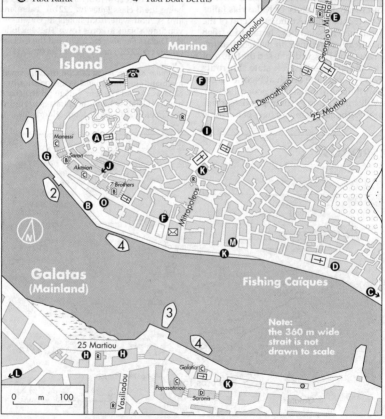

POROS
POROS TOWN

Key

- **A** Campanile
- **B** Bus Stop
- **C** Police / Supermarket
- **D** National Bank
- **E** Doctor
- **F** Pharmacies
- **G** Taxi Rank
- **H** Grocery Stores
- **I** Bakery
- **J** Newspapers
- **K** Restaurants
- **L** Camping (700 m)
- **M** Museum
- **N** Nautical School

- **1** Large Ferries
- **2** Hydrofoils
- **3** Landing Craft Berths
- **4** Taxi Boat Berths

Trireme Berth

Poros Island

Marina

Papadopoulou

Latsi

Georgiou Michail

Demosthenous

25 Martiou

Manessi

Saron

Aktaion

7 Brothers

Mitropoleos

Galatas (Mainland)

Fishing Caïques

Note:
the 360 m wide
strait is not
drawn to scale

25 Martiou

Galatia

Papasahiriou

Saronis

Vasiliadou

0   m   100

∞

Poros Town has little of sightseeing interest beyond the waterfront itself and a small **Archaeological Museum** south-east of the ferry quay (the Venetians preferring to fortify one of the Bourtzi islets rather than build in the town). On the north side of Sphalria lies Greece's **Naval Cadet School** in the former home of the 19 c. Arsenal. As a result, when she isn't on goodwill voyages up the Thames, it is occasionally possible to see the replica **Greek Trireme** (so named because such vessels were powered by three banks of oars) tied up at the end of the ferry dock (a nightwatchman is kept permanently aboard to stop tourists doing untold damage). Now officially part of the Hellenic Navy, the cadets have the dubious pleasure of rowing her each summer along with parties of invited foreign oarsmen.

Once out of the town you will find Poros is all pine trees and hills with an inland road around Kaleureia. This circuit offers a day's gentle strolling, taking in the views from the hills as well as the remains of the ancient city of Kaleureia. This settlement was home to one of ancient Greece's premier religious centres in the form of the 6 c. BC **Temple of Poseidon** (later demolished to furnish the masonry for Hydra Town's quayside monastery); here the great orator Demosthenes committed suicide in 322 BC (by nibbling on his poisoned pen while writing a farewell epistle — the original poison pen letter — to his family when his creditors seized him from the temple where he had sought sanctuary).

Porto Helio
ΠΟΡΤΟ ΧΕΛΙ

CODE ☎ 0754
PORT POLICE ☎ 51408

An extremely large tourist town that is better avoided. This resort has become the natural terminus for ferries and hydrofoils running down the islands in the gulf — so most depart northwards (up to ten daily). Irregular smaller craft do put in occasionally, but the local market is insufficient to generate much traffic.

◄

Pre-booked hotels predominate; but some pricey rooms available.

Spetses
ΣΠΕΤΣΕΣ; 22.5 km²; pop. 3,500.

CODE ☎ 0298
PORT POLICE ☎ 72245
TOURIST POLICE ☎ 73100
FIRST AID ☎ 72472

Sufficiently far from the capital to escape the worst of the day-trippers, yet still close enough to be served by daily Piraeus ferries (just), Spetses is a gentle, small, pine-forested island particularly popular with English tourists (suburbia rather than the fish-and-chips brigade). This is in part due to the island being the setting for John Fowles' novel *The Magus*; a popular tome that has ensured that many holiday-makers come to Spetses disposed to admire the place. The horses and traps that run along the waterfront of Spetses Town don't hurt either, though the paucity of good beaches results in a daily mass migration around the island that is not conducive to relaxed holiday-making.

Mansioned **Spetses Town** is apt to disappoint on first acquaintance: considering that it is the only settlement of any size on the island, the centre area is poorly laid out without the natural charm of most of the Cycladic island choras. It is also comparatively expensive. The tourist area is firmly focused around the streets near the new port. This is rather sad, as the too shallow old port is now reduced to a little visited yacht marina. In fact, it is much the more attractive of the two; with the headland to the south graced with three windmills for good measure.

An island-wide ban on cars has served to increase the suburbs of Spetses Town while restricting the growth of other tourist centres. Movement around the island is thus greatly restricted. As a result, crowded buses run along the northern coast hotel strip as well as to the most popular beach on Spetses — at Ag. Anargiri. Better reached by beach boat (you don't have to fight for a place like you do on the afternoon buses heading

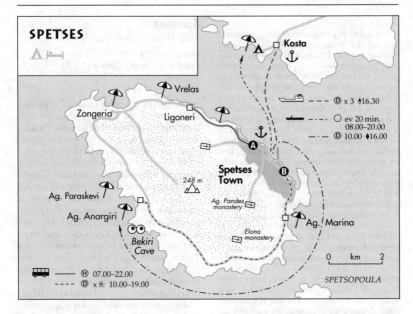

SPETSES

Vrelas

Kosta

Zongeria

Ligoneri

Ⓓ x 3 ◆16.30

O ev 20 min.
08.00–20.00

Ⓓ 10.00 ◆16.00

Spetses Town

Ⓐ

Ⓑ

248 m

Ag. Paraskevi

Ag. Pandes monastery

Ag. Anargiri

Ag. Marina

Bekiri Cave

Elona monastery

0   km   2

Ⓗ 07.00–22.00

Ⓓ x 8: 10.00–19.00

SPETSOPOULA

back to Spetses Town), it offers the best sand beach on the island. Beach boats also run across the straits from Spetses Town to the adjacent beach near the quiet village of **Kosta**; supplementing the landing craft ferry running to the village itself several times a day. Tourist boats also make the crossing to here and Porto Helio. Be very wary of some of these boats: they divide up into 'normal' multi-passenger beach boats and so-called sea 'taxis' individually hired and charging ludicrous 'tourist' fares.

Arrive early: block bookings by package tour operators means that beds are scarce. Tourist agencies east of the ferry dock have lists, and one, *Takis Travel* (☎ 72888) — sited near the ferry quay — acts as an agent for most of the island hoteliers; the residue being covered by *Pine Island Tours* (☎ 72464). Close by the ferry quay are a number of hotels worth a try. These include the budget E-class *Alexandri* (☎ 73073), the D-class *Saronikon* (☎ 73741), and the C-class *Faros* (☎ 72613). Near the town beach are

the D-class *Klimis* (☎ 73777) and *Stelios* (☎ 72364); the latter complete with restaurant. Those with money to spend should try the A-class Edwardian *Posidonion* (☎ 72308).

A

Camping Kosta (☎ 51571). Reasonable site on the mainland 1 km west of Kosta village. A member of the *Harmonie* camping club scheme.

∞

Spetses, like Aegina and Hydra, played an important part in the struggle for Greek independence, furnishing the rebels with a cross between a Greek Boudicca and Lord Nelson in the form of a female admiral, Laskarina Bouboulina. Spetses Town has a **Museum** in one of the 18 c. mansions housing her bones and other independence material. The 8th of September also sees the commemoration of an 1822 naval victory when a Greek fireship forced an attacking Turkish fleet to withdraw from Spetses. This is re-enacted with the burning of a cast-adrift taxi-boat each year. Apart from the Bekiri sea cave at Ag. Anargiri beach, Spetses lacks sights: ticket agencies make a killing selling tours to attractions on the Peloponnese such as Epidavros and Corinth.

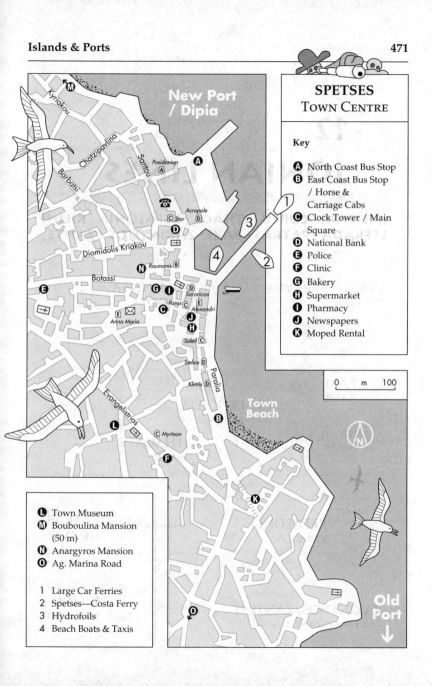

SPETSES
TOWN CENTRE

Key

Ⓐ North Coast Bus Stop
Ⓑ East Coast Bus Stop / Horse & Carriage Cabs
Ⓒ Clock Tower / Main Square
Ⓓ National Bank
Ⓔ Police
Ⓕ Clinic
Ⓖ Bakery
Ⓗ Supermarket
Ⓘ Pharmacy
Ⓙ Newspapers
Ⓚ Moped Rental

Ⓛ Town Museum
Ⓜ Bouboulina Mansion (50 m)
Ⓝ Anargyros Mansion
Ⓞ Ag. Marina Road

1 Large Car Ferries
2 Spetses—Costa Ferry
3 Hydrofoils
4 Beach Boats & Taxis

New Port / Dipia

Kyriakou
Chatzipavlina
Barbatsi
Samou
Posidonion Ⓐ
Acropole Ⓓ
Ⓒ Star
Ⓓ
Diomidolis Kriakou
Botassi
Ⓔ
Ⓝ Roumanis Ⓑ
Ⓖ Ⓘ
Ⓒ Faros Ⓓ
Saronicos
Ⓒ Alexandri
Ⓔ Anna Maria
Ⓙ
Ⓗ
Soleil Ⓒ
Stelios Ⓓ
Klimis Ⓓ
Paralia
Evangelistras
Ⓛ
Ⓒ Myrtoon
Ⓕ
Ⓑ
Town Beach
Ⓚ
Ⓞ
Old Port

0   m   100

N

12
IONIAN LINES

**ANTIPAXI · CORFU · ITHACA · KEFALONIA · KILINI
LEFKADA · PATRAS · PAXI · ZAKINTHOS / ZANTE**

CORFU/KERKYRA
ΚΕΡΚΥΡΑ

IGOUMENITSA
ΗΓΟΥΜΕΝΙΤΣΑ

+2

+9 HOURS

+2

PAXI
ΠΑΞΟΙ

LEFKADA
ΛΕΥΚΑΔΑ

ANTIPAXI
ΑΝΤΙΠΑΞΟΙ

ITHACA
ΙΘΑΚΗ

+2

+1

KEFALONIA
ΚΕΦΑΛΟΝΙΑ

PATRAS
ΠΑΤΡΑ

+3

+3

ZAKINTHOS/ZANTE
ΖΑΚΥΝΘΟ / ΖΑΝΤΗ

KILINI
ΚΥΛΛΗΝΗ

+1½

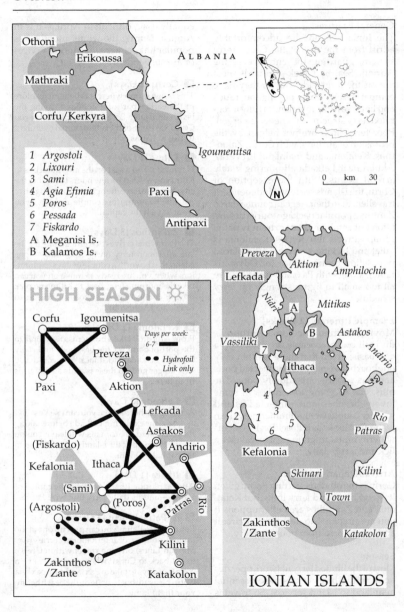

Othoni
Erikoussa
Mathraki
ALBANIA
Corfu/Kerkyra
Igoumenitsa

1 *Argostoli*
2 *Lixouri*
3 *Sami*
4 *Agia Efimia*
5 *Poros*
6 *Pessada*
7 *Fiskardo*
A Meganisi Is.
B Kalamos Is.

Paxi
Antipaxi

0 km 30

N

Preveza Aktion *Amphilochia*
Lefkada
Mitikas
A
Niдri B *Astakos*
Vassiliki 7 *Andirio*
Ithaca
4
2 1 3
6 5
Rio
Kefalonia *Patras*
Kilini
Skinari
Town
Zakinthos /Zante *Katakolon*

IONIAN ISLANDS

HIGH SEASON ☼

Corfu Igoumenitsa
Days per week:
6-7
Preveza
Paxi Aktion
Hydrofoil Link only
Lefkada
Astakos
(Fiskardo) Andirio
Kefalonia Ithaca
(Sami)
(Argostoli) (Poros) Patras Rio
Kilini
Zakinthos /Zante Katakolon

General Features
The Ionian islands lie uncomfortably adrift from the rest of the Greek ferry system, guarding the entrance to the Adriatic Sea. By Greek standards most are on the large side, but as they have comparatively small population ratios and lie close to the mainland, a fully integrated ferry structure has never emerged. Poor ferry links are not helped by the profusion of airports; with Corfu, Zakinthos, Kefalonia and mainland Preveza/ Aktion near Lefkada all offering viable arrival points. With the exception of Corfu, the islands see fewer independent travellers than their Aegean counterparts. Zante is a popular package tourist destination but at the southern extremity of the group attracts few ferries. Kefalonia is quiet and lacking a conveniently placed population centre. Ithaca (of Odysseus fame), along with Paxi and Antipaxi, are all too small to figure strongly on ferry schedules.

Example Itinerary [2 Weeks]
Moving around the Ionian group is difficult but practicable on a one-hop a day basis; given that there is often only one boat between poorly connected ports and bus services are equally poor. The plus side to going Ionian lies in some lovely beaches and pine-clad island scenery coupled with shimmeringly clean water that looks as if Poseidon has set his waternymphs to giving each wavelet a lick and a rub daily.

Arrival/Departure Point
Corfu is the obvious starting point: given its good flight and ferry links, but Kefalonia and Zakinthos are better options if you are prepared to do a smaller circuit and drop Corfu from your itinerary.

Season
Most of the limited ferry network operates on an annual basis; consisting of essential mainland to island services. So travel is equally easy/difficult in April as it is in August. During the winter months less popular links either see reduced services or are suspended.

1 Corfu [2 Days]
This is one group where it is better to explore in the earlier part of a holiday; leaving the beach until later. So, after a couple of days on Corfu, take one of the international overnight ferries to Patras.

2 Patras [1 Day]
Having booked a seat on the afternoon bus to Kilini you will have a few hours to explore the city. You also have the option of heading on to Athens (3½ hours) for a couple of nights if you want to visit the capital.

3 Zakinthos [3 Days]
The Patras bus arrives at Kilini in time for the late afternoon ferry on to Zakinthos — one island that is worth a couple of days exploration, when you are ready to move on you can take the morning ferry back to Kilini and pick up the connecting afternoon service on to Kefalonia (Argostoli).

4 Kefalonia [2 Days]
From Argostoli take a bus across Kefalonia to the port of Sami for the best beds and daily boats to Lefkada and Ithaca. You could also stay longer and do these islands as day trips from here.

5 Lefkada [2 Days]
Arriving on the first boat you can use Vassiliki as a base for exploring Lefkada before taking the ferry on to Ithaca. This will leave you on the northern tip of the island. Take a bus on to the capital — Vathi.

6 Ithaca [1 Day]
After exploring Ithaca, finish in the capital of Vathi — and its daily ferry link with Patras.

2 1 Patras/Corfu [3 Days]
Returning to Patras you can pick up one of the limited number of international ferries (e.g. Minoan Lines) offering travel within Greece to get back to Corfu, where you will have a couple of days to take in Paxi and Antipaxi via Corfu pleasure boats, or lie on the beach before your flight home.

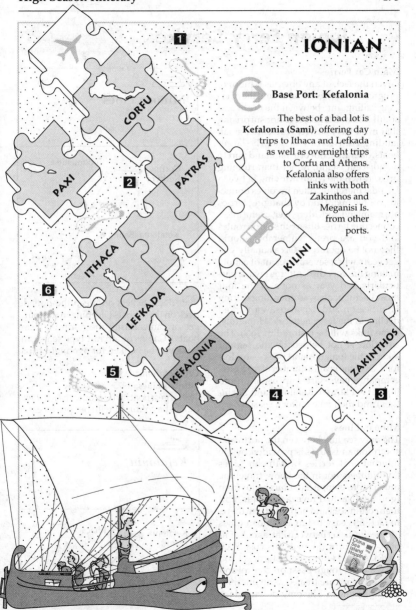

IONIAN

Base Port: Kefalonia

The best of a bad lot is **Kefalonia (Sami)**, offering day trips to Ithaca and Lefkada as well as overnight trips to Corfu and Athens. Kefalonia also offers links with both Zakinthos and Meganisi Is. from other ports.

CORFU

PAXI

PATRAS

ITHACA

KILINI

LEFKADA

KEFALONIA

ZAKINTHOS

Ionian Ferry Services

Main Car Ferries

Given the lack of any obvious pattern of progression between islands and the over-long sailing time between the north and south Ionian islands, it is not surprising that most ferry services are either small landing-craft ferries or elderly larger boats, operating out of a mainland port to an adjacent island, rather than running up or down the chain. Moving between islands, therefore, often involves bouncing off the mainland by changing ferries at a mainland port. Moreover, useful interconnecting ferries often run solo on routes and you are pretty vulnerable should they not be operating. Occasionally you get years when several are out of action, making life very difficult: 1991 was a particularly bad year as none of the four most useful boats was operating during High Season, and 1997 also saw a marked decline in the ferry network. Hopefully, some links will be restored in 1999. The situation is not helped by the regular joker in the Ionian island pack — hydrofoils. Over the years a number of hydrofoil companies have started up (usually running out of Patras to Kefalonia and Zakinthos) and then failed after a season.

Minoan Lines

The only sea link between the north and south Ionian islands is provided by the international ferries of Minoan Lines (landlubbers not in the know travel the much more complicated bus route from Igoumenitsa to Preveza/Lefkada and then continue island hopping from there. In fact, it is easy to buy a Minoan Lines 'domestic' ticket between Patras or Kefalonia and Corfu (in 1998 this cost 5,000 GDR). Armed with a domestic ticket you are waved through passport control and once on board are treated as an international passenger. The only down side is

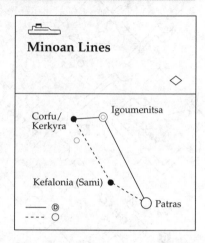

that 'deck' tickets do mean the outside deck on these boats (sleeping in the lounges or canteen isn't the norm on these boats). Cabins or aircraft type seats can, however, be booked for overnight trips.

C/F Kefalonia

Strintzis Lines; 1975; 3472 GRT.
The largest boat in the group, the *Kefalonia* (not to be confused with her predecessor

the late C/F *Kefallinia*), was the new arrival in the Ionian Sea in 1995. With a tried and tested timetable (times have remained unchanged over the lifetime of three ferries on the route), this boat operates the main morning service from the islands to Patras. In High Season she occasionally operates to Argostoli via Kilini. Changes are unlikely in 1999. Her onboard facilities are the best of any domestic boat in the group, with escalators and an open plan passenger saloon.

C/F *Eptanisos*
Strintzis Lines; 1965; 2963 GRT.

The Strintzis Line *Eptanisos* (ex SNCF *Valencay*) followed arrived the Ionian Sea in 1992 from the Cyclades North line operating the Ithaca—Sami—Patras service. Replaced by the larger *Kefalonia* in 1995, she took over the Argostoli—Kilini route while her sister ship — the C/F *Delos* — operated from Kilini to the Kefalonian port of Poros. However, in 1997 the *Delos* was sold, leaving the *Eptanisos* to run the Poros service, with other boats covering the Argostoli route (it is not clear if a replacement ferry will run in 1999). Although an old ferry with distinctly utilitarian facilities by today's standards, the *Eptanisos* is well maintained, and commendably clean. She offers ferry buffs a wonderful opportunity to sail in an unaltered 60s cross-Channel ferry.

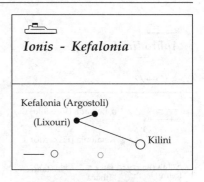

Ionis - Kefalonia

Kefalonia (Argostoli)

(Lixouri)

Kilini

C/F *Dimitrios Miras* - C/F *Ionis* - C/F *Proteus* - C/F *Zakinthos I*
Dimitrios Miras; 1972; 2160 GRT.
Ionis; 1977; 2963 GRT.
Proteus; 1973; 1160 GRT.
Zakinthos I; 1973; 2157 GRT.

Four ferries provide the link between the mainland and Zakinthos. The service runs eight times daily to the capital in the summer, but only four times a day in the Low Season. All independently operated, the boats do the route by rota, and you thus buy a ticket for a particular crossing rather than a specific boat. The *Ionis* is the biggest and best boat on the route, followed by the *Zakinthos I*. The *Proteus* follows grubbily on, while the *Dimitrius Miras* is a converted cargo vessel used for heavy goods vehicle runs.

Eptanisos

Kefalonia (Poros)

Kilini

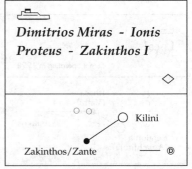

Dimitrios Miras - Ionis Proteus - Zakinthos I

Kilini

Zakinthos/Zante

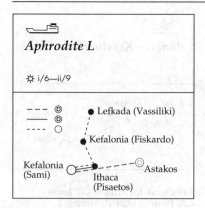

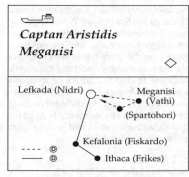

C/F *Aphrodite L*

For over a decade this useful small ferry (oddly decked-out with passenger seating on extended gangways either side of the car deck) has provided a morning and evening link between the port of Sami on Kefalonia and the quay of Pisaetos on Ithaca. In past years the *Aphrodite L* has then undertaken a twice daily run up to Vassiliki on Lefkada via Fiskardo. Since 1997, however, she has been obliged to cover on the Kefalonia—Astakos mainland route (the previous ferry having run into the 'not more than 35 years old' ferry law). This made life difficult for travellers as the Fiskardo—Lefkada link is awkward. One can only hope the *Aphrodite L* will be back on her old route in 1999.

C/F *Captan Aristidis* - C/F *Meganisi*

These two landing-craft ferries combine to run a daily service from Lefkada to northern Kefalonia and Ithaca as well as providing the small island of Meganisi with its main link with the outside world. The *Captan Aristidis* is easily the better of the pair and usually takes the Ithaca run, while the pitifully small *Meganisi* is usually confined to the Meganisi run. In 1996 she had to combine both as the *Captan Aristidis* was deputizing elsewhere. In the summer both boats are swamped by Italian motorists; car owners should arrive on the quayside early to secure a passage.

C/F *Ionion Pelagos*

Each summer sees this stumpy landing-craft ferry operate the shortest crossing

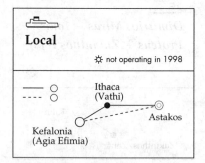

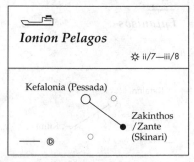

between Kefalonia and Zakinthos (Skinari alias Agios Nikolaos). Services have remained unchanged in years. However, unless you have your own transport, this is a poor link given the absence of bus services (out of High Season) to both ports of call.

C/F *Theologos*

This ferry has provided the daily Corfu—Paxi service for the last few years (often running via Igoumenitsa for the benefit of Athens-bound islanders). For a long time threatened by the arrival of stiff competition from the late catamaran *Nearchos* and the advertised, but invisible, ferry *Panagia Paxon*, her future appeared to be rather bleak. However, she has been the only significant boat operating to Paxi since 1997. Her only competition comes via a small tourist boat — the P/S *Pegassus* — which has been running to Corfu town daily for years.

Corfu—Amphilochia Links

For most of the 1990s a daily link existed between Corfu and the mainland port of Amphilochia (a route that cuts the Athens bus journey time by almost half). In the past a catamaran — the *Nearchos* — ran this service. However, in 1997 she was scared away by the advertised arrival of a ferry on the route; though in the event this rival never appeared. It is unclear if this route will be in operation in 1999.

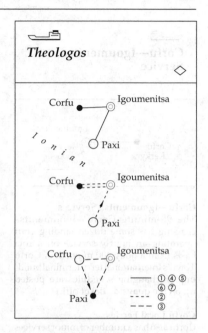

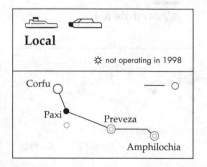

C/F *Agios Spiridon*

Kerkira Lines; 1972; 2574 GRT.
Formerly the *Hellas Express*, this ferry has done time in the Cyclades and Northern Aegean for many years. Docking at Corfu's international port she now runs to Igoumenitsa several times daily, coming into her own during the winter months when poor weather conditions prevent the landing-craft ferries from operating.

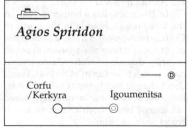

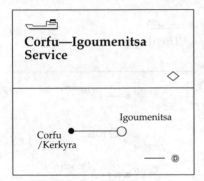

Corfu—Igoumenitsa Services

The 90-minute Corfu—Igoumenitsa crossing has some dozen landing craft operating an hourly service on a rota basis from a quay 400 m north of Corfu Town's International ferry terminal building. Unchanging schedules are posted up on the quayside ticket office.

Corfu Local Ferries

Corfu also has a number of minor services with limited tourist appeal. The most useful of the mainland links is the 5 × ⑩ service between the island's second port of Lefkimi and Igoumenitsa. Lefkimi also has had an inconsistent link with Paxi, though this has diminished in recent years. Tourist boats (the P/S's *Rena S/II*, *Petrakis*, *Sotirakis*, and *Sotirakis II*) also offer extra Paxi, Antipaxi and Plataria connections as well as an Albania service.

P/S *Alexandros K II*

Corfu Town also has a limited service to the three minor islands to the north of Corfu. The *Alexandros K II*—a small passenger boat that can also manage a couple of cars—departs soon after dawn several days a week from Corfu's Old Port. Times don't change much, but (Orthoni aside) these islets are more frequently visited via tourist boats from the north Corfu resort town of Sidari.

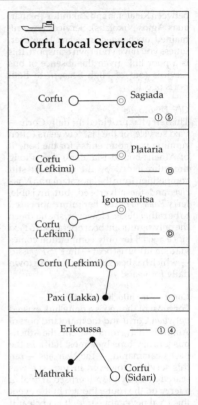

Ionian Islands & Ports

Astakos

ΑΣΤΑΚΟΣ

CODE ☎ 0646

A small village on the mainland west coast, Astakos is the home port of a single ferry running daily to Ithaca and Kefalonia. It is also the departure point for the produce caïques that keep the small fishing community that struggles along on the isolated island of Kalamos (which lies to the north-west) supplied with essentials. However, its connections aside, Astakos has little going for it. In truth, the beach aside, the most interesting thing in town is the bus stop.

⊨

Astakos has three hotels that cater for the few that get caught here. Top of the range is the B-class *Stratos* (☎ 41096). There are also two budget hotels in town: the D-class *Beach* (☎ 41135) and the *Byron* (☎ 41516).

Corfu / Kerkyra

ΚΕΡΚΥΡΑ; 592 km²; pop. 89,600.

TOWN CODE ☎ 0661
NTOG/TOURIST POLICE ☎ 30265
EMERGENCY ☎ 100
PORT POLICE ☎ 34036
HOSPITAL ☎ 25400

Long considered the most beautiful of Greek islands thanks to the abundant rainfall and vegetation, Corfu (or Kerkyra as it is known locally) is now among the most package-touristy parts of Greece. This being so, you have to venture quite far to escape the crowds, but on the plus side the island doesn't attract millions each year without good reason: it is beautiful, people and all. Ruled by the British between 1815 and 1864, the island retains a colonial feel — thanks in part to it being wetter than other islands out of High Season, and the large number of holiday homes scattered around. On the down side, Corfu keeps making the news thanks to attacks by Albanian pirates (a British tourist was killed in 1996). Overlooking the Albanian coast, lush Corfu is proving to be too tempting; even the local *Club Med* resort has come under fire from automatic weapons. The Greek authorities have provided a 50-strong task force to try to prevent further incidents.

As with the other large Ionian islands, the main settlement — **Corfu Town** — lies on the east coast along with most of the tourist development (patronized largely by Brits). On Corfu this is particularly heavy, with a hotel strip running from **Pirgi** down to **Benitses** (the booze and snooze resort of Greece) that contrives to place Corfu close to the top of the 'expensive island' rankings. Luckily, both island and capital are sufficiently attractive to overcome this handicap; with even the worst resorts having the kernel of a former fishing village at their heart.

Unless nightlife is a priority, the overcrowding to be found in Corfu Town and the east coast villages will soon tempt you into venturing further afield. The north and west coasts of the island have most to offer. Along the north coast Kassiopi (the centre of Corfu in Roman times) is an attractive fishing village resort over-looked by the remains of a 12 c. castle built on the site of a Temple of Zeus. **Sidari**, backed by rich farmland, is a less picturesque but equally lively village offering excursion boats to the islets north of Corfu as well as several reasonable beaches. However, the west coast has by far the best of Corfu's beaches, including Agios Georgios (both north and south), Glifada, Agios Gordis, Pelekas and **Mirtiotissa** (arguably the best beach: its isolation ensures it gets the thumbs — among other things — up from nudists).

The cliffs around **Paliokastritsa** are also a great draw — particularly at sunset.

The southern limb of Corfu is quieter with the exception of the large resort at **Messoighi** and the youth-dominated **Kavos**: a beach and disco village — now the 'Ios Town' of Corfu. Nearby **Lefkimi** sees a limited number of ferry services, though the bulk of these operate to Corfu Town. Most ferries that call are international boats, and the island sees an irritating stacking of services with most ferries departing in the same direction within a couple of hours of each other and then nothing for the rest of the day.

⊨

The NTOG/EOT (☎ 37520) and Tourist Police in Corfu Town offer free town as well as hotel, and room information. Hotel beds are adequate for the bulk of the year; but there is pressure on bed space in High Season. Near the New Port are a few rooms and the elderly, but just bearable *Ionian* (☎ 39915), while the Old Port has the over-popular budget *Constantinoupolis* (☎ 39826) and *Acropolis* (☎ 39569). Nearer the top end of the market is the delightfully placed (and pricey) *Arcadion* (☎ 37670) overlooking the cricket pitch. Out of town there is a poor *IYHF Hostel* (☎ 91292) at Kontokali, but best of all — and the current Corfu 'hot-spot' — is the *Pink Palace* (☎ 53103/4) on the west coast at Agios Gordis. offering US$ 19 rooms, built in night-life and a free mini-bus service to and from Corfu Town. Agents meet boats.

A

Nearest camping to Corfu Town is *Camping Kontokali* (☎ 91170) 5 km to the north: a basic site, it scores on convenience rather than the facilities on offer. There are many better sites around: mini-buses lay siege to the ferry terminal when the morning ferries come in and are thereafter conspicuous by their absence. The best of these sites lie away from the tourist strip: *Vatos Camping* (☎ 94393) and *Paliokastritsa Camping* (☎ 0663 41204) on the west coast are attractive, along with the clutch of sites abutting the northern beaches. Nightlife lovers usually stick to the sites on the tourist strip north of Corfu Town. These include Dassia's *Kada Beach Camping* (☎ 93595) and *Corfu Camping* (☎ 93246) at Ipsos. Those seeking quiet days and loud nights could do worse than try *Ippokambos Camping* (☎ 55364) at Messoighi.

∞

Corfu Town is the premier tourist attraction thanks to a delightful mix of Venetian, French and British Georgian buildings straddled by a couple of fortresses partially demolished by the British when they left the islands in the 1860s. The focus of the town is park-like **Spinada** Square or Esplanade and is the site of the famous cricket pitch now used early Saturday mornings as a practice marching ground by the local High School band. The square is bounded on the western side by the **Liston**: a row of tall arcaded houses-cum-cafés built during the brief period of French rule (1807–14), and on the east side by the moated **Old Fortress** — built on the Corfu ('two hills') promontory, and once the site of a Temple of Hera. North of the cricket pitch lies the **Royal Palace**, looking like a Georgian English country house, it was built in 1819 to house a series of British High Commissioners who considered themselves sufficiently high to require a throne room of the regal rather than the convenience variety. These days the recently refurbished building is home to a display of Chinese and Japanese porcelain and bronzes (the collection of a former Greek ambassador in the Far East).

Some 50 m south of the square lies Corfu's **Archaeological Museum**: home to the famous pedimental sculptures (dominated by a primitive figure of a Gorgon — considered to be among the greatest Archaic-period sculptures) from the Temple of Artemis (580 BC) in the ancient town. The museum is also home to an assorted collection of classical and Roman sculpture recovered from various sites on the island. The best of these lies just south of Corfu Town: the ancient city of Kerkyra (now little more than foundations — including the Temple of Artemis). Beyond the ruins lies Kanoni; jumping-off point for a couple of monastery topped islets. The first — **Vlakerani** — is linked to Corfu by a picture-postcard causeway, while **Pontikonissi** (or Mouse Island) is reached by regular caïque and is said to be the boat of Odysseus turned into stone by the wrathful Poseidon.

Further afield, Corfu has a disparate collection of other sights. Nearest to Corfu Town is the 1891-built **Royal Palace** (now a casino) at Achillion; the summer home of Kaiser Wilhelm II from 1908–14, it was the birthplace of Prince Phillip. Far prettier is the cliff and beach beauty

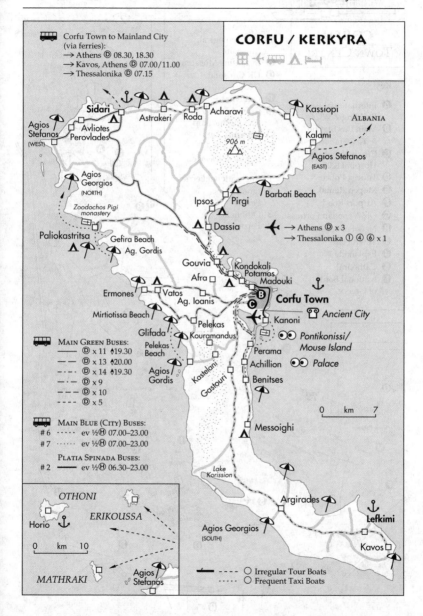

CORFU / KERKYRA

Corfu Town to Mainland City
(via ferries)
→ Athens Ⓓ 08.30, 18.30
→ Kavos, Athens Ⓓ 07.00/11.00
→ Thessalonika Ⓓ 07.15

Sidari
Agios Stefanos (WEST)
Avliotes
Perovlades
Astrakeri
Roda
Acharavi
Kassiopi
ALBANIA
906 m
Kalami
Agios Stefanos (EAST)
Agios Georgios (NORTH)
Zoodochos Pigi monastery
Ipsos
Pirgi
Barbati Beach
Paliokastritsa
Gefira Beach
Ag. Gordis
Dassia
→ Athens Ⓓ x 3
→ Thessalonika ① ④ ⑥ x 1
Gouvia
Kondokali
Potamos
Madouki
Afra
Ermones
Vatos
Ag. Ioanis
B
C
Corfu Town
Ancient City
Mirtiotissa Beach
Pelekas
Kanoni
Glifada
Kouramandus
Pontikonissi/
Mouse Island

MAIN GREEN BUSES:
── Ⓓ x 11 ♦19.30
── Ⓓ x 13 ♦20.00
─·─ Ⓓ x 14 ♦19.30
─··─ Ⓓ x 9
── Ⓓ x 10
---- Ⓓ x 5
Pelekas Beach
Agios Gordis
Kastelani
Gastouri
Perama
Achillion
Palace
Benitses

MAIN BLUE (CITY) BUSES:
#6 ···· ev ½Ⓗ 07.00–23.00
#7 ···· ev ½Ⓗ 07.00–23.00
PLATIA SPINADA BUSES:
#2 ── ev ½Ⓗ 06.30–23.00
Messoighi
0   km   7
Lake Korission

OTHONI
ERIKOUSSA
Horio
Argirades
Lefkimi
0   km   10
Agios Georgios (SOUTH)
Kavos
MATHRAKI
Agios Stefanos
●─ --- ○ Irregular Tour Boats
···· ○ Frequent Taxi Boats

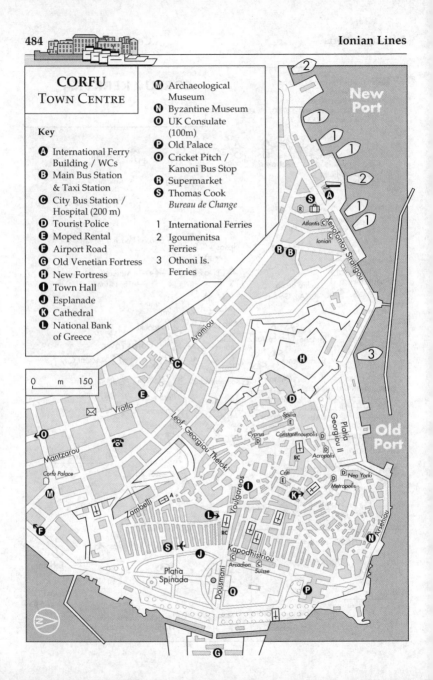

CORFU
TOWN CENTRE

Key

- **A** International Ferry Building / WCs
- **B** Main Bus Station & Taxi Station
- **C** City Bus Station / Hospital (200 m)
- **D** Tourist Police
- **E** Moped Rental
- **F** Airport Road
- **G** Old Venetian Fortress
- **H** New Fortress
- **I** Town Hall
- **J** Esplanade
- **K** Cathedral
- **L** National Bank of Greece
- **M** Archaeological Museum
- **N** Byzantine Museum
- **O** UK Consulate (100m)
- **P** Old Palace
- **Q** Cricket Pitch / Kanoni Bus Stop
- **R** Supermarket
- **S** Thomas Cook *Bureau de Change*

- 1 International Ferries
- 2 Igoumenitsa Ferries
- 3 Othoni Is. Ferries

0   m   150

New Port

Old Port

Eleftherios Stratigou

Atlantis
Ionian

Aramiou

Leof. Georgiou Theloki

Vratla

Mantzarou

Corfu Palace

Zambelli

Spilia

Cyprus
Constantinoupolis

RC

Criti

Acropolis

Nea Yorki

Metropolis

Platia Georgiou II

Voulgareos

Arseniou

Kapodhistriou

Arcadion
Suisse

Platia Spinada

Dousmani

spot of **Paliokastritsa**, home to a castle (c. 1200 AD) and a monastery (1228) replete with icons (Icon fans should also check out the **Byzantine Museum** in Corfu Town).

To the north-east of Corfu lie three islets also open to island hoppers. They see few tourists, but those that call usually end up raving about them. Regular ferries leave from Corfu Town, but given that each can be 'done' in a couple of hours it is better to visit by excursion boat from Sidari. Arid and hilly **Othoni** is the largest of them, and the only one with a resident summer tourist population. Even so, it is very quiet with nothing to do except lounge on the beach and make the dusty walk to the inland Horio. **Erikoussa** is the main objective for the Sidari excursion boats thanks to a good sand beach at the island port village. **Mathraki**, the small-est of the three, sees few tourists and her beaches are home to nesting Loggerhead Turtles each summer. Rooms are available on all three islets. Erikoussa has the only hotel.

Gulf of Corinth Ports

Running north of the Peloponnese from the Corinth Canal to the entrance to the Ionian Sea lies the Gulf of Corinth. Two landing-craft ferry links make the crossing; foot passengers are a rarity. The easterly link runs from **Agios Nikolaos** on the north coast to **Egion** on the Peloponnese roughly 30 times a day. The western link is from **Andirio** to **Rio** (10 km north-east of Patras), running frequently day and night, and used by the Corfu—Athens bus. There is also a regular ferry service between the mainland ports of **Aktion**, just north of Lefkada, and **Preveza** (home to the remains of a notable Roman city), a town on the headland to the north (see p. 495). This service is far less frequent and, if you are bussing up or down the coast between Corfu and Astakos or the Peloponnese, you might well have to stay the night at Preveza (there are a goodly number of hotels on the waterfront). Finally, the small town of **Amphilochia** — deep inside the Preveza Gulf — has had a Corfu catamaran link in previous years.

Igoumenitsa
ΗΓΟΥΜΕΝΙΤΣΑ; pop. 6,500.

CODE ☎ 0665
WATERFRONT GNTO/EOT ☎ 22227
TOURIST POLICE ☎ 22222
POLICE ☎ 22100

Set within the inner recesses of a deep and steamy calm bay, this is one of those places which always prompt the question 'Where are we?' from puzzled ferry passengers. In fact, Igoumenitsa — despite being a surprisingly small place — is Greece's major western port north of the Gulf of Corinth and thus on the itineraries of many ferries (though in practice few foot passengers choose to set down here). The long waterfront is fairly pleasant — given its commercial role — with a park of sorts (filled with bushes used for highly dubious purposes — given the absence of a public WC) and a frontier town air, but walk a street inland and you will find a dusty collection of drab Greek streets of the kind that bedevils many an otherwise pretty town. If you are stuck in town the day then you would do well to head 5 km north to the beach at **Drepanos** which is a much nicer part of the world. Igoumenitsa meantime, offers nothing to do except catch the ferry to Corfu or Italy, or a bus to another Greek destination.

Buses run (from the bus station a block in from the waterfront) direct to Athens (⊙ 08.30, 11.00, 13.30, 19.45), Thessalonika (⊙ 11.45) and also to Prevenza (⊙ 11.45, 15.30) — with its short ferry hop to Aktion and the bus link to Lefkada (last bus 16.10).

⊨

Most folks head for Corfu Town rather than stay in the dozen odd hotels in Igoumenitsa. However, there are advantages in staying here; not least because there is far less pressure on beds. In a pinch try the D-class *Egnatias* (☎ 23648) and *Lux* (☎ 22223) or the C-class *Epirus* (☎ 22504), all on or near the waterfront. Ticket agents also offer some rooms.

Λ

Kalami Beach Camping (☎ 71245); 4 km south of the town. Quite awful — avoid it.

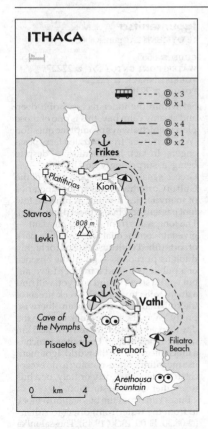

Ithaca

IΘAKH; 96 km²; pop. 4,000.

CODE ☎ 0674
PORT POLICE ☎ 32209
POLICE ☎ 32205
HOSPITAL ☎ 32282

A small and very hilly island, Ithaca lies steeped in the romance of myth rather than offering much in reality beyond a quiet tranquillity. The legendary home of Odysseus (alias Ulysses), hero of the *Odyssey* — and the siege of Troy, too, in a way (he was the devious hero who came

up with the idea of the wooden horse), there is little to do here except walk the hills, indulge in a little quiet romance and wonder why he spent ten years trying to get back. Indeed, there is little to show that he was ever here at all: no dead dogs on the beaches, no remains of a palace (home to his wife Penelope), and no sign of the suitors and attendant orgy girls — Ithaca has yielded little significant archaeological evidence to suggest it was a centre of power at the time. The modern centre, such as it is, consists of the red-tile house village of **Vathi** tucked deep into a bay in the middle of the island. Devastated in the 1953 earthquake that rocked all the southern Ionian islands, it has been rebuilt sympathetically, and offers a taste of rural island life, spiced with the more tourist orientated waterfront looking onto the prison islet of **Lanroito** that graces the mouth of the bay.

Ferry links are good, considering the insignificance of Ithaca as a tourist island (thanks largely to poor pebble beaches and few obvious sights), with boats running to three island ports. The majority of large ferries head for Vathi, with daily High Season landing-craft ferries serving both the small northern port of **Frikes** (from Lefkada) and at **Pisaetos** (from Kefalonia). Pisaetos also sees occasional international boats that can't find the time to steam round to Vathi. This 'port' is no more than an isolated quay below a steep hillside decorated with a switchback dirt track road, that defies the island bus and sees as few taxis. Ithaca has a solitary bus that teeters along the precipitous hill roads to uninspiring **Stavros** (complete with several places offering rooms) and the hamlet villages on the northern half of the island, as well as to **Perahori**, the former centre in pirate-troubled days. High Season also sees taxi boats running from Vathi to the attractive pebble beach villages of **Kioni** and Frikes. Formerly quiet fishing villages, they now offer a gentle spot in which to spend a day or two.

ITHACA
VATHI TOWN

0   m   100

S Sarakiniko Bay Road

F

D

Evmeou

C

V

Petsion
R

H

M

J

An. Kallinikou

Q

Mendor
B

N **I**

L **E**

L

B

Fishing
Caiques

P

3

M

Georgiou Dracouli

K

N

G

P

R

Marina

E *Akeaeon*
R *Koulouri*

A

Vathi
Harbour

2

1

Odisseos

Odysseys

Georgiou Gratsou

T

N

Lazareto
Islet

R

U **O**

*Pebble
Beach*

EVENING ARGOS

**LOST HERO'S
DOG SNUFFS IT**

BODY FOUND ON BEACH BY CASTAWAY

WANTED!

**FAITHFUL
POOCH !**

DELPHI ORACLE
LATEST —

With only one man
of her crew alive
what get to sea
why Twenty five

WHAT DOES IT MEAN?

GROT GIRL

Key

A Tourist Information
B Bus Stop & Taxi Rank
C Police
D Tourist Police
E National Bank of Greece
F Hospital
G Town Hall
H Archaeological Museum

I Pharmacy
J Bakery
K Public WCs
L Ticket Agent
M Moped Rental
N Tavernas
O Circe Club
P Pl. Elastathiou
   Dracouli

Q Cathedral
R Former Prison
S Sarakiniko Bay Road
T North Ithaca Road
U Loutsa / Skinos Bay Road
V Perakhori Road

1 Ferry Berth
2 Irregular Hydrofoils
3 Beach Boats

◻

Accommodation on Ithaca is pretty limited, and what there is tends to be expensive. **Vathi** has some rooms and two B-class hotels: the *Mendor* (☎ 32433), on the waterfront near the caïque harbour, and the western edge of town the hotel/pension *Odysseus* (☎ 32381) — also on the waterfront. There is also a C-class hotel in **Frikes**: the *Nostos* (☎ 31644), and a B-class hotel in Kioni: the *Kioni* (☎ 31362). A few rooms are also on offer at both.

∞

Vathi is host to a small **Archaeological Museum** which in truth has limited appeal. More interesting by far is the **Cave of the Nymphs** — a large cavern 1 km west of Vathi, said to have been used by Odysseus and the goddess Athena to hide the treasure the Phaeacians gave him immediately prior to his return from Troy. A second site with Homeric associations lies on the south-east corner of the island: the **Arethousian Fountain** offers a splendid excuse for some pleasant hill walking, but bring liquid with you as your objective is often drunk dry.

Katakolon
ΚΑΤΑΚΟΛΟ

CODE ☎ 0621

A sleepy little port on the west coast of the Peloponnese, Katakolon hovers on the fringe of the ferry system, appearing every other year or so on a new boat's itinerary before commercial realities set in and it returns to somnolent isolation. The reason for these calls by irregular ferries and cruise ships is the port's ready access to the site of ancient Olympia (27 km), home to the most important Temple of Zeus and the Olympic games. Actually, the port is quite attractive itself, with an impressively long beach, several tavernas and hotels. Buses connect with the town of Pirgos (12 km away) and its links with Olympia (where you will find three campsites and a youth hostel).

◻

Accommodation options in town are confined to three establishments: the A-class pension *Zefyros* (☎ 41170), the C-class hotel *Ionio* (☎ 41494), and the D-class *Delfini* (☎ 41214).

Kefalonia
ΚΕΦΑΛΛΩΝΙΑ; 781 km²; pop. 31,800.

ARGOSTOLI CODE ☎ 0671
SAMI CODE ☎ 0674
ARGOSTOLI NTOG OFFICE ☎ 22248
SAMI PORT POLICE ☎ 22031
POLICE ☎ 22200
HOSPITAL ☎ 22434

The second largest island in the Ionian group, mountainous Kefalonia is a quiet beach-holiday destination now enjoying a very high profile. This is in large part because the island is the setting for Louis de Bernières' recent best selling novel *Captain Corelli's Mandolin*, but Kefalonia also hit the headlines in 1998 thanks to the murder of a couple of British residents in their home (allegedly by a couple of Albanian refugees) and the discovery of a British WW2 submarine off the southeast coast from which the one survivor of its sinking made a record-breaking deep sea escape (though until the wreck was discovered — with its escape hatch open — his story wasn't believed). This latest WW2 tale has simply added to Kefalonia's ability to promote itself on the back of the events of the last half century rather than its previous 3,000 years of history. The most significant of these episodes were the Italian occupation of the island in WW2 and its bloody conclusion (when all but 33 of the Italian garrison of 9,000 were massacred by German forces during their take-over following the surrender of Italy in 1943), and the devastating earthquake that rocked the Ionian islands in 1956, during which almost all the buildings on Kefalonia collapsed. These events provide the setting for (and are excellently described in) *Captain Corelli's Mandolin*.

Kefalonia is very much an island of visual contradictions. On the one hand it boasts some spectacular mountain scenery with a coastline of green pine-clad hills and sandy beach lined coves, all bathed in a timeless light that makes one feel as if one is walking around in a

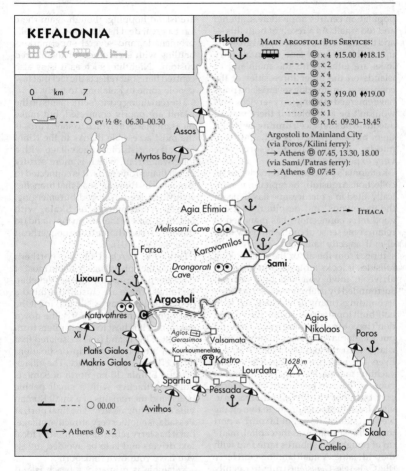

KEFALONIA

0   km   7

⌲ ---- ○ ev ½ ⓓ: 06.30–00.30

Fiskardo

MAIN ARGOSTOLI BUS SERVICES:

——	ⓓ x 4 ♦15.00 ♦♦18.15
----	ⓓ x 2
—·—	ⓓ x 4
····	ⓓ x 2
— —	ⓓ x 5 ♦19.00 ♦♦19.00
—··—	ⓓ x 3
······	ⓓ x 1
——	ⓓ x 16: 09.30–18.45

Argostoli to Mainland City
(via Poros/Kilini ferry):
⟶ Athens ⓓ 07.45, 13.30, 18.00
(via Sami/Patras ferry):
⟶ Athens ⓓ 07.45

Assos

Myrtos Bay

Agia Efimia

Melissani Cave ⊙⊙

Farsa

Karavomilos

Drongorati Cave ⊙⊙

Sami

⟶ ITHACA

Lixouri

Argostoli

Katavothres ⊙⊙

Xi

Agios. Gerasimos Valsamata

Agios Nikolaos

Poros

Platis Gialos
Makris Gialos

Kourkoumenelata

Kastro

1628 m

Lourdata

Spartia

Pessada

— ·— · ○ 00.00

Avithos

✈ ⟶ Athens ⓓ x 2

Skala

Catelio

polarized photograph, on the other hand the island has been shorn of almost every attractive building that it once possessed. Unfortunately, the hurried rebuilding after the 1956 earthquake was more practical than poetic, leaving a result best summed up by Captain Corelli: 'Everything here used to be so pretty, and now everything is concrete.' Don't, however, be put off by this lament: even without its

old architecture Kefalonia is a very attractive place, though you will encounter considerable difficulties in exploring the island if you are without your own transport. Kefalonia's fans tend divide their time between a small hotel, a quiet beach, and a good book (an estimated one in five visitors now come armed with *the* novel).

Size disparities are Kefalonia's great problem: the island is too big while the population centres are widely scattered and too small. As a result of both this — and the misfortune of the capital growing up on the far west side when all ferry links are either with the mainland or islands on the other three sides of the compass — an amazing seven island ports have emerged offering ferry services. This wouldn't be a problem if there was an adequate bus service running between them but sadly there is not, and from midday on, you have to resort to the very expensive taxis.

Kefalonia's ports are a pretty disparate collection. **Argostoli**, the capital, is majestically sited in a picturesque bay beneath the mountains, and despite the lack of good ferry connections has managed to retain some sense of centre but very little else; it abjectly fails to do justice to its setting. From the air or the overlooking hillsides it looks fantastic, but once you arrive in town you will find yourself surrounded by drab concrete structures : its buildings (many deliberately left with half-built top floors — so that the owners don't have to pay the local roof tax) would put Kefalonia very high in any 'Greek island with the ugliest capital' contest. Even the waterfront, complete with a yachting marina, lacks sparkle. There is a good EOT office just south of the ferry port, but otherwise there is little reason to visit. Even the locals prefer to live on the western side of the bay at **Lixouri**, a port town almost as large as the capital, made up of nought but suburbs tarted up with the odd statue. A small landing-craft ferry (the C/F *Agios Gerasimus*) runs frequently between the two.

Of the other ports: the village of **Sami** has become the 'international' berth and the nearest thing Kefalonia has to a main ferry port and tourist resort. With a pleasant, taverna-lined waterfront that is atmospheric enough at night (though a bit too bland for comfort during the day), and a fine pebble beach to the north of the port, it is the easiest place to stay if you are island hopping, though again there isn't a great deal here beyond the hotels, promenade, and several supermarkets battling with each other for the limited custom. Nightlife, such as it is, is also centred here, but reflects the fact that few people come to Kefalonia to party.

The remaining ports/settlements on the island are poorly connected, but make pleasant places in which to stay; **Poros** is the most accessible thanks to the Kilini ferry. It consists of a large village with a long waterfront, which is more scruffy beach than promenade. It is connected to Argostoli by the same road that branches south to the less developed, but emerging, tourist resort village of **Skala**, with beaches (some of the best on the island) to the east a second home to the Loggerhead turtles (see p. 504).

Fiskardo, perched on the northern finger, is the only village to retain most of its attractive, pre-earthquake Venetian buildings. These are clustered around a petite tree-lined bay, easily making it the most photogenic of the ports; the down side is that it is host to day-trippers from the rest of the island (it is so isolated that it is an attractive day trip destination) and Lefkada in consequence. The village of **Agia Efimia**, 10 km north of Sami, is quietly attractive with a small pebble beach and the remains of a small Roman villa crumbling nearby. The final port, at **Pessada**, is another very attractive village, but it has ferry schedules written by local taxi drivers and is to be avoided unless you have your own transport.

Kefalonia is primarily a beach island and has them in abundance. Finding one isn't difficult. Among the best known are those at **Makris Gialos** and **Platis Gialos**. These end at the small islet of **Tourkopodaro** (connected to Kefalonia by a beach). Taverna-backed **Avithos** is also justifiably popular thanks to its fine red sand. Lixouri also has a notable red sand beach at **Xi**. The beach at **Spartia** is more isolated and is backed by picturesque steep white cliffs.

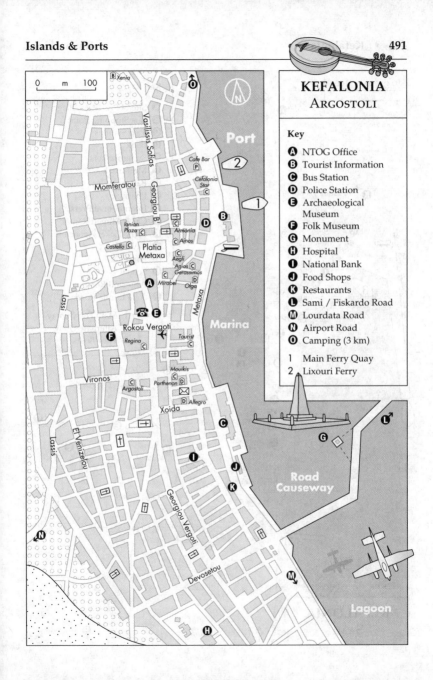

0   m   100

Ⓑ Xenia

Ⓞ

Ⓝ N

Port

Vasilissis Sofias

Momferatou

Georgiou B'

Cafe Bar Ⓟ

Cefalonia Star Ⓒ

Ionian Plaza Ⓒ

Castello Ⓒ

Platia Metaxa

Armonia Ⓒ

Ⓒ Ainos

Ⓒ Aegli

Agios Gerassimos Ⓒ

Ⓐ Mirabel

Ⓓ Olga

Ⓔ

☎

Rokou Vergoti

Ⓕ

Regina Ⓒ

Tourist Ⓒ

✈

Lassi

Metaxa

Marina

Vironos

Mouikis

Parthenon Ⓓ

Argostoli Ⓒ

Ⓓ Allegro

Xoida

El Venizelou

Ⓒ

Ⓘ

Ⓙ

Ⓚ

Lassis

Georgiou Vergoti

Ⓝ

Road Causeway

Ⓛ↗

Ⓖ

1

2

Devosetou

Ⓜ

Lagoon

Ⓗ

KEFALONIA

ARGOSTOLI

Key

Ⓐ NTOG Office
Ⓑ Tourist Information
Ⓒ Bus Station
Ⓓ Police Station
Ⓔ Archaeological Museum
Ⓕ Folk Museum
Ⓖ Monument
Ⓗ Hospital
Ⓘ National Bank
Ⓙ Food Shops
Ⓚ Restaurants
Ⓛ Sami / Fiskardo Road
Ⓜ Lourdata Road
Ⓝ Airport Road
Ⓞ Camping (3 km)

1   Main Ferry Quay
2   Lixouri Ferry

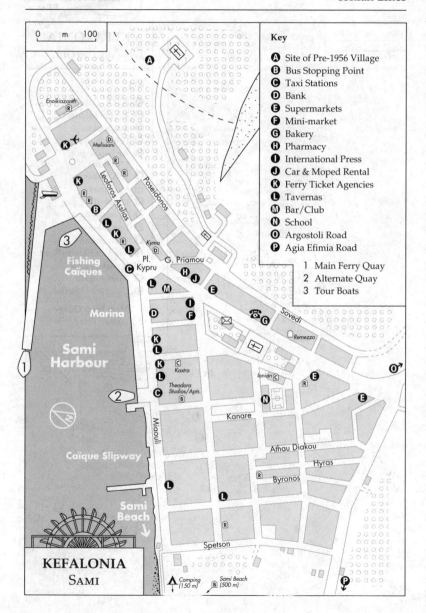

0　m　100

Key

- **A** Site of Pre-1956 Village
- **B** Bus Stopping Point
- **C** Taxi Stations
- **D** Bank
- **E** Supermarkets
- **F** Mini-market
- **G** Bakery
- **H** Pharmacy
- **I** International Press
- **J** Car & Moped Rental
- **K** Ferry Ticket Agencies
- **L** Tavernas
- **M** Bar/Club
- **N** School
- **O** Argostoli Road
- **P** Agia Efimia Road

1　Main Ferry Quay
2　Alternate Quay
3　Tour Boats

Enoikiazonth

Melissani

Leoforos Assias

Poseidonos

Kyma

Pl. Kypru

G. Priamou

Fishing Caïques

Marina

Sami Harbour

Sovedi

Remezzo

Kastro

Theodora Studios/Apts.

Ionian

Caïque Slipway

Miaouli

Kanare

Sami Beach

Athau Diakou

Hyras

Byronos

Spetson

KEFALONIA
SAMI

Camping (150 m)

Sami Beach (500 m)

⊢

Bed supply is reasonably good on Kefalonia, despite the island being well off the backpacker trail and popular with Italian motorists hopping across the Adriatic (the tragic fate of the Italian WW2 garrison has left the islanders with a soft spot for the citizens of this occupying nation). However, beds on Kefalonia are pricey. The EOT office in Argostoli offers help in tracking spare beds down, along with free maps, bus timetables, and ferry information.

Sami has several convenient hotels. Two, the C-class *Ionion* (☎ 22035) and D-class *Kyma* (☎ 22064), both one block behind the promenade (the latter off the town square). Several blocks further back, with good bay views across to Ithaca, is the D-class *Melissani* (☎ 22464). There are also several houses offering rooms in the backstreets of Sami. **Poros** also has a good number of rooms advertised.

Argostoli has hotels aplenty; for a good budget hotel try the D-class *Allegro* (☎ 22268) or *Parthenon* (☎ 22246). More up-market are the C-class *Tourist* (☎ 22510), *Agios Gerasimos* (☎ 28697) or more expensive *Mouikis* (☎ 230 32). If you want to splash out, then there is a B-class *Xenia* (☎ 22233) at the north end of town.

A

There are two reasonable sites on the island: most convenient is *Caravomilos Beach* (☎ 0674 22480) at **Sami**. A nice, mature tree-filled site behind a pebble beach, but (thanks to the large number of Italian motorists) very expensive. It is also very much a 'family' site. *Argostoli Beach* (☎ 0671 23487) — a member of the *Sunshine Camping Club* scheme — is 2 km north of **Agostoli** and offers marginally better value.

∞

Apart from a poor **Archaeological Museum**, the only 'sight' Argostoli has on offer is a small monument on the causeway across the neck of the bay south of the town — built to commemorate the glory of the British Empire (the British built most of the island's roads during 50 years of rule in the 19th century); it is now inscription-less but otherwise intact. During 1992, the mayor of Sami (a part time archaeologist) discovered a major 14 c. BC Mycenaean beehive-shaped tomb on the outskirts of town, reopening speculation as to whether Kefalonia was the true 'Ithaca' of Odysseus — given the absence of finds there and the better topographical 'fit' of Kefalonia to the island described by Homer. This discovery will presumably be open to the

public at some point. Meantime, **island bus tours** out of Argostoli are very popular. These take in the **Venetian Kastro** of St. George, 9 km south of Argostoli, and the **Monastery of Agios Gerasimos** (home to the body of a monk who is now the island's little known patron saint).

Fans of *Captain Corelli's Mandolin* are also visiting the island in increasing numbers with the express purpose of finding the Kefalonia described in the book. Needless to say the earthquake hasn't left much. The old village of **Farsa** is now a deserted ruin on a hillside above the Argostoli—Lixouri road, while Argostoli has lost the attractive tavernas that once lined Metaxa Square. As a result of this dearth of sites, many fans have to make do with visiting the beach beyond the village of **Spartia** from where Captain Corelli (and his mandolin strings) made his bid for freedom, and imbibing the odd beverage at the *Café Tselenti* (supposedly the model for Drosoula's taverna) in **Fiskardo**.

The most impressive sightseeing Kefalonia has to offer—beyond the island's lush mountain and coastal scenery — are its caves. These include the red-walled **Drongarati Cave** (entrance fee 750 GDR) 4 km south-west of Sami (which has such good acoustics that concerts are occasionally held in it), and the 100 m long **Melissani Cave** (entrance fee 950 GDR) on the Sami—Agia Efimia road (complete with a subterranean lake and tour boats). En route you will find a **Tide-Mill Wheel** at **Karavomilos** — one of a number scattered around the Kefalonian coastline. The best known is at **Katavothres**, just north of Argostoli. For many years this (now somewhat over touristed) site attracted interest thanks to the odd phenomenon of the sea seemingly flowing into the apparently inexhaustible sink hole found here. Attempts to track where the water went, with everything from dyes to petrol and saw-dust, proved fruitless until 1963, when a party of Austrian geologists put 140 kg of a water soluble green dye down the sink hole. 14 days later faint traces appeared 20 km away on the other side of the island at Karavomilos and Melissani cave.

Tour buses also combine with ferries to provide excursions to (1) **Zakinthos** (via Pessada), (2) the ruins of ancient **Olympia** — home to the original Olympic Games and the famous Temple of Zeus (via Poros and Kilini), and (3) day trips to **Ithaca** and **Lefkada**.

Kilini
КΥΛΛΗΝΗ

CODE ☎ 0623

The major jumping-off point to the island of Zante, Kilini is a dusty little port with a beach on the west coast of the Peloponnese some 30 km south of Patras. Overland connections are poor; simply getting to this port is apt to be a pain. Two buses a day leave Patras during the week (08.00, 14.55), with only the first running during the weekends. At Kilini they stop at the ticket office block behind the ferry quay, usually only skidding into town at breakneck speed a few minutes before ferries are due to depart. An indifferent train service also runs between the ports.

⊢⊣

Tourist Police (☎ 92211) office on the quay will point you in the direction of the limited (but rarely full) rooms in the port. The nearest hotels are 5 km to the south at **Kastro**.

Lefkada / Lefkas
ΛΕΥΚΑΔΑ; 303 km²; pop. 23,000.

CODE ☎ 0645
POLICE / TOURIST OFFICE ☎ 22346
HOSPITAL ☎ 22336

An island sufficiently close to the mainland to have a road link (via a bridge to the capital of Lefkada Town), Lefkada is barren and austere but spectacular thanks to its mountains and islet-littered coast. Tourist development has largely confined itself to the east and southern coasts, but is comparatively restrained; offering an appealing mix of taverna and tradition. Unusually for a Greek island, the capital — Lefkada Town — is not a ferry port. With the lagoon to the north now home to a yachting marina, and salt flats between it and the mainland, it doesn't feel like a coastal town. Tradition has it that the Lefkada was joined to the mainland until a canal was dug in the 5 C. BC separating the town from the mainland. Earthquake

damage is also all too evident here, but fortunately most of the Venetian churches that make the town have survived, and the ad hoc rebuilding of houses (now limited to a maximum of two storeys high) has produced a charming tin roof and plaster touch. This is one town that has actually been enhanced by earthquake 'repairs'. Unfortunately, accommodation is limited in the town and it is best visited as a day trip from one of Lefkada's ports.

Buses run frequently between the capital and main island towns; most passing through the resort port of **Nidri**, the starting point for boat tours circumnavigating a number of islets including **Skorpios** — owned by the Onassis family. A number of boats (a caïque done up as a mock Odysseus boat — the T/B *Boat Odysseia*) advertise swims *on* the island. Even if this was physically possible, in practice you are not allowed to land and swim from the boat just offshore. Despite this, these excursions offer value for money thanks to the visit to the sea cave on Meganisi. One boat even goes to Lefkada's best sand beach at **Porto Katsiki** — also visited by caïques from the port of **Vassiliki.** Home to the best windsurfing in Europe off a poor pebble beach, this village gets very crowded, but is worth a look in the late afternoon when up to 100 windsurfers are skimming effortlessly up and down the bay. The best beaches on Lefkada are all on the remoter west side. In addition to Porto Katsiki there is an excellent sand beach behind the headland at **Ag. Nikitas**.

⊢⊣

High package tourist presence (courtesy of the airport at Aktion: sometimes advertised as Lefkada airport) has driven up prices and reduced the available accommodation. **Lefkada** is the most likely town to have beds on offer. The E-class *Patrae* (☎ 22359) near the Agricultural bank in the central square has a good reputation, as does the C-class *Santa Mavra* (☎ 22342) and the nearby E-class *Vyzantion* (☎ 22629). More up-market are the expensive promenade B-class *Niricos* (☎ 24132) and *Lefkas* (☎ 23916). **Vassiliki** also has some budget hotels: the C-class *Lefkatas* (☎ 31229)

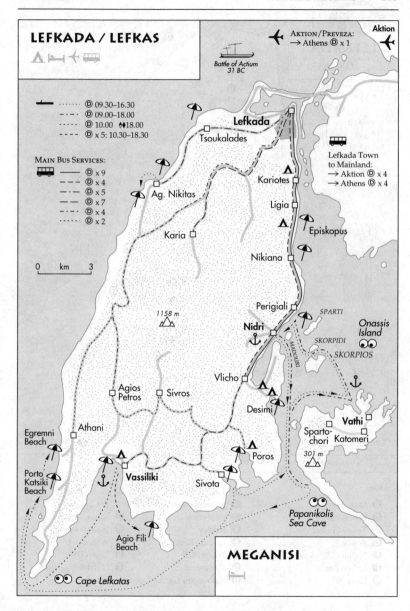

LEFKADA / LEFKAS

🏕 🛏 ✈ 🚌

Battle of Actium
31 BC

AKTION/PREVEZA:
→ Athens Ⓓ x 1

Aktion ✈

········ Ⓓ 09.30–16.30
—·—· Ⓓ 09.00–18.00
········ Ⓓ 10.00 ◆18.00
— — — Ⓓ x 5: 10.30–18.30

MAIN BUS SERVICES:
🚌
——— Ⓓ x 9
— — — Ⓓ x 4
—·—· Ⓓ x 5
— — Ⓓ x 7
— — Ⓓ x 4
········ Ⓓ x 2

0   km   3

Lefkada Town
to Mainland:
→ Aktion Ⓓ x 4
→ Athens Ⓓ x 4

Lefkada

Tsoukalades

Ag. Nikitas

Kariotes

Ligia

Episkopus

Karia

Nikiana

Perigiali

SPARTI

Onassis
Island 👀

Nidri ⚓

SKORPIDI

SKORPIOS

1158 m 🏔

Vlicho

Desimi

Agios
Petros   Sivros

Vathi

Egremni
Beach

Athani

Sparto-
chori   Katomeri

Poros

301 m 🏔

Porto
Katsiki
Beach

Vassiliki

Sivota

Agio Fili
Beach

*Papanikolis
Sea Cave* 👀

👀 *Cape Lefkatas*

MEGANISI

🛏

MADOURI

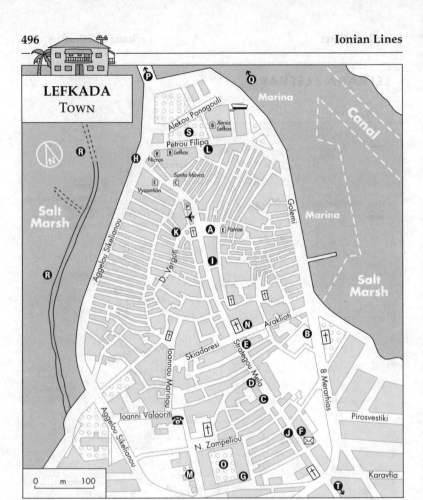

LEFKADA
TOWN

Key

- **A** Main Square
- **B** Bus Station
- **C** Tourist Police
- **D** Police
- **E** National Bank of Greece
- **F** Ionian Bank
- **G** Hospital
- **H** Taxi Station
- **I** Supermarket
- **J** Pharmacy
- **K** Bakery
- **L** Moped Rental
- **M** Town Hall
- **N** Cathedral
- **O** Valaoritou Garden
- **P** Chain Bridge & Causeway
- **Q** Santa Maura Fort
- **R** Line of Roman Aqueduct
- **S** Town Park
- **T** Nidri & Vassiliki Road

and E-class *Paradissos* (☎ 31256), and a plentiful supply of B-class hotels full of package tourists.

Λ

There are six sites on the island: *Camping Vassiliki Beach* (☎ 31308) full-to-bursting with windsurfers is the most convenient, *Camping Desimi Beach* (☎ 95225), 3 km south of Nidri, is less so but offers more space. *Camping Kariotes Beach* (☎ 23594) is the nearest to Lefkada Town. The other sites — *Episkopos Beach* (☎ 92410), *Santa Mavra Camping* (☎ 95493) and *Poros Beach* (☎ 95452), running down the east coast, are primarily geared to motorists.

∞

Lefkada's sights are more made up of places where things happened rather than things to see; the island being a veritable shrine to the sticky side of romance. Story has it that Aristotle, when a very old man, was asked if he regretted that his manly 'powers' had waned. He is said to have observed that it was the best thing that had ever happened to him, as it was 'like being unchained from a lunatic'. Lefkada is, from top to tail, a testament to the acuteness of this observation. **Cape Lefkatas** (formerly Cape Doukato) became the Beachy Head of the ancient world after Sappho (the famous lesbian poet of antiquity) jumped off after experiencing a touch of unrequited love — for a middle-aged man. The tip of this peninsula housed a **Temple of Apollo** (fragmentary remains are extant) whose priests thought this action a terribly good idea and took to chucking sacrificial victims — with symbolic lover's dove wings tied to their limbs — over the edge in years thereafter (there is some evidence that they were collected by boat after they hit the water). Given the close proximity of this lover's leap, it is surprising that Anthony and Cleopatra didn't take advantage of it in 31 BC after the disastrous naval **Battle of Actium** against Octavian, which took place just to the north of Lefkada near the airport of Preveza / Aktion. Instead, they winged it to Egypt and jumped into the next world from there. Romance struck again in the 19 c. when the German archaeologist Wilhelm Dörpfeld hit upon the idea that Lefkada was Homer's Ithaca and then spent futile years trying to prove it. Dying of old age before the total discrediting of his theory could prompt him to test the merits of Sappho's leap, he left some **Bronze Age Tomb** excavations south of Nidri and a commemorative statue of himself on the town waterfront.

Meganisi
ΜΕΓΑΝΗΣΙ; 23 km²; pop. 250.

CODE ☎ 0645

A small island off the south-east coast of Lefkada, Meganisi is linked by a daily ferry from Nidri as well as several tour boats. If you are not planning to stay overnight then the latter are a better way of quickly seeing this gentle island. Most boats also call at the fishing village of **Vathi**, the largest settlement on the north coast, and occasionally at its tidier neighbour — **Spartochori** — as well.

⊨

A reasonable supply of rooms exist in all three villages. There is also an expensive hotel in Katomeri: the A-class *Meganissi* (☎ 51639).

∞

Nidri tourist boats run daily to the **Papanikolis Cave** on the west coast; said to be the second largest sea cave in Greece, the locals claim that they successfully hid a Greek submarine in it for much of the last war, but appealing as this idea is, the more cynical will perceive that it must have been a very small submarine.

Patras
ΠΑΤΡΑ; pop. 141,530.

CODE ☎ 061
TOURIST OFFICE ☎ 22 0902
NTOG OFFICE ☎ 65 3368
FIRST AID ☎ 150

The busiest international port in Greece after Piraeus, Patras is a popular port of for ferries running down the length of the Adriatic or south from Italy. However, the presence of thousands of holiday-makers passing through daily brings out the worst rip-off merchants in Greece; the practical upshot being that if you want either a top-class meal or bed you have to look pretty hard to find it.

The third largest city in Greece, Patras's fate was sealed with the decision to re-build the centre (following its destruction during the War of Independence) using an uninteresting grid pattern. The grime

PATRAS
CITY CENTRE

Key

- **A** International Ferry Terminal / NTOG
- **B** Main Bus Station
- **C** Railway Station
- **D** Public WCs
- **E** Tourist Police / National Bank
- **F** Local Bus Station
- **G** Bakery
- **H** Newspapers
- **I** Roman Odeon
- **J** Acropolis
- **K** Cathedral
- **L** Hospital
- **M** Museum
- **N** Ticket kiosks

1   Domestic Ferries
2   Hydrofoils (if any)

International Ferries (typical locations):
3   Ventouris Ferries
4   Minoan Lines
5   ANEK Lines
6   H.M.L. Ferries
7   Strintzis
8   Superfast
9   Vergina Ferries
10   Adriatica
11   Marlines
12   Agoudimos Lines
13   Poseidon Lines
14   A. K. Ventouris

Gate 6
Gate 5
Gate 4
Gate 3
Gate 2
Gate 1

Hostel (1.5 km)
Aihinon
Favierou
Norman
Karolou
Adonis
Mesonos
Splendid
Acropole
Platia Olgas
Zaimi
Platia Tri. Sym.
Rannia
Othonos Amalias
Mediterranee
Agios Nikolaou
Kolokotroni
Agios Andreou
Pension Nicos
Ermou
Platia Georgiou
Marie
Leoforos Dimitrios Gounari
Riga Fereou
Filopimenos
Korinthou
Kanakari
Patreos
Sachtouri
Trion Navarkhon

0   m   150

laden buildings, relieved only by attractive park-like squares, offer little incentive to hang around, and few tourists do. Fortunately, all facilities and means of escape are on or near the waterfront. The down side of this is that, alongside the ferry terminus and the railway and bus stations, the quayside road is loaded with the worst 'restaurants' in Greece (offering warmed-up greasy — rather than Grecian — cuisine) and the usual collection of ticket agents. Given this, the best advice has to be to feed and change money before you arrive in the port area of town; that way you can still enjoy your holiday without being ripped off. Take care too, if you are getting your currency converted: ticket agents are to be avoided as they will convert your currency — at a price. Most ticket agencies are only interested in selling international tickets, so (tickets to Corfu aside) you will find tickets for domestic ferries and hydrofoils on sale from kiosks at ❶ (if any).

A recent change at Patras has been the introduction of signpost 'Gates' along the waterfront. Your ticket agent should be able to indicate from which your boat will depart, but all international travellers still have to clear passport control in the International Ferry Terminal (❹) to get their boarding pass and have it stamped (this is checked on boarding). Domestic ticket holders just show their tickets.

Patras is naturally a major destination for both trains and buses. The former depart from a quayside station every couple of hours and then crawl to Athens or the Peloponnese, the latter are based at a waterfront bus station (complete with a pricey, but popular, snack and drink shop) and offer a far wider variety of destinations. The most important of these are: to Athens (⊕ 05.00–21.00), Thessalonika (⊚ 08.30, 15.00) and Kilini (⊚ 08.00, 14.45). Finally, the big Adriatic ferry lines run ultra-smooth air-conditioned buses to and from the centre of Athens. Seats can be booked along with your ticket.

⊨
The friendly NTOG office (☎ 42 3866) located in the ferry terminal can point you in the direction of a room. The port area of town has the greatest concentration, with the waterfront D-class *Splendid* (☎ 27 6521) along with the C-class *Acropole* (☎ 27 9809) offering tolerable rooms at better than most prices. Near the bus station you will find the noisy C-class *Adonis* (☎ 22 4213), and another C-class establishment — the *Mediterranee* (☎ 27 9602) is located on Ag. Nikolaou, the main shopping street. The up market *Rannia* (☎ 22 0114) lies on the next block east. Patras also has a couple of good pensions at the southern end of the port; the *Marie* (☎ 33 1302) and the *Nicos* (☎ 27 6183). There is also an IYHF *Youth Hostel* (☎ 42 7278) 2 km north at 68 Iroon Polytechniou.

▲
Kavouri Camping (☎ 42 8066): 2 km east of the port and crowded. Better by far is *Camping Rhion* (☎ 99 1585): on the beach 7 km north.

👓
Patras has just enough sights to keep you occupied while you await your ferry. Locals tend to head for **St. Andrew's Cathedral**; a major shrine thanks to its role as the repository of **St. Andrew's head**. Others head for the **Venetian Castle** on the site of the ancient **Acropolis**. Classical remains are confined to a restored **Odeon**. Patras also has a small **Archaeological Museum** (② to ⑦ 08.30–15.00).

Paxi / Paxos
ΠΑΞΟΙ; 25 km²; pop. 3,000.

CODE ☎ 0662
POLICE ☎ 31222
PORT POLICE ☎ 31259
FIRST AID ☎ 31466

Lying just south of Corfu, tiny Paxi (also known as 'Paxos') is largely the domain of up-market English and Italian tourists; its tranquil atmosphere is severely tested by daily invasions of day-trippers from both Corfu town and the mainland resort of Parga. These two tourist groups combine to make Paxi a comparatively expensive destination. Backpackers are a rarity thanks to the island's pricey reputation, and a lack of budget accommodation.

PAXI / PAXOS

- - - - Ⓗ 09.00–20.00
- - - Ⓓ 10.00 Seven Sea Cave boat tour
· · · · · Ⓗ 10.00–18.00

Lakka

Ipapanti
(Sea
Cave)

(Porto)
Longos

Magazia

Fountana

Bogdanatika

Stachai
(Sea
Caves)

Gaios
Town
Old Port

New
Port

AG. NIKOLAOS

PANAGIA

Ortholithos Stack

Porto
Sputzo

KATSIO-
NISSI

MOGONISI

🚌 —— Ⓓ x 4
- · - Ⓓ x 6
No ⑦ Bus Service

Vrikes
Beach

Voutoumi
Beach

ANTIPAXI

Ormos
Agrapidias

0   km   2

The residents won't thank this book for saying it, but in High Season day-tripping is the best way for island-hoppers to get a taste of the main town. The rest of the year (and once day-trippers have gone) it is a much more tranquil spot, reverting to a Patmos-like cosiness.

The main centre is at **Gaios Town**. Protected by two pine-clad islets (one topped with the remains of a Venetian fortress) nestling within the port bay, it has more charm than many island capitals, despite the inevitable 1953 earthquake damage. Fortunately, most of the lovely red-tiled houses that line the horse-shoe waterfront survived unscathed, and contrast attractively with the sea-canal and islets. Because of the narrowness of the channel the town now has an 'Old Port' harbouring caïques and tour boats, while ferries now dock at the 'New Port'; a quay 600 m along the coast road. The waterfront aside, the town is little more than the main square with a couple of major streets behind; adding greatly to the village feel of the place. The town's only major weakness is the beach; a tiny pebble affair, it does little more than encourage visitors to opt for the caïques that head for two south coast beaches.

The rest of Paxi (along with Antipaxi to the south) is characterized by low hills on the east side and dramatic cliffs and views on the west. Add to this the carpet of ancient olive groves — containing 200,000 trees — and Paxi's homely size and the result is a near perfect walking island.

Buses run regularly from a dusty square at the back of Gaios Town across the island to the small hamlet ports of Lakka and Longos (both of which have seen local ferry links with Corfu in the past). **Longos** is the more attractive settlement of the two, with a couple of tavernas overlooking a small caïque harbour. **Lakka** (also a popular destination for Corfu tour boats) is larger, but relies more on its narrow pine-lined bay for its not inconsiderable scenic appeal.

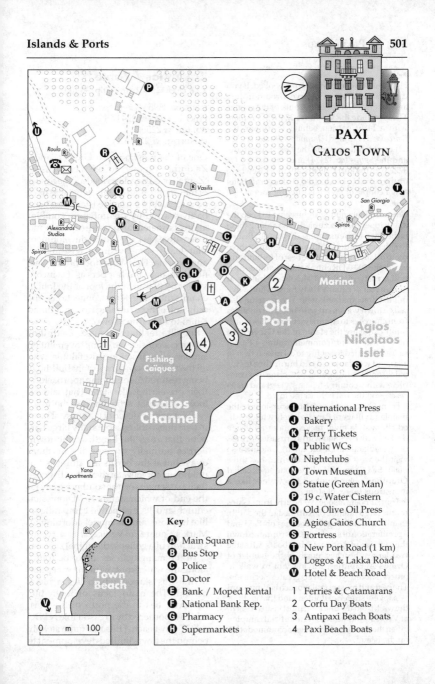

PAXI
GAIOS TOWN

Roula

Vasilis

San Giorgio

Spiros

Alexandros
Studios

Spiros

Marina

Old
Port

Agios
Nikolaos
Islet

Fishing
Caïques

Gaios
Channel

Yana
Apartments

Town
Beach

0   m   100

Key

ⓐ Main Square
ⓑ Bus Stop
ⓒ Police
ⓓ Doctor
ⓔ Bank / Moped Rental
ⓕ National Bank Rep.
ⓖ Pharmacy
ⓗ Supermarkets

ⓘ International Press
ⓙ Bakery
ⓚ Ferry Tickets
ⓛ Public WCs
ⓜ Nightclubs
ⓝ Town Museum
ⓞ Statue (Green Man)
ⓟ 19 c. Water Cistern
ⓠ Old Olive Oil Press
ⓡ Agios Gaios Church
ⓢ Fortress
ⓣ New Port Road (1 km)
ⓤ Loggos & Lakka Road
ⓥ Hotel & Beach Road

1 Ferries & Catamarans
2 Corfu Day Boats
3 Antipaxi Beach Boats
4 Paxi Beach Boats

Hotels are few and usually pre-booked. If you can, phone ahead to reserve a room in July and August. **Gaios** has the bulk of the rooms. These include the *Vasilis* (☎ 32404), complete with a leafy garden behind the town, the *Spiros* (☎ 31172) and *Alexandros Studios* (☎ 321 33) on the hill opposite the bus stop square, and the *Spiros* (☎ 32434) and *San Giorgio* (☎ 32223) on the Port Police headland. Elsewhere on the island **Lakka** has the D-class *Erida* hotel and a couple of tavernas offering rooms.

Gaios has just enough sightseeing to keep the day-trippers fully occupied. First among these is the town **Museum** housed in the old British Residency building. Although it is only a three room affair, it is among the best of its kind and worth the 300 GDR entrance fee. Exhibits include a rusty pistol that shoots six bullets at once, a pair of equally rusty forceps and a five million drachma bank-note. The museum also sells a town walk map with notes on notables from churches to chimneys. Other sites worth hunting out are the statue of the **Green Man** on the waterfront (commemorating a Paxiot sailor who tried to set fire to a Turkish fleet in 1821 and was captured and burnt alive for his pains) and the intriguing 19 c. cistern — complete with a country-house style grand staircase — on the hill behind the town.

From Gaios there are also excursions to the mainland village of **Parga**, a lovely whitewashed chora-style town tucked under a hillside decked with trees and with a Crusader fortress on a headland beside the town). Caïques also visit the west coast of Paxi, which has three major **Sea Caves** and a limestone stack called **Orolithos** poking out of the waters like a monstrous finger of stone.

Tourist boats also leave hourly from Gaios for the large satellite of **Antipaxi** to the south, thanks to a lack of good beaches on Paxi and a proliferation of sandy strands running down the east side of Antipaxi. Most boats call at the two largest beaches, north of the hamlet of **Ormos Agrapidias**, leaving you to walk to others should you covet greater seclusion. The best and most popular beach is **Voutoumi** — a lovely stretch of golden sand that justifies the walk from the first (and most visited beach) at **Vrikes** — home to some unofficial camping given the absence of any other accommodation on the island.

Zakinthos / Zante

ΖΑΚΥΝΘΟΣ; 402 km²; pop. 30,200.

CODE ☎ 0695
PORT POLICE ☎ 22417
POLICE ☎ 22550
HOSPITAL ☎ 22514

One of the most popular Greek islands, Zakinthos (known to the Venetians as 'Zante') was once described as 'the flower of the Orient'. Regrettably, what was once an undeniably attractive island has been badly scarred by the unhappy combination of a major earthquake (in 1953) and insensitive package tourist development that leads some visitors wishing for another one. The island does not see vast numbers of island hoppers as it is inconveniently placed at the foot of the Ionian chain with poor ferry connections: the only link of note running from mainland Kilini to Zakinthos Town.

Rebuilt after the earthquake, **Zakinthos Town** is a considerable improvement on similar reconstruction on Kefalonia, with all the churches and important buildings being restored to something approaching their pre-earthquake state. That said, all look somewhat artificial and the town could never be described as cosy. This is in part due to the exceptionally large harbour that runs the length of the town. Ferries normally dock on the northern quay, but if the berths are full it is not unknown for new arrivals to disgorge their passengers on the southern quay (at the end of which stands Ag. Dionissiou church and its distinctive campanile — like its more famous model adorning St. Mark's Square in Venice, it is a reconstruction of a collapsed original).

All the main facilities are to be found along the waterfront; with the exception of the bus station which lies a block behind. The main focus of town life, however, lies to the north of the port, which is bordered by a reasonable NTOG / EOT pay beach. Hills rise quite steeply behind the town, limited development to

ZAKINTHOS / ZANTE

Blue Caves

Skinari

Smuggler's Cove

Volimes

Anafonitrias
Katastari

Alikanas
Drosia
Tsilivi

Apo
Gerakari
Tragaki
Planos

756 m

Zakinthos Town

Galarou

Macherado

Argassi
Kalamaki

Ag. Leontos

Laganas
Vassilikos

Lithakia

SLOW
PELUZO

Agalas

MARATHONISI

Caves
Keri

Laganas/Turtle (soup) Bay

08.00–18.00

10.00

Speed Boats
(now banned)

→ Athens ⓓ x 3

MAIN BUS SERVICES:
—— ⓓ x 15
---- ⓓ x 8
-·-· ⓓ x 9
— — ⓓ x 3
--- ⓓ x 2
-··- ⓓ x 9
······ ⓓ x 4

Zakinthos Town to Mainland City
(via ferries):
→ Athens ⓓ 07.30, 12.30, 14.15, 17.30

0   km   3

the coastal strip. On a crest above the town are the remains of a Venetian kastro. Severely damaged by the earthquake, it is no longer a major attraction, though the views over the town are impressive.

Zakinthos offers an enjoyable combination of a fertile plain running the length of the island's east side, and a mountainous western half, made more accessible via regular coach excursions. Tourist activity is spread along the southern bay and the east coast (popular with cyclists) either side of Zakinthos Town itself. To the

north it is centred on the resortified villages of **Planos/Tsilivi** and more attractive **Alikanas**, to the south at **Argassi**. Argassi aside, the southern peninsula is arguably the prettiest part of the island — offering a succession of cove beaches backed by a wooded interior that climbs to the summit of Mt. Skopos that rises up between **Kalamaki** and Argassi. The low peak is adorned with the scant remains of a temple of Artemis. Marring all this, on the south coast lies the truly awful disco and beach resort of **Laganas**. Now the second largest settlement after Zakinthos Town, its main arteries resemble a giant 'T'; the upper stroke running along the beach, with an over-long hotel and restaurant alley running inland.

The island bus service is good; serving all the major tourist areas as well as running twice daily to all the other villages on the map opposite — with the notable exception of the northern hamlet of **Skinari** from whence the ferry to Kefalonia departs. Zakinthos Town is also the starting point for popular tour boats and a catamaran (book in advance) service to sights on the scenic north of the island. With fares from around 4,000 GDR for a typical day tour around Zakinthos, this is one instance when forking out for an excursion is worth it.

🛏

The absence of large numbers of backpackers has limited the number of rooms on offer in the town. Hotels there are in profusion on the island. Most, however, are pre-booked solid by package tour operators. **Zakinthos Town** has the bulk of hotels likely to have empty beds. At the top end of the range is the waterfront B-class *Xenia* (☎ 22232), with the pricey new C-class *Palatino* (☎ 27780) 100 m behind. Nearby lies the *Diana* (☎ 28547). Cheaper options are the *Apollon* (☎ 22838) and *Aegli* (☎ 28317). Budget options are the D-class *Ionian* (☎ 22511) north of the Post Office and the *Omonia* (☎ 22113) in the southern suburbs.

▲

The nearest to Zakinthos Town is the good *Camping Zante* (☎ 24754) — a member of the *Sunshine Camping Club* scheme — at Tsilivi Beach (reached via regular bus from the bus station). Further up the coast is *Camping Paradise* (☎ 61888), near the village of Meso-Gerakari and Drosia Beach. Laganas Bay is also home to a couple of sites: *Camping Laganas* (☎ 51585) in an olive grove 1 km west of the end of the town beach is one of the worst sites in Greece. Further west lies the better *Tartarouga Camping* (☎ 51417), a quiet site down the road from the village of Lithakia.

👓

All over Greece you will find postcards of a rusty wreck of a cargo-ship set in a crescent beach of golden sand backed by towering cliffs: a catamaran (the C/M *Love Boat* — Sic)

runs daily to **Smuggler's Cove** (for such is its name) as well as the **Blue Caves** on the northern tip of the island—generally reckoned to be among the best sea caves in Greece.

Coach tours are popular as they enable tourists to take in the island sights without recourse to the main bus routes that tend to head direct to the their destination. Most tours include a mountain monastery, cliff-edge sunset views and the salt-pans on the beach north of Alikanas (known as Alikes beach).

Laganas Bay (also known as **Turtle Bay**) offers you a sight of the unacceptable face of package tourism. Blessed with a number of gently shelving beaches of a particularly fine sand, it has been the nesting area for some 80% of the Mediterranean's population of the shy **Loggerhead Turtle** for thousands of years, only to find a disco-city tourist resort of the tackiest kind (**Laganas**) develop on the main beach. Unfortunately the tourist and turtle nesting seasons are the same, with dire consequences for the turtles. Coming ashore at night they lay eggs in the sand a mere 50 cm below the surface (when they can find a spot where the sand hasn't been packed hard by tourists). These hatch (assuming they haven't had a sun-umbrella pole rammed through the nest) at night, some eight weeks later, and the baby turtles then crawl towards the nearest bright light (in years past this was the moonlit sea: these days it is more likely to be the nearest disco). Meantime the female turtles, in between laying batches of eggs (or jettisoning them at sea rather than approach a neon-lit shore), bask in the bay; only to be regularly run down and killed, or lose limbs to the tour boats' propellers. Be warned: the 'guaranteed' turtle spotting tours are a cynical rip-off. At best you will be looking at a plastic look-a-like that — according to one newspaper report — are so life-like that 'even aficionados have been fooled'; at worst you will be disturbing a very shy reptile at a very vulnerable time. The situation is so bad that the World Wildlife Fund and Greenpeace have called for the entire bay to be declared a marine national park. Some locals disagree: the stringent zoning laws aimed at protecting the beaches are regularly flouted, while boat operators engage in sporadic beach punch-ups with outraged conservationists. All in all you will do better to avoid Laganas; there are plenty of good beaches on the east coast and less environmentally destructive nightlife elsewhere.

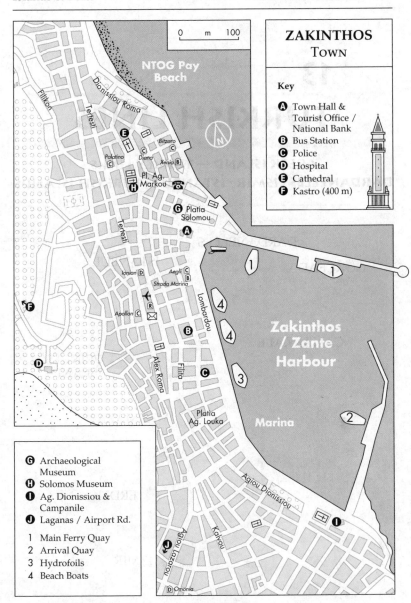

0 m 100

NTOG Pay
Beach

ZAKINTHOS
TOWN

Key

A Town Hall &
Tourist Office /
National Bank
B Bus Station
C Police
D Hospital
E Cathedral
F Kastro (400 m)

Filikon

Dionissiou Roma

Terfesif

E

Bitzaro

C

Palatina

Diana

C

C

Xenia

B

Pl. Ag.
Markou

H

G Platia
Solomou

A

Terfesti

Ionian **D**

Aegli **C**

B

Strada Marina

R

Apallon **C**

F

Lombardou

B

Alex Roma

Filita

C

Platia
Ag. Louka

D

Zakinthos
/ Zante
Harbour

1

1

4

4

3

2

Marina

Agiou Dionissiou

Agiou Lazarou

Koivou

I

J

D Omonia

G Archaeological
Museum
H Solomos Museum
I Ag. Dionissiou &
Campanile
J Laganas / Airport Rd.

1 Main Ferry Quay
2 Arrival Quay
3 Hydrofoils
4 Beach Boats

13
TURKISH LINES

GREEK ISLAND — TURKEY LINKS
DARDANELLES · İSMİR · İSTANBUL · TURKISH ISLANDS

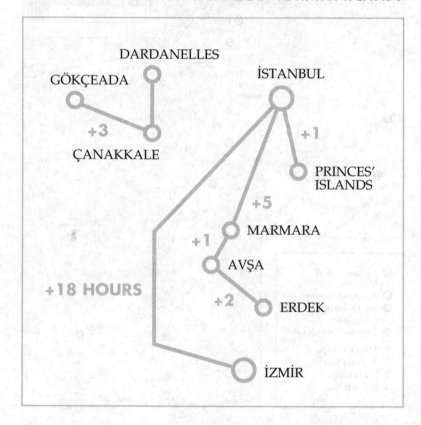

General Features

Given its size, Turkey is endowed with a remarkably poor ferry system. This is a historical accident born out of modern Turkey's failure to retain any of the large Aegean islands (apart from those guarding the entrance to the Dardanelles) once controlled by the Ottoman empire. As a result, ferries on the Turkish Aegean seaboard are — with the odd exception — confined to small international boats providing day trip excursions to adjacent Greek islands: the on-going political tension between Greece and Turkey preventing the emergence of more substantial links. Such islands where Turkey has sovereignty are tiny affairs that serve only to encourage local taxi boats bringing day-trippers from nearby resorts, rather than acting as the necessary catalyst for the emergence of a ferry system. South of the Dardanelles, Turkey is the land of the local bus rather than the ferry. This absence of anything that could remotely be called an Aegean ferry system means that hopping in Turkish waters is, for most tourists, usually a day trip option while following a Greek domestic route.

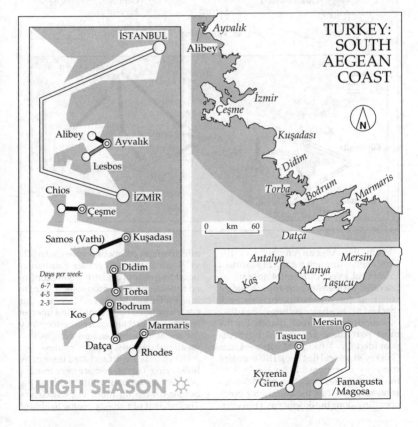

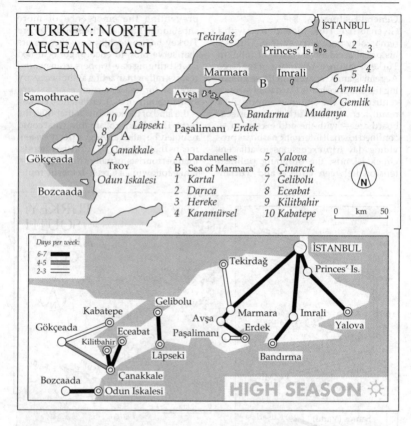

TURKEY: NORTH AEGEAN COAST

A	Dardanelles	5	Yalova
B	Sea of Marmara	6	Çınarcık
1	Kartal	7	Gelibolu
2	Darıca	8	Eceabat
3	Hereke	9	Kilitbahir
4	Karamürsel	10	Kabatepe

Days per week:
6-7
4-5
2-3

HIGH SEASON

From the Aegean entrance of the Dardanelles through the Sea of Marmara to İstanbul, a very different state of affairs prevails, with something approaching a coherent ferry network in existence (backed up by short bus hops), courtesy of some dozen ex-'Greek' islands. For the most part these are served by boats provided by Turkish Maritime Lines (Turkey's national flag line). This excellent company is responsible for the bulk of the Dardanelles and Sea of Marmara services as well as the commuter boats operating along the Bosphorus. However,

effective ferry competition does not really exist since the only other companies operating out of Turkish ports are confined to routes and ships too insignificant to interest Turkish Maritime. Moreover, this company often has a controlling interest in Turkish ports and charges a steep levy for use which discourages competition on all but the most popular routes.

The islands are little visited (except by holidaying Turks), and are very much a product of the messy aftermath of the border drawn up following the Greco-Turkish war of 1920–23. Home to almost exclusively ethnic Greek populations, the inhabitants found themselves on the 'wrong' side of the border, and though largely exempted from the forced population exchanges that occurred between the World Wars, most have subsequently left for Greece (thanks in part to cultural intimidation — something ethnic Turks 'stranded' in Greece also encountered). Home to new Turkish populations, they all have something of a 'someone's-sleeping-in-my-bed' air; with churches either abandoned or converted into mosques and the old Greek place names replaced with suitably Turkish successors.

From the Greek perspective these are very much the 'unlucky Greek islands' — all 13 of them — and reflect the fact that the modern border between Greece and Turkey is historically and archaeologically a very artificial one; something akin to a cultural Berlin Wall enhanced by enforced population exchanges. For most of history the power that reigned supreme on one side of the Aegean also held sway on the other. The Turkish Aegean seaboard is thus littered with cities that to the ancients were as 'Greek' as Athens or Corinth are today. Ironically, the archaeological remains tend to be better preserved than their Western Aegean counterparts, for deforestation of the mountains of Asia Minor caused extensive silting up of harbours on the Eastern Aegean seaboard leading to these cities being abandoned by the end of Roman rule, while prominent Greek cities elsewhere remained inhabited and grew into the built-over population centres of today. Hopping across to Turkey for a day for a spot of ancient 'Greek' city sightseeing combined with a Turkish coffee, and — it has to be said — a good whiff of the Orient besides, has thus become a popular feature of Greek island-hopping holidays.

In the past the omnipresent threat of hostilities between Turkey and Greece — that reached its peak with the 1974 Turkish invasion of Cyprus after a military

Cypriot regime sought union with Greece — has severely limited, and for a time curtailed, ferry links. This uncomfortable situation has eased in recent years, but a number of reciprocal measures enforced after the Cyprus invasion have had a impact on Greek island—Turkey services. Decrees that passengers could only travel to the other country on the ship of the country they were departing from (producing two fleets at every crossing point) are no longer enforced (though the competing fleets remain). A second charter-flight ticket issuing requirement that tourists who have entered Greece cannot spend a night in Turkey without losing their right to use the return half of their ticket is more serious and *remains in force*.

Fares
Turkey offers very good value for money, with the general cost of living about 25% cheaper than Greece. However, even small boats running between the islands and Turkey attract international port taxes and these are kept high by a Greek government intent on discouraging 'their' tourists from visiting the old enemy (day trips to Turkish coast towns are usually around the UK£ 20 / US$ 35 level).

Language
Modern Turkish is not the easiest of tongues to grapple with. Along the coast tourists can happily get by with a mix of English and German, but place names are often a bit of a mouthful. If you are planning to do more than a day trip or hop to Istanbul you should bring a language guide with you. Otherwise you can just about get by pronouncing:

Turkish	English
C	J
Ç	Ch
I	U
İ	E
J	S
Ö	Eu
Ş	Sh

Example Itineraries

Turkey has justly become a popular Greek-island-hopping day-excursion destination. If you find yourself on one of those islands offering excursions you should hop across; the contrast in culture and atmosphere is an experience well worth the cost of tickets. If you are on something longer than a two-week charter flight return ticket, then Turkey offers some interesting island hopping possibilities too.

Arrival/Departure Point

The lack of anything other than local boats making the crossing to Turkey means that the islands of the Dodecanese and Eastern Aegean are the best starting points. Rhodes, Kos and Samos all have frequent charter flights.

A: Day Trips to Turkey

Day trips operate from Rhodes to Marmaris, Kos to Bodrum, Samos to Kuşadası, Chios to Çeşme and Lesbos to Ayvalık. Fares tend to be broadly similar regardless of which crossing you use and reflect the fact that most of the 'ferries' are expensive day-tripper boats. You are usually left to your own devices in Turkey, but you can travel from Samos as part of a tour if so minded. Greek craft from Kos and Rhodes tend to be excursion boats, while their Turkish counterparts are closer to ferries. This distinction can become quite important, for if you travel by ferry you will be deemed an independent traveller and your passport will be stamped on entering and leaving the country. Travellers on excursion boats, because they have a return ticket, are issued with a landing pass while passports (unstamped) are held by passport control. Ferries also have well-advertised return times. Excursion boats don't — so be careful to establish when excursion boats depart for home; they do NOT wait for late passengers. Miss the boat and you'll have to stay overnight; thereby jeopardising your right to your charter

flight home. Finally, it is all but impossible to change Greek currency in Turkish banks or vice versa. Have another currency on you if you want to change cash. Traveller's cheques are no problem. If you do return from a day trip armed with wads of Turkish bank notes the best way of changing them is to offer them to day-trippers boarding the next day's boat.

B: Turkish Excursion [10 Days]

Those with time to hand will find that a trip to Troy and Constantinople (both dear to Greek hearts) is easily achieved:

■ Lesbos

The closest crossing point to Troy, Lesbos offers regular ferries to Ayvalık. Crossing points further south are also practicable options if you don't mind changing buses up the Turkish coast.

■ Ayvalık [1 Day]

Worth a day's exploration; with nearby Alibey to visit. Thereafter you can get a bus on to Çanakkale.

■ Çanakkale [3 Days]

Easily the best base for exploring the region, with plenty of accommodation and easy access to Troy and the battlefields of Gallipoli. Each offers a day of leisurely tourism, before heading on to Bandırma by bus.

■ ■ Bandırma / Princes' Is. [1 Day]

From Bandırma you have several options. You can either take a regular ferry to İstanbul or break the journey with a visit to the Princes' Islands or travel via Erdek and Avşa.

■ İstanbul [3 Days]

Three days gives you time to do the sights and hop up the Bosphorus. Thereafter you can consider the options for returning to Greece.

Return [2 Days]

Most direct route out of High Season is the weekly ferry from İstanbul to Piraeus. Otherwise the fastest return is via ferry to İzmir (though you can always return via ferry to Bandırma and then an İzmir train) and then bus to Çeşme and ferry to Chios.

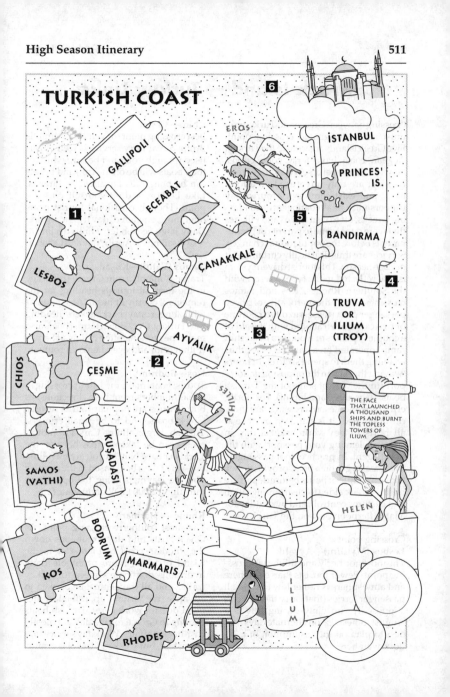

Greek Island — Turkey Links

Crossing between Greece and Turkey you must use a designated crossing point. Five Greek islands adjacent to the Turkish Aegean coast have ferry connections. However, the level of service varies greatly. Most are only advertised on a local basis, and exist courtesy of tourist day trippers and a small contingent of holidaying Greeks, off to visit towns and villages that were once home to parents or grandparents before the population exchanges. Services are thus drastically curtailed out of High Season. This tourist driven system is also reflected in the type of ferry, with the southern Rhodes, Kos and Samos crossings largely the prerogative of pricey passenger craft (these can often take one or two cars driven aboard with the aid of a couple of planks of wood as a makeshift ramp) operated on a day trip basis; thus enabling them to spend six to eight hours 'waving the flag' in the opposing nation's port (in the case of some of the Turkish boats: flags, large and lots of). The northern Chios and Lesbos crossings are more car orientated. It is standard practice at all ports to buy your ticket a day in advance, leaving your passport with the ticket agent. In practice, foot passengers can usually get on a boat, provided they arrive a couple of hours before departure on the Greek side (to clear immigration and customs control); and by midday for a late afternoon boat on the Turkish.

Crossing points:
Lesbos (Mytilini)—Ayvalık
The most northerly and utilitarian crossing point. Fewer tourists than elsewhere and atmosphere is rather low key. Small passenger ferries (that carry the odd car) supposedly run daily during July and August, otherwise on alternate days. It is best to plan on the assumption of a 24-hour wait here.

Chios—Çeşme
Best crossing point for vehicles. Miniotis Brothers' car ferry service is well advertised (though you can't be sure which of their boats will be on the run) and tickets can be bought as far afield as Piraeus. Like Lesbos, a do-it-yourself crossing point. Though occasional tourist boats offer more 'sheltered' day trips at a price. Daily High Season ferry links decline to ① ③ ⑤ sailings in April/May and October.

Samos (Vathi)—Kuşadası
Traffic is mainly from Greece to Turkey in the form of tourists heading for the remains of nearby Ephesus. Also popular with longer stay backpackers heading into Turkey. Occasional tourist boats also make the crossing often calling at Samos (Pithagorio) and even Leros en route.

Kos—Bodrum
Tourist boats make the 1-hour crossing in equal numbers from both directions, as both centres are popular tourist resorts. Greek boats tend to be small cruisers, Turkish, larger affairs. Cars and motorcycles can be taken across here on the Turkish boats. Note: if you are travelling one-way take a boat based in the country you are leaving: taking the opposition puts up to 2,000 GDR on to your fare.

Rhodes—Marmaris
The most southerly crossing point. As Greek boats find day excursions down the Rhodian coast to Lindos or to the island of Symi, more profitable daily hydrofoils dominate Greece to Turkey traffic, and all travel must be booked in advance (the turning up at the last moment doesn't work here). Turkish boats coming to Greece for the day are mostly rust-bucket affairs. Weekday services are consistent, but weekend travel is erratic.

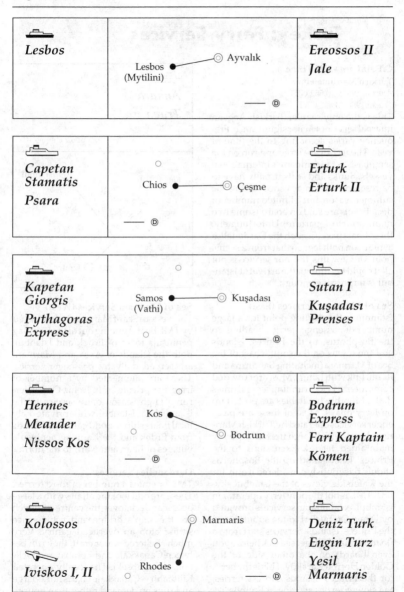

Lesbos

Lesbos (Mytilini) ● —— ◎ Ayvalık

—— Ⓓ

Ereossos II
Jale

Capetan Stamatis
Psara

○

Chios ● —— ◎ Çeşme

—— Ⓓ

Erturk
Erturk II

Kapetan Giorgis
Pythagoras Express

○

Samos (Vathi) ● —— ◎ Kuşadası

○   —— Ⓓ

Sutan I
Kuşadası
Prenses

Hermes
Meander
Nissos Kos

○

Kos ●
○   ◎ Bodrum
—— Ⓓ

Bodrum Express
Fari Kaptain
Kömen

Kolossos

Iviskos I, II

◎ Marmaris
○   ○
Rhodes ●
○   —— Ⓓ

Deniz Turk
Engin Turz
Yesil Marmaris

Turkey: Ferry Services

C/F *Ankara* - C/F *Truva*
Turkish Maritime Lines
Ankara; 1983; 10,552 GRT
Truva; 1966; 3,422 GRT
This is the only regular Turkish Aegean internal service of major significance. Frequency varies according to the time of year. The ferries are large and run on the same basis as the company's international vessels. Bunks and seats usually have to be reserved well in advance during the summer season, but a limited number of deck tickets are sold on board (some two hours prior to departure). Unfortunately, these boats pass through the Dardanelles at night on both legs so that from a scenic point of view this 18-hour service is not all it could be; though the arrival at İstanbul is impressive enough.

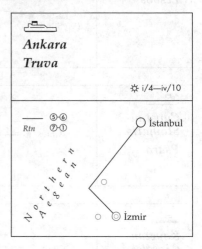

Sea of Marmara Services (East)
İstanbul is the starting point for a large number of passenger ferries heading up the Bosphorus, to the Princes' Islands and the towns on the south coast of the Sea of Marmara (including Bandırma and its rail link with İzmir). Most are crowded commuter services running several times daily. Monthly timetables are posted up on ferry quays. Most of these are passenger services operated by Turkish Maritime Lines with a large fleet of superbly maintained ferries. Excursions to the Princes' Islands and up the Bosphorus should be seriously considered if only for the waterside views of the İstanbul skyline. TML is not the only ferry operator in İstanbul. A catamaran service is provided by Deniz Otobüsleri to the suburbs and the Princes' Islands. Services start from a floating quay (you get sea sick before you even board) on the other side of the Golden Horn at Karaköy. This is the berth for the Princes' Islands express ferries; the slower ferries starting at Eminönü.

Sea of Marmara Services (West)
The western Sea of Marmara is dominated by TML boats running out of the Kapıdağ peninsula town of Erdek and İstanbul. Both the islands of Avşa and Marmara are served daily by passenger ferries. These are augmented by a number of irregular private craft: Deniz Otobüsleri run a High Season daily service to the islands from İstanbul, while private daily local boats ship the odd car to the islands from Erdek and the Kapıdağ peninsula villages of Ilhan and Narli to the north.

Dardanelles Services
TML operates a number of ro-ro ferries. These are odd looking affairs with a large open car deck, over the centre of which are the ship's bridge and cabin-space sitting atop an overhead gantry. Very much sheltered water craft, they run between Çanakkale and Eceabat and Gelibolu and Lâpseki. The locally operated Kilitbahir—Çanakkale boat is not as large and runs on demand rather than hourly.

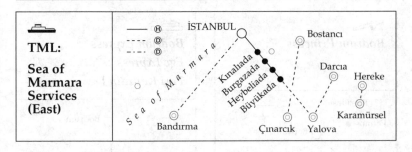

TML:

Sea of Marmara Services (East)

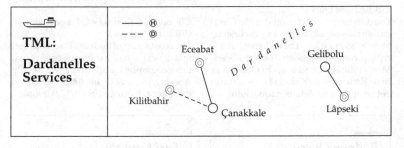

TML:

Sea of Marmara Services (West)

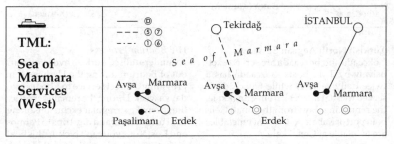

TML:

Dardanelles Services

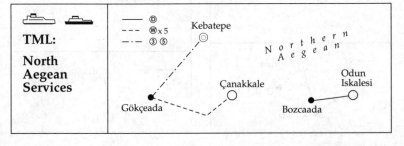

TML:

North Aegean Services

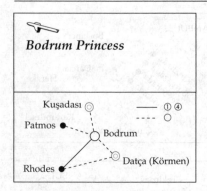

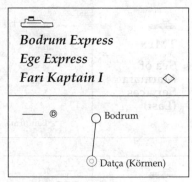

Turkish North Aegean Services

Gökçeada and Bozcaada are served exclusively by TML boats. Bozcaada has a twice daily service, while Gökçeada is served five days a week from Çanakkale; the remaining days from the small Gelibolu port of Kabatepe. Current timetables are available at Çanakkale.

T/B *Bodrum Queen*

Bodrum harbour is cluttered with wooden tourist boats offering pricey excursions to the adjacent islets. The *Bodrum Queen* is typical, running to assorted offshore islets. Most common are sailings to **Otok Is.** or two-island trips to **Korada Is.** (beach and hot springs) and **Ada Is.** (aquarium).

H/F *Bodrum Princess*

An under-utilised Turkish hydrofoil runs out of Bodrum during the High Season, providing a direct service to Rhodes two days a week. During the remainder of her life she makes irregular excursions along the Turkish coast and day trips to Patmos and Kos. Note: you can't pick up this boat except at her starting point (i.e. Bodrum).

C/F *Bodrum Express* - C/F *Ege Express* - C/F *Fari Kaptain I*

The coast south of Bodrum is so indented that several small car ferries profit from this geography by offering a twice-daily crossing from Bodrum (09.00, 17.00) to the quay at **Körmen** (09.00, 17.00) some 7

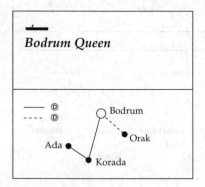

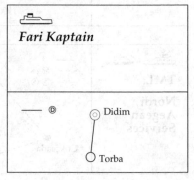

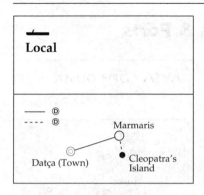

km north of Datça (bus service into town included in the price of the ferry ticket). A second summer service operates twice daily (09.00, 17.00) between Torba (again, ferry-ticket buses depart from Bodrum) to Didim (alias Didyma) to the north; home to a major temple of Apollo.

Marmaris Taxi Boats

Daily taxi boats run from Marmaris along the coast of the Datça peninsula to the town of Datça (some even continuing on to the ancient city of Knidos). In doing so they open up the possibility of doing a loop running Rhodes—Marmaris—Datça—Bodrum—Kos—Rhodes.

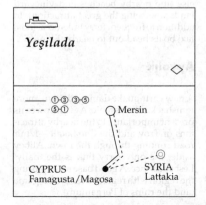

Turkey—North Cyprus Services: Mersin—Famagusta

Occupied northern Cyprus is served by boats out of two Turkish south coast ports. From the Turkish perspective these are full blown international services. However, as Turkey is the only country which recognises the legitimacy of the so-called Turkish Republic of Northern Cyprus, these ferry links are de facto internal Turkish services. Mersin (ancient Tarsus) — a large noisy seaport with nothing to recommend it beyond the ferry link — is the best of the Turkish ports with the thrice-weekly Turkish Maritime Lines' elderly C/F *Yeşilada* operating to the war-ruined derelict resort of Famagusta (now Turkish **Magosa**). Weekend sailing continues on to Syria (Lattakia).

Taşucu—Kyrenia

Slightly closer to the Aegean is the resort town of Silifke and its port Taşucu. Again there is nothing of any interest in the place except the means of leaving it. Small ferries (*Liberty* and *Ertürk*) and hydrofoils make the 7- and 3½-hour crossings respectively to the once attractive port of Kyrenia (now **Girne**) daily in High Season, three times weekly during the rest of the year (though days and times are never very consistent).

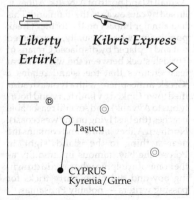

Turkish Islands & Ports

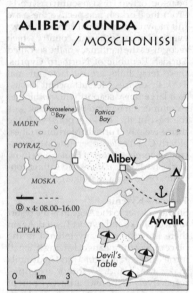

ALIBEY / CUNDA / MOSCHONISSI

Poroselene Bay — *Patrica Bay* — MADEN — POYRAZ — **Alibey** — MOSKA — Ⓓ x 4: 08.00–16.00 — CIPLAK — **Ayvalık** — *Devil's Table* — 0 km 3

AVŞA / OPHIOUSSA

EKİNLİK ADASI — Ekinlik — **Türkeli** — Yiğitier — No bus service — O Irreg. Service — 0 km 3

Alibey / Cunda
ΜΟΣΧΟΝΙΣΣΙ

A small island north of Ayvalık, Alibey is linked by causeway to the mainland. This had a major impact on the former Greek population, who unusually, were forced out and replaced by displaced Cretans of Turkish stock between the wars. This at least ensures that the island retains a 'Greek' atmosphere, with a typical resort-ified town (linked by both ferry and hourly bus to Ayvalık), and several reasonable beaches (the best lying on the west coast). Northern Alibey is quiet and contains the nearest thing to the island 'sight' in Poroselene bay: famous in antiquity as the home of a dolphin who saved a drowning boy and did other party tricks for passing writers — notably Pausanias.

Avşa
ΟΦΙΟΥΣΣΑ

The most popular central Sea of Marmara island, Avşa has emerged in recent years as the getaway destination for the better off in İstanbul and its environs. The only town is a mass of hotels and not much else (the nearby beaches and vineyard landscape being the great attraction). In addition to frequent ferry links occasional taxi boats head out to nearby Ekinlik.

Ayvalık

A new earthquake damaged town, more ramshackle than scenic, Ayvalık owes its present importance to the nearby attractions of Troy and the Çanakkale—İzmir road running through the town. Alibey aside, the only ferry link is the 'daily' Lesbos service. A good base for exploring the region with regular buses to Bergama (and the ruins of Pergamum).

Bandırma

The main city on the Sea of Marmara south coast, Bandırma is a major transportation hub, with regular buses to all the major Aegean and Marmarian towns, an important rail link to İzmir, and regular ferries to İstanbul. Home to both cement and sulphuric acid factories, the city is not likely to be in many visitor's lists of Turkish trip highlights, but is tolerable enough if you are just passing through.

Bodrum
ΑΛΙΚΑΡΝΑΣΣΟΣ

A resort town built on the ancient city of Halicarnassus opposite the island of Kos. These days it is the large, intact crusader castle of St. Peter along with the ruins of the original Mausoleum that are the main attractions, but the mosque and bazaar-filled town is one of the prettiest in the Aegean (the quayside girl selling drinks from inside a large plastic orange aside) and worth a day's visit in its own right. In addition to the daily half-dozen boats that head for Kos or the Datça peninsula, boats also head for beaches and islands nearby. These should be avoided by day trippers because they don't return before Kos boats return.

Bozcaada
ΤΕΝΕΔΟΣ

A small Aegean island a few kilometres south-west of Troy, Bozcaada was known for over two millennia by the name recorded by Homer: Tenedos. Closed to tourists until the late 80s for military reasons (check with the tourist office in Çanakkale for the latest information regarding the need for possible visitor's permits), the island is one of the least spoilt and most attractive around. The only town lies on the north-east corner and is dominated by a well-preserved

BOZCAADA / TENEDOS

No bus service
No beach boat service
Genoese Castle
Bozcaada
230 m
Agiana
Habbelle
Sullubahçe
Tuzburnu
Agazma
Siege of Troy 1250 BC ?
0   km   4

Genoese castle the equal of any in the Aegean. It lies on the site of Justinian's warehouses; for the island was used as a granary storage base in the Byzantine era. South of the town the shoreline is fringed by a succession of sand beaches; the best on the south coast proper, and it was to here that the Greek fleet retreated out of sight when they left the wooden horse outside the gates of Troy. The island economy depends on viticulture; mass tourism has yet to discover the delights of the — still very Greek — cobbled town, with its restaurant-fronted waterfront and dusty hotels in the streets behind.

Çanakkale

The largest port and best stopping point on the Dardanelles (known to the Greeks as the Hellespont), Çanakkale is a pretty town offering plenty to do thanks to the combination of a well-preserved castle (home to a naval museum), a well-stocked archaeological museum, the Dardanelles ferry link, and the half-hourly buses from the town centre to Truva (the modern name for ancient Troy). The centre of town boasts a conspicuous clock tower, and in close proximity to this landmark you will find all the essentials — including the city tourist office. Nearby tour operators offer day packages to both Troy and the Galli-poli battlefields across the Dardanelles (tours to this latter destination are the best way to visit given the absence of a good peninsula bus service).

Çeşme

A quaint little town with a pretty castle and interesting waterfront. Out on a limb at the end of the İzmir peninsula, it has become the main port for large international ferries along with the regular Chios boats — the pull of İzmir (a 90-minute bus ride away) being great. An appealing place to spend one's time with plenty of accommodation and camping to hand.

Datça

Deftly placed on one of the most attractive stretches of the Turkish coast, this quiet town and surrounding green pine forest and turquoise bay-lined Datça peninsula, is the real reason to hop from Rhodes to Marmaris. Taxi boats (and hourly buses) to Datça from there. The town has plenty of rooms, a campsite and is the jumping-off point (via tour boat or taxi) for Knidos 34 km away on the tip of the peninsula. A major city in classical times, it was home to the masterpiece of the sculptor Praxiteles — a (lost) statue of Aphrodite.

Eceabat

Main destination for Çanakkale ferries crossing to the Gelibolu peninsula. Not much here beyond the ferry terminal itself: Kilitbahir being the traditional landing point adjacent to Çanakkale.

Erdek

An attractive (courtesy of a lack of modern building) town on the Kapidağ peninsula, Erdek is the main jumping-off point for the Sea of Marmara islands. The town has all the necessary tourist facilities (behind the tree- and restaurant-lined waterfront). Dolmuş taxis run frequently to nearby Bandirma, with its bus links to Çanakkale and other major centres.

Gelibolu

Known to most by its former name of Gallipoli, Gelibolu is the major port on the European side of the Dardanelles, giving its name to the whole peninsula (and of course, the disastrous WW1 Gallipoli campaign in which the allies fought the Turks). Ferries dock on the outer quay, behind which lie two inner harbours bisected by a bridge. Pretty enough in a quiet sort of way, the town is home to a castle and also boasts a quayside statue of its most famous son, Piri Reis, a 16 c. cartographer and navigator. Hourly buses to İstanbul make Gelibolu more accessible than ferry links would suggest.

Gökçeada
ΙΜΡΟΣ; 597 km².

The only large Aegean island in Turkish hands, Gökçeada is still widely known by its former Greek name of Imbros (or Imroz). Heavily fortified thanks to its strategic position at the entrance of the Dardanelles, tourist access was prohibited until the late 80s when visitors with permits were admitted (information regarding any current requirements can be obtained from the tourist office in Çanakkale). Red tape has relaxed further since, but the number of tourists remains very small. Visits to Gökçeada remain the preserve of the dedicated island hopper intent on 'doing' every Greek or Aegean

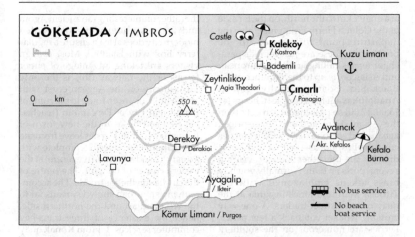

GÖKÇEADA / IMBROS

0 km 6

Castle
Kaleköy / Kastron
Bademli
Kuzu Limanı
Zeytinlikoy / Agia Theodori
Çınarlı / Panagia
550 m
Dereköy / Derakioi
Aydıncık / Akr. Kefalos
Kefalo Burno
Lavunya
Ayagalip / Ikteir
Kömur Limanı / Purgos

No bus service
No beach boat service

island rather than the casual tourist. Green and very hilly, there is little disguising that of all the Turkish islands, this one more than any other feels — thanks to the heavy military presence — like an occupied island. Although exempted from the 1920s population exchanges, the exclusively Greek inhabitants have been driven out over the last 30 years — unsung casualties of the Cyprus conflict. In the absence of a bus service, tourism is confined to the former chora (now Çinarli), and the town of Kaleköy — home to the island's best beach and an impressive castle. Both are linked by dolmuş taxi to the port at Kazu Limanı.

Imrali
ΚΑΛΟΛΙΜΝΟ

The former Greek island of Kalolimno, Imrali is very much the unlucky 13th of the inhabited Turkish islands. Home to a high security prison (from where the 'hero' of the film *Midnight Express* swam to freedom), the island is a latter-day Alcatraz. Ferries running from İstanbul to Gemlik do call; but unless you are dressed as a warder or have done a murder you won't be allowed to disembark.

İstanbul
ΚΩΝΣΤΑΝΤΙΝΟΥΠΟΛΗ / ΒΥΖΑΝΤΙΟ

Still one of the great cities of the world, İstanbul is well worth almost any amount of effort involved in getting there. The combination of the Topkapı Palace (home to the Sultans and their harems and one of the greatest displays of crown jewels), the Agia Sophia (the great cathedral church of the Byzantine Empire), the beautiful Blue Mosque, the ancient Hippodrome and City Walls, and the bustle of the Grand Bazaar is hard to beat. The city owes so much to the sea and boasts a skyline so atmospheric that arrival by boat easily remains the most attractive way to approach. This can be done either by taking the ferry from İzmir or one of the boats operating between İstanbul and the islands and ports on the southern shore of the Sea of Marmara. İstanbul's principal port is located at Eminönü adjacent to the Galata bridge over the Golden Horn. All large ferries depart from here (a convenient quay as it backs on to the old part of the city that is home to all the major sights and the bulk of the budget accommodation). However, the İzmir ferry often lands its passengers at a quay 2 km to the north, on the far side of the Golden Horn. Eminönü is also the departure point for cruises up the Bosphorus. These are just regular passenger ferries calling at all the European and Asian ports up to the entrance of the Black Sea. Boats normally stop at **Anadolukavağı** for a couple of hours (♦♦ 15.00, 17.00) so passengers can get off on the Asian shore and buy over-priced kebabs and seafood dishes. Other ferries cross the Bosphorus — either to the port directly on the other side or visiting several ports on both. Normally you buy brass tokens emblazoned with the Turkish Maritime Lines insignia at the quay or from street traders. A one-way crossing will set you back a few pence. Ferries are numerous on the southern crossings. Timetables can be found on quaysides (European ports shown in black; Asian in red).

⊨

Most budget accommodations are in the Old City in the small streets backing on to Agia Sophia and the Blue Mosque. The total of five youth hostels includes one IYHF hostel at 6 Caferige Cad. The helpful City Tourist Office is at 31. Divan Yolo on the old Hippodrome and can advise on accommodation as well as offer plenty of blurb on the major sights.

A

Noisy short-stay site at *Londra Mocamp* near the city airport.

İzmir
ΣΜΥΡΝΑ

The largest city on the Turkish Aegean coast İzmir (formerly the Greek Smyrna) is now a major metropolis. Sadly, little architecture of character remains in what is now one of the ugliest cities (not many Aegean towns are lumbered with a 'Park of Culture') in one of the Mediterranean's most attractive bays: the Gulf of İzmir. The bulk of the old town was burnt down with the collapse of the abortive Greek attempt to take the coast of Asia minor between 1919–22. The sheer size of the rather uninteresting (an ancient Agora and Fortress aside) wide-boulevarded modern city does at least ensure a regular ferry link with İstanbul. Most foreign visitors are taking advantage of either ferries or the railway (this is the only Turkish city on the Aegean coast with such a link), or are en route to the ruins of the ancient city of Pergamum (reached via frequent buses to the new town of Bergama). İstanbul ferries leave from the international ferry berth (complete with a dusty locked-up duty-free centre) at the eastern corner of the gulf. The centre of the city lies on the south side. The accompanying suburban sprawl spreads far to the west and around the northern side, hence the existence of three trans-bay commuter services: 1. From **Konak** quay (west of city centre) to **Urla** (south side of the gulf midway between İzmir and Çeşme). 2. From Konak quay to **Karşıyaka** (on the north of the gulf). 3. From **Pasaport** quay (centre of the city seafront) to **Alsancak** (200 m west of the International Ferry dock).

⊨

Finding a bed for the night in İzmir is rarely a problem. Cheap pensions and hotels are densest around the railway station. The city bus station also houses a helpful tourist office.

A

Nearest sites are at Çeşme. The village has several sites: notably *Fener Mocamp* on the promontory north of the harbour.

Kabatepe

A small town on the west side of the Gelibolu peninsula, Kabatepe has an infrequent ferry link with Gökçeada, an excellent beach backed by a museum dedicated to the 1915–16 Gallipoli campaign. Local taxis run to nearby ANZAC cove and the many cemeteries that house the 200,000 dead. Local public transport is relatively poor over the whole peninsula: buses or dolmuş taxis from Eceabat are the best means of getting to the town.

Kilitbahir

The narrowest crossing point on the Dardanelles runs between Kilitbahir and Çanakkale (1300 m) — hence the minor ferry link. Worth a visit thanks to the castle, built by Mehmet the Conqueror in 1452, that gives substance to the town's name, which means 'Key to the sea'.

Kuşadası

A rapidly growing tourist resort midway down Turkey's Aegean coast, Kuşadası is named 'Pigeon Island'—after a fortified islet linked to the town via a causeway. It draws the hordes thanks to its role as the jumping-off point to the nearby ruins of Ephesus, the best preserved of ancient Greek cities. Its appeal is such that a stream of cruise ships call, upping prices to Greek levels. The port used to figure more prominently on ferry schedules until the last couple of years.

⊢

Plentiful supply of rooms via ticket agencies.

Λ

Camping Önder: 2 km north of the town.

Lâpseki

A small port that owes its existence to adjacent Gelibolu on the opposite side of the Dardanelles, Lâpseki is very much of an overspill town, relying on the ferry link between the two.

Marmara

The largest island in the Sea of Marmara, and from which it takes its medieval name, Marmara is a mountainous, and rather inhospitable-looking place. The island was famous in the ancient world as one of the best sources of white marble: the whole northern half is composed of little else, leaving a wind-swept landscape with little vegetation and well scarred with three thousand years of quarrying. Southern Marmara has more going for it, with a fringe of pine trees and the best of the small population centres. Ferries stop at assorted points around the coast. Boats to Marmara town (home to two budget hotels and the island bank) often stop at Gundoğdu en route, and the former capital at Saraylar sees boats running north.

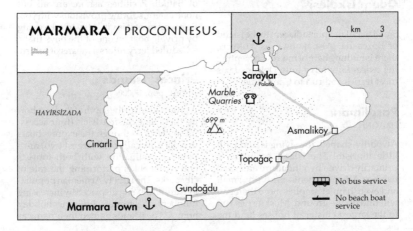

MARMARA / PROCONNESUS

⚓

0   km   3

Saraylar / Palatia

Marble Quarries ♔

HAYİRSİZADA

699 m ⛰

Asmaliköy □

Cinarli □

Topağaç □

🚌 No bus service

⛵ No beach boat service

Gundoğdu □

Marmara Town ⚓

Marmaris

The most southerly Turkey—Greece crossing point, Marmaris has grown from a small fishing village to one of Turkey's leading tourist resorts. The town ribbons along the coast at the head of an islet-littered bay against an attractive backdrop of mountains and pine trees, but lacking anything approaching a major 'sight', seeing is reduced to 'souking' up tourism with a Turkish flavour. There is enough going on to keep you happily occupied for a day but this is arguably the least interesting of Turkey's day-tripper ports. The ferries and hydrofoils to Rhodes are now the only regular services; though previous years have seen long-haul international ferries calling. Taxi boats run along the coast to Datça and to nearby **Cleopatra's Island** (sand imported from Egypt courtesy of one Marcus Antonius). Now sadly overrated and overcrowded.

Tourist Office opposite the ferry quay offers maps and a room-finding service.

Nearest site is *Camping Berch* west of the port.

Odum Iskalesi

Small mainland port adjacent to the island of Bozcaada. Also known as Yukyeri, there is nothing here of interest, excepting the twice-daily ferry link. Dolmuş taxis meet ferries and run to Çanakkale.

Paşalimanı
HAΛONI

An oddly-shaped, low-lying island with little tourism. The island economy is primarily driven by viticulture and shell fishing. All settlements are very small and even 'hamlet' implies more than you will find on the ground. Most ferries run to the largest cluster of houses (and the

PAŞALİMANI / HALONI

No bus service
No beach boat service

KOYUN ADASI

Poyrazlı
Paşalimanı
Harmanlı   170 m
Tuzla
Balikli

0   km   4

island mosque) at Paşalimanı, but you should be aware that boats (especially those operating out of the small village ports north of Erdek on the Kapıdağ Peninsula often prefer to dock at other points — notably the wooded settlement of Balikli. Facilities ashore are all but nonexistent, so bring provisions with you. Best way to visit is via a day trip; crossing by private boat on one of the days that a scheduled ferry offers a means of return.

Princes' Islands
10 km²; pop. 15,000.

A group 20 km to the south of the Bosphorus, these nine car-free islets (four accessible by ferry — though the express boats usually only call at the largest two) are a popular destination with both tourists and locals alike; performing the role of city parks. The largely Armenian populations are now being displaced by increasing numbers of jetsetters building holiday homes. The islands gained their name as places of exile for Byzantine nobles and then members of the Sultan's family. Sadly, these days harems are few on the ground — though one island was briefly used as a rabbit farm. **Büyük** is the largest of the islands, and its Greek title (Prinkipo) gave the name to the group. Today it has a plethora of restaurants, hotels, horses and carriages, and gardens. **Heybeli**, is a quieter version of the same, with a naval college and a Greek Orthodox school of Theology. The interiors of both are wooded, as is smaller **Burgaz**, the only other island to boast a reasonably sized settlement. Northerly **Kınalı** is home to one tiny hamlet, and along with **Sedef**, exists as a beach destination. The remaining islands are little more than rocks with only **Kaşik** readily accessible (via Heybeli beach boats). **Yassi** is now a prison and thus closed to tourists, while **Sivri** has an odd history as dumping ground for stray dogs rounded up from the streets of İstanbul, and **Tavsan** is uninhabited.

Tekirdağ

The only port of note on the northern Sea of Marmara coast, Tekirdağ is poorly connected with the rest of the Turkish ferry system, but offers good bus links with İstanbul. A growing resort town, outlying beaches are the main attraction.

Yalova

The destination of a number of İstanbul—Princes' Island ferries, Yalova is a commuter town on the southern Sea of Marmara coast. Yalova also has daily links with **Darıca** and **Kartal** on the adjacent coast, as does **Çınarcık**, which also sees occasional Princes' Island boats. These are best of the local services (the service between the towns of **Hereke** and **Karamürsel** being the other link) between equally uninspiring towns off the tourist map.

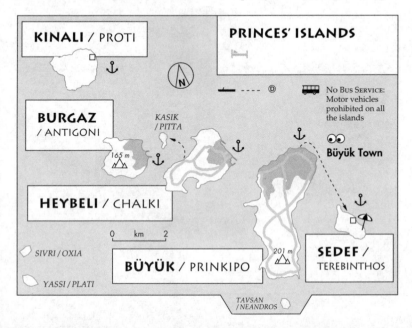

PORT TABLES

& REFERENCE:
FERRY COMPANIES · USEFUL GREEK · INDEX

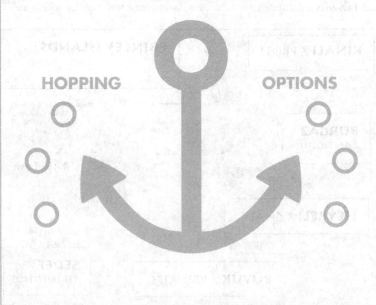

Note:

The following Port Tables show *typical* High Season ferry times. Islands and ports are listed alphabetically. Those islands that are known by two common names (eg. Santorini / Thira) are listed under the first (eg. Santorini). Island ports are not listed separately by name but appear under their respective island's name. Minor ferry services already shown on island maps are not listed again here.

Aegina

Argo-Saronic   p. 452

○ Typical daily departures:

06.10	Poseidon Co.	Piraeus.
07.30	Mirage	Piraeus.
07.40	Keravnos	Piraeus.
08.40	Express Danae	Methana. Poros.
08.45	Poseidon Co.	Piraeus.
08.55	Express Danae	Methana. Poros. Hydra. Spetses. Porto Helio.
09.00	Poseidon Co.	Methana. Poros.
09.10	Eftichia	Methana. Poros. Hydra. Ermioni. Spetses.
09.10	Georgios 2	Methana. Poros. Spetses. Porto Helio.
09.30	Moschos Express	Angistri.
10.00	Keravnos	Angistri.
10.00	Poseidon Co.	Piraeus.
11.45	Keravnos	Piraeus.
12.00	Moschos Express	Angistri.
12.20	Express Danae	Piraeus.
12.30	Poseidon Co.	Piraeus.
14.00	Moschos Express	Angistri.
15.15	Keravnos	Angistri.
15.45	Poseidon Co.	Piraeus.
15.50	Moschos Express	Angistri.
17.00	Poseidon Co.	Piraeus.
17.20	Express Danae	Methana. Poros.
17.30	Express Danae	Piraeus.
17.55	Eftichia	Piraeus.
18.30	Georgios 2	Piraeus.
19.00	Moschos Express	Angistri.
20.30	Express Danae	Piraeus.

① ③ ⑤
| 13.30 | Poseidon Co. | Angistri. Epidavros. |

⑤ ⑥ ⑦
14.15	Poseidon Co.	Piraeus.
16.30	Poseidon Co.	Piraeus.
18.00	Poseidon Co.	Piraeus.
19.15	Poseidon Co.	Piraeus.

⑥ ⑦
| 10.45 | Poseidon Co. | Angistri. Epidavros. |
| 16.00 | Poseidon Co. | Epidavros. |

〜 *Flying Dolphins* include:

Ⓗ 08.00–19.00   Piraeus (Great Harbour).
Ⓓ 09.45 17.15   Poros. Hydra. Spetses.
     09.15 19.15   Epidavros.

Aegina (Agia Marina)

Ⓓ
06.30	Elvira	Piraeus.
09.30	Michael	Piraeus.
13.00	Agios Nektarios B	Piraeus.
17.00	Michael	Piraeus.
18.45	Agios Nektarios B	Piraeus.

〜 *Sea Falcons* include:
Ⓓ 07.30 09.15 12.30 15.15
     17.15 19.15 21.00   Piraeus.

Aegina (Souvala)

Ⓓ
| 08.15 | Poseidon Co. | Piraeus. |
| 12.00 | Poseidon Co. | Piraeus. |

Ⓓ ex ⑥
| 17.30 | Poseidon Co. | Piraeus. |
| 19.30 | Poseidon Co. | Piraeus. |

⑥
| 16.30 | Poseidon Co. | Piraeus. |

〜 *Sea Falcons* include:
Ⓓ 06.40 08.00 09.45 12.45
     14.15 16.15 18.15 21.15   Piraeus.

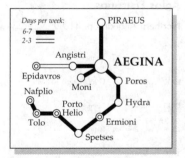

Agathonisi

Dodecanese p. 311

②
| 08.30 | Miniotis | Arki. Lipsi. Patmos. |
| 15.00 | Miniotis | Samos (Pithagorio). |

③
| 13.30 | *Nissos Kalimnos* | Samos (Pithagorio). |
| 16.45 | *Nissos Kalimnos* | Arki. Patmos. Lipsi. Leros. Kalimnos. |

④ ⑤
| 11.00 | Hydrofoil | Samos (Pithagorio). |
| 14.40 | Hydrofoil | Patmos. Leros (Agia Marina). |

⑥
| 08.35 | Samos H/F | Patmos. Lipsi. Leros (Agia Marina). Kalimnos. Kos. |
| 17.25 | Samos H/F | Samos (Pithagorio). |

⑦
| 13.05 | *Nissos Kalimnos* | Samos (Pithagorio). |
| 16.05 | *Nissos Kalimnos* | Patmos. Lipsi. Leros. Kalimnos. |

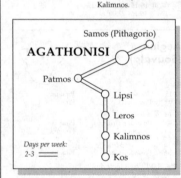

Samos (Pithagorio)

AGATHONISI

Patmos

Lipsi

Leros

Kalimnos

Days per week:
2-3

Kos

Agios Efstratios

Northern Aegean p. 410

② ⑥
| 06.15 | *Alcaeos* | Limnos. Kavala. |

④
| 03.30 | *Alcaeos* | Lesbos (Sigri). Rafina. |

⑤
| 07.15 | *Alcaeos* | Limnos. |

⑥ ⑦
| 23.30 | *Alcaeos* | Rafina. |

○
| 12.00 | *Aeolis* | Limnos. |

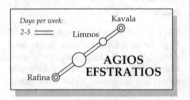

Days per week:
2-3

Kavala

Limnos

AGIOS EFSTRATIOS

Rafina

Agios Konstantinos

Northern Aegean p. 410

① ③ ⑤
| 09.00 | *Macedon* | Skiathos. Skopelos. Alonissos. |
| 19.00 | *Macedon* | Skiathos. Skopelos. (Glossa). |

②
| 13.00 | *Skopelos* | Skiathos. Skopelos (Glossa). Skopelos. Alonissos. |

④
| 08.00 | *Skopelos* | Skiathos. Skopelos (Glossa). |
| 18.00 | *Skopelos* | Skiathos. Skopelos. Alonissos. |

⑥
08.30	*Macedon*	Skiathos. Skopelos. Alonissos.
19.00	*Macedon*	Skiathos. Skopelos.
20.00	*Lemnos*	Skiathos. Skopelos (Glossa).

⑦
| 09.00 | *Lemnos* | Skiathos. Skopelos (Glossa). Skopelos. Alonissos. |
| 12.00 | *Macedon* | Skiathos. Skopelos. Alonissos. |

Flying Dolphins:
| ⑩ x 3 | | Skiathos. Skopelos. Alonissos. |

Days per week:
6-7

Skiathos

Skopelos (Town)

(Glossa)

Alonissos

AGIOS KONSTANTINOS

Agios Nikolaos

Ionian p. 485

⑩
08.30   12.00   15.30   18.00   20.30
    Panagia T. II   Egion.

Alexandria

Egypt   p. 83

○
00.00   *Princesa Amorosa*   Cyprus (Limassol). Haifa.

Alexandroupolis

Northern Aegean   p. 410

①
08.00	*Arsinoe*	Samothrace.
08.30	*Niki H/F*	Samothrace.
12.30	*Saos*	Samothrace.
14.00	*Niki H/F*	Samothrace.
15.30	*Arsinoe*	Samothrace.
15.30	*Niki H/F*	Samothrace. Thassos.

②
08.00	*Arsinoe*	Samothrace.
12.00	*Saos*	Samothrace.
12.30	*Niki H/F*	Samothrace.
15.15	*Niki H/F*	Samothrace.
16.00	*Arsinoe*	Samothrace.

③ ④ ⑥
08.00	*Saos*	Samothrace.
09.30	*Niki H/F*	Samothrace.
15.30	*Saos*	Samothrace.
18.00	*Niki H/F*	Samothrace.

⑤
08.00	*Arsinoe*	Samothrace.
09.30	*Niki H/F*	Samothrace.
15.30	*Niki H/F*	Samothrace.
16.00	*Saos*	Samothrace.

⑦
01.00	*Romilda*	Limnos. Lesbos (Mytilini). Chios. Samos (Vathi). Kos. Rhodes.
07.45	*Niki H/F*	Samothrace.
08.00	*Saos*	Samothrace.
11.00	*Niki H/F*	Samothrace.
13.00	*Niki H/F*	Samothrace. Limnos.
15.00	*Saos*	Samothrace.
19.30	*Niki H/F*	Samothrace.

○
| 07.00 | *Thraki III H/F* | Samothrace. |
| 13.00 | *Thraki III H/F* | Samothrace. |

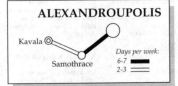

ALEXANDROUPOLIS

Kavala

Samothrace

Days per week:
6-7 ▬▬
2-3 ═══

Alonissos

Northern Aegean   p. 412

①
| 14.35 | *Macedon* | Skopelos. Skiathos. Ag. Konstantinos. |
| 19.10 | *Papadia. II* | Skopelos. Skopelos (Glossa). Skiathos. Volos. |

②
06.00	*Skopelos*	Skopelos. Skiathos. Ag. Konstantinos.
18.45	*Macedon*	Skiathos. Ag. Konstantinos.
19.15	*Skopelos*	Skopelos.

③
07.00	*Lemnos*	Skopelos. Skopelos (Glossa). Volos.
14.35	*Macedon*	Skopelos. Skiathos. Ag. Konstantinos.
17.30	*Skopelos*	Skopelos. Skopelos (Glossa). Skiathos. Ag. Konstantinos.

④
| 15.20 | *Lemnos* | Skopelos. Volos. |
| 18.45 | *Macedon* | Skiathos. Ag. Konstantinos. |

⑤
| 05.30 | *Skopelos* | Skopelos. Skiathos. Volos. |
| 18.30 | *Lemnos* | Thessalonika. |

⑥
00.25	*Macedon*	Ag. Konstantinos.
05.30	*Papadia. II*	Skopelos. Skiathos. Volos.
14.00	*Macedon*	Ag. Konstantinos.
19.30	*Skopelos*	Skopelos (Glossa). Skiathos. Volos.

⑦
14.05	*Skopelos*	Skopelos (Glossa). Skiathos. Volos.
15.15	*Lemnos*	Skopelos. Volos.
17.30	*Macedon*	Skopelos. Skiathos. Ag. Konstantinos.

🐬 *Flying Dolphins* include:
Ⓓ 07.15 13.45 16.00
    Skopelos. Skopelos (Glossa). Skiathos. Ag. Konstantinos.
11.00 Skopelos. Skiathos. Volos.

Thessalonika

Volos

ALONISSOS

Skiathos

(Glossa) Skopelos (Town)

Agios Konstantinos

Skyros

Days per week:
6-7 ▬▬
4-5 ▬▬

Amorgos (Egiali)

Cyclades East
p. 256

①
03.00	Ionian Sun	Amorgos (Katapola). Koufonissia. Schinoussa. Iraklia. Naxos. Paros. Syros. Rafina.
10.50	Speed H/F	Koufonissia. Schinoussa. Iraklia. Naxos. Mykonos.
17.00	Speed H/F	Amorgos (Katapola). Santorini. Ios.

②
01.40	Super Naias	Amorgos (Katapola).
06.35	Super Naias	Naxos. Paros. Syros. Piraeus.
07.15	Ex. Skopelitis	Donoussa. Koufonissia. Schinoussa. Iraklia. Naxos.
19.45	Ex. Skopelitis	Amorgos (Katapola).

④
03.25	Ex. Santorini	Amorgos (Katapola). Astipalea.
07.15	Ex. Skopelitis	Donoussa. Koufonissia. Schinoussa. Iraklia. Naxos.
10.50	Speed H/F	Koufonissia. Schinoussa. Iraklia. Naxos. Mykonos. Syros.
11.00	Ex. Santorini	Donoussa. Naxos. Paros. Piraeus.
18.20	Speed H/F	Amorgos (Katapola). Santorini. Ios.
19.45	Ex. Skopelitis	Amorgos (Katapola).

⑤
| 15.35 | Express Paros | Amorgos (Katapola). Koufonissia. Schinoussa. Iraklia. Naxos. Paros. Syros. |
| 21.45 | Ariadne | Naxos. Paros. Piraeus. |

⑥
| 02.00 | Ionian Sun | Amorgos (Katapola). Naxos. Paros. Syros. Rafina. |

⑦
| 05.50 | Naias Express | Amorgos (Katapola). Koufonissia. Iraklia. Naxos. Mykonos. Tinos. Syros. Piraeus. |

PIRAEUS

Syros   Tinos

Paros   Mykonos

Naxos   Donoussa

Iraklia Schinoussa Koufonissia Amorgos (Katapola)

AMORGOS (Egiali)

Astipalea

Days per week:
4-5
2-3

Amorgos (Katapola)

Cyclades East
p. 255

①
05.00	Ionian Sun	Koufonissia. Schinoussa. Iraklia. Naxos. Paros. Syros. Rafina.
06.00	Ex. Skopelitis	Koufonissia. Schinoussa. Iraklia. Naxos. Mykonos.
10.20	Speed H/F	Amorgos (Egiali). Koufonissia. Schinoussa. Iraklia. Naxos. Mykonos.
17.30	Speed H/F	Santorini. Ios.

②
05.45	Super Naias	Amorgos (Egiali). Naxos. Paros. Syros. Piraeus.
06.00	Ex. Skopelitis	Amorgos (Egiali). Donoussa. Koufonissia. Schinoussa. Iraklia. Naxos.
14.45	Sea Jet I	Naxos. Paros. Syros. Mykonos. Tinos. Andros. Rafina.

③
06.00	Ex. Skopelitis	Koufonissia. Schinoussa. Iraklia. Naxos. Mykonos.
06.30	Supercat Haroulla	Naxos. Paros. Syros. Mykonos. Tinos. Andros. Rafina.
13.15	Speed H/F	Santorini. Ios. Naxos. Paros. Mykonos. Tinos. Syros.
14.40	Romilda	Mykonos. Piraeus.

④
04.10	Ex. Santorini	Astipalea.
06.00	Ex. Skopelitis	Amorgos (Egiali). Donoussa. Koufonissia. Schinoussa. Iraklia. Naxos.
10.00	Ex. Santorini	Amorgos (Egiali). Donoussa. Naxos. Paros. Piraeus.
10.20	Speed H/F	Amorgos (Egiali). Koufonissia. Schinoussa. Iraklia. Naxos. Mykonos. Syros.
13.00	Athina 2004	Naxos. Paros. Mykonos. Tinos. Andros. Rafina.
18.50	Speed H/F	Santorini. Ios.

⑤
04.30	Penelope A	Koufonissia. Schinoussa. Iraklia. Naxos. Paros. Syros. Mykonos. Tinos. Andros. Rafina.
06.00	Ex. Skopelitis	Koufonissia. Schinoussa. Iraklia. Naxos. Mykonos.
16.25	Express Paros	Koufonissia. Schinoussa. Iraklia. Naxos. Paros. Syros.
16.35	Ariadne	Astipalea.

⑥
00.30	Romilda	Astipalea. Kalimnos. Kos. Nissiros. Tilos. Rhodes.
06.00	Ex. Skopelitis	Koufonissia. Schinoussa. Iraklia. Naxos. Mykonos.
08.45	Ionian Sun	Naxos. Paros. Syros. Rafina.

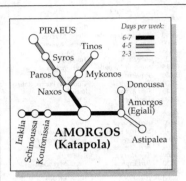

PIRAEUS

Days per week:
6-7
4-5
2-3

Tinos
Syros
Paros　　Mykonos
Naxos　　　　　Donoussa
　　　　　　　　Amorgos
　　　　　　　　(Egiali)
Iraklia　Schinoussa　Koufonissia
AMORGOS　　Astipalea
(Katapola)

⑦
04.00	*Express Athina*	Astipalea.
06.00	*Ex. Skopelitis*	Koufonissia. Schinoussa. Iraklia. Naxos. Mykonos.
09.00	*Naias Express*	Koufonissia. Iraklia. Naxos. Mykonos. Tinos. Syros. Piraeus.
10.00	*Express Athina*	Naxos. Paros. Piraeus.
13.15	Speed H/F	Santorini. Ios. Naxos. Paros. Mykonos. Tinos. Syros.

Amphilochia

Ionian　p. 485

○
| 00.00 | | Preveza. Paxi. Corfu. |

Anafi

Cyclades Central
p. 259

①
| 09.00 | *Express Olympia* | Santorini. Ios. Naxos. Paros. Piraeus. |

②
10.00	Speed H/F	Santorini. Ios.
18.10	Speed H/F	Santorini. Ios.
18.40	*Express Paros*	Santorini. Ios. Sikinos. Folegandros. Naxos. Paros. Syros.

③
05.00	*Maria PA*	Santorini. Folegandros. Sikinos. Ios.
05.35	*Super Naias*	Astipalea.
09.30	*Super Naias*	Santorini. Ios. Naxos. Paros. Piraeus.

⑤
| 10.00 | Speed H/F | Santorini. Ios. |
| 18.10 | Speed H/F | Santorini. Ios. |

⑥
| 04.55 | *Panagia Ekatonta.* | Santorini. Ios. Naxos. Paros. Piraeus. |

⑦
| 05.30 | *Express Apollon* | Santorini. Ios. Naxos. Paros. Piraeus. |

Ancona

Italy　p. 83

Ⓓ
19.00	*Superfast III/IV*	Patras.
14.00	*Kriti II*	Patras.
20.00	*Ikarus*	Igoumenitsa. Patras.

②
| 16.00 | *Kriti I* | Igoumenitsa. Patras. |
| 20.00 | *Pasiphae* | Igoumenitsa. Patras. |

③
| 12.00 | *Ionian Island* | Corfu. Igoumenitsa. Patras. |
| 22.00 | *Kriti I* | Patras. |

④
| 16.00 | *Ikarus* | Igoumenitsa. Patras. |

⑤
12.00	*Ionian Star*	Corfu. Igoumenitsa. Patras.
16.00	*Kriti II*	Igoumenitsa. Patras.
16.00	*Pasiphae*	Igoumenitsa. Patras.

⑥
| 18.00 | *Ikarus* | Igoumenitsa. Patras. |
| 19.00 | *Kriti I* | Igoumenitsa. Patras. |

⑦
| 18.00 | *Pasiphae* | Igoumenitsa. Patras. |
| 23.00 | *Ionian Victory* | Corfu. Igoumenitsa. Patras. |

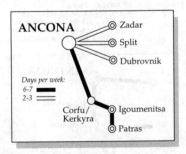

ANCONA　　　◎ Zadar
　　　　　　　　◎ Split
　　　　　　　　◎ Dubrovnik

Days per week:
6-7
2-3

Corfu/　　◎ Igoumenitsa
Kerkyra
　　　　　◎ Patras

Andros

Cyclades North
p. 187

①
09.00	*Bari Express*	Tinos.
09.40	*Supercat Haroulla*	Tinos. Mykonos. Paros.
09.55	*Penelope A*	Tinos. Mykonos.
11.00	*Superferry II*	Rafina.
12.45	*Bari Express*	Rafina.
17.00	*Penelope A*	Rafina.
17.00	*Superferry II*	Tinos. Mykonos.
18.30	*Supercat Haroulla*	Rafina.
19.00	*Bari Express*	Tinos. Mykonos.

②
01.45	*Superferry II*	Rafina.
05.00	*Agios Rafail*	Piraeus.
09.00	*Superferry II*	Tinos. Mykonos.
09.40	*Supercat Haroulla*	Tinos. Mykonos. Syros. Paros. Naxos. Amorgos (Katapola).
09.55	*Penelope A*	Tinos. Mykonos.
10.00	*Bari Express*	Rafina.
17.00	*Penelope A*	Rafina.
17.30	*Bari Express*	Tinos. Mykonos.

③
01.45	*Superferry II*	Rafina.
08.55	*Penelope A*	Tinos.
09.45	*Bari Express*	Rafina.
12.00	*Penelope A*	Rafina.
16.00	*Supercat Haroulla*	Rafina.
17.30	*Bari Express*	Tinos. Mykonos.
19.00	*Penelope A*	Tinos. Mykonos.
19.00	*Superferry II*	Tinos. Mykonos.
23.00	*Penelope A*	Rafina.
23.45	*Agios Rafail*	Syros. Chios. Lesbos (Mytilini).

④
08.55	*Penelope A*	Tinos.
09.40	*Supercat Haroulla*	Tinos. Mykonos. Paros.
10.00	*Bari Express*	Rafina.
10.00	*Superferry II*	Tinos. Mykonos.
12.00	*Penelope A*	Rafina.
17.00	*Superferry II*	Rafina.
17.30	*Bari Express*	Tinos. Mykonos.
18.30	*Supercat Haroulla*	Rafina.
19.00	*Penelope A*	Tinos. Mykonos. Syros. Paros. Naxos. Amorgos (Katapola). Koufonissia. Schinoussa. Iraklia.

⑤
09.00	*Bari Express*	Tinos.
09.40	*Supercat Haroulla*	Tinos. Mykonos.
10.00	*Superferry II*	Tinos. Mykonos.
14.45	*Penelope A*	Rafina.
18.30	*Bari Express*	Tinos. Mykonos.
19.15	*Supercat Haroulla*	Lavrion. Kea.
19.30	*Penelope A*	Tinos. Mykonos.
21.00	*Superferry II*	Tinos. Mykonos. Rafina.
23.45	*Bari Express*	Rafina.
24.00	*Penelope A*	Rafina.

⑥
09.00	*Bari Express*	Tinos.
09.40	*Supercat Haroulla*	Tinos. Mykonos. Paros.
10.00	*Superferry II*	Tinos. Mykonos.
12.00	*Bari Express*	Rafina.
17.00	*Superferry II*	Rafina.
18.30	*Bari Express*	Tinos. Mykonos.
18.30	*Supercat Haroulla*	Rafina.
19.00	*Penelope A*	Tinos. Mykonos.
23.45	*Bari Express*	Rafina.

⑦
09.00	*Bari Express*	Tinos.
09.40	*Supercat Haroulla*	Tinos. Mykonos.
10.00	*Superferry II*	Tinos. Mykonos.
11.00	*Penelope A*	Rafina.
14.00	*Bari Express*	Rafina.
16.00	*Supercat Haroulla*	Rafina.
21.30	*Superferry II*	Rafina.
23.00	*Penelope A*	Rafina.

Andros (Batsi)

Cyclades North
p. 188

Ⓓ
00.00	*ILIO H/F*	Rafina.
00.00	*ILIO H/F*	Tinos. Mykonos. Paros. Naxos. Ios. Santorini.
18.00	*Mega Dolphin*	Kea. Piraeus (Zea).

①
09.00	*Bari Express*	Tinos.
09.15	*Athina 2004*	Tinos. Mykonos. Naxos. Paros.
14.25	*Athina 2004*	Rafina.

②
| 08.45 | *Sea Jet I* | Syros. Mykonos. Syros. Paros. Naxos. Amorgos (Katapola). |
| 20.00 | *Sea Jet I* | Rafina. |

③
| 09.15 | *Athina 2004* | Tinos. Mykonos. Naxos. Paros. |
| 14.25 | *Athina 2004* | Rafina. |

④
| 09.15 | *Athina 2004* | Tinos. Mykonos. Paros. Naxos. Donoussa. Amorgos (Katapola). |
| 17.15 | *Athina 2004* | Rafina. |

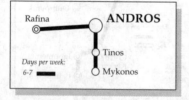

Rafina

ANDROS

Tinos

Days per week:
6-7 ▬▬

Mykonos

ⓢ
09.15	*Athina 2004*	Tinos. Mykonos. Naxos. Paros.
11.15	*Mega Dolphin*	Kea. Piraeus (Zea).
14.25	*Athina 2004*	Rafina.

⑥
| 11.15 | *Mega Dolphin* | Kea. Piraeus (Zea). |

⑦
| 18.15 | *Athina 2004* | Tinos. Mykonos. |

Angistri

Argo-Saronic p. 456

Ⓓ
07.00	*Moschos Express*	Aegina.
07.15	*Keravnos*	Aegina. Piraeus.
10.00	*Moschos Express*	Aegina.
11.20	*Keravnos*	Aegina. Piraeus.
13.00	*Moschos Express*	Aegina.
15.00	*Moschos Express*	Aegina.
18.00	*Moschos Express*	Aegina.

①
05.55	*Manaras Express*	Piraeus.
07.10	*Kitsolakis Express*	Piraeus.
09.45	*Manaras Express*	Piraeus.
14.30	Poseidon Co.	Epidavros.
16.10	*Manaras Express*	Piraeus.
17.15	Poseidon Co.	Aegina. Piraeus.

②
| 07.10 | *Kitsolakis Express* | Piraeus. |

② ③ ④
| 06.10 | *Manaras Express* | Piraeus. |
| 16.40 | *Manaras Express* | Piraeus. |

③
07.10	*Kitsolakis Express*	Piraeus.
14.30	Poseidon Co.	Epidavros.
17.15	Poseidon Co.	Aegina. Piraeus.

④
| 07.10 | *Kitsolakis Express* | Piraeus. |

⑤
09.45	*Manaras Express*	Piraeus.
12.40	*Kitsolakis Express*	Piraeus.
14.30	Poseidon Co.	Epidavros.
15.30	*Manaras Express*	Piraeus.

| 17.15 | Poseidon Co. | Aegina. Piraeus. |
| 20.15 | *Manaras Express* | Piraeus. |

⑥
06.15	*Kitsolakis Express*	Piraeus.
09.00	*Manaras Express*	Piraeus.
11.45	Poseidon Co.	Epidavros.
12.10	*Kitsolakis Express*	Piraeus.
15.45	Poseidon Co.	Aegina. Piraeus.
17.00	*Manaras Express*	Piraeus.

⑦
12.00	Poseidon Co.	Epidavros.
15.00	*Manaras Express*	Piraeus.
16.00	*Kitsolakis Express*	Piraeus.
19.10	*Manaras Express*	Piraeus.
19.45	Poseidon Co.	Aegina. Piraeus.

Antikithera

Argo-Saronic p. 456

③
| 12.00 | *Nissos Kithera* | Kithera (Agia Pelagia). Gythio. |

② ③
| 03.45 | *Kantia* | Crete (Kasteli). |

④
| 15.30 | *Kantia* | Kithera. Piraeus. |

Antiparos

Cyclades Central
p. 136

Ⓓ Ⓗ
| 07.00–24.00; ev. 30 min 10.30–20.30 | *Agioi Anargiri* | Paros (Punta). |

Ⓓ
| x 10 | *Antiparos Express/ Kasos Express/ Panagia Parou* | Paros. |

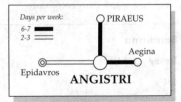

Days per week:
6-7
2-3

PIRAEUS

Aegina

Epidavros

ANGISTRI

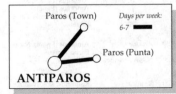

Paros (Town)   *Days per week:*
6-7

Paros (Punta)

ANTIPAROS

Arki

Dodecanese p. 311

②
10.00 Miniotis   Lipsi. Patmos.
13.30 Miniotis   Agathonisi.
                         Samos (Pithagorio).

③
12.15 *Nissos Kalimnos* Agathonisi.
                         Samos (Pithagorio).
17.55 *Nissos Kalimnos* Patmos. Lipsi. Leros.
                         Kalimnos.

Ashdod

Israel p. 83

○
18.00 *Princesa Amorosa* Limassol. Port Said.

Astakos

Ionian Line p. 481

Ⓓ
13.00   *Aphrodite L*   Kefalonia (Sami).

Astipalea

Cyclades East p. 261

②
22.15 *Nissos Kalimnos* Kalimnos.

②
22.20 *Nissos Kalimnos* Kalimnos.

③
07.30 *Super Naias*   Anafi. Santorini. Ios.
                         Naxos. Paros. Piraeus.
11.20 *Romilda*   Amorgos (Katapola).
                         Mykonos. Piraeus.

④
07.30 *Express Santorini* Amorgos (Katapola).
                         Amorgos (Egiali).
                         Donoussa. Naxos. Paros.
                         Piraeus.

⑤
19.30 *Ariadne*   Amorgos (Egiali). Naxos.
                         Paros. Piraeus.
22.20 *Nissos Kalimnos* Kalimnos.

⑥
04.00 *Romilda*   Kalimnos. Kos. Nissiros.
                         Tilos. Rhodes.

PIRAEUS   *Days per week:*
                              4-5 ▬▬▬
Syros   2-3 ═══
        Tinos
                        Naxos
Mykonos
                              Kalimnos
Amorgos

ASTIPALEA

                    Rhodes

15.00 Dode. H/F   Kalimnos. Kos. Symi.
                        Rhodes.

⑦
07.30 *Express Athina* Amorgos (Katapola).
                         Naxos. Paros.
                         Piraeus.

Avşa

Turkey p. 518

Ⓓ
00.00 TML   Marmara. İstanbul.

Ⓓ ex ⑦
00.00 TML   Marmara.
00.00 TML   Erdek.

Ⓓ x ④
00.00 Deniz Otobusleri Marmara. İstanbul.

⑤ ⑦
00.00 TML   Marmara. Tekirdağ.

Ayvalık

Turkey p. 518

Ⓓ
08.00 *Jale*   Lesbos (Mytilini).
17.00 *Aeolis/Eresos II* Lesbos (Mytilini).

Bandırma

Turkey p. 519

Ⓓ
01.15 TML   İstanbul.
14.30 TML   İstanbul.

Bari

Italy   p. 83

ⓓ
17.00	Ventouris	Corfu.
20.00	*Superfast I/II*	Igoumenitsa. Patras.
20.00	Ventouris	Patras.
20.00	Ventouris	Igoumenitsa.

ⓐ
| 19.00 | Ventouris | Kefalonia (Sami). |

①
| 20.00 | *Dame M/Duchess M* | Igoumenitsa. |

③
| 20.00 | *Dame M/Duchess M* | Igoumenitsa. |

⑤
| 09.00 | *Dame M/Duchess M* | Igoumenitsa. |

⑥
| 22.00 | *Dame M/Duchess M* | Igoumenitsa. |

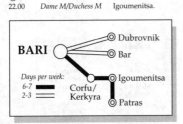

BARI — Dubrovnik, Bar, Igoumenitsa, Corfu/Kerkyra, Patras

Days per week:
6-7 ▬▬
2-3 ═══

Bodrum

Turkey   p. 519

ⓓ
09.00	*Bodrum Princess*	Kos.
09.00	*Fari Kaptain I*	Kos.
09.30	*Bodrum Express*	Datca (Körmen).
11.00	Bodrum T/Bs	Orak Is.
11.00	Bodrum T/Bs	Korada Is. Ada Is. Orak Is.
16.00	*Hermes*	Kos.
17.00	*Bodrum Express*	Datca (Körmen).

Bozcaada

Turkey   p. 519

| ⓓ x 2 | TML | Odum Iskalesi. |

Brindisi

Italy
p. 83

ⓓ
09.00	HML Ferries	Igoumenitsa. Corfu.
10.00	*Ionian Bridge*	Corfu. Igoumenitsa.
14.00	*Santa Eleonora*	Corfu. Paxi.
19.00	*Brindisi/ Valentino*	Igoumenitsa. Patras.
20.00	HML Ferries	Corfu. Igoumenitsa. Kefalonia (Sami). Patras.
20.00	Med Link Lines	Patras.
20.45	*Ouranos*	Igoumenitsa. Corfu.
22.00	*Kapetan Alexandros*	Igoumenitsa.

ⓐ
20.00	Adriatica	Patras.
20.00	Med Link Lines	Igoumenitsa.
21.00	HML Ferries	Paxi. Patras.
22.30	Adriatica	Corfu. Igoumenitsa. Patras.

②
| 20.00 | *Maria G* | Çeşme. |

③
| 20.00 | *Poseidon* | Çeşme. |

⑥
| 16.00 | *Maria G* | Çeşme. |
| 20.00 | *Poseidon* | Çeşme. |

ⓦ
| 00.00 | *Bosphorus* | Çeşme. |

○
| 20.00 | HML Ferries | Ithaca (Pisaetos).
Patras. |
| 20.00 | HML Ferries | Zakinthos.
Patras. |

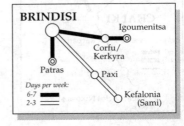

BRINDISI — Igoumenitsa, Corfu/Kerkyra, Patras, Paxi, Kefalonia (Sami)

Days per week:
6-7 ▬▬
2-3 ═══

Çeşme

Turkey
p. 520

Ⓓ
| 08.00 | *Erturk I* | Chios. |
| 18.00 | *Capetan Stamatis* | Chios. |

①
| 20.00 | *Poseidon* | Brindisi. |

④
| 22.00 | *Maria G* | Brindisi. |

⑤
| 04.00 | *Poseidon* | Brindisi. |

⑦
| 24.00 | *Maria G* | Brindisi. |

Chalki

Dodecanese
p. 312

Ⓓ ex ⑦
| 05.30 | *Chalki/* | |
| | *Nikos Ex.* | Rhodes (Kamiros Skala). |

②
02.15	*Romilda*	Karpathos (Diafani).
		Karpathos (Town).
		Kassos.
		Crete (Sitia).
21.45	*Romilda*	Rhodes.

③
| 20.45 | *Daliana* | Rhodes. |

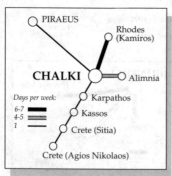

PIRAEUS

Rhodes
(Kamiros)

CHALKI   Alimnia

Days per week:
6-7
4-5
1

Karpathos

Kassos

Crete (Sitia)

Crete (Agios Nikolaos)

④
03.30	*Daliana*	Karpathos (Diafani).
		Karpathos (Town).
		Kassos.
		Crete (Iraklion).
		Santorini.
		Paros.
		Piraeus.

⑤
| 15.00 | Dode. H/F | Rhodes. |
| | | Kos. |

⑦
| 09.00 | *Chalki/* | |
| | *Nikos Express* | Rhodes (Kamiros). |

Chios

Eastern Line
p. 377

Ⓓ
| 08.00 | *Capetan Stamatis* | Çeşme. |
| 14.00 | *Inousse II* | Oinousses. |

①
01.00	*Sappho*	Piraeus.
07.30	*Mytilene*	Lesbos (Mytilini).
09.00	*Miniotis*	Oinousses.
20.30	*Agios Rafail*	Syros.
		Andros.
		Piraeus.
22.00	*Mytilene*	Piraeus.

②
03.00	*Sappho*	Lesbos (Mytilini).
		Limnos.
		Thessalonika.
07.00	*Miniotis*	Psara.
22.00	*Theofilos*	Piraeus.

③
04.00	*Mytilene*	Lesbos (Mytilini).
		Limnos.
06.00	*Agios Rafail*	Piraeus.
09.00	*Miniotis*	Oinousses.
22.00	*Sappho*	Piraeus.

④
04.30	*Theofilos*	Lesbos (Mytilini).
07.00	*Miniotis*	Psara.
08.30	*Agios Rafail*	Lesbos (Mytilini).
22.00	*Theofilos*	Piraeus.

⑤
04.00	*Mytilene*	Lesbos (Mytilini).
09.00	*Miniotis*	Oinousses.
21.00	*Sappho*	Piraeus.

⑥
03.30	*Theofilos*	Lesbos (Mytilini).
		Limnos.
		Thessalonika.

07.00	Miniotis	Psara.
09.30	*Romilda*	Lesbos (Mytilini).
		Limnos.
		Alexandroupolis.
12.00	*Mytilene*	Piraeus.
17.30	*Sappho*	Lesbos (Mytilini).
		Limnos.
		Kavala.

⑦

06.30	*Mytilene*	Lesbos (Mytilini).
09.00	Miniotis	Oinousses.
15.30	*Romilda*	Samos (Vathi).
		Kos.
		Rhodes.
18.00	Miniotis	Samos (Karlovassi).
		Samos (Vathi).
21.30	*Theofilos*	Piraeus.

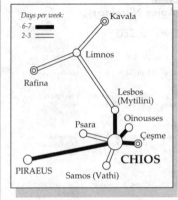

Days per week:
6-7 ▬▬▬
2-3 ═══

Kavala
Limnos
Rafina
Lesbos (Mytilini)
Oinousses
Psara
Çeşme
CHIOS
PIRAEUS
Samos (Vathi)

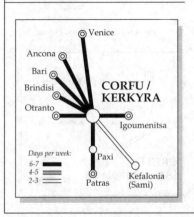

Venice
Ancona
Bari
Brindisi
Otranto
CORFU / KERKYRA
Igoumenitsa
Paxi
Patras
Kefalonia (Sami)

Days per week:
6-7 ▬▬▬
4-5 ═══
2-3 ═══

Corfu / Kerkyra

Ionian Line   p. 481

International Services:

Ⓓ

01.00	*Ionian Bridge*	Brindisi.
07.00	HML Ferries	Igoumenitsa.
		Kefalonia (Sami).
		Patras.
08.00	HML Ferries	Brindisi.
08.30	*Ouranos*	Brindisi.
09.00	*Santa Eleonora*	Brindisi.
18.00	*Ionian Bridge*	Igoumenitsa.
18.30	*Santa Eleonora*	Paxi.
23.00	HML Ferries	Brindisi.

Ⓐ

07.00	Adriatica	Igoumenitsa. Patras.
09.00	Adriatica	Brindisi.

①

06.30	*Aretousa*	Igoumenitsa.
		Venice.
21.00	*Ionian Victory*	Igoumenitsa. Patras.
23.30	*Daedalus/Fedra*	Patras.

②

06.30	*Daedalus/Fedra*	Igoumenitsa.
		Venice.
07.30	*Ionian Island*	Igoumenitsa. Ancona.
09.00	*Petrakis/Sotirakis*	Sarandë.
22.30	*Erotokritos*	Patras.
23.30	*Ionian Star*	Patras.

③

06.30	*Daedalus/Fedra*	Igoumenitsa. Venice.
07.00	*Ionian Victory*	Venice.
23.30	*Aretousa*	Patras.

④

05.15	*Erotokritos*	Igoumenitsa.
		Venice.
07.30	*Ionian Star*	Igoumenitsa. Ancona.
09.30	*Ionian Island*	Igoumenitsa. Patras.
23.30	*Daedalus/Fedra*	Patras.

⑤

06.30	*Aretousa*	Igoumenitsa. Venice.
07.00	*Ionian Island*	Venice.
11.00	*El. Venizelos*	Trieste.
23.30	*Daedalus/Fedra*	Patras.
23.30	*Ionian Victory*	Patras.

⑥

06.30	*Daedalus/Fedra*	Igoumenitsa. Venice.
09.00	*Petrakis/Sotirakis*	Sarandë.
09.30	*Ionian Star*	Igoumenitsa. Patras.
13.00	*Erotokritos*	Igoumenitsa. Patras.
22.30	*Ionian Victory*	Ancona.

⑦

08.00	*Erotokritos*	Igoumenitsa. Venice.
09.00	*Petrakis/Sotirakis*	Sarandë.
12.00	*Aretousa*	Igoumenitsa. Patras.
23.30	*El. Venizelos*	Patras.
23.30	*Ionian Island*	Patras.

Domestic Services:

ⓗ
06.00–22.00   Local C/F   Igoumenitsa.

ⓓ
09.30	Agios Spyridon	Igoumenitsa.
14.00	Agios Spyridon	Igoumenitsa.
14.00	Pegasus T/B	Paxi (Old Port).
19.30	Agios Spyridon	Igoumenitsa.

①
12.45   Theologos   Igoumenitsa. Paxi.

②
12.45   Theologos   Igoumenitsa. Paxi.

② ⑥
06.30   P/S   Erikoussa. Mathraki.
                      Orthoni.

③
| 07.30 | Theologos | Igoumenitsa. Paxi. |
| 17.00 | Theologos | Paxi. |

④ ⑤ ⑥
12.45   Theologos   Igoumenitsa. Paxi.

⑦
12.45   Theologos   Igoumenitsa. Paxi.

○
| 00.00 | Panagia Paxon | Paxi. Preveza. Amphilochia. |
| 00.00 | Nearchos | Paxi. Preveza. Amphilochia. |

Corfu (Lefkimi)

ⓓ
06.00   09.00   12.00
16.00   18.00
        Local C/F   Igoumentisa.

Corfu (Sidari)

① ④
11.00   Orthoni Line   Erikoussa.
                               Mathraki. Orthoni.

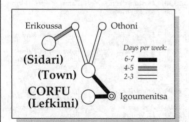

Crete
(Agia Roumeli)

Crete
p. 293

ⓓ
09.30	14.00	15.45	17.00		
		South Crete Line		Lutro.
				Sfakia.
18.00	South Crete Line			Sfakia.
16.30	South Crete Line			Sougia.
				Paleochora.

Crete
(Agios Nikolaos)

Crete   p. 280

ⓓ
10.00   Tour Boats   Spinalonga.

②
07.30	Vitsentzos Kornaros	Crete (Sitia).
18.00	Vitsentzos Kornaros	Milos.
		Piraeus.

④
06.45	Vergina Sky	Santorini.
07.30	Vitsentzos Kornaros	Crete (Sitia).
18.00	Vitsentzos Kornaros	Milos.
		Piraeus.

⑥
08.30	Vitsentzos Kornaros	Crete (Sitia).
		Kassos.
		Karpathos (Town).
		Karpathos (Diafani).
		Rhodes.

⑦
18.00   Vitsentzos Kornaros   Milos. Piraeus.

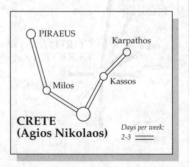

Crete (Chania)

Crete   p. 282

Ⓓ
20.00   *Lato/Lissos*   Piraeus.

Ο
20.30   *Kantia*   Piraeus.

Crete (Iraklion)

Crete   p. 284

International Services:

②
11.00   *Sea Harmony*   Rhodes. Limassol. Haifa.

⑥
23.00   *Sea Harmony*   Piraeus.

Domestic Services:

Ⓓ
19.15   *King Minos/*
       N. Kazantzakis   Piraeus.
07.15   *Artemis/*
       Minoan Prince/
       Vergina Sky   Santorini.

①
08.45   *Maria PA*   Santorini. Ios. Naxos. Paros.
       Mykonos. Tinos. Syros.
14.30   *El Greco*   Santorini. Paros. Tinos.
       Volos.
       Thessalonika.
19.30   *Rethimno*   Piraeus.

②
19.30   *Aptera*   Piraeus.
19.30   *Dimitroula*   Santorini. Naxos. Paros.
       Mykonos.
       Thessalonika.

③
08.00   *Daliana*   Kassos. Karpathos (Town).
       Karpathos (Diafani).
       Chalki. Rhodes.
19.30   *Rethimno*   Piraeus.
21.30   *El Greco*   Santorini. Naxos. Syros.
       Skiathos.
       Thessalonika.

④
16.30   *Daliana*   Santorini. Paros. Piraeus.
19.30   *Aptera*   Piraeus.
21.00   *Dimitroula*   Santorini. Paros. Mykonos.
       Syros. Thessalonika.

⑤
08.45   *Maria PA*   Santorini. Naxos. Paros.
       Mykonos. Syros.

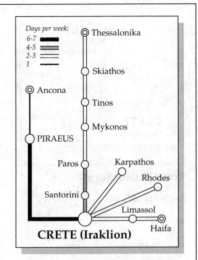

Days per week:
6-7
4-5
2-3
1

Thessalonika
Skiathos
Ancona
Tinos
Mykonos
PIRAEUS
Paros   Karpathos
Rhodes
Santorini
Limassol
CRETE (Iraklion)   Haifa

19.30   *Rethimno*   Piraeus.
22.00   *El Greco*   Santorini. Paros. Tinos.
       Skiathos.
       Thessalonika.

⑥
06.30   *Aptera*   Piraeus.

⑦
01.45   *Dimitroula*   Santorini. Ios. Naxos. Paros.
       Mykonos. Tinos. Syros.
       Volos. Skiathos.
       Thessalonika.
19.30   *Aptera*   Piraeus.

Crete (Kasteli)

Crete
p. 291

②
08.00   *Kantia*   Kithera. Gythio.
24.00   *Kantia*   Kalamata.

④
13.00   *Kantia*   Antikithera. Kithera. Piraeus.

⑥
12.30   *Kantia*   Kalamata.

⑦
13.00   *Kantia*   Kithera. Gythio.
19.00   *Kantia*   Kithera. Piraeus.

PIRAEUS
Monemvassia
Neapoli
Kithera
Antikithera
CRETE
(Kasteli)
Days per week:
2-3 ═══

CRETE (South Coast)
(Agia Roumeli)
(Paleochora)   (Sougia)   (Loutro)   (Sfakia)
Gavdos
Days per week:
6-7 ▬▬▬
2-3 ═══

⑤
18.30   South Crete Line   Gavdos.

⑥ ⑦
09.00   South Crete Line   Gavdos.

Crete (Paleochora)

Crete   p. 292

Ⓓ
08.15   South Crete Line   Sougia.
                                  Agia Roumeli.
10.00   South Crete Line   Elafonisi.

① ③ ④ ⑥
08.30   South Crete Line   Gavdos.

Crete (Rethimno)

Crete   p. 294

Ⓓ
19.30   *Arkadi/Preveli*   Piraeus.

②
06.45   *Vergina Sky*   Santorini.

② ⑥
19.30   *Arkadi/Preveli*   Sifnos. Piraeus.

PIRAEUS
Days per week:
6-7 ▬▬▬
CRETE
(Rethimno)

Crete (Sitia)

Crete   p. 296

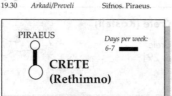

②
13.00   *Romilda*   Kassos.
                              Karpathos (Town).
                              Karpathos (Diafani).
                              Chalki. Rhodes.
15.30   *Vitsentzos Kornaros*   Crete (Agios Nikolaos).
                              Milos. Piraeus.

④
15.30   *Vitsentzos Kornaros*   Crete (Agios Nikolaos).
                              Milos. Piraeus.

⑥
10.00   *Vitsentzos Kornaros*   Kassos.
                              Karpathos (Town).
                              Karpathos (Diafani).
                              Rhodes.

⑦
15.30   *Vitsentzos Kornaros*   Crete (Agios Nikolaos).
                              Milos. Piraeus.

Crete (Sfakia)

Crete   p. 293

Ⓓ
10.30   11.45   13.45   15.45
      South Crete Line   Lutro. Agia Roumeli.

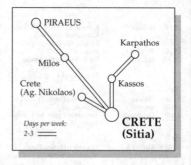

PIRAEUS
Karpathos
Milos
Crete
(Ag. Nikolaos)
Kassos
Days per week:
2-3 ═══
CRETE
(Sitia)

Cyprus (Larnaca)

Cyprus   p. 83

○
Service Suspended   Jounieh.

Cyprus (Limassol)

Cyprus   p. 83

①
14.00	Nissos Kypros	Rhodes. Piraeus.
14.00	Sea Symphony	Rhodes. Piraeus.
15.00	Princesa Marissa	Port Said.

③
15.00	Princesa Amorosa	Port Said.
19.30	Princesa Marissa	Haifa. Port Said.
20.00	Sea Harmony	Haifa.

④
| 20.00 | Princesa Cypria | Haifa. |

⑤
| 13.00 | Sea Harmony | Rhodes. Crete (Iraklion). Piraeus. |
| 17.00 | Princesa Amorosa | Port Said. |

⑥
15.00	Princesa Cypria	Rhodes. Lesbos (Mytilini). Tinos. Piraeus.
18.00	Nissos Kypros	Haifa.
19.30	Princesa Marissa	Haifa.
20.00	Sea Symphony	Haifa.

⑦
| 17.00 | Princesa Amorosa | Port Said. Ashdod. |

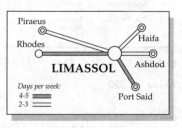

Piraeus
Rhodes
Haifa
LIMASSOL   Ashdod
Days per week:
4-5
2-3
Port Said

Turkish Occupied Ports:

Famagusta / Magosa

② ④ ⑦
| 22.00 | Yeşilada | Mersin. |

Kyrenia / Girne

Ⓓ
| 13.00 | Hydrofoil | Taşucu. |

② ③ ④
| 13.00 | Liberty / Ertürk | Taşucu. |

Datça (Körmen)

Turkey   p. 520

Ⓓ
| 09.00 | Bodrum Express | Bodrum. |
| 17.00 | Bodrum Express | Bodrum. |

Delos

Cyclades North
p. 192

Ⓓ ex ①
11.45	Delos Express	Mykonos.
12.20	Hera	Mykonos.
12.30	Delos Express	Mykonos.
12.30	Niki	Mykonos.
13.45	Hera	Mykonos.
14.15	Delos Express	Mykonos.
14.15	Niki	Mykonos.
15.00	Delos Express	Mykonos.
15.00	Hera	Mykonos.

Donoussa

Cyclades East   p. 264

①
| 01.30 | Ionian Sun | Amorgos (Egiali). (Katapola). Koufonissia. Schinoussa. Iraklia. Naxos. Paros. Syros. Rafina. |

②
00.40	Super Naias	Amorgos (Egiali). Amorgos (Katapola).
08.30	Express Skopelitis	Koufonissia. Schinoussa. Iraklia. Naxos.
18.30	Express Skopelitis	Amorgos (Egiali). Amorgos (Katapola).

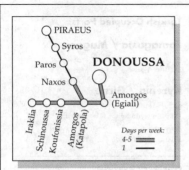

Donoussa route map

PIRAEUS
Syros
Paros
DONOUSSA
Naxos
Amorgos (Egiali)
Iraklia
Schinoussa
Koufonissia
Amorgos (Katapola)

Days per week:
4-5
1

④
02.25	*Express Santorini*	Amorgos (Egiali). Amorgos (Katapola). Astipalea.
08.30	*Express Skopelitis*	Koufonissia. Schinoussa. Iraklia. Naxos.
12.00	*Express Santorini*	Naxos. Paros. Piraeus.
12.30	*Athina 2004*	Amorgos (Katapola). Naxos. Paros. Mykonos. Tinos. Andros. Rafina.
18.30	*Express Skopelitis*	Amorgos (Egiali). Amorgos (Katapola).

⑤
14.30	*Express Paros*	Amorgos (Egiali). Amorgos (Katapola). Koufonissia. Schinoussa. Iraklia. Naxos. Paros. Syros.

⑦
05.00	*Naias Express*	Amorgos (Egiali). Amorgos (Katapola). Koufonissia. Iraklia. Naxos. Mykonos. Tinos. Syros. Piraeus.

Durrës

Albania p. 84

② ④
12.00	Adriatica	Bari.

③ ⑥
19.00	Adriatica	Trieste.

⑦
12.00	Adriatica	Ancona.

Eceabat

Turkey p. 520

Ⓓ ev 2Ⓗ 08.00–03.00   Çanakkale.

Egion

Ionian p. 485

Ⓓ
07.30 10.30 13.30 17.00 19.00
        Panagia T. II   Agios Nikolaos.

Elafonissos

Argo-Saronic p. 458

Ⓓ
x 10   Neapoli.

Ⓞ
22.40   Neapoli. Monemvassia. Piraeus.

Ⓞ
01.25   Kithera (Agia Pelagia). Crete (Kasteli).

Epidavros

Argo-Saronic p. 458

①
09.50	*Flying Dolphin*	Aegina.
16.00	Poseidon Co.	Angistri. Aegina. Piraeus.
19.55	*Flying Dolphin*	Aegina.

③
17.15	Poseidon Co.	Angistri. Aegina. Piraeus.

⑤
16.00	Poseidon Co.	Angistri. Aegina. Piraeus.

⑥
14.00	Poseidon Co.	Angistri. Aegina. Piraeus.

⑦
14.00	Poseidon Co.	Aegina. Piraeus.
18.30	Poseidon Co.	Angistri. Aegina. Piraeus.

Erdek

Turkey p. 520

Ⓓ ex ⑦
00.00   TML   Avşa. Marmara.

① ⑥
00.00   TML   Paşalimanı.

⑤ ⑦
00.00   TML   Avşa. Marmara. Tekirdağ.

Ermioni

Argo-Saronic   p. 458

Ⓓ
12.30   *Saronikos*   Spetses.
14.30   *Saronikos*   Hydra. Poros.
                        Methana.
                        Aegina. Piraeus.

③ ⑥
12.40   *Georgios 2*   Spetses. Porto Helio.
15.30   *Georgios 2*   Poros. Methana. Aegina.
                        Piraeus.

🐬 *Flying Dolphins* include:
Ⓓ
x 6   Hydra. Piraeus (Zea).
x 4   Poros.

Evia (Kimi)

Northern Aegean
p. 197

Ⓓ ex ⑦
11.00   *Lykomides*   Skyros.
17.00   *Lykomides*   Skyros.

⑦
13.00   *Lykomides*   Skyros.
19.00   *Lykomides*   Skyros.

◯
22.15   *Skopelos*   Skopelos.
                        Alonissos.

Volos   *Days per week:*
  ◎   6-7 ▬▬▬▬
      Skiathos   2-3 ════
         ◯
           Skopelos
              ◯
                 ◯ Alonissos
  EVIA   ◯
  (Kimi)   ◯ Skyros

Evia (Marmari)

Cyclades North   p. 197

Ⓓ
06.00   *Express Karystos*   Rafina.

① ② ③ ④
10.30   *Express Karystos*   Rafina.
13.45   *Express Karystos*   Rafina.
17.17   *Express Karystos*   Rafina.

⑤
10.30   *Express Karystos*   Rafina.
13.30   *Express Karystos*   Rafina.
15.30   *Express Karystos*   Rafina.
18.30   *Express Karystos*   Rafina.

⑥
09.30   *Express Karystos*   Rafina.
10.30   *Express Karystos*   Rafina.
13.45   *Express Karystos*   Rafina.
17.17   *Express Karystos*   Rafina.

⑦
14.00   *Express Karystos*   Rafina.
17.17   *Express Karystos*   Rafina.
20.45   *Express Karystos*   Rafina.

Folegandros

Cyclades West   p. 222

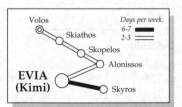

①
03.45   *Express Apollon*   Santorini.
14.00   *Speed H/F*   Sikinos. Ios. Santorini.
20.35   *Panagia Ekatonta.*   Sikinos. Ios. Naxos.
                               Paros. Piraeus.

②
02.30   *Pegasus*   Sikinos. Ios. Santorini.
09.05   *Poseidon Express 2* Sikinos. Ios. Naxos.
                               Paros. Piraeus.
10.30   *Pegasus*   Kimolos. Milos. Sifnos.
                               Serifos. Kythnos.
                               Piraeus.
12.30   *Speed H/F*   Santorini.
13.15   *Express Paros*   Sikinos. Ios. Santorini.
                               Anafi.
15.30   *Speed H/F*   Milos. Sifnos. Paros.
                               Mykonos. Tinos. Syros.
24.00   *Express Paros*   Naxos. Paros. Syros.

③
09.00   *Maria PA*   Sikinos. Ios. Santorini.
10.40   *Speed H/F*   Paros. Naxos. Mykonos.
                               Syros.
16.30   *Panagia Ekatonta.*   Santorini.
18.10   *Speed H/F*   Sikinos. Ios. Santorini.

④
01.15   *Pegasus*   Sikinos. Santorini.
14.00   *Speed H/F*   Sikinos. Ios. Santorini.

⑤
03.05   *Panagia Ekatonta.*   Santorini.
12.30   *Speed H/F*   Santorini.

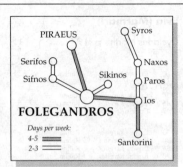

Days per week:
4-5
2-3

15.30	Speed H/F	Milos. Sifnos. Paros. Mykonos. Tinos. Syros.
23.50	*Milos Express*	Serifos. Piraeus.

④
02.00	*Pegasus*	Santorini.
03.45	*Poseidon Express 2*	Santorini.
10.40	Speed H/F	Paros. Naxos. Mykonos.
16.55	*Milos Express*	Sikinos. Santorini.
17.30	Speed H/F	Sikinos. Ios. Santorini.
20.40	*Milos Express*	Kimolos. Milos. Sifnos. Piraeus.

⑦
17.00	*Express Paros*	Milos. Sifnos. Paros. Syros.

Fourni

Eastern Line   p. 381

Ⓓ
07.00	*Maria Express*	Ikaria (Agios Kyrikos).

①
08.00	Miniotis	Ikaria (Agios Kyrikos). Samos (Karlovassi). Samos (Vathi).
10.50	Samos H/F	Ikaria (Agios Kyrikos). Samos (Pithagorio).
16.05	Samos H/F	Patmos. Leros (Agia Marina). Kalimnos. Kos.
20.30	Miniotis	Samos (Pithagorio).

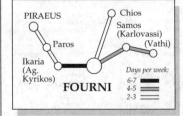

Days per week:
6-7
4-5
2-3

---

③
06.15	*Anemos*	Samos (Karlovassi). Samos (Vathi). Patmos. Lipsi.
08.55	Samos H/F	Ikaria (Agios Kyrikos). Patmos. Lipsi. Leros (Agia Marina). Kalimnos. Kos.
18.30	Samos H/F	Samos (Pithagorio). Samos (Vathi).
20.25	*Anemos*	Ikaria (Agios Kyrikos). Mykonos. Piraeus.

④
06.15	*Golden Vergina*	Samos (Karlovassi). Samos (Vathi).
18.10	*Golden Vergina*	Ikaria (Evdilos). Paros. Piraeus.

⑤
08.55	Samos H/F	Ikaria (Agios Kyrikos). Patmos. Lipsi. Leros (Agia Marina). Kalimnos. Kos.
13.00	Dode. H/F	Ikaria (Agios Kyrikos).
14.55	Dode. H/F	Patmos. Kos. Rhodes.
18.30	Samos H/F	Samos (Pithagorio). Samos (Vathi).

⑥
05.30	*Daliana*	Samos (Karlovassi). Samos (Vathi).
19.00	*Daliana*	Ikaria (Agios Kyrikos). Naxos. Piraeus.

⑦
08.55	Samos H/F	Ikaria (Agios Kyrikos). Patmos. Lipsi. Leros (Agia Marina). Kalimnos. Kos.
18.30	Samos H/F	Samos (Pithagorio). Samos (Vathi).

Gavdos

Crete   p. 298

① ③
16.00	South Crete Line	Sfakia.

④
10.00	South Crete Line	Paleochora.

⑥
06.00	South Crete Line	Sfakia.

⑥ ⑦
07.00	South Crete Line	Paleochora.

Gelibolu

Turkey
p. 520

Ⓓ x 7   06.00–23.00   Lâpseki.

Gökçeada

Turkey
p. 520

Ⓦ x 5   TML   Çanakkale.

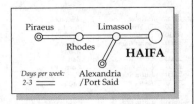

Piraeus   Limassol

Rhodes

HAIFA

Days per week: Alexandria
2-3 ===   /Port Said

Gythio

Argo-Saronic   p. 459

②
15.30   *Kantia*   Crete (Kasteli).

⑦
20.00   *Kantia*   Crete (Kasteli).

○
07.30   *Nissos Kithera*   Kithera (Agia Pelagia).

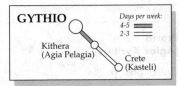

GYTHIO   *Days per week:*
                        4-5 ===
                        2-3 ===
Kithera
(Agia Pelagia)   Crete
                       (Kasteli)

Hydra

Argo-Saronic   p. 459

Ⓓ
09.30   *Mirage*   Spetses. Porto Helio.
11.40   *Mirage*   Poros.
                           Piraeus.
12.00   *Eftichia*   Ermioni. Spetses.
12.00   *Express Danae*   Spetses. Porto Helio.
15.00   *Express Danae*   Poros. Methana.
                           Aegina. Piraeus.
15.15   *Eftichia*   Poros. Methana.
                           Aegina. Piraeus.
17.50   *Mirage*   Spetses. Porto Helio.
20.00   *Mirage*   Piraeus.

🠒 *Flying Dolphins* include:
Ⓓ x 10   Piraeus (Zea).
   x 7   Poros. / Spetses. Porto Helio.

Haifa

Israel   p. 84

④
19.00   *Princesa Marissa*   Port Said. Limassol.
20.00   *Sea Harmony*   Limassol. Rhodes.
                              Crete (Iraklion). Piraeus.

⑤
20.00   *Princesa Cypria*   Limassol. Rhodes.
                              Lesbos (Mytilini). Tinos.
                              Piraeus.

⑦
20.00   *Nissos Kypros*   Limassol. Rhodes.
                              Piraeus.

20.00   *Princesa Marissa*   Limassol. Port Said.
20.00   *Sea Symphony*   Limassol. Rhodes.
                              Piraeus.

○
20.00   *Countess M*   Limassol. Rhodes.
                              Crete (Iraklion).
                              Piraeus.

20.00   *Sea Serenade*   Limassol. Rhodes.
                              Crete (Iraklion).
                              Piraeus.

Igoumenitsa

Ionian Line   p. 485

International Services:

Ⓓ
06.30   HML Ferries   Corfu. Brindisi.
06.30   *Superfast I/II*   Patras.
07.00   *Ouranos*   Corfu. Brindisi.
08.00   *Brindisi/Valentino* Patras.
08.00   HML Ferries   Kefalonia (Sami).
                              Patras.
11.00   *Kapetan Alexandros* Brindisi.
20.30   HML Ferries   Corfu. Brindisi.
21.00   *Ventouris*   Bari.
23.20   *Ionian Bridge*   Corfu. Brindisi.
24.00   *Superfast I/II*   Bari.

Ⓐ
06.30   Med Link Lines   Brindisi.
07.00   Adriatica   Corfu. Brindisi.

①
02.00   *Ikarus*   Ancona.
09.30   *Aretousa*   Venice.
10.00   *Pasiphae*   Patras.
10.30   *Kriti I*   Ancona.
21.30   *Daedalus/Fedra*   Corfu. Patras.
22.30   *Ionian Victory*   Patras.

②		
02.00	Pasiphae	Ancona.
07.00	El. Venizelos	Trieste.
08.30	Daedalus/Fedra	Venice.
10.00	Ionian Island	Ancona.
12.00	Ikarus	Patras.
21.00	Dame M/Duchess M	Bari.
21.00	Erotokritos	Corfu. Patras.
22.00	Ionian Star	Corfu. Patras.
23.00	Talos	Patras.

③		
05.00	Ionian Victory	Corfu. Venice.
08.30	Daedalus/Fedra	Venice.
12.00	Pasiphae	Patras.
13.00	Kriti I	Patras.
21.00	Aretousa	Corfu. Patras.
22.00	Ikarus	Ancona.

④		
07.30	Erotokritos	Venice.
08.00	Talos	Trieste.
10.00	Ionian Star	Ancona.
10.30	Kriti II	Ancona.
11.00	Ionian Island	Patras.
15.00	El. Venizelos	Patras.
19.00	Dame M/Duchess M	Bari.
21.30	Daedalus/Fedra	Corfu. Patras.
22.00	Pasiphae	Ancona.

⑤		
05.00	Ionian Island	Corfu. Venice.
08.00	Ikarus	Patras.
09.00	El. Venizelos	Corfu. Trieste.
09.30	Aretousa	Venice.
21.30	Daedalus/Fedra	Corfu. Patras.
22.00	Ionian Victory	Corfu. Patras.
24.00	Dame M/Duchess M	Bari.
24.00	Ikarus	Ancona.

⑥		
08.00	Pasiphae	Patras.
08.30	Daedalus/Fedra	Venice.
11.00	Ionian Star	Patras.
14.30	Erotokritos	Patras.
20.30	Ionian Victory	Corfu. Ancona.
24.00	Pasiphae	Ancona.

⑦		
06.30	Ionian Star	Venice.
08.00	Talos	Trieste.
10.00	Ikarus	Patras.
10.30	Erotokritos	Venice.
10.30	Kriti II	Ancona.
13.30	Aretousa	Patras.
21.00	Dame M/Duchess M	Bari.
21.30	·El. Venizelos	Corfu. Patras.
22.00	Ionian Island	Corfu. Patras.

Domestic Services:

Ⓓ Ⓗ 05.00–22.00		Corfu.

Ⓓ		
07.30	11.00 14.00	
16.00	19.30	Corfu (Lefkimi).
05.45	11.30 16.15	
	Agios Spyridon	Corfu.

○		
09.30	Theologos	Corfu.
15.00	Theologos	Paxi.

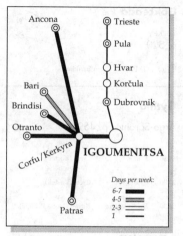

Days per week:
6-7
4-5
2-3
1

Ikaria (Agios Kyrikos)

Eastern Line   p. 384

Ⓓ		
13.00	Maria Express	Fourni.

①		
04.15	Daliana	Samos (Karlovassi).
		Samos (Vathi).
09.00	Miniotis	Samos (Karlovassi).
		Samos (Vathi).
11.20	Samos H/F	Samos (Pithagorio).
15.30	Samos H/F	Fourni. Patmos. Leros (Agia Marina). Kalimnos. Kos.
19.30	Daliana	Naxos. Paros. Piraeus.
19.30	Miniotis	Fourni. Samos (Pithagorio).

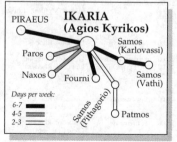

Days per week:
6-7
4-5
2-3

②
| 04.15 | *Milena* | Samos (Karlovassi). Samos (Vathi). |
| 19.20 | *Milena* | Naxos. Paros. Piraeus. |

③
05.20	*Anemos*	Fourni. Samos (Karlovassi). (Vathi). Patmos. Lipsi.
09.25	Samos H/F	Patmos. Lipsi. Leros (Agia Marina). Kalimnos. Kos.
17.25	Samos H/F	Fourni. Samos (Pithagorio). Samos (Vathi).
21.20	*Anemos*	Mykonos. Piraeus.

④
| 04.15 | *Milena* | Samos (Karlovassi). Samos (Vathi). |
| 19.20 | *Milena* | Naxos. Paros. Piraeus. |

⑤
09.25	Samos H/F	Patmos. Lipsi. Leros (Agia Marina). Kalimnos. Kos.
14.00	Dode. H/F	Fourni. Patmos. Kos. Rhodes.
17.25	Samos H/F	Fourni. Samos (Pithagorio). Samos (Vathi).

⑥
04.30	*Daliana*	Fourni. Samos (Karlovassi). Samos (Vathi).
11.05	*Anemos*	Piraeus.
20.00	*Daliana*	Naxos. Piraeus.

⑦
08.20	*Anemos*	Samos (Karlovassi). Samos (Vathi).
09.25	Samos H/F	Patmos. Lipsi. Leros (Agia Marina). Kalimnos. Kos.
11.10	Dode. H/F	Samos (Pithagorio).
14.30	Dode. H/F	Patmos. Leros (Agia Marina). Kos. Kalimnos.
17.25	Samos H/F	Fourni. Samos (Pithagorio). Samos (Vathi).

Ikaria (Evdilos)

Eastern Line   p. 386

②
01.50	*Golden Vergina*	Samos (Karlovassi). Samos (Vathi).
03.10	*Anemos*	Samos (Karlovassi). Samos (Vathi).
08.55	*Golden Vergina*	Piraeus.
10.20	*Anemos*	Piraeus.

③
| 02.50 | *Golden Vergina* | Samos (Karlovassi). Samos (Vathi). |
| 09.55 | *Golden Vergina* | Piraeus. |

④
| 05.00 | *Golden Vergina* | Fourni. Samos (Karlovassi). Samos (Vathi). |
| 19.30 | *Golden Vergina* | Paros. Piraeus. |

⑤
| 02.25 | *Anemos* | Samos (Karlovassi). Samos (Vathi). |
| 09.10 | *Anemos* | Piraeus. |

Days per week: 2-3 ═══

IKARIA (Evdilos)

PIRAEUS — Paros — Samos (Karlovassi) — Samos (Vathi)

⑥
01.50	*Golden Vergina*	Samos (Karlovassi). Samos (Vathi).
04.10	*Anemos*	Samos (Karlovassi). Samos (Vathi).
09.30	*Golden Vergina*	Syros. Piraeus.

⑦
05.00	*Golden Vergina*	Samos (Karlovassi). Samos (Vathi).
12.20	*Golden Vergina*	Paros. Piraeus.
19.30	*Anemos*	Mykonos. Syros. Piraeus.

Ios

Cyclades Central   p. 140

Ⓓ
08.15	Speed H/F	Santorini.
14.00	*Syros Express*	Santorini.
17.55	*Syros Express*	Naxos. Paros. Mykonos.

Ⓓ ex ②
| 05.30 | *Express Olympia* | Santorini. |

①
02.30	*Express Apollon*	Sikinos. Folegandros.
03.00	*Poseidon Express 2*	Santorini.
05.30	*Express Olympia*	Santorini. Anafi.
08.15	Speed H/F	Santorini. Amorgos (Katapola). Amorgos (Egiali). Koufonissia. Schinoussa. Iraklia. Naxos. Mykonos.
08.35	*Poseidon Express 2*	Naxos. Paros. Piraeus.
09.15	*Express Apollon*	Naxos. Paros. Piraeus.
11.15	Speed H/F	Santorini.
12.15	*Express Olympia*	Naxos. Paros. Piraeus.
12.45	Speed H/F	Sikinos. Folegandros.
15.10	Speed H/F	Santorini.
15.10	*Panagia Ekatonta*.	Santorini.
15.15	*Maria PA*	Naxos. Paros. Mykonos. Tinos. Syros.
15.30	*Express Santorini*	Santorini.
16.15	Speed H/F	Naxos. Paros. Mykonos. Tinos. Syros.
21.15	*Express Santorini*	Naxos. Paros. Piraeus.
21.55	*Panagia Ekatonta*.	Naxos. Paros. Piraeus.

②
02.30	*Poseidon Express 2*	Santorini.
04.00	*Pegasus*	Santorini.
05.30	*Express Apollon*	Santorini.

08.15	Speed H/F	Santorini. Anafi.
09.10	*Pegasus*	Sikinos. Folegandros. Kimolos. Milos. Sifnos. Serifos. Kythnos. Piraeus.
09.15	*Express Apollon*	Naxos. Paros. Piraeus.
10.30	*Poseidon Express 2*	Naxos. Paros. Piraeus.
11.50	Speed H/F	Paros. Naxos. Mykonos.
14.45	*Express Paros*	Santorini. Anafi.
15.00	*Maria PA*	Santorini. Anafi.
15.10	*Panagia Ekatonta.*	Santorini.
15.30	*Express Santorini*	Santorini.
15.55	*Ariadne*	Sikinos. Santorini.
16.30	Speed H/F	Santorini. Anafi.
20.30	*Panagia Ekatonta.*	Naxos. Paros. Piraeus.
21.15	*Express Santorini*	Naxos. Paros. Piraeus.
22.05	*Ariadne*	Naxos. Paros. Piraeus.
22.30	*Express Paros*	Sikinos. Folegandros. Naxos. Paros. Syros.
24.00	*Express Athina*	Santorini.

③

02.35	*Super Naias*	Santorini. Anafi. Astipalea.
08.30	*Express Athina*	Naxos. Paros. Piraeus.
09.55	Speed H/F	Sikinos. Folegandros. Paros. Naxos. Mykonos. Syros.
10.45	*Maria PA*	Santorini.
11.00	*Express Olympia*	Naxos. Paros. Piraeus.
11.30	Speed H/F	Santorini. Amorgos (Katapola).
13.30	*Super Naias*	Naxos. Paros. Piraeus.
15.10	*Panagia Ekatonta.*	Sikinos. Folegandros. Santorini.
15.30	*Express Apollon*	Santorini.
16.30	*Maria PA*	Naxos. Paros. Mykonos. Syros.
19.00	Speed H/F	Santorini.
20.35	*Panagia Ekatonta.*	Naxos. Paros. Piraeus.
21.15	*Express Apollon*	Naxos. Paros. Piraeus.

④

02.30	*Poseidon Express 2*	Santorini.
08.15	Speed H/F	Santorini. Amorgos (Katapola). Amorgos (Egiali). Koufonissia. Schinoussa. Iraklia. Naxos. Mykonos. Syros.
08.35	*Poseidon Express 2*	Naxos. Paros. Piraeus.
11.00	*Express Olympia*	Naxos. Paros. Piraeus.
11.15	Speed H/F	Santorini.
12.45	Speed H/F	Sikinos. Folegandros.
15.10	Speed H/F	Santorini.
15.30	*Express Apollon*	Santorini.
15.40	*Super Naias*	Santorini.
16.15	Speed H/F	Naxos. Paros. Mykonos. Tinos. Syros.
16.55	*Ariadne*	Santorini.
20.30	*Super Naias*	Naxos. Paros. Piraeus.
21.15	*Express Apollon*	Naxos. Paros. Piraeus.
22.05	*Ariadne*	Naxos. Paros. Piraeus.
24.00	*Express Athina*	Santorini.

⑤

01.45	*Panagia Ekatonta.*	Sikinos. Folegandros. Santorini.
02.30	*Poseidon Express 2*	Santorini.
08.15	Speed H/F	Santorini. Anafi.
08.20	*Panagia Ekatonta.*	Naxos. Paros. Piraeus.
08.30	*Express Athina*	Naxos. Paros. Piraeus.
08.35	*Poseidon Express 2*	Naxos. Paros. Piraeus.
11.00	*Express Olympia*	Naxos. Paros. Piraeus.

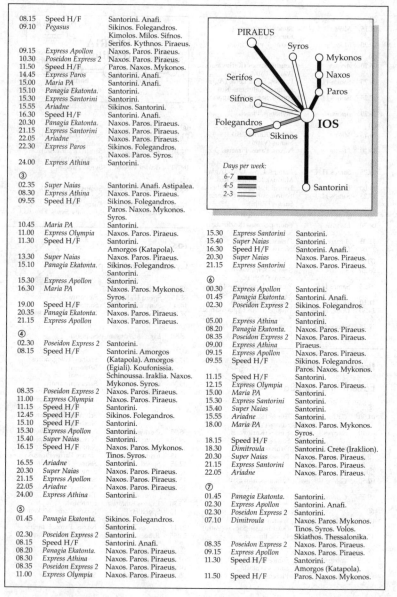

PIRAEUS

Syros

Mykonos

Serifos

Naxos

Panagia Ekatonta.

Paros

Sifnos

Folegandros

IOS

Sikinos

Days per week:

6-7

4-5

2-3

Santorini

15.30	*Express Santorini*	Santorini.
15.40	*Super Naias*	Santorini.
16.30	Speed H/F	Santorini. Anafi.
20.30	*Super Naias*	Naxos. Paros. Piraeus.
21.15	*Express Santorini*	Naxos. Paros. Piraeus.

⑥

00.30	*Express Apollon*	Santorini.
01.45	*Panagia Ekatonta.*	Santorini. Anafi.
02.30	*Poseidon Express 2*	Sikinos. Folegandros. Santorini.
05.00	*Express Athina*	Santorini.
08.20	*Panagia Ekatonta.*	Naxos. Paros. Piraeus.
08.35	*Poseidon Express 2*	Naxos. Paros. Piraeus.
09.00	*Express Athina*	Piraeus.
09.15	*Express Apollon*	Naxos. Paros. Piraeus.
09.55	Speed H/F	Sikinos. Folegandros. Paros. Naxos. Mykonos.
11.15	Speed H/F	Santorini.
12.15	*Express Olympia*	Naxos. Paros. Piraeus.
15.00	*Maria PA*	Santorini.
15.30	*Express Santorini*	Santorini.
15.40	*Super Naias*	Santorini.
15.55	*Ariadne*	Santorini.
18.00	*Maria PA*	Naxos. Paros. Mykonos. Syros.
18.15	Speed H/F	Santorini.
18.30	*Dimitroula*	Santorini. Crete (Iraklion).
20.30	*Super Naias*	Naxos. Paros. Piraeus.
21.15	*Express Santorini*	Naxos. Paros. Piraeus.
22.05	*Ariadne*	Naxos. Paros. Piraeus.

⑦

01.45	*Panagia Ekatonta.*	Santorini.
02.30	*Express Apollon*	Santorini. Anafi.
02.30	*Poseidon Express 2*	Santorini.
07.10	*Dimitroula*	Naxos. Paros. Mykonos. Tinos. Syros. Volos. Skiathos. Thessalonika.
08.35	*Poseidon Express 2*	Naxos. Paros. Piraeus.
09.15	*Express Apollon*	Naxos. Paros. Piraeus.
11.30	Speed H/F	Santorini. Amorgos (Katapola).
11.50	Speed H/F	Paros. Naxos. Mykonos.

12.15	*Express Olympia*	Naxos. Paros. Piraeus.
12.45	*Express Paros*	Santorini. Sikinos. Folegandros. Milos. Sifnos.
13.20	*Panagia Ekatonta.*	Naxos. Paros. Piraeus.
13.30	*Maria PA*	Santorini. Crete (Iraklion).
15.30	*Express Santorini*	Santorini.
15.40	*Super Naias*	Santorini.
15.55	*Ariadne*	Santorini.
16.30	Speed H/F	Santorini.
20.30	*Super Naias*	Naxos. Paros. Piraeus.
21.15	*Express Santorini*	Naxos. Paros. Piraeus.
22.05	*Ariadne*	Naxos. Paros. Piraeus.

Iraklia

Cyclades East   p. 265

Ⓓ

Ferries and Catamarans as **Schinoussa**
Times for boats to:

Naxos & Piraeus:
Schinoussa departure time +30 minutes.

Amorgos:
Schinoussa departure time –30 minutes.

İstanbul

Turkey   p. 521

Ⓓ Ⓗ
06.45–21.00   Princes' Islands.
                               [x 5 steaming on to
                               Yalova or Çinarcik.]

Ⓓ
09.30 20.00   Bandırma.
10.30 13.30   Bosphorus 'Tour'.
08.00   Armutlu. Mudanya.
08.00   Marmara. Avşa.

x 4   Deniz Otobusleri   Marmara. Avşa.

⑤
17.30   TML   İzmir. [② August only]

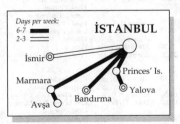

Days per week:
6-7
2-3
İSTANBUL
İsmir
Princes' Is.
Marmara
Yalova
Avşa   Bandırma

Ithaca (Frikes)

Ionian Line   p. 486

Ⓓ
11.00   *Meganisi*   Kefalonia (Fiskardo). Lefkada (Nidri).
13.00   *Nidri*   Lefkada (Nidri).
17.45   *Nidri*   Kefalonia (Fiskardo). Lefkada (Nidri).

Ithaca (Pisaetos)

Ionian Line   p. 486

Ⓓ
07.40   *Aphrodite L*   Kefalonia (Sami).
09.35   *Aphrodite L*   Astakos.
17.00   *Aphrodite L*   Kefalonia (Sami).

Ⓞ
21.00   HML Ferries   Brindisi.

Ithaca (Vathi)

Ionian Line   p. 486

Ⓓ
07.00   *Kefalonia*   Kefalonia (Sami). Patras.
16.30   *Kefalonia*   Kefalonia (Sami). Patras.

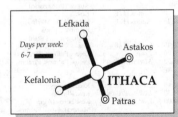

Lefkada
Days per week:
6-7
Astakos
Kefalonia   ITHACA
Patras

İzmir

Turkey   p. 522

② ⑦
14.00   TML   İstanbul.
③
16.00   *Ankara*   Venice.

Kabatepe

Turkey p. 522

③ ⑦
13.00   TML   Gökçeada.

Kalamata

Argo-Saronic p. 461

③ ⑥
23.00   *Kantia*   Kithera. Crete (Kapsali).

Kalimnos

Dodecanese p. 315

Ⓓ
07.00 15.30 18.30
       Olympios Apollon   Kos (Mastihari).

①
05.00   *Marina/Rodanthi*   Kos. Rhodes. Symi.
07.00   Dode. H/F   Kos. Leros (Agia
                            Marina). Lipsi. Patmos.
07.00   *Nissos Kalimnos*   Kos. Nissiros. Tilos.
                            Symi. Rhodes.
                            Kastelorizo.
08.15   Samos H/F   Leros (Agia Marina).
                            Patmos. Fourni.
                            Ikaria (Agios Kyrikos).
                            Samos (Pithagorio).
10.40   Samos H/F   Kos.
14.45   Samos H/F   Leros (Agia Marina).
                            Patmos. Samos
                            (Pithagorio). (Vathi).
18.45   Samos H/F   Kos.
20.00   *Rodos*   Leros. Patmos. Piraeus.
21.30   *Marina/Rodanthi*   Leros. Patmos. Piraeus.

②
02.40   *Leros*   Kos. Rhodes.
04.30   *Marina/Rodanthi*   Kos. Rhodes.
07.00   Dode. H/F   Kos. Leros (Agia
                            Marina). Lipsi. Patmos.
                            Samos (Pithagorio).
08.15   Samos H/F   Leros (Agia Marina).
                            Lipsi. Patmos.
                            Samos (Pithagorio).
10.50   Samos H/F   Kos.
14.45   Samos H/F   Leros (Agia Marina).
                            Lipsi. Patmos. Samos
                            (Pithagorio). (Vathi).
17.55   Samos H/F   Kos.
18.45   *Leros*   Leros. Patmos. Piraeus.
19.00   *Nissos Kalimnos*   Astipalea.

③
02.30   *Marina/Rodanthi*   Kos. Rhodes.
04.30   *Ialyssos*   Kos. Rhodes.

PIRAEUS   Samos (Pithagorio)

                 Days per week:
Patmos   Leros   6-7
                  2-3

Telendos   Lipsi

Astipalea   **KALIMNOS**

Pserimos   Kos

Nissiros   Symi

Tilos   Rhodes

07.00   Dode. H/F   Kos. Nissiros. Tilos.
                            Rhodes.
07.00   *Nissos Kalimnos*   Leros. Lipsi. Patmos.
                            Arki. Agathonisi.
                            Samos (Pithagorio).
08.15   Samos H/F   Leros (Agia Marina).
                            Lipsi. Patmos.
                            Samos (Pithagorio).
08.30   *Romilda*   Astipalea.
                            Amorgos (Katapola).
                            Mykonos. Piraeus.
12.20   Samos H/F   Kos.
14.45   Samos H/F   Leros (Agia Marina).
                            Lipsi. Patmos. Ikaria
                            (Agios Kyrikos). Fourni.
                            Samos (Pithagorio).
17.25   Samos H/F   Kos.
21.30   *Ialyssos*   Leros. Patmos. Piraeus.
21.30   *Marina/Rodanthi*   Piraeus.

④
02.30   *Marina/Rodanthi*   Kos. Rhodes.
03.15   *Leros*   Kos. Rhodes.
07.00   Dode. H/F   Kos. Rhodes.
07.00   *Nissos Kalimnos*   Kos. Nissiros. Tilos.
                            Symi. Rhodes.
                            Kastelorizo.
08.15   Samos H/F   Leros (Agia Marina).
                            Lipsi. Patmos.
                            Samos (Pithagorio).
10.50   Samos H/F   Kos.
14.45   Samos H/F   Leros (Agia Marina).
                            Lipsi. Patmos.
                            Samos (Pithagorio).
17.55   Samos H/F   Kos.
18.45   *Leros*   Leros. Lipsi. Patmos.
                            Piraeus.
21.30   *Marina/Rodanthi*   Piraeus.
21.30   *Marina/Rodanthi*   Leros. Patmos. Piraeus.

⑤
02.30   *Marina/Rodanthi*   Kos. Rhodes.
                            Karpathos (Town).
04.30   *Ialyssos*   Kos. Rhodes.
07.00   Dode. H/F   Kos. Leros (Agia Marina).
                            Lipsi. Patmos.
                            Samos (Pithagorio).

08.15	Samos H/F	Leros (Agia Marina). Lipsi. Patmos. Agathonisi. Samos (Pithagorio).
12.20	Samos H/F	Kos.
14.45	Samos H/F	Leros (Agia Marina). Lipsi. Patmos. Ikaria (Agios Kyrikos). Fourni. Samos (Pithagorio). (Vathi).
17.45	Samos H/F	Kos.
19.00	*Nissos Kalimnos*	Astipalea.
21.30	*Ialyssos*	Leros. Patmos. Piraeus.
21.30	*Marina/Rodanthi*	Piraeus.

⑥
06.30	*Romilda*	Kos. Nissiros. Tilos. Rhodes.
07.00	Dode. H/F	Kos. Leros (Agia Marina). Patmos. Samos (Pithagorio).
08.20	Samos H/F	Leros (Agia Marina). Lipsi. Patmos. Samos (Pithagorio).
08.50	*Milena*	Leros. Patmos. Naxos. Paros. Piraeus.
11.15	Samos H/F	Kos.
11.30	Dode. H/F	Astipalea.
14.45	Samos H/F	Leros (Agia Marina). Lipsi. Patmos. Agathonisi. Samos (Pithagorio).
16.55	Samos H/F	Kos.
17.00	Dode. H/F	Kos. Symi. Rhodes.
21.30	*Marina/Rodanthi*	Leros. Patmos. Piraeus.

⑦
04.30	*Ialyssos*	Kos. Rhodes.
05.30	*Marina/Rodanthi*	Kos. Rhodes.
07.00	Dode. H/F	Kos. Leros (Agia Marina). Patmos. Ikaria (Agios Kyrikos). Samos (Pithagorio).
07.00	*Nissos Kalimnos*	Leros. Lipsi. Patmos. Agathonisi. Samos (Pithagorio).
08.20	Samos H/F	Leros (Agia Marina). Lipsi. Patmos. Samos (Pithagorio).
12.20	Samos H/F	Kos.
14.45	Samos H/F	Leros (Agia Marina). Lipsi. Patmos. Ikaria (Agios Kyrikos). Fourni. Samos (Pithagorio).
17.55	Samos H/F	Kos.
20.20	*Milena*	Leros. Patmos. Naxos. Piraeus.
21.30	*Ialyssos*	Leros. Patmos. Piraeus.

Karpathos (Diafani)

Dodecanese p. 320

②
| 04.50 | *Romilda* | Karpathos (Town). Kassos. Crete (Sitia). |
| 19.20 | *Romilda* | Chalki. Rhodes. |

③
| 18.00 | *Daliana* | Chalki. Rhodes. |

④
| 06.00 | *Daliana* | Karpathos (Town). Kassos. Crete (Iraklion). Santorini. Paros. Piraeus. |

⑥
| 15.30 | *Vitsentzos Kornaros* | Rhodes. |

Karpathos (Town)

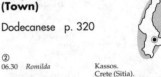

Dodecanese p. 320

②
| 06.30 | *Romilda* | Kassos. Crete (Sitia). |
| 18.00 | *Romilda* | Karpathos (Diafani). Chalki. Rhodes. |

③
| 16.30 | *Daliana* | Karpathos (Diafani). Chalki. Rhodes. |

④
| 08.00 | *Daliana* | Kassos. Crete (Iraklion). Santorini. Paros. Piraeus. |

⑤
| 13.00 | *Marina/Rodanthi* | Rhodes. Kos. Kalimnos. Piraeus. |

⑥
| 14.30 | *Vitsentzos Kornaros* | Karpathos (Diafani). Rhodes. |

⑦
| 09.30 | *Vitsentzos Kornaros* | Kassos. Crete (Sitia). Crete (Agios Nikolaos). Milos. Piraeus. |

Kassos

Dodecanese　p. 322

②
| 08.30 | Romilda | Crete (Sitia). |
| 16.00 | Romilda | Karpathos (Town). Karpathos (Diafani). Chalki. Rhodes. |

③
| 14.10 | Daliana | Karpathos (Town). Karpathos (Diafani). Chalki. Rhodes. |

④
| 10.00 | Daliana | Crete (Iraklion). Santorini. Paros. Piraeus. |

⑥
| 12.45 | Vitsentzos Kornaros | Karpathos (Town). Karpathos (Diafani). Rhodes. |

⑦
| 11.00 | Vitsentzos Kornaros | Crete (Sitia). Crete (Agios Nikolaos). Milos. Piraeus. |

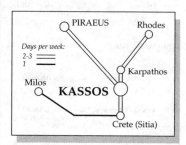

PIRAEUS

Rhodes

Days per week:
2-3 ═══
1 ───

Milos

KASSOS

Karpathos

Crete (Sitia)

Kastelorizo / Megisti

Dodecanese　p. 324

①
| 22.30 | Nissos Kalimnos | Rhodes. Symi. Tilos. Nissiros. Kos. Kalimnos. |

③
| 12.00 | Rodos | Rhodes. Kos. Piraeus. |

④
| 22.30 | Nissos Kalimnos | Rhodes. Symi. Tilos. Nissiros. Kos. Kalimnos. |

Kavala

Northern Aegean　p. 415

Ⓓ
07.50	09.30	12.00		
14.00	16.00	18.00	19.30	
		ANET Line	Thassos (Skala Prinos).

| 07.00 | 12.30 | 14.00 | 18.30 | |
| | | Hydrofoil | Thassos (Town). |

| 08.30 | 15.30 | | |
| | Hydrofoil | Thassos (Limenaria). |

②
| 17.00 | Alcaeos | Limnos. Lesbos (Mytilini). |

③
| 15.30 | Arsinoe | Samothrace. |
| 20.30 | Alcaeos | Limnos. Agios Efstratios. Lesbos (Sigri). Rafina. |

④
| 14.00 | Arsinoe | Samothrace. |

⑤
| 16.30 | Arsinoe | Samothrace. |

⑥
| 15.30 | Arsinoe | Samothrace. |
| 16.00 | Alcaeos | Limnos. Agios Efstratios. Rafina. |

⑦
10.00	Sappho	Limnos. Lesbos (Mytilini). Chios. Piraeus.
14.30	Arsinoe	Samothrace.
15.30	Hydrofoil	Thassos (Skala Marion).

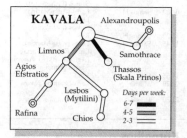

KAVALA　Alexandroupolis

Limnos　　Samothrace

Agios Efstratios　　Thassos (Skala Prinos)

Lesbos (Mytilini)　Days per week:
6-7 ▬▬▬
4-5 ▬▬▬
2-3 ═══

Rafina　　Chios

Kea

Cyclades West　p. 225

Ⓓ x ①
| 10.05 | Mega Dolphin | Andros. |
| 20.25 | Mega Dolphin | Piraeus (Zea). |

①

06.00	*Mirina Express*	Lavrion.
08.15	*Mega Dolphin*	Piraeus (Zea).
11.45	*Express Paros*	Kythnos.
		Syros.
17.00	*Mirina Express*	Lavrion.

②

07.00	*Mirina Express*	Lavrion.

③

07.00	*Mirina Express*	Lavrion.
10.30	*Mirina Express*	Kythnos.
17.00	*Mirina Express*	Lavrion.
18.30	*Express Paros*	Kythnos.
		Syros.

④

07.00	*Mirina Express*	Lavrion.
17.00	*Mirina Express*	Lavrion.

⑤

07.00	*Mirina Express*	Lavrion.
11.00	*Mirina Express*	Lavrion.
12.15	*Mega Dolphin*	Piraeus (Zea).
16.30	*Mirina Express*	Lavrion.
16.35	*Mega Dolphin*	Andros.
19.45	*Mirina Express*	Lavrion.
22.30	*Supercat Haroulla*	Rafina.

⑥

07.00	*Mirina Express*	Lavrion.
10.30	*Mirina Express*	Lavrion.
12.15	*Mega Dolphin*	Piraeus (Zea).
16.00	*Mirina Express*	Lavrion.
16.35	*Mega Dolphin*	Andros.
19.30	*Mirina Express*	Lavrion.

⑦

12.00	*Mirina Express*	Lavrion.
15.30	*Mirina Express*	Lavrion.
19.00	*Mirina Express*	Lavrion.
21.00	*Supercat Haroulla*	Rafina.
22.15	*Mirina Express*	Lavrion.

PIRAEUS — Lavrion — KEA — Andros

Days per week: 6-7

Kefalonia (Agia Efimia)

Ionian Line p. 490

Service Suspended

○		
09.15		Ithaca. Astakos.

○		
18.00		Astakos. [Ithaca].

Kefalonia (Argostoli)

Ionian Line p. 490

Ⓗ	Local	Kefalonia (Lixouri).

Ⓓ		
14.15	*Eptanisos*	Kilini.
14.15	*Ionis*	Kilini.

Kefalonia (Fiskardo)

Ionian Line p. 490

Ⓓ		
10.30	*Meganisi*	Lefkada (Nidri).
12.00	*Nidri*	Ithaca (Frikes).
		Lefkada (Nidri).
17.00	*Meganisi*	Lefkada (Vathi).
19.00	*Nidri*	Lefkada (Nidri).

Kefalonia (Lixouri)

Ionian Line p. 490

Ⓗ	Local	Kefalonia (Argostoli).

Ⓓ		
13.40	*Ionis*	Kefalonia (Argostoli).
13.45	*Eptanisos*	Kefalonia (Argostoli).

Kefalonia (Pessada)

Ionian Line p. 490

Ⓓ		
07.45	*Ionion Pelagos*	Zakinthos (Skinaria).
17.30	*Ionion Pelagos*	Zakinthos (Skinaria).

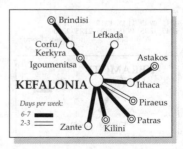

Brindisi • Lefkada • Corfu/Kerkyra • Igoumenitsa • Astakos • KEFALONIA • Ithaca • Piraeus • Zante • Kilini • Patras

Days per week: 6-7 2-3

Kefalonia (Poros)

Ionian Line   p. 490

Ⓓ
05.00	Eptanisos	Kilini.
15.30	Eptanisos	Kilini.
20.30	Eptanisos	Kilini.

Kefalonia (Sami)

Ionian Line   p. 490

International Services:

Ⓓ
| 10.00 | HML Ferries | Patras. |
| 20.30 | HML Ferries | Igoumenitsa. Corfu. Brindisi. |

Ⓐ
| 22.00 | Ventouris | Bari. |

Domestic Services:

Ⓓ
06.45	Aphrodite L	Ithaca (Pisaetos).
08.30	Kefalonia	Patras.
08.45	Aphrodite L	Ithaca (Pisaetos). Astakos.
15.30	Kefalonia	Ithaca.
15.50	Aphrodite L	Ithaca (Pisaetos).
17.45	Kefalonia	Patras.
23.30	Kefalonia	Ithaca.

Ⓞ
| 08.00 | Aphrodite L | Ithaca (Pisaetos). Kefalonia (Fiskardo). Lefkada (Vassiliki). |

Keramoti

Northern Aegean   p. 416

Ⓓ
07.15	09.15	11.15	13.15	15.15	16.45
17.45	18.45	19.45	20.45	21.45	22.30
ANET Line				Thassos (Town).

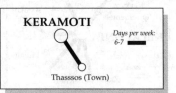

KERAMOTI

Days per week:
6-7 ▬▬

Thasssos (Town)

Kilini

Ionian Line   p. 494

Ⓓ
10.15	Dimitiros Miras/Ionis/ Proteus/Zakinthos I	Zakinthos.
11.00	Ionis	Kefalonia (Lixouri). Kefalonia (Argostoli).
12.00	Eptanisos	Kefalonia (Lixouri). Kefalonia (Argostoli).
14.30	Dimitiros Miras/Ionis/ Proteus/Zakinthos I	Zakinthos.
17.30	Dimitiros Miras/Ionis/ Proteus/Zakinthos I	Zakinthos.
18.30	Eptanisos	Kefalonia (Poros).
20.15	Dimitiros Miras/Ionis/ Proteus/Zakinthos I	Zakinthos.
22.30	Eptanisos	Kefalonia (Poros).

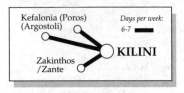

Kefalonia (Poros)
(Argostoli)

Days per week:
6-7 ▬▬

Zakinthos
/Zante

KILINI

Kilitbahir

Turkey   p. 523

Ⓓ x 6
| 00.00 | TML | Çanakkale. |

Kimolos

Cyclades West   p. 229

Ⓓ
x 4
| | Taxi Boat | Milos (Apollonia). |

①
| 21.05 | Milos Express | Milos. Sifnos. Serifos. Kythnos. Piraeus. |

②
11.30	Mega Dolphin	Milos.
11.55	Pegasus	Milos. Sifnos. Serifos. Kythnos. Piraeus.
21.05	Milos Express	Milos. Sifnos. Piraeus.

③
| 14.50 | Milos Express | Milos. Kythnos. Piraeus. |
| 15.35 | Mega Dolphin | Serifos. Sifnos. Kythnos. Piraeus. |

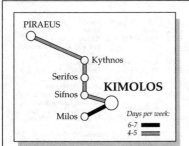

PIRAEUS

Kythnos

Serifos

KIMOLOS

Sifnos

Milos

Days per week:
6-7 ▰▰▰
4-5 ▰▰▰

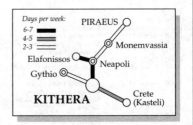

Days per week:
6-7 ▰▰▰
4-5 ▭▭▭
2-3 ═══

PIRAEUS

Monemvassia

Elafonissos

Neapoli

Gythio

KITHERA

Crete
(Kasteli)

④
13.55	Express Paros	Milos.
14.50	Milos Express	Milos. Sifnos. Serifos. Kythnos. Piraeus.
16.15	Express Paros	Sifnos. Serifos. Paros. Syros.

⑤
| 03.00 | Pegasus | Milos. |

⑥
13.55	Express Paros	Milos.
15.30	Milos Express	Folegandros. Sikinos. Santorini.
16.15	Express Paros	Sifnos. Serifos. Paros. Syros.
22.00	Milos Express	Milos. Sifnos. Piraeus.

⑦
| 10.00 | Pegasus | Sifnos. Serifos. Kythnos. Piraeus. |

Kiparissi

Argo-Saronic p. 462

○
| 00.00 | | Kithera (Agia Pelagia). Antikithera. Crete (Kasteli). |

🐬 *Flying Dolphins* include:
| Ⓓ x 1 | | Piraeus. |

Kithera
(Agia Pelagia)

Argo-Saronic p. 462

①
| 11.00 | Maria PA | Antikithera. |
| 23.30 | Maria PA | Gythio. |

②
| 01.10 | Kantia | Antikithera. Crete (Kasteli). |
| 12.10 | Kantia | Gythio. |

④
| 03.30 | Kantia | Crete (Kapsali). |
| 18.00 | Kantia | Piraeus. |

⑦
| 17.10 | Kantia | Gythio. |
| 23.00 | Kantia | Piraeus. |

🐬 *Flying Dolphins*
② ③ ⑥
| 14.05 | | Monemvassia. Gerakas. Kiparissi. Spetses. Hydra. Piraeus (Zea). |

Kos

Dodecanese
p. 328

Ⓓ
08.00	Dode. H/F	Rhodes.
10.00	Tour Boat	Kalimnos.
10.00	Tour Boat	Pserimos.
10.00	Tour Boat	Nissiros.
16.00	Bodrum Princess	Bodrum.
18.00	Hydrofoil	Rhodes.

①
06.30	Marina/Rodanthi	Rhodes. Symi.
07.30	Samos H/F	Kalimnos. Leros (Agia Marina). Patmos. Fourni. Ikaria (Agios Kyrikos). Samos (Pithagorio).
08.00	Dode. H/F	Rhodes.
08.15	Dode. H/F	Leros (Agia Marina). Lipsi. Patmos.
08.30	Nissos Kalimnos	Nissiros. Tilos. Symi. Rhodes. Kastelorizo.
10.15	Dode. H/F	Leros (Agia Marina). Patmos. Samos (Pithagorio).
14.00	Samos H/F	Kalimnos. Leros (Agia Marina). Patmos. Samos (Pithagorio). (Vathi).
18.00	Dode. H/F	Rhodes.
19.15	Dode. H/F	Kalimnos.
20.00	Marina/Rodanthi	Kalimnos. Leros. Patmos. Piraeus.

②
03.50	Leros	Rhodes.
06.00	Marina/Rodanthi	Rhodes.
07.30	Samos H/F	Kalimnos. Leros (Agia Marina). Lipsi. Patmos. Samos (Pithagorio).
08.00	Dode. H/F	Rhodes.
08.15	Dode. H/F	Leros (Agia Marina). Lipsi. Patmos. Samos (Pithagorio).
14.00	Samos H/F	Kalimnos. Leros (Agia Marina). Lipsi. Patmos. Samos (Pithagorio). (Vathi).
17.00	Nissos Kalimnos	Kalimnos.
17.30	Leros	Kalimnos. Leros. Patmos. Piraeus.
18.00	Dode. H/F	Rhodes.
19.15	Dode. H/F	Kalimnos.

③
03.45	Rodos	Rhodes. Kastelorizo.
04.00	Marina/Rodanthi	Rhodes.
05.45	Romilda	Kalimnos. Astipalea. Amorgos (Katapola). Mykonos. Piraeus.
07.30	Samos H/F	Kalimnos. Leros (Agia Marina). Lipsi. Patmos. Samos (Pithagorio).
08.00	Dode. H/F	Nissiros. Tilos. Rhodes.
08.00	Dode. H/F	Rhodes. Symi.
10.15	Dode. H/F	Leros (Agia Marina). Patmos. Samos (Pithagorio).
14.00	Samos H/F	Kalimnos. Leros (Agia Marina). Lipsi. Patmos. Ikaria (Agios Kyrikos). Fourni. Samos (Pithagorio).
18.00	Dode. H/F	Rhodes.
18.00	Romilda	Kalimnos. Astipalea. Amorgos (Katapola). Mykonos. Piraeus.
19.15	Dode. H/F	Kalimnos.
20.00	Ialyssos	Kalimnos. Leros. Patmos. Piraeus.
20.00	Marina/Rodanthi	Kalimnos. Piraeus.
21.00	Rodos	Piraeus.

PIRAEUS

Days per week:
6-7
4-5
2-3

Patmos

Lipsi

Leros

Kalimnos

Pserimos

KOS

Bodrum

Symi

Nissiros

Tilos

Rhodes

Kastelorizo

④
04.00	Marina/Rodanthi	Rhodes.
04.30	Leros	Rhodes.
07.30	Samos H/F	Kalimnos. Leros (Agia Marina). Lipsi. Patmos. Samos (Pithagorio).
08.00	Dode. H/F	Rhodes.
08.15	Dode. H/F	Leros (Agia Marina). Patmos. Agathonisi. Samos (Pithagorio).
08.30	Nissos Kalimnos	Nissiros. Tilos. Symi. Rhodes. Kastelorizo.
14.00	Samos H/F	Kalimnos. Leros (Agia Marina). Lipsi. Patmos. Samos (Pithagorio). Samos (Vathi).
17.30	Leros	Kalimnos. Leros. Lipsi. Patmos. Piraeus.
18.00	Dode. H/F	Rhodes.
19.15	Dode. H/F	Kalimnos.
20.00	Marina/Rodanthi	Kalimnos. Piraeus.
20.00	Marina/Rodanthi	Kalimnos. Leros. Patmos. Piraeus.

⑤
03.45	Rodos	Rhodes.
04.00	Marina/Rodanthi	Rhodes. Karpathos (Town).
06.00	Ialyssos	Rhodes.
07.30	Samos H/F	Kalimnos. Leros (Agia Marina). Lipsi. Patmos. Agathonisi. Samos (Pithagorio).
08.00	Dode. H/F	Rhodes. Chalki.
08.15	Dode. H/F	Leros (Agia Marina). Lipsi. Patmos. Samos (Pithagorio).
10.15	Dode. H/F	Leros (Agia Marina). Patmos. Fourni. Ikaria (Agios Kyrikos).
14.00	Rodos	Patmos. Samos (Vathi). Thessalonika.
14.00	Samos H/F	Kalimnos. Leros (Agia Marina). Lipsi. Patmos. Ikaria (Agios Kyrikos). Fourni. Samos (Pithagorio). Samos (Vathi).
17.00	Nissos Kalimnos	Kalimnos.
18.00	Dode. H/F	Rhodes.
19.15	Dode. H/F	Kalimnos.
20.00	Ialyssos	Kalimnos. Leros. Patmos. Piraeus.
20.00	Marina/Rodanthi	Kalimnos. Piraeus.

⑥
03.30	Marina/Rodanthi	Rhodes.
03.45	Leros	Rhodes.
07.30	Milena	Kalimnos. Leros. Patmos. Naxos. Paros. Piraeus.
07.30	Samos H/F	Kalimnos. Leros (Agia Marina). Lipsi. Patmos. Samos (Pithagorio).
08.00	Dode. H/F	Rhodes. Symi.
08.00	Romilda	Nissiros. Tilos. Rhodes.
08.15	Dode. H/F	Leros (Agia Marina). Patmos. Samos (Pithagorio).
10.45	Dode. H/F	Kalimnos. Astipalea.
14.00	Samos H/F	Kalimnos. Leros (Agia Marina). Lipsi. Patmos. Agathonisi. Samos (Pithagorio). Vathi).
18.00	Dode. H/F	Symi. Rhodes.
19.15	Dode. H/F	Kalimnos.

20.00	*Marina/Rodanthi*	Kalimnos. Leros. Patmos. Piraeus.
20.30	*Leros*	Piraeus.
22.30	*Romilda*	Samos (Vathi). Chios. Lesbos (Mytilini). Limnos. Alexandroupolis.

⑦
06.00	*Ialyssos*	Rhodes.
07.00	*Marina/Rodanthi*	Rhodes.
07.30	Samos H/F	Kalimnos. Leros (Agia Marina). Lipsi. Patmos. Samos (Pithagorio).
08.00	Dode. H/F	Rhodes. Tilos.
08.15	Dode. H/F	Leros (Agia Marina). Patmos. Ikaria (Agios Kyrikos). Samos (Pithagorio).
10.00	*Rodos*	Rhodes.
10.15	Dode. H/F	Nissiros.
14.00	Samos H/F	Kalimnos. Leros (Agia Marina). Lipsi. Patmos. Ikaria (Agios Kyrikos). Fourni. Samos (Pithagorio). Samos (Vathi).
18.00	Dode. H/F	Rhodes.
19.00	*Milena*	Kalimnos. Leros. Patmos. Naxos. Piraeus.
19.15	Dode. H/F	Kalimnos.
20.00	*Ialyssos*	Kalimnos. Leros. Patmos. Piraeus.
21.30	*Marina/Rodanthi*	Piraeus.
22.00	*Rodos*	Piraeus.
22.00	*Romilda*	Rhodes.

Kos (Kardamena)

Dodecanese
p. 332

Ⓓ
| 09.00 | *Nissiros Express* | Nissiros. |

Kos (Mastihari)

Dodecanese
p. 333

Ⓓ
| 09.00 17.00 21.30 | | |
| | *Olympios Apollon* | Kalimnos. |

Kosta

Argo-Saronic p. 470

Ⓓ
| 10.30 13.30 17.00 | *Alexandros M* | Spetses. |

① ② ③ ④ ⑤
| 06.50 08.00 18.30 | *Alexandros M* | Spetses. |

Koufonissia

Cyclades East p. 267

①
06.00	*Ionian Sun*	Schinoussa. Iraklia. Naxos. Paros. Syros. Rafina.
07.00	*Express Skopelitis*	Schinoussa. Iraklia. Naxos. Mykonos.
11.30	Speed H/F	Schinoussa. Iraklia. Naxos. Mykonos.
16.20	Speed H/F	Amorgos (Egiali). Amorgos (Katapola). Santorini. Ios.
19.15	*Express Skopelitis*	Amorgos (Katapola).

②
09.30	*Express Skopelitis*	Schinoussa. Iraklia. Naxos.
13.25	ILIO H/F	Amorgos (Katapola). Santorini.
17.30	*Express Skopelitis*	Donoussa. Amorgos (Egiali). Amorgos (Katapola).

③
| 07.00 | *Express Skopelitis* | Schinoussa. Iraklia. Naxos. Mykonos. |
| 19.15 | *Express Skopelitis* | Amorgos (Katapola). |

④
01.25	*Express Santorini*	Donoussa. Amorgos (Egiali). Amorgos (Katapola). Astipalea.
09.30	*Express Skopelitis*	Schinoussa. Iraklia. Naxos.
11.30	Speed H/F	Schinoussa. Iraklia. Naxos. Mykonos. Syros.
17.30	*Express Skopelitis*	Donoussa. Amorgos (Egiali). Amorgos (Katapola).
17.35	Speed H/F	Amorgos (Egiali). Amorgos (Katapola). Santorini. Ios.

⑤
05.10	*Penelope A*	Schinoussa. Iraklia. Naxos. Paros. Syros. Mykonos. Tinos. Andros. Rafina.
07.00	*Express Skopelitis*	Schinoussa. Iraklia. Naxos. Mykonos.
13.25	ILIO H/F	Amorgos (Katapola). Santorini.
17.30	*Express Paros*	Schinoussa. Iraklia. Naxos. Paros. Syros.
19.15	*Express Skopelitis*	Amorgos (Katapola).

⑥
| 07.00 | *Express Skopelitis* | Schinoussa. Iraklia. Naxos. Mykonos. |
| 19.15 | *Express Skopelitis* | Amorgos (Katapola). |

⑦
07.00	*Express Skopelitis*	Schinoussa. Iraklia. Naxos. Mykonos.
10.05	*Naias Express*	Iraklia. Naxos. Mykonos. Tinos. Syros. Piraeus.
19.15	*Express Skopelitis*	Amorgos (Katapola).

Kuşadası

Turkey   p. 523

Ⓓ
| 08.00 | Fari Kaptain/Sultan I | Samos (Vathi). |
| 17.00 | Kapetan Giorgis | Samos (Vathi). |

Kythnos

Cyclades West   p. 232

①
09.30	Mega Dolphin	Serifos. Sifnos. Milos.
10.10	Express Paros	Kea.
13.20	Express Paros	Syros.
14.00	Pegasus	Piraeus.
14.55	Mega Dolphin	Piraeus.
17.50	Milos Express	Serifos. Sifnos. Kimolos. Milos.

②
02.05	Milos Express	Piraeus.
09.30	Mega Dolphin	Serifos. Sifnos. Milos.
14.55	Mega Dolphin	Piraeus.
17.00	Pegasus	Piraeus.
17.50	Milos Express	Serifos. Sifnos. Kimolos. Milos.

③
09.30	Mega Dolphin	Serifos. Sifnos. Milos.
11.30	Milos Express	Serifos. Sifnos. Kimolos. Milos.
15.00	Mirina Express	Kea. Lavrion.
17.05	Express Paros	Kea.
17.25	Mega Dolphin	Piraeus.
17.35	Milos Express	Piraeus.
20.20	Express Paros	Syros.

④
| 09.30 | Mega Dolphin | Serifos. Sifnos. Milos. |
| 11.30 | Milos Express | Serifos. Sifnos. Kimolos. Milos. |

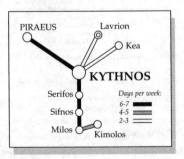

| 14.55 | Mega Dolphin | Piraeus. |
| 23.45 | Pegasus | Serifos. Sifnos. Kimolos. Milos. |

⑤
09.20	Milos Express	Piraeus.
12.00	Pegasus	Piraeus.
17.15	Mega Dolphin	Sifnos. Milos.
19.30	Milos Express	Serifos. Sifnos. Folegandros.

⑥
| 09.30 | Mega Dolphin | Sifnos. Milos. |
| 11.00 | Milos Express | Sifnos. Milos. Kimolos. Folegandros. Sikinos. Santorini. |

⑦
00.15	Pegasus	Serifos. Sifnos. Milos.
11.00	Milos Express	Serifos. Sifnos. Milos.
13.20	Pegasus	Piraeus.
13.40	Mega Dolphin	Piraeus.
18.55	Milos Express	Piraeus.
21.55	Mega Dolphin	Piraeus.

Lâpseki

Turkey   p. 523

Ⓓ x 7   07.30–24.00   Gelibolu.

Lavrion

Athens & Piraeus   p. 121

①
| 09.00 | Mirina Express | Kea. |
| 19.00 | Mirina Express | Kea. |

②
| 19.00 | Mirina Express | Kea. |

③
| 09.00 | Mirina Express | Kea. Kythnos. |
| 19.00 | Mirina Express | Kea. |

④
| 09.00 | Mirina Express | Kea. |
| 19.00 | Mirina Express | Kea. |

⑤
09.00	Mirina Express	Kea.
15.00	Mirina Express	Kea.
18.15	Mirina Express	Kea.
21.30	Mirina Express	Kea.
21.30	Supercat Haroulla	Kea.

⑥
09.00	Mirina Express	Kea.
12.30	Mirina Express	Kea.
16.00	Mirina Express	Kea.

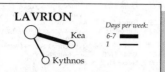

LAVRION

Kea

Kythnos

Days per week:
6-7 ▬
1 ▬

⑦
09.00	*Mirina Express*	Kea.
13.30	*Mirina Express*	Kea.
17.00	*Mirina Express*	Kea.
20.30	*Mirina Express*	Kea.
23.45	*Mirina Express*	Kea.

Lefkada (Nidri)

Ionian Line   p. 494

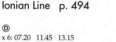

Ⓓ
x 6: 07.20 11.45 13.15
     17.00 18.30 20.00

	Meganisi	Meganisi (Vathi).
		Meganisi (Spartohori).
08.30	*Meganisi*	Kefalonia (Fiskardo).
10.00	*Nidri*	Kefalonia (Fiskardo).
		Ithaca (Frikes).
15.30	*Meganisi*	Kefalonia (Fiskardo).
16.30	*Nidri*	Ithaca (Frikes).
		Kefalonia (Fiskardo).

Lefkada (Vassiliki)

Ionian Line   p. 494

○
01.00	HML Ferries	Brindisi.
11.10	*Aphrodite L*	Kefalonia (Fiskardo).
		Ithaca (Pisaetos).
		Kefalonia (Sami).
12.45	HML Ferries	Corfu.
17.00	*Aphrodite L*	Kefalonia (Fiskardo).
		Ithaca (Pisaetos).
		Kefalonia (Sami).

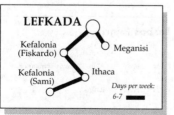

LEFKADA

Kefalonia
(Fiskardo)

Meganisi

Kefalonia
(Sami)

Ithaca

Days per week:
6-7 ▬

Leonidio

Argo-Saronic   p. 465

② ③ ④ ⑥ ⑦
| 11.40 | Monemvassia. Gerakas. Kiparissi. |
| 15.50 | Spetses. Hydra. Piraeus (Zea). |

Leros

Dodecanese   p. 338

①
03.20	*Marina/Rodanthi*	Kalimnos. Kos.
		Rhodes. Symi.
22.00	*Rodos*	Patmos. Piraeus.
23.00	*Marina/Rodanthi*	Patmos. Piraeus.
②
01.20	*Leros*	Kalimnos. Kos. Rhodes.
02.30	*Marina/Rodanthi*	Kalimnos. Kos. Rhodes.
20.00	*Leros*	Patmos. Piraeus.
③
03.00	*Ialyssos*	Kalimnos. Kos. Rhodes.
08.45	*Nissos Kalimnos*	Lipsi. Patmos. Arki.
		Agathonisi.
		Samos (Pithagorio).
21.15	*Nissos Kalimnos*	Kalimnos.
22.50	*Ialyssos*	Patmos. Piraeus.
④
02.05	*Leros*	Kalimnos. Kos. Rhodes.
20.00	*Leros*	Lipsi. Patmos. Piraeus.
23.00	*Marina/Rodanthi*	Patmos. Piraeus.
⑤
03.00	*Ialyssos*	Kalimnos. Kos. Rhodes.
22.50	*Ialyssos*	Patmos. Piraeus.
⑥
04.30	*Milena*	Kos. Kalimnos.
10.20	*Milena*	Patmos. Naxos. Paros.
		Piraeus.
23.00	*Marina/Rodanthi*	Patmos. Piraeus.
⑦
03.00	*Ialyssos*	Kalimnos. Kos. Rhodes.
04.00	*Marina/Rodanthi*	Kalimnos. Kos. Rhodes.
08.45	*Nissos Kalimnos*	Lipsi. Patmos. Agathonisi.
		Samos (Pithagorio).
14.50	*Milena*	Kos. Kalimnos.
20.30	*Nissos Kalimnos*	Kalimnos.
21.50	*Milena*	Patmos. Naxos. Piraeus.
22.50	*Ialyssos*	Patmos. Piraeus.

Leros (Agia Marina)

Dodecanese   p. 338

①
| 09.10 | Samos H/F | Patmos. Fourni. Ikaria |
| | | (Agios Kyrikos). Samos. |

09.30	Dode. H/F	Lipsi. Patmos.
09.45	Samos H/F	Kalimnos. Kos.
11.25	Dode. H/F	Patmos. Samos (Pithagorio).
15.40	Samos H/F	Patmos. Samos (Pithagorio).
16.30	Dode. H/F	Kos. Kalimnos.
17.50	Samos H/F	Kalimnos. Kos.

② ④
09.10	Samos H/F	Lipsi. Patmos. Samos (Pithagorio).
09.30	Dode. H/F	Lipsi. Patmos. Samos (Pithagorio).
09.55	Samos H/F	Kalimnos. Kos.
15.40	Samos H/F	Lipsi. Patmos. Samos (Pithagorio). Samos (Vathi).
16.30	Dode. H/F	Kos. Kalimnos.
17.00	Samos H/F	Kalimnos. Kos.

③ ⑤
09.10	Samos H/F	Lipsi. Patmos. Samos (Pithagorio).
11.25	Dode. H/F	Patmos. Samos (Pithagorio).
11.25	Samos H/F	Kalimnos. Kos.
15.40	Samos H/F	Lipsi. Patmos. Ikaria (Agios Kyrikos). Fourni. Samos (Pithagorio). Samos (Vathi).
16.30	Samos H/F	Kalimnos. Kos.
16.50	Dode. H/F	Kos. Rhodes.

⑥
09.20	Samos H/F	Lipsi. Patmos. Samos (Pithagorio).
09.25	Dode. H/F	Patmos. Samos (Pithagorio).
10.20	Samos H/F	Kalimnos. Kos.
15.40	Samos H/F	Lipsi. Patmos. Agathonisi. Samos (Pithagorio). Samos (Vathi).
16.00	Samos H/F	Kalimnos. Kos.
16.20	Dode. H/F	Kos. Kalimnos.

⑦
09.20	Samos H/F	Lipsi. Patmos. Samos (Pithagorio).

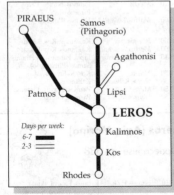

PIRAEUS

Samos (Pithagorio)

Agathonisi

Patmos

Lipsi

LEROS

Days per week:
6-7 ▬▬▬
2-3 ═══

Kalimnos

Kos

Rhodes

09.25	Dode. H/F	Patmos. Ikaria (Agios Kyrikos). Samos (Pithagorio).
11.25	Samos H/F	Kalimnos. Kos.
15.40	Samos H/F	Lipsi. Patmos. Ikaria (Agios Kyrikos). Fourni. Samos (Pithagorio). Samos (Vathi).
16.20	Dode. H/F	Kos. Kalimnos.
17.00	Samos H/F	Kalimnos. Kos.

Lesbos (Mytilini)

Eastern Line   p. 387

Ⓓ
08.00	Aeolis/Eresos II	Ayvalık.

①
16.00	Agios Rafail	Chios. Syros. Andros. Piraeus.
18.00	Mytilene	Chios. Piraeus.
21.00	Theofilos	Piraeus.

②
09.00	Sappho	Limnos. Thessalonika.
18.00	Theofilos	Chios. Piraeus.

③
07.00	Alcaeos	Limnos. Kavala.
08.00	Mytilene	Limnos.
18.00	Sappho	Chios. Piraeus.
21.00	Mytilene	Piraeus.

④
18.00	Agios Rafail	Psara. Piraeus.
18.00	Theofilos	Chios. Piraeus.

⑤
09.00	Mytilene	Piraeus.
17.00	Sappho	Chios. Piraeus.

⑥
05.00	Agios Rafail	Piraeus.
08.00	Mytilene	Chios. Piraeus.
09.00	Theofilos	Limnos. Thessalonika.
14.00	Romilda	Limnos. Alexandroupolis.
22.00	Sappho	Limnos. Kavala.

⑦
10.30	Agios Rafail	Volos.
11.00	Mytilene	Piraeus.
11.30	Romilda	Chios. Samos (Vathi). Kos. Rhodes.
17.00	Theofilos	Chios. Piraeus.
21.00	Sappho	Chios. Piraeus.

Lesbos (Sigri)

②
03.00	Alcaeos	Agios Efstratios. Limnos. Kavala.

④
08.00	Alcaeos	Rafina.

⑤
04.00	Alcaeos	Agios Efstratios. Limnos.

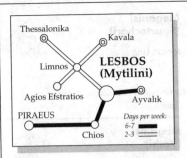

14.30	*Sappho*	Lesbos (Mytilini). Chios. Piraeus.
16.20	*Niki H/F*	Samothrace. Alexandroupolis.
22.00	*Alcaeos*	Agios Efstratios. Rafina.

○
| 15.00 | *Aeolis* | Agios Efstratios. |
| 16.00 | *Thraki III* | Samothrace. |

Lipsi

Dodecanese p. 340

Ⓓ
| 08.00 | *Captain Makis* | Leros. |
| 16.00 | *Megalo./Pat. Ex* | Patmos. |

①
| 10.00 | Dode. H/F | Patmos. |
| 16.00 | Dode. H/F | Leros (Agia Marina). Kos. Kalimnos. |

② ④
09.25	Samos H/F	Leros (Agia Marina). Kalimnos. Kos.
09.40	Samos H/F	Patmos. Samos (Pithagorio).
10.10	Dode. H/F	Patmos. Samos (Pithagorio).
10.30	Miniotis	Patmos.
13.00	Miniotis	Arki. Agathonisi. Samos (Pithagorio).
16.00	Dode. H/F	Leros (Agia Marina). Kos. Kalimnos.
16.05	Samos H/F	Patmos. Samos (Pithagorio). Samos (Vathi).
16.30	Samos H/F	Leros (Agia Marina). Kalimnos. Kos.

③ ⑤
09.40	Samos H/F	Patmos. Samos (Pithagorio).
10.05	*Nissos Kalimnos*	Patmos. Arki. Agathonisi. Samos (Pithagorio).
10.55	Samos H/F	Leros (Agia Marina). Kalimnos. Kos.
13.55	*Anemos*	Samos (Vathi). (Karlovassi). Fourni. Ikaria (Agios Kyrikos). Mykonos. Piraeus.
16.00	Samos H/F	Leros (Agia Marina). Kalimnos. Kos.
16.05	Samos H/F	Patmos. Ikaria (Agios Kyrikos). Fourni. Samos (Pithagorio). Samos (Vathi).
20.00	*Nissos Kalimnos*	Leros. Kalimnos.

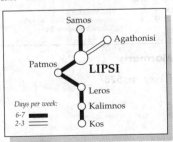

Limnos

Northern Aegean p. 417

②
08.30	*Alcaeos*	Kavala.
14.30	*Sappho*	Thessalonika.
22.30	*Alcaeos*	Lesbos (Mytilini).

③
09.00	*Mytilene*	Lesbos (Mytilini). Piraeus.
09.00	*Sappho*	Lesbos (Mytilini). Chios. Piraeus.
13.30	*Alcaeos*	Kavala.

④
| 02.00 | *Alcaeos* | Agios Efstratios. Lesbos (Sigri). Rafina. |

⑤
| 09.30 | *Alcaeos* | Rafina. |

⑥
09.00	*Alcaeos*	Kavala.
15.00	*Theofilos*	Thessalonika.
20.00	*Romilda*	Alexandroupolis.
22.00	*Alcaeos*	Agios Efstratios. Rafina.

⑦
03.30	*Sappho*	Kavala.
05.45	*Romilda*	Lesbos (Mytilini). Chios. Samos (Vathi). Kos. Rhodes.
09.30	*Theofilos*	Lesbos (Mytilini). Chios. Piraeus.

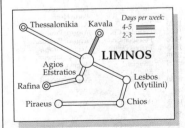

⑥

09.50	Samos H/F	Patmos. Samos (Pithagorio).
09.55	Samos H/F	Leros (Agia Marina). Kalimnos. Kos.
15.30	Samos H/F	Leros (Agia Marina). Kalimnos. Kos.
16.05	Samos H/F	Patmos. Agathonisi. Samos (Pithagorio). Samos (Vathi).

⑦

09.50	Samos H/F	Patmos. Samos (Pithagorio).
10.05	Nissos Kalimnos	Patmos. Agathonisi. Samos (Pithagorio).
10.55	Samos H/F	Leros (Agia Marina). Kalimnos. Kos.
16.05	Samos H/F	Patmos. Ikaria (Agios Kyrikos). Fourni. Samos (Pithagorio). Samos (Vathi).
16.30	Samos H/F	Leros (Agia Marina). Kalimnos. Kos.
19.10	Nissos Kalimnos	Leros. Kalimnos.

Marmara

Turkey   p. 523

ⓓ

00.00	TML	Istanbul.
00.00	TML	Avşa.

ⓓ x 4

00.00	Deniz Otobusleri	Avşa.
00.00	Deniz Otobusleri	İstanbul.

⑤ ⑦

00.00	TML	Avşa. Erdek.
00.00	TML	Tekirdağ.

Marmaras

Northern Aegean   p. 419

ⓓ

08.00	Taxi boat	Mt. Athos boat tour.

🏊 *Flying Dolphins*:

② ④ ⑤ ⑦

20.15	Nea Moudania.
20.15	Alonissos. Skopelos. Skopelos (Glossa). Skiathos. Volos.

Marmaris

Turkey   p. 523

ⓓ

09.00	16.00	Yesil Marmaris	Rhodes.

◯

00.00	TML	Venice.

Meganisi (Spartochori)

Ionian Line
p. 497

ⓓ

08.00	14.00	Meganisi	Lefkada (Nidri).

Meganisi (Vathi)

Ionian Line   p. 497

ⓓ

07.45	Meganisi	Meganisi (Spartochori). Lefkada (Nidri).
13.45	Meganisi	Meganisi (Spartochori). Lefkada (Nidri).
17.00	Meganisi	Lefkada (Vathi).

Mersin

Turkey   p. 517

① ③ ⑤

22.00	Yeşilada	Famagusta.

Methana

Argo-Saronic   p. 465

ⓓ

06.30	Poseidon Co.	Aegina. Piraeus.
09.40	Eftichia	Poros.
09.55	Express Danae	Poros. Hydra. Spetses. Porto Helio.
10.00	Saronikos	Poros. Hydra. Ermioni. Spetses.
10.25	Georgios 2	Poros. Spetses. Porto Helio.
11.20	Eftichia	Aegina. Piraeus.
11.20	Poseidon Co.	Aegina. Piraeus.
14.00	Poseidon Co.	Aegina. Piraeus.
16.45	Express Danae	Aegina. Piraeus.
17.10	Saronikos	Aegina. Piraeus.
17.25	Georgios 2	Aegina. Piraeus.
18.20	Eftichia	Poros.
19.30	Eftichia	Aegina. Piraeus.

⑤

18.55	Poseidon Co.	Aegina. Piraeus.

⑦

18.00	Poseidon Co.	Aegina. Piraeus.

Milos

Cyclades West
p. 235

PIRAEUS

MILOS

Kythnos
Serifos
Sifnos
Kimolos
Folegandros
Sikinos
Santorini
Rhodes
Karpathos
Kassos
Crete (Ag. Nikolaos)
Crete (Sitia)

Days per week:
6-7
2-3
1

①

00.40	*Pegasus*	Piraeus.
01.15	*Vitsentzos Kornaros*	Piraeus.
12.40	*Mega Dolphin*	Sifnos. Serifos. Kythnos. Piraeus.
15.20	*Mega Dolphin*	Sifnos. Paros. Mykonos. Tinos. Syros.
22.15	*Milos Express*	Sifnos. Serifos. Kythnos. Piraeus.

②

00.15	*Vitsentzos Kornaros*	Crete (Agios Nikolaos). Crete (Sitia).
00.30	*Pegasus*	Folegandros. Sikinos. Ios. Santorini.
11.30	*Speed H/F*	Folegandros. Santorini.
12.40	*Mega Dolphin*	Sifnos. Serifos. Kythnos. Piraeus.
13.00	*Pegasus*	Sifnos. Serifos. Kythnos. Piraeus.
15.20	*Mega Dolphin*	Sifnos. Paros. Mykonos. Tinos. Syros.
16.30	*Speed H/F*	Sifnos. Paros. Mykonos. Tinos. Syros.
23.00	*Milos Express*	Sifnos. Piraeus.

③

01.15	*Vitsentzos Kornaros*	Piraeus.
15.00	*Mega Dolphin*	Sifnos. Serifos. Kythnos. Piraeus.
15.20	*Mega Dolphin*	Sifnos. Paros. Mykonos. Tinos. Syros.
15.30	*Milos Express*	Kythnos. Piraeus.
22.45	*Pegasus*	Folegandros. Sikinos. Santorini.

④

00.15	*Vitsentzos Kornaros*	Crete (Agios Nikolaos). Crete (Sitia).
11.00	*Pegasus*	Sifnos. Piraeus.
12.40	*Mega Dolphin*	Sifnos. Serifos. Kythnos. Piraeus.
15.05	*Express Paros*	Kimolos. Sifnos. Serifos. Paros. Syros.
15.20	*Mega Dolphin*	Sifnos. Paros. Mykonos. Tinos. Syros.
22.00	*Milos Express*	Sifnos. Serifos. Kythnos. Piraeus.

⑤

01.15	*Vitsentzos Kornaros*	Piraeus.
08.00	*Pegasus*	Sifnos. Serifos. Kythnos. Piraeus.
11.30	*Speed H/F*	Folegandros. Santorini.
16.30	*Speed H/F*	Sifnos. Paros. Mykonos. Tinos. Syros.
19.10	*Mega Dolphin*	Sifnos. Piraeus.
23.55	*Pegasus*	Folegandros. Santorini.

⑥

00.15	*Vitsentzos Kornaros*	Crete (Agios Nikolaos). Crete (Sitia). Kassos. Karpathos (Town). Karpathos (Diafani). Rhodes.
12.00	*Pegasus*	Sifnos. Piraeus.
13.15	*Mega Dolphin*	Sifnos. Piraeus.
14.25	*Milos Express*	Kimolos. Folegandros. Sikinos. Santorini.
15.05	*Express Paros*	Kimolos. Sifnos. Serifos. Paros. Syros.
19.10	*Mega Dolphin*	Piraeus.
19.45	*Mega Dolphin*	Sifnos. Piraeus.
23.10	*Milos Express*	Sifnos. Piraeus.

⑦

09.00	*Pegasus*	Kimolos. Sifnos. Serifos. Kythnos. Piraeus.
12.30	*Mega Dolphin*	Sifnos. Kythnos. Piraeus.
15.00	*Milos Express*	Sifnos. Serifos. Kythnos. Piraeus.
19.35	*Express Paros*	Sifnos. Paros. Syros.

Monemvassia

Argo-Saronic   p. 465

○

| 01.10 | | Piraeus. |
| 22.35 | | Kithera (Agia Pelagia). Crete (Kasteli). |

Ⓓ

| 17.00/ 18.05 | *Flying Dolphin* | Spetses. Piraeus (Zea). |

Mykonos

Cyclades North
p. 201

Ⓓ

08.30	Syros Express	Paros. Naxos. Ios. Santorini.
09.30	Niki	Delos.
10.45	Niki	Delos.
14.30	Naias II	Tinos. Syros. Piraeus.
15.00	Express Aphrodite	Tinos. Syros. Piraeus.

Ⓓ ex ①

08.30	Delos Express	Delos.
09.00	Hera	Delos.
09.30	Delos Express	Delos.
09.30	Niki	Delos.
09.55	Delos Express	Delos.
10.15	Hera	Delos.
10.45	Niki	Delos.
11.00	Delos Express	Delos.
11.40	Hera	Delos.

①

05.00	Naias Express	Naxos. Paros.
08.00	Superferry II	Tinos. Andros. Rafina.
08.30	Speed H/F	Paros. Naxos. Ios. Santorini.
09.00	Mega Dolphin	Paros. Naxos.
09.30	Naias Express	Tinos. Syros. Piraeus.
10.35	Athina 2004	Naxos. Paros.
12.00	Supercat Haroulla	Paros.
13.00	Athina 2004	Tinos. Andros. Rafina.
14.00	Express Skopelitis	Naxos. Iraklia. Schinoussa. Koufonissia. Amorgos (Katapola).
14.00	Speed H/F	Naxos. Iraklia. Schinoussa. Koufonissia. Amorgos (Egiali). (Katapola). Santorini. Ios.
14.00	Penelope A	Tinos. Andros. Rafina.
15.45	Supercat Haroulla	Tinos. Andros. Rafina.
17.30	Express Paros	Naxos. Paros. Syros.
18.10	Mega Dolphin	Tinos. Syros.
18.30	Speed H/F	Tinos. Syros.
19.30	Athina 2004	Tinos. Rafina.
21.30	Maria PA	Tinos. Syros.
22.00	Superferry II	Tinos. Andros. Rafina.
22.30	Express Athina	Naxos. Paros. Piraeus.

②

00.05	Anemos	Ikaria (Evdilos). Samos (Karlovassi). Samos (Vathi).
08.00	Dimitroula	Paros. Naxos. Santorini. Crete (Iraklion).
08.30	Speed H/F	Paros. Sifnos. Milos. Folegandros. Santorini.
08.45	Bari Express	Tinos. Andros. Rafina.
09.00	Mega Dolphin	Paros. Naxos.
09.30	Naias Express	Tinos. Syros. Piraeus.
09.45	Maria PA	Paros. Naxos. Ios. Santorini. Anafi.
10.15	Sea Jet I	Syros. Paros. Naxos. Amorgos (Katapola).
10.20	Athina 2004	Naxos. Paros.
12.00	Supercat Haroulla	Syros. Paros. Naxos. Amorgos (Katapola).
13.00	Athina 2004	Tinos. Rafina.

14.00	Penelope A	Tinos. Andros. Rafina.
14.30	Speed H/F	Naxos. Paros. Ios. Santorini. Anafi.
18.10	Mega Dolphin	Tinos. Syros.
18.30	Sea Jet I	Tinos. Andros. Rafina.
19.30	Athina 2004	Tinos. Rafina.
19.30	Express Athina	Paros. Naxos. Ios. Santorini.
19.30	Speed H/F	Tinos. Syros.
22.00	Superferry II	Tinos. Andros. Rafina.

③

02.00	Anemos	Ikaria (Agios Kyrikos). Fourni. Samos (Karlovassi). Samos (Vathi). Patmos. Lipsi.
05.15	Dimitroula	Thessalonika.
08.00	Bari Express	Tinos. Andros. Rafina.
08.30	Speed H/F	Paros. Naxos. Ios. Santorini. Amorgos (Katapola).
09.00	Mega Dolphin	Paros. Naxos.
09.30	Naias Express	Tinos. Syros. Piraeus.
10.35	Athina 2004	Naxos. Paros.
12.00	Supercat Haroulla	Tinos. Andros. Rafina.
12.30	Express Paros	Tinos. Syros. Kythnos. Kea.
13.00	Athina 2004	Tinos. Andros. Rafina.
13.45	Speed H/F	Syros.
14.00	Express Skopelitis	Naxos. Iraklia. Schinoussa. Koufonissia. Amorgos (Katapola).
15.15	Speed H/F	Naxos. Paros. Folegandros. Sikinos. Ios. Santorini.
18.00	Romilda	Piraeus.
18.10	Mega Dolphin	Tinos. Syros.
19.30	Athina 2004	Tinos. Rafina.
19.30	Speed H/F	Tinos. Syros.
20.30	Penelope A	Tinos. Andros. Rafina.
22.40	Maria PA	Syros.
24.00	Express Athina	Piraeus.

④

00.40	Anemos	Piraeus.
07.45	Maria PA	Paros. Naxos. Santorini. Crete (Iraklion).
08.30	Speed H/F	Paros. Naxos. Ios. Santorini.
08.45	Bari Express	Tinos. Andros. Rafina.
09.00	Mega Dolphin	Paros. Naxos.
09.30	Naias Express	Tinos. Syros. Piraeus.
09.50	Dimitroula	Paros. Naxos. Santorini. Crete (Iraklion).
10.30	Athina 2004	Paros. Naxos. Donoussa. Amorgos (Katapola).
12.00	Supercat Haroulla	Paros.
14.00	Speed H/F	Syros.
14.00	Superferry II	Tinos. Andros. Rafina.
15.30	Speed H/F	Naxos. Iraklia. Schinoussa. Koufonissia. Amorgos (Egiali). (Katapola). Santorini. Ios.
15.45	Supercat Haroulla	Tinos. Andros. Rafina.
16.00	Athina 2004	Tinos. Andros. Rafina.
18.10	Mega Dolphin	Tinos. Syros.
18.30	Speed H/F	Tinos. Syros.
19.30	Express Athina	Paros. Naxos. Ios. Santorini.
21.30	Penelope A	Syros. Paros. Naxos. Amorgos (Katapola). Koufonissia. Schinoussa. Iraklia.
23.20	Anemos	Ikaria (Evdilos). Samos (Karlovassi). Samos (Vathi).

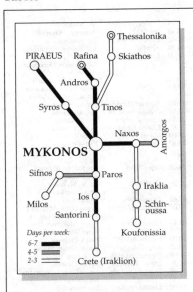

Thessalonika

PIRAEUS Rafina Skiathos

Andros

Syros Tinos

Naxos Amorgos

MYKONOS

Sifnos Paros

Iraklia

Ios Schin-
Milos oussa
Santorini

Days per week: Koufonissia
6-7
4-5
2-3 Crete (Iraklion)

⑤

06.00	Dimitroula	Syros. Thessalonika.
08.30	Express Paros	Paros. Naxos. Donoussa. Amorgos (Egiali). Amorgos (Katapola). Koufonissia. Schinoussa. Iraklia.
08.30	Speed H/F	Paros. Sifnos. Milos. Folegandros. Santorini.
09.30	Naias Express	Tinos. Syros. Piraeus.
10.35	Athina 2004	Naxos. Paros.
12.00	Penelope A	Tinos. Andros. Rafina.
12.30	Supercat Haroulla	Rafina.
13.00	Athina 2004	Tinos. Andros. Rafina.
14.00	Express Skopelitis	Naxos. Iraklia. Schinoussa. Koufonissia. Amorgos (Katapola).
14.30	Speed H/F	Naxos. Paros. Ios. Santorini. Anafi.
16.00	Romilda	Amorgos (Katapola). Astipalea. Kalimnos. Kos. Nissiros. Tilos. Rhodes.
19.30	Athina 2004	Tinos. Rafina.
19.30	Speed H/F	Tinos. Syros.
20.30	Maria PA	Syros.
21.30	Penelope A	Tinos. Andros. Rafina.
22.00	Bari Express	Tinos. Andros. Rafina.
23.00	Naias Express	Syros. Piraeus.
24.00	Superferry II	Rafina.

⑥

| 01.00 | Anemos | Ikaria (Evdilos). Samos (Karlovassi). Samos (Vathi). |
| 08.30 | Speed H/F | Paros. Naxos. Ios. Santorini. |

09.15	Maria PA	Paros. Naxos. Ios. Santorini.
10.15	Penelope A	Tinos. Rafina.
10.20	Athina 2004	Naxos. Paros.
12.00	Supercat Haroulla	Paros.
13.00	Athina 2004	Tinos. Rafina.
13.45	Dimitroula	Paros. Naxos. Ios. Santorini. Crete (Iraklion).
13.45	Naias Express	Tinos. Piraeus.
14.00	Express Skopelitis	Naxos. Iraklia. Schinoussa. Koufonissia. Amorgos (Katapola).
14.00	Superferry II	Tinos. Andros. Rafina.
14.30	Speed H/F	Naxos. Paros. Folegandros. Sikinos. Ios. Santorini.
15.45	Supercat Haroulla	Tinos. Andros. Rafina.
18.30	Speed H/F	Tinos. Syros.
19.30	Athina 2004	Tinos. Rafina.
22.00	Bari Express	Tinos. Andros. Rafina.
22.30	Express Athina	Paros. Naxos. Amorgos (Katapola). Astipalea.
23.30	Maria PA	Syros.

⑦

02.55	Naias Express	Donoussa. Amorgos (Egiali). Amorgos (Katapola). Koufonissia. Iraklia. Naxos.
05.00	Anemos	Ikaria (Agios Kyrikos). Samos (Karlovassi). Samos (Vathi).
07.45	Maria PA	Paros. Naxos. Ios. Santorini. Crete (Iraklion).
08.00	Penelope A	Tinos. Andros. Rafina.
08.30	Speed H/F	Paros. Naxos. Ios. Santorini. Amorgos (Katapola).
11.55	Dimitroula	Tinos. Syros. Volos. Skiathos. Thessalonika.
13.00	Athina 2004	Tinos. Rafina.
13.00	Supercat Haroulla	Tinos. Andros. Rafina.
14.00	Express Skopelitis	Naxos. Iraklia. Schinoussa. Koufonissia. Amorgos (Katapola).
14.00	Naias Express	Tinos. Syros. Piraeus.
14.30	Speed H/F	Naxos. Paros. Ios. Santorini.
19.30	Athina 2004	Tinos. Rafina.
19.30	Speed H/F	Tinos. Syros.
22.00	Bari Express	Tinos. Rafina.
23.00	Anemos	Syros. Piraeus.

Nafplio

Argo-Saronic p. 465

✈ Flying Dolphins
② ③ ④ ⑤ ⑥ ⑦
08.00   Tolo. Porto Helio. Spetses. Ermioni. Hydra. Poros. Aegina. Piraeus (Zea).

Naxos

Cyclades Central
p. 145

Ⓓ
08.45	*Ionian Sun*	Paros. Syros. Rafina.
10.00	Speed H/F	Ios. Santorini.
11.50	*Syros Express*	Ios. Santorini.
12.45	Speed H/F	Mykonos.
15.00	Speed H/F	Paros. Ios. Santorini.
20.00	*Syros Express*	Paros. Mykonos.

Ⓓ ex ②
04.00	*Express Olympia*	Ios. Santorini.
16.50	Speed H/F	Paros. Mykonos. Tinos. Syros.

①
00.15	*Daliana*	Ikaria (Agios Kyrikos). Samos (Karlovassi). (Vathi).
01.00	*Express Apollon*	Ios. Sikinos. Folegandros. Santorini.
01.15	*Poseidon Express 2*	Ios. Santorini.
04.00	*Express Olympia*	Ios. Santorini. Anafi.
06.30	*Naias Express*	Paros. Mykonos. Tinos. Syros. Piraeus.
10.30	*Poseidon Express 2*	Paros. Piraeus.
10.35	*Mega Dolphin*	Paros. Sifnos. Milos.
10.45	*Express Apollon*	Paros. Piraeus.
11.00	*Express Skopelitis*	Mykonos.
11.20	*Highspeed I*	Paros. Piraeus.
11.30	*Athina 2004*	Paros. Mykonos. Tinos. Andros. Rafina.
13.10	*Panagia Ekatonta.*	Ios. Santorini.
13.45	*Express Olympia*	Paros. Piraeus.
14.00	*Express Santorini*	Ios. Santorini.
15.30	*Express Skopelitis*	Iraklia. Schinoussa. Koufonissia. Amorgos (Katapola).
17.00	*Maria PA*	Paros. Mykonos. Tinos. Syros.
19.20	*Express Paros*	Paros. Syros.
21.00	*Express Athina*	Mykonos.
22.45	*Express Santorini*	Paros. Piraeus.
23.10	*Super Naias*	Donoussa. Amorgos (Egiali). (Katapola).
23.30	*Daliana*	Paros. Piraeus.
23.30	*Panagia Ekatonta.*	Paros. Piraeus.
24.00	*Express Athina*	Paros. Piraeus.

②
00.30	*Milena*	Ikaria (Agios Kyrikos). Samos (Karlovassi). (Vathi).
00.30	*Poseidon Express 2*	Ios. Santorini.
04.00	*Express Apollon*	Ios. Santorini.
08.50	*Super Naias*	Paros. Syros. Piraeus.
10.35	*Express Paros*	Folegandros. Sikinos. Ios. Santorini. Anafi.
10.35	*Mega Dolphin*	Paros. Sifnos. Milos.
10.45	*Express Apollon*	Paros. Piraeus.
10.55	*Dimitroula*	Santorini. Crete (Iraklion).
11.30	*Athina 2004*	Paros. Mykonos. Tinos. Rafina.
11.45	*Highspeed I*	Paros. Syros. Piraeus.
12.00	*Poseidon Express 2*	Paros. Piraeus.
13.00	*Maria PA*	Ios. Santorini. Anafi.

13.35	*Panagia Ekatonta.*	Ios. Santorini.
13.40	*Sea Jet I*	Amorgos (Katapola).
14.00	*Express Santorini*	Ios. Santorini.
14.20	*Ariadne*	Ios. Sikinos. Santorini.
15.00	*Express Skopelitis*	Iraklia. Schinoussa. Koufonissia. Donoussa. Amorgos (Egiali). Amorgos (Katapola).
15.45	*Sea Jet I*	Paros. Syros. Mykonos. Tinos. Andros. Rafina.
16.00	*Supercat Haroulla*	Amorgos (Katapola).
22.15	*Panagia Ekatonta.*	Paros. Piraeus.
22.30	*Express Athina*	Ios. Santorini.
22.45	*Express Santorini*	Paros. Piraeus.
23.00	*Milena*	Paros. Piraeus.
23.40	*Ariadne*	Paros. Piraeus.

③
01.00	*Super Naias*	Ios. Santorini. Anafi. Astipalea.
02.20	*Dimitroula*	Paros. Mykonos. Thessalonika.
02.40	*Express Paros*	Paros. Syros.
09.00	*Supercat Haroulla*	Paros. Syros. Mykonos. Tinos. Andros. Rafina.
09.45	*Express Paros*	Paros. Mykonos. Tinos. Syros. Kythnos. Kea.
10.00	*Express Athina*	Paros. Piraeus.
10.35	*Mega Dolphin*	Paros. Sifnos. Milos.
11.00	*Express Skopelitis*	Mykonos.
12.30	*Express Olympia*	Paros. Piraeus.
13.35	*Panagia Ekatonta.*	Ios. Sikinos. Folegandros. Santorini.
14.00	*Express Apollon*	Ios. Santorini.
14.20	*Ariadne*	Syros. Piraeus.
15.25	*Super Naias*	Paros. Piraeus.
15.30	*Express Skopelitis*	Iraklia. Schinoussa. Koufonissia. Amorgos (Katapola).
18.30	*Maria PA*	Paros. Mykonos. Syros.
22.15	*Panagia Ekatonta.*	Paros. Piraeus.
22.45	*Express Apollon*	Paros. Piraeus.
23.00	*Express Santorini*	Iraklia. Schinoussa. Koufonissia. Donoussa. Amorgos (Egiali). (Katapola). Astipalea.

④
00.30	*Milena*	Ikaria (Agios Kyrikos). Samos (Karlovassi). (Vathi).
00.30	*Poseidon Express 2*	Ios. Santorini.
04.30	*El Greco*	Syros. Skiathos. Thessalonika.
10.30	*Poseidon Express 2*	Paros. Piraeus.
10.35	*Mega Dolphin*	Paros. Sifnos. Milos.
11.20	*Highspeed I*	Paros. Piraeus.
12.00	*Athina 2004*	Donoussa. Amorgos (Katapola).
12.00	*Maria PA*	Santorini. Crete (Iraklion).
12.30	*Express Olympia*	Paros. Piraeus.
12.45	*Dimitroula*	Santorini. Crete (Iraklion).
14.00	*Express Apollon*	Ios. Santorini.
14.00	*Express Santorini*	Paros. Piraeus.
14.00	*Super Naias*	Ios. Santorini.
14.30	*Athina 2004*	Paros. Mykonos. Tinos. Andros. Rafina.
15.00	*Express Skopelitis*	Iraklia. Schinoussa. Koufonissia. Donoussa. Amorgos (Egiali). Amorgos (Katapola).
15.20	*Ariadne*	Ios. Santorini.

22.15	*Super Naias*	Paros. Piraeus.
22.30	*Express Athina*	Ios. Santorini.
22.45	*Express Apollon*	Paros. Piraeus.
23.00	*Milena*	Paros. Piraeus.
23.40	*Ariadne*	Paros. Piraeus.

⑤

00.10	*Panagia Ekatonta.*	Ios. Sikinos. Folegandros. Santorini.
00.30	*Poseidon Express 2*	Ios. Santorini.
01.30	*Penelope A*	Amorgos (Katapola). Koufonissia. Schinoussa. Iraklia.
08.30	*Penelope A*	Paros. Syros. Mykonos. Tinos. Andros. Rafina.
09.55	*Panagia Ekatonta.*	Paros. Piraeus.
10.00	*Express Athina*	Paros. Piraeus.
10.30	*Poseidon Express 2*	Paros. Piraeus.
11.00	*Express Paros*	Donoussa. Amorgos (Egiali). (Katapola). Koufonissia. Schinoussa. Iraklia.
11.00	*Express Skopelitis*	Mykonos.
11.20	*Highspeed I*	Paros. Piraeus.
12.30	*El Greco*	Santorini. Crete (Iraklion).
12.30	*Express Olympia*	Paros. Piraeus.
14.00	*Express Santorini*	Ios. Santorini.
14.00	*Super Naias*	Ios. Santorini.
14.20	*Ariadne*	Amorgos (Katapola). Astipalea.
15.30	*Express Skopelitis*	Iraklia. Schinoussa. Koufonissia. Amorgos (Katapola).
16.30	*Maria PA*	Paros. Mykonos. Syros.
19.30	*Express Paros*	Paros. Syros.
22.15	*Super Naias*	Paros. Piraeus.
22.45	*Express Santorini*	Paros. Piraeus.
23.00	*Express Apollon*	Ios. Santorini.
23.15	*Ionian Sun*	Amorgos (Egiali). Amorgos (Katapola).
23.55	*Ariadne*	Paros. Piraeus.

⑥

00.10	*Panagia Ekatonta.*	Ios. Santorini. Anafi.
00.30	*Milena*	Patmos. Leros. Kos. Kalimnos.
00.30	*Poseidon Express 2*	Ios. Sikinos. Folegandros. Santorini.
01.10	*Daliana*	Ikaria (Agios Kyrikos). Fourni. Samos (Karlovassi). (Vathi).
09.55	*Panagia Ekatonta.*	Paros. Piraeus.
10.30	*Poseidon Express 2*	Paros. Piraeus.
10.45	*Express Apollon*	Paros. Piraeus.
11.00	*Express Skopelitis*	Mykonos.
11.20	*Highspeed I*	Paros. Piraeus.
11.30	*Athina 2004*	Paros. Mykonos. Tinos. Rafina.
13.30	*Maria PA*	Ios. Santorini.
13.45	*Express Olympia*	Paros. Piraeus.
14.00	*Express Santorini*	Ios. Santorini.
14.20	*Ariadne*	Ios. Santorini.
15.30	*Express Skopelitis*	Iraklia. Schinoussa. Koufonissia. Amorgos (Katapola).
16.00	*Milena*	Paros. Piraeus.
16.40	*Dimitroula*	Ios. Santorini. Crete (Iraklion).
20.00	*Maria PA*	Paros. Mykonos. Syros.
22.15	*Super Naias*	Paros. Piraeus.
22.45	*Express Santorini*	Paros. Piraeus.
23.40	*Ariadne*	Paros. Piraeus.

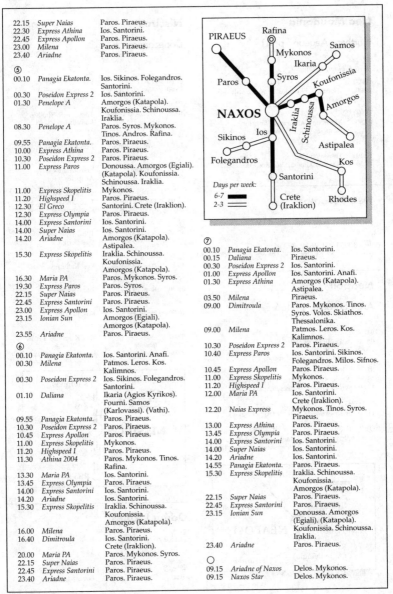

PIRAEUS Rafina
Samos
Mykonos
Ikaria
Paros Syros Koufonissia
NAXOS Amorgos
Iraklia Schinoussa
Sikinos Ios
Astipalea
Folegandros Kos
Santorini

Days per week:
6-7 ▄▄▄
2-3 ═══
Crete (Iraklion) Rhodes

⑦

00.10	*Panagia Ekatonta.*	Ios. Santorini.
00.15	*Daliana*	Piraeus.
00.30	*Poseidon Express 2*	Ios. Santorini.
01.00	*Express Apollon*	Ios. Santorini. Anafi.
01.30	*Express Athina*	Amorgos (Katapola). Astipalea.
03.50	*Milena*	Piraeus.
09.00	*Dimitroula*	Paros. Mykonos. Tinos. Syros. Volos. Skiathos. Thessalonika.
09.00	*Milena*	Patmos. Leros. Kos. Kalimnos.
10.30	*Poseidon Express 2*	Paros. Piraeus.
10.40	*Express Paros*	Ios. Santorini. Sikinos. Folegandros. Milos. Sifnos.
10.45	*Express Apollon*	Paros. Piraeus.
11.00	*Express Skopelitis*	Mykonos.
11.20	*Highspeed I*	Paros. Piraeus.
12.00	*Maria PA*	Ios. Santorini. Crete (Iraklion).
12.20	*Naias Express*	Mykonos. Tinos. Syros. Piraeus.
13.00	*Express Athina*	Paros. Piraeus.
13.45	*Express Olympia*	Paros. Piraeus.
14.00	*Express Santorini*	Ios. Santorini.
14.00	*Super Naias*	Ios. Santorini.
14.20	*Ariadne*	Ios. Santorini.
14.55	*Panagia Ekatonta.*	Paros. Piraeus.
15.30	*Express Skopelitis*	Iraklia. Schinoussa. Koufonissia. Amorgos (Katapola).
22.15	*Super Naias*	Paros. Piraeus.
22.45	*Express Santorini*	Paros. Piraeus.
23.15	*Ionian Sun*	Donoussa. Amorgos (Egiali). (Katapola). Koufonissia. Schinoussa. Iraklia.
23.40	*Ariadne*	Paros. Piraeus.

○

| 09.15 | *Ariadne of Naxos* | Delos. Mykonos. |
| 09.15 | *Naxos Star* | Delos. Mykonos. |

Nea Moudania

Northern Aegean   p. 419

〜 *Flying Dolphins*

① ③ ⑥
08.00   Alonissos. Skopelos. Skopelos (Glossa).
Skiathos.

② ④ ⑤ ⑦
07.30   Marmaras. Alonissos. Skopelos.
Skopelos (Glossa). Skiathos.

① ③ ⑤ ⑦
10.10   Thessalonikia.
17.20   Skiathos. Glossa. Skopelos. Alonissos.

Nea Peramos

Northern Aegean   p. 419

Ⓓ 08.30   12.30   16.30   20.45
ANET Line   Thassos (Skala Prinos).

Neapoli

Argo-Saronic   p. 466

Ⓓ
08.30   09.45   10.45   12.00
13.45   16.45   19.00
Local   Elafonissos.

Ⓓ
08.00   *Nissos Kithera*   Kithera (Agia Pelagia).
17.00   *Nissos Kithera*   Kithera (Agia Pelagia).

① ④ ⑤ ⑥ ⑦
11.00   *Nissos Kithera*   Kithera (Agia Pelagia).

③ ⑤ ⑥ ⑦
00.00   *Flying Dolphin*   Kithera (Agia Pelagia).
Monemvassia. Piraeus (Zea).

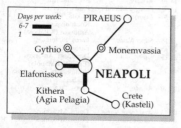

Days per week:
6-7 ▬▬▬
1 ▬▬▬

PIRAEUS ○

Gythio ○   ○ Monemvassia

Elafonissos ▬▬● **NEAPOLI**

Kithera
(Agia Pelagia) ○   ○ Crete
(Kasteli)

Nissiros

Dodecanese   p. 342

Ⓓ
07.00   Taxi boat   Kos (Kardamena).
16.00   *Nissiros Express*   Kos (Kardamena).

①
10.35   *Nissos Kalimnos*   Tilos. Symi. Rhodes.
Kastelorizo.

②
15.20   *Nissos Kalimnos*   Kos. Kalimnos.

③
04.50   *Romilda*   Kos. Kalimnos.
Astipalea.
Amorgos (Katapola).
Mykonos. Piraeus.
09.00   Dode. H/F   Tilos. Rhodes.
20.20   Dode. H/F   Kos.

④
10.35   *Nissos Kalimnos*   Tilos. Symi. Rhodes.
Kastelorizo.

⑤
15.20   *Nissos Kalimnos*   Kos. Kalimnos.

⑥
09.30   *Romilda*   Tilos. Rhodes.

⑦
16.50   Dode. H/F   Kos. Rhodes.

○
00.00   *Ialyssos*   Kos. Kalimnos. Leros.
00.00   *Ialyssos*   Tilos. Rhodes.
00.00   *Ialyssos*   Kos. Astipalea. Piraeus.

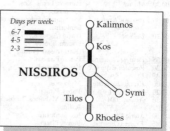

Days per week:
6-7 ▬▬▬
4-5 ▬▬▬
2-3 ══════

○ Kalimnos

○ Kos

NISSIROS ●

Tilos ○   ○ Symi

○ Rhodes

Odum Iskalesi

Turkey   p. 524

Ⓓ x ②
00.00   TML   Bozcaada.

Oinousses

Eastern Line   p. 391

Ⓓ
08.00   *Inousse II*   Chios.

② ④ ⑥
16.00   Miniotis   Chios.

Otranto

Italy   p. 85

① ③ ④ ⑥
22.30   Rainbow Lines   Igoumenitsa. Corfu.

Paros

Cyclades Central
p. 152

Ⓓ
09.45   10.30   11.30
12.30   13.30   14.30
16.00   17.30   19.00
         Antiparos Express
         Kasos Express
         Panagia Parou   Antiparos.

09.30   Speed H/F   Naxos. Ios. Santorini.
10.00   *Ionian Sun*   Syros. Rafina.
10.30   *Syros Express*   Naxos. Ios. Santorini.
11.50   Speed H/F   Naxos. Mykonos.
17.30   Speed H/F   Mykonos. Tinos. Syros.
21.30   *Syros Express*   Mykonos.
21.45   *Ionian Sun*   Naxos.

Ⓓ ex ②
03.00   *Express Olympia*   Naxos. Ios. Santorini.

Ⓓ ex ③
10.30   *Highspeed I*   Naxos.
12.00   *Highspeed I*   Piraeus.

①
00.10   *Poseidon Express 2* Naxos. Ios. Santorini.
00.45   *Ariadne*   Piraeus.
03.00   *Express Olympia*   Naxos. Ios. Santorini.
                               Anafi.
07.35   *Naias Express*   Mykonos. Tinos. Syros.
                               Piraeus.
09.50   *Mega Dolphin*   Naxos.
11.40   *Poseidon Express 2* Piraeus.
12.00   *Athina 2004*   Mykonos. Tinos.
                               Andros. Rafina.
12.00   *Express Apollon*   Piraeus.
12.20   *Mega Dolphin*   Sifnos. Milos.
12.30   *Panagia Ekatonta.*   Naxos. Ios. Santorini.
13.00   *Express Santorini*   Naxos. Ios. Santorini.

13.45   *Supercat Haroulla*   Mykonos. Tinos. Andros.
                               Rafina.
15.00   *Express Olympia*   Piraeus.
17.20   *Mega Dolphin*   Mykonos. Tinos. Syros.
19.00   *Maria PA*   Mykonos. Tinos. Syros.
20.00   *Express Athina*   Naxos. Mykonos.
20.10   *Express Paros*   Syros.
21.45   *El Greco*   Tinos. Volos.
                               Thessalonika.
22.00   *Super Naias*   Naxos. Donoussa.
                               Amorgos (Egiali).
                               Amorgos (Katapola).
22.05   *Golden Vergina*   Ikaria (Evdilos). Samos
                               (Karlovassi). (Vathi).
22.45   *Milena*   Naxos. Ikaria (Agios
                               Kyrikos). Samos
                               (Karlovassi). (Vathi).
23.20   *Poseidon Express 2* Naxos. Ios. Santorini.
24.00   *Express Santorini*   Piraeus.

②
00.30   *Daliana*   Piraeus.
00.30   *Panagia Ekatonta.*   Piraeus.
01.00   *Express Athina*   Piraeus.
03.00   *Express Apollon*   Naxos. Ios. Santorini.
09.30   *Express Paros*   Naxos. Folegandros.
                               Sikinos. Ios. Santorini.
                               Anafi.
09.30   Speed H/F   Sifnos. Milos.
                               Folegandros. Santorini.
09.40   *Dimitroula*   Naxos. Santorini.
                               Crete (Iraklion).
09.50   *Mega Dolphin*   Naxos.
10.00   *Super Naias*   Syros. Piraeus.
11.00   *Maria PA*   Naxos. Ios. Santorini.
                               Anafi.
12.00   *Athina 2004*   Mykonos. Tinos. Rafina.
12.00   *Express Apollon*   Piraeus.
12.20   *Mega Dolphin*   Sifnos. Milos.
12.30   *Panagia Ekatonta.*   Naxos. Ios. Santorini.
13.00   *Express Santorini*   Naxos. Ios. Santorini.
13.00   *Sea Jet I*   Naxos.
                               Amorgos (Katapola).
13.10   *Poseidon Express 2* Piraeus.
13.15   *Ariadne*   Naxos. Ios. Sikinos.
                               Santorini.
14.30   *Supercat Haroulla*   Naxos. Amorgos
                               (Katapola).
16.00   Speed H/F   Ios. Santorini. Anafi.
16.25   *Sea Jet I*   Syros. Mykonos. Tinos.
                               Andros. Rafina.
17.20   *Mega Dolphin*   Mykonos. Tinos. Syros.
21.30   *Express Athina*   Naxos. Ios. Santorini.
21.45   *Daliana*   Santorini. Crete
                               (Iraklion). Kassos.
                               Karpathos (Town).
                               (Diafani). Chalki. Rhodes.
23.20   *Panagia Ekatonta.*   Piraeus.
23.55   *Super Naias*   Naxos. Ios. Santorini.
                               Anafi. Astipalea.
24.00   *Express Santorini*   Piraeus.

③
00.15   *Milena*   Piraeus.
00.45   *Ariadne*   Piraeus.
03.30   *Express Paros*   Syros.
03.35   *Dimitroula*   Mykonos. Thessalonika.
09.30   Speed H/F   Amorgos (Katapola).
09.50   *Mega Dolphin*   Naxos.
10.00   *Supercat Haroulla*   Syros. Mykonos. Tinos.
                               Andros. Rafina.

10.45	*Express Paros*	Mykonos. Tinos. Syros. Kythnos. Kea.
11.00	*Express Athina*	Piraeus.
12.00	*Athina 2004*	Mykonos. Tinos. Andros. Rafina.
12.00	*El Greco*	Santorini. Crete (Iraklion).
12.20	*Mega Dolphin*	Sifnos. Milos.
12.30	*Panagia Ekatonta.*	Naxos. Ios. Sikinos. Folegandros. Santorini.
13.00	*Express Apollon*	Naxos. Ios. Santorini.
13.15	*Ariadne*	Naxos.
13.45	*Express Olympia*	Piraeus.
16.45	Speed H/F	Folegandros. Sikinos. Ios.
17.00	*Super Naias*	Piraeus.
17.20	*Mega Dolphin*	Mykonos. Tinos. Syros.
20.15	*Maria PA*	Mykonos. Syros.
22.00	*Express Santorini*	Naxos. Iraklia. Schinoussa. Koufonissia. Donoussa. Amorgos (Egiali). (Katapola). Astipalea.
22.45	*Milena*	Naxos. Ikaria (Agios Kyrikos). Samos (Karlovassi). (Vathi).
23.20	*Poseidon Express 2*	Naxos. Ios. Santorini.
23.30	*Panagia Ekatonta.*	Piraeus.
24.00	*Express Apollon*	Piraeus.

④

01.20	*Golden Vergina*	Ikaria (Evdilos). Fourni. Samos (Karlovassi). Samos (Vathi).
09.30	*Express Paros*	Serifos. Sifnos. Kimolos. Milos.
09.50	*Mega Dolphin*	Naxos.
10.00	*Maria PA*	Naxos. Santorini. Crete (Iraklion).
11.25	*Athina 2004*	Naxos. Donoussa. Amorgos (Katapola).

PIRAEUS — Thessalonika
Rafina — Skiathos
Tinos — Samos
Mykonos
Syros — Ikaria
Naxos
PAROS
Antiparos — Kou. — Don.
Amorgos
Milos — Sifnos — Ira. Sch.
Sikinos — Ios — Astipalea
Folegandros — Santorini — Rhodes
Karpathos
Crete (Iraklion)

Days per week:
6-7 ▬▬▬
4-5 ▬▬
2-3 ═══

11.30	*Dimitroula*	Naxos. Santorini. Crete (Iraklion).
11.40	*Poseidon Express 2*	Piraeus.
12.20	*Mega Dolphin*	Sifnos. Milos.
12.45	*Super Naias*	Naxos. Ios. Santorini.
13.00	*Express Apollon*	Naxos. Ios. Santorini.
13.45	*Express Olympia*	Piraeus.
13.45	*Supercat Haroulla*	Mykonos. Tinos. Andros. Rafina.
14.15	*Ariadne*	Naxos. Ios. Santorini.
15.00	*Express Santorini*	Piraeus.
15.05	*Athina 2004*	Mykonos. Tinos. Andros. Rafina.
17.20	*Mega Dolphin*	Mykonos. Tinos. Syros.
20.30	*Express Paros*	Syros.
21.30	*Express Athina*	Naxos. Ios. Santorini.
23.00	*Panagia Ekatonta.*	Naxos. Ios. Sikinos. Folegandros. Santorini.
23.05	*Golden Vergina*	Piraeus.
23.20	*Poseidon Express 2*	Naxos. Ios. Santorini.
23.30	*Super Naias*	Piraeus.
24.00	*Express Apollon*	Piraeus.

⑤

00.15	*Milena*	Piraeus.
00.30	*Daliana*	Piraeus.
00.30	*Penelope A*	Naxos. Amorgos (Katapola). Koufonissia. Schinoussa. Iraklia.
00.45	*Ariadne*	Piraeus.
04.10	*Dimitroula*	Mykonos. Syros. Thessalonika.
09.20	*Penelope A*	Syros. Mykonos. Tinos. Andros. Rafina.
09.30	Speed H/F	Sifnos. Milos. Folegandros. Santorini.
09.50	*Express Paros*	Naxos. Donoussa. Amorgos (Egiali). (Katapola). Koufonissia. Schinoussa. Iraklia.
11.00	*Express Athina*	Piraeus.
11.05	*Panagia Ekatonta.*	Piraeus.
11.40	*Poseidon Express 2*	Piraeus.
12.00	*Athina 2004*	Mykonos. Tinos. Andros. Rafina.
12.45	*Super Naias*	Naxos. Ios. Santorini.
13.00	*Express Santorini*	Naxos. Ios. Santorini.
13.15	*Ariadne*	Naxos. Amorgos (Katapola). Astipalea.
13.45	*Express Olympia*	Piraeus.
16.00	Speed H/F	Ios. Santorini. Anafi.
18.30	*Maria PA*	Mykonos. Syros.
21.00	*Express Paros*	Syros.
21.20	*Marina/Rodanthi*	Kos. Rhodes.
21.45	*Ionian Sun*	Naxos. Amorgos (Egiali). Amorgos (Katapola).
22.00	*Express Apollon*	Naxos. Ios. Santorini.
22.05	*Golden Vergina*	Ikaria (Evdilos). Samos (Karlovassi). Samos (Vathi).
23.00	*Panagia Ekatonta.*	Naxos. Ios. Santorini. Anafi.
23.20	*Poseidon Express 2*	Naxos. Ios. Sikinos. Folegandros. Santorini.
23.30	*Super Naias*	Piraeus.
24.00	*Express Santorini*	Piraeus.

⑥

| 01.00 | *Ariadne* | Piraeus. |
| 05.15 | *El Greco* | Tinos. Skiathos. Thessalonika. |

09.30	Express Paros	Serifos. Sifnos. Kimolos. Milos.
11.05	Panagia Ekatonta.	Piraeus.
11.30	Maria PA	Naxos. Ios. Santorini.
11.40	Poseidon Express 2	Piraeus.
12.00	Athina 2004	Mykonos. Tinos. Rafina.
12.00	Express Apollon	Piraeus.
12.45	Super Naias	Naxos. Ios. Santorini.
13.00	Express Santorini	Naxos. Ios. Santorini.
13.15	Ariadne	Naxos. Ios. Santorini.
13.45	Supercat Haroulla	Mykonos. Tinos. Andros. Rafina.
15.00	Express Olympia	Piraeus.
15.25	Dimitroula	Naxos. Ios. Santorini. Crete (Iraklion).
16.45	Speed H/F	Folegandros. Sikinos. Ios. Santorini.
18.00	Milena	Piraeus.
20.30	Express Paros	Syros.
21.20	Marina/Rodanthi	Patmos. Leros. Kalimnos. Kos. Rhodes.
21.30	Maria PA	Mykonos. Syros.
23.00	Panagia Ekatonta.	Naxos. Ios. Santorini.
23.20	Poseidon Express 2	Naxos. Ios. Santorini.
23.30	Super Naias	Piraeus.
24.00	Express Apollon	Naxos. Ios. Santorini. Anafi.
24.00	Express Santorini	Piraeus.

⑦

00.30	Express Athina	Naxos. Amorgos (Katapola). Astipalea.
00.45	Ariadne	Piraeus.
01.15	Golden Vergina	Ikaria (Evdilos). Samos (Karlovassi). Samos (Vathi).
08.00	Milena	Naxos. Patmos. Leros. Kos. Kalimnos.
09.30	Express Paros	Naxos. Ios. Santorini. Sikinos. Folegandros. Milos. Sifnos.
09.30	Speed H/F	Amorgos (Katapola).
10.00	Maria PA	Naxos. Ios. Santorini. Crete (Iraklion).
10.15	Dimitroula	Mykonos. Tinos. Syros. Volos. Skiathos. Thessalonika.
11.40	Poseidon Express 2	Piraeus.
12.00	Express Apollon	Piraeus.
12.45	Super Naias	Naxos. Ios. Santorini.
13.00	Express Santorini	Naxos. Ios. Santorini.
13.15	Ariadne	Naxos. Ios. Santorini.
13.45	El Greco	Santorini. Crete (Iraklion).
14.00	Express Athina	Piraeus.
15.00	Express Olympia	Piraeus.
16.00	Golden Vergina	Piraeus.
16.00	Speed H/F	Ios. Santorini.
16.05	Panagia Ekatonta.	Piraeus.
21.45	Daliana	Naxos. Ikaria (Agios Kyrikos). Samos (Karlovassi). (Vathi).
21.45	Ionian Sun	Naxos. Donoussa. Amorgos (Egiali). (Katapola). Koufonissia. Schinoussa. Iraklia.
23.00	Express Paros	Syros.
23.30	Super Naias	Piraeus.
24.00	Express Apollon	Naxos. Ios. Sikinos. Folegandros. Santorini.
24.00	Express Santorini	Piraeus.

Paros (Piso Livadi)

Cyclades Central   p. 158

○
| 00.00 | Express Skopelitis | Naxos. Mykonos. |
| 00.00 | Express Skopelitis | Iraklia. Schinoussa. Koufonissia. Amorgos (Katapola). |

Paros (Punta)

Cyclades Central   p. 158

Ⓗ
07.00–10.00,		
21.00–24.00;		
ev. 30 min		
10.30–20.30	Agioi Anargiri	Antiparos.

Paşalmanı

Turkey   p. 524

① ⑥
| 00.00 | TML | Erdek. |

Patmos

Dodecanese   p. 346

Ⓓ Tourist boats:
10.00	Anna Express	Lipsi. / Arki.
10.00	Megalohori/ Patmos Express	Lipsi.
16.00	Cassandra/ Hydrofoil	Samos (Pithagorio).

①
00.30	Ialyssos	Piraeus.
01.45	Marina/Rodanthi	Leros. Kalimnos. Kos. Rhodes. Symi.
08.55	Samos H/F	Leros (Agia Marina). Kalimnos. Kos.
10.00	Samos H/F	Fourni. Ikaria (Agios Kyrikos). Samos (Pithagorio).
15.30	Dode. H/F	Lipsi. Leros (Agia Marina). Kos. Kalimnos.
16.00	Dode. H/F	Kos. Rhodes.
16.30	Samos H/F	Samos (Pithagorio). Samos (Vathi).
17.00	Samos H/F	Leros (Agia Marina). Kalimnos. Kos.
23.30	Rodos	Piraeus.
23.50	Leros	Leros. Kalimnos. Kos. Rhodes.

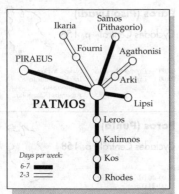

PIRAEUS

Ikaria
Samos (Pithagorio)
Fourni
Agathonisi
Arki

PATMOS   Lipsi

Leros

Kalimnos

Kos

Rhodes

Days per week:
6-7 ▬▬▬
2-3 ═══

②
00.45	*Marina/Rodanthi*	Piraeus.
08.55	Samos H/F	Lipsi. Leros (Agia Marina). Kalimnos. Kos.
10.10	Samos H/F	Samos (Pithagorio).
12.00	Miniotis	Lipsi. Arki. Agathonisi. Samos (Pithagorio).
15.00	Samos H/F	Lipsi. Leros (Agia Marina). Kalimnos. Kos.
15.30	Dode. H/F	Lipsi. Leros (Agia Marina). Kos. Kalimnos.
16.30	Samos H/F	Samos (Pithagorio). Samos (Vathi).
22.00	*Leros*	Piraeus.

③
01.30	*Ialyssos*	Leros. Kalimnos. Kos. Rhodes.
10.10	Samos H/F	Samos (Pithagorio).
10.25	Samos H/F	Lipsi. Leros (Agia Marina). Kalimnos. Kos.
11.10	*Nissos Kalimnos*	Arki. Agathonisi. Samos (Pithagorio).
12.00	*Princesa Cypria*	Limassol. Haifa.
12.15	Dode. H/F	Samos (Pithagorio).
13.00	*Anemos*	Lipsi. Samos (Vathi). Samos (Karlovassi). Fourni. Ikaria (Agios Kyrikos). Mykonos. Piraeus.
15.00	Samos H/F	Lipsi. Leros (Agia Marina). Kalimnos. Kos.
16.00	Dode. H/F	Leros (Agia Marina). Kos. Rhodes.
16.30	Samos H/F	Ikaria (Agios Kyrikos). Fourni. Samos (Pithagorio). Samos (Vathi).
19.00	*Nissos Kalimnos*	Lipsi. Leros. Kalimnos.
23.50	*Leros*	Lipsi. Leros. Kalimnos. Kos. Rhodes.

④
| 00.30 | *Ialyssos* | Piraeus. |
| 08.55 | Samos H/F | Lipsi. Leros (Agia Marina). Kalimnos. Kos. |

10.10	Samos H/F	Samos (Pithagorio).
10.15	Dode. H/F	Agathonisi. Samos (Pithagorio).
15.00	Samos H/F	Lipsi. Leros (Agia Marina). Kalimnos. Kos.
15.30	Dode. H/F	Leros (Agia Marina). Kos. Kalimnos.
16.30	Samos H/F	Samos (Pithagorio). Samos (Vathi).
22.30	*Leros*	Piraeus.

⑤
00.45	*Marina/Rodanthi*	Piraeus.
01.30	*Ialyssos*	Leros. Kalimnos. Kos. Rhodes.
10.10	Samos H/F	Agathonisi. Samos (Pithagorio).
10.25	Samos H/F	Lipsi. Leros (Agia Marina). Kalimnos. Kos.
12.15	Dode. H/F	Samos (Pithagorio).
12.15	Dode. H/F	Fourni. Ikaria (Agios Kyrikos).
15.30	Dode. H/F	Lipsi. Leros (Agia Marina). Kos. Kalimnos.
15.50	Samos H/F	Lipsi. Leros (Agia Marina). Kalimnos. Kos.
16.00	Dode. H/F	Kos. Rhodes.
16.30	*Rodos*	Samos (Vathi). Thessalonika.
16.30	Samos H/F	Ikaria (Agios Kyrikos). Fourni. Samos (Pithagorio). (Vathi).

⑥
00.30	*Ialyssos*	Piraeus.
03.30	*Milena*	Leros. Kos. Kalimnos.
09.30	Samos H/F	Lipsi. Leros (Agia Marina). Kalimnos. Kos.
10.15	Dode. H/F	Samos (Pithagorio).
10.30	Samos H/F	Samos (Pithagorio).
12.00	*Milena*	Naxos. Paros. Piraeus.
15.00	Samos H/F	Lipsi. Leros (Agia Marina). Kalimnos. Kos.
15.30	Dode. H/F	Leros (Agia Marina). Kos. Kalimnos.
16.30	Samos H/F	Agathonisi. Samos (Pithagorio). (Vathi).

⑦
00.45	*Marina/Rodanthi*	Piraeus.
01.30	*Ialyssos*	Leros. Kalimnos. Kos. Rhodes.
02.30	*Marina/Rodanthi*	Leros. Kalimnos. Kos. Rhodes.
06.30	*Rodos*	Kos. Rhodes.
10.15	Dode. H/F	Ikaria (Agios Kyrikos). Samos (Pithagorio).
10.25	Samos H/F	Lipsi. Leros (Agia Marina). Kalimnos. Kos.
10.30	Samos H/F	Samos (Pithagorio).
11.10	*Nissos Kalimnos*	Agathonisi. Samos (Pithagorio).
13.30	*Milena*	Leros. Kos. Kalimnos.
15.30	Dode. H/F	Leros (Agia Marina). Kos. Kalimnos.
16.00	Samos H/F	Lipsi. Leros (Agia Marina). Kalimnos. Kos.
16.30	Samos H/F	Ikaria (Agios Kyrikos). Fourni. Samos (Pithagorio). (Vathi).
18.05	*Nissos Kalimnos*	Lipsi. Leros. Kalimnos.
23.30	*Milena*	Naxos. Piraeus.

Patras

Ionian Line p. 497

International Services:

ⓓ

17.00	HML Ferries	Kefalonia (Sami). Igoumenitsa. Corfu. Brindisi.
18.00	*Superfast I/II*	Igoumenitsa. Bari.
19.00	*Brindisi/ Valentino*	Igoumenitsa. Brindisi.
20.00	Med Link Lines	Brindisi.
20.00	*Superfast III/IV*	Ancona.
20.30	Ventouris	Bari.

Ⓐ

09.00	HML Ferries	Paxi. Brindisi.
19.00	Adriatica	Brindisi.
22.00	Adriatica	Igoumenitsa. Corfu. Brindisi.

①

20.00	*Pasiphae*	Igoumenitsa. Ancona.
22.00	*Daedalus/Fedra*	Corfu. Igoumenitsa. Venice.
23.00	*El. Venizelos*	Igoumenitsa. Trieste.
23.00	*Ionian Island*	Corfu. Igoumenitsa. Ancona.

②

19.00	*Kriti I*	Ancona.
21.30	*Ionian Victory*	Igoumenitsa. Corfu. Venice.
22.00	*Daedalus/Fedra*	Corfu. Igoumenitsa. Venice.

③

16.00	*Ikarus*	Igoumenitsa. Ancona.
22.00	*Erotokritos*	Corfu. Igoumenitsa. Venice.
23.00	*Ionian Star*	Corfu. Igoumenitsa. Ancona.
23.00	*Kriti II*	Igoumenitsa. Ancona.
23.00	*Talos*	Igoumenitsa. Trieste.

④

16.00	*Pasiphae*	Igoumenitsa. Ancona.
21.30	*Ionian Island*	Igoumenitsa. Corfu. Venice.
24.00	*Aretousa*	Corfu. Igoumenitsa. Venice.
24.00	*El. Venizelos*	Igoumenitsa. Corfu. Trieste.

⑤

16.00	*Kriti I*	Ancona.
18.00	*Ikarus*	Igoumenitsa. Ancona.
22.00	*Daedalus/Fedra*	Corfu. Igoumenitsa. Venice.

⑥

13.00	*Ionian Victory*	Igoumenitsa. Corfu. Ancona.
18.00	*Pasiphae*	Igoumenitsa. Ancona.
22.30	*Ionian Star*	Igoumenitsa. Venice.
23.00	*Kriti II*	Igoumenitsa. Ancona.
24.00	*Erotokritos*	Corfu. Igoumenitsa. Venice.

⑦

20.00	*Ikarus*	Igoumenitsa. Ancona.
24.00	*Aretousa*	Corfu. Igoumenitsa. Venice.
24.00	*Kriti I*	Igoumenitsa. Ancona.

○

09.00	HML Ferries	Zakinthos. Brindisi.

Domestic Services:

ⓓ

12.30	*Kefalonia*	Kefalonia (Sami). Ithaca.
20.00	*Kefalonia*	Kefalonia (Sami). Ithaca.

Paxi / Paxos

Ionian Line p. 499

ⓓ

07.00	*Santa Eleonora*	Corfu. Brindisi.

ⓓ ex ③

07.15	*Theologos*	Igoumenitsa. Corfu.

ⓓ ex ⑦

07.30	*Pegasus* T/B	Corfu.

Ⓐ

07.00	HML Ferries	Patras.
18.30	HML Ferries	Brindisi.

③

12.00	*Theologos*	Igoumenitsa. Corfu.

○

00.00		Preveza. Amphilochia.
00.00		Corfu.

Piraeus (Great Harbour)

Athens & Piraeus   p. 118

Note:
Current weekly domestic schedules (running Thursday to Wednesday) are available from the central
Athens (Amerikas St.) and airport branches of the NTOG/EOT. A 48-hour Saronic Gulf ferry schedule (in
Greek) is posted up on the Port Police kiosk on the Saronic Gulf ferry quay. Full Saronic Gulf hydrofoil
timetables are available from the Zea Marina ticket kiosk. International ferry information is obtained from
respective agents.

International Services:

①
| 19.00 | Sea Harmony | Crete (Iraklion). Rhodes. Limassol. Haifa. |

②
| 20.00 | Princesa Cypria | Patmos. Limassol. Haifa. |

④
| 19.00 | Sea Symphony | Rhodes. Limassol. Haifa. |
| 20.00 | Nissos Kypros | Rhodes. Limassol. Haifa. |

Domestic Services:

1. Cyclades, Crete, Dodecanese, Eastern & Northern Aegean

Ⓓ
08.00	Naias II	Syros. Tinos. Mykonos.
08.15	Express Aphrodite	Syros. Tinos. Mykonos.
19.15	King Minos/	
	N. Kazantzakis	Crete (Iraklion).
19.30	Arkadi/Preveli	Crete (Rethimno).
20.30	Lato/Lissos	Crete (Chania).

Ⓓ ex ①
| 22.00 | Express Olympia | Paros. Naxos. Ios. Santorini. |

Ⓓ ex ②
| 16.45 | Highspeed I | Syros. Mykonos. |

①
07.30	Panagia Ekatontapiliani	Paros. Naxos. Ios. Santorini.
07.30	Pegasus	Sifnos. Serifos. Kythnos.
07.35	Highspeed I	Paros. Naxos.
07.45	Mega Dolphin	Kythnos. Serifos. Sifnos. Milos.
08.00	Express Santorini	Paros. Naxos. Ios. Santorini.
11.00	Rodos	Kalimnos. Leros. Patmos.
13.00	Theofilos	Lesbos (Mytilini).
14.00	Express Athina	Syros. Paros. Naxos. Mykonos.
14.00	Leros	Patmos. Leros. Kalimnos. Kos. Rhodes.
15.00	Milos Express	Kythnos. Serifos. Sifnos. Kimolos. Milos.
16.00	Marina/Rodanthi	Leros. Kalimnos. Kos. Rhodes.
16.00	Super Naias	Syros. Paros. Naxos. Donoussa. Amorgos (Egiali). Amorgos (Katapola).
16.45	Golden Vergina	Paros. Ikaria (Evdilos). Samos (Karlovassi). Samos (Vathi).
17.00	Naias Express	Syros. Tinos. Mykonos.
17.30	Milena	Paros. Naxos. Ikaria (Agios Kyrikos). Samos (Karlovassi). Samos (Vathi).
18.00	Anemos	Syros. Mykonos. Ikaria (Evdilos). Samos (Karlovassi). Samos (Vathi).
18.00	Kantia	Kithera. Antikithera. Crete (Kasteli).
18.00	Sappho	Chios. Lesbos (Mytilini). Limnos. Thessalonika.
18.30	Pegasus	Serifos. Sifnos. Milos. Folegandros. Sikinos. Ios. Santorini.
18.30	Poseidon Express 2	Paros. Naxos. Ios. Santorini.
19.00	Vitsentzos Kornaros	Milos. Crete (Agios Nikolaos). Crete (Sitia).
19.30	Aptera	Crete (Iraklion).

19.30	*Arkadi/Preveli*	Sifnos. Crete (Rethimno).
22.00	*Express Apollon*	Paros. Naxos. Ios. Santorini.
22.45	*Arkadi/Preveli*	Sifnos. Crete (Rethimno).

②

07.30	*Panagia Ekatontapiliani*	Paros. Naxos. Ios. Santorini.
07.35	*Highspeed I*	Syros. Paros. Naxos.
07.45	*Mega Dolphin*	Kythnos. Serifos. Sifnos. Milos.
08.00	*Express Santorini*	Paros. Naxos. Ios. Santorini.
08.30	*Ariadne*	Paros. Naxos. Ios. Sikinos. Santorini.
14.00	*Express Athina*	Syros. Mykonos. Paros. Naxos. Ios. Santorini.
14.00	*Ialyssos*	Patmos. Leros. Kalimnos. Kos. Rhodes.
14.00	*Theofilos*	Lesbos (Mytilini). Chios.
15.00	*Milos Express*	Kythnos. Serifos. Sifnos. Kimolos. Milos.
16.00	*Daliana*	Paros. Santorini. Crete (Iraklion). Kassos. Karpathos (Town). Karpathos (Diafani). Chalki. Rhodes.
16.00	*Marina/Rodanthi*	Kalimnos. Kos. Rhodes.
17.00	*Naias Express*	Syros. Tinos. Mykonos.
17.00	*Rodos*	Kos. Rhodes. Kastelorizo.
18.00	*Agios Rafail*	Chios.
18.00	*Super Naias*	Syros. Paros. Naxos. Ios. Santorini. Anafi. Astipalea.
19.00	*Golden Vergina*	Syros. Ikaria (Evdilos). Samos (Karlovassi). Samos (Vathi).
19.00	*Mytilene*	Chios. Lesbos (Mytilini). Limnos.
19.30	*Rethimno*	Crete (Iraklion).
20.00	*Anemos*	Syros. Mykonos. Ikaria (Agios Kyrikos). Fourni. Samos (Karlovassi). Samos (Vathi). Patmos. Lipsi.

③

07.30	*Panagia Ekatontapiliani*	Paros. Naxos. Ios. Sikinos. Folegandros. Santorini.
07.45	*Mega Dolphin*	Kythnos. Serifos. Sifnos. Milos.
08.00	*Express Apollon*	Paros. Naxos. Ios. Santorini.
08.15	*Milos Express*	Kythnos. Serifos. Sifnos. Kimolos. Milos.
08.30	*Ariadne*	Paros. Naxos.
14.00	*Leros*	Patmos. Lipsi. Leros. Kalimnos. Kos. Rhodes.
16.00	*Marina/Rodanthi*	Kalimnos. Kos. Rhodes.
17.00	*Express Santorini*	Paros. Naxos. Iraklia. Schinoussa. Koufonissia. Donoussa. Amorgos (Egiali). Amorgos (Katapola). Astipalea.
17.00	*Naias Express*	Syros. Tinos. Mykonos.
17.30	*Milena*	Paros. Naxos. Ikaria (Agios Kyrikos). Samos (Karlovassi). Samos (Vathi).
18.00	*Pegasus*	Sifnos. Milos. Folegandros. Sikinos. Santorini.
18.30	*Poseidon Express 2*	Paros. Naxos. Ios. Santorini.
19.00	*Agios Rafail*	Andros. Syros. Chios. Lesbos (Mytilini).
19.00	*Express Athina*	Syros. Mykonos.
19.00	*Theofilos*	Chios. Lesbos (Mytilini).
19.00	*Vitsentzos Kornaros*	Milos. Crete (Agios Nikolaos). Crete (Sitia).
19.30	*Aptera*	Crete (Iraklion).
20.00	*Golden Vergina*	Paros. Ikaria (Evdilos). Fourni. Samos (Karlovassi). Samos (Vathi).

④

07.30	*Super Naias*	Paros. Naxos. Ios. Santorini.
07.35	*Highspeed I*	Paros. Naxos.
07.45	*Mega Dolphin*	Kythnos. Serifos. Sifnos. Milos.
08.00	*Express Apollon*	Paros. Naxos. Ios. Santorini.
08.15	*Milos Express*	Kythnos. Serifos. Sifnos. Kimolos. Milos.
08.30	*Ariadne*	Syros. Paros. Naxos. Ios. Santorini.
14.00	*Express Athina*	Syros. Mykonos. Paros. Naxos. Ios. Santorini.
14.00	*Ialyssos*	Patmos. Leros. Kalimnos. Kos. Rhodes.
16.00	*Marina/Rodanthi*	Kalimnos. Kos. Rhodes. Karpathos (Town).
17.00	*Naias Express*	Syros. Tinos. Mykonos.
17.00	*Rodos*	Kos. Rhodes.
17.15	*Anemos*	Syros. Mykonos. Ikaria (Evdilos). Samos (Karlovassi). Samos (Vathi).
18.00	*Panagia Ekatontapiliani*	Paros. Naxos. Ios. Sikinos. Folegandros. Santorini.
18.30	*Poseidon Express 2*	Paros. Naxos. Ios. Santorini.
19.00	*Mytilene*	Chios. Lesbos (Mytilini).
19.30	*Rethimno*	Crete (Iraklion).
20.00	*Sappho*	Lesbos (Mytilini). Chios.
21.00	*Pegasus*	Kythnos. Serifos. Sifnos. Kimolos. Milos.

⑤

| 07.30 | *Super Naias* | Paros. Naxos. Ios. Santorini. |
| 07.35 | *Highspeed I* | Paros. Naxos. |

Piraeus (Great Harbour):

08.00	*Express Santorini*	Paros. Naxos. Ios. Santorini.
08.30	*Ariadne*	Paros. Naxos. Amorgos (Katapola). Astipalea.
14.00	*Agios Rafail*	Psara. Lesbos (Mytilini).
15.00	*Romilda*	Mykonos. Amorgos (Katapola). Astipalea. Kalimnos. Kos. Nissiros. Tilos. Rhodes.
15.20	*Mega Dolphin*	Kythnos. Sifnos. Milos.
16.00	*Marina/Rodanthi*	Paros. Kos. Rhodes.
16.00	*Milena*	Naxos. Patmos. Leros. Kos. Kalimnos.
16.15	*Milos Express*	Kythnos. Serifos. Sifnos. Folegandros.
16.45	*Golden Vergina*	Paros. Ikaria (Evdilos). Samos (Karlovassi). Samos (Vathi).
17.00	*Express Apollon*	Paros. Naxos. Ios. Santorini.
17.00	*Leros*	Kos. Rhodes.
17.00	*Naias Express*	Syros. Tinos. Mykonos.
17.30	*Daliana*	Naxos. Ikaria (Agios Kyrikos). Fourni. Samos (Karlovassi). Samos (Vathi).
18.00	*Panagia Ekatontapiliani*	Paros. Naxos. Ios. Santorini. Anafi.
18.00	*Pegasus*	Sifnos. Milos. Folegandros. Santorini.
18.00	*Theofilos*	Chios. Lesbos (Mytilini). Limnos. Thessalonika.
18.30	*Poseidon Express 2*	Paros. Naxos. Ios. Sikinos. Folegandros. Santorini.
19.00	*Anemos*	Syros. Mykonos. Ikaria (Evdilos). Samos (Karlovassi). Samos (Vathi).
19.00	*Vitsentzos Kornaros*	Milos. Crete (Agios Nikolaos). Crete (Sitia). Kassos. Karpathos (Town). Karpathos (Diafani). Rhodes.
19.30	*Aptera*	Crete (Iraklion).
21.00	*Kantia*	Crete (Chania).
21.00	*Mytilene*	Lesbos (Mytilini). Chios.
22.00	*Express Athina*	Ios. Santorini.

⑥

07.30	*Naias Express*	Syros. Tinos. Mykonos.
07.30	*Super Naias*	Paros. Naxos. Ios. Santorini.
07.35	*Highspeed I*	Paros. Naxos.
07.45	*Milos Express*	Kythnos. Sifnos. Milos. Kimolos. Folegandros. Sikinos. Santorini.
08.00	*Express Santorini*	Paros. Naxos. Ios. Santorini.
08.30	*Ariadne*	Paros. Naxos. Ios. Santorini.
09.00	*Mega Dolphin*	Kythnos. Sifnos. Milos.
09.00	*Sappho*	Chios. Lesbos (Mytilini). Limnos. Kavala.
14.00	*Ialyssos*	Patmos. Leros. Kalimnos. Kos. Rhodes.
15.00	*Mega Dolphin*	Serifos. Sifnos. Milos.
16.00	*Marina/Rodanthi*	Paros. Patmos. Leros. Kalimnos. Kos. Rhodes.
17.00	*Express Athina*	Syros. Mykonos. Paros. Naxos. Amorgos (Katapola). Astipalea.
18.00	*Panagia Ekatontapiliani*	Paros. Naxos. Ios. Santorini.
18.30	*Poseidon Express 2*	Paros. Naxos. Ios. Santorini.
19.00	*Express Apollon*	Paros. Naxos. Ios. Santorini. Anafi.
19.30	*Aptera*	Crete (Iraklion).
20.00	*Golden Vergina*	Paros. Ikaria (Evdilos). Samos (Karlovassi). Samos (Vathi).
21.00	*Naias Express*	Syros. Tinos. Mykonos. Donoussa. Amorgos (Egiali). Amorgos (Katapola). Koufonissia. Iraklia. Naxos.
21.00	*Pegasus*	Kythnos. Serifos. Sifnos. Milos.
22.00	*Mytilene*	Chios. Lesbos (Mytilini).
23.00	*Anemos*	Syros. Mykonos. Ikaria (Agios Kyrikos). Samos (Karlovassi). Samos (Vathi).

⑦

01.00	*Agios Rafail*	Lesbos (Mytilini).
02.30	*Milena*	Paros. Naxos. Patmos. Leros. Kos. Kalimnos.
07.30	*Super Naias*	Paros. Naxos. Ios. Santorini.
07.35	*Highspeed I*	Paros. Naxos.
07.45	*Mega Dolphin*	Sifnos. Milos.
07.45	*Milos Express*	Kythnos. Serifos. Sifnos. Milos.
08.00	*Express Santorini*	Paros. Naxos. Ios. Santorini.
08.30	*Ariadne*	Paros. Naxos. Ios. Santorini.
10.00	*Mega Dolphin*	Serifos. Sifnos. Kythnos.
16.00	*Marina/Rodanthi*	Patmos. Leros. Kalimnos. Kos. Rhodes. Symi.
16.45	*Daliana*	Paros. Naxos. Ikaria (Agios Kyrikos). Samos (Karlovassi). Samos (Vathi).
18.00	*Pegasus*	Serifos. Sifnos. Milos.
18.30	*Poseidon Express 2*	Syros. Paros. Naxos. Ios. Santorini.
19.00	*Express Apollon*	Paros. Naxos. Ios. Sikinos. Folegandros. Santorini.
19.30	*Rethimno*	Crete (Iraklion).
22.00	*Express Olympia*	Paros. Naxos. Ios. Santorini. Anafi.
23.00	*Mytilene*	Chios. Lesbos (Mytilini).
24.00	*Naias Express*	Mykonos. Naxos. Paros.

Piraeus (Great Harbour):

2. Saronic Gulf

Ⓓ
06.45	*Mirage*	Aegina.
07.30	*Express Danae*	Aegina. Methana. Poros.
07.45	*Express Danae*	Aegina. Methana. Poros. Hydra. Spetses. Porto Helio.
08.00	*Eftichia*	Aegina. Methana. Poros. Hydra. Ermioni. Spetses.
08.00	*Georgios 2*	Aegina. Methana. Poros. Spetses. Porto Helio.
08.30	*Mirage*	Hydra. Spetses. Porto Helio.
09.00	*Keravnos*	Aegina. Angistri.
14.30	*Keravnos*	Aegina. Angistri.
14.30	*Mirage*	Aegina.
16.00	*Express Danae*	Aegina. Methana. Poros.
16.30	*Mirage*	Poros. Hydra. Spetses. Porto Helio.

🐬 *Flying Dolphins/Sea Falcons:*

Ⓓ Ⓗ
| 06.00–19.00 | Aegina (Town). |
| 06.00–20.00 | Aegina (Souvala). Aegina (Agia Marina). |

○ Typical daily ferry departures:

| 06.30 | Poseidon Co. | Aegina (Souvala). |
| 06.30 | Poseidon Co. | Aegina (Souvala). |

07.30	Poseidon Co.	Aegina. Methana. Poros.
08.00	*Manaras Express*	Aegina. Angistri.
08.00	*Elvira*	Aegina (Agia Marina).
09.15	Poseidon Co.	Aegina (Souvala). Aegina.
09.30	*Agios Nektarios B*	Aegina (Agia Marina).
10.30	Poseidon Co.	Aegina. Methana. Poros.
10.45	Poseidon Co.	Aegina.
13.30	*Manaras Express*	Aegina. Angistri.
14.00	*Michael*	Aegina (Agia Marina).
14.00	Poseidon Co.	Aegina (Souvala). Aegina.
15.00	Poseidon Co.	Aegina. Methana. Poros.
15.30	Poseidon Co.	Aegina (Souvala).
16.00	*Agios Nektarios B*	Aegina (Agia Marina).
18.00	Poseidon Co.	Aegina.
18.30	*Manaras Express*	Aegina. Angistri.
19.00	*Michael*	Aegina (Agia Marina).
20.30	Poseidon Co.	Aegina.

Additional services include:

① ③ ⑤
| 00.00 | Poseidon Co. | Aegina. Angistri. Epidavros. |

⑥ ⑦
| 14.00 | Poseidon Co. | Aegina. Angistri. Epidavros. |

Piraeus (Zea Marina)

Athens & Piraeus p. 121

Ⓓ
| 00.00 | *Flying Cat* | Poros. Hydra. Spetses. Porto Helio. |
| 00.00 | *Flying Dol. 2000* | Poros. Hydra. Spetses. Porto Helio. |

🐬 *Flying Dolphins* include:
Ⓓ
x 12	Hydra.
x 12	Poros.
x 12	Spetses.
00.00	Epidavros.
08.00	Poros. Hydra. Ermioni.
08.25	Hydra. Spetses. Porto Helio.
09.00	Aegina (Town). Methana. Poros. Hydra. Ermioni. Spetses. Porto Helio.
13.45	Poros. Hydra. Ermioni.
14.30	Hydra. Spetses. Porto Helio.
16.00	Aegina (Town). Methana. Poros. Hydra. Ermioni. Spetses. Porto Helio. Tolo.

① ④ ⑥ ⑦
| 08.15 | Spetses. Monemvassia. Kithera (Agia Pelagia). |

③
| 08.15 | Aegina. Methana. Poros. Ermioni. Leonidio. Kiparissi. Monemvassia. Kithera (Agia Pelagia). |

🐬 *Mega Dolphins* include:

Ⓓ x ①
| 08.30 | *Mega Dolphin* | Kea. Andros. |
①
| 05.20 | *Mega Dolphin* | Andros. Kea. |
⑤ ⑥
| 15.00 | *Mega Dolphin* | Kea. Andros. |

Poros

Argo-Saronic p. 466

Ⓓ ev 20 min:
06.00–22.00   *Elpis I*   Galatas.

Ⓓ
00.00   *Flying Dol. 2000*   Hydra. Spetses.
                             Porto Helio.
00.00   *Flying Dol. 2000*   Piraeus (Zea).
10.30   *Saronikos*   Hydra. Ermioni.
10.30   *Eftichia*   Hydra. Ermioni. Spetses.
10.45   Poseidon Co.   Methana. Aegina. Piraeus.
10.50   *Express Danae*   Methana. Aegina. Piraeus.
10.50   *Georgios 2*   Spetses. Porto Helio.
11.00   *Express Danae*   Hydra. Spetses.
                             Porto Helio.
12.10   *Mirage*   Piraeus.
14.00   Poseidon Co.   Methana. Aegina. Piraeus.
16.00   *Express Danae*   Methana. Aegina. Piraeus.
16.40   *Eftichia*   Methana. Aegina. Piraeus.
17.00   *Georgios 2*   Methana. Aegina. Piraeus.
17.20   *Mirage*   Hydra. Spetses.
                             Porto Helio.
18.00   Poseidon Co.   [⑦ 16.20]
                             Methana.
                             Aegina. Piraeus.
19.00   *Eftichia*   Methana. Aegina.
                             Piraeus.

① ② ③ ④ ⑤
06.30   Poseidon Co.   Methana. Aegina.
                             Piraeus.

⑥ ⑦
07.00   Poseidon Co.   Methana. Aegina.
                             Piraeus.
10.00   Poseidon Co.   Methana. Aegina.
                             Piraeus.
19.00   Poseidon Co.   Methana. Aegina.
                             Piraeus.

🚤 *Flying Dolphins* include:
Ⓓ
x 6   Hydra
x 7   Piraeus (Zea).
x 4   Spetses.

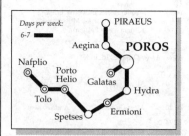

Days per week:
6-7 ▬

PIRAEUS
Aegina
POROS
Nafplio
Porto Helio
Galatas
Tolo
Hydra
Spetses
Ermioni

Port Said

Egypt p. 85

◯
20.00   *Princesa Amorosa*   Ashdod. Limassol.
                             Haifa.

Porto Helio

Argo-Saronic p. 469

Ⓓ
10.40   *Mirage*   Spetses. Hydra. Poros.
                             Piraeus.
13.30   *Express Danae*   Spetses. Hydra. Poros.
                             Methana. Aegina. Piraeus.
19.00   *Mirage*   Spetses. Hydra. Piraeus.

🚤 *Flying Dolphins* include:
Ⓓ x 6 Hydra. Spetses. Piraeus (Zea).

Preveza

Ionian Line p. 487

◯
00.00   Amphilochia.
00.00   Paxi. Corfu.

Princes' Islands

Turkey p. 524

Ⓓ x 6
06.45–21.00   TML   İstanbul.
00.00–00.00   TML   Yalova.

Psara

Eastern Line p. 392

②
12.00   Miniotis   Chios.

④
12.00   Miniotis   Chios.
22.15   *Agios Rafail*   Piraeus.

⑤
23.00   *Agios Rafail*   Lesbos (Mytilini).

⑥
12.00   Miniotis   Chios.

Rafina

Athens & Piraeus p. 122

ⒹD

07.45	ILIO H/F	Evia (Nea Styra).
07.45	*Sea Jet I*	Tinos. Mykonos.
08.30	*Ex. Karystos*	Evia (Marmari).
16.00	ILIO H/F	Andros (Batsi). Tinos. Mykonos. Paros. Naxos. Ios. Santorini.
17.00	*Ionian Sun*	Syros. Paros. Naxos.

Ⓓ ex ②

16.00	*Sea Jet I*	Tinos. Mykonos.

①

05.00	*Athina 2004*	Andros.
07.00	*Bari Express*	Andros. Tinos.
07.30	*Supercat Haroulla*	Andros. Tinos. Mykonos. Paros.
07.35	ILIO H/F	Andros (Batsi). Tinos. Mykonos. Paros. Sifnos. Milos.
08.00	*Karistos*	Evia (Karystos).
08.00	*Penelope A*	Andros. Tinos. Mykonos.
08.15	*Athina 2004*	Andros. Tinos. Mykonos. Naxos. Paros.
12.00	*Ex. Karystos*	Evia (Marmari).
14.15	*Karistos*	Evia (Karystos).
15.00	*Superferry II*	Andros. Tinos. Mykonos.
15.30	*Ex. Karystos*	Evia (Marmari).
17.00	*Bari Express*	Andros. Tinos. Mykonos.
17.15	*Athina 2004*	Tinos. Mykonos.
18.00	*Alcaeos*	Lesbos (Sigri). Agios Efstratios. Limnos. Kavala.
18.30	*Karistos*	Evia (Karystos).
19.00	*Ex. Karystos*	Evia (Marmari).

②

07.00	*Superferry II*	Andros. Tinos. Mykonos.
07.30	*Supercat Haroulla*	Andros. Tinos. Mykonos. Syros. Paros. Naxos. Amorgos (Katapola).
07.45	*Sea Jet I*	Andros. Syros. Mykonos. Syros. Paros. Naxos. Amorgos (Katapola).
08.00	*Karistos*	Evia (Karystos).
08.00	*Penelope A*	Andros. Tinos. Mykonos.
08.15	*Athina 2004*	Tinos. Mykonos. Naxos. Paros.
12.00	*Ex. Karystos*	Evia (Marmari).
14.15	*Karistos*	Evia (Karystos).
15.00	*Bari Express*	Andros. Tinos. Mykonos.
15.30	*Ex. Karystos*	Evia (Marmari).
17.15	*Athina 2004*	Tinos. Mykonos.
18.30	*Karistos*	Evia (Karystos).
19.00	*Ex. Karystos*	Evia (Marmari).

③

07.00	*Penelope A*	Andros. Tinos.
08.00	*Karistos*	Evia (Karystos).
08.15	*Athina 2004*	Andros. Tinos. Mykonos. Naxos. Paros.
12.00	*Ex. Karystos*	Evia (Marmari).
14.15	*Karistos*	Evia (Karystos).
15.00	*Bari Express*	Andros. Tinos. Mykonos.
15.30	*Ex. Karystos*	Evia (Marmari).
17.00	*Penelope A*	Andros. Tinos. Mykonos.
17.00	*Superferry II*	Andros. Tinos. Mykonos.
17.15	*Athina 2004*	Tinos. Mykonos.
18.30	*Karistos*	Evia (Karystos).
19.00	*Ex. Karystos*	Evia (Marmari).

④

07.00	*Penelope A*	Andros. Tinos.
07.30	*Supercat Haroulla*	Andros. Tinos. Mykonos. Paros.
08.00	*Karistos*	Evia (Karystos).
08.00	*Superferry II*	Andros. Tinos. Mykonos.
08.15	*Athina 2004*	Andros. Tinos. Mykonos. Paros. Naxos. Donoussa. Amorgos (Katapola).
12.00	*Ex. Karystos*	Evia (Marmari).
14.15	*Karistos*	Evia (Karystos).
15.00	*Bari Express*	Andros. Tinos. Mykonos.
15.30	*Ex. Karystos*	Evia (Marmari).
17.00	*Penelope A*	Andros. Tinos. Mykonos. Syros. Paros. Naxos. Amorgos (Katapola). Koufonissia. Schinoussa. Iraklia.
18.30	*Karistos*	Evia (Karystos).
19.00	*Alcaeos*	Lesbos (Sigri). Agios Efstratios. Limnos.
19.00	*Ex. Karystos*	Evia (Marmari).

⑤

07.00	*Bari Express*	Andros. Tinos.
07.30	*Supercat Haroulla*	Andros. Tinos. Mykonos.
08.00	*Karistos*	Evia (Karystos).
08.00	*Superferry II*	Andros. Tinos. Mykonos.
08.15	*Athina 2004*	Andros. Tinos. Mykonos. Naxos. Paros.
12.00	*Karistos*	Evia (Marmari).
14.00	*Ex. Karystos*	Evia (Marmari).
14.15	*Karistos*	Evia (Karystos).

RAFINA

Kavala
Limnos
Ag. Efstratios
Evia (Marmari)
Evia (Karystos)
Syros
Andros
Paros
Tinos
Naxos
Mykonos
Little Cyclades
Amorgos

Days per week:
6-7
2-3

16.00	*Bari Express*	Andros. Tinos. Mykonos.
16.30	*Supercat Haroulla*	Andros. Lavrion. Kea.
17.00	*Ex. Karystos*	Evia (Marmari).
17.00	*Ionian Sun*	Syros. Paros. Naxos. Amorgos (Egiali). Amorgos (Katapola).
17.15	*Athina 2004*	Tinos. Mykonos.
17.30	*Penelope A*	Andros. Tinos. Mykonos.
19.00	*Karistos*	Evia (Karystos).
19.00	*Superferry II*	Andros. Tinos. Mykonos.
20.30	*Ex. Karystos*	Evia (Marmari).
22.00	*Alcaeos*	Agios Efstratios. Limnos. Kavala.

⑥

07.00	*Bari Express*	Andros. Tinos.
07.30	*Supercat Haroulla*	Andros. Tinos. Mykonos. Paros.
07.50	*Penelope A*	Tinos. Mykonos.
08.00	*Karistos*	Evia (Marmari).
08.00	*Superferry II*	Andros. Tinos. Mykonos.
08.15	*Athina 2004*	Tinos. Mykonos. Naxos. Paros.
11.00	*Karistos*	Evia (Karystos).
12.00	*Ex. Karystos*	Evia (Marmari).
15.30	*Ex. Karystos*	Evia (Marmari).
15.30	*Karistos*	Evia (Marmari).
16.00	*Bari Express*	Andros. Tinos. Mykonos.
17.00	*Karistos*	Evia (Marmari).
17.00	*Penelope A*	Andros. Tinos. Mykonos.
17.15	*Athina 2004*	Tinos. Mykonos.
19.00	*Ex. Karystos*	Evia (Marmari).
20.00	*Karistos*	Evia (Karystos).

⑦

07.00	*Bari Express*	Andros. Tinos.
07.30	*Supercat Haroulla*	Andros. Tinos. Mykonos.
08.00	*Karistos*	Evia (Karystos).
08.00	*Superferry II*	Andros. Tinos. Mykonos.
08.15	*Athina 2004*	Tinos. Mykonos.
14.15	*Karistos*	Evia (Karystos).
15.30	*Ex. Karystos*	Evia (Marmari).
16.00	*Alcaeos*	Limnos. Agios Efstratios.
17.00	*Ionian Sun*	Syros. Paros. Naxos. Donoussa. Amorgos (Egiali). Amorgos (Katapola). Koufonissia. Schinoussa. Iraklia.
17.15	*Athina 2004*	Andros. Tinos. Mykonos.
17.30	*Bari Express*	Mykonos. Tinos.
18.00	*Karistos*	Evia (Karystos).
18.30	*Supercat Haroulla*	Kea.
19.00	*Ex. Karystos*	Evia (Marmari).
19.00	*Superferry II*	Andros.
20.30	*Penelope A*	Andros.
22.00	*Ex. Karystos*	Evia (Marmari).
22.15	*Karistos*	Evia (Karystos).
23.00	*Superferry II*	Syros. Tinos. Mykonos.

○

15.45	ILIO H/F	Evia (Nea Styra). Evia (Aliveri). Skala Oropou.

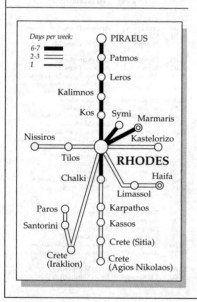

Days per week:
6-7
2-3
1

PIRAEUS
Patmos
Leros
Kalimnos
Kos
Symi — Marmaris
Nissiros
Kastelorizo
Tilos
RHODES
Chalki
Haifa
Limassol
Paros
Karpathos
Santorini
Kassos
Crete (Sitia)
Crete (Iraklion)
Crete (Agios Nikolaos)

Rhodes

Dodecanese   p. 350

International Services:

Ⓓ

08.00	Hydrofoil	Marmaris.
17.00	*Deniz Turk*	Marmaris.

②

13.00	*Sea Symphony*	Piraeus.
14.00	*Nissos Kypros*	Piraeus.
21.00	*Sea Harmony*	Limassol. Haifa.

⑤

15.00	*Sea Symphony*	Limassol. Haifa.
17.00	*Nissos Kypros*	Limassol. Haifa.

⑥

11.00	*Sea Harmony*	Crete (Iraklion). Piraeus.

⑦

15.00	*Princesa Cypria*	Lesbos (Mytilini). Tinos. Piraeus.

Domestic Services:

Ⓓ

08.00	Dode. H/Fl	Kos.
09.00	*Symi II*	Symi.
17.00	Dode. H/F	Kos.

①		
08.00	Dode. H/F	Kos. Leros (Agia Marina). Patmos. Samos.
09.30	*Marina/Rodanthi*	Symi.
16.00	*Marina/Rodanthi*	Kos. Kalimnos. Leros. Patmos. Piraeus.
17.00	*Nissos Kalimnos*	Kastelorizo.
22.00	*Romilda*	Chalki. Karpathos (Diafani). (Town). Kassos. Crete (Sitia).

②		
09.00	*Nissos Kalimnos*	Symi. Tilos. Nissiros. Kos. Kalimnos.
14.00	*Leros*	Kos. Kalimnos. Leros. Patmos. Piraeus.
18.00	*Symi I*	Symi.

③		
01.00	*Romilda*	Tilos. Nissiros. Kos. Kalimnos. Astipalea. Amorgos (Katapola). Mykonos. Piraeus.
08.00	Dode. H/F	Kos. Leros (Agia Marina). Patmos. Samos.
09.00	*Rodos*	Kastelorizo.
14.00	*Ialyssos*	Kos. Kalimnos. Leros. Patmos. Piraeus.
16.00	*Marina/Rodanthi*	Kos. Kalimnos. Piraeus.
17.00	*Rodos*	Kos. Piraeus.
18.00	Dode. H/F	Tilos. Nissiros. Kos.
18.00	*Symi I*	Symi.

④		
01.00	*Daliana*	Chalki. Karpathos (Diafani). (Town). Kassos. Crete (Iraklion). Santorini. Paros. Piraeus.
08.00	Dode. H/F	Kos.
14.00	*Leros*	Kos. Kalimnos. Leros. Lipsi. Patmos. Piraeus.
16.00	*Marina/Rodanthi*	Kos. Kalimnos. Leros. Patmos. Piraeus.
17.00	*Nissos Kalimnos*	Kastelorizo.

⑤		
08.00	Dode. H/F	Kos. Leros (Agia Marina). Patmos. Fourni. Ikaria (Agios Kyrikos).
08.30	*Marina/Rodanthi*	Karpathos (Town).
09.00	*Nissos Kalimnos*	Symi. Tilos. Nissiros. Kos. Kalimnos.
10.00	*Rodos*	Kos. Patmos. Samos (Vathi). Thessalonika.
10.30	Dode. H/F	Chalki.
14.00	*Ialyssos*	Kos. Kalimnos. Leros. Patmos. Piraeus.
16.00	*Marina/Rodanthi*	Kos. Kalimnos. Piraeus.
17.00	*Symi I*	Symi.

⑥		
08.00	Dode. H/F	Symi. Kos. Kalimnos. Astipalea.
10.15	Dode. H/F	Symi.
16.00	*Marina/Rodanthi*	Kos. Kalimnos. Leros. Patmos. Piraeus.
17.00	*Leros*	Kos. Piraeus.
17.30	*Romilda*	Kos. Samos (Vathi). Chios. Lesbos (Mytilini). Limnos. Alexandroupolis.
18.00	*Symi I*	Symi.

⑦		
06.00	*Vitsentzos Kornaros*	Karpathos (Town). Kassos. Crete (Sitia). Crete (Agios Nikolaos). Milos. Piraeus.
08.00	Dode. H/F	Kos. Nissiros.
10.15	Dode. H/F	Tilos.
14.00	*Ialyssos*	Kos. Kalimnos. Leros. Patmos. Piraeus.
17.30	*Marina/Rodanthi*	Kos. Piraeus.
18.00	*Rodos*	Kos. Piraeus.
18.00	*Symi I*	Symi.
18.00	*Symi II*	Symi.

Rhodes (Kamiros Skala)

Dodecanese   p. 360

⑩ ex ⑦		
14.30	*Chalki/Nikos Express*	Chalki.
⑦		
18.00	*Chalki/Nikos Express*	Chalki.

Salamina / Salamis (Paloukia)

Athens & Piraeus   p. 123

⑩ ⑭		
06.30–21.30	Taxi Boat	Piraeus.

Samos (Karlovassi)

Eastern Line   p. 395

①		
06.00	Miniotis	Fourni. Ikaria (Agios Kyrikos).
06.10	*Daliana*	Samos (Vathi).
11.00	Miniotis	Samos (Vathi).
17.30	Miniotis	Ikaria (Agios Kyrikos). Fourni.
17.40	*Daliana*	Ikaria (Agios Kyrikos). Naxos. Paros. Piraeus.

②		
03.40	*Golden Vergina*	Samos (Vathi).
05.00	*Anemos*	Samos (Vathi).
06.30	*Milena*	Samos (Vathi).
07.10	*Golden Vergina*	Ikaria (Evdilos). Piraeus.
08.30	*Anemos*	Ikaria (Evdilos). Piraeus.
17.30	*Milena*	Ikaria (Agios Kyrikos). Naxos. Paros. Piraeus.
20.30	Miniotis	Chios.

③		
04.40	*Golden Vergina*	Samos (Vathi).

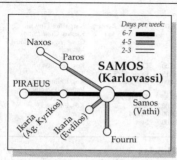

07.30 *Anemos* Samos (Vathi). Patmos. Lipsi.
08.10 *Golden Vergina* Ikaria (Evdilos). Piraeus.
19.00 *Anemos* Fourni.
Ikaria (Agios Kyrikos).
Mykonos. Piraeus.

④
06.30 *Milena* Samos (Vathi).
07.35 *Golden Vergina* Samos (Vathi).
16.55 *Golden Vergina* Fourni. Ikaria (Evdilos).
Paros. Piraeus.
17.30 *Milena* Ikaria (Agios Kyrikos).
Naxos. Paros. Piraeus.

⑤
04.15 *Anemos* Samos (Vathi).
07.15 *Anemos* Ikaria (Evdilos). Piraeus.

⑥
03.40 *Golden Vergina* Samos (Vathi).
06.00 *Anemos* Samos (Vathi).
06.45 *Daliana* Samos (Vathi).
07.45 *Golden Vergina* Ikaria (Evdilos). Syros.
Piraeus.
09.30 *Anemos* Ikaria (Agios Kyrikos).
Piraeus.
17.40 *Daliana* Fourni.
Ikaria (Agios Kyrikos).
Naxos. Piraeus.

⑦
06.25 *Golden Vergina* Samos (Vathi).
10.05 *Anemos* Samos (Vathi).
10.35 *Golden Vergina* Ikaria (Evdilos). Paros.
Piraeus.
18.00 *Anemos* Ikaria (Evdilos).
Mykonos.
Syros. Piraeus.
21.30 *Miniotis* Samos (Vathi).

Samos (Pithagorio)

Eastern Line   p. 395

○
09.00 *Cassandra* Patmos.

①
07.50 Samos H/F Patmos. Leros (Agia Marina). Kalimnos. Kos.
14.00 Dode. H/F Patmos. Kos. Rhodes.
14.00 Samos H/F Ikaria (Agios Kyrikos). Fourni. Patmos. Leros (Agia Marina). Kalimnos. Kos.

②
07.00 Miniotis Agathonisi. Arki. Lipsi. Patmos.
07.50 Samos H/F Patmos. Lipsi. Leros (Agia Marina). Kalimnos. Kos.
14.00 Dode. H/F Patmos. Lipsi. Leros (Agia Marina). Kos. Kalimnos.
14.30 Samos H/F Patmos. Lipsi. Leros (Agia Marina). Kalimnos. Kos.
19.00 Miniotis Samos (Karlovassi). Chios.

③
07.50 Samos H/F Fourni. Ikaria (Agios Kyrikos). Patmos. Lipsi. Leros (Agia Marina). Kalimnos. Kos.
14.15 Samos H/F Patmos. Lipsi. Leros (Agia Marina). Kalimnos. Kos.
14.45 Dode. H/F Patmos. Leros (Agia Marina). Kos. Rhodes.
15.00 *Nissos Kalimnos* Agathonisi. Arki. Patmos. Lipsi. Leros. Kalimnos.

④
07.50 Samos H/F Patmos. Lipsi. Leros (Agia Marina). Kalimnos. Kos.
14.00 Dode. H/F Agathonisi. Patmos. Leros (Agia Marina). Kos. Kalimnos.
14.30 Samos H/F Patmos. Lipsi. Leros (Agia Marina). Kalimnos. Kos.

⑤
07.50 Samos H/F Fourni. Ikaria (Agios Kyrikos). Patmos. Lipsi. Leros (Agia Marina). Kalimnos. Kos.
14.00 Dode. H/F Patmos. Lipsi. Leros (Agia Marina). Kos. Kalimnos.
14.30 Samos H/F Agathonisi. Patmos. Lipsi. Leros (Agia Marina). Kalimnos. Kos.

⑥
07.50 Samos H/F Agathonisi. Patmos. Lipsi. Leros (Agia Marina). Kalimnos. Kos.
13.30 Samos H/F Patmos. Lipsi. Leros (Agia Marina). Kalimnos. Kos.
14.00 Dode. H/F Patmos. Leros (Agia Marina). Kos. Kalimnos.

⑦
07.50 Samos H/F Fourni. Ikaria (Agios Kyrikos). Patmos. Lipsi. Leros (Agia Marina). Kalimnos. Kos.
13.10 Dode. H/F Ikaria (Agios Kyrikos). Patmos. Leros (Agia Marina). Kos. Kalimnos.
14.30 Samos H/F Patmos. Lipsi. Leros (Agia Marina). Kalimnos. Kos.
14.35 *Nissos Kalimnos* Agathonisi. Patmos. Lipsi. Leros. Kalimnos.

Samos (Vathi)

Eastern Line   p. 394

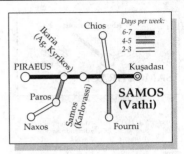

Ⓓ
| 08.00 | *Kapetan Giorgis* | Kuşadası. |
| 17.00 | *Fari Kaptain/Sultan I* | Kuşadası. |

①
07.00	Samos H/F	Samos (Pithagorio). Patmos. Leros (Agia Marina). Kalimnos. Kos.
16.00	*Daliana*	Samos (Karlovassi). Ikaria (Agios Kyrikos). Naxos. Paros. Piraeus.
16.00	*Miniotis*	Samos (Karlovassi). Ikaria (Agios Kyrikos). Fourni.

②
06.00	*Golden Vergina*	Samos (Karlovassi). Ikaria (Evdilos). Piraeus.
07.00	Samos H/F	Samos (Pithagorio). Patmos. Lipsi. Leros (Agia Marina). Kalimnos. Kos.
07.30	*Anemos*	Samos (Karlovassi). Ikaria (Evdilos). Piraeus.
16.00	*Milena*	Samos (Karlovassi). Ikaria (Agios Kyrikos). Naxos. Paros. Piraeus.

③
07.00	*Golden Vergina*	Samos (Karlovassi). Ikaria (Evdilos). Piraeus.
07.00	Samos H/F	Samos (Pithagorio). Fourni. Ikaria (Agios Kyrikos). Patmos. Lipsi. Leros (Agia Marina). Kalimnos. Kos.
10.00	*Anemos*	Patmos. Lipsi.
18.00	*Anemos*	Samos (Karlovassi). Fourni. Ikaria (Agios Kyrikos). Mykonos. Piraeus.

④
07.00	Samos H/F	Samos (Pithagorio). Patmos. Lipsi. Leros (Agia Marina). Kalimnos. Kos.
15.45	*Golden Vergina*	Samos (Karlovassi). Fourni. Ikaria (Evdilos). Paros. Piraeus.
16.00	*Milena*	Samos (Karlovassi). Ikaria (Agios Kyrikos). Naxos. Paros. Piraeus.

⑤
06.15	*Anemos*	Samos (Karlovassi). Ikaria (Evdilos). Piraeus.
07.00	Samos H/F	Samos (Pithagorio). Fourni. Ikaria (Agios Kyrikos). Patmos. Lipsi. Leros (Agia Marina). Kalimnos. Kos.
20.00	*Rodos*	Thessalonika.

⑥
| 06.30 | *Golden Vergina* | Samos (Karlovassi). Ikaria (Evdilos). Syros. Piraeus. |
| 06.30 | *Romilda* | Chios. Lesbos (Mytilini). Limnos. Alexandroupolis. |

07.00	Samos H/F	Samos (Pithagorio). Agathonisi. Patmos. Lipsi. Leros (Agia Marina). Kalimnos. Kos.
08.30	*Anemos*	Samos (Karlovassi). Ikaria (Agios Kyrikos). Piraeus.
16.00	*Daliana*	Samos (Karlovassi). Fourni. Ikaria (Agios Kyrikos). Naxos. Piraeus.

⑦
05.00	*Rodos*	Patmos. Kos. Rhodes.
07.00	Samos H/F	Samos (Pithagorio). Fourni. Ikaria (Agios Kyrikos). Patmos. Lipsi. Leros (Agia Marina). Kalimnos. Kos.
09.30	*Golden Vergina*	Samos (Karlovassi). Ikaria (Evdilos). Paros. Piraeus.
17.00	*Anemos*	Samos (Karlovassi). Ikaria (Evdilos). Mykonos. Syros. Piraeus.
18.45	*Romilda*	Kos. Rhodes.
23.00	*Miniotis*	Samos (Karlovassi).

Samothrace

Northern Aegean   p. 420

① ②
08.00	*Niki H/F*	Alexandroupolis.
11.30	*Arsinoe*	Alexandroupolis.
12.00	*Niki H/F*	Alexandroupolis.
17.00	*Saos*	Alexandroupolis.
19.00	*Arsinoe*	Alexandroupolis.

③
09.00	*Arsinoe*	Kavala.
11.30	*Saos*	Alexandroupolis.
12.30	*Niki H/F*	Alexandroupolis.
19.00	*Saos*	Alexandroupolis.

④
07.30	*Niki H/F*	Alexandroupolis.
09.00	*Arsinoe*	Kavala.
12.30	*Saos*	Alexandroupolis.
17.30	*Niki H/F*	Alexandroupolis.
19.00	*Arsinoe*	Alexandroupolis.

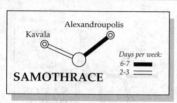

SAMOTHRACE

Days per week:
6-7 ▰▰▰
2-3 ══

⑤

08.00	Niki H/F	Alexandroupolis.
09.00	Saos	Alexandroupolis.
11.30	Arsinoe	Kavala.
12.00	Niki H/F	Alexandroupolis.
20.00	Saos	Alexandroupolis.

⑥

08.00	Niki H/F	Alexandroupolis.
09.30	Arsinoe	Kavala.
11.30	Saos	Alexandroupolis.
12.00	Niki H/F	Alexandroupolis.
19.00	Saos	Alexandroupolis.
19.30	Niki H/F	Alexandroupolis.

⑦

08.30	Niki H/F	Alexandroupolis.
09.00	Arsinoe	Kavala.
11.30	Saos	Alexandroupolis.
18.15	Saos	Alexandroupolis.
20.00	Arsinoe	Alexandroupolis.

○

08.30	Thraki III H/F	Alexandroupolis.
14.15	Thraki III H/F	Limnos.
18.00	Thraki III H/F	Alexandroupolis.

Santorini / Thira (Athinios)

Cyclades Central   p. 163

ⓓ

10.00	Theoskepasti	Santorini (Old Port).
		Nea Kameni.
		Thirasia (Korfos).
		Thirasia. Santorini (Oia).
16.00	Syros Express	Ios. Naxos. Paros. Mykonos.

ⓓ ex ②

08.00	Express Olympia	Ios. Naxos. Paros. Piraeus.

①

07.00	Express Olympia	Anafi.
07.30	Poseidon Express 2	Ios. Naxos. Paros. Piraeus.
08.00	Express Apollon	Ios. Naxos. Paros. Piraeus.
09.00	Speed H/F	Amorgos (Katapola).
		Amorgos (Egiali).
		Koufonissia. Schinoussa.
		Iraklia. Naxos. Mykonos.
11.00	Express Olympia	Ios. Naxos. Paros. Piraeus.
12.00	Speed H/F	Ios. Sikinos. Folegandros.

13.30	Maria PA	Ios. Naxos. Paros.
		Mykonos. Tinos. Syros.
15.30	Speed H/F	Ios. Naxos. Paros.
		Mykonos. Tinos. Syros.
18.30	El Greco	Paros. Tinos. Volos.
		Thessalonika.
19.00	Speed H/F	Ios.
19.00	Panagia Ekatonta.	Folegandros. Sikinos. Ios.
		Naxos. Paros. Piraeus.
20.00	Express Santorini	Ios. Naxos. Paros. Piraeus.

②

07.30	Poseidon Express 2	Folegandros. Sikinos. Ios.
		Naxos. Paros. Piraeus.
07.45	Pegasus	Ios. Sikinos. Folegandros.
		Kimolos. Milos. Sifnos.
		Serifos. Kythnos. Piraeus.
08.00	Express Apollon	Ios. Naxos. Paros. Piraeus.
09.00	Speed H/F	Anafi.
13.50	Dimitroula	Crete (Iraklion).
14.30	Speed H/F	Folegandros. Milos.
		Sifnos. Paros. Mykonos.
		Tinos. Syros.
16.25	Express Paros	Anafi.
17.15	Maria PA	Anafi.
17.15	Vergina Sky	Crete (Rethimno).
17.20	Speed H/F	Anafi.
19.00	Panagia Ekatonta.	Ios. Naxos. Paros. Piraeus.
19.10	Speed H/F	Ios.
20.00	Express Santorini	Ios. Naxos. Paros. Piraeus.
20.45	Ariadne	Ios. Naxos. Paros. Piraeus.
20.55	Express Paros	Ios. Sikinos. Folegandros.
		Naxos. Paros. Syros.
23.25	Dimitroula	Naxos. Paros. Mykonos.
		Thessalonika.

③

02.00	Daliana	Crete (Iraklion). Kassos.
		Karpathos (Town).
		Karpathos (Diafani).
		Chalki. Rhodes.
04.00	Super Naias	Anafi. Astipalea.
07.00	Express Athina	Ios. Naxos. Paros. Piraeus.
07.00	Maria PA	Folegandros. Sikinos. Ios.
08.00	Express Olympia	Ios. Naxos. Paros. Piraeus.
09.00	Speed H/F	Ios. Sikinos. Folegandros.
		Paros. Naxos. Mykonos.
		Syros.
12.00	Super Naias	Ios. Naxos. Paros. Piraeus.
12.15	Speed H/F	Amorgos (Katapola).
15.00	Maria PA	Ios. Naxos. Paros.
		Mykonos. Syros.
15.15	El Greco	Crete (Iraklion).
15.30	Speed H/F	Ios. Naxos. Paros.
		Mykonos. Tinos. Syros.
19.00	Panagia Ekatonta.	Thirasia. Ios. Naxos.
		Paros. Piraeus.
19.50	Speed H/F	Ios.
20.00	Express Apollon	Ios. Naxos. Paros. Piraeus.

④

01.30	El Greco	Naxos. Syros. Skiathos.
		Thessalonika.
07.30	Poseidon Express 2	Ios. Naxos. Paros. Piraeus.
07.45	Pegasus	Milos. Sifnos. Piraeus.
08.00	Express Olympia	Ios. Naxos. Paros. Piraeus.
09.00	Speed H/F	Amorgos (Katapola).
		Amorgos (Egiali).
		Koufonissia. Schinoussa.
		Iraklia. Naxos. Mykonos.
		Syros.

12.00	Speed H/F	Ios. Sikinos. Folegandros.
15.00	*Maria PA*	Crete (Iraklion).
15.30	Speed H/F	Ios. Naxos. Paros. Mykonos. Tinos. Syros.
15.35	*Dimitroula*	Crete (Iraklion).
17.15	*Vergina Sky*	Crete (Agios Nikolaos).
19.00	*Super Naias*	Ios. Naxos. Paros. Piraeus.
20.00	*Express Apollon*	Ios. Naxos. Paros. Piraeus.
20.10	Speed H/F	Ios.
20.45	*Ariadne*	Ios. Naxos. Paros. Piraeus.
21.00	*Daliana*	Paros. Piraeus.

ⓢ

01.10	*Dimitroula*	Paros. Mykonos. Syros. Thessalonika.
07.00	*Express Athina*	Ios. Naxos. Paros. Piraeus.
07.00	*Panagia Ekatonta.*	Ios. Naxos. Paros. Piraeus.
07.30	*Poseidon Express 2*	Ios. Naxos. Paros. Piraeus.
08.00	*Express Olympia*	Ios. Naxos. Paros. Piraeus.
09.00	Speed H/F	Anafi.
11.00	Speed H/F	Ios. Paros. Naxos. Naxos. Paros. Mykonos.
13.30	*Maria PA*	Naxos. Paros. Mykonos. Syros.
14.30	Speed H/F	Folegandros. Milos. Sifnos. Paros. Mykonos. Tinos. Syros.
15.30	*El Greco*	Crete (Iraklion).
17.20	Speed H/F	Anafi.
19.00	*Super Naias*	Ios. Naxos. Paros. Piraeus.
19.10	Speed H/F	Ios.
20.00	*Express Santorini*	Ios. Naxos. Paros. Piraeus.

⑥

02.00	*El Greco*	Paros. Tinos. Skiathos. Thessalonika.
03.10	*Panagia Ekatonta.*	Anafi.
07.00	*Express Athina*	Ios. Piraeus.

07.00	*Panagia Ekatonta.*	Ios. Naxos. Paros. Piraeus.
07.30	*Poseidon Express 2*	Ios. Naxos. Paros. Piraeus.
08.00	*Express Apollon*	Ios. Naxos. Paros. Piraeus.
08.00	*Pegasus*	Sikinos. Milos. Sifnos. Piraeus.
09.00	Speed H/F	Ios. Sikinos. Folegandros. Paros. Naxos. Mykonos.
11.00	*Express Olympia*	Ios. Naxos. Paros. Piraeus.
13.00	Speed H/F	Ios. Paros. Naxos. Mykonos. Tinos. Syros.
17.00	*Maria PA*	Ios. Naxos. Paros. Mykonos. Syros.
19.00	*Super Naias*	Ios. Naxos. Paros. Piraeus.
19.10	*Milos Express*	Folegandros. Kimolos. Milos. Sifnos. Piraeus.
20.00	*Dimitroula*	Crete (Iraklion).
20.00	*Express Santorini*	Ios. Naxos. Paros. Piraeus.
20.45	*Ariadne*	Ios. Naxos. Paros. Piraeus.

⑦

04.00	*Express Apollon*	Anafi.
05.40	*Dimitroula*	Ios. Naxos. Paros. Mykonos. Tinos. Syros. Volos. Skiathos. Thessalonika.
07.30	*Poseidon Express 2*	Ios. Naxos. Paros. Piraeus.
08.00	*Express Apollon*	Ios. Naxos. Paros. Piraeus.
11.00	*Express Olympia*	Ios. Naxos. Paros. Piraeus.
11.00	Speed H/F	Ios. Paros. Naxos. Mykonos.
12.00	*Panagia Ekatonta.*	Ios. Naxos. Paros. Piraeus.
12.15	Speed H/F	Amorgos (Katapola).
14.20	*Express Paros*	Sikinos. Folegandros. Milos. Sifnos.
15.30	Speed H/F	Ios. Naxos. Paros. Mykonos. Tinos. Syros.
15.30	*Maria PA*	Crete (Iraklion).
17.00	*El Greco*	Crete (Iraklion).
17.30	Speed H/F	Ios.
19.00	*Super Naias*	Ios. Naxos. Paros. Piraeus.
20.00	*Express Santorini*	Ios. Naxos. Paros. Piraeus.
20.45	*Ariadne*	Ios. Naxos. Paros. Piraeus.

Days per week:
6-7 ▬▬▬
4-5 ▬▬
2-3 ═══

Santorini (Fira / Old Port)

Cyclades Central p. 161

Ⓓ

09.15	Tour Boat	Nea Kameni.
10.30	*Theoskepasti*	Nea Kameni. Thirasia (Korfos). Thirasia (Riva). Santorini (Oia).
10.30	*Nissos Thirassia*	Nea Kameni. Thirasia (Korfos). Thirasia (Riva). Santorini (Oia).
15.20	Tour Boat	Nea Kameni.
16.50	*Theoskepasti*	Santorini.
17.00	*Nissos Thirassia*	Santorini.

②

07.45	*Theoskepasti*	Thirasia (Riva).

④

07.45	*Theoskepasti*	Thirasia (Riva).

Schinoussa

Cyclades East   p. 269

①
06.30	Ionian Sun	Iraklia. Naxos. Paros. Syros. Rafina.
07.45	Ex. Skopelitis	Iraklia. Naxos. Mykonos.
11.50	Speed H/F	Iraklia. Naxos. Mykonos.
16.00	Speed H/F	Koufonissia. Amorgos (Egiali). Amorgos (Katapola). Santorini. Ios.
18.30	Ex. Skopelitis	Koufonissia. Amorgos (Katapola).

②
| 10.15 | Ex. Skopelitis | Iraklia. Naxos. |
| 17.00 | Ex. Skopelitis | Koufonissia. Donoussa. Amorgos (Egiali). Amorgos (Katapola). |

③
| 07.45 | Ex. Skopelitis | Iraklia. Naxos. Mykonos. |
| 18.30 | Ex. Skopelitis | Koufonissia. Amorgos (Katapola). |

④
00.45	Ex. Santorini	Koufonissia. Donoussa. Amorgos (Egiali). Amorgos (Katapola). Astipalea.
10.15	Ex. Skopelitis	Iraklia. Naxos.
11.50	Speed H/F	Iraklia. Naxos. Mykonos. Syros.
17.00	Ex. Skopelitis	Koufonissia. Donoussa. Amorgos (Egiali). (Katapola).
17.15	Speed H/F	Koufonissia. Amorgos (Egiali). (Katapola). Santorini. Ios.

⑤
05.30	Penelope A	Iraklia. Naxos. Paros. Syros. Mykonos. Tinos. Andros. Rafina.
07.45	Ex. Skopelitis	Iraklia. Naxos. Mykonos.
13.00	ILIO H/F	Koufonissia. Amorgos (Katapola). Santorini.
18.10	Express Paros	Iraklia. Naxos. Paros. Syros.
18.30	Ex. Skopelitis	Koufonissia. Amorgos (Katapola).

⑥
| 07.45 | Ex. Skopelitis | Iraklia. Naxos. Mykonos. |
| 18.30 | Ex. Skopelitis | Koufonissia. Amorgos (Katapola). |

⑦
| 07.45 | Ex. Skopelitis | Iraklia. Naxos. Mykonos. |
| 18.30 | Ex. Skopelitis | Koufonissia. Amorgos (Katapola). |

Serifos

Cyclades West p. 240

①
10.25	Mega Dolphin	Sifnos. Milos.
12.35	Pegasus	Kythnos. Piraeus.
14.00	Mega Dolphin	Kythnos. Piraeus.
19.25	Milos Express	Sifnos. Kimolos. Milos.
22.35	Pegasus	Sifnos. Milos. Folegandros. Sikinos. Ios. Santorini.

②
00.35	Milos Express	Kythnos. Piraeus.
10.25	Mega Dolphin	Sifnos. Milos.
14.00	Mega Dolphin	Kythnos. Piraeus.
15.25	Pegasus	Kythnos. Piraeus.
19.25	Milos Express	Sifnos. Kimolos. Milos.

③
10.25	Mega Dolphin	Sifnos. Milos.
13.00	Milos Express	Sifnos. Kimolos. Milos.
16.30	Mega Dolphin	Kythnos. Piraeus.

④
10.25	Mega Dolphin	Sifnos. Milos.
11.30	Express Paros	Sifnos. Kimolos. Milos.
13.00	Milos Express	Sifnos. Kimolos. Milos.
13.20	ILIO H/F	Sifnos. Paros. Mykonos.
14.00	Mega Dolphin	Kythnos. Piraeus.
17.45	Express Paros	Paros. Syros.

⑤
01.00	Pegasus	Sifnos. Kimolos. Milos.
07.50	Milos Express	Kythnos. Piraeus.
10.20	Pegasus	Kythnos. Piraeus.
21.00	Milos Express	Sifnos. Folegandros.

⑥
01.15	Milos Express	Piraeus.
11.30	Express Paros	Sifnos. Kimolos. Milos.
17.20	Mega Dolphin	Sifnos. Milos.
17.45	Express Paros	Paros. Syros.

⑦
01.45	Pegasus	Sifnos. Milos.
12.00	Pegasus	Kythnos. Piraeus.
12.30	Milos Express	Sifnos. Milos.
17.25	Milos Express	Kythnos. Piraeus.
18.35	Mega Dolphin	Sifnos. Kythnos. Piraeus.
22.15	Pegasus	Sifnos. Milos. Piraeus.

PIRAEUS

Days per week:
6-7
4-5
2-3

Syros
Paros
Mykonos
Naxos
Donoussa

IRAKLIA
SCHINOUSSA
KOUFONISSIA   Amorgos (Katapola) (Egiali)

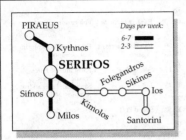

Sifnos

Cyclades West   p. 244

①
11.00	Mega Dolphin	Milos.
11.45	Pegasus	Serifos. Kythnos. Piraeus.
13.25	Mega Dolphin	Serifos. Kythnos. Piraeus.
13.30	Mega Dolphin	Milos.
16.10	Mega Dolphin	Paros. Mykonos. Tinos. Syros.
20.15	Milos Express	Kimolos. Milos.
23.25	Pegasus	Milos. Folegandros. Sikinos. Ios. Santorini.
23.45	Milos Express	Serifos. Kythnos. Piraeus.

②
10.30	Speed H/F	Milos. Folegandros. Santorini.
11.00	Mega Dolphin	Milos.
13.25	Mega Dolphin	Serifos. Kythnos. Piraeus.
13.30	Mega Dolphin	Milos.
14.30	Pegasus	Serifos. Kythnos. Piraeus.
16.10	Mega Dolphin	Paros. Mykonos. Tinos. Syros.
17.30	Speed H/F	Paros. Mykonos. Tinos. Syros.
20.15	Milos Express	Kimolos. Milos.

③
00.30	Milos Express	Piraeus.
02.30	Arkadi/Preveli	Piraeus.
11.00	Mega Dolphin	Milos.
13.30	Mega Dolphin	Milos.
14.00	Milos Express	Kimolos. Milos.
16.00	Mega Dolphin	Serifos. Kythnos. Piraeus.
16.10	Mega Dolphin	Paros. Mykonos. Tinos. Syros.
21.15	Pegasus	Milos. Folegandros. Sikinos. Santorini.

④
11.00	Mega Dolphin	Milos.
12.30	Pegasus	Piraeus.
12.45	Express Paros	Kimolos. Milos.
13.25	Mega Dolphin	Serifos. Kythnos. Piraeus.
13.30	Mega Dolphin	Milos.
14.00	Milos Express	Kimolos. Milos.
16.10	Mega Dolphin	Paros. Mykonos. Tinos. Syros.
17.25	Express Paros	Serifos. Paros. Syros.

⑤
01.50	Pegasus	Kimolos. Milos.
02.30	Milos Express	Serifos. Kythnos. Piraeus.
09.30	Pegasus	Serifos. Kythnos. Piraeus.
10.30	Speed H/F	Milos. Folegandros. Santorini.

17.30	Speed H/F	Paros. Mykonos. Tinos. Syros.
18.15	Mega Dolphin	Milos.
19.30	Arkadi/Preveli	Crete (Rethimno).
19.45	Mega Dolphin	Piraeus.
22.00	Milos Express	Folegandros. Serifos. Piraeus.
22.25	Pegasus	Milos. Folegandros. Santorini.
22.45	Arkadi/Preveli	Crete (Rethimno).

⑥
11.35	Mega Dolphin	Milos.
12.45	Express Paros	Kimolos. Milos.
13.00	Milos Express	Milos. Kimolos. Folegandros. Sikinos. Santorini.
13.30	Pegasus	Piraeus.
14.10	Mega Dolphin	Piraeus.
17.25	Express Paros	Serifos. Paros. Syros.
17.55	Mega Dolphin	Milos.

⑦
00.40	Milos Express	Piraeus.
02.30	Arkadi/Preveli	Piraeus.
02.40	Pegasus	Milos.
10.20	Mega Dolphin	Milos.
11.05	Pegasus	Serifos. Kythnos. Piraeus.
13.25	Mega Dolphin	Kythnos. Piraeus.
13.25	Milos Express	Milos.
16.30	Milos Express	Serifos. Kythnos. Piraeus.
18.50	Mega Dolphin	Kythnos. Piraeus.
21.20	Express Paros	Paros. Syros.
23.10	Pegasus	Milos. Piraeus.

Sikinos

Cyclades West   p. 248

①
02.50	Express Apollon	Folegandros. Santorini.
14.50	Speed H/F	Ios. Santorini.
21.20	Panagia Ekatonta.	Ios. Naxos. Paros. Piraeus.

⑤
| 02.20 | *Panagia Ekatonta.* | Folegandros. Santorini. |

⑥
02.50	*Poseidon Express 2*	Folegandros. Santorini.
09.15	*Pegasus*	Milos. Sifnos. Piraeus.
10.15	*Speed H/F*	Folegandros. Paros. Naxos. Mykonos.
17.45	*Milos Express*	Santorini. Folegandros. Kimolos. Milos. Sifnos. Piraeus.
17.50	*Speed H/F*	Ios. Santorini.

⑦
| 16.00 | *Express Paros* | Folegandros. Milos. Sifnos. Paros. Syros. |

②
03.30	*Pegasus*	Ios. Santorini.
09.40	*Pegasus*	Folegandros. Kimolos. Milos. Sifnos. Serifos. Kythnos. Piraeus.
09.45	*Poseidon Express 2*	Ios. Naxos. Paros. Piraeus.
14.10	*Express Paros*	Ios. Santorini. Anafi.
16.30	*Ariadne*	Santorini. Ios. Naxos. Paros. Piraeus.
23.05	*Express Paros*	Folegandros. Naxos. Paros. Syros.

③
10.00	*Maria PA*	Ios. Santorini.
10.15	*Speed H/F*	Folegandros. Paros. Naxos. Mykonos. Syros.
15.45	*Panagia Ekatonta.*	Folegandros. Santorini.
18.35	*Speed H/F*	Ios. Santorini.

④
02.15	*Pegasus*	Santorini.
13.10	*Speed H/F*	Folegandros.
14.50	*Speed H/F*	Ios. Santorini.

Skiathos

Northern Aegean   p. 424

①
00.15	*Skopelos*	Skopelos.
01.30	*Dimitroula*	Thessalonika.
07.45	*Skopelos*	Volos.
10.55	*Lemnos*	Skopelos.
12.15	*Macedon*	Skopelos. Alonissos.
13.40	*Lemnos*	Volos.
16.15	*Papadia. II*	Skopelos (Glossa). Skopelos. Alonissos.
17.00	*Macedon*	Ag. Konstantinos.
20.25	*Lemnos*	Skopelos. Thessalonika.
22.00	*Papadia. II*	Volos.
22.45	*Skopelos*	Skopelos. Alonissos.

②
00.15	*Macedon*	Skopelos. Skopelos (Glossa).
08.30	*Skopelos*	Ag. Konstantinos.
09.00	*Macedon*	Volos.
11.10	*Papadia. II*	Skopelos.
14.00	*Papadia. II*	Volos.
15.40	*Lemnos*	Volos.
15.55	*Macedon*	Skopelos (Glossa). Skopelos. Alonissos.
20.30	*Macedon*	Ag. Konstantinos.
21.10	*Papadia. II*	Skopelos (Glossa).
22.45	*Papadia. II*	Volos.
23.20	*Lemnos*	Skopelos. Alonissos.

③
08.00	*Skopelos*	Volos.
11.10	*Papadia. II*	Skopelos.
12.15	*Macedon*	Skopelos. Alonissos.
14.00	*Papadia. II*	Volos.
15.15	*Skopelos*	Skopelos. Alonissos.
15.55	*Lemnos*	Volos.
17.00	*Macedon*	Ag. Konstantinos.
20.00	*Skopelos*	Ag. Konstantinos.
21.10	*Papadia. II*	Skopelos (Glossa).
22.20	*Lemnos*	Skopelos. Thessalonika.
22.45	*Papadia. II*	Volos.

④
09.00	*Macedon*	Volos.
11.10	*Papadia. II*	Skopelos.
12.15	*Skopelos*	Skopelos (Glossa).

13.15	El Greco	Thessalonika.
13.45	Skopelos	Ag. Konstantinos.
14.00	Papadia. II	Volos.
15.55	Macedon	Skopelos (Glossa). Skopelos. Alonissos.
20.30	Macedon	Ag. Konstantinos.
21.10	Papadia. II	Skopelos (Glossa).
21.35	Skopelos	Skopelos. Alonissos.
22.45	Papadia. II	Volos.
23.20	Lemnos	Skopelos. Skopelos (Glossa).

⑤
03.30	El Greco	Syros. Naxos. Santorini. Crete (Iraklion).
08.00	Skopelos	Volos.
09.00	Lemnos	Volos.
11.10	Papadia. II	Skopelos.
12.15	Macedon	Skopelos.
14.00	Papadia. II	Volos.
15.15	Macedon	Ag. Konstantinos.
15.30	Skopelos	Volos.
15.50	Lemnos	Skopelos (Glossa). Skopelos. Alonissos. Thessalonika.
21.10	Papadia. II	Skopelos. Alonissos.
22.15	Macedon	Skopelos. Alonissos.
23.15	Skopelos	Skopelos.

⑥
04.30	Dimitroula	Syros. Tinos. Mykonos. Paros. Naxos. Ios. Santorini. Crete (Iraklion).
08.45	Papadia. II	Volos.
08.45	Skopelos	Volos.
11.45	Macedon	Skopelos. Alonissos.
14.15	El Greco	Thessalonika.
15.10	Papadia. II	Skopelos (Glossa).
16.00	Lemnos	Ag. Konstantinos.
16.35	Skopelos	Skopelos. Alonissos.
16.40	Papadia. II	Volos.
21.50	Skopelos	Volos.
22.15	Macedon	Skopelos.
23.15	Lemnos	Skopelos (Glossa).
23.40	Papadia. II	Skopelos.

⑦
04.45	El Greco	Tinos. Paros. Santorini. Crete (Iraklion).
08.00	Macedon	Ag. Konstantinos.
08.45	Papadia. II	Volos.
11.15	Skopelos	Skopelos (Glossa). Skopelos. Alonissos.
12.15	Lemnos	Skopelos (Glossa). Skopelos. Alonissos.
15.15	Macedon	Skopelos. Alonissos.
16.05	Papadia. II	Skopelos. Skopelos (Glossa).
16.30	Skopelos	Volos.
19.30	Papadia. II	Volos.
20.00	Macedon	Ag. Konstantinos.
22.55	Lemnos	Volos.

〜 *Flying Dolphins* include:

Ⓓ
07.50	Thessalonikia.
x 8	Volos/Agios Konstantinos.
x 8	Skopelos (Glossa). Skopelos. Alonissos.

Ⓓ ex ③ (High Season only)
| 09.40 | Skopelos (Glossa). Skopelos. Alonissos. Skyros. |

Skopelos

Northern Aegean
p. 427

①
06.15	Skopelos	Skiathos. Volos.
12.15	Lemnos	Skiathos. Volos.
13.45	Macedon	Alonissos.
15.25	Macedon	Skiathos. Ag. Konstantinos.
18.15	Papadia. II	Alonissos.
20.00	Papadia. II	Skopelos (Glossa). Skiathos. Volos.
21.50	Lemnos	Thessalonika.

②
00.20	Skopelos	Alonissos.
01.45	Macedon	Skopelos (Glossa).
06.50	Skopelos	Skiathos. Ag. Konstantinos.
12.35	Papadia. II	Skiathos. Volos.
14.30	Lemnos	Skiathos. Volos.
17.55	Macedon	Alonissos.
18.30	Skopelos	Alonissos.

③
00.40	Lemnos	Alonissos.
06.30	Skopelos	Skiathos. Volos.
07.45	Lemnos	Skopelos (Glossa). Volos.
12.35	Papadia. II	Skiathos. Volos.
13.45	Macedon	Alonissos.
15.25	Macedon	Skiathos. Ag. Konstantinos.
16.40	Skopelos	Alonissos.
18.20	Skopelos	Skopelos (Glossa). Skiathos. Ag. Konstantinos.
23.40	Lemnos	Thessalonika.

④
01.45	Macedon	Skopelos (Glossa).
12.35	Papadia. II	Skiathos. Volos.
14.30	Lemnos	Alonissos.
17.00	Lemnos	Volos.
17.55	Macedon	Alonissos.
23.00	Skopelos	Alonissos.

⑤
| 00.50 | Lemnos | Skopelos (Glossa). |
| 06.20 | Skopelos | Skiathos. Volos. |

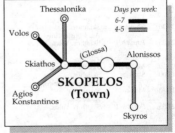

Thessalonika

Days per week:
6-7
4-5

Volos

Skiathos

(Glossa)

Alonissos

**SKOPELOS
(Town)**

Agios
Konstantinos

Skyros

12.35	*Papadia. II*	Skiathos. Volos.
13.45	*Macedon*	Skiathos.
		Ag. Konstantinos.
17.45	*Lemnos*	Alonissos.
		Thessalonika.
22.35	*Papadia. II*	Alonissos.
23.40	*Macedon*	Alonissos.

⑥

06.15	*Papadia. II*	Skiathos. Volos.
07.15	*Skopelos*	Skiathos. Volos.
13.15	*Macedon*	Alonissos.
14.30	*Lemnos*	Skiathos.
		Ag. Konstantinos.
18.40	*Skopelos*	Alonissos.

⑦

07.30	*Papadia. II*	Skiathos. Volos.
13.15	*Skopelos*	Alonissos.
14.10	*Lemnos*	Alonissos.
16.05	*Lemnos*	Volos.
16.35	*Macedon*	Alonissos.
17.20	*Papadia. II*	Skopelos (Glossa).
18.20	*Macedon*	Skiathos.
		Ag. Konstantinos.

🐾🌊 *Flying Dolphins* include:
ⓓ

06.55	Thessalonikia.
x 8	Volos. / Agios Konstantinos.
x 8	Alonissos.
x 4	Skopelos (Glossa).

ⓓ ex ③ (High Season only)
10.30	Alonissos. Skyros.

Skopelos (Glossa)

Northern Aegean   p. 428

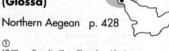

①
17.00	*Papadia. II*	Skopelos. Alonissos.
21.10	*Papadia. II*	Skiathos. Volos.

②
08.10	*Macedon*	Skiathos. Volos.
16.40	*Macedon*	Skopelos. Alonissos.
17.15	*Skopelos*	Skopelos. Alonissos.
21.55	*Papadia. II*	Skiathos. Volos.

③
09.00	*Lemnos*	Volos.
19.30	*Skopelos*	Skiathos.
		Ag. Konstantinos.
21.55	*Papadia. II*	Skiathos. Volos.

④
08.10	*Macedon*	Skiathos. Volos.
13.00	*Skopelos*	Skiathos.
		Ag. Konstantinos.
16.40	*Macedon*	Skopelos.
		Alonissos.
21.55	*Papadia. II*	Skiathos. Volos.

⑤
08.10	*Lemnos*	Skiathos. Volos.

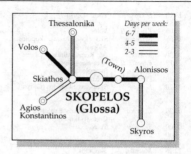

16.30	*Lemnos*	Skopelos. Alonissos.
		Thessalonika.

⑥
15.50	*Papadia. II*	Skiathos. Volos.
21.00	*Skopelos*	Skiathos. Volos.
24.00	*Lemnos*	Ag. Konstantinos.

⑦
07.10	*Macedon*	Skiathos.
		Ag. Konstantinos.
12.00	*Skopelos*	Skopelos.
		Alonissos.
12.55	*Lemnos*	Skopelos.
		Alonissos.
15.40	*Skopelos*	Skiathos. Volos.
18.45	*Papadia. II*	Skiathos. Volos.

🐾🌊 *Flying Dolphins* include:
ⓓ

x 6	Volos. / Skopelos.
	Alonissos.
07.30	Skiathos. Thessalonikia.
09.55	Alonissos. Skyros.

Skyros

Northern Aegean
p. 430

ⓓ ex ⑦
08.00	*Lykomides*	Evia (Kimi).
14.00	*Lykomides*	Evia (Kimi).

⑦
10.00	*Lykomides*	Evia (Kimi).
16.00	*Lykomides*	Evia (Kimi).

○
00.00		Tinos. Mykonos. Paros.
		Santorini. Crete (Iraklion).
00.00		Thessalonika.

🐾🌊 *Flying Dolphins*:
② ③ ⑤ ⑥ ⑦
17.00	Alonissos. Skopelos. Skopelos (Glossa).
	Skiathos. Volos.

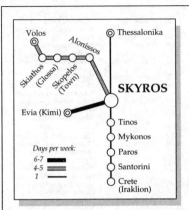

Volos
Thessalonika
Alonissos
Skiathos (Glossa)
Skopelos (Town)

SKYROS

Evia (Kimi)

Tinos
Mykonos
Paros
Santorini
Crete (Iraklion)

Days per week:
6-7
4-5
1

Spetses

Argo-Saronic p. 469

Ⓓ		
x6	*Alexandros M*	Kosta.
00.00	*Flying Dol. 2000*	Porto Helio.
00.00	*Flying Dol. 2000*	Hydra. Poros. Piraeus (Zea).
10.10	*Mirage*	Porto Helio.
11.00	*Mirage*	Hydra. Poros. Piraeus.
13.00	*Express Danae*	Porto Helio.
13.30	*Eftichia*	Ermioni. Hydra. Poros. Methana. Aegina. Piraeus.
14.00	*Express Danae*	Hydra. Poros. Methana. Aegina. Piraeus.
14.45	*Georgios 2*	Poros. Methana. Aegina. Piraeus.
18.30	*Mirage*	Porto Helio.
19.20	*Mirage*	Hydra. Piraeus.

🐬 *Flying Dolphins*:

Ⓓ x 6   Poros. Piraeus (Zea).

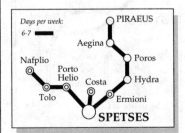

Days per week:
6-7

PIRAEUS
Aegina
Nafplio
Poros
Porto Helio
Costa
Hydra
Tolo
Ermioni
SPETSES

Symi

Dodecanese p. 361

Ⓓ		
06.00	*Symi I*	Rhodes.
16.00	*Symi II*	Rhodes.
①		
10.40	*Marina/Rodanthi*	Rhodes.
14.45	*Nissos Kalimnos*	Rhodes. Kastelorizo.
②		
11.05	*Nissos Kalimnos*	Tilos. Nissiros. Kos. Kalimnos.
③		
15.30	Dode. H/F	Rhodes. Kos. Kalimnos.
④		
14.45	*Nissos Kalimnos*	Rhodes. Kastelorizo.
⑤		
11.05	*Nissos Kalimnos*	Tilos. Nissiros. Kos. Kalimnos.
⑥		
09.00	Dode. H/F	Kos. Kalimnos. Astipalea.
15.30	Dode. H/F	Rhodes. Kos.
19.40	Dode. H/F	Rhodes.
⑦		
20.00	*Symi II*	Rhodes.

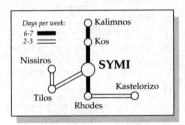

Days per week:
6-7
2-3

Kalimnos
Kos
Nissiros
SYMI
Kastelorizo
Tilos
Rhodes

Syros

Cyclades North p. 206

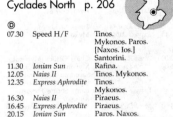

Ⓓ		
07.30	Speed H/F	Tinos. Mykonos. Paros. [Naxos. Ios.] Santorini.
11.30	*Ionian Sun*	Rafina.
12.05	*Naias II*	Tinos. Mykonos.
12.35	*Express Aphrodite*	Tinos. Mykonos.
16.30	*Naias II*	Piraeus.
16.45	*Express Aphrodite*	Piraeus.
20.15	*Ionian Sun*	Paros. Naxos.

Ⓓ ex ②
| 19.10 | Highspeed I | Mykonos. |
| 20.40 | Highspeed I | Piraeus. |

①
00.25	Anemos	Piraeus.
03.00	Superferry II	Tinos. Mykonos.
07.15	Express Paros	Kythnos. Kea.
08.00	Mega Dolphin	Tinos. Mykonos. Paros. Naxos.
11.10	Naias Express	Piraeus.
16.00	Express Paros	Tinos. Mykonos. Naxos. Paros.
18.15	Express Athina	Paros. Naxos. Mykonos.
20.30	Super Naias	Paros. Naxos. Donoussa. Amorgos (Egiali). Amorgos (Katapola).
21.05	Naias Express	Tinos. Mykonos.
22.45	Anemos	Mykonos. Ikaria (Evdilos). Samos (Karlovassi). (Vathi).

②
02.45	Agios Rafail	Andros. Piraeus.
06.40	Dimitroula	Mykonos. Paros. Naxos. Santorini. Crete (Iraklion).
07.15	Express Paros	Paros. Naxos. Folegandros. Sikinos. Ios. Santorini. Anafi.
08.00	Mega Dolphin	Tinos. Mykonos. Paros. Naxos.
08.00	Maria PA	Mykonos. Paros. Naxos. Ios. Santorini. Anafi.
10.00	Highspeed I	Paros. Naxos.
11.10	Naias Express	Piraeus.
11.30	Super Naias	Piraeus.
13.15	Supercat Haroulla	Paros. Naxos. Amorgos (Katapola).
13.20	Highspeed I	Piraeus.
18.15	Express Athina	Mykonos. Paros. Naxos. Ios. Santorini.
21.05	Naias Express	Tinos. Mykonos.
22.25	Super Naias	Paros. Naxos. Ios. Santorini. Anafi. Astipalea.
23.15	Golden Vergina	Ikaria (Evdilos). Samos (Karlovassi). Samos (Vathi).

③
00.45	Anemos	Mykonos. Ikaria (Agios Kyrikos). Fourni. Samos (Karlovassi). Samos (Vathi). Patmos. Lipsi.
07.15	Express Paros	Naxos. Paros. Mykonos. Tinos.
08.00	Mega Dolphin	Tinos. Mykonos. Paros. Naxos.
11.10	Naias Express	Piraeus.
11.45	Supercat Haroulla	Mykonos. Tinos. Andros. Rafina.
14.25	Express Paros	Kythnos. Kea.
17.00	Ariadne	Piraeus.
21.05	Naias Express	Tinos. Mykonos.
23.15	Express Athina	Mykonos. Piraeus.

④
02.00	Agios Rafail	Chios. Lesbos (Mytilini).
06.00	Maria PA	Mykonos. Paros. Naxos. Santorini. Crete (Iraklion).
06.15	El Greco	Skiathos. Thessalonika.
07.15	Express Paros	Paros. Serifos. Sifnos. Kimolos. Milos.
08.00	Mega Dolphin	Tinos. Mykonos. Paros. Naxos.

08.30	Dimitroula	Mykonos. Paros. Naxos. Santorini. Crete (Iraklion).
11.10	Naias Express	Piraeus.
12.45	Ariadne	Paros. Naxos. Ios. Santorini.
18.15	Express Athina	Mykonos. Paros. Naxos. Ios. Santorini.
21.05	Naias Express	Tinos. Mykonos.
22.00	Anemos	Mykonos. Ikaria (Evdilos). Samos (Karlovassi). (Vathi).
22.15	Penelope A	Paros. Naxos. Amorgos (Katapola). Koufonissia. Schinoussa. Iraklia.

⑤
07.20	Dimitroula	Thessalonika.
08.00	Express Paros	Mykonos. Paros. Naxos. Donoussa. Amorgos (Egiali). Amorgos (Katapola). Koufonissia. Schinoussa. Iraklia.
10.45	El Greco	Naxos. Santorini. Crete (Iraklion).
11.10	Naias Express	Piraeus.
11.15	Penelope A	Mykonos. Tinos. Andros. Rafina.
20.15	Ionian Sun	Paros. Naxos. Amorgos (Egiali). (Katapola).
21.05	Naias Express	Tinos. Mykonos.
23.45	Anemos	Mykonos. Ikaria (Evdilos). Samos (Karlovassi). (Vathi).

⑥
00.05	Naias Express	Piraeus.
07.15	Express Paros	Paros. Serifos. Sifnos. Kimolos. Milos.
07.30	Maria PA	Mykonos. Paros. Naxos. Ios. Santorini.
11.35	Naias Express	Tinos. Mykonos.
11.50	Dimitroula	Tinos. Mykonos. Paros. Naxos. Ios. Santorini. Crete (Iraklion).
13.00	Golden Vergina	Piraeus.
21.15	Express Athina	Mykonos. Paros. Naxos. Amorgos (Katapola). Astipalea.

PIRAEUS Rafina

Days per week:
6-7
4-5
2-3

Tinos
Mykonos
SYROS
Naxos
Paros
Amorgos
Ira
Ios
Sch
Sikinos
Kou
Folegandros
Astipalea
Santorini

Ferry Company Colours

Ferry	Livery				
Agia Methodia	5	Festos	28	Papadiamantis II	19
Agios Andreas	26	Georgios Express	42	Pasiphae	28
Agios Rafail	30	Golden Vergina	3	Patmos	16
Agios Spiridon	21	Grace M	25	Pegasus	41
Alcaeos	30	Ialyssos	16	Penelope A	4
Anemos	31	Ikarus	28	Polaris	41
Ankara	39	Igoumenitsa Ex.	5	Poseidon	26
Anna V	5	Ionian Bridge	36	Poseidon Ex. 2	14
Aphrodite II	26	Ionian Galaxy	36	Poseidonia	20
Apollonia II	20	Ionian Island	36	Preveli	15
Aptera	9	Ionian Star	36	Princessa Cypria	24
Aretousa	28	Ionian Sun	36	Princessa Marissa	24
Ariadne	28	Ionian Victory	36	Proteus	40
Arkadi	15	Iskenderun	39	Psara	27
Arsinoe	6	Kantia	9	Rethimno	15
Athens Express	41	Kapetan Alex. A	4	Rodanthi	17
Bari Express	41	Kefalonia	36	Romilda	17
Brindisi	43	King Minos	28	Rodos	16
Capetan Stamatis	27	Kriti I–II	9	Samsum	39
Chioni	27	Lato	9	Sansovino	1
Countess M	25	Laurana	1	Saos	7
Crown M	25	Lemnos	31	Sappho	30
Daedalus	28	Leros	16	Saronikos	13
Daliana	17	Lissos	9	Saturnus	41
Dame M	25	Lykomides	34	Sea Harmony	32
Dimitroula	17	Macedon	31	Sea Serenade	32
Duchess M	25	Maria PA	18	Sea Symphony	32
Eftichia	13	Marina	17	Skopelos	31
Egitto Express	1	Media II	20	Super Ferry II	36
Egnatia II	20	Megistanas	14	Superfast I–IV	37
El Greco	28	Milena	17	Super Naias	3
El. Venizelos	9	Milos Express	23	Symi I	38
Eptanisos	35	Mirina Express	19	Syros Express	8
Erotokritos	28	Mytilene	30	Talos	9
Espresso Grecia	1	Naias II	3	Thassos I–IV	11
Espresso Venezia	1	Naias Express	3	Theofilos	30
Express Aphrodite	2	Neptunia	20	Theseus	29
Express Apollon	2	Nissos Kalimnos	10	Truva	39
Express Athina	2	Nissos Kypros	33	Valentino	43
Express Danae	2	N. Kazantzakis	28	Vega	41
Express Olympia	2	Palladio	1	Venus	41
Express Paros	8	Panagia		Vicountess M	25
Express Santorini	2	Ekatonapiliani	3	Vit. Kornaros	22
Fedra	28	Panther	20	Zakinthos I	12

Car & Passenger Ferry Liveries

International Line Only

Funnel Logo

Hull Logo

1 **ADRIATICA**

 2 **AGAPITOS EXPRESS FERRIES**

 3 **AGAPITOS LINES**

 4 **AGOUDIMOS LINES**

 5 **A. K. VENTOURIS**

 6 **ΑΡΣΙΝΟΗ LINES**
ALEX.—SAMOTHR. CON.

 7 **ALEX.—SAMOTHR. CON.**

8 **AMORGOS FERRIES**

 9 **ANEK LINES**

 10 **ANEK SEA LINES**

 11 **A. N. E. O.**
ANE THASSOS

 12 **ANEZ**

 13 **ARGOSARONIC LINE**

 14 **ARKADIA LINES**

 15 **CRETAN FERRIES**

 16 **D.A.N.E. SEA LINE**

 17 **GA FERRIES**

 18 **GOLDEN FERRIES**

 19 **GOUTOS LINES**

20   HML FERRIES

21   KERKIRA LINES

22   LANE LINES

23   LINDOS LINES

24   LOUIS CRUISE LINES

25   MARLINES

26   MED LINK LINES

27   MINIOTIS LINES

28   MINOAN LINES

29   MIRAS FERRIES

30   NEL LINES

31   NOMIKOS LINES

32   POSEIDON LINES

33   SALAMIS LINES

34   SKYROS LINE

35   STRINTZIS LINES

36   STRINTZIS LINES

37   SUPERFAST

38   SYMI ANE

39   TURKISH MARITIME LINES

40   TYROGALAS

41   VENTOURIS FERRIES

42   VENTOURIS SEA LINES   DEFUNCT

43   VERGINA FERRIES

Hydrofoil Liveries

44 A. N. E. THASSOS
Thission Dolphin

45 BODRUM EXPRESS LINES
Bodrum Princess

46 CERES H/F GROUP
Flying Dolphin/ Mega Dolphin I–XXXII

47 DODECANESE H/Fs
Aristea M Georgios M Gina I, II; Mazilena I, II

48 ILIO LINES
Delfini I–XIV

49 NEK AE
Marina II

50 SAMOS HYDROFOILS
Samos Flying Dolphin I–IV

51 SEA FALCON LINES
Falcon I–III

52 SPEED LINES
Ios Dolphin Santorini Dolphin Santorini Dolphin II

53 UNION SHIPPING Co.
Asklepios Hippokrates

Catamaran Liveries

Hydrofoil & Catamaran
Logos & Colours

54 CERES LINES
Flying Cat I

55 CERES LINES
Flying Dolphin 2000

56 GOUTOS LINES
Athina 2004 Supercat Haroulla

57 MINOAN LINES
Highspeed I

58 MISANO ALTA VELOCITA
Santa Eleonora

59 PARASKEVAS NAFTILIAKI
Keravnos

60 STRINTZIS LINES
Mirage

61 STRINTZIS / SEA JET
Sea Jet I

⑦
01.15	Naias Express	Tinos. Mykonos. Donoussa. Amorgos (Egiali). (Katapola). Koufonissia. Iraklia. Naxos.
03.45	Anemos	Mykonos. Ikaria (Agios Kyrikos). Samos (Karlovassi). Samos (Vathi).
06.00	Maria PA	Mykonos. Paros. Naxos. Ios. Santorini. Crete (Iraklion).
07.15	Express Paros	Paros. Naxos. Ios. Santorini. Sikinos. Folegandros. Milos. Sifnos.
13.50	Dimitroula	Volos. Skiathos. Thessalonika.
15.45	Naias Express	Piraeus.
20.15	Ionian Sun	Paros. Naxos. Donoussa. Amorgos (Egiali). Amorgos (Katapola). Koufonissia. Schinoussa. Iraklia.
22.35	Poseidon Ex. 2	Paros. Naxos. Ios. Santorini.

Tekirdağ

Turkey   p. 525

⑤ ⑦
| 14.00 | TML | Marmara. Avşa. Erdek. |

Thassos (Skala Prinos)

Northern Aegean   p. 434

Ⓓ
06.00 07.20 12.00
14.15 16.00 18.00 19.00   Kavala.

10.30 14.30 19.00
        ANET Line   Nea Peramos.

Thassos (Town)

Ⓓ
05.45 08.15 10.15 12.15
14.00 15.30 16.30 17.30
18.30 19.30 20.30 21.30
        ANET Line   Keramoti.

Ⓓ x 4   Hydrofoil   Kavala.

Ο
00.00   Hydrofoil   Samothrace. Alexandroupolis.

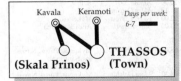

Kavala   Keramoti   *Days per week:*
                     6-7 ▬▬

THASSOS
(Skala Prinos) (Town)

Thessalonika

Northern Aegean   p. 437

①
| 14.00 | Dimitroula | Volos. Syros. Mykonos. Paros. Naxos. Santorini. Crete (Iraklion). |

②
| 07.30 | Lemnos | Skopelos. Skiathos. Volos. |
| 18.00 | El Greco | Volos. Tinos. Paros. Santorini. Crete (Iraklion). |

③
| 01.00 | Sappho | Limnos. Lesbos (Mytilini). Chios. Piraeus. |
| 20.00 | Dimitroula | Syros. Mykonos. Paros. Naxos. Santorini. Crete (Iraklion). |

④
| 07.30 | Lemnos | Skopelos. Alonissos. |
| 21.30 | El Greco | Skiathos. Syros. Naxos. Santorini. Crete (Iraklion). |

⑤
| 22.30 | Dimitroula | Skiathos. Syros. Tinos. Mykonos. Paros. Naxos. Ios. Santorini. Crete (Iraklion). |

⑥
07.30	Lemnos	Skopelos. Skiathos. Ag. Konstantino.
15.00	Rodos	Samos (Vathi). Patmos. Kos. Rhodes.
23.00	El Greco	Skiathos. Tinos. Paros. Santorini. Crete (Iraklion).

⑦
| 01.00 | Theofilos | Limnos. Lesbos (Mytilini). Chios. Piraeus. |

〰️ *Flying Dolphins*:
Ⓓ
16.00   Skiathos. Skopelos. Glossa. Alonissos.

THESSALONIKA

Lesbos

Skiathos

Skopelos   Alonissos

Chios

Skyros

Tinos   Piraeus

Mykonos

Paros

Days per week:
4-5 ▨▨▨
2-3 ═══

Santorini

Crete (Iraklion)

Thirasia

Cyclades Central   p. 174

Ⓓ
| 16.00 | Theoskepasti | Santorini (Oia). Santorini (Old Port). Santorini. |
| 16.00 | Nissos Thirassia | Santorini (Oia). Santorini (Old Port). Santorini. |

② ④
| 13.30 | Theoskepasti | Santorini. |

③
| 19.30 | Panagia Ekatontapiliani | Ios. Naxos. Paros. Piraeus. |

Tilos

Dodecanese   p. 365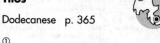

①
| 12.25 | Nissos Kalimnos | Symi. Rhodes. Kastelorizo. |

②
| 13.30 | Nissos Kalimnos | Nissiros. Kos. Kalimnos. |

③
03.30	Romilda	Nissiros. Kos. Kalimnos. Astipalea. Amorgos (Katapola). Mykonos. Piraeus.
09.50	Dode. H/F	Rhodes.
19.30	Dode. H/F	Nissiros. Kos.

④
| 12.25 | Nissos Kalimnos | Symi. Rhodes. Kastelorizo. |

⑤
| 13.30 | Nissos Kalimnos | Nissiros. Kos. Kalimnos. |

⑥
| 11.00 | Romilda | Rhodes. |

⑦
| 15.00 | Dode. H/F | Rhodes. Kos. |

○
| 00.00 | Ialyssos | Rhodes. |
| 00.00 | Ialyssos | Nissiros. Kos. Kalimnos. Leros. Patmos. Piraeus. |

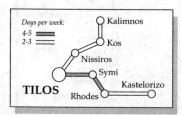

Days per week:
4-5 ▬▬
2-3 ═══

Kalimnos
Kos
Nissiros
Symi
TILOS   Kastelorizo
Rhodes

Tinos

Cyclades North   p. 210

Ⓓ
09.00	Megalochori	Mykonos. Delos.
09.30	Sea Jet I	Mykonos.
12.55	Naias II	Mykonos.
13.30	Express Aphrodite	Mykonos.
15.20	Naias II	Syros. Piraeus.
15.45	Express Aphrodite	Syros. Piraeus.

Ⓓ ex ②
12.00	Sea Jet I	Rafina.
17.15	Sea Jet I	Mykonos.
19.00	Sea Jet I	Rafina.

①
04.00	Superferry II	Mykonos.
08.00	Speed H/F	Mykonos. Paros. Naxos. Ios. Santorini.
08.30	Mega Dolphin	Mykonos. Paros. Naxos.
09.00	Superferry II	Andros. Rafina.
10.10	Athina 2004	Mykonos. Naxos. Paros.
10.15	Naias Express	Syros. Piraeus.
11.15	Supercat Haroulla	Mykonos. Paros.
11.45	Bari Express	Andros. Rafina.
11.45	Penelope A	Mykonos.
13.30	Athina 2004	Andros. Rafina.
15.00	Penelope A	Andros. Rafina.
16.30	Express Paros	Mykonos. Naxos. Paros.
16.30	Supercat Haroulla	Andros. Rafina.
18.50	Athina 2004	Mykonos.
19.00	Speed H/F	Syros.
19.00	Superferry II	Mykonos.
20.00	Athina 2004	Rafina.
21.00	Bari Express	Mykonos.
22.00	Naias Express	Mykonos.
22.15	Maria PA	Syros.
23.00	Superferry II	Andros. Rafina.
23.30	El Greco	Volos. Thessalonika.

②
08.00	Speed H/F	Mykonos. Paros. Sifnos. Milos. Folegandros. Santorini.
08.30	Mega Dolphin	Mykonos. Paros. Naxos.
09.00	Bari Express	Andros. Rafina.
09.55	Athina 2004	Mykonos. Naxos. Paros.
10.15	Naias Express	Syros. Piraeus.
11.00	Superferry II	Mykonos.
11.15	Supercat Haroulla	Mykonos. Syros. Paros. Naxos. Amorgos (Katapola).
11.45	Penelope A	Mykonos.
13.30	Athina 2004	Rafina.
15.00	Penelope A	Andros. Rafina.
18.30	Bari Express	Mykonos.
19.00	Sea Jet I	Andros. Rafina.
20.00	Athina 2004	Rafina.
21.15	Mega Dolphin	Syros.
22.00	Naias Express	Mykonos.
23.00	Superferry II	Andros. Rafina.

③
08.00	Speed H/F	Mykonos. Paros. Naxos. Ios. Santorini. Amorgos (Katapola).
08.30	Mega Dolphin	Mykonos. Paros. Naxos.
08.45	Bari Express	Andros. Rafina.

10.10	*Athina 2004*	Mykonos. Naxos. Paros.
10.15	*El Greco*	Paros. Santorini.
		Crete (Iraklion).
10.15	*Naias Express*	Syros. Piraeus.
10.15	*Penelope A*	Andros. Rafina.
12.50	*Supercat Haroulla*	Andros. Rafina.
13.00	*Express Paros*	Syros. Kythnos. Kea.
13.30	*Athina 2004*	Andros. Rafina.
18.30	*Bari Express*	Mykonos.
19.45	*Penelope A*	Mykonos.
20.00	*Athina 2004*	Rafina.
20.00	*Speed H/F*	Syros.
21.00	*Superferry II*	Mykonos.
21.15	*Mega Dolphin*	Syros.
21.30	*Penelope A*	Andros. Rafina.
22.00	*Naias Express*	Mykonos.

④

08.00	*Speed H/F*	Mykonos. Paros. Naxos.
		Ios. Santorini.
08.30	*Mega Dolphin*	Mykonos. Paros. Naxos.
09.00	*Bari Express*	Andros. Rafina.
10.05	*Athina 2004*	Mykonos. Paros. Naxos.
		Donoussa.
		Amorgos (Katapola).
10.15	*Naias Express*	Syros. Piraeus.
10.15	*Penelope A*	Andros. Rafina.
11.15	*Supercat Haroulla*	Mykonos. Paros.
11.55	*Superferry II*	Mykonos.
15.00	*Superferry II*	Andros. Rafina.
16.30	*Supercat Haroulla*	Andros. Rafina.
18.30	*Bari Express*	Mykonos.
19.00	*Speed H/F*	Syros.
20.40	*Penelope A*	Mykonos. Syros. Paros.
		Naxos. Amorgos (Katapola).
		Koufonissia. Schinoussa.
		Iraklia.
21.15	*Mega Dolphin*	Syros.
22.00	*Naias Express*	Mykonos.

⑤

08.00	*Speed H/F*	Mykonos. Paros. Sifnos.
		Milos. Folegandros.
		Santorini.
10.10	*Athina 2004*	Mykonos. Naxos. Paros.
10.15	*Naias Express*	Syros. Piraeus.
10.45	*Bari Express*	Rafina.
11.30	*Supercat Haroulla*	Mykonos. Rafina.
11.55	*Superferry II*	Mykonos.
12.45	*Penelope A*	Andros. Rafina.
18.50	*Athina 2004*	Mykonos.
19.30	*Bari Express*	Mykonos.
20.00	*Athina 2004*	Rafina.
20.00	*Speed H/F*	Syros.
20.20	*Penelope A*	Mykonos.
22.00	*Naias Express*	Mykonos. Syros. Piraeus.
22.15	*Penelope A*	Andros. Rafina.
22.45	*Bari Express*	Andros. Rafina.
23.00	*Superferry II*	Mykonos. Rafina.

⑥

07.00	*El Greco*	Skiathos. Thessalonika.
08.00	*Speed H/F*	Mykonos. Paros. Naxos.
		Ios. Santorini.
09.30	*Penelope A*	Mykonos.
09.55	*Athina 2004*	Mykonos. Naxos. Paros.
11.00	*Bari Express*	Andros. Rafina.
11.15	*Penelope A*	Rafina.
11.15	*Supercat Haroulla*	Mykonos. Paros.
11.55	*Superferry II*	Mykonos.
12.30	*Naias Express*	Mykonos.

12.50	*Dimitroula*	Mykonos. Paros. Naxos.
		Ios. Santorini.
		Crete (Iraklion).
13.30	*Athina 2004*	Rafina.
14.30	*Naias Express*	Piraeus.
15.00	*Superferry II*	Andros. Rafina.
16.30	*Supercat Haroulla*	Andros. Rafina.
18.50	*Athina 2004*	Mykonos.
19.00	*Speed H/F*	Syros.
19.30	*Bari Express*	Mykonos.
19.50	*Penelope A*	Mykonos.
20.00	*Athina 2004*	Rafina.
22.45	*Bari Express*	Andros. Rafina.

⑦

02.10	*Naias Express*	Mykonos. Donoussa.
		Amorgos (Egiali).
		Amorgos (Katapola).
		Koufonissia.
		Iraklia. Naxos.
08.00	*Speed H/F*	Mykonos. Paros. Naxos.
		Ios. Santorini.
		Amorgos (Katapola).
09.00	*Penelope A*	Andros. Rafina.
09.55	*Athina 2004*	Mykonos.
11.15	*Supercat Haroulla*	Mykonos.
11.55	*Superferry II*	Mykonos.
12.00	*El Greco*	Paros. Santorini.
		Crete (Iraklion).
12.50	*Dimitroula*	Syros. Volos. Skiathos.
		Thessalonika.
13.00	*Bari Express*	Andros. Rafina.
14.00	*Supercat Haroulla*	Andros. Rafina.
14.45	*Naias Express*	Syros. Piraeus.
19.05	*Athina 2004*	Mykonos.
20.00	*Speed H/F*	Syros.
20.15	*Athina 2004*	Rafina.
22.45	*Bari Express*	Rafina.

Days per week:
6-7
4-5
2-3

Thessalonika
Rafina
PIRAEUS
Andros
Skiathos
Syros
TINOS
Mykonos
Naxos
Paros
Iraklia
Ios
Schinoussa
Koufonissia
Santorini
Amorgos
Crete (Iraklion)

Trieste

Italy p. 85

①⑤
| 16.00 | Talos | Igoumenitsa. Patras. |

③
| 12.30 | El. Venizelos | Igoumenitsa. Patras. |

⑥
| 18.00 | El. Venizelos | Igoumenitsa. Corfu. Patras. |

Venice

Italy p. 85

①
| 17.00 | Ionian Star | Igoumenitsa. Corfu. Patras. |
| 19.00 | Erotokritos | Igoumenitsa. Corfu. Patras. |

②
| 21.00 | Aretousa | Igoumenitsa. Corfu. Patras. |

③ ④ ⑦
| 17.00 | Daedalus/Fedra | Igoumenitsa. Corfu. Patras. |
| 17.00 | Ionian Victory | Igoumenitsa. Corfu. Patras. |

⑤
| 12.00 | Erotokritos | Corfu. Igoumenitsa. Patras. |

⑥
| 13.00 | Aretousa | Corfu. Igoumenitsa. Patras. |
| 17.00 | Ionian Island | Igoumenitsa. Corfu. Patras. |

Ⓦ
| 00.00 | TML | İzmir. |
| 00.00 | TML | Marmaris./Antalya. |

Volos

Northern Aegean p. 441

①
01.00	Agios Rafail	Lesbos (Mytilini).
08.00	Lemnos	Skiathos. Skopelos.
12.00	Skopelos	Skiathos.
13.00	Papadia. II	Skiathos. Skopelos (Glossa). Skopelos. Alonissos.
17.00	Lemnos	Skiathos. Skopelos. Thessalonika.
19.30	Skopelos	Skiathos. Skopelos. Alonissos.
21.30	Dimitroula	Syros. Mykonos. Paros. Naxos. Santorini. Crete (Iraklion).

②
08.00	Papadia. II	Skiathos. Skopelos.
08.30	El Greco	Thessalonika.
13.00	Macedon	Skiathos. Skopelos (Glossa). Skopelos. Alonissos.
18.00	Papadia. II	Skiathos. Skopelos (Glossa).
20.30	Lemnos	Skiathos. Skopelos. Alonissos.

③
| 01.20 | El Greco | Tinos. Paros. Santorini. Crete (Iraklion). |

| 19.30 | Lemnos | Skiathos. Skopelos. Thessalonika. |

② ④
08.00	Papadia. II	Skiathos. Skopelos.
13.00	Macedon	Skiathos. Skopelos (Glossa). Skopelos. Alonissos.
18.00	Papadia. II	Skiathos. Skopelos (Glossa).
20.30	Lemnos	Skiathos. Skopelos. Skopelos (Glossa).

⑤ ⑥
12.00	Papadia. II	Skiathos. Skopelos (Glossa).
13.30	Skopelos	Evia (Nisi). Skiathos. Skopelos. Alonissos.
20.30	Papadia. II	Skiathos. Skopelos.

⑦
08.00	Skopelos	Skiathos. Skopelos (Glossa). Skopelos. Alonissos.
13.00	Papadia. II	Skiathos. Skopelos. Skopelos (Glossa).
21.00	Skopelos	Skiathos. Skopelos.
23.00	Dimitroula	Skiathos. Thessalonika.

🐬 Flying Dolphins include:

Ⓓ x 4   Skiathos. Skopelos (Glossa). Skopelos. Alonissos.

Zakinthos / Zante (Town)

Ionian Line p. 502

Ⓓ
05.30	08.00	09.00	10.45	13.00	14.30
18.00	19.45				
	Dimitrios Miras/ Ionis/Proteus/ Zakinthos I				Kilini.

○
| 12.00 | HML Ferries | Patras. |
| 12.00 | HML Ferries | Brindisi. |

Zakinthos / Zante (Skinari)

Ionian Line p. 504

Ⓓ
| 09.15 | Ionion Pelagos | Kefalonia (Pessada). |
| 19.30 | Ionion Pelagos | Kefalonia (Pessada). |

Kefalonia (Pessada)

Zakinthos (Skinari)

Kilini

ZAKINTHOS

Days per week: 6-7

Ferry Companies: UK/US Agents

Line	Agent	
Adriatica	UK: **Serena Holidays**	40-42 Kenway Rd, London. SW5 0RA ☎ (0171) 373 6548
ANEK	UK: **Viamare Travel Ltd.**	Graphic House, 2 Sumatra Rd, London. NW6 1PU ☎ (0171) 431 4560. Fax (0171) 431 5456
Arkadia Lines	UK: **Golden Sun Holidays**	15 Kentish Town Road, London. NW1 8NH ☎ (0171) 267 2657. Fax (0171) 267 6138
G.A. Ferries	UK: **Hellenic MacTravel Ltd.**	36 King Street, London. WC2 8JS ☎ (0171) 836 8216
Hellenic Mediterranean. Lines Co. Ltd.	UK: **Med. Pass. Services Ltd.** US: **All Leisure Travel**	PO Box 9942, London W6 0DF ☎ (0181) 748 3664 1 Hallidie Plaza, Suite 701, San Francisco, CA 94102 ☎ (415) 989 7434
Jadrolinija	UK: **Viamare Travel Ltd.** US: **OdessAmerica Cruise Co.**	(Address: see above) 170 Old Country Road Suite 608, Mineola, NY 11501 ☎ (516) 747 8880
Marlines	UK: **Viamare Travel Ltd.**	(Address: see above)
Minoan Lines	UK: **Magnum Travel Co. Ltd.** US: **Sea Connections Center**	729 Green Lanes, Winchmore Hill, London. N21 3SA ☎ (0181) 360 5353 757 Deep Valley Drive, Rolling Hills Estates, Los Angeles, CA 90274-3607 ☎ (310) 544 3551
Poseidon Lines	UK: **Viamare Travel Ltd.**	(Address: see above)
Salamis Cruise Lines	UK: **Viamare Travel Ltd.**	(Address: see above)
Strintzis Lines	UK: **Viamare Travel Ltd.** US: **Sea Connections Center**	(Address: see above) (Address: see above)
Superfast Ferries	UK: **Viamare Travel Ltd.** US: **Kompas Holidays** **International**	(Address: see above) 2826 E. Commercial Blvd., Fort Lauderdale, FL 33308 ☎ (954) 771 9200
Turkish Maritime Lines	UK: **Sunquest Holidays Ltd.**	23 Princes Street, London. W1R 7RG ☎ (0171) 499 9919

Main Ferry Companies

| Company | Livery No. | (See Colour Liveries between pages 592–593) |

ADRIATICA   **1**
de Navigazione S.p.A.
30123 Venezia, ITALY
Zattere 1411.
P.O.B. 705
☎ (041) 781611
Web http://www.adriatica.it
Tlx 410045 ADRNAV I

Egitto Express, Laurana, Palladio,
Sansovino.

AGAPITOS EXPRESS FERRIES   **2**
99, Kolokotroni Street
185 35 Piraeus (2nd floor), GREECE
☎ (01) 4130566, 4123159
Tlx 24-1679
Web http://www.united-hellas.com
          /agapitos

Express Aphrodite, Express Apollon,
Express Athina, Express Danae,
Express Olympia, Express Santorini.

AGAPITOS LINES   **3**
Akti Miaouli & Skouze 1
185 35 Piraeus, GREECE
☎ (01) 429 5020

Golden Vergina, Naias II, Naias Express,
Panagia Ekatontapiliani, Super Naias.

A.K. VENTOURIS   **5**
73 Possidonos Av.
175 62 P. Faliro, GREECE
☎ (01) 9389280
Fax (01) 9389289

Agia Methodia, Igoumenitsa Express.

ANEK LINES   **9**
N. Plastria-Apokoronou,
Chania, GREECE
☎ (0821) 27600-10
Fax (0821) 27611
Web http://conceptum.com.gr/anek
Tlx 29-1106

Aptera, El. Venizelos, Kantia, Kriti I,
Kriti II, Lato, Lissos, Rethimno, Talos.

ARKADIA LINES   **14**
Akti Miaouli 93, Piraeus, GREECE
☎ (01) 4186583-89
Fax 4516945

Megistanas, Poseidon Express 2.

CRETAN FERRIES   **15**
(RETHIMNIAKI S.A.)
2 Akti Possidonos,
Piraeus, GREECE.
☎ (01) 4177770
Fax 4178980

Arkadi, Preveli.

DANE SEA LINES   **16**
(DODEKANISSIAKI SHIPPING Co)
Parodos Amerikis,
851 00 RODOS
☎ (0241) 30930
Web http://www.helios.gr/dane

Iylassos, Leros, Patmos, Rodos.

G.A. FERRIES   **17**
Akti Kondili & 2, Aitolikou,
Piraeus, GREECE
☎ (01) 4110007, 4110254
Fax 4232383
Tlx 241986

Daliana, Dimitroula, Marina,
Milena, Rodanthi, Romilda.

GOUTOS LINES   **19, 56**
43, Konitsis Street,
152 35 Athens, GREECE
☎ 8028334

Mirina Express, Papadiamantis II,
C/M Athina 2004, C/M Super Cat Haroulla.

HELLENIC MEDITERRANEAN   **20**
LINES Co. Ltd.
Electric Railway Station Building,
P.O. Box 80057, 18510 Piraeus, GREECE
☎ (01) 4174341-5
WEB http://www.hml.it
TLX 21 2517
⛴

Apollonia II, Egnatia II, Media II,
Panther, Poseidonia.

LINDOS SHIPPING Co.   **23**
4, Akti Tzelepi, 18531 Piraeus, GREECE
☎ (01) 4121679, 4113956
⛴

Milos Express.

LOUIS CRUISE LINES   **24**
54-58 Evagoras Avenue,
P.O. Box 1301 Nicosia, CYPRUS
☎ (02) 442114
TLX 2341
⛴

Princesa Cypria, Princesa Marissa.

MARLINES   **25**
38 Akti Possidonas, 18531
Piraeus, GREECE
☎ (01) 411 0777
TLX 241691
⛴

Countess M, Crown M, Dame M, Duchess M,
Grace M, Vicountess M.

MINOAN LINES S.A.   **28, 57**
28, Akti Possidonos, Piraeus, GREECE
☎ (01) 4118211-6 Tlx 21-3265
Passenger Office and Bus Terminal:
2, Leoforos Vassileos Konstantinou (Stadion)
116 35 Athens, GREECE
☎ 7512356
FAX (01) 7520540
WEB http://www.minoan.gr
⛴

Aretousa, Ariadne, Daedalus, El Greco,
Erotokritos, Fedra, Festos, Ikarus, King Minos,
Knossos, Pasiphae, N. Kazantzakis.
C/M Highspeed 1.

NEL LINES   **30**
(MARITIME Co. of LESVOS S.A.)
47, Kountouriotou Street,

811 00 Mytilini, Lesbos, GREECE
☎ (0251) 23097, 29087
TLX 297-152
⛴

Agios Rafail, Alcaeos, Mytilene,
Sappho, Theofilos.

NOMIKOS LINES   **31**
120, Karaiskou Street, 185 35
Piraeus, GREECE
☎ (01) 4172415, 4178080
TLX 21-2446
⛴

Anemos, Lemnos, Macedon, Skopelos.

POSEIDON LINES   **32**
166 73 Voula,
Athens, GREECE
☎ 8958923
TLX 215926
⛴

Sea Harmony, Sea Serenade,
Sea Symphony.

STRINTZIS LINES   **35, 36, 60**
26 Akti Possidonos, 185 31
Piraeus, GREECE
☎ (01) 4129815
WEB http://www.strintzis.gr
⛴

Eptanisos, Ionian Bridge, Ionian Galaxy,
Ionian Island, Ionian Star, Ionian Sun,
Ionian Victory, Kefalonia, Super Ferry II.
C/M Mirage.

SUPERFAST FERRIES   **37**
Amalias 30,
105 58 Athens, GREECE
☎ (01) 331 3252
FAX (01) 331 0369
⛴

Superfast I, Superfast II, Superfast III,
Superfast IV.

VENTOURIS FERRIES   **41**
91 Pireos Av. & Kithiron 2
185 41 Piraeus, GREECE
☎ (01) 4825815
WEB http://www.ventouris.gr
⛴

Athens Express, Bari Express, Pegasus,
Saturnus, Vega, Venus.

Useful Greek

The Greek Alphabet — Transliteration

Greek Capital	Small	English Equivalent	Name	Pronounced like
A	α	A	Alpha	c*a*t
B	β	B/V	Beta	*v*an
Γ	γ	G	Gamma	su*g*ar/*y*es
Δ	δ	D	Delta	*th*is
E	ε	E	Epsilon	*e*gg
Z	ζ	Z	Zeta	*z*oo
H	η	E	Eta	f*ee*t
Θ	θ	TH	Theta	*th*ick
I	ι	I	Iota	f*ee*t
K	κ	K	Kappa	*k*ing
Λ	λ	L	Lamtha	*l*ong
M	μ	M	Mu	*m*an
N	ν	N	Nu	*n*ot
Ξ	ξ	TS/KS	Tsi/Xi	bo*x*
O	o	O	O-mikron	*d*ot
Π	π	P	Pi	*p*ick
P	ρ	R	Rho	*r*ed
Σ	σ, ς	S	Sigma	*s*it (ς only at the end of a word)
T	τ	T	Tau	*t*ap
Y	υ	U	Upsilon	m*ee*t
Φ	φ	PH/F	Phi	*f*at
X	χ	CH/H	Chi	lo*ch*
Ψ	ψ	PS	Psi	la*ps*e
Ω / Ω	ω	O	O-mega	*d*ot

Combinations & Dipthongs

AI	αι	AI	*e*gg
AY	αυ	AV/AF	h*a*ve
EI	ει	I	s*ee*n
EY	ευ	EV/EF	*e*ver/*e*ffort
OI	οι	I	s*ee*n
OY	ευ	OU	m*oo*n
ΓΓ	γγ	NG	go/ri*ng*
ΓK	γκ	G/NG	go/ri*ng*
ΜΠ	μπ	B	*b*oat
NT	ντ	D/ND	*d*og/se*nd*
TZ	τζ	TS	dee*ds*
ΤΣ	τσ	TS	dee*ds*
YI	υι	I	s*ee*n

Greek   Pronunciation   English

Basics:

Ναι	Ne	Yes
Οχι	ochi	No
Παρακαλω	parakalo	Please
Ευχαριστω	efcharisto	Thank You
Με συγχωρειτε	me sinkhorite	Excuse Me
Φυγετε	fiyete	Hop It!
Βοηθεια	voithia	Help!
Γεια σας	yassas (pl.)	Hello/
Γεια σου	yassoo (s.)	Goodbye
Καλημερα	Kalimera	Good morning
Καληνυχτα	Kalinihta	Good night
Συγνωμη	signomi	Sorry
Ποτε;	pote	When?
Ποσο;	posso	How much?
Που;	pu	Where?

Signs:

ΑΦΙΤΕΙΣ	Afitese	Arrivals
ΑΝΔΡΩΝ	Andron	Gentlemen
ΑΝΑΧΩΡΗΣΕΙΣ	Anachoresis	Departures
ΓΥΝΑΙΚΩΝ	Ginekon	Ladies
ΕΙΣΟΔΟΣ	Eisodos	Entrance
ΕΞΟΔΟΣ	Exodos	Exit
ΣΤΑΣΙΣ	Stasis	Bus Stop
ΤΟΥΑΛΕΤΕΣ	Toualetes	Toilets
ΦΑΡΜΑΚΕΙΟΝ	Farmakion	Pharmacy
ΞΕΝΟΔΟΧΕΙΟ	Zenodokhio	Hotel

Miscellaneous:

Αγια	Agia	Saint
Αστυνομια	Astinomia	Police Stn.
Εισιτηρια	Isitiria	Tickets
Λεωφορειο	Leoforio	Bus
Λιμανι	Limani	Port
Νησι / Νισι	Nissi	Island
Οδος	Odhos	Street
Πλατεια	Platia	Square
Πλοιο	Plio	Boat/Ferry
Σπηλαιο	Spileo	Cave
Τραινο	Treno	Train
Χωριο	Horio/Hora	Village

Numbers:

Ενας	enas	1
Δυο	deo	2
Τρεις / Τρια	tris/tria	3
Τεσσερεις	tesseres	4
Πεντε	pende	5
Εξι	exi	6
Επτα	epta	7
Οκτω	okto	8
Εννεα	ennea	9
Δεκα	deka	10
Ενδεκα	andeka	11
Δωδεκα	dodeka	12
Δεκατρια	deka tria	13
Δεκατεσσερα	deka tessera	14
Εικοσι	ikosi	20
Πενηντα	peninda	50
Εκατο	ekato	100
Χιλια	chilia	1000

Days:

Δευτερα	deftera	Monday
Τριτη	triti	Tuesday
Τεταρτη	tetarti	Wednesday
Πεμπτη	pempti	Thursday
Παρασκευη	paraskevi	Friday
Ζαββατο	savato	Saturday
Κυριακη	kiriaki	Sunday
Σημερα	simera	Today
Αυριω	avrio	Tomorrow
Χθες	hthes	Yesterday

Accommodation:

Εχετε δωματια	ehete domatia	Do you have rooms?
Θελω ενα	thelo enna	I want a…
μονο	mono	single…
διπλο	thiplo	double…
δωματιο	domatio	room
για	yia	for…
δυο μερεζ	deo meres	two days
τρειζ μερεζ	tris meres	three days

Index

Abbreviations:

Al — Albania, Cy — Cyprus, Eg — Egypt, Isr — Israel, It — Italy, Leb — Lebanon,
N Cy — Northern Cyprus, Sy — Syria, Tk — Turkey.

C/F — Car Ferry, C/M — Catamaran, H/F — Hydrofoil, P/S — Passenger Ship,
T/B — Tourist Boat or Taxi Boat.

Ferry Names are listed in *Italics*.
Ferry and Island Maps are indicated by **bold** page numbers; Street/Site Maps by <u>**underlined bold**</u> numbers.

CRUISE THE FAMOUS GREEK ISLANDS AND MEDITERRANEAN WITH YOUR OWN YACHT

Quality yachts for chartering

Alpha Yachting has been in existence for 28 years, arranging thousands of successful, reliable yacht charters. Let us help you discover the beauty of the Greek Islands and make your Yachting Vacation in the Mediterranean a truly cultural experience. We are proud to charter clean, reliable yachts and provide personalized service. Alpha Yachting is managed by Manos Komninos, who is not only a Yacht Broker, but an established Naval Architect with over 28 years experience.

Alpha yachting

INTERNATIONAL BROKERS - CHARTER AGENTS - NAVAL ARCHITECTS - OWNERS

67, Posidonos Av., 166 75 Glyfada,
Athens - Greece
Tel.: 9680486-7, Fax: 9680488 & 8945142
E-mail: mano@otenet.gr

THE BEST COMPETITIVE PRICES DIRECT FROM THE GREEK OFFICE